W9-CNW-643

Academic American Encyclopedia

Grolier Incorporated

Danbury, Connecticut

Library of Congress Cataloging-in-Publication Data

Academic American encyclopedia.
      p.   cm.
    "Titles of other English language editions: Lexicon Universal
Encyclopedia, Grolier Academic Encyclopedia, Academic International,
Grolier International Encyclopedia"—CIP data sheet.
    Includes bibliographical references and index.
    ISBN 0-7172-2053-2 (set)
    1. Encyclopedias and dictionaries.
AE5.A23   1994
031—dc20   93–8360
                                                CIP

F

F/f is the sixth letter of the English alphabet. Both the letter and its position in the alphabet derive from the Latin, which in turn derived it from the Greek by way of the Etruscan. The Greeks took the letter from a Semitic writing system, where the name of the sound was *waw*, used for the consonant *w*. The corresponding Greek letter *digamma* probably represented the *w* sound but disappeared before the development of the classical Greek alphabet. Through a series of complex transitions the *digamma* came to represent the *f* sound in Western alphabets—a voiceless, labiodental fricative made by expelling the breath between the lower lip and upper teeth. The voiced counterpart of *f* is *v*, and the two sounds interchange at times, as in the English *of*, where written *F/f* is pronounced as *v*. I. J. GELB AND R. M. WHITING

F-15 Eagle

The McDonnell Douglas F-15 Eagle is a U.S. jet fighter plane that was deployed in western Europe by NATO forces in 1977. A two-seat, dual-role version, the F-15E, was delivered to the U.S. Air Force in 1988. Powered by either two Pratt and Whitney or two General Electric turbofans, it can reach speeds in excess of Mach 2.5 or 2,600 km/h (1,615 mph) with a ceiling of 18,300 m (60,000 ft). Early versions fire cannons and heat-seeking missiles. The ground attack models also carry ordnance payloads. With the development of the Advanced Tactical Fighter (ATF) the F-15 will be phased out of production.

F-16 Fighting Falcon

The General Dynamics F-16 Fighting Falcon is a highly maneuverable, all-weather, multirole jet fighter aircraft. Since reaching combat readiness status in 1980, the F-16 has become a mainstay of NATO air forces. Basic configurations are the single-seat F-16A fighter and the two-seat F-16B fighter/trainer. The F-16A is powered by one turbofan engine with a static thrust of 25,000 lb (11,340 kg), which enables the aircraft to exceed Mach 2, or 2,452 km/h (1,524 mph). Its armament includes a 20-mm multibarrel cannon and the new advanced medium-range air-to-air missile (AMRAAM).

F-86 Sabre

The North American F-86 Sabre was the first swept-wing U.S.A.F. fighter. When the prototype was ordered in 1944, the F-86 was intended to have unswept wings, but following post-war study of German research into swept wings, the design was revised to incorporate 11.3-m (37-ft 1-in) span surfaces with a 35-degree sweepback. The Sabre featured a pressurized cockpit, power-boosted ailerons, and automatic wing slots. Developed as a single-seat fighter, fighter-bomber, and all-weather interceptor, the various models were equipped with turbojet engines of power ratings from 5,200 to 8,920 lb (2,340 to 4,013 kg) of static thrust. Several world air speed records were set by the F-86, which performed well in the Korean War. PETER M. H. LEWIS

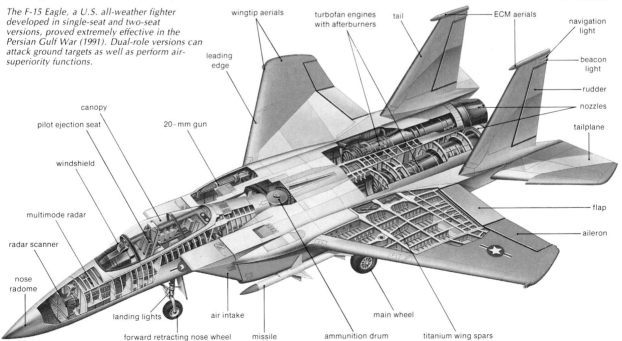

The F-15 Eagle, a U.S. all-weather fighter developed in single-seat and two-seat versions, proved extremely effective in the Persian Gulf War (1991). Dual-role versions can attack ground targets as well as perform air-superiority functions.

F-117A stealth fighter

The F-117A stealth fighter has a conventional all-metal construction with several coatings of radar-absorbing material. Unlike the smoothly contoured B-2 stealth bomber, the fighter uses sharp angles to deflect and disperse its radar signature.

The Lockheed F-117A stealth fighter is a U.S. aircraft designed to be undetectable by enemy radar defense systems. Despite its name the plane is actually intended as an attack aircraft, a role it performed well during the Gulf War (1991), delivering "smart bombs" against sensitive Iraqi installations and suppressing air defenses. The F-117A became fully operational in 1983 and saw action during the invasion of Panama in 1989. It is powered by two General Electric turbofans, each producing 10,000 lb (4,536 kg) of static thrust, giving it a maximum speed just in excess of mach 1, or 1,220 km/h (758 mph).

Fa-hsien (Faxian) [fah-shee-en']

Fa-hsien was a Chinese Buddhist monk and scribe of the 4th–5th century. From 399 to 414, he and several companions made a pilgrimage through India and Central Asia gathering and copying sacred texts of various schools of Buddhism. After returning to China, Fa-hsien began translating the sacred texts into Chinese, with the goal of compiling a complete canon of Buddhist scriptures. His account of his travels *Fo Kuo Chi* (*c.*414; Record of Buddhist Kingdoms) is an invaluable source of information on India in the early 5th century. There are several English translations of the work.

Bibliography: Giles, H. A., *The Travels of Fa-hsien* (1923; repr. 1959).

Fabergé, Peter Carl [fah-bair-zhay']

Peter Carl Fabergé, b. May 30 (N.S.), 1846, d. Sept. 24, 1920, was a Russian goldsmith whose work has often been compared with that of Benvenuto Cellini. Of French Huguenot ancestry, Fabergé inherited (1870) the directorship of the jewelry firm established by his father, Gustave, in 1842. Under his leadership the Fabergé studios achieved international reputation for the skill exemplified in the objets d'art created by its artisans who worked in gold, silver, enamel, and precious stones, set in ingenious designs.

The Fabergé firm was in its heyday during the reigns of tsars Alexander III and Nicholas II; it employed more than 500 artisans, with branches in Moscow (1887), Kiev (1905), and London (1906). Some of the most imaginative pieces turned out from the studios were for the Russian court, including decorated enamel Easter eggs given as presents by the tsars.

The firm did not survive the Revolutions of 1917; it was nationalized and then closed down (1918) by the Bolsheviks. Fabergé died in exile in Lausanne.

Bibliography: Hill, G., et al., eds., *Fabergé and the Russian Master Goldsmiths* (1989); Pfeter, S., *Fabergé Eggs* (1990); Snowman, A. K., *Fabergé, Jeweler to Royalty* (1983); Van Habsburg-Lothringen, G., and Von Solodkoff, A., *Fabergé* (1988).

Fabian Society [fay'-bee-uhn]

The Fabian Society is a British organization that was founded in 1883–84 with the aim of spreading socialist ideas among the educated public and ultimately establishing a socialist government. Among its more prominent members have been George Bernard Shaw, Sidney and Beatrice Webb, and Annie Besant. The Fabians rejected revolutionary Marxism, favoring a program of education fostered by research, publications, and seminars. After the appearance (1889) of the *Fabian Essays*, the society became an influential political force. It was a key constituent of the Labour Representation Committee, founded in 1900, which subsequently became the British LABOUR PARTY. It is now a specialized research agency of the Labour party.

Bibliography: Bosanquet, N., and Townsend, P., *Labour and Equality* (1980); Britain, I., *Fabianism and Culture* (1982); Cole, C. D. H., *Fabian Socialism* (1943; repr. 1971); MacKenzie, N. I., *The Fabians* (1977).

See also: SOCIALISM.

Fabius (family) [fay'-bee-uhs]

The Roman patrician clan (*gens*) of the Fabi was prominent from the 5th century BC on. Its most famous member was **Quintus Fabius Maximus Verrucosus**, d. 203 BC, who was consul five times (233, 228, 215, 214, 209) and dictator twice (*c.*221, 217). He was nicknamed Cunctator (delayer) for his delaying tactics against HANNIBAL in the Second PUNIC WAR. He first used these tactics of harassing Hannibal's army and not joining battle after the Roman defeat (217) at Lake Trasimene; he was overshadowed, however, by the more aggressive Marcus Minucius Rufus. After the even greater Roman disaster at Cannae (216), Fabius's tactics were resumed and wore down Hannibal's strength. Fabius unsuccessfully opposed SCIPIO AFRICANUS MAJOR's invasion (204) of Africa.

Quintus Fabius Maximus Aemilianus, *c.*186–130 BC, was the oldest brother of SCIPIO AFRICANUS MINOR but was adopted into the Fabian gens. Consul in 145, he fought Viriathus (145–44) and was the legate (134–33) of Scipio at Numantia. **Quintus Fabius Pictor**, fl. 216 BC, wrote a history of Rome in Greek that traced the beginnings of Rome to Aeneas; now lost, this work set the pattern for Roman historiography.

ALLEN M. WARD

fable

Although the term *fable* can be applied to any work of fiction, it most frequently denotes a brief tale in which animals or inanimate objects speak and behave like humans, usually to advance a moral point. The term is derived from the Latin *fabula*, "a telling."

Like other myths and legends, fables appear in the earliest records of widely separated cultures. In the 16th century, Sanskrit tales came to Europe via Persia. Earlier versions of similar tales, however, had probably reached classical Greece and were reflected in the tales of AESOP (about 6th century BC). They were transmitted into Latin by Phaedrus in the 1st century AD.

Although a complete text of Aesop was not known until much later, writers in the Middle Ages had an interest in imparting moral lessons through simple stories. Consequently, a large body of fables, based more or less directly on Aesopian models, resulted. The medieval beast epic REYNARD THE FOX introduced a cast of animal characters that were adapted by later poets to contemporary situations. Examples are the vain cock Chauntecleer of Geoffrey CHAUCER's "Nun's Priest's Tale" (in *The Canterbury Tales*, *c.*1387–1400) and the fox and ape in Edmund SPENSER's more openly satirical *Mother Hubberds Tale* (1591).

France, in particular, showed a continuing interest in the fable from the 13th century onward, as seen in the works of MARIE DE FRANCE. This interest culminated in the *Fables* (1668–94) of Jean de LA FONTAINE, which remain popular to the present day. Within natural settings, they comment on human folly, and many may be read as satires—tolerant but shrewd commentaries on French society.

A reaction against La Fontaine was expressed by the German Gotthold Lessing, whose *Fables* (1759) presented a more vigorous moral analysis. Lessing advocated a return to the ex-

The 17th-century French fabulist Jean de la Fontaine created the tale of the fox and the raven, in which the clever fox tricks the raven out of a choice piece of cheese. The fable illustrates a moral or satiric point within an allegorical framework.

ample of Aesop, in which the story existed primarily for the moral, and he accused La Fontaine of relying too heavily on the charm of the tale itself. The tradition of the fable was continued in the 17th and 18th centuries by such writers as John Dryden and John Gay.

Modern authors often use the expanded fable, a book-length story involving an animal population, such as George Orwell's *Animal Farm* (1945). In such works isolated moral lessons are less important than the larger fiction, and fable merges with ALLEGORY. Other modern examples of the fable are James Thurber's *Fables of Our Time* (1940) and William Golding's *Pincher Martin* (1950). DONALD CHENEY

Bibliography: Blackham, J. J., *The Fable as Literature* (1985); Chance, J., ed., *The Mythographic Art* (1990); Hanning, R., and Ferrante, J., trans., *The Lais of Marie de France* (1978); Henryson, R., *The Moral Fables of Aesop* (1987); Jacobs, J., ed., *The Fables of Aesop* (1889; repr. 1987); Kennerly, K., ed., *Hesitant Wolf and Scrupulous Fox* (1987); Rice, S. P., *Ancient Indian Fables and Stories* (1924; repr. 1974).

fabliau   [fa-blee-oh']

The fabliaux (singular, fabliau) constitute a genre of short narrative verse composed in France primarily from the 12th to the 14th century. The conventional form consisted of eight-syllable lines with rhyming couplets.

The narrative formula and subject matter of the fabliau were exploited by Giovanni BOCCACCIO and Geoffrey CHAUCER, among others. The genre is distinct from the FABLE and miracle story in its realism. It is concerned with everyday events, real customs, minor disasters, and human folly. The subjects, often drawn from folklore, are sometimes serious but usually oriented toward comedy and amusing satire, mocking avid monks, imperious women, charlatans, and their dupes.

Fabliaux are thought to represent a reaction to the more serious medieval literary genres such as the epic, lives of the saints, and courtly love lyrics. FRANCIS J. CARMODY

Bibliography: Eichmann, R., and DuVal, J., *The French Fabliau* (1984); Hellman, R., and O'Gorman, R., trans., *Fabliaux* (1965; repr. 1976).

Fabre, Jean Henri   [fah'-bruh]

The French entomologist Jean Henri Fabre, b. Dec. 22, 1823, d. Oct. 11, 1915, provided the first detailed study of insect be-

havior from his countless observations of insects in their natural habitats. After an early period of teaching and writing, Fabre, in 1879, retired to the village of Serignan, where he researched insects, not as mounted specimens, but as they lived in their natural surroundings. His 10-volume *Souvenirs entomologiques* gained wide recognition; parts translated into English include *The Life of the Fly* (1913), *The Life of the Spider* (1914), and *The Life of the Weevil* (1922).

Bibliography: Fabre, J. Henri, *The Insect World of J. Henri Fabre*, trans. by A. T. deMattos (1991).

Fabricius, David   [fuh-brish'-uhs]

The German astronomer and Protestant minister David Fabricius, b. Mar. 9, 1564, d. May 7, 1617, is best known for his discovery, with the naked eye, of the first VARIABLE STAR, known today as Mira Ceti. Fabricius was one of the earliest astronomers, after Galileo, to use the telescope in astronomy. He denied the existence of Kepler's elliptical planetary orbits, however, clinging instead to the Greek belief in the importance of uniform circular motion. Fabricius was murdered by one of his parishioners. STEVEN J. DICK

Fabricius ab Aquapendente, Hieronymus
[ahb ak-wuh-pen-den'-tay, hee-yair-ahn'-i-muhs]

Hieronymus Fabricius ab Aquapendente, b. *c.*1533, d. May 21, 1619, an Italian anatomist-surgeon, exerted considerable influence on the development of medicine in Europe. He improved surgical techniques and wrote the first works in comparative embryology: *De formato foetu* (Of the Formation of the Fetus, 1604) and *De Formatione ovi et pulli* (Of the Formation of Eggs and Chicks, 1621). The former provided comparative studies of the intrauterine environment of dogs, cats, horses, and humans. He also described the semilunar valves of veins in detail, providing his pupil William HARVEY with an important clue to how blood circulated.

facade   [fuh-sahd']

Façade is a French word meaning "face" or "front." In architecture, the term identifies the side of a structure, normally the front, that is architecturally or visually more significant than the others. The term *facade* may designate any prominent outer facet or surface of a building.

facsimile   [fak-sim'-uh-lee]

A facsimile, or fax, machine is a device capable of transmitting or receiving an exact copy of a page of printed or pictorial matter over telephone lines in, usually, less than 60 seconds. In the early 1990s fax transmission had become the preferred method for the rapid sending of printed material.

Facsimile transmission in some form has been available since the turn of the century. From the 1920s, newspapers used large, slow facsimile devices, equipped with photoelectric cells that scanned material placed on rotating drums, to transmit photographs. Police departments, the military, and some businesses sent printed matter via matched facsimile machines. Fax remained a relatively specialized communications device, however, until the development of sophisticated scanning and digitizing techniques in computer and communications technologies, and the establishment of standards that make it possible for all fax machines to communicate with one another over ordinary telephone lines. Most contemporary fax machines conform to a set of standards, known as Group III, that were implemented in 1980, and that require digital image scanning and data compression. Machines built to conform to Group III standards can transmit data at a maximum 9,600 bits per second (bps).

To transmit, the original document is fed into the machine, where it is scanned by a mirror-and-lens-aided CHARGE-COUPLED DEVICE, or, in some faxes, by a series of light-emitting DIODES (LEDs). Light and dark picture elements—pixels, or pels—are described digitally; the message is shortened by compressing much of the white space. The receiving machine, which is addressed through its telephone number, translates the code it receives back into a pattern of grays, blacks, and white. The reconstituted message is printed out on heat-sensitive paper, using techniques similar to those for copying machines. Some fax machines can actually double as copiers.

Bibliography: Banks, M., *Understanding FAX and Electronic Mail* (1990); Fishman, D., and King, E., *The Book of Fax* (1988).

See also: DIGITAL TECHNOLOGY.

factor

In mathematics, a given NUMBER or other quantity can sometimes be written as the product of two or more other numbers. These latter numbers are then called factors of the given number. For example, suppose the given number is 12. This number can also be written as the product of 1×12, of 2×6, and of 3×4. The numbers 1, 2, 3, 4, 6, and 12 are therefore all factors of 12. This mathematical process of breaking a number or other quantity into factors is referred to as factorization, or factoring.

Conversely, if a number is a factor of a given number a, it is also a divisor of a. Take the above example again. When $a = 12$, then $12 \div 1 = 12$, $12 \div 2 = 6$, $12 \div 3 = 4$, $12 \div 6 = 2$, and $12 \div 12 = 1$. Because the only divisors of 12 are 1, 2, 3, 4, 6, and 12, it can be concluded that these are the only factors of 12.

In general, if a is any positive integer, then the integers b and c are factors of a if $a = b \times c$. Any positive integer a has at least the two distinct factors a and 1, except for 1 itself. If the integer has only these two factors, it is called a PRIME NUMBER. If it has more than these two factors, it is known as a composite number. In using EXPONENTS, the concept of factors is also involved. For example, the positive integer a^n indicates that a is to be multiplied by itself to n factors, or n number of times. Thus, in the example, if $n = 3$, $a^n = a \times a \times a$.

In ALGEBRA, factors of POLYNOMIALS are defined in a similar manner. For example, take the polynomial $2x^2 - 10x + 12$. This can be broken down into the divisors 2, $x - 2$, and $x - 3$. The latter three expressions are therefore said to be the factors of the given polynomial.   ROY DUBISCH

factor analysis

Factor analysis is a statistical method that attempts to explain the common dependence of a set of response variables on a smaller number of unobservable FACTORS. The usual practice is to assume only a few factors at first, gradually increasing their number until the data are adequately explained. This makes interpretation difficult, and the results of factor analysis are rarely more than suggestive. The development of factor analysis has been closely associated with PSYCHOLOGICAL MEASUREMENT.

factorial   [fak-tohr'-ee-ul]

In mathematics, a number followed by an exclamation point is called a factorial. A factorial indicates the end product obtained after multiplying the given number by all the preceding whole numbers, on down to 1. Thus $1! = 1 \times 1 = 1$; $2! = 2 \times 1 = 2$; $3! = 3 \times 2 \times 1 = 6$; $4! = 4 \times 3 \times 2 \times 1 = 24$; $5! = 5 \times 4 \times 3 \times 2 \times 1 = 120$; $6! = 6 \times 5 \times 4 \times 3 \times 2 \times 1 = 720$; and so on. Expressions containing factorials arise in the SERIES expansions of many quantities, in the BINOMIAL THEOREM, in PERMUTATIONS AND COMBINATIONS, and in PROBABILITY THEORY.

factory farming

Factory farming, or confinement rearing, is a method of raising large numbers of POULTRY or livestock in relatively small areas, under conditions that ensure rapid growth. Confinement practices include bringing feed to the animals rather than allowing them to forage, and controlling feed rations—often through computerization and automation—to attain the most efficient ratio of growth-time to feed cost. In general, factory farming produces meat, milk, or eggs in less time than is possible with traditional ANIMAL HUSBANDRY practices. Confinement facilities range from barns that may contain several hundred pens for VEAL calves to chicken houses holding 100,000 broiler chickens penned in groups of 10,000 or more. Dairy farms may house large numbers of cows in small confined lots; PIGS may be fattened in droves of several hundreds; and cattle FEEDLOTS containing up to 100,000 animals are not uncommon. Animals raised in confinement conditions receive rations containing high proportions of protein and high percentages of grains. Cattle ordinarily require 10 pounds of feed to produce one pound of weight gain; under confinement they gain one pound with only 6 pounds of enriched feed.

The large concentrations of animals in confinement pens or feedlots would once inevitably have caused lethal epidemics of disease. To prevent such epidemics and to improve feed/weight-gain efficiency ratios, minute quantities of various growth stimulants and of antibiotics and other drugs are added to feed or injected directly into the animals. Pigs, for example, receive antibiotics and sulfa drugs for weight gain and to prevent respiratory infections, and arsenic compounds against parasitic diseases. The female hormone estrogen promotes growth in livestock. Other substances, such as the synthetic estrogen diethylstilbestrol (see DES) and antibiotics such as chloramphenicol have been banned for use as animal drugs because they are suspected carcinogens or may have other toxic effects when ingested by humans. In recent years the U.S. Department of Agriculture has found that beef and poultry test virtually free of illegal drug residues, while some pork and veal still show high levels of antibiotics and banned sulfa drugs. An equally pressing problem has been the creation of antibiotic-resistant bacteria as the result of the routine administration of small quantities of antibiotics to farm animals. Several outbreaks of food poisoning in the mid-1980s involved antibiotic-immune strains of *Salmonella* bacteria.

Factory farming has greatly reduced the labor required to raise farm animals. In broiler-chicken rearing, for example, it took 16 labor hours to raise a flock of 100 broilers in 1945. It is now 1.4 labor hours due to automated confinement facilities and advances in poultry breeding and nutrition.

Nevertheless, some farmers are beginning to question the fundamental economics of factory farming. In Europe especially—where concerns over cruelty to animals and the health hazards associated with intensive rearing have been more publicized than in the United States—some studies suggest that although production of meat, poultry, milk, and eggs is greatly enhanced by factory-farming practices, the high costs of erecting buildings and buying equipment and the expenses necessary to chemically maintain herds and flocks may, in the end, erode profits to a level comparable with conventional rearing practices.

Bibliography: Bogart, R., and Taylor, R. E., *Scientific Farm Production*, 3d ed. (1988); Brown, R. A., *Environmental Management in Animal Agriculture* (1981); Schell, O., *Modern Meat: Antibiotics, Hormones, and the Pharmaceutical Farm* (1984).

factory system

The factory system is the most advanced of the four principal types of industrial organization.

Simpler Industrial Organizations. Of these forms, the simplest and least specialized is the undiversified household, in which members of the family provide for their own needs. The second is the handicraft system, in which skilled independent craft workers, working in small shops or with the assistance of apprentices or journeymen, specialize in making particular products. Third is the domestic, or putting-out system, in which an employer owns the materials and distributes them to various craft workers who carry the goods through the various steps in a production process.

The Advanced Organization. The factory system, when fully developed, differs from the other three forms of industrial organization in several important respects. It brings sizable groups of laborers together in a building or rooms wholly devoted to their work. It is marked by an extensive use of power-driven machines. Further, the system is characterized by a high degree of coordination. This coordination is achieved within the factory by causing the work to flow through a series of processing steps and by the imposition of discipline and supervision upon the workers.

Origins. The factory system played a key role in the INDUSTRIAL REVOLUTION that originated in Britain and later spread to other parts of the world. First utilized in the British cotton textile industry during the 1770s, the system was initially slow to move into other sectors of British industry, largely because of the workers' hostility to the discipline imposed. As power-driven machinery came to be used more widely, however, the cost advantages of the factory over other forms of industrial organization served to force workers into the system. Well before the end of the 19th century, the factory had become the predominant form of industrial organization in Britain, Western Europe, and the United States.

Social Effects. The factory system, which is in large part responsible for the spectacular increase in the output of manufactured products over the past 200 years, has had important social as well as economic effects. It has led, for example, to the emergence of a capitalist-owner class whose members finance the machinery and equipment that ordinarily would be too expensive for workers to acquire. It is responsible both for the decline in the relative importance of self-employed artisans and craft workers and for the emergence of a labor class dependent for income upon the sale of their services to employers. Moreover, because factories have to be located near markets or close to sources of energy or raw materials, the factory system has contributed significantly to the urbanization of modern industrial society.   HAROLD F. WILLIAMSON

Bibliography: Dodd, G., *Days at the Factories: Manufacturing in the 19th Century* (1843; repr. 1975); Dubofsky, M., *Industrialism and the American Worker, 1865–1928*, 2d ed. (1985); Glen, R., *Urban Workers in the Industrial Revolution* (1984); Perrin, N., and Breisch, K., *Mills and Factories of New England* (1988); Wilson, R. G., et al., *The Machine Age in America, 1918–41* (1986).

See also: ASSEMBLY LINE; AUTOMATION; INDUSTRIAL ENGINEERING; INDUSTRIAL MANAGEMENT; MANUFACTURING, HISTORY OF.

facula   [fak'-yuh-luh]

A facula is a bright, irregularly shaped magnetic area of the photosphere of the SUN. It is visible in white light, most clearly near the solar limb. Dimensions of faculae range up to 100,000 km (62,100 mi) or more in diameter, and their lifetimes are typically several months.   PETER FOUKAL

Fadeyev, Aleksandr Aleksandrovich   [fuhd-yay'-uhf]

Aleksandr Fadeyev, b. Dec. 24, 1901, d. May 13, 1956, was a Soviet novelist and bureaucrat. He is remembered chiefly for his early novel *The Rout* (1927; Eng. trans., 1957), an account of a Communist guerrilla unit's fight against the Japanese and White Russians in the Far East during Russia's civil war. The most successful of Fadeyev's other writings was *The Young Guard* (1945; Eng. trans., 1959), which describes the struggle of a group of Soviet adolescents against the Nazis. After the novel was criticized for its failure to credit the Communist party with a stellar role, Fadeyev rewrote (1951) the text. As secretary general of the Union of Soviet Writers from 1946 to 1954, Fadeyev was in part responsible for the arrest and execution of scores of his colleagues. After the revelations of state crimes following Stalin's death, Fadeyev committed suicide.   MAURICE FRIEDBERG

Bibliography: Brown, E. J., *Russian Literature since the Revolution* (1982); Rzhevsky, N., *Russian Literature and Ideology* (1983).

fado   [fah'-doo]

The fado (derived from the Latin *fatum*, "fate") is a Portuguese urban folksong, best known in the cities of Lisbon and Coimbra but also heard elsewhere. The songs embody the mood called in Portugal *saudade*, which has been described as an indolent dreaming wistfulness. The music is in duple meter and generally in the minor mode. A Portuguese lute and a guitar support the solo singer. The first of these follows or embellishes the vocal line, while the second provides an accompaniment of alternating tonic and dominant seventh chords. In contrast to the strict rhythm of the guitars is the free and subtle rhythm of the singer, or *fadista*, who may be either male or female and who traditionally is clothed in black.

The origins of the fado are disputed: Angolan, Arabic, South African, or gypsy ancestry has been proposed. The term is found in Brazil as early as 1819, and appears in Portugal by 1833. The poorer quarters of Lisbon, where fado houses still abound, enjoyed a monopoly on the form until about 1870, when its popularity began to spread. In Coimbra the fado was taken up by university students and given a character more aristocratic and sentimental than in Lisbon. The most celebrated *fadista*, Amalia Rodrigues, won an international audience through tours and recordings.   LAWRENCE FUCHSBERG

Bibliography: Gallop, R., *Portugal: A Book of Folk Ways* (1936; repr. 1961); Nettl, B. et al., *Folk and Traditional Music of the Western Continents*, 3d ed. (1990).

Faerie Queene, The

The Faerie Queene is an epic poem by Edmund SPENSER, planned as a chivalric allegory praising England and Queen Elizabeth I (1533–1603). The first installment was published in 1590 in 3 books of 12 cantos each. A dedicatory letter to Sir Walter Raleigh proposes a complete poem of 12 books on the moral virtues followed by 12 on the political.

Each book has its own protagonist, and in each Prince Arthur personifies magnificence, or "greatness of soul." Books 1–3 are devoted to Holiness, Temperance, and Chastity; 4–6 (1596), to Friendship, Justice, and Courtesy. A fragment was published posthumously in 1609 as "Cantos of Mutabilitie" with an indication that it was part of a seventh book on Constancy. The poem is written in Spenserian stanzas—eight lines of iambic pentameter and a final alexandrine, rhyming *a b a b, b c b c, c* (see VERSIFICATION).

Although *The Faerie Queene* is unfinished, it has been said to possess a certain completeness in its present form. *The Faerie Queene* had a powerful influence on later poets, especially Milton and the romantics.   DONALD CHENEY

Bibliography: Dundas, J., *The Spider and the Bee: The Artistry of Spenser's Faerie Queene* (1985); Heale, E., *The Faerie Queene* (1987); Lewis, C. S., *The Allegory of Love* (1936); Lockerd, B., Jr., *The Sacred Marriage* (1987); O'Connell, M., *Mirror and Veil: The Historical Dimension of Spenser's Faerie Queene* (1977); Tonkin, H., *Faerie Queene* (1989); Williams, K., *Spenser's World of Glass* (1966).

Faeroe Islands   [fair'-oh]

The Faeroe Islands, located in the North Atlantic about halfway between the Scottish Shetland Islands and Iceland, constitute a self-governing unit within Denmark. With a total land area of only 1,399 km² (540 mi²), the archipelago comprises 17 inhabited and 5 uninhabited islands. The population is 47,653 (1989 est.). Thorshavn (1988 est. pop., 14,547), on the island of Streymoy, is the capital. The people speak their own language, Faeroese, which is related to Danish.

The Faeroes are volcanic, rocky, and precipitous, with mountains rising to 882 m (2,894 ft). There is little flat land or natural vegetation. Winters are long and dark, and summer nights are short. Rainfall is heavy, averaging 1,525 mm (60 in) annually, and storms are frequent. Temperatures are mild, however, modified by the warm North Atlantic Drift. The traditional occupations of shepherding, wool working, fowling, and potato growing are still pursued, but large-scale deep-sea fishing and fish processing are now the major economic activities, and tourism is being developed.

The islands were first settled by Irish monks about 700 and by Vikings about 800. They belonged to Norway until 1380, when they were ceded to Denmark. The islands were granted home rule in 1948. The Faeroes have their own legislature and flag. They send two representatives to the Danish parliament.

Fafnir   [fahf'-neer]

In Norse mythology, Fafnir was a giant who assumed the form of a dragon to guard a golden hoard he had obtained by killing his father. In Richard Wagner's opera cycle, The RING OF THE NIBELUNG, the same character kills his brother in order to gain the gold that the gods have paid him and his brother for building Valhalla. Fafnir himself is killed by Sieg-fried. Many versions of this legend exist.

Fahd, King of Saudi Arabia

Fahd ibn Abd al-Aziz, b. 1922, succeeded to the throne of Saudi Arabia upon the death (June 13, 1982) of his half brother King KHALID. One of the many sons of Ibn Saud, founder of the kingdom, Fahd received a traditional education at court and held several official posts before becoming crown prince and first deputy prime minister in 1975. Fahd, who supervised Saudi Arabia's economic modernization, is regarded as a moderate among Arab leaders. He backed the allied coalition in the GULF WAR against Iraq and in April 1991 announced plans to form a consultative assembly for Saudi Arabia.

Fahrenheit, Gabriel Daniel   [fah'-ren-hyt]

Gabriel Daniel Fahrenheit, b. May 24, 1686, d. Sept. 16, 1736, introduced the first practical mercury THERMOMETER and in-vented the meteorological HYGROMETER. He spent most of his life in Amsterdam (the Netherlands) as a manufacturer of weather instruments.

Fahrenheit scale   [fair'-en-hyt]

The Fahrenheit scale is a TEMPERATURE scale still widely used in England and the United States (although seldom in scientific work), in which the melting point of ice is specified as 32° and the normal boiling point of water 212°. It was introduced about 1720 by Gabriel Daniel Fahrenheit.

Fahrenheit's original scale was evidently based on two fixed points: the lowest temperature he could achieve, and "the 96th degree when the thermometer is held in the mouth or un-der the armpit." Why Fahrenheit chose 96° for body heat is not known.
HENRY A. BENT

Bibliography: McGee, T. G., *Principles and Methods of Temperature Measurement* (1988); Smorodinsky, Y. A., *Temperature* (1985).

Faidherbe, Louis Léon César   [fay-dairb']

Louis Léon César Faidherbe, b. June 3, 1818, d. Sept. 28, 1889, was a French colonial administrator who helped to establish France's African empire. A military engineer, Faidherbe served (1854–61, 1863–65) as governor of Senegal, where he founded Dakar. He fought off Hajj UMAR and greatly extended France's possessions in the region. He was appointed (1870) commander in northern France in the later stages of the Fran-co-Prussian War and later served in the National Assembly.

faïence   [fay-ens' or fay-ahns']

Faïence refers generally to a type of tin-glazed earthenware that became popular throughout Europe from the 16th centu-ry. The term, which was current by 1610, is probably a French corruption of Faenza, an Italian city celebrated for its produc-tion of MAJOLICA, the earliest European tin-glazed earthenware, which had been copied from the earthenware produced in Moorish Spain beginning in the 11th century. DELFTWARE is an-other popular form of faïence.

Tin glaze is a white, opaque glaze resembling a fine enamel paint. In the 16th and 17th centuries, colored designs were applied to the glaze before the piece was fired, but after 1750 a new technique was introduced whereby the designs were added after the first firing; the piece was then fired again. This technique permitted ornate decoration.

Faïence was at the height of its popularity during the early and mid-18th century, when factories in Italy, France, and Holland produced a great variety of wares—including table-ware, tiles, and jardinieres. Individual centers of production evolved their own distinctive styles, and Bologna, Padua, Rouen, Moustiers, and Nevers produced particularly fine pieces. In the late 18th century the use of faïence declined as more delicate porcelain from French factories and English Staffordshire earthenware became available.

Bibliography: Cooper, Emmanuel, *A History of World Pottery*, rev. ed. (1989); Ketchum, William C., Jr., *Pottery and Porcelain* (1983).

faint object detection

Detection of faint celestial objects requires the use of optical instruments such as binoculars and telescopes along with pho-tographic plates and photoemissive devices.

Photography. The photographic technique allows large areas of the sky to be covered with one exposure, achieves a high resolution useful in examining structural details of extended celestial objects or of stellar spectra, offers a variety of emul-sions sensitive to various wavelength regions, and provides a permanent record (see ASTROPHOTOGRAPHY). Most emulsions have a quantum efficiency of 1 percent or less, however, meaning that about 100 photons must fall on a point on the emulsion before one will be recorded. To improve quantum efficiency, astronomers have employed a variety of hypersen-sitization techniques, including baking in nitrogen and wash-ing with water or ammonia. Photographic emulsions, com-bined with hypersensitization, have yielded quantum efficien-cies of up to 4 percent.

Photoemissive Devices. Photoemissive detectors involve the production of free electrons by incident photons, and the measurement of the resulting flow. The primary attribute of photoemissive devices is relatively high quantum efficiency (from 10 to 80 percent). Photoemissive devices do not yet pro-vide the resolution possible with photography. Because of their high quantum efficiency, sensitivity to wide-spectrum ra-diation, large dynamic range, and processing speed, however, they have become useful for a variety of astronomical obser-vations.

Two types of photoemissive detectors are the PHOTOMULTIPLI-ER and the CHARGE-COUPLED DEVICE. The photomultiplier focuses electrons onto an emission surface, which releases a stream of electrons that can be easily detected. The much-smaller charge-coupled device commonly uses a photosensitive sili-con chip; photons striking the chip's surface trigger the re-lease of electrons to an electron receptor, which converts the electrical impulses into a digital code. Faint images received via photoemissive detectors can be enhanced by a computer.
CYNTHIA E. IRVINE

fainting

Fainting, or syncope, is a brief loss of consciousness resulting from a temporary decrease in the flow of blood to the brain. It can result from emotional shock, severe pain, a rapid change in the body's position, or certain drugs. Sometimes, immedi-ately before fainting, a person becomes pale and begins to perspire, and may feel light-headed. Frequent fainting can be a sign of cardiovascular disease or disturbance of the organs of balance.
PETER L. PETRAKIS

Fair Deal

The Fair Deal was the name given to the domestic programs of U.S. president Harry S. Truman. First used in 1949, the term generally refers to Truman's entire presidency (1945–53). Included among the Fair Deal proposals were a full employ-ment law, a national health insurance plan, extended social security, aid to education, civil rights legislation, public hous-ing, universal military training, an increase in the minimum wage, and a fair employment practices act. Many of these programs had to wait for action until later administrations; others were never realized at all. In response to Truman's pro-posals, however, Congress passed the Employment Act of 1946, which established the COUNCIL OF ECONOMIC ADVISERS; the Housing Act of 1949, which was the first to provide federal funds for urban renewal; the Fair Labor Standards Act Amend-ments of 1949, which raised the minimum wage from 40 to 75 cents an hour; and the Social Security Act Amendments of 1950, which increased Social Security benefits and extended their coverage to include an additional 10 million persons, in-cluding agricultural and domestic workers, state and local government employees, and self-employed persons.

Bibliography: Hamby, Alonzo L., *Beyond the New Deal: Harry S. Tru-man and American Liberalism* (1973); Lacey, Michael J., ed., *The Tru-man Presidency* (1989).

Fair Labor Standards Act: see MINIMUM WAGE.

Fairbairn, Sir William

The English metallurgist, civil engineer, and shipbuilder Sir William Fairbairn, b. Feb. 19, 1789, d. Aug. 18, 1874, pioneered the use of iron in bridges, building structures, and ship hulls, as well as techniques for testing iron. A millwright in Manchester, Fairbairn set up a shipyard in London in 1835 to build iron ships. In 1845 he helped Robert Stephenson design two tubular railway bridges in Wales, the Britannia Bridge and the Conway Bridge, which employed wrought iron in a revolutionary type of box girder. Fairbairn was the first builder to fabricate wrought-iron beams by riveting, and he invented a steam riveter for that purpose.   FRANCES GIES

Fairbanks

Fairbanks, a city in central Alaska, lies on the Chena River, about 180 km (110 mi) south of the Arctic Circle. Its population is 30,843 (1990). Fairbanks is a transportation and trade center for Alaska's interior; its major industries include mining and lumbering. Fort Wainwright and Eielson Air Force Base are nearby, and the University of Alaska (established 1917) is at College, 5 km (3 mi) to the northwest. Alaskaland, a 16-ha (40-acre) civic and cultural center, includes the Pioneer Museum and a reproduction of an Indian village. Fairbanks was founded in 1902 after gold was discovered nearby.

Fairbanks, Charles Warren

Charles Warren Fairbanks, b. near Unionville Center, Ohio, May 11, 1852, d. June 4, 1918, was an Indiana lawyer who served in the U.S. Senate (1897–1905) and as the 26th vice-president of the United States (1905–09). A conservative Republican, Warren was chosen in 1904 to run for the vice presidency as a balance to the presidential nominee, Theodore Roosevelt, a progressive.

Fairbanks, Douglas

Douglas Fairbanks was the stage name of Douglas Elton Ullman, b. New York City, May 23, 1883, d. Dec. 12, 1939, an American actor who starred in silent films including *The Mark of Zorro* (1920) and *The Thief of Bagdad* (1924). Fairbanks supervised every detail of his films and often wrote the scripts. His most successful sound film was *The Taming of the Shrew* (1929), costarring his wife Mary PICKFORD. His son by a previous marriage, Douglas Fairbanks, Jr., b. Dec. 9, 1909, also appeared in action films and has been an independent television producer in England.   LESLIE HALLIWELL

Bibliography: Fairbanks, Douglas, Jr., and Schickel, Richard, *The Fairbanks Album* (1975); Herndon, Booton, *Mary Pickford and Douglas Fairbanks* (1977); Schickel, Richard, *Schickel on Film* (1989).

Fairbanks, Thaddeus

The American mechanic Thaddeus Fairbanks, b. Brimfield, Mass., Jan. 17, 1796, d. Apr. 12, 1886, built and patented (1831) the first successful platform scales, later adapted in many forms and used worldwide. He entered the foundry business with his brother in 1823 and invented a plow, a cookstove, and a flax and hemp-dressing machine.
                        FRANCES GIES

Fairchild, David Grandison

The American botanist and agricultural explorer David Grandison Fairchild, b. East Lansing, Mich., Apr. 7, 1869, d. Aug. 6, 1954, helped introduce over 200,000 new plants into the United States while an administrator for the Department of Agriculture (USDA). With an extensive background in botany—his graduate studies included work in Italy, Germany, and Java—Fairchild joined the USDA in 1889. He helped organize its section of Foreign Seed and Plant Introduction, served as agricultural explorer on many foreign plant-research expeditions, and was chief administrator of the section from 1904 to 1928. In 1938 he opened a large BOTANICAL GARDEN, the Fairchild Tropical Garden, near Miami, Fla.   FRANCES GIES

Fairchild, Sherman Mills

The American inventor and aircraft manufacturer Sherman Mills Fairchild, b. Oneonta, N.Y., Apr. 7, 1896, d. Mar. 28, 1971, began designing aerial-photography equipment as a young man. In 1922 he organized Fairchild Aerial Camera Company, and in 1924, Fairchild Aerial Surveys. Forming still another company in 1925, he built the first U.S. airplane with hydraulic landing gear and an enclosed pilot's cabin. His companies produced trainers, aircraft engines, aerial cameras, precision instruments, and semiconductor devices.

Fairfax of Cameron, Thomas Fairfax, 6th Baron

Lord Fairfax, b. England, Oct. 22, 1693, d. Dec. 9, 1781, was one of the principal landowners of 18th-century Virginia. A descendant of the 3d Baron Fairfax (1612–71), who was commander in chief of the parliamentary forces in the English Civil War, the 6th baron inherited about 2 million ha (5 million acres) of land between the Potomac and Rappahannock rivers, the so-called Northern Neck of Virginia, and settled there in 1747. The only peer residing in America at the time of the American Revolution, Fairfax, although a staunch loyalist, was not harassed.

Bibliography: Brown, Stuart E., *Virginia Baron: The Story of Thomas, Sixth Lord of Fairfax* (1965); Morrison, Charles, *The Fairfax Line: A Profile in History and Geography* (1970).

Fairleigh Dickinson University

Established in 1942, Fairleigh Dickinson University is a private coeducational institution in New Jersey with campuses in Rutherford (1942; enrollment: 2,266; library: 150,000 volumes), Teaneck-Hackensack (1954; enrollment: 5,841; library: 251,000 volumes), and Florham-Madison (1958; enrollment: 3,800; library: 150,000 volumes).

Fairless, Benjamin

Benjamin Franklin Fairless, b. Pigeon Run, Ohio, May 3, 1890, d. Jan. 1, 1962, was for years a leading figure in the U.S. steel industry. The son of a coal miner, he worked his way through Ohio Northern University and was hired as a civil engineer for a steel company. His ensuing career was a steady ascent through the executive ranks until at 47 he became president of the U.S. Steel Corporation. He ran the company until his retirement at 65, after which he continued to be a spokesman for the steel industry and also served on government advisory committees.

fairs: see CARNIVALS AND FAIRS; TRADE FAIRS; WORLD'S FAIRS.

fairy

In folklore, a fairy is a preternatural creature that lives on the Earth and may be either helpful or harmful to human beings. Fairies are common to folklore all over the world. They resemble humans but are usually much smaller and possess powers of magic. They can become invisible at will and thus live unseen in the midst of human society.

According to tradition, some fairies live in an organized community, called fairyland, which is free of sickness and the passage of time. Mortals occasionally discover fairyland by accident, are the lovers of fairies, or are abducted and taken there. A famous Japanese FAIRY TALE illustrates some of the elements that seem to be common to fairy lore throughout the world. The fisherman Urashima is beguiled by a beautiful fairy into her underwater kingdom. After spending one night with her, he returns to the upper world and discovers that his family has vanished and he is now an old man.

Some types of fairies are associated with particular places or occupations. Kelpies, mermaids, and nixies live in water; dwarfs and gnomes populate underground places and are great experts in mining and metal smithing. Other popular fairy workers include the leprechaun shoemaker and the many varieties of fairies who are the secret inhabitants and helpers of households: brownies and silkies in Great Britain, kobolds

The painting Titania, Bottom and the Fairies *(1794) by Henry Fuseli depicts a scene from Shakespeare's comedy* A Midsummer Night's Dream. *Fantasy and reality blend in the play when mortal lovers enter an enchanted world ruled by Queen Titania.*

in Germany, the nissen and tomte in Scandinavia.

Although the majority of fairy types are the product of European FOLKLORE, beings with magical powers appear throughout the world, although not all resemble the "little people" of Celtic or Saxon legend. Some Arabic JINNI are described as monstrous demons, while others perform good deeds for humans. The Japanese kappa are malicious spirits who capture swimmers in rivers and lakes. In China, the wicked hu hsien, or fox spirits, are fairies with great powers over nature; they can transform their shape, pass through solid matter, and live in air, water, or earth.

Different peoples ascribe different origins to their fairies. Many groups believe that fairies are the spirits of the dead. Often their origin is described as divine: they might be gods from earlier times who have lost their powers or fallen angels who have been trapped in the regions of earth. The word *fairy* is believed to have been derived from the Latin *fatae,* the three fates who are present at every human birth and decide its destiny.

Bibliography: Briggs, K. M., *The Fairies in English Tradition and Literature* (1967); Froud, Brian, and Lee, Alan, illus., *Faeries,* ed. by David Larkin (1978); South, Malcolm, ed., *Mythical and Fabulous Creatures* (1987).

fairy bluebird

Fairy bluebirds comprise two species of birds in the family Irenidae, order Passeriformes. The blue-backed fairy bluebird, *Irena puella,* is found in India, Indochina, and Malaysia and is about 25 cm (10 in) long. The male is velvety black below with the top of the head, back, and rump iridescent blue; the female is a duller greenish blue, with black primaries. In the Philippine species, *I. cyanogaster,* the sexes are more similar, and both are colored blue and black. Forest dwellers, fairy bluebirds feed mainly on fruits, particularly berries. The female lays two eggs into a flat, cuplike nest. Fairy bluebirds live in pairs or small troops.   ROBERT J. RAIKOW

fairy ring mushroom

The fairy ring mushroom, *Marasmius oreades,* is a member of the gill-bearing order Agaricales of FUNGI. Found growing in circles in grassy fields, it is leathery, with an ivory to tan cap 1.3–5.1 cm (0.5–2 in) across. The name is derived from the superstition that mushroom circles represent the path of dancing fairies.

fairy slipper

Fairy slipper, *Calypso bulbosa,* family Orchidaceae, is an orchid found in bogs in temperate regions. A bulbous herb, it has a single leaf petiole and a single flower that is borne at the top of a bare stalk. The lip of the flowers is large and pouchlike, with the sac marked with purple and bearing a patch of yellow hairs.   K. B. PAUL

fairy tale

A fairy tale is a traditional story whose events are magically caused. Folklorists distinguish two narrative types: the folk fairy tale, best known in the West through the works of the brothers Grimm (see GRIMM'S FAIRY TALES); and the literary fairy tale, popular in Europe since the 18th century. Although each form has its own history and style, they share two important traits: both represent a distinct art form, and both evoke a sense of wonder and enchantment.

The folk fairy tale belongs to the oral tradition of FOLKLORE, but it differs in several respects from other types of folktales such as the FABLE, LEGEND, and myth. It is, for example, a complex tale with several episodes; it takes place in a world that seems to be free of the constraints of time, space, and

The fairy tale is a synthesis of oral and written folktale traditions. Fairy tales are distinct from myths and legends in the timelessness of their settings. Charles Perrault published 80 tales from European oral tradition, popularly known as the Tales of Mother Goose *(1697). Two of his tales are illustrated here: a 19th-century illustration by Gustave Doré of* Little Red Riding Hood *(above) and a scene from* Sleeping Beauty *(below).*

causality; its hero or heroine has neither historical nor mythical significance; and it does not pretend to be true.

The Folk Fairy Tale. The origin of European folk fairy tales is obscure. The same tales have appeared at different times in different countries of Europe, Asia, and North Africa, and many date back centuries in oral tradition (see ORAL LITERATURE). Because of the highly developed style of the European tales, however, scholars believe that in their present form they were transmitted as written, rather than oral, narratives. The earliest collections containing motifs of the European folk fairy tale are the *Gesta Romanorum* (written about the 14th century), the ARABIAN NIGHTS (c.1450), Giovanni Francesco STRAPAROLA's *The Facetious Nights* (1550–53; Eng. trans., 1901), and Charles PERRAULT's *Tales of Mother Goose* (1697; Eng. trans., c.1729).

Working with polarities—good and bad, beautiful and ugly—the fairy tale tells of the wondrous adventures of a hero or heroine who, after a series of struggles with supernatural forces, attains his or her wish and lives happily ever after. In most of these stories, the protagonists are either royal themselves or of royal descent. Such stories as *Little Red Riding Hood* and *Jack the Giant Killer*, however, differ in two important respects. First, their protagonists are often ordinary people, not kings and princesses. Second, in addition to entertaining, most of these stories teach some fairly hard lessons about the ways of the world.

The Literary Fairy Tale. In contrast to the folk fairy tale, the literary fairy tale has no set patterns of plot or character. The genre became popular in France beginning in the late 17th century with the published stories of the Comtesse d'Aulnoy (1650–1705). Later it was popularized in Germany by Goethe and Wieland, and, in the 19th century, by a group of romantic writers including E. T. A. Hoffman, John Ruskin, Charles Kingsley, and Oscar Wilde. Of all the authors who aspired to write fairy tales, however, Hans Christian ANDERSEN was and remains the most successful, and his work has acquired the same "traditional" aura as that of the Grimm brothers.

Fairy tales have been a source of inspiration for artists of all kinds. Numerous artists have illustrated innumerable editions of Grimm and Andersen; Walt Disney's animated versions are world-famous. Fairy tales have also inspired operas, such as Engelbert Humperdinck's *Hansel and Gretel* (1893), and ballets, such as *Sleeping Beauty* by Sergei Prokofiev.

MARY B. CORCORAN

Bibliography: Bettelheim, Bruno, *The Uses of Enchantment: The Meaning and Importance of Fairy Tales* (1976; repr. 1989); Darnton, Robert, "Peasants Tell Tales: The Meaning of Mother Goose," in *The Great Cat Massacre* (1984); Gose, Elliott, *Mere Creatures: A Study of Modern Fantasy Tales for Children* (1988); Hearn, Betsy, *Beauty and the Beast: Visions and Revisions of an Old Tale* (1989); Luthi, Max, *The European Folktale*, trans. by J. D. Niles (1982; repr. 1986), and *The Fairy Tale as an Art Form and Portrait of Man*, trans. by J. Erickson (1987); Morgan, Jeanne, *Perrault's Morals for Moderns* (1985); Stein, Murray, and Corbett, Lionel, eds., *Psyche's Stories* (1991); Thalmann, Marianne, *The Romantic Fairy Tale*, trans. by M. B. Corcoran (1964); Zipes, Jack, ed., *Victorian Fairy Tales* (1989).

Faisal, King of Saudi Arabia   [fy'-sul]

Faisal ibn Abd al-Aziz ibn Abd al-Rahman al Saud, b. c.1906, d. Mar. 25, 1975, succeeded his brother SAUD, who was peacefully deposed from the throne of Saudi Arabia in 1964. Faisal had become crown prince and premier after his brother took the throne in 1953. He was not given full executive power, however, until an economic crisis in 1958. Except for a brief period (1960–62), Faisal continued as premier until his death. A moderate reformer, he made Saudi Arabia a leading conservative power in Arab politics, opposing revolutionary movements in Yemen and elsewhere in the Arab world. He did, however, join left-wing Arab regimes in the 1967 Arab-Israeli War. Thereafter he was more concerned with Arab unity, supporting the Arab oil embargo in the fall of 1973. He was assassinated by his nephew Prince Faisal ibn Masaid and succeeded by his brother KHALID.

ROBIN BUSS

Bibliography: Hudson, Michael C., *Arab Politics* (1977); Sheean, Vincent, *Faisal* (1975); Stefoff, R., *Faisal* (1989).

Faisal I, King of Iraq

Faisal I, b. May 20, 1885, d. Sept. 8, 1933, first king of the Iraqi state that emerged after World War I, contributed significantly to the maturing of Arab national consciousness. The third son of HUSAYN IBN ALI of Mecca, he abandoned his youthful vision of a reformed Ottoman Empire to lead his father's armies in the Arab Revolt (1916–18) during World War I. He was elected king of Syria in 1920 but was forced to abdicate by the French. In 1921, however, the British installed him as king of Iraq under their mandate. Shrewdly balancing British against local interests, Faisal gained legal independence for Iraq in 1932.

ROBERT G. LANDEN

Bibliography: Longrigg, Stephen H., *Iraq, 1900 to 1950* (1953); Simon, R. S., *Iraq between the Two World Wars* (1986).

See also: LAWRENCE, T. E.

faith healing

Faith healing is the cure or relief of physical or mental ills by prayer or religious rituals that may either supplement or replace medical treatment. The practice has been common in most cultures and religious traditions. Primitive peoples turned to a shaman or medicine man to cure their ills. The ancient Greeks and Romans erected temples to Asclepius, the god of medicine. In biblical times, sickness was considered the result of sin or the work of the devil. According to the New Testament, Jesus Christ sometimes brought about physical cures through the forgiveness of sin (Matthew 9:2–7). The early Christians followed his example and prayed for the healing of the sick (James 5:14–16). A sacrament of healing, the ANOINTING OF THE SICK, developed in the Catholic tradition, and faith-healing services continue to be a part of some branches of evangelical Protestantism; one well-known Protestant faith healer was Kathryn Kuhlman. LOURDES and other shrines noted for claims of cures attract many sick people each year. Faith healing is also related to the principles of NEW THOUGHT and those of Mary Baker Eddy in the founding of CHRISTIAN SCIENCE.

JOAN A. RANGE

Bibliography: Frazier, Claude, *Faith Healing* (1973); Jackson, Edgar N., *The Role of Faith in the Process of Healing* (1982); Peel, Robert, *Spiritual Healing in a Scientific Age* (1987).

faith: see RELIGION.

Faiyum: see AL-FAIYUM.

Fakhr al-Din   [fah'-kur ahl-deen']

Fakhr al-Din al-Razy, 1149–1209, was a Muslim theologian and philosopher and the author of one of the greatest commentaries on the Koran. Born in Persia, he traveled in Central Asia and later settled in Herat (in present-day Afghanistan) under the protection of the Ghorid sultans. Best known as an exponent of orthodox Islam, he wrote *Mafatih al-Ghayb* (The Keys of the Mystery, 1279–89), a 6-volume commentary on the Koran. He set out the bases of Muslim jurisprudence in his *Encyclopedia of the Sciences*. Fakhr al-Din's other writings include a manual on metaphysics. His bold opinions made him many enemies, one of whom is said to have poisoned him.

Bibliography: Kraus, P., *The Controversies of Fakr al-Din Razi in Islamic Culture* (1938).

fakir   [fah-keer']

Fakir (Arabic, "poor") refers to a Muslim or Hindu ascetic or mendicant monk who belongs to a religious order but lives by begging and may be adept in magic and miracle working. In Islamic cultures the term is often synonymous with DERVISH.

Falange: see FASCISM.

Falashas   [fah-lah'-shuhz]

The Falashas are a group of Ethiopians who claim Jewish origin as descendants of Menelik, the alleged son of King Solomon and the Queen of Sheba. Numbering about 30,000, until recently they lived a segregated life in villages north of Lake Tana. The Falashas observe the traditions of Judaism: they practice monogamy, obey the biblical laws of purity and circumcision, observe the Sabbath and biblical holidays, recite traditional prayers, and follow biblical dietary customs. In their synagogues they read the Bible in the Geez (an Ethiopian dialect) translation; it includes the Old Testament and some Apocrypha. They do not know the Talmud. The name *Falasha* (Amharic for "stranger") was given to them by other Ethiopians; they call themselves *Beta Israel* ("House of Israel").

The Falashas suffered great hardship in the civil wars and famines that afflicted Ethiopia in the 1970s and 1980s, and many sought refuge in the Sudan. In 1984, 1985, and 1991, almost all of them were airlifted to Israel in a rescue operation sponsored by the Israeli government.   NAHUM N. GLATZER

Bibliography: Ashkenazi, M., and Weingrod, A., *Ethiopian Jews and Israel* (1987); Gruber, R., *Rescue* (1988); Shelemay, K. K., *Music, Ritual, and Falasha History,* rev. ed. (1989).

Falco, Louis

Louis Falco, b. New York City, Aug. 2, 1942, d. Mar. 26, 1993, was a modern dancer, choreographer, and dance director who worked in both abstract and dramatic terms. He danced with the José Limón company (1960–70) and had his own company (1967–83). His works include *Argot* (1967), *Caviar* (1970), *Eclipse* (1974), *Early Sunday Morning* (1979), and *Service Compris* (1980). During the 1980s he was active as a choreographer for advertising, videos, and films, including *Fame* (1980), *Angel Heart* (1987), and *Leonard Part 6* (1987).   BARBARA BARKER

falcon   [fal'-kuhn]

Falcons are any of about 60 species of birds of prey that constitute the family Falconidae in the order Falconiformes, which also includes eagles, hawks, kites, and vultures. The true falcons are typified by a bullet-shaped body, long and pointed wings, a medium to long tail, long toes with sharply hooked claws, a short neck, and a short, hooked, and usually notched bill. Coloration may vary widely, but the sexes of any one species are usually similar in appearance, except that the females are larger. Certain species of falcons are also known as caracaras, falconets, gyrfalcons, hobbies, kestrels, and peregrines; a number of falcons are also called hawks.

Falcons are strong, fast fliers with great aerial agility. They

The peregrine falcon, Falco peregrinus, once highly prized for the sport of falconry, ranges throughout the world, particularly in open country. It flies swiftly, diving from high altitudes to attack its prey.

seldom soar in the manner of hawks. The peregrine has been clocked at 290 km/h (180 mph) in a dive. This speed and agility make falcons successful hunters of birds, reptiles, and small mammals. Some species, however, are insectivorous or eaters of carrion. Although falcons strike or grasp their prey with their claws, they generally kill the captured prey with their beaks, whereas hawks kill with their claws.

Falcons are usually solitary or live in pairs. They nest in trees or on cliffs and often occupy the nests of other species of birds. Females generally lay two to six eggs, and both the male and female incubate the eggs and care for the young. The falcon passes through four periods during its life cycle. The nestling period occupies the time from hatching to first flight, during which the young bird gains all its feathers. The postnestling stage is the fledgling; during this period the parents still hunt food for the young falcon. When the bird leaves the nest to be on its own, it is considered a juvenile until it reaches sexual maturity. Then it is considered an adult. Falcons seldom live more than 20 years.

The falcons' only serious enemy is humankind. For many years falcons were considered vermin because they were thought to exact a heavy toll on chickens and other livestock. In recent times pesticides have been responsible for decimating and endangering several species. Research has shown that organochlorine pesticides (DDT, dieldrin) reduce the ability of certain birds to produce sufficient calcium for their eggs; consequently, the eggs are thin shelled and susceptible to breakage. At least one of the living species is considered endangered, the Seychelles kestrel, *F. araea,* and one other species, the Mauritius kestrel, *F. punctatus,* may be extinct.

The earliest fossil record of the falcon family is from the Miocene Epoch of Argentina, about 15 million years ago. There are 11 known fossil species.   STEPHEN FAUER

Bibliography: Ferguson-Lees, J., et al., *Birds of Prey* (1991); Liotta, P. H., *Learning to Fly: A Season with the Peregrine Falcon* (1989); Miller, M., and Nelson, C., *Talons: North American Birds of Prey* (1993); Ratcliffe, D., *The Peregrine Falcon* (1980); Savage, C., *Peregrine Falcons* (1992); Scholz, F., *Birds of Prey* (1993).

Falconet, Étienne Maurice   [fahl-koh-nay']

Étienne Maurice Falconet, b. Dec. 1, 1716, d. Jan. 24, 1791, was a French rococo sculptor characterized by artistic individuality and independence. A pupil of Jean Baptiste Lemoyne, he was called to Russia by Empress Catherine II in 1766 and worked there until 1778. In Russia he executed his masterpiece, a bronze equestrian monument to Peter the Great (The Hermitage, Saint Petersburg), which was unveiled in 1782. The energetic movement expressed in this work breaks with classical equestrian traditions. It also reflects Falconet's belief in the superiority of the vital realism of contemporary art over the art of the ancients. Falconet's most famous work, the *Menacing Cupid* (1757; Louvre, Paris), exhibits a more conventional rococo playfulness.

Bibliography: Levitine, George, *The Sculpture of Falconet* (1972).

falconry   [fal'-kuhn-ree]

Falconry, or hawking, is the sport of hunting with FALCONS and HAWKS. Believed to have originated in Central Asia about 2000 BC, it has had a devoted following in the Middle East ever since. In Europe it was popular among nobility between the 10th and 17th centuries, but it declined with the introduction of guns. Interest in the sport revived after World War I, particularly in Great Britain and Europe. An organization for falconry, established in the United States in 1942, was succeeded by the North American Falconers' Association.

In strict falconry usage, the terms *falcon* and *tiercel* were reserved for the female and male peregrine, respectively, but with qualifying terms they were also applied to falcons such as the gyrfalcon, kestrel, and merlin and to hawks such as the goshawk and sparrow hawk. (In the Western Hemisphere, the bird called a sparrow hawk is actually a falcon, and some hawks are occasionally called merlins.)

The style of hunting varies, depending somewhat on the kind of hawk available to the hunter. Short-winged hawks, such as the goshawk and Cooper's hawk, hunt ground-level prey from a high perch. Long-winged hawks, such as the peregrine, gyrfalcon, and merlin, hunt from the air and take flying prey. Short-winged hawks are trained to return to the falconer's glove, but long-winged birds are trained to return to a lure—a mock bird swinging on a cord.

Bibliography: Glasier, Phillip, *Falconry and Hawking,* 2d ed. (1987); Perry-Jones, J., *Falconry* (1989).

Falkenhayn, Erich von   [fahl'-ken-hyn, ay'-rik fuhn]

Erich Georg Anton Sebastian von Falkenhayn, b. Sept. 11, 1861, d. Apr. 8, 1922, was chief of the German general staff (1914–16) during World War I. Succeeding Helmuth Johannes Ludwig von Moltke, Falkenhayn adopted the strategy of a war of attrition on the western front. Believing that the war would be won there, he opposed the plans of Generals Paul von Hindenburg and Erich Ludendorff for an offensive against Russia but was overruled by Emperor William II. To break the deadlock in the west, Falkenhayn planned a major assault on Verdun, which began on Feb. 21, 1916 (see VERDUN, BATTLE OF). Six months later, as the unsuccessful and costly battle continued, he was relieved of his command. He subsequently commanded forces in Romania, Palestine, and Lithuania.

Bibliography: Horne, Alistair, *The Price of Glory: Verdun 1916* (1962).

Falkland Islands

The Falkland Islands (Spanish: Islas Malvinas) are a British crown colony, located in the South Atlantic Ocean about 770 km (480 mi) northeast of Cape Horn. There are two large islands, East and West Falkland; about 200 smaller, mostly uninhabited islets; and several other widely scattered islands that are dependencies of the Falklands. The total land area is about 12,000 km^2 (4,700 mi^2). Stanley, located on East Falkland, is the capital. The population of 1,958 (1990 est.) is primarily of British origin. Sheep raising is the mainstay of the economy. The annual mean temperature is 6° C (42° F), and precipitation averages about 685 mm (27 in) yearly.

The Falklands were probably discovered by John Davis, a British navigator, in 1592. The first colony was established (1764) by the French, but it soon passed to Spain and, after abandonment, was resettled by Argentina in 1820. The British occupied the islands in 1833. Argentina's continuing claim to sovereignty finally prompted UN-initiated negotiations in 1966. Negotiations were halted when Argentine troops seized the islands on Apr. 2, 1982. Britain dispatched a large task force, retook (April 25) South Georgia, and, after intense naval and air battles, landed (May 21) troops on East Falkland. Heavy fighting ensued until the Argentines, entrenched at Port Stanley, surrendered on June 14, 1982. Over 250 British and 650 Argentines were killed, and both sides suffered heavy losses of matériel. South Georgia and the South Sandwich Islands, formerly dependencies of the Falklands, became a separate British dependent territory in 1985. Britain and Argentina reestablished diplomatic links in 1990, although Argentina did not formally renounce sovereignty over the islands.

RICHARD W. WILKIE

Bibliography: Beck, P., *The Falkland Islands* (1989).

The Falkland Islands in the South Atlantic have a damp, cool, and windy climate that discourages natural tree growth. The landscape consists mostly of open moors with tundralike vegetation.

Fall of the House of Usher, The

''The Fall of the House of Usher'' (1839) is a tale by Edgar Allan POE that incorporates autobiographical elements, tonal and plot unity, and an eerie Gothicism to make it his most popular and frequently reprinted story. In it the sensible narrator visits his demented friend, Roderick Usher, in Usher's symbolically cracked house. Usher places his cataleptic twin sister, Madeline, in a basement coffin while she is still barely alive. One stormy night, she noisily emerges to fall on him; both then die as the house (family and dwelling together) collapses. The work concerns sentient materiality, spiritual listlessness, possible incest and vampirism, premature burial, and revenge.

ROBERT L. GALE

Bibliography: Dayan, J., *Fables of the Mind* (1987); Thompson, G. R., *Poe's Fiction, Romantic Irony in the Gothic Tales* (1973).

fall line

A fall line, also called a fall zone, is the line at which streams make a sudden descent, for example, over the edge of a plateau. Falls or rapids occur as the waters descend from a zone of erosion-resistant uplands to lowlands or plains composed of softer, less resistant rock. This imaginary line on each river, which usually marks the head of navigation and a source of significant waterpower, is a natural site for settlement. A notable example is found in the eastern United States from New York to Alabama in the zone where the major rivers descend from the Appalachian foothills to the Atlantic coastal plain. Here, the fall line is marked by such cities as Trenton, N.J., Philadelphia, Pa., Baltimore, Md., Washington, D.C., Richmond, Va., Raleigh, N.C., Columbia, S.C., and Macon, Ga.

Fall River

Fall River is a port city in eastern Massachusetts. Its population is 92,703 (1990). Located at the mouth of the Taunton River on Mount Hope Bay, the city harbors the World War II battleship U.S.S. *Massachusetts* as a war memorial; it also has a marine museum.

First settled in 1656, Fall River was incorporated in 1803. It provided one of the earliest sites for the manufacture of cotton because of its good harbor and the presence of the rapidly flowing Quequechan River to power the mills. Its first cotton mill was constructed in 1811. The city was hard hit by the Depression of the 1930s and competition from southern textile mills. The current economy is more diversified, but cotton goods and clothing are still manufactured. Plastics, rubber goods, and textile machinery are also produced. The murder trial of Lizzie BORDEN was held there in 1892–93.

Falla, Manuel de   [fah'-ee-ah, mahn-wayl day]

Manuel de Falla, b. Nov. 23, 1876, d. Nov. 14, 1946, a famous Spanish composer, is admired for his brilliant and colorful evocations of Spain in his music. He studied piano at the Royal Conservatory in Madrid and composition with Felipe Pedrell, who urged Falla to write music of true Spanish character. He spent the years 1907–14 in Paris, where he was befriended and encouraged by Claude Debussy. His only published opera, *La Vida Breve* (The Short Life), was performed at the *Opéra Comique* in 1914. Thereafter, Falla lived mainly in Granada, which is evoked in the symphonic impressions for piano and orchestra, *Nights in the Gardens of Spain* (1911–15). Falla's greatest successes were two ballets reflecting the dances and folklore of his native province of Andalusia. The first, *El Amor Brujo* (Love, the Sorcerer), composed in 1914–15 and drawn from legends of the Gypsies of Granada, includes "Ritual Fire Dance" and "Dance of Terror," two numbers frequently performed in piano versions. The second, *The Three-Cornered Hat* (1918–19), tells the humorous story of a miller, his attractive wife, and an amorous magistrate.

In *Four Spanish Pieces* (1906–07), for piano, and *Seven Spanish Popular Songs* (1914), for voice and piano, Falla evokes the regional folk music of Spain. With *El Retablo de Maese Pedro* (Master Peter's Puppet Show, 1919–22), he turned to a scene from Cervantes' *Don Quixote*. His concerto for harpsichord and five instruments (1923–26) draws largely on Spanish music of the 16th century. In 1939, Falla went to Argentina. He died there, leaving unfinished a cantata, *Atlántida*, which was completed by his former pupil, Ernesto Halffter, and first performed in 1961.   GILBERT CHASE

Bibliography: Chase, G., and Budwig, A., *Manuel de Falla* (1986); Crichton, R., *Falla* (1983); Pahissa, J., *Manuel de Falla* (1986); Trend, J. B., *Manuel de Falla and Spanish Music* (1929).

fallacy   [fal'-uh-see]

In logic, a fallacy is a form of reasoning that is illogical or that violates the rules of valid argumentation. A formal fallacy makes strict violations of the rules of logic. An informal fallacy does not violate the rules of logic, but it violates the rules of valid reasoning or arrives at unsound conclusions, because of unsound reasoning.

A common formal fallacy involves affirming the consequent or denying the antecedent in hypothetical reasoning. That is, if A, then B, affirming B as the proof of A, or denying A as the basis for denying B. In either case, it does not follow that the affirmation or the denial proves what is claimed. Thus, if all Americans are bald (A), then all Americans require no hairdressers (B)—the affirmation of A, that is, saying it is true, does not prove B; neither does the denial of B prove the denial of A. Two other kinds of formal fallacies that are important are the argument from the undistributed middle and the conversion of a universal positive proposition. In the first, it is argued that "all A is B" and "all C is B"; therefore, "all A is C." If "Americans" is substituted for "A", "human beings" for "B", and "Hungarians" for "C", it is easily seen that the argument is fallacious. In the other case, it is argued that if "all A is B," then "all B is A"; this is obviously fallacious if the same substitutions are made.

Because informal fallacies occur much more frequently in ordinary discussions, in political speeches, and in advertising, they are, in some ways, more important. Some of these fallacies are a result of the ambiguity of the terms used; people often slip unconsciously from one meaning of a term to another. Other major informal fallacies are the *ignoratio elenchi*, that is, arguing for something different from the question asked; and the *tu quoque* argument, in which an unsound argument is justified by claiming the unsoundness of another. These soon degenerate into the argument *ad hominem*, in which the argument of an opponent is countered by pointing to his or her personal faults rather than by considering the substance of the argument; and the argument from authority, which appeals to famous or important people who agree with a particular point of view.   RICHARD H. POPKIN

Bibliography: Engel, S. Morris, *With Good Reason: An Introduction to Informal Fallacies*, 3d ed. (1985); Fearnside, W. Ward, and Holther, William B., *Fallacy: The Counterfeit of Argument* (1959).

Fälldin, Thorbjörn   [fel-deen', toor'-bee-urn]

Nils Olof Thorbjörn Fälldin, b. Apr. 24, 1926, became, in 1976, Sweden's first non-Socialist prime minister in more than 40 years. After working as a farmer, he was elected to parliament in 1958, representing the agrarian Center party. Defeated in the 1964 election, Fälldin was reelected in 1967. He became the Center party leader in 1971 and prime minister when the non-Socialist coalition triumphed in the September 1976 election. Fälldin resigned in October 1978 over a nuclear power plant dispute but again became prime minister in Oc-

In 1976, Thorbjörn Fälldin led a non-Socialist coalition to victory over Sweden's long-dominant Social Democratic party. A self-educated sheep farmer, he had gained popularity for opposing nuclear energy, high taxes, and a centralized economy. Fälldin resigned as prime minister in 1978 but was reelected in 1979. His government was defeated in the 1982 elections.

tober 1979. In May 1981 a dispute over tax policy led Fälldin to resign; two weeks later he was reappointed. In September 1982 his coalition was defeated in the general elections.

Fallen Timbers, Battle of

The Battle of Fallen Timbers was fought on Aug. 20, 1794, near present-day Maumee, Ohio. A well-trained American army under Gen. Anthony WAYNE defeated an Indian force, thus demonstrating the strength of the U.S. government. The Indians subsequently signed the Treaty of Greenville (1795), which opened much of the NORTHWEST TERRITORY to settlers.

Bibliography: Downes, Randolph C., *Frontier Ohio, 1788–1803* (1935); Nelson, Paul D., *Anthony Wayne* (1985).

falling star: see METEOR AND METEORITE.

fallout

Fallout is radioactive material that falls through the atmosphere as a result of natural causes, the explosion of ATOMIC BOMBS or HYDROGEN BOMBS, or possible nuclear accidents (see NUCLEAR ENERGY). It can cause serious health problems in humans and animals exposed to high levels of radiation (see RADIATION INJURY). Natural fallout occurs when radioactive elements in the Earth's crust diffuse into the atmosphere or when COSMIC RAYS from the Sun produce radioactive isotopes of carbon and hydrogen in the atmosphere.

Fallout produced by bomb explosions is of three kinds: local, tropospheric, and stratospheric. Local fallout, which occurs in the vicinity of the explosion, is usually heavy but lasts only a short time. Tropospheric fallout is produced by fine radioactive particles from an explosion that becomes trapped in the troposphere, the atmospheric belt that extends from 11 to 16 km (7 to 10 mi) above the Earth. These tropospheric particles fall out well after the explosion and cover a much wider area. Stratospheric fallout results from the largest bombs, which produce particles that may travel above the troposphere to the stratosphere, remain there for years, and later fall all over the Earth. Prominent among the radioisotopes in stratospheric fallout are cesium-137 and strontium-90, which have half-lives of 27 and 28 years, respectively.

In theory, nuclear reactor designs incorporate safety features to keep fallout to a minimum should some accident occur, such as a loss of coolant. In the world's worst reactor accident, however—at the USSR's CHERNOBYL power plant, in 1986—significant fallout was spread across parts of Europe.

Bibliography: Fradkin, P. L., *Fallout* (1989); International Atomic Energy Agency, *Environmental Contamination by Radioactive Materials* (1969); Medvedev, Z. A., *Legacy of Chernobyl* (1990); Solomon, F., et al., eds., *The Medical Implications of Nuclear War* (1987).

fallout shelter

A major consideration in any CIVIL DEFENSE program is the establishment of a shelter system to protect against the heat, blast, and radioactive fallout that would result from an attack with nuclear weapons. A shelter should ideally be large enough to accommodate at least 50 people and should have the capacity to reduce radiation by a factor of at least 100 for a 2-week period and to protect against heat and blast effects. The protective value of a shelter, however, depends on a large number of variables, among them its distance from the blast center and the length of the HALF-LIFE of the radioactive elements created by the blast. (No shelter, of course, can protect against ingestion of such long-lived radioactive elements as strontium-90 and cesium-137.)

In some nations, including the United States, shelters of a sort have been created in buildings and such structures as tunnels and mines. The U.S. National Shelter Survey, begun in 1961, identified sites—principally basements, subways, and the like—that might shelter some 250 million people. Unfortunately, most of these sites are in large urban centers and are not readily accessible to a majority of the population. In addition, shelters should contain at least a 2-week supply of food, water, sanitation kits, radiological-monitoring kits, and medical supplies. The federal program that was to assure stocking of shelter sites ended in 1970.

According to estimates by the Federal Emergency Management Agency (FEMA)—which is responsible for integrating federal and state planning for emergencies such as nuclear war—it would cost some $60 billion to build shelters to protect the entire U.S. population.

Few nations maintain ongoing shelter programs. Only Switzerland claims to have built shelters sufficient to house almost all its people. Finland, Norway, and Sweden supported some shelter construction, and China also embarked on a program of shelter building. Soviet civil-defense programs, which, after the Swiss, were considered the most extensive in the world and have been in operation since the 1960s, were said to provide protection for most levels of its leadership (about 110,000 people), for the on-duty shift of its workers at key installations, and for perhaps 10% of its urban population.

JAMES M. McCULLOUGH

Bibliography: Clayton, Bruce, *Fallout Survival: A Guide to Radiological Defense* (1984); Kerr, Thomas J., *Civil Defense in the U.S.: Band-Aid for a Holocaust?* (1983); Scheer, Robert, *With Enough Shovels: Reagan, Bush, and Nuclear War* (1982).

false paca

The false paca, or pacarana, D. branickii, is a rare species of rodent native to the Andes. It resembles the paca, a forest-dwelling rodent that is also native to South America.

The false paca, or pacarana, *Dinomys branickii*, in the family Dinomyidae, is a chunky, fat-tailed rodent that resembles a huge guinea pig. The largest false pacas weigh about 15 kg (33 lb), are about 80 cm (30 in) long, and have a 20-cm (8-in) tail. The coat is brown or black with white stripes and spots. Each of the four digits of every foot is armed with a long, powerful claw. False pacas live on the lower Andean slopes and feed on plants. They are nearly extinct.

EVERETT SENTMAN

false sunbird

False sunbird is the common name for two species of small birds in the family Philepittidae, found only in Madagascar. They are so named because of their resemblance to SUNBIRDS,

and they were originally classified with them. The wattled false sunbird, *Neodrepanis coruscans*, has a short tail and long down-curving bill with which it sips nectar and catches small insects. The male is blue above and yellow below, with a bare wattle around the eye; the female is duller. A second species, *N. hypoxantha*, is known only from a few museum specimens.

ROBERT J. RAIKOW

false teeth: see DENTURES.

falsetto   [fawl-set'-oh]

Falsetto is the light, treble "head voice" of the male singer, achieved by a technique that causes the vocal cords to vibrate at a shorter length. Although a distinction is sometimes made between the sound of the falsetto voice when it is produced by a bass or baritone, and that of the COUNTERTENOR, who normally sings within the falsetto range, both types of singer evidently produce their sounds in a physiologically identical manner. Falsetto was once much used in all-male choirs. The style has been revived by contemporary pop-music stars.

Falstaff   [fawl'-staf]

Sir John Falstaff, who appears in William Shakespeare's two-part history play *Henry IV* (1598), is perhaps the most celebrated of all English literary characters. The amiable, bibulous old knight, who resembles the braggart soldier of Plautus's comedies, plays the role of Prince Hal's surrogate father but is cast aside when Hal becomes king. Falstaff's death is reported in *Henry V* (1600), but, according to tradition, Shakespeare wrote *The Merry Wives of Windsor* (1602) to gratify Queen Elizabeth's wish to see Sir John in love. Falstaff also figures in operas by Giuseppe Verdi and Ralph Vaughan Williams.

Bibliography: Wilson, John Dover, *The Fortunes of Falstaff* (1943).

Falwell, Jerry

A Baptist minister and television evangelist, the Rev. Jerry Falwell, b. Lynchburg, Va., Aug. 11, 1933, is a leading advocate of religious and political conservatism in the United States. His "Old Time Gospel Hour," on the air since 1956, has been televised nationally since 1971. Falwell founded (1979) and served as president (until 1987) of MORAL MAJORITY, a conservative political action group, which he expanded into the larger Liberty Federation in 1986. An upholder of traditional morality, he wrote *Strength for the Journey: An Autobiography* (1987).

Bibliography: Smolla, R. A., *Jerry Falwell v. Larry Flynt: The First Amendment on Trial* (1989; repr. 1991); Snowball, D., *Continuity and Change in the Rhetoric of the Moral Majority* (1991).

Familists

Originally called the *Familia Caritatis* (Family of Love), Familists were members of a Christian sect founded at Emden in East Friesland (Germany) by Hendrik Niclaes (1502–80). Initiated by a rite of adult baptism, they believed that they were liberated by grace from observing laws and freed by the spirit of love from professing creeds. The sect spread to England but was suppressed there in 1580. By 1700 the Familist movement had been absorbed by the Quakers and other groups.

family

The family, among the oldest and most fundamental of human institutions, consists of a man and a woman who are generally expected to produce children, care for them, and help train them in the ways of their culture. This simple family, known as the conjugal, elementary, or nuclear family, is present in virtually all known societies.

Long before the emergence of tribal society, people regulated themselves by elaborating rules governing sexual pairing. These rules were, and remain, extremely diverse, although prohibitions against incest—sexual relations between close family members—have been virtually universal. The in-

The nuclear family has formed the fundamental unit of nearly all human societies. The nuclear family of these Brazilian Indians comprises two adults and their children and serves three important functions: regulating reproduction, caring for and educating the children, and sharing economic duties.

simple in structure. There are two general sources of complexity in family structure. The first originates in the custom of taking more than one spouse. A few preliterate cultures have practiced polyandry, the system by which one woman takes more than one husband. Much more common, and not limited to preliterate societies, has been polygyny, one husband having more than one wife. In many Islamic cultures polygyny is still practiced, and family structures as a result tend to be quite complex. Even in Islam, however, relatively few men in fact practice polygyny because they cannot afford to maintain more than one wife and the children she bears. (See also POLYGAMY.)

The second source of complexity in family structure hinges on the manner in which the relations between kin and the nuclear family are ordered. In various societies children are encouraged to remain closely attached to their family of orientation, bringing their spouses to live in or near their parents' home. This arrangement, known as the EXTENDED FAMILY, consists generally of several nuclear families arrayed around parents.

The extended family structure is well suited to subsistence economies because the expansive network of kin provides any given couple with access to goods and services that they alone could not provide. Once widespread, it is characteristic

(Left) *The extended family consists of at least two nuclear families spanning three or more generations and living in or near the parents' home. Although common in agricultural societies, the extended family household is rare in the industrial West, where large family gatherings, such as the one in this turn-of-the-century photograph, are usually reserved for special occasions.*

(Below) *The form and functions of the modern nuclear family in many ways resemble those of its preliterate Indian counterpart (top).*

cest taboo requires individuals to find and marry mates from outside their own family group, thus reducing the possibilities for serious conflict within the family and also increasing the social interaction between family groups.

Generally speaking, all people encounter two families: the family they are born into, called the family of orientation, and the family they form when they take a spouse, called the family of procreation. KINSHIP bonds link these two families into more-complex family systems.

In traditional, preindustrial societies, kinship ties constitute the primary forms of social organization, regulating the transfer of property, providing structures of authority, and forming the basis for the organization of production and distribution. In such societies the NUCLEAR FAMILY tends to be overshadowed by the larger network of kin.

In other societies, including that of the modern industrial state, kinship matters less in shaping human lives. Individuals rely on a complex array of institutions, including the state, industries and commercial institutions, and churches and schools, to organize their activities into orderly and socially useful endeavors. In such societies the nuclear family tends to be predominant, and kin relations tend to be secondary.

FAMILY STRUCTURE

All families begin with a mated pair, but they rarely remain so

of almost all preindustrial societies, large or small. In modern industrial societies variations of the extended family and the kin network persist among the poor and within ethnic or religious minority groups, in part because such a family structure helps to sustain individuals in the face of economic hardship and helps to lessen the demoralization that often accompanies minority status.

FAMILY FUNCTIONING

In preliterate cultures, and even in Western society until fairly recently, the family was an all-purpose institution. The network of kin provided the nuclear family with economic assistance; the household was the principal unit of production as well as of consumption; and the complex rules of kinship regulated sexual behavior and helped assure the orderly reproduction of society. The family head was typically also its religious leader and the spokesperson for the family in public matters. Countless aspects of daily life were thus organized in terms of families, kin groups, and the residence and descent rules that prevailed.

In contemporary industrial societies the family is a much less comprehensive institution. Specialized institutions have taken over many of the responsibilities that were once the family's. For administration and production, the home has been replaced by the office and the factory. The church and the school carry much of the burden of sacred and secular training. The legal, medical, and other professions provide much of the specialized assistance, counseling, and support that the extended family once supplied. Nevertheless, the family continues to play an important role in modern life. It remains the primary group where intimacy and affection can be freely expressed; it is still the most broadly satisfactory setting for the primary care of infants. In a sense, the family has itself become a specialized institution whose unique mission is to provide the emotional support that the larger, more impersonal worlds of education, work, and politics do not.

With this transformation in family functioning, momentous changes have occurred in the nature of the husband-wife bond and in the relations between parents and children. In traditional societies marked by extensive kin relations, the nuclear family is only a small component of a large system. Until comparatively recent times, parents had the most powerful voice in deciding when and whom their children would marry. The nuclear family was neither economically nor emotionally self-sufficient. It was embedded in a thick web of social obligations that made the nuclear family, and the wishes of the people in it, subordinate to the larger family of which it was a part. Furthermore, the nuclear family traditionally was not the intensely emotional relationship that it characteristically is today. Infants were indulged to the extent that hard work and scarce resources permitted, but at what today would be regarded a very tender age, children were expected to begin to shoulder serious adult responsibilities.

This pattern of family functioning began to unravel with the beginnings of the Enlightenment and the Industrial Revolution. Aspirations for greater personal freedom blended with and reinforced changing economic conditions to produce a slow but accelerating movement toward more independent nuclear families that depended less on the expanded kin network. As a result, the expanded kin network slowly lost power. The change began among the more wealthy and secure. With the advance of industrialism and the rapid rise in standards of living, more and more couples broke away from the kin network. Emphasis shifted to the couple and their needs: the nuclear family began to become more self-sufficient in both economic and emotional ways. Husbands and wives were expected to be loving companions, not just helpmates. Children assumed a more prominent place in the family relations as attention shifted to themes of emotional maturity and personal development.

The entire character of family functioning has undergone change in the last several centuries. Changes that first swept Western societies are now also affecting non-Western cultures and the modernizing sectors of the developing world. The practice of child marriage, for example, is no longer officially sanctioned in India; the traditional extended family of

China has been almost completely dismantled in favor of nuclear families; all but the most remote villages show signs of these changes. As industry spreads, as markets grow, as wage labor replaces subsistence agriculture, the nuclear family begins to predominate, and ties to relatives weaken. Couples tend to become more autonomous, and family functions turn inward, focusing more and more on private concerns.

PATTERNS OF CONTEMPORARY FAMILY LIFE

Except during wartime and depressions, the marriage rate in the United States has remained consistently high; more than 90 percent of Americans marry at least once. In selecting a spouse, most people choose from groups of people similar to themselves, a tendency that social scientists term *homogamy*. Such factors as religion and ethnicity continue to play a role in mate selection, although their impact has been slowly diminishing.

After many decades of a declining age at first marriage, the trend to more youthful marriage has begun to reverse, and since 1955 the average age at first marriage has been increasing. By 1978 the average man and woman were 24.2 and 21.8 years of age at the time of their first marriage, closer to the averages for the 1890s than for the 1950s.

More and more men and women are postponing marriage in order to establish themselves in occupational pursuits or simply to enjoy the relative freedom that remaining single offers. The relaxation of norms governing premarital sex and the increased acceptance of cohabitation also reduce pressures that lead to early marriages. Expectations for married life are changing rapidly, and the resulting uncertainties may also contribute to the growing reluctance to rush into marriage. Similarly, as divorce rates rise, many people respond by being more cautious and more hesitant about marriage for fear of its dissolving in a painful divorce. These changing expectations for marriage and family life have led to three broad trends: greater equality in marital roles; declining size of families; and increasing acceptance of divorce.

Changing Roles. For many generations of American families, the customary role for wives was exclusively that of homemaker and mother, and the primary role of husbands was that of breadwinner. As recently as 1970 the majority of American men, according to public-opinion polls, were opposed to their wives' working outside the home. Economic pressures and a growing insistence on equal treatment for women, however, have led to rapid change. The majority of American wives now work outside the home. In fact, very near a majority of mothers with preschool-aged children work outside the home. Opinion polls now record that most husbands approve of their wives' working. Patterns in the performance of domestic duties have been much slower to change, but even here traditional roles are giving way to greater sharing and reduced sexual segregation of tasks.

Much of this greater flexibility has come about because parents now are choosing to have fewer children than did earlier generations of parents. The birthrate has been declining fairly steadily for some time now, to the point where the statistically average American family has slightly less than two children. If the present pattern prevails, large families, once a standard, will have become oddities.

Researchers also report that parents are less inclined to defer their own aspirations in favor of their children's. Some feel that this reflects a growth in the emphasis on personal autonomy and a heightened concern for personal growth and satisfaction. Such changes in attitudes toward family life have made families more fragile. This is reflected most obviously in the dramatic increase in divorce in recent years. If the present divorce rate persists, within another generation roughly half of all marriages will be ended by divorce. Nearly half of all children can now be expected to live some portion of their childhood years in a single-parent family.

While divorce is generally upsetting for all concerned and is often the source of serious social problems, it does not follow that the low divorce rates of the past meant that couples were somehow happier than they are now. The opposite might well have been the case. Some social scientists maintain that divorce may be the inevitable accompaniment to the increased emphasis on personal development and mutually rewarding intimacy within the nuclear family that marks contemporary U.S. culture.

The New Diversity. The family has been subject to enormous pressures as Western and non-Western cultures alike have changed from a largely rural to an increasingly urbanized, industrial orientation. The changes have altered aspirations, but they do not appear to have greatly diminished the desire for entering into intimate relationships. To be sure, the number of people who are choosing to live on their own has dramatically increased in the past decade, and the increasing age at first marriage may suggest a growing wariness of becoming committed to a long-term relationship. Nonetheless, the vast majority of people will eventually marry or in some other way enjoy another's affections on a sustained basis.

As the family continues to undergo change new forms of family living as well as alternatives to family living have emerged. Various communal experiments enjoyed a recent, but apparently short-lived, flurry of attention. Cohabitation has become more common, as has the decision to remain childless. In recent years the number of single-parent families has dramatically increased, reflecting not only rising divorce rates but also a growing tendency not to remarry. Each of these developments raises its own problems—problems rooted in moral concepts as well as in concerns for physical and emotional well-being.

In recognition of the simultaneous fragility and importance of the nuclear family many industrial nations have moved in the direction of developing comprehensive programs of support for the nuclear family. State-funded day-care centers and homemaker programs help to make it easier for both husband and wife to work. In some countries, notably Sweden, programs have been introduced that offer fathers paid paternity leaves in order that they may assist in caring for their newborn children. Many societies are also attempting to devise ways to help the elderly be less reliant on their children while not being brushed aside into impersonal and largely custodial institutions. The future of the family, whatever else it may hold, will almost certainly depend to a large extent on enlightened support from other institutions in the society.

JAN DIZARD

Bibliography: Apter, T., *Altered Loves: Mothers and Daughters during Adolescence* (1990); Leslie, G. R., and Korman, S. K., *The Family in Social Context* (1985); Louv, R., *Childhood's Future* (1991); Mintz, S., and Kellog, S., *Domestic Revolutions: A Social History of American Family Life* (1988); Rothman, D. J., and Rothman, S. M., eds., *The Family* (1979); Rubin, L., *Worlds of Pain* (1977; repr. 1990); Spiro, M. E., *Is the Family Universal?* (1991); Stacey, J., *Brave New Families* (1990).

See also: MARRIAGE; OLD AGE; WOMEN IN SOCIETY; YOUNG PEOPLE.

Family Compact

In Canadian history, Family Compact is the name given to a small oligarchy that ruled Upper Canada (Ontario) in the early 19th century. A group of wealthy men who dominated the governor's council and the legislature, the compact was conservative and pro-British in outlook. Its influence declined in the 1830s. In European history, the name is applied to three treaties (1733, 1743, 1761) between France and Spain, both ruled by branches of the Bourbon dynasty.

family planning: see BIRTH CONTROL; POPULATION.

famine

A famine is a shortage of food of sufficient duration to cause widespread privation and a rise in mortality. Famine has recurred since at least as early as the beginnings of agriculture, which laid the foundation for settled, civilized society. Very little is known, however, of the frequency and severity of famines in the past. History is replete with allusions—no fewer than ten famines are mentioned in the Bible—but the listing is incomplete and quantification sketchy. Even within this century the exact number of people who have perished during major famines is unknown.

Natural Causes of Famine. Shortfalls in food availabilities can be of both natural and human-caused origin. DROUGHT is the most common natural cause, although hurricanes and their accompanying floods can cause disaster in intensively cultivated coastal areas. Historically, drought has been most crippling in the more arid portions of densely populated monsoonal Asia, especially in China and India.

Periodic pest infestations and epidemics of plant and animal diseases have also been important natural causes of famine. Among the latter, the potato blight that struck Ireland in the 1840s is the best known. The potato is native to South America. Introduced into Ireland in the 18th century, it proved an ideal crop and by the end of the 1700s supplied some 80% of the calories in the peasant diet. The blight, caused by a fungus, appeared three times in the 1840s, each time destroying most of the crop. Relief efforts were only partially effective. Perhaps 1.5 million people died, and an equal number emigrated, reducing the population by about one-fourth. Today, with 4.9 million people, Ireland's population remains much lower than its 1840 level.

War-Induced Famines. Warfare from earliest times has been destructive to crops and animals, and blockades and sieges of cities have been responsible for countless famines, as they were for hundreds of thousands of deaths in Leningrad, Warsaw, the Netherlands, and Greece during World War II. War-induced famine resulted in 3–5 million deaths in China's Henan (Honan) province in 1943 and untold suffering in Cambodia (Kampuchea) in the late 1970s. Civil war, followed by uncontrolled looting of food by the forces of rival clans, led to starvation in Somalia in the early 1990s.

Control of the food supply can also be used by political leaders to force their will during peacetime. The Soviet famine of the early 1930s was the result of a ruthless drive to force a reluctant peasantry onto collective farms.

Few famines are general, in the sense that all people within a given area suffer equally. Rather, food scarcity causes a rise in prices, and the poor find their access to food cut off. The Bengal famine of 1943 had several causes: the conquest of Burma by the Japanese, depriving India of a traditional source of surpluses; the removal of rice stocks from rural Bengal to deny them to a potential invader; a series of hurricanes that did heavy damage to the main 1942 harvest; and unprecedented war-induced prosperity in Calcutta. These factors combined to bring about a sixfold increase in the price of rice. For the rural poor such prices were utterly beyond reach. Estimates of the total deaths range from 1.5 to 3 million.

Physiological Effects of Famine. The rise in the death rate caused by famine can result either from outright starvation or from diseases that afflict the undernourished (see NUTRITIONAL-DEFICIENCY DISEASES). Controlled studies have shown that, if caloric intake is reduced to 50 percent of normal, body weight will drop within a few months by about a quarter. Thereafter, a reduced level of activity can be maintained for many months. With prolongation or further drops in intake, however, additional weight losses will occur, and the incidence of diseases that traditionally accompany famine (typhus, cholera, and the plague have historically been the most closely linked) will rise. Although starvation will occur mainly among the poor, epidemics of disease can afflict all.

With restoration of normal supplies of food, recovery can be rapid, and most adults will show no lasting aftereffects. Young children, however, can be permanently impaired, both mentally and in the height and weight they will ultimately attain. KWASHIORKOR and MARASMUS are widely prevalent childhood diseases caused by insufficient protein intake.

Scientific and technical advances during the last 150 years have greatly enhanced the ability to grow more food and to move it quickly from abundant to deficient areas. Crop yields per unit area are now many times what they were only 50 years ago, and the potential for additional gains, particularly in the world's poorer regions, remains enormous. Extensive works of irrigation in many of these areas have reduced the impact of year-to-year variations in rainfall.

Because famines have always been localized, the effect of improved communications has been especially dramatic. The isolation of most communities formerly could turn a regional crop failure into a calamity. Today assistance can be speedily mounted from substantial distances. That no serious famines occurred in India between 1899–1901 and 1943 is attributable to the construction of that country's rail network; that none occurred in the mid-1960s following the successive crop failure caused by the failure of two monsoons was due to the ability of the United States, Canada, and Australia to rush almost 20 million tons of wheat to India's relief.

Obstacles to Relief Efforts. Despite the current abundance of grains and other foods that can be airlifted to countries suffering from famine, political conditions within the starving nations may often frustrate relief efforts. The 1984–85 Ethiopian famine provides examples of many of the problems associated with relief. The Ethiopian government denied the existence of the famine for many months. When it finally acknowledged the need for help, it seized and held shipments destined for the north of the country because it was fighting against a separatist movement there. Much of the food was stolen and sold by government officials; much of the rest spoiled before it could reach starving populations. Transport arrangements often broke down. Only when famine victims fled to refugee camps was it possible to feed them adequately.

International organizations have discussed various plans for dealing with famine crises when they occur. A fundamental necessity for the prevention of famine would be the establishment of a system of world food reserves. No such system as yet exists. It was fortunate for India that the 1965–67 crisis coincided with large surpluses among the world's major food exporters. Had similar failures occurred in the early 1970s, a time of tight supplies, the world would have been hard-pressed to come to India's aid.

The breakthroughs that have permitted the great increases in agricultural productivity have focused on a small number of crops—no more than 15 plants account for three-quarters of the plant calories now consumed—and in breeding for yield, genetic variation has suffered. Unless steps are taken to maintain the pool of natural germ plasm, dangerous new diseases and pests could emerge.   THOMAS T. POLEMAN

Bibliography: Dreze, J., and Sen, A., eds., *The Political Economy of Hunger* (1991); Glanz, M. H., ed., *Drought and Hunger in Africa* (1987); Heiden, D., *Dust to Dust: A Doctor's View of Famine in Africa* (1992); Lappé, F. M., and Collins, J., *World Hunger: 12 Myths* (1986); Ravallion, M., *Markets and Famines* (1990); Sen, A., *Poverty and Famine* (1981); Walter, J., and Schofield, R., eds., *Famine, Disease, and the Social Order in Early Modern Society* (1986; repr. 1991).

MAJOR FAMINES SINCE WORLD WAR I

Year	Place	Cause
1928–29	Northwest China	Drought; more than 3 million deaths
1932–34	Union of Soviet Socialist Republics	Forced collectivization; up to 5 million deaths
1941–43	Greece	War; 200,000–400,000 deaths
1943	Honan, China	War, drought; 3–5 million deaths
1943–44	Bengal, India	War; 1.5-3 million deaths
1944–45	German-occupied Europe; Japanese-occupied Southeast Asia	War
1967–70	Nigeria (Biafra)	Civil war; 2–3 million deaths
1968–74	Sahelian zone of sub-Saharan Africa	Drought; number of deaths unknown
Late 1970s	Kampuchea	War; number of deaths unknown
1979–81	Uganda	Civil war, drought; more than 250,000 deaths
1983–	Sahelian zone and Horn of Africa	Drought and war; number of deaths unknown

fan

Fans are devices for agitating the air and have been in use since prehistoric times. The earliest fans were made of

Hand-painted fans are often exemplars of the artistic style of their period. This 18th-century French brisé fan, set in an intricately carved ivory frame, displays a single pastoral scene on one side and separate paintings on classical themes on its paneled side.

palmetto leaf, bound grasses, or feathers fixed to a wood or bone handle. They were used to cool the face, fan fires, and keep flies away during religious rituals or other ceremonies.

Representations of fans can be found in the art of many ancient peoples, and legends in China trace the fan's origins back to perhaps the 2d millennium BC. Chinese fans were introduced into Japan in the 6th century AD, and the folding fan is a 7th-century Japanese invention—a pleated, decorated leaf of paper mounted on a radiating framework of thin sticks.

The popularity of folding fans spread rapidly to China; they were introduced into Europe in the 14th century. Later, fan parts were often imported from China and assembled in Europe. The leaves were painted with mythological, biblical, classical, or historical motifs.

The popularity of the fan reached its zenith in Europe during the 17th and 18th centuries, and France became the center of fan manufacture. Leaves were now made of vellum, fabric, and lace as well as paper; designs were often printed and hand colored or embroidered; and mother-of-pearl sticks began to be used frequently. Folding fans without leaves were called "brisé" fans. Their thin sticks of ivory, shell, or wood were held in place by ribbons or strings. During this period the fan became a necessary component of dress and a means of discreet flirtation. Books were written to teach the "language of the fan." Variations such as lorgnette fans with mounted eyeglasses and domino fans with inset eyeholes became popular. Mass production in the 19th century popularized the cockade fan, which opened to reveal a circular leaf, and purse-size fans with retractable sticks.

With the 20th-century development of large floor or ceiling-mounted electric fans—some of them capable of cooling entire rooms—and later of AIR CONDITIONING, hand-held fans lost their function as cooling devices and gradually fell out of fashion.   MATTHEW X. KIERNAN

Bibliography: Armstrong, N., *The Book of Fans* (1979); Bennett, A. G., *Unfolding Beauty* (1988); Green, B. D., *A Collector's Guide to Fans through the Ages* (1979); Mayor, S., *The Collector's Guide to Fans* (1990).

Fan K'uan   (Fan Kuan)   [fahn kwahn]

Fan K'uan, fl. late 10th–early 11th century, was a master of Chinese landscape painting during the Northern Sung dynasty (960–1126). His monumental hanging scroll entitled *Traveling among the Streams and Mountains* (National Palace Museum, Taiwan) is among the first surviving Chinese masterpieces.

fan-tan   [fan'-dan]

Fan-tan, also known as sevens, parliament, or card dominoes, is a card game for two to eight players. All 52 cards in a standard deck are dealt and each player antes one chip. The player to the dealer's left must place a seven faceup in the center of the table or pass and pay a one-chip penalty. The next player tries to build a sequence in the suit played or lay down another seven. Sequences are built downward to the ace or upward to the king. The first to play out his or her hand wins. *Fan-tan* is also the name of a Chinese gambling game that uses beans for counters.

Bibliography: Ainslie, Tom, *Ainslie's Complete Hoyle* (1975; repr. 1979).

fandango   [fan-dang'-goh]

Possibly the oldest existing Spanish dance, dating from the 7th century, the fandango is a dance of courtship or of friendly competition in brisk $6/8$ or $3/4$ time. Without touching and with arms held high, two dancers flirt as they stamp their feet and hop in elaborate patterns as counterpoint to the rhythm of castanets and guitar. Sudden pauses punctuate the intricate footwork, which increases in tempo as the dancers challenge one another to greater virtuosic displays.   BARBARA NEWMAN

Bibliography: Sachs, Curt, *A World History of the Dance* (1937).

Faneuil Hall   [fan'-yul]

Faneuil Hall was built as a market and meeting hall and given (1742) to the city of Boston by Peter Faneuil, a merchant. It became famous as the "Cradle of Liberty" because it was the site of public protests against British policies before the American Revolution. During the 19th century Wendell Phillips and Daniel Webster addressed antislavery meetings held in the hall. The building was restored after a fire in 1761 by the architect Charles BULFINCH and enlarged in 1805. Designated a national historical landmark in 1967, Faneuil Hall, undergoing renovations in the early 1990s, is still in use as a marketplace and for forums.

Bibliography: Freely, John, *Boston and Cambridge* (1984).

Fanfani, Amintore   [fahn-fah'-nee, ah-meen-toh'-ray]

Amintore Fanfani, b. Feb. 6, 1908, has five times been premier of Italy. Fanfani gained his doctorate in political economy in 1932 and has been a teacher and writer in the field of eco-

Amintore Fanfani, a leader of the Italian Christian Democratic party, was a dominant political figure in Italy after World War II. Between 1954 and 1963, Fanfani served four terms as premier and later distinguished himself both as foreign minister and as president of the Italian senate before becoming premier for a fifth time (1982–83).

nomic history. In 1946 he was elected to the Constituent Assembly as a Christian Democrat. He served in various ministerial posts from 1947 to 1953. He was premier in 1954, 1958–59, 1960–62, and 1962–63, minister of foreign affairs in 1965 and 1966–68, president of the Senate in 1968–73 and 1976–82, premier again in 1982–83, and president of the Senate again in 1985. He has been a life senator since 1972.

Fang

The Fang are a people of west central Africa who live principally in the rain forest of Gabon and Cameroon and speak a Bantu language of the Benue-Niger subfamily of Niger-Congo stock. A subdivision of the Pahouin peoples, they number more than 300,000.

Fang live in compact villages and are led by headmen with little authority. They are subsistence farmers who grow primarily root crops and bananas. The Fang also keep domestic animals and supplement their farming with hunting and fishing. Recently some have become settled farmers and grow cacao for export. Because many young men have become migratory workers in the timber industry, the traditional social cohesion of the Fang has tended to break down.

Descent, inheritance, and residence after marriage are traced through the paternal line. Marriage is polygamous and is arranged by payment of bride price or by sister exchange. Fang have several types of secret societies that play an important role in social and religious rituals.

Traditionally the Fang were a warring people, and their exploits and conquests are kept alive in legend. They are known for their poetry, their spectacular dancing, and for various types of wood carving, such as drums, stools, masks, and especially, their blackened *bieri*, or reliquary figures.

Bibliography: Balandier, G., *The Sociology of Black Africa: Social Dynamics in Central Africa*, trans. by D. Garman (1970); Delange, J., *The Art and Peoples of Black Africa*, trans. by C. F. Jopling (1974); July, R. W., *A History of the African People*, 4th ed. (1980).

Fangio, Juan Manuel   [fahn'-hee-oh]

Juan Manuel Fangio, b. June 24, 1911, is an Argentine automobile racer who won the world driving championship five times in the 1950s. Fangio drove mostly American-built cars and was little known until 1948, when he went to Europe to race. Driving Alfa Romeos, he finished second (1950) and first (1951) in the world driving championship. Fangio won again (1954) in a Maserati, in a Mercedes (1955), in a Ferrari (1956), and in a Maserati (1957). He last raced in 1958, bringing to an end the driving career of a basically shy man who was one of auto racing's most aggressive performers.

Bibliography: Borgeson, Griffith, *Grand Prix Championship Courses and Drivers* (1968).

Fanny Hill, or The Memoirs of a Woman of Pleasure

John Cleland's *Fanny Hill, or The Memoirs of a Woman of Pleasure* (1748–49) is a classic erotic novel. Although the author attempted to avoid vulgarity by using poetic diction and euphemisms, the novel was suppressed shortly after its publication because of its frankly sexual scenes.

The story of a prostitute, *Fanny Hill* parodies the novels of the time, particularly Daniel Defoe's *Moll Flanders* (1722).
                                                          JANE COLVILLE BETTS

Fanon, Frantz   [fah-nohn', frahnts]

Frantz Omar Fanon, b. 1925, d. Dec. 6, 1961, a West-Indian–born psychiatrist, became involved in the Algerian nationalist movement and wrote several seminal works on racism and colonial liberation. Born on Martinique, he was educated there and in France. After taking a psychiatric post in an Algerian hospital in 1953, Fanon joined (1954) the liberation movement and became (1957) editor of its newspaper. In 1960 he was appointed ambassador to Ghana by the rebel Algerian government.

Fanon's first book, *Black Skin, White Masks* (1952; Eng. trans., 1967), was a study of the psychology of racism and colonial domination. Just before his death from leukemia he published *The Wretched of the Earth* (1961; Eng. trans., 1968), in which he called for revolutions to liberate Third World peoples from dehumanizing colonialism. This work became a classic of modern revolutionary theory.

Bibliography: McCulloch, J., *Black Soul White Artifact* (1983); Onwuanibe, Richard C., *A Critique of Revolutionary Humanism* (1983); Perinbam, B. Marie, *Holy Virtue* (1982).

fantasy   (literature)

Fantasy is the treatment of events that the rational mind considers impossible or highly unlikely. As a so-called literary genre, however, it is hard to define. Writings since ancient times have incorporated elements of myth and legend for purposes ranging from satire and allegory to simple storytelling. The 18th-century movement known as the Enlightenment brought critical attention to bear on the uses of the probable and the possible in fiction. In the early 19th century the English writer Samuel Taylor Coleridge formulated the influential view that "fancy, or fantasy," is a poorer echo of the higher workings of the "imagination." This view entered into later speculations on fantasy writing and is still reflected in the distinction sometimes—and sometimes unfairly—made between "high" and "low" fantasy, the former taken to include works of literary skill and psychological depth, and the latter generally indicating the so-called "sword and sorcery" books that make up the bulk of titles in the fantasy section of bookstores.

Modern fantasy and its subgenre, SCIENCE FICTION, developed from the GOTHIC ROMANCES of the later 18th century. (Science fiction is now usually concerned with creating alternative realities, whereas fantasy aims more toward the suspension of disbelief in the unreal.) Equally important were such 19th-century figures as Lewis CARROLL and George MACDONALD, who exemplified the urge of many writers to explore the imagination along routes alternative to those followed in realistic writing. The difficulty in considering fantasy as a distinct field in literature is seen in the fact that writers as disparate as Jorge Luis BORGES, Ray BRADBURY, James Branch CABELL, Italo CALVINO, Lord DUNSANY, Ursula LE GUIN, C. S. LEWIS, H. P. LOVECRAFT, J. R. R. TOLKIEN, and Charles WILLIAMS have all been called fantasists.

Bibliography: Brooke-Rose, C., *A Rhetoric of the Unreal* (1983); Hunter, L., *Modern Allegory and Fantasy* (1989); Manlove, C. N., *The Impulse of Fantasy Literature* (1983); Moorcock, M., *Wizardry and Wild Romance* (1988); Olson, L., *Eclipse of Uncertainty* (1987).

fantasy   (psychology)

Fantasy is a form of consciousness that lies between ordinary thought processes and an uncontrolled state of awareness. The mind is released from the strictures of objective reality, and the imagination is allowed to roam freely—although usually guided by more or less unconscious urges, concerns, and memories. Such distinctions take time to develop; in children, it is often hard to distinguish between fantasy and other modes of thought. Fantasy is also apparent in the PLAY activities that are part of normal growth. Fantasizing is perhaps most familiar in the form of daydreams, often of a wish-fulfilling nature. Although sometimes called fantasies, night dreams are a distinct phenomenon occurring in a different physiological state (see DREAMS AND DREAMING). Fantasy activity is frequent in creative thought and also helps in rehearsing future actions, but excessive fantasizing is considered a sign of maladjusted personality. Various PSYCHOSES are characterized by an inability to distinguish fantasy from reality, and drug-disoriented persons may similarly experience HALLUCINATIONS. Fantasies are a common object of psychological studies, and personality tests often use fantasizing as a technique. (See also HYPNOTISM.)

Bibliography: Klinger, Eric, *Daydreaming* (1990); Watkins, May, *Waking Dreams*, 3d ed. (1984).

Fanti   [fan'-tee]

The Fanti, or Fante, are an Akan-speaking people of the coastal area of Ghana. Numbering about 500,000, they live in compact villages where they grow yams and other vegetables and keep livestock. Descent and inheritance are traced through the mother's line, but the soul is thought to come from the father.

Traditionally the Fanti formed a confederation of small military states that competed with the ASHANTI kingdom to the north in the trade of gold, slaves, and European imports. In this rivalry they were allied with the British, whereas the Ashanti allied themselves with the Dutch. After the British broke the strong Fanti confederation, the Fanti became (1874) part of the British Gold Coast colony; together with the British, they defeated the Ashanti.

Each of the former Fanti states was ruled by a combination of a paramount chief, divisional chiefs, and subchiefs. Patrilineal, military companies played an important role in the political, social, and religious life of the states.

Traditional Fanti religious beliefs are concerned with a creator god, a host of lesser deities served through priests, and ancestral spirits. Art forms include a rich body of folklore, wood carvings, and objects cast in bronze through the lost-wax process.   PHOEBE MILLER

Fantin-Latour, Henri   [fahn-tan'-lah-toor']

Henri Fantin-Latour, b. Jan. 14, 1836, d. Aug. 25, 1904, was a French painter best known for his flower studies executed in a meticulous "Dutch" manner. His works include still lifes, romantic figures and portrait groups. Believing color to be analogous to sound, Fantin-Latour painted compositions inspired by the music of Hector Berlioz, Robert Schumann, and Richard Wagner. Although his work subsequently appeared regularly at the Paris Salon, he was rejected in 1859 and exhibited at the Salon des Refusés in 1863 with other artists frequently spurned by the Salon jury. Fantin-Latour was friendly with most of the advanced artists of the day, including Édouard Manet and James McNeill Whistler. Though he never exhibited with the impressionists, he painted them. In his best-known group portrait, *Studio in the Batignolles Quarter* (1870; Louvre, Paris), Frédéric Bazille, Claude Monet, and Pierre Auguste Renoir are grouped around Manet.   PEARL GORDON

Bibliography: Hediard, G., *Fantin-Latour's Lithographs* (1986); Layton, Gustave, *The Dreamy, Romantic and Symbolic Art by Fantin-Latour* (1983); Verrier, Michelle, *Fantin-Latour* (1978).

Far East

The term *Far East*, referring to eastern Asia, was first used by Western Europeans in the early 17th century, during the Age of Exploration. It refers primarily to China, Japan, Korea, Mongolia, and eastern Siberia but sometimes includes the countries of the Indochinese and Malay peninsulas (Burma, Kampuchea, Laos, Malaysia, Singapore, Vietnam, and Thailand) and the entire Malay Archipelago, comprising Indonesia and the Philippines. The designation is not exact, and the western boundaries, between Central and South Asia and the Far East, are vague.

Far from the Madding Crowd

Far from the Madding Crowd (1874), an early novel by Thomas HARDY in which he first used the ancient term *Wessex* to describe the Dorset of his youth, represents the author's attempt to create a setting more atmospheric than geographic. In the novel, Hardy deals with a favorite theme: the opposition between selfless and selfish love. Selfless love is here embodied in the patience and natural goodness shown by the bailiff Gabriel Oak, and selfish love, illustrated by Farmer Boldwood and the soldier-bounder Sergeant Troy. Bathsheba Everdene, the object of the three suitors' attentions and the unwitting cause of a series of Hardyesque mishaps, finally rewards the steadfastness of Gabriel.

Bibliography: Kramer, D., *Critical Essays on Thomas Hardy* (1990).

Farabi, al-   [fah-rah'-bee, ahl]

Al-Farabi, c.870–c.950, was the greatest philosopher of Islam before Avicenna. He wrote commentaries on a number of Aristotelian texts and composed many original treatises on psychology, mathematics, and the occult sciences. In both his commentaries and original compositions, al-Farabi attempted to demonstrate the unity of Plato and Aristotle and to prove the primacy of philosophy. He maintained that, in contrast to philosophy, religion represents the truth in a symbolic form for nonphilosophers. In all his writings, which reveal the influence of a mystical NEOPLATONISM, he attempted to reconcile Islam with philosophy.   TAMARA GREEN

Bibliography: Rescher, Nicholas, *Al-Farabi: An Annotated Bibliography* (1962).

farad   [fair'-uhd]

The farad is the unit of CAPACITANCE, named for Michael Faraday. A CAPACITOR has a capacitance of 1 farad (1F) if there is a potential difference of 1 volt between its plates when it is charged to 1 coulomb of electricity on each plate. Thus, 1 farad is 1 coulomb/volt. The farad is a relatively large amount of capacitance, and most of the capacitors used in electronics have capacitances measured in microfarads (μF) or micromicrofarads ($\mu\mu$F).

Faraday, Michael   [fair'-uh-day]

The English chemist and physicist Michael Faraday, b. Sept. 22, 1791, d. Aug. 25, 1867, is known for his pioneering experiments in electricity and magnetism. Many consider him the greatest experimentalist who ever lived. Several concepts that he derived directly from experiments, such as lines of magnetic force, have become common ideas in modern physics.

Faraday was born at Newington, Surrey, near London. He received little more than a primary education, and at the age of 14 he was apprenticed to a bookbinder. There he became interested in the physical and chemical works of the time. After hearing a lecture by the famous chemist Humphry DAVY, he sent Davy the notes he had made of his lectures. As a result Faraday was appointed, at the age of 21, assistant to Davy in the laboratory of the Royal Institution in London.

During the initial years of his scientific work, Faraday occupied himself mainly with chemical problems. He discovered two new chlorides of carbon and succeeded in liquefying chlorine and other gases. He isolated benzene in 1825, the year in which he was appointed director of the laboratory.

Michael Faraday, whose experiments in electrical chemistry and magnetism led to his discovery (1831) of electromagnetic induction, laid the groundwork for the developing field of electromagnetism. Largely self-educated, Faraday was offered the presidency of the Royal Society in recognition of his achievements.

Davy, who had the greatest influence on Faraday's thinking, had shown in 1807 that the metals sodium and potassium can be precipitated from their compounds by an electric current, a process known as ELECTROLYSIS. Faraday's vigorous pursuit of these experiments led in 1834 to what became known as Faraday's laws of electrolysis (see ELECTROCHEMISTRY).

Faraday's research into electricity and electrolysis was guided by the belief that electricity is only one of the many manifestations of the unified forces of nature, which included heat, light, magnetism, and chemical affinity. Although this idea was erroneous, it led him into the field of electromagnetism (see MAGNETISM), which was still in its infancy. In 1785, Charles Coulomb had been the first to demonstrate the manner in which electric charges repel one another, and it was not until 1820 that Hans Christian OERSTED and André Marie AMPÈRE discovered that an electric current produces a magnetic field. Faraday's ideas about conservation of energy led him to believe that since an electric current could cause a magnetic field, a magnetic field should be able to produce an electric current. He demonstrated this principle of INDUCTION in 1831. Faraday expressed the electric current induced in the wire in terms of the number of lines of force that are cut by the wire. The principle of induction was a landmark in applied science, for it made possible the dynamo, or GENERATOR, which produces electricity by mechanical means.

Faraday's introduction of the concept of lines of force was rejected by most of the mathematical physicists of Europe, since they assumed that electric charges attract and repel one another, by action at a distance, making such lines unnecessary. Faraday had demonstrated the phenomenon of electromagnetism in a series of experiments, however. This experimental necessity probably led the physicist James Clerk MAXWELL to accept the concept of lines of force and put Faraday's ideas into mathematical form, thus giving birth to modern field theory. Faraday's discovery (1845) that an intense magnetic field can rotate the plane of polarized light is known today as the Faraday effect. The phenomenon has been used to elucidate molecular structure and has yielded information about galactic magnetic fields.

Faraday described his numerous experiments in electricity and electromagnetism in three volumes entitled *Experimental Researches in Electricity* (1839, 1844, 1855); his chemical work was chronicled in *Experimental Researches in Chemistry and Physics* (1858). Faraday ceased research work in 1855 because of declining mental powers, but he continued as a lecturer until 1861. A series of six children's lectures, published in 1860 as *The Chemical History of a Candle,* has become a classic of science literature.   STEVEN J. DICK

Bibliography: Gooding, David, and James, F. A., eds., *Faraday Rediscovered* (1986); Pearce, L., *Michael Faraday* (1987); Ronan, Colin, *Faraday and Electricity* (1968).

farce

Farce is a dramatic form that derives much of its comic appeal from broad physical humor, improbable situations, and exaggerated characters. Its name, from the Latin *farcire* (''to stuff''), suggests its often chaotic nature. Unlike more refined and rational COMEDY, farce delights in the theatrical and the fantastic. The typical farce makes us laugh at situations that in real life would cause extreme pain or embarrassment. Thus, physical abuse, sexual impropriety, exposure, and even death are staples of farce.

The many forms of farce can be grouped into two broad categories. The first, characterized by a loose, improvisational structure, is dominated by the presence of clowns (often masked), who usually retain the same name or distinctive appearance and behavior in every play in which they appear. Italian COMMEDIA DELL'ARTE takes this form, as, in modern times, do the films of Charlie CHAPLIN and the MARX BROTHERS. Plays of the second category are more regular in structure, with carefully controlled plots that often seem to reduce the characters to the status of puppets. Shakespeare's *Comedy of Errors* and the bedroom farces of Georges FEYDEAU are examples of this type.

Although elements of farce can be found in the comedies of ARISTOPHANES and PLAUTUS, farce developed as a distinct form both in antiquity and in the Middle Ages. French medieval farces were short and simple, mere interludes between the religious dramas with which they appeared. A more complex form, the commedia dell'arte, developed in Italy during the Renaissance; its stock characters were freely borrowed by MOLIÈRE. Farce has never ceased to be popular, but 19th-century France was especially favorable to the genre. Eugène LABICHE and Feydeau developed farce into a complex art of involved plots and absurd situations. In the 20th century, farce has been given a serious turn by such writers for the THEATER OF THE ABSURD as Eugène IONESCO and Harold PINTER.

STUART E. BAKER

Bibliography: Bermel, A., *Farce: A History* (1990).

Farel, Guillaume   [fah-rel', gee-yohm']

Guillaume Farel, b. 1489, d. Sept. 13, 1565, was a French reformer and associate of John CALVIN. A leader of the Protestant REFORMATION in French-speaking Switzerland, Farel came to his Protestant convictions by way of his studies in biblical humanism at the University of Paris. Banished from France in 1523 for his Protestant leanings, Farel formed (1526) a traveling band of Protestants who worked for reform in several Swiss provinces. He participated in the disputation that turned (1528) Bern to the Reformation and led (1530) the Reform in Neuchâtel. His greatest triumph came in 1535 when, with his assistant Pierre Viret, he brought Geneva into the Reformed camp. Farel is best known, however, for convincing John Calvin to come to Geneva as minister and teacher in 1536. Farel and Calvin worked together until 1538, when they were expelled from Geneva. Calvin eventually returned, but Farel settled in Neuchâtel.

MARK A. NOLL

Farewell, My Lovely

Farewell, My Lovely (1940), the second Raymond CHANDLER novel featuring private detective Philip Marlowe, is considered an example of mystery writing at its best. Chandler's portrayal here of the seedier aspects of the Los Angeles and southern California milieu is particularly effective. Marlowe sets out to find a missing woman; he is also hired as bodyguard for a man who is trying to recover a stolen necklace. The two cases are ultimately revealed to be connected, and in unraveling them, Marlowe exposes the corruption of an entire town. Marlowe is a prototype of the hard-boiled detective, since made familiar in countless movies and television series.

CHARLOTTE D. SOLOMON

Farewell to Arms, A

A Farewell to Arms (1929), Ernest HEMINGWAY's third novel, helped popularize the author's spare, deceptively simple prose. Set on the Italian front during the disastrous years 1915–17, *A Farewell to Arms* relates the story of Lt. Frederic Henry, a U.S. ambulance driver, and his love for Catherine Barkley, a British nurse, who has helped him recuperate from leg wounds. Following the Italian retreat from Caporetto, during which Henry barely escapes execution for desertion, they flee to Switzerland. Their Swiss idyll terminates tragically, however, when Catherine dies in childbirth. Hemingway drew partly on personal experience for the brilliantly recreated war sequences, and the amatory episodes, though much fictionalized, recall his abortive love for Agnes von Kurowsky, his American nurse in Milan. The novel was filmed in 1932 and again in 1958.

CARLOS BAKER

Bibliography: Baker, Carlos, *Hemingway: The Writer as Artist*, 4th ed. (1973); Bloom, Harold, ed., *Ernest Hemingway's A Farewell to Arms* (1987); Donaldson, Scott, ed., *New Essays on A Farewell to Arms* (1991); Gellens, Jay, ed., *Twentieth Century Interpretations of "A Farewell to Arms"* (1970); Reynolds, Michael S., *Hemingway's First War* (1976).

Fargo   [fahr'-goh]

Fargo is the seat of Cass County, North Dakota, and the state's largest city. It is located on the west bank of the Red River of the North, which separates North Dakota from Minnesota. The city (1990 pop., 74,111) is a trade and distribution center for the wheat and livestock produced in the surrounding region. Local industries manufacture farm machinery, construction materials, and fertilizer. Legalized casino gambling also has made Fargo a regional tourist center. North Dakota State University (1890) is there.

Fargo was established in 1871 at the point where the Northern Pacific Railway crossed the Red River. First called Centralia, the name was changed in 1872 to honor William George Fargo, founder of Wells, Fargo and Company and one of the railroad's directors. Low railroad freight rates and the discovery of the land's immense wheat-producing potential attracted settlers.

Fargo, William George

William George Fargo, b. Pompey, N.J., May 20, 1818, d. Aug. 3, 1881, was an American leader in long-distance express services. He began carrying mail over a 48-km (30-mi) route when he was 13 years old. After working at a number of jobs, he formed (1844) a partnership, Wells and Company, to operate an express service between Buffalo, N.Y., and Chicago. He helped organize the American Express Company (1850) and WELLS, FARGO AND COMPANY (1852) to provide express service between the East Coast and California. The latter company soon dominated the express business west of the Mississippi. From 1862 to 1866, Fargo was mayor of Buffalo. In the 1870s he was president both of Wells, Fargo and Company and of American Express.

Bibliography: Beebe, Lucius, and Clegg, Charles, *U.S. West: The Saga of Wells Fargo* (1949).

Fargue, Léon Paul   [fahrg]

Léon Paul Fargue, b. Mar. 4, 1876, d. Nov. 27, 1947, called the "poet of Paris," went through symbolist, surrealist, and cubist phases in his poetry, which includes *Tancrède* (1911), *Poèmes* (1912), and *Sous la Lampe* (Under the Lamp, 1929). *Le Piéton de Paris* (A Wanderer in Paris, 1939) is his memoir of Paris literary life in the pre–World War I era.

Farinelli   [fah-ree-nel'-lee]

Farinelli was the professional name of Carlo Broschi, b. Andria, Italy, Jan. 24, 1705, d. Bologna, July 15, 1782, the most famous CASTRATO singer of the 18th century. He studied singing with Nicola Antonio Porpora in Naples and then enjoyed a brilliant operatic career in Italy, Austria, and England. In 1737 he went to Spain, where his singing so captivated Philip V, and later Ferdinand VI, that he gained great political power there. By converting the Spaniards to Italian opera, Farinelli retarded the development of native Spanish music for nearly a quarter of a century. In 1759, Charles III ordered Farinelli to leave Spain, and the singer retired to a villa near Bologna.

WILLIAM HAYS

Bibliography: Hamilton, Mary Neal, *Music in Eighteenth-Century Spain* (1937; repr. 1971); Heriot, Angus, *The Castrati in Opera* (1956; repr. 1974); Toye, Francis, *Italian Opera* (1952; repr. 1988).

Farley, James A.

James Aloysius Farley, b. Rockland County, N.Y., May 30, 1888, d. June 9, 1976, was a New York businessman who managed Franklin D. Roosevelt's campaigns for the presidency in 1932 and 1936. Farley served as chairman of the Democratic National Committee (1932–40) and postmaster general (1933–40), but he broke with Roosevelt in 1940 when the latter decided to run for a third term.

Farm Bureau: see AMERICAN FARM BUREAU FEDERATION.

Farm Credit Administration

The Farm Credit Administration (FCA) is an independent agency of the U.S. government that was established under the

Farm Credit Act of 1933. It regulates, coordinates, and examines the institutions comprising the Farm Credit System, a nationwide system of banks and associations that exists to make loans to farmers, ranchers, and agricultural cooperatives. Initially capitalized by the U.S. government, these institutions are now owned by their borrowers.

In 1985, an economically depressed year for U.S. farmers, the system held about one-third of the nation's $210 billion farm debt. Congress that year passed a farm credit bill that established a new unit, the Farm Credit System Capital Corp., to assume responsibility for bad loans as well as for transferring funds from healthier districts to weaker ones. The same legislation authorized the U.S. Treasury to provide a line of credit for the system, and it also strengthened the regulatory powers of the Farm Credit Administration over the system. The structure of the system—which had initially been composed of land banks, credit banks, and banks for cooperatives in each of the 12 Farm Credit districts—has been changed as well. Since 1988, however, the system has shown net gains. In 1990 it produced profits of $608 million.

Bibliography: Cochrane, W. W., *The Development of American Agriculture* (1977); Nelson, Aaron G., et al., *Agricultural Finance: Principles and Practice of Farm Credit,* 8th rev. ed. (1988).

See also: AGRICULTURAL ECONOMICS.

farm machinery: see COMBINE; FARMS AND FARMING; HARROW; HARVESTER; PLOW; REAPER; TRACTOR.

Farmer, Fannie

Fannie Merritt Farmer, an American author and teacher, wrote (1896) the popular Boston Cooking School Cook Book and in 1902 founded a cooking school called Miss Farmer's School of Cookery. Her teaching methods and recipes, intended to familiarize unskilled cooks with kitchen procedures, emphasized the use of standard measurements.

The American culinary expert Fannie Merritt Farmer, b. Boston, Mar. 23, 1857, d. Jan. 15, 1915, is best known as the author of *The Boston Cooking School Cook Book,* published in 1896 and considered by many the most useful cookbook ever written. Updated for the modern kitchen, and called *The Fannie Farmer Cookbook,* it remained in print for many years. Farmer began teaching herself to cook after she suffered a paralytic stroke that forced her to discontinue high school. She enrolled in the Boston Cooking School, and in 1891, two years after graduating, she was named director. Her own school, Miss Farmer's School of Cookery, opened in 1902.

As a teacher and writer, Farmer emphasized the actual practice of cooking. She was among the first to indicate precise measurements in recipes, using standardized measuring implements such as the teaspoon and cup. Her careful descriptions of basic cooking processes enabled even a novice cook to follow her recipes.

Bibliography: *The Original Boston Cooking-School Cook Book,* a facsimile of the first edition of the *Boston Cooking-School Cook Book* (1988).

Farmer, Moses

Moses Gerrish Farmer, b. Boscawen, N.H., Feb. 9, 1820, d. May 25, 1893, was a versatile American inventor who conducted pioneer experiments with electricity and telegraphy. He helped build early telegraph lines in Massachusetts, installed the first electric fire alarm system in Boston, discovered the principle of MULTIPLEXING, and developed a process for ELECTROPLATING aluminum.

In 1858–59, anticipating Thomas EDISON by 20 years, Farmer produced electric lamps. He lighted his own house and in 1868 fitted out a house in Cambridge, Mass., with 40 electric lamps and his own patented generator.

Farmer-Labor party

The Farmer-Labor party was a Minnesota political party (1918–44) founded to represent the interests of farmers and urban laborers. An offshoot of the NONPARTISAN LEAGUE, the party first placed candidates on the ballot in 1918 and subsequently elected two U.S. senators and three U.S. representatives as well as a number of state and local officials. In 1930 its candidate, Floyd B. Olson, was elected to the first of three terms as governor. The party supported the NEW DEAL policies of President Franklin D. Roosevelt, and in 1944 it merged with Minnesota's Democratic party to form the Democratic-Farmer Labor party.

The Minnesota party had little connection with the National Farmer-Labor party, formed as the National Labor party in 1919. The latter fielded a number of state and national candidates, including its 1920 presidential candidate, Parley P. Christensen. Its platform called for widespread public ownership of the nation's resources, but its strength was largely limited to such states as Montana, South Dakota, and Washington. A lack of finances and poor organization contributed to its eclipse during the 1920s.

Bibliography: Mitau, G. Theodore, *Politics in Minnesota,* 2d rev. ed. (1970); Nye, Russel B., *Midwestern Progressive Politics: A Historical Study of Its Origins and Development, 1870–1958,* rev. ed. (1959).

farms and farming

The production of food and fiber from the soil, farming is a slow biological process involving soil cultivation, planting, harvesting, and the disposition of the harvest. Closely related to farming are herding, ranching, the cultivation of orchards, tree farming, and FISH FARMING, or aquaculture.

Throughout history, farming has been the occupation of nine-tenths or more of humankind. Painfully slow progress in farming techniques eventually provided surpluses beyond the needs of the producers, freeing many for the nonfarming pursuits that eventually created societies based on technology rather than food production. The farmer's surplus, then, is fundamental to civilization. Even today, however, more than half the world's population of about five billion people are still engaged in farming.

Farming can be carried on only where climate and soil are favorable. It is necessarily limited to areas of productive soils, tillable topography, adequate moisture from precipitation or irrigation, and a growing season long enough for plant germination and maturation. There are a few especially advantaged areas that have the natural resources to build an extensive system of highly productive farms. Taken overall, the United States is one such area.

Within the natural environmental conditions necessary for farming there are wide variations that determine the crops produced, the techniques employed, and the type of farm organization. In addition, regional history, tradition, folk wisdom, level of knowledge, and incentive for gain have multiplied the differences among farming practices from place to place and time to time. Today, however, diminishing isolation has resulted in the diffusion and exchange of plants, animals, tools, and knowledge, and—at least where economic and agricultural conditions are similar—a growing similarity of agricultural practices. Nevertheless, crop belts like the corn-hog belt in the midwestern United States, special niches

(Above) *American farms in moderately hilly areas, such as those in Pennsylvania, are plowed along the natural contours of the land to prevent excessive water runoff and soil erosion. Mixed crops are planted to permit maximum use of moisture and nutrients.*

(Below) *Rice, the most important food crop in Asian countries, has been cultivated for thousands of years in wet, tropical areas, such as the Indonesian island of Bali. A plant requiring much water for nourishment, rice is usually grown in flat, flooded fields.*

like the Rhine vineyards of Germany or the rubber tree groves of Malaysia, along with hundreds of other distinctive farm areas, continue to produce immensely diverse patterns among the world's farms.

Primitive SLASH AND BURN farming is still practiced in remote areas. Subsistence and small-village agriculture is the pattern in much of the developing Third World. Mixed or general-family farms with crops and livestock interrelated, and with the resources to reach commercial markets, have dominated agriculture in the developed countries in the 19th and 20th centuries. Plantations producing staple crops for sale in world markets are a feature of tropical and subtropical regions. Highly capitalized farming operations, they are not significantly different from large-scale one-crop corporation farms.

Farming is a production process that requires much care and attention, and farms have usually been family operations, where all the family members contribute as much labor as is needed to produce crops. Other forms of organization—communes, collective farms, cooperative farms, special structures like the Israeli kibbutz, and corporation farms—have appeared where government authority or cultural or ideological pressure has intervened.

FARMING IN THE WESTERN WORLD

Techniques of farming evolved in response to population pressure, invention, selection of crops and animals, available human and animal or mechanical power, supply of arable land, and, eventually, the pull of market demand.

Beginning with the digging stick, the hoe, the sickle, and the earliest domesticated plants of the NEOLITHIC PERIOD about 10,000 years ago, farming evolved with painful slowness, as animals were domesticated, the ard (a primitive plow) and the flail were invented, fruit and nut trees cultivated, and irrigation became a standard practice. Shifting slash-and-burn techniques were succeeded in Europe by a two-field system that alternated crops with fallow fields. The succeeding three-field system used late in the Middle Ages increased production nearly 17 percent. Along the way, the ard was replaced by a real moldboard PLOW made of wood and iron, which turned over rather than simply scratched the earth. The scythe improved upon the sickle, and the horse-collar allowed the quicker horse to replace the ox has a draft animal. The narrow strips of land cultivated by medieval village farmers provided bare subsistence. The ENCLOSURE of these divided fields into larger fields devoted to a single crop led to more efficient production of marketable crops. The enclosure movement eventually brought about the elimination of fallow fields and the introduction of the practice of crop rotation.

19th-Century Farm Technology. The great progress in science and technology during the late 18th and 19th centuries transformed agriculture in Western Europe and North America. Expanded knowledge of agricultural chemistry led to improved practices of fertilization and of livestock feeding. Plant and animal breeding by selection of desirable features increased productivity (see ANIMAL HUSBANDRY). Growing urban markets that could now be reached by canals, railroads, and steamboats invited farmers to maximize production for material gain. The cotton gin and steam-powered sugar mills and grain-threshing machines transformed methods of growing crops that had once been highly labor-intensive.

A great age of horse-powered farm machinery dominated Western European and American agriculture until early in the twentieth century. Horses pulled steel plows, harrows, cultivators, mowers, hay rakes, and reapers; they activated threshing machines and combines and performed many other farm jobs. Elaborate horse-powered farm machinery vastly increased labor productivity and brought new lands under cultivation. Horse power applied to farming had developed as far as it could by the time horses were replaced by the internal combustion engine early in the 20th century.

Mechanical power led to another farming revolution in the developed countries. In the United States between 1910 and 1960 about 36,420,000 ha (90,000,000 acres) were freed from growing the hay that fueled horses, and were shifted to other crops. Tractors, autos, trucks, combines, irrigation pumps, milkers, aerial crop dusters, and vegetable harvesters further increased labor productivity and gross volume while allowing farm size to grow and encouraging farm specialization.

At the same time as the mechanical revolution was taking place in farming, the application of biological and chemical science to crop improvement was increasing both the quality and quantity of agricultural output. The science of genetics produced hybrid corn, more productive poultry and dairy cattle, and—since World War II—the "miracle" rices and wheats of the GREEN REVOLUTION. Recently developed techniques of genetic engineering hold out promise for still greater gains. Insecticides, fungicides, herbicides, growth regulators, and antibiotics have made farming a "high tech" enterprise. Chemical fertilizer applications soared with cheapened production by the petrochemical industries.

The U.S. Family Farm. About 1900 the family farm (at least, the farm that has remained in the American collective memory as the "ideal" family farm) measured about 65 ha (160 acres), was largely self-sufficient, and produced modest quantities of surplus products for sale. The farm family provided most, if not all, of the labor required except during harvest, when a harvesting crew might be assembled from the neighborhood. Horses for power and other livestock were bred and fed on the farm. Established routines allowed for the field rotation of hay, pasture, oats, corn, and wheat that conserved soil resources. Dairy cattle, pigs, and poultry provided salable goods as well as farm food. Livestock manure fertilized the fields. Basic machinery—the plow, harrow, harvester, and mower—was relatively simple, and might be repaired and maintained on the farm itself. Farm structures—house, privy, barn and silo, corn crib, hoghouses, equipment shed, fences—were equally uncomplicated, and some could be built by the farmer and his family. Crop production, upkeep of harness, machinery, and structures, the care of the animals, milking, and housekeeping kept the family labor force fully occupied and tied to daily and seasonal rounds of toil.

Farm families lived on their farms and not in villages, as was (and is) common in much of Europe and the Third World. When farms averaged 65 ha, the distance between farmhouses was 0.8 km (0.5 mi). Such dispersed settlement isolated farm families. Yet these distances could be overcome by trading labor at harvest time, exchanging special skills like butchering and horse training, and by participating in community schools and churches.

The norm primarily in the Midwest for the generations between the Civil War and World War II, the 65-ha family farm exemplified the American ideal of independence. Equally numerous in other sections of the country, however, were small, poor farms on the margins of good land, and tenant farms—particularly in the cotton-raising South—where farmers worked land they did not own in exchange for a share of the crops they raised. As a symbol of rural poverty, the Southern sharecropper vanished in the years following World War II (largely as the result of the mechanization of cotton cultivation). The rental of land for cash, or for a share of the crop, however, is a practice that still persists.

Changes in U.S. Farm Structure. Technological change in farming has proceeded hand in hand with industrialization and urbanization. In fact, progress in farming was long considered a measure of society's modernization.

The increase in field size and farm size to accommodate innovative technologies—such as harvester combines or tomato harvester machines—has meant a decline in the number of farms and a reduction of the farm labor force. Gains in gross production volume and production per worker, per acre, and per animal unit released labor for nonfarm pursuits and provided ample and relatively cheap food for urban populations.

The United States provides the most notable measurements of the changes in farming that have occurred throughout the industrialized West. From 1950 to 1980, U.S. farm output doubled. The average size of farms grew from 87 to 182 ha (215 to 450 acres), the number of farms fell from 5.6 to 2.4 million, and the farm population shrank from 23 to 6 million (from 15 percent to 2.7 percent of the total population). At the same time, the number of persons supplied with farm products grew from 15 to 65 for each farm worker.

Among the 2.4 million farms that exist at present, the top 20 percent in terms of size produce almost 80 percent of farm output. At the other end, the smallest farms—representing almost 50 percent of all farms—produce only 10 percent of total farm output.

Although the decline in the number of farms began to slow after 1980, the number of people who earned their livelihoods solely from farming continued to shrink. About one-half of all U.S. farm families now derive more income from nonfarm sources than from the sale of farm products.

Today, a successful family farm is a commercialized and specialized business, highly capital- and energy-intensive. It concentrates on the production of one or two commercial crops (corn, for example, or soybeans, pigs, beef cattle, or milk). It utilizes machinery to the fullest extent on ever-larger fields, and depends on borrowed capital for the purchase of equipment, seeds, fertilizer, and pesticides to maximize yields on expensive land. Management skills of a high order are required to succeed in this type of farming. A representative midwestern farmer, for example, could have a capital investment in land and equipment of $1.5 million and sell crops worth $300,000. Net income on such a farm—depending on production costs, weather, market demand, and other factors—might be $30,000 or less.

Commercial family farms are sometimes incorporated to gain tax and management advantages, but they remain family businesses. Public corporations have ventured into specialized farming operations that benefit from expansion of scale. Big corporation farms grow fruits and vegetables in California, and cotton in California, Texas, and Mississippi; they fatten thousands of cattle in feedlots and raise poultry in factories. The displacement of family farms by corporations has inspired some public concern; although an increasing percentage of products are grown by corporation farms, high capital and operating costs have restrained their growth somewhat (see AGRIBUSINESS).

Changes in Farm Economics. The increase in farm size and productivity has been both the cause and the result of the increased dependence on the input industries that supply machinery, chemicals, and feed and seed. In the United States particularly, the temptation to buy more acreage in order to use farm machinery to its full potential (and to buy larger machinery so that the increased acres can be efficiently cultivated) has brought many farmers close to bankruptcy, especially in periods of lowered farm income.

Farm products today are no longer directly consumable goods. Rather, they are raw materials that will be factory processed, packaged, and merchandised. For example, much of the corn grown in the United States is used for livestock feed for the meat-packing and distributing industry. Wheat is shipped long distances to flour mills, then to mass-production bakeries, then to retail stores. Fruits and vegetables—when not processed and canned or frozen—move from the farmer to packers and middlemen handlers before reaching store shelves. In the United States, distribution charges interposed between the farmer and the consumer have reduced the farmer's share of the consumer's food dollar to about 36 cents.

Farming is necessarily a slow process, even where two or three crops can be grown annually. In the United States, one crop a year is the norm in most areas. Trees and vines require three or more years to come into bearing. The pig crop takes nearly a year from breeding to sale weight; beef cattle require two or more years. The farmer's turnover is slow compared to that of commerce and industry, and in addition, the hazards of nature bear heavily upon farms.

Unlike industry, in farming increase in size does not necessarily produce increased efficiency. Optimum farm size varies with differing crops and locations. The most efficient U.S. dairy farms in 1984, for example, maintained about 300 cows on about 120 ha (300 acres). Larger herds increase volume but do not raise efficiency or lower costs.

More than 200 commercial crops are grown on U.S. farms under widely different geographical and economic conditions. Wheat farmers of the Great Plains and the Palouse region of Washington and Oregon have arrangements for seed-ing, irrigation, and harvest that are unique to their climate, soil, and geography. Wine-grape farmers in California and upper New York State cope with the vagaries of consumer tastes, as well as with the weather. Citrus farmers in California, Texas, and Florida depend on organized marketing to maintain prices. Farmers who produce processing tomatoes and potatoes plan their crops in response to the demand of fast-food outlets for ketchup and tomato paste, French fries and chips.

Areas of Specialized Farm Production. Farms tend to specialize according to climatic and soil conditions, and according to their location with respect to markets and sources of production materials. Dairy farms are concentrated in the Northeast, around the Great Lakes, and near large cities. Cattle and sheep ranches are located in arid regions from the Rocky Mountains westward and in other regions where there are large supplies of hay and grasses. Specialized wheat farms are found in the Great Plains and in the Northwest.

Corn and soybean production is the foundation of farming on the rich lands of the central region known as the Corn Belt. Many farms specialize in producing only these two grains. However, since soybeans and corn are the main feed for hogs and for fattening cattle, many Corn Belt farms also produce hogs and import beef cattle from ranches in the West for fattening. In recent years cattle fattening has become more concentrated in large-scale specialized units of the Corn Belt and in the sorghum-grain and irrigated regions of the Southern Plains.

Cotton is limited by climate to the southern and southwestern states. Fruits and vegetables are produced mainly where local climate is favorable. Year-round vegetable production is found primarily in Florida and California. Poultry is produced in large specialized units concentrated especially in states that have access both to feed supplies and to consuming centers. However, some farms produce several commodities throughout the year, in order to utilize labor and other resources efficiently.

THE ROLE OF GOVERNMENT

Farming figures importantly in the governmental policies of most nations. Farms are the source of strategic food supplies, of important raw materials for industry, and of major commodities for trade and commerce. Farming interests, especially in the United States, possess considerable political power and influence.

Farm welfare has therefore had the solicitous attention of the United States government for many decades. In the 19th century it was assumed that easy distribution of land would encourage the development of productive farms. This idea culminated in the HOMESTEAD ACT of 1862, which gave 160 acres (65 ha) of public land each to settlers who declared their intention of building farms. By establishing support for research and education, the government hoped to make farms more productive and farm life more fulfilling. The creation of the U.S. Department of Agriculture (see AGRICULTURE, U.S. DEPARTMENT OF, and the passing of the MORRILL LAND GRANT COLLEGE ACT, both in 1862, were followed by the Hatch Act of 1887, which subsidized state agricultural experiment stations, and the Smith-Lever Act of 1914, which supported agricultural extension services in the states (see AGRICULTURAL EDUCATION).

The disadvantages of small-scale farming in an industrialized economy, especially evident at the time of the Great Depression of the 1930s, gave rise to federal efforts to support farm prices. A program to restrain the production of price-depressing surpluses and to raise prices to parity levels began with the Agricultural Adjustment Act of 1933 and became a central feature of government farm policy. The act declared that farm commodities should have the same purchasing power (parity) as they had in the period 1910–14. For example, the parity price of a bushel of corn should buy as much fertilizer, machinery, or other materials as a bushel of corn would have purchased during the base period. The base period for determining parity has changed several times since 1933, and the 1977 Food and Agricultural Act uses the cost of production rather than parity as a means of setting price supports.

At different times the government has also paid farmers

to withhold land from production, has provided commodity loans above market prices to persuade farmers to keep crops off the market, and has paid farmers the difference between the target prices it considers fair and actual market prices. The 1983 PIK (Payment in Kind) program attempted to shrink government surplus commodity holdings by paying farmers who reduced their plantings of wheat, rice, and cotton from government stockpiles of these commodities. The program, which cost about $12 billion, did little to reduce the size of harvests or of government surpluses.

Importance of Farm Exports. American farmers produce commercial crops in quantities that are far in excess of domestic needs. Much of the excess is stockpiled, while much more has been sold in foreign markets.

Since the beginning of colonial development, food and commodity exports have bolstered American growth. Tobacco, rice, indigo, and foodstuffs were major colonial exports. Exported cotton, wheat, and livestock products sustained the U.S. economy through the 19th and into the 20th centuries. After World War II, swelling farm productivity caused a great accumulation of surpluses, which were reduced through the Food for Peace program, begun in 1954, and through subsidized sales to Third World countries. Renewed demand for American wheat and feed grains during the decade 1970–80 moved surpluses abroad at good prices and encouraged U.S. farmers to plant more hectares. The first half of the 1980s, however, saw a U.S. grain embargo imposed against the USSR in retaliation for its invasion of Afghanistan; a world economic recession; and growing competition from other grain producers, such as Argentina. Wheat farmers, particularly, felt the negative economic effects of shrinking export markets. Nevertheless, one-quarter of U.S. farm production is still exported. Its receipts total an annual $35–40 billion.

FARMING IN WESTERN EUROPE

Western Europe has moved at a slower pace than the United States toward more efficient, larger, commercialized family farming operations. Specialized dairying, livestock, and poultry farmers, especially in Britain and the Netherlands, draw heavily upon purchased feed grain, much of it imported from North America. In France and Italy, and most of the other European Mediterranean countries, however, land consolidation as a means of using machinery effectively has not taken place, and the traditional small holding remains the norm.

The European Common Market (the EC, or EUROPEAN COMMUNITY) was organized in 1958. Its principal purpose was to establish open markets for European products within the European community and to permit more efficient export marketing of farm surpluses. The price subsidies provided farmers by the EC, combined with more productive farming techniques, have made the EC a serious competitor with the United States and other food-exporting nations. The subsidies have also been one of the obstacles to the increased sale of U.S. food products within the EC and a source of U.S.–EC controversy.

NON-WESTERN TYPES OF FARMING ORGANIZATIONS

Under central planning farming in the countries of Eastern Europe was organized in accord with Communist ideology. Big industrialized farms, state farms, and collective farms aimed to achieve economies of scale by covering great acreages of cropland with massive machinery and large numbers of workers. Efficiency was elusive under bureaucratic management, and production per worker and per acre in the USSR averaged about half that of Great Britain's farms. Since the collapse of Communist regimes in the late 1980s, efforts to privatize farming have worked relatively well in such countries as Poland and Hungary but have been far less successful in the republics of the former USSR.

The giant commune in China, which might take in the land and populations of several villages, became the standard Chinese farm organization after the 1949 revolution. It brought an initial sharp decline in production, although China later managed to regain near self-sufficiency in food. By the late 1980s, however, many Chinese farmworkers were being allowed to own their own plots of land, and the commune system seemed viable only for commercial crops like wheat.

Israel pioneered the KIBBUTZ, a form of cooperative farm that has been highly productive of food and specialty crops both for local consumption and export. The Mexican ejido is a cooperative village enterprise that leaves production to individual farmers but centralizes purchasing and marketing. The Israeli moshav functions in a similar fashion.

Plantations produce single crops—rubber, coffee, sisal, bananas, palm oil, pineapples, cacao—for sale to distant markets. Today, plantation farming is found primarily in tropical and semitropical countries. It is usually organized on a large scale and may be exploitive both of labor and, because only one type of crop is raised, of soil resources. Plantations growing profitable crops for export have often displaced small peasant farms, pushing small farmers back on marginal land or off the land altogether. Especially in regions of Central and South America and in parts of Africa, plantation economies have taken over so much land that not enough is left to raise food for local populations.

Village farming in the past, and in many regions in the present, has involved peasants cultivating small plots of land intensively, producing a diversity of intertilled food and fiber crops, and sustaining a large rural population. It rarely produces great surpluses. Many areas of subsistence peasant farming are close to maximum land productivity, and many peasant villages may live on the edge of malnutrition. Depleted soil and unfavorable climatic conditions have decimated peasant populations in many regions of Africa and Asia.

The GREEN REVOLUTION produced high-yielding strains of rice, wheat, and corn and has transformed agriculture in Mexico and India, but the cultivation of these new grains is confined to wealthy farmers with large fields. The development of indigenous plants as crops for food and export, however, offers the possibility of new wealth for village farmers, especially in tropical regions. Little-known tropical fruits (the carambola or the pummelo, for example), the high-protein seeds quinoa and AMARANTH, and desert shrubs such as PRICKLY PEAR or kenaf (a hibiscus grown for its fiber)—as well as many other plants now ignored or grown only in small quantities—might become major crops in the future.   JAMES H. SHIDELER

Bibliography: Cochrane, Willard W., *The Development of American Agriculture* (1979); Critchfield, R., *Villages* (1981); Diamanti, Joyce, et al., *Amber Waves of Grain* (1991); Grigg, D. B., *Agricultural Systems of the World* (1974); Jager, Ronald, *Eighty Acres* (1990); Nygaard, D. F., and Pellett, P. L., eds., *Dry Area Agriculture* (1986); Prothero, Rowland E., *English Farming Past and Present* (1917; repr. 1968); Rhodes, Richard, *Farm: A Year in the Life of an American Farmer* (1989; repr. 1990); Ruthenberg, H., *Farming Systems in the Tropics*, 3d ed. (1980; repr. 1983); Ucko, P. J., and Dimbleby, G. W., eds., *The Domestication and Exploitation of Plants and Animals* (1969); Usherwood, N. R., ed., *Transferring Technology for Small Scale Farming* (1981).

See also: AGRICULTURAL ECOLOGY; AGRICULTURAL ECONOMICS; AGRICULTURE, HISTORY OF; AGRICULTURE AND THE FOOD SUPPLY.

Farnese, Alessandro   [fahr-nay'-zay, ahl-es-sahn'-droh]

Alessandro Farnese, 3d duke of Parma, b. Aug. 27, 1545, d. Dec. 3, 1592, was a diplomat and one of the greatest generals of the 16th century. The son of Ottavio Farnese, 2d duke of Parma, and Margaret of Austria, he grew up in the court of PHILIP II of Spain. Farnese fought the Turks in the Battle of LEPANTO (1571) and in 1578 became governor-general of the Netherlands, then in armed revolt against Spanish rule (see DUTCH REVOLT).

With the capture (1585) of Antwerp, Farnese finally subdued the largely Catholic southern Netherlands (modern Belgium). Plans to conquer the northern provinces were diverted in favor of preparations for a Spanish invasion of England, which was thwarted by the defeat (1588) of the Spanish Armada. During the French Wars of Religion (see RELIGION, WARS OF), Farnese led Spanish troops into France to aid the Catholics at Paris (1590) and Rouen (1592).

Bibliography: Grierson, Edward, *The Fatal Inheritance* (1969); Parker, Geoffrey, *The Army of Flanders and the Spanish Road, 1567–1659* (1972); Solari, Giovanna R., *The House of Farnese*, trans. by Simona Morini and Frederic Tuten (1968).

Farnese, Elizabeth

Elizabeth Farnese, b. Oct. 25, 1692, d. July 11, 1766, was the second queen consort of PHILIP V of Spain, whom she married in 1714. Aided initially by the able Cardinal Alberoni (1664–1752), she soon dominated her husband and involved Spain in several wars. As a result of these, her son Charles (later Charles III of Spain) became (1734) king of Naples, and her son Philip received (1748) Parma by reversion from Charles. Elizabeth lost power after the succession (1746) of her stepson FERDINAND VI.

Farnese Heracles

The Farnese Heracles (3d century AD; Museo Nazionale, Naples), a Hellenistic statue by the Roman sculptor Glycon, is a marble copy of a bronze statue executed (c.340 BC) by the late-classical Greek sculptor LYSIPPUS. It was found (c.1540–47) in the Baths of Caracalla. The much-admired statue inspired such artists as Peter Paul Rubens, Hendrick Goltzius, the Carracci brothers, and the neoclassicist Antonio Canova.
JOHN STEPHENS CRAWFORD

Bibliography: Vermeule, C., *Greek Sculpture and Roman Taste* (1977).

Farnese Palace

The Farnese Palace, or Palazzo Farnese, in Rome, now the French Embassy, was begun in 1534 by Cardinal Alessandro Farnese when he became Pope Paul III. He commissioned Antonio da SANGALLO the Younger, who produced an essentially Florentine design, with an interior court and a crisply differentiated facade. Construction had begun when Sangallo died in 1546, and the work was continued by MICHELANGELO, who made many changes. He unified the facade, adding a weighty cornice and a large central window. Inside, above the columns of the court, he completed two additional stories, increasing the density of the Mannerist window decoration as it mounted. The Galleria was frescoed (1597–1604) by Annibale CARRACCI with mythological scenes.   DAVID CAST

Bibliography: Ackerman, James S., *The Architecture of Michelangelo*, rev. ed. (1971).

Farnsworth, Philo Taylor

Philo Taylor Farnsworth, b. Beaver, Utah, Aug. 19, 1906, d. Mar. 11, 1971, was a U.S. research engineer and executive who was a pioneer in TELEVISION. Farnsworth was a 15-year-old high school student when he designed his first television system. Six years later he obtained his first patent. In 1935 he demonstrated his complete television system. Farnsworth held 165 patents, mostly in radio and television. He founded and spent his career as head of the Farnsworth Television & Radio Corporation and its successors.

Bibliography: Farnsworth, E. G., *Distant Vision* (1989).

faro   [fair'-oh]

Faro is a card game in which up to ten players bet that a certain card will win or lose. A 52-card deck is used, and the 13 spade cards from another deck are placed faceup. Two cards from the deck are exposed. The first card is the loser, the second the winner. All bets on either card are paid. Faro is a 17th-century gambling game named for the pharaoh on French playing cards. Banned (1739) by law in England, it later became the most popular card gambling game in America.

Bibliography: Scarne, John, *Scarne on Cards* (1974; repr. 1989).

Faroe Islands: see FAEROE ISLANDS.

Farouk, King of Egypt   [fuh-rook']

Farouk, b. Feb. 11, 1920, d. Mar. 17, 1965, was king of Egypt from 1936 until July 1952, when he was overthrown in the revolution led by General Muhammad Naguib. Succeeding his father, FUAD I, Farouk was initially popular. His authority crumbled, however, as a result of confrontations with domestic political opponents (especially the powerful WAFD party), of gossip about his lurid private life, and of his ambitious nationalist foreign policy that brought conflict with Britain and the disastrous ARAB-ISRAELI WAR of 1948. By 1952, Farouk symbolized a corrupt, uncaring regime that shamed patriotic Egyptians. Gamal Abdul NASSER, who played a leading role in the coup against the king, soon displaced Naguib as ruler of Egypt.   ROBERT G. LANDEN

Bibliography: McBride, Barrie St. Clair, *Farouk of Egypt: A Biography* (1968); McLeave, Hugh, *The Last Pharaoh: Farouk of Egypt* (1970).

Farquhar, George   [fahr'-kwur]

The Irish-born English dramatist and actor George Farquhar, b. 1678, d. Apr. 29, 1707, is often considered the last of the Restoration playwrights. His popular comedies of manners, notably *The Recruiting Officer* (1706) and *The Beaux' Stratagem* (1707), have often been successfully revived. The first of these draws on Farquhar's own military experiences. The second, with its ingenious plot, middle-class characters, and happy ending, was a success when first produced, yet Farquhar died in poverty during the play's first run.   ROBIN BUSS

Farragut, David Glasgow   [far'-uh-guht]

Admiral David Farragut entered the U.S. Navy as a midshipman at the age of nine and became one of the outstanding naval commanders of the Civil War. A seasoned veteran of both the War of 1812 and the Mexican War, Farragut gave the North an important victory in 1862 by capturing New Orleans. Two years later he led a Union fleet into Mobile Bay, sealing off the vital port of Mobile from Confederate shipping for the duration of the war.

David Glasgow Farragut, b. July 5, 1801, d. Aug. 14, 1870, was an American naval officer who led the Union assaults upon New Orleans and Mobile Bay during the Civil War. Adopted by David Porter after the death of his parents, Farragut served as a midshipman at the age of nine. He served under Porter on the frigate *Essex* in the War of 1812 and was made prize master of a captured ship. From 1815 until 1861, Farragut alternated between routine sea duty and shore duty, with periods of leave. At the outbreak of the Civil War he was a senior officer with a long but undistinguished record of service.

A resident of Norfolk, Va., Farragut left for New York on Apr. 18, 1861, the day after Virginia seceded from the Union. Once satisfied with Farragut's loyalty to the Union, the Navy Department chose him to capture New Orleans, a major Northern objective. Farragut boldly led his ships past Forts Jackson and St. Philip, the principal obstacles on the Mississippi River below New Orleans. He arrived at the city on Apr. 25, 1862, and the army occupied it on May 1. Farragut's feat electrified the North, opened the lower Mississippi to Federal forces, and discouraged European intervention on behalf of the Confederacy. It also earned Farragut promotion to rear admiral; he was the first to hold that rank in the U.S. Navy.

On Aug. 5, 1864, Farragut similarly bypassed strongly defended forts in Mobile Bay to attack and destroy the Confederate warships defending Mobile, Ala. Although the city itself was not captured until April 1865, Farragut effectively closed the Confederacy's last major Gulf port. During a critical moment of this assault, when one ship's captain hesitated out of fear of Confederate mines—then called torpedoes—Farragut shouted, "Damn the torpedoes, full speed ahead." Between 1865 and 1870, Farragut was twice promoted, becoming the U.S. Navy's first four-star admiral.   KENNETH J. HAGAN

Bibliography: Farragut, Loyall, *The Life of David Glasgow Farragut* (1879); Lewis, Charles L., *David Glasgow Farragut*, 2 vols. (1941, 1943); Mahan, Alfred Thayer, *Admiral Farragut* (1892; repr. 1970).

Farrar, Geraldine   [fuh-rahr']

Geraldine Farrar, b. Melrose, Mass., Feb. 28, 1882, d. Mar. 11, 1967, was one of the most glamorous American operatic sopranos. Farrar studied in Boston, Paris, and Germany, making her operatic debut (1901) in Berlin as Marguerite in Gounod's *Faust*. She also sang in Monte Carlo, Paris, London, and Brussels before her triumphant debut in Gounod's *Roméo et Juliette* at the Metropolitan Opera (1906). Farrar was the Metropolitan's principal lyric soprano for 15 years, appearing in nearly 500 performances, often as a partner to Enrico Caruso. She created the operatic roles of the Goosegirl in Humperdinck's *Königskinder* (1910) and the title part in Puccini's *Suor Angelica* (1918). Farrar retired from opera in 1922. Her autobiography, *Such Sweet Compulsion,* was published in 1938.
STEPHANIE VON BUCHAU

Bibliography: Briggs, John, *Requiem for a Yellow Brick Brewery: A History of the Metropolitan Opera* (1969).

Farrell, Eileen

Dramatic soprano Eileen Farrell, b. Willimantic, Conn., Feb. 13, 1920, was noted for the power and warmth of her voice. She began as a singer on radio in 1940, gaining her own half-hour show in 1941. In 1947 she embarked on a long international career as a recitalist and as a singer with major orchestras and choral groups. She first appeared in a staged opera in 1956, and she made her debut at the Metropolitan Opera in the title role of Gluck's *Alcestis* in 1960. Farrell made many recordings, including several in the blues and popular music fields.

Farrell, James T.   [far'-ul]

James Thomas Farrell, b. Chicago, Feb. 27, 1904, d. Aug. 22, 1979, was an American author best known for his novels about Irish-American families on Chicago's South Side. He first received recognition for his Studs Lonigan trilogy (*Young Lonigan,* 1932; *The Young Manhood of Studs Lonigan,* 1934; *Judgment Day,* 1935) and subsequently published more than 50 works of fiction, criticism, poetry, and journalism. In the 1930s and '40s he was active in left-wing social causes; *A Note on Literary Criticism* (1936) delineated his brand of independent Marxism.

Photo Jill Krementz © 1973

The American author James T. Farrell became controversial during the late 1930s, partly because of his Marxist views and the stark realism of his literary style. Farrell's most important work, the Studs Lonigan trilogy, chronicles the gradual brutalization and corruption of a young man growing up in the Irish Catholic neighborhoods of Chicago.

Farrell's fiction is a part of the tradition of naturalistic writing established by Sherwood Anderson and Theodore Dreiser, and the force of his work derives from the uncompromising realism of his technique. He was especially inspired by the pragmatist thinkers John Dewey and George Mead in his effort to reveal the social basis of human character and destiny in his fiction. Although naturalism became less important as a literary technique after World War II, Farrell continued to write in that tradition. ALAN M. WALD

Bibliography: Fried, Lewis, *Makers of the City* (1990); Wald, Alan, *James T. Farrell: The Revolutionary Socialist Years* (1978).

Farrell, Suzanne

Suzanne Farrell, b. Cincinnati, Aug. 16, 1945, is the archetypal American ballerina. She was trained at the School of American Ballet, where she was discovered by George Balanchine. She joined the New York City Ballet in 1961, rising to principal in 1965. After a row with Balanchine over her marriage, she resigned in 1969 and joined Maurice Béjart's Ballet of the 20th Century, before returning to New York City Ballet in 1975. She retired from the company in 1989 and soon after joined the Fort Worth Ballet as an artistic advisor. Her autobiography, *Holding on to the Air,* was published in 1990.

fasces [fas'-eez]

In ancient Rome, fasces were rods of elm or birch tied together with leather thongs around an ax with projecting blade, used as a symbol of authority. They were carried by lictors (guards) walking in advance of public officials including praetors, consuls, proconsuls, victorious generals, dictators, and emperors. The Italian Fascist party adopted the fasces as its emblem and took its name from them.

fascism [fash'-izm]

Fascism was an authoritarian political movement that developed in Italy and other European countries after 1919 as a reaction against the political and social changes brought about by World War I and the spread of socialism and communism. Its name was derived from the fasces, an ancient Roman symbol of authority consisting of a bundle of rods and an ax.

Italian fascism was founded in Milan on Mar. 23, 1919, by Benito MUSSOLINI, a former revolutionary socialist leader. His followers, mostly war veterans, were organized along paramilitary lines and wore black shirts as uniforms. The early Fascist program was a mixture of left- and right-wing ideas that emphasized intense NATIONALISM, productivism, antisocialism,

elitism, and the need for a strong leader. Mussolini's oratorical skills, the postwar economic crisis, a widespread lack of confidence in the traditional political system, and a growing fear of socialism, all helped the Fascist party to grow to 300,000 registered members by 1921. In that year it elected 35 members to parliament. Mussolini became prime minister in October 1922 following the "march on Rome" and 3 years of bloody violence. In 1926 he seized total power as dictator and ruled Italy until July 1943, when he was deposed. A puppet Fascist regime with Mussolini at its head nominally controlled northern Italy under the Germans until Mussolini's execution by partisans in 1945 (see ITALY, HISTORY OF). A neo-Fascist party, the Italian Social Movement, was founded after World War II, but its influence was small.

The Philosophy of Fascism. Fascist ideology, largely the work of the neoidealist philosopher Giovanni GENTILE, emphasized the subordination of the individual to a "totalitarian" state that was to control all aspects of national life. Violence as a creative force was an important aspect of the Fascist philosophy. A special feature of Italian fascism was the attempt to eliminate the class struggle from history through nationalism and the corporate state. Mussolini organized the economy and all "producers"—from peasants and factory workers to intellectuals and industrialists—into 22 corporations as a means of improving productivity and avoiding industrial disputes. Contrary to the regime's propaganda claims, the totalitarian state functioned poorly. Mussolini had to compromise with big business, the monarchy, and the Roman Catholic church. The Italian economy experienced no appreciable growth. The corporate state was never fully implemented, and the expansionist, militaristic nature of fascism contributed to imperialist adventures in Ethiopia and the Balkans and ultimately to World War II.

The intellectual roots of fascism can be traced back to voluntaristic philosophers such as Arthur SCHOPENHAUER, Friedrich NIETZSCHE, and Henri BERGSON and to SOCIAL DARWINISM with its emphasis on the survival of the fittest. Its immediate roots, however, were in certain irrational, socialist, and nationalist tendencies of the turn of the century that combined in a protest against the liberal bourgeois ideas then holding sway in Western Europe. Gabriele D'ANNUNZIO, Georges SOREL, and Maurice BARRÈS were particularly influential.

European Fascism. Closely related to Italian fascism was German National Socialism, or NAZISM, under Adolf HITLER. It won wide support among the unemployed, the impoverished middle class, and industrialists who feared socialism and communism. In Spain the Falange Española (Spanish Phalanx), inspired by Mussolini's doctrines, was founded in 1933 by José Antonio Primo de Rivera (1903–36). During the SPANISH CIVIL WAR, the Falange was reorganized as the Falange Española Tradicionalista by Gen. Francisco FRANCO, who made it the official party of his regime. Of less importance were the Fascist movements in France and the British Union of Fascists under Sir Oswald MOSLEY. Fascist movements sprang up in many other European countries during the 1930s, including Romania (see IRON GUARD), Belgium, Austria, and the Netherlands. Fascist groups rose to power in many of the countries under German occupation during World War II. In France the VICHY GOVERNMENT of Marshal Philippe Petain was strongly influenced by the ACTION FRANÇAISE, a movement that shared many ideas with fascism. The collaborationist Quisling government in occupied Norway also espoused a fascistlike ideology. The defeat of Italy and Germany in the war, however, spelled the end of fascism as an effective, internationally appealing mass movement.

Reviewed by PHILIP CANNISTRARO

Bibliography: Arendt, Hannah, *The Origins of Totalitarianism,* rev. ed. (1966); Blinkhorn, Martin, ed., *Fascists and Conservatives* (1990); Cassels, Alan, *Fascist Italy,* 2d ed. (1985); De Felice, Renzo, *Interpretations of Fascism,* trans. by Brenda Everett (1977); Gregor, James, *Young Mussolini and the Intellectual Origins of Fascism* (1979); Payne, Stanley G., *Fascism: A Comparative Approach toward a Definition* (1980); Smith, Dennis M., *Mussolini* (1982); Snowden, Frank, *Fascist Revolution in Tuscany* (1990); Thurlow, Richard, C., *Fascism in Britain* (1987).

See also: TOTALITARIANISM.

The Fascist dictator Benito Mussolini (center) *of Italy reviews an elite corps of German troops with the Nazi leader Adolf Hitler. The alliance of these dictators in the 1930s reflected the close relationship between fascism and National Socialism in ideology and practice.*

fashion design

The term *fashion,* applied to dress, refers to modes or styles that are popular at any particular time. Factors that impinge on fashion are manifold, ranging from impressive events (the bikini bathing suit was named for the Pacific atoll of Bikini, where the United States conducted atom-bomb tests in the 1940s) to the popularity of generals and politicians (the Eisenhower jacket; the disappearance of men's hats during the presidency of the always-hatless John F. Kennedy). However, the influence of French clothing designers and, in this century, of the major fashion houses that constitute the haute couture (high-quality design and dressmaking) has been a decisive factor in fashion in the West since the Renaissance.

Paris. Since the 14th century the acknowledged center of the fashion industry has been Paris, largely because of the predominance of fabric manufacturing and the number of merchants of fashionable goods. Much of France's fashion industry, especially silk weaving, was encouraged by the patronage of the king. To promote their wares the French manufacturers would dispatch dolls, dressed in the latest styles, to the cities and courts throughout Europe, where they were eagerly awaited by the privileged ladies who would make their selection of styles from them. This custom continued into the 19th century. In the 17th century, fashion engravings appeared in France; these were the forerunners of modern fashion magazines. The most influential 18th-century Parisian publications were *Courier de la mode* (1768), *Galerie des modes et costumes français* (1778–87), and *Journal de la mode et du goût,* which lasted until 1793.

The first French fashion designer of eminence was Rose Bertin (1747–1813), who by 1776 was modiste to Queen Marie Antoinette of France. During the French Revolution, Bertin fled to England; from there she continued to send out fashion dolls dressed in the new high-waisted neo-Greek styles. During the Napoleonic age the designer Louis Hippolyte Leroy created apparel for the Empress Josephine. The man who created the Parisian fashion industry as it is known today, however, was an Englishman working in Paris, Charles Frederick WORTH, who rose from obscurity to become (1858) the fashion arbiter to the Empress Eugénie. He continued to dominate the fashion scene after the fall of Napoleon III in 1870. Worth created the first couture, or fashion, house with its fashion shows, mannequins, sales staff, dressmakers, and Paris labels; the house of Worth continued in the family until 1956.

Other fashion houses followed to rival the Maison Worth. Jacques Doucet endeavored to return to the elegant style of the 18th century, and Madame Paquin, Madame Cheruit, and the Callot sisters were influential about 1900. Paul POIRET, however, created the first revolution in 20th-century dress about 1910 when he freed women from corsets and introduced oriental-style costumes of turbans and hobble skirts.

In the 1920s, Coco CHANEL replaced Poiret's exoticisms with simple classic suits and dresses of restrained color. Other women with a more romantic approach were Jeanne LANVIN and Madelaine Vionnet (1878–1982). Jeanne Lanvin's career began with her designs for her daughter's clothes, and this free and innocent effect, which was often created with costly brocades and lamés, became her métier. Vionnet was one of the most skilled couturieres. She cut and sewed her own de-

(Left) *Charles Frederick Worth, one of the most brilliant and influential designers of the 19th century, founded the first couture house in 1858. He was the first couturier to dictate changes in style.*
(Below) *Worth's designs were imitated throughout the world. This fashion plate shows different views of the American version of a Worth gown (1874). By the 1870s, due to Worth's influence, the bustle had replaced the crinoline. (Harper's Bazaar.)*

(Left) *The elaborate gowns of Queen Marie Antoinette, seen with King Louis XVI in this 18th-century French fashion plate, were designed by the court dressmaker, Rose Bertin. Bertin, designated "Minister of Fashion" by the queen, was the first notable French fashion designer. (Louvre, Paris.)*

(Left) *Paul Poiret's loosely fitted, brightly colored evening gown (1915), seen in the Gazette du Bon Ton, reveals the influence of the Far East on his designs. Poiret, one of the most innovative couturiers of the early 20th century, discarded the bulky and restrictive corset and restored a natural silhouette to women's fashion.*

Coco Chanel dominated the haute couture of the mid-20th century with such simple, elegant styles as the "little black dress" (1930), at one time a wardrobe staple, and the tweed suit (1930). Chanel's tailored fashions, designed for office wear, reflected the increasing emancipation of women. (Fashion Institute of Technology, New York City.)

signs and introduced the bias cut—cutting the fabric against the weave—to create a free-flowing effect, as well as the cowl and halter necklines. Her work was so well structured that it was impossible to copy.

Jean PATOU brought an end to the 1920s look in 1929 when he introduced a collection with natural waistlines and longer hemlines for daytime dresses and floor-length skirts for evening wear. The other designers immediately followed this conservative yet natural look.

The English designer Captain Edward Molyneux and the American MAINBOCHER were prominent during the 1930s. Molyneux's clothes were elegant and uncomplicated, correct for spectator sports and practical for traveling. Mainbocher's padded shoulders and "wasp" waists anticipated the styles of the 1940s. Lucien Lelong introduced a ready-made department, *robes d'édition*, in 1933. Ready-made clothes had been available from mail-order houses and department stores before 1900, but Lelong's innovation was unique in a Paris *haute couture* ("high fashion") house. Lelong was one of the greatest businessmen since Worth. During the Nazi occupation of France in World War II, he persuaded the Germans to allow the fashion industry to remain in Paris rather than to move it to Berlin or Vienna. Elsa SCHIAPARELLI's designs in bright colors, especially shocking pink, also emphasized the shoulders and minimized the waist. She added unusual surrealist-inspired touches to her collection: junk jewelry that glowed in the dark and handbags that lit up inside. Schiaparelli was also not averse to such practical ideas as zippers or synthetic fabrics.

During World War II, Paris was in danger of losing its position of fashion eminence to America. In 1947, however, Christian DIOR's triumphant entry into couture and his romantic "New Look," with its slim waist, full bust, and long wide skirt, reestablished French domination of the world of fashion. Other French couturiers who brought a brilliant glamour to postwar Paris were Jacques Fath and Pierre Balmain. The Spanish designer Cristobal BALENCIAGA was renowned for his "architectural" skills with a dress. The soft ease of his puffed gowns and unfitted chemises, in vogue during the 1950s, belied the complexities of their structure.

The 1960s saw the rise of the *prêt-à-porter*, or ready-to-wear, market, as well as the decline of the fashion house that limited itself to creating designs for individual customers. Since the days of Worth couture designers had permitted and

profited from a limited copying of their fashions by manufacturers in other countries, particularly the United States. By the 1960s, this practice had increased. Yves SAINT-LAURENT expanded the limits of the fashion house by opening boutiques with inexpensive ready-to-wear clothes, as well as perfumes, cosmetics, and accessories.

The 1960s revolutionaries André Courrèges and Pierre Cardin designed for the youth explosion, offering boots, miniskirts, and pantsuits in a space-age style. They also produced for the ready-to-wear market, and their clothes and accessories were sold internationally under their labels. Also part of the international market were the fashions of Karl Lagerfeld, who designs for Chanel, and Christian Lacroix, who captured attention in the 1980s with his bold colors and innovative silhouettes, particularly the "pouf" or bubble dress.

International Fashions. Since the 1960s other nations—particularly Britain, Italy, the United States, and in the 1980s, Japan—have produced designers with international reputations to match those of the Paris couturiers. Mary Quant of London created (1965) the miniskirt before Cardin or Courrèges adopted it. Among the Italian designers, Emilio Pucci and Valentino have achieved international success, and Japan's Issey Miyake has gained a following with his flowing, unstructured designs.

Designers in the United States, perhaps unjustifiably, have taken second place to Paris designers, yet some have gained international prestige. Mainly, they have taken a less traditional and more practical approach to style, which seems to be a forecast of future fashion trends. Claire McCARDELL brought a new practicality and puritanical simplicity to women's clothing; in 1938 she created a dress with no inner construction, years ahead of its time. Charles James rivaled Balenciaga and Schiaparelli with his avant-garde ideas. Other notable designers in America include Norman Norell, Pauline Trigère, Valentina, and, more recently, James Galanos, Rudi Gernreich, Halston, Adolfo, Perry Ellis, Calvin Klein, and Donna Karan. Ralph Lauren and Bill Blass have promoted the idea of a whole environment, creating designs for clothing, housewares, eyeglasses, and auto interiors. By the late 1980s, fashion catering to the needs of professional working women was a priority for some designers. Most international designers now also create clothing for men.

Prêt-à-Porter. In 1970 the French government built on the edge of Paris a large glass exhibition hall, the Salon du Prêt-à-Porter (meaning ready-to-carry or ready-to-wear) to accom-

The American couturiere Claire McCardell, seen modeling one of her gowns (1945), created clothing noted for simplicity of both style and construction. American designers now receive international recognition for fashions that are as beautiful as they are practical. (Fashion Institute of Technology, New York City.)

modate the growing industry of ready-to-wear clothing. The elegant haute couture house is giving way to the work of designers whose output is sold to boutiques and department stores and purchased by women who care about clothes of designer quality, even if they have neither the time nor the money to buy couturier fashions.   E. M. Plunkett

Bibliography: Batterby, Michael and Ariane, *Mirror, Mirror: A Social History of Fashion* (1977); Boucher, François, *20,000 Years of Fashion* (1967); Coleridge, N., *The Fashion Conspiracy* (1988); Daria, I., *The Fashion Cycle* (1990); Ewing, Elizabeth, *History of Twentieth-Century Fashion*, rev. ed. (1986); Frings, V. S., *Fashion: From Concept to Consumer* (1982); Gold, Annalee, *Ninety Years of Fashion* (1990); Mulvagh, Jane, *The ''Vogue'' History of Twentieth Century Fashion* (1989); Squire, Geoffrey, *Dress and Society 1560–1970* (1974); Steele, Valerie, *Paris Fashion: A Cultural History* (1988); Tate, Sharon, *Inside Fashion Design* (1977).

See also: CLOTHING INDUSTRY; COSTUME.

fashion photography

Fashion photography illustrates and documents styles of dress and is used both as a sales tool in advertising and as a means of legitimizing and establishing new fashions as they emerge. The many highly talented photographers in the field have produced a level of work that is often well above the commercial and is studied and ranked as a form of social documentation, if not as art.

The roots of modern fashion photography can be traced to the 18th-century sketches known as fashion plates and the 19th-century drawings used to illustrate catalogs. Like the modern photograph these drawings were used to disseminate ideas about style and sophistication. Among the first fashion photographs were those taken by Baron Adolph de Meyer, Edward STEICHEN, and Cecil BEATON during the 1920s. In many of these photographs style was opulently linked with social status and famous clothing designers. Such magazines as *Vogue* and *Harper's Bazaar* devoted their pages almost exclusively to photo illustrations. Photographers like Richard AVEDON and Irving PENN carried on the tradition of studio photography that these magazines had fostered—although, by the 1950s and '60s, the posed, highly stylized, somewhat tense fashion portrait was shot in front of an empty backdrop that removed the distinction between floor and wall, emphasizing the difference between fashion and reality. More contemporary photographers—Bruce Weber, Herb Ritt, and many others—shoot on location, looking for spontaneity and a more potent connection with the real.

Bibliography: Devlin, P., *The Vogue Book of Fashion Photography* (1979); Farber, R., *The Fashion Photographer* (1981); Harrison, M., *The Art of Vogue Covers* (1984); Randall, R., *Fashion Photography* (1984).

Fashoda Incident   [fuh-shoh'-duh]

The Fashoda Incident was a confrontation between Great Britain and France in 1898 that arose from the rivalry of the two powers for territory in Africa. The British aim to link Egypt with South Africa by a Cape-to-Cairo railway was challenged by a French drive to establish a belt across the continent from Senegal to Somaliland. A French military party advancing eastward was met at Fashoda (now Kodok) on the White Nile by a British force under Sir Herbert KITCHENER on Sept. 18, 1898. Although the two countries hovered on the brink of war, diplomatic negotiations in Europe resolved the issue. France withdrew its force and accepted the watershed between the Congo and the Nile basins as the boundary between its sphere of influence and Britain's.   D. M. L. Farr

Bibliography: Bates, D., *The Fashoda Incident of 1898* (1984).

Fassbinder, Rainer Werner   [fahs'-bin-dur, ry'-nur vair'-nur]

Rainer Werner Fassbinder, b. May 31, 1946, d. June 10, 1982, was one of Germany's greatest and most prolific film directors as well as a stage and screen actor and scriptwriter. He joined the Munich Action Theater in 1967 and began making films two years later, using a permanent ensemble of experienced actors. Fassbinder's work reflects the influence of Bertolt

Brecht and Karl Marx, and of Freudian psychology; his choice of material was influenced by the American filmmaker Douglas Sirk. His subject matter ranges from the failure of friends to communicate, as portrayed in *Katzelmacher* (1969), to the dullness of daily existence, depicted in *Warum läuft Herr R. Amok?* (Why Does Herr R. Run Amok?, 1969) and *Die bitteren Tränen der Petra von Kant* (The Bitter Tears of Petra von Kant, 1972). Particularly admired are the bittersweet *Der Händler der vier Jahreszeiten* (Merchant of the Four Seasons, 1971), the stylish *Effi Breist*, and *Ali: Angst essen Seele auf* (Ali: Fear Eats the Soul, 1974), a study in adversity. Fassbinder's *Faustrecht der Freiheit* (1975), released in English as *Fox and His Friends*, created a new wave of interest in his films in both the United States and Europe. In 1978, Fassbinder released his first English language film, *Despair*, starring Dirk Bogarde. His most commercially successful film was *The Marriage of Maria Braun* (1979).   Gautam Dasgupta

Bibliography: Katz, R., *Love Is Colder than Death* (1987).

Fast, Howard

Howard Melvin Fast, b. New York City, Nov. 11, 1914, is a prolific American writer of novels, short stories, plays, and essays. During the 1940s and early '50s he was prominently associated with left-wing politics, which he described in *The Naked God* (1957). His best-known works are historical novels, including *Citizen Tom Paine* (1943), *Freedom Road* (1944), and *Spartacus* (1952; film, 1960). In 1950, before his public break with the Communist party, he was imprisoned on a charge of contempt of Congress. He received the Stalin International Peace Prize in 1953. His later novels include *The Immigrants* (1977) and *The Dinner Party* (1987).   Marcus Klein

fast foods: see FOOD SERVICE SYSTEMS.

fasting

Fasting is the practice of abstaining from food, either completely or partially, for a specified period. It is an ancient practice found in most religions of the world. Recent scientific research suggests that fasting may be healthful and, when engaged in carefully, may bring about heightened states of consciousness and sensibility. Traditionally, fasting has been a widely used form of ASCETICISM and a penitential practice observed for the purpose of purifying the person or of atoning for sins and wrongdoing. Most religions designate certain days or seasons as times of fasting for their adherents, such as LENT, YOM KIPPUR, and RAMADAN. Certain events are considered appropriate times for fasting, such as the day or night before a major personal commitment. The vigil of knighthood is an historical instance of this practice. Prayer is supposed to accompany fasting.   Joan A. Range

fat

Fat, or LIPIDS, is a family of chemical compounds stored by plants and animals as a source of energy. In most animals fats are stored in special cells that tend to form pads of tissue under the skin and around certain organs and joints, the locations depending on the species. Stored fat, or adipose tissue, serves as a fuel reserve for METABOLISM. Fat protects the body from shocks and jolts and provides insulation. In plants, fats in the form of oil are found in the stems, seeds, and fruit.

All fats are made up of units of GLYCEROL and fatty acids. The kind of fatty acids eaten can affect a person's health. Saturated fatty acids found in butter, milk, and other animal products can raise the level of CHOLESTEROL in the blood, thus leading to ARTERIOSCLEROSIS. Unsaturated fats found in vegetable oils can reduce high levels of blood cholesterol.

Fat is a concentrated source of energy. The breakdown of stored fat during metabolism yields fatty acids, the source of metabolic energy for muscle contraction. The body's adipose tissue is in a constant state of buildup and breakdown, thus ensuring a continual supply of fatty acids. A normal human male has about 15 kg (33 lb) of stored fat, which theoretically can support life for about two months. Obese people may have 100 kg (220 lb) of fat—a year's supply. Research has shown that fat distribution in men and women serves different purposes: abdominal fat, found more often in men, provides fuel for quick energy, while the fat in the thighs and buttocks of women provides energy for pregnancy and nursing.

Bibliography: Vergroesen, A. J., and Crawford, M., eds., *The Role of Fats in Human Nutrition*, 2d ed. (1989).

See also: NUTRITION, HUMAN.

fata morgana   [fah'-tuh mor-gah'-nah]

A fata morgana is a complex MIRAGE that causes distant coastlines and buildings to appear as castles in the sky. It is a combination of an inferior mirage, in which the false image appears below the true position, and a superior mirage, in which a double image appears, one image inverted below the other. The fata morgana is named for the magical powers of Morgan le Fay, the sorceress of Arthurian legend. It was first described in the Strait of Messina, Italy, but also occurs across Toyama Bay, Japan, and on Lake Geneva, Switzerland.

Fatehpur Sikri   [fuh-tuh-poor' see'-kree]

Fatehpur Sikri (1981 pop., 17,908), a town about 40 km (25 mi) southwest of Agra in Uttar Pradesh state, north India, was from 1569 to 1584 the site of the Mogul emperor AKBAR's capital. Founded to honor the Muslim saint Salim Chishti, who had prophesied the birth of Akbar's son and heir, Jahangir, the city is one of the finest extant examples of Mogul architecture in India. Among its magnificent palace buildings and halls of state are numerous architectural conceits, such as the Diwani-Am, a five-storied pavilion the stepped tiers of which diminish in scale as they rise toward a kiosk on top; and a courtyard transformed by its paving into a gigantic functional chessboard. The Great Mosque complex contains the ornate marble tomb of Salim and a triumphal gateway memorializing Akbar's military conquests.

Fatehpur Sikri was originally bounded on its northwest side by a large artificial lake. This proved to be an inadequate water supply for the city, and the capital was abandoned less than 20 years after it was laid out.   DIRAN KAVORK DOHANIAN

Fates

In Greek mythology, the three Fates, or Moirai, were the offspring of ZEUS and the Titan Themis. Though robed in white, they are described as daughters of the night and equated with the obscure darkness of human destiny. Each had her separate duty to perform: Clotho spun the thread of life; Lachesis fixed the length of the thread as she held it; and Atropos cut the thread with her shears when the span of life was done. In Roman mythology, the Fates were also known as the Parcae.

Fath, Jacques: see FASHION DESIGN.

Fathers of the Church

During the first three centuries of Christian history only bishops were called Fathers of the Church. The title was later extended to all learned church writers of antiquity recognized for their orthodoxy of doctrine and holiness of life. The last of the fathers are generally considered to be Saint ISIDORE OF SEVILLE (d. 636) in the West and Saint JOHN DAMASCENE (d.c.750) in the East. Some of the preeminent fathers have also been designated as DOCTORS OF THE CHURCH, a title of later origin.

See also: APOSTOLIC FATHERS; PATRISTIC LITERATURE.

Fathers and Sons

In *Fathers and Sons* (1862), the Russian novelist Ivan TURGENEV deals with the age-old theme of a conflict between generations. The theme is made more poignant by being placed in a contemporary context—the generation gap created by the government reforms of 1856 to 1861. In the novel the nihilist

sons, represented by Bazarov, believe only in science and its rational application to human affairs; at the same time, they despise the values of their fathers, upheld by Kirsanov: honor, patriotism, love, and beauty.   VICTOR TERRAS

Bibliography: Costlow, Jane, *Worlds within Worlds* (1990).

fatigue: see MUSCLE CONTRACTION; SLEEP.

Fátima   (city)   [fah'-tee-mah]

Fátima (1981 pop., 525) is a village in central Portugal located 115 km (70 mi) north of Lisbon. It is one of the world's foremost Roman Catholic pilgrimage centers. In 1917 the Virgin Mary reportedly appeared on several occasions to three children there. Authorized pilgrimages have taken place since 1927 by those seeking cures and offering prayers. A basilica was begun in 1928 and consecrated in 1953.

Fatima   (daughter of Muhammad)   [fat'-i-muh]

Fatima, c.616–33, was the only daughter of the Prophet MUHAMMAD, the wife of ALI, and in Muslim tradition, the ancestor of the Fatimid caliphs and the imams of the SHIITE branch of Islam. The subject of many legends, she is revered by all Muslims, but especially by the Shiites.

Fatimids   [fat'-i-midz]

The Fatimids were an Islamic dynasty that reigned in North Africa and later in Egypt from 909 until 1171. The Fatimid CALIPHATE was the political pinnacle of the ISMAILIS, a group of SHIITES who expected the appearance of a messiah descended from the marriage of ALI, the fourth caliph, and Fatima, the daughter of the Prophet Muhammad.

The Fatimids initially established a North African empire centered in Tunisia, from which they planned to move eastward and supplant the ABBASIDS. Consequently, they conquered Egypt in 969 and created Cairo as their capital. They then extended their influence to Syria, Palestine, and Arabia. They reached the zenith of their power in the reign of al-Mustansir (1036–94). The dynasty enjoyed generally peaceful relations with the Byzantines and cooperated with the Turkish rulers of Syria against the Crusades.

From the mid-12th century, the Fatimid kingdom began to crumble internally; the caliphs lost most of their power, and the viziers, at the head of a highly centralized government, assumed much of the executive and military leadership. Therefore, SALADIN found it easy to end Fatimid rule in 1171. Despite the religious unorthodoxy of the dynasty, most of its subjects remained orthodox Muslims. In this period Egypt enjoyed extraordinary economic and cultural vitality.

MICHAEL W. DOLS

Bibliography: Lewis, Bernard, *The Origin of Isma'ilism* (1975); O'Leary, De Lacy, *A Short History of the Fatimid Kaliphate* (1923).

fats and oils

Fats and oils are an important, diverse class of animal and vegetable compounds used extensively as foods, cleansers, and lubricants. Various fats are the raw materials for many industrial processes. Originally, fats and oils were distinguished by their physical state: fats are solid at room temperature, oils are liquids. Chemists now classify both as fats to avoid possible confusion with petroleum and ESSENTIAL OILS.

Chemistry of Fats.   Fats are triglycerides—ESTERS comprising three molecules of FATTY ACIDS and one of the alcohol GLYCEROL. Natural triglycerides are usually mixed; that is, they contain more than one kind of fatty acid. Natural fats are composed of different glycerides, the specific composition being determined by the species and the function.

The common fatty acids have between 12 and 20 carbon atoms in even numbers. Both saturated and unsaturated acids are present. The unsaturated acids contain one or more carbon-carbon double bonds, which lead to a decrease in the melting temperature. Unsaturation is most often found in the oils. These compounds are more reactive to oxygen, resulting in oil that is less stable and is subject to rancidity.

Sources. A relatively small number of plants and animals yield commercial quantities of fat.

Hogs yield lard from their fatty tissue. Major producers are the United States, Canada, Brazil, France, and Germany. Approximately 14% of the live weight of the hog can be obtained as lard and rendered into pork fat, a darker grade with a characteristic flavor and better keeping quality. A process to improve lard as a shortening has been developed, involving the rearrangement of triglyceride structures.

Cow's MILK (goat and buffalo in some countries) is an important ingredient of butter. The commercial product contains about 81% butterfat along with small amounts of salt and curd. Natural bacteria have been largely replaced by special strains that add a pleasing flavor and aroma.

Whale oil, in Europe, is used as a substitute for margarine or lard. Its major current application is in soap.

SOYBEAN oil, the world's largest-volume oil product, is a food. Much of the oil, which constitutes about 16% to 18% of the bean's weight, is modified before use. Soybean oil, often a constituent of paints and printing inks, is basic to the preparation of resins and plastics.

PEANUT oil is the world's second largest-volume oil product. A high-quality edible oil, it is widely used for cooking, in mayonnaise, or as a salad oil.

COCONUT oil, from copra, the dried nutmeat of many palm trees, represents approximately 8% of the world's trade in fats and oils. The Philippines, Sri Lanka, and Indonesia are the principal producers and exporters of copra. After World War II copra use shifted from food to production of soap, chemical detergents, alcohols, amines, and acids.

LINSEED OIL, derived from flaxseeds grown mainly in Canada, Argentina, and the United States, is a drying oil because of the large amount of unsaturation present. Drying oils are used in protective coatings such as paints and varnishes. Linseed oil is also used in making linoleum and alkyd resins.

Other commercial vegetable oils are derived from CORN, OLIVES, RAPE plants (canola oil), SAFFLOWERS, and SUNFLOWERS, among other sources, and synthetic oils are being developed.

Processing. Processes for obtaining fats are of two general types: extraction from the natural source, and processing or modification. Three basic modes of extraction are used. (1) In *rendering*, the seeds or fatty tissues are heated with water and steam, often under pressure, and the nearly insoluble fat is separated by skimming or centrifuging. Lard from hogs, and whale and olive oils are derived this way. (2) In *pressing*, mills or screw presses are used to break down the cell walls and liberate the oil. This method is effective for soybean, peanut, coconut, and linseed oils. (3) Extraction with hydrocarbon solvents takes advantage of their power to dissolve fats. These solvents are volatile and may be removed and recycled. Nuts and seeds of high oil content lend themselves well to pressing and extraction. Soybean, linseed, and peanut oils are obtained by either method.

Raw fat is processed to improve the quality of the product. The number of steps used depends upon the type of raw fat and its ultimate application. *Refining* removes the nonglyceride material consisting mostly of hydrolyzed fatty acids. Their presence imparts a disagreeable taste to foods such as salad oil. The nonglycerides may be removed by treatment with bases such as sodium hydroxide or sodium carbonate. *Bleaching* makes fat white and can be accomplished chemically, by physical adsorption with activated carbon or clays, or by heating. *Winterizing* is rapid or slow chilling to remove waxes, stearic acid, or higher-melting glycerides. Peanut-based salad oil is winterized so that it will remain a liquid at cooler temperatures. *Hydrogenation*, often called hardening, involves the addition of hydrogen to the carbon-carbon double or triple bonds of unsaturated fats. It produces a desirable solid fat for margarine and shortening. Hardened fats have less susceptibility to slow oxidation, which would cause them to turn rancid.

Function. Fats play two principal roles in plant and animal physiology: as sources of stored energy and as protection against thermal and physical injury. Research shows, however, that they are also associated with the sterols, vitamins, and other substances vital to the organism's well-being. The greater solubility of these chemicals in fats assists in their necessary transfer from one location in the organism to another.

K. THOMAS FINLEY

Bibliography: Finnegan, John, *Understanding Oils and Fats* (1989); Ihde, Aaron J., *The Development of Modern Chemistry* (1964; repr. 1983); Kent, J. A., ed., *Riegel's Handbook of Industrial Chemistry*, 8th ed. (1983); Morrison, R. T., and Boyd, R. N., *Organic Chemistry*, 5th ed. (1987).

See also: CARBOXYLIC ACID; SAPONIFICATION.

fatty acid

Certain CARBOXYLIC ACIDS, particularly those with longer carbon chains (12–20 carbon atoms), are often called fatty acids because they are constituents of animal FATS AND OILS. The fatty acids may be released from the fat by hydrolysis, as in the following example:

$$CH_2O_2C(CH_2)_{14}CH_3 \qquad\qquad CH_2OH$$
$$|$$
$$CHO_2C(CH_2)_{14}CH_3 \xrightarrow[H^+ \text{ or } OH^-]{3H_2O} CHOH + 3\ CH_3(CH_2)_{14}COOH$$
$$|$$
$$CH_2O_2C(CH_2)_{14}CH_3 \qquad\qquad CH_2OH$$

tripalmitin   glycerol   palmitic acid

Fatty acids may be easily prepared from other organic compounds by oxidation of the corresponding alcohol, aldehyde, or unsaturated hydrocarbon. They have the acidic properties and chemical reactivity typical of carboxyl compounds. Salts of long-chain fatty acids (14 or more carbon atoms), or soaps, are important because of their ability to form emulsions with oils. A number of unsaturated fatty acids, such as oleic acid, occur in natural materials.

$$CH_3(CH_2)_7 \overset{H}{\underset{}{C}} = \overset{H}{\underset{}{C}} (CH_2)_7CO_2H$$

oleic acid
(*cis*-9-octadecenoic acid)

The olefinic bonds lower the melting point of the acid and increase its reactivity, especially toward oxidation and addition.

Vinegar is a dilute aqueous solution of ACETIC ACID (Latin: *acetum*, vinegar; CH_3CO_2H). Butyric (Latin: *butyrum*, butter) acid ($CH_3CH_2CH_2CO_2H$) is one of the 14 fatty acids found in butter. Formic (Latin: *formica*, ant) acid (HCO_2H) is a protective chemical found in many ants.

K. THOMAS FINLEY

See also: ACIDS AND BASES; SAPONIFICATION.

SELECTED FATTY ACIDS

Common Name	Systematic Name	Formula	Melting Point (°C)	Source (%)
Lauric	Dodecanoic	$CH_3(CH_2)_{10}CO_2H$	44	Coconut (48), palm kernel (52)
Myristic	Tetradecanoic	$CH_3(CH_2)_{12}CO_2H$	55	Coconut (18), whale blubber (8)
Palmitic	Hexadecanoic	$CH_3(CH_2)_{14}CO_2H$	63	Palm (42), beef tallow (32)
Stearic	Octadecanoic	$CH_3(CH_2)_{16}CO_2H$	70	Peanut (5), lard (18)
Oleic	*cis*-9-Octadecenoic	$CH_3(CH_2)_7CH{=}CH(CH_2)_7CO_2H$	14	Olive (83), beef tallow (48)
Linoleic	9,12-Octadecadienoic *(cis)*	$CH_3(CH_2)_3(CH_2CH{=}CH)_2(CH_2)_7CO_2H$	−9	Palm (10), whale blubber (9)
Linolenic	9,12,15-Octadecatrienoic *(cis)*	$CH_3(CH_2CH{=}CH)_3(CH_2)_7CO_2H$	−11	Linseed (58), lard (1)

Faulkner, Brian   [fawk'-nur]

Arthur Brian Deane Faulkner, b. Feb. 18, 1921, d. Mar. 3, 1977, was the last prime minister of Northern Ireland under the constitution established in 1920. Elected to the Northern Ireland Parliament in 1949, he held several cabinet posts between 1959 and March 1971, when he succeeded James Chichester-Clarke as prime minister. At this time the IRISH REPUBLICAN ARMY (IRA) was increasing its terrorist activities against the British Army, which had been in Northern Ireland since 1969. Faulkner initiated (Aug. 9, 1971) the policy of interning suspected IRA members, but this had the effect of increasing, rather than decreasing, the violence and further alienated the Catholic minority in religion-torn Ulster.

On Mar. 30, 1972, the British government suspended the constitution and assumed direct rule. In 1973 a new provincial legislature and executive board were established, and after elections based on proportional representation, Faulkner became (Jan. 1, 1974) head of the new coalition administration, the first in Ulster's history. The coalition was brought down in May 1974 by a general strike organized by Protestant extremists, and the British government resumed direct rule. Faulkner retired as leader of the Protestant party in August 1976.

Faulkner, William

William Cuthbert Faulkner, b. New Albany, Miss., Sept. 25, 1897, d. July 6, 1962, was one of America's most innovative novelists. He lived most of his life in Oxford, Miss., and his works combine regional traditions and culture with masterly characterization and technical experimentation.

In a career lasting more than three decades, Faulkner published 19 novels, more than 80 short stories, 2 books of poems, and numerous essays. Like Thomas Mann and James Joyce, writers he greatly admired, Faulkner depicted traditional society not only in its own terms but also in terms of ageless human dramas.

Early Life and Works. Faulkner's principal setting is Yoknapatawpha County, a fictional domain loosely based upon places and subjects near to him in his youth. His family had played a significant role in Mississippi history. His great-grandfather, the model for the senior John Sartoris of several novels, was a lawyer, soldier, painter, railroad builder, poet, and novelist and was twice acquitted of murder charges. Faulkner grew up surrounded by traditional lore—family and regional stories, rural folk wisdom and humor, heroic and tragic accounts of the War Between the States, and tales of the hunting code and the Southern gentleman's ideal of conduct. In his lifetime and

American author William Faulkner, a major figure in contemporary literature, wrote novels and short stories combining stream-of-consciousness narrative with linguistic innovations and vivid characterization. Faulkner's fictional Yoknapatawpha County, although set in his native South, is a microcosm of universal human experience.

in his works, Faulkner bore witness to great political, economic, and social changes in the life of the South.

Although Oxford, Miss., was in some ways rural, it was also the seat of the state university, the county government, and the federal district court, and it had ties to major cultural centers. A voracious reader, more schooled than he would ever admit, Faulkner began writing in his early teens. As a young man he produced hand-lettered and hand-illustrated books for his friends, including books of poems, at least one esoteric play, an allegorical story, and a children's tale. These works show his early commitment to a writer's life.

Faulkner's early years were not confined to the countryside that he eventually shaped into Yoknapatawpha. Before the 1918 armistice, he trained in Toronto as a fighter pilot with the Royal Air Force. He traveled to New York City, New Orleans, and Europe. He read and wrote, absorbing the modernist influences that were changing the face of 20th-century art. In the mid-1920s, Faulkner lived among writers and artists in the French Quarter of New Orleans and received encouragement for his fiction, most notably from Sherwood Anderson. He had come to New Orleans with a book of poems to his credit, *The Marble Faun* (1924), and he there completed his first novel, *Soldiers' Pay* (1926), about the homecoming of a fatally wounded aviator.

The Mature Years. After travel abroad and the publication of his second novel, *Mosquitoes* (1927), about bohemian life in New Orleans, Faulkner returned to Oxford, Miss., apparently on Anderson's advice, to begin a remarkable decade of writing. *Sartoris* (1929) was his first major exploration of Yoknapatawpha County, what he called his "little postage stamp of native soil," and he exploited it fictionally during the following 24 years, with occasional side trips.

Faulkner's next novel, THE SOUND AND THE FURY (1929), displayed startling progress. It showed that he had mastered his material, demonstrated a rich variety of styles, and brought to bear techniques and ideas then pervasive in literature and art. Established as an author, Faulkner continued to write novels, always experimenting with new forms. As I Lay Dying (1930) was a tour de force in stream of consciousness. Subsequent works included the tightly knit novel LIGHT IN AUGUST (1932), the monumentally complex narrative ABSALOM, ABSALOM! (1936), and the episodic *Go Down, Moses* (1942), containing his most famous short piece, "The BEAR." *A Fable* (1954) and *The Reivers* (1962) each won the Pulitzer Prize for fiction, but Faulkner's later novels were generally considered less successful.

Faulkner set ambitious goals for himself and often considered his books failures because they did not measure up to his expectations. Others thought differently, however. Faulkner received the 1949 Nobel Prize for literature. A humanist, he repeatedly explored the question of human freedom and the obstacles to it—racism, regimentation, shame, fear, pride, and overly abstract principles. In his Nobel Prize acceptance speech, Faulkner summed up a lifetime of writing: "The poet's voice need not merely be the record of man, it can be one of the props, the pillars to help him endure and prevail."

THOMAS L. MCHANEY

Bibliography: Adams, Richard P., *Faulkner: Myth and Motion* (1968); Blotner, Joseph, *Faulkner: A Biography*, 2 vols. (1972; repr. 1991); Brooks, Cleanth, *Essays on the Prejudices, Predilections, and Firm Beliefs of William Faulkner* (1987), *William Faulkner: The Yoknapatawpha County* (1964; repr. 1990), and *William Faulkner: Toward Yoknapatawpha and Beyond* (1978; repr. 1990); Howe, Irving, *William Faulkner: A Critical Study*, 3d ed. (1975); Karl, Frederick, *William Faulkner: An American Writer* (1989; repr. 1990); McHaney, Thomas, *William Faulkner: A Reference Guide* (1976); Meriwether, James B., ed., *Essays, Speeches, and Public Letters of William Faulkner* (1965); Millgate, Michael, *The Achievement of William Faulkner* (1966; repr. 1989); Oates, Stephen B., *William Faulkner: The Man and the Artist* (1987); Wagner, Linda, ed., *William Faulkner: Four Decades of Criticism* (1973).

fault

A fault is a fracture in the Earth's crust along which measurable movement has occurred. Generally, one block of the crust moves past another, the distance moved varying from a

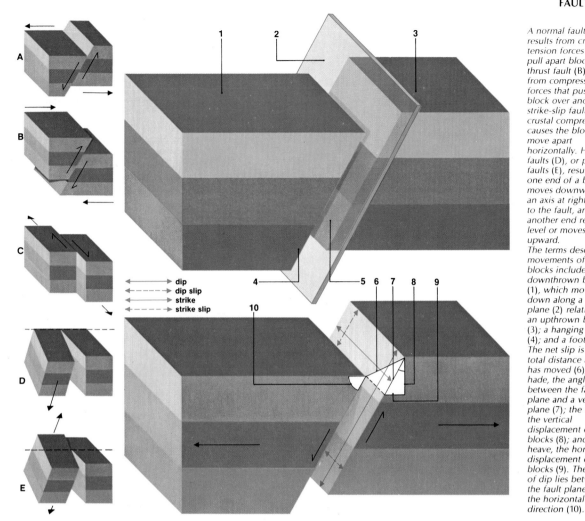

dip
dip slip
strike
strike slip

A normal fault (A) results from crustal tension forces that pull apart blocks. A thrust fault (B) results from compressional forces that push one block over another. In strike-slip faults (C), crustal compression causes the blocks to move apart horizontally. Hinge faults (D), or pivotal faults (E), result when one end of a block moves downward on an axis at right angles to the fault, and another end remains level or moves upward.

The terms describing movements of fault blocks include a downthrown block (1), which moves down along a fault plane (2) relative to an upthrown block (3); a hanging wall (4); and a footwall (5). The net slip is the total distance a block has moved (6); the hade, the angle between the fault plane and a vertical plane (7); the throw, the vertical displacement of the blocks (8); and the heave, the horizontal displacement of the blocks (9). The angle of dip lies between the fault plane and the horizontal direction (10).

few meters to hundreds of kilometers, but because it is usually not possible to say with certainty which block moved and which remained still, geologists can generally describe only the sense of movement, not the direction and magnitude.

Types. Two general classes of faults exist, distinguished by whether the movement is up and down (dip-slip) or parallel to (strike-slip) the fault plane. Dip-slip faults are further classified as normal or thrust (reverse) faults. The difference between these is determined by relative movement. In a dip-slip fault, the fault plane is commonly not vertical. Consequently, one block rests above the other. The block on top is the hanging wall, that beneath is the footwall. If the hanging wall moves down relative to the footwall, the fault is a normal fault; if the hanging wall moves up, the fault is a thrust fault. Normal faults are produced by tensional (pull-apart) forces; thrust faults are produced by compressional (push-together) forces.

Faults are produced by the forces that build MOUNTAIN systems. Major thrust and strike-slip faults are more common than major normal faults, however, because mountain chains are produced by compressional forces. Normal faults may form later, following the compressional phase of mountain building (OROGENY), as in the Great Basin region of the western United States. Normal faults also occur in the interior of continents and in coastal regions such as North America's Gulf Coast, where fault movement occurs in response to gravitational forces on accumulating sediment.

Fault Movement. Although most faults are inactive, and have been so for millions of years, some faults, such as the SAN ANDREAS FAULT in California, have remained active. When such an active fault moves sporadically and suddenly, an EARTH-

QUAKE results. In the case of the San Andreas, a strike-slip fault, portions are creeping (moving very slowly), while others are locked. Strain energy accumulates in the locked portions, where earthquakes are likely to occur. The largest earthquakes occur along compressional faults, smaller earthquakes along tensional faults. The reason for this is that the force of friction is more easily overcome in a tensional system.

Measurements are made along active faults to determine the rate of movement. Various techniques are employed, some of which involve the use of sophisticated and expensive LASER measuring devices and others merely an iron bar placed athwart the fault plane and anchored at only one end. Rates of continuous movement on a creeping fault are usually about 1-10 cm (0.4-4.0 in) a year. Active faults that produce earthquakes may not move for several decades, then move 1 m (3 ft) or more in a fraction of a second. If averaged over the period of time since the last movement, however, the rate of such movement may be about the same as that of a fault that has been continuously creeping.

Faults that have a history of recent movement or that are still active generally affect the surface TOPOGRAPHY. Offset streams, fault scarps (cliffs coincident with fault planes; see ESCARPMENT), flatirons (truncated ridge spurs), and stream valleys that follow fault traces are all features related to recent fault movement. These features are generally eroded away along inactive faults; resistant rock layers, however, may be offset and brought into relief, forming a fault-line scarp.

Construction along Faults. Construction along faults may pose complex problems. If the fault is active, special building or foundation designs, or both, may be necessary to ensure that the structure can withstand shaking or other movement.

Construction of large buildings, bridges, or dams directly on active faults is commonly avoided, although many such structures have been built directly on the San Andreas and other active faults in California.

Construction on inactive faults may present problems of other kinds. GROUNDWATER may open up a fault zone by dissolving the gouge or fault BRECCIA; or it may precipitate minerals that cement the fault zone together. An ancient fault may have brought rocks of different mechanical properties into contact, posing unique problems for foundation construction.

R. D. HATCHER, JR.

Bibliography: Jaroszewski, Wojciech, *Fault and Fold Tectonics* (1984); Scholtz, C. H., *The Mechanics of Earthquakes and Faulting* (1990).

See also: HORST AND GRABEN; JOINT (in geology); RIFT VALLEYS; TRANSFORM FAULT.

Faunus   [fawn'-uhs]

In Roman mythology, Faunus was a fertility and woodland god. An agricultural deity, Faunus protected crops, fields, flocks, and shepherds and invented a rustic musical instrument, the shawm. The Roman festival known as the LUPERCALIA was closely identified with Faunus, who, as Lupercus, was worshiped in a temple on the Palatine Hill. Faunus also functioned as a prophetic god. Some scholars have suggested that Faunus may have been an early king of Latium who was subsequently deified.

Fauré, Gabriel Urbain   [foh-ray', gah-bree-el' uer-ban']

Gabriel Urbain Fauré, b. May 12, 1845, d. Nov. 4, 1924, was an eminent French composer, organist, and teacher. He attended (1855–66) the Niedermeyer School in Paris, where he studied with Camille Saint-Saëns. Fauré later became a church organist in Brittany. He served briefly in the French army in 1870 and taught at the Niedermeyer School from 1872. In 1896 he became professor of composition at the Paris Conservatory and principal organist at the Church of the Madeleine. Later he was a music critic for *Le Figaro*. In 1905 he was appointed director of the Paris Conservatory. Many of Fauré's pupils achieved fame, among them Nadia Boulanger, Georges Enesco, Maurice Ravel, and Florent Schmitt.

Fauré's outstanding works include much chamber music, particularly the Piano Quartet in C minor (1879), *Requiem* (1886), and nearly 100 songs. Few other compositions have become popular outside France, despite their excellence, melodic beauty, and harmonic originality. Fauré's music represents the best in the French tradition, in which restraint and balance, simplicity and lyricism, and subtle detail are characteristic. He also wrote two operas; orchestral works, including *Pavane* (1887); and piano pieces.

HOMER ULRICH

Bibliography: Jones, J. B., ed., *Gabriel Fauré* (1989); Koechlin, Charles, *Gabriel Fauré* (1945; repr. 1976); Nectou, Jean-Michel, ed., *Gabriel Fauré* (1984); Orledge, Robert, *Gabriel Fauré* (1982).

Faust   [fowst]

A Dr. Johann Faust—who lived in Germany in the first half of the 16th century and was a student of magic, astrology, and alchemy—provided the model for the protagonist of *The History of Dr. Johann Faustus* (anon., c.1580). The German book was the first printed collection of the legends attached to the name *Faust,* the scholar who sells his soul to the devil in exchange for knowledge and power. The story, in translation, appeared throughout Europe and inspired—among other, lesser works—Christopher Marlowe's great play DOCTOR FAUSTUS (publ. 1604) and Johann Goethe's dramatic poem *Faust: A Tragedy* (1808, 1832). For many, the Faust figure embodies a human dilemma, where the search for and possession of knowledge inevitably poisons or corrupts one's relationship to God and nature. Authors such as Heinrich Heine and Thomas Mann, composers such as Hector Berlioz and Charles Gounod, and Eugène Delacroix and Max Beckmann among artists have all found Faust a tragic symbol of central importance.

Bibliography: Butler, E. M., *The Fortunes of Faust* (1952; repr. 1979); Dieckmann, L., *Goethe's Faust: A Critical Reading* (1972); Faustus, Johann, *The Historie of the Damnable Life and Deserved Death of Dr. John Faustus* (1592; repr. 1969); Grim, W., *The Faust Legend in Music and Literature* (1987); Grimm, R., and Hermond, J., eds., *Our Faust? Roots and Ramifications of a Modern German Myth* (1987); Palmer, P. M., and Moore, R. P., *Sources of the Faust Tradition* (1936; repr. 1969); Smeed, John W., *Faust in Literature* (1987).

Fauvism   [foh'-vizm]

Maurice de Vlaminck's painting Street Scene in Marly-le-Roi *(1904) is representative of the style of painting known as Fauvism, which arose in Paris during the years 1905-07. The work exhibits the typical Fauvist combination of spontaneous execution, emotively expressive colors, and distorted composition. (Musée National d'Art Moderne, Paris.)*

At the 1905 Salon d'Automne in Paris a group of painters under the leadership of Henri MATISSE shocked the art world with their paintings characterized by brilliant color, expressive brushwork, and flat composition, as in Matisse's *The Green Stripe, Portrait of Mme. Matisse* (1905; Statens Museum fur Kunst, Copenhagen). The critic Louis Vauxcelles, on visiting the show, called the painters the "Wild Beasts," or "Les Fauves"; the pejorative remark was exploited by hostile critics, and the name stuck.

Vincent VAN GOGH, Paul GAUGUIN, the NABIS, and the neoimpressionists (see NEOIMPRESSIONISM) were the most important influences on the Fauves. Some of them had been students of Gustave MOREAU at the École des Beaux-Arts; these included Matisse, Albert Marquet, Georges ROUAULT, Charles Camoir, Jean Puy, and Henri Manguin. André DERAIN and Maurice de VLAMINCK had painted together at Chatou. A contingent from Le Havre, Achille Émile Orthon Friesz, Raoul DUFY, and Georges BRAQUE, joined the group after seeing Matisse's work. Kees van DONGEN, a Dutch painter, joined them when he settled in Paris.

The Fauves never issued a theoretical manifesto. By the time Matisse wrote his "Notes of a Painter" in 1908, the peak of Fauvism was over. Matisse himself moved from the spontaneous and exuberant use of color that characterized Fauvism to a more decorative formalism. Although Fauvism was a short-lived movement, it was influential; the German expressionists, particularly Wassily KANDINSKY and Alexey von JAWLENSKY in Munich, and the Die BRÜCKE group in Dresden were heavily indebted to it. (See EXPRESSIONISM.)

The Fauves represented the first break with the artistic traditions of the past. The movement's emphasis on formal values and expressive use of color, line, and brushwork helped liberate painting from the representational expectations that had dominated Western art since the Renaissance. Fauvism was the first explosive 20th-century art movement.

IDA K. RIGBY

Bibliography: Diel, Gaston, *The Fauves* (1975); Elderfield, John, *The Wild Beast: Fauvism and Its Affinities* (1976); Freeman, Judi, et al., *The Fauve Landscape* (1990); Leymarie, Jean, *Fauves and Fauvism* (1986); Whitfield, Sarah, *Fauvism* (1990).

favorite son

In U.S. politics a favorite son is a person favored for nomination by a state delegation to a presidential nominating convention (SEE POLITICAL CONVENTION). Although he or she has little chance of being nominated, the favorite son controls a block of votes that can be released at a crucial moment to gain the election of a preferred candidate.

Fawkes, Guy [fawks, gy]

Guy Fawkes, b. Apr. 13, 1570, was instrumental in the Gunpowder Plot of 1605 to blow up the English Parliament and King James I. An English Roman Catholic convert, he enlisted in the Spanish army in 1593 and fought in the Netherlands. In 1604 he was engaged by the Catholic conspirators who planned to overthrow the Protestant monarchy in England to stow gunpowder barrels in a vault under the House of Lords and to explode them on Nov. 5, 1605, when the king opened Parliament. An anonymous letter warned the government, however, and during a search on Nov. 4, 1605, Fawkes was arrested. Under torture he revealed the plot and was executed on Jan. 31, 1606. November 5 continues to be celebrated in Britain as Guy Fawkes Day.

Bibliography: Garnett, Henry, *Portrait of Guy Fawkes* (1962); Langdon-Davies, John, ed., *Gunpowder Plot* (1964); Parkinson, C. Northcote, *Gunpowder, Treason, and Plot* (1977).

fax: see FACSIMILE.

Fayetteville [fay'-et-vil]

Fayetteville, seat of Cumberland County, is a city in central North Carolina at the head of navigation on the Cape Fear River. It has a population of 75,695 (1990). Settled (1739) by Highland Scots, it was incorporated (1783) from two settlements and named for the marquis de Lafayette. Serving as state capital (1789–93), it was the scene of the state's ratification of the U.S. Constitution (Nov. 21, 1789). The economy is based primarily on textiles and wood products. Fort Bragg and Pope Air Force Base are nearby.

FDIC: see FEDERAL DEPOSIT INSURANCE CORPORATION.

fear

Fear is an EMOTION characterized by unpleasant, often intense feelings and by a desire to flee or hide. Although it is generally believed to be related to ANXIETY, there is no consensus about how it is related. When recurring fear is out of proportion to any real danger, it is called a PHOBIA. Fear is accompanied by activity of the sympathetic nervous system, the system that shifts blood flow and energy to the functions needed for fight or flight. Electrical stimulation of certain areas of the brain in animals will cause flight.

The most common symptoms of fear are pounding heart, rapid pulse, muscle tension, irritability, dry throat, nervous perspiration, and "butterflies" in the stomach. Some of these symptoms, such as pulse and heart changes, also occur when other emotions are experienced. Other features, though not unique to fear, are more characteristic; among these are increases in muscle tension, skin conductance, and respiration rate. These features are associated with the hormone epinephrine, whereas the symptoms characteristic of anger are associated with the additional action of norepinephrine. Rabbits show more epinephrine; lions, more norepinephrine.

Although most causes of fear are learned, some things cause fear the first time they are seen. Chimpanzees fear the first snake or skull they see. Both chimp and human infants in certain stages show an innate fear of strangers.

Bibliography: Coles, Robert, *A Study of Courage and Fear* (1967), vol. 1 in *Children of Crisis*; Cramer, K., and Pautz, P. D., eds., *The Architecture of Fear* (1989); Doctor, R. M., and Kahn, A. P., *The Encyclopedia of Phobias, Fears, and Anxieties* (1989); Kleinknecht, Ronald A., *The Anxious Self: Diagnosis and Treatment of Fears and Phobias* (1986); Marks, Isaac, *Fears, Phobias, and Rituals* (1987).

Fearing, Kenneth

Kenneth Fearing, b. Chicago, July 28, 1902, d. June 26, 1961, was an American poet and a prolific writer of mystery novels. His poems satirize the evils found in middle-class urban life. Collections include *Afternoon of a Pawnbroker* (1943), *Stranger at Coney Island* (1948), and *New and Selected Poems* (1956). Fearing's most successful psychological thriller was *The Big Clock* (1948); other works include *The Loneliest Girl in the World* (1951) and *The Crozart Story* (1960).

Bibliography: French, Warren, ed., *The Thirties: Fiction, Poetry, Drama*, rev. ed. (1976).

feather

A feather is a specialized epidermal outgrowth unique to birds. It is composed of pigments and keratin, a protein that constitutes horny substances such as hair, nails, claws, and hooves. Strong, lightweight, and flexible, feathers cover and shape a bird's body, make flying possible, serve as attractive displays in courtship and mating rituals, and provide balance, protective coloration, and insulation. Feathers presumably are an evolutionary development from reptilian scales.

The main types are body contour feathers, which include flight feathers and wing coverts, down, and filoplumes. All feathers grow from papillae, which are nipplelike structures that anchor the quill. The quill, which is hollow, emerges from a follicle and connects to a shaft, the center of which contains spongy, air-filled cells.

Primary (A) and secondary (B) wing feathers, as well as the tail feather (C), are strong enough to lift and guide a bird in flight. Contour feathers (D) define the bird's body shape, and down feathers (E), the first type of feather grown by a young bird, provide insulation. A filoplume (F) is a hairlike feather usually interspersed among contour feathers. Feathers have a hollow quill (1) that is embedded in the bird's skin. The quill extends into a central shaft (2), from which barbs (3) project to form a vane (4). Each barb of the first four types of feather has numerous barbules (5), which hook onto barbules of adjacent barbs. These hooked barbules strengthen the feather for flight. The down and filoplume feathers appear fluffy because they lack hooked barbules. The fluffy down feathers provide warmth.

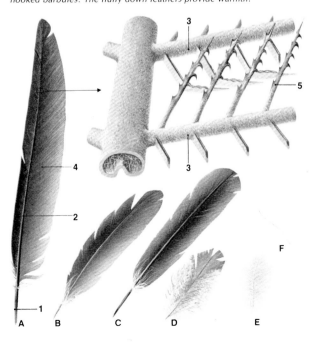

Body contour feathers shape a bird's body into a characteristic form. A contour feather has downy barbs at the shaft's base and a vane at the tip. A typical flight feather has a tightly structured vane, which is the flat, bladelike part of the feather. Long rows of barbs constitute a vane and in turn comprise rows of overlapping barbules. The barbules are held in place by hooklike structures known as barbicels. Barbs can be separated from each other and smoothed back into place because barbules and barbicels act somewhat like a zipper. Primary and secondary flight feathers of the wing, as well as tail feathers, allow a bird to control lift, steering, and braking during flight. Wing coverts, which grow over the quills of flight feathers, are similarly structured.

A down feather has barbules that lack hooks and as a result has a loose, fluffy appearance. Down feathers cover all young birds before wing and body feathers grow in and provide insulation to most adult birds. Filoplumes are hairlike feathers that have a slender shaft with few or no barbs.

Feathers of most birds grow in tracts, or patterns, along the body. The tracts are placed so that overlapping feathers cover bare patches of skin. The most general tract sites are the upper half of the head, the spine region, the shoulders to the wings, and the legs.

Birds molt, or shed their feathers, one or more times a year, depending on the species. New feathers grow from papillae of previously molted feathers. Chicks molt several times before assuming adult plumage. Some birds molt an equal number of feathers on each wing so they can maintain balance during flight. Many waterfowl, such as ducks, molt their flight feathers all at once and cannot fly until the feathers are renewed.

Coloration results from chemical pigments and from the refraction of light from the structural irregularities of the feathers. Red, yellow, and black colors are due to pigment, and blue and iridescent colors are caused by light refraction. White occurs when no pigment is present and the barbs equally reflect all wavelengths of light.   JULIE WHITAKER

Bibliography: King, A. S., and McLelland, J., eds., *Form and Function in Birds*, 3 vols. (1980–85); Voitkevich, A. A., *The Feathers and Plumage of Birds* (1966).

feather star

Feather stars are ECHINODERMS that, along with the sea lilies, constitute the class Crinoidea. Ten or more featherlike branching arms, with numerous tube feet, arise from the cup-shaped body, or theca. The animal anchors itself to a solid substratum by means of a ring of clawlike structures called cirri. During feeding the arms are extended to catch small organisms; prey is carried to the mouth in a rope of mucus. Dense aggregations of feather stars occur where food material is abundant. Some are brilliantly colored. Feather stars swim by rapidly thrashing their arms.   DAVID L. PAWSON

featherbedding

Featherbedding is a method of maintaining the employment of some LABOR UNION members by imposing rules or limitations on employers that result in their retaining or hiring "redundant" workers or that arbitrarily lengthen the period of time in which work is performed. A classic example of featherbedding was the insistence of the railroad unions in the 1960s that firemen continue to ride diesel locomotives, which have no fires to tend. Although unions generally dispute the charge of featherbedding, officials often defend the practice as the only way to protect workers whose jobs may be threatened by improved technology.

feces [fee'-seez]

Feces, also called excreta and stool, are the waste products of digestion. They take form as they are moved along the large INTESTINE by involuntary muscular contractions called PERISTALSIS (see also DIGESTION, HUMAN). The normal daily stool of human adults is about 250 g (9 oz). Besides food products, up to 20 percent of this weight is intestinal bacteria. Other constituents are digestive secretions, enzymes, fats, cell debris, elec-

trolytes, water, and small amounts of protein. The characteristic odor of feces is caused by certain organic chemicals, primarily skatole.

Medical examination of feces aids in diagnosing many gastrointestinal disorders. Very dark stools, for example, may indicate an ulcerative lesion in the higher digestive tract. Heavy, fat-rich stools can indicate various intestinal and pancreatic disorders, and so forth. Feces are also examined to detect internal parasites.

See also: COPROLITE; GUANO; MANURE.

Fechner, Gustav Theodor   [fek'-nur, gus'-tahf tay'-oh-dor]

Gustav Theodor Fechner, b. Apr. 19, 1801, d. Nov. 18, 1887, was a German physicist and psychologist and a founder of PSYCHOPHYSICS. He developed experimental methods for studying the relation of sensation to physical stimuli and put into mathematical form Ernst Weber's findings about just-noticeable differences (WEBER-FECHNER LAW). He also did pioneer work in experimental aesthetics.

Federal Aviation Administration

A part of the U.S. Department of Transportation since 1967, the Federal Aviation Administration (FAA) is responsible for regulating the technical aspects of civil air transportation. (The economic supervision of airlines was a responsibility of the CIVIL AERONAUTICS BOARD until deregulation in 1981.) The FAA establishes safety standards for aircraft and medical standards for personnel, operates and maintains communications equipment and control towers at airports, develops and tests navigation equipment and improved aircraft, and investigates airplane crashes. The FAA also helps plan and develop public airports and provides numerous other technical services. Until 1967 it was called the Federal Aviation Agency.

Federal Bureau of Investigation

The Federal Bureau of Investigation (FBI), a division of the U.S. Department of Justice, is one of the most powerful and influential law enforcement organizations in the world. With more than 8,000 special agents scattered across the country in both large cities and small towns or based at headquarters in Washington, D.C., the FBI is responsible for enforcing hundreds of federal criminal laws. Its cases include kidnappings and bank robberies, efforts to locate fugitives, and analyses of frauds against the government. It also has jurisdiction over counterintelligence matters (finding and apprehending foreign spies working in the United States), and at various times in American history it has fulfilled a vaguely defined mandate to protect the so-called internal security of the country. Since World War II, it has also been responsible for conducting background investigations of certain people under consideration for federal jobs. By the example of its own procedures and the thorough training courses that it conducts, the FBI has a profound influence on local police forces.

The FBI Identification Division, established in 1924, maintains the world's largest fingerprint files. Like those of the agency's scientific laboratory, established in 1932, its services are available to other law enforcement agencies.

Beginning as the Bureau of Investigation in 1908, the FBI originally had few responsibilities. It first attracted notice when new federal laws, such as those forbidding the interstate transportation of stolen motor vehicles, were adopted to deal with problems that had traditionally been handled by the states. The bureau was soon exploited for political purposes. It was used in the Palmer raids (1919–20; see PALMER, A. MITCHELL) to arrest immigrants who were thought to be subversives, and its agents later spied on political adversaries of President Warren G. Harding.

J. Edgar HOOVER was named director of the bureau in 1924 with a mandate to eliminate corruption and to get the agency out of politics. Hoover reduced the number of agents and established professional qualifications for the bureau's members. His own ambitions for national celebrity and the adoption of dozens of federal criminal laws by Congress combined to increase the bureau's prestige. Hoover's death in 1972, however, was followed by the gradual revelation of a series of abuses that occurred both during his tenure and in subsequent years. They included disruptive activities against leftist and civil rights organizations; extensive illegal wiretapping and bugging; the use of the agency files for political purposes by U.S. presidents beginning with Franklin Delano Roosevelt; and the keeping of extensive secret dossiers on politicians, on people perceived as FBI adversaries (for example, Martin Luther King, Jr.), and on many important U.S. authors.

In 1993, President Bill Clinton dismissed FBI director William S. Sessions (1987–93) for alleged ethical misconduct and named Federal District Judge Louis J. Freeh of New York to succeed him.   SANFORD J. UNGAR

Bibliography: Mitgang, H., *Dangerous Dossiers* (1988); O'Reilly, K., *Hoover and the Un-Americans* (1983) and *Racial-Matters* (1989); Sorrentino, F. M., *Ideological Warfare* (1985); Ungar, S. J., *FBI* (1976).

Federal Communications Commission

The Federal Communications Commission, an independent U.S. government agency, regulates interstate and foreign communications by radio, television, wire, and cable. It grants licenses to radio and television broadcasters and assigns frequencies. The five-member commission, appointed by the president, is responsible to Congress.

The FCC has three main bureaus. The Mass Media Bureau regulates most RADIO AND TELEVISION BROADCASTING. It issues construction permits and operating licenses and oversees cable television operators. The Common Carrier Bureau regulates public services such as telephone, telegraph, and satellite communications. The Private Radio Bureau regulates such services as police and taxicab radios and CITIZENS BAND RADIO.

The commission was created by the Federal Communications Act of 1934, succeeding the Federal Radio Commission established in 1927. Its decisions aided the development of FM and of color television broadcasting and have determined the amount of regulation and—in the 1980s—deregulation of TV advertising. In 1987 the Commission abolished the Fairness Doctrine, which required radio and TV stations to present opposing viewpoints. The FCC is still responsible, however, for enforcing the equal-time provision, which is intended to ensure equal noncommercial broadcast time to political candidates running for the same office.

Bibliography: Paglin, M. D., ed., *A Legislative History of the Communications Act of 1934* (1990); Stern, R. H., *The Federal Communications Commission and Television* (1989).

Federal Deposit Insurance Corporation

Created in 1933 during the Great Depression, when many banks failed, the U.S. Federal Deposit Insurance Corporation (FDIC) protects depositors by insuring their bank accounts, up to $100,000. All national banks are required to belong, and most state banks are voluntary members. In 1989 the Resolution Trust Corporation (RTC) and the Savings Association Insurance Fund were formed under the FDIC to resolve or rescue troubled savings associations. By October 1990 the FTC had taken over nearly 500 insolvent thrift institutions. By 1993, Congress had approved expenditures of nearly $200 billion to pay off depositors and dispose of assets. Estimates of the ultimate cost of the rescue, including interest payments, ran to $500 billion. (See SAVINGS INDUSTRY.)

Federal Home Loan Bank Board

The Federal Home Loan Bank Board (FHLBB) was established in 1932 to provide credit reserves for savings and loan associations engaged in home mortgage lending. It was dismantled by the extensive savings-and-loan bailout and reorganization legislation of 1989, when its regulatory functions went to the new Office of Thrift Supervision under the Treasury. Until then the FHLBB had directed 12 regional Federal Home Loan Banks. It also had operated the Federal Savings and Loan Insurance Corporation, which in 1989 became the Savings Association Insurance Fund run by the Federal Deposit Insurance Corporation. (See SAVINGS INDUSTRY.)

Federal Housing Administration

The Federal Housing Administration (FHA) was created in 1934 as a U.S. government agency whose function was to insure MORTGAGES, thus providing (a) banks and other lending institutions with a guarantee that their HOUSING loans would be adequately secured and (b) the housing industry with a new stimulus during a time when almost no new homes were being built. Because FHA-insured mortgages, and the houses they buy, must conform to certain standards, the agency has had a great influence on the housing and mortgage-lending industries. In 1965 the FHA was incorporated into the new Department of Housing and Urban Development (HUD). The Office of Housing continued its role as mortgage guarantor and widened its area of responsibility to include mortgages lent to the owners of multifamily dwellings and to public housing authorities as well as to individual home owners.

Federal Mediation and Conciliation Service

The Federal Mediation and Conciliation Service is an independent federal agency that offers its services in handling disputes between labor and management. The agency was created by the Labor-Management Relations (Taft-Hartley) Act of 1947. It may enter into the negotiation process when interstate commerce is vitally affected or at the request of either labor or management.

This agency has a roster of several hundred qualified mediators. After evaluating the positions of both labor and management, the mediators offer recommendations for overcoming the labor-management differences. Neither side is obligated to accept the mediators' suggestions. Mediators, who must be impartial to maintain the confidence of both labor and management, include attorneys, professors, distinguished national figures, and community leaders.

Federal National Mortgage Association

The Federal National Mortgage Association—nicknamed Fannie Mae—was created (1938) by the U.S. Congress. Now a private corporation, it seeks to encourage the fluidity of the home-mortgage market by buying and selling mortgages. Its sister organization—Ginnie Mae, or Government National Mortgage Association—was established in 1968. A government-owned corporation under the control of the Department of Housing and Urban Development, it helps finance public-housing programs.

Federal Reserve System

The Federal Reserve System, nicknamed the Fed, is the CENTRAL BANK of the United States. It has two main functions: to be a "bankers' bank," holding deposits of the commercial banks and operating a nationwide check-clearing system; and to serve as the basic controller of credit in the U.S. economy, thus determining the size of the money supply and the ease or difficulty of borrowing. All national banks must belong to the Federal Reserve System, and many state banks belong voluntarily. The system was established in 1913.

Unlike the central banks of other countries, the Federal Reserve is divided into 12 privately controlled, separate central banks located in Atlanta, Boston, Chicago, Cleveland, Dallas, Kansas City, Minneapolis, New York City, Philadelphia, Richmond, St. Louis, and San Francisco. Each bank serves a designated district. The system was organized this way to diffuse the power of the central bank. The independence of the Federal Reserve banks is limited, however; power is centralized in a board of governors, with offices in Washington, D.C. The 7 governors are appointed for terms of 14 years by the president of the United States, subject to confirmation by the Senate. The president also appoints one of the governors as chairperson.

The governors of the Federal Reserve Board and the presidents of the 12 Federal Reserve banks are often referred to as monetary authorities. They control the issuance of paper currency and coins, regulate the banks that are members of the Federal Reserve System, decide whether member banks may establish branches or buy other banks, and regulate the operations of bank-holding companies. They also determine monetary policy, which, by affecting interest rates and the money supply, results in a measure of indirect influence on the level of economic activity, unemployment, and inflation.

All member banks are required to maintain non-interest-bearing reserve deposits based on a percentage of their transaction balances at the district Federal Reserve Bank. The monetary authorities implement monetary policy primarily by changing the size of the reserves. By raising legal reserve requirements, the Federal Reserve tightens credit, that is, reduces the size of the money supply generated by the BANKING SYSTEM. By lowering reserve requirements, it can increase the money supply. More often, however, the Federal Reserve controls reserves indirectly, through the operations of the Federal Open Market Committee (consisting of the 7 governors and 5 of the 12 reserve-bank presidents), which directs the buying and selling of U.S. government securities on the open market. When the Federal Reserve wishes to decrease reserves in this way, it sells federal securities; the checks it receives in payment have the effect of removing funds from the banking system. When it wishes to expand the money supply, it buys securities, issuing checks drawn on itself; these checks enable banks receiving them to obtain increased reserve deposits with their reserve banks, which lets them expand the money supply.

The Federal Reserve regulates the money supply in a third way: through the discount rate, the interest rate at which it lends money to members. In practice, however, changes in the discount rate act as a signal of the Federal Reserve's intentions, which are carried out mainly by changing reserve requirements or through open-market operations.

The Federal Reserve acts as the government's official buyer and seller of foreign currencies. It also holds gold deposited in the United States by other countries and handles purchases and sales of U.S. government securities on behalf of foreign governmental bodies.

The Federal Reserve's ability to implement monetary policy has been adversely affected by state banks' leaving the system to invest their reserves more profitably. In 1980, to counteract this trend, the U.S. Congress passed legislation requiring all commercial banks to establish reserves with the Federal Reserve over an 8-year phase-in period, although membership is not required. It was hoped that by increasing the Federal Reserve's influence it could control monetary policy more effectively. In 1981 about 5,500 of the 15,000 U.S. commercial banks belonged to the Federal Reserve; in 1991 there were more than 6,000 members out of fewer than 14,000 commercial banks.   PAUL S. NADLER

Bibliography: De Rosa, P., and Stern, G. H., *In the Name of Money* (1980); Garcia, G. R., and Plautz, E., *The Federal Reserve* (1986); Greider, W., *Secrets of the Temple: How the Federal Reserve Runs the Country* (1988); Kettl, D. F., *Leadership at the Fed* (1986; repr. 1988); Livingstone, J., *The Origins of the Federal Reserve System* (1986); Maisel, S. J., *Managing the Dollar* (1973); Nadler, P. S., *Commercial Banking in the Economy*, 4th ed. (1986).

federal style

The federal style is a style of architecture, furniture, and decoration produced in the United States in the years 1780 through 1820. The style is best characterized as an aspect of NEOCLASSICISM, influenced by the Scottish architect Robert ADAM, with American motifs added. The original source of the style lay in the architecture and ornament of late Roman antiquity. In 1773, just before the American Revolution, the first volume of *The Works of Robert and James Adam* appeared in London and soon became the most influential manual for architectural design in England and, subsequently, in the newly established United States.

The most important architect of the federal style was Charles BULFINCH of Boston, who designed the Massachusetts State House (1795–98) and various churches and houses in that city before being called to Washington to complete the national Capitol building. Characteristics of the style include light, classical geometry; use of slender Ionic or Corinthian orders, frequently in white against a background of red brick or clapboard; and use of a delicate fanlight (half-circle window with sash bars in the shape of a fan) above doorways.

RON WIEDENHOEFT

Bibliography: Middleton, Robin, and Watkin, David, *Neoclassical and 19th Century Architecture* (1980; repr. 1987).

Federal Theatre Project

A program of the WORKS PROGRESS ADMINISTRATION, the Federal Theatre Project (1935–39) was developed during the presidency of Franklin D. Roosevelt and employed thousands of theater artists and technicians who were on relief rolls. Under the leadership of Hallie Flanagan, the FTP became the largest theatrical endeavor ever undertaken by the federal government, with a congressional appropriation of $46 million for over 1,200 productions of more than 800 works and the publication of *Federal Theatre Magazine*.

The United States was divided into five regions to administer the program, and regional playwriting and staging experimentation were encouraged. New York had five units of its own, including units for new plays, a black theater, and a "living newspaper" of documented current events. The FTP also presented circuses, children's programs, and puppetry. In 1936 it simultaneously staged Sinclair Lewis's *It Can't Happen Here* in 20 theaters in 17 states, produced several plays by George Bernard Shaw and Eugene O'Neill, and presented John Houseman and Orson Welles's production of *Macbeth*. The project was discontinued in 1939 by an act of Congress.

BONNIE MARRANCA

Bibliography: Bentley, J., *Hallie Flanagan* (1988); Buttitta, Tony, and Witham, B. B., *Uncle Sam Presents* (1982); Flanagan, Hallie, *Arena: The History of the Federal Theatre* (1940; repr. 1965); Mathews, J. D., *The Federal Theatre, 1935–1939* (1967; repr. 1971); O'Connor, John, and Brown, Lorraine, *Free, Adult, Uncensored: The Living History of the Federal Theatre Project* (1978).

Federal Trade Commission

Established in 1914, the Federal Trade Commission (FTC) is charged with maintaining free and fair competition in U.S. business. It takes action against monopoly, restraints on trade, and unfair or deceptive trade practices by issuing advisory opinions and other guidance materials for business to comply with voluntarily. It also takes legal action in cases where there appears to be a persistent violation of the law. This may begin with the issuance of a formal complaint by the commission, followed by hearings before an FTC administrative law judge. The judge's decision may be appealed by the respondent to the commission itself, to a U.S. court of appeals, and even to the U.S. Supreme Court.

The laws administered by the FTC include the Federal Trade Commission Act, the CLAYTON ANTI-TRUST ACT, the Fair Packaging and Labeling Act, the Truth in Lending Act, the Fair Credit Reporting Act, and the ROBINSON-PATMAN ACT. It shares responsibility for the administration of the Clayton Act with the antitrust division of the Department of Justice, which also enforces the SHERMAN ANTI-TRUST ACT.

The FTC has 5 commissioners, appointed by the president for 7-year terms.

Bibliography: Hasin, B. R., *Consumer, Commissions and Congress: Law Theory and the Federal Trade Commission, 1968–1985* (1986); Mackay, R. J., et al., eds., *Public Choice and Regulation* (1987).

Federal Writers' Project

The Federal Writers' Project was a federally funded arts program that supported out-of-work writers during the Depression of the 1930s. A project of the WORKS PROGRESS ADMINISTRATION and directed by Henry G. Alsberg, it began in 1935 and continued for four years. Although the wages were modest, writers flocked to the program, and over 6,000 were involved during its life. The Federal Writers' Project eventually published 378 books and pamphlets. These include a series of state guidebooks, studies of American folklore, and special individual projects. The state guidebooks are perhaps the most impressive achievement, although *These Are Our Lives* (1939), an oral history of workers' lives during the Depression, received critical acclaim and initiated a genre that is still popular today. Among the writers who participated in the project were John Cheever, Kenneth Patchen, Richard Wright, Tillie Olsen, Nelson Algren, and Studs Terkel.

Bibliography: Mangione, Jerre, *The Dream and the Deal: The Federal Writers' Project, 1935–43* (1972); Penkower, Monty N., *The Federal Writers' Project: A Study in Government Patronage* (1977).

federalism

Federalism is a form of GOVERNMENT in which power is divided between a central government and several formerly independent regional governments. The regional governments maintain partial autonomy after being subsumed into the larger central government. The central government is responsible for matters of mutual concern to all regions, such as foreign affairs, defense, and currency, while the regional governments are entrusted with authority over other matters, such as education. In the United States, for example, the individual states surrender partial sovereignty but retain all rights and prerogatives not specifically assigned the federal government under the Constitution. In all modern federal systems the authority of the central and regional governments is specified in a written constitution, and conflicts of authority between the two are decided by a judicial authority. A federation differs from a confederation, in which the central authority normally has little power over member states and almost none over individuals within those states.

Early examples of federalism can be found among the Israeli tribes in the 2d millennium BC, the Greek city-states of the 3d and 2d centuries BC, and the Swiss cantons of the 13th century AD, all of which united against foreign opponents for mutual survival. In the 17th and 18th centuries the United Provinces of the Netherlands maintained a federal form of government.

Modern federalism stems from the federal type of government instituted by the founders of the United States. The federalist ideas underlying the U.S. Constitution were delineated in *The Federalist,* a series of papers written (1787–88) by Alexander HAMILTON, James MADISON, and John JAY, but the major problem of federalism—the allocation of power between central and regional governments—was only resolved in the United States by the Civil War (see STATE RIGHTS). In the 19th century the success of the American federalist system led a number of other countries to institute federalist systems. Modern federal governments include Australia, Canada, Germany, India, Mexico, Nigeria, Switzerland, and the USSR.

FRANCIS S. PIERCE

Bibliography: Anton, T. J., *American Federalism and Public Policy* (1989); Boogman, J. C., and Van Der Plaat, G. N., eds., *Federalism* (1980); Duchacek, I. D., *Comparative Federalism* (1970; repr. 1987); Elazar, D. J., *American Federalism*, 2d ed. (1972; repr. 1985).

Federalist, The

The Federalist is the collective title for 85 essays signed "Publius" and published (1787–88) in various New York newspapers to convince New York voters to support ratification of the new Constitution of the United States. Sometimes called the *Federalist Papers,* they were published in book form in 1788. Although the authorship of certain essays is still disputed, the consensus is that Alexander Hamilton wrote 52, James Madison 28, and John Jay 5.

The first 14 are a general discussion of the importance of union to the "political prosperity" of America. Essays 15–22 contain arguments to show the inadequacy of confederations and of the Articles of Confederation, and in 23–36 evidence is presented to show the need for a government "at least

Alexander Hamilton wrote at least 52 of the 85 essays constituting The Federalist, *also called the* Federalist Papers. *The essays were published anonymously in 1787–88 to rally support in New York for ratification of the federal Constitution. Hamilton argued that the Constitution would preserve individual liberties while providing effective central government.*

equally energetic" as that provided by the Constitution. Numbers 37–51 contain explanations of the republican principles underlying the document, and 52–66 are an analysis of the legislative power and the regulation of elections. The remainder, written by Hamilton, contain the analysis of the executive (67–77) and judicial branches (78–83) and of the question of a bill of rights.

The essays failed in their immediate purpose, for New York voted against ratification. They endured, however, as the classic analysis of the Constitution and an influential treatise on federalism.

FORREST McDONALD

Bibliography: Dietze, G., *The Federalist* (1960; repr. 1977); Epstein, D. F., *The Political Theory of "The Federalist"* (1986); Kesler, C. R., ed., *Saving the Revolution* (1987).

Federalist party

The Federalist party, in U.S. history, is a name that was originally applied to the advocates of ratification of the Constitution of the United States of 1787. Later, however, it came to designate supporters of the presidential administrations of George Washington and John Adams and especially of the fiscal policies of Treasury Secretary Alexander Hamilton.

Until 1795 the Federalists were not a political organization in any modern sense. Rather, Federalism was a frame of mind, a set of attitudes that included belief in a strong and activist central government, public credit, the promotion of commerce and industry, and strict neutrality in the French Revolutionary Wars—all of which were generally reflected in government policy. Opposition arose on all these points, however, and became increasingly organized around James Madison and Thomas Jefferson. Federalists began to adopt the tactics of the opposition Democratic-Republicans in response to attacks on JAY'S TREATY with Britain (1794), which Federalists believed preserved neutrality and Democratic-Republicans charged was anti-French. Although parties were widely regarded as inimical to free government, and although Washington, Hamilton, and Adams deplored their rise (together with the tendency toward a North versus South and pro-British versus pro-French polarization of political opinion), parties were an established fact by the presidential election of 1796.

During Adams's presidency the Federalists attempted to stifle dissent by the ALIEN AND SEDITION ACTS (1798). These, however, had the effect of stiffening the opposition at the time when the Federalists themselves were splitting into "High" and "Low" wings over the issue of the XYZ AFFAIR and the ensuing Quasi-War with France. By the election of 1800, therefore, the Democratic-Republicans gained control of the federal government. The death of Washington in 1799 and of Hamilton in 1804 left the Federalists without a powerful leader, and they proved inept at the highly organized popular politics of the Democratic-Republicans. Although the party continued to have strength in New England, expressing the opposition of commercial interests to the EMBARGO ACT of 1807 and the WAR OF 1812, it never made a comeback on the national level. After the HARTFORD CONVENTION of 1815, the Federalists were a dying anachronism.   FORREST McDONALD

Bibliography: Chambers, William Nisbet, and Burnham, Walter Dean, eds., *The American Party Systems,* 2d ed. (1975); Fischer, D. H., *The Revolution of American Conservatism* (1965); Kerber, Linda K., *Federalists in Dissent* (1970); Ladenburg, T., *The Federalist Era* (1989).

See also: DEMOCRATIC PARTY.

federation: see FEDERALISM.

Federation of American Scientists

The Federation of American Scientists, whose headquarters are in Washington, D.C., was founded in 1946 to act on public issues with scientific implications. Its members testify before congressional committees and issue public statements. It has approximately 5,000 members and holds annual meetings. It publishes *Public Interest Report.*

Fedin, Konstantin Aleksandrovich   [fee-ed-een']

Konstantin Aleksandrovich Fedin, b. Feb. 24 (N.S.), 1892, d. July 15, 1977, was a Russian writer. His first stories and his novel *Cities and Years* (1924; Eng. trans., 1962) identified him as one of the Serapion Brothers, a group dedicated to a literature free from state control. With the tightening of literary controls under Stalin, however, Fedin began following the orthodoxy of socialist realism and wrote in support of the Soviet regime. His novel *The Rape of Europe* (1933–35) contrasts the decadence of the West with the progressiveness of the USSR. His postwar trilogy—*Early Joys* (1944; Eng. trans., 1948), *No Ordinary Summer* (1947–48; Eng. trans., 1950), and *The Bonfire* (1961; Eng. trans., 1962–65)—is less political. The first two novels were awarded the Stalin Prize.

As secretary general of the Soviet Writer's Union (1959–71), Fedin was instrumental in imposing restrictions on such dissident writers as Andrei Sinyavsky, Yuli Daniel, and Aleksandr Solzhenitsyn.   LAZLO M. TIKOS

Bibliography: Blum, Julius M., *Konstantin Fedin* (1967).

fee

In PROPERTY law, a fee is a freehold estate that belongs to a person and his or her heirs until they convey (transfer by deed) or devise (transfer by will) it or until it is divested (taken away) on the occurrence of some previously specified condition. It is to be distinguished from a life estate, where the land is held only during the life of a specified person, and a tenancy, where the land is leased from another for a period of time. A fee simple, also called a fee simple absolute or a fee, can only be lost through a conveyance, devise, or a superior interest. Determinable and conditional fees are also forfeitable on the occurrence of specified events or conditions.

feedback

Feedback refers to a system, process, or machine in which part of the output is fed back—that is, returned—to the input in order to regulate the operation. The returned part of the output is called feedback. When the feedback signal reinforces the trend of the system, it is said to be positive. When it opposes the trend of the system, it is called negative feedback. Negative feedback is employed to stabilize systems. More rigorously, a negative feedback system can be said to maintain an output equal to a desired value. It does this by comparing measurements of input and output and using the results of the comparison to control input. Negative feedback is used in AMPLIFIERS and is basic to AUTOMATION and PROCESS CONTROL. Positive feedback finds an application in OSCILLATORS.

In mechanical systems, one early example of the application of the feedback principle was that of James Watt's flyball governor for his steam engine (1788). The device contained two balls that were attached in such a way that they rotated at

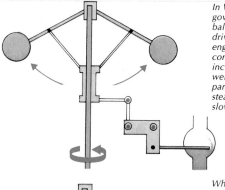

In Watt's flyball governor two heavy balls are linked to the drive shaft of a steam engine and to a control linkage. With increasing speed the weights move out, partially closing the steam valve and slowing the engine.

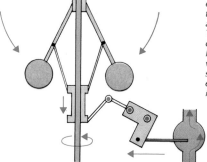

When the steam engine slows down, the heavy balls fall and move inward. The moving weights cause the control linkage to open the valve, allowing more steam to enter the engine and speed it up.

engine speed and moved in or out by centrifugal force, a force that is proportional to the speed of rotation. The outward motion of the balls controlled the steam inlet valve to the engine, shutting the valve as the speed increased. The feedback consisted of the transmission of ball position (a function of engine speed) to the input valve. Deviations from the desired speed were automatically corrected by a change in steam input, and the engine became self-regulating.

In the 1920s the U.S. telephone industry was seeking an accurate amplifier for use in the long-distance telephone system, where several hundred amplifiers might be used along a telephone line, and the effects of distortion would be cumulative. Harold S. BLACK of the Bell Telephone research staff, who was studying the problem, saw that feedback might solve the problem. On Aug. 6, 1927, he developed the mathematical theory of a feedback amplifier, which led to the actual design of a feedback system. He recognized that a sample from the amplifier output should be compared to the amplifier input in such a way that a difference in the waveforms creates an error signal; this signal is put into such a form that when it is fed back to the input, it reduces the error so that the output waveform is made to correspond more closely with the input waveform. The principle is now universally used in transistor power amplifiers and in automatic control systems.

The above discussion has been of feedback systems in electromechanical devices, but feedback also occurs in living organisms. The production of ENZYMES and the maintenance of HORMONE levels in the body, for example, involve complex biochemical feedback systems, and BIOFEEDBACK is a general term for efforts to gain psychological control over physiological processes. The concept of feedback also plays a significant role in INFORMATION THEORY.   J. D. RYDER

Bibliography: Mayr, Otto, *The Origins of Feedback Control* (1970); Van De Vegte, John, *Feedback Control Systems,* 2d ed. (1990).

feedlot

A feedlot is a plot of land where cattle, lambs, or pigs are confined in large groups to be fattened for slaughter. Cattle are the principal livestock in feedlots, and large lots in only 13 U.S. states account for 85 percent of the total feed-fattened cattle produced annually. A majority of these feedlots are located in the Midwestern corn-producing states, such as Iowa, Nebraska, and Illinois.

Most feedlots have a capacity of 1,000 or fewer cattle at one time, but some in Arizona, Colorado, California, and Texas have capacities of more than 100,000. The larger feedlots have their own feed-mixing facilities and veterinary services. Some environmentalists are concerned that these large concentrations of livestock and the drainage of materials from feedlots will pollute the environment, especially surface and subsurface waters.　　REX GILBREATH

Feiffer, Jules　[fy'-fur]

Jules Feiffer, b. New York City, Jan. 26, 1929, popularized the satirical comic strip. His cartoons, which feature wonderfully illogical monologues issuing from the mouths of anguished figures, were first published in the New York *Village Voice* in 1956 and quickly attained nationwide distribution. Feiffer won an Academy Award (1961) for his animated cartoon *Munro* and has written several screenplays, notably *Carnal Knowledge* (1971) and *Popeye* (1980). His work for the theater includes *The Explainers* (1961), a musical revue based on his cartoons; *Little Murders* (1967); *The White House Murder Case* (1970); and *Elliot Loves* (1990).　　DIANA KURZ

Feininger, Lyonel　[fy'-ning-ur]

In *Woman in Mauve* (1922), the American cubist painter Lyonel Feininger breaks the figural and architectural images into planes of translucent color that frequently overlap and complement one another. (Private collection, Lugano, Switzerland.)

Lyonel Charles Adrian Feininger, b. New York City, July 17, 1871, d. Jan. 13, 1956, was one of America's important expatriate artists. Sent to Germany in 1887 to study music, he studied art instead, and became a successful cartoonist and illustrator in Berlin. Turning to serious painting, he traveled to Paris in 1906–07 and again in 1911, when he came under the influence of the cubists, particularly Robert Delaunay. He soon established a reputation as one of the most lyrical interpreters of the cubist manner. In 1919 he was invited by Walter Gropius

to teach at the Bauhaus and remained there until the Nazis forced its closing in 1933. Four years later he returned to New York, where he worked until he died.

In his most memorable paintings—such as the series of 13 scenes of the village church at Gelmeroda, begun in 1913—Feininger employs the cubist techniques of planar fragmentation and multiple views. He goes beyond cubism, however, in suggesting a haunting, translucent light that seems to dissolve forms even as it defines them, as in *The Church of Gelmeroda XII* (1929; Rhode Island School of Design, Providence). After his return to America, Feininger interpreted the towering skyline of Manhattan—with such works as *Manhattan, Dawn* (1944; Collection Julia Feininger, New York)—in much the same way he had the village church, transforming the modern city into a poetic vision of great subtlety and nuance.　　IRMA B. JAFFE

Bibliography: Hess, Hans, *Lyonel Feininger* (1961); Luckhardt, Ulricht, *Lyonel Feininger* (1989); Ness, June L., ed., *Lyonel Feininger* (1974); Prasse, Leona E., *Lyonel Feininger: A Definitive Catalog of His Graphic Work, Etchings, Lithographs, Woodcuts* (1972).

Feke, Robert　[feek]

Robert Feke, a native-born American painter of the colonial period, painted Isaac Royall and His Family *in 1741. In the dignified poses of his sitters, Feke's work resembles the early portraits of Thomas Gainsborough. (Fogg Museum, Cambridge, Mass.)*

The first native American artist to create a substantial body of paintings of high merit, Robert Feke, c.1707–52, developed a restrained but eloquent version of the British baroque portrait style. Though largely self-taught, he was influenced in his early work by the painter John Smibert. His group portrait *Isaac Royall and His Family* (1741; Fogg Museum, Cambridge, Mass.) is one of his earliest works and one of the most ambitious by any colonial American artist. His two self-portraits (c.1742; Museum of Fine Arts, Boston; and c.1750; Rhode Island Historical Society, Providence) are remarkable for their penetrating characterization. Although he traveled widely, Feke painted chiefly in Boston and Philadelphia.　　DAVID TATHAM

Bibliography: Foote, Henry W., *Robert Feke: Colonial Portrait Painter* (1930; repr. 1969); Goodrich, Lloyd, *Robert Feke* (1946); Wilmerding, John, ed., *The Genius of American Painting* (1973).

Feld, Eliot

Eliot Feld, b. Brooklyn, N.Y., July 5, 1942, is a ballet choreographer and the founder (in 1974) of the Eliot Feld Ballet (now Feld Ballets NY). He created his first ballet, *Harbinger* (1967), while still a soloist for American Ballet Theatre. His early works were largely about mood: aloneness in *At Midnight* (1967) and dreamy romanticism in *Intermezzo* (1969). Feld ballets in the mid- and late 1970s focused on dramatic or comic themes, Americana, Latin American culture, and his own Jewish heritage. Important recent works include *Contra Pose* (1990) and *Common Ground* (1991).

Feld founded the American Ballet Company in 1968 and disbanded it because of financial difficulty in 1971. His present company, the Feld Ballet, was formed in 1974.

feldspar [feld'-spahr]

The feldspars are the most abundant and widespread minerals of the crust, or outermost part, of the Earth. Because of their abundance, feldspars are used in the classification of IGNEOUS ROCKS. They are also abundant in METAMORPHIC ROCKS and in some sediments and SEDIMENTARY ROCKS, especially those formed in arid and semiarid regions. Feldspars are also major constituents of moon rocks, which are similar to rocks of the Earth's crust. Feldspars are used in the manufacture of ceramics and ceramic glazes and as mild abrasives. A few varieties, including labradorite and orthoclase, are occasionally used as gems because they show an iridescent play of colors or a milky translucence. Milky varieties are termed moonstone.

Minerology. Feldspars are aluminosilicates, containing silicon and aluminum ions bound together by oxygen ions to form a three-dimensional framework of atoms (see SILICATE MINERALS). Other ions, principally potassium, sodium, and calcium, occupy sites within the framework and give rise to the three pure, or end-member species: orthoclase ($KAlSi_3O_8$), albite ($NaAlSi_3O_8$), and anorthite ($CaAl_2Si_2O_8$). Extensive chemical variation, or solid solution, occurs between orthoclase and albite, with potassium and sodium substituting for each other. Feldspars in this range are called alkali feldspars. Complete solid solution between albite and anorthite is also possible, with calcium substituting freely for sodium. Because these two ions have different charges, the proportions of aluminum to silicon in the aluminosilicate framework must also vary to maintain electrical-charge neutrality. Feldspars between albite and anorthite in composition are termed plagioclase. There is little solid solution between orthoclase and anorthite.

Feldspars are generally light-colored minerals, white or buff to gray in color. One species, microcline, may also be light brick-red or even the green to blue green variety called amazonite. Feldspars are slightly translucent and have a glassy, or vitreous, luster rather like that of glazed porcelain. Because their atomic framework has planes of weakness, feldspars exhibit good cleavage, breaking readily into blocky pieces with smooth sides. On the Mohs mineral hardness scale, feldspars are 6—slightly harder than a steel knife blade and about as hard as porcelain.

The high-temperature potassium feldspars, sanidine and orthoclase, are monoclinic in their crystal symmetry; the others are triclinic, although they retain the general atomic pattern of the monoclinic species. Because triclinic feldspars have nearly monoclinic symmetry, they commonly occur in complex intergrowths of crystals called twins, which mimic the higher monoclinic symmetry (see TWIN LAW). Plagioclase in particular exhibits a prominent twinning called albite twinning. Thin, platelike crystals, oriented so as to be mirror images of each other, are intergrown. On a cleavage surface, this intergrowth causes a finely striped pattern characteristic of plagioclase. About a dozen different patterns of twinning have been recognized in the feldspars.

Plagioclase feldspars, the most abundant minerals in the Earth's crust, are mixtures of sodium and calcium aluminum silicates. They show finely striped patterns on cleaved surfaces. Usually gray, pink, or white, they are found as irregular grains or as granular masses.

Microcline feldspar, usually found as large, white-to-pale-yellow or, more rarely, red or green, prismatic crystals, is a potassium aluminum silicate. Translucent blue-green microcline, or amazonite, is a semiprecious stone used in jewelry.

Alkali Feldspars. The three different but closely related species of alkali feldspar are sanidine, orthoclase, and microcline. The differences among these feldspars result from details of their atomic structures, principally the different ways in which aluminum is distributed, or ordered, in the aluminosilicate frameworks of each. Sanidine is the form stable at the highest temperatures. It can accommodate sodium in all proportions, and a complete compositional series (with a slight structural change) runs from pure potassium sanidine ($KAlSi_3O_8$) to pure albite ($NaAlSi_3O_8$). Members of this series that are more than two-thirds sodium are called anorthoclase and have triclinic symmetry. At lower temperatures orthoclase is more stable than sanidine, and many igneous rocks contain orthoclase. The compositional range of orthoclase extends only partway to albite, and orthoclase may occur with albite in rocks. In some igneous rocks and in most metamorphic rocks, microcline is the common potassium feldspar. Microcline can accommodate only a little sodium and, like orthoclase, may occur with albite.

All the potassium feldspars can contain more sodium at high temperatures than at low. As a high-temperature feldspar cools, albite separates and appears as small grains, bleb, or streaks within it. This process of separation is called exsolution, and the mixtures are termed perthites. The perthitic texture may be coarse and easily visible as slight variations in color in the crystal, or it may be microscopic and practically invisible. The coarseness of the texture depends mostly on the rate at which the feldspar was cooled—the slower the cooling, the coarser the texture.

Alkali feldspars occur in many rocks. They are abundant in GRANITES, a family of intrusive igneous rocks composed chiefly of alkali feldspars and quartz. Granites constitute the cores of mountain ranges; they are formed by the melting of the Earth's crust as mountains are built. Sanidine is found chiefly in some lavas, where it is preserved by rapid chilling. When cooled slowly, sanidine changes to orthoclase. Crude crystals of microcline several feet wide (among the largest of any mineral) are commonly found in PEGMATITES, coarse-grained, granitelike rocks found in mountains. Pockets yield beautiful, sharp crystals, sometimes of the green variety amazonite. Pegmatites in the granite near Pikes Peak in Colorado are famous for such crystal groups.

Alkali feldspars are also common in many metamorphic rocks that have crystallized at high temperatures. Micas and other minerals common in lower temperature rocks tend to break down into feldspar as the temperature increases during metamorphism. Alkali feldspars weather to clays, forming important deposits of china clay or kaolin. In arid regions, however, alkali feldspars accumulate in the sand and gravel formed by mechanical breakdown of rock. A SANDSTONE formed from this sand with more than 25 percent feldspar grains is called an ARKOSE.

Plagioclase. Plagioclase feldspars are those ranging from albite to anorthite in composition. Plagioclase feldspars are even more abundant than the alkali species and are found in many igneous and metamorphic rocks.

Crystallization of plagioclase from a melt or molten-rock magma has been studied in detail. As the melt cools, the feldspar that forms is richer in calcium than the melt itself. On further cooling, feldspar that is richer in sodium forms, and the feldspar already formed tends to react with the melt and become richer in sodium as well. If cooling takes place slowly, the feldspar will be homogeneous and have the same composition as the starting melt. Under conditions of relatively rapid cooling, however, the feldspar grains will not have fully reacted and will be zoned, richer in calcium in the centers and in sodium on the outsides.

Igneous rocks that crystallize at high temperatures contain calcic plagioclase (rich in calcium), and rocks forming at lower temperatures contain sodic plagioclase (rich in sodium). A partly crystallized magma is separated into a solid rock containing calcic plagioclase and a still molten residue richer in sodium. If this residue is removed from the already solid rock, perhaps by a volcanic eruption, it forms a rock containing sodic plagioclase upon cooling. Thus a magma may be divided by igneous-differentiation processes to form igneous rocks of different compositions.

Plagioclases are among the most common minerals in igneous rocks; a few examples may show their variety. Anorthosite is a rock composed principally of calcic plagioclase, usually bytownite or labradorite. Anorthosite is uncommon on the Earth, but may constitute a substantial part of the mountainous or highland regions of the Moon. BASALT rocks contain plagioclase, magnesium, and iron-rich minerals, such as olivine or pyroxene. The sea floors and many oceanic islands, including Iceland and Hawaii, are composed of basalt. Basalt also makes up the lunar mare, or lowlands. ANDESITE, the volcanic rock of the Andes, the Cascades, and many other mountain ranges, contains substantial plagioclase.

Plagioclase weathers more readily than alkali feldspars and is less common in sediments and sedimentary rocks. Albite, considered either an alkali feldspar or a plagioclase, is found in some sedimentary rocks; in some sodium-rich sediments it has actually grown as crystals rather than being detritus from the breakdown of other rocks. Plagioclase is widespread in metamorphic rocks. Albite is characteristic of metamorphic rocks formed below about 500° C; at higher temperatures more calcic species are characteristic. Pure anorthite is found in some highly metamorphosed marbles.   PETER B. LEAVENS

Bibliography: Barth, Tom F., *Feldspars* (1969); Kraus, E. H., and Hunt, W. F., *Mineralogy,* 5th ed. (1959); MacKenzie, W. J., ed., *The Feldspars* (1974); Smith, J. V., *Feldspar Minerals,* 2 vols. (1974; repr. 1988).

feldspathoid   [feld'-spuh-thoyd]

Feldspathoids are a group of SILICATE MINERALS that are typical of rocks relatively rich in the alkali elements sodium and potassium and relatively poor in silica (SiO$_2$). In such alkaline rocks, as they are called, the feldspathoids occur with, or instead of, the more common feldspar minerals and are never found in rocks containing the mineral QUARTZ. The feldspathoids are framework silicates, in which tetrahedral groups of silica and alumina atoms are joined to form three-dimensional networks. Sodium, potassium, and other ions and ionic groups are housed in cavities within the frameworks. Of the dozen or so feldspathoids and related minerals, all but a few are extremely rare.

Types. Nepheline (Na, K)(AlSiO$_4$), the most common of the group, is a white to gray mineral that is distinguished from the feldspars, which it resembles, by its poorer cleavage and slightly greasy luster. It occurs as grains or large masses in many alkaline IGNEOUS ROCKS ranging from magnesium-rich nepheline BASALTS to granitelike but quartz-free nepheline SYENITES. It is also found in some METAMORPHIC ROCKS, particularly the nepheline GNEISSES of Ontario, Canada.

Sodalite, a sodium-aluminum silicate, is one of several feldspathoid minerals closely related chemically to the feldspars; sodalite, however, contains less silica. Sodalite is generally found as transparent-to-opaque, rounded masses of irregular shape or as scattered grains.

Leucite (KAlSi$_2$O$_6$), next to nepheline in abundance, is usually found in fine-grained LAVAS in the form of chalky, well-formed, trapezohedral crystals up to several centimeters across. Because its atoms are loosely packed, leucite is less dense than the feldspars or nepheline. This makes it unstable at great depths and pressures, which is why leucite is found only in shallow intrusives and in volcanic deposits, but never in deep-seated PLUTONS. The most notable occurrence of leucite is in the volcanic rocks of central Italy.

The SODALITE group of feldspathoids (sodalite, nosean, Haüyne, and lazurite) contain sodium and sometimes calcium. In addition, they contain such extra ions as chloride (Cl$^-$), sulfate (SO$_4^{2-}$), and sulfide (S^{2-}). They are found, usually in small amounts, in many of the rocks that contain nepheline. Other, rarer feldspathoids include kalsilite (KAlSiO$_4$), petalite (LiAlSi$_4$O$_{10}$), and cancrinite [Na$_6$Ca$_2$(CO$_3$)(AlSiO$_4$)$_6$].

Uses. NEPHELINE is used in ceramics. Sodalite provides an opaque, purplish blue GEM, and the related species lazurite is the blue LAPIS LAZULI. Lazurite is ground in oil and used to make ultramarine blue pigment. Most feldspathoids, however, have no commercial uses.   PETER B. LEAVENS

Bibliography: Deer, W. A., et al., *Rock Forming Minerals* (1963), vol. 4 in *Framework Silicates;* Webster, R., *Gems,* 4th ed. (1983).

fellahin   [fel-uh-heen']

The term *fellahin* (from Arabic *fellāh,* "farmer") is used in Arab lands to refer to peasant agriculturalists as opposed to nomadic desert dwellers (Bedouin). In English usage it more frequently refers to the inhabitants of the Egyptian Delta, the largest agricultural area in the Middle East. The men and women of this densely populated region between Cairo and the Mediterranean Sea cultivate three crops a year on land that is formed from the silt of the Nile and is irrigated by the same source. More fellahin have gained ownership of land since the Egyptian social revolution of the 1950s and the completion of the ASWAN HIGH DAM, but most remain small-scale farmers whose ancient life-style has only recently begun to change through the advent of mechanized cultivation and government-sponsored social services.   ROBERT A. FERNEA

Bibliography: Adams, Richard H., Jr., *Development and Social Change in Rural Egypt* (1986); Blackman, Winifred S., *The Fellahin of Upper Egypt* (1927; repr. 1968).

Feller, Bob

Robert William Andrew Feller, b. Van Meter, Iowa, Nov. 3, 1918, was an American baseball pitcher known for his famous strikeout records in the 1930s, '40s, and '50s. Nicknamed "Rapid Robert," Feller reached the major leagues with the Cleveland Indians as a 17-year-old in 1936. That season he struck out 17 men in a single game. He continued tò set records, including 3 no-hitters, 12 one-hitters, and 348 strikeouts in a season and 18 in a game, compiling 266 victories before he retired from the Indians in 1956. As he lost his fastball with age, Feller developed into one of the finest all-around pitchers. He is a member of the Baseball Hall of Fame.

Fellini, Federico   [fel-lee'-nee, fay-day-ree'-koh]

Italian filmmaker Federico Fellini, b. Jan. 20, 1920, d. Oct. 31, 1993, is best known for flamboyant, often grotesque film fantasies, many scored by composer Nino Rota and often starring Fellini's wife, Giulietta Masina. Fellini collaborated as a scriptwriter with Roberto Rossellini on the neorealist films *Open City* (1945) and *Paisan* (1946), directing some of the latter. He debuted as solo director with *The White Sheik* (1952) and followed with *I Vitelloni* (1953). *La Strada* (1954), a powerful fable starring Masina, won international recognition and an Oscar for best foreign film. Fellini's second Oscar was awarded for *Nights of Cabiria* (1956), again starring Masina. The notoriety of *La Dolce Vita* (1960), an indictment of contemporary Roman decadence, launched Fellini as an international media star.

Fellini's third Oscar winner, *8½* (1963), used stream-of-consciousness techniques to explore the anxieties of a film director and the process of filmmaking itself. In the opulent *Juliet of the Spirits* (1965), Masina portrayed a fantasy-driven housewife. *Fellini-Satyricon* (1969) became a cult object for much of late 1960s North American university film culture. *Roma* (1972), though largely ignored, may well be Fellini's most artistically

Gelsomina (played by Giulietta Masina) is swept up in a small-town religious celebration in La Strada *(1954), the film that marked Fellini's break with neorealism and first gained him international recognition.*

ambitious film. His final Oscar-winner, *Amarcord* (1974), was a vibrant reconstruction of adolescence under fascism in Rimini, Fellini's hometown.

Fellini's later work was less enthusiastically received. Nonetheless, *Fellini's Casanova* (1976), *City of Women* (1980), *And the Ship Sails On* (1983), and *Ginger and Fred* (1985) are interesting "postmodern" perceptions of the loss of social and personal reality and its replacement by meaningless simulations, some provided by television. Although Fellini expressed his dislike of the medium, *The Clowns* (1970) and *Orchestra Rehearsal* (1979) were made for Italian television. *Intervista* (1986) is a fictional documentary featuring the director and the film studio Cinécittà. *La voce della luna* (1989), a fantasy about the inmates of an insane asylum, has not been released in North America.

Although film academics now often dismiss Fellini as self-indulgent, sexist, and apolitical, from the 1950s into the 1970s he was considered a major film innovator.   FRANK BURKE

Bibliography: Bondanella, P., and Degli-Esposti, C., eds., *Critical Essays on Federico Fellini* (1993); Burke, Frank, *Federico Fellini: "Variety Lights" to "La Dolce Vita"* (1984); Grazzini, G., *Federico Fellini: Comments on Film* (1988); Murray, E., *Fellini the Artist*, 2d ed. (1985); Stritch, C., ed., *Fellini's Faces* (1982); Tornabene, F., *Federico Fellini* (1990).

felony

In criminal law, a felony is a serious crime that in the United States is punishable by death or confinement in state or federal prison, usually for more than one year. Under the old English COMMON LAW, felons had to forfeit either their lands or their goods or both and were subject to possible capital punishment. Under modern law, forfeiture no longer exists, but felons can lose certain legal rights, such as the right to vote, either temporarily or permanently. Many states follow modern common law or federal law in classifying offenses as felonies or as MISDEMEANORS, a less serious category of crime, punishable by less than one year in prison. Crimes most often classified as felonies include murder, arson, and rape.

felsite   [fel'-syt]

A felsite is an extremely fine-grained, light-colored IGNEOUS ROCK. It is composed of microscopic grains of FELDSPAR and QUARTZ, with very few ferromagnesian minerals, such as pyroxene or hornblende. The term *felsite,* commonly used in mining and field geology, is normally applied to dikes or sills that have crystallized at shallow depths.   JAMES A. WHITNEY

felt

Nonwoven felt is a fabric produced from a matted sheet of tangled wool, hair, or fur, often combined with cotton or synthetic fibers. The felting process has been known since antiquity, and felted materials were probably made before woven fabrics. Heat, combined with pressure, moisture, and other chemical action, causes the tangling and shrinkage of the wool fibers. Felts of various materials are used for hats, as padding in apparel, mattresses, and furniture, and as insulation. Woven felts are woven fabrics of cotton or wool that are compressed by shrinkage and then napped on both sides so that the weave is barely discernible.   ISABEL B. WINGATE

Felton, William Harrell

William Harrell Felton, b. Oglethorpe County, Ga., June 19, 1823, d. Sept. 24, 1909, was an American politician who gained fame by battling almost single-handedly the reactionary political machine of Georgia. He was elected to Congress in 1874 in one of the bitterest campaigns in Georgia's history. After defeating the state's Democratic organization, Felton became the central figure in Georgia politics and served three terms in Congress. His wife, Rebecca Latimer Felton (1835–1930), was the first female member of the U.S. Senate, where she served briefly by appointment in 1922.

femininity: see SEXUAL DEVELOPMENT.

feminism

Generally, feminism means the advocacy of women's rights to full citizenship—that is, political, economic, and social equality with men. Feminism encompasses some widely differing views, however, including those advocating female separatism.

Modern feminism, which was born with the great democratic revolutions of the 18th century (American and French), differed from its precursors in applying the democratic implications of "the rights of man and the citizen" to women as a group. Abigail ADAMS asked her husband, John, to "remember the ladies" in framing the Constitution; Mary WOLLSTONECRAFT, inspired by the French Revolution, wrote the premier feminist treatise, A VINDICATION OF THE RIGHTS OF WOMEN (1792). Beginning with the SENECA FALLS CONVENTION in 1848, American women schooled in reform struggles began a serious fight for the rights of women to control their persons, property, and earnings and for the right to vote (see SUFFRAGE, WOMEN'S). Elizabeth Cady STANTON's Declaration of Rights and Sentiments established a blueprint. American women would not gain the vote until 1920, but throughout the remainder of the 19th century many feminist goals were gradually realized, especially the rights of married women to control their own property (New York State, 1848 and 1860; South Carolina, 1868; and so on).

Throughout the 19th and early 20th centuries the women's movement primarily reflected white middle-class values and never satisfactorily answered the ex-slave Sojourner Truth's challenge: "Ain't I a woman?" The goals of black and working-class women remained inseparable from their racial and class oppression. The goals of middle-class women centered on obtaining the opportunities available to the men of their own class, such as education or reforming society as a whole. Thus some women sought to improve the position of women through temperance (see TEMPERANCE MOVEMENT; WCTU), social reform, and protective legislation for working women. After women won the vote, the women's movement waned, and the first EQUAL RIGHTS AMENDMENT (ERA), introduced by Alice PAUL in 1923, failed to pass.

The women's movement did not reemerge until the 1960s, when the example of the civil rights movement and the dissatisfactions of college-educated women converged. Betty FRIEDAN's *The Feminine Mystique* (1963) called national attention to women's plight. The founding (1965) of the NATIONAL ORGANIZATION FOR WOMEN provided a focus for the struggle for women's rights. In 1973 the ERA was reintroduced. Since the passage of the Civil Rights Act of 1964, women have won the right to abortion and some guarantees for equal opportunity and pay in employment. During the 1980s, however, the ERA was defeated, the right to abortion came under attack, and growing numbers of women were finding the ad hoc employment measures inadequate to guarantee equality. The decline in alimony and child support, combined with the rising divorce rate, made women's rights to economic equality pressing. As Friedan's *The Second Stage* (1981) suggested, many feminists were also interested in building a new kind of family life.

Despite differences, most feminists seek equal economic rights; support reproductive rights, including the right to abortion; criticize traditional definitions of gender roles; and favor raising children of both genders for similar public achievements and domestic responsibilities. Many wish to reform language so that it does not equate *man* with *humanity*. Many also campaign vigorously against violence against women (wife battering, rape) and against the denigration of women in the media.   ELIZABETH FOX-GENOVESE

Bibliography: Adams, Parveen, and Cowie, Elizabeth, *The Woman in Question* (1990); Alberti, Johanna, *Beyond Suffrage: Feminists in War and Peace* (1989); Black, Naomi, *Social Feminism* (1988); Cohen, Marcia, *The History of Feminism* (1989); Epstein, Barbara Leslie, *The Politics of Domesticity: Women, Evangelism, and Temperance in Nineteenth-Century America* (1981); Evans, Sara, *Personal Politics: The Roots of Women's Liberation in the Civil Rights Movement and the New Left* (1979); Riley, Maria, *Transforming Feminism* (1989); Rossi, Alice, ed., *The Feminist Papers* (1973); Stempel, Laura, *Women's Issues* (1989).

fencing

Fencing, once exclusively a form of combat, is now enjoyed as a competitive sport worldwide. Modern fencers frown on identifying their sport with dueling, as in motion-picture sequences portraying acrobatic combatants engaged in reckless, devil-may-care swordplay. The sport of fencing calls for precision, coordination, and strategy, among other skills. First introduced as a sport on a small scale in the 14th century, fencing was one of the few events included in the first Olympic Games in 1896, and it has been included in every Olympic competition ever since.

The basic equipment used in fencing consists of a mask, a padded jacket, glove, and one of three weapons—the foil, épée, or sabre. Techniques and target areas for valid hits differ according to the weapon used. While some fencers may compete in each of the three weapons, generally skills are honed in one particular weapon. Until recently women were permitted to compete only in foil, but the United States Fencing Association now offers national competitions for women in sabre and épée, and the international federation has added women's épée to the World Championships.

The foil, which is the basic weapon of the sport, is a direct offshoot of the short dress sword introduced in the last half of the 17th century, probably at the court of France's Louis XIV. Weighing about one pound, it has a flexible, rectangular blade, about 35 inches in length, and a bell guard to protect the hand. Touches are scored with the point of the blade and must land within the torso of the body, from the neckband of the fencer's uniform to the hipline, the groin, and back.

The épée is the weapon most closely resembling the old-style dueling sword. It is similar in length to the foil but weighs about 27 oz., with a larger hand guard and a stiffer, triangular blade. Touches are scored with the point of the blade, and the entire body is a valid target area.

The sabre has a flexible rectangular blade with cutting edges along the entire front and one-third of the back edge. Its hand guard has one section attached to the pommel at the back of the handle. Touches are scored with the point as well as the length of the blade, and the target area includes the front and back torso, arms, hands, neck, and head.

Electric judging equipment is now used in all fencing matches. For foil and épée, a spring-loaded tip is attached to the point of the weapon and is connected to a wire that runs inside the blade, through the sleeve of the contestant's jacket,

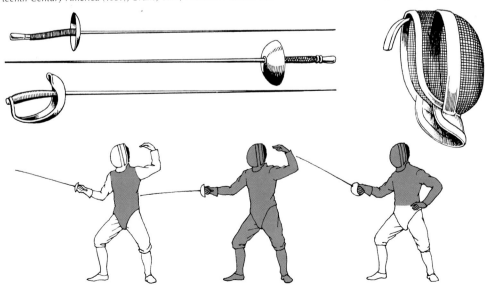

The three basic weapons used in competitive fencing are the foil, the épée, and the sabre. The foil and the épée, or dueling sword, have long, flexible blades and are used for thrusting attacks. The sabre's blade, unlike that of the foil or épée, has two cutting edges and is used for either thrusting or slashing. The diagram of fencers in the on-guard position indicates the differing technique required by each weapon. The shaded portion of the fencers represents accepted target zones. Fencers are required to wear a face mask and throat bib.

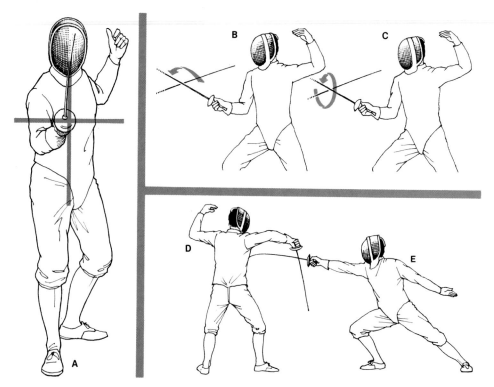

Crosslines imposed over the diagram of a fencer (A) indicate quadrants into which the target area is divided. (Right) Four basic maneuvers of swordsmanship are illustrated. To parry (B), a fencer employs a sideward sweep of his weapon to deflect an attack. The counterparry (C) is used to deflect an attack by means of a rapid circular movement of the weapon. The prime parry (D), which involves a swift, downward sweep of the weapon, is used to fend off an attack to the upper central target area. The lunge (E), the fundamental technique of attack, is executed with a swift forward stride with the right foot in an attempt to reach the opponent before a defensive reaction can occur.

and into a central scoring machine that registers hits. In the sabre, a sensor in the hand guard connects to the scoring machine.

Each time a fencer scores a touch, a point is gained. In a fencing bout, the objective is to be the first to score five touches on the opponent. Bouts are officiated by a president, sometimes with the assistance of a number of judges. The playing area is the "strip," or "piste," an area 14 m (46 ft) long and 2 m (6.6 ft) wide.

Bibliography: Alaux, Michel, *Modern Fencing: Foil and Saber from Initiation to Competition* (1975); Bower, Muriel, *Fencing*, 6th ed. (1990).

Fénelon, François de Salignac de la Mothe
[fay-nuh-lohn']

François de Fénelon, b. Aug. 6, 1651, d. Jan. 7, 1715, was a French Roman Catholic churchman, theologian, and writer, whose works had considerable influence on the political and educational theories of the ENLIGHTENMENT. After his ordination in 1676, he directed an institute for the instruction of converts from Protestantism. Later, he became tutor to the grandson of Louis XIV, and in 1695 he was consecrated archbishop of Cambrai. His sympathy for the mystical doctrine of QUIETISM and his treatise *Télémaque* (1699), an implicit criticism of Louis XIV's government, earned him numerous enemies at court and in the church. He also wrote (1687) an important treatise on the education of girls.   T. TACKETT

Bibliography: Little, Katherine Day, *François de Fénelon: A Study of a Personality* (1951); Raymond, M., *Fénelon* (1967).

Feng Yü-hsiang   (Feng Yuxiang)   [fuhng'-yoo'-shee-ahng']

Feng Yü-hsiang, the "Christian General," b. Sept. 26, 1882, d. Sept. 1, 1948, was a Chinese warlord who held the balance of power in North China from 1924 to 1930. He seized Peking in 1924 and, although driven out (1926) by CHANG TSO-LIN, reoccupied the city in 1928 after throwing his support to the KUOMINTANG. He broke with CHIANG KAI-SHEK in 1929 and thereafter fluctuated between opposing and supporting Chiang.

Bibliography: Sheridan, James, *Chinese Warlord* (1966).

Fenian cycle   [fen'-ee-uhn]

The Fenian cycle is a body of early Irish heroic tales centering on the exploits of FINN MAC CUMHAIL and the Fianna, bands of warriors known as Fenians. Other characters include Finn's son OSSIAN, Ossian's son Oscar, and Diarmuid and Grania, young lovers who are pursued by Finn, Grania's fiancé. Diarmuid, Grania, and Finn are analogous to another famous trio, Tristan, Isolde, and King Marc of the Arthurian legends.

DAVID H. GREENE

Fenians

The Fenians, or Irish Republican Brotherhood, was a revolutionary society founded in 1858 to overthrow British rule in Ireland. Its American wing, which led raids on Canada in 1866 and 1870, was an important center of Irish-American politics in the late 19th century. In Ireland, the brotherhood declined after an abortive rebellion in 1867. Many of its adherents drifted over to the more promising constitutional methods of Charles Stewart PARNELL's Home Rule movement. Nevertheless, the IRB survived to organize the EASTER RISING of 1916, and its spirit lives on in the IRISH REPUBLICAN ARMY. In Northern Ireland the term *fenians* is used as a derogatory synonym for Catholics.   DAVID W. MILLER

Bibliography: O'Broin, Leon, *Revolutionary Underground: The Story of the Irish Republican Brotherhood, 1858–1924* (1976).

See also: IRELAND, HISTORY OF.

fennel

Fennel, *Foeniculum vulgare* var. *dulce,* is a perennial herb of the parsley family, Umbelliferae. It is cultivated as an annual and grown for its licorice-flavored fennel seeds, which are used as food seasoning. The large-leaf bases of *finocchio,* or Florence fennel, *F. vulgare* var. *azoricum,* are eaten as a vegetable. Fennel oil is used in liqueurs, candies, and perfumes. The plant is native to southern Europe and widely cultivated in temperate and subtropical regions.   ARTHUR O. TUCKER

Fenollosa, Ernest Francisco   [fen-uh-loh'-suh]

The American educator and orientalist Ernest Francisco Fenollosa, b. Feb. 18, 1853, d. Sept. 21, 1908, pioneered Western studies of Far Eastern art and literature and also made contributions in American art education. Graduated (1874) from Harvard, he taught philosophy and economics at the newly founded Imperial University in Tokyo from 1878 to 1886 and later (1887–90) was on the staff of Tokyo's Imperial Museum. He undertook studies of the traditional arts of the Orient and urged the preservation of ancient art treasures in Japan, then preoccupied with emulating modern Western traditions. With Arthur Dow of Columbia Teacher's College, he later developed a system of art education that incorporated Far Eastern aesthetics, which was implemented in American public schools in the early 20th century. Among his principal works are *East and West: The Discovery of America and Other Poems* (1893) and *Epochs of Chinese and Japanese Art* (2d ed., 1912). Fenollosa's poetic theory and translations of Oriental poetry had a strong influence on Ezra Pound's English haiku and monumental *Cantos*.   BARBARA BRENNAN FORD

Bibliography: Chisolm, Lawrence W., *Fenollosa: The Far East and American Culture* (1963).

Fenrir   [fen'-rir]

In Norse mythology Fenrir was a ferocious wolf, the offspring of LOKI and the giantess Angerboda. The gods subdued him with a magical chain, Gleipher, but in the process he bit off the hand of the god Tyr.

Fens, The   [fenz]

The Fens is a large area of reclaimed marshland in eastern England, located primarily in southern LINCOLNSHIRE. The area is about 115 km (70 mi) long and 55 km (35 mi) wide. The elevation is generally at sea level, but some spots are lower. The Ouse River, which flows through the area, is embanked to prevent flooding. Reclaimed gradually between the 17th and 19th centuries from unproductive marshes, the Fens contains some of the best agricultural land in England, producing grains, potatoes, and sugar beets.

Fenton, Roger

Roger Fenton, b. March 1819, d. Aug. 8, 1869, an outstanding 19th-century English photographer, was among the first to photograph war under combat conditions. He initially studied law and art, and his early photographic work includes views of Moscow (1852) and portraits of the British Royal Family, beginning in 1853. From March to June 1855, Fenton documented the Crimean War. Limited to the lengthy exposures required for posed portraits and still landscapes, Fenton nonetheless effectively recorded the details of the war and its aftermath.   KEITH F. DAVIS

Bibliography: Fenton, Roger, *Roger Fenton, Photographer of the Crimean War* (1954); Hannavy, John, *Roger Fenton of Crimble Hall* (1975).

fenugreek   [fen'-yuh-greek]

Fenugreek is the annual herb, *Trigonella foenum-graecum*, in the pea family, Leguminosae. Native to the Mediterranean region and northern India, fenugreek is widely cultivated there and in China for its small, fragrant seeds. It is a common ingredient of curry and chutney. Fenugreek extract has a maple flavor and is used in imitation maple syrups and in butterscotch and rum flavorings. The seed is also an important source of diosgenin, a widely used raw material in the manufacture of steroids.   ARTHUR O. TUCKER

Feoktistov, Konstantin P.   [fee-awk'-tis-tawf]

The Soviet space engineer and cosmonaut Konstantin Petrovich Feoktistov, b. Feb. 29, 1926, participated in the world's first multipersonnel spaceflight in 1964. Feoktistov was a prominent engineer in the spacecraft design bureau headed by Sergey Korolev and helped design the Vostok and Voskhod spaceships. He and a doctor were chosen to be passengers on board the *Voskhod 1* flight and received four months of specialized training before blasting off on Oct. 12, 1964. After the 24-hour flight, Feoktistov returned to management

duties at the design bureau, where he became one of the principal designers of the Salyut space station.
                    JAMES OBERG

fer-de-lance   [fair-duh-lans']

The fer-de-lance, B. atrox, inhabits sugarcane fields and normally feeds on rodents. Its bite is almost always fatal to humans.

Fer-de-lance, *Bothrops atrox*, is a venomous pit viper in the family Crotalidae related to the RATTLESNAKE. Its name is derived from Creole-French *fer-de-lance*, meaning "head of a lance," which refers to the shape of the snake's head. Its habitat extends from southern Mexico into tropical South America, but it is also found in some islands of the Lesser Antilles. Maximum size is 1.5 to 1.8 m (5 to 6 ft). The coloration is olive-gray crossed by dark bands with dull yellow or greenish margins. The young are born live, with as many as 70 in a brood.

feral children   [fair'-ul]

Feral children are those said to have been nurtured and reared by animals in the wild. Children who have wandered off and survived on their own and children who have been deliberately deprived of human contact may also be described as feral. These children are of interest to the scientific community because they may shed light on the origins of language and on the interrelation of culture and biology. There have been more than 40 recorded cases of children being reared by animals, from a 14th-century Hessian wolf child to such 20th-century cases as a gazelle boy in the Western Sahara and a wolf boy in Sultanpur, India. Most of the evidence for these cases, however, has been secondhand and lacking in essential detail, and no one case has afforded conclusive proof. Because feral children are often severely retarded when restored to human society, it is speculated that they are victims of AUTISM who have been abandoned by their parents.

The best documented account of feral children is that of the wolf children of Midnapore, India, who were dug out of a wolf den by an Anglican missionary, the Reverend J. A. L. Singh, in 1920. Singh claimed that he personally rescued the children after having seen them living with the wolves. Although the children developed some social skills and the rudiments of language, they never became completely normal, and they died young. There is, however, no way of knowing to what extent their limitations were a result of cultural deprivation.

Fictionalized accounts of feral children have recurred throughout history, from the legend of ROMULUS AND REMUS to the more recent fictions of Mowgli in Rudyard Kipling's JUNGLE BOOK (1894) and TARZAN OF THE APES in several works by Edgar Rice Burroughs. They have been the themes of the films *The Wild Child* (1970) by François Truffaut and *The Mystery of Kaspar Hauser* (1974) by Werner Herzog. The latter, derived from the novel by Jakob WASSERMAN, is also based on a true case.   CHARLES MACLEAN

Bibliography: Armen, Jean-Claude, *Gazelle-Boy*, trans. by J. Stephen Hardman (1974); Itard, Jean-Marc-Gaspard, *Wild Boy of Aveyron*, trans. by George and Muriel Humphrey (1962); Lane, Harlan, *The Wild*

Boy of Aveyron (1976); Maclean, Charles, *The Wolf Children* (1978); Malson, Lucien, and Itard, Jean-Marc-Gaspard, *Wolf Children and the Problem of Human Nature* (1972); Singh, Joseph, and Zingg, Robert, *Wolf-Children and Feral Man* (1942; repr. 1966).

Ferber, Edna

Edna Ferber, b. Kalamazoo, Mich., Aug. 15, 1887, d. Apr. 16, 1968, was an American writer whose popular novels describe the diversity and sweep of American life. *So Big* (1924), about a Midwestern farming community, won a Pulitzer Prize. *Showboat* (1926), adapted by Jerome Kern and Oscar Hammerstein II, became a classic American musical play and film. Many of Ferber's other novels—including *Cimarron* (1930), *Saratoga Trunk* (1941), *Giant* (1952), and *Ice Palace* (1959)—were made into films. With George S. Kaufman she wrote several popular stage comedies (*The Royal Family,* 1927; *Dinner at Eight,* 1932; and *Stage Door,* 1936) that also became films. *A Peculiar Treasure* (1939) and *A Kind of Magic* (1963) are her autobiographies.

Ferber, Herbert

Herbert Ferber, b. New York City, Apr. 30, 1906, d. Aug. 20, 1991, was one of America's first nonrepresentational sculptors. He moved in his work from sculpture as object to sculpture as environment. In the 1940s he turned to openwork compositions and experimented with welding techniques. In the 1950s he began making what he called "cages" or "roofed" sculptures, and in the 1960s he created room-size sculpture through which spectators could move. He attempted, in his own words, "to fuse an acknowledgement of urban and industrial society . . . with a lyrical and humanist ingredient."

DIANA KURZ

Bibliography: Goldwater, R., *What is Modern Sculpture?* (1972); Rose, B., *American Art Since 1900* (1964; rev. ed. 1975).

Ferdinand II, King of Aragon   (Ferdinand the Catholic)

Ferdinand II, b. Mar. 10, 1452, d. Feb. 23, 1516, was king of Aragon (1479–1516) and king of Castile (as Ferdinand V, 1474–1504). He was the second son of John II, king of Aragon. The death of Ferdinand's elder brother in 1461 made him heir to the throne, and in 1469 he was married to ISABELLA I, who in 1474 succeeded her brother Henry IV and became queen of Castile and León. In spite of Ferdinand's early and unsuccessful attempt to claim full rights as king of Castile, the marriage was a political success that made possible the later unification of Spain.

Ferdinand helped Isabella restore order in Castile after the civil wars of the preceding reign, and he was also the chief architect of the conquest (1492) of Granada, the last Moorish state in Spain. In his native Aragon, he was forced to act with greater caution because of the limits of his royal prerogative,

Ferdinand II of Aragon and Isabella I of Castile make their triumphal entry into Granada, the last Moorish stronghold in Spain. Ferdinand's victory over the Moors on Jan. 2, 1492, united all of Spain under the joint rule of the "Catholic kings." (Royal Chapel, Granada, Spain.)

and in general he maintained the traditional liberties of his subjects. When he instituted reforms, as in his settlement of the agrarian difficulties in Catalonia (the *Senténcia* of Guadalupe of 1484), he did so by strengthening traditional institutions. Lacking the religious fervor of Isabella, he nevertheless supported the INQUISITION and the expulsion of the Jews (1492) for political reasons.

Although his domestic policies were very important for the development of Spain, Ferdinand's primary interest was in diplomacy and war. Cold, calculating, and devious, he was one of the models for Machiavelli's PRINCE. His greatest diplomatic achievement was the establishment of Spanish predominance in Italy through a complex series of campaigns (part of the ITALIAN WARS) and negotiations that brought him Naples in 1504 and greatly weakened his arch-rivals, the French. He also developed an elaborate system of matrimonial alliances to isolate France and prepare for the eventual unification of Spain and Portugal; but these proved less successful, and his connection with the Habsburgs led to a bitter struggle within Spain itself.

After Isabella's death in 1504, Ferdinand claimed the regency of Castile on behalf of his daughter JOAN THE MAD but was opposed by her Habsburg husband, PHILIP I, and a majority of the Castilian nobles. When Philip died in 1506, Ferdinand gained his prize but spent the remainder of the reign working against the succession of Philip's son, the future emperor CHARLES V. As Aragon did not recognize descent in the female line, he tried to conceive a son by his second wife Germaine de Foix in the hope of detaching his ancestral kingdom from Charles's inheritance. Fortunately for Spanish unity, he failed to do so.

WILLIAM S. MALTBY

Bibliography: Fernández-Armesto, Felipe, *Ferdinand and Isabella* (1975); Mariéjol, J. H., *The Spain of Ferdinand and Isabella,* trans. by Benjamin Keen (1961); Prescott, W. H., *History of the Reign of Ferdinand and Isabella,* abridged and edited by C. H. Gardiner (1963).

Ferdinand I, Emperor of Austria

Ferdinand I, b. Apr. 19, 1793, d. June 29, 1875, succeeded his father, Francis I (earlier Holy Roman Emperor FRANCIS II), as emperor of Austria in 1835. Subject to fits of insanity, he was an ineffectual ruler, and the empire was governed by a council under Klemens von METTERNICH. Unable to deal with the REVOLUTIONS OF 1848, Ferdinand abdicated in favor of his nephew FRANCIS JOSEPH in December of that year.

Ferdinand I, Tsar of Bulgaria

Ferdinand I, b. Feb. 26, 1861, d. Sept. 10, 1948, was a German prince who was elected ruler of the principality of Bulgaria, then under Turkish sovereignty, in 1887. In 1908 he proclaimed Bulgaria's independence, with himself as tsar. His army fought the Turks victoriously in the first phase of the BALKAN WARS (1912–13), but he turned against his Serbian and Greek allies, and the second phase ended disastrously for Bulgaria. To achieve his expansionist ambitions, Ferdinand joined (October 1915) the Central Powers of World War I. The Bulgarian Army was defeated in September 1918, and Ferdinand abdicated on Oct. 4, 1918.   K. M. SMOGORZEWSKI

Bibliography: Constant, Stephen, *Foxy Ferdinand, Tsar of Bulgaria* (1979); Crampton, R. J., *Bulgaria, 1878–1918* (1983).

Ferdinand I, Holy Roman Emperor

Ferdinand I, Holy Roman emperor (1558–64) and king of Hungary and Bohemia (1526–64), was one of the most successful of HABSBURG rulers. Born in Spain on Mar. 10, 1503, he was the younger son of Philip of Habsburg and Joan the Mad of Castile. Ferdinand's elder brother, CHARLES V, gave him the Habsburg duchy of Austria and made him his representative in the imperial government of Germany (1522). In 1530, Charles had the German electors designate Ferdinand king of the Romans (heir presumptive to the imperial title).

Ferdinand had already succeeded (1526) through his wife Anne, sister of LOUIS II of Hungary and Bohemia, to those two crowns. His relations with the local estates remained difficult, but in both countries Ferdinand established effective rule and a hereditary succession. The Turks continued to occupy a large part of Hungary, however, and the prince of Transylvania, John Zápolya, who also claimed the crown as JOHN I, occupied another part. In a bitter quarrel with Charles V, Ferdinand insisted successfully on his succession to the imperial title, against the claims of Charles's son, who became PHILIP II of Spain. In 1555 he negotiated the Peace of Augsburg, by which the German princes were given the right to choose between Roman Catholicism and Lutheranism. This agreement preserved peace in Germany for over 50 years. Ferdinand died in Vienna on July 25, 1564, and was succeeded in all his titles by his son MAXIMILIAN II.   H. G. KOENIGSBERGER

Bibliography: Betts, R. R., "Constitutional Development and Political Thought in Eastern Europe," and Spooner, F. C., "The Habsburg-Valois Struggle," in *The New Cambridge Modern History*, vol. 2 (1958); Dillon, K. J., *King and Estates in the Bohemian Lands, 1526–1564* (1976).

See also: AUGSBURG, PEACE OF.

Ferdinand II, Holy Roman Emperor

Ferdinand II, b. July 9, 1578, d. Feb. 15, 1637, was Holy Roman emperor from 1619 to 1637 and the principal champion of the Roman Catholic cause in the THIRTY YEARS' WAR. Educated by the Jesuits, Ferdinand was determined to reign as a Roman Catholic monarch. As archduke of Styria he banished the Protestant leaders of the Styrian estates. As king of Bohemia (from 1617) and as emperor he worked to crush the rebellion of the Bohemian Protestants, who elected (1619) the elector palatine, FREDERICK V, as a rival king of Bohemia. Ferdinand crushed this rebellion with military help from the Spanish Habsburgs and from Bavaria but thereby precipitated the Thirty Years' War.

After 1626, Albrecht von WALLENSTEIN organized a huge imperial army that made Ferdinand the virtual military master of Germany. Ferdinand and his advisors, however, had failed to think out a rational and consistent imperial policy. Ferdinand was therefore content with the restoration of ecclesiastical property through the Edict of Restitution (1629) and with supporting Spanish ambitions in the Netherlands.

The jealous imperial electors blackmailed Ferdinand into dismissing Wallenstein in 1630; but the victories of GUSTAV II ADOLF, king of Sweden, forced him to recall his hated general. After Gustav's death, Wallenstein's enemies accused him of treason, and Ferdinand consented to Wallenstein's murder in 1634. The Spanish-imperial victory of Nördlingen in 1634 led most German princes to conclude (1635) the Peace of Prague with Ferdinand. By this agreement, the Edict of Restitution was rescinded, but the princes' armies were placed under imperial command. Ferdinand's son, Ferdinand III, succeeded to this apparently strong position but also inherited the hostility of Sweden and France and the doubtful loyalty of the German princes.   H. G. KOENIGSBERGER

Bibliography: Bireley, Robert, *Religion and Politics in the Age of the Counter-Reformation* (1981); Koenigsberger, H. G., *The Hapsburgs and Europe 1516–1660* (1971).

Ferdinand III, Holy Roman Emperor

Ferdinand III, b. July 13, 1608, d. Apr. 2, 1657, was the Holy Roman emperor who ended the THIRTY YEARS' WAR in Germany. During the lifetime of his father, Ferdinand II, he succeeded to the thrones of Hungary (1625) and Bohemia (1627). He was an opponent of Albrecht von WALLENSTEIN, whom he succeeded as imperial commander in chief in 1634. In that year he won the battle of Nördlingen against the Swedes. As emperor (from 1637), Ferdinand endured a series of imperial defeats and took the lead in the negotiations that finally led to the Peace of Westphalia in 1648. The settlement forced on Ferdinand a virtual retreat from Germany. From then on, the Austrian HABSBURGS concentrated more and more on their ethnically diverse, Catholic, Danubian dominions.   H. G. KOENIGSBERGER

Bibliography: Koenigsberger, H. G., *The Hapsburgs and Europe 1516–1660* (1971); Parker, Geoffrey, *The Thirty Years' War* (1985).

See also: WESTPHALIA, PEACE OF.

Ferdinand I, King of Naples

Ferdinand I, king of Naples, b. 1423, d. Jan. 25, 1494, was the illegitimate son of ALFONSO V of Aragon, who seized Naples in 1442. Succeeding to the Neapolitan throne in 1458, Ferdinand was faced with a baronial revolt in favor of the rival king, RENÉ OF ANJOU. This was suppressed in 1462, but Ferdinand's viciously authoritarian policies provoked another unsuccessful revolt (1485–87). In the tumultuous affairs of Italy as a whole, Ferdinand allied himself chiefly with Florence, with whose help he expelled (1481) the Turks from Otranto.

Ferdinand I, King of Portugal

Ferdinand I, b. Oct. 31, 1345, d. Oct. 22, 1383, succeeded his father, PETER I, to the Portuguese throne in 1367. Laying claim to the Castilian throne, Ferdinand fought two humiliating wars (1369–71, 1372–73) against Henry II of Castile and a third (1381–82) against Henry's successor, John I. English help from JOHN OF GAUNT in the last two wars was to little avail. By the final peace (1382), John I of Castile married Ferdinand's only legitimate child, Beatrice. This marriage would have given Portugal to Castile on Ferdinand's death but for the revolution led by Ferdinand's half brother, JOHN I.

Ferdinand, King of Romania

Ferdinand, b. Aug. 24, 1865, d. July 20, 1927, succeeded his uncle, CAROL I, as king of Romania in October 1914, shortly after the outbreak of World War I. Although a Hohenzollern, and thus related to the German royal family, he was induced to enter (August 1916) the war on the Allied side by promises of major territorial concessions as well as by the influence of his English wife, Marie. Romania was soon overrun by Austro-German forces, and Ferdinand was forced to conclude a separate peace in May 1918. However, he reentered the war on its conclusion, Nov. 10, 1918, just before its conclusion, and thus won the promised territories—Transylvania and much of the Hungarian plain—in the peace settlement. Ferdinand was crowned king of Greater Romania in 1922.   K. M. SMOGORZEWSKI

Ferdinand III, Spanish King of Castile

Ferdinand III, c.1200–1252, was king of the Spanish realm of Castile from 1217 to 1252. After inheriting the neighboring kingdom of León in 1230, he permanently united the two kingdoms. He gained renown for his reconquest of much of southern Spain from the Moors. By a series of sieges he captured Córdoba (1236), Jaén (1245), and Seville (1248); he also received the submission of the Moors of Murcia (1243). As a result, Muslim Spain was reduced to the kingdom of Granada, whose ruler paid an annual tribute to Castile. Ferdinand also initiated some of the cultural developments that were brought to completion by his son, ALFONSO X. Ferdinand was canonized in 1671. Feast day: May 30.

JOSEPH F. O'CALLAGHAN

Ferdinand VI, King of Spain

Ferdinand VI, b. Sept. 23, 1713, d. Aug. 10, 1759, became king of Spain in 1746 and ruled until his death. His reign was a time of reform, prosperity, and peace. In 1729, Ferdinand married Maria Bárbara de Bragança, daughter of King John V of Portugal. They had no children. In 1746 he succeeded his father, PHILIP V, on the throne. He was a good ruler but was timid and melancholy. Ably assisted by his prime minister, the marqués de ENSENADA, he improved the tax and customs administrations, strengthened the armed forces, and developed the nation's economy. He pursued a foreign policy of neutrality between France and Britain. By the Concordat of 1753, he reduced the influence of the Roman Catholic church in the secular life of Spain. He founded (1752) the Academy of Fine Arts and encouraged culture and science through generous subsidies. He was succeeded by his half-brother, Charles III.

DANIEL R. HEADRICK

Ferdinand VII, King of Spain

Ferdinand VII of Spain, portrayed here by Francisco Goya, first assumed the throne by forcing his father's abdication in 1808. Imprisoned in France for six years, Ferdinand returned to Spain in 1814 and immediately suspended the liberal constitution adopted in his absence. A rebellion in 1820 forced him to accept the constitution, but the French intervened to restore him to absolute power.

Ferdinand VII, b. Oct. 14, 1784, d. Sept. 29, 1833, was king of Spain from 1808 to 1833. The son of CHARLES IV, he was an absolutist monarch whose reign was marked by discontent and rebellion. In 1807, Ferdinand was arrested for plotting to overthrow the chief minister, Manuel de GODOY, who was keeping him ignorant of state affairs. A riot in March 1808 forced Godoy to flee and frightened Charles IV into abdicating his crown to Ferdinand. Soon thereafter, Ferdinand and Charles were lured to a meeting with NAPOLEON I at Bayonne. Napoleon forced Ferdinand to return the crown to Charles and forced Charles to surrender his rights to Napoleon. Thereupon Ferdinand was imprisoned in France until 1814, while French troops ravaged Spain.

When Ferdinand returned to Spain as king in 1814, he repudiated the revolutionary Constitution of 1812, reestablished the Inquisition, and embarked on a reign of terror against all suspected liberals. Repeated uprisings by liberal officers failed. After one such uprising in 1820, Ferdinand was captured and forced to respect the constitution. Meanwhile he secretly plotted with royalist insurgents and appealed for help from abroad. When a French army swept out the liberals in 1823, Ferdinand used his restored absolute power to persecute his enemies so cruelly that even his supporters were horrified.

Ferdinand ignored ordinary matters of government and continually changed ministers, thereby hindering the reconstruction of his war-torn country. In his last years, old age and the influence of his fourth wife, María Cristina, led him to soften his policies. She persuaded him to revoke the Salic Law provision forbidding female rulers so that their daughter, the future ISABELLA II, might succeed Ferdinand to the throne. Isabella's succession, however, was contested by Ferdinand's brother, Carlos, and the CARLIST wars resulted.   DANIEL R. HEADRICK

Bibliography: Carr, Raymond, *Spain 1808–1975,* 2d ed. (1982); Lovett, Gabriel, *Napoleon and the Birth of Modern Spain,* 2 vols. (1965).

Ferdinand I, King of the Two Sicilies

Ferdinand I, b. Jan. 12, 1751, d. Jan. 4, 1825, was a Spanish Bourbon who ruled (1816–25) as king of the Two Sicilies. When his father became king of Spain in 1759 as CHARLES III, Ferdinand inherited the thrones of Naples (as Ferdinand IV) and Sicily (as Ferdinand III). In 1768 he married the Austrian Maria Carolina, sister of Marie Antoinette of France, and she exerted a reactionary and pro-Austrian influence on his reign. In 1799 the French revolutionary armies took Naples, and the couple fled briefly to Sicily but quickly returned. In 1806, NAPOLEON I again took Naples and again the couple fled to Sicily. The Congress of Vienna restored Naples to Ferdinand

in 1815; he then combined Naples and Sicily to form the kingdom of the Two Sicilies and ruled as Ferdinand I. In 1820 a liberal revolt forced him to establish a constitutional monarchy, but he restored absolute rule with Austrian aid in 1821.

Ferdinand II, King of the Two Sicilies

Ferdinand II, b. Jan. 12, 1810, d. May 22, 1859, king of the Two Sicilies from 1830, was the son and successor of Francis I. He began his reign with an amnesty for political prisoners and various reforms but gradually became more reactionary. Although forced to grant a constitution when revolution began in 1848, he subsequently rescinded it. The use of artillery to crush the rebellion won him the nickname "King Bomba"; his severity toward opponents was denounced abroad.

Bibliography: Acton, H. M., *The Last Bourbons of Naples* (1961).

Ferdowsi: see FIRDAWSI.

Ferguson, James Edward   [fur'-guh-suhn]

James Edward Ferguson, b. Bell County, Tex., Aug. 31, 1871, d. Sept. 21, 1944, was a governor of Texas who, after being impeached and removed from office, exercised power through his wife, Miriam A. Wallace Ferguson (1875–1961), who was twice governor (1925–27, 1933–35). "Pa" Ferguson was elected governor in 1914 as a populist and especially as the champion of the small farmer. Accused of corruption, he was removed in 1917 and prohibited from running for public office again. In 1924, "Ma" Ferguson ran and won a notable victory. She was elected to a second term in 1932.

Fergusson, Francis

Francis Liesseline Fergusson, b. Albuquerque, N.Mex., Feb. 21, 1904, d. Dec. 19, 1986, was a noted American critic and scholar and the author of several influential works on literature and drama. The best known is *The Idea of a Theatre* (1949), an innovative work that continues to shape the ideas and practices of dramatic criticism. Other works include *Dante's Drama of the Mind* (1953), on the *Purgatorio,* and *Trope and Allegory: Themes Common to Dante and Shakespeare* (1977).   COLETTE BROOKS

Fergusson, Robert

The Scottish poet Robert Fergusson, b. Sept. 5, 1750, d. Oct. 16, 1774, helped lead the 18th-century revival of poetry in the Scots dialect. His *Poems* (1773 and 1779) were an important influence on Robert Burns. His powerful and spirited satirical verse, first published in Ruddiman's *Weekly Magazine* and collected in 1773, includes "Auld Reekie." Fergusson's tragic life, which was clouded by illness and poverty, further interested Burns, who raised a memorial on his predecessor's grave. Fergusson died in a lunatic asylum.   ROBIN BUSS

Ferlinghetti, Lawrence   [fur-lin-get'-ee]

Lawrence Ferlinghetti, b. Yonkers, N.Y., Mar. 24, 1919 or 1920, is an American poet who became associated with the beat movement of the 1950s. In 1953 he and Peter D. Martin founded City Lights, the first all-paperbound bookstore in the United States. Located in San Francisco, it became a cultural center for young writers of the BEAT GENERATION. With profits from that enterprise, the two men began to publish City Lights Books and the Pocket Poets Series. Their first publication was *Pictures of the Gone World* (1955), Ferlinghetti's first book of poems. His second and best-known work was *A Coney Island of the Mind* (1958). In the 1950s, Ferlinghetti gave poetry readings to support the American poetry revival in San Francisco, a movement dedicated to bringing poetry out of the university and into the street. Later works include *Starting from San Francisco* (1961), *Back Roads to Far Places* (1971), and *Wild Dreams of a New Beginning* (1988).

Bibliography: Skau, Michael, *Constantly Risking Absurdity: Essays on the Writings of Lawrence Ferlinghetti* (1987); Silesky, Barry, *Ferlinghetti* (1990); Smith, Larry, *Lawrence Ferlinghetti* (1983).

Fermanagh [fur-man'-uh]

Fermanagh (1991 pop., 54,290) is a county and district in south central Northern Ireland. It has an area of 1,877 km² (725 mi²). Enniskillen is the county town. Fermanagh is bisected from northwest to southeast by island-dotted Lough Erne. The land is hilly, rising to elevations of over 600 m (2,000 ft). Quarrying, potato growing, and stock farming are principal occupations. Settled during the prehistoric period, the area has numerous early Celtic remains. During the early 17th century many English and Scottish immigrants settled there.

Fermat, Pierre de [fair-mah']

Pierre de Fermat, a French mathematician of the 17th century, pursued mathematics as an avocation while serving as a jurist and government official. One of the most productive mathematicians of his time, Fermat made significant contributions to the development of differential calculus, number theory, optics, and probability theory.

Pierre de Fermat, b. Aug. 17, 1601, d. Jan. 12, 1665, was a French mathematician who made important discoveries in ANALYTIC GEOMETRY and NUMBER THEORY and also worked on probability theory and optics. For Fermat, a Toulouse lawyer and government official, mathematics was only a hobby.

In 1636, Fermat presented a system of analytic geometry similar to the one that René DESCARTES would propose a year later. Fermat's work, based upon an attempted reconstruction of the work of the Greek mathematician APOLLONIUS OF PERGA, made use of the algebra of François VIÈTE. A similar attempt to reconstruct an ancient work led to methods, similar to differentiation and integration, for finding the MAXIMA AND MINIMA points of curves and the areas enclosed by curves.

Fermat's greatest work was in number theory. He was especially interested in the properties of PRIME NUMBERS and in the determination of families of solutions to sets of similar problems. His most famous theorem, known as Fermat's last theorem, states that the equation $x^n + y^n = z^n$, where x, y, and z are positive integers, has no solution if n is an integer greater than 2. Fermat wrote in the margin of his copy of the works of Apollonius: "I have discovered a truly remarkable proof [of this theorem] which this margin is too small to contain." Search for a general proof thereafter occupied many mathematicians, with success finally announced only in 1993 by a British mathematician, Andrew Wiles.

Fermat worked with Blaise PASCAL on the theory of probabilities. Together, they formulated the principles on which Christiaan HUYGENS founded the calculus of probabilities. Fermat published almost nothing during his lifetime: he usually announced his discoveries in letters to friends or simply noted results in the margins of his books. His work was largely forgotten until the mid-1800s.   STEVEN LUBAR

Bibliography: Cipra, Barry, "Fermat's Last Theorem Finally Yields," *Science*, July 2, 1993; Mahoney, Michael, *The Mathematical Career of Pierre de Fermat* (1973).

Fermat's last theorem: see FERMAT, PIERRE DE.

fermentation

Fermentation is the chemical process by which living cells degrade sugar in the absence of air to yield part or all of the energy needed by an organism. Fermentation is also called anaerobic respiration, or anaerobic glycolysis. Certain microorganisms, such as YEAST and some bacteria, exist in the absence of oxygen and are called ANAEROBES. Most living things, however, possess—in addition to anaerobic respiration—a subsequent chemical process called aerobic respiration, which requires molecular oxygen.

In fermentation, the sugar molecules are converted to alcohol and lactic acid. Beer, wine, and cheese production and several other commercial processes require fermentation of certain kinds of yeast, bacteria, and molds.

The major chemical steps in fermentation involve the breakdown of a sugar, such as glucose, into pyruvic acid. This conversion involves the sequential action of at least a dozen enzymes. About 40 years of intensive research were devoted to discovering the details of this process. The METABOLISM of glucose to form pyruvic acid occurs in all cells, and chemical energy is extracted and stored in a compound called adenosine triphosphate for use in metabolism (see ATP).

Fermentation yields relatively small amounts of energy, and for this reason large amounts of glucose must be degraded by aerobic organisms to maintain life under oxygen-poor conditions. The aerobic respiratory process uses the chemical products formed in fermentation and is called the tricarboxylic acid cycle, or the KREBS CYCLE. In this next stage of metabolism, namely, the breakdown of pyruvic acid in the presence of oxygen, much larger amounts of energy are liberated.

Bibliography: McNeil, B. M., and Harvey, L. M., eds., *Fermentation* (1990); Stanbury, P. F., and Whitaker, A., *Principles of Fermentation Technology* (1984); Stryer, L., *Biochemistry*, 3d ed. (1988); Ward, O. P., *Fermentation Biotechnology* (1989).

Fermi, Enrico [fair'-mee, ayn-ree'-koh]

Enrico Fermi conducted the experiments in radioactivity that won him the 1938 Nobel Prize for physics before emigrating from Italy to the United States and commencing work on the atomic bomb. An exceptional researcher and theorist, Fermi developed a statistical method for predicting the behavior of atomic particles and later led the group that achieved the first self-sustaining fission reaction.

The Italian physicist Enrico Fermi, b. Sept. 29, 1901, d. Nov. 28, 1954, is best known as a central figure in the MANHATTAN PROJECT to build the first ATOMIC BOMB. Fermi received his doctorate from the University of Pisa in 1922. After working under Max BORN at Göttingen and Paul EHRENFEST at Leiden, he returned to Italy in 1926 and became professor of theoretical physics at the University of Rome. In 1938, on the eve of World War II, he escaped to the United States.

Fermi's early work on the statistical distribution of elementary particles led him to divide these atomic constituents into two groups, known as fermions and bosons, depending on their spin characteristics. This division is now accepted as standard. His subsequent work on radioactivity and atomic structure involved experiments on the production of artificial radioactivity by bombarding matter with neutrons, for which he received the 1938 Nobel Prize for physics (see NUCLEAR ENERGY). In collaboration with other eminent scientists, Fermi experimented with nuclear fission at Columbia University. This work culminated in the first sustained nuclear reaction, on Dec. 2, 1942, at the University of Chicago. Further work at Los Alamos Scientific Laboratory led to the construction of the ATOMIC BOMB. After the war, Fermi accepted a post at the newly established Institute for Nuclear Studies at the University of Chicago and continued his work in the field of neutron physics.

STEVEN J. DICK

Bibliography: Fermi, Laura, *Atoms in the Family: My Life with Enrico Fermi* (1954); Segrè, Emilio, *Enrico Fermi, Physicist* (1970).

Fermi National Accelerator Laboratory

The Fermi National Accelerator Laboratory, or Fermilab, is a high-energy physics research center that was founded in 1967 near Chicago and named for Enrico Fermi. Fermilab is operated by Universities Research Association, and it is funded by the U.S. Department of Energy. The facility houses a 500 billion, or giga, electron-volt (500-GeV) proton synchrotron ACCELERATOR. The addition to the accelerator in 1983 of a superconducting magnetic ring, the Tevatron, increased the potential to 1,000 GeV (1 TeV), and the later addition of an antiproton storage ring enabled researchers to achieve collision energies of about 1.8 TeV by 1987 (see DETECTOR, PARTICLE).

BRIAN SOUTHWORTH

fermion   [fur'-mee-ahn]

A fermion is any FUNDAMENTAL PARTICLE that has half-odd-integral spin; that is, its angular momentum is an odd multiple of the quantity $h/2\pi$. Fermions, unlike bosons, obey the Pauli EXCLUSION PRINCIPLE. Light fermions, such as electrons, are called LEPTONS; heavy fermions, such as protons and neutrons, are called BARYONS.

fermium   [fur'-mee-uhm]

The chemical element fermium, named for Enrico Fermi, is a metal of the ACTINIDE SERIES in Group IIIB of the periodic table. Its symbol is Fm, its atomic number is 100, and the atomic weight of its stablest isotope is 257. Like other TRANSURANIUM ELEMENTS, fermium does not occur naturally. It and einsteinium were first produced in a thermonuclear explosion in the South Pacific in 1952 and identified by the American chemist Glenn Seaborg and his collaborators. All of its isotopes are radioactive, their half-lives ranging from a few milliseconds to about 100 days.

fern

Ferns are vascular plants often placed in the class Filicineae in the five-kingdom system of classification. Their distinguishing features include conducting tissue, reproduction by spores, and leaves with a branching vein system. So-called fern allies (CLUB MOSSES, HORSETAILS, QUILLWORTS, and spike mosses) differ in having needlelike or scalelike leaves, each with but a single unbranched vein.

Ferns are found in all regions of the world except for the most severe deserts. They occur well above the Arctic Circle as well as in dry, rocky regions, high mountains, and lowland forests. Ferns are most richly developed in wet forests of tropical mountainous regions, generally at middle elevations (900–2,000 m/3,000–7,000 ft). In these regions the ferns are predominantly EPIPHYTES, which grow on the trunks and branches of trees and derive moisture and nutrients from mosses and humus accumulated on the trees.

About 12,000 fern species are known to exist, with many still being discovered. They are arranged in about 350 genera in 28 families. The precise numbers are strongly debated among botanists and depend on opinions regarding the relative importance of certain characteristics.

Structure and Size. The most conspicuous part of the fern is its leaves, or fronds; the stem and roots are relatively inconspicuous. The stem is usually specialized as a rhizome, which

creeps on or just beneath the soil level. The form of a fern varies considerably. Many have the typical dissected fronds associated with ferns, but other species have fronds that are undivided and straplike, grasslike, or star shaped. One of the most distinctive features of ferns is the way in which the leaves are developed during growth. In most other plant groups the leaves enlarge in all directions at once, but in ferns they mature progressively from the base to the tip, resulting in a coiled juvenile leaf, called a crosier or fiddlehead. As the frond matures at the base, it gradually unrolls.

Most ferns are between 10 and 91 cm (4 and 36 in) long, but the giants of the fern world are the tree ferns: their stems are often 18-m-high (60-ft) trunks, crowned with fronds measuring 3 m (10 ft) long. Tree ferns do not have the largest leaves, however, for other species that grow from creeping rhizomes gradually unroll to lengths of 4.5–6 m (15–20 ft) or even 21 m (70 ft). At the other extreme, a number of the tropical rain-forest ferns have fronds only one cell thick, adapted to a climate having nearly 100 percent humidity at all times. These ''filmy ferns'' may be extremely small, with fronds less than 13 mm (0.5 in) long.

Aquatic Ferns. Various ferns occupy aquatic habitats. The water clover, *Marsilea,* has rhizomes rooted in the mud with fronds like four-leaf clovers above the water. The mosquito fern, *Azolla,* and water spangles, *Salvinia,* float on the surface with roots or rootlike appendages dangling beneath. Their fronds are round or oval and in *Azolla* are only 2 mm (0.08 in) long. *Azolla* is especially interesting because its leaves have a small pouch containing a blue-green alga, *Anabaena azollae,* which is believed to fix nitrogen from the water into usable form for plants, thus increasing the rice production in the paddies that contain the *Azolla* (see NITROGEN CYCLE). The floating fern, *Ceratopteris,* is a popular aquarium plant used by tropical-fish hobbyists.

The Reproductive Cycle. A noteworthy feature of the fern's REPRODUCTION cycle is that two very different reproductive forms exist in every species, a phenomenon known as the ALTERNATION OF GENERATIONS. The familiar form of the fern is the sporophyte generation, in which each cell is diploid, containing a normal number of chromosomes. The other form, the gametophyte generation, exists as an inconspicuous plant, called a prothallus, which is less than 5 mm (0.2 in) in length. The prothallus is haploid, each cell having half the normal number of chromosomes.

Stout, erect stems and large fronds characterize many ferns of the genus Marattia, *which includes 60 species found in the tropics and in New Zealand. These ferns bear their sporangia in clusters, known as synangia, which occur in pairs along each side of many leaf veins.* Marattia *ferns belong to the primitive order Marattiales.*

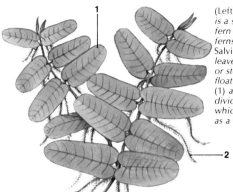

(Left) Salvinia natans is a small, floating fern of Europe. Water ferns of the genus Salvinia bear three leaves at each node, or stem joint: two floating, or air, leaves (1) and one finely divided water leaf (2), which may function as a root.

The adder's-tongue fern, Ophioglossum vulgatum (right), and moonwort, Botrychium lunaria (left), belong to the family of succulent ferns, Ophioglossaceae, which is not closely related to other fern groups. Adder's-tongue, common in fields and woodlands, bears a single green leaf and a fertile stalk that resembles a snake's tongue. Moonwort, found on dry meadows and hillsides, has leaflets shaped like half-moons and a stalk topped by long, spore-bearing clusters. Both species are small, usually less than 15 cm (6 in) tall, and produce fronds annually from underground stems.

(Right) The mosquito fern, Azolla filiculoides, is a North American water fern that has been introduced into Europe. It bears minute air leaves (1) and has roots (2) that hang freely in the water. The leaves of Azolla contain a symbiotic blue-green alga, Anabaena azollae, which apparently fixes atmospheric nitrogen for its host.

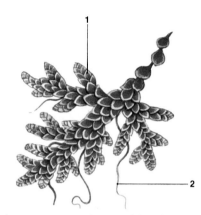

A mature fern plant bears spore cases (sporangia) on its frond, usually on the lower surface. In most ferns the sporangia are found in clusters called sori, of several to 100 sporangia or more. Each sporangium, consisting of a stalk and capsule, generally produces 64 spores—more, in the primitive groups. A central cell divides until 16 cells are formed, each cell with two sets of chromosomes, one set from each parent. A special nuclear division, called MEIOSIS, occurs in each cell to reduce the chromosome number by half and form four spores, making a total of 64, each with 1 set of chromosomes. The spores are discharged from the sporangia and fall to the ground or float some distance in the air. Those falling in moist regions germinate, sending out a green filament of cells that broadens with further growth to form the heart-shaped prothallus, which obtains water and minerals from the soil by hairlike rhizoids. Antheridia, containing sperms, and archegonia, each containing an egg, are produced on the lower surface of the prothallus. The sperms require water, such as rain or dew, in which to swim to the egg. The fertilized egg divides many times to form the new fern; thus completing the life cycle.

Vegetative Reproduction. In addition to reproduction by spores, many ferns reproduce vegetatively. Some produce buds on the roots (as in *Asplenium, Platycerium,* and *Ophioglossum*) or on the frond (as in *Asplenium, Tectaria, Diplazium,* and *Woodwardia*). The members of the Boston fern genus, *Nephrolepis,* send out slender, hairlike stems (stolons) that produce new plants when they touch the soil. Many ferns multiply through rhizome branching. Some ferns are propagated commercially by tissue culture; this is done by removing a living stem tip and growing it on nutrient agar. With special sterile treatment it will grow and divide, creating hundreds of plants from a single stem tip.

Evolution of Ferns. Ferns are an ancient group of plants. They had their beginnings in the Devonian Period, nearly 390–340 million years ago. During the Carboniferous Period (the Coal Age), ferns and seed ferns, which may have evolved from a common ancestral group, were a major part of the vegetation, along with the fern allies and early conifers. Few ferns of that

The royal fern, Osmunda regalis, grows in the wetlands, bogs, and meadows of North America and northwestern Europe. Under favorable conditions it may reach a height of more than 1.8 m (6 ft). Feathery, light-brown, spore-bearing leaflets (1) occur at the tips of fertile leaves; the sterile leaflets (2) are oblong and widely spaced.

time have evolved to modern forms. The great coal swamps disappeared in the drier times of the Permian, Triassic, and Jurassic periods, and there are relatively few fern fossils from those times. The Cretaceous Period marks the appearance of modern ferns, as well as the flowering plants. The seed ferns, although extinct today, probably gave rise to the flowering plants and to the cycads.   JOHN T. MICKEL

Bibliography: Dunbar, L., *Ferns of the Coastal Plains* (1989); Jones, D., *Encyclopedia of Ferns*, vol. 1 (1987); Lellinger, D. B., *A Field Manual of the Ferns and Fern-Allies of the United States and Canada* (1985); Mickel, J. T., *How to Know the Ferns and Fern Allies* (1979).

Fernandel [fer-nahn-del']

Fernandel was the stage name of French actor and vaudeville entertainer Fernand Joseph Désiré Contandin, b. May 8, 1903, d. Feb. 26, 1971. Possessor of a long face and toothy grin, Fernandel was a leading performer in French, Italian, and occasional U.S. films from the 1930s until his death. Best known for his sly and earthy comic roles, such as that of an embattled priest in the series initiated by *The Little World of Don Camillo* (1952), he successfully played tragic characters also.

Fernández, Gregorio [fair-nahn'-dayth, gray-gor'-yoh]

Gregorio Fernández, c.1576–1636, was an important sculptor of the Spanish baroque who worked mainly in Valladolid. His polychromed wood images reflect the influence of the naturalistic style of Juan de JUNI and are characterized by their dramatic intensity. Among his best-known works is the *Pietà* of 1617 (National Museum, Valladolid), in which the figure of Mary has glass eyes, thereafter a regular feature of Spanish sculpture. Many of Fernández's religious figures, such as *The Dead Christ* (1605; Capuchinos del Pardo, Madrid), were carved and painted with strikingly realistic details. Fernández executed many altarpieces, including the high altar of the Cathedral of Plasencia (1624–34).   EDWARD J. SULLIVAN

Bibliography: Kubler, George, and Soria, Martin, *Art and Architecture in Spain and Portugal and Their American Dominions, 1500–1800* (1959).

Fernández de Córdoba, Gonzalo [fair-nahn'-dayth day kohr'-doh-bah, gohn-thah'-loh]

Gonzalo Fernández de Córdoba, b. Sept. 1, 1453, d. Dec. 1 or 2, 1515, was a Spanish general known as el Gran Capitán. He fought in the wars to drive the Muslims from Spain and helped negotiate the surrender (1492) of the Moorish kingdom of Granada. After France had invaded the Kingdom of Naples in the ITALIAN WARS, Fernández de Córdoba was sent (1495) to Italy with an army; he soon forced the French to withdraw. When the Treaty of Granada (1500), which divided Naples between France and Spain, proved unworkable, the war was resumed. Fernández de Córdoba's brilliant victories at Cerignola and at Garigliano in 1503 brought all of Naples under Spanish rule. He was viceroy of Naples from 1504 to 1507.

Bibliography: De Gaury, Gerald, *The Grand Captain: Gonzalo de Córdoba* (1955); Purcell, Mary, *The Great Captain: Gonzalo Fernández de Córdoba* (1962).

Fernández de Lizardi, José Joaquín [fair-nahn'-dayth day lee-thahr'-dee, hoh-say' hoh-ah-keen']

José Joaquín Fernández de Lizardi, b. Nov. 15, 1776, d. June 21, 1827, was a Mexican novelist, poet, dramatist, and avid supporter of Mexico's independence from Spain. His literary reputation is based on three novels, *The Itching Parrot* (1816; Eng. trans., 1942), *La Quijotita y su prima* (Miss Quixote and Her Cousin, 1819), and *Don Catrín de la Fachenda* (1832). *The Itching Parrot*, a scathing satire of Mexico's middle class, reflects both the influence of the 18th-century French *philosophes* and the form of the Spanish picaresque novel. It is considered the first Latin American novel.   EDWARD MULLEN

Fernando Po: see BIOKO.

Ferrar, Nicholas [fair'-ur]

Nicholas Ferrar, b. Feb. 22, 1592, d. Dec. 4, 1637, was an English religious figure who founded the community of Little Gidding. Giving up a brilliant political career, he settled (1625) at Little Gidding, Huntingdonshire, where he led his household, consisting of his mother and about 30 others, through a schedule of regulated prayer, work, and neighborhood assistance. His Anglican lay community incurred Puritan hostility and was broken up during the English Civil War. T. S. Eliot used the community as the setting for his poem *Little Gidding*.

Bibliography: Maycock, A. L., *Nicholas Ferrar of Little Gidding* (1938).

Ferrara [fer-rah'-rah]

Ferrara (1988 est. pop., 143,046) is the capital city of Ferrara province in the Emilia-Romagna region in northern Italy. Situated in the Emilian Plain on the Po di Volano River, 45 km (28 mi) northeast of Bologna, it is an important center for fruit production and the manufacture of chemicals, plastics, shoes, and sugar. Monuments include the medieval Este Castle (begun 14th century), the Cathedral of San Giorgio (begun 1135), and the Renaissance Schifanoia and Diamanti palaces.

First mentioned in 8th-century sources, Ferrara was, from the early 13th century, a principality of the ESTE family, which hosted one of the great Renaissance courts. The Council of Ferrara was held there in 1438. In 1598, Ferrara became part of the Papal States. The pope ceded it to the French in 1797 but regained it in 1815. In 1860, Ferrara became part of united Italy.   DANIEL R. LESNICK

Bibliography: Dean, T., *Land and Power in Late Medieval Ferrara* (1987).

Ferrara-Florence, Council of

The Council of Ferrara-Florence (1438–45), held successively at Ferrara, Florence, and Rome, was an ecumenical council of the Roman Catholic church convened for the primary purpose of ending the schism between that church and the Eastern ORTHODOX CHURCH. Officially, it was the second part of a council transferred from Basel (see BASEL, COUNCIL OF), although a group of dissident churchmen remained in Basel and continued a rival council until 1449. Both the Byzantine emperor John VIII and the patriarch of Constantinople Joseph II were present at Ferrara-Florence, in part to seek aid from the West against the Turks. After much discussion of their theological differences, the two churches were formally reunited in 1439. The Orthodox leaders had difficulty, however, winning approval from the clergy at home, and all semblance of unity dissolved after the fall of the Byzantine Empire to the Ottoman Turks in 1453.

The council also negotiated reunion with several smaller eastern churches (see ARMENIAN CHURCH, NESTORIAN CHURCH, JACOBITE CHURCH, and EASTERN RITE CHURCHES) and challenged the conciliar theory (see CONCILIARISM) enunciated at the councils of Constance and Basel.   T. TACKETT

Bibliography: Halecki, Oscar, *From Florence to Brest, 1439–1596*, 2d ed. (1968).

Ferrari, Giuseppe [fer-rah'-ree]

Giuseppe Ferrari, b. Mar. 7, 1811, d. July 2, 1876, was an Italian historian and political philosopher whose work influenced the Italian RISORGIMENTO. He received doctorates from the universities of Pavia and Paris. During the 1840s and 1850s he wrote and taught philosophy in France. Returning to Italy in 1859, Ferrari was elected to Parliament and given several university chairs. His works include *Essay on the Principle and Limits of the Philosophy of History* (1843) and *History of the Italian Revolutions* (4 vols., 1858).

Ferrari, Lodovico

Lodovico Ferrari, b. Feb. 2, 1522, d. Oct. 5, 1565, was an Italian mathematician who discovered the solution, or ROOT, of the quartic EQUATION (fourth-degree polynomial equation). He was a pupil of Gerolamo CARDANO and succeeded him as public lecturer on mathematics in Milan in 1540. There, in 1548, he defended Cardano in a debate with Niccolò TARTAGLIA, even though Cardano had published without permission Tartaglia's solution of the cubic equation (third-degree equation). This debate brought Ferrari public attention and gained him a position as tax assessor in Mantua. In 1565 he became professor of mathematics at Bologna.   STEVEN LUBAR

Ferraro, Geraldine

Geraldine Anne Ferraro, b. Newburgh, N.Y., Aug. 26, 1935, was nominated as the first woman vice-presidential candidate of a major U.S. party in 1984. The daughter of an Italian immigrant, Ferraro graduated (1956) from Marymount College in Manhattan and earned a law degree (1960) from Fordham University. She practiced law privately until 1974, when she became an assistant district attorney in Queens, N.Y. In 1978 she won election to Congress as a Democrat. Twice reelected, she gained (1983) a seat on the House budget committee and in 1984 chaired the Democratic platform committee. Describing herself as a "moderate," she sponsored women's economic equity legislation, opposed mandatory school busing, and supported tuition tax credits.

Before the 1984 convention, the almost-certain Democratic presidential candidate, Walter Mondale, chose Ferraro as his running mate; at the convention (July 16–19) they both were nominated. Ferraro became a national figure as she campaigned vigorously and debated her Republican opponent, Vice-President George Bush, on television. The Mondale-Ferraro ticket, however, was badly defeated by President Ronald Reagan and Bush in November. In 1992 she ran unsuccessfully in the New York Democratic primary for a U.S. Senate seat.

Ferrel cell

The Ferrel cell, in models of the circulation of the ATMOSPHERE, was proposed as a mid-latitude "wheel" of wind circulating in each hemisphere between a polar and an equatorial HADLEY CELL. The wind in a Ferrel cell moved eastward and poleward near the Earth's surface, but westward and equatorward at higher altitudes. This is now known to be an oversimplification of actual wind patterns. The Ferrel cell was named for the American meteorologist William Ferrel (1817–91), the first to link the CORIOLIS EFFECT with air-circulation patterns.

Ferrer, José   [fair-air']

José Ferrer, b. Santurce, Puerto Rico, Jan. 8, 1912, d. Jan. 26, 1992, was an American actor, director, and producer noted for his Academy Award–winning performance in the film *Cyrano de Bergerac* (1950). Active both in the theater and films, Ferrer portrayed Iago in a stage production of *Othello* (1943) and Toulouse-Lautrec in the film *Moulin Rouge* (1952). He directed the plays *Stalag 17* (1951) and *The Shrike* (1952). Later films include *Dune* (1984); he also appeared on television.

ferret   [fair'-et]

The endangered status of the black-footed ferret, M. nigripes, *probably results from reduced populations of prairie dogs, its main prey. These ferrets may use prairie dog burrows for shelter.*

Ferrets are members of the WEASEL family, Mustelidae. In Europe, the ferret is the domesticated form of the polecat *Mustela putorius*. Since ancient times it has been used to kill rats and drive rabbits from their burrows. The black-footed ferret of the western United States, *M. nigripes*, feeds mostly on prairie dogs. Once considered extinct, ferrets bred in captivity have been reintroduced in Wyoming.   EVERETT SENTMAN

Bibliography: Seal, U.S., *Conservation Biology and the Black-Footed Ferret* (1989); Wellstead, Graham, *Ferrets and Ferreting* (1989).

Ferrier, Kathleen   [fair'-ee-ur]

Kathleen Ferrier, b. Apr. 22, 1912, d. Oct. 8, 1953, was an English contralto whose brilliant singing career was cut short by cancer. Although she sang few operatic roles (Gluck's *Orfeo* was one, and her 1947 Glyndebourne recording was one of her most famous) she became a leading concert artist, and her voice lost little of its richness on records. Ferrier's recording (1952) of Mahler's *Das Lied von der Erde* with Bruno Walter was particularly notable and led to her fame as a Mahler specialist.

Bibliography: Cardus, Neville, ed., *Kathleen Ferrier: A Memoir* (1954; rev. 1969); Ferrier, Winifred, *Kathleen Ferrier* (1955).

Ferris wheel

A favorite ride at amusement parks and carnivals, the Ferris wheel is a huge, upright double wheel supported by one or two towers, powered to revolve, with seats, or cars, set at intervals between the two rims. It was invented by the American engineer G. W. Ferris for the 1893 World's Columbian Exposition in Chicago. Ferris's wheel could carry more than 2,000 people, giving them a splendid view of the exposition grounds from a vantage point at the top, which was 76 m (250 ft) aboveground. A wheel built in London in 1894 was 100 m (328 ft) high. Most modern fairground wheels are 12 to 14 m (40 to 45 ft) in diameter.

Ferriss, Hugh   [fair'-is]

Hugh Ferriss, b. St. Louis, Mo., July 12, 1889, d. Jan. 28, 1962, is known for his drawings of futuristic skyscraper cities. His training as an architect included an apprenticeship with Cass Gilbert, after which he served as a consultant to a number of agencies, including the United Nations headquarters planning staff (1947–50).

Bibliography: Leich, Jean F., and Goldberger, Paul, *Architectural Visions: The Drawing of Hugh Ferriss* (1980).

ferrite   [fair'-yt]

Ferrites are ceramiclike, magnetic materials consisting of magnetic oxides, often ferric oxide combined with one or more other metals such as magnesium, zinc, or nickel. Ferrites exhibit a permanent MAGNETISM known as ferrimagnetism. Because of their magnetic properties, ferrites are used extensively in electronics and in radio technology. Memory cores in computers, cores for high-frequency coils, transformers, and antenna rods for AM radios are made of ferrites.

ferromagnetism: see MAGNETISM.

ferrotype   [fair'-oh-typ]

The ferrotype, or tintype, was a photograph made by exposing a thin, black-enameled metal plate that had been coated with collodion, the same photosensitive substance used in the CALOTYPE. Unlike the calotype, however, the ferrotype required no paper print; the plate was itself the photograph, and the black background created the illusion of a positive image. (Another positive-appearing negative image was produced by the AMBROTYPE.) Popularly labeled "tintypes," small ferrotypes were the least inexpensive and the most common form of portrait photography in the mid-19th century, especially in the form of the miniature "Little Gem" portraits (see CARTE DE VISITE).

ferry

A ferry is a boat designed to carry passengers, vehicles, and goods across relatively protected waters. Early ferries were rafts or barges propelled by oars; river ferries were often attached to a cable and pulled from shore to shore. John FITCH operated (1787) the first steam-powered ferry, on the Delaware River at Philadelphia. Nineteenth-century ferry types included some that are still seen today, particularly the double-ended vessel with double rudders and reversible engines, used where crossings are short and turnaround room limited; and train ferries, with tracks built into decks, for ferrying whole trains across waterways. Modern ferries may be built with large holds that can accommodate several lanes of automobiles and are usually double-ended for easy loading and unloading.

In the past, ferries were largely confined to short passages across rivers, lakes, and bays. Today, however, the distinction is made between coastwise ferries, those traveling 20 nautical miles (37 km/23 mi) or less from shore, and ocean ferries, vehicles that navigate more than 20 naut mi from the coast. Modern ocean ferries, such as some that operate on the English Channel, are often HYDROFOILS or hovercraft (see AIR-CUSHION VEHICLE), vessels that employ nontraditional propulsion methods. By the mid-1990s, a new fleet of wave-piercing catamarans—high-speed vessels capable of transoceanic voyaging—will be in service crossing the English Channel.

Ferry accidents almost always involve older vessels that have been overloaded. The most notorious recent ferry disaster among modern western ferry fleets, however, occurred on the English Channel in 1987, when the bow doors on the vehicle deck of the British ferry *Herald of Free Enterprise* were left open and the vessel capsized, sinking almost immediately. In response, new ferries have been built with watertight doors and sealed-off vehicle decks.

Ferry, Jules François Camille   [fair-ee′]

The French statesman Jules Ferry, b. Apr. 5, 1832, d. Mar. 17, 1893, reformed France's public school system and laid the foundation of the French colonial system. Entering politics by attacking the alleged peculations of the Parisian official Baron HAUSSMANN in the late 1860s, Ferry served (1870–71) as mayor of Paris during the Prussian siege of the city and while the COMMUNE OF PARIS was in control. Ferry was a government minister during most of the period from 1879 to 1885, serving twice as premier (1880–81, 1883–85). Seeking to secularize the schools, he was responsible for the laws of 1882 that established free and compulsory primary education and outlawed clerical teachers. He also helped acquire Tunisia, Tonkin, Madagascar, and part of the Congo as French colonial holdings. His government fell after a French setback in Tonkin (now part of Vietnam). In 1893, Ferry became president of the senate, but in the same year he was assassinated by a religious fanatic.   P. M. EWY

Bibliography: Power, Thomas F., *Jules Ferry and the Renaissance of French Imperialism* (1944; repr. 1966).

Fertile Crescent

Coined by the orientalist James BREASTED in 1916, the name *Fertile Crescent* is given to the area of the Middle East where the earliest known civilizations of the ancient world began. The region extends like an arc from the Nile valley of Egypt north along the coast of the Mediterranean Sea, then east and south through the Tigris and Euphrates valley to the head of the Persian Gulf, passing through present-day Israel, Lebanon, Syria, Iraq, and western Iran. A cultivatable area characterized (in the area north of Egypt) by dry summers and rainy winters, the Fertile Crescent is where farming originated in the Middle East in the 9th millennium BC. Later, in the late 5th millennium, the oldest urban and literate societies emerged around the same time in Egypt, at the western end of the crescent, and in Sumer, at the eastern end. On the Mediterranean coast the Canaanite kingdoms arose in the centuries that followed; these were succeeded by Phoenicia and ancient Israel,

while MESOPOTAMIA was dominated by the Babylonians and Assyrians.   RALPH S. SOLECKI

Bibliography: Breasted, James H., *Ancient Times,* 2d ed. (1935); Nissen, Hans, *The Early History of the Ancient Near East,* trans. by E. Lutzeier and K. Northcott (1988).

fertility, human

In humans fertility is a medical term for a woman's capacity to conceive or a man's capacity to induce conception. Human fertility begins during puberty, when females start menstruating and males develop viable sperm. Men can remain fertile into their 70s, but a woman's fertility peaks in her mid-20s and decreases sharply after 35, ending at menopause, around age 51. Humans are fertile year-round, but recent studies suggest that annual fertility peaks when there are 12 hours of sunlight and temperatures between 10° to 21° C (50 to 70° F). Others attribute this to close timing with holidays and vacations.

Fertility can be affected by health and environmental problems. Sexually transmitted diseases (STDs) such as human papillomavirus (causing genital warts) or chlamydia can cause scarring of the reproductive tissues in women and men, keeping the sperm or egg apart or preventing implantation of the embryo in the uterus. Women's fertility can also be affected by hormone and ovulation disturbances, scar tissue from previous abdominal surgery, use of the intrauterine device for birth control, and antibodies to sperm. Psychological stress can temporarily stop ovulation. A woman can stop menstruating if her proportion of body fat goes below 20 percent of body weight, a condition affecting athletes such as runners, ballet dancers, and women with anorexia nervosa.

In men, low or no sperm count can result from physical conditions such as varicocele (varicose veins in the scrotum), alcohol and drug use, exposure to certain chemicals, some medications, and higher temperatures around the testicles, caused by tight clothing.

Some fertility problems can be treated with surgery or drugs, as well as techniques like ARTIFICIAL INSEMINATION and IN VITRO FERTILIZATION.

Bibliography: Bellina, J. H., and Wilson, J., *You Can Have a Baby* (1985); Harrison, R. F., and Bonnar, J., *Fertility and Sterility* (1983); Kass-Annese, B., and Danzer, H. C., *Fertility Awareness Workbook* (1986).

See also: INFERTILITY.

fertility rites

Fertility rites are ceremonies of a magic-religious nature performed to ensure the continuity of life. From earliest time humans have performed these rites in an attempt to control the environment. Expressed as invocations, incantations, prayers, hymns, processions, dances, and sacred dramas, these ritual activities were believed to be closely connected with the processes of nature. If the enactment of fertility rites could induce fertility in the animal and human worlds, the vegetable world would also be stimulated to reproduction, resulting in an abundant harvest. The basis for such rites was usually a belief in sympathetic MAGIC, based on the assumption that the principle of life and fertility was one and indivisible.

A persistent theme of primitive fertility rituals was the freeing of the waters and the subsequent regeneration of the earth. Many hymns of the *Rig-Veda* are supplications to Indra, in his role as god of weather and war, to slay the giant who had imprisoned the great rivers of India (see VEDAS). Such personification of natural phenomena was common. Another prevalent myth of pastoral societies, often enacted as sacred drama, was the search of the earth goddess for her lost lover, brother, or child who either has been killed or has disappeared from Earth. Symbolizing death and the return of vegetation and life, this myth was recorded as early as 3000 BC in the Babylonian cult of ISHTAR (Inanna) and Tammuz, and it is traceable through the Sabeans at Harran (present-day Yemen). Another example is the death and resurrection of the Phoenician-Greek deity ADONIS, beloved of Aphrodite. The Greek myth of Demeter and Persephone (Kore) represents the same theme, as does the Egyptian myth of Osiris and Isis.

Sacred marriages frequently have formed part of the fertility ritual; the effectiveness of this symbolic union at times depended on the chastity of the participants. Ritual prostitution, human and animal sacrifice, and displays of phallic symbols were also sometimes believed to stimulate fertility. In a number of preliterate societies the role of the god was combined with that of the king, and the fertility of the land and people was linked with the king's state of perfection and purification.

Processions and dances also play a fundamental part in fertility rites: the sword dance of the Maruts in the *Rig-Veda;* of the Greek Kouretes, a band of youths of semidivine origin; and of the Corybantes, Bacchantes, and Maenads are all intimately linked with the worship of the vegetation spirit. In Britain, May Day celebrations and the MAYPOLE DANCE originate in spring fertility festivals. Many similar rites are recalled in the folk traditions of various European nations.

Bibliography: Frazer, James G., *The New Golden Bough,* ed. by Theodor H. Gaster (1959; repr. 1975).

fertilization

Fertilization is the stage of sexual REPRODUCTION in which a male reproductive cell, or sperm, fuses with a female reproductive cell, or egg, resulting in the mixing of the genetic information carried in the parent cells. Fertilization in plants or animals initiates the development of the embryo and begins the events in the development of the adult individual.

Two basic patterns of mating and fertilization occur among animals. In external fertilization in fish, frogs, and toads, for example, mating partners come close to each other and simultaneously spawn—that is, release sperm and eggs directly into the water. Frequent chance collisions among the closely spaced reproductive cells, or gametes, then lead to many fertilizations. The second pattern is internal fertilization, which is characteristic of such land animals as mammals, birds, reptiles, insects, spiders, and many worms. Mating partners come into physical contact, and an orifice or copulating organ of the male ejects flagellated, or swimming, sperm into the female's reproductive system.

Fertilization in the higher plants occurs as the POLLEN grain contacts the stigma of a FLOWER of the same species. The pollen tube, after penetrating the tissues of the flower, produces two sperm cells; one sperm will fuse with an egg cell within the stigma to complete fertilization.

Bibliography: Dale, B., *Fertilization in Animals* (1983); Meeuse, B., and Morris, J., *The Sex Life of Flowers* (1988).

See also: ARTIFICIAL INSEMINATION; DEVELOPMENT, HUMAN; IN VITRO FERTILIZATION; REPRODUCTIVE SYSTEM, HUMAN.

fertilizer

A fertilizer is any natural or manufactured material that is added to soil to increase plant growth. Plants cannot live without the primary nutritional elements, nitrogen, phosphorus, and potassium; the secondary elements, calcium, magnesium, and sulfur; and small amounts of boron, chlorine, cobalt, copper, iron, manganese, molybdenum, and zinc—called micronutrients or trace elements. Plants obtain all these nutritional elements from the soil. They must be added to soils deficient in them because of natural conditions, leaching, or intensive crop cultivation. Natural fertilizers such as manure are bulky, difficult to transport, and in short supply outside cattle-raising areas. Consequently, manufactured fertilizers have become essential in modern agriculture. Their wide use has significantly improved the production and quality of crops.

HISTORY OF FERTILIZER USE

The value of animal MANURE for improving the productivity of land was recognized perhaps as early as the beginnings of AGRICULTURE. Greco-Roman agricultural writers enumerated the merits of using the dung of birds and poultry and the excreta of horses, cows, goats, sheep, and humans for different soils and crops, as well as describing the benefits of COMPOST prepared from dung, vines, straw, stalks, leaves, weeds, and oth-

er trash. Pliny the Elder, writing in the 1st century AD, explored the use of green manures (legumes and other plants that are plowed back into the soil to enrich it) and the value of ashes, which contain potash, a source of potassium. The Elizabethan philosopher, Sir Francis BACON, was the first to describe scientific research on fertilizers made from composts and manures. The 17th-century German alchemist Johann Rudolf GLAUBER discovered a method of preparing SALTPETER (potassium nitrate) and commented on its use as a fertilizer. His "fattening salt," which contained lime, potash, phosphoric acid, and nitrogen, might be called the first complete mineral fertilizer.

The second John Winthrop (1606–76), a founder of the Connecticut colonies, established a stock company for manufacturing saltpeter from the excreta of farm animals, thus becoming the first fertilizer manufacturer in North America. Most of the early fertilizer products, however, were made from agricultural and industrial residues: animal manures, blood and bones from butchered cattle, cottonseed meal, fish scraps, and castor pomace (the pulp remaining after the castor bean has been pressed). Peruvian GUANO was first imported for use as a fertilizer in 1849. The German chemist Justus von LIEBIG demonstrated the importance of mineral elements in the soil to the healthy growth of plants, and worked to develop artificial fertilizers. In 1842, the English agriculturalist Sir John LAWES received a patent for producing a more soluble, and hence more effective, form of phosphate by treating bones with sulfuric acid. His method, with which the first SUPERPHOSPHATE was produced, marked the beginning of the chemical fertilizer industry.

The production of synthetic nitrate, for use primarily in explosives, began during World War I. After the war, facilities for manufacturing nitrate were shifted to the production of nitrogen fertilizer. The first commercial source of potash was the mineral kainite that was produced in European potash mines. When World War I cut off potash supplies, sources were found in the United States, notably in the brine from Searles Lake in California, which contains the potassium chloride from which potash is made.

COMPOSITION AND GRADES OF FERTILIZERS

The usefulness of a fertilizer for crop production depends on its chemical composition. Although the value of a fertilizer is dependent chiefly on its content of nitrogen (N), phosphate (P_2O_5), and potassium (K_2O), the presence or absence of other elements may be a factor in its choice for a particular crop. For example, the presence of high concentrations of chloride ions results in a tobacco leaf that burns poorly. To be suitable for tobacco crops, fertilizers, therefore, must not contain chlorides. Fertilizers are numbered according to the proportion of nitrogen, phosphate, and potassium, respectively. Thus a 10–20–20 fertilizer contains 10% nitrogen, 20% phosphate, and 20% potassium. Other nutrients are not included in the grade designation, although information about the proportion of secondary and trace elements may appear on the product label.

The term *simple* is normally used to denote a fertilizer containing a single plant nutrient. For example, ammonium sulfate is a simple nitrogen fertilizer, and superphosphate is a simple phosphate fertilizer. Some fertilizer compounds contain two of the primary plant nutrients and are called multiple nutrient materials. Examples are ammonium phosphates and potassium nitrates.

The choice of fertilizers also involves the physical condition of the material. Many fertilizers readily absorb moisture from the air and tend to become sticky. Loss of moisture, or the pressure resulting from the piling of large quantities of the material, may cause caking; both conditions inhibit the uniform application of fertilizers, particularly where machinery is used.

Phosphates and potassium compounds are usually applied in solid form, since they rarely present caking problems. Solid nitrogen fertilizers, on the other hand, frequently cake or absorb moisture. Large-scale applications of nitrogenous fertilizers are usually applied in the form of anhydrous AMMONIA, a pressurized, liquid ammonia that is injected about 15 cm (6 in) under the soil's surface to prevent the liquid from vaporizing. The machinery for applying anhydrous ammonia is complex and expensive; therefore liquid nitrogen solutions, often containing additional fertilizer ingredients, are used in many areas.

Sophisticated new methods of applying fertilizers include the use of pellets compounded of a fertilizer mixture that breaks down and is absorbed by the soil at a rate adjusted to the crop requirements.

PROBLEMS ASSOCIATED WITH FERTILIZER USE

The problems involved in the heavy use of fertilizers are related to pollution and the quality of crops.

Eutrophication. When a body of water is overly rich in plant nutrients, the growth of algae and other aquatic vegetation expands far beyond normal limits. If this process, called EUTROPHICATION, continues for a considerable length of time, the water may eventually silt up and the area will become bog. The important nutrients involved in this process are nitrogen and phosphorus. Excess nitrogen is readily leached from soil in the form of nitrates. Much of the nitrogen content of water in agricultural areas, particularly after heavy spring rains, may come from fertilizers used in the area. Because phosphorus becomes "fixed" in the soil, however, it is usually not leached. Phosphorus runoffs that are present in sewage and industrial wastes are often caused by the heavy use of phosphorus-containing detergents and by other nonagricultural activities.

Effects on Crop Quality. The extensive use of fertilizers may have a noticeable negative effect on both the growth and the quality of plants and crops. Excessive amounts of the primary nutrients may result in potatoes that have too much water, in inferior tobacco, or in forage grasses that cause nutritional problems in cattle. When micronutrients are added to the soil in quantities larger than the minute amounts needed by plants, they may have toxic effects. In addition, although excess nitrates leach out of the soil, other fertilizer elements may remain and build up in the form of mineral salts in areas of low rainfall, eventually lowering soil quality.

NEW SOURCES IN THE FUTURE

Technologies are being developed that may soon make possible new fertilizer materials and methods for applying them.

Sewage Sludge. Liquid SLUDGE—the end product of sewage treatment—has great potential as a fertilizer, and some areas have experimented with sludge composting. Sludge contains soluble nitrogen and phosphorus compounds and many of the secondary and trace elements necessary for plant nutrition. But the levels of these elements, as well as the presence of certain toxic elements such as cadmium, mercury, and lead, are often too high for routine use of sludge on farmland. New methods for treating sludge, to remove the unwanted elements and ensure that all infectious matter has been destroyed, are being tried. Sludge, like manure, contains considerable organic material that acts as a soil improver by building up the organic matter in soil.

Manures. Huge quantities of manure accumulate in regions where large numbers of cattle or poultry are found. Techniques are being developed for processing this manure, for removing disease microorganisms by sterilization, and for converting manure into a form that can be transported more easily. Thus far, large-scale methods for handling manure have proved too expensive, and manure fertilizers cannot yet compete with artificial fertilizers.   CHARLES T. LICHY

Bibliography: Archer, J., *Crop Nutrition and Fertilizer Use* (1985); Cooke, G. W., *Fertilizing for Maximum Yield*, 3d ed. (1988); Engelsted, O. P., ed., *Fertilizer Technology and Use*, 3d ed. (1986); Hignett, T. P., ed., *Fertilizer Manual* (1985); Schmid, O., and Klay, R., *Green Manuring: Principles and Practice*, 2d ed. (1984); Simpson, K., *Fertilizers and Manures* (1986); Wines, R., *Fertilizers in America: From Waste Recycling to Resource Exploitation* (1985).

fescue   [fes'-kue]

Fescue, *Festuca*, comprises more than 100 species of annual and perennial grasses in the grass family, Gramineae. Fescue is worldwide in distribution but more abundant in temperate or cold regions. Some species have become naturalized in North America. Fescue grows well in sandy soil and moderate shade, and it is sometimes included in lawn-seed mixture. Chewing fescue, a variety of red fescue, *F. rubra*, forms a low, dense, matlike turf that is popular for golf putting greens.

Fessenden, Reginald Aubrey   [fes'-en-den]

The American physicist and electrical engineer Reginald Aubrey Fessenden, b. East Bolton, Quebec, Oct. 6, 1866, d. July 22, 1932, is known for his early work in wireless communication. He began his research at the University of Pittsburgh; after designing a high-frequency alternator, he broadcast (1906) the first program of speech and music ever transmitted by radio. That same year, he established two-way transatlantic wireless telegraph communication. Fessenden also invented the heterodyne system of radio reception, the sonic depth finder, the radio compass, submarine signaling devices, the smoke cloud (for tank warfare), and the turbo-electric drive (for battleships).

Bibliography: Abbott, D., ed., *The Biographical Dictionary of Scientists, Engineers, and Inventors* (1986).

Fessenden, William Pitt

William Pitt Fessenden, b. Boscawen, N.H., Oct. 16, 1806, d. Sept. 8, 1869, was a leading senator during the U.S. Civil War and Reconstruction period. Elected U.S. senator from Maine in 1854, Fessenden, who opposed extension of slavery into the western territories, was an organizer of the Republican party. A member of the Senate Finance Committee from 1857 and its chairman from 1861, he played a major role in the financial administration of the Civil War. In 1864–65 he was secretary of the treasury. Returning to the Senate in 1865, Fessenden chaired the Joint Congressional Committee on Reconstruction and wrote most of the report (1866) that asserted congressional control over RECONSTRUCTION. In 1868 he was one of seven Republican senators who voted for acquittal in the impeachment trial of President Andrew Johnson.

Bibliography: Jellison, Charles A., *Fessenden of Maine* (1962).

festival plays: see MEDIEVAL DRAMA.

Festival of Two Worlds: see SPOLETO FESTIVAL.

fetal alcohol syndrome

Fetal alcohol syndrome (FAS) is a grouping of defects that may occur in infants born to women who drink alcohol during pregnancy. Signs of FAS include low birth weight and an abnormally small head; facial deformities such as small and narrow or very round eyes, flattened midface and widely spaced nose, very narrow upper lip, and oddly set ears; and mild to moderate mental retardation. As FAS children develop, they also often exhibit behavioral and cognitive problems. In some cases the defects are severe and are accompanied by other systemic abnormalities. When some but not all of these signs are observed, they are more generally known as fetal alcohol effects (FAE).

FAS has been observed worldwide. In the United States, perhaps one out of every 750 newborn infants displays the full range of FAS symptoms, indicating that 30% to 40% of mothers who drink heavily give birth to such children. No safe lower limits can be placed on drinking levels, however, because even women who drink as little as two drinks a week have given birth to children with FAE.

Bibliography: Dorris, Michael, *The Broken Cord* (1989); Light, W. J., *Alcoholism and Women, Genetics, and Fetal Development* (1988); Plant, Moira, *Women, Drinking, and Pregnancy* (1985).

Fétis, François Joseph   [fay-tees']

François Joseph Fétis, b. Mar. 25, 1784, d. Mar. 26, 1871, was an illustrious Belgian musicologist, critic, teacher, conductor, and composer. He received his first lessons in violin, piano, and organ from his father, an organist, and in 1800 entered the

Paris Conservatory. In 1821, Fétis was appointed professor of counterpoint and fugue at the conservatory; in 1827 he became its librarian. That same year, he founded the *Revue musicale*, a critical journal of contemporary music. He became the director of the Brussels Conservatory and chapel master to King Leopold I in 1833. Fétis wrote numerous treatises on music. Among his historical works is *Histoire générale de la musique* (1869–76).　　　　　　ROBERT M. CAMMAROTA

fetish　[fet'-ish]

The African fetish figure wears or bears magical objects believed to contain powerful spirits. The many objects on this Kongo fetish include small wood sculptures, bits of cloth, nails, and pieces of metal. This fetish is malevolent: when its spirits are released, they do harm.

A fetish is an object believed to have magical powers; it may be either a natural object, such as a shell, or an artifact, such as a wood carving. The word is derived from the Portuguese *feitico*, meaning a charm, talisman, or AMULET. Portuguese sailors coined the term in the 15th century when they observed the veneration that West-Coast Africans had for such objects, which they wore on their persons.

The most important aspects of the fetish are that it is believed to embody the power of the sacred and that it is portable, making it always accessible to the bearer. Auguste Comte and Charles de Brosses interpreted the fetish as a basis for their theories concerning the origin of religion. Today the term is popularly used to refer to an object or idea that receives superstitious or unquestioning trust or reverence. It is also used in psychiatry to refer to the inordinate or pathological fascination a person may have for an inanimate object.
　　　　　　CHARLES H. LONG

Bibliography: Milligan, Robert H., *Fetish Folk of West Africa* (1912; repr. 1970); Nassau, Robert H., *Fetishism in West Africa: Forty Years' Observation of Native Customs and Superstitions* (1904; repr. 1977).

fetishism　[fet'-ish-izm]

Fetishism is sexual interest focused on an object, symbol, or body part. Articles of clothing such as panties, bras, shoes, stockings, or handkerchiefs may be objects of intense sexual interest. Fetishists, usually male, also fixate upon body parts such as eyes, ears, hair, hands, or feet.

A minimal degree of fetishism can probably be found in most people. Fetishism as a psychosexual abnormality exists when individuals have strong preferences for a fetish, or believe they must have the fetish in order to achieve sexual gratification. The fetish may even be preferred to a sexual partner.
　　　　　　STEPHEN P. McCARY

Bibliography: Carson, R. C., and Butcher, J. N., *Abnormal Psychology and Modern Life*, 8th ed. (1987); McCary, S. P. and J. L., *McCary's Human Sexuality*, 3d ed. (1984).

fetterbush　[fet'-ur-bush]

Fetterbush is the common name for about 50 species of usually evergreen shrubs in the genus *Leucothoë*, distributed throughout eastern Asia, Madagascar, and the Americas. Most species grow to about 1.8 m (6 ft) in height and have alternate leaves and simple, white to pink flowers. The fetterbush is propagated by cutting or seed.　　　　　　K. B. PAUL

fetus:　see EMBRYO; PREGNANCY AND BIRTH.

Feuchtmayer, Joseph Anton　[foysht'-my-ur]

A sculptor and stucco decorator in southwestern Germany, Joseph Anton Feuchtmayer, b. June 3, 1696, d. Jan. 2, 1770, was descended from a family of artists from Upper Bavaria. In 1706 his father, Franz Joseph Feuchtmayer, also a sculptor, moved the family workshop to Mimmenhausen on Lake Constance; young Feuchtmayer took over this workshop after his father's death in 1718. A prolific worker, he made numerous statues, altars, decorations, and fittings for many Swabian churches, including his painted wood statue *The Virgin Immaculate* (c.1770; Staatliche Museum, Berlin). He moved away from the traditional concept of sculpture as a solid mass, opening up his figures with deeply cut, swirling draperies, torturous elongations, and violent gestures, carrying the dynamism of the rococo style to an extreme.
　　　　　　ELIZABETH PUTZ

Bibliography: Hempel, Eberhard, *Baroque Art and Architecture in Central Europe* (1965).

Feuchtwanger, Lion　[foysht'-vahng-ur, lee'-ohn]

Lion Feuchtwanger, b. July 7, 1884, d. Dec. 21, 1958, was a German historical novelist and playwright. To actualize themes for the present, he combined psychological insights with historical parallels to contemporary events. His most famous work, *Jud Süss* (1925; trans. as *Power*, 1926), depicts the rise of a ruthless 18th-century Jew who regains his humanity by resisting conversion to Christianity. In addition to writing plays and such successful historical novels as the "Josephus trilogy" (published 1932, 1935, 1941; Eng. trans., 1932, 1936, 1942), Feuchtwanger was the translator, with Bertolt Brecht, of Marlowe's *Edward II* and of the works of Aeschylus, Aristophanes, and Calderón.　　　　　　JACK ZIPES

Bibliography: Kahn, Lothar, *Insight and Action: The Life and Work of Lion Feuchtwanger* (1975); Spalek, John M., ed., *Lion Feuchtwanger: The Man, His Ideas, His Work* (1972).

feud

A feud is an ongoing exchange of hostilities between two closely related groups of people. Antagonisms are fueled by intermittent acts ranging from insults to physical violence. Only rarely are all parties to the conflict involved in fighting, however, and strict rules of conduct usually exclude women and children from the hostilities. Actual fighting may be rare, but adult men must be prepared to offend and defend at all times lest their personal honor or that of their group or lineage be defamed. In long-standing feuds, every social issue may become a new source of disagreement.

Feuds have generally occurred between groups of people sharing the same occupations and religious and civil institutions but who retain a high degree of local autonomy. A well-known example is the 19th-century feud between the Hatfields and the McCoys of the Appalachian Mountain region of the eastern United States. Feuds were also common in the FRONTIER areas of 19th-century America. Although feuding has been outlawed in most countries of the West, the hostile exchanges of the feud still occur in various non-Western societies and even among some neighboring urban groups in America today. Especially in the urban ghetto, acts of violence sometimes help to sustain strong social ties and to define social relationships among the young men of such groups as they pass from boyhood to manhood.　　　　　　ROBERT A. FERNEA

Bibliography: Donnelly, Shirley, *The Hatfield-McCoy Feud Reader* (1971); Jones, Virgil C., *The Hatfields and the McCoys* (1948); Waller, Altina, *Feud* (1988).

feudalism

Feudalism was a medieval contractual relationship among the European upper classes, by which a lord granted land to his man in return for military service. Feudalism was further characterized by the localization of political and economic power in the hands of lords and their vassals and by the exercise of that power from the base of castles, each of which dominated the district in which it was situated. The term *feudalism* thus encompasses a division of governmental power spreading over various castle-dominated districts. It does not, however, refer to the social and economic relationships between the peasants and their lords, which are defined as MANORIALISM.

Analogies to European feudalism have been sought in non-European countries, and medieval Japan is commonly described as a feudal society. The cited similarities, however, are less striking than the dissimilarities. The Japanese had no contract theory (or practice) between ruler and ruled, proceeded by unwritten (rather than clear oral or written) custom, and had no schematic hierarchy clearly defining the roles of lords and underlords.

Origins and Early History. The origins and early history of feudalism defy precise accounting. Clearly, feudalism was, in its nascence, a blend of Roman custom (for example, conditional tenure of land dependent upon the fulfilling of named obligations) and Germanic elements (for example, sworn fealty, or faithfulness). Because the military service of KNIGHTS was a central element of feudalism, some historians find the introduction of heavy cavalry during the 8th century a key factor in its development; others point to the introduction of the stirrup, which greatly increased the efficiency of fighting on horseback. Both schools agree that the knight had to be able to maintain expensive equipment and a horse. Moreover, he could practice fighting only if he was supported by land and labor and was thus free to engage in the martial skills.

Systematic feudalism is generally thought to have emerged in the Frankish territories during the 9th and 10th centuries. Civil wars and the last wave of invasions of Europe by the Magyars and the Vikings accelerated the devolution of de-

This 14th-century manuscript shows King Philip VI of France, flanked by his vassals, hearing a case against Robert of Artois. In feudal society, lords were expected to take counsel from their vassals when planning war or sitting in judgment. (Bibliothèque Nationale, Paris.)

fense to the local level. These developments were catalyzed by the abandonment of royal rights into the hands of lesser officials, usurpation of these rights even against the monarch's will, and willing submission of people to men of local power who could defend them. During this period of breakdown of centralized royal control, the church came to govern its own holdings, and effective secular government contracted to the small units ruled by castles, in which lords and their men were bound together by service-and-protection contracts.

In theory, diagrammatic feudalism resembles a pyramid, with the lowest vassals at its base and the lines of authority flowing up to the peak of the structure, the king. In practice, however, this scheme varied from nation to nation. In the East Frankish (German) kingdom, which became the nucleus of the HOLY ROMAN EMPIRE, the pyramid ended at the level below king or emperor, that of the great princes. In other words, the German kings were never able to impose themselves at the top of a system that had developed out of royal weakness. They were recognized as feudal suzerains but did not exercise sovereignty. In the West Frankish kingdom (France) the kings finally overcame the same handicap, using their positions as feudal suzerains to become feudal sovereigns. In England, where feudalism was imposed by the Normans (although some elements were already present), the kings were at the top of the pyramid, ruling by grace of their offices rather than by the grace of their feudal positions. The extent of feudalism must not be exaggerated, however. Many portions of Europe were never feudalized; feudalism as described here was largely confined to northern France, western Germany, England, the Norman kingdom of Sicily, the Crusader states, and northern Spain. Other parts of Europe experienced some feudalism, but it was never a dominant form of sociopolitical organization.

Institutions. Feudal institutions varied greatly from region to region, and few feudal contracts had all the features here described. Common to all, however, was the process by which one nobleman (the vassal) became the man of another (the lord) by swearing homage and fealty. This was originally done simply to establish a mutually protective relationship, but by the early 11th century vassalage brought with it a fief—land held in return for military service. With the vassal's holding of a fief went rights of governance and of jurisdiction over those who dwelt on it.

Lord and vassal were interlocked in a web of mutual rights and obligations, to the advantage of both. Whereas the lord owed his vassal protection, the vassal owed his lord a specified number of days annually in offensive military service and in garrisoning his castle. The lord was expected to provide a court for his vassals, who, in turn, were to provide the lord with counsel before he undertook any initiative of importance to the feudal community as a whole—for example, arranging his own or his children's marriages or planning a crusade. In addition, the lord frequently convened his vassals "to do him honor."

Financial benefits accrued largely to the lord. A vassal owed his lord a fee known as relief when he succeeded to his fief, was expected to contribute to the lord's ransom were he captured and to his crusading expenses, and had to share the financial burden when the lord's eldest son was knighted and his eldest daughter married. In addition, a vassal had to seek his lord's permission to marry off his daughter (lest the land conveyed as dowry fall into the hands of an antagonist) and for himself to take a wife. Should the vassal die leaving a widow or minor children, they were provided for by the lord, who saw to their education, support, and marriage. Should the vassal die without heirs, his fief escheated, or reverted to the lord.

Decline. The decline of feudalism is both more complex and better understood that its origins and rise. Indeed, feudalism had hardly begun before its first important sign of decline appeared. This was the inheritance of fiefs, replacing the previous original individual feudal contract; when a lord was no longer able to enter into an agreement with his vassal, freely accepted by both parties, then the personal nature of the feudal contract was seriously undermined. This transformation occurred before 1100, as did the beginning of the commutation of personal military service into money payments (called scutage in England), which further undermined the personal loyalty central to original feudalism. A late medieval outgrowth of this commutation was contract service in return for land or money, embodying loyalty to a lord in return for help (maintenance) and protection—what was known in England as bastard feudalism. This form of social bond enabled wealthy lords to field an army quickly when needed and gave them tangible and effective means to assert their own private influence in political and social life, to the detriment of orderly central government. Something else that appeared early in the history of feudalism was liege homage, by which a man who was the vassal of more than one lord chose one as his paramount lord, thus again subverting the original feudal idea of personal loyalty between lord and vassal.

The centralization of strong lordships, whether as kings (as in England and France) or territorial rulers (as in the Holy Roman Empire), obviously undercut the localization of government so essential to feudalism. So too did new forms of warfare during the 14th and 15th centuries, which made the limited service of the feudal army of knights anachronistic. Other reasons for feudalism's decline were familial and social. Family ties came to be seen as more important than particularistic territorial concerns; the economic and social gulf between greater and lesser nobles grew wider; and respect for historical ties of mutual relationships between lord and vassal steadily weakened. These circumstances, as well as the increasing division of inheritances, all combined to destroy feudalism, slowly and inexorably. The process was largely complete by the end of the 14th century.

Significance. The historical significance of feudalism defies brief statement; it was a trunk with deep and wide-spreading roots. Feudalism afforded the structure by which most medieval European monarchies centralized. Constitutionally, the English-speaking world owes to feudalism the right of opposition to tyranny, representative institutions, resistance to taxation levied without consultation, and limited monarchy— since the king was bound by custom, by his own law, and by the necessity to practice self-restraint lest he be restrained by the community. Feudalism also contributed the contract theory of government—the idea that both the government and its citizens have reciprocal rights and obligations. Feudal legacies in cultural matters include CHIVALRY, from which many modern standards of a gentleman are derived; CASTLE architecture; and the epic, romance, and courtly literature.

JAMES W. ALEXANDER

Bibliography: Bloch, Marc, *Feudal Society,* trans. by L. A. Manyon (1961; repr. 1964); Coulbourn, Rushton, *Feudalism in History* (1956; repr. 1965); Ganshof, François L., *Feudalism,* trans. by P. Grierson (1952); Herlihy, David, ed., *The History of Feudalism* (1970); Holton, R. J., *The Transition from Feudalism to Capitalism* (1985); Poly, Jean-Pierre, and Bouenagel, Eric, *The Feudal Transformation, 900–1200* (1990); Stephenson, Carl, *Medieval Feudalism* (1942); Ullmann, Walter, *The Individual and Society in the Middle Ages* (1966).

Feuerbach, Anselm   [foy'-ur-bahk, ahn'-selm]

Anselm Feuerbach, b. Sept. 12, 1829, d. Jan. 4, 1880, was a leading German academic painter, one of a group known as the "German-Romans" that included Arnold BÖCKLIN, Franz von Lenbach, and Hans von Marées. Born into an intellectual family, Feuerbach studied at the academies of Düsseldorf, Munich, and Antwerp, as well as in the studio of Thomas Couture in Paris. Much of Feuerbach's life was spent in Rome and Venice, where he was especially attracted to the art of Titian and Veronese.

Feuerbach's portraits, particularly those of his mistress and model Nanna Risi, are highly esteemed. Idealism and lofty, classical themes characterize Feuerbach's mythological paintings, such as *Medea* (1870; Staatsgemäldesammlungen, Vienna) and *Orpheus and Eurydice* (1869; Kunsthistorisches Museum, Vienna). After 17 years in Rome, Feuerbach was appointed professor of painting at the Vienna Academy in 1873. He remained there for three years, working on decorations for the assembly hall, but he resigned after a nervous breakdown that

Iphigenia, *painted by Anselm Feuerbach in 1862, is a monumental representation of his mistress and model, Nanna Risi. The subject, from Greek mythology, is the ill-fated daughter of Clytemnestra and Agamemnon. (Hessisches Landesmuseum, Darmstadt.)*

was probably caused by bureaucratic difficulties and unenthusiastic response to his paintings.   JEFFREY HOWE

Bibliography: Novotny, Fritz, *Painting and Sculpture in Europe, 1780–1880* (1971); Schiff, Gert, "Teutons in Togas" in *Academic Art,* ed. by T. B. Hess and J. Ashberry (1968).

Feuerbach, Ludwig

Ludwig Andreas Feuerbach, b. July 28, 1804, d. Sept. 13, 1872, was a German philosopher noted for his highly critical psychological analysis of religious belief and for his contribution to MATERIALISM. A theology student at Heidelberg and Berlin, he was drawn into philosophy through the influence of G. W. F. HEGEL. Feuerbach received his doctorate at Erlangen; he remained there until 1832 when he was dismissed for his *Thoughts Concerning Death and Immortality,* published anonymously in 1830, which portrayed Christianity as being both inhumane and dehumanizing. In 1836, Feuerbach moved to Bruckberg and collaborated with Arnold Ruge on the *Hallische Jahrbücher,* a review in which many of Feuerbach's writings were first published. During this period most of Feuerbach's significant books appeared: *The Essence of Christianity* (1841), *Principles of the Philosophy of the Future* (1843), and *The Essence of Religion* (1846). In his later years Feuerbach became a symbol for German liberals. His philosophical anthropology became a new point of departure for Hegelians such as Friedrich ENGELS and Karl MARX.

The German idealist Hegel maintained that reality is the result of thought; Feuerbach maintained that thought is the result of reality. Hegel believed in the primacy of an absolute reason that realized itself through nature and humanity; Feuerbach believed in the primacy of human reason, which creates the only authentic reality a person can know and the only selfhood he or she can use. Hegel had placed reality in abstract thought; Feuerbach placed reality in people.

This criticism of IDEALISM led Feuerbach to a critique of religion. God and an absolute reason, Feuerbach held, are merely projections of the human mind. When they are credited with the best attributes, people are left with only the lesser ones. The resulting sense of sin and impotence impoverishes human life. Religion, Feuerbach conceded, had made a contribution to human evolution; but he held that religion was just another unconscious product of the human faculty for mythmaking. This faculty, Feuerbach said, could now become conscious through a knowledge of anthropology, psychology, and physiology. With such knowledge, humanity could create true health and happiness here on Earth. Feuerbach concluded that theology and philosophy should properly be concerned only with the nature of humankind and with the humanization of God.

In synthesizing anthropology and theology, Feuerbach made humanity an end in itself. Feuerbach was not promoting a form of egoism, however. Instead, he maintained that a person's social nature is manifested in love, which is fulfilled in an I-Thou relationship. PETE A. Y. GUNTER

Bibliography: Marx, Karl, *Feuerbach* (1973); Wartofsky, Marx W., *Feuerbach* (1977; repr. 1982); Wilson, C. A., *Feuerbach and the Search for Otherness* (1989).

Feuillade, Louis [fuh-ee-yahd']

The film director Louis Feuillade, b. Feb. 19, 1873, d. Feb. 26, 1925, was one of the masters of French cinema during World War I. He found his ideal form in the serials *Fantômas* (1913–14), *Les Vampires* (1915–16), and *Tih Minh* (1918). Praised by the surrealists at the time, these films, with their mixture of fantasy and banality, were rediscovered during the 1940s and '50s and greatly influenced filmmakers such as Alain Resnais and Georges Franju. ROY ARMES

Feuillants [fuh-ee-yahn']

The Feuillants, founded in 1791, constituted one of the political clubs of the French Revolution. Its members, who broke away from the JACOBINS, favored preservation of a constitutional monarchy. The club was officially closed in January 1792 on the pretext that its meeting place, the old monastery of the Feuillants (a reformed Cistercian order), was within the precincts of the Legislative Assembly. After the overthrow of the monarchy in August 1792, however, the former Feuillants were proscribed.

fever

Fever, or pyrexia, is a BODY TEMPERATURE that is elevated above the normal range: normal oral temperatures range from 98.6° F (37° C) in persons confined to bed to 99.0° F (37.4° C) in active persons; temperatures taken rectally usually register slightly higher. Body temperature is usually kept within the normal range by several mechanisms, which are controlled and integrated mainly in the hypothalamus region of the brain. Fever is not a disease itself but a symptom of disease. It is a sign of infectious disease, such as pneumonia, and may accompany certain kinds of cancers, a stroke or heart attack, and various other disorders. Because many microorganisms cannot survive elevated temperatures, fever is generally considered a defense mechanism against infections. Temperatures above 112° F (44.5° C) are usually fatal because they cause irreversible damage to the nervous system. In most cases, fever can be reduced by aspirin or other fever-reducing drugs, called antipyretics. PETER L. PETRAKIS

Bibliography: Kluger, M. J., *Fever: Its Biology, Evolution, and Function* (1979); Lawson, J. H., *A Synopsis of Fevers and Their Treatment,* 12th ed. (1977); Lipton, J. M., ed., *Fever* (1980).

feverfew [fee'-vur-fue]

Feverfew, Chrysanthemum parthenium, is a strongly scented, summer-flowering chrysanthemum. It has historically found many uses—as an herb, for relief of fever, as an insect repellent, and as a flavor in tea or wine.

Feverfew, *Chrysanthemum parthenium*, is a bushy, hardy perennial plant in the family Compositae. Long a garden favorite, it is also found in the wild. Feverfews are erect and leafy, growing to a height of 90 cm (3 ft). The leaves are strongly aromatic and pinnate, with three to seven oval leaflets, each of which is further divided into lobed segments. Flower heads are numerous, barely 2 cm (0.8 in) in diameter, and buttonlike, with a yellow disk and white rays. The plant blooms during the summer and grows readily from seed. K. B. PAUL

feverwort [fee'-vur-wurt]

Feverwort, or horse gentian, *Triosteum*, comprises five or six species of coarse, upright perennial herbs in the honeysuckle family, Caprifoliceae. Native to eastern Asia and eastern North America, feverworts are 90 to 120 cm (3 to 4 ft) high; their leaves are opposite, oval to oblong-ovate, and dark green. The small flowers are yellowish or purplish; the fruit is a dry, green to red drupe with three seeds. K. B. PAUL

Feydeau, Georges [fay-doh']

Georges Feydeau, b. Dec. 8, 1862, d. June 5, 1921, was a French dramatist who wrote popular farces about extramarital intrigues and domestic strife. His intricate, well-constructed plots are filled with complex deceptions, farfetched schemes, misunderstandings, and cases of mistaken identity that he always resolved ingeniously. Feydeau used elaborate stage settings and props to give credence to his plots. His best-known play is *La Dame de chez Maxim* (The Lady from Maxim's, 1899); others include *Hotel Paradiso* (1894; Eng. trans., c.1957), *A Flea in Her Ear* (1907; Eng. trans., 1968), and *Occupe-toi d'Amélie* (Keep an Eye on Amélie, 1908). STUART E. BAKER

Bibliography: Esteban, Manuel A., *Georges Feydeau* (1983).

Feynman, Richard Phillips [fyn'-muhn]

The American physicist Richard Phillips Feynman, b. New York City, May 11, 1918, d. Feb. 15, 1988, contributed to the joining of relativity and quantum theory with electromagnetism to form QUANTUM ELECTRODYNAMICS. He is also known for his reformulation of QUANTUM MECHANICS and his research on liquid helium. In 1965 he shared the Nobel Prize for physics with Julian SCHWINGER and Sin Itiro Tomonago for their contributions to electrodynamics.

Feynman earned his Ph.D. from Princeton University in 1942, worked on the MANHATTAN PROJECT during World War II, and served on the faculty of Cornell University before going to the California Institute of Technology in 1950. In 1986 he was a member of the presidential commission that investigated the Space Shuttle *Challenger* disaster. A writer of scientific works such as *The Character of Physical Law* (1967) and *Statistical Mechanics* (1972), Feynman was also a popular lecturer and author of a two-volume informal memoir of his career as a physicist, *Surely You're Joking, Mr. Feynman!* (1985) and *What Do You Care What Other People Think?* (1988).

Fez

Fez (French: Fès; Arabic: Fas), the capital city of Fez province, north central Morocco, lies about 195 km (120 mi) southeast of Tangier; its population is 933,000 (1987 est.). Located on the Oued Fez river in the northern foothills of the Middle Atlas Mountains, Fez is a sacred Islamic city and center of learning and was once the northern capital of Morocco. The main industry is tourism, and local craftspeople are known for their leatherwork and textiles. The city consists of an old walled section, Fez el-Bali, which includes ancient mosques and the mazelike medina (native quarter), and a new section to the south.

Founded as early as 790, Fez became the capital of Arab Morocco in 808 under Idris II. He built the famous Quarawiyin Mosque (859), which houses Al Quarawiyin University (859). The Marinids, who captured Fez in 1250, erected the Royal Palace complex (begun 1276) and a series of elaborate tombs in the hills on the northwest side of the city. The city was under French protection from 1912 to 1956.

Fianna Fáil   [fee'-uh-nuh foyl]

Fianna Fáil (Gaelic, ''Warriors of Ireland'') is one of the two major political parties in the Republic of Ireland, the other being FINE GAEL. Fianna Fáil, organized in 1926 by Eamon DE VALERA, advocates an independent and united Ireland. The party held power from 1932 until 1973, except for the years 1948–51 and 1954–57. It was again in office from 1977 to 1981, in 1982, and from 1987.

fiber, natural

Fibers obtained from a plant or an animal are classed as natural fibers (for other types, see SYNTHETIC FIBERS). The majority of these fibers are used in weaving textiles, although the coarser plant fibers are also used for rope and twine. Plant fibers come from the seed hairs, leaves, stems (bast fibers), or husks of the plant. Animal fibers are provided, generally, by animal hair and, in the case of silk, by the secretion of the silkworm.

Plant Fibers. The most abundant and commonly used plant fiber is cotton, gathered from the cotton boll, or seed pod, when it is mature. The short, fluffy fibers must be ''ginned'' to separate fiber from seed. After the fibers are combed to align them all in one direction, they can be spun into yarn. Spinning, an operation most natural fibers undergo, is accomplished by twisting the short fibers into strong, continuous strands of yarn or thread. Other seed-hair fibers include kapok, used for pillow stuffing.

Fibers taken from the plant leaf are called ''hard,'' or cordage, fibers because they are used principally to make rope. The most important leaf fibers are those from the sisal, or agave, plant grown in Brazil and Africa, and a Mexican agave that produces a fiber called henequen. Both sisal and henequen fibers are stiff, strong, and rough textured. Abaca, or manila hemp, is a fiber from the leafstalk of a banana plant,

Jute (left), flax (center), and cotton (right) yield important vegetable fibers. Jute and flax fibers are derived from the stems; cotton fibers are the seed hairs of the plant. Flax grows best in damp, temperate climates; cotton and jute thrive in warm, humid regions.

Musa textilis, which grows in the Philippines. Abaca is the strongest of the leaf fibers and is used primarily for cordage. Most leaf fibers come from tropical areas. The palmetto, the only native U.S. leaf fiber plant, grows in the southeast; its fibers are used in brushes.

Stem, or bast, fibers include the important flax, hemp, and jute plants. Softer and more flexible than the leaf fibers, they are stripped from the plant stems after the stems have been softened in water. Hemp comes from the stems of the *Cannabis sativa* plant—the same plant that produces marijuana. Until it was replaced by abaca and sisal, hemp was the principal cordage fiber. It is used today for twine and for rough fabrics, such as burlap. Flax stems produce that fiber which is woven into linen. Jute, a plant growing primarily in India and Bangladesh, provides fiber for twine, burlap, and sacking. Ramie,

Under magnification, goat hair (1) is coarse and brittle. Sheep's wool (2) is fine, soft, and elastic. Camel's hair yarn (3), from the fine underhair of Asian camels, yields a fabric that is softer and warmer than wool. Angora rabbit hair (4) is lightweight and springy. Cashmere (5), from the undercoats of Kashmir goats, is prized for its softness and silky luster. Horsehair (6) is round, coarse, and bristly.

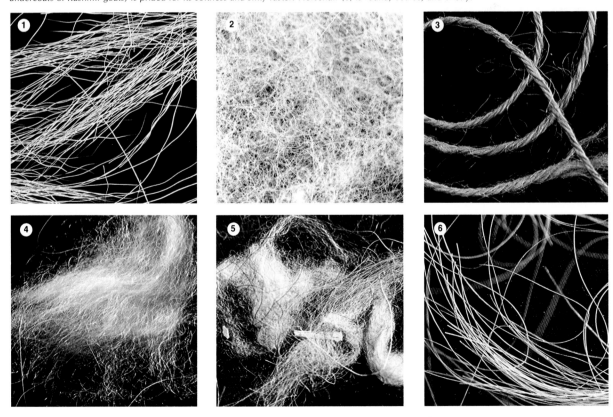

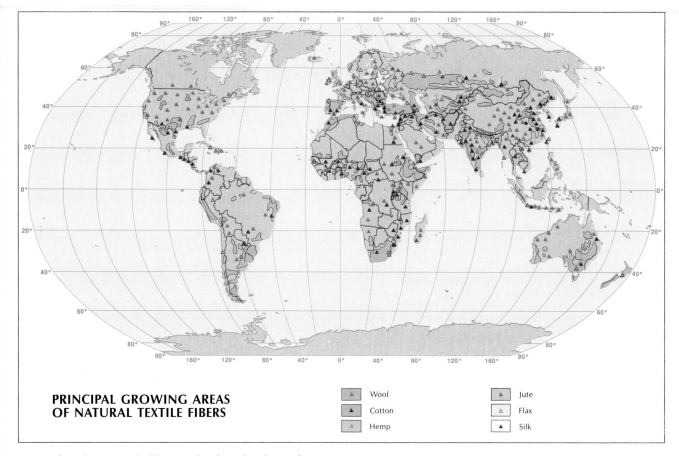

**PRINCIPAL GROWING AREAS
OF NATURAL TEXTILE FIBERS**

Wool Jute

Cotton Flax

Hemp Silk

a relatively new textile fiber, is taken from the plant *Bohmeria nivea,* grown principally in the People's Republic of China. Kenaf, from a hibiscus grown mainly in India, is used for canvas and cordage.

Coir is the rough-textured fiber that comes from the husk of coconuts. It is used as a brush bristle, or is spun into a thick twine for weaving into doormats and other floor coverings.

Animal Fibers. Wool, the long fine hair of sheep, is the most important animal fiber. The fine underhair of the angora and cashmere goats, the angora rabbit, the camel, the alpaca, and the vicuña have a special softness and, often, high bulk (as in mohair, from the angora goat).

Silk is a protein extruded in long, continuous strands by the silkworm as it weaves its cocoon. The fine strands of several cocoons are unwound and twisted together to make silk thread, which produces fabrics of a unique softness and luster.

Bibliography: Grayson, M., ed., *Encyclopedia of Textiles, Fibers, and Non-Woven Fabrics* (1984); Lyle, D. S., *Modern Textiles,* 2d ed. (1982); Needles, H. L., *Textile Fibers, Dyes, Finishes, and Processes* (1986).

fiber optics

A relatively new technology with vast potential importance, fiber optics is the channeled transmission of light through hair-thin glass fibers. The light is prevented from escaping the fiber by total internal reflection—a process that takes place when a light ray travels through a medium with an INDEX OF REFRACTION higher than that of the medium surrounding it. In this case the fiber core has a higher refractive index than the material around the core, and light hitting that material is reflected back into the core, where it continues to travel down the fiber.

Fiber-optic technology has been applied in many areas, although its greatest impact has come in the field of telecommunications, where optical fiber offers the ability to transmit audio, video, and data information as coded light pulses. In

fact, fiber optics is rapidly becoming the preferred mode of transmitting communications of all kinds. Its advantages over older methods—all of which involve the movement of electrons through metallic cables—are many, and include vastly increased carrying capacity (due to the very high frequency of light), lower transmission losses, lower cost of basic materials, much smaller cable size, and almost complete immunity from stray electrical fields (interference). Other applications include the simple transmission of light for illumination in awkward places, image guiding for remote viewing, and sensing—the measurement of various properties of materials, structures, or living things.

Although the possibility of lightwave communications occurred to Alexander Graham Bell, inventor of the telephone, the feasibility of such a system had to await the invention (1960) of the LASER and the subsequent development of reliable ways to generate light pulses and to reamplify and detect them. Most of these advances occurred in the 1970s, and by 1977 glass-purifying and fiber-drawing techniques had also reached the stage where interoffice lightwave communications were possible. With further technological development, many intercity routes were in operation by 1985, and some transoceanic routes had been completed by 1990.

A Long-Distance Fiber-Optics Communications System. AT&T's Northeast Corridor Network, which runs from Virginia to Massachusetts, utilizes fiber cables carrying upward of 50 fiber pairs. Using a semiconductor laser or a light-emitting DIODE as the light source, a transmitter codes the audio or visual input into a series of light pulses, called bits. These travel along a fiber at a bit-rate of 90 million bits per second (the equivalent of 1,340 voice circuits per fiber pair). Pulses need reamplifying, or boosting, about every 10 km (6.2 mi), and finally reach a receiver, containing a semiconductor photodiode detector, which amplifies, decodes, and regenerates the original audio or visual information. Silicon integrated circuits control and modulate both transmitter and receiver operations.

Light Propagation and Signal Loss. The glass fibers used in present-day fiber-optic systems are based on ultrapure fused silica. Fiber made from ordinary glass is so dirty that impurities reduce signal intensity by a factor of one million in only about 5 m (16 ft) of fiber. These impurities must be removed—often to the parts-per-billion level—before useful long-haul fibers can be drawn. But even perfectly pure glass is not perfectly transparent. It attenuates, or weakens, light in two ways. One, occurring at shorter wavelengths, is a scattering caused by unavoidable density fluctuations within the fiber. The other is a longer wavelength absorption by atomic vibrations (phonons). For silica, the minimum attenuation, or the maximum transparency, occurs in wavelengths in the near infrared, at about 1.5 μm (micrometers).

Light injected into a fiber can adopt any of several zigzag paths, or modes. When a large number of modes are present they may overlap, for each mode has a different velocity along the fiber (modal dispersion). Mode numbers decrease with decreasing fiber diameter and with a decreasing difference in refractive index between the fiber core and the surrounding region. Fibers are therefore made very thin, with a core region having an index value about one percent larger than that of the surrounding region. Single, or monomode, fiber production is quite feasible, and today most high-capacity systems use monomode fibers. The present pace of technological advance remains impressive, with the fiber capacity of new systems doubling every 18 to 24 months. The newest systems operate at more than 2 billion bits per second per fiber pair. During the 1990s optical fiber technology is expected to extend to include both residential telephone and cable television service.

Other Applications of Fiber Optics. Noncommunication advances in fiber optics have fallen into two main areas, flexible and rigid fibers. Sensors are a major flexible fiber application, and uses include the measurement of pressure, temperature, rotation, fluid flow, and electric current. Fiber-optics sensitivity is excellent, and measurements are made without electrical connections. Other flexible fiber applications concern high-intensity illumination in general, instrument illumination for automotive and avionic systems, power transmission for use with robotics, surgical and dental procedures, and image guiding. The last involves fiber bundles that are spatially aligned from end to end, and the technique is used for direct viewing of otherwise inaccessible areas, as in medical ENDO-SCOPES. In rigid fiber optics, thousands of fibers are fused into a solid block. These optic plates are used for image transfer from a cathode-ray tube to a permanent photographic recording. Applications are manifold: in facsimile systems, phototypesetting, recording oscilloscopes, computer graphics, and many others. MALCOLM E. LINES

Bibliography: Chaffee, G., *The Rewiring of America* (1988); Edwards, T., *Fiber Optics Systems: An Introduction* (1989); Kotte, E. V., et al., eds., *Technologies of Light* (1988); Ungar, Serge, *Fiber Optics* (1990).

fiberglass

Fiberglass consists of glass fibers drawn or blown directly from a GLASS melt. Blown fibers are usually 15–38 cm (6–15 in) long, while drawn fibers may be several kilometers long. Fiberglass is most commonly used in a composite with a plastic polymer. Such composites are similar to wood but resistant to moisture and rot, and they are easy to form into complex shapes. They are used in automobile bodies, boats, and other structural applications requiring light weight, strength, and corrosion resistance. Fiberglass can also be used for thermal and electrical insulation and is woven into fabrics for drapes.

Long glass fibers are made by melting glass "marbles" in an electric furnace, then drawing the fibers continuously through holes in a platinum bushing and winding them onto a revolving drum. As the fibers cool, they are sprayed with a polymer, which protects the freshly formed surface from abrasion and inhibits the development of surface flaws, which can reduce the strength of the fibers. The shorter blown fibers are made by air-steam or flame-blowing processes that pull streams of melted glass into fibers. Drawn fibers are typically 10–25 mi-crons (0.0004–0.001 in) in diameter, depending upon drawing speed and temperature; blown fibers may be as little as about two-millionths of a centimeter in diameter.

A typical composition of fiberglass ("E" glass) is 54% silica, 15% alumina, 16% calcia, 5% magnesia, 9.5% boron oxide, and 0.5% sodium oxide by weight. This glass has good chemical durability and strength because of low alkali (sodium) content and can be melted at a reasonably low temperature because of the boron. ROBERT H. DOREMUS

Bibliography: Safford, E. L., and McCann, J. A., *Fiberglass and Laser Handbook*, 2d ed. (1988).

Fibiger, Johannes   [fee'-bee-gur]

Johannes Andreas Grile Fibiger, b. Apr. 23, 1867, d. Jan. 30, 1928, Danish pathologist, was awarded the 1926 Nobel Prize for physiology or medicine for his work on inducing cancer experimentally. Although the apparent results of his work came to be doubted—he had tried to link parasite infestations with cancers—Fibiger's efforts to induce cancer in the laboratory encouraged later researchers in this field.

Fibonacci, Leonardo: see LEONARDO PISANO.

Fibonacci sequence   [fee-boh-nah'-chee]

A Fibonacci sequence is a SEQUENCE in which each term is the sum of the two terms immediately preceding it. It is named for its discoverer, Leonardo Fibonacci (LEONARDO PISANO). The Fibonacci sequence that has 1 as its first term is 1, 1, 2, 3, 5, 8, 13, 21, 34, 55. . . . The numbers may also be referred to as Fibonacci numbers. The defining property can be given symbolically as $C_n = C_{n-1} + C_{n-2}$. This equation is a recursion relation, or recurrence relation, which relates different terms of a sequence or of a series. Fibonacci sequences have proved useful in number theory, geometry, the theory of continued fractions, and genetics. They also arise in many seemingly unrelated phenomena, for example, the GOLDEN SECTION, a shape valued in art and architecture because of its pleasing proportions, and the spiral arrangement of petals and branches on certain types of flowers and trees.

Bibliography: Garland, T. H., *Fascinating Fibonaccis* (1987); Vorob'ev, N. N., *Fibonacci Numbers* (1961; repr. 1983).

fibrillation: see PALPITATION.

Ficciones   [feek-see-oh'-nes]

Ficciones (1944; Eng. trans., 1962) is, with *The Aleph* (1949; Eng. trans., 1970), the most important collection of short stories by the Argentinian writer Jorge Luis BORGES. Because Borges believes that philosophy and theology are superior forms of fiction, his major themes are often derived from metaphysical arguments. Sometimes Borges rewrites old stories, but they are always given a masterly twist that transforms them into new and highly original pieces. In the frequently used image of the labyrinth, he expresses the idea that, for humans, the world is chaos, and all attempts to solve God's maze are bound to fail. JAIME ALAZRAKI

Bibliography: Lusky-Friedman, M., *The Emperor's Kites* (1987).

Fichte, Johann Gottlieb   [fik'-te]

Johann Gottlieb Fichte, b. May 19, 1762, d. Jan. 27, 1814, was a German transcendental idealist philosopher. After studying theology and philosophy at the universities of Jena and Leipzig, he became a private tutor. Fichte's interest in Immanuel KANT led him to write *Essay towards a Critique of All Revelations* (1792), an unsigned work in which he developed Kant's justification of faith in the name of practical reason. Some reviewers thought Kant was the author. It was through this work, which received Kant's praise, that Fichte became known. His *Addresses to the German Nation* (1807–08) influenced the development of German nationalism. Fichte taught at the University of Berlin from 1810 until his death.

Crucial to the metaphysics of Fichte is his concept of the creative ego. According to him, this ego is neither subjective nor personal but, instead, is the universal and absolute ego from which all objective reality is derived. The ego is not an object of experience, although it is responsible for experience and is known through its activity within the consciousness itself. Because the activity of the ego is ethical, its major manifestation is in human ethical activity. Ultimately, in Fichte's view, the moral order of reality is identified as God, which is neither personal nor providential. Some viewed the philosophy of Fichte as an expression of atheism, whereas others considered it a form of pantheism.

Fichte deduced the nature and function of the state, with its system of rights and duties, from the moral nature of reality. The rights of all people, and the growth of the state as the necessary condition of the fulfillment of these rights and their corresponding duties, are derived from individuals' freedom and moral consciousness. If all people were fully developed morally, a state would be unnecessary. Fichte considered the state as a necessary instrument of social and moral progress, required by the basic nature of the human condition.

Fichte's concept of the state and of the ultimate moral nature of society and reality directly influenced F. W. J. von SCHELLING and G. W. F. HEGEL, who took a similarly idealistic view of the human realm and reality as a whole (see IDEALISM). The collected works of Fichte were edited and published (1845–46) by his son Immanuel.   J. T. MOORE

Bibliography: Adamson, Robert, *Fichte* (1881; repr. 1976); Engelbrecht, Helmuth C., *J. G. Fichte: A Study of His Political Writing with Special Reference to His Nationalism* (1933; repr. 1968); Neuhouser, F., *Fichte's Theory of Subjectivity* (1990).

Ficino, Marsilio   [fee-chee'-noh, mahr-seel'-ee-oh]

The Italian philosopher and theologian Marsilio Ficino, b. Oct. 19, 1433, d. Oct. 1, 1499, was the most influential Christian Platonist of the Italian Renaissance. In 1462 he became the head of the Platonic Academy near Florence, where he spent most of his life translating the works of Plato from Greek into Latin and writing commentaries on them and the principal Neoplatonists (see NEOPLATONISM). Ficino believed that true philosophy and true religion are in harmony with each other. He stressed themes of good, love, humanity, and immortality, and conceived the universe as a hierarchy of beings from God down to prime matter, with humankind, the microcosm, as the center and bond of the universe. In his *Theologia Platonica* (Platonic Theology, 1482), he combined Christian theology with Platonic philosophy.   JOHN P. DOYLE

Bibliography: Allen, M. J., *The Platonism of Marsilio Ficino* (1984); Collins, A. B., *The Secular Is Sacred* (1974); Kristeller, P. O., *The Philosophy of Marsilio Ficino*, trans. by V. Conant (1943).

Ficke, Arthur Davison

An American poet and critic, Arthur Davison Ficke, b. Davenport, Iowa, Nov. 10, 1883, d. Nov. 30, 1945, opposed modernism in poetry. With the poet Witter Bynner (1881–1968), he published *Spectra* (1916)—a collection of verse parodying such modernist movements as IMAGISM—which was taken by many readers to be serious poetry. *Sonnets of a Portrait Painter* (1914) reflects Ficke's interest in art. His horror of modernism may be seen in such works as *Out of Silence* (1924) and *Tumultuous Shore* (1942).   JAMES HART

Bibliography: Smith, William, *The Spectra Hoax* (1961).

fiddler crab

Fiddler crabs are any of a group of small beach-dwelling crabs of genus *Uca*. They are so named because the males have one extremely large claw that may weigh as much as half the weight of the entire animal; the second claw is relatively diminutive. Widely distributed, especially in tropical regions, fiddler crabs live in mud or sand burrows. The varied courtship behavior of fiddler species includes ritualized waving

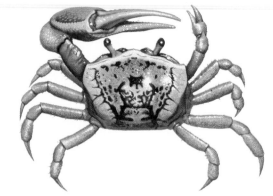

A male fiddler crab, Uca, *waves its enlarged "fiddle claw" as part of its courtship display; the movements vary from species to species.*

of claws, display of vivid colors, production of sounds by rubbing parts of bodies together, and dancing movements.
                DAVID L. PAWSON

Bibliography: Crane, Jocelyn, *Fiddler Crabs of the World* (1975).

Fiedler, Arthur   [feed'-lur]

The American conductor Arthur Fiedler began his musical career as a violist with the Boston Symphony Orchestra (1915). From 1930 to 1979, he conducted the Boston Pops Orchestra, delighting audiences with his innovative repertoire of light classical music.

The conductor Arthur Fiedler, b. Boston, Dec. 17, 1894, d. July 10, 1979, celebrated a half century as leader of the BOSTON POPS ORCHESTRA in 1979. He attended (1911–15) the Royal Academy of Music in Berlin. Returning to the United States, he became a violist with the Boston Symphony. Fiedler organized the Boston Sinfonietta, a chamber orchestra, in 1925 and inaugurated the Esplanade Concerts, free summer concerts held on the shores of Boston's Charles River, in 1929. He became permanent conductor of the Boston Pops a year later. He was also guest conductor of the San Francisco Symphony, the New York Philharmonic, and the NBC Symphony. His deft handling of the light classic and popular repertoire endeared him to a large audience, and in 1977 he was awarded the Presidential Medal of Freedom.   ELLA A. MALIN

Bibliography: Holland, James R., *Mr. Pops* (1972); Moore, Robin, *Fiedler: The Colorful Mr. Pops* (1968; repr. 1980).

Fiedler, Leslie A.

Leslie A. Fiedler, b. Newark, N.J., Mar. 8, 1917, is an American critic, fiction writer, and teacher whose provocative analyses of literature seem to constitute impassioned psychoanalyses of of American society as well. His two major studies of American fiction, *An End to Innocence* (1955) and *Love and Death in the American Novel* (1960), assert that racism, repressed homosexuality, and misogyny are primary influences in American art and life. Fiedler provokes disagreement but is respected for his insights into subjects as wide-ranging as his own Jewish heritage, science fiction, and the American Indian. *Freaks* (1978) is an exhaustive catalog of the grotesque in art, science, nature, and the "normal." *What Was Literature?* (1982) asserts that traditional literary standards are obsolete, and truth should be sought instead in popular literature. In *Fiedler on the Roof* (1991) the critic himself is the main subject.   C. CANTALUPO

Bibliography: Kenner, Hugh, "Who Was Leslie Fiedler?" *Harper's*, November 1982.

Field (family)

An American business family, the Fields have been associated since the 1880s with Chicago's leading department store, Marshall Field. The family's enterprises also once included a large newspaper and publishing business.

Marshall Field I, b. Conway, Mass., Aug. 18, 1834, d. Jan. 16, 1906, was a clerk in a Pittsfield, Mass., dry-goods store before moving to Chicago in 1856. In 1865 he organized the firm of Field, Palmer and Leiter, which, in 1881, became Marshall Field and Company. An innovator in merchandising methods, Field increased the store's annual business to $40 million by 1895. The company stocked merchandise on an enormous scale, began manufacturing certain products, sold wholesale and retail, and opened offices in New York, Europe, and Japan. A noted philanthropist, Field made large gifts to the University of Chicago and founded what is now the Field Museum of Natural History in Chicago.

His grandson, **Marshall Field III**, b. Chicago, Sept. 28, 1893, d. Nov. 8, 1956, founded (1941) the *Chicago Sun*, which he later merged (1948) into the *Sun-Times*. His communications ventures were consolidated (1944) in Field Enterprises Inc., which also published *The World Book Encyclopedia*. Marshall Field III established (1940) the Field Foundation, which funds programs in social welfare and education.

Marshall Field IV, b. New York City, June 15, 1916, d. Sept. 18, 1965, and **Marshall Field V**, b. Charlottesville, Va., May 13, 1941, expanded the family enterprises in communications, education, real estate, and energy. The *Chicago Daily News*, bought in 1959 by Marshall Field IV, ceased publishing in March 1978 due to financial losses, however, and in September 1978, the *World Book Encyclopedia* was sold.

Bibliography: Mahoney, Tom, and Sloane, Leonard, *The Great Merchants* (1974).

field

In mathematics, a field is an arithmetically closed system that may be defined in various ways, depending upon the kind of mathematics being performed. Most directly, a field can be defined as a set of elements and the mathematical properties that they obey—that is, the mathematical operations that can be performed with the given set (see SET THEORY). For example, take the set of RATIONAL NUMBERS. Together with the operations of addition and multiplication, they form an infinite field. Fields also exist whose underlying sets of elements are finite.

The concept of fields was developed in the course of 19th-century studies of algebraic equations (see ALGEBRA) and NUMBER THEORY. Related mathematical concepts include the group, a set of elements along with only one operation (see GROUP THEORY), and the RING, a more general concept than the field. A field, that is, may be considered a special type of ring: a commutative ring whose elements obey the COMMUTATIVE LAWS of addition and multiplication.

Fields and other algebraic structures are studied in modern, or abstract, algebra. Besides the set of rational numbers, the sets of REAL NUMBERS and of COMPLEX NUMBERS are important examples of infinite fields. Perhaps the most important use of fields is in the theory of equations.   AVNER ASH

Field, Cyrus W.

Cyrus Field, an American businessman, posed for this Matthew Brady photograph, holding a length of the transatlantic telegraph cable that made him famous. After four abortive attempts, Field's scheme to lay more than 2,980 km (1,852 mi) of submarine telegraph cable succeeded in 1866, a feat that provided a near-instantaneous communications link between Great Britain and the United States.

Cyrus West Field, b. Nov. 30, 1819, d. July 12, 1892, was a promoter who laid the first transatlantic telegraph cable. He was a successful merchant who retired at the age of 33 to devote himself to his great dream. Field formed the New York, Newfoundland, and London Telegraph Company with charters from the British and American governments and with financial backing from Peter COOPER and others on both sides of the Atlantic. Three attempts in 1857 to lay a cable between Newfoundland and Ireland failed, but a fourth attempt in 1858 succeeded long enough to make Field a hero before the cable stopped functioning. In 1866 he tried again, chartering the world's largest steamship, the *Great Eastern*. His success this time brought him fame and a new fortune. During the 1870s he bought control of the New York Elevated Railroad Company and served as its president. In his later years he lost his wealth as a result of bad investments.

Bibliography: Carter, Samuel, *Cyrus Field: Man of Two Worlds* (1968).

Field, David Dudley, Jr.

David Field, b. Feb. 13, 1805, d. Apr. 13, 1894, was an American lawyer and legal reformer. After setting up practice in New York City, he began (1837) to work for reform of the New York State legal system. The result was the 1848 Code of Civil Procedure, adopted or used as a model by many other states and by foreign countries. He also helped formulate a code for criminal procedure that was adopted by New York State a few years later.

Bibliography: Reppy, Alison, ed., *David Dudley Field: Centenary Essays Celebrating 100 Years of Legal Reform* (1949).

Field, Eugene

Eugene Field, b. St. Louis, Mo., Sept. 3, 1850, d. Nov. 4, 1895, an American journalist and poet, was a columnist for the Denver *Tribune* and for Melville Stone's Chicago *Morning News*, where he wrote the popular and whimsical column "Sharps and Flats," a mixture of commentary and verse. Widely read as a journalist in his time, Field is best remembered today as the author of the poems "Little Boy Blue" and "Dutch Lullaby" ("Wynken, Blynken, and Nod"), which have been set to music; he is sometimes called "the poet of childhood." His publications include *A Little Book of Western Verse* (1889) and the anthologies *A Little Book of Profitable Tales* (1890) and *With Trumpet and Drum* (1892). *Echoes from the Sabine Farm* (1892) was written in collaboration with his brother, Roswell Martin Field.   RICHARD F. HIXSON

Bibliography: Thompson, Slason, *Eugene Field: A Study in Heredity and Contradictions* (1901; repr. 1974).

Field, John

John Field, b. July 26, 1782, d. Jan. 23, 1837, was an Irish composer and pianist best known as the inventor of the name and piano style of the NOCTURNE. Trained by Muzio Clementi, Field made his London debut as a pianist in 1794. Field settled (1803) in St. Petersburg, Russia, and lived out his life in that country, though he did make an extended tour (1831–35) of western Europe. He died in Moscow. Field's piano music was admired by Robert Schumann and Franz Liszt, and the style of his 20 nocturnes for piano was appropriated by Frédéric Chopin. Field's other works include seven piano concertos, sonatas, and chamber music.   F. E. KIRBY

Bibliography: Nikolayev, Aleksandr, *John Field* (Eng. trans., 1973); Piggott, Patrick, *The Life and Music of John Field, 1782–1837* (1973).

Field, Marshall: see FIELD (family).

Field, Stephen Johnson

Stephen Johnson Field, b. Haddam, Conn., Nov. 4, 1816, d. Apr. 9, 1899, was a justice of the U.S. Supreme Court. In 1849 he left New York City, where he had practiced law with his brother, David Dudley, and settled in California. He was elected to the California state legislature in 1850 and played a leading role in setting up the state's civil and criminal codes, adapted from his brother's codes for New York. In 1857, he was appointed to the state supreme court and in 1863 to the U.S. Supreme Court, remaining there until 1897. During his long tenure Field was noted for his dissents, many of which reflected a strict-conservative view of the law.

Bibliography: Black, C. F., and Smith, S. B., eds., *Some Account of the Work of Stephen J. Field . . .* (1882; repr. 1986); Swisher, Carl B., *Stephen J. Field: Craftsman of the Law* (1930; repr. 1969).

field artillery: see ARTILLERY.

field hockey

Field hockey, a stick and ball game related to ICE HOCKEY and LACROSSE, originated in ancient Egypt, Persia, and Greece and assumed its present form after its spread to Europe. The English organized the game, which they called *hockie* and the French called *hoquet*, and instituted most of the modern rules. The first field hockey club, Blackheath, was formed sometime before 1861. Because of its extreme popularity in British colonies, particularly in India, Britain and its former possessions have dominated field hockey in the Olympics.

In the United States, the game is played primarily by women. One of America's greatest women players was Anne Townsend, who was selected for the All-America team from 1924 to 1939.

Field hockey has been a women's team sport in the northeastern United States since its introduction in 1901. The goalkeeper, who wears protective clothing, may block the ball with any part of the body; the other players may block only with their hands or sticks.

The field hockey playing field measures 100 yd (91.5 m) long and 60 yd (54.9 m) wide. The center of the field contains a circle 1 yd (92 cm) in diameter in which the face-off (called a "bully") takes place. At each end of the field is a goal, consisting of two upright poles 7 ft (2.13 m) high, 4 yd (3.66 m) apart, and backed by a net attached to the poles and crossbar. A semicircular striking area extends 16 yd (14.64 m) around the goal. A point is scored by hitting the ball into the net from within the striking circle. A stick with a crook is used to maneuver the ball. The ball—white, usually leather covered—weighs between 5½ and 5¾ oz (155 and 163 g) and is between 2⅞ and 3⅜ in. (7.3–7.7 cm) in diameter. Teams consist of 11 players: five forwards, three halfbacks, two fullbacks, and a goalkeeper. A goalkeeper may stop a shot with his or her stick or body, while other players may use their sticks or hands.   HOWARD LISS

Bibliography: Barnes, M. J., and Kentwell, R. G., *Field Hockey: The Coach and the Players,* 2d ed. (1978); Kentwell, Richard, *Field Hockey Techniques and Tactics, 1986* (1986).

Field Museum of Natural History

The Field Museum of Natural History, located in Chicago, Ill., and known from 1943 to 1966 as the Chicago Natural History Museum, was founded in 1893 by the wealthy businessman Marshall FIELD. The museum's extensive collections originated with the World's Columbian Exposition held in Chicago in 1893, and have since been sustained by gifts from the Field family and other private and public benefactors. Divided into departments of anthropology, geology, botany, and zoology, the museum's 13 million objects include displays of artifacts from ancient civilizations, gems and jewels, fossils, meteorites, and animals from around the world in lifelike settings.

field spaniel

The field spaniel, a hunting dog used to flush game, was developed in England in the late 1800s. Crosses with English springer spaniels in the early 1900s improved the breed, which had become so low and elongate that its field performance was hampered.

The field spaniel is a rare gundog. Only a few are registered each year in the United States and in Britain, its native land. The breed was created by crossing Sussex spaniels with cocker spaniels that were apparently a type called the Welsh cocker. Field spaniels are medium-sized dogs, standing about 45 cm (18 in) high at the shoulder and weighing 16–23 kg (35–50 lb). They have moderately long pendant ears. The coat is flat or slightly wavy, never curly, and should be silky in texture and long enough to provide protection from the elements. The ears, chest, legs, and underbody are moderately feathered. Field spaniels are black, liver, golden liver, red, or roan, with or without tan markings over the eyes and on the cheeks, feet, and pasterns. Markings are discouraged.   JOHN MANDEVILLE

Bibliography: American Kennel Club, *The Complete Dog Book,* 17th ed. (1985).

Fielding, Henry

Henry Fielding, an 18th-century English satirist, mocked contemporary morals in his comic novels Joseph Andrews *(1742) and* Tom Jones *(1749). Before turning to prose fiction, Fielding enjoyed popularity as a playwright; but he was forced to abandon the theater when his plays aroused the wrath of powerful political figures.*

Henry Fielding, b. Apr. 22, 1707, d. Oct. 8, 1754, one of the greatest artists among English novelists of the 18th century, and an important playwright and essayist, was largely responsible for the emergence of the novel as a prominent literary form.

After attending Eton and Leyden University, Fielding earned his living as a dramatist. His first play, *Love in Several Masques,* was produced in 1728, when he was 21 years old. For a decade such farces as *Tom Thumb* (1730) made Fielding England's most successful playwright. His political satires, however, such as *Pasquin* (1736), about the corrupt administration of Sir Robert WALPOLE, led to the Licensing Act of 1737, which effectively ended Fielding's dramatic career.

The success of the novel *Pamela: or Virtue Rewarded* (1740–41) by the London printer Samuel RICHARDSON provoked Fielding to write (1741) a satire, dubbed *Shamela,* on its bourgeois morality. A more thoughtful comic romance about Pamela's reputed brother, *Joseph Andrews,* followed in 1742. The famous preface to JOSEPH ANDREWS called upon the artistic tradition of the "comic epic in prose," exemplified by Cervantes' *Don Quixote.* The novel's favorable reception may have inspired Fielding to publish a collection of essays, poems, plays, and prose fiction under the title *Miscellanies* (1743). The third and last volume of this work was the satiric *Jonathan Wild,* called "the finest example of sustained irony in English fiction." Purporting to celebrate the rise and fall of a "Great Man" (Wild was an actual London rogue who was hanged in 1725), the novel would have been understood by Fielding's contemporaries as something of a political allegory on the recently ended career of Walpole as first minister.

For almost a decade thereafter Fielding devoted himself largely to political pamphlets and essays. His periodicals the *True Patriot* (1745–46) and *Jacobite's Journal* (1747–48) responded to the Jacobite threat posed by the exiled house of Stuart. The so-called Jacobite Rebellion of "Bonnie Prince Charlie" in 1745 also served as historical background in Fielding's greatest fictional work, TOM JONES (1749). Essentially a comic romance, this account of the coming of age of a vital but imprudent young hero was rooted in the ancient conventions of myth and romance. By writing about an "ordinary" person, however, Fielding made many of those high conventions freshly accessible to the new bourgeois world of the novel.

Fielding's last essay-periodical, *The Covent-Garden Journal* (1752), includes some of his most humorous pieces; but the tone of his final novel, *Amelia* (1751), is equivocal. Its narrative of domestic problems created by another improvident (but now married) hero, Booth, and suffered by his level-headed wife, Amelia, does not always seem consistent with Fielding's "comic-epic" style and romance conventions. *Amelia* has nevertheless interested modern readers precisely because of its ambiguous texture.

Failing health resulting from his strenuous duties as a principal magistrate of London caused Fielding in 1754 to seek relief in Lisbon, where he died and was buried. His painful trip there is recorded with great good humor in his final work, *Journal of a Voyage to Lisbon* (1755).

Fielding's enduring reputation and influence in prose fiction have varied only with varying modes of critical taste in the later novel. He has never lost his reading audience; and his two finest works have been popularized anew in the rollicking films *Tom Jones* (1963) and *Joseph Andrews* (1977).

HENRY KNIGHT MILLER

Bibliography: Battestin, M. C., *The Moral Basis of Fielding's Art* (1959); Battestin, M. C., and Ruther, R., *Henry Fielding: A Life* (1990); Cleary, T., *Henry Fielding: Political Writer* (1984); McCrea, B., *Henry Fielding and the Politics of Mid-18th Century England* (1981); Miller, H. K., *Henry Fielding's Tom Jones and the Romance Tradition* (1976); Varey, S., *Henry Fielding* (1986).

Fielding, William Stevens

The Canadian political leader William Stevens Fielding, b. Nov. 24, 1848, d. June 23, 1929, began his career as a journalist in Halifax, Nova Scotia. A Liberal, he was elected (1882) to the Nova Scotia legislature and served (1884–96) as premier of that province. As federal minister of finance (1896–1911) under Sir Wilfrid Laurier, Fielding negotiated the reciprocity agreement with the United States that caused the fall of the Laurier government in 1911. In 1917 he broke with the Liberals over the issue of military conscription, which he supported. Reconciled with his party, he served (1921–25) again as finance minister under Mackenzie KING.

Fields, Dorothy

Dorothy Fields, b. Allenhurst, N.J., July 15, 1905, d. Mar. 28, 1974, a writer of musical lyrics, collaborated with her brother Herbert Fields on such Broadway musicals as *Annie Get Your Gun* (1946). She also wrote such songs as "On the Sunny Side of the Street" (1930) with composer Jimmy McHugh, and with Jerome Kern wrote the Oscar-winning song "The Way You Look Tonight" (1936).

Fields, Lew: see WEBER, JOSEPH, AND FIELDS, LEW.

Fields, W. C.

W. C. Fields, b. William Claude Dukenfield, Philadelphia, Jan. 29, 1879 or 1880, d. Dec. 25, 1946, was known on stage, screen, and radio for the highly original, misanthropic cast of his humor. Whether in the role of unscrupulous con man or henpecked, hard-drinking husband, Fields would brag of his

W. C. Fields introduces himself to Mae West in this scene from their comedy classic, My Little Chickadee *(1940). Both on screen and in real life, Fields maintained the image of a cynical rogue mocking middle-class values with false pomposity and irreverent humor.*

hatred for dogs, children, policemen, bankers, wives, and mothers-in-law. A talented comic juggler, Fields had become a success in stage revues and in silent movies in the 1920s. In the 1930s, his raspy voice and inimitable persona were captured in such favorite sound films as *You Can't Cheat an Honest Man* (1939), *The Bank Dick* (1940), *My Little Chickadee* (1940), with Mae West, and *Never Give a Sucker an Even Break* (1941). Fields wrote the screenplays for many of his films and contributed numberless ad-libs. In a famous characterization, he portrayed Mr. Micawber in the 1935 film version of *David Copperfield*.   FRANK MANCHEL

Bibliography: Deschner, D., *The Complete Films of W. C. Fields* (1989); Everson, W. K., *The Art of W. C. Fields* (1967); Fields, Ronald, *W. C. Fields: A Life in Film* (1984); Monti, Carlotta, and Rice, Cy, *W. C. Fields and Me* (1973); Yanni, N., *W. C. Fields* (1974).

Fiesole, Mino da: see MINO DA FIESOLE.

Fife

Fife is a former county, now an administrative region, in east central Scotland. Situated on the North Sea coast between the firths of Tay and Forth, it has an area of 1,308 km² (505 mi²) and a population of 344,700 (1988 est.).

The land undulates upward from the low, fertile coastline to the Lomond and Ochil hills. Agriculture is highly developed along the coast and in the Eden River valley. The chief crops are grains, potatoes, sugar beets, and other vegetables. In the south, Fife's cities, including DUNFERMLINE, KIRKCALDY, and Burntisland, manufacture ships, linen, and electronics. The coastal towns have fishing fleets, and tourism is important in SAINT ANDREWS, an old university town and former ecclesiastical seat as well as the ancestral home of golf.

Fife was occupied by the Picts, the Romans, and the Danes before becoming part of the kingdom of Scotland in the 11th century. The county was reorganized as a region in 1975.

fife

The fife, a small FLUTE with six to eight holes on top, has been known since the time of the Crusades. It was introduced into the British military from Switzerland during the 16th century. Displaced by other instruments in the 17th century, the fife reappeared during the 18th century, when it was used to play military calls accompanied by drums. Because it can play only the diatonic scale, its use has been limited. George Frideric Handel and Giacomo Meyerbeer did, however, write operatic scores with parts for the fife.   ELWYN A. WIENANDT

15th Amendment

The 15th Amendment to the CONSTITUTION OF THE UNITED STATES, ratified in 1870, prohibits federal or state governments from infringing on a citizen's right to vote "on account of race, color, or previous condition of servitude." This amendment is the last of three so-called RECONSTRUCTION amendments ratified in the aftermath of the Civil War to abolish slavery and firmly establish minority CIVIL RIGHTS (see 13TH AMENDMENT; 14TH AMENDMENT). The 15th Amendment allowed the federal government to legislate qualifications for voting, a right formerly left to the states. Its ratification, however, had little impact for almost a century and had virtually no effect in the South where various methods—from terrorism to the poll tax and grandfather clause—were employed to keep blacks from voting. Various actions of Congress and the Supreme Court eventually struck down voting restrictions. In *Smith* v. *Allwright* (1944), for example, the Court held voting rights discrimination in primaries to be unconstitutional on the basis of the 15th Amendment. Other cases blocked the discriminatory use of reapportionment and property and residence requirements. Congress passed the CIVIL RIGHTS ACT of 1957, establishing a commission to investigate voting discrimination, and in 1965 the VOTING RIGHTS ACT (extended in 1970, 1975, and 1982) was passed to increase black voter registration by empowering the Justice Department to closely monitor voting qualifications.

5th Amendment

The 5th amendment to the CONSTITUTION OF THE UNITED STATES, a provision of the BILL OF RIGHTS, provides several important protections for persons accused of a crime. It requires INDICTMENT by a GRAND JURY on a federal offense and protection against DOUBLE JEOPARDY and SELF-INCRIMINATION. It also forbids deprivation of life, liberty, or property without DUE PROCESS of law and prohibits the taking of private property for public use without just compensation (see EMINENT DOMAIN). These guarantees against abuses by the federal government were extended to cover acts of state governments by various Supreme Court decisions interpreting the 14TH AMENDMENT.

The 5th Amendment has been widely identified with the phrase "take the 5th" used by witnesses testifying before congressional investigating committees or judicial bodies. The right to refuse to answer questions, in any government proceeding, on the grounds of possible self-incrimination reflects a judicial interpretation broader than that intended when Congress proposed the amendment in 1789. The amendment has also been extended to such issues as involuntary or coerced confessions and the treatment of private papers.

Bibliography: Levy, Leonard W., *Origins of the Fifth Amendment: The Right against Self-Incrimination* (1968); Peltason, J. W., *Corwin and Peltason's Understanding of the Constitution*, 10th ed. (1985).

See also: ESCOBEDO V. ILLINOIS; MIRANDA V. ARIZONA.

fifth disease

Erythema infectiosum, or fifth disease, is a mild, flulike illness common in children aged five to nine. It is one of the few human diseases known to be caused by a PARVOVIRUS, one of a group of small, DNA-containing viruses. Symptoms in children usually develop in late winter and spring and include a low-grade fever, fatigue, and redness of the cheeks. Within two days a rash appears on the arms, legs, and trunk. Occasionally adults who were not exposed to the parvovirus as children may acquire the infection and develop more serious symptoms, such as persistent joint pain that can be mistaken for arthritis or Lyme disease. Pregnant women who become infected are at risk for miscarriage or stillbirth. People with serious anemia or immune system deficiencies who become infected may develop life-threatening anemia that can lead to congestive heart failure. There is no treatment for the disease, but a blood test can determine if a person has been infected and how recently. Fifth disease derives its name from an early 20th-century list of pediatric diseases that show similar rash symptoms. Erythema infectiosum was the fifth entry on that list.   WILLIAM A. CHECK

Bibliography: Krugman, Saul, and Katz, Samuel L., *Infectious Diseases of Children* (1990).

fifth force: see FUNDAMENTAL INTERACTIONS.

Fifth Republic: see FRANCE, HISTORY OF.

Fifty-Four Forty or Fight: see OREGON QUESTION.

fig

Figs comprise a large genus, *Ficus*, of deciduous and evergreen tropical and subtropical trees, shrubs, and vines belonging to the mulberry family, Moraceae. Commercially, the most important fig is *Ficus carica*, the tree that produces the edible fig fruit. Among the most ancient cultivated fruit trees, the fig is indigenous to the eastern Mediterranean and the southwest region of Asia, where its cultivation probably began. It is now grown in warm, semiarid areas throughout the world.

The fruit-bearing fig ranges from a bushlike 1 m (3 ft) to a moderately tall tree that may grow up to 12 m (39 ft) in height. It is characterized by its dark green, deeply lobed leaves. The fig bears no visible flowers; instead, its flowers

The common orchard fig, F. carica, a bushlike tree with deeply lobed leaves, originated in the Middle East. Its fruit is a fleshy receptacle (cross section, center) containing numerous small seeds.

are borne within a round, fleshy structure, the syconium, which matures into the edible fig. The common fig bears only female flowers, but develops its fruits without pollination. Varieties of the Smyrna type also bear only female flowers, but in order to produce fruit, they must be pollinated by a process known as caprification.

Caprifigs. The caprifig is a wild form of fig tree whose male flowers produce inedible fruits that are host to the fig wasp, *Blastophaga psenes*. Fig wasps lay their eggs in the caprifig flowers; the eggs hatch within the developing caprifig, and the mature female wasps seek new flowers in which to lay their eggs. When caprifigs are hung among the branches of a cultivated fig, the pollen-dusted wasps squeeze through the narrow openings at the ends of the syconia and pollinate the flowers inside. The wasps die within the syconia, and their bodies are absorbed into the developing fruit. Figs produced by caprification are usually larger than the common fig.

Fig Cultivation. Fig trees are propagated through rooted cuttings taken from the wood of older trees. They grow best in moderately dry areas that have no rain during the period of fruit maturation, when humidity might hinder the process of fruit drying. The partially dried fruit drops to the ground, where it is gathered and the drying process completed. Some fruit may be picked before it dries and eaten as fresh fruit. Figs are classified either as Smyrna type, Common type, or San Pedro type figs. Smyrna figs produce only a summer crop. Common and San Pedro figs may also produce a spring, or breba, crop which requires caprification.

Other Important Fig Species. The rubber plant, *F. elastica*, is a popular houseplant. Grown as a tree in tropical regions, it produces a latex sold as Assam rubber. The pipal, or BO TREE, *F. religiosa*, is considered sacred by Buddhists. The gigantic BANYAN tree, *F. benghalensis*, often produces edible fruits.

Bibliography: Childers, Norman F., *Modern Fruit Science*, 9th ed. (1983); Stefanile, Felix, *Fig Tree in America* (1970).

Figaro, Le   [fee-gah-roh', luh]

Le Figaro is France's oldest newspaper. Founded in 1854, it has been a daily since 1866, although it suspended publication (1942–44) when censorship was imposed during World War II. Traditionally of moderate right-wing leanings, with a scrupulously independent news staff, the paper became considerably more conservative after a change of ownership in 1975.
JOHN D. MITCHELL

fighting fish: see SIAMESE FIGHTING FISH.

Figueiredo, João Batista de Oliveira
[fee-gay-ray'-doh]

The Brazilian army general João Batista de Oliveira Figueiredo, b. Jan. 15, 1918, succeeded Ernesto GEISEL as president of Brazil in March 1979. The son of a general, Figueiredo entered the military academy at Pôrto Alegre in 1928. In 1953 he joined the National Information Service, an intelligence-gathering organization. He advanced to head the military staff of President Emilio G. Medici in 1969 and then led the Information Service (1974–78). He relinquished the presidency in 1985 to the first civilian elected in 21 years.

Figueroa   (family)   [fee-gay-roh'-ah]

The Figueroa family of Spanish architects worked mainly in Seville in Spain during the late 17th and 18th centuries. **Leonardo de Figueroa**, *c.*1650–1730 and his son **Ambrosio**, 1700–75, are best known for the facades of their buildings, in which brick was employed as a decorative element against white or yellow walls trimmed in red. This style became characteristic throughout southern Spain. Leonardo's first known work is the Hospital de los Venerables Sacerdotes (1687–97), the first building in Seville in which the structural elements were not disguised by stucco. His design for the interior was more conservative; the clear lines of the arcade in the patio of the Venerables Church are attractively simple. At times, Leonardo's style was somewhat *retardataire* (recalling past styles), as in the Salvador Church, Seville (1696–1711), where the facade is derived from Sebastiano SERLIO and the flying buttresses recall Gothic structures. Ambrosio continued his father's manner of surface articulation in the public Chapel of the Cartuja in Seville (1752–58).
EDWARD J. SULLIVAN

Bibliography: Kubler, George, and Soria, Martin, *Art and Architecture in Spain and Portugal and Their American Dominions, 1500–1800* (1959).

figured bass

Figured bass, also known as thoroughbass or continuo from the Italian *basso continuo*, refers to a bass line in the music of the 17th and 18th centuries and also to the method of chordal accompaniment using that bass line as a basis for improvisation. The bass notes are often "figured"—marked with numerals or musical signs that indicate the harmonies intended by the composer, while allowing the performer considerable scope for invention. With few exceptions, most music of the baroque and early classical periods contained a figured bass. Usually either harpsichord or organ was used, although lute, guitar, harp, theorbo, and other instruments were possible. The figured bass was normally strengthened by a second performer playing the same bass notes.

A figured bass suggests only a general harmonic outline, but the harmonic support of the improvisation was essential to the sound of baroque and later 18th-century music because it supplied the tonal direction and structural organization of each composition. The figured bass was in use for more than 150 years, during which many treatises on the subject, some by eminent composers, were written for the instruction of students.
GEORGE J. BUELOW

Bibliography: Arnold, F. T., *The Art of Accompaniment from a Thorough-Bass*, 2 vols. (1931; repr. 1961); Buelow, George J., *Thorough-Bass Accompaniment According to J. D. Heinichen* (1966; repr. 1986); Williams, Peter, "Continuo," in *The New Grove Dictionary of Music and Musicians* (1980).

figurehead

In the age of sailing vessels, the brightly polychromed or gilded wooden figurehead, perched prominently on the front or bow of the vessel, under the bowsprit, helped establish a ship's identity. From the earliest times, the prows of ships have been embellished with imaginative carved figures, including dolphins, sea serpents, and mermaids. From about 1760 to about 1880, however, these figures were often life-size human forms, either realistic portraits of prominent historical figures or mythic ideal types, carved to stride, point, or look forward with serious mien. Professional carvers, such as the SKILLIN family of Boston, were located principally in urban shipbuilding centers, and their art often involved designing the figurehead, the principal ship ornament, at the same time as the decorative stern carving. By the end of the 19th century the art of elaborate large-scale figurehead carving had almost disappeared as steamships replaced the wooden sailing vessels.

Particularly fine examples of American work include *Pocahontas* (c.1800–20; Kendall Whaling Museum, Sharon, Mass.), which is attributed to William RUSH of Philadelphia, and a superb naturalistic figure of a woman (c.1820; Bostonian Society, Old State House, Boston) by Isaac Fowle of Boston. Other excellent examples of American figurehead carving can be found at the Abby Aldrich Rockefeller Folk Art Center (Williamsburg, Va.), the Mariners' Museum (Newport News, Va.), Mystic Seaport (Mystic, Conn.), the Peabody Museum (Salem, Mass.), and a number of other museums devoted primarily to the study of American FOLK ART and maritime history.

MARGARETTA M. LOVELL

Bibliography: Brewington, M. V., *Shipcarvers of North America* (1962); Hamilton, G., *Silent Pilots* (1984); Norton, Peter, *Ships' Figureheads* (1976); Pickney, Pauline, *American Figureheads and Their Carvers* (1940).

See also: WOOD CARVING.

figures of speech

In its broadest sense a figure of speech is any intentional departure from the ordinary form, use, or arrangement of words for the purpose of making expression more striking or effective. Ancient rhetoricians identified about 250 such figures of speech. These included such devices as *antithesis,* the expression of contrasting ideas in parallel form ("Better to reign in hell than serve in heaven"); *alliteration,* most often defined as the close repetition of initial consonant sounds in important words ("hell" and "heaven" in the preceding example); and *repetition,* the repeating of any element in an utterance, including sound (as in alliteration and RHYME), a word or phrase, a pattern of accents (as in meter), or an arrangement of lines (as in stanzas). Under a broad definition, even variant spellings of a word, as in contractions (" 'tis," "o'er," "t'other"), qualify as figures of speech.

Under a narrower definition, a figure of speech, or *trope,* is an expression that means something else or something more than what it says; it is language that departs from its literal meaning. In this sense—the sense usually intended when we speak of figurative language—a figure of speech bypasses logic and appeals to the imagination. Thus, paradoxically, it makes possible the expression of meanings more forcefully and more fully than can be accomplished by using literal language.

A simple example is SIMILE, a stated comparison between things essentially unlike, as in "My love is like a red, red rose." This comparison sounds almost logical, but in fact it is not, for a woman could never be confused literally with a rose; the meaning, however, is more vividly and fully conveyed than in the literal paraphrase, "My beloved is beautiful." If the word *like* is removed from this simile, it becomes a METAPHOR, an unstated comparison between things essentially unlike and, in a literal sense, illogical. In metaphor, the things compared may be either named or implied. "Sheathe thy impatience" compares impatience to a sword. "Night's candles are burnt out" compares stars to candles. Emily Dickinson's poem, "I like to see it lap the miles," compares a railroad train to a horse, although neither is named.

Personification, the attribution of human characteristics to something nonhuman ("So when he calls me, Death shall find me ready"), is a subtype of metaphor, comparing the thing meant to a person. Closely related to personification, and often used with it, is *apostrophe,* in which someone absent or dead, or something nonhuman, is addressed as if it were human, present, alive, and could respond ("Ring out, wild bells, to the wild sky"; "Milton! thou shouldst be living at this hour").

Although classification is difficult and imperfect, the tropes mentioned above all rest, in some way, on comparison. Based on contiguity are *synecdoche,* the use of the part for the whole ("Everyone who wants a roof should have one"), or occasionally, of the whole for the part; and *metonymy,* substitution for the thing meant of something closely associated with it ("The palace should not scorn the cottage"). Metonymy and synecdoche are so nearly alike that the distinction between them is disappearing, and both are often referred to as metonymy.

Related to metonymy and metaphor is the *literary symbol*—an object, person, situation, or action that means more than what it is. Unlike the figurative term in a metaphor (candles in "Night's candles are burnt out"), a symbol means itself and something more too. It has both literal and metaphorical meanings ("Two men look out through the same bars;/One sees the mud, and one the stars"). A peculiar value of symbol is that, although it may have a single ulterior meaning, it often suggests a variety of possible other meanings. It is thus an especially rich figure of speech.

Opposed to the figures based on comparison or contiguity are those based on contrast. Two of these are *verbal irony,* which states the opposite of what is meant; and *paradox,* an apparent contradiction that is somehow true. A paradox is usually resolved by seeing that one (or both) of its contradictory terms is itself used figuratively or has a double meaning ("Believe him, he has known the world too long,/And seen the death of much immortal song"). The paradox of the immortal song that dies is resolved when it is recognized that the word *immortal* is used ironically. The aged reader has seen the death of many poems once falsely proclaimed by the critics as "immortal." A special kind of paradox is the *oxymoron,* a compact figure in which successive words apparently contradict each other ("Women! my strongest weakness"). Closely related to verbal irony are *hyperbole,* or overstatement, saying more than is actually meant ("At every word a reputation dies"); and *litotes,* or understatement, saying less than what is meant or saying it with less force than seems warranted, frequently using a negative assertion ("One could do worse than be a swinger of birches").

Figurative language serves to convey thoughts, feelings, and perceptions that cannot be adequately expressed in literal language. Indeed, language evolves largely through metaphor. The word *astonishment,* for example, is derived from roots meaning "struck by thunder." The invention of fresh metaphors today still makes possible the expression of emotions and concepts for which no names exist.

LAURENCE PERRINE

Bibliography: Barfield, Owen, *Poetic Diction: A Study in Meaning,* 4th ed. (1984); Beckson, Karl, and Ganz, Arthur, *Literary Terms: A Dictionary,* rev. ed. (1975); Holman, C. Hugh, *A Handbook to Literature,* 5th ed. (1986); Perrine, Laurence, *Sound and Sense,* 7th ed. (1987); Preminger, Alex, et al., eds., *The Princeton Handbook of Poetic Terms* (1986); Quinn, Arthur, *Figures of Speech* (1983); Welleck, R., and Warren, A., *The Theory of Literature;* 3d ed. (1949).

See also: PUN; VERSIFICATION.

figwort [fig'-wurt]

The figwort family, Scrophulariaceae, contains about 3,000 species of herbs, shrubs, and trees found worldwide. This family contains many medicinal plants, such as FOXGLOVE, the source of the heart drug DIGITALIS, as well as flowering plants like the SNAPDRAGON. The genus *Scrophularia* contains about 200 species of strong-smelling herbs native to the Northern Hemisphere and named for their supposed medicinal usefulness in cases of scrofula, tuberculosis of the lymph nodes. Maryland figwort, *S. marilandica,* is found from Maine to Georgia and produces greenish purple flowers in midsummer.

Fiji [fee'-jee]

Fiji is an independent nation in the South Pacific Ocean, about 2,100 km (1,300 mi) north of New Zealand. It is an archipelago of more than 800 islands spread over about 1,600,000 km² (1,000,000 mi²). A British colony for nearly a century, Fiji became independent in 1970.

REPUBLIC OF FIJI

LAND. Area: 18,274 km² (7,056 mi²). Capital and largest city: Suva (1986 pop., 69,665).

PEOPLE. Population (1993 est.): 800,000; density: 43.8 persons per km² (113.4 per mi²). Distribution (1993 est.): 39% urban, 61% rural. Annual growth (1993 est.): 2.0%. Official language: English. Major religions: Protestantism, Hinduism.

EDUCATION AND HEALTH. Literacy (1986): 87% of adult population. Universities (1993): 1. Hospital beds (1990): 1,747. Physicians (1990): 300. Life expectancy (1992): women—67; men—62. Infant mortality (1992): 19 per 1,000 live births.

ECONOMY. GDP (1991 est.): $1.3 billion; $1,700 per capita. Labor distribution (1987): agriculture and fishing—67%; other—33%. Foreign trade (1991 est.): imports—$840 million; exports—$646 million; principal trade partners—Australia, New Zealand, Japan. Currency: 1 Fiji dollar = 100 cents.

GOVERNMENT. Type: republic. Legislature: Parliament. Political subdivisions: 4 provinces.

COMMUNICATIONS. Railroads (1990): 595 km (370 mi) total. Roads (1991): 4,821 km (2,996 mi) total. Major ports: 4. Major airfields: 1.

LAND AND PEOPLE

Only about 105 of Fiji's islands are inhabited. The larger islands are volcanic and mountainous except in the river valleys; the smaller islands are mostly coral. The largest island, Viti Levu, where almost 80% of the population live, covers 10,386 km² (4,010 mi²); Suva, the capital and largest city, is located on its southeast coast. The climate is tropical, with an annual mean temperature of 27° C (80° F); rainfall varies from 1,780 mm (70 in) in the west to more than 2,540 mm (100 in) in the east. Vegetation varies according to rainfall, with dense forests in the mountains, tropical savanna grasslands in the west,

and dense vegetation in the east. Mount Tomaniivi (1,323 m/4,341 ft), on Viti Levu, is Fiji's highest point. Mangrove trees dominate coastal areas.

Native Fijians, who were a minority in their own country at independence, are mainly of Melanesian stock. The former Indian majority (only 46% of the population by 1991) is descended from field workers brought by the British. Although the Indians are forbidden land ownership, they operate most of the sugar plantations. Although English is the official language, Fijians speak their own language and are primarily Christian (85% Methodist). The Indian population, which is 70% Hindu and 25% Muslim, speaks a dialect of Hindi. There are also small Chinese and white minorities. Fiji experiences tensions as a result of its diverse ethnic composition. Primary education is neither free nor compulsory, but the literacy rate is high. The University of the South Pacific (1968) is at Suva.

ECONOMIC ACTIVITY

Fiji's economy is primarily agricultural. Sugarcane, produced for export, normally constitutes about 80% of total agricultural output. Coconuts and ginger are also raised for export; cassava, sweet potatoes, and rice are grown for domestic consumption. In 1990, 279,000 visitors came to Fiji, although sugar production and tourism were adversely affected by two coups in 1987. Gold is the leading mineral product. The underdeveloped industrial sector produces some consumer goods, garments, and food products. Fiji is trying to diversify exports and increase manufacturing. Exploration for offshore oil is being conducted, and pine forests (for timber) are being planted. The fishing industry has grown rapidly.

HISTORY AND GOVERNMENT

Fiji was probably settled by about 500 BC. The first European discovery was by the Dutch navigator Abel Janszoon TASMAN, in 1643. During the first half of the 19th century, shipwrecked sailors and missionaries settled in Fiji. Their influence led first to conflicts and then warfare between Fiji's indigenous tribes. Finally, in 1874, Paramount Chief Cakobau invited Great Britain to assume sovereignty of the islands. Under British rule, sugarcane plantations were established.

Suva, the capital and chief port of Fiji, is located near the mouth of the Rewa River on the southeastern coast of Viti Levu, the largest of the nation's islands. Because of its harbor, Suva was chosen as Fiji's capital in 1882 and is now the largest city in the South Pacific.

Fiji gained independence on Oct. 10, 1970. In May 1987, after the ruling Fijian-dominated National Alliance party was defeated by an Indian-backed coalition, tensions between Fijians and Indians contributed to a military coup led by Lt. Col. (later Col.) Sitiveni Rabuka. Fiji's Supreme Court declared the coup illegal, and the governor-general assumed executive power. His plans to establish a caretaker government including all major groups prompted another coup by Rabuka. On Oct. 6, 1987, Rabuka declared Fiji a republic; he turned power over to a civilian government on December 5. In 1990 a new constitution guaranteeing Fijians a permanent legislative majority was approved. Elections for the lower house of a new Parliament were held in 1992.   MICHAEL MCINTYRE

Bibliography: Lal, B. V., *Fiji: Coups in Paradise* (1989); Lawson, S., *The Failure of Democratic Politics in Fiji* (1991); Scaar, D., *The Politics of Illusion* (1988; repr 1989); Wright, R., *On Fiji Islands* (1986).

Fikret, Tevfik: see TEVFIK FIKRET.

Filarete, Antonio Averlino   [fee-lah-ret'-tay, ahn-tohn'-ee-oh ah-vair-lee'-noh]

Antonio Averlino, known as Filarete, c.1400–c.1469, was an Italian architect, sculptor, and theoretician who worked (1433–48) in Rome where he designed the bronze doors for the old Saint Peter's Basilica. From 1452 he worked in Milan for Francesco Sforza at the Castello and then at the Ospedale Maggiore, where he was superintendent until 1465. During this time he wrote a 25-chapter architectural treatise that supports the principles of ancient architecture; it also includes the first Renaissance plan for an ideal city, Sforzinda.   DAVID CAST

Bibliography: Murray, P., *The Architecture of the Italian Renaissance*, rev. ed. (1986).

filariasis   [fil-uh-ry'-uh-sis]

Filariasis is a collective term for the PARASITIC DISEASES caused by the roundworms called filariids, which constitute the superfamily Filariodea (see NEMATODE). The diseases are observed in all vertebrates except fish. Many infestations are mild, producing no symptoms or minor dermatitis and inflammation. A few filariasis diseases in humans can be serious, although rarely fatal; in dogs—and sometimes cats—the infestation known as heartworm, caused by *Dirofilaria immitis*, is often fatal (see DOG; DISEASES, ANIMAL).

Human filariasis diseases are largely restricted to tropical and subtropical regions. They are transmitted from person to person by any of several genera of mosquitoes or biting flies, which introduce the larval stage of the worm into the bloodstream. The adult worms live in various body tissues; the elongated embryos, called microfilariae, circulate in the bloodstream, where they frequently show a diurnal or nocturnal periodicity in their numbers.

The disease most commonly known as filariasis occurs in Africa, Asia, and the South Pacific region. It is caused by *Wuchereria bancrofti*, *Brugia malayi*, and a few other roundworm species and is transmitted by mosquitoes. The adult worms live within the lymph ducts or glands, where they may eventually obstruct lymph circulation. This leads to edema, or the abnormal accumulation of tissue fluid. The extremities and scrotum are most often affected and may swell to enormous proportions, a condition commonly called elephantiasis; the skin over the swollen areas becomes dark, thick, and coarse. The original infestation is dealt with fairly successfully by drugs that attack the adult worms, microfilariae, or both, but treatments for elephantiasis are less effective. Eradication of the mosquito vectors of the disease is the key to control of filariasis, but this has been difficult or impossible.

Another filarial disease, onchocerciasis (RIVER BLINDNESS), can cause loss of vision if untreated; it occurs in Africa and Central and South America. African EYE WORM, *Loa loa*, by contrast, is rarely serious.   DAVID FRANCIS METTRICK

Bibliography: Cahill, K. M., and O'Brien, W., *Tropical Medicine* (1990); CIBA Foundation Staff, *Filariasis, No. 127* (1987).

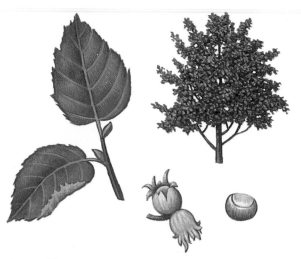

The giant filbert tree, C. maxima, native to southeastern Europe, grows to 9 m (30 ft) in height and bears heart-shaped leaves. Leafy husks (bottom center) cover the large, edible nuts (bottom right).

filbert

The filbert, or hazelnut, is the fruit of plants belonging to the genus *Corylus* of the birch family, Betulaceae. Of the ten major species, the most widely grown are the European filbert (*C. avellana*), the American filbert (*C. americana*), the Turkish filbert (*C. colurna*), and the beaked filbert (*C. cornuta*). Filberts are deciduous shrubs or small trees (although some varieties may reach heights of 18 m/60 ft) native to the temperate zone. Native varieties grow wild throughout America but are cultivated only in areas that do not have late spring frosts, since the flowers, which open in mild-winter and early-spring weather, are vulnerable to frost-kill.

Most filberts require more than one variety for pollination. They grow in a wide range of soils and are propagated by seed, layering, or grafting. Commercial production of filberts in the United States is centered in Oregon and Washington. The major filbert-exporting countries are Turkey, Italy, and Spain.   DONALD K. OURECKY

filefish   [fyl'-fish]

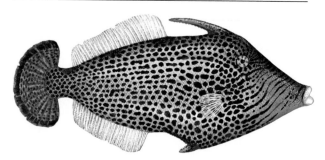

The fan-tailed filefish, Pervagor spilosoma, has a strikingly flat body and rough skin, hence the name.

Filefish is the common name of about 85 species of plant-eating fish constituting the subfamily Monacanthinae in the TRIGGERFISH family, Balistidae. Common in warm ocean waters, filefish are named for the sandpaperlike skin of most of the species. The small-mouthed, flattened body generally reaches a length of 25 cm (10 in), but *Aluterus scriptus* grows to 1 m (3 ft) long.   ALFRED PERLMUTTER

Filene, Edward Albert   [fy-leen']

Edward Albert Filene, b. Sept. 3, 1860, d. Sept. 26, 1937, built his father's dry-goods and clothes store into a great Boston department store, William Filene's Sons. Among his innovations was the "bargain basement," which was designed as a means of selling slow-moving items. Filene was also a civic reformer and organized Boston's first chamber of commerce. Believing that the future lay in a high-wage, mass-distribution economy, he promoted consumer cooperatives and employee credit unions. He left most of his fortune to the Twentieth Century Fund, an organization devoted to economic research.

filibuster   [fil'-uh-buhs-tur]

A filibuster, in politics, is an effort made by a minority of members in a representative assembly to prolong debate in order to delay a vote. Filibustering tactics are often used in the U.S. Senate, which until 1917 had no provision for limiting debate on an issue. In that year a rule was passed to permit closing of debate (CLOTURE) by a vote of two-thirds of the members present and voting. The rule was amended in 1949 and 1959; in 1975 it was changed again to require an affirmative vote by three-fifths of the total Senate membership. Filibustering senators from the South were able to block civil rights legislation on several occasions. They were defeated in 1964 when, after 75 days of delay, the Senate invoked cloture to pass the Civil Rights Act of 1964.

The term *filibuster* (from the Spanish *filibustero*, "free-booter") was originally applied during the 17th century to buccaneers who raided the Spanish colonies in the Americas. In the 19th century it was used for U.S. adventurers and soldiers of fortune who led military expeditions into Mexico and Central America, mainly during the 1850s. The most famous of these was William WALKER, who established a short-lived state in Baja California in 1853 and briefly installed himself as president of Nicaragua (1856–57).

Bibliography: Brown, C. H., *Agents of Manifest Destiny* (1980); Burdette, F. L., *Filibustering in the Senate* (1940; repr. 1965).

Filipchenko, Anatoly V.   [fee-leep-chen'-koh]

The Soviet cosmonaut Anatoly Vasilyevich Filipchenko, b. Feb. 26, 1928, commanded space missions that served as a prelude for the Salyut and Apollo-Soyuz projects. A Soviet air force jet pilot and graduate of the air force academy, he joined the cosmonaut corps in 1963. Filipchenko commanded the three-man *Soyuz 7* spaceship in October 1969, during which Salyut rendezvous maneuvers were tested. He later trained for Salyut missions but was switched to the APOLLO-SOYUZ TEST PROJECT in 1973. He commanded (Dec. 2–8, 1974) the two-man *Soyuz 16* flight, which was a rehearsal for the actual Soviet-American linkup.   JAMES OBERG

Fillmore, Millard   [fil'-mohr, mil'-urd]

Millard Fillmore was the 13th president of the United States (1850–53), succeeding to that office on the death of Zachary TAYLOR.

Fillmore was born in Cayuga County, N.Y., on Jan. 7, 1800. His parents were poor, and as a child he had little schooling. An apprentice wool carder, he gained his first formal education in 1819, when a slow period at work enabled him to attend New Hope Academy for 6 months. He then purchased a release from his apprenticeship, worked in a law office, and passed the bar examination in 1823. His law practice flourished, first in East Aurora, N.Y., and then in Buffalo, N.Y., which in 1830 he made his permanent home.

Early Political Career. Fillmore began his political career in the mid-1820s, as one of the many young men swept up in the ANTI-MASONIC movement of western New York. Elected to the state assembly in 1828, Fillmore successfully sponsored a bill to end imprisonment for debt. In 1832 he was elected to the U.S. Congress as an Anti-Mason. In Congress, Fillmore joined the WHIG PARTY, the coalition opposed to Andrew Jackson. He served as a Whig congressman from Buffalo from 1837 to 1843 and became a strong advocate of internal improvements and of the protective tariff. A man of solid character and diplomatic temperament, Fillmore won the respect of his colleagues, who in 1840 named him chairman of the House Ways and

MILLARD FILLMORE
13th President of the United States (1850–53)

Nickname: "The American Louis Philippe"
Born: Jan. 7, 1800, Summerhill, N.Y.
Profession: Lawyer
Religious Affiliation: Unitarian
Marriage: Feb. 5, 1826, to Abigail Powers (1798–1853); Feb. 10, 1858, to Caroline Carmichael McIntosh (1813–81)
Children: Millard Powers Fillmore (1828–89); Mary Abigail Fillmore (1832–54)
Political Affiliation: Whig
Died: Mar. 8, 1874, Buffalo, N.Y.
Buried: Forest Lawn Cemetery, Buffalo, N.Y.

Vice-President and Cabinet Members

Vice-President: None
Secretary of State: John M. Clayton (1850); Daniel Webster (1850–52); Edward Everett (1852–53)
Secretary of the Treasury: William M. Meredith (1850); Thomas Corwin (1850–53)
Secretary of War: George W. Crawford (1850); Charles M. Conrad (1850–53)
Attorney General: Reverdy Johnson (1850); John J. Crittenden (1850–53)
Postmaster General: Jacob Collamer (1850); Nathan K. Hall (1850–52); Samuel D. Hubbard (1852–53)
Secretary of the Navy: William B. Preston (1850); William A. Graham (1850–52); John P. Kennedy (1852–53)
Secretary of the Interior: Thomas Ewing (1850); Thomas M. T. McKennan (1850); Alexander H. H. Stuart (1850–53)

Means Committee. He led passage of the Whig Tariff Act of 1842.

During the 1840s, Fillmore became identified with the conservative wing of the Whig party in New York. The liberal faction, led by Thurlow WEED and William H. SEWARD, was sympathetic to the growing antislavery movement. Seward and Weed also sought to attract to the Whigs voters from the great numbers of immigrants who flooded into New York after 1842. Fillmore, although against slavery, opposed the abolitionists as disruptive of the Whig party and of the nation itself. He was similarly skeptical about the quick naturalization of foreigners, who voted in droves for the Democratic party. As the Whig nominee for governor of New York in 1844, Fillmore attributed his narrow defeat to the hostile votes of abolitionists and Irish Roman Catholics. He returned (1847) to office when elected comptroller of the state of New York.

Vice-Presidency and Presidency. In 1848 the Whigs chose an outsider, Gen. Zachary Taylor, a Louisiana slaveholder who had never voted and was not a Whig, as their presidential candidate. To reconcile the more traditional elements of the party, the convention named Fillmore as the Whig vice-presidential candidate. Despite rising animosity over the question of the expansion of slavery into territories won in the MEXICAN WAR, the narrow victory of Taylor and Fillmore held out hope of a conciliatory national solution to the problem. The hope proved false. Taylor was fiercely resistant to the proposals that emerged in 1850 to resolve the dispute over slavery, although the measures had the strong support of Whig founders Henry CLAY and Daniel WEBSTER.

At the height of the sectional crisis Taylor died unexpectedly, and on July 9, 1850, Fillmore became president. Dramatically and decisively, the new president committed himself to sectional compromise. Accepting the resignations of Taylor's cabinet, he appointed Daniel Webster, the major Northern advocate of compromise, as his secretary of state, and also named Whigs favorable to compromise to the other cabinet posts. As fast as Congress could approve the bills making up the COMPROMISE OF 1850, Fillmore signed them into law. His administration strictly enforced the most controversial of the new measures, the FUGITIVE SLAVE LAW, which required Northerners to collaborate in the return of escaped slaves to their Southern owners. During the remainder of his term, Fillmore became the first president to approve federal aid for the building of railroads and the first to send a trade mission (led by Commodore Matthew C. PERRY) to Japan.

Because of his enforcement of the Fugitive Slave Law, Fillmore was the favorite of Southern delegates to the divided Whig presidential convention of 1852. His antagonists were Northern Whigs, led by his old New York rivals Seward and Weed, who favored the choice of an antislavery presidential candidate. The Southerners achieved a pro-Compromise party platform, but after 53 ballots, the Northerners succeeded in pushing through an antislavery nominee, Gen. Winfield SCOTT. The divided Whigs were defeated by Democrat Franklin Pierce in the election, and the Whig party thereafter began to disintegrate.

Later Life. Fillmore returned to Buffalo but remained active in politics and again sought the presidency in 1856. He profited from the rapidly rising nativist movement, which opposed the deepening influence of Catholic immigrants in U.S. life and politics. The KNOW-NOTHING PARTY, founded on nativism, named Fillmore its presidential nominee in 1856. He also won the nomination of the remnant of the Whig party, now dominated by Southerners. Pitted against both Democrats and Republicans, Fillmore carried only Maryland in the election but won over 40 percent of the vote in ten other Southern states.

Fillmore supported the Union during the Civil War but felt that the conflict was needless. He was critical of President Abraham Lincoln's administration and supported Democrat George B. McClellan in the presidential contest of 1864. After retiring from politics, he became active in the civic life of Buffalo and died there at age 74 on Mar. 8, 1874.

SYDNEY NATHANS

Bibliography: Barre, W. L., *The Life and Public Services of Millard Fillmore* (1856; repr. 1971); Crawford, J. E., *Millard Fillmore* (1991); Rayback, Robert J., *Millard Fillmore* (1959); Smith, E. B., *The Presidencies of Zachary Taylor and Millard Fillmore* (1988).

film: see ANIMATION; CINEMATOGRAPHY; DOCUMENTARY; FILM, HISTORY OF; FILM PRODUCTION.

film, history of

The history of film has been dominated by the discovery and testing of the paradoxes inherent in the medium itself. Film uses machines to record images of life; it combines still photographs to give the illusion of continuous motion; it seems to present life itself, but it also offers impossible unrealities approached only in dreams.

The motion picture was developed in the 1890s from the union of still PHOTOGRAPHY, which records physical reality, with the persistence-of-vision toy, which made drawn figures appear to move. Four major film traditions have developed since then: fictional narrative film, which tells stories about people with whom an audience can identify because their world looks familiar; nonfictional documentary film, which focuses on the real world either to instruct or to reveal some sort of truth about it; animated film, which makes drawn or sculpted figures look as if they are moving and speaking; and experimental film, which exploits film's ability to create a purely abstract, nonrealistic world unlike any previously seen.

Film is considered the youngest art form and has inherited much from the older and more traditional arts. Like the novel, it can tell stories; like the drama, it can portray conflict between live characters; like painting, it composes in space with light, color, shade, shape, and texture; like music, it moves in time according to principles of rhythm and tone; like dance, it presents the movement of figures in space and is often underscored by music; and like photography, it presents a two-dimensional rendering of what appears to be three-dimensional reality, using perspective, depth, and shading.

Film, however, is one of the few arts that is both spatial and temporal, intentionally manipulating both space and time. This synthesis has given rise to two conflicting theories about film and its historical development. Some theorists, such as S. M. EISENSTEIN and Rudolf Arnheim, have argued that film must take the path of the other modern arts and concentrate not on telling stories or representing reality but on investigating time and space in a pure and consciously abstract way. Others, such as André Bazin and Siegfried KRACAUER, maintain that film must fully and carefully develop its connection with nature so that it can portray human events as excitingly and revealingly as possible.

Because of his fame, his success at publicizing his activities, and his habit of patenting machines before actually inventing them, Thomas EDISON received most of the credit for having

Eadweard Muybridge, an early pioneer of motion picture development, used a series of sequential cameras to photograph the movements of a running horse. This study, published in 1878 as The Horse in Motion, *prompted further experiments with the photography of motion and influenced the development of both motion picture cameras and projectors.*

invented the motion picture; as early as 1887, he patented a motion picture camera, but this could not produce images. In reality, many inventors contributed to the development of moving pictures. Perhaps the first important contribution was the series of motion photographs made by Eadweard MUYBRIDGE between 1872 and 1877. Hired by the governor of California, Leland Stanford, to capture on film the movement of a racehorse, Muybridge tied a series of wires across the track and connected each one to the shutter of a still camera. The running horse tripped the wires and exposed a series of still photographs, which Muybridge then mounted on a stroboscopic disk and projected with a magic lantern to reproduce an image of the horse in motion. Muybridge shot hundreds of such studies and went on to lecture in Europe, where his work intrigued the French scientist E. J. MAREY. Marey devised a means of shooting motion photographs with what he called a photographic gun.

Edison became interested in the possibilities of motion photography after hearing Muybridge lecture in West Orange, N.J. Edison's motion picture experiments, under the direction of William Kennedy Laurie Dickson, began in 1888 with an attempt to record the photographs on wax cylinders similar to those used to make the original phonograph recordings. Dickson made a major breakthrough when he decided to use George EASTMAN's celluloid film instead. Celluloid was tough but supple and could be manufactured in long rolls, making it an excellent medium for motion photography, which required great lengths of film. Between 1891 and 1895, Dickson shot many 15-second films using the Edison camera, or Kinetograph, but Edison decided against projecting the films for audiences—in part because the visual results were inadequate and in part because he felt that motion pictures would have little public appeal. Instead, Edison marketed an electrically driven peep-hole viewing machine (the Kinetoscope) that displayed the marvels recorded to one viewer at a time.

Edison thought so little of the Kinetoscope that he failed to extend his patent rights to England and Europe, an oversight that allowed two Frenchmen, Louis and Auguste LUMIÈRE, to manufacture a more portable camera and a functional projector, the Cinématographe, based on Edison's machine. The movie era might be said to have begun officially on Dec. 28, 1895, when the Lumières presented a program of brief motion pictures to a paying audience in the basement of a Paris café. English and German inventors also copied and improved upon the Edison machines, as did many other experimenters in the United States. By the end of the 19th century vast numbers of people in both Europe and America had been exposed to some form of motion pictures.

The earliest films presented 15- to 60-second glimpses of real scenes recorded outdoors (workmen, trains, fire engines, boats, parades, soldiers) or of staged theatrical performances shot indoors. These two early tendencies—to record life as it

These early-20th-century projectionists are cranking the projector and rewinding the filmstrip by hand. Manually operated camera-projectors, derived from Edison's kinetoscope and developed in France by the Lumière brothers, could be used anywhere. Edison's kinetograph camera was electrically powered, limiting his film sequences to staged indoor productions.

is and to dramatize life for artistic effect—can be viewed as the two dominant paths of film history.

Georges MÉLIÈS was the most important of the early theatrical filmmakers. A magician by trade, Méliès, in such films as *A Trip to the Moon* (1902), showed how the cinema could perform the most amazing magic tricks of all: simply by stopping the camera, adding something to the scene or removing something from it, and then starting the camera again, he made things seem to appear and disappear. Early English and French filmmakers such as Cecil Hepworth, James Williamson, and Ferdinand Zecca also discovered how rhythmic movement (the chase) and rhythmic editing could make cinema's treatment of time and space more exciting.

AMERICAN FILM IN THE SILENT ERA (1903-1928)

A most interesting primitive American film was *The Great Train Robbery* (1903), directed by Edwin S. PORTER of the Edison Company. This early western used much freer editing and camera work than usual to tell its story, which included bandits, a holdup, a chase by a posse, and a final shoot-out. When other companies (Vitagraph, the American Mutoscope and Biograph Company, Lubin, and Kalem among them) began producing films that rivaled those of the Edison Company, Edison sued them for infringement of his patent rights. This so-called patents war lasted 10 years (1898–1908), ending only when nine leading film companies merged to form the Motion Picture Patents Company.

One reason for the settlement was the enormous profits to be derived from what had begun merely as a cheap novelty. Before 1905 motion pictures were usually shown in vaudeville houses as one act on the bill. After 1905 a growing number of small, storefront theaters called nickelodeons, accommodating

The kinetoscope, invented (1888) by William Dickson in Thomas Edison's laboratory, was an early peep-show machine. Almost 12 m (40 ft) of celluloid film was needed to present 46 pictures per second.

The Great Train Robbery (1903), directed by Edwin S. Porter, was the first film to contain two concurrent story lines. Porter's innovative editing and camera work imparted unprecedented vitality to this film.

(Below) *The Edison Company, although a major contributor to the development of motion pictures, declined in importance as a studio because of its insistence on single-reel films and its unsuccessful attempt to monopolize film production and distribution.*

(Above) *D.W. Griffith's innovative film techniques and dramatic expression culminated in his Civil War-era epic,* The Birth of a Nation *(1915).*

less than 200 patrons, began to show motion pictures exclusively. By 1908 an estimated 10 million Americans were paying their nickels and dimes to see such films. Young speculators such as William Fox and Marcus Loew saw their theaters, which initially cost but $1,600 each, grow into enterprises worth $150,000 each within 5 years. Called the drama of the people, the early motion pictures attracted primarily working-class and immigrant audiences who found the nickelodeon a pleasant diversion; they might not have been able to read English, but they understood the silent language of pictures.

The popularity of the moving pictures led to the first attacks against it by crusading moralists, police, and politicians. Local censorship boards were established to eliminate objectionable material from films. In 1909 the infant U.S. film industry waged a counterattack by creating the first of many self-censorship boards, the National Board of Censorship (after 1916 called the National Board of Review), whose purpose was to set moral standards for films and thereby save them from costly mutilation.

A nickelodeon program consisted of about six 10-minute films, usually including an adventure, a comedy, an informational film, a chase film, and a melodrama. The most accomplished maker of these films was Biograph's D. W. GRIFFITH, who almost singlehandedly transformed both the art and the business of the motion picture. Griffith made over 400 short films between 1908 and 1913, in this period discovering or developing almost every major technique by which film manipulates time and space: the use of alternating close-ups, medium shots, and distant panoramas; the subtle control of rhythmic editing; the effective use of traveling shots, atmospheric lighting, narrative commentary, poetic detail, and visual symbolism; and the advantages of understated acting, at which his acting company excelled. The culmination of Griffith's work was *The Birth of a Nation* (1915), a mammoth (and racist) 3-hour epic of the Civil War and Reconstruction. Its historical detail, suspense, and passionate conviction made the 10-minute film obsolete.

The decade between 1908 and 1918 was one of the most important in the history of American film. The full-length feature film replaced the program of short films; World War I destroyed or restricted the film industries of Europe, promoting greater technical innovation, growth, and commercial stability in America; the film industry was consolidated with the founding of the first major studios in Hollywood, Calif. (Fox, Paramount, and Universal); and the great American silent comedies were born. Mack SENNETT became the driving force behind the Keystone Company in 1912; Hal Roach founded his comedy company in 1914; and Charlie CHAPLIN probably had the best-known face in the world in 1916.

During this period the first movie stars rose to fame, replacing the anonymous players of the short films. In 1918, America's two favorite stars, Charlie Chaplin and Mary PICKFORD, both signed contracts for over $1 million. Other familiar stars of the decade included comedians Fatty ARBUCKLE and John Bunny, cowboys William S. HART and Bronco Billy Anderson, matinee idols Rudolph VALENTINO and John Gilbert, and the alluring females Theda BARA and the "It Girl," Clara BOW. Along with the stars came the first movie fan magazines, beginning with *Photoplay* in 1912. That same year also saw the first of the FILM SERIALS, *The Perils of Pauline,* starring Pearl White.

The next decade in American film history, 1918 to 1928, was a period of stabilization rather than expansion. Films were made within studio complexes, which were, in essence, factories designed to produce films in the same way that Henry Ford's factories produced automobiles. Film companies became monopolies in that they not only made films but distributed them to theaters and owned the theaters in which they were shown as well. This vertical integration provided the commercial foundation of the film industry for the next 30 years. Two new producing companies founded during the decade were Warner Brothers (1923), which would rise with its early conversion to synchronized sound, and Metro-Goldwyn (1924; later Metro-Goldwyn-Mayer), the producing arm of Loew's, under the direction of Louis B. MAYER and Irving Thalberg.

Attacks against immorality in films intensified during this Jazz Age decade, spurred by the sensual implications and sexual practices of the movie stars both on and off the screen. In 1921, after several nationally publicized sex and drug scandals, the industry headed off the threat of federal CENSORSHIP by creating the office of the Motion Picture Producers and Distributors of America (now the Motion Picture Association of America), under the direction of Will H. HAYS. Hays, who had been postmaster general of the United States and Warren G. Harding's campaign manager, began a series of public relations campaigns to underscore the importance of motion pictures to American life. He also circulated several lists of practices that were henceforth forbidden on and off the screen.

Hollywood films of the 1920s became more polished, subtle, and skillful, especially imaginative in handling the absence of sound. It was the great age of comedy. Chaplin retained a hold on his world-following with full-length features such as *The Kid* (1920) and *The Gold Rush* (1925); Harold LLOYD climbed his way to success—and got the girl—no matter how great the obstacles, in *Grandma's Boy* (1922) and *The Freshman* (1925); Buster KEATON remained deadpan through a

Charlie Chaplin's first sound film, City Lights *(1931), attracts a large crowd at the Broadway Theatre, here displaying the familiar image of "The Little Tramp." Chaplin used music but no dialogue to underscore a highly successful mixture of comedy and pathos.*

Stars and directors became synonymous with their genres for many early film audiences. Valentino personified romance, Chaplin comedy, and De Mille the spectacle, in such films as The Sheik *(1921) (left),* City Lights *(1931) (center), and* The Ten Commandments *(1923) (right).*

succession of wildly bizarre sight gags in *Sherlock Jr.* (1924) and *The General* (1926); Harry Langdon was ever the innocent elf cast adrift in a mean, tough world; and director Ernst Lu-BITSCH, fresh from Germany, brought his "touch" to understated comedies of manners, sex, and marriage. The decade saw the United States's first great war film (*The Big Parade*, 1925), its first great westerns (*The Covered Wagon*, 1923; *The Iron Horse*, 1924), and its first great biblical epics (*The Ten Commandments*, 1923, and *King of Kings*, 1927, by Cecil B. De MILLE). Other films of this era included Erich Von STROHEIM's sexual studies, Lon CHANEY's grotesque costume melodramas, and the first great documentary feature, Robert J. FLAHERTY's *Nanook of the North* (1922).

EUROPEAN FILM IN THE 1920s
In the same decade, the European film industries recovered from the war to produce one of the richest artistic periods in film history. The German cinema, stimulated by EXPRESSIONISM in painting, poetry, and the theater and by the design theories of the BAUHAUS, created bizarrely expressionistic settings for such fantasies as Robert Wiene's *The Cabinet of Doctor Caligari* (1919), F. W. MURNAU's *Nosferatu* (1922), and Fritz LANG's *Metropolis* (1927). The Germans also brought their sense of decor, atmospheric lighting, and penchant for a frequently moving camera to such realistic political and psychological studies as Murnau's *The Last Laugh* (1924), G. W. PABST's *The Joyless Street* (1925), and E. A. Dupont's *Variety* (1925).

Innovation also came from the completely different approach in the USSR, where movies were intended not only to

entertain but also to instruct the masses in the social and political goals of their new government. The Soviet cinema used montage, or complicated editing techniques that relied on visual metaphor, to create excitement and richness of texture and, ultimately, to shape ideological attitudes and to provide its semiliterate people with a history that offered a rationale for the revolution. The most influential Soviet theorist and filmmaker was Sergei M. Eisenstein, whose *Potemkin* (1925) had a worldwide impact. Other innovative Soviet filmmakers of the 1920s included V. I. PUDOVKIN, Lev Kuleshov, Abram Room, and Alexander DOVZHENKO.

Fritz Lang's Metropolis *(1927) exemplifies the German expressionist movement, in which fantastic sets, stylized acting, and eerie lighting were used to create emotional, political, or social allegories.*

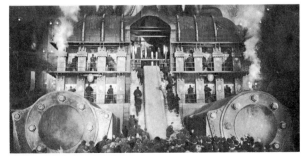

The Swedish cinema of the 1920s relied heavily on the striking visual qualities of the northern landscape. Mauritz Stiller and Victor Sjöström mixed this natural imagery of mountains, sea, and ice with psychological drama and tales of supernatural quests. French cinema, by contrast, brought the methods and assumptions of modern painting to film. Under the influence of SURREALISM and dadaism, filmmakers working in France began to experiment with the possibility of rendering abstract perceptions or dreams in a visual medium. Marcel DUCHAMP, René CLAIR, Fernand LÉGER, Jean RENOIR—and Luis BUÑUEL and Salvador DALI in *Un Chien andalou* (1928)—all made antirealist, antirational, noncommercial films that helped establish the avant-garde tradition in filmmaking. Several of these filmmakers would later make significant contributions to the narrative tradition in the sound era.

THE ARRIVAL OF SOUND

The era of the talking film began in late 1927 with the enormous success of Warner Brothers' *The Jazz Singer,* a part talkie. The first 100% sound film, *Lights of New York,* followed in 1928. Although experimentation with synchronizing sound and picture was as old as the cinema itself (Dickson, for example, made a rough synchronization of the two for Edison in 1894), the feasibility of sound film was widely publicized only after Warner Brothers purchased the Vitaphone from Western Electric in 1926. The original Vitaphone system synchronized the picture with a separate phonographic disk, rather than using the more accurate method of recording (based on the principle of the OSCILLOSCOPE) a sound track on the film itself. Warners originally used the Vitaphone to make short musical films featuring both classical and popular performers and to record musical sound tracks for otherwise silent films (*Don Juan,* 1926). For *The Jazz Singer,* Warners added four synchronized musical sequences to a silent film. When Al JOLSON sang and then delivered several lines of dialogue, audiences were electrified. The silent film was dead within a year.

The conversion to synchronized sound caused serious problems for the film industry. Sound recording was difficult; cameras had to shoot from inside glass booths; studios had to build special soundproof stages; theaters required expensive new equipment; writers had to be hired who had an ear for dialogue; and actors had to be found whose voices could deliver it. Many of the earliest talkies were ugly and static, the visual images serving merely as an accompaniment to endless dialogue, sound effects, and musical numbers. Serious film critics mourned the passing of the motion picture, which no longer seemed to contain either motion or picture.

The most effective early sound films were those which played most adventurously with the union of picture and sound track. Walt DISNEY's cartoons combined surprising sights with inventive sounds, carefully orchestrating the animated motion and musical rhythm. Ernst Lubitsch also played very cleverly with sound, contrasting the action depicted visually with the information on the sound track in dazzlingly funny or revealing ways. By 1930 the U.S. film industry had conquered both the technical and the artistic problems involved in using sight and sound harmoniously, and the European industry was quick to follow.

HOLLYWOOD'S GOLDEN ERA

The 1930s was the golden era of the Hollywood studio film. It was the decade of the great movie stars—Greta GARBO, Marlene DIETRICH, Jean HARLOW, Mae WEST, Katharine HEPBURN, Bette DAVIS, Cary GRANT, Gary COOPER, Clark GABLE—and some of America's greatest directors thrived on the pressures and excitement of studio production. Josef von STERNBERG became legendary for his use of exotic decor and sexual symbolism; Howard HAWKS made driving adventures and fast-paced comedies; Frank CAPRA blended politics and morality in a series of comedy-dramas; and John FORD mythified the American West.

American studio pictures came in cycles, the liveliest of which could not have been made before synchronized sound. The gangster film introduced Americans to the tough doings and tougher talk of big-city thugs, as played by James CAGNEY, Paul MUNI, and Edward G. ROBINSON. Musicals included the

(Left) *The famous "fight scene" between Una Merkel* (left) *and Marlene Dietrich* (right), *interrupted by James Stewart* (center), *in* Destry Rides Again *(1939) was considered daring in its time.* Destry Rides Again *remains a popular Western.*

(Above) The Public Enemy *(1931), featuring James Cagney* (right), *is a classic gangster film, a genre prevalent during the 1930s.*

witty operettas of Ernst Lubitsch, with Maurice CHEVALIER and Jeanette MacDonald (see EDDY, NELSON, AND MACDONALD, JEANETTE); the backstage musicals of Busby BERKELEY, with their dazzling kaleidoscopic dance numbers; and the smooth, more natural song-and-dance comedies of Fred ASTAIRE and Ginger ROGERS. Synchronized sound also produced screwball comedy, which explored the dizzy doings of fast-moving, fast-thinking, and, above all, fast-talking men and women.

The conflict between artistic freedom and censorship rose again with the talking picture. Spurred by the depression and by the threat of economic boycott by the newly formed Catholic Legion of Decency, the motion picture industry adopted an official Production Code in 1934. Written in 1930 by Daniel Lord, S.J., and Martin Quigley, a Catholic layman who was publisher of *The Motion Picture Herald,* the code explicitly prohibited certain acts, themes, words, and implications. Will Hays appointed Joseph I. Breen, the Catholic layman instrumental in founding the Legion of Decency, head of the Production Code Administration, which awarded the industry's seal of approval only to films that met the code's moral standards. The result was the curtailment of explicit violence and sexual innuendo, as well as much of the flavor that had characterized films earlier in the decade.

EUROPE DURING THE 1930s

The 1930s abroad did not produce films as consistently rich as those of the previous decade. With the coming of sound, the British film industry was reduced to a Hollywood satellite. The most stylish British productions were the historical dramas of Sir Alexander KORDA and the mystery-adventures of Alfred HITCHCOCK. The major Korda stars, as well as Hitchcock himself, left Britain for Hollywood before the decade ended. More innovative were the government-funded documentaries and experimental films made by the General Post Office Film Unit under the direction of John Grierson.

Soviet filmmakers had problems with the early sound-film machines and with the application of montage theory (a totally visual conception) to sound filming. They were further plagued by restrictive Stalinist policies, which kept ambitious film artists like Pudovkin and Eisenstein from making films

(Left) *Fred Astaire and Ginger Rogers, one of the most successful partnerships in film history, execute a dance sequence in the great Hollywood musical comedy* Top Hat *(1935), directed by Mark Sandrich and with music by Irving Berlin.*

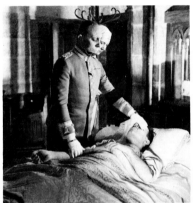

(Above) *Complex cinematography was brilliantly exploited by Busby Berkeley in lavish productions such as* Dames *(1934)* (left)*, by Orson Welles in his masterpiece,* Citizen Kane *(1941)* (center)*, and by Jean Renoir in France's prewar classic,* Grand Illusion *(1937)* (right)*.

altogether. The style of the German cinema was perfectly suited to sound filming, and German films of the period 1928–32 show some of the most creative uses of the medium in the early years of sound. When the Nazis came to power in 1933, however, almost all the creative film talent left Germany. An exception was Leni RIEFENSTAHL, whose theatrical documentary *Triumph of the Will* (1934) represents a highly effective example of Nazi propaganda translated into cinematic terms.

French cinema, the most exciting alternative to Hollywood in the 1930s, produced many of France's most classic films. The decade found director Jean Renoir—in *Grand Illusion* (1937) and *Rules of the Game* (1939)—at the height of his powers; René Clair mastered both the musical fantasy and the sociopolitical satire (*À Nous la liberté*, 1931); Marcel PAGNOL brought to the screen his trilogy of Marseilles life, *Fanny*; the young Jean VIGO, in only two films, brilliantly expressed youthful rebellion and mature love; and director Marcel CARNÉ teamed with poet Jacques Prévert to produce haunting existential romances of lost love and inevitable death in *Quai des brumes* (1938) and *Le Jour se lève* (1939).

HOLLYWOOD AND WORLD WAR II
During World War II, films were required to lift the spirits of Americans both at home and overseas. Many of the most accomplished Hollywood directors and producers went to work for the War Department. Frank Capra produced the "Why We Fight" series (1942–45); Walt Disney, fresh from his *Snow White* (1937) and *Fantasia* (1940) successes, made animated informational films; and John Ford, Garson KANIN, John HUSTON, and William WYLER all made documentaries about important battles. Among the new American directors to make remarkable narrative films at home were three former screenwriters, Preston STURGES, Billy WILDER, and John Huston. Orson WELLES, the boy genius of theater and radio fame, also came to Hollywood to shoot *Citizen Kane* (1941), the complicated and tragic story of a newspaper magnate.

POSTWAR DECLINE
Between 1946 and 1953 the movie industry was attacked from many sides. As a result, the Hollywood studio system totally collapsed. First, the U.S. House of Representatives' Committee on Un-American Activities investigated alleged Communist infiltration of the motion picture industry in two separate sets of hearings. In 1948, The HOLLYWOOD TEN, 10 screenwriters and directors who refused to answer the questions of the committee, went to jail for contempt of Congress. Then, from 1951 to 1954, in mass hearings, Hollywood celebrities were forced either to name their associates as fellow Communists or to refuse to answer all questions on the grounds of 5th Amendment protection against self-incrimination. These hearings led the industry to blacklist many of its most talented workers and also weakened its image in the eyes of America and the world.

In 1948 the United States Supreme Court, ruling in *United States* v. *Paramount* that the vertical integration of the movie industry was monopolistic, required the movie studios to divest themselves of the theaters that showed their pictures and thereafter to cease all unfair or discriminatory distribution practices. At the same time, movie attendance begun a steady decline; the film industry's gross revenues fell every year from 1947 to 1963. The most obvious cause was the rise of television, (see VIDEO), as more and more Americans each year stayed home to watch the entertainment they could get most comfortably and inexpensively. In addition, European quotas against American films bit into Hollywood's foreign revenues.

While major American movies lost money, foreign art films were attracting an enthusiastic and growing audience, and these foreign films created social as well as commercial difficulties for the industry. In 1951, *The Miracle*, a 40-minute film by Roberto ROSSELLINI, was attacked by the New York Catholic Diocese as sacrilegious and was banned by New York City's commissioner of licenses. The 1952 Supreme Court ruling in the *Miracle* case officially granted motion pictures the right to free speech as guaranteed in the Constitution, reversing a 1915 ruling by the Court that movies were not equivalent to speech. Although the ruling permitted more freedom of expression in films, it also provoked public boycotts and repeated legal tests of the definition of obscenity.

Postwar foreign filmmakers, such as Rossellini, in The Miracle *(1948)* (left), *De Sica, in* Umberto D *(1952)* (center), *and Kurosawa, in* Rashomon *(1950)* (right), *experimented with form, content, and technique while confronting serious social issues.*

Hollywood attempted to counter the effects of television with a series of technological gimmicks in the early 1950s: 3-D, Cinerama, and CinemaScope. The industry converted almost exclusively to color filming during the decade, aided by the cheapness and flexibility of the new Eastman color monopack, which came to challenge the monopoly of Technicolor. The content of postwar films also began to change as Hollywood searched for a new audience and a new style. There were more socially conscious films—such as Fred ZINNEMANN's *The Men* (1950) and Elia KAZAN's *On the Waterfront* (1954); more adaptations of popular novels and plays; more independent (as opposed to studio) production; and a greater concentration on FILM NOIR—grim detective stories in brutal urban settings. Older genres such as the Western still flourished, and MGM brought the musical to what many consider its pinnacle in a series of films produced by Arthur Freed and directed by Vincente MINNELLI, Gene KELLY, and Stanley Donen.

EUROPEAN FILM IN THE POSTWAR WORLD

The stimulus for defining a new film content and style came to the United States from abroad, where many previously dormant film industries sprang to life in the postwar years. The defection of mass American audiences to television, their replacement by those willing to experience more unsettling film entertainment, the film festivals where international films competed for commercial distribution, and foreign governmental support of film production all contributed to the growth of non-American film industries in the postwar years.

Italy. The European film renaissance can be said to have started in Italy with such masters of NEOREALISM as Roberto Rossellini in *Open City* (1945), Vittorio DE SICA in *The Bicycle Thief* (1948) and *Umberto D* (1952), and Luchino VISCONTI in *La Terra Trema* (1948). Federico FELLINI broke with the tradition to make more poetic and personal films such as *I Vitelloni* (1953) and *La Strada* (1954), then shifted to a more flamboyant style in the 1960s with *La Dolce Vita* (1960), *8 1/2* (1963), and *Fellini-Satyricon* (1968). A new departure—both artistic and thematic—was evidenced by Michelangelo ANTONIONI in his subtle psychosocial trilogy of films that began with *L'Aventura* (1960). The vitality of Italian filmmaking continued through the 1970s and '80s with the political and sexual allegories of Pier-Paolo PASOLINI (*The Gospel According to St. Matthew,* 1964; *Teorema,* 1968; *Salo,* 1977); with Bernardo BERTOLUCCI's fusing a radical political consciousness with a stunning visual style (*The Conformist,* 1970; *Last Tango in Paris,* 1972; *1900,* 1977); and with retrospective glimpses of Italian history and cinema by Paolo and Vittorio Taviani (*Padre Padrone,* 1977; *The Night of the Shooting Stars,* 1983).

France. With the coming of NEW WAVE films in the late 1950s, the French cinema reasserted the artistic primacy it had enjoyed in the prewar period. Applying a personal style to radically different forms of film narrative, New Wave directors included Claude CHABROL (*The Cousins,* 1959), François TRUFFAUT (*The 400 Blows,* 1959; *Jules and Jim,* 1961), Alain RESNAIS

(*Hiroshima Mon Amour,* 1959), and Jean Luc GODARD, who, following the success of his offbeat *Breathless* (1960), became progressively more committed to a Marxist interpretation of society in *Two or Three Things I Know about Her* (1966), *Weekend* (1967), and *La Chinoise* (1967). While Truffaut became obsessively concerned with the value of cinema as art, education, and communication (*The Wild Child,* 1969; *Day for Night,* 1973; *The Last Metro,* 1980), Godard became obsessively concerned with the way cinema—like all media of popular culture—masks the covert operations of ideology in bourgeois society (*Tout va bien,* 1972; *Sauve qui peut,* 1980; *First Name: Carmen,* 1983). Louis MALLE audaciously explored such charged subjects as incest and collaborationism in *Murmur of the Heart* (1971) and *Lacombe Lucien* (1974).

Sweden. From Sweden Ingmar BERGMAN emerged in the 1950s as the master of introspective, often death-obsessed studies of complex human relationships. Although capable of comedy, as in *Smiles of a Summer Night* (1955), Bergman was at his most impressive in more despairing, existentialist dramas such as *The Seventh Seal* (1957), *Wild Strawberries* (1957), *Persona* (1966), and *Cries and Whispers* (1972), aided by a first-rate acting ensemble and brilliant cinematography. In later color films, such as *The Magic Flute* (1974) and *Fanny and Alexander* (1982), Bergman cast off his fatalistic obsessions to reaffirm the magic of theater and cinema.

Great Britain. The British cinema, struggling in the shadow of Hollywood's English-language domination, had been largely reduced to inexpensive comedies by the early 1950s, usually starring Alec GUINNESS. Over the next decade, however, English directors produced compelling cinematic translations of Harold PINTER's existentialist dramas, and of classic British novelists from Fielding to Fowles. Britain regained a healthy share of the world market with films such as Jack Clayton's *Room at the Top* (1958); Tony RICHARDSON's *Look Back in Anger* (1959), *The Entertainer* (1960), *A Taste of Honey* (1961), and *Tom Jones* (1963); Joseph LOSEY's *The Servant* (1963) and *Accident* (1967); and Ken Russell's *Women in Love* (1969). The popularity of the James Bond spy series, which began in 1962, gave the British film industry an added boost.

Eastern Europe and the Soviet Union. The postwar cinemas of Eastern Europe walked a tightrope between their rich artistic tradition and official Soviet policies of artistic suppression. The Polish cinema enjoyed two major periods of creative freedom—in the late 1950s and early 1960s, and two decades later, in the late 1970s and early 1980s, which saw the rise of the Solidarity worker's movement. Roman POLANSKI began with psychological studies of obsessed or neurotic characters (*Knife in the Water,* 1962; *Repulsion,* 1965), only to leave Poland for both American genre films and European literary adaptations (*Rosemary's Baby,* 1968; *Macbeth,* 1971; *Chinatown,* 1974; *Tess,* 1979). Andrej WAJDA remained in Poland to direct films in both periods of expressive freedom (*Kanal,* 1957; *Ashes and Diamonds,* 1958; *Man of Marble,* 1977; *Man of Iron,* 1981).

With sketches of Czech life, films from tiny Czechoslovakia dominated the international festivals for much of the 1960s. The major directors either remained silently in Czechoslovakia after the 1968 Soviet invasion (Jiri Menzel, *Closely Watched Trains*, 1966) or emigrated to the West (Jan Kadar, *The Shop on Main Street*, 1965). Most successful of Czech émigrés has been Milos FORMAN (*Loves of a Blonde*, 1965; *The Firemen's Ball*, 1967), who found a home in Hollywood with his off-beat sketches of oddballs and loners (*One Flew over the Cuckoo's Nest*, 1975; *Amadeus*, 1984; *Valmont*, 1989).

Soviet films have never since equaled the international reputation of the silent classics by Eisenstein and Pudovkin. During the era of repression that ended only in the late 1980s, the few films to make an impact beyond the Soviet sphere of influence were sentimental recollections of the struggle against the Nazis (*The Cranes are Flying*, 1959; *Ballad of a Soldier*, 1960) or the Boris Pasternak translations of Shakespeare classics, directed by Grigory KOZINTSEV (*Hamlet, 1963; King Lear*, 1971). The most adventurous Soviet directors made films with difficulty (Andrei Tarkovsky: *Andrei Rublev*, 1966; *Solaris*, 1971); or, once made, their work was locked up and forgotten. With the era of glasnost, however, many of these films began to surface. Audiences in the USSR and elsewhere can now see Aleksandr Askoldov's *The Commissar* (1967), or Tengiz Abuladze's epic satire of Stalin, *Repentance* (made in 1982, released finally in 1986). Some of the new Soviet films bear unsettling resemblances to Hollywood films: the adolescent characters in *Little Vera* (1989), for example, behave exactly like their counterparts in the West.

Germany. The rise of a postwar generation of German filmmakers, nurtured almost exclusively on American films and actively supported by the German government, produced the most impressive new national cinema of the 1970s—rich in its output and diverse in its styles. Volker Schlondorf specialized in literary adaptations (*Young Torless*, 1966; *The Tin Drum*, 1981) while Wim WENDERS made German echoes of the American genre films that shaped his own view of both film and the world (*The American Friend*, 1977; *Paris, Texas*, 1984; *Wings of Desire*, 1988). Werner HERZOG directed psychological studies of obsessed characters who try to dominate their landscapes but are instead dominated by them (*Aguirre, the Wrath of God*, 1972; *Kaspar Hauser*, 1974; *Fitzcarraldo*, 1982). Rainer Werner FASSBINDER was the most eclectic of the new German group, specializing in political allegories that mixed a radical critique of bourgeois society, a sadomasochistic view of sexual power relationships, and references to the Hollywood cinema that he both loved and distrusted (*Ali: Fear Eats the Soul*, 1972; *Fox and His Friends*, 1974; *The Marriage of Maria Braun*, 1978; *Berlin Alexanderplatz* [made for television], 1980). Among other German films to attract international attention were the operatic epics of Hans Jurgen Syberberg (*Our Hitler*, 1977; *Parsifal*, 1981).

Spain. A promising national cinema emerged in Spain where, until the late 1970s, the regime of Generalissimo Francisco Franco had restricted expression in all the arts. The most distinguished Spanish filmmaker, Luis BUÑUEL, rarely worked in Spain but produced his films largely in Mexico and France. Buñuel broke new ground with ironic examinations of the internal contradictions of religious dogma (*Nazarin*, 1958; *Viridiana*, 1961; *The Milky Way*, 1969) and middle-class life *The Discreet Charm of the Bourgoisie*, 1972; *That Obscure Object of Desire*, 1977). Succeeding generations of Spanish filmmakers have been greatly influenced by Buñuel. They include Carlos Saura (*Cria*, 1976; *Carmen*, 1983; *Ay! Carmela*, 1990) and Pedro Almodóvar (*Women on the Verge of a Nervous Breakdown*, 1987; *Tie Me Up! Tie Me Down!*, 1990).

NONWESTERN FILM PRODUCTION
In the postwar era, directors outside the Western tradition for the first time brought their regional perceptions and concerns to an international audience.

Japan. From Japan came Akira KUROSAWA, whose exploration of the elusive nature of truth in *Rashomon* (1950) opened the way for subsequent acceptance of his samurai dramas (*Seven Samurai*, 1954; *Yojimbo*, 1961) and literary adaptations (*Throne of Blood*, 1957; *Ran*, 1985). He was joined by Kenji MIZOGUCHI, known for his stately period films *Ugetsu* (1953) and *Sansho the Bailiff* (1955), and Yasujiro OZU, whose poetic studies of modern domestic relations introduced Western audiences to a personal sensitivity that was both intensely national and universal. The major figure of a new generation of Japanese filmmakers is Nagisa Oshima (*Death by Hanging*, 1968; *In the Realm of the Senses*, 1976), who shares many of the political and stylistic concerns of Jean Luc Godard. Juzo Itami makes comic movies that place the Japanese squarely between the horns of their tradition-v.-modernism dilemma. They include *Tampopo* (1987) and *Taxing Woman* (1988)—both films that were as popular in the United States as in Japan.

India. The Indian film industry produces more feature films than any other in the world for a vast population of moviegoers. While most of these films follow clear and cheap formulas, the problems of an India in transition have been vividly brought to life in the quiet, reflective films of Satyajit RAY, particularly in the trilogy *Pather Panchali* (1955), *Aparajito* (1956), and *The World of Apu* (1958).

Third World. Many other nations of Asia, Africa, and Latin America have begun to produce films, primarily for their own regions but occasionally in the international market. Cuba possesses a vast government-funded film school and studio. Its most distinguished director has been Tomas Gutierrez Alea (*Memories of Underdevelopment*, 1968). With the loosening of political restrictions, the Brazilian and Argentinian cinemas emerged in the 1980s with such films as Hector Babenco's *Pixote* (1981) and *Kiss of the Spider Woman* (1985), and—among many others—Fernando Solanas's *Tango* (1986).

In the 1980s, films from the People's Republic of China began to circulate throughout the West. Other Far Eastern films include those from Hong Kong, most of them of the kung fu variety.

Australia. Although essentially Western, the Australian cinema shares many thematic concerns with nations that see themselves as colonized and economically exploited by the West. After a series of successes directed by Peter Weir (*The Last Wave*, 1977; *The Year of Living Dangerously*, 1982), Bruce Beresford (*Breaker Morant*, 1980), Gillian Armstrong (*My Brilliant Career*, 1979), Fred Schepisi (*The Chant of Jimmie Blacksmith*, 1978), and George Miller (*Mad Max*, 1979; *The Road Warrior*, 1981), many directors and stars (Judy Davis, Mel Gibson) left Australia for Hollywood.

AMERICAN FILM OF THE 1960s AND 1970s
Throughout the 1960s and '70s the American film industry accommodated itself to the competition of the world market, to a film audience that had shrunk from 80 million to 20 million weekly, to the tastes of an increasingly young and educated audience, and to the new social and sexual values sweeping the United States and much of the rest of the industrialized world. Major Hollywood studios became primarily offices for film distribution, and were often subsidiaries of huge conglomerates like Coca Cola. (A decade later, however, ownership began to move overseas, notably to Japan, where the Sony Corp. bought Columbia and Matsushita purchased MCA.) Hollywood began to produce far more material for television than for movie theaters; and increasingly, films were shot in places other than Hollywood. New York City, for example, recovered its early status as a filmmaking center.

American movies of the period, from the beginning of the Kennedy presidency to the era of Watergate, moved strongly into social criticism (*Doctor Strangelove*, 1963; *The Graduate*, 1967; *Bonnie and Clyde*, 1967; *2001: A Space Odyssey*, 1968; *The Wild Bunch*, 1969; *M*A*S*H*, 1970; *McCabe and Mrs. Miller*, 1971; *The Godfather*, 1972; *The Conversation*, 1974; *One Flew over the Cuckoo's Nest*, 1975). Challenging the traditional norms and institutions of American life—law, order, decency, and sexual purity—these films searched for spiritual meaning in an American society that had become entangled in Viet Nam, enslaved by the rigidly institutional and merely material. The collapse of the 1930 Hollywood Production Code and its 1968 replacement by the Motion Picture Rating System (G, PG, PG-13, R, and X), which indicated the level of audience maturity each film demanded, was an effect of these

In Return of the Jedi *(1983), the third of director-producer George Lucas's popular* Star Wars *series of science fantasy films, good triumphs over evil amid amazing galactic special effects.*

new themes. The X rating proved unworkable, and in 1990 was replaced by a new label, NC-17 (no children under 17).

The most successful directors of the period—Stanley KUB-RICK, Robert ALTMAN, Francis Ford COPPOLA, Woody ALLEN, Arthur PENN—played most imaginatively with the tools of film communication itself, perhaps influenced by such vital experimental cinema makers as Stan BRAKHAGE, Kenneth Anger, and Bruce Baillie. The new stars of the 1960s and 1970s (with the exceptions of Paul NEWMAN and Robert REDFORD), like the content of their films, were more offbeat and less glamorous than their predecessors—Robert DE NIRO, Woody Allen, Jane Fonda (see FONDA family), Dustin HOFFMAN, Jack NICHOLSON, Al PACINO, Barbra STREISAND, Diane KEATON, Meryl STREEP.

The same two decades saw the rebirth of U.S. documentary films in the work of Fred WISEMAN, the Maysles brothers, Donn Pennebaker, and, in Europe, Marcel OPHULS.

CONTEMPORARY AMERICAN FILM

Since the late 1970s there has been a radical change in both film content and the distribution of the film product. While films of the previous decade challenged the myths of American life and movies, films of the late 1970s and the 1980s reaffirmed those myths and sought new ones. The epics of Steven SPIELBERG and George LUCAS (The *Star Wars* trilogy, 1977–83; *Close Encounters of the Third Kind*, 1977; *Raiders of the Lost Arc*, 1981; *E.T.: The Extraterrestrial*, 1982) offered an escape

from social reality into a movieland Oz of myth and magic, aided by the often beautiful, sometimes awesome effects of visual technology (see CINEMATOGRAPHY; COMPUTER GRAPHICS). If many of the epics evoked the childhood wonder of space and magic, others called up the darker myths of horror, terror, and irrational menace (the *Halloween* and *Friday the 13th* series; *Alien*, 1979; *Poltergeist*, 1982). Many films that remained earthbound returned to earnest or comic investigations of the dilemmas of everyday life (divorce and male parenting in *Kramer vs. Kramer*, 1979; a troubled family in *Ordinary People*, 1980; women in a male world in *Tootsie*, 1982; a nostalgic return to lost youth in *The Big Chill*, 1983; mother-daughter relationships in *Terms of Endearment*, 1983). The *Dirty Harry* series of Clint EASTWOOD films, as well as the Rocky and Rambo films of Sylvester Stallone, affirmed the power of assertive individualism. The newest popular genre, the "Teen Pic," in which a youth comes of age by discovering the value of social and sexual relationships, both acknowledged the age of the majority of the movie audience and adapted the classic *bildungsroman* (a novel, usually about the moral or intellectual maturing of youth) into optimistic teenage American terms (*Saturday Night Fever*, 1977; *Flashdance*, 1983; *Risky Business*, 1983; *The Breakfast Club*, 1985). Vietnam has been revisited (*Platoon*, 1986; *Full Metal Jacket*, 1987; *Born on the Fourth of July*, 1990). Classics from other media are still being translated into cinema (*The Bostonians*, 1984; *Passage to India*, 1984; *Room with a View*, 1986; *The Dead*, 1987). In recent years, nostalgia has come in two versions: baseball mythologizing (*The Natural*, 1984; *Bull Durham*, 1988; *Field of Dreams*, 1989), and live-actor reproductions of revered comic strips (the *Superman* series, which began in 1978 but continued well into the 1980s; *Batman*, 1989; *Dick Tracy*, 1990).

Since the 1980s, the film and television industries of the 1980s have become virtually indistinguishable. Not only do feature films use television technologies (videotape, video cameras, and video monitors), but every feature film is composed for eventual viewing on television. The simultaneous arrival of cable television and videocassette recorders (VCRs) increased both the need and the audience for feature films in the home. The conversion of feature films to the VCR has almost totally eliminated CinemaScope and other striking visual technologies—reversing the visual tendency of four decades toward complex, contrapuntal compositions in extreme depth and width. (Imax, a recent big-screen system, uses 70-millimeter film and fills a screen area ten times as big as the standard. But its use has been restricted, primarily, to specialty showings, such as those at museums.) Visual complexity simply cannot be seen on the small television screen. Instead, movies have invested in stereo soundtracks, which sound tremendous in the theater and on high-fidelity VCRs. To make

Werner Herzog's Nosferatu *(1979) retells the Dracula story, first filmed by F. W. Murnau in 1922. The many other versions include Tod Browning's classic* Dracula *(1931), with Bela Lugosi as the evil count.*

The forced evacuation (1975) of Cambodia's capital Phnom Penh by the fanatic Khmer Rouge is pictured in The Killing Fields *(1984), a devastatingly vivid and convincing re-creation of a country in chaos.*

their older films more attractive for television, the industry has invented a method for adding color to black and white films.

GERALD MAST

Bibliography:
GENERAL HISTORIES AND CRITICISM: Allen, Robert C., and Gomery, Douglas, *Film History: Theory and Practice* (1985); Brownlow, Kevis, *The Parade's Gone By* (1968); Cook, David A., *A History of Narrative Film, 1889–1979* (1981); Eisenstein, Sergei M., *Film Form* (1949); Ellis, J. C., *A History of Film*, 3d ed. (1990); Kawin, Bruce, *How Movies Work* (1987); Mast, Gerald, *A Short History of the Movies*, 4th ed. (1986); Mast, Gerald, and Cohen, Marshall, *Film Theory and Criticism*, 3d ed. (1985); Monaco, James, *How to Read a Film* (1977).
AMERICAN, CANADIAN, AND LATIN AMERICAN FILM: Bogle, Donald, *Toms, Coons, Mulattoes, Mammies, and Bucks: An Interpretive History of Blacks in American Films* (1973); Burton, Julianne, *The New Latin Cinema* (1976); Gabler, Neal, *An Empire of Their Own: How the Jews Invented Hollywood* (1988); Hamilton, Ian, *Writers in Hollywood, 1915–51* (1990); Haskell, Molly, *From Reverence to Rape* (1974); Jowett, Garth, *Film: The Democratic Art* (1976); Mast, Gerald, ed., *The Movies in Our Midst* (1982); Monaco, James, *American Film Now* (1979); Morris, Peter, *Embattled Shadows: A History of the Canadian Film* (1979); Nevares, B. R., *The Mexican Cinema* (1976); Quart, Leonard, and Auster, Albert, *American Film and Society since 1945* (1985); Russo, Vito, *The Celluloid Closet* (1981); Sarris, Andrew, *The American Cinema* (1968); Sklar, Robert, *Movie-Made America* (1975).
EUROPEAN FILM: Abel, R., *French Cinema: The First Wave, 1915–29* (1987); Armes, Roy, *A Critical History of British Cinema* (1978); Barlow, John D., *German Expressionist Film* (1980); Cowie, Peter, *Swedish Cinema* (1969); Durgnat, Raymond, *A Mirror for England* (1971); Elsaessar, T., *New German Cinema* (1989); Hull, D. S., *Film in the Third Reich* (1969); Kracauer, S., *From Caligari to Hitler* (1959); Kurzewski, S., *Contemporary Polish Cinema* (1980); Leprohon, P., *The Italian Cinema* (1972); Leyda, Jan, *Kino: A History of the Russian and Soviet Film* (1960); Liehm, Antonin J. and Mira, *The Most Important Art: East European Film after 1945* (1977); Manvell, Roger, *New Cinema in Britain* (1969); Monaco, James, *The New Wave* (1976); Phillips, Klaus, ed., *New German Filmmakers* (1984); Rondi, Gian, *Italian Cinema Today* (1965); Witcombe, Roger, *The New Italian Cinema* (1982).
ASIAN AND AUSTRALIAN FILM: Barnouw, Erik, and Krishnaswamy, S., *Indian Film*, 2d ed. (1980); Bertrand, Ina, ed., *Cinema in Australia* (1990); Bock, Audie, *Japanese Film Directors* (1978); Clark, Paul, *Chinese Cinema* (1988); Downing, John D., *Third World Cinema* (1988); Eberhard, Wolfram, *The Chinese Silver Screen* (1972); Mellen, Joan, *The Waves at Genji's Door: Japan through Its Cinema* (1976); Murray, Scott, ed., *The New Australian Cinema* (1981); Rhode, Eric, *History and Heartburn: The Saga of Australian Film* (1981); Richie, Donald, *The Japanese Cinema* (1971; repr. 1990); Richie, Donald, and Anderson, Joseph, *Japanese Film* (1960); Sato, Tadao, *Currents in Japanese Cinema* (1982); Stratton, David, *The Last New Wave: The Australian Film Revival* (1981).

See also: ANIMATION; DOCUMENTARY; FILM PRODUCTION.

film noir [film nwar]

The term *film noir* ("dark cinema") was first used by French critics to describe a genre of American suspense film of the 1940s and '50s whose urban, often nighttime settings and fatalistic themes suggested an unstable world full of danger and moral corruption. The oblique lighting and off-balance compositions typical of the visual style of such films heightened the effect of disillusionment and bitter realism. Famous examples of film noir include *Double Indemnity* (1944), *The Big Heat* (1953), and *Touch of Evil* (1958).

Bibliography: Silver, Alain, and Wald, Elizabeth, eds., *Film Noir: An Encyclopedic Reference to the American Style* (1978).

film production

As a general term, film production is all the work that goes into the making of a film, including its planning and realization. What is actually produced during this period is an approved, final negative. During the distribution phase that follows production, multiple prints are struck from the negative, and the movie is released, marketed, and exhibited.

As a more specific term, production is one phase of overall production activity, essentially the shooting phase. Every film goes through the following stages: development, when the project is conceived, written, and financed; pre-production, when the shooting is prepared for; production, when most of the script is staged, shot, and recorded; and post-production, when the picture and sound are edited and polished.

On location for The Big Chill *(1983)*, director Lawrence Kasdan checks the camera viewfinder. Mounted on a movable platform, the camera can be positioned high enough to get a long shot of the scene below.

Terminology. A few definitions are necessary here. A *shot* is a continuously exposed piece of film, or the continuous view that is presented between one cut and another. One may not get a perfect shot on the first trial, or take. A *take* is an attempt to photograph and/or record a particular shot. Most industry CINEMATOGRAPHY is done on 35-mm negative film. Takes approved by the director are printed, evaluated (in the form of *dailies* or *rushes*—that is, daily rolls of rush-produced picture and transferred synchronous sound—so that the director, cinematographer, and actors can see and hear the results of the previous day's shooting), and eventually cut by the editor into a *workprint* (a trial version of picture and sound, to which the original camera negative may be matched and cut). A shot, then, may also be thought of as a printed and edited take. A particular shot is taken by one camera, equipped with one lens, from a particular vantage point—that is, from a particular camera *setup*. An entire scene could well be photographed from three or four setups and then edited into ten or twenty shots.

In an edited film a *scene* will usually consist of more than one shot, and a full-fledged dramatic encounter in a given location (in dramatic and narrative terms, a *scene*) may entail a variety of setups and as many shots as desired. A *sequence* is a consecutive series of shots and/or scenes, and it is not restricted to covering action in a single location. In the climactic baptism sequence in *The Godfather* (1972), for example, the scene in the church is cut together with scenes of the preparation and execution of several murders in widely dispersed locations. Each of those scenes comprises several shots, and all the shots and scenes together make up that particular sequence. On the other hand, a sequence may also be made up of individual shots that have no necessary relationship to any scene, as is the case in the avalanche of images concluding Abel Gance's *Napoléon* (1927).

Independent and Studio Production. In the so-called Golden Age of Hollywood (approximately the late 1920s through the early 1950s), a major studio had vast resources, a regular audience, and self-contained facilities that allowed it to develop, produce, and release as many as 50 pictures a year. A studio like MGM, for example, had a lot the size of a small town, and it included the studio office buildings, the script vaults, a world-class film laboratory, thousands of costumes worth thousands of dollars each, a virtual lumberyard, prop-making shops, standing outdoor sets, editing and mixing rooms, a restaurant, and a large number of *sound stages* (windowless, soundproofed buildings in which interiors—and some apparent exteriors—are shot) lined up like great concrete barns.

Today, however, many studios survive by renting out their facilities to independent filmmakers and to those in the business of making movies for television. It is common for a studio to participate in the financing of a picture, or to buy it when it is completed, and then to release it under the studio logo. Thus a virtually independent production, or even a foreign import, may well be released as "A Paramount Picture," even if Paramount had little creative input. Nevertheless, most of the studios do release several of their own pictures each year, and to that extent "the studio system" of doing things still prevails in Hollywood.

A truly independent producer is one who finances and realizes a picture without help from a studio, and who is then free to license the film to an independent distributor. Many independent producers raise money by borrowing against presold distribution rights, and by showing the script, budget, and the proposed *talent package*—usually the director and the stars—to a bank or loan company.

Development. Development begins when someone gets an idea for a movie. That person might be the head of a studio's story department, a producer who anticipates demand for a certain type of picture, or an agent who is skilled at putting people and properties together. Most often, it is a writer. Legally, development begins when the producer hires a writer.

The writer may begin with a *treatment,* or scene-by-scene story outline, which is eventually expanded into a full-length screenplay. The writer's key contribution is the structuring of the narrative. While the director is more responsible for the style of the movie, the writer is the one who determines the tale to be told. The screenwriter has far less creative autonomy than the novelist, however, and surrenders all control over the script when it is sold.

The script is then *broken down,* or analyzed as to its production requirements: how much each scene is liable to cost, what props and costumes will be necessary, and how efficiently the scenes may be arranged into an economical shooting schedule. It is normal for the scenes in a movie to be shot out of sequence, that is, in an order that is convenient rather than in the order of the script. All the scenes on a given set or location, for example, will most likely be shot at one time.

Once the script has been written, legally researched for possible libel or other actionable qualities, approved, and broken down, and budgeting and financing has been secured, a start date is set—or the project is, for one reason or another, denied final approval and put in *turnaround* (offered to anyone who will reimburse the costs of development).

Pre-Production. Pre-production is the period of converting the screenplay into a blueprint for the production of specific scenes; finding locations, hiring the cast, fixing the final budget, and determining the shooting schedule; designing and constructing the sets, making or buying the costumes, designing the makeup; researching to determine the accuracy of details; and working out the mechanical special effects—those which can be staged before the camera, as opposed to optical special effects, which are done in the laboratory.

The essential collaboration during the development period is between the writer and the producer. During pre-production

the creative collaborators are the director, the designer, and the cinematographer. The work of breaking down the script and drafting the shooting schedule is done by the production manager, who is the producer's representative on the set.

The production designer integrates the sets, costumes, and color schemes into a comprehensive design. A soundtrack may be designed just as comprehensively, by a sound designer, and that work begins in pre-production even though the bulk of it is done in post-production. The cinematographer evaluates and tests how well the sets, costumes, locations, and so on will look on film. The director both supervises and collaborates with these people, who in turn supervise extensive crews of creative and skilled professionals.

Of particular importance are the casting of the principal actors and the determination of the shooting location. A sound stage may be made to look like anything from a city street to a closet; it is an ideal location for the control of lighting and for the recording of a live, perfectly synchronized ("lip sync") soundtrack that is free of background noise. It is also an artificial environment and may prove to offer a poor substitute for the natural and authentic. The majority of nonfiction films are shot *on location*—that is, outside the studio, in what may be made to pass for authentic story environments—and so are a great many narrative films. The sweep of the wheat fields in *Days of Heaven* (1978) could not have been shot in a studio any more successfully than the claustrophobic *Cabinet of Dr. Caligari* (1919) could have been shot on location.

Production. Production is the period of principal photography—essentially the shooting and recording, by the first unit, of those scenes in the script which involve the principal actors, under the supervision of the director. A second or third unit, each with its own director and crew, may shoot scenes with crowds or stunt doubles, big action sequences, or landscape and aerial shots. An insert unit shoots close-ups that are cut in, such as inserts of maps, documents, and so forth. The core of the picture is what is shot by the first (and, in many cases, the second) unit.

The director is the coordinator of the production team, working closely with the actors, with the power of approval or disapproval over their efforts and those of everyone else (subject to the ultimate control of the producer). The director is primarily responsible for the integration of camerawork, performance, and editing, and his or her creative control extends until the completion of the first edited version. The composition of a given shot may be chosen by the cinematographer or the director.

In consultation with the director, the cinematographer determines how the shots will be lit. The actual work is executed by electricians under the supervision of the *gaffer* (the principal electrician). Most of the moving and hauling is done by *grips,* who are supervised by the key grip.

Live sound is recorded by the production sound team; in most cases one person is in charge of the microphones, another takes care of the tape recorder. Sound tracks may be recorded with or without camera synchronization.

The script supervisor keeps track of which scenes have been shot, as well as of *continuity,* the details within scenes that must match (or relate together logically) from one shot to another. The actors, too, are concerned with continuity, but in their case the challenge is to perform their roles in fragments and out of sequence.

Post-Production. The fragments of picture and sound that have been so carefully planned and executed are assembled into a whole during post-production. The rolls of negative exposed by the production camera are printed (creating the positive daily rolls that are then cut up for the workprint) and then broken down—cut, rolled up, and stored—into labeled scenes. When the workprint has been edited, or cut to the film editor's, director's, and producer's satisfaction, the original negative footage that corresponds to the workprint footage (and bears the same numbers along its edge) is trimmed and assembled. The workprint may be spliced and respliced until each cut has been perfected. One never experiments with the negative, however, which is handled as little as possible and is spliced permanently with cement.

In preparation for filming a scene in Ran *(1985), a tale of medieval battles for kingship and power, Japanese director Akira Kurosawa plots the movements of his actors. This rough choreography is essential, especially when the camera must photograph moving masses of people—the several large armies in* Ran, *for example.*

Actor David Naughton turns into a werewolf in An American Werewolf in London *(1981), one of the most terrifying transformation scenes in all horror films. Here, Naughton is being inserted into his costume.*

The daily sound rolls (reels of magnetic tape in sync with the camera rolls) are transferred to *mag film* (sprocketed film base of the same gauge as the picture, and coated with magnetic oxide), so that there is one *frame* of sound for each frame of picture. The sound may be cut and spliced just as easily as the picture. The dialogue track is cut along with the picture by the film editor.

Optical special effects are made by an independent unit, and titles are prepared by the art department. Visual devices like fades, dissolves, and wipes are created in the laboratory on an optical printer; and all of these shots are cut into the edited negative at virtually the last moment.

The soundtrack consists of dialogue, music, and effects. The typical soundtrack includes dialogue, and other tracks that are created during post-production and synchronized with the picture. A good deal of dialogue is post-synchronized (particularly if the original has been marred by background noise), as are virtually all music and the majority of effects.

In most cases the composer begins to score a movie only when it has reached the workprint stage. The composer works with the music editor, who prepares, times, and cuts the music track. The sound effects editor, who works with the greatest number of tracks, assembles all those sounds which are neither dialogue nor music. When all of the tracks have been edited and re-recorded, the final soundtrack is mixed, in sync with the workprint. Then its final product, a sound composite on mag stock, is transferred to an optical or magnetic soundtrack master, from which the soundtrack on the release print is photographically copied or magnetically re-recorded.

Once the negative has been cut, its light and color values are corrected *(timed)* so that they will match from scene to scene. The negative is copied, with computer-triggered changes in printing exposure, to produce a corrected intermediate positive (IP), from which an intermediate negative (IN) is generated. The IN, and subsequent IPs and INs, may incorporate further corrections. Ideally, very few intermediates separate the release print from the negative, because contrast increases and detail is lost with each printing generation.

The cinematographer, the director, and the editor work closely with the laboratory until a final trial composite print, or *answer print*, meets their approval. The negative that produced that print becomes "*the* negative" from which, at the onset of the distribution phase, release prints will be struck.

BRUCE KAWIN

Bibliography: Chase, Donald, ed., *Filmmaking: The Collaborative Art* (1975); Goldman, William, *Adventures in the Screen Trade* (1983); Kawin, Bruce F., *How Movies Work* (1987); Russo, John A., *Making Movies: The Inside Guide to Independent Movie Production* (1989).

film serials

Film serials, the bulk of which were produced in Hollywood between 1913 and the late 1940s, were interrupted melodramas or mysteries ("cliffhangers") that typically consisted of 12 to 15 episodes varying in length from 18 to 30 minutes. Up to 1930, approximately 300 silent serials appeared—the first was *The Adventures of Kathlyn* (1913); the most popular was Pathé's *The Perils of Pauline* (1914), starring Pearl White. At least a part of their charm derived from carefully timed dramatic sequences that substituted for a lack of narrative depth. Among the best-known serials of the sound era, during which Westerns, space stories, and fantasy dominated, were *The Lone Ranger, Captain Video, Flash Gordon, Zorro, The Masked Marvel,* and *The Green Hornet.*   BRUCE BERMAN

Bibliography: Barbour, A. G., *Cliffhanger* (1972); Cline, W. C., *In the Nick of Time* (1984); Kinnard, R., *Fifty Years of Serial Thrills* (1983); Lahue, K. C., *Bound and Gagged* (1968) and *Continued Next Week* (1964); Stedman, R. W., *The Serials,* 2d ed. (1977).

filter, electronic

A filter is an electronic circuit that selectively passes or rejects electrical signals according to their frequency by means of a network of capacitors, resistors, and inductors. Filters are classified according to their function. A low-pass filter transmits signals that have a frequency below a specified level; a high-pass filter transmits only high-frequency signals. Band-pass filters pass a narrow range of frequencies while rejecting signals having higher or lower frequencies. Band-elimination filters transmit all but a narrow band of frequencies.

An important class of filter is the active filter. Whereas a conventional or passive filter attenuates some of the signal it is designed to transmit as well as much of the signal it is designed to reject, active filters use one or more OPERATIONAL AMPLIFIERS to restore the level of the desired signal to its original amplitude.

Filters are widely used in electronic circuits. They are used to reduce or eliminate electrical NOISE, enhance the quality of speech transmission systems, and eliminate fluctuations in the amplitude of an electrical current.   FORREST M. MIMS, III

Bibliography: Grob, Bernard, *Basic Electronics,* 6th ed. (1988); Harper, Charles A., *Handbook of Components for Electronics* (1977).

filtration

In analytical chemistry filtration is a separation method used mostly to separate a precipitate from the solution in which it was formed. A solid-liquid mixture is transferred onto a porous material, such as paper, that allows passage of the liquid (filtrate) but retains the solid.

Common analytical filtration media include different kinds of paper and filter crucibles of various types (sintered glass, porous porcelain or aluminum oxide, and Gooch), all of which are available with different porosities for retaining precipitates having different particle sizes and properties. Filter paper used for quantitative analyses must be of the "ashless" type; it is always destroyed by ignition and leaves less than 0.0001 g of ash. Filter paper is especially suitable for gelatinous precipitates and those which require high-temperature ignition before weighing.

Most filter crucibles have porous bottoms built in. A Gooch crucible, however, has a removable mat (usually asbestos) supported on a perforated bottom. Suction is applied to draw solution through the filter; consequently, filtration and washing require less time. Drying or heating of the precipitate is simple. Sintered glass crucibles cannot be used above 500° C. Unless there is a special objection to its use, a filter crucible is preferred over filter paper for gravimetric analysis (see QUANTITATIVE CHEMICAL ANALYSIS).   LAURANCE A. KNECHT

fin de siècle   [fan duh see-ek'-luh]

Fin de siècle is a term, with connotations of decadence, applied especially to certain examples of late 19th-century art, literature, and mores. English representatives of the style include *The Yellow Book* (1894–97), the drawings of Aubrey Beardsley, Oscar Wilde's *Salomé* (1893) and *The Picture of Dorian Gray* (1891), and Ernest Dowson's "Cynara." French examples include the art of Henri de Toulouse-Lautrec, and J. K. Huysmans's novel *Against the Grain* (1884; Eng. trans., 1922). Vienna is the city most closely associated with the notions implied by the phrase *fin de siècle,* however, because Viennese culture achieved particular international renown at that time—as exemplified by Sigmund Freud, Arnold Schoenberg, the Secession movement, and Hugo von Hofmannsthal.

Bibliography: Pierrot, Jean, *The Decadent Imagination, 1880–1900* (1981); Teich, M., and Porter, R., eds., *Fin de Siècle and Its Legacy* (1990); Schorske, Carl E., *Fin de Siècle Vienna* (1980).

finance, state and local

State and local finance is the science and practice of raising and expending public revenues by subnational units of government. In federal systems, sovereignty is shared between the central (that is, federal) government and a number of state (or provincial) governments. Local governments, in contrast, are not sovereign but are the creations of the state or provincial governments. In democratic systems, citizens of states and localities vote to provide certain public services and to tax themselves to pay for these services.

State Finance. In the United States the major objects of state government expenditure are education, highways, public welfare, and health and hospitals. Although states differ, a substantial portion of some of these expenditures (especially education) is administered through grants to local governments. Individual and corporate INCOME TAXES, general SALES TAXES, and selective sales taxes (including motor-fuel taxes) are the major sources of internal revenue for state governments. About one-fourth of their revenue comes from the federal government. BOND financing also is available to many states, though often restricted by the state constitution.

Local Finance. Local governments in the United States include counties, townships, municipalities, school districts, and special districts. Counties, townships, and municipalities provide a wide variety of services, whereas school districts deal with public-education services. Special districts are formed for particular purposes, such as transportation, irrigation, sewer service, harbor facilities, and so on. School and special districts overlap other local governments. PROPERTY TAXES are the major source of internal revenue for local governments, although municipalities and special districts obtain significant amounts from local income taxes, local sales taxes, and user or service charges. Revenues from both state and federal governments are also important, and most local governments can sell bonds to finance public construction.

Problems. State and local governments, as the levels of government closest to the people, face an especially strong challenge to provide desired public services at least tax cost. Local governments compete with one another to attract business and industry and their tax revenues. Since World War II the revenue base for central cities has been eroded by migrations of industry and citizens to suburban areas while INNER CITY service demands have increased. Severe financial crises have arisen for many cities.

Relations with the federal government also involve problems. Many public services (such as education and welfare) are a mixture of local and national interests, and the precise division of authority and responsibility is difficult to establish and subject to revision with changing economic and political conditions. In the 1960s and '70s, federal grants-in-aid to states and localities expanded greatly both on a categorical (program-by-program) basis and as general REVENUE SHARING (sometimes called block grants; revenue sharing ended in 1986). Matching requirements committed state and local money to these programs. The Bush administration in 1991 called for a plan whereby federal funds allocated to the states would be administered by the states themselves without federal earmarking. Critics charged, however, that such an arrangement might jeopardize certain social programs. Recent cutbacks at all levels have forced policymakers to reappraise existing funding guidelines.   WAYLAND D. GARDNER

Bibliography: Bahl, Roy, *Financing State and Local Government in the 1980's* (1984); Break, G. F., et al., *State and Local Finance* (1984); Gianaris, Nicholas V., *Contemporary Public Finance* (1989); Harrison, Anthony, ed., *The Control of the Public Expenditure* (1989); Holcombe, Randall G., *Public Finance and the Political Process* (1983).

finance, U.S. government: see BUDGET; INCOME, NATIONAL.

finance company

Finance companies make cash loans to consumers and also make loans for purchases of durable goods, which are then security for the loans. In addition, they finance consumer purchases by purchasing installment credit contracts (see INSTALLMENT PLAN) that retailers have negotiated with buyers. Finance companies in the United States hold total assets of approximately $500 billion.

finch

Finch is a general term popularly applied to more than 1,000 species of stout-billed, seed-eating birds that are classified in several different families and subfamilies. Among the weaverbirds, Ploceidae, for instance, are many species called finches (see WEAVER FINCH). The WAXBILLS, Estrildidae, are also a type of finch. Charles Darwin based much of his theory of evolution on birds now known as DARWIN'S FINCHES (Geospizidae). In a more restricted sense, however, finches belong primarily to the subfamily Carduelinae of the great family Fringillidae, which also includes the cardinals, buntings, grosbeaks, towhees, sparrows, and many other birds. Other carduelines, which are not specifically named finch, include the siskins, redpolls, crossbills, and pine grosbeaks.

The purple finch, Carpodacus purpureus, *is a sparrow-sized bird native to North America. The male* (top left) *is purple red, particularly on the head, breast, and rump; the female* (lower left) *is flecked with brown. Similar in size, both the male* (top right) *and the female* (lower right) *gray-crowned rosy finch,* Leucosticte tephrocotis, *have brown-to-black plumage with red or grayish white areas.*

Most finches, regardless of their classification, are primarily seedeaters, with stout bills and a well-developed gizzard. But even the seedeaters usually feed their young, for a few days at least, on more easily digested insects. Exceptions occur among the GOLDFINCHES, redpolls, and some other carduelines. Goldfinches, for instance, delay nesting until new thistledown is available for building their compact, waterproof nests and until the softer, pulpier new seeds of the year are available for feeding their young. Then the young are fed by regurgitation of partially digested seeds.

Many finches are brightly colored with red, yellow, or blue predominating, as in the purple (royal red) finch, goldfinch, and indigo bunting. The painted bunting is an extreme example of bizarre coloration, sporting a breathtaking combination of red, blue, green, and yellow. Most finches are very musical, with songs that vary from the soft twittering of goldfinches and canaries to the spirited warble of the purple finches in flight. Many authorities consider finches the highest and latest development on the avian evolutionary ladder.

GEORGE J. WALLACE

Bibliography: Dunham, T., *The ABC's of Finches* (1986); Koepf, C., *The New Finch Handbook* (1984); Nicolai, J., *A Complete Introduction to Finches* (1987); Vriends, M. M., *The Complete Book of Finches* (1987).

Fine Gael   [fin'-e gayl]

The Fine Gael, or United Ireland party, is one of the two major political parties of Ireland. Before 1935 it was called Cuman na nGaedheal (Society of the Gaels). Formed by those who supported the 1921 treaty creating the Irish Free State, it was the ruling party from 1923 to 1932, when the republican FIANNA FÁIL won power. Since then Fine Gael has formed five coalition governments (1948–51, 1954–57, 1973–77, 1981–82, 1982–87). Traditionally a more moderate party than Fianna Fáil, it draws much of its support from the middle class.

finfoot

The African finfoot, Podica senegalensis, *40 cm (16 in) long, is an aquatic bird that lives in densely wooded tropical streams.*

The finfoots, or sun-grebes, are medium-size, long-bodied birds of the family Heliornithidae. They use their large, lobed toes as paddles when diving and swimming in pursuit of fish and other aquatic life. They inhabit streams in the tropics of South America, Asia, and Africa.   GEORGE J. WALLACE

Finger Lakes

The Finger Lakes are a series of long, narrow glacial lakes in west central New York State. From west to east the lakes are Conesus, Hemlock, Canadice, Honeoye, Canandaigua, Keu-

ka, Seneca, Cayuga, Owasco, Skaneateles, and Otisco. The lakes vary in length from 18 to 64 km (11 to 40 mi) and are up to 6 km (3.7 mi) wide.

Formed by successive continental ice sheets expanding southward along the paths of preexisting stream valleys, the lakes occupy steep, narrow rock troughs. Seneca, which is 174 km^2 (67 mi^2) in area and 188 m (617 ft) deep, is the largest. The Finger Lakes add much to the natural beauty of a region in which resorts and state parks attract many vacationers. Fruits and vegetables are produced there, including the grapes that make the region the center of New York State's wine industry.

fingerprinting

Fingerprinting is the science of using the friction ridge patterns on the fingertips for identification purposes and is one of the earliest forms of scientific evidence to be recognized by courts of law. A person's fingerprints form an indelible, unchangeable signature, and fingerprint records can be used for identification, despite changes in appearance or age.

The present system of fingerprint classification is derived from the system published in 1900 by Sir Edward Henry of Scotland Yard. It is based on the classification of three general patterns—arches, loops, and whorls—which are subdivided into types. This subdivision is extended by ridge counts. Fingerprint cards are filed according to classification type, and the cards can be retrieved by computer networks for comparison with new, unidentified fingerprints.

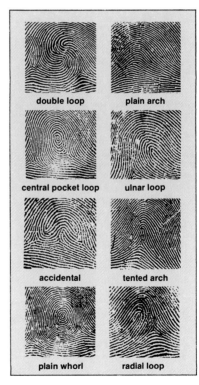

The Henry system, one of several systems devised for classifying fingerprints, is used in most English-speaking countries. It was developed early in the 20th century by an Englishman, Sir Edward Henry, who classified fingerprints according to eight types, based on three fundamental ridge patterns of loops, arches, and whorls. Complete classification requires a knowledge of the type and number of ridges on all ten fingers. The U.S. Federal Bureau of Investigation holds the world's largest collection of fingerprints. Classified and filed by computer, the collection includes the prints not only of criminals, but also of members of the armed forces, federal employees, and others.

One of the most important uses of fingerprints is to prove a suspect's presence at a crime scene. Oil or perspiration on the friction ridges is often transferred to objects handled at a crime scene. These latent prints may be developed by dusting them with fine powder or, if they are on porous material, by treating them with chemicals. Special chemicals are used for various surface materials. A gold-particle solution, for example, can highlight protein residues left by fingers on adhesive tape and some other types of substances. Lasers may also be employed. Laser light augments the natural fluorescence of organic residues, so that photographic time exposures can record faint ridge patterns that may be several years old.

Fingerprint security systems make use of devices called laser locks. Persons seeking access to a secured area must press their fingers against a plate where a laser can compare the prints to those in a file of security-cleared personnel. The medical use of fingerprints is also being explored, since some genetic conditions such as Down's syndrome have long been associated with certain types of print patterns. The technique known as ''genetic fingerprinting'' (see GENETIC ENGINEERING), based on the unique DNA profile of an individual, has nothing to do with fingerprints.   ROBERT F. BORKENSTEIN

Bibliography: Clements, W. W., *The Study of Latent Fingerprints* (1987); Collins, C. G., *Fingerprint Science,* 2d ed. (1989).

Finiguerra, Maso   [fee-nee-gwair'-rah, mah'-zoh]

The Florentine goldsmith, designer, and engraver Maso Finiguerra, 1426–64, was one of the first Italian printmakers and a master of *niello,* a technique of decorating incised silver with a black metallic compound. Finiguerra was highly regarded by Giorgio VASARI and Benvenuto CELLINI, but few works can be attributed to him with certainty. He is thought to have assisted Lorenzo GHIBERTI in the creation of the east door of the Baptistery in Florence, and he later associated himself with Antonio Pollaiuolo (see POLLAIUOLO family), whose paintings he may have reproduced in a series of copper-plate engravings made between 1459 and 1464.

Bibliography: Levenson, J. A., et al., *Early Italian Engravings for the National Gallery of Washington* (1973); Phillips, J. G., *Early Florentine Engravers* (1955).

Finisterre, Cape   [fin-is-tair']

Cape Finisterre, a promontory on the Atlantic Ocean, is the westernmost point in Spain. The British won important naval battles against the French off its shores during the War of the Austrian Succession (1747) and the Napoleonic Wars (1805).

Fink, Mike

Mike Fink, c.1770–1823, an American frontier hero, was a keelboatman on the Ohio and Mississippi rivers whose physical prowess became legendary in oral and written folklore. A formidable brawler dubbed ''king of the keelboatmen,'' he was also known for his skill in telling tall tales.

Bibliography: Blair, Walter, and Meine, Franklin J., eds., *Half Horse, Half Alligator: The Growth of the Mike Fink Legend* (1956; repr. 1981).

Finland

Finland (Finnish: Suomi) is the fifth largest country in Europe, excluding the USSR. Its population center is farther north than that of any other country except Iceland; its capital, Helsinki, is, after Reykjavik, Iceland, the world's northernmost capital city. About one-third of the country lies north of the Arctic Circle. Finland is bordered on the north by Norway, on the east by the USSR, on the south by the Gulf of Finland, and on the west by the Gulf of Bothnia and Sweden. The country is one of the leading manufacturers and exporters of timber and paper products in the world, and its economy depends heavily on the forestry industry.

LAND AND RESOURCES

Most of Finland is lowland. One-third of its area lies below 100 m (330 ft), two-thirds below 200 m (660 ft), and almost nine-tenths below 300 m (985 ft). The highest elevations are in the extreme northwest where Haltia (Lapp: Haldetšokka), the highest point on Finland, rises to 1,328 m (4,357 ft). An ancient granite bedrock shield underlies Finland and is crossed by numerous major fracture lines that appear as gorges, long, narrow lakes, or elongated bays at the coast.

Physical Regions. Finland has three main physical regions: the coastal lowlands, the lake district, and the northern uplands. The coastal lowlands, about 65–130 km (40–80 mi) wide, extend along the indented coastlines of the Gulf of Finland on the south and the Gulf of Bothnia on the west. Thousands of rocky islands lie off the coasts, the principal group being the Åland (Finnish: Ahvenanmaa) Islands. The lake district is the interior plateau of southern central Finland. This

REPUBLIC OF FINLAND

LAND. Area: 338,145 km^2 (130,558 mi^2). Capital and largest city: Helsinki (1989 pop., 485,800).

PEOPLE. Population (1988 est.): 4,954,359. Density (1988 est.): 14.65 persons per km^2 (38 per mi^2). Distribution (1989 est.): 62% urban, 38% rural. Annual growth (1980–87): 0.5%. Official languages: Finnish, Swedish. Major religion: Evangelical Lutheranism.

EDUCATION AND HEALTH. Literacy (1989): 99% of adult population. Universities (1989): 10. Hospital beds (1988): 66,616. Physicians (1988): 9,614. Life expectancy (1987): women—78.7; men—70.7. Infant mortality (1987): 6.2 per 1,000 live births.

ECONOMY. GNP (1988): $92 billion; $18,610 per capita. Labor distribution (1990): agriculture and forestry—10%; industry and construction—30%; services—60%; unemployed (1988 average)—4.6%. Foreign trade (1990): imports—$33.0 billion; exports—$31.1 billion; principal trade partners—Sweden, Germany, USSR, United Kingdom. Currency: 1 markaa = 100 pennia.

GOVERNMENT. Type: republic. Legislature: Eduskunta. Political subdivisions: 12 provinces.

COMMUNICATIONS. Railroads (1989): 5,863 km (3,643 mi) total. Roads (1990): 45,696 km (28,394 mi) paved; 30,675 km (19,060.5 mi) unpaved. Major ports: 12. Major airfields: 20.

lake-studded region is heavily forested and has numerous swamps and bogs. Many lakes are connected by short rivers. The northern upland, much of which lies north of the Arctic Circle, has poor soils and is the most sparsely populated region of Finland. In the far north, arctic forests and swamps give way to tundra—a frozen, forestless region.

Soils. The most common soil is till—an unstratified mixture of clay, sand, and gravel—which covers the bedrock almost everywhere. Large areas of clay are found in south and southwest Finland. Peat covers more than 30% of the land area. The soil is usually 3–4 m (10–13 ft) thick but in some places is as thick as 110 m (360 ft). Clay is best suited for agriculture, till and rocky soil for forestry.

Climate. Finland's climate exhibits both maritime and continental influences. Surrounding seas cool the climate on the coast in spring but warm it in fall. The climate becomes more continental, that is, more extreme, toward the east and north. The extreme north, however, exhibits a marine climate because of the influence of the Arctic Ocean. Rainfall decreases from 700 mm (28 in) in southern Finland to 400 mm (16 in) in northern Finland. The heaviest rainfall is from August to September, the lightest from February to April. The summer lasts 2 to 4 months, the growing season 4 to 6.

Drainage. Finland is known as a land of lakes and islands. The 60,000-odd lakes average 7 m (23 ft) deep and usually have indented shorelines and islands. They are connected by rivers and canals to form long lake-systems. Finland's largest lake, Saimaa, is actually a system of more than 100 interconnected smaller lakes. Finland's rivers are short and shallow, the longest being located in the north.

The coast of Finland is more than 1,100 km (700 mi) long, but because it is heavily indented, the shoreline measures nearly 5,000 km (3,000 mi). Finland has about 30,000 coastal islands, of which the southwest archipelago is unusual for its natural beauty.

Vegetation and Animal Life. Finland is situated entirely within the northern zone of coniferous forests. Forests cover about 65% of the total area. Pines constitute 45% of the forests, spruces 37%, and birches 15%. Southern deciduous trees such as oaks, lindens, elms, and ashes, appear in the southwest. Flora includes 1,227 different species of herbaceous plants and shrubs, 800 species of moss, and more than 1,000 species of lichen. Among the fauna are 67 species of mammals, including bear, elk (moose), and wolf; 370 species of birds; and 77 species of fish, 33 of which are economically valuable.

Resources. Forests are Finland's most important natural resource, and forest products are a major source of national income. The underlying bedrock contains a diversity of minor mineral deposits, including copper, nickel, iron, zinc, chromium, lead, and iron pyrites. In addition, limestone and granite are quarried for building materials. The small mineral de-

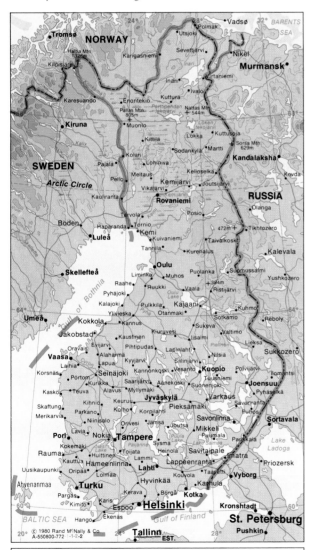

FINLAND

	Meters	Feet			
—— Railroad	2000	6562		Meters	Feet
+ Spot Elevation	1000	3281		0	0
Scale 1:8,634,000	500	1640		200	656
0 50 100 150 km	200	656		2000	6562
0 50 100 mi	0	0			

Helsinki, the nation's capital and largest city, is located on the Gulf of Finland. A major seaport, Helsinki receives almost half of the nation's imports. During the 9-month winter, icebreakers are necessary to keep the harbor open to navigation.

posits make mining uneconomical, although a large mine in eastern Finland produces quantities of copper and zinc. The country has abundant water supplies, but water must often be transported over long distances to the population centers.

PEOPLE

Racially the Finns are mixed, most being either of East Baltic stock (living mainly in eastern Finland) or of Nordic stock (in the west and south, especially on the coast and in Ahvenanmaa). A small number of Lapps live in northern Finland (see LAPLAND). Other ethnic groups include about 2,800 Russian speakers, 2,500 English speakers, 2,200 German speakers, 5,500 Gypsies, and 1,000 Jews.

The Finnish language belongs to the Finno-Ugric family of the URAL-ALTAIC LANGUAGES; it is related to Estonian and Hungarian. At least seven main dialects can be distinguished, each of which has numerous local accents. Finnish is spoken by 93.6% of the population, Swedish by 6%. Most of the Swedish-speaking people live in the southern coastal area, Ahvenanmaa, and on the coast of Ostrobothnia. About 1,726 persons speak Lapp, which is also of Finno-Ugric origin. Finnish and Swedish are both official languages.

The constitution of Finland allows freedom of worship. Members of the Evangelical Lutheran church constitute 88.4% of the population; the Orthodox church, 1.1%; the Roman Catholic church, 0.1%; other denominations, 0.8%; and those with no church affiliation, 9.6%. The Lutheran and Orthodox churches are recognized as official state churches.

Demography. Although Finland is about ten times the size of the Netherlands, its population is only about one-third as large. The southern, industrialized third of the country is the most densely populated, with 46.8 persons per km^2 (121.2 per mi^2); the northern two-thirds of the country averages 9.1 inhabitants per km^2 (23.6 per mi^2).

Scattered settlements are characteristic of the countryside. Rapid urbanization began after World War II, when 425,000 refugees from Soviet-occupied land were resettled, mostly in the cities. The largest cities are HELSINKI, TAMPERE, TURKU and Lahti in the south, and Oulu in the north.

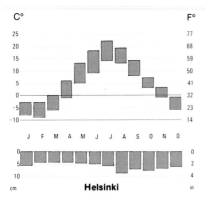

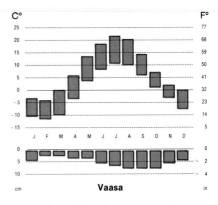

Annual climate charts of two cities in Finland illustrate the distinct climate zones in that country. Bars indicate the monthly ranges of temperatures (red) and precipitation (blue). Helsinki, at the southern extreme of Finland, has a subcontinental humid climate. Vaasa, a port city on the Gulf of Bothnia, has a subarctic climate. Although one-third of Finland lies north of the Arctic Circle, its climate is tempered by the warming influences of the North Atlantic current and the Baltic Sea.

Education and Health. The first stage in education is a compulsory 9-year comprehensive school. The second stage comprises a 3-year senior secondary school or a vocational school. Graduates of senior secondary schools must take a matriculation examination. Those who pass it can apply to universities, technical schools, or other institutions of higher education.

The standard of national health care is high in Finland. The National Health Act of 1972 abolished physicians' fees and provided for the creation of municipal health-care centers throughout the country. Individual licensed physicians also exist. The number of hospital beds in relation to population is one of the highest in the world.

The Arts. The oldest FINNISH LITERATURE is in the form of epic poetry, legends, stories, and proverbs. Elias Lönnrot (1802–84) collected folk literature and published the KALEVALA, the Finnish national epic. Important writers include Aleksis Kivi (1834–72), Minna CANTH, Frans Emil SILLANPÄÄ, Mika WALTARI, and Väinö Linna. Eiono Leino (1879–1926) is perhaps the best-known poet; Edith Södergran (1892–1923) was a pioneer of the modernist movement in Scandinavia. Important contemporary poets include Paavo Haavikko, Eeva-Liisa Manner, and Pentti Saarikoski.

The best-known Finnish composer outside Finland is Jean SIBELIUS. Others include Fredrik Pacius (1809–91), Oskar Merikanto (1868–1924), Aarre Merikanto (1893–1958), Leevi Madetoja (1887–1947), and Uuno Klami (1900–61). Aulis Sallinen and Joonas Kokkonen are major contemporary composers. The Kaustinen Folk Festival draws large crowds every summer. (See also SCANDINAVIAN MUSIC.)

The high standard of imaginative Finnish architecture can be seen even in old church buildings. Eero SAARINEN, Eliel SAA-

RINEN, Wivi Lönn (1872–1966), and Lars Sonck (1870–1956) were pioneers of the national romantic style. Neoclassicism was introduced by J. S. Sirén (1889–1961), and functionalism by Alvar AALTO. Aalto is also well known as an urban planner, interior designer, and industrial and furniture designer. Raimo and Raili Pietilä are contemporary architects well known for their unconventional, expressionistic style.

Albert Edelfelt (1854–1905) and Akseli Gallen-Kallela (1865–1931) are representatives of the golden era of Finnish painting; their ideas were derived from history and the *Kalevala*. Helene Schjerbeck (1862–1946) was a leader in the break with realism; Hugo Simberg (1873–1917) was one of the first symbolic painters; Tvko Sallinen (1879–1955) was a well-known expressionist; and Vilho Lampi (1898–1936) represented primitivism.

ECONOMIC ACTIVITY

Finland's most important industry has traditionally been wood processing, including production of pulp and paper. The metal and engineering industries have developed rapidly and today are the largest source of industrial employment. The chemical, graphics, and food industries are also significant to the economy, followed by textile and electrochemical enterprises. Mining activity has decreased in importance, although Finland still produces one-half of the copper and nickel needed for the domestic market.

Power. Largely because Finnish industry, particularly the forest industry, is energy intensive, Finland's energy consumption is one of the highest per capita in the world. Of this energy 44% is supplied by imported oil and coal and 11% by imports of natural gas and electricity. Four nuclear power plants furnish another 16%; 11% is supplied by hydropower, 3% by peat, and 15% by other indigenous fuels.

Agriculture. In 1960, 30% of Finland's work force was engaged in farming; by 1990 the figure was less than 10%, and only 7% of the total land area was cultivated. Nevertheless, the agricultural sector produces a surplus of dairy products, meat, and eggs. Wheat and rye are the most important bread grains; other major crops include hay, potatoes, oats, and barley. Finland's climate and small farms favor dairy and livestock production, which accounts for most of the farm income. The problems created by overproduction have led to soil banking (a policy of purposely leaving farmland uncultivated) and reforestation.

Forestry. Forests cover about 65% of the total land area, or about 26.4 million ha (65.2 million acres), of which 20 million ha (49.4 million acres) are productive. Since the 1950s large-scale swamp drainage, fertilizing, and reforestation have improved production. The state owns 20% of the forests; the rest are privately controlled. Owners of small farms work in the forests during winter, but mechanization has reduced the need for this seasonal work force.

Transportation. Roads are the leading means of transportation in Finland. Automobiles number about 360 per 1,000 inhabitants. Railways connect the country with Sweden and the USSR, and Helsinki has a subway system. In the past, waterborne traffic was hampered by ice during the winter, but the use of icebreakers has eased this problem.

Trade. Finland is dependent on foreign trade. Although exports are diverse, forest products and metal and engineering

Finlandia House, or Finlandia Hall (1962–75), Helsinki's principal concert and convention center, was one of the later works of the internationally renowned Finnish architect Alvar Aalto.

(Above) *Finland's thousands of lakes and extensive coniferous forests are dominant features of the country's natural landscape and contribute greatly to its scenic beauty. The lakes, rivers, and streams are used to generate hydroelectric power. The forests, too, are an important economic resource, the production of lumber and other wood products being a traditional mainstay of the Finnish economy. (Right) After harvesting, the timber is floated along a network of inland waterways to the mills, where it is processed. Although the forest industry employs a declining number of Finnish workers, the paper and paper products derived from it still constitute the most important single item in the manufacturing sector, measured by the gross value of output.*

products account for more than three-fourths of the total value of exported goods. Raw materials represent nearly half of the total value of imports; next in importance are consumer goods and investment goods; fuels and crude oil make up the remainder. Finland is an associated member of the European Free Trade Association (EFTA), but most of its trade is with the nations of the European Economic Community (EEC).

GOVERNMENT

The Finnish constitution was adopted in 1919. Finland is a republic, headed by a president elected for a 6-year term. The president is normally chosen by the general electorate (all citizens over 18), but if no candidate receives a majority vote, the winner is picked by a 301-member electoral college. Supreme executive power is vested in the president, who is responsible for the country's foreign relations. Legislative power

is shared by the president and the one-chamber parliament of 200 members. The council of state (cabinet), which is headed by a prime minister, is responsible for the country's general administration. Judicial power is vested in independent courts of justice. The country is divided into 12 provinces, which are subdivided into municipalities. The unit of local government is the commune.

HISTORY

The first settlements in Finland were probably made by people moving east after the Ice Age and date back to about 7000 BC. It is believed that the Finns are descendants of these original settlers and others who migrated into the area in the following millennia. Beginning in the 12th century, Sweden gradually conquered Finland and introduced Christianity to the Finns. The Pähkinansäari peace treaty in 1323 established the bound-

Olavinlinna (Saint Olav's Castle) is a fortress built in 1475 by the Swedes to guard their eastern frontier in Finland. Situated on a rocky island in Pihlaja Lake, part of the Lake Saimaa system, today the castle is surrounded by the popular resort town of Savonlinna.

ary between Sweden and Novgorod, the Russian power to the east. In the 16th century, as Sweden consolidated its authority in Finland, Lutheranism was proclaimed the official religion. The peace treaty of Stolbovo (1617) gave Sweden the eastern parts of Finland and Inkerinmaa (Ingria). These, however, were lost to Russia in the Uudenkaupunki peace treaty (Treaty of Nystad) in 1721. During the 18th century a growing separatist movement in Finland demanded independence.

As a result of the war of 1808–09, Sweden surrendered Finland to Russia. Finland became an autonomous grand duchy with the tsar assuming the title grand duke of Finland. The Russian governor-general represented the supreme executive power, and Finland was allowed to retain its old constitution. It had its own parliament, government, administration, law and

The Lapps, a seminomadic people who inhabit northern Finland and much of subarctic Scandinavia, have traditionally herded the reindeer that inhabit the region. The Lapps' way of life is changing as many Lapps adopt modern, more sedentary herding methods.

courts, postal services, army (until 1904), and currency. In 1906 the Finnish diet was replaced by the unicameral parliament, and simultaneously universal suffrage was adopted.

At times, strong attempts were made to Russianize Finland, provoking a growing desire for complete independence. After the Russian Revolution of November (N.S.) 1917, Finland declared its independence on Dec. 6, 1917. Civil war broke out in 1918, with Soviet-supported Communist troops fighting German-supported non-Communists, the latter led by Carl Gustaf Emil MANNERHEIM. In 1920 peace was concluded with the USSR following a territorial war over KARELIA, but relations between the two countries remained cool. By the outbreak of World War II, Finland had adopted a policy of neutrality, and when the USSR demanded Finnish territory and military bases for defense against Germany, Finland refused. On Nov. 30, 1939, Soviet troops invaded Finland, beginning the RUSSO-FINNISH WAR. In March 1940, by the Treaty of Moscow, Finland ceded Karelian territories to the USSR. When Germany invaded the USSR in 1941, Finland reoccupied its former territories. In 1944, however, Soviet troops staged a counterinvasion, and by the armistice signed in September 1944, Finland was forced to cede the Karelian Isthmus and other eastern lands, including the corridor in the extreme north to the Barents Sea, and to grant a 50-year lease to a military base at Porkkala. The USSR returned the military base in 1955 in exchange for the renewal of a friendship treaty signed in 1948. Since World War II, Finland has maintained a careful neutrality, often with special regard to the USSR, its powerful neighbor to the east. Finland's policy of neutrality was largely formulated by Urho Kaleva KEKKONEN, who served as president from 1956 until 1982. The breakup of the USSR in 1991 freed Finland from the threat of Soviet influence in its affairs; it also brought hard economic times, however, the Soviet Union having been one of the country's chief export markets. In March 1992, Finland, following the example of Sweden, applied for membership in the European Community, offering to abandon its neutral status in exchange for admission.

TOIVE AARTOLAHTI
Reviewed by RITVA POOM

Bibliography: Engman, Max, and Kirby, David, eds., *Finland: People, Nation State* (1989); Kirby, D. G., *Finland in the 20th Century* (1980); Pentikainen, Juha, *Kalevala Mythology*, trans. by R. Poom (1990); Rinehart, Robert, ed., *Finland and the United States* (1993); Singleton, Fred, *A Short History of Finland* (1990).

See also: SCANDINAVIA, HISTORY OF.

Finland, Gulf of

The Gulf of Finland is an arm of the Baltic Sea that extends east-west for some 400 km (250 mi) between Finland and Russia and Estonia. The largest cities on the gulf are Helsinki, the capital of Finland, and Saint Petersburg, the second largest city in Russia. At its eastern end the gulf is connected by the Saimaa Canal to several lakes, the largest of which, Ladoga, is in Russia. The canal is used for shipping cargo.

Finley, Robert

An American Presbyterian clergyman, Robert Finley, b. Princeton, N.J., Feb. 15, 1772, d. Oct. 3, 1817, organized (1816) the AMERICAN COLONIZATION SOCIETY, which raised funds to send free blacks to Africa. After serving as a pastor and as headmaster of a school for boys, he was appointed (1817) president of the University of Georgia. He wrote *Thoughts on the Colonization of Free Blacks* (1816).

Finn mac Cumhail   [fin muh-kool']

In Irish folklore, Finn mac Cumhail is the hero of a group of ballads and tales known as the FENIAN CYCLE, set in about the 3d century AD. The posthumous son of Cumhail, Finn was reared by peasants and entered the service of the seer Finn Eger. Finn mac Cumhail accidentally tasted the salmon of Lynn Feic, which was the source of all wisdom, when he burned his thumb while cooking the salmon and sucked on the thumb to soothe it. Thereafter, Finn was able to obtain wisdom merely by chewing his thumb. The stories deal primarily with the struggle of Finn, his son Oisin, his grandson Oscar, and the Fianna warriors against the Fomors, giants representing the forces of darkness.

Bibliography: Gantz, J., *Early Irish Myths and Sagas* (1982); Gregory, Isabella, *Gods and Fighting Men* (1904; repr. 1970); Matthews, J., *Fionn Mac Cumhail: Champion of Ireland* (1988).

finnan haddie: see COD.

Finnegans Wake

Massive in size, dauntingly obscure, and full of verbal extravagance, James JOYCE's novel *Finnegans Wake* (1939), centering on a Dublin family, proceeds by analogy and parallel to incorporate virtually all history and much of art, psychology, and mythology. For his structure, Joyce relies on Giambattista VICO's cyclical view of history, which posits four ages: the divine, the heroic, the human, and the age of confusion. The novel, accordingly, is divided into four parts, each corresponding to a particular age with its characteristic features and attributes. In this richly experimental work, begun in 1923, Joyce joins the local and the universal through his portrayal of the creative father of the Earwicker family, his quarreling sons, and his renovating wife. MAURICE HARMON

Bibliography: Atherton, J. S., *The Books at the Wake* (1960; rev. ed., 1974); Attridge, D., ed., *The Cambridge Companion to James Joyce* (1990); Glasheen, Adeline, *A Third Census of Finnegans Wake* (1977); Gordon, John, *Finnegans Wake: A Plot Summary* (1987); McHugh, Roland, *The Finnegans Wake Experience* (1981).

Finney, Albert

Albert Finney, b. May 9, 1936, is an English actor. Following early stage triumphs, he made his screen debut in *Saturday Night and Sunday Morning* (1961). Thereafter Finney made only a few films, including *Tom Jones* (1963) and *Charlie Bubbles* (1968), which he also directed. After *Murder on the Orient Express* (1974), he worked exclusively on the stage until he made such films as *Wolfen* (1981), *Shoot the Moon* (1982), *The Dresser* (1983), *Under the Volcano* (1984), and *Miller's Crossing* (1990).

Finney, Charles G.

Charles Grandison Finney, b. Warren, Conn., Aug. 29, 1792, d. Aug. 16, 1875, was an American lawyer, theologian, and revivalist. After practicing law in upstate New York, he experienced a dramatic conversion and became (1824) a Presbyterian minister. His revivals were immensely successful. They featured daring, new methods of evangelism—protracted meetings of nightly gatherings and the "anxious bench," where souls under conviction could pray for salvation. Finney encouraged people to exert themselves in becoming Christians and in overcoming social ills such as slavery. In 1835 he became professor of theology at Oberlin College, where he taught until 1875. He was president of the college from 1851 to 1866. His books include his memoirs (1876) and *Lectures on Revivals of Religion* (1835). MARK A. NOLL

Bibliography: Drummond, L., *The Life and Ministry of Charles Finney* (1985); Hardman, K. J., *Charles Grandison Finney, 1792 to 1875* (1987).

Finnish language: see URAL-ALTAIC LANGUAGES.

Finnish literature

Finland, which did not achieve independence until 1918, had little indigenous literature until the end of the 19th century. Folk poetry, both epic and lyric, existed but had scant influence on literature until the end of the 18th century. In the 19th century, Elias Lönnrot and other scholars collected and compiled the KALEVALA, the Finnish national epic.

The first great Finnish prose writer, Aleksis Kivi (1834–72), was a novelist and playwright who was largely ignored during his lifetime; he died in poverty. Minna CANTH, an energetic fighter for women's rights and social justice, was a contempo-

rary of Juhani Aho (1861–1921), a novelist and short-story writer known for his humorous sketches and lyrical, dreamy descriptions of nature. Joel Lehtonen, Volter Kilpi, and especially Nobel Prize–winner Frans Eemil SILLANPÄÄ dominated naturalistic prose in the first half of the 20th century. Also important are Toivo Pekkanen, who wrote about the plight of industrial workers, and Pentti Haanpää, who portrayed with a bitter but defiant humor the struggle of humans against harsh nature in northern Finland. After World War II, Väinö Linna had great success with a war novel and a fictional trilogy on the struggles of poor farmers that culminated in the Civil War of 1918. More recently, Veijo Meri has described the violence and absurdity of human life, especially during times of war. Mika WALTARI, the Finnish prose writer best known to an international audience, wrote his most successful novels in the 1940s and '50s. From the 1960s, social issues became central to novelists Hannu Salama and Pentti Sorikoski and to such younger writers as Alpo Ruuth and Antti Tuuri.

In poetry, after the mythical evocations of the great Finnish poet Eino Leino (1878–1926), Veikko Antero Koskenniemi often turned to classical themes. Uuno Kailas wrote verse that unveils the self-analysis of a tortured soul, whereas Kaarlo Sarkia sought solace in aestheticism and fantasy. The personal, abrupt, and humorous poetry of Aaro Hellaakoski and the equally humorous, learned, yet folklike verse of P. Mustapää were only appreciated after 1945. The generation of the 1950s, including Paavo Haavikko and Eeva-Liisa Manner, introduced new poetic forms to which their successors, such as Pentti Saarikoski, often added absurd humor, formalist experimentation, and social criticism. JAAKKO A. AHOKAS

Bibliography: Ahokas, J. A., *History of Finnish Literature* (1973); Dauenhauer, R., and Binham, P., eds., *Snow in May: An Anthology of Modern Finnish Writing 1945–1972* (1978); Lomas, H., intro. by, *Territorial Song: New Writing in Finland* (1981).

Finnish-Russian War: see RUSSO-FINNISH WAR.

Finnish spitz

The Finnish spitz, considered the national dog of Finland, was recognized by the American Kennel Club in 1988. Originally similar to the larger laika-type sled dogs from which it was derived, the Finnish spitz reaches 49.5 cm (19.5 in) in height at the shoulders and about 16 kg (35 lb) in weight. The head is foxlike with a tapered muzzle and erect ears. The double coat, generally in shades of reddish gold, is long and stands out from the body on the back, especially across the shoulders. Finnish spitzes are used in Finland for hunting upland game birds, which they seek out and point by barking.

Finno-Ugric languages: see URAL-ALTAIC LANGUAGES.

Fiorelli, Giuseppe [fee-oh-rel'-lee]

Giuseppe Fiorelli, b. June 8, 1823, d. Jan. 28, 1895, was an Italian archaeologist best known for his excavations of POMPEII, starting in 1860. Unlike his predecessors working there, Fiorelli was not simply interested in locating treasure but began a systematic approach aimed at uncovering the social and economic aspects of the ancient city. He helped pioneer the use of archaeological STRATIGRAPHY and invented the technique of making plaster casts of human bodies and houses from the impressions they left in the ash. At the training school he founded at Pompeii, he taught his rigorous archaeological methods to students of all nationalities. He is the author of *Descrizione di Pompei* (Descriptions of Pompeii, 1875).

fir

Firs are cone-bearing evergreen trees belonging to the pine family, Pinaceae. There are about 40 species of true firs, *Abies;* all are native to the Northern Hemisphere. They grow in cool regions extending southward into the mountains of Guatemala, northern Africa, the Himalayas, and Taiwan.

The fir, genus Abies, is a handsome north temperate evergreen tree grown for its wood and used in landscaping. Two species of fir are the grand fir (left), A grandis, which grows to a height of 90 m (300 ft), and the white fir (right), A. concolor. Firs bear upright cones (center) and needles that are aromatic when crushed.

Fir trees usually have bark with resinous blisters that produce furrows. Needles are usually flattened or sometimes four-angled, pointed or notched, and often arranged in two rows; they live for 7 to 10 years. Cones, which are egg-shaped or cylindrical, usually occur on topmost branches and mature in one season. The genus *Abies* is easily distinguishable from other CONIFERS by disklike leaf scars and erect cones that break up as soon as the seeds are ripe.

The wood of fir is soft and easily worked. Because it is odorless, it is in demand for butter, lard, and grocery boxes. After treatment with a preservative it is sometimes used for telephone poles and for piles. Oleoresins are extracted from some firs and are known in the trade as Canada balsam, or Strasburg turpentine, and leaf oils.

Some firs have been introduced into the United States as landscape trees. The Spanish fir, *A. pinsapo*, is commonly grown in the Pacific Northwest. Another commonly grown ornamental is *A. nordmanniana*.

Firbank, Ronald   [fur'-bank]

Ronald Firbank, whose full name was Arthur Annesley Ronald Firbank, b. Jan. 17, 1886, d. May 21, 1926, was an English writer whose novels combine witty dialogue and artificially contrived plots. The possessor of a highly individual talent and temperament, Firbank was a convert to Catholicism, a homosexual, and an aesthete; he also traveled widely. Among his novels are *Vainglory* (1915), *Caprice* (1917), *Valmouth* (1919), *Prancing Nigger* (1924), and *Concerning the Eccentricities of Cardinal Pirelli* (1926). Their mixture of fantasy, decadence, wit, Catholic ritual, and mannered style has made Firbank a cult figure of some note.   ROBIN BUSS

Bibliography: Benkowitz, Miriam K., *Ronald Firbank: A Biography* (1969); Brophy, Brigid, *Prancing Novelist* (1973).

Firdawsi   [fur-dow'-see]

Firdawsi, *c.*935–*c.*1020, whose original name was Abolqasem Mansur, is considered one of the greatest Persian poets; he is the author of the Iranian national epic, the SHAH NAMAH (Book of Kings). Little is known about his life except that he lived and died in the eastern Iranian province of Khorasan. Most of what is written about him appears to be legend.

The *Shah Namah*, nearly 60,000 couplets long, traces the fortunes of Persia dynasty by dynasty, from the creation of man to the Arab conquest (*c.*637–51). It was based on earlier chronicles by other poets and legends passed down to Firdawsi. He began the work during the Samanid dynasty, worked on it continuously for 35 years, and completed it in 1010, after the conquest of Khorasan by Mahmud of Ghazni, to whom the poem is dedicated. The work had a profound effect on later Persian literature and provided favorite themes for later Persian painters.   JEROME W. CLINTON

Bibliography: Arberry, Arthur John, *Classical Persian Literature* (1958); Ferdowsi, *The Epic of the Kings*, trans. by Reuben Levy (1967).

fire

The development of methods and tools for controlling and using fire was critical in human evolution and is believed to have allowed early humans to spread northward from the warm climates of their origins into the more severe environments of Europe and Asia. The evidence for early fire use is

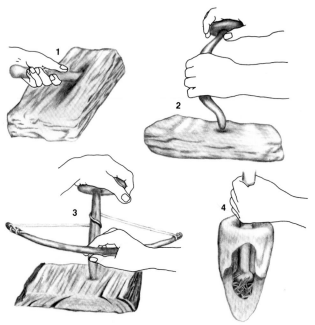

Primitive methods of igniting wood chips enabled Neolithic man to produce at will the essential tool of fire. The fire plow (1), used today among some peoples in Polynesia and parts of Africa, ignites tinder by friction generated when a wood cylinder is rubbed in a groove. The fire drill (2) and the bow drill (3) both generate heat when a stick is revolved rapidly in a wood socket. The fire piston (4), found in Indonesia, uses the heat of quickly compressed air to ignite tinder placed within a wood or bamboo tube.

often ambiguous because of the difficulty in determining whether the archaeological evidence is the result of accidental fire or its deliberate use. Such evidence includes finds of occupation sites with fired or baked soils, bones or stones that have been changed through the application of heat, and areas containing thick layers of ash and charcoal that might have been hearth structures. The earliest finds, in Kenya and Ethiopia, date from about 1.5 million years ago. Less equivocal evidence exists for deliberate fire use in the PALEOLITHIC PERIOD, beginning about 500,000 years ago. NEOLITHIC sites have yielded objects that may have been firemaking tools: drills for producing friction heat in wood and flints for striking sparks from iron pyrites.

With the ability to produce and control fire, early humans could make heat and light, cook foods that were difficult to eat in their raw state, drive game toward killing stands, and keep dangerous animals away from home hearths. With fire, wood could be worked to a strong, sharp point; clay pots could be baked into a stonelike hardness; and land could be cleared for planting (see SLASH-AND-BURN AGRICULTURE).

Eventually, the use of fire brought about the birth of civilizations based on the smelting and forming of metals. The upsurge in the power of technological societies seems to have been controlled, in large part, by the amounts of fuel available for burning: at first wood in the form of CHARCOAL, and, only relatively recently, coal and oil.

In Greek mythology, PROMETHEUS bestowed godlike powers when he stole the gods' fire to give it to humanity. Humans have always worshiped fire for its awesome power in nature and its beneficence when controlled. Fire has played a central role in religion. It has been personified as a god (for example, the Indo-Iranian Agni) and recognized as a symbol of home and family in many cultures. It has also been a symbol of purification and of immortality and renewal; hence, the lighting of flames of remembrance and the myth of the PHOENIX.

See also: COMBUSTION; FLAME.

fire ant: see ANT.

fire engine

Fighting fires in cities requires the use of devices that can carry a source of water to the scene of the fire and direct a stream of water directly into the flames. Huge, water-filled syringes—used, for example, in 1st-century-BC Alexandria—were an ancient form of fire engine. By the time of the Great Fire of London (1666), wooden tubs were wheeled to fires, filled with water by bucket brigades, and emptied by hand-operated pumps. To be effective, the pumps had to operate close to the fire and were often burnt themselves. None could generate enough water to cope with a large fire.

The development of more efficient pumps and of flexible hose improved municipal fire-fighting capabilities, but it was the harnessing of steam power in the 19th century that brought fire fighting into the modern age. The first steam-powered fire engine was built in London in 1829. Its pump, rated at 10 hp, could throw a stream of water some 27 m (88.6 ft). Paul Rapsey Hodge, an English engineer, built America's first steam fire engine in 1840. Although it was self-propelled, it often broke down.

Most early steam fire engines used steam only for powering the water pumps; propulsion was still supplied by horses. The steam-engine *Joe Ross*, built in Cincinnati in the 1850s, rode on two rear wheels and was steered by a single front wheel. It weighed 9 metric tons (10 U.S. tons), and was driven by a team of four horses. By the turn of the century internal-combustion engines had begun to replace horsepower. Early motorized pumpers used two engines, one to propel the machine, the other to drive the pump. The first pumper with a single engine that did both jobs was manufactured in the early 1900s by the Waterous Fire Engine Works of Saint Paul, Minn.

Ladders on fire engines were introduced in the 18th century. At first they were used only to help people escape from the

The earliest fire-fighting devices included the hand-held syringe (left), used since ancient times, and the two-man tub pump (right), developed in Europe during the 17th century. Although maneuverable, these devices had an extremely short range, which limited their effectiveness.

The first steam-pumped fire engine (left) was invented (1829) by George Braithwaite of London. A logical development of the steam engine used to pump water from mines, the steam fire engine was, however, slow to gain acceptance by traditional fire companies. Paul R. Hodge's "Exterminator" (right), the first self-propelled steam fire engine, was introduced in New York in 1841. Weighing eight tons, this inefficient vehicle often broke down and was driven only for a period of a few months before being discontinued.

(Above) *By the late 19th century, manufacturers began to produce relatively lightweight, efficient steam pumps. Horse-drawn steam engines, such as this double vertical piston engine, were widely used until the advent of the internal-combustion engine.*

The self-propelled steam fire engine, developed during the late 19th century, was used primarily for large fires in urban areas, where its relatively high pumping capacity was needed. Called the "Fire King," this engine was built in 1899 by the firm of Merryweather and Sons.

upper floors of burning buildings: they were not used as adjuncts in fire fighting until many years later. In about 1832 sectional ladders that could be joined together to make one long ladder were developed in London. In 1837 the first portable fire-escape ladder was invented. It was mounted on wheels and could reach a height of about 20 m (65.6 ft). The first successful aerial ladder truck was invented in 1868 by Daniel Hayes, a San Francisco fireman. Its ladders were self-contained, readily extendable, and could be directed at almost any angle toward a burning building, something that was not possible with the older types of ladders.

Modern aerial ladders are operated hydraulically. The average fire ladder can reach a height of 30 m (100 ft), although a few can extend as far as about 50 m (164 ft). They are usually mounted on turntablelike disks, allowing great flexibility in fire-fighting and rescue operations. Hoses are often run up the ladder to nozzles mounted at the top so that fire fighters can more accurately direct streams of water.

Today's fire fighters often use elevating platforms and aerial towers. These devices are of two principal designs. With one type, the platform is mounted on a jointed boom that travels in an arc—much the same as the "cherry pickers" used by utility companies. With the other, the platform is mounted on an extendable or telescopic boom similar to an aerial ladder.

NATIONAL FIRE PROTECTION ASSOCIATION

Bibliography: McCall, W. P., ed., *American Fire Engines Since 1900* (1976); Mahoney, G., *Introduction to Fire Apparatus and Equipment*, 2d ed. (1985).

See also: FIRE PREVENTION AND CONTROL.

fire extinguisher

Portable fire extinguishers are devices used to extinguish fires in their early stages. A fire extinguisher consists of a container, an extinguishing agent, a pressure-producing device, and a mechanism, such as a hose and a nozzle, for discharging the contents.

An early type of extinguisher was the "squirt," a pumplike device consisting of a cylinder and a plunger for discharging water. "Fire annihilators" were large containers of water or other liquids that were designed to burst when thrown on a burning object.

The first modern portable extinguisher consisted of a metal cylinder filled with a solution of sodium bicarbonate and water beneath a container of sulfuric acid. When the extinguisher was inverted, the acid mixed with the solution to form carbon dioxide gas, which expelled the liquid through a small, hand-held hose. These soda-acid extinguishers have gradually been replaced—beginning about 1960—by a multipurpose, dry-chemical extinguisher that is effective on a wide range of fires.

To designate the suitability of fire extinguishers for particular fires, fires are classified according to the material that is on fire. Class A fires involve ordinary combustibles such as paper, wood, and cloth; Class B fires cover flammable and combustible liquids, greases, and similar materials; Class C fires are those involving electrical equipment; and Class D fires are limited to combustible metals such as magnesium.

Class A fires are extinguished by the heat-absorbing effect of water or of water-based liquids or by smothering the fires with certain dry chemicals.

Class B fires can be extinguished by excluding air, by inhibiting the release of combustible vapors, or by interrupting the combustion chain reaction. Class B extinguishers usually employ dry chemicals, carbon dioxide, foam, or liquefied gas (also known as halon).

Class C fires must be extinguished with an agent that is electrically nonconducting, in order to avoid shock hazard to the user. Dry chemical, carbon dioxide, and halon extinguishers are used.

Class D fires require a smothering and heat-absorbing extinguishing agent that does not react with the burning metal.

NATIONAL FIRE PROTECTION ASSOCIATION

Bibliography: Colburn, Robert E., *Fire Protection and Suppression*, ed. by Carlton Williams (1975); Haessler, Walter M., *The Extinguishment of Fire*, rev. ed. (1974); National Fire Protection Association, *Portable Fire Extinguishers* (1984).

See also: FIRE PREVENTION AND CONTROL.

fire fighting: see FIRE PREVENTION AND CONTROL.

fire insurance

Fire insurance is insurance against loss from fire, lightning, and removal of property from premises endangered by those perils. It belongs within the large category of property/casualty insurance, which, along with life and health insurance, forms the major portion of the INSURANCE industry. Generally, fire insurers agree to pay the cost of replacing lost property, less deductions for depreciation. Separate agreements may be drawn up to cover other losses, such as the loss of rent to a landlord or the loss of business revenue as the result of fire. Many fire insurance policies also provide extended coverage, which may include damage caused by windstorm and hail, explosion, riot, automobiles, and aircraft. Comprehensive, or multiple-peril, homeowners policies often cover for losses from theft and vandalism; most also include liability coverage, which will pay for certain damages suffered by others from accidents that occur on the property of the insured.

The costs of fire insurance depend on the likelihood of loss. In determining premiums, insurance underwriters consider a number of factors, such as the location of the building and its construction, the presence or absence of smoke detectors and other alarms, the kind of business conducted or the type of occupancy, and the proximity of fire hydrants.

Fire Next Time, The

With his two-part essay *The Fire Next Time* (1963), a passionate and probing examination of the black American experience, James BALDWIN won even higher acclaim than he had as a novelist. In the essay, Baldwin articulates the idea that "black has become a beautiful color because it is feared." Reflecting a common theme in black American literature—the invisibility of the black man—the author also argues that it is necessary for blacks to make whites aware of their reality.

CHARLOTTE D. SOLOMON

Bibliography: Porter, Horace A., *Stealing the Fire* (1988); Standley, F. L., and Burt, N. V., *Critical Essays on James Baldwin* (1988).

fire prevention and control

In the United States more than 2.4 million fires occur each year, causing thousands of deaths—some 6,000 annually—hundreds of thousands of injuries, and billions of dollars in property damage. Despite a dramatic drop in recent years, the U.S. rate of fire-caused deaths is the highest of the industrialized nations. Comparative figures are telling: Chicago, half the size of Hong Kong, suffers triple the number of fire-caused deaths; Baltimore, Md., has 13 times as many deaths by fire as Amsterdam, a city of the same size.

Yearly, about 100,000 U.S. fires are deliberately set. ARSON in the United States, which has the highest rate of deliberate burning in the world, has contributed to the virtual abandonment of whole areas of many cities. The crime of arson causes almost 1,000 deaths yearly, and contributes over $1.5 billion

Large fires often produce billows of smoke, fumes, and flame and are extremely difficult and dangerous to extinguish. Despite advances in fire-fighting equipment and techniques, it is estimated that fires claim 6,000 lives annually in the United States alone.

to fire-related damage. Arson may be a factor in every type of fire and is therefore a central concern of insurance companies, police forces, and fire departments.

FIRE DEPARTMENTS

Until the mid-18th century, city dwellers had only the fire watchman and the volunteer bucket brigade to protect them from fires. Benjamin Franklin organized the first permanent fire company in 1736 in Philadelphia; New York City followed suit in 1737. By the late 1800s, however, a series of devastating fires had claimed thousands of lives and destroyed whole sections of many U.S. cities. The principal causes for these conflagrations were poor building construction and shoddy materials, insufficient water supplies, and a fragmented system of fire fighting that created fierce rivalries between volunteer fire departments, which often fought one another rather than the fires they were called to put out.

The waste and tragedy of major city fires hastened the development of modern fire-protection techniques. By 1900, salaried fire departments, steam-propelled fire engines, telegraph fire-alarm systems, and fire hydrants were in use in the largest U.S. cities. Today nearly every community is served by an organized fire department; there are more than 30,000 in the United States. Of the 1 million U.S. fire fighters, some 250,000 are full-time, career professionals. Others are either "call" fire fighters who are paid for each alarm they answer or volunteers who receive no pay. The 23,000 all-volunteer fire departments serve about 25% of the population; the 1,800 all-professional departments protect 44% of the population, primarily in the nation's cities. The remainder mix professional and volunteer staffs. Fire fighting is an extremely hazardous occupation, with over 100 fire-fighter deaths and more than 100,000 injuries every year.

FIRE FIGHTING

Modern fire communications systems range from the pull alarms in street boxes that alert a local department to a fire's location, to voice boxes from which a caller can talk directly with the department, to radio systems between departments.

The basic fire-fighting vehicle is a self-propelled truck, the FIRE ENGINE, adapted for a variety of functions and carrying an extensive assortment of tools and equipment: pumps, hoses, water tanks, ladders, and portable tools and appliances. The type of engine equipment will vary with the intended service. A pumper has a hose, water tanks, and pumps and is used as an auxiliary source of water at a fire. A ladder truck houses the long aerial ladders used for rescue and fire fighting and also carries such special equipment for rescue and salvage operations as breathing apparatuses and tools for forcible entry.

Other fire-fighting equipment that may be brought to the scene of the fire, or fireground, includes portable FIRE EXTINGUISHERS, radio equipment, electric lights and generators, portable pumps, and water-additive equipment to make foam for smothering fires burning in flammable liquids.

PREVENTIVE TECHNOLOGY

Increased scientific knowledge about the nature of fires now permits accurate computer simulation of the progress of a fire in a particular site. Computer simulation can also measure the effectiveness of such preventive devices as smoke detectors, sprinklers, and fire-resistant materials. The period before a fire within a room "flashes over"—that is, grows from a small fire into one where the entire room is ablaze—may be only a few minutes. A simulation can predict whether a single smoke detector, for example, is sufficient to give ample warning, and it can demonstrate the most efficient escape routes.

Well over three-quarters of all U.S. homes now have at least one SMOKE DETECTOR, and local fire ordinances usually require the installation of detectors in all new homes. Heat and fire sensors are additional devices for detecting fire and alerting people to the danger.

The most effective means of controlling fire in large buildings are automatic fire sprinkler systems. Water pipes are positioned behind the ceilings; at intervals, sprinkler heads protrude into the room. Sufficient heat destroys the seals in the sprinklers, releasing a steady stream of water. The newest sprinklers have automatic shutoff valves and may be equipped to transmit fire alarms to local fire departments.

In Yellowstone National Park, a fire fighter shovels dirt to smother flaming underbrush during the great fire of the summer of 1988. Almost 180,000 ha (450,000 acres) were touched by the fire. Half of that area was completely burned in canopy fires that swept through the tops of forest stands, killing everything underneath. For many years, fire-management policy in the park had been to allow fires to burn themselves out, creating a mosaic of partially and totally burned areas where new forests with different tree species would eventually grow and offer new habitats to a variety of plants and animals. A combination of drought and high winds, however, increased the size and ferocity of the 1988 fire to almost unmanageable proportions. When flames threatened homes outside the park, fire fighters were called in. The fires were not completely extinguished until the rains came in November.

Fire Suppressants. Water is still the most commonly used extinguishing agent. It cools the burning material and smothers the fire. For special situations, however, other extinguishing agents are more effective. Fire-fighting foam is used primarily to fight fires involving flammable liquids. Carbon dioxide suppresses fires involving gas, flammable liquids, electrical equipment, and ordinary combustible material such as paper and wood. Halon was a preferred extinguishing agent for fire suppression on airplanes and in installations of electronic equipment, because its dense vapor left little residue. Its use, however, is being phased out because of its destructive effect on the atmosphere's ozone layer.

Fire-Safety Codes and Standards. Major elements of fire-prevention technology are the codes and standards developed to prevent fires. The National Fire Protection Association (NFPA) publishes fire-safety standards for such diverse areas as nuclear plants, high-rise buildings, shipyards, dry-cleaning establishments, and hospitals. NFPA standards are developed by committees of experts from the appropriate fields with the help of engineers specially trained in fire-prevention techniques.

Building Design. Three principal elements determine the degree of fire hazard in a building: its structure, its contents, and the interior finishes. Every element of the structural framework must be planned with fire safety in mind. The interior finishes, such as wood paneling, wallboard, acoustical tile, furniture, and carpeting fabrics must all be evaluated for their flammability characteristics. In many cases, local codes give minimum fire-resistance standards for interior-finish materials; many materials carry flammability information.

A building's contents may also determine the type and severity of a fire. Local fire departments should be made aware of the storage of volatile chemicals or other highly flammable materials, or of products that produce toxic gases when they burn.

FOREST FIRES

The responsibility for forest-fire control is shared by the states and the federal government, whose U.S. Forest Service guards the national forests. Because the majority of U.S. forest fires are believed to begin through human intent or carelessness, the most effective preventive technique is disseminating information on the dangers.

All forest fires begin on the floor of the forest, where the most easily flammable debris—leaves, twigs, and small growth—burns first. Forests may sometimes be cleared of this debris, often by carefully controlled burning. Where the danger of fire seems imminent, as in hot, dry seasons, firebreaks—clear channels that have been emptied of all flamma-ble materials—are bulldozed through.

In heavily forested areas a firewatch system is usually maintained during dry periods. Consisting of a chain of lookout towers often supplemented by small aircraft, the system is linked by radio to a central office that can dispatch fire-fighting crews as soon as a blaze is spotted.

Although fighting a large forest fire requires large crews, heavy equipment, and considerable knowledge of how fire behaves under the rapidly changing conditions within a forest, fire-fighting techniques are basic and simple. In order to stop the fire, it is necessary to remove the fire's fuel—by creating firebreaks, spreading chemicals that decrease the flammability of wood, pumping water, or spreading smothering materials such as dirt or sand.

Under difficult conditions—when the forest is unusually dry and winds are high—even the most well-organized fire-fighting crew may be unable to stop a forest fire. Where communities are built in such areas as the dry hills of southern California, small brush or forest fires may spread to engulf residential areas.   NATIONAL FIRE PROTECTION ASSOCIATION

Bibliography: Hall, G., and Burks, J., *Working Fire* (1985); James, D., *Fire Prevention Handbook* (1986); Nao, T., *Forest Fire Prevention and Control* (1982); O'Hagen, J. T., *High-Rise Fire and Life Safety* (1977); Pyne, S. J., *Fire in America* (1982) and *Fire on the Rim* (1989; repr. 1990); Robertson, J. C., *Introduction to Fire Prevention*, 3d ed. (1989); Roblee, C. L., and McKechnie, A., *The Investigation of Fires*, 2d ed. (1988).

See also: COMBUSTION; FLAME; FLAME RETARDANTS.

fire thorn

Fire thorn, *Pyracantha,* is any of several thorny shrubs belonging to the rose family, Rosaceae. They are native to southern Europe and Asia and are grown in temperate regions as landscape plants. They produce white blooms in early summer and become studded with long-lasting orange red fruits.

firearms

A firearm is a weapon that uses the force of an explosive propellant to project a missile. Firearms, or small arms, are distinguished by caliber (the width of the barrel opening), and comprise weapons up to and including those of .60 caliber (0.6-in/15.24-mm bore), and all gauges of SHOTGUN. (CANNON is the term for those weapons with calibers greater than 0.8 in, or 20 mm. Larger-caliber weapons are usually categorized as ARTILLERY.) Among small arms, the RIFLE and shotgun are both long-barreled weapons used for long-range shooting; the PISTOL has a shorter barrel and is accurate only at relatively short ranges. The REVOLVER, usually a pistol, has a revolving cylinder that allows repeat firing. The MACHINE GUN is an automatic firearm, the first of a line of weapons including assault rifles and submachine guns.

Early Firearms. The precise origin of firearms is unknown, although they were certainly in use by the early 14th century and were fairly common in Europe by mid-century. These early guns were little more than large-caliber tubes of wrought iron or cast bronze, closed at one end and loaded by placing GUNPOWDER and projectile in the muzzle, or open end. They were fired by touching a burning wick, or match, to the powder at a "touch-hole" bored in the top of the barrel. To make certain that the powder would ignite, a recess was incised around the hole into which additional powder—the primer—was poured.

Firing Mechanisms. The first major improvement in small arms was the introduction of a mechanical firing mechanism, or lock, which lowered the match to the touch hole with a pull of the trigger. This matchlock improved accuracy by permitting the gunner to concentrate on aiming the weapon, rather than having to guide the match to the primer. In use by the early 15th century, matchlock guns were the first small arms to have a significant impact on the conduct of warfare. Matchlock mechanisms became increasingly sophisticated over the next two centuries, but all required a smoldering match to ig-

nite the primer. The principle of self-ignition was introduced in the early 16th century with the invention of the wheel-lock, which fired the powder by mechanically generated sparks. Wheel-locks were the weapon of choice for cavalrymen of the time.

The problem of protecting the primer from rain while making it easy to fire was partially solved by the development of the flash pan, a small covered dish that held the primer. The invention of the flintlock improved on the flash-pan design. The flintlock was a spark-generating mechanism in which a flint, actuated by the trigger, struck the metal handle of the pan cover, at the same time pushing the cover back so that the powder was exposed to receive the sparks. The flintlock was the dominant ignition system from the early 1600s. The British "Brown Bess" MUSKET was introduced in the 1690s and remained in service without significant modification until the 1840s.

Rifling. Smoothbore muskets were notorious for their short range and poor accuracy. Seeking to improve performance, gun makers etched spiral grooves, or rifling, inside the musket barrel. The grooving imparted a spin to the projectile, thus stabilizing its trajectory. Rifles became popular with hunters in both Europe and America, but they were impractical for most military uses because they were difficult to load. In 1849 the French army captain Claude Minié invented the conical minié ball, which was easily dropped down the barrel of a ri-

The evolution of military firearms is traced by studying selected historical weapons. The matchlock petronel (A), used during the late 16th century, was fired by touching a lighted match to the priming powder through the operation of the trigger; the curved stock helped absorb the recoil. The wheel-lock, as in this 17th-century English pistol (B), was favored by cavalrymen but was too fragile for use by the infantry. The smoldering match was discarded in favor of a spring-wound wheel that struck a piece of iron pyrite, directing sparks to the priming powder. The Kentucky rifle (C), a long-barreled, muzzle-loading weapon, was developed by the Pennsylvania Dutch and was produced first with flintlock and later with percussion firing mechanisms. The Spencer Model 1860 (D), widely used by Union cavalry during the U.S. Civil War, was the first successful repeating carbine. The first practical revolver, the Colt Patterson percussion pistol (E), was manufactured from 1836 to 1842. The lever-action repeating Winchester Model 73 (F) was the favored multipurpose weapon of settlers in the American West. The Maxim gun (G), developed by Hiram S. Maxim, was adopted by the German army in 1908. Firing 450 rounds per minute, it was the first successful automatic machine gun.

fled musket but expanded to engage the rifling when the weapon was fired. Rifles using expandable bullets had four times the range and accuracy of the smoothbore musket. Their introduction to the battlefield began a new and bloody era of warfare.

Metallic Cartridges. The percussion cap, invented in the early 19th century, provided for more reliability than had earlier ignition mechanisms. A small copper cup containing an explosive charge that ignited when it was struck by a small hammer (later, a firing pin), the percussion cap was soon attached directly to metallic cartridges containing gunpowder, thus joining the ignition system, propellant, and projectile in one easily loaded package (see AMMUNITION).

Because the metallic cartridge achieved a gas-tight seal with the barrel, all of the gases generated by the gunpowder explosion were channeled forward, to propel the cartridge, and none could escape to the rear and into the face of the shooter. Breech-loading using loose powder had been impractical, since the gases escaped back into the action. The invention of the cartridge led to the fabrication of the first practical breech-loading weapons. By the late 1860s the muzzle-loader had become obsolete. Ammunition magazines, which could hold many cartridges, and other quick-loading mechanisms were devised for breech-loaders in the last half of the 19th century, producing repeating rifles capable of rapid, accurate fire even at long range.

Machine Guns. Attempts to automate the loading and firing processes resulted in the development, in the 1860s, of the first machine guns. Successful designs were usually multibarreled, crank-operated weapons, of which the Gatling is the most famous. In 1884, Hiram S. Maxim (see MAXIM family) invented a gun that loaded, fired, and extracted spent cartridges using the energy of the weapon's recoil. The Maxim gun, which fired as long as the trigger was held down and the ammunition lasted, was the first true automatic weapon. Powerful "smokeless powder" propellants used from the 1890s allowed the machine gun to fire repeatedly without fouling the weapon and reinforced a trend toward smaller-caliber bullets.

The automatic machine gun had a devastating effect on the armies of World War I, driving them into trenches and forcing the final abandonment of linear offensive tactics. The military had to devise new tactical and technological systems to overcome the dominance of the machine gun–equipped defender. Part of the solution was to make automatic weapons light enough to be easily carried by one soldier in an attack. A number of man-portable light machine guns were introduced toward the end of World War I. Submachine guns, firing short-range pistol ammunition, were also used to boost the firepower of the attacker.

Assault Rifles. The trend toward lighter machine guns and automatic rifles continued during World War II. The lighter a weapon was made, however, the more difficult it was to control during automatic fire. In 1943 the Germans introduced the first true assault rifle, an automatic weapon that used mid-size cartridges that attained ranges approaching those of standard rifle ammunition but produced considerably less recoil. The Soviet Kalashnikov rifle (AK-47) and the U.S. M-16 are contemporary assault rifles. They are fully and semiautomatic and are capable of accurate rapid fire.

Most of the world's armies have adopted automatic rifles. Current research focuses on decreasing weapon weight through the use of plastic parts, smaller or "caseless" ammunition, and burst-limiting mechanisms that can restrict the number of rounds fired with one pull of the trigger.

DOUGLAS P. SCALARD

Bibliography: Adams, R., *Modern Handguns* (1989); Blair, Claude, ed., *Pollard's History of Firearms* (1983); Campbell, H., *History of Firearms* (1977); Hogg, I. V., ed., *Jane's Infantry Weapons* (1990); Smith, W. H., *Small Arms of the World*, 12th ed. (1983); Warner, Ken, *Gun Digest, 1991*, 45th ed. (1991).

See also: SHOOTING.

fireball: see METEOR AND METEORITE.

firebrick: see REFRACTORY MATERIALS.

firefly

Fireflies, also called lightning bugs, are members of the family Lampyridae, order Coleoptera. These beetles are 0.5 to 2 cm (0.2 to 0.8 in) long. The head is largely hidden by an extension of the thorax. Fireflies are named for the cold light emitted as a mating signal by abdominal glands in many species (see BIOLUMINESCENCE). Each species has a unique signal, and females of some species thereby locate males of other species and eat them. Many species have wingless females. These, along with firefly larvae, are often called glowworms.

The firefly species, P. pennsylvanica, *common to the eastern United States, is a long, slender beetle with luminescent abdominal segments. During evenings in June and July, meadows are transformed with the flashing lights of thousands of fireflies.*

fireplace

A fireplace is an area built to hold an open fire. Inside a house, it is usually built at floor level, with heat-reflective walls of stone, brick, or metal. It connects with a CHIMNEY flue for the exhaust of smoke, and its hearth—the floor of the fireplace—is usually made of firebrick or some other REFRACTORY MATERIAL. In a well-designed fireplace the three walls narrow as they rise toward the chimney, so that much of the fire's heat is deflected out into the room. Domestic fireplaces are usually installed for aesthetic reasons, although today they may also be used to augment the heat supply.

To increase efficiency, fabricated units incorporate features to circulate cool air through a series of heat exchangers and reintroduce the warmed air into the room. The efficiency of such a unit is greatly increased by adding a blower to the system.

EUGENE F. TUTT

Bibliography: Amrhein, J. E., *Residential Fireplace and Chimney Handbook*, 5th ed. (1988); Baden-Powell, C., *Fireplace Design and Construction* (1984).

fireproofing: see FIRE PREVENTION AND CONTROL;
FLAME RETARDANTS.

Firestone, Harvey S.

Harvey Samuel Firestone, b. Columbiana, Ohio, Dec. 20, 1868, d. Feb. 7, 1938, was a leader in the U.S. tire and rubber industry. He first became interested in tires while working as a salesman for his uncle's buggy company. In 1896 he formed a company in Chicago to sell tires. He moved to Akron, Ohio, in 1900 and formed the Firestone Tire & Rubber Company, of which he was president until 1932.

In 1906 Firestone became the principal supplier of tires for the Ford Motor Company and subsequently developed a close friendship with Henry Ford. Firestone introduced detachable rims and, in 1923, the balloon tire. In the 1920s the company established huge rubber plantations in Liberia. By the late 1930s Firestone was supplying a quarter of the tires used in the United States.

Bibliography: Lief, Alfred, *Harvey Firestone* (1951).

fireweed

Fireweed, *Epilobium angustifolium,* is a robust perennial herb in the evening primrose family, Onagraceae. Native to North America and Eurasia, it spreads rapidly by underground runners. Flowers are rosy purple on terminal spikes that appear in midsummer. The alternate simple leaves are 5–15 cm (2–6 in) long. When forests are destroyed by fire, fireweed soon appears, which accounts for its name.   CHARLES L. WILSON

fireworks

Fireworks are devices that use explosive, flammable material to create spectacular displays of light, noise, and smoke. Although they are usually thought of today in connection with celebrations, one of their earliest uses was in warfare, which is a role they still play. Pyrotechnics is the art and technology of making and using fireworks.

The Chinese are often credited with the invention and early development of fireworks. The knowledge spread west, through Arabia to Europe. But as late as the 18th century, fireworks still lacked what is now considered an essential characteristic: color. By the early 19th century potassium chlorate was in use; with the addition of various metallic salts to it, brilliant colors could be produced. Various chemical compounds such as potassium chlorate, potassium nitrate, and potassium perchlorate contain the oxygen necessary for COMBUSTION of the pyrotechnic mixture. The salts of these metals produce the colors indicated: strontium produces a red color; copper produces blue; barium, green; and sodium, yellow. Magnesium and aluminum powder add extra sparkle and flash.

Nearly all types of fireworks have a body that is built up by rolling paper around a form until the desired thickness is reached. The casing must be packed so that the pyrotechnic compound is thoroughly compressed, because any cavity left in the mixture can lead to malfunction at the time of ignition.

Civilian, decorative fireworks include rockets, fountains, and sparklers. Special displays are produced by attaching fireworks to a frame in a particular pattern. Military pyrotechnics are used for various purposes. Illumination devices, which normally have a magnesium mixture for the filler, can illuminate a battlefield for short periods. They can be activated by a trip wire, shot by artillery or mortars, or dropped by parachute. Pyrotechnics launched by a small rifle or rocket are available in several colors for SIGNALING. Artillery simulators, which are actually large, smoke-emitting firecrackers, add realism to training maneuvers, and smoke devices are used to screen a unit's movement from the enemy.

DAVID N. BUCKNER

Bibliography: Lancaster, Ronald, et al., *Fireworks Principles and Practice* (1972).

A Roman candle consists of a sealed cardboard cylinder (1) packed with several layers of fuses, metal salt pellets, and gunpowder. A burning taper is used to light a slow-burning fuse (2), which lies above a salt pellet and a gunpowder charge. When the burning fuse reaches the salt pellet (3), the pellet begins to burn, igniting the gunpowder. The gunpowder charge ejects the flaring pellet as a sparkling ball of color (4) and ignites a fuse below it. The entire cycle is then repeated (5).

1   2   3   4   5

The colors, fiery flashes, and star-burst effects of fireworks displays are produced by using metal salts and metal powders in combination with an explosive. Sodium salts produce a yellow flash; barium, a bright green one; and magnesium, brilliant sparks.

firn

Firn, also called névé, is frozen water at a stage intermediate between snow and glacier ice. After it has fallen, powder snow is transformed by sublimation, evaporation, and melting into granular snow, which, after a year or more, becomes firn. Compaction and deformation due to glacial movement change firn into glacier ice.   ROBERT L. NICHOLS

first aid

First aid is the initial care given to a sick or injured person before more formal medical assistance is applied. The goal is to intervene actively to prevent further damage, to provide life support, and to begin effective treatment of the victim's condition, to minimize injury and prevent death. Those trained in first aid should be able to assess the nature and the extent of an emergency and to determine the best course of action to take until professional medical help arrives.

The need for training in first aid is evident, considering that injury is the fourth leading cause of death. Falls are the most common cause of injury, but motor vehicle accidents are the most lethal, accounting for 22 percent of injury deaths.

First aid begins with a scene survey. Before approaching a victim, a survey of the area is necessary to determine if conditions surrounding the incident may place the victim and the rescuer in danger. Next, the primary survey will determine if lifesaving procedures must be immediately performed to save the victim's life. The primary survey involves checking the ABCs: A: Is the airway opened and the victim's neck stabilized? B: Is the patient breathing? C: Is the victim's blood circulating? Is there a pulse? Or is there active bleeding?

Lifesaving procedures include CARDIOPULMONARY RESUSCITATION (CPR), which may be needed to provide basic life support when a victim has no pulse and is not breathing. The Heimlich maneuver aids choking victims by forcing ejection of obstructing material from the windpipe. The severity of spi-

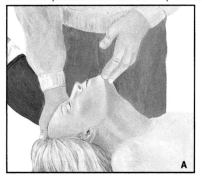
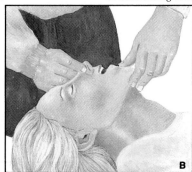
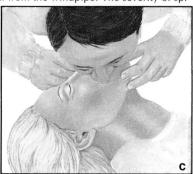

To start CPR, tilt the victim's head back and push the chin up to open the airway (A); check for breathing, and clear any visible obstructions. Pinch the nose shut (B), seal the mouth and give two breaths (C), then look for the rise and fall of the chest to indicate breathing, and check the carotid artery on the neck for a pulse (D). If there is no pulse, find the notch of the breastbone with two fingers and place the heel of the other hand above the notch (E). Put the heel of the first hand on top of the second hand and pump down about 4–5 cm (1.5–2 in) 15 times in 10 to 12 seconds (F). After one minute of CPR check the pulse. If there is no pulse, and the victim has not begun breathing, continue the cycle of two breaths and 15 compressions until the victim starts to breathe or until help arrives.

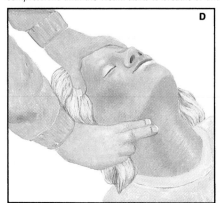

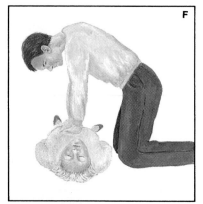

(G) For CPR on a child one to eight years of age, use the heel of one hand to give 80 to 100 compressions per minute. An infant (H) needs only the index and middle fingers for 100 2.5-cm (1-in) deep compressions per minute.

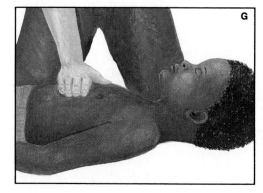
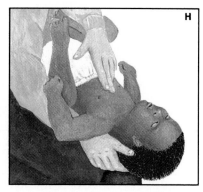

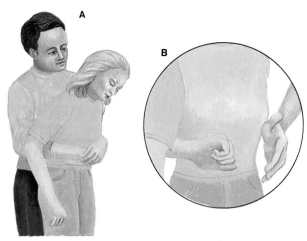

The Heimlich maneuver aids choking victims by forcing ejection of the obstructing material from the windpipe. (A) The person giving first aid should wrap arms about the standing or sitting victim. (B) One fist, thumb down, is grasped by the other hand and pressed into the abdomen just below the rib cage with a quick, strong, upward thrust.

nal cord injuries has decreased 30–45 percent due to awareness that the neck must be stabilized before moving the accident victim. External bleeding is controlled by direct pressure and elevation of the bleeding site.

The secondary survey is a total body examination, a pulse check, respiration count (breaths per minute), and observation of skin conditions. The only outward sign of severe medical problems, such as cardiac disease, stroke, or internal bleeding, may be shock. Those in shock will have pale, cool, and clammy skin, a rapid (over 100 beats per minute) and weak pulse, more than 20 respirations per minute, weakness, and confused behavior. Treatment involves minimizing body heat loss, elevating the legs without disturbing the rest of the body, and getting help as quickly as possible.

First aid for fractures, sprains, and strains includes ice packs, crutches, elevation, and splinting. These first aid measures diminish pain, reduce swelling, and minimize the possibility of further damage. Poisonings account for 3 percent of all injuries. The local poison control center, listed in the phone book, should be consulted for specific first aid measures for the toxic material swallowed or inhaled.

First aid for first-degree and second-degree burns with no open blisters involves flushing the area with cool running water and applying moist dressings, loosely bandaged. For second-degree burns with open blisters and third-degree burns, a dry dressing should be applied and the area bandaged. Blisters should not be popped, nor should greasy creams or ointments be put on the wound. If the burn is due to a chemical, the area should be rinsed with cool water, dry dressed, and a physician consulted.

Seizures are treated by minimizing the possibility of inadvertent injury. Nothing should be placed in a seizing person's mouth. Following the seizure, when the person is relaxed, the airway should be checked to be sure it is open and CPR should be started if pulse and breathing are absent.

Animal and human bites easily become infected and must be carefully cleaned and washed. The possibility of tetanus and rabies must be considered, and a physician should be consulted. Snake bites are best treated in an emergency room. There is some controversy over the best method of field treatment, but most experts now agree that the wound should be gently washed clean, splinted, and kept lower than the heart during transport to the emergency room. Tourniquets, "cutting and sucking," and ice packs are not recommended.

Heatstroke, heat exhaustion, and heat cramps are common on hot days with no breeze. Those particularly susceptible include the very young, the elderly, obese people, and athletes. These heat illnesses are best treated by removing victims from the heat and cooling them rapidly without precipitating shiv-

ering. Heatstroke can be life threatening, and emergency medical help should be called.

Those administering first aid are protected from legal liability for negligence by Good Samaritan Laws in 14 states, as long as they use first aid to the best of their ability and knowledge. In the other states there is an unwritten law to this effect, and the court system has never found anyone guilty of negligence as long as they used good common sense and there was no intent to do harm when they gave first aid. The American Red Cross offers a full spectrum of first aid courses in most communities. All are encouraged to obtain a certificate in a standard first aid course.   DONALD J. GORDON, M.D.

Bibliography: American National Red Cross, *The American Red Cross Standard First Aid* (1988); Auerbach, Paul S., and Geehr, Edward C., *Management of Wilderness and Environmental Emergencies,* 2d ed. (1989).

1st Amendment

The 1st Amendment to the CONSTITUTION OF THE UNITED STATES is the best-known provision of the BILL OF RIGHTS. It prohibits Congress from making any laws that abridge or restrict FREEDOM OF RELIGION, FREEDOM OF SPEECH, FREEDOM OF THE PRESS, or the right to assemble peaceably and to petition the government for redress of grievances. In GITLOW V. NEW YORK (1925)—and in other important cases (*Near v. Minnesota*, 1931; *DeJonge v. Oregon*, 1937; *Cantwell v. Connecticut*, 1940)—the Supreme Court held that the protection of these fundamental liberties applied also to the states under the DUE PROCESS clause of the 14TH AMENDMENT.

Differences and difficulties in interpretation have characterized much of the later history of the 1st Amendment. For example, the amendment prevents Congress from making any law regarding the "establishment of religion," but this clause has been interpreted either as barring the government from giving preferment to any particular religion or as requiring a complete and total separation of CHURCH AND STATE. Moreover, in spite of the apparent absolute prohibition in the amendment's language "Congress shall make no law . . .," Congress has, in fact, many times passed laws "in the public interest" that restrict freedom of speech and press. Among the most famous of these acts are the ALIEN AND SEDITION ACTS (1798), the SMITH ACT (1940), and the McCARRAN ACT (1950). In addition, federal agencies and prosecutors have initiated actions that, where allowed, have resulted in certain limitations on freedom of speech and press.

In ruling on the constitutionality of various restrictions on these CIVIL RIGHTS, the Supreme Court has at various times tended to support either the rights of the individual or the interest of society. Since the early 1950s, however, the Court has also followed a balancing approach whereby the private and public interests are weighed in each case.

Bibliography: Berns, Walter, *The First Amendment and the Future of American Democracy* (1976); Levy, Leonard W., et al., eds., *Encyclopedia of the American Constitution,* 4 vols. (1986); Mickelson, S., and Teran, E. M., eds., *The First Amendment and the Challenge of New Technology* (1989); Rutland, Robert A., *The Birth of the Bill of Rights, 1776–1791*, rev. ed. (1983); Van Alystyne, William, *Interpretations of the First Amendment* (1984).

See also: CENSORSHIP; CIVIL DISOBEDIENCE; DENNIS V. UNITED STATES; MILLER V. CALIFORNIA; NEW YORK TIMES COMPANY V. SULLIVAN; NEW YORK TIMES COMPANY V. UNITED STATES; PORNOGRAPHY; ROTH V. UNITED STATES; SCHENK V. UNITED STATES.

Firth, Sir Raymond

Raymond Firth, b. Mar. 25, 1901, is a distinguished British social anthropologist and professor emeritus of the University of London. A student of Bronislaw Malinowski, he is known for his extensive and detailed ethnographic reporting. His major field studies are of Malay fishermen and the Polynesians of Tikopia, which Firth visited first in 1928–29 and again in an important restudy in 1952. *We the Tikopia* (1936; abr. ed., 1983) is the best known of his many writings on Tikopia society. Other works include *Elements of Social Organization* (1951; 3d ed., 1981) and *Symbols: Public and Private* (1973).
                                              STEPHEN KOWALEWSKI

fiscal policy

Fiscal policy is one course of action that a government follows to stabilize the national economy by adjusting levels of spending and TAXATION. (The other major type of stabilizing action is MONETARY POLICY.) In a modern industrial economy, government spending is one major component of the aggregate demand for goods and services that directly affects EMPLOYMENT AND UNEMPLOYMENT. Changes in tax rates influence private investment and consumption, the other two major components of aggregate demand. When the economy is operating at less than full employment—a situation of deficient aggregate demand—fiscal policy theory indicates that government spending should be increased and taxes reduced to stimulate business investment and consumer spending. The intended result is higher levels of aggregate demand, national production, and employment. Government spending should be reduced and tax rates increased to diminish investment and consumption when aggregate demand is excessive and the economy experiences INFLATION. In conditions of both inflation and unemployment (STAGFLATION), as experienced during the late 1970s, fiscal policy decisions become problematic. As experienced during the late 1970s, fiscal policy decisions become problematic. Likewise they pose difficulties when, as in the 1990s, they threaten inflation by increasing an already-huge national debt.

Primarily as the result of the theoretical work of John Maynard KEYNES, discretionary fiscal policy—deliberate government action to change taxes and expenditures in order to correct for RECESSION or inflation—has been a much-used tool of government economists since the 1930s. In the 1970s and 1980s, however, proponents of monetary policy argued that Keynesian fiscal policy creates stagflation through excessive public spending and an investment-reducing tax-transfer system. Discretionary monetarism advocates adjusting the money supply and interest rates as a means of controlling economic activity. The influence of the pro-monetarist Reagan administration, however, did not signal an end to fiscal policy. The fiscal-monetary debate has fallen on partisan lines, and, as a result, federal policymakers have formed an integrated approach to economic matters.   CAMPBELL R. MCCONNELL

Bibliography: Arestis, P., and Chick, V., *Recent Development in Post-Keynesian Economics* (1992); Brems, H., *Fiscal Policy* (1983).

Fischart, Johann Baptist   [fish'-ahrt]

Johann Baptist Fischart, 1546–c.1590, was a German satirist and humanist writer who wrote under the pseudonym Mentzer. He was outspoken in his support of Calvinism and in his attacks on the Roman Catholic church. Educated in the major European centers of learning, he received a law degree from the University of Basel in 1574. He freely translated and adapted François Rabelais's *Gargantua* in 1575 and attacked the Jesuits in *Jesuiterhütlein* (Jesuit's Hat, 1580). *Das Glückhafft Schiff von Zürich* (Lucky Boat of Zurich, 1577) is his most famous narrative poem.   HUGO BEKKER

Fischer, Bobby

Robert James Fischer, b. Mar. 9, 1943, Chicago, Ill., was world chess champion and one of the most talented players in the history of the game. Fischer became an international grandmaster by age 15 and left high school to devote himself to professional competition. He was United States champion (1957–61, 1963–67) and world champion (1972–75), becoming the first American to win the world title since its establishment in 1886. Fischer snapped the Russian monopoly of the title by defeating then-champion Boris SPASSKY, with a convincing victory in a match that began in July of 1972 in Reykjavik, Iceland. He forfeited the title in April 1975 following a dispute over conduct of the world title tournament. The title was awarded to the Russian challenger Anatoly KARPOV. Fischer withdrew entirely from the chess world until 1992, when he and Spassky had a rematch, won by Fischer.

Bibliography: Brady, Frank, *Profile of a Prodigy: The Life and Games of Bobby Fischer*, rev. ed. (1989); Burger, Robert E., *The Chess of Bobby Fischer* (1975); Fischer, Bobby, *My Sixty Memorable Games* (1989); Waitzkin, Fred, *Searching for Bobby Fischer* (1988).

Fischer, Emil Hermann

The German chemist Emil Hermann Fischer, b. Oct. 9, 1852, d. July 15, 1919, made important contributions to organic chemistry. As early as 1875 he had prepared phenylhydrazine, and in 1884 he demonstrated that it could be used as an agent for separating and identifying sugars that have the same empirical formula. His greatest success was the synthesis of glucose, mannose, and fructose in 1890 and the determination of their projection formulas (showing the spatial relation of atoms in molecules with the same structural formula) and those of all possible aldohexoses. He extended his work to the disaccharides and GLYCOSIDES and to the enzymes that split them.

In 1897, Fischer recognized that uric acid and xanthine are oxides of the base purine. From xanthine he synthesized theobromine and caffeine and determined their structures. For his work on carbohydrates and purines, Fischer received the 1902 Nobel Prize for chemistry.

Fischer then turned to the study of proteins, and between 1899 and 1908 found effective ways of separating the AMINO ACIDS derived from them. He also obtained the various amino acids in optically active forms, united them in chains, and built di- and polypeptides. In 1914, Fischer prepared the first synthetic nucleotide, a component of the nucleic acids found in the proteins of cell nuclei.

During World War I, Fischer took an active part in the effort to develop a way of converting fatty acids to serve as food, the result of which was ester margarine. It was largely by the inspiration of Fischer that the Kaiser-Wilhelm Institute für Chemie, the first of the pure research laboratories, was created. Despondent over the war and illness, Fischer committed suicide in 1919.   VIRGINIA F. MCCONNELL

Bibliography: Farber, Edward, ed., *Great Chemists* (1961).

Fischer, Ernst Otto

The German chemist Ernst Otto Fischer, b. Nov. 10, 1918, was awarded the Nobel Prize for chemistry in 1973 jointly with Geoffrey Wilkinson for his contribution to the understanding of the structure of ferrocene, a crystalline compound of iron. X-ray crystallographic analysis of ferrocene indicated that the iron was sandwiched between two five-sided carbon rings to form an organometallic compound.   O. B. RAMSAY

Fischer, Hans

The German chemist Hans Fischer, b. July 27, 1881, d. Mar. 31, 1945, was noted for his studies on the structure and synthesis of many of the class of compounds called PORPHYRINS, which includes CHLOROPHYLL in plants and HEMOGLOBIN in animals. For this work he received the Nobel Prize for chemistry in 1930. Fischer was educated at Marburg and taught at Innsbruck, at Vienna, and, for most of his life, at the Polytechnic Institute in Munich.   HENRY M. LEICESTER

Fischer, Johann Michael

Johann Michael Fischer, b. 1692, d. May 5, 1766, was one of the most productive southern German rococo architects. The son of a mason, he himself became a master mason in Munich in 1722. Fischer's Church of Saint Anna am Lehel in Munich (1727–39), in the form of an elongated oval, recalls Dominikus ZIMMERMANN's work. Large windows admit a calculated profusion of light; the upward movement of the piers enhances the vitality of the whole, and the spirited decoration of the ASAM BROTHERS complements the interior. Fischer's Saint Mary at Ingolstadt (1736–39; now destroyed), an octagon with unequal sides, was an excellent example of his brilliant use of interior light and color. Often employing the standard oval plan during his early career, he later rejected it for more austere longitudinal plans.

Fisher's greatest accomplishment, begun by Simpert Kramer in 1737, is the abbey church at Ottobeuren (1748–62). The magnificent interior of this church achieves its dynamic effect through decoration rather than structure. The Church of Rott am Inn (1759–63), one of his last works, is characterized by airiness and transparency. Fischer is credited with having completed more than 50 churches.   ROBERT F. CHIRICO

Bibliography: Hempel, Eberhard, *Baroque Art and Architecture in Central Europe* (1965); Hitchcock, H. R., *Rococo Architecture in Southern Germany* (1968).

Fischer-Dieskau, Dietrich   [fish'-ur dees'-kow, deet'-rik]

The German baritone Dietrich Fischer-Dieskau, b. Berlin, May 28, 1925, is considered by many the greatest lieder singer of his generation. He learned to play the piano as a child. In 1942 he began to study singing with Hermann Weissenborn, but his training was interrupted a year later by army service. While he was a prisoner of war in Italy in 1945, the Americans recognized his talent and sent him on a singing tour of POW camps. After the war he resumed studies with Weissenborn and started his professional career. Having recorded some Bach cantatas and Schubert's song cycle *Die Winterreise*, he developed such a large following that his recital debut in 1947 was sold out. He made his operatic debut (1948) at the Berlin State Opera in Verdi's *Don Carlos.* He has appeared with the Munich and Vienna State Operas and, from 1951, at all the major European music festivals. He first toured the United States in 1954. His repertoire ranges from Heinrich Schütz to Arnold Schoenberg, Hans Werner Henze, and Benjamin Britten. He has recorded more than 450 Schubert songs and has written books on Schubert and on Wagner and Nietzche, as well as a volume of memoirs.   ELLA A. MALLIN

Bibliography: Fischer-Dieskau, Dietrich, *The Fischer-Dieskau Book of Lieder*, trans. by George Bird and Richard Stokes (1977), *Schubert: A Biographical Study of His Songs*, trans. and ed. by Kenneth S. Whitton (1976), and *Reverberations: The Memoirs of Dietrich Fischer-Dieskau*, trans. by Ruth Hein (1989).

Fischer von Erlach, Johann Bernhard   [fuhn air'-lahk]

Johann Bernhard Fischer von Erlach, b. July 20, 1656, d. Apr. 5, 1723, was one of the most intellectual and influential Austrian architects of the baroque period (see BAROQUE ART AND ARCHITECTURE). His work encompassed a variety of European trends, but he assimilated them into a personal style, giving impetus to the Austrian baroque. He traveled to Italy (c.1673–85) and possibly studied with Carlo Fontana in Rome; he may also have been in contact with Giovanni Lorenzo Bernini's workshop. The impact of ceiling painting was evidenced in his interior decorations for the mausoleum of Ferdinand II in Graz (1687). He tutored the crown prince (later Holy Roman Emperor Joseph I) in 1689 and established a position for himself in court architecture. Schloss Frain in Moravia (1690–94), with its dominating oval plan and great hall, was his first major baroque building. He was ennobled in 1696, and in 1705 he became surveyor general of imperial buildings.

His Church of the Holy Trinity (1694–1702) in Salzburg reflects Francesco Borromini's Saint Agnese (1653–57) in Rome, but Fischer gave his church a sense of depth not possible at Saint Agnese. His crowning achievement was the Karlskirche in Vienna (begun 1716), completed by his son Joseph Emanuel (1693–1742). A unique structure, Karlskirche includes numerous decorative and iconographic motifs. The elliptical plan continues in the elevation, and Johann Michael Rottmayr's (1654–1730) ceiling fresco further enhances an upward movement, causing a unified spatial organization. The exterior is an eclectic combination of a Roman temple portico similar to that of the Pantheon, a pair of imitation Trajan's columns, and imperial Austrian baroque towers.

Among his secular architecture were SCHÖNBRUNN PALACE (c.1696), Palais Trautson (1700–12), and the Imperial Library of Vienna (1723–35). Completed by his son, the library exhibits an imposing interior of complex spatial units determined by differentiated vaulting zones. The influence of French classicism caused an effective moderation and articulation of surfaces. Fischer von Erlach wrote *A Plan of Civil and Historical Architecture* (1721; Eng. trans., 1730), a thorough history of architecture, including that of Egypt and the Orient.   ROBERT F. CHIRICO

Bibliography: Aurenhammer, Hans, *J. B. Fischer von Erlach* (1973); Bourke, John, *Baroque Churches of Central Europe*, 2d ed. (1962; repr. 1978).

Fischinger, Oskar   [fish'-ing-ur]

The German animator Oskar Fischinger, b. July 22, 1900, d. Jan. 31, 1967, made films that used abstract forms to interpret music. Examples are the numbered series *Studien 1–12* (1925–36), *An American March* (1940), and *Motion Painting No. 1* (1947). Fischinger also created special effects for Hollywood films and invented the lumigraph light-producing device (1951).

Fish   (family)

The Fish family of New York has been prominent in public life since the Revolutionary War.

Nicholas Fish, b. Aug. 28, 1758, d. June 20, 1833, was an officer in the Revolutionary army. He was a New York City alderman from 1806 to 1817 and later served as state adjutant general, director of federal revenue, and as chairman of the board of trustees of Columbia University. He ran unsuccessfully for lieutenant governor as a Federalist in 1810.

His son, **Hamilton Fish**, b. Aug. 3, 1808, d. Sept. 6, 1893, entered politics as a Whig and was elected to the U.S. House of Representatives in 1842. He became governor of New York in 1849 and was a U.S. senator from 1851 to 1857. He joined the Republican party in 1856, after the Whigs disbanded. Fish was appointed secretary of state by President Ulysses S. Grant in 1869 and served with distinction through both of Grant's terms. He negotiated the Treaty of Washington (1871), which settled the Alabama Claims dispute with Britain.

Other prominent members of the Fish family include the sons of Hamilton: **Nicholas** (1848–1902), a diplomat who served as minister to Belgium; **Hamilton** (1849–1936), a lawyer and Republican politician who was elected to the House of Representatives in 1909; and **Stuyvesant** (1851–1923), a banker and businessman who served as director of the Illinois Central Railroad. The younger Hamilton's son, also named **Hamilton** (1888–1991), served as a Republican in Congress from 1920 to 1945. A vocal anti-Communist and isolationist, he was a leading opponent of the policies of President Franklin Roosevelt who, ironically, was one of Fish's constituents. His son, **Hamilton** (1926–   ), was elected to repeated terms in the U.S. House of Representatives as a Republican from New York beginning in 1968; a grandson, also named **Hamilton** (1951–   ), is a liberal who was publisher of *The Nation* from 1977 to 1987.

Bibliography: Nevins, Allan, *Hamilton Fish: The Inner History of the Grant Administration*, 2 vols. (1957).

fish

Fish are cold-blooded aquatic animals with backbones, gills, and fins. Most fishes are torpedo-shaped (fusiform) for efficient travel through water, but much variation in shape occurs, from flattened and rounded, as in flounders, to vertical and angular, as in sea horses. Fishes range in size from the pygmy goby, *Pandaka pygmaea*, of the Philippines, which reaches only 12 mm (0.5 in) long and about 1.5 g (0.05 oz) in weight and is sexually mature at 6 mm (0.25 in), to the whale shark, *Rhincodon typus*, which grows to 18 m (60 ft) long and more than 20 U.S. tons in weight.

Fish were among the first animals systematically hunted by primitive humans. Even today, relatively primitive societies in the South Pacific and South America depend largely on fish for food, while in many industrialized nations, fish still constitute a major part of the diet. It is said that the search for codfish led French fishermen to the discovery of Canada and that villages sprang up on the coasts of Norway, Scotland, Japan, and other countries wherever shoals of herrings regularly came close to shore. Today fishes are harvested for unprocessed human food, fish meal, animal feed, and oil. They also are pursued avidly by sport anglers, who contribute to the economy of fishing areas and to specific industries. Currently, however, the increasing human population, overfishing to supply this population, and pollution of the world's waters are all cutting heavily into the world supply of fish, and threatening the existence of a number of species. At the same time, regulations to curtail the taking of certain species or sizes are virtually unenforceable on an international level.

DISTRIBUTION

Fish are found throughout the world, from altitudes of more than 5,000 m (3 mi), as in Lake Titicaca, located 3,800 m (2.3 mi) above sea level in the Andes, to depths of about 10 km (6 mi) in the Pacific Ocean. Some, like certain killifishes, *Cyprinodon*, inhabit hot springs, where the water temperature may reach 45° C (113° F); others, like the icefishes, *Chaenocephalus*, are found in Antarctic seas, where water temperature may fall below 0° C (32° F). About 107 species, including the swordfish, *Xiphias*, are distributed worldwide in tropical and subtropical waters, but many species have very limited ranges, among the smallest being that of the killifish *Cyprinodon diabolis*, which is confined to a single spring in Nevada.

About 70% of the Earth's surface is covered by oceans and seas, and about 3.5% of the land surface (1% of the Earth's total surface) is covered by fresh water. Inhabiting these waters are an estimated 20,000 or more fish species, equal to or exceeding the number of all other vertebrate species combined. Bird species number approximately 8,600; reptiles, 6,000; mammals, 4,500; and amphibians, 2,500. About 60% of the fish species live in marine waters; the remaining 40% are found in fresh water.

Most of the world's fishes are continental in orientation, living either as part of the freshwater systems on land or as sea-dwellers staying near and influenced by the coastal environment. High densities of marine fish populations occur near coasts, because the waters there are extremely rich in nutrients. Coastal benefits include chemical and organic enrichment discharged by rivers, upwellings from the ocean depths that recycle previously deposited nitrates and phosphates, aeration caused by surf and tide, and the penetration of sunlight.

ANATOMY

The living species of fish are usually divided into three classes: the Agnatha, the jawless fishes, comprising the hagfishes and lampreys; the Chondrichthyes, the cartilaginous-skeleton fishes, such as sharks and rays; and the Osteichthyes,

the bony-skeleton fishes, comprising all other living fishes. The skeletons of these three groups vary in fundamental ways. In the hagfishes and lampreys the backbone is basically a notochord, a rodlike structure composed of unique notochordal tissue. In sharks and rays the notochord is surrounded and constricted by spaced rings of cartilage, the vertebrae, to form a backbone. The remainder of the skeleton is also cartilaginous, not bony, but in many forms the cartilage is partly calcified, and thereby hardened, by the addition of calcareous salts. In primitive bony fishes, such as the sturgeon, the vertebrae spaced along the notochord are still largely cartilaginous, but in most advanced bony fishes the vertebrae are bony and are united to form the backbone, and the notochord is no longer present.

Some fishes, such as lampreys, lack ribs; others have either a single or a double pair of ribs attached to each trunk vertebra. Among the higher bony fishes there also may be small, riblike intermuscular bones, which often render such fish difficult to eat.

The body apppendages of fish are of two kinds, cirrhi and fins. Cirrhi are flaps of flesh that may appear on any part of the body; they often serve as camouflage. Fins are either median or paired. Median fins are situated along the centerline of the body, at the top, the bottom, and the end. The top, or dorsal, fin may consist of one to several fins, one behind the other, and may include a fleshy fin, called the adipose fin, near the tail. The bottom, or anal, fin is located on the belly behind the vent, or anus. The end fin is called the tail, or caudal, fin.

The dorsal and anal fins may be supported by cartilaginous rods, as in the lampreys, by cartilaginous rods and horny rays, as in sharks, by horny rays, as in the spiny-finned fishes, or by bony rays (derived from scales) in the soft-rayed fishes. The tail fin may be protocercal, the body continuing straight back as a middle support between the upper and lower lobes of the tail; heterocercal, with the end of the body turning up and continuing to the tip of the upper lobe; or homocercal, in which the last few vertebrae are fused and joined with other bony elements (hypurals) to support the tail-fin rays. A modification of the heterocercal tail so as to resemble the protocercal type is called diphycercal.

The paired fins correspond to the arms and legs of land vertebrates. The pectoral fins are situated at the front of the body behind the gill openings and generally function to provide maneuverability, but may be highly modified to fulfill other functions. The simplest internal support for the pectoral

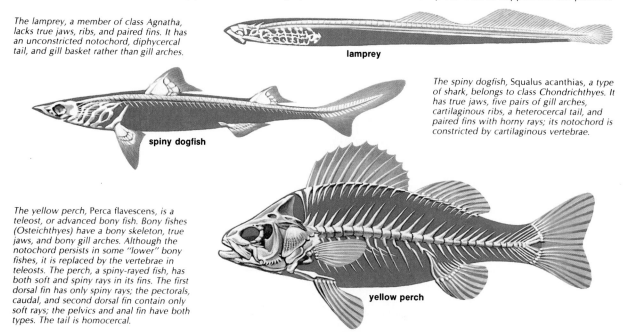

The lamprey, a member of class Agnatha, lacks true jaws, ribs, and paired fins. It has an unconstricted notochord, diphycercal tail, and gill basket rather than gill arches.

lamprey

spiny dogfish

The spiny dogfish, Squalus acanthias, a type of shark, belongs to class Chondrichthyes. It has true jaws, five pairs of gill arches, cartilaginous ribs, a heterocercal tail, and paired fins with horny rays; its notochord is constricted by cartilaginous vertebrae.

The yellow perch, Perca flavescens, is a teleost, or advanced bony fish. Bony fishes (Osteichthyes) have a bony skeleton, true jaws, and bony gill arches. Although the notochord persists in some "lower" bony fishes, it is replaced by the vertebrae in teleosts. The perch, a spiny-rayed fish, has both soft and spiny rays in its fins. The first dorsal fin has only spiny rays; the pectorals, caudal, and second dorsal fin contain only soft rays; the pelvics and anal fin have both types. The tail is homocercal.

yellow perch

fins occurs in the sharks, where a U-shaped cartilaginous skeletal structure, called the pectoral girdle, joins and helps support the two pectoral fins. In the higher bony fishes the pectoral girdle is composed of bone and is more complex in structure. The pelvic fins, also called the ventral fins, are located along the bottom of the body but vary considerably in their placement. They may be located in the middle of the belly, as in salmon; below the pectorals, as in the largemouth bass; or in front of the pectorals, as in cods. Pelvic fins also serve as maneuvering structures and also may be modified to serve other uses. The supporting pelvic girdle is lacking in many bony fishes; in most fishes in which the pelvic girdle is present it is represented by a single skeletal element on each side of the body.

The scales of fish are colorless; a fish's coloring arises from structures beneath or closely associated with the scales. Not all species of fishes have scales, or the scales may be so small as to make the fish appear scaleless. Scales also may be present only on small areas of the body. The arrangement of scales may be imbricate (overlapping like the shingles on a roof) or mosaic (fitting closely together or just minutely separated).

Four basic scale types can be distinguished on the basis of structure. Placoid scales, also called dermal denticles, are found on sharks and rays and are toothlike in structure. Indeed, modified and enlarged placoid scales have become the teeth of sharks. The placoid scale consists of an upper layer of enamellike substance called vitrodentine, a lower layer of dentine, a pulp cavity, and a disklike basal plate embedded in the skin. Placoid scales do not increase in size as do the scales of bony fishes, and new scales must be added as a shark grows.

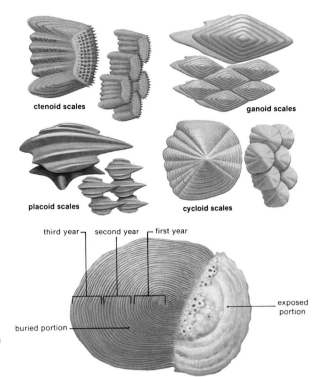

ctenoid scales

ganoid scales

placoid scales

cycloid scales

third year second year first year

buried portion

exposed portion

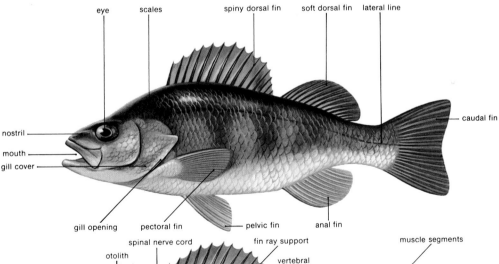

eye scales spiny dorsal fin soft dorsal fin lateral line

nostril

mouth

gill cover

caudal fin

gill opening pectoral fin pelvic fin anal fin

Drawings (above) show scale types on the basis of shape: ctenoid, ganoid, placoid, and cycloid. Most often, scales form an overlapping pattern like shingles on a roof. The cycloid scale (enlarged) of a salmon shows concentric bony ridges, or circuli, which reflect the growth patterns of the individual; clusters of ridges, called annuli, mark each yearly growth cycle.

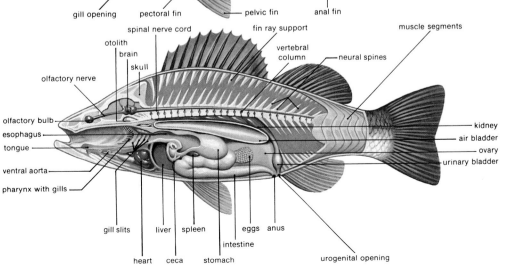

spinal nerve cord fin ray support muscle segments

otolith
brain
skull

vertebral column

neural spines

olfactory nerve

olfactory bulb

esophagus

tongue

ventral aorta

pharynx with gills

kidney

air bladder

ovary

urinary bladder

gill slits liver spleen eggs anus

heart ceca stomach intestine

urogenital opening

External and internal features of the yellow perch are illustrated (left). Most fishes are covered by scales; not all fishes have all the fins shown here. Muscles, needed for swimming, account for much of a fish's body weight. Sensory organs include lateral line system, nostrils, lidless eyes, and otoliths (ear stones) for equilibrium. The drawings also show gas exchange, digestive, excretory, and female reproductive organs.

Cosmoid scales are found on the primitive coelacanth. They also occur on lungfishes, but in a highly modified, single-layered form. The cosmoid scale of the coelacanth is a four-layered bony scale. The upper layer is enamellike vitrodentine; the second layer is a hard, dentinelike substance called cosmine; the third layer is spongy bone, and the lowest layer is dense bone.

Ganoid scales, as found on gars, are typically squarish (rhombic) in shape and consist of a single bony layer, a layer of cosmine, and a covering of a very hard enamellike substance called ganoin.

Leptoid scales are believed to have been derived from ganoid scales by the loss of the ganoin layer; they consist of a single layer of bone. Leptoid scales are found on the higher bony fishes and occur in two forms: cycloid (circular) and ctenoid (toothed), the latter bearing tiny comblike projections. The single-layered cosmoid scale of lungfishes also may be classified as leptoid, although of a different derivation.

CIRCULATION

The blood of the fish serves, as does the blood of other vertebrates, to transport oxygen, nutrients, and wastes. The typical fish's circulation is a single circuit: heart-gills-body-heart. In contrast, mammals have two circuits: heart-lungs-heart and heart-body-heart. The fish heart proper is two-chambered, consisting of an upper atrium and a lower ventricle. Amphibians, basically, have a three-chambered heart, two atria and one ventricle; reptiles have a three- or four-chambered heart; and mammals and birds have a four-chambered heart consisting of two atria and two ventricles. The fish heart, however, has two accessory chambers, and all four chambers are contained within a single pericardial sac. One accessory chamber is the thin-walled sinus venosus, which collects blood and leads into the atrium; the other accessory chamber is the conus arteriosus, an enlargement of the main artery leading out of the ventricle. In some fishes, such as sharks, the conus arteriosus is muscular and pumps blood in the manner of the ventricle.

RESPIRATION

In order to live, fish must extract oxygen from the water and transfer it to their bloodstream. This is done by gills, lungs, specialized chambers, or skin, any of which must be richly supplied with blood vessels in order to act as a respiratory organ. Extracting oxygen from water is more difficult and requires a greater expenditure of energy than does extracting oxygen from air. Water is a thousand times more dense (heavier per unit volume) than air, and at 20° C (68° F) it has 50 times more viscosity (resistance to flow) than air and contains only 3% as much oxygen as an equal volume of air. Fishes, therefore, have necessarily evolved very efficient systems for extracting oxygen from water; some fishes are able to extract as much as 80% of the oxygen contained in the water passing over the gills, whereas humans can extract only about 25% of the oxygen from the air taken into the lungs.

Gills are made efficient in a number of ways. (1) A large surface area for gaseous exchange means that more oxygen can enter the bloodstream over a given period of time. A single gill of a bony fish consists of a curved gill arch bearing a V-shaped double row of gill filaments. Each filament has many minute folds in its surface, giving it a sort of fuzzy appearance and increasing the amount of surface area along a given length of filament. Consequently, the surface area of the gills is commonly 10 to 60 times more than that of the whole body surface. (2) A short diffusion, or travel, distance for the oxygen increases the rate of oxygen entry into the blood. The blood traveling in the folds of the filaments is very close to the oxygen-containing water, being separated from it by a very thin membrane usually 1 to 3 microns (4/100,000 to 1/10,000 in) thick, and possibly less. (3) By using countercurrent circulation in the gill, the blood in the filament folds travels forward, in the opposite direction to the water flow, so that a constant imbalance is maintained between the lower amount of oxygen in the blood and the higher amount in the water, ensuring passage of oxygen to the blood. If the blood were to flow in the same direction as the water, oxygenated blood at the rear of the gills would be traveling with deoxy-

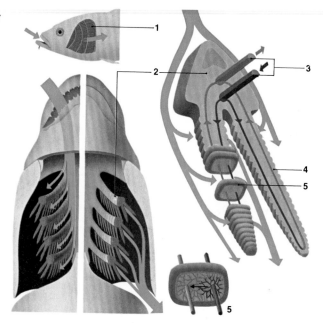

In most bony fishes oxygen and carbon dioxide are exchanged in the gills (1). Four bony gill arches (2) on either side of the head bear arteries (3), which run through V-shaped gill filaments (4). Each filament is formed into platelike sections (5) filled with capillaries that are near the gill surface, bringing the blood close to the oxygen-rich water. Water (blue green) taken in through the mouth flows over the filaments in only one direction. Blood circulating within the filaments flows in the opposite direction, ensuring that deoxygenated blood (blue) comes in contact with fully oxygenated water. This countercurrent circulation system facilitates the efficient intake of oxygen and the release of excess carbon dioxide into the water.

genated water and not only could not extract oxygen from the water but would even lose oxygen to it. (4) Gills have little physiological dead space. The folds of the filament are close enough together so that most of the water passing between them is involved in the gas-exchange process. (5) Water flows continuously in only one direction over the gills, as contrasted with the interrupted, two-way flow of air in and out of lungs of mammals.

AIR BREATHING

A fish out of water usually dies because its gills collapse, reducing the area of the respiratory surface, and become dry, effectively stopping the diffusion of oxygen into the blood. Many fishes, however, have evolved methods of extracting oxygen from air. Such adaptations permit these fishes to live in oxygen-poor waters, where they come to the surface to gulp air, or in waters subjected to drying; or they may enable a species to exploit environments, such as damp beaches, unavailable to other fishes. One method of air breathing is the development of gills that either secrete mucus or trap moisture that supports the gills and keeps them wet. Another method is to breathe through a damp skin, as do the freshwater eels. Very commonly, special chambers have been developed in the mouth, throat, or head in which inspired air is brought into contact with moist tissues richly supplied with blood vessels. Some fishes have thin-walled areas in the intestine where oxygen can be extracted from swallowed air. In still others, the swim bladder, often mistaken for a lung because of its inflated shape and shiny, silvery white walls, is modified into an air-breathing apparatus. Air breathing has become so important to some species that they will drown if not allowed access to air.

BODY TEMPERATURE

Fish are described as cold-blooded, meaning that their body temperature varies with the external temperature. Fish do, however, produce metabolic heat (that is, heat derived from the oxidation, or "burning," of food and from other processes), but much of this heat is lost to the outside at the gills. Blood passing through the gills loses heat to the water quite rapidly, so that a fish's body temperature is usually within a degree or so of the water temperature. Tunas and mackerel sharks, however, are warm-bodied fishes. They have evolved countercurrent circulatory networks that consist basically of paired ingoing and outgoing blood vessels. In this way the heat of the warm blood going to the gills is transferred to the cooled blood coming from the gills, and the heat is kept within the fish's body. By using these networks, yellowfin and skipjack tuna are able to keep their body temperature from about 5° to almost 12° C (9° to 21° F) above the water temperature. One skipjack taken in warm waters registered a body temperature of 37.8° C (100° F). The bluefin tuna does even better and might qualify as a warm-blooded (as opposed to warm-bodied) fish. It is able to maintain a fairly constant body temperature across different water temperatures, its body temperature varying only about 5 C degrees (9 F degrees) over a 20 C degree (36 F degree) range of water temperatures.

One of the advantages of warm-bodiedness is an increase in muscle power. Muscles contract more rapidly when warm without loss of force. If with a 10 C degree (18 F degree) rise in body temperature a muscle can contract three times as fast, then three times the power is available from that muscle. More muscle power means more speed in pursuing prey, escaping enemies, and shortening the time required for long-distance migration.

WATER BALANCE

The blood of freshwater fishes is typically more salty than the water in which they live. Osmotic pressure, the force that tends to equalize differences in salt concentrations, causes

water to diffuse, or enter, into the fish's body, primarily through the gills, mouth membranes, and intestine. To eliminate this excess water, freshwater fishes produce a large amount of very dilute urine. Lampreys, for example, may daily produce an amount of urine equal to as much as 36% of their total body weight; bony fishes commonly produce amounts of urine equaling from 5 to 12% of their body weight per day. As these fishes are gaining water, they are losing salts. Salts contained in their foods are insufficient to maintain the proper salt balance. Freshwater fishes have therefore developed the capacity to absorb salts from water by means of their gills.

Marine bony fishes, in contrast, have blood that is less salty than sea water, and consequently they lose water and absorb salts. To offset this loss of fluid, marine fishes drink seawater and produce very little urine. The drinking of seawater, however, adds to the concentration of salts. These salts are eliminated in several ways. Calcium, magnesium, and sulfates are passed out through the anus along with wastes. Sodium, potassium, chloride, and nitrogenous compounds, such as urea, are excreted through the gills.

The hagfishes and the sharks have approached the problem of fluid balance in other ways. Hagfish blood has a total salt concentration approximately equal to that of seawater. Sharks' gills do not excrete the nitrogenous waste product urea, retaining it instead in the blood. The presence of urea and another waste product, trimethylamine oxide, as well as various salts, keeps the shark's blood at a slightly higher solute concentration than that of seawater.

SWIMMING

Many fishes swim by contracting and relaxing a succession of muscle blocks, called myomeres, alternately on each side of

(Left) A marine fish, such as the jack (above), loses water by osmosis through gills and skin; it drinks seawater (dark arrow) to offset this loss. A freshwater fish, such as the Alaska blackfish (below), absorbs much water, and excretes the excess (dark arrow) as dilute urine.

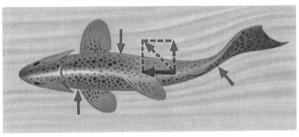

Arrows indicate the forces that water exerts on a swimming fish. As the tail moves from side to side, the water pushes against it (diagonal arrow). The forward component of this force (heavy arrow) propels the fish forward. The lateral component (broken vertical arrow), which would turn the fish to the side, is offset by the force of the water that acts upon the fish's sides (solid vertical arrows).

Tuna and related fishes swim by moving the tail fin from side to side with powerful strokes; only the tail stalk bends. At the other end of the spectrum of swimming motions, the eel moves with a series of distinct waves which travel down its body. Most fishes, as illustrated by the dogfish, exhibit intermediate characteristics: they swim with reduced body waves and amplified tail movements.

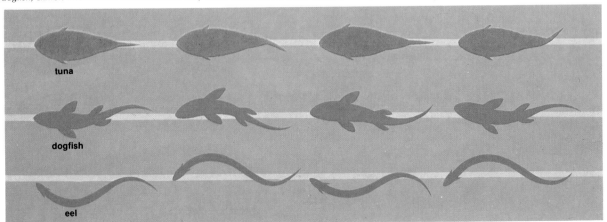

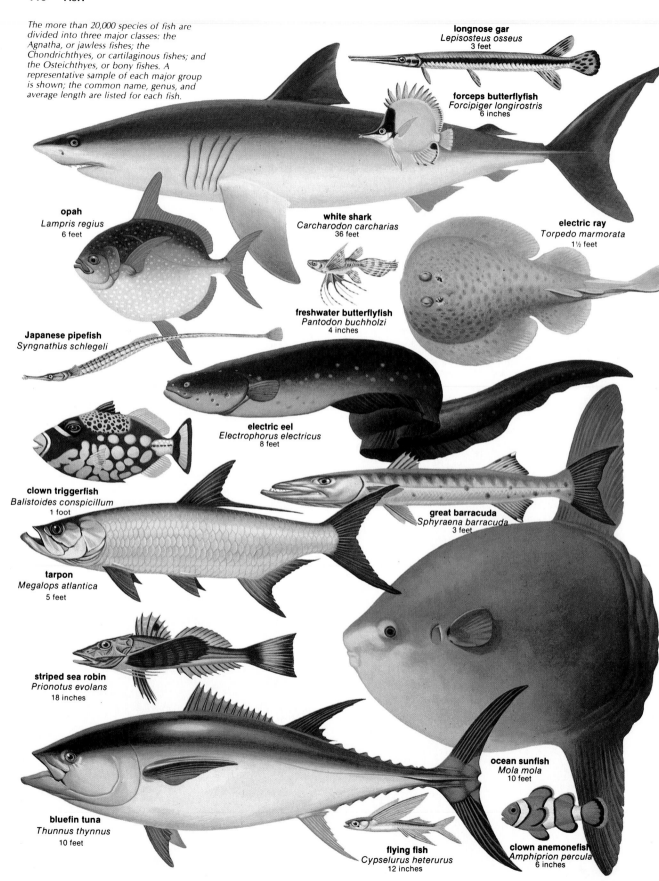

The more than 20,000 species of fish are divided into three major classes: the Agnatha, or jawless fishes; the Chondrichthyes, or cartilaginous fishes; and the Osteichthyes, or bony fishes. A representative sample of each major group is shown; the common name, genus, and average length are listed for each fish.

longnose gar
Lepisosteus osseus
3 feet

forceps butterflyfish
Forcipiger longirostris
6 inches

opah
Lampris regius
6 feet

white shark
Carcharodon carcharias
36 feet

electric ray
Torpedo marmorata
1½ feet

Japanese pipefish
Syngnathus schlegeli

freshwater butterflyfish
Pantodon buchholzi
4 inches

electric eel
Electrophorus electricus
8 feet

clown triggerfish
Balistoides conspicillum
1 foot

great barracuda
Sphyraena barracuda
3 feet

tarpon
Megalops atlantica
5 feet

striped sea robin
Prionotus evolans
18 inches

ocean sunfish
Mola mola
10 feet

bluefin tuna
Thunnus thynnus
10 feet

flying fish
Cypselurus heterurus
12 inches

clown anemonefish
Amphiprion percula
6 inches

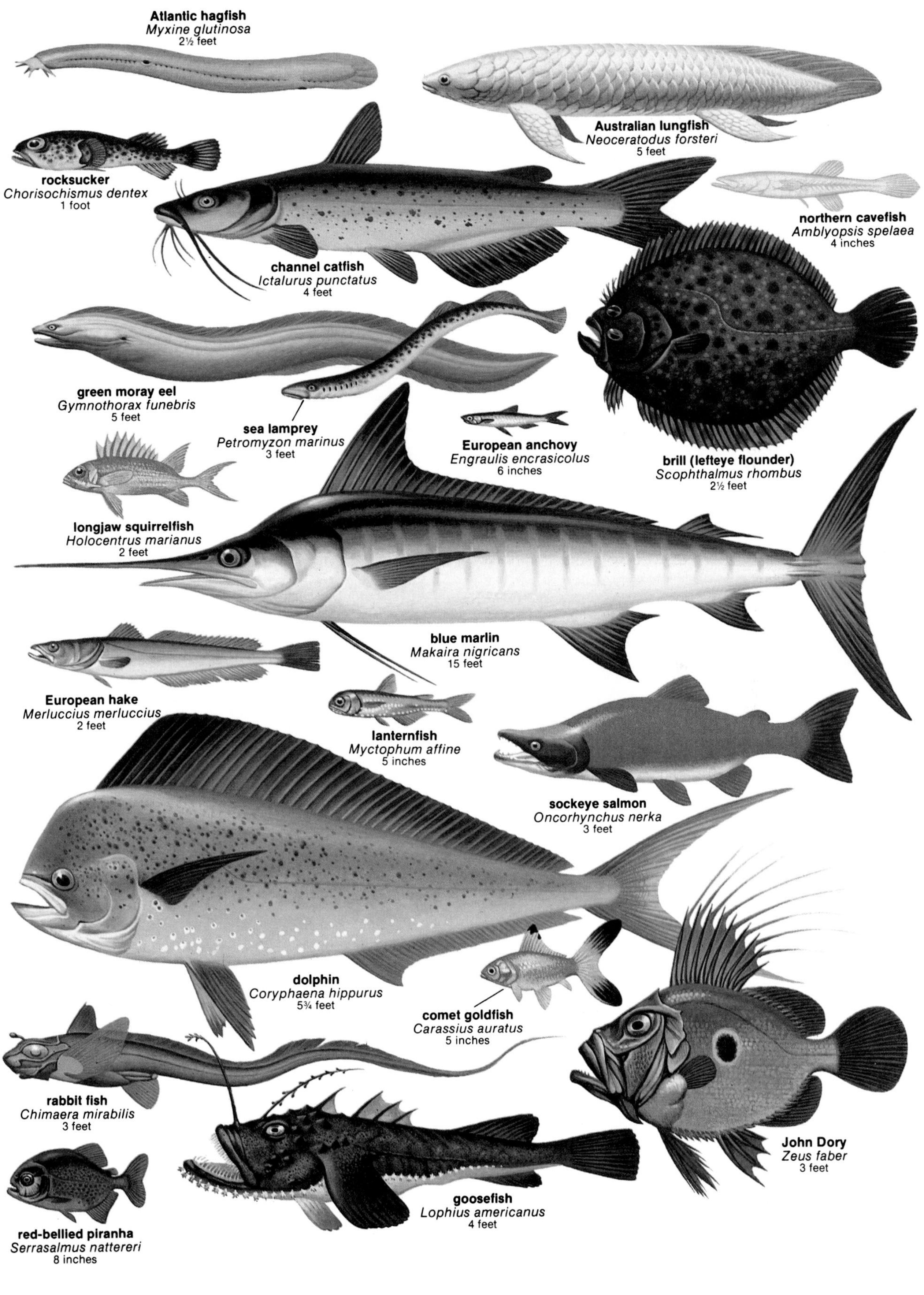

Atlantic hagfish
Myxine glutinosa
2½ feet

Australian lungfish
Neoceratodus forsteri
5 feet

rocksucker
Chorisochismus dentex
1 foot

channel catfish
Ictalurus punctatus
4 feet

northern cavefish
Amblyopsis spelaea
4 inches

green moray eel
Gymnothorax funebris
5 feet

sea lamprey
Petromyzon marinus
3 feet

European anchovy
Engraulis encrasicolus
6 inches

brill (lefteye flounder)
Scophthalmus rhombus
2½ feet

longjaw squirrelfish
Holocentrus marianus
2 feet

blue marlin
Makaira nigricans
15 feet

European hake
Merluccius merluccius
2 feet

lanternfish
Myctophum affine
5 inches

sockeye salmon
Oncorhynchus nerka
3 feet

dolphin
Coryphaena hippurus
5¾ feet

comet goldfish
Carassius auratus
5 inches

John Dory
Zeus faber
3 feet

rabbit fish
Chimaera mirabilis
3 feet

goosefish
Lophius americanus
4 feet

red-bellied piranha
Serrasalmus nattereri
8 inches

the body, starting at the head and progressing down toward the tail. The alternate shortening and relaxing of successive muscle blocks, which bends part of the body first toward one side and then toward the other, results in a series of waves traveling down the fish's body. The rear part of each wave thrusts against the water and propels the fish forward. This type of movement is quite clearly seen in the freshwater eel. Because movement of the head back and forth exerts drag, which consumes additional energy and slows travel, a great many fishes have modified this snakelike motion by keeping the waves very small along most of the length of the body, in some cases showing no obvious movement at all, and then increasing them sharply in the tail region. It is the end of the traveling waves that moves the tail forcefully back and forth, providing the main propulsion for forward motion. A simpler form of tail propulsion is seen in such inflexible-bodied fishes as the trunkfish, which simply alternates contractions of all the muscle blocks on one side of the body with those on the other side, causing the tail to move from side to side like a sculling paddle.

Some of the predatory bony fishes are the fastest swimmers; they can cruise at speeds that are between three and six times their body length per second and may be able to reach 9 to 13 body lengths per second in very short bursts. Some fishes, such as the blenny, which has been timed at 0.8 km/hr (0.5 mph), swim very slowly; others, such as the salmon, which may reach a sustained speed of 13 km/hr (8 mph), move much faster; and it has been estimated that tuna may reach speeds of 80 km/hr (50 mph), and swordfish, 97 km/hr (60 mph).

GAS BLADDER

Because a weightless, or buoyant, body requires a minimum of energy to keep it at a given depth, and because a weightless body requires less energy than a weighted body to move at a given speed, many fishes have evolved means of reducing their body weight, or density, relative to the density of water. A fish whose total body density equaled that of water would be effectively weightless, neither rising nor sinking. Because fat is less dense than water, one method of reducing body density would be to increase the proportion of fat within the body. Theoretically, about one-third of a fish's body weight would have to be made up of fat in order to make the fish weightless in seawater. This condition is approached in some species of deep-sea sharks having very large livers that contain a great amount of squalene, a fatty substance that is significantly less dense than seawater.

Another method of reducing density is to include gases within the body. Many fishes have a gas-filled bladder that serves this function. The gases within the bladder are similar to those in air but are present in different and widely varying

Drawing of a deep sea snaggletooth, Astronesthes, *indicates the position of the gas bladder and rete mirabile. The gas bladder (detail below), which lies just below the kidney, regulates bouyancy. The rete mirabile, with its countercurrent system of capillaries, and gas gland, which secretes lactic acid, act to inflate the gas bladder.*

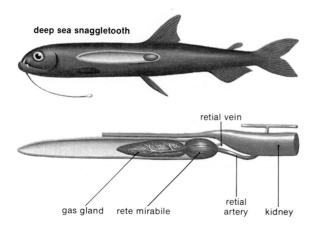

deep sea snaggletooth

retial vein

gas gland   rete mirabile   retial artery   kidney

proportions. The degree of body volume that must be taken up by gas in order to achieve weightlessness depends mainly upon whether the fish is freshwater or marine. Fresh water is less dense than seawater and consequently provides less buoyancy. Freshwater fishes, therefore, require a larger gas bladder than do marine fishes to keep them from sinking. According to calculations, the capacity of a gas bladder should be about 7% of body volume for a freshwater fish and 5% for a marine fish. In actual measurements, freshwater fishes' gas bladders have been found to range from 7 to 11% of body volume, while those of marine fishes have ranged from 4 to 6% of body volume.

If the gas bladder contained an unchanging quantity of gas, the fish possessing it would be weightless at only one depth. The reason for this is that as pressure increases with depth, the gas in the bladder is compressed, decreasing the bladder's volume and increasing the relative density of the fish. The fish would then have to use considerable energy to stop its increasingly denser body from sinking. Conversely, when a fish rises from great depths and pressure is decreased, the volume of the bladder expands and the fish becomes too light to remain at a given depth without considerable effort (in extreme cases, such as with certain deep-water fishes, excessive expansion of gases in the bladder can cause the bladder to burst). The quantity of gas within a fish's bladder must therefore be adjustable. If, as in the carp, the gas bladder is connected by a duct to the gullet, gas may be expelled through the mouth and gill cavities as the fish rises, and, in a similar manner, gas may be added to the bladder by swallowing air at the water surface.

For most fishes, however, coming to the surface to gulp air prior to going deeper is impractical, and in many fishes the gas bladder has no connection to the outside. In these fishes there must be another means of adjusting the quantity of gas within the bladder. This is done by transferring gases from the gas bladder to adjoining blood vessels and back again.

Deflating the gas bladder is a passive operation, working under the higher pressures building up within the gas bladder. This pressure forces the gas into surrounding blood capillaries, which then carry the gas away. These blood vessels may be scattered through the walls of the gas bladder, they may be confined to a compartment at the rear of the bladder, or they may be restricted to a region at the top of the bladder, which is separated from the bladder by a constrictive muscle and is known as the oval organ.

Inflating the gas bladder is an active, or dynamic, operation because it is done against the high pressures within the bladder. The gases may be forced into the bladder by blood vessels covering large areas of the bladder walls, or, more commonly, by a combination of two units known as the gas gland and the rete mirabile. The gas gland is a modification of the inner lining of the bladder; the rete mirabile is a dense bundle of capillaries arranged side by side in countercurrent fashion. Blood leaving the gas bladder would be carrying a gas, such as oxygen, at a high pressure equal to that within the gas bladder. Blood arriving at the gas bladder would be carrying oxygen at quite a low pressure, equal to that within the water passing over the gills. The oxygen therefore diffuses from the outgoing blood into the incoming blood. This process is repeated continuously, with greater and greater concentrations and higher and higher pressures of oxygen collecting at the junction point of the outgoing and incoming capillaries, the gas gland. The gas gland may facilitate this buildup by secreting lactic acid, which acts to increase the pressure of oxygen within the blood. When the pressure of the oxygen in the gas gland exceeds that within the gas bladder, the oxygen diffuses into the bladder.

LATERAL LINE SYSTEM

The lateral line system, found in many fishes and in some aquatic amphibians, is sensitive to differences in water pressure. These differences may be due to changes in depth or to the currentlike waves caused by approaching objects. The basic sensory unit of the lateral line system is the neuromast, which is a bundle of sensory and supporting cells whose projecting hairs are encased in a gelatinous cap. The nueromasts

The lateral line system (red) of a red mullet (A) is located in the head and along the sides of the body. It consists of fluid-filled canals (B) under the skin, which open through small pores (C). Within the canals (D) are groups of sensory cells (1) with projecting hairs (2) surrounded by a gelatinous cap (3), which send continuous trains of impulses along nerves (4) to the brain. Pressure waves in the water stimulate the sensory cells, changing the frequency of the nerve impulses and allowing the fish to detect objects and other fishes. By comparing the pressure waves reaching different parts of its body (E), a fish can locate an object. Fighting fish (F) respond to pressure waves, caused by body movements.

continuously send out trains of nerve impulses. When pressure waves cause the gelatinous caps of the neuromasts to move, bending the enclosed hairs, the frequency of the nerve impulses is either increased or decreased, depending on the direction of bending.

Neuromasts may occur singly, in small groups called pit organs, or in rows within grooves or canals, when they are referred to as the lateral line system. The lateral line system runs along the sides of the body onto the head, where it divides into three branches, two to the snout and one to the lower jaw.

A swimming fish sets up a pressure wave in the water that is detectable by the lateral line systems of other fishes. It also sets up a bow wave in front of itself, the pressure of which is higher than that of the wave flow along its sides. These near-field differences are registered by its own lateral line system. As the fish approaches an object, such as a rock or the glass wall of an aquarium, the pressure waves around its body are distorted, and these changes are quickly detected by the lateral line system, enabling the fish to swerve or to take other suitable action. Because sound waves are waves of pressure, the lateral line system is also able to detect very low-frequency sounds of 100 Hz or less.

An interesting adaptation of the pressure-sensitive systems is seen in the modified groups of neuromasts called the ampullae of Lorenzini, which are found in sharks and certain bony fishes. The ampullae of Lorenzini act as electroreceptors and are able to detect electrical charges, or fields, in the water. Most animals, including humans, emit a DC field when in seawater. This is presumably caused by electrical potential differences between body fluids and seawater and between different parts of the body. An AC field is also set up by muscular activity (contractions). A wound, even a scratch, can markedly alter these electrical fields. The cat shark, *Scyliorhinus*, is known to catch prey by using its ampullae of Lorenzini to detect the electrical field generated by flatfish (plaice) buried beneath the sand.

REPRODUCTION

Most fishes are egg-layers, but many bear living young. Live-bearing fishes may be ovoviviparous, in which the eggs essentially simply hatch within the female, or viviparous, in which the unborn young are supplied nourishment through the mother's tissues. In some ovoviviparous fishes the embryo develops in the egg while the egg is still within its follicular covering within the ovary, and ovulation (or release of the egg) and birth occur at the same time. In other ovoviviparous forms the eggs are released from the protective follicles into the cavity of the hollow ovary, where development continues. In some viviparous fishes the walls of the egg follicle are in intimate contact with the embryo, supplying it with nourishment. In the viviparous sharks, a part of the oviduct, or egg channel, is developed into a uterus, where the modified yolk sacs of the young are closely joined to pockets within the uterus.

In live-bearing fishes and in some egg-layers, fertilization occurs internally, and methods have been evolved for introducing the sperm into the female's body. In sharks the pelvic fins of the male are modified into intromittent organs called myxopterygia, and in the male topminnows the anal fin is modified into a similar-functioning intromittent organ called the gonopodium.

At least three modes of reproduction—heterosexual, hermaphroditic, and parthenogenetic—are found in fishes. In the

Although some Osteichthyes, or bony fishes, are live bearers, the majority lay eggs that are fertilized externally. In typical egg-laying fish, such as perch, family Percidae, the female (A) produces many small eggs in the ovary; the eggs pass through the oviduct and the urogenital opening and are deposited in the water. Similarly, the male (B) produces sperm in the testis; the sperm then passes through the vas deferens and the urogenital opening into the water, where fertilization occurs.

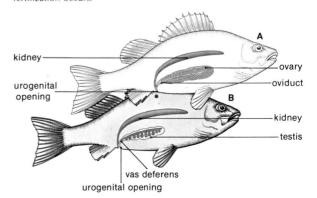

most common form, heterosexual reproduction, there are separate male and female parents, but even here there is considerable variation. In some live-bearing fishes, the female is able to store sperm for up to 8 or even 10 months, and this sperm is used to fertilize new batches of eggs as they develop. In some cases, a female may carry sperm from several males at once.

In hermaphroditic reproduction, a single fish is both male and female, produces both eggs and sperm (either at the same time or at different times), and mates with other similar hermaphroditic fishes. External self-fertilization occurs in one hermaphroditic fish, which sheds egg and sperm simultaneously. In another, internal self-fertilization may occur. In certain fishes there is a time sequence of hermaphroditism, young fishes reversing their sex as they grow older.

In parthenogenetic reproduction, unfertilized eggs develop into embryos. This is known to exist in at least one fish species, *Poecilia formosa*, of the Amazon River; however, even though development proceeds without fertilization in some of these females, mating with a male is still required to stimulate egg development.

Parental care also shows great diversity. Some fishes, like the Atlantic herring, form huge schools of males and females and freely shed their eggs and sperm (milt), and then abandon the eggs. Other fishes build nests and care for both the eggs and newly hatched young. Others have evolved methods of carrying the eggs with them, commonly in their mouths, but also in gill cavities or in special pouches on the body.

EVOLUTION
The first fishes, and indeed the first vertebrates, were the os-

The Atlantic salmon, Salmo salar *(closely related to the trout), stays in fresh water for 1 to 5 years before migrating to the sea as an adult. It returns to fresh water only to spawn and die. Fertile eggs about 6 mm (0.24 in) in diameter are translucent (A), and infertile eggs are opaque white. The developing embryo has prominent eyes (B). Newly hatched larvae (C) depend on the yolk sac (1) for food. Larvae are about 24 mm (1 in) long when the yolk sac is almost consumed (D). Larvae 4 cm (1.6 in) long have fully formed mouths and feed on small aquatic organisms (E). A young fish, about 10 cm (4 in) long, is called a parr and is marked with about 10 mauve blotches (parr marks) along its flank (F). Parr marks are lost when the freshwater period is complete (G). At this stage the fish is called a smolt and measures some 20 cm (8 in) in length. Large, aged males (H) returning to fresh water to spawn have a crooked lower jaw, or kype (1).*

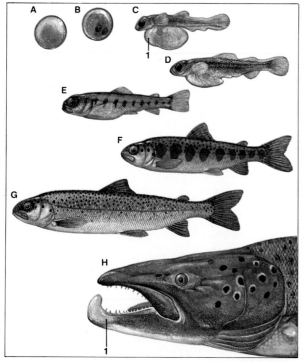

Like other cichlids, male and female Jack Dempseys, C. biocellatum *(top),* share parental duties, such as guarding and fanning their eggs. Newly hatched fry stay close to the parents. Mouth brooders, including Tilapia *cichlids (bottom),* protect the fry in their mouths.

tracoderms, which appeared in the Cambrian Period, about 510 million years ago, and became extinct at the end of the Devonian, about 350 million years ago. Ostracoderms were jawless fishes found mainly in fresh water. They were covered with a bony armor or scales and were often less than 30 cm (1 ft) long. The ostracoderms are placed in the class Agnatha along with the living jawless fishes, the lampreys and hagfishes, which are believed to be descended from the ostracoderms.

The first fishes with jaws, the acanthodians, or spiny sharks, appeared in the late Silurian, about 410 million years ago, and became extinct before the end of the Permian, about 250 million years ago. Acanthodians were generally small sharklike fishes varying from toothless filter-feeders to toothed predators. They are often classified as an order of the class Placodermi, another group of primitive fishes, but recent authorities tend to place the acanthodians in a class by themselves (class Acanthodii) or even within the class of modern bony fishes, the Osteichthyes. It is commonly believed that the acanthodians and the modern bony fishes are related and that either the acanthodians gave rise to the modern bony fishes or that both groups share a common ancestor.

The placoderms, another group of jawed fishes, appeared at the beginning of the Devonian, about 395 million years ago, and became extinct at the end of the Devonian or the beginning of the Mississippian (Carboniferous), about 345 million years ago. Placoderms were typically small, flattened bottom-dwellers. The upper jaw was firmly fused to the skull, but there was a hinge joint between the skull and the bony plating of the trunk region.

The cartilaginous-skeleton sharks and rays, class Chondrichthyes, which appeared about 370 million years ago in the middle Devonian, are generally believed to be descended from the bony-skeleton placoderms. The cartilaginous skeletons are considered to be a later development.

The modern bony fishes, class Osteichthyes, appeared in the late Silurian or early Devonian, about 395 million years ago. The early forms were freshwater fishes, for no fossil remains of modern bony fishes have been found in marine deposits older than Triassic time, about 230 million years ago. The Osteichthyes may have arisen from the acanthodians. A subclass of the Osteichthyes, the ray-finned fishes (subclass Actinopterygii), became and have remained the dominant group of fishes throughout the world. It was not the ray-finned fishes, however, that led to the evolution of the land vertebrates.

The ancestors of the land vertebrates are found among another group of bony fishes called the Choanichthyes or Sarcopterygii. Choanate fishes are characterized by internal nostrils, fleshy fins called lobe fins, and cosmoid scales. The choanate fishes appeared in the late Silurian or early Devo-

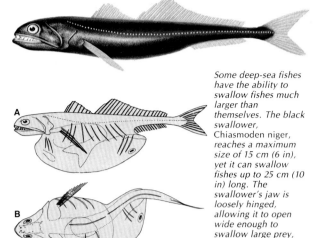

Some deep-sea fishes have the ability to swallow fishes much larger than themselves. The black swallower, Chiasmoden niger, reaches a maximum size of 15 cm (6 in), yet it can swallow fishes up to 25 cm (10 in) long. The swallower's jaw is loosely hinged, allowing it to open wide enough to swallow large prey, which is then passed into the expansible stomach (A, side view; B, top view).

nian, more than 390 million years ago, and possibly arose from the acanthodians. The choanate fishes include a group known as the Crossopterygii, which has one living representative, the coelacanth *Latimeria*. During the Devonian Period some crossopterygian fishes of the order (or suborder) Rhipidistia evolved to become the first amphibians.

Classification. The classification of fishes is a subject of considerable debate. The living fishes are often divided into three different classes. Divisions within these classes, however—particularly within the bony fishes (Osteichthyes)—are much in dispute. Different names are applied to the same group, and any given group may be regarded as either a subclass, order, or some other rank, depending upon the authority consulted. The following general classification includes as many alternative definitions as space allows:

Class Agnatha or Cephalaspidomorphi, the jawless fishes
Subclass (or order) Cyclostomata, the lampreys and hagfishes (*In certain classifications, the lampreys and hagfishes are each considered separate superclasses: Cephalaspidomorphi and Pteraspidomorphi, respectively.*)

Class Chondrichthyes, the cartilaginous-skeleton fishes
Subclass Holocephali, the chimaeras, or ratfishes
Subclass Elasmobranchii, the sharks, skates, and rays

Class Osteichthyes, the bony fishes
Subclass (or order) Crossopterygii, the coelacanth
Subclass (or order) Dipnoi or Dipneusti, the lungfishes
(*In some classifications, the above two subclasses are treated as orders of a single subclass, the Choanichthyes or Sarcopterygii, the lobe-finned fishes.*)
Subclass Actinopterygii, the ray-finned fishes
Infraclass (or superorder) Chondrostei, the primitive ray-finned bony fishes: sturgeons, paddlefish, and bichirs (*In some classifications, the bichirs are placed in a subclass of their own, the Brachiopterygii.*)
Infraclass (or superorder) Holostei or Neopterygii, the intermediate ray-finned fishes: gars and the bowfin (*In certain classifications, the gars are treated as a separate superorder, the Ginglymodi. The term Ginglymodi also has been used to designate the gars as an order, but this term has been replaced at the ordinal level by the term Lepisosteiformes; orders are now indicated by the ending -formes.*)
Infraclass (or superorder) Teleostei or Neopterygii, the advanced bony fishes: herring, salmon, perch

EDWIN E. ROSENBLUM

Bibliography: Alexander, R. M., *Functional Design in Fishes,* 3d ed. (1974); Blake, R. W., *Fish Locomotion* (1983); Bone, Q., and Marshall, N. B., *Biology of Fishes* (1983); Hauser, H., *Book of Marine Fishes* (1988); Kennlyeside, M. H., *Diversity and Adaptation in Fish Behaviour* (1979); Madsen, Kjeld, *Aquarium Fishes in Color* (1982); McClane, A. J., *McClane's Field Guide to Freshwater Fishes of North America* (1978); Migdaklsi, E. C., and Fichter, G. S., *The Fresh and Salt Water Fishes of the World* (1976); Moyle, P. B., and Cech, J. J., *Fishes: An Introduction to Ichthyology,* 2d ed. (1988); Nelson, J. S., *Fishes of the World* (1984); Norman, J. R., *A History of Fishes,* 3d ed. (1975); Smith, Lynwood S., *Introduction to Fish Physiology* (1982); Weatherly, A. H., and Gill, H. S., *The Biology of Fish Growth* (1987).

Fish, Hamilton: see FISH (family).

Fish, Robert L.

Mystery writer Robert L. Fish, b. Cleveland, Ohio, Aug. 21, 1912, d. Feb. 24, 1981, was the author of 40 novels and 100 short stories and articles. A plastics engineer, Fish did not begin writing until his late forties but almost immediately achieved recognition for such works as *The Fugitive* (1962) and *Mute Witness* (1963, written under Fish's pseudonym, Robert L. Pike), on which the film *Bullitt* (1968) was based. Fish won three Edgar Allan Poe awards. His last work, *Rough Diamond* (1981), was published posthumously.

fish farming

Fish farming, or aquaculture, is the raising of food fish and other aquatic life in protected enclosures or in controlled, natural environments. Although the cultivation of fish for commercial harvesting is an ancient practice in some countries—the farming of carp provides a significant proportion of the protein supply in China, for example—in the United States and Europe it is still a relatively small industry. In the coming years, however, new technologies and methods may increase

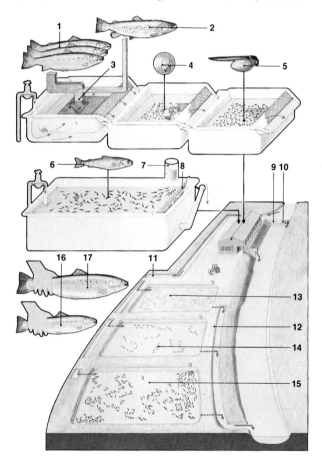

The process of raising brown trout begins when eggs and milt from adult female and male fish (1, 2) are mixed (3). The fertilized eggs are hatched (4) and reared through the larval stage (5) in temperature-controlled incubators. At about 3 weeks, the fry (6) are transferred to fry tanks, where automatic feeders (7) release controlled amounts of food; a fish screen (8) prevents their escape. At 12 weeks, the fry are moved to earth ponds situated on a river; a dam (9) diverts water for the ponds. A fish ladder (10) permits movement of the river fish, and inlet and outlet channels (11, 12) keep the pond water fresh. Ponds (13–15) hold fish at different growth stages. At 24 months (16), trout reach edible size. At 36 months (17), they are mature and can breed.

aquaculture yields, much as poultry production soared in the 1950s after the mechanization of that industry.

In the United States about 5 percent of the fish harvest is produced by aquaculture. Both federal and state agencies are involved in hatchery programs for trout and salmon, but private aquaculture accounts for most of the fish crop. Almost all the commercially marketed U.S. catfish, crawfish, and rainbow trout, and about half the oysters, are aquaculture products.

Catfish is the largest crop, grown primarily in Mississippi, Arkansas, and Louisiana. Catfish cultivation is relatively simple because the fish are omnivorous feeders and reproduce easily. Crawfish—cultivated mainly in Louisiana—is the second-largest fish crop and, like catfish, is relatively easy to grow, requiring no additional food beyond what the crawfish can forage in the ponds where they are stocked. Trout, the third most important crop, is produced almost exclusively in Idaho, where there is an abundant supply of fast-running river water. Pacific salmon are produced annually from hatcheries in the northwestern states. Young salmon smolts are released into the ocean and caught when they return to spawn; or they may be raised in pens and harvested after one year, when they weigh about 0.5 kg (1 lb).

The U.S. oyster crop has been decreasing for many years, in part because of water pollution, overfishing, and the loss of viable habitats. New methods of feeding and cultivation are being tried, but their success depends on conditions that are often beyond the control of the oyster farmer.

Culture systems for other aquatic species—among them, striped bass, sturgeon, clams, and tilapia—are being developed, both in the United States and overseas. Norway has a large and thriving salmon-raising industry. Freshwater shrimp grow in ponds in Hawaii; marine shrimp are raised in Ecuador, Mexico, Taiwan, and Japan, which is also experimenting with domesticated lobsters and crabs. Israel and the Philippines both have large freshwater fish-farming programs.

A new inshore fish-rearing method has been successful in encouraging growth in the numbers of marine fish and crustaceans. When an artificial reef is set up in a barren ocean area where few living creatures exist, there is a rapid increase in the overall number, and often the species, of fish as they find shelter within the reef. An eventual heavy growth of small marine organisms living on the reef itself also occurs. Reefs may consist of building rubble, concrete pipe, old tires, or specially designed structures. Japan has almost doubled its inshore fishing catch by building 2,500 artificial reefs along parts of its coastline.

Bibliography: Landau, Matthew, *Introduction to Aquaculture* (1991); Lee, S. J., and Newman, M. E., *Aquaculture: An Introduction* (1992); Limburg, P. R., *Farming the Waters* (1981); Martin, Roy F., and Flick, George J., Jr., eds., *The Seafood Industry* (1990); Tiddens, Art, *Aquaculture in America* (1990); Walker, Mike, *Aquaculture Engineering* (1989).

See also: FISHING INDUSTRY.

fish hawk: see OSPREY.

fish meal

Fish meal is a product made from dehydrated, ground fish that is used primarily for livestock feed. Roughly 20 percent of the world's fish catch is converted into meal. The principal meal fish are menhaden, mackerel, pilchard, hake, and anchoveta. Fish waste from food fish processing is also used for meal.

Meal made from such white-fleshed fish species as hake, and manufactured under controlled conditions, is called fish protein concentrate (FPC). Although it has so far proved uneconomic, it is hoped that FPC may someday be used as a protein supplement in human diets.   FELIX FAVORITE

Fisher, Andrew

Andrew Fisher, b. Aug. 29, 1862, d. Oct. 22, 1928, was Labor prime minister of Australia in 1908–09, 1910–13, and 1914–15. Born in Scotland, he emigrated to Queensland in 1885, becoming a coal miner and union leader. Elected to the first Federal Parliament in 1901, he became Labor party leader in 1907. His Labor governments created the Commonwealth Bank and national navy and began the transcontinental railroad. Fisher also led his country into World War I.

Fisher, Dorothy Canfield

Dorothy Canfield Fisher, b. Lawrence, Kans., Feb. 17, 1879, d. Nov. 9, 1958, was a popular American novelist. *The Squirrel-Cage* (1912) was her first widely read work. Others include *The Bent Twig* (1915), *The Brimming Cup* (1921), and *The Deepening Stream* (1930).

Bibliography: Washington, Ida H., *Dorothy Canfield Fisher* (1982).

Fisher, Geoffrey Francis

Geoffrey Francis Fisher, b. May 5, 1887, d. Sept. 14, 1972, was archbishop of Canterbury from 1945 to 1961. Educated at Oxford, he was headmaster of Repton School (1914–32), bishop of Chester (1932–39), and bishop of London (1939–45). A keen ecumenist and able administrator, he was a president of the World Council of Churches from 1946 to 1954. He visited Pope John XXIII in 1960, the first meeting of an archbishop of Canterbury with a pope since the Reformation.

Fisher, Irving

Irving Fisher, b. Saugerties, N.Y., Feb. 27, 1867, d. Apr. 29, 1947, was an economist who worked in monetary theory and index numbers. He taught (1895–1935) at Yale University. Fisher also had evangelistic interests in social welfare reform, mental health, and the temperance movement.

Fisher, Saint John

Saint John Fisher, b. 1469, d. June 22, 1535, was an English Roman Catholic prelate and humanist executed for treason during the Reformation. He became bishop of Rochester in 1504 and confessor to Lady Margaret Beaufort, the mother of Henry VII. His humanist interests persisted throughout his life; he brought his friend ERASMUS to England to teach Greek.

The situation arising from HENRY VIII's dissatisfaction with his wife, CATHERINE OF ARAGON, dominated Fisher's last eight years. Fisher was openly opposed to the dissolution of Henry's marriage to Catherine. He also refused to recognize royal supremacy and the end of papal jurisdiction over the church in England. After he failed to take the oath required by the Act of Succession (1534), he was imprisoned in the Tower of London. When Pope Paul III showed his support for Fisher by naming him a cardinal on May 20, 1535, Fisher's fate was sealed; he was tried for treason and executed. He was canonized in 1935. Feast day: June 22.   THOMAS E. MORRISSEY

Bibliography: Bradshaw, B., and Duffy, E., eds., *Humanism, Reform, and the Reformation* (1989); Rex, R., *The Theology of John Fisher* (1991).

Fisher, M. F. K.

The American writer Mary Frances Kennedy Fisher, b. Albion, Mich., July 3, 1908, d. June 22, 1992, reflected on food and life with erudition and humor. Five of her early books are collected in *The Art of Eating* (1954; repr. 1990). Her autobiographical writings include *Among Friends* (1971), *Sister Age* (1983), and *Long Ago in France* (1991). A selection of prefaces is reprinted in *Dubious Honors* (1988).

Fisher, Sir Ronald Aylmer

Sir Ronald Aylmer Fisher, b. Feb. 17, 1890, d. July 29, 1962, was a British statistician, biologist, and mathematician who developed SAMPLING techniques and randomization procedures now used throughout the world. Fisher received a B.A. in astronomy from Cambridge in 1912. His interest in the theory of errors in astronomy eventually led him to investigate statistical problems. In 1919 he left a position as a mathematics teacher in the public schools in order to work at the Rothamsted Agricultural Experiment Station, where he made extensive contributions to both statistics and genetics.

The significant contributions made by Fisher and his associates included the development of methods appropriate for small samples, the discovery of the exact distributions of many sample statistics, the formulation of logical principles for testing hypotheses, the development of criteria for choice among various possible estimators for a population parameter, and the invention of the technique known as analysis of VARI-ANCE. Because of his many important contributions to the field, Fisher is considered one of the founders of modern statistics.   H. HOWARD FRISINGER

Bibliography: Hacking, Ian, *Logic of Statistical Inference* (1965).

Fisher, Rudolph

An American writer and physician, Rudolph Fisher, b. Washington, D.C., May 9, 1897, d. Dec. 26, 1934, is best known for two novels of black life in Harlem in the 1920s. In *The Walls of Jericho* (1928), Fisher's gift for satire sharpens his portraits of three classes of black society and several types of whites. *The Conjure-Man Dies* (1932), the first mystery novel by a black American, takes as its hero a Harvard-educated African prince who practices psychiatry in Harlem and uses his insight into paranoia to catch a murderer. Fisher's short stories are collected in *The City of Refuge* (1987).

Bibliography: Bontemps, Arna, *The Harlem Renaissance Remembered* (1972); Davis, A. P., and Redding, Saunders, eds., *Cavalcade* (1971).

Fisher, Vardis

Vardis Fisher, b. Annis, Idaho, Mar. 31, 1895, d. July 9, 1968, was an American writer whose novels, set in the Rocky Mountains, have been praised for their psychological realism and historical accuracy. Among the best known are *Children of God* (1939), on the history of Mormonism; *The Mothers* (1943), on the Donner Party; and four autobiographical novels: *In Tragic Life* (1932), *Passions Spin the Plot* (1934), *We Are Betrayed* (1935), and *No Villain Need Be* (1936). Fisher also completed a 12-volume series of novels on humankind's spiritual and intellectual history, called collectively *The Testament of Man* (1943–60). He was a close friend of Thomas Wolfe, with whom he is often compared.

Bibliography: Flora, J. M., *Vardis Fisher* (1965); Grover, D. C., *The Novelist as Poet* (1973) and *A Solitary Voice* (1973); Woodward, T., *Tiger on the Road* (1989).

Fisher of Kilverstone, John Arbuthnot Fisher, 1st Baron

The British admiral Lord Fisher, b. Jan. 25, 1841, d. July 10, 1920, entered the Royal Navy in 1854 and became admiral of the fleet in 1905. As first sea lord in the Admiralty (1904–10), Fisher improved the military preparedness of the navy, introducing, among other things, a new class of battleship, the DREADNOUGHT (1906), and converting the fleet from coal to oil, a step that led the British to acquire oil interests in the Middle East. Fisher's policies enabled the Royal Navy to match the German naval buildup under Admiral von TIRPITZ and to neutralize the German fleet during World War I. Brought back as first sea lord under Winston CHURCHILL in 1914, Fisher opposed the disastrous GALLIPOLI CAMPAIGN and resigned in May 1915.

Bibliography: Hough, Richard, *Admiral of the Fleet: The Life of John Fisher* (1970); Jameson, William, *The Fleet that Jack Built* (1962); Mackay, R. F., *Fisher of Kilverstone* (1973); Marder, A. J., *From the Dreadnought to Scapa Flow*, 5 vols. (1961–70).

fishing

The sport of fishing has been practiced widely throughout the world for countless years. In the United States alone, about 36.5 million fishing licenses are issued each year. That number does not include children or saltwater fishermen, neither of whom require licenses.

Types of Fish. Anglers fish for thousands of species. The larger species are found in salt water. A 1,208-kg (2,664-lb) white shark was caught by rod off Australia in 1959. The largest freshwater fish for sportsmen is the white sturgeon. Among the most popular saltwater fish are flounder, bluefish, cod, striped bass, tuna, sea trout, porgies, red snapper, halibut, and haddock. The popular freshwater fish include black bass, various types of trout, sunfish, crappies, salmon, perch, pike, muskies, sturgeon, and shad. Some fish live in both fresh and salt water. Amphidromous species (milkfish, snook) move from fresh to salt water, but not for the purpose of spawning. Anadromous species (Atlantic salmon, alewife, shad) move from oceans to rivers in order to spawn. Catadromous fish (American eel) move from fresh to salt water in order to spawn.

Methods of Fishing. There are three general methods of sport fishing—trolling, casting, and still fishing. To troll, the angler lets out line attached to a baited hook or lure, which is pulled along as the fisherman's boat moves through the water. To cast, the angler flips his baited hook toward an area where the fish are likely to lurk, such as in a weed bed or under a fallen tree. For still fishing, the angler sits on shore or anchors his boat and sinks a weighted line with bait and hook into the water; often a bobber is attached to the line to indicate movement if the fish should nibble. Sometimes the boat anchor is not dropped, so that the boat can drift. Other less frequently practiced methods of fishing include harpooning and fishing with bow-and-arrow. In wintertime many anglers ice-fish by cutting holes in the ice; they sometimes fish from inside a small enclosure called a fish shanty.

Bait. Fish are attracted to hooks by either natural or artificial baits. For freshwater fish, natural baits include worms, night crawlers, minnows, small baitfish (such as shiners and suckers), hellgramites, and crickets. The most popular saltwater baits are crayfish, clams, or small pieces of fish. Hundreds of artificial lures, shaped as small fish, worms, flies, or colorful objects, are also used.

Fishing Poles and Reels. Most fishing rods are made of graphite, fiberglass, or boron, although some expensive fly rods are made of split bamboo. Fishing reels come in five general classifications: fly reel, bait-casting reel, spin-casting reel, opened-face reel, and larger reels for saltwater fish and more powerful freshwater fish such as sturgeon or muskies. The reels allow the fisherman to cast, or throw out his line, and

These sport fishermen are in the Gulf of Mexico off Biloxi, Miss. In these warm Gulf Stream waters, game fishes include bonito, marlin, bluefish, sailfish, tuna, and several types of trout.

Fishing techniques differ according to the species of fish being sought. (Above) Carp, catfish, and panfish can be caught in still water by casting a baited hook to rest on the bottom, where those species feed. (Right) Many varieties of trout and salmon, which prefer fast-moving water, are caught with spinning lures and small artificial flies.

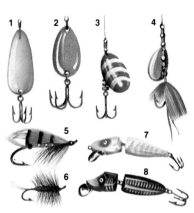

(Left) Artificial lures, such as spoons (1, 2) and spinners (3, 4), attract fish with their wobbling action and flashing colors. The streamer (5), a wet fly, is designed to sink swiftly; the dry fly (6), which resembles a larval insect, floats on the surface. Jointed plugs (7, 8) feature an erratic motion similar to that of an injured minnow.

retrieve it untangled. Sport fishing is one of the largest and most profitable recreation businesses in the United States.

HOWARD LISS

Bibliography: Baughman, M., *Ocean Fishing* (1986); Benn, Timothy, *The Almost Compleat Angler* (1988); Blaisdell, Harold F., *The Art of Fishing with Worms and Other Live Bait* (1978); Buller, F., and Falkus, H., *Falkus and Buller's Freshwater Fishing* (1988); McClane, A. J., *Complete Book of Fishing* (1987); Stoker, Hugh, et al., *Fishing with the Experts* (1978); Swainbank, T., et al., *Taking Freshwater Game Fish* (1988); Thiffault, Mark, ed., *Illustrated Guide to Better Fishing*, 3d ed. (1990); Walton, Izaac, *The Compleat Angler* (1659; repr. 1988); Waterman, Charles F., *History of Angling* (1981); Wright, L., *First Cast: The Beginner's Guide to Fly Fishing* (1988).

fishing industry

Commercial fishing is a worldwide enterprise that involves the capture of ocean and freshwater fish, shellfish, and marine mammals and their processing for market. Fishing equipment ranges from small boats whose nets are cast and hauled in by hand to factory ships equipped with the most advanced technologies for finding, harvesting, and processing huge quantities of fish. These large catches are very expensive, however, not only in the cost of the equipment (some advanced fishing vessels are nearly as expensive as warships) and fuel, but also in the potential depletion of fishery resources.

The major portion of the total fish harvest consists of relatively few fish species, which are divided into two groups. Pelagic species—those which inhabit the near-surface layers of the oceans—include several species of herring, tuna, salmon, anchovies, pilchard, sardines, menhaden, and mackerel. Demersal species—fish that inhabit the near bottom layers of the ocean—include cod, sole, halibut, haddock, hake, and flounder. Large catches are also made of a group of fish classed commercially as SHELLFISH—shrimp, lobster, scallops, oysters, clams, crabs, mussels, and squid. The most important marine mammal is the whale. Although WHALING is a specialized area within the fishing industry, it has lost most of its former importance.

Almost all large pelagic and demersal fish catches are made over the continental shelf, the underwater plateau surrounding the continents and large islands. In these waters temperatures, water depths, and the currents that influence the quantities of available food create an environment that is highly favorable to the existence of large schools of fish.

The animals living in and on the bottom of the continental shelf serve as additional food sources for demersal fish. Furthermore, most species spawn on continental shelves, and the main nursery grounds of many species are also in coastal regions. The main fishing grounds are located on the wider continental shelves of the mid and high latitudes. These include

Of the hundreds of species of fish that inhabit the sea, the anchoveta (A), cod (B), herring (C), haddock (D), and sardine (E) are among the most important commercially for the fishing industry. The anchovies and sardines are smaller members of the herring family; all three are pelagic fish. Codfish and haddock are related and are usually caught near the bottom. The herring and codfish families combined account for 40 percent of the world's total annual catch of fish.

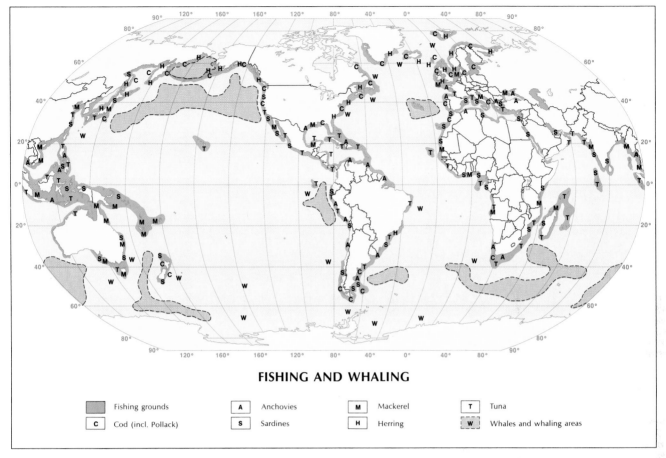

FISHING AND WHALING

▨ Fishing grounds	**A** Anchovies	**M** Mackerel	**T** Tuna
C Cod (incl. Pollack)	**S** Sardines	**H** Herring	**W** Whales and whaling areas

the Grand Banks, Bering Sea, and North Sea, the resources of which are exploited by many nations.

THE DEVELOPMENT OF THE FISHING INDUSTRY

Prehistoric peoples were hunters and food collectors, and they found much of their food in lakes, rivers, and shallow coastal ocean waters. Shellfish were the most accessible food fish, and the large shell heaps found throughout the world bear witness to the first fishing technique, the use of bare hands.

During the Mesolithic Period (c.10,000–6000 BC) certain cultures that depended almost entirely on a diet of fish developed primitive fishing technologies. The Scandinavian Maglemosian culture, for example, used stone-pointed fishing spears, stone fishhooks, fishing lines and nets, and bone harpoons. Improved equipment increased the size of catches, and preservation techniques were developed for drying, smoking, salting, and pickling fish.

As larger fishing craft were built, vessels ventured farther into the oceans, and sea fishing developed into a well-defined vocation, with settlements whose central occupation was the catching of fish.

Early ocean fisheries were confined to the coastal regions of settled areas and to the Mediterranean Sea, which had been the traditional fishing grounds for large numbers of fish species, especially tuna. Gradually, the rich fishing regions of the Atlantic Ocean and the North and Baltic seas began to be exploited. The opening of these new fishing grounds had a significant influence on the spread of trade during the Middle Ages and on the establishment of new trade routes—for example, the herring fisheries in the southern Baltic and North seas that helped to establish the HANSEATIC LEAGUE.

The opening of the fishing areas around Nova Scotia and Newfoundland had a considerable effect on European history. First fished by the French in the early 1500s, by the beginning of the 17th century the North Atlantic fisheries had become the principal source of New World wealth for England.

PRINCIPAL FISHERIES

The most important world fisheries are located in waters less than 400 m (1,300 ft) in depth. The major fishing grounds are in the North Atlantic (including the GRAND BANKS and the Georges Banks off the New England coast), the North Sea, the waters over the continental shelves of Iceland and Norway, and the Barents Sea; in the North Pacific, particularly the Bering Sea, the Gulf of Alaska, and the coastal areas around Japan; and in the Pacific waters off the coasts of China and Malaysia. Other important fishing grounds are found off the Peruvian coast and off the coast of the southeastern United States.

Fishing is often restricted to the spawning periods of a particular species. Fortunately, different stocks of the same spe-

After being beheaded and de-tailed, fresh-caught tuna are numbered and arranged in rows in a Tokyo wholesale fish market. The large yellowfin tuna, T. albacares, is particularly prized for sushi, the Japanese raw fish cuisine.

A

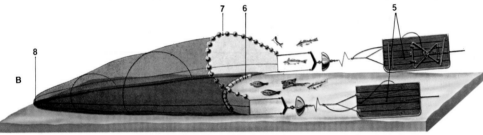

B

C

Otter trawling is an important form of commercial fishing. An otter trawl is a net that is towed along the ocean bottom by long cables called warps. On the side trawler (A), the warp cables pass through fore and aft gallows (1, 2) mounted on one side of the ship, then through a towing block (3). When full, the trawl is hauled to the surface by powerful winches (4). On the trawl itself (B), the towing cables are attached to otter boards (5), iron-shod wood panels that pull sideways as they are dragged forward, keeping the trawl mouth open horizontally; heavy rollers on the net's bottom lip (6), and floats along the top (7), keep the mouth open vertically. The trawl net tapers to a narrow end (the cod end) that is laced closed (8). When the trawl is hoisted on deck, the end-lacing is released and the catch is dropped into the ship. Otter trawling requires great lengths of cable (C).

cies often have different spawning times on different grounds, and this fact enables the fishery to be extended over longer periods. For example, the Norwegian "spring herring" gathers for spawning mainly in January and February; the "big herring" (stors-ild) spawns in September to December. The herring stock size caught along the Norwegian coast has fluctuated throughout the centuries, and documents indicate that from about 1500 there have been four good herring periods, each lasting from 50 to 80 years. The last good period began about 1885 and declined rapidly in the late 1960s. At present, herring stocks throughout the North Atlantic are low, and their harvesting is regulated through national quotas.

Another example of a seasonal fishery is the Norwegian cod fishery, where cod migrating to the Norwegian coast to spawn are harvested in the winter, and immature cod from the Barents Sea are caught in the spring as they migrate to feed in the regions off the northern coast of Norway.

The local fisheries of the African coast, and many of those found elsewhere in the tropics, remain relatively undeveloped. The principal limiting factors are: first, the narrowness of the continental shelf, which limits the presence of demersal fish, and the existence of a straight coastline that offers few possibilities for good harbors; second, the high temperatures, which affect the keeping quality of the fish catch; and third, limited access to the interior, making marketing difficult. Fish landings from these areas are usually dried, smoked, or salted immediately.

Major Fishing Countries. Catches of fish and shellfish throughout the world have risen within the decade of the '80s from about 77 million metric tons (1982) to over 90 million metric tons (1986). Almost half the catch, 40.5 million metric tons, is taken by Asian countries, principally Japan, which today captures the world's largest catches. The USSR follows Japan; China is third, but with a catch only half the size of the Soviets'; and the United States and Chile share fourth place.

The total catch of marine fish and shellfish in the United States throughout the 1980s averaged about 3 million metric tons annually. About one-quarter of the marine fish catch is taken in the Northwest Atlantic, some 40% in the Southwest Atlantic and the Gulf of Mexico, and another quarter in the Northeast Pacific and Alaskan coastal waters. Tuna and shrimp are the most valuable catches. The haddock fishery off the New England coast is another important fishery, although haddock landings have decreased sharply in recent years because of overfishing. The same fishery yields cod and flounder. Salmon and halibut are harvested in the Northeast Pacific, and the anchovy fishery off the coast of California produces fish for processing and for live bait.

About 250,000 fishermen are engaged in marine fisheries in the United States. Most U.S. fishing vessels are smaller than 50 gross tons and less than 20 m (65 ft) long, with only a few hundred vessels of significantly larger size in the U.S. fleet. Principal ports are San Pedro, Calif. (tuna), Kodiak, Alaska (crab and groundfish), and Cameron, La. (menhaden).

The profitable crab fishery in the Bering Sea collapsed in 1983 and is not expected to yield higher catches until the mid-1990s. Much of the crab fleet were converted to trawlers, which yielded higher catches of Pacific cod and pollock in joint-venture fisheries with foreign processors (mainly Japanese and Russian).

The catches of Pacific salmon have decreased in recent years despite increased efforts in release of smolt (young salmon) produced in coastal hatcheries.

FISHING TECHNOLOGIES
In most modern fishing fleets the basic fishing vessel is the trawler, equipped with a diesel engine and outfitted with a variety of equipment for fish finding and capturing.

Echo sounders and sonar devices detect the presence of fish in waters up to 400 fathoms deep (730 m/2,400 ft) and are also used to ascertain water depths and the roughness on the ocean bottom. Airplanes are used to scout scattered shoals of pelagic fish.

Fish Harvesting. The standard methods of catching fish involve either nets, hooked lines, or traps. Pelagic fish are most often harvested using purse seine nets, which are set in a wide circle around the school and then closed (or pursed) and drawn up. Straight drift or gill nets—whose mesh is just large enough to allow the heads of fish to pass through while trapping them at their gills—are used to catch salmon, tuna, cod, and other fish. (Since the 1980s, however, the use of immense assemblies of drift nets has exacerbated the overfishing of valuable fisheries and caused the accidental deaths of thousands of such noncommercial species as porpoises.) Demersal fish may be netted in otter trawl nets pulled along the ocean bottom or with beam trawls that are used in more shallow waters, primarily for shrimp.

In halibut fishing, hooked groundlines, called longlines, may reach lengths of many miles, with baited hooks attached at intervals of 6 to 9 m (20 to 30 ft). Floating longlines are used primarily in tuna and salmon fishing, as are trolling lines, shorter lines towed behind a moving boat. Lights may be lowered into fresh and brackish waters to attract fish, which are then sucked up into the ship by vacuum pumps.

Fish Processing. Large fishing vessels on long voyages are equipped to keep their catch edible by storing it in refrigerated facilities or by quick-freezing it. A fully equipped factory ship will also have machinery on board for fish filleting and freezing or canning. Fish fillets are frozen at sea into large blocks weighing up to 45 kg (100 lb); these are later reprocessed on shore into individual portions. Some ships may also have facilities for drying and grinding fish into fish meal.

Factory ships are huge vessels operated by crews of 500 to 650 and accompanied by their own fleets of smaller ships called catcher boats.

FISHERIES MANAGEMENT
As early as the 1890s it was acknowledged that fishery resources are limited and that they must be managed through international agreements. In 1902 the International Council for Exploration of the Sea (ICES) was formed by the major European fishing countries. The founding of ICES led to several conventions for the regulation of fisheries by mesh size of nets and by quotas, in order to obtain "maximum sustainable yields"—the highest yields consistent with the maintenance of fish stocks. Although such conventions have been effective in the Northeast Atlantic, they have not operated as well in other regions. The extension of national jurisdictions over fisheries

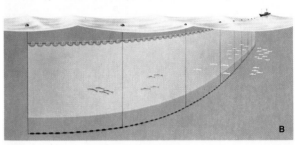

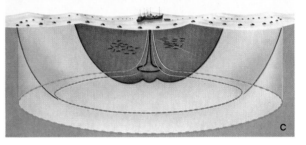

The beam trawl (A) *is a net bag used to catch demersal fish and shrimp in relatively shallow water. The bag's mouth is held open by a beam, and the bag is dragged over the seabed on metal skids. The gill net* (B) *is a long, floating net attached to the end of a drifting boat. Pelagic fish are trapped by their gills as they try to pass through the net's mesh. The purse seine* (C) *is used to trap pelagic schools of fish. The long, float-suspended net is towed in a wide circle around a shoal until the two ends of the net meet. The net is then pursed, or closed, by drawing in a line that runs through loops on the lower edge, to form a huge bag that can be hauled aboard.*

resources to a 200-naut-mi (370-km/230-mi) zone, beginning in the 1970s, has further limited the effectiveness of many international conventions.

In the United States the Fishery Conservation and Management Act of 1976 places all marine resources from the coast to 200 naut mi offshore under U.S. jurisdiction. Management is effected through regional fisheries councils, which also grant permits to foreign countries to harvest specified quantities of certain fish species in return for a fee. Countries that have fished under U.S. license include Japan, South Korea, the USSR, and Poland.

In addition to these quotas for foreign fishing vessels, quotas on commercially important fish such as salmon have been set for the American fishing fleet, which is restricted in terms of both the total catch of any particular species and the season when such fish may be harvested.

WORLD CATCHES
In 1948 the total world fish catch was about 19 million metric tons. With the introduction of advanced harvesting technologies, the total catch rose to over 60 million metric tons by 1970. Although there have been major fluctuations, since 1970 the trend has been upward: almost 77 million metric tons in 1982, more than 92 million metric tons in the late 1980s.

The causes for fluctuating—and, in some species groups, diminishing—catches are varied and include factors that are beyond human control: for example, the change in the ocean currents that caused the disappearance of the anchovy from the coastal waters off Peru (see El Niño). Overfishing, which

A bulging net of fish is thrown into a fish hatch of a modern, stern-fishing trawler. In ships close to port the fish are stored in refrigerated brine or melting crushed ice. In ships far from port, the fish are cleaned and quick-frozen to preserve them.

is the harvesting of a species to a point where it cannot reproduce itself in significant numbers, is partly responsible for decline of California sardines. Species that are now in danger of being overfished include cod, haddock, halibut, salmon, and several species of tuna and whale. International agreements and quotas are effective to some extent in preventing the extinction of some of these species.

Beginning in the early 1980s, Japanese, Taiwanese, and South Korean fishing fleets began to use a new fishing technique to make large-scale squid catches in the North Pacific. Huge, 15-m-deep (50-ft) drift nets made of unbreakable nylon, each stretching 90 m (295 ft), are lowered off the boats each evening. Together, the nets from a single boat form a great wall just under the surface of the ocean. The nets drift all night, entangling any sea creatures that happen to swim into their meshes—not only the desired squid, but quantities of salmon, steelhead trout, and ocean mammals as big as seals.

Illegal catches of immature salmon have appeared regularly in Asian markets. (Legally salmon belong to the country where they originated.) Because these fish have been taken before they can return to their native waters to spawn, the use of drift nets threatens the survival of the salmon as well as the steelhead trout populations in the northern Pacific area. As they "strip-mine" the ocean the nets kill vast numbers of unwanted species; for example, they may be responsible for the decline in the numbers of young humpback whales.

Fishing nations in South Pacific regions have asked for an end to the taking of albacore TUNA with drift nets, and in 1989, the United Nations called for the end of drift net use in the South Pacific by the summer of 1991. Japan and Taiwan agreed; but in 1990, Asian ships had begun moving drift net operations to fisheries in the South Atlantic.

FUTURE POSSIBILITIES

Most present fishery resources are fished to their limits, at least for those species having commercial importance. Many species exist, however, for which there has been no commercial demand, although some of these fish—notably whiting, hake, and pollack—offer great commercial possibilities if

markets can be developed for them. Many of the pelagic fish now used for the production of fish meal may be sold for direct human consumption in the future.

KRILL, a pelagic crustacean, exists in huge numbers in the Antarctic, where it is the principal food of whales. Krill resources offer great possibilities for exploitation, although when krill-processing technology is perfected, the fishing nations must agree on the optimal amounts of the harvest.

The improved cultivation of marine resources offers another possibility for increasing the number of food fish. Salmon have been artificially propagated in Norway and North America and in the Baltic Sea, and sea trout have been transplanted into coastal areas, where it is hoped that they will form less migratory, local stocks that can be easily harvested (see FISH FARMING). Lagoon cultivation of shrimp has been successful in Ecuador, which is now a large supplier of shrimp to the United States, and in China, Taiwan, and Indonesia. The cultivation of species of inland fish is an advancing technology that may also provide an important protein source.

FELIX FAVORITE AND TAIVO LAEVASTU

Bibliography: Allen, P., ed., *The U.S. Fishing Industry* (1982); Johnston, D. M., *The International Law of Fisheries* (1987); Johnston, P. F., *The New England Fisheries* (1984); Kawaky, J., ed., *Commercial Fisherman's Guide*, 3 vols. (1990); Laevastu, T., and Hayes, M. L., *Fisheries Oceanography and Ecology* (1981); Martin, R. F., and Flick, G. J., Jr., eds., *The Seafood Industry* (1990); Neilson, L. A., and Johnson, D. L., eds., *Fisheries Techniques* (1983); Royce, W. F., *Fisheries Development* (1987); Sainsbury, J., *Commercial Fishing Methods* (1986).

See also: FISH; WHALING; separate articles on individual fish species.

Fisk, James

James Fisk, b. Bennington, Vt., Apr. 1, 1834, d. Jan. 7, 1872, was a financier and stock speculator who became known as the "Barnum of Wall Street." He left school at an early age and worked at odd jobs before becoming a buyer for Jordan and Marsh, a Boston dry goods firm. After the Civil War he was an agent for the financier Daniel DREW, who helped him open a brokerage firm. With Drew and Jay GOULD, Fisk was a principal in the "Erie War," the struggle to prevent Cornelius Vanderbilt from gaining control of the Erie Railroad. In 1869, Fisk and Gould attempted to corner the gold market, an adventure that ended in the BLACK FRIDAY panic of September 24. Fisk lived licentiously, without regard for his reputation. He died the day after he was shot by a business associate following a quarrel that involved Fisk's favorite mistress.

Bibliography: Ackerman, K. D., *The Gold Ring: Jim Fisk, Jay Gould, and Black Friday, 1869* (1988); Swanberg, W. A., *Jim Fisk* (1959).

The business tactics and stock speculations of the American financier James Fisk secured him a vast fortune. Working closely with Jay Gould and Daniel Drew, Fisk manipulated the stock of the Erie Railroad for personal gain. The attempt of these men to corner the gold market resulted in the "Black Friday" panic of Sept. 24, 1869.

Fisk University

Founded in 1865 as a college for blacks, and still having a large black enrollment, Fisk University (enrollment: 900; library: 186,174 volumes) is a private coeducational liberal arts school affiliated with the United Church of Christ. It is located in Nashville, Tenn.

Fiske, John

The American historian and philosopher John Fiske, b. Hartford, Conn., Mar. 30, 1842, d. July 4, 1901, popularized SOCIAL DARWINISM—Herbert SPENCER's interpretation of Charles Darwin's ideas on evolution—and applied it to U.S. history. Fiske's *Outlines of Cosmic Philosophy* (2 vols., 1874) contended that societies, like biological organisms, develop according to laws of evolution.

In 1880 Fiske delivered a series of lectures that treated the United States as the culmination of the historical evolution toward democracy. In *The Critical Period of American History, 1783–1789* (1888), Fiske argued that the U.S. Constitution had saved the nation from the impending catastrophe of interstate struggles.

Bibliography: Berman, Milton, *John Fiske* (1961).

Fiske, Minnie Maddern

Minnie Maddern Fiske is the stage name of Marie Augusta Davey, b. New Orleans, Dec. 19, 1865, d. Feb. 13, 1932, an American actress who made her stage debut at the age of three. She appeared in serious drama, such as a stage adaptation (1897) of Thomas Hardy's *Tess of the D'Urbervilles*, as well as in light comedy. An advocate of stage realism, Fiske championed Henrik Ibsen's plays at a time when they were considered scandalous.   ANDREW J. KELLY

Bibliography: Binns, Archie, *Mrs. Fiske and the American Theatre* (1955; repr. 1983).

fission, nuclear

Nuclear fission is a special type of nuclear reaction in which a heavy nucleus breaks up into two smaller nuclei or fragments. Fission may occur spontaneously or by the bombardment of a nucleus with a particle such as a neutron or a proton or with gamma radiation. Many different nuclei may undergo fission, but all have some common characteristics. Fission is a complex process, and it creates many different products. In addition to the two fragments, NEUTRONS, beta particles, NEUTRINOS, and GAMMA RAYS are also emitted in a fission process.

The phenomenon of fission is a statistical process in the sense that there are about 50 different ways a nucleus may undergo fission, producing a different pair of primary fragments each time, and creating some one hundred different nuclei. Some modes of fission are more probable than others. One characteristic of the process is that the fissioning nucleus breaks into two unequal parts, creating a lighter fragment and a heavier fragment. These nuclei are formed with excess energy that they do not have in their normal, or ground, states, and they must deexcite, or lose energy, usually by the emission of gamma radiation and sometimes by neutron emission. Each primary fragment formed is rich in neutrons and is radioactive. It undergoes successive BETA DECAY, each time creating a new element until a stable final nucleus is formed. The radioactive nuclei can be separated and can be used in research, NUCLEAR MEDICINE, engineering, and agriculture.

Some nuclei, such as URANIUM-235, which contains 92 protons and 143 neutrons, are more apt than others to undergo fission when bombarded by low-energy neutrons. For this reason uranium-235 is used as the fissionable material in the construction of a NUCLEAR REACTOR. Each fission process causes additional neutrons to be emitted. The excess neutrons thus produced can cause more fissions in the fissionable material, generating a CHAIN REACTION in the reactor.   R. R. ROY

Bibliography: Badash, L., et al., *Nuclear Fission* (1985); Cameron, I. F., *Nuclear Fission Reactors* (1982); Cohen, B. L., *The Nuclear Energy Op-*

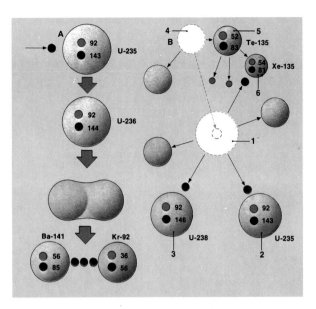

(A) A thermal, or low-energy, neutron (black) may be absorbed by a uranium-235 (U-235) nucleus, containing 92 protons (red) and 143 neutrons, to form an unstable uranium-236 nucleus. The U-236 nucleus fissions, or splits, into two smaller nuclei, such as barium-141 (Ba-141) and krypton-92 (Kr-92), and 2 or 3 neutrons. (B) Neutrons from a fissioned nucleus (1) may strike another U-235 nucleus (2) and cause it to fragment and release more neutrons, producing a chain reaction if enough U-235 neutrons are present. Neutrons may also be absorbed by nonfissionable U-238 nuclei (3) or previously created fission products (4). A fission product such as tellurium-135 (5), for example, decays to xenon-135 (6), which absorbs neutrons without splitting.

tion (1990); Gibson, W. M., *The Physics of Nuclear Reactions* (1980); Hamilton, W. D., and Pearson, J. M., eds., *Nuclear Physics* (1986); Kocherga, O. K., ed., *Theory of Nuclear Reactions* (1980); Kruschke, E. R., and Jackson, B. M., *Nuclear Energy Policy* (1990).

See also: ATOMIC BOMB; NUCLEAR ENERGY; RADIOACTIVITY.

Fitch, Clyde

A versatile American dramatist, William Clyde Fitch, b. Elmira, N.Y., May 2, 1865, d. Sept. 4, 1909, wrote or adapted more than 40 plays, ranging from farces and melodramas to historical and problem plays. Many of his works were written as vehicles for particular stars, including *Barbara Frietchie* (1899) for Julia Marlow and *Captain Jinks of the Horse Marines* (1901) for Ethel Barrymore. *The Girl with the Green Eyes* (1902), *The Truth* (1906), and *The City* (1909) are considered his best plays.

Fitch, John

John Fitch, b. Jan. 21, 1743, d. July 2, 1798, is best known as the builder of the first practical STEAMBOAT, which he built 21 years before Robert Fulton's commercially successful CLERMONT. Fitch read about Thomas Newcomen's STEAM ENGINE in 1785 and then experimented with steam propulsion, navigating a paddle-propelled steam craft on the Delaware River in 1787. He built a 13.7-m-long (45-ft) steamboat, which he demonstrated on the Delaware to delegates to the Constitutional Convention.

In 1790, with a larger boat, Fitch inaugurated the first regularly scheduled steamboat service in the world, between Philadelphia and Burlington, N.J. After trying unsuccessfully to obtain the necessary financial backing for other projects, Fitch ceased his efforts and retired to Bardstown, Ky., where he died destitute and despondent after suffering from a prolonged illness.   FRANCES GIES

Bibliography: Boyd, Thomas, *Poor John Fitch, Inventor of the Steamboat* (1935; repr. 1971).

Fitz, Henry

The American instrument maker Henry Fitz, b. Newburyport, Mass., Dec. 31, 1808, d. Nov. 6, 1863, earned a notable reputation for his construction of equatorially mounted achromatic telescopes. Originally a locksmith who traveled a circuit between New York, Philadelphia, Baltimore, and New Orleans, Fitz became interested in telescopes, astronomy, and daguerreotype photography. In 1840 he opened a studio in Baltimore, where he took photographs and built cameras and telescopes. Five years later he moved to New York, where he exhibited a 6-in (15.2-cm) refracting telescope at the American Institute Fair. This award-winning instrument brought Fitz numerous orders and a good income.   DAVID HOUNSHELL

FitzGerald, Edward

In translating the work of the Persian poet OMAR KHAYYAM, Edward FitzGerald, b. Mar. 31, 1809, d. June 14, 1883, created one of the best-loved and most memorable poems in the English language. A friend of Tennyson and Carlyle, FitzGerald devoted himself to Oriental studies after 1850, publishing his freely adapted RUBAIYAT OF OMAR KHAYYAM in 1859. This reflective poem, with its haunting stanzas on love, death, and the passage of time, did not become widely known until after the translator's death. FitzGerald also wrote aphorisms and translated Spanish and Greek playwrights.   ROBIN BUSS

Bibliography: Benson, A. C., *Edward FitzGerald* (1905; repr. 1988); Jewett, I. B., *Edward FitzGerald* (1977); Terhune, A. M. and A. B., eds., *The Letters of Edward FitzGerald*, 4 vols. (1980).

Fitzgerald, Ella

The singer Ella Fitzgerald, b. Newport News, Va., Apr. 25, 1918, is second only to Billie Holiday in the influence she has had over several generations of pop-music singers. Her career began (1934–39) with Chick Webb's band, which she led for a year after his death. After recording (1938) ''A-tisket, A-tasket,'' she had countless hits, sang with Duke Ellington, Count Basie, and other major bands, and appeared as a soloist with more than 40 symphony orchestras. A great scat singer and ballad interpreter, she consistently lifted often trivial material to the level of high jazz art.   JONATHAN KAMIN

Bibliography: Kliment, Bud, *Ella Fitzgerald* (1988).

Fitzgerald, F. Scott

Francis Scott Key Fitzgerald, b. Saint Paul, Minn., Sept. 24, 1896, d. Dec. 21, 1940, was an American writer of fiction whose work spanned the years between World Wars I and II. A master of the short story and the novel of manners, Fitzgerald is recognized by the public and literary critics alike as one of the most important writers of his time, especially for helping to create the image of the Jazz Age. Both his life and his works also offer an acute commentary on the disillusion and depression of the 1930s. His style, in the great tradition of English prose, is notable for its grace, lucidity, and aptness of phrase.

Fitzgerald was of Irish ancestry on both sides, and he was distantly related to Francis Scott Key, for whom he was named, and to Maryland aristocracy. His mother's father, Philip McQuillan, was a successful wholesale merchant. The grandfather's early death and the father's failure to hold a job left the family dependent on the McQuillan wealth. Young Scott's mixed feelings of hostility and love, guilt and shame, toward his parents are seen to underlie his psychic conflicts.

Because of his mother's ambitions, Fitzgerald was sent east to a Catholic prep school in 1911, but he always retained something of the wonder and defensiveness of the provincial coming into a more worldly society. Similarly, although he was never more than a nominal Catholic after his youth, Catholicism plays a part in his early fiction and in the values and attitudes he held throughout his life. He went on to Princeton University in 1913 but left in his junior year, partly because of ill health but chiefly because of low grades resulting from his

F. Scott Fitzgerald, an American author, chronicled the social climate of the 1920s. Fitzgerald's works contain many autobiographical elements; his personal life was marred by the unsatisfying affluence and empty hedonism depicted in his novels.

inattention to academic work. Although he returned the next fall, he did not stay to receive a degree. Instead, he entered the army as a second lieutenant in 1917.

Nevertheless, Fitzgerald's Princeton years were important. They provided an outlet for his writing talent, introduced him to more and better literature than he had known before, and brought him together with other literary young men, notably Edmund Wilson. Princeton also furnished most of the material for *This Side of Paradise* (1920), which launched his career.

Throughout the 1920s Fitzgerald's life and much of his fiction was preoccupied with Zelda Sayre, the Alabama girl he married immediately after the publication of his first novel (see FITZGERALD, ZELDA SAYRE). The central characters of *The Beautiful and Damned* (1922), his second novel, are a couple like the Fitzgeralds, who lead a life of drinking, partying, and endless talk. But while the Fitzgeralds' disorderly lives both mirrored and created the pattern for others of the 1920s generation, it was increasingly damaging to Fitzgerald's work. Going to Europe, first in 1921, was both an adventure and an escape. It was during their second period there, from 1924 to 1926, that he completed what many consider his best work, THE GREAT GATSBY (1925). In *Gatsby*, Fitzgerald was able to reach beyond the details of his romance with Zelda to explore the nature and internal ramifications of the romantic quest itself. It is the powerful association of that pursuit with the development of the United States as a land of promise and the subsequent conflicts between materialism and idealism that provide the novel with its substance and stature.

As the 1920s advanced, Fitzgerald's drinking became regarded as alcoholism, while Zelda's erratic behavior was diagnosed (1930) as schizophrenia. His difficulty in organizing his novel TENDER IS THE NIGHT (1934) was largely due to the strain that his own and Zelda's conditions placed upon him, accompanied by his trying to understand and utilize the conflicts created by these conditions as the substance of the book.

Fitzgerald's life reached a low point in 1935, when he suffered the nervous collapse that he later brilliantly described in three essays called *The Crack-Up* (1945). By that time Zelda's mental illness had begun to require hospitalization, and she was in and out of mental institutions for the rest of her life. (She died in a fire at Highland Hospital, Asheville, N.C., in 1948.) The couple lived apart during much of the decade, their daughter, Scotty (1921–86), becoming increasingly Fitzgerald's charge. His work, off and on, as a movie scriptwriter marks his last years; at his death he was working on a novel about Hollywood, *The Last Tycoon* (1941). Although his literary reputation had declined drastically before his death, its revival since 1950 has been phenomenal, and the Fitzgeralds' lives have made a permanent claim upon the American imagination.   KENNETH EBLE

Bibliography: Bloom, H., ed., *F. Scott Fitzgerald* (1988); Bruccoli, M., *Some Sort of Epic Grandeur* (1981) and, as ed., *The Correspondence of F. Scott Fitzgerald* (1980); Chambers, J. B., *The Novels of F. Scott Fitzgerald* (1989); Eble, K., *F. Scott Fitzgerald*, rev. ed. (1977); Mellow, J., *Inverted Lives* (1984); Mizener, A., ed., *F. Scott Fitzgerald: A Collection of Critical Essays* (1963); Phillips, G., *Fiction, Film, and F. Scott Fitzgerald* (1986).

FitzGerald, Garret

Garret FitzGerald, b. Feb. 9, 1926, was prime minister of Ireland from June 1981 to February 1982, and from December 1982 until February 1987. FitzGerald served (1973–77) as foreign minister under Liam Cosgrave and became leader of the Fine Gael party in 1977. Governing as head of a Fine Gael–Labour coalition, he concluded (1985) an agreement with Britain establishing a common Anglo-Irish policy for Northern Ireland during his second term of office but failed to deal effectively with Ireland's rising unemployment. FitzGerald's coalition fell when Labour withdrew its support in January 1987. He was replaced as premier by Fianna Fáil's Charles Haughey, and as Fine Gael leader by Alan Dukes.

Fitzgerald, George Francis

The Irish physicist George Francis Fitzgerald, b. Aug. 3, 1851, d. Feb. 21, 1901, was professor of physics at Trinity College in Dublin and is known as a profound analyst of 19th-century developments in electromagnetic theory. Two years after the MICHELSON-MORLEY EXPERIMENT of 1887, which shattered classical physics, Fitzgerald suggested that the shrinkage of a body due to motion at speeds close to that of light would account for the astonishing result of that experiment. This concept, the FITZGERALD-LORENTZ CONTRACTION, plays a key role in the modern theory of RELATIVITY.   CARL A. ZAPFFE

Fitzgerald, Lionel LeMoine

The Canadian painter Lionel LeMoine Fitzgerald, b. Mar. 17, 1890, d. Aug. 5, 1956, studied briefly at the Art Students League in New York City before returning to Canada in 1922 and painting his prairie environment in an impressionistic style. Later, under the influence of Georges Seurat, he became absorbed in the problem of form, which resulted in many carefully composed still lifes executed with a painstaking technique in muted colors. He also painted a series of self-portraits. Fitzgerald joined the GROUP OF SEVEN in 1932 but exhibited with them only once.   DAVID WISTOW

Bibliography: Harper, J. Russell, *Painting in Canada: A History* (1966); Mellen, Peter, *The Group of Seven* (1970); Winnipeg Art Gallery, *Lionel LeMoine Fitzgerald: The Development of an Artist* (1978–79).

Fitzgerald, Robert

Translator, poet, critic, and Harvard professor Robert Stuart Fitzgerald, b. Geneva, N.Y., Oct. 12, 1910, d. Jan. 16, 1985, was best known for his expressive blank-verse translations of classical Greek authors. With Dudley Fitts, Fitzgerald produced notable English versions of Euripides' *Alcestis* (1936) and Sophocles' *Antigone* (1939) and *Oedipus Rex* (1949). His reputation, however, rests mostly on his translations of three epics: Homer's *Odyssey* (1961; Bollingen Prize) and *Iliad* (1974) and Vergil's *Aeneid* (1983). Fitzgerald also published four collections of his own poetry, as well as a book about literary criticism, *Enlarging the Change* (1984).

FitzGerald, Robert David

Robert David FitzGerald, b. Feb. 22, 1902, is an Australian poet whose philosophical poems involve a search for the truths of consciousness and memory. His works include *To Meet the Sun* (1929); *Moonlight Acre* (1938), which won the Australian Literature Society's gold medal; *Forty Years Poems* (1965); and the prose work *Of Places and Poetry* (1976).

Bibliography: Day, Arthur Grove, *Robert D. FitzGerald* (1974).

Fitzgerald, Zelda Sayre

Zelda Sayre Fitzgerald, b. Montgomery, Ala., July 24, 1900, d. Mar. 10, 1948, was a writer who was married to and overshadowed by the celebrated author F. Scott FITZGERALD. Although her life was marred by schizophrenia, her short stories, essays, and novel (*Save Me the Waltz*, 1932) indicate talent of a high order. Some of the material in her journals was used by Fitzgerald, particularly in his novel *Tender Is the Night* (1934).

Bibliography: Milford, Nancy, *Zelda* (1970; repr. 1983).

Fitzgerald-Lorentz contraction

The Fitzgerald-Lorentz contraction is an effect first postulated in 1892 by George F. FITZGERALD and amplified in 1895 by Hendrik A. LORENTZ. It was proposed in an attempt to explain the null result of the MICHELSON-MORLEY EXPERIMENT, performed in 1887, which measured the time taken for a light beam to travel a distance d and back when the direction of motion of the beam was parallel to the supposed direction of motion of the laboratory, or observer, through the "ETHER." The time was compared with that for the same trip when the laboratory moved perpendicular to the light's direction. In this case, the laboratory's motion was the Earth's motion through space. The ether was the medium through which light was presumed to travel with speed c.

According to classical theory, the time taken for both round trips should be different. The Michelson-Morley experiment, however, demonstrated no difference in travel times. Fitzgerald suggested that if the length of the parallel arm d were contracted to $d\sqrt{1 - v^2/c^2}$ (where v is the speed of the laboratory) while that of the perpendicular arm remained unchanged, the prediction would agree with the experiment.

Lorentz later proposed a model for matter that incorporated this effect. He stated that the atoms and molecules that compose matter would, under the effect of motion, be compressed along the direction of motion. It would be impossible to measure this deformation; a ruler placed alongside a speeding object would be similarly shortened.

Albert Einstein showed, in his theory of RELATIVITY, that the contraction was a fundamental consequence of the assumption that the speed of light is the same in all reference frames. The effect is only significant at speeds that are a sizable fraction of the speed of light.   CLIFFORD M. WILL

Bibliography: Taylor, E. F., and Wheeler, J. A., *Spacetime Physics* (1966).

Fitzmaurice, George

George Fitzmaurice, b. Jan. 28, 1877, d. May 12, 1963, was an Irish playwright whose comedy *The Country Dressmaker* (1907) was a favorite of the early Abbey Theatre. His tragicomic short plays, *The Pie-Dish* (1908) and *The Magic Glasses* (1913), by contrast, baffled audiences. Fitzmaurice's posthumously produced fantasies, such as *The Enchanted Land* (1966), suggest the playwright's affinity with J. M. Synge.   ROBERT HOGAN

Bibliography: McGuinness, A. E., *George Fitzmaurice* (1975); Slaughter, H. K., *George Fitzmaurice and His Enchanted Land* (1972).

Fitzpatrick, Sir Charles

Sir Charles Fitzpatrick, b. Dec. 19, 1853, d. June 17, 1942, was a Canadian jurist who first won attention defending the insurgent Louis RIEL in 1885. Elected (1896) to the Canadian House of Commons as a Liberal, he served as federal minister of justice from 1902 to 1906, when he was named chief justice of the Canadian Supreme Court. He was later lieutenant governor of Quebec (1918–23).

Fitzpatrick, Thomas

The American fur trapper, guide, and Indian agent Thomas Fitzpatrick, b. 1799, d. Feb. 7, 1854, was one of the famous MOUNTAIN MEN of the Rockies. Born in Ireland, he emigrated to the United States as a youth. He joined several trapping expeditions, and, during the 1830s, operated the Rocky Mountain Fur Company with James BRIDGER and others. In 1836, Fitzpatrick began to serve as a guide; he escorted the missionary parties of Marcus WHITMAN and Pierre Jean DE SMET to the Northwest, guided (1841) the first wagon train of settlers to California, and accompanied John C. FRÉMONT's 1843–44 expedition. After 1846, Fitzpatrick was Indian agent for the Upper Platte River region; he negotiated (1851) the Fort Laramie Treaty, which established boundaries for the Plains tribes and guaranteed the safety of whites traveling the Oregon Trail.

ELLIOTT WEST

Bibliography: Hafen, Leroy R., *The Life of Thomas Fitzpatrick, Mountain Man, Guide and Indian Agent,* rev. ed. (1973; repr. 1981).

Fitzsimmons, Frank Edward

The U.S. trade union leader Frank Edward Fitzsimmons, b. Jeannette, Pa., Apr. 7, 1908, d. May 6, 1981, became president of the Teamsters Union in 1971. He joined the Teamsters in 1934 after working as a bus driver and truck driver and rose to international vice-president in 1961 and general vice-president in 1967. He became acting president in 1967 when Teamsters president James R. Hoffa was imprisoned.

Fitzsimons, Thomas

Thomas Fitzsimons, b. Ireland, 1741, d. Aug. 26, 1811, was a U.S. political and business leader who signed the Constitution. An active supporter of the American Revolution, Fitzsimons led a company of home guards during the war and became a member (1782–83) of the Continental Congress. After serving in the Pennsylvania state legislature (1786–87), he was a delegate to the 1787 Constitutional Convention. Fitzsimons was elected as a Federalist to the U.S. House of Representatives (1789–95), where he supported Alexander Hamilton's bank and tariff policies. For many years a member of the Philadelphia Chamber of Commerce, he founded the Bank of North America.

Fitzwilliam Museum

The Fitzwilliam Museum in Cambridge, England, is the art gallery and museum of Cambridge University. The museum was founded in 1816 by Richard, 7th viscount Fitzwilliam of Merrion, who donated his collection of paintings, medieval manuscripts, and Rembrandt etchings. The building was begun in 1837, completed in 1875, and has since been extended. The museum's collection has been enlarged by several important bequests and now includes Greek and Roman sculpture, Greek coins, and English ceramics. All periods of European paintings are represented, and the collection is particularly noted for its 17th-century Dutch and Flemish works.

CARTER RATCLIFF

Fiume: see RIJEKA.

Five, The

The Five were a group of Russian composers formed around and influenced by Mily BALAKIREV, and including Aleksandr BORODIN, César CUI, Modest MUSSORGSKY, and Nikolai RIMSKY-KORSAKOV. The group was active during the 1860s and '70s. They were strongly influenced by the critic Vladimir Stassov, who encouraged them and coined the nickname "the mighty handful" for the group. Stassov worked for their ideal of a national Russian music based on the folk and church music of the past—as opposed to the "Westernizing" ideals of Anton Rubinstein and his pupils. By a strange paradox, these Westernizers were associated with the old capital, Moscow, whereas the nationalist "five" were based in the comparatively modern and Westernized city of St. Petersburg. The members of the group went their own ways after Mussorgsky's death in 1881 and Balakirev's withdrawal from public life.

MARTIN COOPER

Bibliography: Abraham, G., *Essays on Russian and East European Music* (1985); Seroff, Victor I., *The Mighty Five* (1948); Zetlin, Mikhail O., *The Five,* trans. by George Panin (1959).

Five Civilized Tribes

The Five Civilized Tribes was a loose confederation, formed in 1859, of North American Indians in what was then INDIAN TERRITORY (in present-day Oklahoma). The group comprised the Iroquoian-speaking CHEROKEE and the Muskogean-speaking CHICKASAW, CHOCTAW, CREEK, and SEMINOLE. They were described as "civilized" because of their early adoption of many of the white man's ways. Under the Indian Removal Act of 1830, the Five Tribes were deported from their traditional homelands east of the Mississippi and forced to settle in Indian Territory. Each organized an autonomous state modeled after the U.S. federal government, established courts and a formalized code of laws, constructed schools and Christian churches, and developed a writing system patterned on the one earlier devised by the Cherokee.

Members of the Five Tribes absorbed many cultural features of their white neighbors, including plow agriculture and animal husbandry, European-style houses and dress, and even the ownership of black slaves. Some tribesmen joined the Confederate forces during the Civil War. Thereafter the United States instituted a policy of detribalization and gradually curtailed Indian control of tribal lands. The tribal nations remained independent until 1907, when statehood was granted to Oklahoma and the federal government opened Indian Territory to white settlement. Today, many descendants of the Five Tribes live on reservations in Oklahoma.

Before forced settlement in Indian Territory, the members of the Five Tribes, some of which were traditionally enemies, shared many culture traits. All relied primarily on maize agriculture, with fishing, hunting, and foraging an important but subsidiary means of subsistence. Village life was highly developed. Households generally included small extended families, with kinship based on a matrilineal clan system. Among the more western tribes, notably the Creek, social stratification existed in the form of noble and common classes that were marked by their mode of dress. Independent communities were politically integrated into confederacies. Temple architecture, ceremonial centers, and elaborate rituals—such as the CORN DANCE—existed, centered on the growing of corn and worship of the Sun. Traditional crafts included coiled pottery, woven blankets, and articles of wrought copper.

JAMES W. HERRICK

Bibliography: Bailey, M. T., *Reconstruction in Indian Territory* (1972); Cotterill, R. S., *The Southern Indians* (1954); Debo, A., *And Still the Waters Run* (1984); Foreman, G., *The Five Civilized Tribes* (1934; repr. 1966) and *Indian Removal* (1934; repr. 1966); Perdue, T., *Nations Remembered* (1980); Swanton, J. R., *The Indians of the Southeastern United States* (1946).

Five Nations: see IROQUOIS LEAGUE.

five-spice powder

Five-spice powder is a pungent, sweet-smelling blend of spices used in Chinese and Vietnamese cooking for pork, chicken, and duck dishes. It contains approximately equal proportions of finely ground fennel seed, cloves, star anise, cinnamon, and Szechuan pepper. To make Chinese eight-spice powder, ground ginger, anise, and licorice root are added.

ARTHUR O. TUCKER

fixation   [fik-say'-shuhn]

In psychology, the term *fixation* is used in a number of ways. In classic psychoanalytic theory, a fixation is any process that tends to delay or distort an individual's progression through the so-called oral, anal, and genital stages of personality development toward maturity. The individual is then said to be "fixated" at one of these stages. The term also refers more specifically to a person's unreasonable or even pathological attachment to another person. In LEARNING THEORY, the strengthening, or reinforcement, of a learned response is sometimes called a fixation as well.

Bibliography: Fenichel, Otto, *The Psychoanalytic Theory of Neurosis* (1945); Russell, Gerald F., ed., *The Neuroses and Personality Disorders* (1984).

Fizeau, Armand Hippolyte Louis [fee-zoh']

French physicist Armand Hippolyte Louis Fizeau, b. Sept. 23, 1819, d. Sept. 18, 1896, contributed significantly to the field of optics. A wealthy scientific amateur, Fizeau first collaborated with Léon Foucault in improving, for scientific applications, the recently developed daguerreotype method of photography. The two scientists then studied the wave nature of light and showed that infrared light can also produce interference fringes. Working separately with the reflector-rotating mirror device they had developed, both men proved that light travels more swiftly in air than in a denser medium. Fizeau later developed a system for measuring the absolute velocity of light; his results, although not quite accurate, proved the usefulness of his method. In 1848 he published a paper on sound waves, describing what is now known as the Doppler effect—unknown to Fizeau, Doppler's paper had appeared 6 years earlier—and suggesting that light waves would show the same effect. His experimental demonstration of this was later confirmed by A. A. Michelson and E. W. Morley, a result that was to be of profound importance in astrophysics.

fjord [fee-ohrd']

Fjords are long, narrow, deep, and relatively straight arms of the ocean that may project many kilometers inland. Bordered by steep walls commonly thousands of meters high, and by truncated spurs, their beauty is enhanced by waterfalls that drop from great heights. Some fjords terminate landward in tidewater glaciers from which icebergs calve; others terminate in steep bedrock slopes. Found in high latitudes along mountainous coasts, they are glacially eroded valleys, differing from glaciated valleys like Yosemite in California only in that they are submerged. After the valleys had been cut and deglaciated, they were invaded by the ocean. The depth of the fjords, more than a thousand meters in some places, is due mainly to the depth of glacial erosion below sea level, not to a rise of sea level after the valleys were formed.

Fjords are found in Greenland, Norway, Alaska, British Columbia, New Zealand, and elsewhere. Some of them are part of the most spectacular scenery in the world. Perhaps those in Norway are best known; cruise ships regularly schedule trips along the Norwegian coast. ROBERT L. NICHOLS

Bibliography: Hurdle, B. G., ed., *The Nordic Seas* (1986); Syvitski, J. P., et al., *Fjords* (1986).

Flacius Illyricus, Matthias [flay'-shuhs il-ir'-i-kuhs, muh-thy'-uhs]

Matthias Flacius Illyricus, b. Mar. 3, 1520, d. Mar. 11, 1575, was a German Protestant reformer and theologian. After studying at the universities of Basel and Tübingen, he went to Wittenberg, where he was influenced by Philipp Melanchthon and by Martin Luther. Appointed professor of Hebrew in 1544, Flacius became a strict dogmatist; he opposed the concessions proposed in 1548 between Roman Catholics and Protestants in the Augsburg Interim and in the Leipzig Interim, on the ground that they were dangerous to the integrity of Lutheranism. In 1557, Flacius became professor of New Testament at the University of Jena. Among his major writings are *Ecclesiastica historia* (1562–74), a multivolume study of church history that was renamed *Centuriae Magdeburgenses* (Magdeburg Centuries) from its third edition in 1757, and *Clavis scripturae sacrae* (Key to Sacred Scripture, 1567).

Flack, Audrey

Audrey Flack, b. May 30, 1931, a noted American photorealist painter, was one of the first artists to openly acknowledge the use of photographs as the basis for her compositions in the early 1960s (see PHOTOREALISM). In 1969, Flack developed a technique of airbrushing paint over images that were projected from color slides onto a canvas, thus eliminating the need for preliminary drawing. Her cluttered still-life paintings engage the viewer with their exaggerated scale, minute detail, and trompe l'oeil spatial effects, as well as their kitsch subject matter. *Gambler's Cabinet* (1976; Collection Meisel Gallery, New York City) is typical of her work. LISA M. MESSINGER

Bibliography: Coke, Van Deren, *The Painter and the Photograph*, 2d ed. (1972); Kultermann, Ugo, *New Realism* (1972); Nemser, Cindy, "Conversations with Audrey Flack," *Arts Magazine* (February 1974); Siegel, Jeanne, "Audrey Flack's Object" *Arts Magazine* (June 1976).

flag

A flag is a piece of colored fabric that serves as a symbol or a signaling device. Some flags are used only for decoration, but those are rare. Basically, flags are messages from a person or a group of people. This may be seen in everyday phrases such as "show the flag," that is, display the military power of a country without actually threatening to use it; "run it up the pole and see who salutes it," that is, express an idea in a clear graphic form in order to elicit reactions to it; and "win the pennant," that is, be highly successful in a competitive endeavor.

Flags express numerous kinds of messages—protection, victory, challenge, submission, pride, honor, threat, loyalty, and hope. Patriots express their love of country by hoisting flags; victorious armies humiliate their enemies by displaying captured flags; dictators use flags to help mold public opinion; and activists challenge the government by flaunting outlawed banners. Ships fly flags both for identification (by nation, shipping line, or both) and for SIGNALING.

As a form of political expression, flags are closely related to other symbols. Official seals and coats of arms authenticate the acts of governments; armbands and uniforms unite demonstrators in their common cause; emblems such as the American eagle, the hammer and sickle of Soviet Communism, or the swastika of Nazism appear on posters, ballots, and lapel pins. Groups of all sizes—even private individuals—may have flags that serve to state and affirm their beliefs in the face of opposing beliefs. The most important flags of the modern era are those that identify the nation-state.

Flags are normally of cloth or other flexible material and are made in such a way as to be displayed, temporarily or permanently, from a rigid staff. Today, flags are usually made of cotton, wool, or synthetic fabrics; however, they are sometimes metal, plastic, or paper. Formerly, flags were made of silk or linen. The size of a flag depends on its intended use. For example, small ones are used as table decorations, and the largest flag in regular use, in Brazil, is 70 by 100 m (more than 200 by 300 ft). Military flags of today, carried only in ceremonies and parades, are much smaller than the flags of centuries past used for rallying troops and giving directions in the midst of combat.

The importance of a flag lies in its symbolism rather than in its material or size; its color and design are the basis for expressing that symbolism. Although all colors may be and have been used, most nonmilitary flags use one or more of six colors—red, yellow, blue, green, black, and white. Designs are of every imaginable form, from the solid red of revolution to the intricate painted or embroidered patterns incorporating hundreds of individual elements; but the majority of flags are simple. For ready identification, especially at sea or at a great distance, the following basic geometric patterns are popular: an emblem centered on a plain field, with or without a border; quartered or crosswise divisions; a plain field with a distinctive rectangular area in the upper hoist area (known as the canton); and vertical or horizontal stripes. Combinations of these patterns are also used.

A specialized vocabulary has developed to describe the parts and the uses of flags. Some societies emphasize flags and have elaborate rituals surrounding them; others consider flags casually or even largely ignore them. The study of all aspects of flag design, history, symbolism, etiquette, terminology, and development is known as vexillology (from the Latin *vexillum*, meaning "flag").

ORIGIN

The date of the earliest flag is not known. Apparently the first vexilloids (flaglike objects) came into use when people began to live in cities and to organize regular military forces.

Archaeological records from the ancient Middle East, Egypt, China, and America suggest that the use of flags was nearly universal among early civilizations. These earliest flags frequently consisted of a carved emblem at the top of a pole, sometimes with ribbons attached below. Natural subjects, especially wild animals, were felt to be appropriate symbols and indeed are still found in modern heraldry—from the lions in the royal standard of Britain to the bison on the state flag of Wyoming. Very early the practical uses of flags became evident; they could identify the rank of a commander, indicate tactical directions on the battlefield, signal the intentions of a ship or its place of registration, or inspire men and women undertaking difficult and dangerous tasks.

The use of cloth flags attached along the side of a pole may have been a Chinese invention, since woven silk was developed very early in the Far East. The beginnings of modern flag design, that is, the combination of colors and forms on cloth to transmit certain ideas, may be seen in the development of HERALDRY during the 12th century in Europe and slightly later in Japan. Heraldry was the design of coats of arms to distinguish individuals, families, and institutions. Although not all flags are heraldic, many of the rules that developed in European heraldry furnish the basis for the most expressive flags. Preference was given to designs of two or three colors, with a single emblem set against a plain or simply divided background. Colors had to be contrasting for easy visibility. As the heraldic tradition developed, more or less consistent meanings were recorded to prevent their being used by more than one person or group.

One of the most important developments in flag history has been the proliferation of national flags, which began in the late 18th century and still continues. The American and French revolutions of 1775 and 1789, respectively, associated specific designs and colors with the concepts of liberty, independence, democracy, nationalism, and political mobilization of the masses. Since then, most of the great multinational empires have vanished. The organization of the world on the basis of countries characterized by a single nationality and national ideology has spread successively to Europe, Latin America, Asia, Africa, and the Pacific. The royal standard of a monarch representing many different peoples has given way to the national flag of a distinctive people with its own language, culture, territory, and aspirations.

FLAG SYMBOLISM

The UNION JACK of the United Kingdom combines the crosses of St. George, St. Andrew, and St. Patrick, the patron saints of England, Scotland, and Ireland, respectively. The five points of the star in the national flag of Somalia represent a claim to the five territories in which the Somalis live. The yellow-blue-red flag of Venezuela symbolizes the wealth of the New World (yellow) separated from Spain (red) by the blue ocean. The red of revolution and communism serves as the background for the national flag of China, and its five gold stars reflect not only the old Chinese imperial color but the importance the Chinese have traditionally assigned to the symbolism of five. When Adolf Hitler came to power in Germany in the 1930s, he replaced the black-red-gold of German liberal democracy with the black-white-red "blood and iron" flag of the 19th-century German Empire. Later he substituted the swastika banner of his own Nazi party.

Different as the national flags of the world are, major patterns can be discerned in the ways they are used, in the symbolism of their designs and colors, and even in their origins. For example, those who struggled against Spanish rule in Latin America achieved one of their early successes in Argentina. The blue-white-blue flag adopted by that country (then called the United Provinces of La Plata) in 1816 was also flown by privateers who harassed Spanish ports and ships along the coasts of South and Central America. The same flag was adopted by the leaders of Central America after Spanish rule was thrown off in 1821. As individual republics emerged from the Central American federation (1825–38), they modified the flag but still retained its basic colors. The Revolutions of 1848 in Europe inspired Costa Rica to add a stripe of red through the center of the blue-white-blue; Guatemala changed to vertical stripes; and Honduras, Nicaragua, and El Salvador added distinctive emblems on the central white stripe.

The struggle of the Arab countries for independence and unity is also reflected in their flags. The first national flag (1947–51) of Cyrenaica was that of the conservative Sanusi religious sect; it was black with a white star and a crescent in the center. Stripes of red and green, symbolizing the Fezzan and Tripolitania, were added when they joined Cyrenaica as the independent country of Libya in 1951. A revolution in 1969 replaced the monarchy and its conservative policies; the flag was altered to red-white-black, the recognized "Arab liberation colors." In 1971, Libya joined Egypt and Syria in the Confederation of Arab Republics and added its emblem, the gold hawk of the tribe of Quraish, to the center stripe. In 1977, infuriated by attempts of the Egyptian president Anwar al-Sadat to negotiate peace with Israel, Libya again changed its flag. It chose a field of plain green, the fourth traditional Islamic color.

FLAGS OF THE UNITED STATES

In the United States, cities, counties, states, military units, businesses, churches, scout organizations, labor groups, political parties, private yachtsmen, and many others have distinctive flags. The histories of the flags of Hawaii, Texas, and South Carolina would require entire books to recount.

Surprisingly, the origins of the national flag, the Stars and Stripes, are somewhat obscure. The flag was officially adopted on June 14, 1777, when the Continental Congress resolved that "the Flag of the united states be 13 stripes alternate red and white, that the Union be 13 stars white in a blue field representing a new constellation." Its immediate predecessor, the Continental Colors, had consisted of 13 horizontal red and white stripes for the 13 colonies represented in the Continental Congress, with the British Union Jack as a canton to indicate that the rebels were demanding the historic rights of British citizens. How and why stars were chosen to replace the Union Jack is not known. Stars were uncommon in flags in that era, although the American example has since made them popular.

The colors red, white, and blue were clearly derived from British sources; many English flags had red and white stripes. Americans at the time of the national centennial in 1876 warmed to the popular story about the young seamstress Betsy ROSS, who supposedly sewed the first flag for George Washington. Although according to historical records she did indeed make flags, no evidence indicates that she was involved in making or designing the first Stars and Stripes, and the validity of the traditional story is doubtful.

After Vermont and Kentucky joined the Union, 2 stars and 2 stripes were added (1795) to the flag. Such a 15-star, 15-stripe flag—now preserved in the Smithsonian Institution—inspired Francis Scott KEY to write "The Star-Spangled Banner." The design of the flag was changed again in 1818, when the decision was made to keep the 13 stripes permanently and add stars to indicate the current number of states in the Union.

Altogether the Stars and Stripes has been through 27 versions, the most recent introduced on July 4, 1960, when Hawaii was admitted to statehood. Until 1912 no official pattern existed for the arrangement of the stars. Flags of the 19th century varied greatly in their star patterns, in the number of points on the stars, in the shades of red and blue, in the width-to-length ratio of the flag, and in other details. Design and color were first standardized in the 20th century.

ETIQUETTE OF THE FLAG

Traditionally flags have been respected, and rules have governed their display. During the 20th century, however, flag etiquette has received particular attention, especially in the United States and other countries where the flag is a primary focus of patriotism. In the United States the anniversary of the flag's adoption (June 14) has been celebrated as Flag Day since 1916; it is a legal holiday in Pennsylvania.

In 1942 the U.S. Congress adopted a Flag Code, subsequently amended, setting forth uniform procedures for displaying the flag in a respectful manner. The two most important guides are tradition and common sense. For example, the

FLAGS FROM WORLD HISTORY

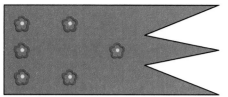

CHARLEMAGNE

WILLIAM I (THE CONQUEROR) OF ENGLAND

GENGHIS KHAN

PEASANTS' WAR (16TH-CENTURY GERMANY)

PETER I (THE GREAT) OF RUSSIA

JOSÉ DE SAN MARTIN

HUDSON'S BAY COMPANY

CHINA UNDER THE CH'ING DYNASTY (19TH-CENTURY)

FLAG PROPOSED BY CECIL RHODES FOR BRITISH AFRICA

UNION OF SOVIET SOCIALIST REPUBLICS

FLAGS FROM AMERICAN HISTORY

VIKINGS

CHRISTOPHER COLUMBUS

HENRY HUDSON

BRITISH EXPLORERS AND SETTLERS (FIRST UNION JACK)

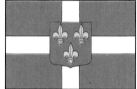

FRENCH EXPLORERS AND SETTLERS (17TH AND 18TH CENTURIES)

CONTINENTAL COLORS (1776)

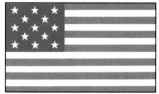

FIRST STARS AND STRIPES (1777-95)

ESEK HOPKINS, FIRST COMMANDER IN CHIEF OF THE CONTINENTAL NAVY

FIRST STAR-SPANGLED BANNER (1795-1818)

OLIVER HAZARD PERRY (WAR OF 1812)

TEXAS REPUBLIC (1836)

BEAR FLAG REPUBLIC (1846)

STARS AND BARS OF THE CONFEDERACY (1861-63)

FORT SUMTER FLAG (1861)

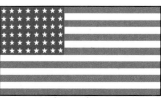

STARS AND STRIPES (OLD GLORY) IN 48-STAR VERSION (1912-59)

FLAGS OF AFRICA

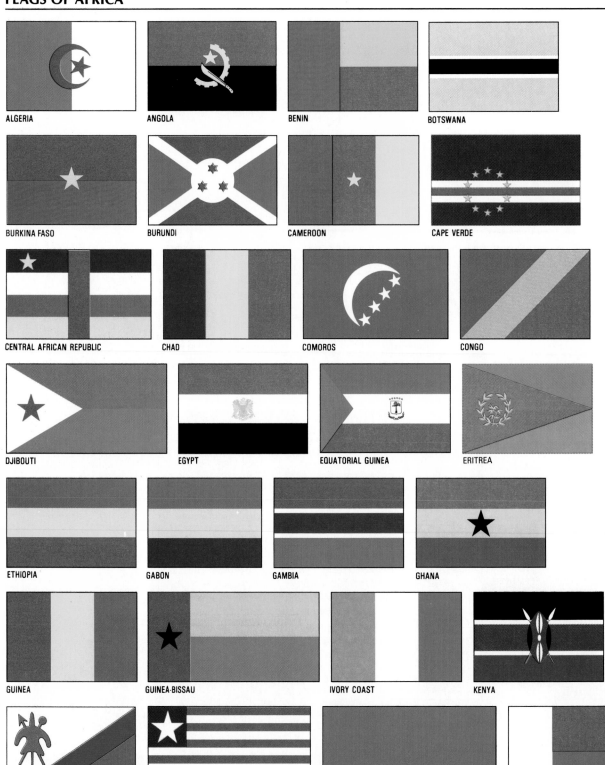

ALGERIA

ANGOLA

BENIN

BOTSWANA

BURKINA FASO

BURUNDI

CAMEROON

CAPE VERDE

CENTRAL AFRICAN REPUBLIC

CHAD

COMOROS

CONGO

DJIBOUTI

EGYPT

EQUATORIAL GUINEA

ERITREA

ETHIOPIA

GABON

GAMBIA

GHANA

GUINEA

GUINEA-BISSAU

IVORY COAST

KENYA

LESOTHO

LIBERIA

LIBYA

MADAGASCAR

FLAGS OF AFRICA (continued)

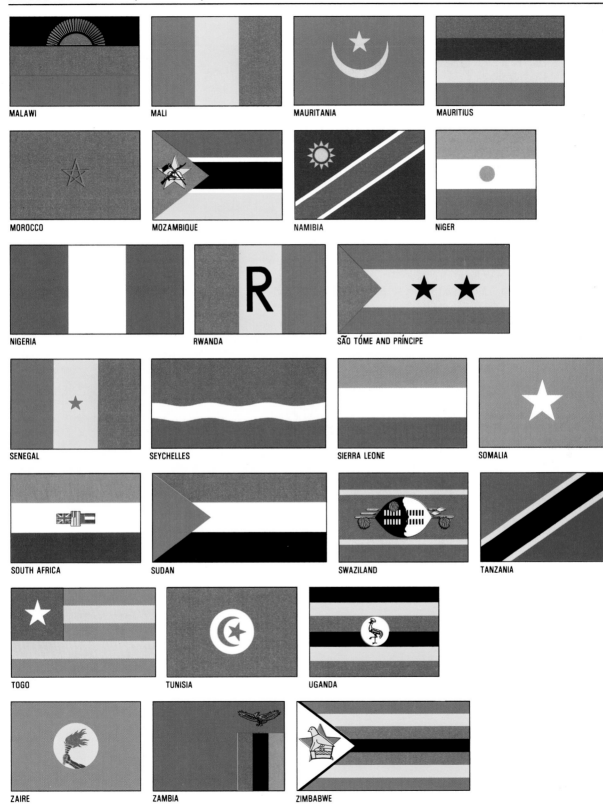

MALAWI

MALI

MAURITANIA

MAURITIUS

MOROCCO

MOZAMBIQUE

NAMIBIA

NIGER

NIGERIA

RWANDA

SÃO TÓME AND PRÍNCIPE

SENEGAL

SEYCHELLES

SIERRA LEONE

SOMALIA

SOUTH AFRICA

SUDAN

SWAZILAND

TANZANIA

TOGO

TUNISIA

UGANDA

ZAIRE

ZAMBIA

ZIMBABWE

FLAGS OF ASIA

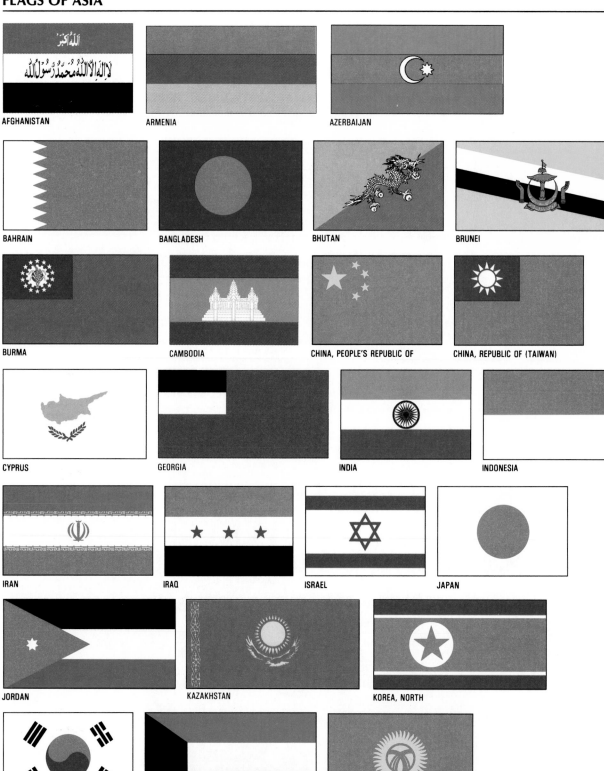

AFGHANISTAN

ARMENIA

AZERBAIJAN

BAHRAIN

BANGLADESH

BHUTAN

BRUNEI

BURMA

CAMBODIA

CHINA, PEOPLE'S REPUBLIC OF

CHINA, REPUBLIC OF (TAIWAN)

CYPRUS

GEORGIA

INDIA

INDONESIA

IRAN

IRAQ

ISRAEL

JAPAN

JORDAN

KAZAKHSTAN

KOREA, NORTH

KOREA, SOUTH

KUWAIT

KYRGYZSTAN

FLAGS OF ASIA (continued)

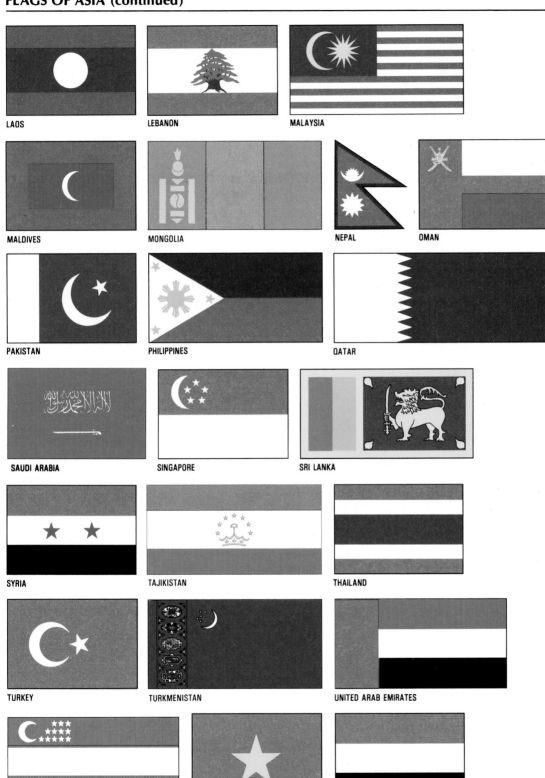

LAOS

LEBANON

MALAYSIA

MALDIVES

MONGOLIA

NEPAL

OMAN

PAKISTAN

PHILIPPINES

QATAR

SAUDI ARABIA

SINGAPORE

SRI LANKA

SYRIA

TAJIKISTAN

THAILAND

TURKEY

TURKMENISTAN

UNITED ARAB EMIRATES

UZBEKISTAN

VIETNAM

YEMEN

FLAGS OF EUROPE

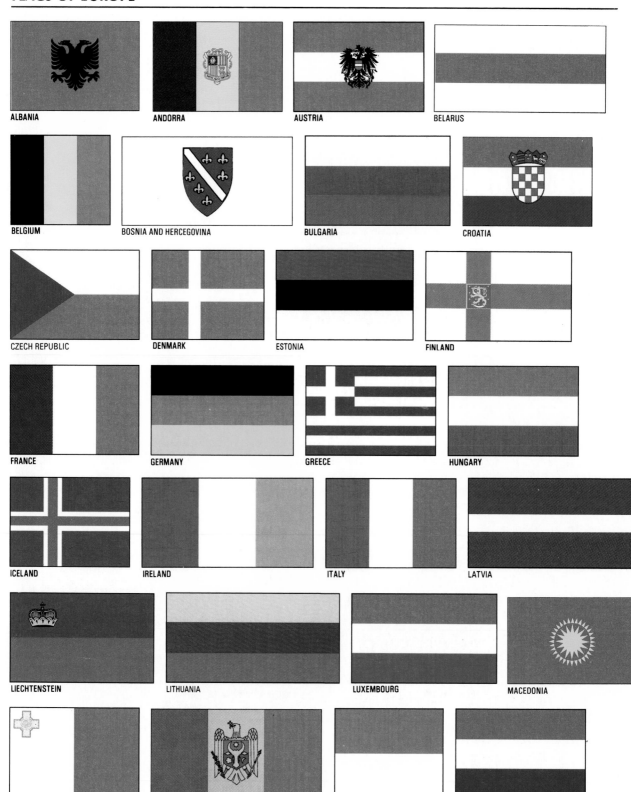

ALBANIA

ANDORRA

AUSTRIA

BELARUS

BELGIUM

BOSNIA AND HERCEGOVINA

BULGARIA

CROATIA

CZECH REPUBLIC

DENMARK

ESTONIA

FINLAND

FRANCE

GERMANY

GREECE

HUNGARY

ICELAND

IRELAND

ITALY

LATVIA

LIECHTENSTEIN

LITHUANIA

LUXEMBOURG

MACEDONIA

MALTA

MOLDOVA

MONACO

NETHERLANDS

FLAGS OF EUROPE (continued)

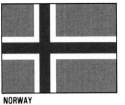
NORWAY

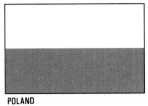
POLAND

PORTUGAL

ROMANIA

RUSSIAN FEDERATION

SAN MARINO

SLOVAKIA

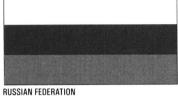
SLOVENIA

SPAIN

SWEDEN

SWITZERLAND

UKRAINE

UNITED KINGDOM

VATICAN CITY

YUGOSLAVIA

FLAGS OF SOUTH AMERICA

ARGENTINA

BOLIVIA

BRAZIL

CHILE

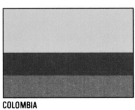
COLOMBIA

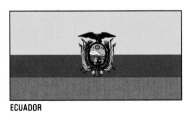
ECUADOR

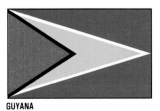
GUYANA

PARAGUAY

PERU

FLAGS OF SOUTH AMERICA (continued)

SURINAME

URUGUAY

VENEZUELA

FLAGS OF NORTH AMERICA

CANADA

MEXICO

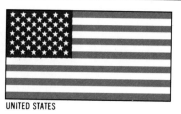
UNITED STATES

FLAGS OF THE CARIBBEAN

ANTIGUA AND BARBUDA

BAHAMAS

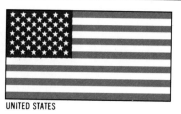
BARBADOS

CUBA

DOMINICA

DOMINICAN REPUBLIC

GRENADA

HAITI

JAMAICA

SAINT KITTS-NEVIS

SAINT LUCIA

SAINT VINCENT AND THE GRENADINES

TRINIDAD AND TOBAGO

FLAGS OF CENTRAL AMERICA

BELIZE

COSTA RICA

EL SALVADOR

GUATEMALA

HONDURAS

NICARAGUA

PANAMA

FLAGS OF OCEANIA

AUSTRALIA

FIJI

KIRIBATI

MARSHALL ISLANDS

FEDERATED STATES OF MICRONESIA

NAURU

NEW ZEALAND

PAPUA NEW GUINEA

SOLOMON ISLANDS

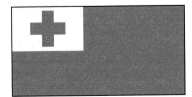

TONGA

TUVALU

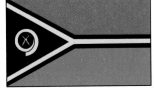

VANUATU

WESTERN SAMOA

FLAGS OF AUSTRALIA

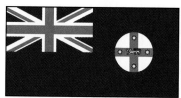

NEW SOUTH WALES

NORFOLK ISLAND

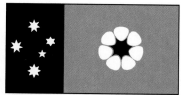

NORTHERN TERRITORY

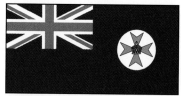

QUEENSLAND

SOUTH AUSTRALIA

TASMANIA

VICTORIA

WESTERN AUSTRALIA

FLAGS OF CANADA

ALBERTA

BRITISH COLUMBIA

MANITOBA

NEW BRUNSWICK

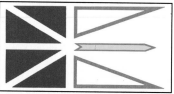

NEWFOUNDLAND

NORTHWEST TERRITORIES

NOVA SCOTIA

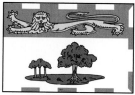

ONTARIO

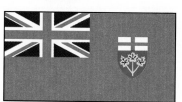

PRINCE EDWARD ISLAND

QUEBEC

SASKATCHEWAN

YUKON TERRITORY

FLAGS OF INTERNATIONAL ORGANIZATIONS

UNITED NATIONS

RED CROSS

RED CRESCENT

RED MAGEN DAVID

OLYMPICS

NATO

ORG. OF AMERICAN STATES

COMECON

ORG. OF AFRICAN UNITY

ARAB LEAGUE

FLAGS OF UNITED STATES TERRITORIES

AMERICAN SAMOA

PALAU (BELAU)

GUAM

NORTHERN MARIANAS

PUERTO RICO

U.S. VIRGIN ISLANDS

FLAGS OF THE UNITED STATES

ALABAMA

ALASKA

ARIZONA

ARKANSAS

CALIFORNIA

COLORADO

CONNECTICUT

DELAWARE

DISTRICT OF COLUMBIA

FLORIDA

GEORGIA

HAWAII

IDAHO

ILLINOIS

INDIANA

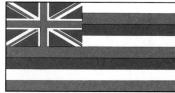

IOWA

KANSAS

KENTUCKY

LOUISIANA

MAINE

MARYLAND

MASSACHUSETTS

MICHIGAN

MINNESOTA

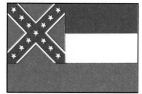

MISSISSIPPI

MISSOURI

MONTANA

NEBRASKA

FLAGS OF THE UNITED STATES (continued)

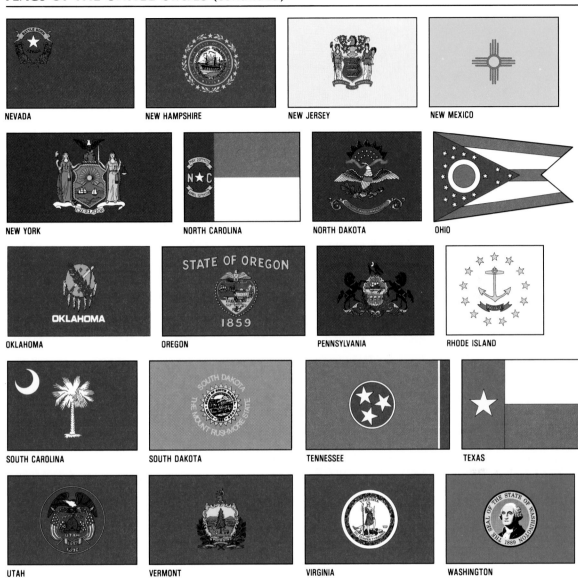

NEVADA

NEW HAMPSHIRE

NEW JERSEY

NEW MEXICO

NEW YORK

NORTH CAROLINA

NORTH DAKOTA

OHIO

OKLAHOMA

OREGON

PENNSYLVANIA

RHODE ISLAND

SOUTH CAROLINA

SOUTH DAKOTA

TENNESSEE

TEXAS

UTAH

VERMONT

VIRGINIA

WASHINGTON

WEST VIRGINIA

WISCONSIN

WYOMING

FLAGS OF THE U.S. GOVERNMENT

PRESIDENT

VICE-PRESIDENT

SECRETARY OF STATE

DEPT. OF THE TREASURY

SECRETARY OF DEFENSE

ATTORNEY GENERAL

DEPT. OF THE INTERIOR

DEPT. OF AGRICULTURE

SECRETARY OF COMMERCE

DEPT. OF LABOR

DEPT. OF TRANSPORTATION

DEPT. OF HEALTH AND
HUMAN SERVICES

DEPT. OF HOUSING AND
URBAN DEVELOPMENT

DEPT. OF ENERGY

DEPT. OF EDUCATION

U.S. ARMY

U.S. MARINE CORPS

U.S. NAVY

U.S. AIR FORCE

U.S. COAST GUARD

JACK OF U.S. WARSHIPS

U.S. flag had traditionally been flown only during daytime, but since the activities of the nation go on 24 hours a day, and because raising and lowering the flag every day is expensive, in recent years it has become common to fly the flag at night. In that case, the flag should be spotlighted, as the revised code recommends. Likewise, because of improved manufacturing techniques, flags can now withstand moisture and need not be lowered in harsh weather.

In the United States when the U.S. flag is hoisted with other flags, it should take precedence; the way in which this status is achieved depends on the circumstances. For example, international custom dictates that the flag of one nation should not be displayed above that of another nation; nor should the flag of one nation be larger than that of another when they are raised together. When the flag of the United States is displayed with other national flags within the United States, therefore, its precedence is established by its being placed at the head of the line of flags or to its own extreme right. It is also placed to the right when flown with flags of states, military officers, and companies, but then it may also be larger and flown higher. The Flag Code includes rules for displaying the flag at half-staff to mourn the dead and for displaying the flag on special holidays, in parades, with the flag of the United Nations, in meeting halls, and in other similar circumstances. The following is the official salute to the flag: "I pledge allegiance to the flag of the United States of America and to the Republic for which it stands, one Nation under God, indivisible, with liberty and justice for all."

A number of political and legal battles have been waged over the so-called desecration of the flag. For example, members of the Jehovah's Witness religious sect refuse on principle to salute the flag, and they have been prosecuted for it. Political protesters, like those opposed to the Vietnam War in the 1960s, tried to dramatize their cause by burning the flag or otherwise defacing it. In the late 1980s the issue found its way to the Supreme Court, which ruled that a protester who had burned the flag at the 1988 Republican National Convention was merely expressing free speech. The Court later ruled that a congressional law protecting the flag from desecration was unconstitutional.

The symbolism of flags has caused emotions to run high in other countries. Canadians debated for several decades whether the nation should have a distinctive flag and, if so, what its design should be. The debate subsided only gradually after the present national flag was adopted in 1965. A similar discussion took place in South Africa in the 1920s. In South Vietnam in the early 1960s, the refusal of President Ngo Dinh Diem to allow the display of Buddhist flags was a political decision that contributed to his overthrow and assassination. Elsewhere flags have been potent emblems of revolutionary movements and of authoritarian political parties.

Their potential for expressing deep-felt emotions in a condensed but obvious form, and with great public visibility, has made flags an important medium of political communication.

WHITNEY SMITH

Bibliography: Furlong, W. R., and McCandless, B., *So Proudly We Hail: The History of the United States Flag* (1981); Mastai, B. and M. L., *The History of the United States Flag* (1961); Shearer, B. F. and B. S., *State Names, Seals, Flags, and Symbols* (1987); Smith, W., ed., *Guide to the Flags of the World* (1982).

flag of convenience

A flag of convenience, in maritime usage, signifies the fact that a ship of one nation is registered under the flag of another. Many American merchant ships, for example, are registered in Liberia or Panama and fly their flags. Foreign registry allows shipowners to pay lower wages than those required by U.S. seamen's unions and to avoid adherence to costly safety regulations and the payment of certain taxes.

See also: SHIPPING.

flagella   [fluh-jel'-uh]

Motile, threadlike organelles that project from the surface of a cell are called flagella. They are usually at least as long as the cell body. Flagella function either in moving the cell or in moving fluids or small particles across the cell surface. They are commonly found on unicellular and small multicellular organisms and on the male reproductive cells of most animals and many plants. The number of flagella per flagellated cell varies in different species from one to many, but usually there are only a few. Flagella have two fundamentally different structures. Those of bacteria are simple polymers of one kind of protein (flagellin) attached at the cell surface to a much more complex basal structure. Those of Protozoa and all higher organisms are membrane-bounded bundles of fibers arranged in the same standard pattern as in cilia, which are shorter and more numerous than flagella.

flagellants   [flaj'-uh-lents]

During the Middle Ages, the flagellants were groups of Christians who subjected themselves to ritualized whipping as atonement for sin. Individual flagellation had become a common form of ecclesiastical punishment as early as the 4th century, and monastic communities allowed voluntary group flagellation as a form of penance later in the medieval period. Organized bands of flagellants made their first known appearance in Europe in the mid-13th century. The major factors stimulating this phenomenon seem to have been famine and war, which were interpreted in the prophecies of Joachim of Fiore (c.1132–1202) as a sign of divine displeasure at the sinfulness of the world. The movement died down but revived spontaneously during the plague years of the Black Death (1348–50). Although condemned by Pope Clement IV in 1349 and by the Council of Constance (1414–18), manifestations of flagellant activity continued through the 15th century. Similar practices were found in antiquity among the Spartans and Romans and are a part of some North American Indian initiation rites.

DAVID HARRY MILLER

Bibliography: Chadwick, Owen, *Western Asceticism* (1958).

flageolet   [flaj-uh-let']

The French flageolet was a type of fipple flute (see RECORDER) invented in the 16th century and popular in England in the 1660s and '70s. It had four fingerholes on top and two on bottom. Replaced before the end of the 17th century by the recorder, it was nevertheless used in operas by Handel, Mozart, and Gluck. In the 19th century it and the English flageolet appeared with key mechanisms. The "bird flageolet" was a smaller instrument used to teach tunes to songbirds.

ELWYN A. WIENANDT

Flaget, Benedict Joseph   [flah-zhay']

Called the "bishop of the wilderness," Benedict Joseph Flaget, b. Nov. 7, 1763, d. Feb. 11, 1850, was a French-born Roman Catholic priest who fled the French Revolution and came to the United States in 1792. Appointed bishop of Bardstown, Ky., in 1810, he traveled hundreds of miles on horseback each month, supervising the frontier churches under his care and doing mission work among the Indians. He was a man of great erudition and one of the most influential Roman Catholics in 19th-century America.

Bibliography: Spalding, Martin, *Life, Times and Character of the Right Reverend Benedict Joseph Flaget* (1852; repr. 1969).

Flagg, Ernest

The American architect Ernest Flagg, b. Brooklyn, N.Y., Feb. 6, 1857, d. Apr. 10, 1947, has the dual distinction of being a pioneer in both housing and skyscraper design. The architect's education at the École des Beaux-Arts in Paris was financed by his cousin's husband, the railroad magnate Cornelius Vanderbilt. His European training is reflected in a plan for Saint Luke's Hospital (1891) in New York City, where each ward is isolated as a square pavilion. The same ideas are seen in Flagg's designs for tenements, which improved living conditions in this building type by using a larger lot size to bring more light and air into each apartment. His greatest achievement, the recently demolished Singer Building (1908) in New

York City, was the tallest building in the world (41 stories) when it was built. Flagg also designed the Corcoran Gallery of Art, Washington, D.C. LEON SATKOWSKI

Flagstad, Kirsten [flahg'-staht, kirsh'-tuhn]

Kirsten Flagstad, b. July 12, 1895, d. Dec. 7, 1962, a Norwegian singer, had one of the most beautiful voices of this century, a rich, dark soprano used with unfailing accuracy and musicianship. She studied in Oslo and made her debut there in 1913 in Eugen d'Albert's *Tiefland.* After having specialized in operetta, Flagstad made a successful Bayreuth debut (1934), but it was her sensational appearance (1935) in New York as Sieglinde that established her as one of the greatest Wagnerian sopranos. During World War II she chose to remain with her family in Norway and was later unjustly accused of collaborating with the Nazis. Retiring from the operatic stage in 1955, she continued to sing in Norway and to make recordings and was named director (1958–60) of the Norwegian Opera.

STEPHANIE VON BUCHAU

Bibliography: Flagstad, Kirsten, *The Flagstad Manuscript,* ed. by Louis Biancolli (1952; repr. 1977); McArthur, Edwin, *Flagstad: A Personal Memoir* (1965; repr. 1980); Vogt, Howard, *Flagstad: Singer of the Century* (1988).

Flagstaff

Flagstaff, a city in north central Arizona, is the seat of Coconino County. It is located about 200 km (125 mi) northeast of Phoenix and has a population of 45,857 (1990). Flagstaff is a cultural and educational center: Lowell Observatory (from which the planet Pluto was first observed), Northern Arizona University (1899), and a National Aeronautics and Space Administration (NASA) laboratory and library are all located in or near the city. The economy is based on lumbering, cattle ranching, and tourism. Sunset Crater, Wupatki, and Walnut Canyon national monuments, Coconino National Forest, and the Navajo and Hopi Indian reservations are nearby. The city was settled in 1876.

Flaherty, Robert Joseph [flay'-urt-ee]

Robert Joseph Flaherty, b. Iron Mountain, Mich., Feb. 16, 1884, d. July 23, 1951, was a filmmaker whose originality and poetic vision helped create a romantic tradition in documentary films. Before making *Nanook of the North* (1922), a depiction of Eskimo life and his first and most famous film, Flaherty explored Canada as a mapmaker. His interest in native cultures and the simple agrarian life is reflected in later films—*Moana* (1926), *Tabu* (1931), *Man of Aran* (1934), and *Louisiana Story* (1948).

Bibliography: Barsam, Richard, *The Vision of Robert Flaherty* (1988); Flaherty, Frances H., *The Odyssey of a Film-maker: Robert Flaherty's Story* (1953; repr. 1972); Griffith, Richard, *The World of Robert Flaherty* (1953; repr. 1972); Rotha, Paul, *Robert J. Flaherty* (1984); Weinberg, Herman G., *Robert Flaherty and Hans Richter* (1979).

flake tool: see PALEOLITHIC PERIOD.

Flamboyant Gothic style

Flamboyant, from the French word meaning "flamelike," is a stylistic term used to identify the last major period of GOTHIC ART AND ARCHITECTURE, which began in the reign (1364–80) of Charles V of France and extended to about 1540—a long period of creative renewal in both secular and ecclesiastical architecture after almost a century of decline. Although precedents for the curvilinear tracery and some of the ornamental motifs of this exuberantly decorative style had already occurred in England, the major structural elements were derived more directly from the French RAYONNANT STYLE. But the older architectural formulas were now reinterpreted with unparalleled freedom.

The architect Guy de Dammartin, working at the Palais des Contes (1384–86) in Poitiers and at the Sainte Chapelle (1380–89) in Riom, has been credited with initiating the Flamboyant style. The great surge in building activity, however, came

only with the reunification of France after the victories of Joan of Arc in the Hundred Years' War, culminating at the end of the 15th century and the early decades of the 16th century in the series of grand cathedral facades, such as the west facade of Troyes Cathedral (1506) and the transept facades (1499) of Beauvais Cathedral, created by Martin Chambiges and his son Pierre. Disseminated over much of the continent, the Flamboyant style developed its most extravagant intricacies in Spain, as in the facade of Saint Paul's Church (c.1490–1515) in Valladolid by Simón de Colonia. In Portugal under King Manuel I (r. 1495–1521) it was further enriched by an unrestrained growth of exotic forms, which became known as the Manueline style. WILLIAM M. HINKLE

Bibliography: Frankl, Paul, *Gothic Architecture,* trans. by Dieter Pevsner (1962); Harvey, John H., *The Cathedrals of Spain* (1957) and *The Gothic World, 1100–1600* (1950).

flame

A flame is the region in a gaseous medium where combustion takes place, accompanied by the evolution of heat and, usually, light. (Hydrogen, for example, burns with a nearly invisible flame.) Flames were initially used for heat and illumination but now are used chiefly for heat. The efficient recovery of heat requires its extraction from the hot gases by direct conduction, since very little is transferred by radiation (see HEAT AND HEAT TRANSFER). Fireplaces generally give warmth by radiation, which means that most of the heat from the flames is lost up the chimney; the heating efficiency of a fireplace is greatly improved by circulating air through the fireplace by means of ducts.

A distinction can be made between two types of flames: premixed and diffusion. In a premixed flame, a gaseous fuel is mixed with air or oxygen and fed to a flame holder such as a Bunsen burner or cooking stove. The efficiency of this method typically produces a clean, smokeless flame. Solid and liquid fuels burn in a diffusion flame. Wax, for example, the fuel for a candle, melts and is drawn up by the wick, where it vaporizes. The wax vapor emerges from the wick while air diffuses from the outside; a hollow flame results in the region where they meet. The yellow color is due to the presence of hot, incandescent carbon particles, which subsequently cool and become smoke. STEPHEN FLEISHMAN

Bibliography: Barnard, J. A., and Bradley, J. N., *Flame and Combustion,* 2d ed. (1985); Fristrom, R. M., and Westenberg, A. A., *Flame Structure* (1965); Gaydon, A. G., and Wolfhard, H. G., *Flames: Their Structure, Radiation and Temperature,* 4th ed. (1979).

See also: COMBUSTION; FIRE.

flame retardants

A flame retardant is a chemical applied to a combustible material to reduce the rate at which it burns. There are two classes of flame retardants: those that are most effective for materials containing a substantial amount of oxygen—such as cellulose and certain synthetic polymers—and that carry out their function primarily in the material itself, and those that are effective for materials with all-carbon structures and little oxygen—polymers such as polyethylene or polyvinyl chloride—and that work in the burning vapor above the polymer.

Compounds of phosphoric acid or of sulfuric acid are most frequently used as flame retardants for the first class of materials. As long as the wood, paper, or polymer is in normal use, the acid is neutralized by a fugitive species, a simple organic substance that vaporizes at the onset of fire, leaving behind the relatively nonvolatile acid fragments. On heating, these acids react with the cellulose or synthetic polymer to produce large amounts of carbon char and incombustible gases such as steam and carbon dioxide, which either prevent the fire from starting or smother it. Other simple inorganic materials, such as borax, zinc borate, and boric acid, are also effective in retarding flames. They melt at low temperatures and block diffusion of oxygen to the burning surface.

The second class of flame retardants work by decomposing in fire to produce volatile fragments that intervene in the chemical processes in the burning vapor above the polymer and thereby block the combustion process. The chemicals most frequently used include bromine compounds and antimony oxide. Some fire retardants may themselves produce fairly toxic gases during exposure of the treated material to fire temperatures. If a fire is hot enough to release all of the retardant, the gases may present problems, particularly for fire fighters.   JOHN W. LYONS

See also: FIRE PREVENTION AND CONTROL.

flame test: see QUALITATIVE CHEMICAL ANALYSIS.

flame tree

Flame tree, *Brachychiton acerifolius,* family Sterculiaceae, is native to Australia and is grown as an ornamental in warm climates. It grows to 30 m (100 ft) in the wild and to 12 m (40 ft) in cultivation and blooms in midsummer. Leaves have long stalks and are usually 20–25 cm (8–10 in) wide, deeply lobed, and shiny. The flowers are brilliant scarlet; the fruit is a woody follicle, smooth and black, about 10 cm (4 in) long. Flame trees are propagated by seed or by cuttings from ripened wood.   K. B. PAUL

flamenco   [fluh-meng'-koh]

Flamenco is the term used to designate a particular style of song, dance, and guitar music that originated in Andalusia in southern Spain. The roots of flamenco are not known, but it is believed that Gypsies were primarily responsible for developing and popularizing the style. Musicologists also find significant Arabic influences, particularly in the way the voice is used in singing the *cante hondo,* the "deep song," of flamenco. Both song and dance are accompanied by guitar, which is also used as a solo instrument. Flamenco dance is characterized by intricate toe and heel clicking and by the sinuous arm and hand gestures of the female dancers.

Flamenco songs and dances, which were once confined to café and theatrical performance, have now become part of the Spanish artistic tradition.

Bibliography: Pohren, D. E., *The Art of Flamenco,* 3d ed. (1972; repr. 1985).

flamingo   [fluh-ming'-goh]

The greater flamingo, P. ruber, a wading bird that lives in large colonies, strains mud bottoms of rivers and lakes for algae and small aquatic animals with its crooked beak. The flamingo constructs a cylindrical mud nest (left) for its egg, which both parents care for.

Flamingos are large wading birds with very long legs and neck, an abruptly turned-down bill, and an unfeathered face. They are found in Africa, Asia, Europe, South America, and the Caribbean area. Wild flamingos are sometimes seen in Florida, but they do not naturally nest in the United States. Flamingos are white, pinkish white, or vermilion, with black flight feathers (remiges); they stand from 90 cm to 1.5 m (3 to 5 ft) tall. Flamingos feed on minute animal and vegetable matter, such as algae and diatoms, or on small mollusks or crustaceans. When feeding, the flamingo places its head and bill upside down below the surface of the water. Using its thick, fleshy tongue, the bird forces muddy water through the serrated edges of its bill, thus straining the water and trapping the edible material in it.

Flamingos, highly gregarious throughout the year, nest in colonies; in some species, such as the lesser flamingo (*Phoeniconaias minor*), these colonies may number as many as 2 million birds. The nest is a cone of mud up to about 45 cm (1.5 ft) high, and one or two whitish eggs are laid in a shallow depression at the top of the cone. Both sexes incubate the eggs. The young hatch after about a month and have a straight bill, which begins to develop a bend within a few weeks.

The 4 to 6 living species and 14 extinct species of flamingos constitute the family Phoenicopteridae, which is usually placed in an order of its own—Phoenicopteriformes.
                                            GARY D. SCHNELL

Bibliography: Allen, R. P., *The Flamingos: Their Life History and Survival* (1956); Bent, Arthur C., *Life Histories of North American Marsh Birds* (1926); Brown, L. H., *The Mystery of the Flamingos* (1959).

Flamininus, Titus Quinctius   [flam-i-ny'-nuhs, ty'-tuhs kwink'-shuhs]

Titus Quinctius Flamininus, c.229–174 BC, was a Roman statesman and general. Elected consul for 198 BC, he defeated (197) PHILIP V of Macedonia at Cynoscephalae and proclaimed (196) freedom for Greece. After Cynoscephalae, Flamininus tried to stabilize affairs by preventing war among the Greek states. He forced Nabis, king of Sparta, to surrender Argos and was honored as a liberator when he withdrew (194) Roman troops from Greece. The Aetolian League (see AETOLIA), however, allied with the Seleucid king ANTIOCHUS III, and the Romans soon returned (191) to defeat Antiochus at Thermopylae. Flamininus attempted to preserve Greek local autonomy, but this policy was abandoned soon after his death.
                                            ALLEN M. WARD

Bibliography: Badian, Ernst, *Foreign Clientelae, 264–70 B.C.* (1958), and "Titus Quinctius Flamininus: Philhellenism and Realpolitik," in University of Cincinnati Classical Studies, 2 (1923); Scullard, H. H., *Roman Politics, 220–150 B.C.* (1951).

Flammarion, Camille   [flah-mahr-ee-ohn']

The French astronomer Camille Flammarion, b. Feb. 26, 1842, d. June 3, 1925, was a prolific and widely read popularizer of astronomy. His interests ranged from extraterrestrial life, discussed in *La Pluralité des mondes habités* (The Plurality of Inhabited Worlds, 1862), to parapsychology, explored in *L'inconnu et les problèmes psychiques* (The Unknown and Psychic Problems, 1900). He made many balloon flights to study atmospheric phenomena and, as early as 1876, observed with a telescope the seasonal variations of the dark spots of Mars. His most popular work, *Astronomie populaire* (1880; *Popular Astronomy,* 1894), was translated into many languages.

Flamsteed, John   [flam'-steed]

John Flamsteed, b. Aug. 19, 1646, d. Dec. 31, 1719, was the first director of the ROYAL GREENWICH OBSERVATORY in England. He distinguished himself especially through the compilation of star catalogs. An extremely frail and sickly man throughout his life, Flamsteed nevertheless obtained an M.A. from Cambridge after four years of nonresident enrollment. Upon his appointment as first astronomer royal in 1675, he applied himself

John Flamsteed, a British astronomer of the late 17th century, was instrumental in founding the Royal Greenwich Observatory and was appointed (1675) its first director by Charles II. His accurate observations were the first based on the use of Galileo's telescope.

with single-minded devotion to the task of determining accurate stellar and lunar positions as an aid to navigation. This program of Astrometry was identical to that of Tycho Brahe and Johannes Hevelius, but Flamsteed's innovation was to employ a telescopic sight on his 7-ft (2-m) sextant to make the observations. This method resulted in an approximate 15-fold increase in accuracy, to about 10 seconds of arc, over Brahe's work. After a famous controversy in which Isaac Newton and Edmond HALLEY conspired (1712) to publish parts of Flamsteed's work without his permission, the complete *Historia Coelestis Britannica*, containing the positions of some 3,000 stars, appeared posthumously in 1725. It was followed by the *Atlas Coelestis* (1729).

Bibliography: Baily, Francis, *An Account of the Rev. John Flamsteed and Supplement to the Account* (1835; repr. 1966).

Flanagan, Edward J.

Edward Joseph Flanagan, b. Ireland, July 13, 1886, d. May 15, 1948, was a Roman Catholic priest who worked first with derelict men and then with delinquent and homeless boys in the archdiocese of Omaha, Nebr. Believing that "there is no such thing as a bad boy," he created BOYS TOWN, a community in Douglas County, Nebr., run by the hundreds of boys who live in it. Father Flanagan, as he was known, captured public support for his project and became an authority on juvenile delinquency.

Bibliography: Graves, Charles P., *Father Flanagan, Founder of Boys Town* (1972).

Flanagan, Hallie: see FEDERAL THEATRE PROJECT.

Flanders   (historic region of the Low Countries)
[flan'-durz]

Flanders, a former county on the North Sea, was the heart of economic and political development in the Low Countries during the Middle Ages. At its most extensive, it included the present Belgian provinces of West and East Flanders and parts of modern France and the Netherlands. In the past foreigners often used the name for all of the Low Countries. Now it is used loosely to refer to the Belgian regions in which Flemish, or Dutch, is spoken.

With its favorable location on the sea, Flanders became a wealthy trading center with numerous industrial towns, of which BRUGES and GHENT were the most important. The principal industry, woolen textiles, was heavily dependent on wool imports from England.

Established as a county in the 9th century, most of Flanders was a fief under the French crown until the early 16th century, although the part east of the Scheldt River, added in the 11th century, belonged to the Holy Roman Empire. For several centuries the counts of Flanders were powerful and virtually independent rulers. They played a leading role in the Cru-

sades in the 12th century. By the 14th century, however, rivalry had developed in the towns between the wealthy patricians and the guild members, especially the weavers.

With the outbreak of urban rebellions the counts and nobles turned for support to the French king, and the burghers, led by the ARTEVELDE family of Ghent, repeatedly allied themselves with England during the HUNDRED YEARS' WAR. During this period of turmoil, democratic governments, the first in northern Europe, were introduced. By the end of the 14th century, however, Flanders had come under Burgundian rule and lost its independence.

Although Flanders continued to flourish economically and culturally during the 15th century, it declined under the HABSBURGS, who succeeded to the Burgundian inheritance in 1482. Their harsh rule provoked general revolt in the Low Countries in the mid-16th century (see DUTCH REVOLT). Flanders was soon pacified by the Spanish, but it suffered economically from the separation of the northern provinces and the commercial rivalry of the new Dutch republic. Subsequently, Flanders was the scene of repeated warfare between the Spanish, and, after 1713, the Austrian, Habsburgs and France, which conquered numerous areas in southern Flanders. By the 18th century Flanders was a predominantly agricultural region. In 1815 it became part of the kingdom of the Netherlands, and in 1830 it was incorporated in the new kingdom of Belgium. It was the scene of heavy fighting in World War I.

HERBERT H. ROWEN

Bibliography: Lucas, H. S., *The Low Countries and the Hundred Years' War* (1929); Carson, Patricia, *The Fair Face of Flanders* (1969); Nicholas, D. M., *Town and Countryside: Social, Economic and Political Tensions in Fourteenth-Century Flanders* (1971).

See also: LOW COUNTRIES, HISTORY OF THE.

Flanders   (province in France)

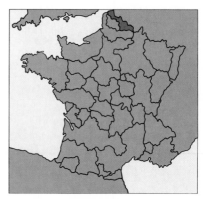

The shaded portion of the map indicates the location of Flanders, a former French province that was incorporated within the département of Nord after the French Revolution. During the Middle Ages, Flanders, which occupied portions of present-day France, Belgium, and the Netherlands, became an important commercial center under the rule of independent counts.

Flanders is a former province of France, situated in the northern part of the country just south of the Belgian border and along the North Sea coast. LILLE was its capital. For most of its history this region was part of the state of Flanders, most of which was located in present-day Belgium and the Netherlands. Flemish is still spoken in northwest Flanders. From 1668 to 1697, LOUIS XIV gradually secured this prosperous area for France. It remained a French province until the French Revolution when it became (1789) the roughly coterminous department of Nord.

Flannagan, John B.   [flan'-uh-gen]

John Bernard Flannagan, b. Fargo, N.D., Apr. 7, 1895, d. Jan. 6, 1942, was an American sculptor who worked in both wood and stone. From 1914 to 1917 he attended the Minneapolis Institute of Art. After five years as a seaman, Flannagan returned to painting and began sculpting in wood. These pieces, which often employ the theme of mother and child, are solid and brooding and recall primitive African and pre-Columbian sculptures. In 1924 and 1925, Flannagan supplemented his income by carving furniture; then in 1926 he began to work in stone, sculpting birds and animals from stones found in fields. With a minimum of carving, he was able to make the stone evoke the desired subject, as if it had always existed in that form. Three months before his first retrospective exhibition, Flannagan committed suicide.   HARRY RAND

Bibliography: Baro, Gene, *John Flannagan: Sculpture and Works on Paper* (1974); Miller, D. C., ed., *The Sculpture of John B. Flannagan* (1942); Sweeney, J. J., et al., *Five American Sculptors* (1935).

flannel

Flannel is a soft, warm fabric with a slightly napped, or brushed, surface. Flannels are napped by brushing wires gently over the fabric surface to raise the fiber ends. The resultant pockets of interlocking fiber trap air, increase the bulk of the fabric, and make it warmer and more absorbent. Flannel, which may be made from wool, cotton, a blend of wool and cotton, or synthetic fibers, is used for clothing, infants' wear, and sheeting.   ISABEL B. WINGATE

flannelbush

The flannelbush, *Fremontodendron californicum,* is an evergreen California shrub in the family Bombacaceae. It grows to a height of 4.5 m (15 ft). The leaves are slightly lobed, about 2.5 cm (1 in) long, and feltlike underneath; the cup-shaped, lemon yellow flowers are 5–6.25 cm (2–2.5 in) across; and the fruit is a capsule.   K. B. PAUL

flap-footed lizard

Flap-footed lizard is the common name for about 30 species of snakelike lizards in the family Pygopodidae that are unique to Australia, New Guinea, and Tasmania. They have hind legs represented by a flap or fold of skin less than 0.6 cm (0.25 in) wide, and no forelegs.

Flap-footed lizards range from 15 to 75 cm (6 to 29 in) in length. Like snakes, they lack moveable eyelids; the eye is covered instead with a transparent scale. Locomotion is by serpentine undulation of the body. Most species are terrestrial, taking refuge under rocks or logs. A few species are burrowers and tend to have pointed heads, small flaps, and a reduced or absent external ear opening. Flap-footed lizards lay eggs and are mostly insectivorous. The exceptions are two species in the genus *Lialis* that have backward-curving teeth for holding lizards, which constitute their primary prey. Like American glass snakes, flap-footed lizards can break off their tails to escape predators.

flare, solar: see SOLAR FLARE.

flare star

Flare stars are cool, red dwarf stars of spectral type M that undergo unpredictable short outbursts of brightness, which sometimes increase the total visual luminosity of the star by several magnitudes. A typical outburst lasts from a few minutes to as long as an hour or so, and may recur several times in a day. The outbursts are not understood; they superficially resemble SOLAR FLARES but are much larger. Radio outbursts have also been detected from several flare stars: the ratio of the radio energy to that in the optical spectrum is much greater for flare stars than it is in solar flares. X-ray emission from flare stars has also been detected. UV Ceti was the first flare star discovered (1948). The nearest known star, Proxima Centauri, is also a flare star.   R. H. GARSTANG

flash flood

Flash floods are characteristic flow patterns of streams that are dry except for a few days each year when an extremely heavy rain falls. Although most common in DESERT regions, they can occur almost anywhere, and they constitute a severe natural hazard. Most are caused by high-intensity convectional storms, usually summer thunderstorms, that either hover briefly above a dry streambed or, while in motion, follow the course of the channel; and by the imperviousness of desert

land surfaces, which allow little or no precipitation to sink into the ground. Such surfaces, known as duricrusts, may allow as much as 100 percent runoff. Flash-flood water may travel down-channel as rapidly as 35 km/h (22 mph), with a viscous forward wall of sediment and water standing 0.3–1.5 m (1–5 ft) in height. Such floods are noted for their ability to move heavy loads. Boulders, vehicles, and even railroad locomotives weighing many tons have been inundated and swept downstream for several kilometers.   DAVID L. WEIDE

See also: FLOODS AND FLOOD CONTROL; RIVER AND STREAM.

flash photography

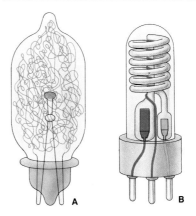

Two basic sources of artificial light are used in modern flash photography. A flashbulb (A) emits light by means of the battery-triggered ignition of its magnesium-aluminum filament. An electronic flashtube (B) produces light by directing an electrical discharge through a glass tube filled with an inert gas, usually xenon.

Flash PHOTOGRAPHY makes use of the artificial light produced by a flash device. It is used for taking pictures when the natural light is insufficient, or to reduce excessive contrast and soften shadows in strong light. The flash apparatus in older cameras was usually a separate device attached to the camera by a wire and set off when the camera's shutter was opened. Newer cameras make provision for the flash to be connected directly to the top of the camera. Most recent camera designs incorporate the flash into the body of the camera. Flash illumination is very limited in range and is useful only for relatively close-up photography.

Flashbulbs. The flashbulb contains fine magnesium wire, or other metallic wire, in oxygen. It is ignited by a brief pulse of electric current at the same moment as, or slightly before, the camera shutter opens. The bulb is backed in its flash container by a reflector, which channels all the light produced by the flash toward the object being photographed. Instructions supplied with the flashbulb help the user to determine the proper lens opening. Each flashbulb may be used only once, because the wire mass inside the bulb is completely burned in producing the flash.

The flash cube is a set of four bulbs in a plastic housing. The bulbs can be used in succession simply by turning the housing, which fits into the camera top.

Electronic Flash. Either as a gas-filled tube that plugs into the top of the camera (in older equipment), or as a unit built into the face of the camera, the electronic flash reaches its peak illumination much faster than the flashbulb, supplies a light more compatible with daylight, and can be used over and over again. A battery supplies power to a capacitor or condenser, which stores electrical energy, then discharges it to trigger the flash. The power supply is usually recharged so rapidly that the flash can be triggered repeatedly over a period of a few seconds. The automatic electronic flash includes a sensor that measures the light of the flash as it is reflected back from the subject and turns off the flash when the proper exposure has been made.

Multiple Flash. A number of rapid-fire flashes, each lasting only hundredths of a second, may be used to photograph a series of stop-action still pictures. The device used is a strobe light, related to the STROBOSCOPE, and is useful in analyzing high-speed phenomena.

flash point

The flash point of a substance is the lowest temperature at which the vapor of the substance can form an explosive mixture with air. Flash point information is valuable in determining the potential fire hazard of chemicals; the lower the flash point, the more hazardous the chemical. The flash points of some common inflammable materials are: butane, $-104°$ C ($-156°$ F); ethyl ether, $-45°$ C ($-49°$ F); and benzene, 10 to $12°$ C (50 to $54°$ F).

flash spectrum

The flash spectrum of the SUN is the spectrum emitted by the outer layer of the Sun known as the chromosphere. It is usually obscured by the light from the rest of the Sun but can be observed during the few seconds of totality of a solar eclipse. A reddish glow is then seen coming from a thin region—the chromosphere—around the solar limb. The red hue is produced by the strong emission of the hydrogen atom at a wavelength of 6,563 angstroms.

Flash spectrum analysis shows that the chromosphere is a layer of rapidly moving gases, at a temperature of about 8,000 K and a density around 10^{-13} gm/cm^3. It extends to a height of about 7,000 km (4,350 mi) above the photosphere of the Sun.

PETER FOUKAL

flat-coated retriever

The flat-coated retriever, an excellent hunting and retrieving dog, was bred in England about the middle of the 19th century. Like other retrievers, this medium-size dog has a flat coat and a keen sense of smell and is willing to pursue game into water.

The flat-coated retriever's principal ancestor was the extinct North American breed known as the St. John's dog, from Newfoundland, yet the breed is almost exclusively English in development and popularity. Only a few flat-coats are registered each year with the American Kennel Club.

The breed was developed during the second half of the 19th century and was originally known as the wavy-coated retriever. It is a sturdy, medium-size dog; it stands about 58 cm (23 in) at the shoulder and weighs 27–32 kg (60–70 lb). The breed is black or liver in color and has a dense, flat coat of fine texture and quality.

JOHN MANDEVILLE

flatbed cylinder press

The flatbed cylinder press or, more simply, cylinder press, is one of three basic types of printing presses used in LETTERPRESS printing. (The others are the platen press and the ROTARY PRESS.) The world's first flatbed press was built by Friedrich König in England in 1811. In the flatbed press there is a flat printing surface, or bed, to hold the printing form, or plate. The paper is fed in sheets, with each sheet wrapped around the impression cylinder. During the printing stroke the cylinder is in contact with the plate and rotates while the bed is moving in a straight line, pressing the paper against the inked printing plate. Since only a small part of the form is under impression at a time, the machine can be much larger than a comparable platen press. On the nonprinting stroke the motion of the bed is reversed, the cylinder is raised away from the bed, the plate is freshly inked, and the printed sheet is withdrawn. The reversing operation imposes a limit on the printing speed—about 5,000 impressions per hour—making cylinder presses slower than rotary presses but faster than platen presses.

M. C. FAIRLEY

Bibliography: Hutchings, Ernest A. D., *Printing by Letterpress* (1964); Moran, James, *Printing Presses* (1973).

See also: PRINTING.

flatfish

Flatfishes are marine bottom-dwelling fish that lie on their left or right sides rather than on their bellies. Their bottom sides are usually white or, if pigmented, much lighter than the upper sides. Both eyes are located on the upper side of their heads. Species of flatfishes inhabit oceans worldwide and are found in both cold and warm waters but are most abundant in temperate waters. Flatfishes are included in the order Pleuronectiformes. Six families in this order are psettodids (Psettodidae), citharids (Citharidae), left-eyed flounder (Bothidae), right-eyed flounder (Pleuronectidae), SOLES (Soleidae), and tonguefish (Cynoglossidae).

Flounder. In the waters of the western north Atlantic, FLOUNDER predominate in the flatfish fauna. Among the right-eyed flounder are Atlantic HALIBUT, *Hippoglossus hippoglossus;* American PLAICE, or dabs, *Hippoglossoides platessoides;* witch flounder, *Glyptocephalus cynoglossus;* yellowtail flounder, *Limanda ferruginea;* and winter flounder, *Pseudopleuronectes americanus.* The Atlantic halibut is found in the subarctic Atlantic, on the American coast from Labrador to Cape Cod. It is reported to reach a length of more than 2.7 m (9 ft) and a weight of more than 320 kg (700 lb). This fish is found in depths of from 55 to 915 m (180 to 3000 ft). The Atlantic halibut is a voracious feeder, preying mostly on fish but also eating many invertebrates. The American plaice is found on both sides of the north Atlantic. In the American Atlantic it is usually found from Labrador to Cape Cod. This fish may reach a length of almost 1 m (3 ft) and a weight of 6.5 kg (14 lb). Like the Atlantic halibut, the American plaice is also a cold-water species and is found in shallow waters near shore to depths of 700 m (2,300 ft). Invertebrates seem to be its principal food. The witch flounder is found on both sides of the Atlantic and, on the American coast, is most abundant north of Cape Cod. It reaches a length of 60 cm (2 ft) and a weight of about 2 kg (4 lb). The witch flounder frequents depths between 100 and 275 m (360 and 900 ft). Its principal food is small invertebrates. Yellowtail and winter flounder are exclusively western Atlantic fish and are common in the waters of the New England and middle Atlantic states. They reach a length of 60 cm (2 ft) and feed primarily on invertebrates.

Along the western Atlantic coast, a common species of left-eyed flounder is the summer flounder, *Paralichthys dentatus.* This species is found from Maine to South Carolina but is most common south of Cape Cod. It is reported to grow to a length of almost 1 m (4 ft) and a weight of 12 kg (26 lb). The summer flounder moves inshore along beaches and into bays in summer and migrates to the continental shelf to depths of 45–150 m (150–500 ft) in winter. It is an active, predaceous species and will follow small fish to the water's surface, frequently jumping clear of the water in the chase.

Sole. Flatfishes belonging to the sole family are less numerous than those belonging to the families of the right-eyed and left-eyed flounder. Because of the epicurean appeal of the European sole, *Solea solea,* and the association of the term *sole* with an excellent-tasting fish, however, many species of flounder have been given the name *sole.* Along the Atlantic coast of the United States, the witch flounder is marketed as gray sole and subspecies of winter flounder as lemon sole. Numerous species of flounder along the Pacific coast of the United States have been marketed as soles. Few species of

The flatfish, order Pleuronectiformes, is a bottom-dwelling marine fish that has both eyes on one side of its head. Many are photochromatic, or color sensitive; they camouflage themselves by spontaneously changing appearance to match that of their environment.

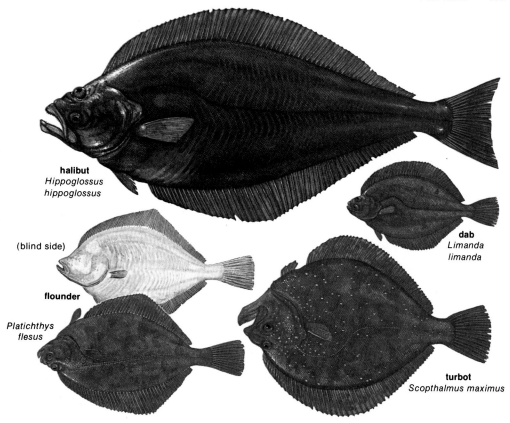

halibut
Hippoglossus hippoglossus

(blind side)

flounder

Platichthys flesus

dab
Limanda limanda

turbot
Scopthalmus maximus

true soles exist along the western Atlantic coast. A common species, the hogchoker, *Trinectes maculatus,* although recorded from Cape Cod to Virginia, is most abundant from Virginia southward. It reaches a length of about 20 cm (8 in) and is unimportant economically. Flatfishes belonging to the tonguefish family are tear-shaped, and most are less than 30 cm (1 ft) long. They are unimportant commercially.

Life Cycle. All species of flatfishes are bottom-dwellers. They are prolific spawners. For example, a 90-kg (200-lb) Atlantic halibut has been estimated to produce more than 2,000,000 eggs, and the smaller American plaice has been reported to produce 60,000 eggs. In most species of flatfishes the eggs are buoyant. The winter flounder's eggs sink to the bottom and adhere to various objects and to one another. Hatching time may vary from several days to weeks, depending on the water temperature. The larval fish floating in the water have a normal appearance, with a single eye on each side of the head.

In the later larval stages, one eye migrates to the opposite side of the head adjacent to the other eye. At the same time, the fish's coloration deepens. Pigment appears on the eyed side, and as the larva grows, it gradually turns over on the noneyed side and settles to the bottom. Metamorphosis from a normal-appearing larval fish with the backside uppermost to the late larval and adult fish with one side facing the bottom appears to have little effect on the symmetry of the internal organs. However, the flatfish's blind side frequently shows poorly developed side fins, a distorted mouth, and fewer and less-developed teeth. The migration of an eye and turning on one side are not the only adaptations to bottom living that these fish have developed. They also can change their color and markings to blend with the bottom and thus hide from predators as well as prey. They dart into the loose sand or mud on the bottom and vigorously move their fins, which swirl the bottom material over their bodies so that only their gill movement betrays their presence.   ALFRED PERLMUTTER

Bibliography: Migdalski, Edward C., and Fichter, George S., *The Fresh and Salt Water Fishes of the World* (1976).

Flathead

The Flathead, a North American Indian people of the Salishan linguistic family, inhabited southwest Montana's Bitterroot River valley, at the easternmost extreme of the Plateau culture area, in the early 19th century. The Plains Indians came to call them Flatheads to distinguish them from more westerly Salishan-speaking groups who practiced ritual head deformation.

Like other Interior SALISH tribes, the Flathead fished during spring; in summer they depended on the women for root and berry foods and in late summer, on the men for deer and elk meat. In the fall they migrated eastward to hunt bison through the winter. Their typical Plateau culture was transformed by Plains traits related to horse riding and organized bison hunting. The Flathead originally lived in long A-frame lean-tos but later also used TEPEES. Horse raids and war honors stimulated the ranking of families by wealth and reputation. A semihereditary chief governed with the assistance of a tribal war leader, a council of lesser chiefs, and an informal police. Enemy tribes included the BANNOCK, BLACKFOOT, and SHOSHONI.

The Flathead began to trade their beaver and bison skins for guns, kettles, beads, needles, and cloth, in the 1820s and '30s, and in 1841 a mission was established among them. The U.S. government began (1855) to consolidate the Flathead, KUTENAI, and Pend d'Oreille and did nothing to halt white settlement in their territory. After agreeing (1872) to migrate north from their aboriginal homeland, the Flathead again suffered substantial land reductions through allotment and sales beginning in 1904. The Flathead numbered between 600 and 1,000 in the early 19th century. In 1990 the tribal enrollment of the Flathead Reservation (including a group of Kutenai) was 6,652. Tribal government is by an elective council of 10.
                                                        FRED W. VOGET

Bibliography: Fahey, John, *The Flathead Indians* (1974); Johnson, Olga, *Flathead and Kootenay* (1969); Turney-High, H. H., *The Flathead Indians of Montana* (1937).

Flatiron Building [flat'-y-urn]

The 20-story Flatiron Building at 175 Fifth Avenue, New York City, erected in 1901–02 by Daniel Hudson BURNHAM and Company, was the tallest building in the world at the time. Its robust articulation and classicizing details, which first appeared in Burnham's work in the late 1890s, contrast with his cagelike, terra-cotta–sheathed Reliance Building (1894) in Chicago. The Land Title Building (1897) in Philadelphia, a key transitional work, displays the solidity and three-dimensionality of masonry form that in the Flatiron Building, Burnham's finest skyscraper, is transformed into a pleasing series of sculptural surface patterns that progress from foundation to cornice, roughly grouped into a base, shaft, and capital resembling those of a classical column. The unique, triangular floor plan of the building was demanded by the wedge-shaped site on which it stands.   ANN VAN ZANTEN

Bibliography: Reynolds, D. M., *Manhattan Architecture* (1988).

Flatt and Scruggs

Guitarist and singer Lester Raymond Flatt, banjoist Earl Eugene Scruggs, and their band, the Foggy Mountain Boys, epitomized BLUEGRASS MUSIC during the 1950s and '60s. Flatt, b. Tennessee, June 28, 1914, d. May 11, 1979, and Scruggs, b. North Carolina, Jan. 6, 1924, met in the early 1940s as performers at the GRAND OLE OPRY. In 1948 they formed their own group and won national acclaim through such recordings as "The Ballad of Jed Clampett," theme music for the television show *The Beverly Hillbillies* (1962), and "Foggy Mountain Breakdown," which became the theme music for the film *Bonnie and Clyde* (1968). In 1969 the team broke up. Flatt continued to play unamplified, traditional bluegrass, while Scruggs turned to country rock.

Bibliography: Rosenberg, N. V., "Lester Flatt and Earl Scruggs," in *Stars of Country Music*, ed. by Bill C. Malone and Judith McCulloch (1975).

Flattery, Cape [flat'-ur-ee]

Cape Flattery is a high, rocky promontory in northwest Washington, at the entrance to the Strait of JUAN DE FUCA. Its cliffs rise 37 m (120 ft) above the Pacific Ocean. Discovered in 1778 by James Cook, it is now marked by a lighthouse and weather station. A Makah Indian reservation is on the cape.

flatware

Flatware, or silverware, are the knives, forks, spoons, and serving utensils used in eating. The most widely used flatware is made of STAINLESS STEEL, a combination of steel, nickel, and chrome. It is also made in sterling silver (92.5% silver and 7.5% strengthening alloy), silver plate (a copper-alloy base metal electroplated with pure silver), gold electroplate (a copper-alloy base metal electroplated with 23-karat gold), and pewter (a blend of tin, copper, and antimony).

Although manufacturing processes vary according to the metal used, certain basic steps are involved in the manufacture of all flatware pieces. Production begins when the metal is cut to the rough outline of the piece. Each piece is then carefully shaped through a variety of rolling and annealing operations. The actual design of the pattern is applied to each piece by means of a mechanical drop hammer that holds hardened steel dies of both the front and back of the pattern. In better-quality flatware, a series of painstaking finishing operations assure such features as smooth and uniform edges around the bowls of the spoons, perfectly uniform tines, or prongs, for each fork, and careful polishing between the tines. Final buffing and polishing bring out the full luster of each piece.   THOMAS B. ROSS

Bibliography: Holland, Margaret, *Silver* (1973); Newman, H., *An Illustrated Dictionary of Silverware* (1987); Turner, Noel, *American Silver Flatware* (1971).

flatworm

Flatworm is the common name for flat-bodied, wormlike animals belonging to the phylum Platyhelminthes and including the free-living flatworms (such as PLANARIA, class Turbellaria) and the parasitic FLUKES, class Trematoda, and TAPEWORMS, class Cestoda. Platyhelminths are considered the most primitive bilaterally symmetric animals (the two lateral halves are mirror images) and the most primitive group of animals possessing a proper excretory system—tubes running down either side of the body and opening to the exterior through pores that link a series of "flame cells" containing cilia (hairs).

Flatworms possess neither a body cavity (coelom) nor a respiratory or circulatory system. The digestive system (absent in tapeworms) has a single opening serving as both mouth and anus. Turbellarians range in size from 0.5 cm (0.2 in) for the majority to 60 cm (2 ft) in length, are usually marine, and glide on a ciliated lower epidermis or swim by body undulation. They are carnivorous and have the ability to grow new parts (regeneration). Trematodes attach by hooks and suckers to their host; the most significant to humans is the genus *Schistosoma*, responsible for SCHISTOSOMIASIS (bilharziasis), a parasitic disease. Most tapeworms consist of a front segment (scolex) with suckers and hooks for attaching to the host's intestine; the rest of the animal is a series of separate segments, or proglottids, produced by budding from the front end.
                    STEPHEN C. REINGOLD

Bibliography: Burt, D. R. R., *Platyhelminthes and Parasitism* (1970).

Flaubert, Gustave [floh-bair']

Gustave Flaubert, b. Dec. 12, 1821, d. May 8, 1880, the author of one of the most influential prose works of the 19th century, produced only five novels and a few shorter works in his lifetime; he devoted years to revising and polishing each one. A master stylist whose novels have the studied perfection of poetry, Flaubert was, paradoxically, hailed as a realist, although his themes were romantic, and his plots and characters were largely secondary to his preoccupation with style.

Even *Madame Bovary*, based on a news item, was a vehicle for his theory that the true concern of literature is literature itself and that even the most banal subject can become the stuff of poetry. Although plagued by the necessity of working within the conventions of fiction—plot and action—Flaubert recognized their function: "A necklace," he wrote, "is composed of pearls, but it is the string that makes the necklace." What he sought was a prose style, arrived at in "ten years or ten centuries," that would be "as rhythmic as verse, as precise as the language of science." He believed that the possibilities of prose, unlike those of poetry, were yet to be discovered. For these views and for the achievement of many of his goals, Flaubert is regarded as the prophet of modern fiction.

Flaubert was raised in the hospital of Rouen where his father was chief resident surgeon. Slow to develop and often compared unfavorably with his older brother, who distinguished himself in medicine, Gustave soon saw himself as others saw him—the idiot of the family. In 1843, having failed his law examinations at the University of Paris, he devoted

The 19th-century French author Gustave Flaubert crafted his writings with a strong sense of realism, precise objectivity, and technical perfection. Flaubert believed that "the author, in his work, must be like God in the Universe, present everywhere and visible nowhere."

himself to writing. A year later, afflicted with epilepsy, he was given an allowance by his father and settled at Croisset, near Rouen. Although he had not yet published anything, Flaubert proceeded to make friends in Parisian literary circles and to work on the preliminary versions of two novels that were not to appear for decades: *A Sentimental Education* and *The Temptation of St. Anthony*.

From 1849 to 1851, Flaubert traveled through the Near East and North Africa, returning to Croisset with notes and memories of exotica that were to be incorporated years later into *Salammbô*. In 1856, after five years of labor, he completed *Madame Bovary* (1857; Eng. trans., 1957), but even before it reached the bookstores in Paris, it was impounded. This novel—the story of Emma Bovary's restless search for a life beyond the dull existence she shares with her doctor husband in a drab Norman farming town, her escape through adultery and finally suicide—caused Flaubert to be brought to trial for its supposedly immoral and irreligious ideas. The notoriety of the charges—of which Flaubert was acquitted—contributed to the novel's immense success.

In 1855, Flaubert returned to *The Temptation of St. Anthony*, begun in the 1840s, and, while completing his research on the ancient world, he decided to create an oriental extravaganza around a Carthaginian priestess who breaks her vows for a young warrior. Though poorly received at first, *Salammbô* (1862; Eng. trans., 1886), the novelist's most romantic work, won for Flaubert official recognition: he was received by the royal family and decorated.

After decades of revising, Flaubert finally published *A Sentimental Education* (1869; Eng. trans., 1964) and *The Temptation of St. Anthony* (1874; Eng. trans., 1910); neither found favor with the public. Flaubert was shattered by the failure of *St. Anthony*, a veritable prose poem that had been his life's work. The novel nonetheless remains a masterpiece, revealing Flaubert's most abiding obsessions.

His lifelong animosity toward the bourgeoisie, which could inspire him to heights of lyricism, led him to begin a bitter comic novel, *Bouvard et Pécuchet* (1881; Eng. trans., 1954), about two aging bachelors who blunderingly rediscover the history of human progress through a series of ill-conceived experiments. He was forced to abandon the novel by the bankruptcy of his niece's husband, whom he saved by virtually divesting himself of all his property. As a distraction from his financial insecurity, as well as from the deaths of his beloved friend, George Sand, and his former mistress, Louise Colet, Flaubert turned to a shorter fictional form. In less than 3 years he produced three splendid novellas: "St. Julian the Hospitaller," "Hérodias," and "A Simple Heart." Published under the title *Three Tales* (1877; Eng. trans., 1967), the book's immediate success did much to bolster his morale but little to ease his financial plight. He managed to complete *Bouvard et Pécuchet* just before his sudden death from apoplexy in 1880.

BETH ARCHER BROMBERT

Bibliography: Bart, B. F., *Flaubert* (1967); Culler, J., *Flaubert*, rev. ed. (1985); Donato, E., *The Script of Decadence* (1991); Knight, D., *Flaubert's Characters* (1985); Lottman, H., *Flaubert* (1989); Porter, L. M., ed., *Critical Essays on Gustave Flaubert* (1986); Roe, D., *Gustave Flaubert* (1989); Steegmuller, F., ed. and trans., *The Letters of Gustave Flaubert*, 2 vols. (1980, 1982), and *Flaubert in Egypt* (1973).

Flavin, Dan [flay'-vin]

The American artist Dan Flavin, b. Apr. 1, 1933, is an innovator in the use of fluorescent lighting to create abstract sculptures. Flavin, often linked with the MINIMAL ART movement, made his first fluorescent work, *The diagonal of May 25, 1963*, in his Brooklyn loft. Both it and subsequent works play with the junction of light and shadow to arrange and rearrange space. Later works used neon and colored fluorescent light as well as white light. In 1977–78, Flavin added fluorescent installations to three railroad tracks in New York City's Grand Central Terminal. BARBARA CAVALIERE

Bibliography: Battcock, Gregory, ed., *Minimal Art: A Critical Anthology* (1968); Calas, Nicolas and Elena, *Icons and Images of the Sixties* (1971); The National Gallery of Canada, Ottawa, *Dan Flavin* (1969).

flavors and fragrances

Flavors and fragrances are substances that stimulate the senses of TASTE AND SMELL. With the exception of the four primary taste sensations—sweet, bitter, salty, and sour—flavor characteristics are the result of our perception of odor; the difference between a flavor and a fragrance is in large part only a semantic distinction. Thus, a substance that provides an odor in PERFUMES may also be used to add flavoring to a food.

Most natural flavorings and fragrances are derived from plant substances—either from the aromatic, volatile vegetable oils known as ESSENTIAL OILS, or from the nonvolatile plant oils called RESINS. The aromatic substances derived from flowers, from herbs and spices, and from animal secretions (musk and ambergris, for example) are usually costly and limited in supply. Over the past century, success in reproducing some of these substances synthetically has created a new industry that today produces hundreds of flavors and fragrances for use in food, perfumes, and other products.

Some fragrant substances are relatively easy to synthesize. Vanillin, the aromatic ingredient in vanilla, can be readily reproduced by synthesis, as can benzaldehyde, the principal component of the odor of wild cherry. Many flavors and fragrances, however, have scores, if not hundreds, of components that contribute to their aroma. Only recently has it become possible to separate these components, using gas chromatography, and to determine their chemical structure with the aid of spectroscopy. Once the chemical identity of the components is known, it is often possible to make them synthetically. The search for new synthetics continues, and some of the most complex, among them the substances that produce the aroma of coffee, have still not been duplicated satisfactorily.

Many of the chemical compounds making up these synthetic materials are identical to those found in nature and are as harmless, or harmful, as the naturally derived essences. New products with unknown toxicology must be tested for safety, and, when used in foods, must be accepted as safe by the U.S. Food and Drug Administration. (See FOOD ADDITIVES.)

The availability of synthetic flavors and fragrances makes possible a large variety of products, from inexpensive beverages, to perfumed soaps, to used cars with an applied "new car odor." To cite two examples: the chemical compound B–phenylethyl alcohol, a vital ingredient in any rose fragrance, may be extracted from natural rose oil at a cost of thousands of dollars per kilogram; or an identical, synthetic substance can be made at one percent of this cost. Synthetic musk is chemically different from the musk derived from animals, but its odor effects are similar, and again the cost is a small fraction of that for the natural extract, and the quantities available are basically unlimited. ERNST THEIMER

Bibliography: Apt, C., *Flavor: Its Chemical, Behavioral and Commercial Aspects* (1977); Heath, H. B., and Reineccius, G. A., *Flavor Chemistry and Technology* (1986); Jouhar, A. J., *The Raw Materials of Perfumery*, 9th ed. (1989); Hornstein, I., ed., *Flavor Chemistry* (1966); Theimer, E. T., ed., *Fragrance Chemistry* (1982).

flax [flaks]

Flax is a group of annual and perennial plants from the Linaceae family that form the genus *Linum*. Several varieties of one species, *L. usitatissimum*, are grown primarily for their fiber, used in making LINEN, or for their seeds, the source of LINSEED OIL. Ornamental flax is cultivated in gardens.

Native to temperate and subtropical regions, flax is one of the oldest cultivated plants. Linen fabrics and bundles of flax fiber have been found among the remains of the Neolithic Swiss Lake Dwellers. Flax was cultivated by the ancient civilizations of the Middle East, by the Romans, and in medieval Europe, where it was the principal vegetable fiber grown. In the 19th century, cotton textiles largely supplanted linen; the 20th-century development of synthetic fibers reduced the need for flax still further. Today, the major producers of fiber flax are the USSR, China, France, Romania, Czechoslovakia, and Poland. Seed flax is grown in Canada, Argentina, India, the USSR, and the United States.

Flax, L. usitatissimum, *has been cultivated since prehistoric times for its stalk fiber* (bottom right), *used to make linen, and for its seed* (top right), *which yields linseed oil. Valued for their delicate blooms, several species of flax are grown as flower borders by home gardeners.*

Fiber flax grows best in a cool, moist climate; seed flax prefers a dry environment. Fiber varieties are planted close together to encourage taller stalks and minimal branching. For seed production, in which the fiber is not extracted, shorter, branching varieties of flax are used.

When the plant turns brown, flaxseed is harvested by machine. Fiber flax is harvested either by hand or by machine, the seeds are removed, and the stalks are bundled and soaked, or retted, to loosen the fibers. Retting may last up to 6 weeks, after which the stalks are dried, beaten, and scraped, or scutched, to remove the fibers. Finally, the long fibers are separated by combing, or hackling, and are spun on equipment similar to that used for cotton. Flax produces a strong thread used for sewing, netting, twine, and toweling, as well as for weaving into linen.   LAURENCE W. MAZZENO, JR.

Bibliography: Bird, John, and Catheral, Ed, *Fibres and Fabrics* (1977); Chapman, C. B., *Fibres* (1974); Hoppe, Elisabeth, and Edberg, Ragnar, *Carding, Spinning, Dyeing* (1975); Linder, O. and H., *Handspinning Flax* (1986).

Flaxman, John   [flaks'-muhn]

John Flaxman, b. July 6, 1755, d. Dec. 7, 1826, was the most influential exponent of NEOCLASSICISM in British sculpture during the late 18th and early 19th centuries. The son of a maker of plaster casts, he was a child prodigy, first exhibiting at the Free Society of Artists in 1767. He entered the Royal Academy Schools in 1770 and began to exhibit in the Academy's galleries the following year. Flaxman continued both as a student and afterward as a regular exhibitor at the Academy until 1787. During this time he became the close friend of William Blake.

In 1775, Flaxman was employed as a modeler for Josiah WEDGWOOD's pottery works, designing reliefs and medallions on classical themes. In addition to his work for Wedgwood, he began (1782) to undertake the first of his many funerary monuments. In 1787 he went to Rome, the center of neoclassical ideas, where he studied the art of Antonio CANOVA and the writings of Johann WINCKELMANN. In Rome he continued to supervise modelers for Wedgwood and undertook important sculpture commissions, including a reconstruction (1792) of the Belvedere Torso as *Hercules and Hebe* (destroyed). He also illustrated many classical texts in a refined linear drawing style, which were engraved and which won him international admiration.

Flaxman returned to London in 1794 and soon exerted an influence on British art similar to that which his contemporary, Jacques Louis David, exerted in France. He became an associate of the Royal Academy in 1797, a full member in 1800, and a professor in 1810. His funeral monuments of this period adorn the crypts of many English cathedrals, including Saint Paul's Cathedral and Westminster Abbey. Among his most successful later works are *Satan Overcome by St. Michael* (1822; Petworth Collection, London) and his illustrations of *Hesiod* (1817), engraved by Blake, which combine his earlier classicism with a religious mysticism that indicates a sympathy for the emerging romantic spirit.

Bibliography: Constable, W. G., *John Flaxman, 1755–1826* (1927); Honour, Hugh, *Neoclassicism* (1968); Whinney, Margaret, *Sculpture in Britain, 1530–1830* (1964).

flea

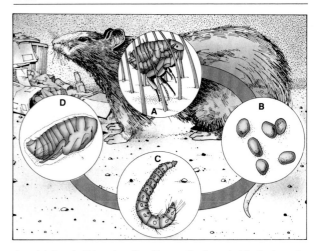

An adult female Oriental rat flea, Xenopsylla cheopis *(A), feeds on the host's blood before laying eggs (B) in the dirt or in the host's nest. The eggs hatch into larvae (C) that feed on organic debris and eventually molt into pupae (D), emerge as adults, and seek new hosts.*

The flea is any wingless, bloodsucking insect of the order Siphonaptera that parasitizes warm-blooded animals. Most are 0.1–0.4 cm (0.04–0.16 in) long and have enlarged, muscular hindlegs adapted for leaping.

Fleas exhibit complete metamorphosis, with a larval form that feeds on organic debris. In the wild, flea larvae subsist on the hair, skin, droppings, and food scraps that accumulate in nests and lairs of animals. They also live in the bedding of livestock and pets, as well as in dirty rugs. The larval stage lasts 15 to 200 days, and the adults may live almost a year.

A few species of fleas are inactive and remain attached to their hosts for long periods. Chigoes infest feet and toes of persons who walk barefoot in tropical and subtropical regions, causing painful swelling and infection. Sticktights cause serious damage to domestic poultry. Chickens and turkeys may have hundreds of sticktights attached to their head, causing irritation, weight loss, and blindness.

The Oriental rat flea is the primary transmitter of *Yersinia pestis,* the bacterium that causes bubonic plague. Plague was a major scourge of civilizations in past centuries. Today small outbreaks periodically occur in the United States, largely resulting from the existence of the disease in populations of wild rodents.   DAVID J. HORN

Bibliography: Fox, Irving, *Fleas of Eastern United States* (1940; repr. 1968); Hubbard, Clarence A., *Fleas of Western North America* (1947; repr. 1968); Weber, W. J., *Fleas, Ticks, and Cockroaches* (1984).

fleabane   [flee'-bayn]

Fleabane, *Erigeron,* is comprised of about 200 species of annual and perennial herbs in the daisy family, Compositae. They occur in fields and open woods; a few are used in rock gardens. Flower heads are solitary or branched in clusters. Their disk flowers are yellow, and the rays mostly rose, violet, or white, rarely yellow.   K. B. PAUL

Fleet, Thomas

Thomas Fleet, b. Shropshire, England, Sept. 8, 1685, d. July 21, 1758, a successful printer in colonial America, published one of Boston's best-known early newspapers, the *Boston Evening-Post*, which he founded in 1735. Fleet's sons, Thomas and James, continued publication of the *Evening-Post* after his death until Apr. 24, 1775. Fleet served (1729–31) as printer to the Massachusetts House of Representatives and published numerous books, including Joseph Addison's *Cato* (1750) and Michael Wigglesworth's *The Day of Doom* (1751).

Fleetwood Hill, Battle of: see BRANDY STATION, BATTLE OF.

Fleetwood Mac

Fleetwood Mac, the English blues-rock music group, was formed in 1967 as a quartet that included drummer Mick Fleetwood, b. June 24, 1947, and bassist John McVie, b. Nov. 26, 1946. Since that year it has changed some of its personnel several times and has had phenomenal successes and lackluster periods when the group seemed almost moribund. Songwriter-keyboardist Christine Perfect McVie, b. July 12, 1943, joined the group in 1970. The 1975 addition of the American singer Stevie Nicks and her husband, guitarist Lindsay Buckingham, resulted in a series of hit albums, including *Fleetwood Mac* (1975), *Rumours* (1977), *Mirage* (1982), and *Tango in the Night* (1987). Mick Fleetwood's memoirs, *Fleetwood,* were published in 1990.

Fleming, Sir Alexander

The Scottish bacteriologist Sir Alexander Fleming, b. Aug. 6, 1881, d. Mar. 11, 1955, discovered penicillin. Fleming received (1906) his medical degree from St. Mary's Hospital in London. During World War I he began searching for antibacterial substances and in 1921 discovered lysozyme, an antibiotic enzyme that attacks many types of bacteria. In 1928 he found that a *Penicillium* mold had accidentally contaminated a staphylococcus culture and stopped the bacteria's growth. The mold's antibacterial substance, which he named PENICILLIN, was nontoxic and effective against many bacteria harmful to humans. Fleming shared the 1945 Nobel Prize for physiology or medicine with British scientists Ernst Boris CHAIN and Sir Howard Walter FLOREY, who were able to purify and obtain enough penicillin for human trials. In 1947, Fleming became director of the Wright-Fleming Institute of St. Mary's Hospital.

Bibliography: Macfarlane, Gwyn, *Alexander Fleming* (1984); Malkin, John, *Sir Alexander Fleming* (1985).

Sir Alexander Fleming, a British bacteriologist, discovered the antibiotic penicillin in 1928 while examining a bacteria culture contaminated with mold. He was knighted in 1944 and shared the 1945 Nobel Prize for physiology or medicine with W. Florey and E. B. Chain, who purified and tested the drug.

Fleming, Sir Ambrose

An electrical engineer who invented the thermionic valve (the first ELECTRON TUBE), Sir John Ambrose Fleming, b. Nov. 29, 1849, d. Apr. 18, 1945, also contributed to the science of photometry (see PHOTOMETER), the measurement of the intensity of light. His work with the thermionic valve in 1904 and 1905 was important to the development of RADIO. From 1885 to 1926, Fleming taught at the University of London. He was knighted in 1929. His books include *The Alternate Current Transformer* (1889, 1892), *The Principles of Electric Wave Telegraphy* (1906), *The Propagation of Electric Currents in Telephone and Telegraph Conductors* (1911), and *Memoirs of a Scientific Life* (1934).

Bibliography: MacGregor-Morris, J. T., *The Inventor of the Valve* (1954).

Fleming, Sir Arthur Percy Morris

Sir Arthur Percy Morris Fleming, b. Jan. 16, 1881, d. Sept. 14, 1960, was a British engineer who is best known for his work in radar and radio. During World War I, Fleming made major improvements in equipment for detecting submarines. In 1920 he started Britain's second radio broadcasting station, in Manchester. During the 1930s he worked on high-power thermionic tubes, which were used in Britain's wartime radar systems. Fleming spent most of his professional career working for British Westinghouse Company.

Fleming, Ian

Ian Fleming, b. May 28, 1908, d. Aug. 12, 1964, at one time a journalist, stockbroker, and British naval intelligence officer, is best known as the creator of James Bond, fiction's most famous spy. The winning formula used in each of 13 Bond novels mixed old-fashioned intrigue and jet-age exoticism with the idiosyncrasies displayed by Agent 007 in his continuing battle against bizarre international conspiracies. *From Russia, With Love* (1957; film, 1963) gained authenticity from Fleming's experience in Moscow as a secret agent. Other Bond novels that enjoyed immense popularity when transferred to the screen include *Dr. No* (1958; film 1963), *Goldfinger* (1959; film 1964), *You Only Live Twice* (1964; film 1967), *The Spy Who Loved Me* (1962, film 1977), and *Moonraker* (1955; film 1979).

Bibliography: Boyd, Ann, *The Devil with James Bond* (1967; repr. 1975); Bryce, Ivar, *You Only Live Once; Memories of Ian Fleming* (1975); Rosenberg, Bruce, and Stewart, Ann H., *Ian Fleming* (1989).

Fleming, Peggy

Peggy Gale Fleming, b. San Jose, Calif., July 27, 1948, is an American figure skater who dominated the sport in the 1960s with her dazzling balletlike moves on ice. A skater from the age of nine, she rose rapidly among the ranks of Americans after a plane crash eliminated the U.S. national team in 1961. She was sixth in the 1964 Olympics, then won national championships five straight years, and culminated her competitive career with the 1968 Olympic singles title at Grenoble, France. Petite and strikingly beautiful, she is one of the most famous in a long line of American skaters. She turned professional in 1968.

Flemish art and architecture

Flemish art and architecture refers to works produced in an area that roughly corresponds to present-day BELGIUM. The correct name of this area is Southern Netherlands, but it is commonly known as Flanders, for the largest of its provinces.

With few exceptions, Flemish artists achieved their most significant successes in painting rather than in sculpture or in architecture. The most creative and influential Flemish artistic activity occurred during the 15th century and the first decades of the 17th century. During the 15th century, Flanders, then ruled by the dukes of Burgundy, was politically and artistically affiliated with France. Artists worked for prosperous local patrons, especially in Ghent, Bruges, and Brussels, and for the

Burgundian court. After the marriage (1477) of Mary of Burgundy to Maximilian of Austria, Flanders became part of the Habsburg empire (see HABSBURG dynasty); the Southern Netherlands was governed by the Spanish Habsburgs through the end of the 17th century.

PAINTING

From the 11th through the 14th century manuscript illumination (see ILLUMINATED MANUSCRIPTS) was the most common form of painting. The finest examples, such as the work of Jean Bondol (fl. 1368–c.1381), date from the second half of the 14th century. Like other Flemish painters who worked in France, Bondol combined the elegant stylization of French manuscripts with a less idealized depiction of landscape and secondary figures. The supreme achievement of this form was the *Trés Riches Heures de Jean duc de Berry*, painted by the LIMBOURG BROTHERS prior to 1416. This manuscript represents the highest development of the International Style (see INTERNATIONAL STYLE, art) and anticipates, in its detailed depictions of everyday life, the Flemish interest in GENRE PAINTING.

In the 15th century manuscript illumination was supplanted in important by painting on wooden panels. The characteristics of these panel paintings can be summarized by contrasting the principal Flemish innovation of the 1420s—the medium of oil paint—with the contemporary Italian development of linear perspective (see PERSPECTIVE, art), by which means Italian artists were able to structure space according to mathematical principles. Flemish artists preferred empirical analysis to mathematical proportion and delighted in representing the visible world in all its variety. Oil paint made possible the depiction of minute still-life details and landscape vistas and permitted representation of the effects of light in shape and texture. Flemish artists applied oil paint in superimposed translucent layers, attaining the unprecedentedly rich, glowing colors that are a hallmark of their painting. Jan van EYCK, in such works as the *Madonna with Chancellor Rolin* (c.1434; Louvre, Paris), was the first to realize the full potential of the new medium.

The symbolic mentality of the Middle Ages was accompanied by a keen interest in the secular, material world, and Flemish late-Gothic paintings, despite their religious subjects, often contained many carefully assembled mundane details.

The Flemish artists of the 15th century were innovators in their use of oil paints to achieve rich colors and shadings. Jan van Eyck's Madonna with Chancellor Rolin *(c.1434), with its distinctive, bright landscape background, exemplifies this technique. (Louvre, Paris.)*

The 15th-century Flemish master Hans Memling painted most of his works for the Hospital of Saint John in Bruges. The Saint Ursula reliquary (1489) is in the form of a chapel with six painted panels narrating the martyrdom of Saint Ursula and her followers. This end panel typifies the compositional balance and simple piety pervading Memling's devotional works.

Even the most commonplace objects were treated as vehicles for religious symbolism. In the *Merode Altarpiece* by the Master of Flémalle (see CAMPIN, ROBERT) (c.1425–27; The Cloisters, New York City), for example, the towel is both a functional household object and a symbol of the Virgin's purity. By uniting the secular and the spiritual, the Flemish artist placed religious events in a contemporary setting and imbued the physical world with spiritual significance.

Although sharing these characteristics, artists worked in individual styles. Jan van Eyck was the first Flemish painter to sign his works. His paintings, dispassionate and calm, are exceptional in their handling of light and detail. Rogier van der WEYDEN was much more concerned with the rendering of human emotions. Whereas his teacher, the Master of Flémalle, depicted robust figures in local settings, van der Weyden detached religious drama from everyday locations and gave his work strong linear rhythms and delicate refinement of form. Hans MEMLING excelled in portraiture, depicting his contemporaries with unaffected simplicity and startling directness of observation. The melancholy, spiritual intensity of Hugo van der GOES, who exploited the symbolic possibilities of realistic detail, has found many 20th-century admirers, and anticipated the work of expressionists such as Vincent van Gogh.

Since the mid-15th century, Italian artists had admired and been inspired by Flemish paintings. The *Portinari Altarpiece* (c.1475; Uffizi, Florence) by Hugo van der Goes, commissioned for a Florentine church, had a particularly forceful impact on Italian painters. With the advent of the 16th century and the spread of humanism in Flanders, however, the direction of artistic influence was reversed. Flemings began to emulate Italian Renaissance art, and artistic pilgrimages to Italy became common. Several changes resulted from this reorientation. New subjects and forms were introduced by Jan GOSSAERT, known as Mabuse, who introduced the Italian manner of depicting nude figures and was the first to bring the true mythological subjects to the Netherlands. Although Quentin MASSYS, the founder of the Antwerp school of painting, remained closely tied to northern tradition, he assimilated Leonardo da Vinci's technique of subtle shading of light and darker tones, as well as some of his compositional ideas.

Bernard van ORLEY emulated RAPHAEL's representation of human figures. Raphael's tapestry cartoons (see CARTOON, art), which were sent to Brussels around 1515, were a major influence on van Orley's work.

Under Italian influence late-Gothic Flemish art began to imitate the style of MANNERISM; in this process, the traditional Flemish fascination with the particular gave way to a desire for generalization and large-scale patterning. This tendency was most marked in the large figural compositions of the late 16th century.

While these developments were taking place, traditional northern interests were not superseded. Flemings continued to be renowned for their talent as portraitists. Moreover, by the mid-16th century landscapes and scenes of everyday life had evolved into independent subjects (see GENRE PAINTING), and still-life painting was moving in the same direction. Peter Bruegel the Elder (see BRUEGEL family) was the greatest painter to concentrate on traditionally northern subject matter. He too absorbed Italian influence, although on the level of pictorial organization rather than that of specific motifs. Unlike the Italians, Bruegel did not idealize human beings but depicted them in minutely detailed realistic settings.

In the revolt, begun during the 1560s, that occurred throughout the Netherlands, only the Northern Netherlands gained independence from Spanish rule; the Southern Netherlands remained part of the Habsburg empire. The two countries, politically separate from 1609, became artistically distinct. In both parts of the Netherlands the 17th century marked a turning away from the abstraction and artificiality of Mannerism, and baroque art had a very different character in Flanders than in Holland (see DUTCH ART AND ARCHITECTURE). Catholicism was reinstated in Flanders, and church patronage of art continued. The aristocratically inclined burghers continued to purchase mythological and historical subjects as readily as scenes of domestic life. With all subjects, Flemish painters used rich colors and decorative compositions and frequently represented dramatic action.

Whereas in the Northern Netherlands several distinct local styles flourished, Flemish painting was dominated by a single genius, Peter Paul RUBENS, a resident of Antwerp. Rubens was the first to synthesize Flemish and Italian traditions. He united the Flemish interest in finely detailed landscape, rich color, and intricate texture with the Italian tendency to generalize and compose in large-scale patterns. From this fusion Rubens produced monumental scenes of great vitality.

Among those influenced by Rubens were Anthony VAN DYCK and Jacob JORDAENS. Van Dyck was one of the most perceptive portraitists in the history of art. He could suggest both the individuality of his sitters and their social distinction. Jordaens did not emulate the magnificence of Rubens's compositions. Instead, whether in his religious and mythological scenes or in his depictions of rustic festivities, he delighted in representing the bustle of the mundane world. His figures, though monumental in scale, are heavier and less energetic than those of Rubens.

The artistic authority of Rubens is also evident in the work of landscape and still-life painters such as Frans SNYDERS, but his influence on those painters who worked on a small scale was less pervasive. Adriaen BROUWER combined a Flemish sense of lively movement with a Dutch emphasis on tonal values. Jan Bruegel the Elder maintained a delicate, miniaturist approach, which was quite distinct from the manner of Rubens.

With the death of Rubens the golden age of Flemish painting came to an end. During the 18th and 19th centuries most Flemish artists followed the trends in French art. Jacques Louis DAVID was exiled to Brussels in 1815, and his form of NEOCLASSICISM had a particularly great impact upon Flemish painting. James ENSOR was exceptional in his originality; his highly personal style, with its eerie colors and macabre, fantastic distortions, influenced the expressionist painters of the 20th century (see EXPRESSIONISM, art).

The most renowned Belgian painters of the 20th century are the surrealists René MAGRITTE, who explored the problematical relations of images and worlds, and Paul DELVAUX (see SURREALISM, art).

SCULPTURE

During the Carolingian period (see CAROLINGIAN ART AND ARCHITECTURE), the valley of the Meuse River became a center for ivory carving and metalwork. Mosan sculptors produced metalwork of exceptionally high quality during the Romanesque period (see ROMANESQUE ART AND ARCHITECTURE). RÉNIER DE HUY and NICHOLAS OF VERDUN, the two greatest Flemish Romanesque sculptors, were both Mosan goldsmiths.

Rénier de Huy's masterpiece is the cast-brass baptismal font (c.1107–18) for the Church of Saint Barthélémy at Liège. Despite their typically Romanesque geometric quality, the relief scenes on the basin show the influence of classical art in the way drapery is handled to suggest human form.

Nicholas of Verdun was the late great goldsmith of the Ro-

(Above) *Pieter Bruegel the Elder, considered the greatest Flemish painter of the 16th century, was known for his genre paintings that realistically portrayed everyday life.* The Peasant Wedding *(1568) captures the action and movement of his subjects and is rich in symbolic detail. (Museum of Art History, Vienna.)*

(Below) *Peter Paul Rubens fused the styles of the Italian and Flemish traditions to produce masterful paintings, such as* The Three Graces *(c.1639). (Prado, Madrid.)*

(Left) *The Town Hall of Antwerp (1561-66) was designed by the Flemish architect Cornelis Floris. Based on Mannerist design, the building, particularly the central block and tower, is heavily ornamented with statuary.* (Below) *The 17th-century sculptor Rombout Verhulst fashioned this terra-cotta bust of Maria van Reygersberg. (Rijksmuseum, Amsterdam.)*

manesque period. His highly influential works, such as the engraved and enameled altar frontal (finished 1181) for Kolsterneuburg, near Vienna, also reveal a knowledge of classical art as well as close observation of life. Nicholas introduced a greater naturalism in the representation of human emotions and used the lines of drapery to suggest the motion of human forms. Both characteristics were adopted and further developed in Gothic art.

During the Gothic period, French sculpture exerted considerable influence on Flemish production. The most accomplished sculptor at the Burgundian court, however, was Claus SLUTER, a Dutchman who spent part of his career in Brussels. Sluter's powerfully individualized figures mark a crucial step in the emanicipation of sculpture from its subordination to architecture.

During the 16th century, Italian works became very influential in the Flemish sculptural centers of Antwerp and Mechelen. The most talented Flemish-born sculptor of the period, Giovanni da BOLOGNA, spent his highly successful career in Italy. The same was true of François DUQUESNOY, the preeminent Flemish sculptor of the 17th century. Another important baroque sculptor was Artus QUELLINUS, whose principal work is the decoration of the Amsterdam Town Hall.

Flemish sculptors continued to be active outside the Southern Netherlands during the 18th century. Michael RYSBRACK, Peter Scheemakers (1691-1781), and Laurent Delvaux (1696-1778) had successful careers in England as portraitists and tomb sculptors. Those sculptors who remained in Flanders and who worked, often anonymously, for local churches produced unusual and distinctive works. In the second half of the 17th century and throughout the 18th century, developments in the traditional art of decorating wooden church furniture culminated in the treatment of confessionals and pulpits as settings for large, complicated figural ensembles, for example, the pulpit (1699) at Brussels Cathedral by Hendrik Verbruggen.

During the 19th century the influence of French sculpture was strong. French-derived neoclassicism was the dominant style of the first half of the century, but the most noteworthy sculptor of the later period was Constantin MEUNIER, a realist who was influenced by the style of Auguste Rodin, as can be seen in his *Monument to Labor* (c.1893-1905; Brussels Museum). During the twentieth century sculpture was a less important art than painting, as has always been the case in the Flemish tradition.

ARCHITECTURE

Artistic and cultural activity during the Romanesque period centered around monasteries and the powerful bishoprics of Tournai and Liège. Saint Barthélemy, Liège (11th-12th century), is one of the few surviving pieces of architecture from this period. Because of local prosperity, Romanesque buildings were replaced throughout the 13th, 14th, and 15th centuries by new, Gothic structures. French influence on Flemish ecclesiastical architecture was especially strong at the beginning of the Gothic period. As *Saints Michael and Gudule* at Brussels (begun c.1226) illustrates, Flemish architects did not emphasize verticality to the same degree as did the French. The most innovative developments occurred with secular architecture, such as market halls, whose existence and size reflected the continuing increase in cloth manufacture and trade. Examples include the Cloth Hall at Ypres (c.1304-80) and the Town Hall at Bruges (begun 1376). Prominent belfries were a characteristic feature of these buildings.

Not until the 16th century did Flemish architects turn away from the Gothic style and begin to imitate Italian Renaissance and Mannerist buildings. The Town Hall in Antwerp (1561-66), designed by Cornelis Floris (1514-75) and others, combines local and imported forms. Strapwork, an interlacing type of Mannerist ornament that originated in northern Europe and was popular with Flemish architects, is used sparingly. The tightly crowded and linear design of the Town Hall indicates its Mannerist character. In contrast the Jesuit Church of Saint Charles Borromeo at Antwerp (begun 1615), designed by Pieter Huyssens (1577-1637) and others, displays the full, flowing forms and the richer play of light and shade that are characteristic of baroque architecture. The facade, which includes sculptural reliefs designed by Rubens, was modeled upon Italian Jesuit examples. Significantly, the finest example of the Flemish baroque is the exuberant, triple-arched portico that Rubens designed for his own house in Antwerp.

Flemish architecture in the 18th, 19th and 20 centuries generally followed European trends. The work of Victor HORTA is an important exception. The buildings in Brussels that he designed during the 1890s are early examples of the style known as ART NOUVEAU. As in Tassel House (1892-93), the linear rhythms of his designs, which emulate natural forms, are carried along by the exposed metal framework. Henri VAN DE VELDE, who also worked in an Art Nouveau style, was important for his early espousal of principles that later informed much 20th-century architecture. He stressed the necessity of discarding excessive architectural ornament, advocated functionalism, and recognized the beauty of mechanical forms.

ZIRKA ZAREMBA FILIPCZAK

Bibliography: Conway, William M., *The Van Eycks and Their Followers* (1921; repr. 1976); Cuttler, Charles D., *Northern Painting, from Pucelle to Bruegel* (1968); Friedlaender, Max J., *From Van Eyck to Bruegel*, ed.

by F. Grossman, 3d ed. (1969); Gerson, Horst, and ter Kuile, E. H., *Art and Architecture in Belgium, 1600–1800* (1960); Held, Julius S., *Reubens and His Circle* (1981); Osten, Gert, and Vey, Horst, *Painting and Sculpture in Germany and the Netherlands, 1500–1600* (1969); Panofsky, Erwin, *Early Netherlandish Painting*, 2 vols. (1964); Puyvelde, Leo and Thierry van, *Flemish Painting*, 2 vols., trans. by Alan Kendall (1970, 1972); Voet, Leon, *The Golden Age of Antwerp* (1973); Whinney, M. D., *Early Flemish Painting* (1968).

Flemish language: see GERMANIC LANGUAGES.

Flemish literature: see DUTCH AND FLEMISH LITERATURE.

Fletcher, Alice

Alice Cunningham Fletcher, b. Mar. 15, 1838, d. Apr. 6, 1923, was an American ethnologist who worked among the Omaha Indians and is noted for the treatise *The Omaha Tribe* (1911), written with Francis La Flesche. She influenced passage of the Dawes Act of 1887 legalizing allotment of Indian land ownership, an act later regarded as deleterious to Indian interests.

BEA MEDICINE

Bibliography: Mark, J., *A Stranger in Her Native Land* (1988).

Fletcher, Giles

Giles Fletcher the Younger, c.1585–1623, was an English poet and the rector of Alderton, Suffolk. His devotional poem *Christ's Victory* (1610), although somewhat contrived in style, is considered a link between the works of Spenser and Milton. It was partly inspired by the French Protestant poet Du Bartas.

ROBIN BUSS

Fletcher, John: see BEAUMONT, FRANCIS, AND FLETCHER, JOHN.

Fletcher, John Gould

The American poet and critic John Gould Fletcher, b. Jan. 3, 1886, d. May 10, 1950, lived for a number of years in England, where he wrote such volumes of free verse as *Irradiations: Sand and Spray* (1915) under the influence of imagism. His later verse, such as the 1939 Pulitzer Prize–winning *Selected Poems* (1938), was more traditional. Besides critical and biographical studies, Fletcher wrote his autobiography, *Life Is My Song* (1937).

PAULA HART

Bibliography: Carpenter, L., *John Gould Fletcher and Southern Modernism* (1990).

Fletcher, Phineas

Phineas Fletcher, 1582–1650, was an English poet whose *Purple Island* (1633), like the work of his brother Giles FLETCHER, influenced Milton and continued the tradition of Spenser. An allegory on the human body and intellect, the poem contains pastoral descriptions. Fletcher also wrote a Spenserian poem entitled *Venus and Anchises*.

ROBIN BUSS

Fletcher v. Peck

The case of *Fletcher* v. *Peck* (1810) involved the first interpretation by the U.S. Supreme Court of the so-called contract clause of the U.S. Constitution: "No State shall . . . pass any . . . Law impairing the Obligation of Contracts." In this instance Robert Fletcher brought suit against John Peck for breach of CONTRACT on land that Peck had sold him in 1804. The property had originally been part of a larger purchase from the state of Georgia by four land companies that had bribed several members of the legislature in order to obtain their votes to authorize the sale (see YAZOO LAND FRAUD). A subsequent legislature rescinded the law selling the land and declared null and void all rights and claims thereunder. Peck had bought the land in 1795 and had later signed the deed over to Fletcher. Fletcher sought to get his money back, contending that the original sale of the land by the legislature was void and that Peck was guilty of a breach of covenant.

Chief Justice John Marshall, in his opinion for the Court ruling against Fletcher, asserted that the sale of the land by the legislature was a contract and that, in spite of the bribery and fraud connected with the sale, a subsequent legislature could not retrieve the land without violating the contract clause of the Constitution.

ROBERT J. STEAMER

Fletcher's Ice Island

Fletcher's Ice Island, or T-3, discovered in the Arctic Ocean in April 1947, was occupied several times in the 1950s and early 1960s as a base for weather reporting and geophysical research. At the time of its original occupation (Mar. 19, 1952) by a party led by Lt. Col. Joseph O. Fletcher (USAF), the ice island was 7 by 14 km (4 by 9 mi) in size, 45 m (150 ft) in thickness, and weighed about 4 billion tons. It drifted about 2.4 to 3.2 km (1½ to 2 mi) per day. A 16-m (52-ft) core from the ice revealed 54 discrete layers of silt with remains of vegetation; this proved its land-based origin, probably from a shelf glacier on Ellesmere Island.

Bibliography: Fletcher, Joseph O., "Three Months on an Arctic Ice Island," *National Geographic Magazine*, April 1953; Weeks, Tim, and Maher, Ramona, *Ice Island* (1965).

fleur-de-lis   [flur-duh-lee']

A fleur-de-lis, or "lily flower," is a heraldic device associated with the French crown, which adopted it as an emblem in the 12th century. It is composed of three vertical petals, the central one erect, the others curving to the right and left, joined near the base by a bar (see HERALDRY). Of obscure origin, the device is commonly believed to represent a lily, signifying purity, supposedly sent from heaven in AD 496 to the Frankish king Clovis. It remained part of the French coat of arms until 1830. A red fleur-de-lis is the heraldic symbol of Florence.

Fleury, André Hercule de   [flur-ee', ahn-dray' air-kuel' duh]

André Hercule de Fleury, b. June 22, 1653, d. Jan. 29, 1743, was a French churchman who rose to royal favor as tutor of the young LOUIS XV and served as his chief advisor from 1726 to 1743. He promoted French prosperity and European peace without solving the Old Regime's problems. The son of a tax collector, Fleury became LOUIS XIV's almoner in 1683. After serving (1698–1715) as bishop at Fréjus, he returned to court as the dauphin's preceptor just before the dauphin ascended the throne as Louis XV (1715). Fleury became a member of the royal council in 1723 and its presiding minister and a cardinal in 1726.

Fleury appointed able ministers and managed to balance budgets by avoiding war. Currency stabilization, government support of trade, extensive road building, and efficient local administration by INTENDANTS contributed to a long cycle of prosperity after 1730. At the same time, however, forced road labor (*corvée*), indirect-tax farming, mercantilist controls over industry, and forced royal compromises with the PARLEMENTS over JANSENISM were mixed blessings. After negotiating France's future acquisition of Lorraine through cautious involvement in the War of the POLISH SUCCESSION (1733–38), Fleury was forced by ministerial rivals into the costly War of the AUSTRIAN SUCCESSION (1742–48). He died in office at the age of 90.

A. LLOYD MOOTE

Bibliography: Wilson, Arthur, *French Foreign Policy during the Administration of Cardinal Fleury* (1936; repr. 1972).

Flexner, Abraham   [fleks'-nur]

Abraham Flexner, b. Nov. 13, 1866, d. Sept. 21, 1959, an American reformer of education, was responsible for major transformations in medical education and for organizing the INSTITUTE FOR ADVANCED STUDY in Princeton, N.J.

Educated as a classicist, Flexner opened (1891) a school in his hometown of Louisville, Ky. His unorthodox methods included the absence of rules, examinations, records, and reports. Students proceeded at their own pace; consequently, many entered college at a relatively young age. Flexner's reputation as an educator grew, and in 1908 he published his first book, *The American College.* It was based on his studies at Harvard and at the University of Berlin and criticized the American system of electives, lectures, and assistantships.

The Carnegie Foundation commissioned Flexner to study medical education, and his report, *Medical Education in the United States and Canada* (1910), rated 155 medical schools. His findings led to the closing of almost half the schools and the modification of many others. While at the General Education Board of the Rockefeller Foundation (1913–28), Flexner administered a large fund given by private donors for the improvement of medical education. The money provided for endowments for teaching and research, and created faculty positions for doctors at university-connected teaching hospitals.

Flexner's proposal for a model school, published as *A Modern School* (1916), was supported by the Rockefeller Foundation, which later established the Lincoln Experimental School of Teachers College, Columbia University, patterned after Flexner's model. In 1930, Flexner wrote *Universities: American, English, German,* in which he advocated the German-university ideal of scholarship rather than teaching. He was instrumental in getting Louis Bamberger, a New Jersey department store owner, to endow the Institute for Advanced Study. Flexner was its director from 1930 to 1939.

Bibliography: Flexner, A., *An Autobiography* (1960); Numbers, R. L., ed., *The Education of American Physicians: Historical Essays* (1980).

flicker

The yellow-shafted flicker, C. auratus auratus, *is a woodpecker that constantly flicks its tail and wing feathers. It feeds on insects, especially ants, that it finds on the ground.*

Flickers are any of six species of woodpeckers belonging to the genus *Colaptes* in the woodpecker family, Picidae. The common flicker, *C. auratus,* found in North America from Alaska to Mexico and in the West Indies, reaches slightly over 30 cm (12 in) in overall length. It has a brown back marked with dark spots and bars, white undersides spotted with black, and a black crescent on the breast. Males and young females have cheek stripes, or a "mustache," behind the bill. An eastern American form, *C. auratus auratus,* known as the yellow-shafted flicker or yellowhammer, has yellow under the wings, black cheek stripes, and a red patch on the back of the head. A western form, known as the red-shafted flicker, is salmon-red under the wings and has red cheek stripes. Once considered a separate species, *C. cafer,* it is now considered a variant, *C. auratus cafer,* of the common flicker. The five other species of flickers are found in Cuba and throughout South America. Unlike other woodpeckers, flickers often feed on the ground, seeking insects, especially ants.

WILLIAM F. SANDFORD

Bibliography: Bent, A. C., *Life Histories of North American Woodpeckers* (1939); Skutch, Alexander F., *Life of the Woodpecker* (1985).

flight

Flight is the ability to move with direction through the air, an ability shared by many animals. Humans can fly only in the machines they have devised.

BATS, most BIRDS, and many INSECTS practice true natural flight: that is, the motions of their wings produce the air lift necessary to take off, fly, and land. A number of other kinds of animals can glide for brief distances through the air. They do so by means of stretchable body membranes, as with various small mammals and some lizards and snakes, or by means of enlarged fins, such as the FLYING FISH. A few species of fish actually flap their fins in the air like birds (see HATCHETFISH).

Many birds have the ability to soar: they can remain airborne by floating without wing movement, supported by a rising column of air. For such birds as the EAGLE and CONDOR, the little energy they expend in soaring may compensate for the very large amounts of energy needed for these birds to launch themselves into the air from a standing position.

The travel range of flying animals can be enormous. The monarch BUTTERFLY can fly 1,000 km (620 mi) without stopping to feed. Bird flights of 650 km (400 mi) in 24 hours have often been recorded.

The machines that carry humans into the air are of two varieties. Lighter-than-air vehicles contain a gas that is more buoyant than air: hydrogen or helium in AIRSHIPS; heated air inside BALLOONS. Heavier-than-air flight is provided by HELICOPTERS, GLIDERS, and AIRCRAFT. The lifting force in an aircraft is generated by the wings; the propulsive force, an engine-driven PROPELLER or a JET PROPULSION engine, moves the vehicle through the air fast enough for the wings to produce sufficient lift. A rocket (see ROCKETS AND MISSILES) is a specialized flight vehicle that can also move beyond the atmosphere by the force of engine thrust alone.

Bibliography: Boyne, Walter J., *The Smithsonian Book of Flight* (1987); Danthanarayana, W., ed., *Insect Flight* (1986); Padian, K., ed., *The Origin of Birds and the Evolution of Flight* (1986); Terres, J. K., *How Birds Fly* (1987).

See also: AERODYNAMICS; ASTRONAUTICS; BIOLOGICAL LOCOMOTION.

flight, human-powered

The concept of human-powered flight dates to ancient times. The societies of the ancient Near East were rife with legends of flying humans. The most enduring of these classic mythological tales is that of DAEDALUS and Icarus. During the Middle Ages various individuals unsuccessfully attempted human-powered flight; the most notable of these early pioneers was the monk Eilmer of Malmesbury (AD c.1000), who succeeded in making a short gliding flight from Malmesbury Abbey in Wiltshire. Many of these individuals envisioned complicated ORNITHOPTER-type flying machines (machines with flapping wings) of the same general type conceived by Leonardo da Vinci. Giovanni Borelli's work *De motu animalium* (On the Movement of Animals, 1685) demonstrated that the muscular structure of a human was inadequate for ornithopter flight. Over the next two centuries, the primary effort in aeronautics was directed toward refining and extending aerodynamic knowledge, deriving lightweight flight structures, and developing engines capable of propelling an aircraft.

A £50,000 prize that was established in 1959 by British industrialist Henry Kremer attracted many well-conceived projects designed for 1- and 2-man crews to pedal an aircraft over a specified 1-mile (1.6-km), figure-8 course. The prize was finally won on Aug. 23, 1977, by the *Gossamer Condor,* an ultralightweight vehicle, constructed of cardboard, piano wire, aluminum tubing, and Mylar clear plastic, with a 29-m (96-ft) wingspan. Bryan Allen, a competitive bicyclist and biologist, piloted the aircraft over the course, making two turns and passing over a 3-m-high (10-ft) barrier in 6.5 minutes.

Human-powered flight represents the coming together of the highest technical standards with great physical stamina and endurance on the part of the pilot. Although physical requirements limit its applicability, the *Gossamer Condor* has inspired a new class of human-powered vehicles. In June 1979,

Aloft on its only flight (Apr. 23, 1988), the Daedalus *resembles an exotic dragonfly. The sparest of aerodynamic designs, it consists of a 34-m (112-ft) wing, cabin pod, pedal-powered propeller, and tail assemblage—all mounted on an 8.8-m (29-ft) hollow rod.*

Bryan Allen pedaled the *Gossamer Albatross,* a 27-kg (60-lb) aircraft with a wingspan of 29.3 m (96 ft), across the English Channel. On Jan. 22, 1987, a new distance record for human-powered flight was set by Glenn Tremml, a 26-year-old medical student, who pedaled the *Eagle* (40 kg/92 lb) for 60 km (37.3 mi) at California's Edwards Air Force Base. Tremml's feat was surpassed (Apr. 23, 1988) by the flight of the *Daedalus,* powered by cycling champion Kanellos Kanellopoulos, who flew 118 km (74 mi) from Crete to a crash landing off the Aegean island Santorini. In 1989 a human-powered helicopter made a first, brief flight.   RICHARD P. HALLION

Bibliography: Grosser, Morton, *Gossamer Odyssey: The Triumph of Human-Powered Flight* (1981); Reay, David A., *The History of Man-Powered Flight* (1977).

Flinders, Matthew

The English seaman Matthew Flinders, b. Mar. 16, 1774, d. July 19, 1814, was one of the world's most accomplished navigators and hydrographers. After serving in the South Pacific with William BLIGH, he sailed (1795) for Australia, where, with naval surgeon George Bass, he circumnavigated Van Diemen's Land (Tasmania). Because of his brilliant hydrographic work he was sent (1801) to chart the Queensland coast. Although dogged by ill luck, he completed the first circumnavigation of Australia in June 1803. Shipwrecked while returning to England, Flinders sought assistance from French-held Mauritius. Because France was at war with Britain, however, he was held prisoner there for seven years (1803–10). Flinders's noteworthy *Voyage to Terra Australis* was published just before his death.   E. J. TAPP

Bibliography: Colwell, M., *The Voyages of Matthew Flinders* (1970); Mack, J. D., *Matthew Flinders* (1966); Perry, T. M., *The Discovery of Australia: The Charts and Maps of the Navigators and Explorers* (1983).

Flinders Range

The Flinders Range is a mountain region in southeastern South Australia. Its greatest elevation, 1,889 m (6,200 ft), is Saint Mary Peak. The mountains yield coal, lead, and copper. Matthew Flinders, a British navigator charting Australia's coasts, sighted the range in 1802.

Flindt, Flemming   [flint]

Flemming Ole Flindt, b. Copenhagen, Sept. 30, 1936, is a ballet choreographer who trained at the Royal Danish Ballet school, joining the company in 1955 and serving as director (1966–78). He danced with the Paris Opera (1960–65) and was artistic director of the Dallas Ballet (1981–88). Flindt's chore-

ography includes *The Lesson* (1963), *The Triumph of Death* (1971), and *Tarantelle Classique* (1985).   M. ROBERTSON

Flint

Flint, a city in eastern Michigan, is a major automobile-manufacturing center and the seat of Genesee County. The population of the city is 140,761 (1990), and 431,000 (1988 est.) persons reside in the metropolitan area. The city began as a fur-trading post that was built on the Flint River in 1819. Early settlers turned to lumbering, which in turn led to a prosperous carriage-making industry. Car manufacturing began in the early 20th century, and today General Motors is the major employer. During the 1980s the city lost thousands of jobs as a result of the economic constriction within that industry.

flint: see CHERT AND FLINT.

Flint, Richard Foster

The American geologist Richard Foster Flint, b. Chicago, Mar. 1, 1902, d. June 6, 1976, was well known for his studies of glacial geology. He served on the staff of Yale University (1925–70) and was chairman (1939–45) of the compilation committee for the Glacial Map of North America sponsored by the National Research Council. Flint also helped establish (1953) what is now the Radiocarbon Laboratory at Yale. His textbooks include *Glacial and Quaternary Geology* (3d rev. ed., 1971), *The Earth and Its History* (1973), and, with Brian Skinner, *Physical Geology* (1932; 2d ed., 1977).

flintlock: see MUSKET.

Flintshire   [flint'-shir]

Flintshire is a former county in northeastern Wales, along the Irish Sea coast. From the seacoast and River Dee estuary, the land gradually rises to the Clwydian Hills. In the fertile Clwyd and Dee river valleys, agriculture is the principal economic activity, with oats and wheat the major crops. Sheep and cattle are raised at higher elevations. Coal, mined in the mountains, supports iron and steel, chemical, textile (especially rayon), and aircraft manufacturing in the vicinity of the city of Flint. Tourism is important because of coastal resorts, numerous Norman castles, and other historic landmarks.

Neolithic and Bronze Age remains indicate the early inhabitation of Flintshire. It was subsequently occupied by the Celts; the Romans; the Saxons of Mercia, who built the earthwork OFFA'S DYKE; and the Normans. In 1284, Edward I made Flintshire a county; in 1974 it became part of CLWYD.

Flood: see DELUGE.

floodplain

Along many rivers there occurs a flat, elongated strip of land called a floodplain. As the name suggests, this landform originates from the periodic flooding of the river, a process that results in widespread deposition of sediment. Floodplains that are inundated every one or two years are commonly referred to as active or living. The unconsolidated sediment, mostly suspended clay and silt, that settles out during flooding is derived from erosion of the surrounding land in the drainage basin (see EROSION AND SEDIMENTATION).

Although deposition of suspended sediment beyond the bank tends to build up the floodplain, raising it as much as 1 cm (0.4 in) a year, the dominant sedimentation process is the formation of wholly or partially submerged bars in the river channel. Point bars characteristically develop around the inner convex banks of MEANDER bends, whereas longitudinal and diagonal bars develop in the channel complex of BRAIDED STREAMS. Point bars are commonly separated from the adjacent floodplain by a slight depression known as a swale.

The current around a meander bend erodes the bank, resulting in a lateral shift of the river course. For a river that has almost reached equilibrium, erosion on the outer (concave) bank is nearly balanced by deposition on inner (point bar) banks downstream. As the river shifts course, the point bar and swale system—hence, the floodplain—grows laterally, a process known as lateral accretion. Alternating point bars and swales on a floodplain surface afford clear evidence of shifts in river course. Lateral shifts in a river channel tend to limit the upward growth of the floodplain caused by overbank deposition. In braided rivers, the stabilization of bars and islands by vegetation contributes to the growth of the floodplain.

Floodplain alluvium is composed mostly of stratified clay, silt, sand, and gravel, generally with some admixture of organic material of vegetal origin. The sand and gravel often display cross-bedding, and the entire alluvial sequence is characterized by a fining upward in grain size. Because of channel migration and the variability of in-channel processes, alluvial fill displays lateral textural variations. Rapid deposition of overbank material in the vicinity of the channel leads to levee formation, especially where vegetation is available to trap sediment.

Floodplains commonly have poor surface and subsurface drainage. They display a variety of morphologic features, including levees, flood basins, backswamps, OXBOW LAKES, and various types of bars and alluvial islands. Downcutting of the river into its floodplain may result in formation of river terraces. Finally, floodplains provide rich agricultural lands that in many parts of the world are highly populated. Their main disadvantage stems from the natural hazard of flooding, sometimes on a catastrophic scale—as in the great floods of 1993 in the Mississippi River floodplain.   A. V. JOPLING

Bibliography: Baker, Victor R., et al., *Flood Geomorphology* (1988); Bridges, E. M., *World Geomorphology* (1990); Carling, P. A., and Petts, C. E., *Lowland Floodplain Rivers* (1992).

See also: RIVER AND STREAM.

floods and flood control

A flood is the inundation of normally dry land resulting from the rising and overflowing of a body of water. The effects of floods, both beneficial and destructive, have been recorded for at least 5,000 years. The most familiar flood story is that in the Book of Genesis. The event upon which this Old Testament tale is based may have occurred about 3000 BC, when the Euphrates River inundated a vast area, including Ur in southern Mesopotamia. According to the Bible, the flood resulted from 40 days of continual rain, producing high water that lasted 150 days and flood depths in excess of 15 cubits (7.5 m/25 ft). (See DELUGE.)

The benefits of *regular* flooding were appreciated in ancient Egypt, where the floodwaters of the Nile brought fertile silt and much-needed water to the fields each year. The earliest records of stream levels are from these annual Nile floods.

Coastal Floods. Coastal flooding can be caused by high, wind-generated WATER WAVES, exceptionally high tides, SUBSIDENCE of coastal areas, and TSUNAMIS (seismic sea waves). Coastal flooding is of special concern because, in many countries, population is concentrated along coastlines. For example, U.S. coastal counties—those bordering oceans or the Great Lakes—contained 53 percent of the population in 1990.

Although exceptionally high tides rarely produce serious and widespread damage on their own, they may significantly increase the hazard of flooding in combination with even moderately severe storms. HURRICANES and major storms produce most coastal floods. In 1970 and again in 1991 cyclones in the Bay of Bengal produced heavy seas that inundated the coastal regions of Bangladesh, killing well over 100,000 people each time. Wind-generated waves over 30 m (100 ft) in height have been observed in the open ocean. Fortunately, these huge waves usually diminish in size before reaching coastlines. On the other hand, tsunamis, caused by EARTHQUAKES, LANDSLIDES, and volcanic eruptions, are low (less than a meter high) in the open ocean. They travel at speeds up to 800 km/h (500 mph), however, and grow higher as they near land; tsunamis 18 to 30 m (60–100 ft) high are not uncommon. Tsunamis occur most often in the Pacific Ocean and have taken many lives in Japan. One of the most spectacular, well-documented tsunamis of recent times occurred at Lituya Bay, Alaska, in 1958. A minor earthquake there caused a rockfall into the sea, producing a 60-m (200-ft) wave that destroyed vegetation, including heavy timber, at heights of as much as 520 m (1,700 ft) above sea level.

River Floods. RIVER flooding results from a variety of causes. Natural causes include rain, snowmelt, and ice jams (see ICE,

The immense force of the 1993 Mississippi River floodwaters broke through the levee (upper left) and carried this house downstream, along with several farm buildings. The destruction in this Illinois scene was repeated throughout the upper sections of the Mississippi Basin.

Levees were reinforced with sandbags, and new levees thrown up—as here, in St. Genevieve, Mo., where pumps were used to drain already-flooded areas behind the levees.

RIVER AND LAKE). Floods on rivers and streams result from prolonged periods of precipitation over broad regions. This was the case in June 1972, when six days of torrential rain from Hurricane Agnes battered the eastern United States. In an area from Virginia to New York, Agnes caused more than $3.5 billion in damage, taking 132 lives and leaving a quarter of a million people homeless. In the same month a notable cloudburst-caused flood occurred in the Black Hills of South Dakota, taking 242 lives and causing $163 million in property damage.

Cloudburst floods are caused by extremely intense rainfall (23 cm/10 in or more an hour), but they are short-lived, rarely continuing for more than a few hours at a given location. They tend to be somewhat more common in mountainous areas, where steep slopes cause water to travel at high speeds, thus eroding and carrying away natural and artificial debris. These floods often occur rapidly and with little warning—hence the name FLASH FLOOD.

Moderate amounts of warm rain falling on a snowpack, particularly if the ground beneath the snow is frozen and unable to absorb the moisture, can cause severe flooding. Such was the case in New England and adjacent states in March 1936, when snowmelt equivalent to 25–75 cm (10–30 in) of rain occurred. Slabs of ice constricted river channels and plugged bridge openings. When the flood was over, 107 people had lost their lives. Damage was estimated at $270 million.

Floods may result from the failure of artificial structures such as dams. One of the most devastating U.S. dam failures occurred in February 1972 at Buffalo Creek in Logan County, W.Va. A dam used to impound coal-mining wastes, as well as water, completely collapsed after 3 days of rain, causing a 3-hour flood that took 118 lives.

Flooding is also caused by the constriction of streams by engineering projects such as landfills; removal of vegetation, which accelerates the rate of rain runoff; and paving and construction, which reduce the land's capacity to absorb rainfall. The 1993 floods in the upper sections of the Mississippi River floodplain were among the most extensive—involving nine states and and about 8 million ha (20 million acres)—and destructive (at least $17 billion in damages) the United States has ever known. Although the floods were triggered by a long period of heavy spring and summer rains, many flood experts also blamed the extensive engineering works that have directed and restricted the course of the great river and its tributaries.

Warning Systems. Deaths caused by flooding in the United States have averaged about 200 annually since 1970, and property losses have reached over $4 billion per year. (1993 must be counted as an exceptional year.) Losses would be far higher were it not for the 50 state offices of the National Weather Service's River and Flood Forecasting Service, which issue flood forecasts and warnings. Flood forecasts are based on meteorological data, upstream information, and estimates (based on previous experience and analysis) of how a particular watershed will respond to precipitation.

The U.S. Coast and Geodetic Survey, with the cooperation of the armed forces and the Federal Aviation Agency, maintains the Seismic Sea Wave Warning System, a network of seismic- and tide-monitoring stations rimming the Pacific Ocean. The warnings, made available to all nations, have proved effective in saving lives and reducing property loss.

Flood frequency analyses are performed by hydrologists, engineers, and planners, using records of past stream flow to estimate the probability of occurrence of floods of various sizes. For example, if a flood of a particular size has a probability of one chance in one hundred of being equaled or exceeded each year, it is said to be a "100-year flood."

Flood Control. Coastal flooding is an almost insoluble problem. Even where major flooding is practically an annual occurrence, the need for land far outweighs the dangers of flood. For example, much of the agricultural area in Bangladesh is a vast, low-lying plain formed by the deltas of three great rivers. If the yearly MONSOON brings heavy rains, or a CYCLONE or hurricane raises water levels, the plain is inundated, settlements disappear, and inhabitants are swept away.

In the Netherlands, after the catastrophic storm of 1953, which destroyed dikes and flooded POLDER lands, the Dutch devised the DELTA PLAN, a 9-km (5.6-m) length of movable steel gates that protects the most vulnerable areas of the southern coast. The THAMES RIVER surge barrier is erected on the river just below London.

Two different and at times competing approaches are used in attempting to prevent or reduce damage caused by river flooding. The structural approach relies on dams and reservoirs, levees or dikes, modification of stream channels, flood-diversion systems, and treatment of watersheds. Flood-control dams impound water at times of flood to mitigate downstream hazard; then, after the threat subsides, water is slowly released. Artificial levees raise the height of streambanks, thus reducing the likelihood of flooding. Straightening of channels to allow floodwaters to flow faster and therefore shallower is yet another method. In some places, floodwaters are diverted into previously prepared holding basins to reduce the flood crest downstream. Another technique diminishes the amount of water entering streams by reforesting watersheds and by detaining runoff high in the headwaters of a river.

Critics of the structural approach note that the cost of flood-control structures often exceeds the value of the property being protected. In addition, such restraining structures as artificial levees tend simply to move the hazard upstream or downstream, and levee failure can be extremely serious. Channel straightening is often temporary. For example, new bends have developed along several hundred kilometers of the Mississippi River since the 1930s, when the U.S. Army Corps of Engineers began extensive channel improvements.

Advocates of the nonstructural approach prefer using zoning, subdivision regulations, and public acquisition to prevent new building in FLOODPLAINS. They encourage using these lands for compatible purposes, such as for agriculture and parks. For areas of existing development, early-warning systems and flood insurance are prescribed.

SIGNIFICANT FLOODS WITHIN THE PAST CENTURY

Year	Location and Cause
1883	Java and Sumatra. Tsunami, following the explosion of Krakatoa. Some 36,000 lives lost.
1887	Henan, China. Huang He, swollen by rains, overflows levees, floods 150,000 km² (50,000 mi²). 900,000 lives lost.
1889	Johnstown, Pa. Dam failure. 2,200 lives lost.
1900	Galveston, Tex. Hurricane flooding. 6,000 lives lost.
1916	The Netherlands. North Sea storms flood lowlands. 10,000 lost.
1928	Florida. Hurricane causes Lake Okeechobee to flood. 2,400 lives lost.
1938	North China. Chinese forces blow up dikes on the Huang He, to impede Japanese advance. Estimated 1 million lives lost.
1960	Chile, Hawaii, Japan. Giant tsunami following a major Chilean earthquake inundates coastal areas in all three countries.
1963	North Italy. Landslide into the reservoir of the Vaiont Dam sends a huge wave into valley below. 2,000 lives lost.
1970	E. Pakistan (now Bangladesh). Cyclone-generated floods inundate coastal regions. 300,000–500,000 lives lost.
1971	Orissa State, India. Cyclone and sea surge hit the coast. 10,000 lives lost.
1979	Morvi, India. Heavy monsoon rains cause collapse of river dam. 7,000 to 10,000 lives lost.
1982	Peru. Torrential rains cause lake to overflow into Chantayacu River valley. 2,500 lives lost.
1985	Northeastern Brazil. Rain-caused floods; 1 million homeless.
1988	Bangladesh. Monsoon flooding inundates 3/4 of country; 2,500 dead, 28 million homeless.
1988	Sudan. Torrential rains flood the Nile. 1.5 million homeless in Khartoum area; numbers of dead unknown.
1991	Bangladesh. Cyclone hits delta region with 145 mph (233 km/h) winds, floods, 5–6-m (16–20-ft) water surges. 125,000 believed lost.
1993	Nine midwestern states. Record spring and summer rains cause prolonged flooding along the Mississippi and its tributaries, leaving 50 dead, 70,000 homeless.

Critics of the nonstructural approach agree that avoidance of flood-prone areas is desirable. They point out, however, that many major cities were sited adjacent to bodies of water for purposes of transportation, power generation, and water supply, and that it is economically unfeasible to abandon these metropolitan areas. Recent trends in flood control have been toward the use of both approaches, as nonstructural methods have gained greater recognition. The National Flood Insurance Act, enacted (1968) by the U.S. Congress, provides affordable flood insurance to the owners of buildings in communities that participate in land-use programs to reduce flood damage risks. Risks can be lessened, for example, by restricting new building in areas that are known to be flood prone. In the early 1990s, almost every eligible U.S. community—those whose precincts lie within flood-prone areas and that have significant development—was participating in the program, with almost two-and-a-half million individual flood insurance policies in force.   DONALD O. DOEHRING

Bibliography: Dudley, W. C., and Lee, M., *Tsunami!* (1988); Fein, J., and Stephens, P. L., eds., *Monsoons* (1986); Frank, A. D., *Development of the Federal Program of Flood Control on the Mississippi River* (1930; repr. 1970); Lillehammer, A., and Saltveit, S. J., eds., *Regulated Rivers* (1985); Purseglove, J., *Taming the Flood* (1988); Saul, A., *Floods and Flood Management* (1992); Stacy, S. M., *When the River Rises: Flood Control on the Boise River* (1992).

Flora

In Roman mythology, Flora was the goddess of flowers and springtime and the wife of the west wind, Zephyr. Her festival, the Floralia, was celebrated in April and May.

Florence

Florence (Italian: Firenze) is the capital city of both Firenze province and the Tuscany region of central Italy; it lies on the Arno River at the foot of the Apennines. The population of the city is 408,403 (1991). Florence's modern importance is in large part a result of the great outburst of artistic and architectural activity that occurred there from the 13th to the 15th century. The city's cultural treasures have made tourism the economic mainstay.

Since the late 19th century, large residential and manufacturing districts have sprung up around the old city core. Florence is famous for its gold and silver jewelry, leatherwork, high-fashion clothing, shoes, ornamental glass, and furniture. Wine, olive oil, perfumes, and precision instruments are other notable products. The city is on Italy's north-south railroad line and is therefore an important rail center.

The Artistic Heritage of Florence. Florence attracts well over 1 million tourists annually, most of them from the United States, who are drawn to the numerous monuments and museums. Many of the best known architectural treasures are religious

buildings, notably the Baptistery of San Giovanni (c.1000), considered the oldest building in the city, and San Miniato, another fine Romanesque church. The bronze-relief baptistery doors, designed by Lorenzo GHIBERTI, were constructed in the first half of the 15th century. The bell tower of the Gothic cathedral of Santa Maria del Fiore was designed by GIOTTO. The cathedral, which contains MICHELANGELO's sculptural masterpiece the *Pietà* (c.1546–50), was begun in 1294 and consecrated in 1436. The dome was designed (c.1420) by Filippo BRUNELLESCHI. Brunelleschi also originally designed the Ospedale degli Innocenti, whose wide arches are decorated with glazed terra-cottas by Luca della Robbia (see DELLA ROBBIA family).

Not far from the cathedral is the Medici parish church of San Lorenzo. Michelangelo constructed one of the church's Medici chapels, and it contains magnificent sculptures he made for the tombs of Giuliano and Lorenzo. The 13th-century Franciscan church of Santa Croce—its interior decorated by Giotto, CIMABUE, DONATELLO, Brunelleschi, and others—has a MICHELOZZO-designed Medici chapel in which Michelangelo, Galileo, Machiavelli, and Rossini are buried.

The Piazzadella Signoria contains the Palazzo Vecchio, built in the 14th century as the seat of Florentine government, and the Loggia dei Lanzi. It was redecorated two centuries later when the Medicis added open-air sculpture galleries and beautiful fountains. The BARGELLO, which also dates from the 14th century, is now a state museum. The enormous PITTI PALACE (begun 1458) was the official home of the king when Florence was Italy's capital (1865–70). The noted Boboli Gardens are behind the palace.

Florence has about 40 art museums, which house the works of such masters as Masaccio, Fra Angelico, Botticelli, Leonardo da Vinci, Raphael, Donatello, Ghiberti, Luca della Robbia, Michelangelo, Titian, Tintoretto, Veronese, and Rubens. The Pitti and the UFFIZI museums, originally the office building of the Medici grand dukes, hold two of the world's greatest collections of medieval and Renaissance art. The city's national library and state archives house incomparable manuscript collections.

History. Originally Etruscan, then Roman (until the 5th century), Gothic, Byzantine, and Lombard, Florence reached its peak of economic, political, and cultural splendor between the 13th and 16th centuries. Commercial power developed in earnest after Florence became a free commune in 1115. Ripped by civil strife until the late 13th century, Florence nevertheless flourished as a trade and industrial center. It was ruled by an oligarchy of merchants and bankers and gradually attained supremacy over the surrounding area. In 1348 more than 60% of the nearly 100,000 inhabitants were killed by the Black Death (BUBONIC PLAGUE), temporarily halting the city's growth.

Three hundred years of domination by the MEDICI family

(Left) The Cathedral of Santa Maria del Fiore's famous dome, designed (c.1420) by Filippo Brunelleschi, dominates this view of Florence. The Campanile of the Gothic cathedral was designed by Giotto; the adjacent cathedral museum houses works by della Robbia and Donatello. (Right) The 14th-century Ponte Vecchio is the oldest bridge in Florence and the only one spared during the destruction of World War II. It is lined with goldsmith and silversmith shops dating from the 16th century, when Florence flourished as the financial and artistic center of Italy.

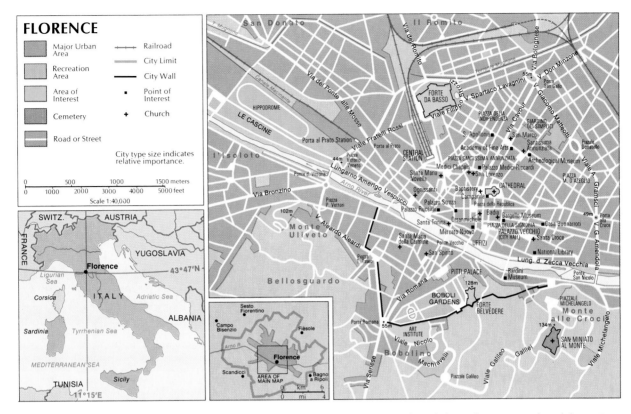

FLORENCE

Major Urban Area

Recreation Area

Area of Interest

Cemetery

Road or Street

Railroad

City Limit

City Wall

■ Point of Interest

✝ Church

City type size indicates relative importance.

0   500   1000   1500 meters
0   1000   2000   3000   4000   5000 feet
Scale 1:40,000

began in 1434 with Cosimo (1389–1464). Medici control, largely the result of financial power and political skill, was interrupted by the revolution of 1494–98, led by the Dominican religious reformer Girolamo SAVONAROLA. In 1527, Emperor CHARLES V restored the Medici, and Alessandro (c.1510–1537) became the first duke of Tuscany. Cosimo I (1519–74), who was created the first grand duke in 1569, brought almost all of Tuscany under his rule. The grand duchy was ruled by the house of Habsburg-Lorraine after the Medici line died out in 1737. Tuscany was annexed to the new kingdom of Italy in 1861, and Florence was the capital of the kingdom from 1865 to 1871. The city later declined.

Threatened for centuries by flooding from the Arno River, the city was devastated by a 1966 inundation. Supported by contributions from all over the world, experts worked for years to salvage the city's art treasures.   DANIEL R. LESNICK

Bibliography: Brucker, Gene, *Renaissance Florence*, rev. ed. (1983); McCarthy, Mary, *The Stones of Florence* (1976); Scott, Rupert, *Florence Explored* (1988).

Flores, Juan José   [floh'-rays]

Juan José Flores, b. July 19, 1800, d. Oct. 1, 1864, was the first president of Ecuador. In 1830 he led Ecuador's secession from Simón Bolivar's Gran Colombia and became president of the new republic. A conservative, he was opposed by the liberals under Vicente ROCAFUERTE, with whom he agreed to alternate office after civil war in 1834. Flores stepped down then, but at the end of his second term (1839–43) refused to do so. In 1845 he was deposed and fled the country. From 1860 to 1864 he was commander of the army in the conservative regime of Gabriel GARCÍA MORENO.

Bibliography: Van Aken, Mark J., *King of the Night: Juan José Flores and Ecuador, 1824–1864* (1989).

Florey, Sir Howard Walter   [flohr'-ee]

Sir Howard Walter Florey, b. Adelaide, Australia, Sept. 24, 1898, d. Feb. 21, 1968, a medical scientist, collaborated with Ernst Boris CHAIN to purify and test PENICILLIN, directing its

production as a clinical drug. The two men shared the 1945 Nobel Prize for physiology or medicine with Alexander FLEMING, who had discovered penicillin. In 1962, Florey became provost of Queen's College, Oxford, a post he held until his death.

Bibliography: Bickel, Lennard, *Rise Up to Life* (1972).

floriculture   [flohr'-i-kuhl-chur]

Floriculture is the branch of HORTICULTURE concerned with the commercial growing of plants for their FLOWERS and with the cultivation and sale of HOUSEPLANTS. The principal commercial flower crops grown in the United States are roses, carnations, chrysanthemums, snapdragons, gladioli, and orchids, although many other flower species are also cultivated. Crops are grown throughout the year in southern California and Florida, and greenhouse crops are raised in every state.

Greenhouse Floriculture. Successful greenhouse floriculture

Ornamental flowers are often cultivated in commercial greenhouses, which are usually long, narrow structures with peaked roofs of glass or plastic. Environmental factors are carefully controlled, frequently by automatic systems, to ensure ideal conditions for plant growth.

(Right) *Workers tend this Dutch tulip field completely by hand. After the flowers are cut, the bulbs are harvested, cleaned, and prepared for sale, just as has been done in Holland for centuries. Daffodils, crocuses, and hyacinths are also grown in the colorful bulb fields. Although the fields are tourist attractions and the growers sell cut flowers, most of their profits come from the sale of bulbs for commercial propagation.*

Although some flowers have been cultivated for as long as 2,500 years, widespread interest in plant breeding began in Europe only about 400 years ago, when scientific expeditions began bringing back many new specimens from different parts of the world. Modern floriculturists have selectively bred plants for desired characteristics, such as color, size, number of blooms, and length of flowering season; flowers are grown both outdoors and in greenhouses. Popular cultivated flowers include daffodils (A), crocuses (B), hyacinths (C), lilacs (D), lilies (E), freesias (F), irises (G), carnations (H), anemones (I), dahlias (J), cyclamens (K), and chrysanthemums (L).

requires the maintenance of a totally managed environment. Such growth factors as soil, temperature, water, and types and amounts of nutrients must be meticulously controlled. Photoperiod, the precise length of daylight that triggers flowering in each plant species, is lengthened by using artificial light or shortened by shutting out sunlight. Soluble fertilizers are added to the watering system according to carefully measured formulas, and the addition of small amounts of carbon dioxide to greenhouse air increases the rate at which flower crops grow. In large, sophisticated greenhouses most of these factors are controlled through automated systems.

Commercial Bulb Growing. In addition to the production of flowers and potted plants, a large industry flourishes, primarily in Holland, that is devoted to the raising of flower bulbs. Tulip, hyacinth, narcissus, crocus, iris, and other flowering plants that produce underground bulbs, corms, or rhizomes are grown on dune sands and polders. After the flowers are cut, the bulbs are harvested and treated with heat and disinfectants to destroy bulb-infesting parasites. Bulbs are produced both for planting in gardens and for commercial flower production.

Transport, the Vital Factor. Since flowers are among the most perishable of all crops, they must be marketed within a short time after they are cut. Until air transport became a feasible shipping mode, most commercially grown flowers were raised in greenhouses near the urban centers that were their main markets. Greenhouse floriculture, however, is probably the most costly form of agriculture. Current costs involve a minimum of $100,000 annually per acre of growing area. Although greenhouse culture continues to be important, flowers grown in the open air at a fraction of greenhouse costs are now cultivated in warm, sunny regions and shipped quickly to urban centers. Carnations, for example, once were grown exclusively in Massachusetts greenhouses but are now an important crop in Colorado. Poinsettias, grown in California and shipped to the East Coast, can be sold more cheaply than those grown in greenhouses on the East Coast. Orchids, which require highly humidified greenhouses and are extremely tender, were once grown only near the cities where they were sold; today orchids are increasingly grown out of doors in Florida, California, and Hawaii and then air-shipped to urban centers.   Donald Wyman

Bibliography: Halpin, Anne M., *The Year-Round Flower Gardener* (1989); Larson, Roy A., *Introduction to Floriculture* (1980); Mastalerz, J. W., *The Greenhouse Environment* (1977); Nelson, Kennard S., *Flower and Plant Production in the Greenhouse*, 3d ed. (1978); Salinger, J. P., *Commercial Flower Growing and Marketing* (1985).

Florida

Florida, a favorite destination of millions of tourists, is a fast-developing state of the southeastern United States. Mostly a peninsula, Florida is bordered by Alabama and Georgia on the north, the Atlantic Ocean on the east, the Straits of Florida on the south, and the Gulf of Mexico and Alabama on the west. The first European to visit the region was the Spanish explorer Juan PONCE DE LEÓN in 1513, who called it *Florida* ("feast of flowers"), either because he saw a profusion of flowers on its coast or because it was Easter week (*Pascua florida*). The first permanent European settlement in the continental United States was at SAINT AUGUSTINE in 1565.

LAND AND RESOURCES

Florida is low-lying and level, with an average elevation of about 30 m (100 ft). The highest point, in Walton County in

FLORIDA

LAND. Area: 170,313 km² (65,758 mi²); rank: 22d. Capital: Tallahassee (1990 pop., 124,773). Largest city: Jacksonville (1990 pop., 672,971). Counties: 67. Elevations: highest—105 m (345 ft), in Walton County; lowest—sea level, at Atlantic coast.

PEOPLE. Population (1990 resident): 12,937,926; rank: 4th; density: 76.9 persons per km² (196.7 per mi²). Distribution (1990): 84.8% urban, 15.2% rural. Average annual change (1980–90): +3.3%.

EDUCATION. Public enrollment (1990): elementary—1,369,934; secondary—491,658; higher—439,818. Nonpublic enrollment (1980): elementary—90,100; secondary—27,500; combined—82,000; higher (1990)—98,571. Institutions of higher education (1988)—98.

ECONOMY. State personal income (1989): $223.6 billion; rank: 4th. Median family income (1989): $32,212; rank: 30th. Nonagricultural labor distribution (1989): manufacturing—541,000 persons; wholesale and retail trade—1,440,000; government—805,000; services—1,502,000; transportation and public utilities—266,000; finance, insurance, and real estate—372,000; construction—341,000. Agriculture: income (1989)—$6.2 billion. Fishing: value (1989)—$185 million. Lumber production (1991): 570 million board feet. Mining (nonfuel): value (1988)—$1.4 billion. Manufacturing: value added (1987)—$27.6 billion. Services: value (1987)—$60.8 billion.

GOVERNMENT (1993). Governor: Lawton Chiles, Democrat. U.S. Congress: Senate—1 Democrat, 1 Republican. House—10 Democrats, 13 Republicans. Electoral college votes: 25. State legislature: 40 senators, 120 representatives.

STATE SYMBOLS. Statehood: Mar. 3, 1845; the 27th state. Nickname: Sunshine State; bird: mockingbird; flower: orange blossom; tree: sabal palmetto palm; motto: In God We Trust; song: "Old Folks at Home" ("Swanee River").

the northwest, is 105 m (345 ft) above sea level. Florida has 2,172 km (1,350 mi) of coastline, more than any other state except Alaska; 933 km (580 mi) of the coastline border the Atlantic, and 1,239 km (770 mi) border the Gulf of Mexico. The uneven coastline is indented with estuaries, bays, inlets, lagoons, and rivers. The FLORIDA KEYS, an arc of islands—mostly either uplifted coral reefs or limestone shoals—lie off the state's southern tip.

Physiographic Regions. The land area of Florida and its continental shelf make up the Florida Plateau, which separates the Atlantic Ocean from the Gulf of Mexico. Volcanic mountains buried during the Paleozoic Era (600 to 225 million years ago) form the base of the Florida Plateau. At present, these volcanic rocks are approximately 3,959 m (13,000 ft) below the surface of central Florida. Sands and other materials that were deposited on the base have formed sedimentary rocks more than 1,200 m (4,000 ft) thick. The plateau has shifted over the centuries, and it is now tilted from east to west, with the eastern part higher than the western part as evidenced by the gulf's broad continental shelf. If the plateau were not tilted and the whole area were dry land, the state of Florida would be twice its present size.

The Florida Plateau is divided into five land regions—the coastal lowlands, the EVERGLADES, the central highlands, the northwestern highlands, and the Marianna lowlands. The coastal lowlands include the Atlantic and Gulf zones and contain 70% of Florida's population. The Everglades were originally a sea bottom. As the area was raised, the Okeechobee Basin remained higher than the area to the south. Because Lake OKEECHOBEE is shallow, has low banks, and is in a wet region, water overflows to the south and southwest, creating a sea of water grasses, open water areas, cypress forests, and mangrove swamps. Human activities, however, have modified the water flow and changed the natural character of the Everglades. The central highlands, narrow in the south and wide in the north, are marked by sinkholes, lakes, and springs. A part of the OKEFENOKEE SWAMP is in the far north, astride the border with Georgia. West of the SUWANNEE RIVER are the northwestern highlands, with elevations rising above 91 m (300 ft) and deeply cut river valleys. The Marianna lowlands bisect the northwestern highlands.

Soils. The coastal lowlands have poorly drained, sandy soils. In the Everglades the soil is primarily peat and muck, often highly sandy and lacking minerals. Well-drained sands, with small amounts of silt and clay, are found in the central highlands. The well-drained soils in the northwestern highlands and Marianna lowlands, with some clay content, are the best agricultural soils.

Rivers and Lakes. Because of Florida's relatively flat topography, most of its rivers are slow moving, and many overflow during periods of heavy rain and dry up in times of drought. The state's longest river, the Saint Johns, flows north from Indian River County to the Atlantic Ocean, near Jacksonville. Other major rivers include the Apalachicola, Kissimmee, Peace, Perdido, St. Marys, Suwannee, and Withlacoochee.

Florida's groundwaters are primarily supplied by the Floridan aquifer, which extends across the entire state, except in the far west. Lake Okeechobee is the largest lake in the state and the fourth-largest natural lake within the United States. Central Florida is the site of numerous sinkhole lakes.

Climate. Florida's climate is influenced by the state's location, its peninsular shape, and its numerous inland water bodies. No place in the state is more than 110 km (70 mi) from open water. Winds that blow over the GULF STREAM (known locally as the Florida Current) moderate the climate.

The Florida Keys have a tropical climate, with average temperatures ranging from 22° C (71° F) in January to 29° C (84° F) in July. Northern Florida has a subtropical to temperate climate; Tallahassee has average temperatures of 12° C (53° F) in January and 27° C (81° F) in July.

The southeastern coast and the northwestern panhandle receive an average of 1,626 mm (64 in) of precipitation each year. In north central Florida the average annual precipitation is approximately 1,321 mm (52 in). Thunderstorms occur frequently, especially in central Florida. Hurricanes usually de-

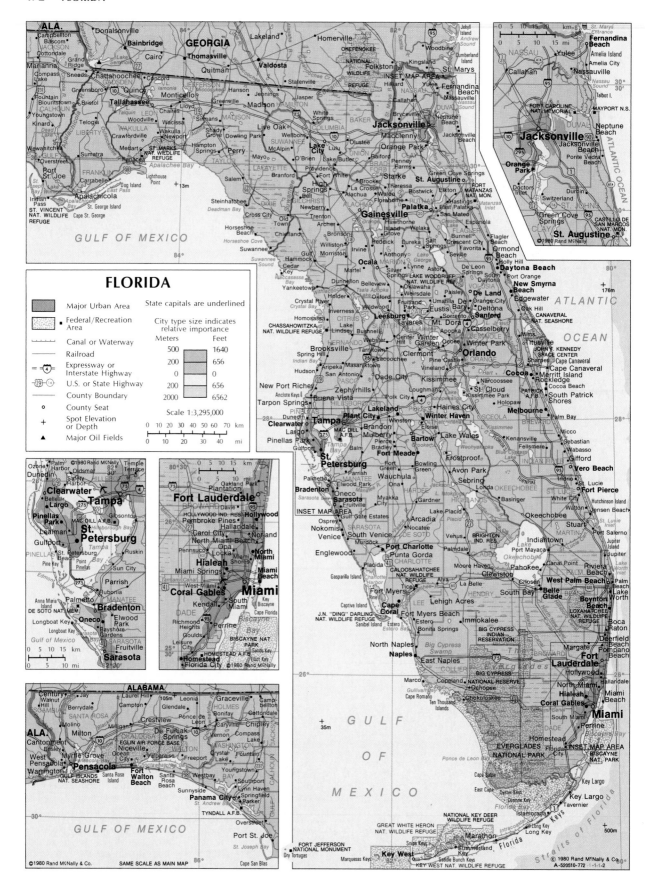

FLORIDA

	Major Urban Area	State capitals are underlined
	Federal/Recreation Area	

City type size indicates relative importance

Meters		Feet
500		1640
200		656
0		0
200		656
2000		6562

Canal or Waterway
Railroad
Expressway or Interstate Highway
U.S. or State Highway
County Boundary
○ County Seat
+ Spot Elevation or Depth
▲ Major Oil Fields

Scale 1:3,295,000

0 10 20 30 40 50 60 70 km
0 10 20 30 40 mi

©1980 Rand McNally & Co.   SAME SCALE AS MAIN MAP

(Left) *Miami, Florida's second largest city and a part of its largest metropolitan area, is a major center of the state's lucrative tourism industry. A large Cuban population has also resulted in a strong Latin influence. A section of the city is known as Little Havana.*

(Below) *Cypress trees, often with Spanish moss hanging from their branches, are common in Florida, frequently growing in swamps. Florida has the most extensive subtropical wilderness areas in the United States. The largest such area, Big Cypress Swamp, is now a national preserve.*

velop in the Caribbean and the Atlantic in late summer and early fall and can cause severe damage if they strike Florida. Since 1900, more than 20 major hurricanes have hit Florida, mostly in the southern and panhandle areas of the state.

Vegetation and Animal Life. About half of Florida's land area is covered with forests, and more than 350 types of trees grow in the state. Common hardwoods include ash, hickory, magnolia, mahogany, and oak. Mangrove and cypress flourish in the southern swamplands, such as Big Cypress Swamp and the Everglades. Pines predominate in the north. Palm trees grow throughout most of the state. The swamplands are noted for their epiphytes (air plants), such as Spanish moss, nonparasitic plants that typically hang from trees (especially oak and cypress); tall saw grass is also common in these wet regions.

Florida has a great variety of wildlife. Large mammals include whitetail deer, black bears, bobcats, and a few cougars. Foxes, muskrats, otters, possums, rabbits, raccoons, and squirrels are abundant. Swamps provide a habitat for alligators. Game birds, such as wild turkeys and quail, and water birds, such as egrets, flamingos, gulls, herons, and pelicans, are found. Common freshwater fish species include black bass, bream, catfish, and trout; marine animals include barracuda, bonito, dolphins, mackerel, marlin, menhaden, black mullet, pompano, tarpon, crabs, shrimp, and large turtles.

Mineral Resources. Florida has extensive phosphate deposits, found mainly in the central part of the state, and limestone, located throughout the state. Kaolin and other clays, sand and gravel, ilmenite, monazite, and zirconium are also found. Petroleum deposits are in the southwest, near Fort Myers, and there is a more significant deposit near Pensacola.

PEOPLE
Florida's resident (excluding overseas) population is 12,937,926 (1990), an increase of 32.7% since 1980. The state's increase from 1980 to 1990 was far higher than the national average of 9.8%, and in absolute numbers Florida's total gain of 3,191,602 inhabitants was surpassed only by California. Between 1960 and 1980, Florida's population nearly doubled. Most of the population increase in recent decades has been due to in-migration. Many new Floridians are retirees, whose presence accounts for the state's high proportion of persons aged 65 or more—19% of the state's population, compared to the national average of about 12%. Florida's population density is well above that of the nation as a whole, and most of the population is classified as urban. The chief cities are (in order of population) JACKSONVILLE, MIAMI, TAMPA, Saint Petersburg, HIALEAH, ORLANDO, FORT LAUDERDALE, TALLAHASSEE, Hollywood, Clearwater, Miami Beach, Gainesville, Pompano Beach, WEST PALM BEACH, Largo City, DAYTONA BEACH, and PENSACOLA. The great majority of Florida's inhabitants are white; blacks make

up about 13.6% of the population. Significant numbers of Hispanics, especially Cubans who immigrated during the 1960s, live primarily in the greater Miami area, as well as in Tampa and other communities. A second major wave of Cuban immigration took place in 1980, when about 115,000 refugees arrived in southern Florida. A Greek community lives in Tarpon Springs, on the west coast. About 36,335 American Indians live in the state. The SEMINOLE Indians live mostly in the Everglades. Roman Catholics form the largest single religious denomination in Florida. Among Protestants, the Baptists and Methodists are particularly strong. Florida also has a sizable Jewish community.

EDUCATION AND CULTURAL ACTIVITY
Education. The 1868 state constitution authorized a statewide system of public education. Attendance is compulsory at elementary and secondary schools in Florida between the ages of 7 and 16. For information on public institutions of higher education, see FLORIDA, STATE UNIVERSITIES OF.

Cultural Institutions. Notable museums include the John and Mabel Ringling Museum of Art, at Sarasota, with a major collection of European paintings; the Florida Museum of Natural History, at Gainesville; the Center for the Fine Arts, at Miami; the Cummer Gallery of Art, at Jacksonville; the Museum of

Florida History, at Tallahassee; and Marineland of Florida, near Saint Augustine, with extensive exhibits on the sea, including two oceanariums. Music and opera are performed by the Florida Symphony (Orlando), the Florida State Opera (Tallahassee), and the Greater Miami Opera (Miami).

Historical Sites. Castillo de San Marcos National Monument contains a masonry fort, begun in 1672, built by the Spanish to protect Saint Augustine. De Soto National Memorial, near Bradenton, commemorates the landing (1539) of the Spanish explorer Hernando de Soto. Fort Jefferson National Monument, in the DRY TORTUGAS islands, is the site of an immense fortification that served as a Federal military prison during and after the U.S. Civil War. Dade Battlefield, near Bushnell, is the site where U.S. troops were defeated (1835) by Indians at the start of the Second Seminole War.

Sports and Outdoor Recreation. Because of its climate and location, Florida offers extensive opportunities for outdoor sports. The state has numerous beach resorts, as well as ample facilities for marine and freshwater fishing, pleasure boating, waterskiing, and other water sports. Each year many major-league baseball teams conduct spring training in the state from February to early April. The Orange Bowl, played at Miami, is a noted annual postseason college football game.

Communications. Florida's first radio station (1920) and first television station (1949) began broadcasting from Miami. Numerous radio and television stations are now in operation as well as educational television and cable systems. The state's first newspaper was the *East Florida Gazette,* established in 1783 in Saint Augustine. Today the *Miami Herald* is considered Florida's most influential newspaper. A leading Spanish-language daily is *Diario Las Americas.*

Walt Disney World is a major travel destination for Florida visitors. Located just outside Orlando, it is one of several entertainment complexes located in the area, all of which have contributed to strong economic and population growth for Orlando and its environs.

ECONOMIC ACTIVITY

Florida's chief economic development began in the early 20th century; today the state has a diversified modern economy. Tourism and other service industries and government (including military installations) are the chief employers. The state's economy benefits from the many retired persons who live in Florida on pensions earned elsewhere.

Agriculture. Florida is a major agricultural state with approximately 41,000 farms having an average size of about 123.8 ha (306 acres). The state's most important products are citrus fruits—especially oranges, which were introduced around 1570 by Spanish settlers and by the early 1800s had become an important commercial product. Other principal crops are vegetables (particularly tomatoes); sugarcane, the state's major field crop; tobacco; soybeans; nuts, especially peanuts and pecans; and noncitrus fruits, mainly watermelons, cantaloupes, and strawberries. Most citrus groves and vegetable farms are in central and southern Florida; sugarcane is grown south of Lake Okeechobee; and nuts and tobacco are produced in the northern part of the state. Income, amounting to about 20% of the total farm marketings, is also derived from livestock. A great number of Florida cattle and calves, hogs, and broiler chickens are marketed each year, and large amounts of dairy products and eggs are produced. The raising of Thoroughbred horses is also a major endeavor in Florida, particularly on the horse farms in Marion County.

Forestry and Fishing. Lumbering is a relatively small but significant industry in Florida; softwoods are the chief trees cut. Florida's commercial fish catch is among the highest in value in the nation. Important species include shrimp, black mullet, and blue crab. Most fish are caught off the west coast.

Mining. Florida is a leading state in nonfuel mineral output. Its principal minerals are phosphate, of which Florida is the nation's leading producer; petroleum and natural gas; stone; clay; sand and gravel; limestone; ilmenite; and dolomite.

Manufacturing. Florida has a growing manufacturing sector but is not a center of heavy industry. Most manufacturing is concentrated around its major cities. Chief manufactures are processed food, especially citrus products, such as frozen orange juice concentrate; transportation equipment; electrical equipment; chemicals; fabricated metals; paper and paper goods; printed materials; and cigars.

Tourism. Tourists in Florida spend billions of dollars each year in the state. The warm climate of southern Florida during the winter is a favorite attraction for vacationers from the northeastern United States and Canada. In addition to the many beach resorts on both coasts, points of interest include CAPE CANAVERAL, the site of the John F. KENNEDY SPACE CENTER; Walt Disney World/Epcot Center and MGM Studios, and Universal Studios, near Orlando (see DISNEYLAND AND WALT DISNEY WORLD); Cypress Gardens, near Winter Haven; Busch Gardens, in Tampa, containing a large zoo; and Everglades National Park. The state has many state parks and recreation areas.

Transportation. Florida has well-developed road and railway systems. Its busiest seaports are Tampa-Saint Petersburg, Jacksonville, Port Everglades (at Fort Lauderdale), and Miami. Important waterways include sections of both the Gulf Intracoastal Waterway and the Atlantic Intracoastal Waterway. Florida has many airports, with Miami International Airport one of the nation's busiest.

Energy. Petroleum is the source of about 60% of the energy produced in Florida. Other sources include natural gas and coal. Most electricity is produced in thermal plants, but the state also has nuclear power facilities and a few small hydroelectric installations.

GOVERNMENT AND POLITICS

Government. Florida is governed under a constitution of 1885, as revised in 1968 and later amended. The chief executive is the governor, popularly elected to a 4-year term; a governor may not serve more than 10 consecutive years. As opposed to most other states, other statewide elected officials have considerable authority independent of the governor and appreciably limit the power of the chief executive. The Florida legislature is made up of a senate, whose 40 members are

Extensive citrus groves cover the landscape near Winter Garden, in central Florida, west of Orlando. Florida leads all states by a considerable margin in the production of oranges, grapefruit, and tangerines. Most of the state's harvest is processed into frozen concentrates.

popularly elected to 4-year terms, and a house of representatives, whose 120 members are popularly elected to 2-year terms. The highest tribunal in the state is the supreme court, composed of 7 justices appointed by the governor to 6-year terms; one of the justices is elected by the court to serve for 2 years as chief justice. The large majority of the state's 67 counties are administered by 5 county commissioners. Most of Florida's 390 (1991) incorporated cities have either a mayor-and-council form or a manager-and-council form of government. The government of some cities, notably Jacksonville and Miami, has been integrated with that of other municipalities or the surrounding county.

Politics. Democrats have dominated Florida politics on the state and local levels since 1876, although in recent decades two Republican governors have been elected—in 1966 and 1986. By the mid-20th century, however, Republicans had made considerable gains in national presidential elections, and since 1952, Democratic presidential candidates have carried Florida only in 1964 and 1976.

HISTORY

At the end of the last ice age, more than 10,000 years ago, Florida was inhabited by groups from the Caribbean and by Indians who had migrated from the north and northwest following the movement of large game animals. At the time of the first European contact in the early 16th century, four major Indian groups (with an estimated total population ranging from 100,000 to 900,000) lived in what is now Florida: the APALACHEE in the northwest; the Calusa in the southwest; the Tequesta along the southeastern coast; and the Timucua in the north central region.

European Rule. In 1513, Juan Ponce de Léon landed on the northeast Florida coast and claimed Florida for Spain. In 1521 he returned to found a colony but was unsuccessful and was killed the same year. In 1528, Pánfilo de NARVÁEZ, another Spanish explorer, anchored in Tampa Bay and then traveled inland. In 1539, Hernando DE SOTO landed near Tampa Bay, exploring that area and then northern Florida. Another Spaniard, Tristán de Luna, attempted, with some 1,600 men and women, to establish a permanent colony on Pensacola Bay in 1559, but after two difficult years the settlement was abandoned.

In 1562 the French Huguenot leader Gaspard de COLIGNY commissioned Jean RIBAUT to found a colony in the territory, and in 1564, Ribaut's aide, René de LAUDONNIÉRE, built Fort Caroline, near present-day Jacksonville. PHILIP II of Spain sent a military expedition, led by Pedro MENÉNDEZ DE AVILÉS, to destroy the French settlement. Arriving in 1565, Menéndez estab-

lished Saint Augustine and massacred the French; he captured Fort Caroline and founded another settlement there. The Spanish subsequently built forts and missions across northern Florida and around the southwestern coast. During the SEVEN YEARS' WAR (1756–63) between Britain and France, Spain sided with France and lost Cuba in 1762. Under the terms of the peace treaty (1763), Spain traded Florida to Britain in exchange for Cuba.

Under British rule Florida was divided into two separate colonies, East Florida and West Florida. During the American Revolution, Floridians remained loyal to Britain; but by the Treaty of Paris (1783), English hegemony in Florida was ended and the region was returned to Spain.

U.S. Acquisition. During the WAR OF 1812, Britain used Pensacola as a naval base, but in 1814 it was captured by American troops. In 1819, Spain agreed to transfer Florida to the United States, which assumed control in 1821. The following year Florida was organized as a territory, and William P. Duval became governor; soon many settlers, including Indians, streamed into Florida from the North. Conflicts erupted with

St. Augustine's Castillo de San Marcos National Monument, a former military fort located in the nation's oldest permanently settled city, is a reminder of the lengthy Spanish presence in early Florida. It is the oldest masonry fort (begun in 1672) in the continental United States.

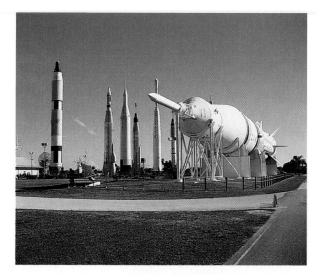

The Kennedy Space Center in Florida is the launch site for all U.S.-manned space missions as well as many unmanned spacecraft and represents an important economic endeavor in the state. Of interest to visitors is the center's Spaceport USA, offering a variety of exhibits.

the Seminole Indians, who were defeated in the Second Seminole War (1835–42). Some of the Seminole were removed to Oklahoma, and a small band migrated to the Everglades.

Statehood. Florida entered the Union as a slave state on Mar. 3, 1845. By 1860 the population was about 140,000, of whom 63,000 were black. Florida seceded from the Union on Jan. 10, 1861, and then joined the Confederacy. Most of Florida's coastal towns were captured early by Union forces, but Tallahassee remained under Confederate control throughout the war. The Battle of Olustee, which took place in Florida on Feb. 20, 1864, was one of the last Confederate victories.

In 1868, after a new constitution guaranteeing blacks the right to vote had been adopted, the state was readmitted to the Union. Republicans held most important elected offices until 1876, when the Democrats returned to power.

An era of rapid economic growth began in the 1880s—great deposits of phosphate were discovered, citrus groves were planted, southern swamplands were drained and converted to farmland, and railroads and tourist facilities were constructed. Several entrepreneurs, notably Henry M. Flagler (1830–1913), Hamilton Disston (1844–96), and Henry B. Plant (1819–99), led Florida's development.

The Modern Era. During the early 1920s, Florida experienced a great land boom. Real estate prices rose spectacularly until 1926, when a combination of factors, especially the well-publicized opinion of respected financial experts that Florida land was vastly overpriced, led to a rapid and severe drop in values. Later in 1926, Miami, one of Florida's chief boom cities (its population had grown from 1,681 inhabitants in 1900 to 69,754 in 1925), was badly damaged by a hurricane. The state's economy had largely recovered by 1929, when the Great Depression began, bringing reverses.

From 1920 to 1930, Florida's population had grown by more than 50%, reaching about 1,468,000 inhabitants. Growth continued during the 1930s and accelerated in the 1940s, when war-related activities spurred additional development. By 1950, Florida had about 2,771,000 inhabitants, and during both the 1950s and '60s its population grew by about 2 million persons. In the postwar period the tourist and retirement industries grew rapidly, as did commercial farming. The aerospace industry developed in association with the Cape Canaveral missile and space-flight center. Floridians adhered gradually to the 1954 U.S. Supreme Court decision outlawing segregated schools, and by the 1970s most public schools were integrated. In the 1970s laws were passed that ensured protection of the state's natural areas. Thousands of Cuban refugees settled in Florida, especially in Miami, in the 1960s and again in

1980. During the 1980s, Florida's economy became more like that of the rest of the nation, with a decrease in agriculture and an increase in the service sector. Ongoing growth in population has encouraged growth-management legislation relating to environmentally sensitive land and beaches. In August 1992, South Florida, especially the Homestead area, was devastated by Hurricane Andrew; the storm killed 38 persons and left 250,000 homeless. After an initially slow official response, the U.S. military began construction of temporary shelters.

EDWARD FERNALD

Bibliography: Carter, L. J., *The Florida Experience: Land and Water Policy in a Growth State* (1975); Douglas, Marjory S., *Florida* (1967); Federal Writers' Project, *Florida* (1939); Fernald, E. A., ed., *The Atlas of Florida,* 2d ed. (1991) and *Water Resources Atlas of Florida* (1984); Morris, A. C., *The Florida Handbook* (biennial); Nulty, W. H., *Confederate Florida* (1990); Patrick, Rembert W., *Florida under Five Flags,* rev. ed. (1967); Tebeau, Charlton W., *A History of Florida* (1971); Terhune, F. W., ed., *1991 Florida Statistical Abstract* (1991).

Florida, state universities of

The **University of Florida** (1853; enrollment: 34,019; library: 2,500,000 volumes) at Gainesville is a land-grant institution that includes colleges of arts and sciences, engineering, dentistry, journalism and communications, agriculture, law, medicine, and veterinary medicine and the school of forest resources and conservation. **Florida State University** (1857; enrollment: 26,037; library: 1,700,000 volumes) at Tallahassee grants degrees in arts and sciences, law, engineering, nursing, home economics, and several other areas. Another land-grant institution is **Florida Agricultural and Mechanical University** (1887; enrollment: 7,469; library: 375,000 volumes) at Tallahassee, founded as a normal school for blacks. Other schools are **Florida Atlantic University** (1961; enrollment: 11,481; library: 1,600,000 volumes) at Boca Raton, **Florida International University** (1965; enrollment: 20,195; library: 786,824) at Miami, the **University of Central Florida** (1963; enrollment: 17,812; library: 700,963 volumes) at Orlando, the **University of North Florida** (1965; enrollment: 7,727; library: 463,721 volumes) at Jacksonville, and the **University of West Florida** (1963; enrollment: 7,576; library: 610,000 volumes) at Pensacola. The **University of South Florida** (1956; enrollment: 25,021; library: 716,970 volumes) is at Tampa; its **New College** in Sarasota serves as the undergraduate honors college of the State university system.

Florida, Straits of

The Straits of Florida connect the Gulf of Mexico with the Atlantic Ocean. The passage (up to 145 km/90 mi wide) is bounded by the Florida Keys on the north and by Cuba and the Bahamas on the south. The Florida Current (part of the Gulf Stream) flows eastward through the straits.

Florida Keys

The Florida Keys are a chain of islands that extend for about 240 km (150 mi) from the tip of Florida into the Gulf of Mexico to Key West, the westernmost island. They are linked to the mainland by the Overseas Highway, whose longest bridge extends for 11 km (7 mi) over the Gulf. Key Largo is the largest island in the chain, whose primary industry is tourism.

Florio, John   [flohr'-ee-oh]

The English translator and lexicographer John Florio, *c.*1553–1625, was the author of several works on the Italian language and compiled the first Italian-English dictionary, *A World of Words* (1598), which he later revised as *Queen Anna's New World of Words* (1611). Florio is chiefly remembered, however, for his translation (1603) of the *Essays* of Michel de Montaigne, which introduced the genre into England.

Floris   (family)

Floris is the name of an Antwerp family of noted stonemasons, architects, sculptors, and painters. Floris de Vriendt, patriarch of the family, was a 15th-century stonemason. His great-grandson, **Cornelis Floris de Vriendt**, c.1514–1575, a sculptor, architect and draftsman, is thought to have designed the Antwerp Town Hall (1561–66), the principal work of architecture in the southern Netherlands of the 16th century. **Frans Floris the Elder** (1516–70), Cornelis's brother, was a painter. A pupil of Lambert Lombard, the Romanist painter, he followed Lombard to Rome in 1538. On his return in 1540, he joined the Antwerp painters' guild and remained active in his native city until his death. Works such as the large *Fall of the Rebel Angels* (1554; Musée Royal des Beaux-Arts, Antwerp) or the *Last Judgment* (1565; Kunsthistorisches Museum, Vienna) are characteristic of his Romanist MANNERISM. Frans's brothers, Jan and Jacob, two sons, two nephews, and a grand-nephew, were also practicing artists.   CHARLES MINOTT

Bibliography: Cuttler, Charles D., *Northern Painting* (1968); Gerson, H., and ter Kuile, E. H., *Art and Architecture in Belgium 1600 to 1800* (1960).

Flory, Paul

The American physical chemist Paul John Flory, b. Starling, Ill., June 19, 1910, d. Sept. 9, 1985, conducted pioneer studies on polymers, for which he won the 1974 Nobel Prize for chemistry. Flory worked as a research chemist in industry and in higher education, holding posts at Du Pont, Standard Oil, Goodyear, and Cornell and Stanford universities. He investigated, both theoretically and experimentally, the steps by which polymerization reactions occur and the structure and properties of plastics, rubbers, and fibers.

ROBERT J. PARADOWSKI

flotation process

The flotation process is a method for concentrating valuable minerals—such as copper, lead, and zinc—from ores by agitating very finely ground ore with water, reagents called oilers or collectors, and other chemicals called frothers and conditioners. The collectors are chosen to react specifically with the desired mineral and make it nonwettable. When air is then bubbled through the mixture, the mineral particles become attached to the bubbles by surface tension and are floated off for collection. The frothers help to stabilize the bubbles, and the conditioners maintain the pH of the solution within desired limits.

The operation of the mechanical flotation cell is simple. The ore-water pulp is fed into the unit and is kept agitated and circulating by an impeller that is mounted at the bottom of the vertical shaft. This rotating impeller generates a sufficient vacuum to draw air down the standpipe that surrounds the impeller shaft and dissipates the air throughout the pulp in the form of tiny bubbles. Those undesired minerals that do not float stay in the main body of the pulp. Automatic scrapers remove the mineral-laden froth containing the concentrate.   MERLE C. NUTT

Bibliography: Ranney, M., ed., *Flotation Agents and Processes* (1981).

Flötner, Peter   [flurt'-nur]

Peter Flötner, c.1490–1546, the most important Nuremberg artist of the generation following Albrecht DÜRER, was an early leader of the German Renaissance. He is best known for his sculpture, but was also an architect, engraver and goldsmith. In his early career, Flötner continued the tradition of late Gothic art; before the early 1530s, however, he had twice visited Italy, where he was influenced by Renaissance art.

Like Dürer, Flötner provided an important link between Gothic Germany and Renaissance Italy. His knowledge of Italian art was communicated to German artists through his sculpture as well as through his numerous preparatory drawings and woodcut illustrations. Flötner's later work anticipates MANNERISM, although he traveled to Italy before the appearance there of Mannerist art.   ERIC G. CARLSON

Bibliography: Osten, Gert von der, and Vey, Horst, *Painting and Sculpture in Germany and the Netherlands: 1500–1600* (1969); Smith, J. C., *Nuremberg* (1983).

Flotow, Friedrich von   [floh'-toh]

Friedrich von Flotow, b. Apr. 27, 1812, d. Jan. 24, 1883, was a German composer of operas. Because his father was in the diplomatic corps, von Flotow spent much of his early years in Paris where he studied under Johann Peter Pixis and Anton Reicha. From 1856 to 1863 he was superintendent of the court theater in Schwerin, after which he lived in Paris. Of his approximately 20 operas, the most popular is the melodic, light-romantic comedy *Martha*, first performed in Vienna in 1847. The opera includes a popular operatic version of "'tis the last rose of summer," which had been adapted earlier by Thomas Moore from an old Irish ballad.   F. E. KIRBY

flotsam, jetsam, and lagan

Under admiralty (maritime) law, the terms *flotsam, jetsam, and lagan* refer to goods that are cast away or otherwise lost at sea in a storm or similar emergency. Flotsam are any goods or parts of a ship found floating at sea. Jetsam (from "jettison") are goods voluntarily cast into the water in an attempt to keep a ship afloat by decreasing its weight. Goods that are thrown overboard and are attached to a cork or buoy to facilitate later recovery are called lagan or ligan. Goods washed ashore are classified as wrack.

Admiralty law holds that rescuing people and property aboard helpless ships is a duty, that anyone who does so is entitled to a reward. The amount of the reward is determined by a court, which takes into account such circumstances as the value of the property saved, how much the property was endangered, and how difficult the rescue was. The reward is divided among the owner, master, and crew of the rescuing ship and is paid for by all the people who owned property on the endangered vessel, regardless of whose property was destroyed or whether it was lost unintentionally or as a result of voluntary efforts to save the ship.

flounder

Flounder are species of chiefly marine, carnivorous FLATFISH belonging to the Bothidae and Pleuronectidae families, order Heterosomata. All have in common a remarkable adaptation: both eyes migrate to either the right or the left side of the head during the larval stage, shortly after hatching. As a result, flounder swim on one side with the eyes pointing up. All are

Adult flounders, such as Platichthys flesus, *have both eyes located on one side of the head* (top); *the lower, colorless side is blind.*

predaceous. Flounders can readily change their coloration and can mimic both the color and pattern of the ocean bottom. Flounder are caught for sport, as well as for their commercial value as a food fish. Some can also live in brackish or even fresh water.   A. R. EMERY

flour

Flour is a food prepared by grinding and sieving grains, primarily WHEAT. Wheat flour is particularly suitable for use as an ingredient in the preparation of baked products. When it is mixed with liquid in the correct proportions, its major protein components (collectively known as gluten) form an elastic network that is capable of holding leavening gases and that will set to a rather firm spongy structure when heated in an oven. Other grains—among them, barley, buckwheat, corn, rice, and rye—are also ground into flour and are often mixed with wheat flour in making certain types of bread. Almost all grain flours are made using the processes described here for wheat flour.

Wheat is divided into hard wheats, whose flours yield doughs that are elastic and have excellent gas-holding or expansion properties, and soft wheat, whose flours are used for cakes, cookies, piecrusts, and similar products where a high volume is not essential and a tender or crumbly texture is desired. Hard wheats have a higher protein content than soft wheats. All-purpose flour, made from a combination of hard and soft wheats, is used to make most home-baked products.

The milling process by which flour is made separates the wheat endosperm (the starchy interior portion of the kernel) from the BRAN layers and the wheat germ and then reduces the endosperm chunks to a fine powder. In conventional modern milling processes, the wheat kernels and their products are passed between several pairs of rotating steel cylinders and the ground material is sifted, thus separating particles of different sizes. The first few sets of roll mills break open the seed coat and strip out the friable endosperm. Subsequent sets of rolls grind the particles finer and perform other essential functions such as flattening the germ, thereby facilitating its separation from the endosperm particles. After each stage of the grinding process, stacks of screens with different mesh sizes separate the ground material into several streams. These streams may be further processed by grinding, or they may be drawn off for feedstuffs or combined to yield flours with different properties. By combining properly selected streams, the miller can make flours of widely varying quality from the same wheat. Ordinarily, about 70 percent of the kernel emerges from the process as flour of some sort.

Whole wheat flour is prepared in much the same way as white flour, except that the ground bran, germ, and endosperm are ultimately combined to produce a material having much the same composition as the original grain. Whole wheat flour is darker, coarser, and stronger in flavor than white flour, and the BREAD made from it is tougher and denser. This flour also becomes rancid more quickly during storage. Most whole wheat breads contain substantial amounts of white flour for improving baking performance.

Like most foods, flour does not provide a complete or well-balanced supply of all essential nutrients. Other ingredients used in making bread, especially milk and yeast, provide some additional amino acids, vitamins, and minerals. Enriched flour contains extra amounts of thiamin, riboflavin, niacin, and iron added by the miller. It may also contain additional calcium or wheat germ.   SAMUEL A. MATZ

Bibliography: Steen, H., *Flour Milling in America* (1963; repr. 1973).

flowchart

A flowchart is a pictorial description of a procedure to be followed in solving a given problem. Frequently used to outline computer programs and ALGORITHMS, flowcharts are made up of boxes connected by arrows. To perform the process described in a flowchart, one begins at start and follows the arrows from box to box, performing the actions indicated. The shape of each box indicates what kind of step it represents, such as processing, decision making, and control.

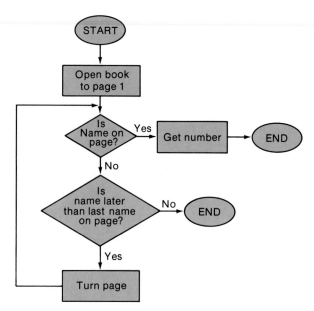

Flowcharts are useful in designing computer programs and for communicating program descriptions because they can suppress unnecessary details and have a precise meaning if carefully used. The standard flowchart forms are not convenient for all programming languages, and many variations are in use. Flowcharts may also be used to represent an overall view of manufacturing processes.

SUSAN OWICKI AND ELLIOTT ORGANICK

Bibliography: Boillot, Michel H., et al., *Essentials of Flowcharting*, 4th ed. (1985).

See also: COMPUTER PROGRAMMING.

flower

The flower is the reproductive structure of ANGIOSPERMS, or flowering plants. Compared to the reproductive structures of other plants, the flower is unique in several ways. It consists of four kinds of modified leaves, two of which (stamens and carpels, the latter sometimes called pistils) bear POLLEN and SEEDS. Several nonflowering plants also produce pollen and seeds on modified leaves, but in the angiosperms the modified leaf called the carpel forms an ovary that completely encloses the ovule, which becomes the seed. In the GYMNOSPERMS, ovules are borne on open modified leaves, such as the scale of a pine cone. The term *angiosperm* is derived from the Greek and means "seed in a vessel"; gymnosperm means "naked seed."

According to the fossil record, flowering plants appeared only about 140 million years ago, during the early Cretaceous Period; the earliest land plants appeared perhaps 600 million years ago. The angiosperms now dominate the world's vegetation. Only the gymnosperms, which form vast coniferous forests in northern temperate zones, offer any substantial competition. There may be more than 250,000 angiosperm species, compared to fewer than 1,000 species of gymnosperms and fewer than about 40,000 other types of vascular plants (ferns and their relatives) and bryophytes (liverworts, mosses, and hornworts). There are fewer than 15,000 species of algae, and perhaps more than 100,000 species of fungi and bacteria.

In modern classification systems, fungi are not considered plants but form a kingdom of their own, and the blue-green ALGAE (cyanobacteria; 1,500 species) and the BACTERIA (1,500 species) also form a separate kingdom. Except for the mosses, ferns, and conifers, most of the plants encountered on land are angiosperms. They predominate in the vegetation of the grasslands, deciduous forests, tropical rain forests, shrubby chaparral, deserts, and tundras.

More than any other major plant group, the flowering plants are ecologically related to animals. Modern animals, in-

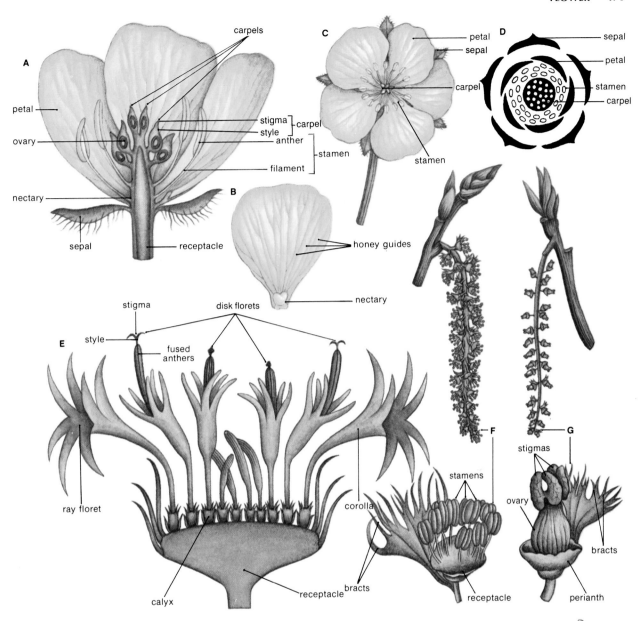

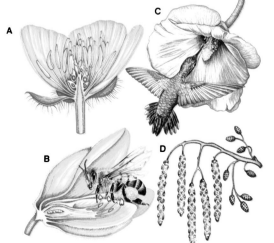

(Above) *Flowers contain the reproductive organs of angiosperms. Some plants have flowers with both male and female appendages and are known as perfect flowers. Others have separate, or imperfect, male and female flowers. As indicated in this cross section, buttercups, Ranunculus (A), have perfect flowers. The carpel, or female reproductive structure, includes the stigma, style, and ovary. The stamen, or male structure, comprises the filament and anther. The sepals, collectively, form the calyx, and the petals form the corolla. Each petal (B) is marked by honey guides, radiating lines that lead insects to the nectary. The arrangement of the various floral parts is shown in a top view (C) and is represented by a floral diagram (D). Plants in the composite family, such as the cornflower, Centaurea cyanus (E), have flowers that consist of two types of florets. The outer ray florets are sterile; the disk flowers contain fertile reproductive organs. Other angiosperms, such as the black poplar, Populus nigra, are dioecious; catkins of male (F) and female (G) flowers grow on separate trees. (Right) Various flowers are adapted to different types of pollination. Buttercups (A) are nonspecialized; they are pollinated by a number of insects. Gorse, Ulex europaeus (B), is specialized for bee pollination. Flowers of this type have brightly colored petals, and their nectaries are accessible only to specialized organs. Hibiscus species (C) are adapted for bird pollination; hummingbirds are among the principal bird pollinators. Hazel, Corylus (D), like most trees, is wind pollinated. Its flowers hang in long, thin catkins.*

cluding humans, and flowering plants are equally dependent upon each other. Most flowering species rely on animals for reproduction. Insects carry pollen from the stamens to the carpels; bats and birds participate in POLLINATION of some species. The dispersal and growth of the seeds are further ensured by animals attracted to their colorful and aromatic flowers and tasty fruits. Many fruits and seeds (the exclusive products of angiosperms) are also collected and consumed by humans, and the seeds are planted in extensive systems of agriculture. Almost all plants used in agriculture are angiosperms. (Mushrooms, fern fiddleheads, and pine nuts are exceptions.) In another relationship between plants and animals, only the special growing cells at the base of a grass (angiosperm) leaf seem well-adapted to animal grazing.

STRUCTURE OF FLOWERS

Four kinds of modified leaves make up a complete flower: carpels and stamens (primary reproductive structures) and petals and sepals (secondary structures). The carpel is the female reproductive structure. It has a stigma, where the pollen becomes attached and germinates; a style, through which the pollen tube grows; and an ovary with one or more ovules. The egg cell that will unite with the sperm cell (delivered by the pollen tube) forms in the ovule. The stamen is the male structure; its filament supports an anther, in which the pollen is formed. The often brightly colored petals are important in attracting pollinators, and the often leaflike sepals enclose the bud before the flower opens. The many species of flowering plants are usually distinguished from one another by the way these four basic flower parts are modified, although closely related species within a genus may have quite similar flowers.

Some flowers have only one carpel, others have two or a few, and still others have many. Several carpels in a single flower may be separate or fused together. If fused, they may be joined only at the ovaries or along their entire length. The ovary may contain one to many ovules, and these may be arranged in various ways. Frequently, the ovaries are attached to the receptacle (the end of the stem, or peduncle, that supports the flower parts) at the same level as the other flower parts, in which case the ovary is said to be hypogynous (or superior). In some cases the other flower parts are attached above the ovary, which is then said to be epigynous (inferior). In the rose family and some of its relatives, the stamens, petals, and sepals are attached around the ring of a cup with the ovaries at the bottom of the cup (perigynous).

Stamens also vary in several ways, although not as markedly as ovaries. Classification schemes often depend on the number of stamens in a given flower and whether they are attached oppositely or alternately with the petals.

The petals together form the corolla, with numerous and often beautiful forms. Besides the number of petals, two other important variations occur. First, petals may be separately attached to the receptacle, or they may be united along their edges to form a tube. Second, the corolla may be radially symmetrical, with petals radiating out in all directions from the center of the flower (as in a buttercup, geranium, lily, or rose), or some petals may have shapes different from others, so that the flower has dorsiventral symmetry—in which a vertical plane divides the flower into two equal, mirror-image halves (as in snapdragon, honeysuckle, or orchid).

Many flower petals have patterns of pigment that absorb only in the ultraviolet part of the spectrum. Insects, which have eyes that are sensitive to ultraviolet light, see patterns on the flower that are not visible to humans. These patterns frequently consist of radiating lines that lead the insect to the nectar. A few flowers (for example, clematis) have no true petals but do have colorful sepals.

If a flower lacks any of the four basic parts, it is called incomplete. If it lacks one of the essential reproductive parts (stamens or carpels), it is called imperfect. Thus, flowers that have both stamens and carpels but lack petals or sepals are perfect incomplete flowers. Imperfect flowers can be male or female. If male and female flowers occur on the same plant, the plant is called monoecious; if male and female flowers are on separate plants, it is dioecious. Maize (corn) is a monoecious plant, with its tassels (stamens) at the top and its ears

(carpels) on the stem below. Cottonwoods are dioecious—the male trees produce pollen, and female trees produce seeds.

In most angiosperms, pollen is transferred by insects. Insect-pollinated flowers often have rather showy corollas, which are often modified to ensure the dusting of pollen onto the insects as they penetrate the flowers in search of nectar. The dusted insects transfer the pollen to the stigma of the next flower they enter. Flowers pollinated by moths, hummingbirds, or bats may have specialized corollas that match the appropriate organs of the animals seeking the nectar.

In some major groups, pollen is transferred by the wind. Some species of wind-pollinated flowers are not at all showy, with the anthers suspended on long filaments so that the pollen dusts freely into the wind. The pollen grains may be winged, which allows them to be carried more easily on the breezes. Styles and stigmas may also extend some distance from the flower, to catch the blowing pollen. Sepals and petals may be either absent or quite small. Grasses, which are some of the most successful plants, are wind-pollinated, as are many trees—for example, maples, oaks, and walnuts.

A few species, including such important crops as wheat, rice, barley, oats, and peas, are self-pollinated. The pollen is transferred directly from stamens to carpels. Such species naturally maintain their genetic purity. To produce new hybrids, cross-pollination must be carried out manually. Some flowers (dandelion, hawkweed, certain grasses) do not require pollination to produce seed. Certain cells in the ovule other than the egg cell develop into seeds in the process called apomixis.

FLOWER ARRANGEMENT ON THE PLANT

A group of flowers on a plant is called an inflorescence. A great variety of inflorescences occur among the angiosperms. The simplest is a single, solitary flower at the end of a stem, with leaves at the base. It is rare for an entire plant to have a single flower, as is true of the tulip; but a solitary, terminal flower at the end of the main stem, with axillary flowers in the angles between leaves and stems, is common.

A number of flowers radiating along a single stem, usually with modified leaves (bracts) at the base of the peduncles, is a

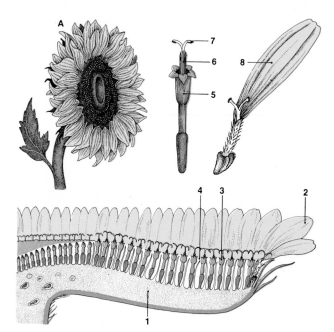

The common sunflower, Helianthus annus (A), has an inflorescence consisting of many smaller flowers, or florets, that act as one large flower. This flower head, borne on a receptacle (1), includes outer ray florets (2) and inner disk florets (3). Pappus scales (4), or modified sepals, separate the florets. The disk florets consist of a fused corolla (5) enclosing fused male anthers (6) and a female stigma (7), which is connected by the style to the ovary. The structure of the ray florets is similar, but the corolla (8) is greatly expanded.

raceme. Most racemes are indeterminate, meaning that the younger flowers are at the tip of the stem in the center of the raceme. A spike occurs when the flowers in the raceme are attached closely to the main stem. For example, a head of wheat is spiked, as are virtually all grass flowers. A compound raceme with several branching stems, each forming a raceme, is called a panicle. In a small number of species, the oldest flowers may occur near the stem tips of a raceme or panicle; this determinate structure is a cyme. When all the peduncles of several flowers in an inflorescence radiate from the same point, they form a flattopped, or sometimes rounded, umbel.

Flowers densely packed together on short peduncles and a short main axis form a head; clover is an example of this formation. The most common flower heads occur in the large aster or sunflower (composite) family. In a sunflower or daisy, two kinds of flowers occur in the head: ray or strap flowers, which consist of one long petal with an ovary and sometimes stamens; and disk flowers, which consist of five greatly reduced, radially symmetrical petals at the tips of a corolla tube, plus an ovary and, usually, stamens. The sepals in a composite flower head may have been modified to form filaments, such as the parachute on a dandelion seed. Two other special inflorescences are the catkins, rather loose, hanging spikes of flowers occurring on birch and other trees; and the spadices, which are spikes of male flowers above female flowers surrounded by large, sometimes colored leaves called spathes, as on calla lily.

THE SEED AND THE FRUIT
The products of the flower are the seed and the fruit. The seed is the mature ovule. It includes a minute embryo plant and, almost always, stored food that will supply the seedling when it begins to grow after sprouting, or germination. Important seeds that humans eat include the cereals, such as wheat, rice, maize; legumes, such as peas, beans, lentils, peanuts; and nuts. Many seeds are rich in fats (including oils), a concentrated form of energy, and are of great commercial importance—for example, soybeans, cottonseed, coconuts, peanuts, rapeseed, sunflower, and linseed (flax). The cereals

store mostly carbohydrate, and many legumes store much protein along with carbohydrate and, often, fat.

In a restricted botanical sense, the fruit is the mature ovary wall, but often food is stored in accessory tissues besides the ovary wall (see FRUITS AND FRUIT CULTIVATION).

FLOWERING TIME
Some plants, called annuals, germinate from seed and then flower and die within one year. Winter annuals may germinate in late autumn, live through the winter as slow-growing seedlings under the snow, and grow and flower in spring or early summer. Many cereals are winter annuals, but often a single species has winter-annual and spring-annual varieties or cultivars (agricultural varieties), as is the case with barley, rye, and wheat. Biennials typically germinate in the spring, grow as a rosette—a circle of leaves close to the ground, as in beets or dandelion—during the first summer, and send up a flowering shoot during the second season. Perennials, which grow and flower for several seasons, are called polycarpic. Monocarpic plants are those that flower only once and then die. These include annuals and biennials but also a few species such as bamboo and the century plant (Agave) that grow for several years, flower once, and then die.

The variety of flowering plants is enormous. Some angiosperm trees challenge the great conifers in size, while some floating flowering plants (Lemna) are smaller than a fingernail. Orchids grow suspended on the trunks of trees in tropical rain forests, and the sausage tree has a huge hanging flower pollinated by bats. Cacti and yucca plants have needles or swords for protection, and some angiosperms trap and consume insects (see CARNIVOROUS PLANTS). A few species of flowering plants grow during a short season in Antarctica; others grow near the tops of all but the highest mountains.

HOW FLOWERS FORM
Although a vast body of descriptive data is available on plant development, many problems remain unsolved. In both plants and animals the cells divide and multiply, under normal conditions, at the right time and place. A precise schedule for development is followed, and the role of genetic material in determining this process is acknowledged; however, the nature of the mechanism of development is not fully understood.

The formation of flowers in plants provides an appropriate model for the study of development. The plant stem grows by the division of a group of cells near the tip of the stem, with a few other dividing cells scattered in the stem down to a few centimeters below the tip. Regions of active cell division and growth in plants are called meristems. When a tree grows, a layer of meristem cells, called the cambium, forms between the bark and the wood. As these cells divide and grow, wood is produced on the inside and bark on the outside.

At some time during the life of the plant the meristems at the stem tips or in the lateral buds stop producing more stems and more leaves and produce flowers instead. Frequently, this occurs in response to changes in the environment. It is as if an environmental signal detected by the plant is translated into a signal within the plant, and this causes buds to grow into flowers instead of into stems and leaves.

In the early part of the 20th century it was thought that flowering resulted from a balance in internal nutrients. This continues to be a valuable concept with a few species. Tomato plants, for example, flower more and bear more fruit when nitrogen fertilizers are withheld after they are mature. Fruit trees respond in much the same way, but many plants flower more instead of less when nitrogen is increased. Other factors have proved to be far more important.

Temperature and Light. Winter annuals and biennials form flowers in response to the low temperatures of winter. This phenomenon was noted in the early 19th century, but it was not until the early 20th century that it was first documented and recognized by scientists. Many species of plants are induced to flower by several days to weeks of temperatures close to or just above the freezing point of water. The flowering of summer vegetables is promoted by a brief exposure to lower temperatures; a few perennials also respond this way.

Light also variously affects flowering plants. A few species seem to flower in response to increased light levels; others re-

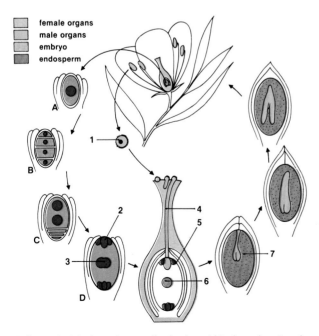

female organs
male organs
embryo
endosperm

Pollen grains (1), the male sex cells, develop within the anther. Female sex cells develop within the ovule by a process of cell division (A–C) that produces an embryo sac (D) containing the egg (2) and a large cell with two polar nuclei (3). The pollen grain adheres to the stigma and sends a pollen tube (4) into the ovule. Two sperm cells pass through the tube; one fertilizes the egg (5), and the other fuses with the polar nuclei (6) to form the endosperm. The ovule becomes the seed. The endosperm supplies food for the embryo (7).

spond to dimmer light. However, most species respond not to the brightness of light but to its duration, or the duration of the dark period (night), or to a combination of both.

In 1920, W. W. Garner and H. A. Allard reported that Maryland mammoth tobacco plants remained vegetative in the fields during the summer but flowered profusely in the winter greenhouse. They tested several different environmental factors, one of which was the length of day. When their test plants were placed in cabinets in midsummer at about 4:00 PM and removed at 8:00 AM the next morning, the plants flowered profusely, just as they had in the winter greenhouses.

Garner and Allard found that several species responded to short days (or, as later studies would suggest, long nights), and they called these short-day plants. Examples are cocklebur, chrysanthemum, poinsettia, and morning glory. Other species had the opposite response: they would bloom when the days got longer. These were called long-day plants. Beets, dill, Darnel ryegrass, spinach, henbane, radish, a tobacco species, and various cereals are good examples. The flowering time of a few species such as tomato, cucumber, globe amaranth, sunflower, a tobacco species, and garden pea, seems to be unaffected by day length, although the number or size of flowers or fruit set may be influenced strongly. Garner and Allard called this phenomenon photoperiodism.

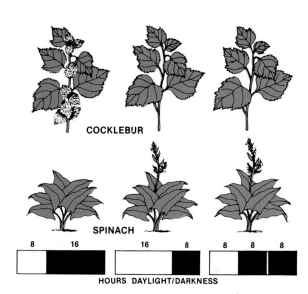

Studies of photoperiodism indicate that plants are especially sensitive to periods of darkness as well as to light. A short-day plant, such as cocklebur, needs a minimum period of uninterrupted darkness to induce flowering; it will not bloom if the darkness is interrupted even briefly. A long-day plant, such as spinach, will not flower when given 16 hours of darkness, but will flower if this period is interrupted.

Photoperiodism. In the 1930s, in the USSR, Mikhail Chailakhyan noted that the leaf was the part of the plant that responded to the length of day or night. If the leaf of a short-day plant is covered with a black bag, for example, the plant will flower, even though the stems and the buds (which will become flowers) remain under long-day conditions. Long-day plants will not flower when their leaves are covered long enough to give the leaf only short-day conditions.

Thus the leaf detects the day length and sends a signal to the bud, where flowers actually form. It is conceivable that this signal is an electrical, or nervous, impulse, but it seems much more likely that it is a chemical substance, or hormone. For one thing, the signal moves quite slowly—only a few centimeters per hour—which seems far too slow for an electrical stimulus. Another evidence for a hormone is that plants that have been induced to flower by the proper environmental treatment can be grafted onto plants that have been maintained in a vegetative condition. This causes the vegetative plants to flower, even if they do not experience the environmental conditions normally required to induce flowering.

Individual species have specific requirements for a minimum light or dark period. Cocklebur, a short-day plant, requires a minimum of about 8.5 hours of darkness to induce flowering (the critical night). The plant flowers maximally with 12 to 16 hours of darkness. Henbane, a long-day plant, requires more than about 12 hours of light to produce flowers.

In 1938, Karl Hamner and James Bonner gave cocklebur plants a 16-hour night and interrupted it briefly with light after about 8 hours. The plants responded as though they were experiencing long days instead of short days, remaining vegetative. This discovery of the night-interruption phenomenon opened up several avenues for future research. The intensity of light required to produce this effect varies from species to species. The light of the full Moon can be slightly effective in certain species if they are exposed to it for the entire night.

Orange-red wavelengths are the most effective in producing this phenomenon. It was discovered in the early 1950s that the effects of a night interruption with orange-red light can be almost completely reversed if that exposure is followed by one to far-red wavelengths. Thus, if a cocklebur plant is given a 16-hour dark period that is interrupted after 8 hours with orange-red light, it remains vegetative; a subsequent exposure to far-red leads again to flowering—unless this is in turn followed by orange-red light. The last exposure determines the response.

The discovery of the night-interruption phenomenon was extremely significant because it was found that many plant responses follow part of the same pattern. If lettuce seeds absorb water and are then exposed to orange-red light, they germinate; if they are later exposed to far-red light, they do not. Orange-red light also causes dark-grown stems to stop elongating, leaves to expand, hooks on seedlings to unfold, apple skins to turn red, and other phenomena to occur. In each case, subsequent exposure to far-red light reverses the effect.

It was postulated that a plant pigment exists that is converted from one form to another by orange-red light and back to the original form by far-red light. This pigment was called

(Right) *General trends in the evolution of the flowers of angiosperms include reduction in number and fusion of floral parts. Specific theories concerning flower development are derived by working backward from observations of primitive modern flowers; fossil evidence is too sketchy to provide positive proof. According to the most widely accepted theory, ancestral flowers (A) were similar to ferns, with separate male (1) and female (2) sporophylls—specialized spore-bearing leaves—arranged on a branchlike axis. The female leaves gradually folded in and fused to form simple ovaries (3) inside carpels (4), and the male spore sacs gradually fused to form stamens (5), resulting in a primitive angiosperm flower (B).*

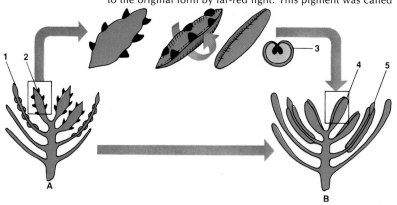

phytochrome, and in 1959 this important protein was first extracted from plant tissues. Phytochrome seems to be the means by which the plant "knows" whether it is in the light or the dark. Most light sources, including sunlight, act primarily as orange-red sources. During the 1970s and 80s much was learned about the action of phytochrome in flowering. It now seems clear that two kinds of phytochrome play separate roles in the flowering process. Time measurement, however, consists of much more than phytochrome.

Biological Clock. Virtually all living organisms (except perhaps the prokaryotes—bacteria and blue-green algae) have a BIOLOGICAL CLOCK. In plants this can be studied not only in the phenomenon of photoperiodism but in such phenomena as the diurnal movements of leaves. A bean plant, for example, has its leaves in a nearly horizontal position at noon and in an almost vertical position after midnight. These leaf movements continue to occur even when plants are placed under constant conditions of light and temperature, receiving no obvious external cues about the daily environmental cycle.

Actually, under such conditions, rhythms of both plants and animals tend to run either fast or slow (usually slow), often as much as an hour or more each day. After just a few days the leaf position of the bean plant is far out of phase with the daily cycle going on outside the laboratory; leaves may be in the midnight position at noon. This is almost conclusive evidence that organisms have an internal clock capable of measuring time, although not very accurately. In the natural environment, accuracy is not necessary because the clock is reset by the daily rising and the setting of the Sun.

Flower formation as exhibited in photoperiodism is an excellent example of both phytochrome action and the biological clock in plants.

THE CLASSIFICATION OF FLOWERING PLANTS
Some of the earliest systems of plant classification were highly artificial. Plants were not grouped according to genetic relationship but with respect to certain arbitrary features, such as number of stamens. One artificial ecological scheme might place all the plants of the prairie in one group and desert plants in another. A useful and long-used artificial approach is to classify plants as herbs, shrubs, or trees. Taxonomists seek to develop a natural system in which species are related to one another on the basis of common ancestry in their evolutionary development (see CLASSIFICATION, BIOLOGICAL).

Within the angiosperms, there are clearly two groups of plants: the Monocotyledonae and the Dicotyledonae, usually called monocots and dicots. (The COTYLEDON is the embryonic seed leaf.) Examples of the monocots are lilies, rushes, sedges, grasses, irises, orchids, and palm trees. Dicots include honeysuckles, sunflowers, buttercups, roses, all deciduous broadleaf trees except the ginkgo, mustards, mallows, primroses, phloxes, snapdragons, mints, goosefoots, and geraniums.

Monocots are characterized especially by having only one cotyledon (often not easy to distinguish) as part of the embryo in the seed; the dicots have two cotyledons (for example, the two halves of a bean seed). The veins in a monocot leaf are typically parallel; those in a dicot leaf typically form a network. Monocot flower parts usually occur in threes; dicot flower parts occur in twos, fours, or usually fives. Monocot stems have their vascular bundles (groups of transporting cells) enclosed in a sheath of cells and scattered in a matrix of pith cells; dicot stems have vascular bundles arranged in a ring, and often there is a cambium (layer of dividing cells) that allows the stem to become thicker in diameter from year to year. Monocot stems, even palm trees, do not grow in thickness from year to year. Dicots often have a branching taproot, while monocots typically have a fibrous root system. A few exceptions occur in each of these generalizations, but for the most part it is easy to distinguish between monocots and dicots by keeping all the characteristics in mind.

One problem in angiosperm taxonomy concerns the manner in which the genera are arranged in relation to one another. It is a convention of both botanists and zoologists that groups of genera should be classified into families, groups of families into orders, groups of orders into classes, groups of classes into divisions (phyla in zoology), and groups of divisions into

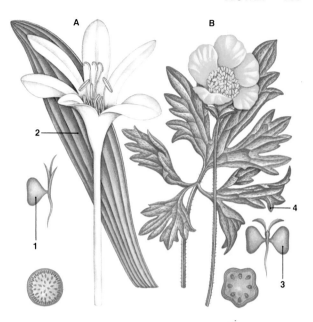

Monocots, such as the autumn crocus, Colchium autumnale (A), have only one cotyledon (1), or seed leaf, in the embryo; most monocots have parallel-veined leaves (2). Dicots, including the creeping buttercup, Ranunculus repens (B), have two cotyledons (3); most dicots have net-veined leaves (4).

kingdoms. Sometimes subclasses, suborders, and other subdivisions are also used.

Taxonomists also disagree as to whether the angiosperms should be considered a division, a class, or a subclass; so even at this level problems remain to be resolved. A few taxonomists consider the dicots and the monocots to represent classes (if the angiosperms form a division), but most taxonomists call the dicots and the monocots subclasses. One system considers them a series between subclasses and orders. All taxonomists agree, however, that the monocots and dicots form logical groups within the angiosperms. There is also general agreement about the arrangement of monocot orders.

The question of how to arrange dicot orders is not entirely resolved. Two systems exist that date almost from the time of Carolus LINNAEUS (1753). One of these assumes that petal structure is especially important. Those plants having united petals would form one major group within the dicots; plants with separate petals would form another group. Within these groups some orders are thought to be more primitive than others in the evolutionary sequence of plants. The second system assumes that ovary position is the most important criterion. Those dicots having superior ovaries would form one evolutionary sequence, while those orders with inferior ovaries would form another line. At present most taxonomists feel that the second system comes the closest to expressing a natural classification scheme. In this scheme united petals with irregular corollas occur in both major lines of evolution and thus would be examples of parallel evolution, having originated independently in each line. In the other scheme inferior ovaries would be an example of parallel evolution.

There is some disagreement about the number of families of flowering plants, but one authority lists a total of 306 families: 249 dicot and 57 monocot families. Nearly half of the species of angiosperms occur in 19 families, which are listed approximately in the order of their size (largest first): aster, orchid, pea, grass, gardenia (coffee, quinine), spurge, sedge, lily, rose, mint, verbena, snapdragon, mustard, myrtle, fig (hemp, mulberry), heath, carrot, potato, and palm.

THE IMPORTANCE OF FLOWERS
Flowers and flowering plants form an exceedingly important part of nature. They also provide color to the surroundings—not only the flowers themselves but also the brilliant colored leaves that cover the hillsides during the autumn in temperate

regions. Gymnosperms, which were predominant until the angiosperms appeared 140 million years ago, have no colorful flowers; a few exhibit autumn colors.

Flowers are used in plantings and in many ceremonies; their seeds, fruits, roots, stems, and leaves also provide food, as has been noted in several examples. In turn, most of the animals that humans eat depend upon flowering plants for their food supply.   FRANK B. SALISBURY

Bibliography: Bell, A. D., *Plant Form: An Illustrated Guide to Flowering Plant Morphology* (1990); Bernier, G., ed., *The Physiology of Flowering* (1983); Cronquist, A., *An Integrated System of Classification of Flowering Plants* (1981) and *The Evolution and Classification of Flowering Plants* (1968); Grant, V., *Genetics of Flowering Plants* (1975); Jensen, W. A., and Salisbury, F. B., *Botany: An Ecological Approach* (1972); Salisbury, F. B., *The Flowering Process* (1963) and *The Biology of Flowering* (1971); Shukla, P., and Misra, S. P., *An Introduction to Taxonomy of Angiosperms* (1979); Vince-Prue, D., and Thomas, B., eds., *Light and the Flowering Process* (1984).

See also: ALTERNATION OF GENERATIONS; BOTANY; EVOLUTION; HOUSEPLANTS; PLANT PROPAGATION.

flowerpecker

Flowerpeckers comprise 7 genera and about 58 species of birds in the family Dicaeidae, order Passeriformes. These small (7.5–19 cm/3–7.5 in), colorful, arboreal birds with square-ended tails occur in India, Southeast Asia, China, the Australasian region, and east to the Solomon Islands. Flowerpeckers have short bills, and the semitubular tongues of many species are adapted for nectar feeding. They feed mainly on insects, nectar, and especially berries. Both sexes take care of the young.   ROBERT J. RAIKOW

flowering rush

Flowering rush is an aquatic perennial herb, *Butomus umbellatus*, in the flowering rush family, Butomaceae. It grows to a height of 1.4 m (4.5 ft) and has a fleshy rootstock and long, narrow leaves similar to those of the rush. Flowering rush bears numerous rose-colored flowers. Native to Eurasia, it grows wild in northeastern North America.

flowerpot snake

Typhlops braminus, a small blind snake of the family Typhlopidae, is sometimes called the flowerpot snake because it occasionally burrows into the soil of flowerpots left in the open. These insect-eating snakes are brown or black in color and about 13 cm (5 in) long, with a cylindrical body and blunt head. Small eyes are visible beneath the head scales. Native to the general area of southeastern Asia, these snakes have been introduced into Hawaii, Mexico, and many islands. It is thought that they reproduce parthenogenetically because no males have been found.   JONATHAN CAMPBELL

Flowers of Evil, The

The 100 poems in the first edition of *The Flowers of Evil* (*Les Fleurs du mal*; Eng. trans., 1909), published in 1857 by the French poet Charles BAUDELAIRE, brought a new sensibility into literature and may be said to mark the beginning of modernism in poetry. Upon their publication, Baudelaire was prosecuted and convicted for producing an offense to public morals, and his poems were censored. (Six of the poems remained banned in France until Baudelaire's conviction was overturned, posthumously, in 1947). In the poems—some of which appeared only with the publication (1861) of the second edition—Baudelaire seeks poetic truth in life's darkest places. He knows himself to be damned yet yearns for death, in hope of finding "the new," whether in heaven or hell.

Bibliography: Baudelaire, Charles, *Les Fleurs du mal*, trans. by Richard Howard (1982).

flowmeter

Flowmeters are devices used in industry to measure the rate of flow of liquids and gases in a pipe under pressure. Displacement flowmeters act like pumps reversed under fluid pressure.

Differential pressure flowmeters operate by measuring the relation of fluid flow to the drop in pressure caused by a restriction in a conduit. The Venturi tube and the Pitot tube, used to measure airspeed and stream velocity, work on this principle in conjunction with a MANOMETER. The rotameter employs a free float that positions itself under its own weight against upward stream flow in an inverted, tapered glass tube. Flowmeters with electrical readout employ electromagnetic or radio-isotope principles or depend on the cooling of resistance wires and of thermopiles.   FRANK J. OLIVER

Floyd, Carlisle

Carlisle Floyd, b. Latta, S.C., June 12, 1926, is a composer best known for his operas, particularly *Susannah*. Based on a libretto by Floyd, *Susannah* won the New York Music Critics Circle citation as the best new opera produced in New York in 1956. Among Floyd's other operas are *Wuthering Heights* (1958), based on the novel by Emily Brontë; *Of Mice and Men* (1970), after the novel by John Steinbeck; and *Willie Stark* (1983), from Robert Penn Warren's novel *All the King's Men*.

Floyd, John Buchanan

John Buchanan Floyd, b. Montgomery County, Va., June 1, 1806, d. Aug. 26, 1863, was President James Buchanan's secretary of war (1857–60) on the eve of the U.S. Civil War. He was accused of transferring funds and weapons to the South, but the charges were never proved. He resigned when Buchanan refused to evacuate federal troops from Fort Sumter, which Floyd said had been occupied on Dec. 26, 1860, against War Department orders. Floyd served as a Confederate brigadier general at Fort Donelson and fled (February 1862) just before the fort fell to Ulysses S. Grant.

Floyd, Pretty Boy

The American gangster Charles Arthur "Pretty Boy" Floyd, b. Akins, Okla., 1901, d. Oct. 22, 1934, robbed many midwestern banks and allegedly killed ten people. The ruggedly handsome Floyd, branded "Public Enemy No. 1," was killed by FBI agents. A folk hero in Oklahoma, he was mentioned sympathetically in John Steinbeck's *Grapes of Wrath*.

Bibliography: Nash, Jay R., *Bloodletters and Badmen* (1973); Quimby, Myron J., *The Devil's Emissaries* (1970).

flu: see INFLUENZA.

flügelhorn   [flue'-gul-hohrn]

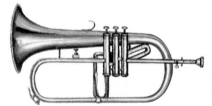

The flügelhorn, a brass wind instrument, was first made in Austria between 1820 and 1830. The three-valved B-flat soprano flügelhorn is the most popular.

The flügelhorn is a member of the BUGLE family of wind instruments that includes the baritone, euphonium, and bass TUBA. It is comparable to the CORNET in size and pitch, but it has a larger bore and bell and a mellower tone. The flügelhorn is not often used in American BANDS, but it is regularly used in England and continental Europe. Ottorino Respighi wrote for it in *The Pines of Rome* to simulate the sound of ancient Roman instruments.   ELWYN A. WIENANDT

fluid mechanics

Fluid mechanics, or hydrodynamics, is the study of the effect of forces on fluids (liquids or gases) at rest or in motion. Although the basic laws of conservation of mass, momentum, and energy hold for fluids just as they do for solids, they exhibit a different mathematical form. The study of fluid mechanics is therefore considered a separate field from that of solid mechanics or the mechanics of particles and rigid bodies. The field of fluid mechanics can be further divided into hydrostatics (fluids at rest), hydraulics (liquids in motion in channels and pipes; see HYDRAULIC SYSTEMS), AERODYNAMICS (the flow of gases), gas dynamics (flow of gases when compressibility is significant), and MAGNETOHYDRODYNAMICS (flow of ionized gases).

DEVELOPMENT OF FLUID MECHANICS

Rational fluid mechanics is thought to have begun with ARCHIMEDES, who in the 3d century BC stated his law of buoyancy (see ARCHIMEDES' PRINCIPLE). Nothing further was accomplished in the field until 1605, when Simon STEVIN published his *Hydrostatics*. In 1644, Evangelista TORRICELLI stated his law of efflux, and in 1663, Blaise Pascal rediscovered Stevin's laws. Twenty-five years later, Sir Isaac NEWTON summed up all of fluid mechanics as it was known at that time in book 2 of his *Principia* and added some original ideas, including his hypothesis of viscosity.

The basic laws of ideal, frictionless fluids were finally given mathematical form by Leonhard EULER in 1755. Euler based his work in part on earlier work by Daniel and Jacques BERNOULLI. In 1827, Claude Navier derived the equations of viscous flow, which were published by Sir George Gabriel STOKES in 1845. The work of Joseph Boussinesq in 1877 and Osborne REYNOLDS in 1883 on laminar (streamlined) flow and turbulent (erratic) flow led to the extension of the Navier-Stokes equations to turbulent flow by including the Reynolds stresses. These equations, however, were too difficult to solve until Ludwig Prandtl and Theodore von KÁRMÁN showed (1904 and 1921, respectively) how the concept of the boundary layer reduces them to a simpler form. Today solutions of the Euler equations, with corrections from the boundary-layer equations, are used to describe the flight of aircraft and spacecraft; to calculate flow past ships, trains, automobiles, and such stationary structures as buildings and bridges; and to describe the flow in pumps, turbines, and chemical-processing plants. They are also used to describe the motion of the atmosphere and the oceans, the flow in channels and pipes and over dams, and the flow of ionized gases (plasmas).

PROPERTIES OF FLUIDS

The distinguishing feature of a fluid, in contrast to a solid, is the ease with which the fluid may be deformed. If a shearing force, however small, is applied to a fluid, the fluid will move and continue to move as long as the shear acts on it. For example, the force of gravity causes water poured from a tilted pitcher to flow. When the pitcher is righted, the flow ceases because the gravitational force is then exactly balanced by the pressure force of the pitcher wall.

Unlike liquids, gases cannot be poured from one open container into another, but they, too, deform under shear stress. Because shear stresses result from relative motion, they are equivalent whether the fluid flows past a stationary object or the object moves through the fluid.

Even though a fluid can deform easily under an applied force, the fluid's viscosity creates resistance to this force. The VISCOSITY of gases, which is much less than that of liquids, increases slightly as the temperature increases, whereas that of liquids decreases when the temperature increases. Highly viscous liquids are more properly the subject of the study of rheology; fluid mechanics is primarily concerned with Newtonian fluids, or those in which stress, viscosity, and rate of strain are linearly related.

Pressure and density are considered mechanical properties of the fluid, although they are also thermodynamical properties that are related to the temperature and entropy of the fluid by means of an equation of state. For a small change in pressure, the density of a gas is essentially unaffected; thus it, as well as all liquids, may be considered incompressible. If density changes are significant in flow problems, however, then the flow must be considered compressible. Compressibility effects result when the speed of the flow approaches the speed of

sound or the speed of flow in a channel approaches $\sqrt{gh}$, where g is the acceleration of gravity and h is the depth of the fluid.

HYDROSTATICS—FLUIDS AT REST

When a fluid is at rest or in equilibrium with the forces acting on it, motion does not have to be considered. Hydrostatics is a special case of how fluids at rest are affected by pressure exerted by external forces, such as the atmosphere or a piston and the body force due to gravity. The gravity force exhibits its effect in the increase in pressure with depth due to the weight of the fluid above the point of observation. Thus the increase in pressure p with depth h below the free surface is equal to the specific weight w times h or $\Delta p = p - p_o = wh$, where p_o is the pressure at the surface. PASCAL'S LAW states that in a fluid at rest the pressure on a surface is independent of the orientation of the surface.

FLUID FLOW—REAL FLUIDS

The equations governing the flow of real fluids are complex; in the case of turbulent flow, they are not completely known. Laminar flow is described by the Navier-Stokes equations, for which solutions can be obtained only in simple cases that nevertheless are of great importance in understanding fluid flow. Approximate solutions in more complex situations can be obtained by using large digital computers.

If the velocity of the flow increases, the flow becomes unstable, and transition from laminar to turbulent flow takes place. The fluid particles begin to flow in highly irregular paths. Eddies form and transfer momentum over distances varying from a few millimeters, as in controlled laboratory experiments, to several meters, as in a large room, around the exterior of buildings or other structures, and in the oceans or the atmosphere. Accordingly, the equations of turbulent flow are more complex; for any solution they require empirical relations obtained from carefully controlled experiments.

Whether a flow is laminar or turbulent generally can be determined by calculating the Reynolds number, Re, of the flow. The Reynolds number is the product of the density ρ, a characteristic length L, and a characteristic velocity V, all divided by the coefficient of viscosity, μ.

$$Re = \frac{\rho L V}{\mu}$$

The Reynolds number is dimensionless; that is, it is a pure number. As long as Re is small, the flow remains laminar; when it becomes greater than a critical value Re_c, the flow becomes turbulent. With ρ, L, and μ constant, Re varies simply as V. For flow in smooth round pipes, Re_c is about 2,000, with L equal to the diameter of the pipe. On the other hand, in flow over flat surfaces $Re_c \approx 500,000$, when L = the distance along the surface from its leading edge.

The key physical process in the flow of real fluids is the conversion of mechanical energy into heat that is the result of viscosity in laminar or turbulent flow. Many practical problems in flow through pipes and channels have been solved by using simple empirical laws that embody a friction factor and that account for energy loss.   ROBERT E. STREET

Bibliography: Cheremisinof, N. P., *Encyclopedia of Fluid Mechanics*, 6 vols. (1985–87); Streeter, V., and Wylie, B., *Fluid Mechanics*, 8th ed. (1985); White, F. M., *Fluid Mechanics*, 2d ed. (1986).

fluidized bed combustion

Fluidized bed combustion (FBC) is a technique for producing heat from low-grade coal. Air is blown into a bed of sand, or of powdered coal and limestone, causing the bed to churn almost like a boiling fluid. The bed is heated red-hot by the injection and ignition of a start-up gas, and more ground or powdered coal is slowly fed in. Steam is generated in boiler tubes laid in the bed, and the exhaust gases are captured under pressure and used to drive a gas turbine.

FBC technology offers the possibility of burning coal without producing pollutants: limestone removes polluting sulfur dioxide in the form of calcium sulfate solids, and FBC furnaces emit less nitrogen oxide than other types. Nevertheless, prospects for large-scale FBC furnaces waned in the late 1980s because of high costs as well as the indestructible slag that is the final by-product of FBC combustion.

fluke

A fluke is a parasitic flatworm of the class Trematoda. The body is shaped like a simple leaf, usually with the mouth at the anterior end. One or more suckers enable the fluke to hold to its host, and a muscular pharynx is used to suck in tissues or body fluids. Eggs are deposited in the host's organ or in tissues where the mature worms reside. They reach the outside by way of the digestive tract and feces.

Some flukes attack only one kind of fish, amphibian, reptile, or mammal and live externally or in its mouth cavity or urinary bladder. Most flukes are internal parasites, living in the lungs, digestive tract, or blood vessels of some vertebrate animal, but have developmental stages in one or more invertebrate animals such as snails or crustaceans. The vertebrate host becomes infected either by eating the invertebrate host or by direct invasion by immature flukes.

Sexual reproduction of the parasite occurs in the vertebrate host, and asexual reproduction may take place in the invertebrate host. Thus each adult fluke may produce up to 500,000 eggs. Of the young that hatch out and enter an invertebrate host, each may produce up to 300 individuals that can infect a vertebrate host.

By far the majority of vertebrates that serve as hosts to flukes are oceanic and freshwater fish. Trematode infestations can be a serious problem in hatcheries, causing blindness and other body damage. A number of trematode species are parasitic on humans and their domestic animals. The most familiar are those that cause SCHISTOSOMIASIS, or snail fever, snails being secondary hosts for these species. Some trematode diseases are more common in certain areas, such as the so-called Chinese liver-fluke disease, which occurs in various Asian nations, and paragonimiasis, a lung-fluke disease of semitropical regions.   LORUS J. AND MARGERY MILNE

Bibliography: Chandler, A. C., *Introduction to Parasitology*, 11th ed. (1988); Crompton, D. W., and Joyner, S. M., *Parasitic Worms* (1980).

flume studies

In the hydrologic sciences, flume studies are studies of water flow in channels called flumes. The channel may be a natural one, with an engineered control structure for monitoring flow and sediment discharge in the channel. Engineers also build artificial flumes, sometimes of a large and elaborate nature. Such channels are used for controlled laboratory studies of the fluid mechanics of water flow and sediment transport.

Laboratory flumes may be designed with either fixed or mobile boundaries. With the latter scientists can study the hydraulic resistance that different boundary conditions or different types of sediment offer to water flow. Such studies provide data useful in channel design and river engineering. Flumes are also used to study the structure of fluid turbulence (see FLUID MECHANICS), a topic that is of importance to boundary-layer theory (see AERODYNAMICS). Geologists use flumes to study the ways in which riverbeds form. Such studies are particularly useful for interpreting the sedimentary structures found in nature and for reconstructing past water flow.

Some special-purpose flumes are of a circular design, others conform to the shape of a river MEANDER bend, and still others are equipped with a wave maker and a porous artificial beach. One large flume at Colorado State University, in Fort Collins, is 61 m (200 ft) long, 1.22 m (4 ft) deep, and 2.44 m (8 ft) wide; it could be described as a flume river, bridging the gap between laboratory experimentation and the natural prototype. Although most flume studies are limited by scale and are confined to two dimensions, they have generated a large body of useful empirical data.   A. V. JOPLING

Bibliography: Bos, M. G., *Flow Measuring Flumes for Open Channel Systems* (1984); Morris, Henry, and Wiggert, J., *Applied Hydraulics in Engineering*, 2d ed. (1972); Pedlosky, Joseph, *Geophysical Fluid Dynamics*, 2d ed. (1987); Smith, Norman, *Man and Water* (1976).

fluorescence   [flohr'-es-ens]

Fluorescence is a form of LUMINESCENCE in which certain substances emit light or other radiation when they are stimulated,

The color of a fluorescent mineral may differ markedly when it fluoresces (bottom) *from when it is seen under normal lighting conditions* (top). *Fluorescence is a widely variable property, as well. The fluorescent colors of a given mineral may differ from one specimen to another, and some specimens may not display the phenomenon at all. These differences depend on variations in impurities within the samples. Among the fluorescent minerals are autunite, calcite, hyalite, fluorspar, scheelite, and willemite.*

or excited, by incoming radiation and then return to their original state. A number of minerals, for example, glow when they are excited by ultraviolet light with colors far different from those of their ordinary appearance. The word *fluorescence,* in fact, comes from the mineral fluorspar, some varieties of which display this phenomenon. Besides solids such as minerals, some liquids and gases also fluoresce. The presence of impurities in a substance makes the occurrence of fluorescence more likely.

Fluorescence is sometimes arbitrarily distinguished from the related phenomenon called PHOSPHORESCENCE by limiting the definition of fluorescence to substances that reemit radiation within about 10^{-8} seconds after being stimulated. Fluorescent substances that continue to reemit radiation for longer periods may then be called phosphors, such as the phosphors in television tubes (see CATHODE-RAY TUBE). Other such familiar applications of fluorescence include fluorescent light and the use in clothing of brightening agents, whose reemitted blue-white colors tend to mask the yellowing of materials with age. Fluorescent dyes are also employed in paints and plastics, and they are useful tagging materials in a wide range of scientific techniques.

Fluorescent emissions are commonly of a longer wavelength than the stimulating radiation. LASER technology, however, has made possible fluorescent emissions that are of shorter wavelengths than the incident laser source. A further application of fluorescent emission in the laser field involves certain organic dyes. These dyes are efficient sources of tunable laser oscillation when excited by other lasers operating at fixed wavelengths.   WM. R. BENNETT, JR.

Bibliography: Lakowicz, J., *Principles of Fluorescence Spectroscopy* (1983); Robbins, M., *Collector's Book of Fluorescent Minerals* (1983).

fluorescent light

A fluorescent light is a highly efficient light source that uses a mercury arc and a fluorescent phosphor coating inside its tube. It is most widely used in factories, offices, stores, and schools. The principles of the fluorescent lamp have been known since the 1860s. The French physicist A. H. BECQUEREL made a primitive fluorescent lamp in 1867, and many other inventors, including Thomas Edison, experimented with fluorescence. The fluorescent lamp did not become practical, however, until about 1939.

The mercury arc in a fluorescent lamp operates between two heated coils called cathodes. Much of the arc's energy is emitted in the invisible ultraviolet range, but the phosphor coating in the tube converts it to visible wavelengths. Different phosphors can produce a range of colors varying from cool to warm.

Fluorescent lamps lack the flexibility of incandescent lamps in that wattage cannot be changed simply by removing one lamp and putting in another. Since the resistance of a mercury arc decreases as current increases, the current would destroy the lamp if not controlled. Therefore a ballast must be used to limit the current and—for most sizes—to increase the voltage for reliable starting and stable operation. Each lamp size requires a different ballast.

The great advantages of a fluorescent light are its high light output per watt and its long life. The new compact fluorescent lamps, which screw into their light sockets like conventional incandescents, consume 75 to 85 percent less electricity than do incandescent bulbs and last up to 13 times longer. A compact 18-watt fluorescent provides the same amount of light as a 75-watt incandescent bulb.   WILLARD ALLPHIN

Bibliography: Lovins, Amory B., *The State of the Art: Lighting* (1988–90); Murdoch, Joseph B., *Illumination Engineering* (1985).

See also: LIGHTING DEVICES.

fluoridation

Fluoridation is the process of adding fluoride to water supplies as a preventive measure against tooth decay (see TEETH). Fluorides—that is, ions of the element fluorine—occur naturally in many waters, often to the extent of 0.1 to 0.2 parts per million (ppm) but sometimes in excess of 4 ppm. U.S. Public Health Service (PHS) studies in the 1930s and 1940s indicated a correlation between higher fluoride concentrations and lower rates of tooth decay. Experimental programs involving artificial fluoridation at selected sites were devised to test this possibility, but before completion of the programs the PHS officially endorsed fluoridation in 1950. Since then, water supplies for about 50% of the U.S. population have come to be fluoridated, with similar or even higher percentages in Canada, Ireland, Australia, and New Zealand. Great Britain and the Soviet Union fluoridate water supplies for less than 20% of their populations, however, and most countries of Western Europe no longer fluoridate their water at all.

Fluoridation has long been a source of controversy, despite the fact that the average child today has decay on 3 tooth surfaces, as opposed to 10 in a child of prefluoridation days. Opponents are concerned about studies that show fluoride may cause some adverse effects. Many critics view fluoridation as a form of medication, imposed on the public in violation of individual choice.

Bibliography: Hileman, Gette, "Fluoridation of Water," *Chemical and Engineering News,* Aug. 1, 1988; Murray, J. J., and Rugg-Gunn, R. J., *Fluorides in Caries Prevention,* 2d. ed. (1982).

fluorine

Fluorine is a pale yellow, poisonous, highly corrosive gas. It is the lightest member of the HALOGENS, Group VIIA of the periodic table, and the most reactive of all elements. Its symbol is F, its atomic weight is 18.99840, and its atomic number is 9. The name *fluorine* is derived from the mineral fluorspar, CaF_2, which, in turn, is derived from the Latin *fluo* ("flow"), because until AD 1500 it was used as a flux in metallurgy.

DISCOVERY

By 1670 the German scientist Heinrich Schwanhard had discovered that glass can be etched by fluorspar treated with a strong acid. This treatment generates hydrofluoric acid, HF, a highly corrosive acid still used for etching glass. Although Carl S. Scheele of Sweden is often credited with the discovery of hydrofluoric acid, it seems apparent that he and most of his contemporaries believed that the acid is an integral part of the fluorspar, not realizing the significance of adding a strong acid when activating the mineral. The true nature of the acid did not begin to emerge until early in the 19th century. Unsuccessful attempts to separate and characterize the unknown element by the electrolysis of fluorspar were made by Edmond Frémy in France and George Gore in England, among others. Success came in 1886 when Henri Moissan, a student of Frémy, used a solution of potassium acid fluoride, KHF_2, in anhydrous hydrofluoric acid as the electrolyte.

NATURAL OCCURRENCE

Fluorine is relatively abundant in the universe. According to some theorists, this may be attributed to the formation of the element by supernova explosions, when neutrinos transform an isotope of neon into one of fluorine. On the Earth, fluorine is widely distributed among natural compounds, but its extreme reactivity precludes its presence in elemental form. Although constituting only 0.065 percent of the Earth's crust, fluorine is found in oceans, lakes, rivers, and all other forms of natural water; in the bones, teeth, and blood of all mammals; and in all plants and plant parts. In spite of its ubiquity, as yet no universally acceptable evidence exists that fluorine is a necessary ingredient of living beings. Fluorine is found most abundantly in nature as the minerals fluorspar (FLUORITE, CaF_2), cryolite (Na_3AlF_6), and fluorapatite ($CaF_2 \cdot 3Ca[PO_4]_2$). Fluorspar is found extensively in Illinois and Kentucky. CRYOLITE occurs extensively in Greenland and Iceland, although its use in the production of aluminum is so extensive that much of the supply needed for other manufacturing must be produced synthetically.

PROPERTIES

Fluorine exists as a diatomic gas, F_2. Highly toxic, it has a characteristic pungent odor that can be detected before hazardous concentrations build up. Fluorine boils at $-188°$ C ($-370°$ F) and its melting point is $-219°$ C ($-426°$ F).

Only one stable isotope of fluorine occurs—^{19}F. The fluorine atom has seven electrons in its outer shell and requires an additional electron for maximum stability. This electron is strongly attracted by the positively charged nucleus because of the small size of the fluorine atom, accounting for the extreme electronegativity of the element. As a result, fluorine has a valence of -1 and forms compounds with all elements except the noble gases helium, neon, and argon. Fluorine salts are called fluorides.

Fluorine is manufactured by electrolyzing a mixture of potassium fluoride and hydrogen fluoride. It is stored and shipped in containers lined with TEFLON or made of a special steel. The latter becomes coated with iron fluoride, thus retarding further reaction.

THE FLUORINE INDUSTRY

The earliest large-scale commercial use of fluorine-containing compounds was probably the result of the work of General Motors Corporation chemists Thomas Midgley and Albert Henne, who, in the 1920s, set out to develop a refrigerant that did not have the drawbacks of those used at the time. The result was a chlorofluorocarbon, dichlorodifluoromethane, CCl_2F_2, now called FREON-12. It is nonflammable, noncorrosive, and nontoxic; it liquefies easily and boils at a low temperature ($-29.8°$ C/$-21.6°$ F). Joint production by General Motors and Du Pont began in 1931, and a whole family of these refrigerants was subsequently developed. The use of chlorofluorocarbons was rapidly expanded into the field of AEROSOL propellants. Their use declined after 1977, however, when it was found that they deplete the ozone in the upper atmosphere, and several nations have proposed banning their use as propellants and refrigerants by the end of the 20th century (see OZONE LAYER).

The fluorochemical industry actually began in the United States about 1940, when the Du Pont Corporation developed a polymer of a tetrafluoroethylene, Teflon TFE. The introduction of this product resulted in a dramatic increase in fluorine requirements (see PLASTICS). Later demands arose for the element, for use in a gaseous diffusion process that concentrated uranium isotopes for the manufacture of nuclear weapons. This was done by the chemical conversion of ore to gaseous uranium hexafluoride, followed by the separation of stable uranium-238 from fissionable uranium-235 by gaseous diffusion. In addition to the resulting demand for fluorine, the corrosive nature of these products meant that fluorocarbon coolants had to be developed for removing the heat generated while pumping the uranium hexafluorides.

USES AND COMPOUNDS

In addition to its use in uranium processing, refrigerants, and aerosol propellants, fluorine is used in dentifrices, as a catalyst in producing the dodecylbenzene used to make detergents, and in alkylating olefins used in refining high-octane gasoline, as well as in the production of polyfluorhydrocarbon resins such as TEFLON, noted for their nonstick properties and resistance to corrosion.

Sodium fluoride, NaF, is used as a sterilant and insecticide and in FLUORIDATION of water. It is also a paint preservative, it renders enamels opaque, and it is used in dyes and in the primary metal and ceramics industries. Boron trifluoride is a catalyst in the alkylation of benzene for detergent production and in making polymers and copolymers for adhesives. Other compounds include antimony trifluoride (SbF_3), a catalyst; sulfur hexafluoride (SF_6), a gaseous insulator; and polymers such as vinylidene fluoride ($CH_2{=}CF_2)_x$. Fluorine compounds are of interest whenever incombustibility or oil and water resistance are important. They are also used in elastomers and in surfactants for coatings applied to fiberboard, paper, and cloth. CHARLES HOWARD

Bibliography: Filler, R., and Kobayashi, Y., eds., *Biomedical Aspects of Fluorine Chemistry* (1983); Liebman, Joel, and Greenberg, Arthur, eds., *Fluorine-Containing Molecules* (1989); Young, A. S., *Sulfur Dioxide, Chlorine, Fluorine and Chlorine Oxides* (1983).

fluorite   [flohr'-yt]

Fluorite is a widely distributed, brittle, transparent-to-translucent calcium fluoride mineral of great industrial importance. Impurities cause fluorite, colorless or white when pure, to vary widely in color. Some samples thermoluminesce, emitting light when heated.

Fluorite, calcium fluoride, CaF_2, is a major industrial mineral used as a flux in steel making as well as in the preparation of hydrofluoric acid and, in the ceramics industry, in glasses and enamels. Fluorite's vitreous, cubic crystals (isometric system) and cleavable, granular masses have a wide color range (often green, blue, or purple) and may fluoresce under ultraviolet light. Hardness is 4, specific gravity 3.0–3.3. Fluorite deposits form under a wide variety of conditions: as veins produced by hydrothermal alteration, as beds and cavities in sedimentary rocks, in hot spring deposits, and in pegmatites.

See also: FLUORESCENCE.

fluorocarbon   [flohr'-oh-kahr-buhn]

A fluorocarbon is an organic chemical that has one or more fluorine atoms. Over one hundred fluorocarbons have been classified, and because a hydrogen atom in any hydrocarbon may be substituted by a FLUORINE atom, the list of potential fluorocarbons is virtually endless. Hydrocarbons containing both chlorine and fluorine are called chlorofluorocarbons, or CFCs. Fully substituted fluorocarbons, called perfluorocarbons, are inert, nontoxic, odorless, and nonflammable.

The FREON group of CFCs includes Freon-11 (CCl_3F), used as an AEROSOL propellant, and Freon-12 (CCl_2F_2), a commonly used refrigerant (see REFRIGERATION). Freon contributes to atmospheric OZONE LAYER depletion, which causes the Earth's surface to be exposed to excessive ultraviolet radiation. The

use of CFCs as aerosol propellants therefore has been in decline since the mid-1970s, and in 1988 the Du Pont Company and the Dow Chemical Company, major producers of the chemicals, agreed to phase out CFC production.

Tetrafluoroethylene ($CF_2{=}CF_2$) can be polymerized by a free-radical agent to form TEFLON, and Fluothane ($CF_3CHClBr$) is used as an ANESTHETIC replacing ether.

fluorometer   [flohr-ahm'-e-tur]

The fluorometer is a photoelectric instrument used primarily in chemistry to measure the wavelength and intensity of fluorescent light (see FLUORESCENCE). Certain chemical substances, called fluorescent or phosphorescent compounds, absorb light energy and reemit it at a different wavelength. By determining the wavelengths at which this light is reemitted and by measuring its intensity, it is possible to identify such compounds and quantitatively measure them.

The intensity of the fluorescent light is measured by using a photoelectric cell to convert its energy to electrical energy. The wavelength, or color, can be determined by establishing which colored filter allows most of its light to pass. More sophisticated instruments identify the wavelength of fluorescent light by breaking it up into its spectrum of component colors, using a prism or grating and photoelectrically measuring the most intense spectral region. LESLIE W. LEE

fluoroscope

The fluoroscope is an instrument designed to allow observation of the internal structure of an opaque body by using X RAYS. In industry it is used to detect flaws in materials and devices. In medicine it is used to view the internal organs of the human body. A fluoroscope consists of an X-ray source and a fluorescent screen. The patient is placed between the source and the screen so that the X rays pass through the patient's body. When they strike the fluorescent screen, they produce visible light by the process of FLUORESCENCE. The intensity of the light produced depends on the nature of the tissue through which the X rays must travel. For example, bone effectively blocks X rays and produces a dark shadow on the screen. An advantage of the fluoroscope is that it allows a physician to view organs in motion, instead of "frozen," as they are in an ordinary X-ray photograph. The photograph, however, gives better clarity. A problem in fluoroscopy is that it requires a large dose of X rays, which may be hazardous to both the patient and the operator. By the use of image intensifiers it is possible to reduce this dosage. Such a procedure has almost completely replaced the standard fluoroscope.

Bibliography: Hiss, Stephen S., *Understanding Radiography*, 2d ed. (1983); Hynes, D. M., and Edmonds, Ernest, *Multiformat Videofluoroscopy* (1990).

See also: RADIOLOGY.

flute

The flute is a woodwind instrument that dates from ancient times. Sound is produced from a flute by blowing onto a

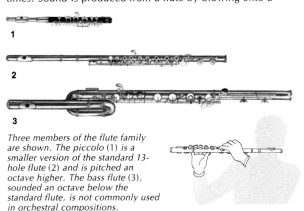

Three members of the flute family are shown. The piccolo (1) is a smaller version of the standard 13-hole flute (2) and is pitched an octave higher. The bass flute (3), sounded an octave below the standard flute, is not commonly used in orchestral compositions.

sharp edge, causing air enclosed in a tube to vibrate. Many types of primitive flutes are known throughout the world. In tropical regions and in the Orient, they are commonly made from bamboo tubes. End-blown flutes may be simple tubes with a sharp edge or notch, or they may have an inserted block, as in RECORDERS and whistles. The widespread side-blown or transverse flute is now common in the West. The term *flute* also refers to certain ORGAN pipes.

Evidence of the side-blown flute in Europe is sporadic until the later Middle Ages, when it was cultivated chiefly by the minnesingers in Germany. Shrill, narrow-bored flutes (FIFES) became common as military instruments, and one-handed, narrow-bored pipes played together with small drums (see PIPE AND TABOR) accompanied dancing in southern France and are still used in northern Spain. By 1500 both recorders and key-less, six-holed, cylindrical transverse flutes were familiar in-struments—the tenor transverse flute, pitched in D, was the ancestor of the modern instrument. About 1670 the transverse flute, like the other basic woodwinds, underwent a transfor-mation. The instrument emerged in three sections—the cylin-drical head joint, the middle joint, and the foot joint with in-verse conical bore—and had six finger holes plus one closed key for D sharp in the foot section. It was usually constructed of boxwood, the joints and ends strengthened by decorative ivory rings. The instrument's lovely, mellow tone was capable of sensitive nuances and inspired a large solo literature, in-cluding more than 500 compositions by Johann Quantz and the concertos and chamber music of Wolfgang Amadeus Mo-zart. Nevertheless, chromatic notes (sharped and flatted tones) were difficult to play in tune in tonalities other than D Major and those closely related. With the addition of more keys late in the century, however, the flute of the baroque and classical eras reached its peak.

Theobald Böhm experimented with the flute from 1832 to 1847, desiring to give it a bigger tone. He finally produced a parabolic (bowl-shaped) head joint attached to a cylindrical body with open-standing keys and finger pads to cover large finger holes. Since then, other minor improvements have been made. The modern flute has a range from middle B^b upward for about three octaves. The basic instrument (without B^b key) is approximately 66 cm (26 in) long. In Europe flutes are often constructed of wood; silver is commonly used in the United States.

Other orchestral flutes are the PICCOLO, a brilliant instrument pitched an octave higher than the standard flute, and the alto flute, pitched a fourth lower than the standard instrument. The rare bass flute, pitched an octave below the standard instru-ment, is not a regular member of the orchestra.

ROBERT A. WARNER

Bibliography: Baines, Anthony, *Woodwind Instruments and Their His-tory*, rev. ed. (1963); Bate, Philip, *The Flute* (1969); Chapman, F. B., *Flute Technique*, 4th ed. (1973); Toff, Nancy, *The Development of the Modern Flute* (1979; repr. 1986).

flux   [fluhks]

Flux is a material used in metal refining to remove undesirable substances, such as sand, ash, or dirt. The flux combines with the waste materials and forms a liquid mass, or slag, which can be drawn off from the surface of the molten metal. Fluxes also aid in the fusion of ore metals being processed, and may be used as protective coverings for certain molten metal baths. They are used, as well, in BRAZING, cutting, soldering, and WELDING to prevent the formation of oxides and other un-desirable substances or to dissolve them and facilitate their re-moval. Selection of a flux is primarily a chemical problem re-quiring knowledge of the properties of all the materials in-volved in a given process.

MERLE C. NUTT

See also: METALLURGY.

fly

Fly is the common name for insects of the order Diptera, or true flies, which includes the small HOUSEFLY, FRUIT FLY, GNAT, MOSQUITO, MIDGE, BLOWFLY, and BOTFLY, and the nearly 2.5-cm-long (1-in) crane fly, DEERFLY and HORSEFLY. Many flies are ei-

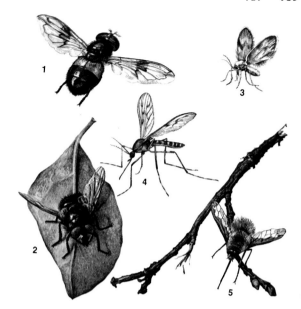

Dipterans, or true flies, belong to the fourth largest order of insects. They possess one pair of functional wings and one pair of modified, knoblike wings that maintain equilibrium during flight. Common flies include the hover fly (1), family Syrphidae; the blowfly (2), family Calliphoridae; the moth fly (3), family Psychodidae; the mosquito (4), family Culicidae; and the bee fly (5), family Bombylidae.

ther harmful as carriers of disease or nuisances because they are voracious biters or bloodsuckers. Some, such as the fruit fly, have been used extensively for laboratory studies of genet-ics, because they breed rapidly and their large chromosomes are easily seen under the microscope.

The term *fly* is applied to such non-Diptera as the butterfly, dragonfly, mayfly, and stone fly. Unlike these and other in-sects, true flies have a single pair of membranous forewings, with knob-shaped vestigial wings instead of hind wings. The vestigial wings are called halteres and are used as balancing organs.

The mouthparts are specialized for lapping or sucking in some flies and for piercing and sucking in others. Almost all species have antennae and large compound eyes. A network of thick veins strengthens the wings; the pattern of these vena-tions is used for identification and classification. One theory is that the veins evolved from tracheae, a system of tubes common in insects that supplies oxygen to the tissues.

All flies develop through metamorphosis in four stages: egg, larva, pupa, and adult. The larvae, commonly called maggots, lack eyes, legs, wings, antennae, and distinct mouthparts and body regions. To accomplish its transformation to the adult, larval muscle and other tissues are broken down into a creamy fluid and resynthesized into the adult structures. The pupa is defenseless but generally escapes predators because it is dark brown and buried in soil or heaps of waste.

FLIES AND DISEASE

Some of the most serious diseases among humans—MALARIA, YELLOW FEVER, DENGUE FEVER, FILARIASIS, and viral ENCEPHALITIS—are transmitted by mosquitoes. Many hundreds of thousands of people living along Africa's rivers are permanently blinded by small roundworms introduced by the bite of the blackfly.

In much of the world today, poor sanitation, domestic flies, and intestinal diseases are constant and related problems. In Latin America, Africa, and India, blowflies and houseflies are especially abundant; they shuttle between feces and human food, carrying the agents of CHOLERA, diarrheal disease, DYSEN-TERY, and gastroenteritis. Some species prefer the eye and transfer the microbes of pinkeye, CONJUNCTIVITIS, and TRACHO-MA from diseased to healthy eyes; others spread YAWS, a skin disease, when they feed on cuts and sores.

Some adult flies are harmless but deposit their eggs in wounds or body openings of livestock and humans. The larval

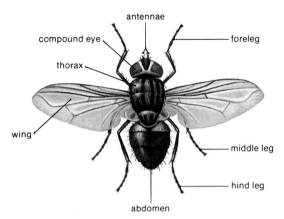

Most adult flies are anatomically similar to the housefly, Musca domestica. *Ranging from 1 mm (0.04 in) to more than 5.5 cm (2 in) in size, they usually have soft bodies, suctorial mouths, compound eyes, antennae, and a network of veins strengthening the wings.*

flies, or maggots, consume living tissue, and the wound enlarges as more females are attracted to the site for oviposition. Such maggot infestations are called MYIASIS. Agricultural crops are also attacked. Maggots of the Hessian fly are a major pest of wheat; other species attack other crops.

BENEFICIAL ROLES
The beneficial activities of flies include pollination, the reduction and recycling of biological wastes, and the contribution of the fruit fly, *Drosophila*, to genetics studies. In the 1930s, before the advent of antibiotics and sulfa drugs, doctors cured stubborn cases of bone infection by using maggots of certain species of bluebottle fly, *Lucilia*, that had been grown under sterile laboratory conditions. The maggots consumed dead and decaying tissue, suppressing harmful bacteria with their secretions and encouraging the growth of healthy tissue. This practice resulted from studies following up on the accidental discovery, during the U.S. Civil War, that wounded soldiers infested with such maggots tended to exhibit better rates of recovery than did uninfested soldiers.

COMMON TYPES AND LIFE CYCLE
The primitive Nematocera, with long antennae, include crane flies, mosquitoes, and midges. The Brachycera have short antennae and include the more evolved horseflies and blackflies. Both groups emerge as adults through straight breaks in the puparial case. The most advanced types, such as common domestic flies, emerge from an opening at the end of the puparial case with crumpled wings, a soft body, and spindly legs. The wings and abdomen soon expand through blood pressure, and within an hour or two the exoskeleton has hardened and darkened and the insect is ready to fly.

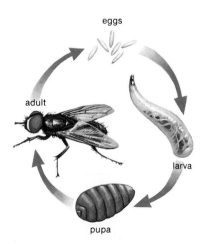

The life cycle of a housefly is typical of all true flies and consists of four stages: egg, larva, pupa, and adult. An adult female lays 100 to 160 eggs at a time, usually in decaying organic matter. Each egg, 1 mm (0.04 in) long, hatches into a larva in 12 to 24 hours. After several days the larva changes into a pupa, which is encased in a tough shell. In 3 to 5 days a full-sized adult fly emerges. During warm weather, it will live about 1 month.

CONTROL OF FLIES
When the insecticide DDT was introduced after 1945, it was hailed as a panacea, until flies became resistant to it and its destructive environmental effects were discovered and carcinogenic effects suspected. The development of other insecticides followed, as flies developed resistance to one after another. Today, it is recognized that chemical insecticides alone cannot do the job. Good sanitation is the best method of fly control. Effective disposal of garbage, manure, and other fly-breeding materials will reduce flies to below annoyance levels, but this is not always feasible in poor countries.

Other control methods are being studied. There has been limited success in reducing certain fly populations, such as the Mediterranean fruit flies in California, by the continual release of irradiated sterile males, which mate with wild females who then produce no offspring. In preliminary studies, scientists have also used GENETIC ENGINEERING techniques to transform some flies, thus altering the inherited traits that make them capable of spreading disease.   BERNARD GREENBERG

Bibliography: Ashburner, M., et al., *The Genetics and Biology of Drosophilia* (1984); Kim, K. C., and Merritt, R. W., eds., *Black Flies* (1988); Oldroyd, H., *The Natural History of Flies* (1964); Shorrocks, B., *Drosophila* (1980); West, L. S., *The Housefly* (1951).

flycatcher (bird)

Flycatcher is the common name for insectivorous songbirds of the Old World family Muscicapidiae and the New World family Tyrannidae. The tyrannids are mainly tropical, but about 30 species occur regularly in North America north of Mexico, and several species have reached Alaska. Most of them return to tropical or subtropical regions for the winter. Among the

Flycatchers snap up insects in midflight and harass larger birds. (Bottom) The great crested flycatcher, Mysiarchus crinitus, *decorates its nest with snake skins, bits of cellophane, and other unusual material. (Center) The scissor-tailed flycatcher,* Muscivora forficata, *common to Texas, used its long tail feathers to maneuver during aerial acrobatics. (Top) The willow flycatcher,* Empidonax trailli, *is often seen along wooded lake shores in North America.*

best-known North American flycatchers are the kingbirds, phoebes, and wood pewees.

Flycatchers feed by darting after insects from their perches. North American forms are characterized by wide, flat bills equipped at the base with bristles for snaring insects. Some flycatchers, especially those in the tropics, build elaborate nests. The nests may be long and sleevelike or large and bulky. North American flycatchers usually lay from 4 to 6 eggs, sometimes more; tropical species may lay only 2. The eggs are white and usually marked with brownish blotches. Incubation periods vary from 13 to 16 or more days in different species.

GEORGE J. WALLACE

Bibliography: Bent, Arthur, C., *Life Histories of North American Flycatchers, Larks, Swallows, and Their Allies* (1942).

flycatcher (plant): see CARNIVOROUS PLANTS.

flying buttress: see BUTTRESS.

Flying Dutchman, The

The *Flying Dutchman* is a three-act opera composed by Richard WAGNER and first produced at the Dresden Opera House in 1843. Based on a legend Wagner found in Heinrich HEINE's *Memoirs of Herr von Schnabelwopski* (1833), the opera is the story of a man doomed to wander the seas eternally in his ship *The Flying Dutchman* until he is redeemed by a woman's love. Wagner conceived the idea for the opera in 1839 after being nearly shipwrecked in a North Sea storm.

flying fish

A typical flying fish, Cypselurus opisthopus *uses its enlarged pectoral fins to produce its gliding flight above the ocean's surface. It is found throughout the open waters of the Pacific.*

Flying fish glide through the air rather than fly. To become airborne, the fish swims at high speed (32 km/h; 20 mph) just beneath the surface. It rises on its tail fin and gains speed by vigorous sculling (50 beats each second). Taking off at 56 km/h (35 mph), it produces lift by stretching its enlarged fins. Glides of 200 m (660 ft) are recorded.

Flying fish are surface-dwelling fishes of the open oceans that belong to the family Exocoetidae. They are easily recognized by their enlarged pectoral fins and the elongation of the lower portion of their tail fin and by their characteristic leaps and glides over the ocean surface. One species, the Atlantic flying fish, *Cypselurus heterurus*, is found in warm waters on both sides of the Atlantic, and in the West Atlantic it is common in the Gulf Stream. It reaches 38 cm (15 in) in length. Flying fish leap into the air, hold their fins rigidly outspread, and glide like flying squirrels.

ALFRED PERLMUTTER

flying gurnard

The flying gurnards are tropical marine fish that belong to the family Dactylopteridae and are said to fly short distances out of the water. Their structure and habits suggest, however, that they are incapable of such flight. They do have remarkably large, winglike pectoral fins but are heavy bodied and walk over the bottom on pectoral spines. These fish average about 30 cm (12 in) in length and have blunt heads and elongated spines.

C. P. IDYLL

flying lemur: see COLUGO.

flying saucer: see UNIDENTIFIED FLYING OBJECT.

flying squirrel

A flying squirrel is a rodent that glides, rather than flies, by means of a thin, furry skin, or membrane, that extends out from the sides of the body and connects the front and hind legs. In North America, Europe, and Asia, these rodents are members of the squirrel family, Sciuridae. They include 35 species and constitute the squirrel subfamily Petauristinae. In Africa, another rodent family, the Anomaluridae, with 12 species, contains squirrellike animals with gliding membranes. These are known as African scaly-tailed flying squirrels. Glides of 450 m (1,500 ft) by the giant flying squirrel *Petaurista* have been recorded.

EVERETT SENTMAN

Flying Tigers: see P-40.

Flynn, Elizabeth Gurley

Elizabeth Gurley Flynn, b. Concord, N.H., Aug. 7, 1890, d. Sept. 5, 1964, was the first woman to lead the U.S. Communist party. She became a labor organizer for the Industrial Workers of the World in 1906 and led important textile strikes in Lawrence, Mass. (1912), and Patterson, N.J. (1913). In 1920, Flynn helped found the American Civil Liberties Union, and during the 1920s she worked on behalf of Sacco and Vanzetti. Flynn joined the Communist party in 1937 and was a member of its national committe during World War II. Arrested (1951) for violating the Smith Act, she was imprisoned from January 1955 to May 1957. She was chairman of the national committee of the Communist party from 1961 until her death.

Bibliography: Flynn, Elizabeth Gurley, *The Rebel Girl: An Autobiography*, rev. ed. (1973); Lamont, Corliss, ed., *Trial of Elizabeth Gurley Flynn by the American Civil Liberties Union* (1968).

Flynn, Errol

Errol Flynn, the stage name of Leslie Thomas Flynn, b. Hobart, Tasmania, June 20, 1909, d. Oct. 14, 1959, was a film star known principally for his roles as a swashbuckling romantic hero. His adventure films include *Captain Blood* (1935) and *The Sea Hawk* (1940). In *Too Much, Too Soon* (1958), he played his friend John Barrymore.

LESLIE HALLIWELL

Bibliography: Flynn, Errol, *My Wicked, Wicked Ways* (1959; repr. 1983); Valenti, P., *Errol Flynn* (1984).

flywheel

A flywheel is a heavy wheel that is rigidly attached to a shaft. Because of its rotary inertia, the flywheel resists changes in the speed of rotation of the shaft; it also can be used to store and deliver mechanical energy on demand.

In a piston engine (see INTERNAL-COMBUSTION ENGINE), a flywheel is used to moderate fluctuations in the speed of rotation of the crankshaft; these fluctuations result from the fact that the impulses transmitted from the pistons to the crankshaft through the connecting rods are intermittent. On machines for punching or forming sheet metal, the large forces that are periodically required are delivered by a flywheel, whose kinetic (rotary) energy is built up by a comparatively low-powered motor while the machine is idling.

Current concern for dwindling sources of energy has stimulated renewed interest in applications of flywheels. A promising recent application is a regenerative braking system in automobiles. When a car is braked by an ordinary braking system, its kinetic energy (energy of motion) must be dissipated as heat in the BRAKES. To accelerate the car again, the engine must supply additional energy. In regenerative braking, most of the energy is stored in a flywheel, instead of being dissipated as heat in the brakes. This flywheel energy is then used to assist the engine in accelerating the car. Flywheels for energy-storage systems must be capable of high speeds because the energy stored increases as the square of the rotational speed. Hence, there is a continuing search for improved materials for such applications.   ALEXANDER COWIE

FM: see FREQUENCY MODULATION.

FM radio

FM radio broadcasting relies on the FREQUENCY MODULATION transmission system developed in 1933 by Edwin Howard ARMSTRONG and is a principal alternative to AM radio broadcasting. FM stations were originally developed in the late 1940s and the 1950s to counter the commercial formats of AM stations, which depended heavily upon saturation advertising and repetitive "playlists" of popular songs. FM catered to a more diversified audience and focused on in-depth news analysis and classical or semiclassical music. Since the 1960s, however—with the availability of inexpensive AM-FM radios, the decline of network radio, and the increase in the number of local FM stations—the differences in programming between AM and FM stations have become less pronounced.

Because FM radio is transmitted in a very high frequency range (88–108 MHz in the United States), the transmission area is limited. The fidelity of the sound is, however, superior to that of the AM signal. Television sound is commonly transmitted on FM bands, and the broadcasting industry has recently introduced radio and TV simulcasts, in which the sound portion of a TV progam is broadcast simultaneously on FM radio, allowing the listener to take advantage of STEREOPHONIC SOUND reproduction.   DAVE BITTAN

Bibliography: Chowning, J., and Bristoe, D., *FM Theory and Applications* (1987); Elving, Bruce, *FM Atlas and Station Directory*, 12th ed. (1989); Kiver, Milton S., *F–M Simplified* (1960).

See also: AMPLITUDE MODULATION; RADIO AND TELEVISION BROADCASTING; TELEVISION TRANSMISSION.

Fo, Dario   [foh, dah´-ree-oh]

Dario Fo, b. Mar. 24, 1926, is an Italian dramatist whose political satires recall the improvisations of COMMEDIA DELL'ARTE. His many plays have been produced successfully in more than 30 countries—although his fame is greatest in Italy, where the objects of his satire often reside. One of his most popular plays is *Mistero Buffo* (1969), a set of black-humor sketches for a single actor. *Accidental Death of an Anarchist* (1970; Eng. trans., 1980), an absurdist satire based on the 1969 murder of an Italian leftist, played to full houses in Rome for over four years. Fo and his wife, the actress Franca Rame, lead the theater cooperative La Comune.

FOB

FOB, an abbreviation for "free on board," is a commercial term indicating that the seller or exporter of a piece of goods is responsible for the cost of its shipment from a specified point to its point of destination.

focal point

In OPTICS, the focal point of a LENS is the point of convergence of incoming parallel light rays. If the lens is of the type that diverges light, its focal point is the apparent point of origin of the diverging rays. By symmetry, every lens has two focal points, one on each side of the lens and at the same distance from the center of the lens (the focal length). Because of the principle of the reversibility of light rays, the diverging light from a point source placed at the focal point of a converging lens will emerge as a parallel beam. This is known as collimating the light.

Foch, Ferdinand   [fawsh]

Marshal of France Ferdinand Foch assumed supreme command of the Allied forces on the western front in April 1918. After halting the German advance at the Marne in July, Foch launched the Allied counteroffensive that ended World War I in November.

Ferdinand Foch, b. Oct. 2, 1851, d. Mar. 20, 1929, was commander in chief of the Allied armies in France in the final stages of WORLD WAR I and helped to bring about the Allied victory. A fervent Roman Catholic with Jesuit training, he joined the army in 1871 and studied at the École Supérieure de Guerre (war college), where he later taught tactics. His lectures were published in two works, *The Principles of War* (Eng. trans., 1918) and *De la conduite de la guerre* ("On the Conduct of War," 1904). From 1908 to 1911 he was the school's director.

In 1914, at the outbreak of World War I, Foch commanded the French Ninth Army in the first Battle of the MARNE. He also commanded an army group in the Battle of the SOMME (1916) but was then forced into retirement until he became chief of the French general staff in 1917. In April 1918, Foch was given unified command of all of the Allied troops in France. Halting the German advance in the Second Battle of the Marne (July 1918), Foch mounted the counteroffensive that turned the tide of the war. He was made a marshal, and three months later he accepted the German surrender (November 1918).

P. M. EWY

Bibliography: King, Jere C., *Foch Versus Clemenceau: France and German Dismemberment* (1960); Liddell Hart, B. H., *Foch: The Man of Orléans* (1932; repr. 1980); Marshall-Cornwall, James, *Foch as Military Commander* (1976).

Focillon, Henri   [faw-see-ohn´]

Henri Focillon, b. Sept. 7, 1881, d. Mar. 3, 1943, was a French art historian who taught at the University of Lyon and the University of Paris, where he was director of the Institute of Art and Archaeology. In 1938 he came to the United States and taught at Yale University until his death. His publications range widely over the fields of Western and Eastern art, though his main contributions were in medieval art and aesthetics. He is especially remembered for his work with problems of morphology, the study of the meaning and character of form in works of visual art.

Of Focillon's works translated into English, the most popular have been *The Art of the West in the Middle Ages* (1963), *The Life of Forms in Art* (1942; repr. 1989), and *The Year 1000* (1969).   JACQUELINE V. FALKENHEIM

fodder

Fodder is the dried parts of plants used for feeding livestock. Corn fodder includes the dried stem, leaves, and ears of the corn plant, and sorghum fodder includes the dried stem, leaves, and grain head of the sorghum plant. If the corn ear or sorghum head is removed, the remaining dried stem and leaves are referred to as stover. The nutritive value of these materials varies, depending on the proportion of stem, leaves, and grain included. In many parts of the world a more general definition of fodder includes any feed or roughage material fed to domestic animals, especially cattle, horses, and sheep. In the United States, during the early part of the 20th century, when there was less mechanical harvesting, feed was frequently stored and handled as fodder. As modern methods of harvesting and silage making developed, the use of fodder declined, and today it is seldom seen.　CONNELL JEAN BROWN

See also: SILO.

foehn　[furn]

A foehn is a warm, dry katabatic WIND that blows down leeward mountain slopes. When deep layers of air ascend mountain slopes, the air cools, and its water vapor condenses to form rain or snow. Because the air that subsequently descends the lee sides is drier, little evaporation takes place to absorb the heat, and the air warms quickly as it travels downslope. The leeward wind is thus warmer and drier than the windward, and the windward slopes receive much more precipitation than the leeward. The foehn wall, a cloud bank marking the upper limit of precipitation, hangs over mountain ridges, often obscuring them.

See also: CHINOOK; MOUNTAIN AND VALLEY WINDS.

fog

Fog consists of water drops formed in air near the Earth's surface as the air cools to its dew point. When, during the evening, the relative humidity is high, the wind is light, and the night is long, the cooling of air by radiation to the dew point at first produces DEW. Later in the evening, however, water begins to condense as fog. Initially, fog tends to be patchy and shallow. If a light breeze stirs the air, the fog may attain a depth of up to 100 m (300 ft). Ice fog may also occur.

Over flat country, fog becomes a solid deck. Radiation fog is most prevalent in autumn and early winter, when nights are longer but the air is still moist from summer. A fog deck will break during morning, but on overcast days and during winters at high latitude, it may break up about noon; sometimes, in mountain valleys and Arctic areas, it does not dissolve for weeks. As stagnant, foggy air is filled with particulate material, it gives rise to the disagreeable condition known as SMOG (smoke plus fog).

During the winter and particularly over snow, warm, moist tropical air driven, or advected, by wind to high latitudes is cooled from below. This can produce a fog deck, or advection fog, that is several kilometers thick. When such fog forms over the sea, it is called tropical air fog. Prevalent in areas where persistent summer winds blow for days and weeks at a time, this type of fog carries tropical air toward the cooler water that is always present in high latitudes.

Fog, when in the form of a cloud on the ground, develops when air from low plains moves gradually upward toward mountains and lower pressures. The rising air will often cool sufficiently from expansion to cause the temperature of the air to fall to the point at which upslope fog forms. Arctic sea smoke, often called fog, is caused by the formation of water vapor when cold, dry air passes over oceans and lakes during the winter. Because air can only hold fairly specific percentages of water at given temperatures, the water that is evaporated soon recondenses, thus giving the appearance of smoke plumes.　HERBERT RIEHL

Bibliography: Barry, R. G., and Chorley, R. J., *Atmosphere, Weather, and Climate,* 5th ed. (1988); Cole, Franklyn W., *Introduction to Meteorology,* 3d ed. (1980).

Fogazzaro, Antonio　[foh-gaht-tsahr'-oh]

Antonio Fogazzaro, b. Mar. 25, 1842, d. Mar. 7, 1911, was an Italian novelist and poet who portrayed characters suffering interior conflicts between reason and religion, passion and duty. His masterpiece, *Piccolo mondo antico* (1895; trans. as *The Patriot,* 1906), was highly successful. The Roman Catholic church condemned most of his later novels, including *The Saint* (1906; Eng. trans., 1906) and *Leila* (1910) because it con-

sidered these works too critical of religion and tainted by modernism.　LOUIS KIBLER

Bibliography: Gallarati-Scotti, Tommaso, *Life of Antonio Fogazzaro* (1922; repr. 1970).

Foggia　[foh'-jah]

Foggia (1988 est. pop., 159,192), a city in southeastern Italy, is located about 130 km (80 mi) northeast of Naples. Situated in the center of the fertile Apulian plain, where sheep and grains are raised, Foggia has been a major wheat market since ancient times and is now the commercial, industrial, and transportation center of the plain.

Foggia was originally settled by Greeks. In the 13th century it became part of the kingdom of Naples, which controlled it until 1860, when Foggia became part of unified Italy. The city suffered heavy Allied bombing during World War II.

Foix　[fwah]

Foix (1982 pop., 9,212), a town in southwestern France, is located at the junction of the Arget and Ariège rivers in the foothills of the Pyrenees. It is a commercial center for the surrounding agricultural region. Textile manufacturing is the principal industry. Foix's 12th-century castle, which overlooks the city, is the major tourist attraction. From the 11th to the 13th century, Foix was the capital of the powerful counts of Foix. It resisted attack during the crusade against the ALBIGENSES but was captured by King Philip III in 1272.

Fokine, Mikhail　[foh-keen']

Mikhail Fokine, b. Saint Petersburg, Russia, Apr. 25 (N.S.), 1880, d. Aug. 22, 1942, is best known for his ballets *Les Sylphides, Firebird,* and *Petrouchka* and ranks as one of the most important and influential choreographers of the 20th century. Fokine studied at the Imperial Ballet School and became a notable soloist in the Maryinsky Ballet (now Kirov). He left the Maryinsky company in 1909 to become chief choreographer for Serge DIAGHILEV's troop of Russian dancers, which was to emerge as the BALLETS RUSSES and change the course of Western ballet history.

From his early days as a student, Fokine had rejected the artificiality of conventional ballets. In 1904 he had conveyed to the authorities of the Maryinsky troupe his desire for greater naturalism of movement and more integration of story, music, choreography, and scenic design. It was in these areas that he was later to serve Diaghilev's similar artistic vision, creating a total of 60 ballets in his lifetime. *Firebird* (1910) and *Petrouchka* (1911), both with scores by Igor Stravinsky, are characteristic of Fokine's innovative work. Both gave him ample scope to portray the artistic essence of the characters in the dancing; and both—departing from the traditional form of a balletic frame used to set off the ballerina in virtuoso technical displays—provided rich parts for the male dancer, who had been relegated to a minor role by the end of the 19th century. Fokine worked with most of the great companies in the first half of the 20th century. He died in New York City.

PETER ROSENWALD

Bibliography: Fokine, Mikhail, *Memoirs of Ballet Master* (1961); Malko, Nicolai, *A Certain Art* (1966).

Fokker, Anthony Hermann Gerard　[fah'-kur]

Anthony Hermann Gerard Fokker, b. Apr. 6, 1890, d. Dec. 23, 1939, was an aircraft designer and manufacturer. He produced more than 40 types of airplanes for the German armed forces during World War I and devised the synchronizing gear system that enabled the pilot to fire a machine gun through the propeller without hitting the blades. After the war, Fokker—who had been born in Java of Dutch parents—became a naturalized citizen of the United States and devoted himself to developing commercial aircraft. He wrote an autobiography, *The Flying Dutchman* (1931).

Bibliography: Hegener, Henri, *Fokker, the Man and the Aircraft,* ed. by B. Robertson (1961).

Fokker D-VII   [fahk'-ur]

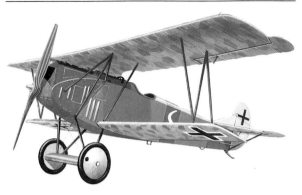

The Fokker D-VII, Germany's best biplane fighter during World War I, differed from most other fighter planes of the period because it had a light, strong fuselage of steel tubing instead of the usual wood fuselage. It had a top speed of 188 km/h (117 mph).

Among the numerous German single-seat fighters of World War I, the Fokker D-VII, designed by Reinhold Platz, became preeminent and was ordered into quantity production immediately after winning a competition in January 1918. A conventional, single-engine biplane with an 8.93 m (29 ft 3.5 in) wingspan, the D-VII was powered by either the 160-hp Mercedes D-III or the 185-hp B.M.W. III 6-cylinder, water-cooled engine. Armament consisted of a pair of synchronized Spandau machine guns mounted on the upper fuselage decking within easy reach of the pilot. The airplane had a top speed of 188 km/h (117 mph) and superb flying qualities. After the Armistice, Anthony Fokker, the manufacturer, managed to smuggle about 120 virtually complete D-VIIs into his native Holland, where he produced the fighter for the Dutch and other air forces.   PETER M. H. LEWIS

fold

A fold is any bent or curved domain in one layer or several stacked layers of rock. In a folded geological surface the region of greatest curvature is its hinge; the less deformed adjacent flanks are its limbs. A fold may include any number of stacked parallel layers. The surface formed by joining the hinge lines of all the stacked folded surfaces is called the axial surface, hinge surface, or axial plane. It may be curved.

Descriptively, folds are classified as SYNCLINES AND ANTI-CLINES. Folds are upright when the axial plane is near vertical, inclined when it dips between 10° and 80°, and recumbent when it averages a dip lower than 10°. In isoclinal folds, the two limbs are parallel to each other. Folds become overturned when the stratigraphic succession in one limb is reversed. In symmetrical folds (not necessarily upright) the axial plane is a plane of symmetry. Folds are also classified according to the mutual relationship of successive folded surfaces. They are parallel when successive folded surfaces remain mutually parallel to each other and similar when successive folded surfaces are ideally congruent. Most naturally occurring folds are, to various degrees, combinations of these two

ideal types. Folds may serve as structural controls or as traps for mineral and fuel deposits.

Folding reflects the ductile behavior of rocks. A thin, flat layer or slab that is stressed can become curved in two basic modes. In bending, compression is at right angles to the slab; in buckling, it is parallel to the slab. Most geological folds are initiated by buckling through two mechanisms. In flexural-slip folding, the layers may slip past each other in much the same way that the pages of a book slip past one another when several are bent together. In passive folding, the layer boundaries may be completely passive, little more than patterns in a homogeneous packet of rock. Flexural-slip folding normally results in parallel folds, whereas passive folding tends to form similar folds. In most naturally occurring examples the two mechanisms act in combination to varying degrees. Ideally, passive folding may involve flow of rock across parallel bedding planes, such that some parts of the folded layers thin out and others thicken. The two limbs of the fold may not approach each other, and lateral shortening may not be necessary; folding is then entirely in simple shear. In most real cases, however, some lateral shortening occurs, along with a pure shear component of deformation. The contrast in ductil-

The terminology used to describe the various features of a fold include a trough, or lowest surface (1); a hinge, or region of greatest curvature (2); a crest, or highest surface (3); limbs, or less-deformed adjacent flanks (4); an anticline, or upward archlike fold (5); a syncline, or inverted anticline (6); a crest plane (7), an axial, or hinge, plane (8), and a trough plane (9).

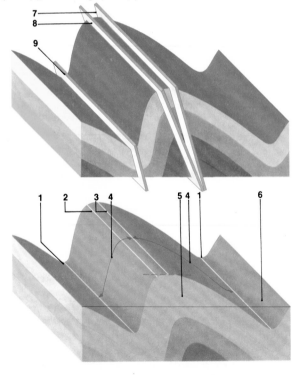

In many places layered rocks, such as sedimentary strata, have been bent or buckled into more or less regular wavelike folds as a result of compressional forces. In a fold, the degree of compression determines the type of folding, or wrinkling, produced in the Earth's crust. When compression begins, a simple, symmetrical anticline, or arched-up fold (A), will probably form. As compression continues, the folding may become asymmetric in shape, developing into an inclined anticline (B) and then into a recumbent fold (C), in which the anticline lies over a syncline, or downfold. If the compressional forces are great, the rocks may fracture and move over the syncline to form an overthrust fold (D). A nappe (E) forms when the movement of the overlying mass of rock continues for more than 1 km (0.6 mi).

A   B   C   D   E

ity between adjacent beds is an important parameter in folding. In diapir folds, active upward movement of cores of anticlines may result in piercing of the outer layers. Salt domes are special cases of diapir folds.

Theoretically, lateral shortening of strata to produce folds can be accomplished in several ways. The sequence of strata may buckle between more rigid basement blocks; they may become folded as they glide under the direct or indirect influence of gravity; or deep-seated ductile rocks may undergo strain in response to stresses at depth. These stresses are not necessarily the result of crustal shortening; they are possibly caused by the emplacement of igneous rocks. In the great majority of cases, folding is related to deformation in orogenic belts (see MOUNTAIN).
JOHN G. DENNIS

Bibliography: Mitra, S., and Fisher, G. W., eds., *Structural Geology of Fold and Thrust Belts* (1992); Ramsay, John G., and Huber, Martin, *Techniques of Modern Structural Geology,* 2 vols. (1984–87); Twiss, R. J., and Moores, E. M., *Structural Geology* (1992).

Foley, Thomas S.

Thomas Stephen Foley, b. Spokane, Wash., Mar. 6, 1929, a Democratic congressman from Washington, became Speaker of the House in June 1989 after Jim WRIGHT resigned. First elected to congress in 1964, Foley gained a reputation as a liberal and conciliator. He was chairman of the agriculture committee (1975–81), majority (Democratic) whip (1981–87), and majority leader (1987–88) before becoming speaker.

Folger Shakespeare Library   [fohl'-jur]

The Folger Shakespeare Library, in Washington, D.C., possesses one of the world's largest collections of Shakespeareana and is a major archival source for students of 16th- and 17th-century British history. Based on the Shakespeare collection of Henry Clay Folger and his wife, Emily, whose bequest established the institution, the library now owns over 250,000 volumes and 55,000 manuscripts. Housed in a building completed in 1932, it is administered by the trustees of Amherst College.
COLIN STEELE

foliation

Foliation is the planar arrangement of minerals or textural features in certain kinds of rock. Primary foliation develops when a rock is formed; secondary, afterward. In metamorphic rocks, foliation is secondary. It forms as minerals under pressure or subjected to movement recrystallize and reorient themselves. In folded rocks, foliation may be parallel to the axial plane of the folds, parallel to the original bedding, or unrelated to preexisting structures. Axial-plane foliation is commonly associated with the movement and elongation of minerals parallel to the lineation on the planes. Bedding foliation develops in distinctly layered rock that is bent to form round folds. Thin layers and their platy minerals slip parallel to the bedding surfaces.

In plutons and dikes the margins of the igneous rock commonly display primary foliation parallel to the margins. This is because platy and prismatic minerals crystallize and align themselves while the magma expands against or moves along its walls. The secondary foliation that develops in slates or slaty rocks is called cleavage.
ANNA HIETANEN

Folies-Bergère   [foh-lee' bair-zhair']

The Folies-Bergère theater, which opened in Paris on May 1, 1869, was the birthplace of the musical revue. It featured comedy acts, partially nude women, and lavishly colorful, spectacular productions. Closed briefly in 1993, the Folies reopened with large ambitions: "to show the limits . . . extravagances . . . and ambiguities of human beings."

folio

In the printer's trade, the term *folio* (from the Latin word for "leaf") denotes a sheet of paper folded once to form two leaves, or four pages. It also refers to editions of Shakespeare's plays, which were published after his death. The First Folio appeared in 1623. Three others followed, in 1632, 1663, and 1685.
J. A. CUDDON

folk art

Folk art is the art of the common people—typically peasants, fishers, and rural artisans—as contrasted with fine art, the art produced by professionally trained artists. The term *folk art* originated during the 19th century and is related to the concepts of FOLKLORE, folk literature, and folk music. As the creation of ordinary people within the framework of a large-scale developed culture, folk art is distinct from so-called PRIMITIVE ART, the art produced by the peoples of preliterate, preurban societies. Folk art differs from commercial decorative art in being a traditional form created in rural areas.

In contrast to the more finished and self-conscious fine arts, folk art is a cruder, more spontaneous expression of the feelings, attitudes, and needs of the lower classes of a society. Most of it is utilitarian in character and is not conceived of as art by those who have made it. Peasant houses, decorated furniture, costumes, pottery, woodwork, metal objects, toys, and painted signs are characteristic examples of folk art. Although some of these objects may be of high artistic quality, revealing the superior skill and inspiration of the individual artisan, by and large folk art is a highly traditional form of art, using clearly defined conventions handed down from generation to generation, often over many centuries.

Whereas some folk artisans are highly skilled and have undergone years of apprenticeship under older masters, most are probably amateurs—in the best sense of the word—who turn out artworks when they are not occupied with the activities that provide their livelihood. Traditionally, wood carving, metalworking, and construction have been the work of men, whereas women have primarily engaged in textile work and often basketry and pottery making, although this kind of specialization varies from culture to culture, depending on the local tradition and the particular social situation. The importance of folk art for a given society and the role it traditionally has played also differ greatly.

It is ironic that the unique beauty and artistic appeal of folk art—characterized everywhere by its simplicity, unpretentiousness, and strength—should have been discovered at the very time when this art form had largely disappeared in most of Europe and North America. Although folk art still exists in

Brightly painted hearts and flowers highlight the ornate surface decoration of this 19th-century Swedish corner cupboard from the province of Skåne. The owner's initials and the year of the piece's construction are prominently displayed on the upper cabinet door. Folk furniture in Sweden, as in most European countries, shows distinct regional variations. (Nordiska Museum, Stockholm.)

Sicilian folk artists cover their donkey carts with colorful painted designs. In this 19th-century example from Palermo, vivid scenes of the legendary rape of the Sabines are portrayed on the side panels. (Lüden Collection, Wyk, West Germany.)

some parts of Eastern Europe, Asia, and Africa, the spread of industrialization is rapidly undermining folk traditions even in these countries, and the time is not far off when this artistic genre will have disappeared altogether. The chief reason for its decline is that the handmade craft productions of the local artisans cannot compete with the cheap, mass-produced, machine-made objects turned out in factories; and as the market for handcrafted goods dwindles, the output declines and ultimately stops altogether. Additionally, as more and more peasants become industrial workers, their ties to the traditional village culture weaken, and they come to value modern machine products more than what they perceive as backward and primitive objects made in rural areas. As folk art declines, however, an awareness of its value and beauty is spreading, and collections of traditional crafts and museums dedicated to their preservation are being formed in all countries to keep this precious heritage alive.

WESTERN TRADITIONS

Europe. A rich and varied folk art existed throughout Europe prior to the Industrial Revolution. Most of the surviving works date from the 18th or 19th century, although some objects may be older and all can be traced to more-ancient traditions, some of which have existed for many centuries.

Among the European folk-art traditions, perhaps the most outstanding from an artistic point of view are those of Scandinavia, Germany, Holland, and Switzerland. In Sweden the wooden peasant houses with their finely carved furnishings are particularly notable, as are the painted or woven wall hangings. Denmark excels in brightly painted peasant furniture displaying ornamental designs of birds and flowers. Much of the folk art of Iceland is distinguished by abstract band-and-scroll patterns that can be traced to the Nordic art of early Germanic times.

Diverse folk-art traditions are found in Germany, where the art of each region is so distinctive that the peasant houses of northern Germany, for example, with their brick construction and steep thatched roofs, are entirely different from those of the Bavarian Alps, with their wood construction, flatter roofs, and colorful painted decorations. In Holland, peasant embroidery and Delft pottery wares are particularly beautiful, but many other types of folk art are also found. Considering its small size and relatively homogeneous population, Switzerland has produced one of the most remarkable European tra-

ditions of folk art in terms of breadth and variety. In addition to gaily decorated houses (including the alpine CHALET), garments, and carved wooden and pottery utensils of all types, Swiss tradition is notable for the fascinating painted masks that are still made in the Lötschenthal region of the Valais canton.

In southern Europe, Italy, Spain, and Portugal are the countries best known for their folk arts, some of which continue to flourish. Examples of local art still made by common people for their own use include the colorful Sicilian donkey carts along with small-scale versions made as toys. The brightly painted pottery of Spain and Portugal is still produced in various places, notably Toledo and Valencia. The colorful motifs used to decorate these wares are quite varied, some of them being purely ornamental floral designs, others religious in character, and still others reflecting the Islamic heritage from the centuries of Moorish rule over the Iberian peninsula. These objects are only a small part of the multifarious folk-art traditions of these countries.

France, too, possesses a rich and varied tradition of folk objects of all types. The peasant furniture is outstanding, especially that of the Alsace region. Also well known is the lacework of Brittany and the pottery of Normandy; each region, however, has its own specialty, and interesting examples of peasant crafts may be found in all the provinces. By contrast, little survives of the various lively folk traditions that existed during the 18th and early 19th centuries in Britain, perhaps because the Industrial Revolution occurred earliest there. Particularly outstanding in England were the sturdy salt-glaze wares and decorated pottery, for which Staffordshire was famous.

Much of the folk art of Eastern Europe reflects on the one hand the influence of ancient Byzantine artistic tradition and on the other the long years of Turkish rule under the Ottomans. Most remarkable, especially in the Slavic countries, are the textiles, particularly the embroidered peasant blouses, which are among the loveliest in Europe. Also distinctively Slavic are the flat-woven rugs and tapestries known as kilims, which are often based on Turkish prototypes, reflecting the Islamic artistic tradition. Similar decorative motifs may also be seen in the folk pottery of Hungary, Czechoslovakia, and Poland. Because Eastern Europe was industrialized later than other parts of the continent, the folk-art tradition lasted longer, extending into the 20th century and even to the present in some areas.

North America. The diverse folk-art traditions of North America stem from a variety of cultural traditions imported by the European settlers. The folk arts that developed in New

Eastern Europe is noted for its folk costumes. This finely embroidered sheepskin vest was crafted in Transylvania (in present-day Romania) in the 1880s. Such garments were worn by both men and women. (Lüden Collection, Wyk, West Germany.)

England and Pennsylvania are particularly notable, with the popular art of Massachusetts, Rhode Island, and Connecticut derived from English sources and the so-called PENNSYLVANIA DUTCH art based on German models.

New England is outstanding for its simple wooden farmhouses, its beautifully designed furniture, and its embroidered samplers. The folk artists of rural Pennsylvania are well known for colorful chests and painted ceramics as well as fraktur documents and charming drawings. Especially renowned are the boldly patterned Amish quilts, considered one of the finest and most distinctively American folk creations in the United States. Other characteristic productions of northeastern American artisans are the furniture of the Shakers, with its severe yet beautiful lines, the stone houses of the Huguenot settlers in the Hudson valley, and the salt-glaze ceramic vessels made in New York and New Jersey. Beautiful pottery was also produced in the mountain states of the upper South, notably in Virginia, Tennessee, and Kentucky.

An early-20th-century pieced quilt, designed in a traditional pattern known as "Sunshine and Shadow" or "Grandmother's Dream," exemplifies the bold geometric patterning and vivid hues found in many Amish quilts. (Metropolitan Museum of Art, New York City.)

Very different is the folk art of the Southwest, where Mexican influences are clearly evident and in some instances elements from the artistic heritage of the native Indian culture are incorporated. Outstanding among the objects reflecting Spanish influence are the 19th-century *santos*—small carved and painted figures representing Christ, Mary, and various Roman Catholic saints—intended to adorn niches in the walls of churches and to be carried in religious processions. Today these highly spiritualized images are considered masterpieces of popular religious carving.

Folk paintings and folk sculptures, often referred to by the terms *naive art* or, especially in describing paintings, *primitivist art*, form another major category of American folk art. Unlike the artisans who have produced utilitarian objects, a number of the folk artists who have made these works are known by name, and some of them have achieved considerable fame despite the fact that they usually have been simple, rural folk with only limited training. Such names as Edward HICKS and Ammi Phillips from the 19th century and Grandma MOSES and Horace PIPPIN from the 20th century are well known today, and their paintings are much admired; however, many of the most charming creations have been the work of anonymous artisans. The painters known as LIMNERS specialized in portraits of local people. Others painted

Girl in a Garden (c.1830), by an anonymous American artist, illustrates the two-dimensional, exaggerated representations often characteristic of portraits by limners. Folk painting depends less on naturalistic portrayal than on pattern and imagery for its lively charm. (Abby Aldrich Rockefeller Folk Art Center, Williamsburg, Va.)

Rearing unicorns flank the text of this Pennsylvania Dutch baptismal certificate, dated 1804. Such fraktur documents, intricately hand-lettered and embellished with animals, figures, and floral motifs, were produced in great numbers during the 18th and 19th centuries. (Abby Aldrich Rockefeller Folk Art Center, Williamsburg, Va.)

Wood carving, an early form of American folk art, found full expression in the creation of ships' figureheads, which often served a symbolic as well as a decorative purpose, representing the name of the ship or its owner. This carved wooden figurehead, Lady with a Rose (c.1800–10), is from Essex, Conn. (Mariners Museum, Newport News, Va.)

the homesteads and landscapes of the region in which they worked.

Among folk sculptures, ship FIGUREHEADS, often depicting enchanting ladies, are the most delightful, but a great variety of carvings of all types were executed. The sailors plying the seas engraved designs on whale teeth, whalebone, and walrus ivory, which are called SCRIMSHAW. Others carved toys and whirligigs, wooden figures of ducks and geese to be used as decoys, and the so-called cigar-store Indians, which were placed outside tobacconists' shops. Of metal sculptures, the weather vanes are often outstanding in both design and imagery. The carved TOMBSTONES of the 17th to early 19th centuries found throughout the eastern United States are not only of great interest historically but often display elaborate graphic design as well.

NON-WESTERN TRADITIONS

The Far East. Enduring folk-art traditions have flourished throughout Asia for centuries. In the Far East, the traditional folk art of China is noted for crudely executed but often charming folk wood-block prints, hand colored in bright hues; intricately formed paper cutouts; and a variety of folk potteries made at provincial kilns.

In Japan, folk art, or *mingei*, historically has played a vital role in the cultural expression of the nation as a whole, and the tradition continues to possess considerable vitality today. Still found all over Japan are austerely beautiful peasant houses with overhanging thatched roofs and simple interiors, testifying to the refined aesthetic taste of the rural population. Wood or stone folk sculptures representing popular deities traditionally were made in many sections of the country, the best known of which are the Jizo images produced on the island of Sado. Of folk paintings, the most characteristic are the votive pictures called *ema* and the charming popular pictures traditionally made for travelers passing through the village of Otsu on Lake Biwa.

The bulk of Japanese *mingei* consists of regionally distinct crafts of every kind produced in huge quantities throughout Japan. The best examples date from the Edo period (1615–1868), before Japan embarked on its industrial development, but in isolated rural areas fine folk crafts are still being made. The finely decorated Seto oil plates used to catch the dripping oil in lanterns are among the most beautiful Japanese folk ceramics and today are highly esteemed by collectors. Also from Seto are the handsome stoneware plates, or *ishizara*, traditionally used in peasant kitchens. Of contemporary folk pottery, the best is being made in northern Kyushu in isolated mountain villages and in the southernmost region of the country in the area of Kagoshima, as well as in the backward district of the Tohoku section of northern Honshu. Outstanding examples of Japanese folk textiles are the mag-

nificent woven or dyed garments from Okinawa, which are famous for the beauty of their colors and design. Other folk textiles include cotton or silk hangings, called *noren;* carrying cloths, or *furoshiki;* and bedspreads, or *futon.* Wood or lacquer bowls, plates, and containers are often decorated in bright colors or with pleasing pictorial designs. Characteristically Japanese are the innumerable ingenious uses of vegetable fibers to form rain capes, snow boots, toy horses, brooms, and baskets of every description. Of Japan's folk toys, the delightful *kokeshi* dolls are the best known today.

Closely related to the folk art of Japan is that of Korea, where traditions of excellent craftsmanship have existed for many centuries. Outstanding examples include the splendid wooden chests, much sought after by modern collectors; the folk lacquers and ceramic wares; and the primitive, strong folk paintings.

Southeast Asia and India. In Southeast Asia, the folk pottery of Vietnam consists largely of rough porcelains decorated in blue and white in imitation of Chinese Ming ware, yet possessing a vigor and simplicity all its own. In Indonesia, the most notable productions are the BATIK folk textiles, celebrated throughout the world for the excellence of their arti-

Among the most expressive forms of Balinese folk art are the painted-leather puppets associated with the wayang shadow play. Used to enact scenes from the Hindu epics, these highly stylized, cutout images are manipulated so as to cast shadows on a canvas backdrop. Music and a narration accompany the movements of the shadow puppets in this millennium-old artistic tradition.

sanship and the beauty of their designs. On the island of Bali, the paper or leather *wayang* puppets made for the shadow plays are the best known and most unique of the folk-art objects. Also impressive are the brilliantly painted peasant houses with steeply gabled roofs and elaborate carvings.

In southern Asia, India possesses the oldest and richest tradition of folk art, which in some regions is still thriving. In keeping with the strong religious traditions of the country, much Indian folk art is connected with the ceremonies performed by pious Hindu worshipers. Numerous folk sculptures made of bronze, wood, and clay represent the gods and goddesses of the Hindu pantheon. The most interesting of the bronzes come from the south of India and Bengal, whereas the best known of the brightly painted wooden statues are those from Puri in Orissa, representing Vishnu in his incarnation as the Jagannath (Lord of the Universe). The most dramatic are the giant clay horses, sometimes as much as 7 m (22 ft) high, which come from Sirunathur in Madras. Unique among Indian textiles is the tradition of embroidered materials with insets of mirror glass from Kutch in western India. Also charming are the folk toys, especially those from Varanasi (Benares) in Uttar Pradesh.

Central and Western Asia. In central and western Asia, areas deeply influenced by Islam, there exists a rich folk tradition of textile, ceramic, and metal work. Throughout this area, carpets are central to the folk-art tradition, and those made in Turkey, the Caucasus, Iran, and Turkestan are rightly looked upon as masterpieces of this genre. The mountain villages of the Caucasus are particularly famous for the beauty and variety of their productions, including both prayer rugs with a religious design as the principal motif and rugs with orna-

Lively folk renderings on wooden plaques, called ema, were traditionally presented as votive offerings at Buddhist temples in Japan. This 19th-century ema from the Kofukuji, a temple in Nara, depicts an animal of the zodiac. (Japan Folk Crafts Museum, Tokyo.)

mental patterns that are purely decorative. Most of these works are pile rugs made of wool from local sheep, but others take the form of flat-woven kilims. All of them are outstanding for the beauty of their natural colors and the excellence of their artisanship, although the more recent production tends to be inferior in quality. Among the folk pottery of western Asia, particularly fine are the Turkish wares from Isnik, with their tulip designs and brilliant blue glazes, and the Iranian ceramics from Arak. Beautiful ceramic tiles are also used in construction throughout this region. Etched or pierced metal is employed extensively for brass bottles and vessels of all types.   HUGO MUNSTERBERG

Bibliography: Bossert, H. T., *Folk Art of Europe* (1990) and *Folk Art of Asia, Africa, Australia, and the Americas* (1990); Glassie, H., *The Spirit of Folk Art* (1989); Johnson, J., and Ketchum, W. C., Jr., *American Folk Art of the Twentieth Century* (1985); Kauffman, H., *Pennsylvania Dutch American Folk Art*, rev. and enl. ed. (1984); Lipman J., and Winchester, A., *The Flowering of American Folk Art* (1974; repr. 1989); Munsterberg, H., *The Folk Arts of Japan* (1958).

See also: ANTIQUE COLLECTING.

folk dance

Dancers at the annual Highland Games at Antigonish, Nova Scotia, perform the complicated steps of a Scottish sword dance above the crossed blades. Sword dances are found throughout the world in various forms, and many include battle mime or swordplay.

Folk dance is not only the oldest form of dance, it is also the basis of all other dance forms, including BALLET, MODERN DANCE, ballroom, disco, and jazz dance. Humans have always used dance for communicating their emotions through movement and rhythm. As time passed, folk dance increasingly acquired the qualities of social recreation. Folk dance reflects the life and times of a culture; it takes on the characteristics of its locale. The famous dancer-choreographer Matteo Vittucci once said, "Show me a dance and I'll show you the kind of king or government you have." A distinguishing feature of folk dance is that it is not a performing art, but a participatory activity. It is a type of traditional, communal dancing, passed down from generation to generation and done in a recreational atmosphere. Another important aspect of folk dance is the use of traditional costumes and accessories, which also aids in preserving a culture's link with its past.

The forms, patterns, and functions of folk dance are varied. The dances can be done without partners in a circle, in a square, or in long lines, or they can be done with couples, threesomes, or, on occasion, as a solo. The types of dances include war dances, contest dances, wedding dances, courtship dances, and dances for the fun of movement alone. The Philippine *rice-planting* dance and the Japanese *coal miner's* dance are types of work dances. Many forms of windmill, spinning wheel, and weaving dances exist. Almost every country has a shoemaker's and a sailor's dance; for example,

the HASAPIKOS is the most popular dance in Greece. Sailors brought the music and dance of their native countries to many foreign lands; therefore, tunes like the "Soldier's Joy," used for hornpipes and sailor's dances, are found throughout the world. The Mexican *El Bolonchon*, which honors the Virgin Mary, is one of the many religious dances. In Israel the dance *David Melech* tells the story of King David of the Bible. Dances have been created for special holidays—for example, the Ukrainian *hayivka* or the Swedish *Christmas Polka*. The rapid movements of the Italian TARANTELLA were traditionally thought to ward off the effects of a spider's bite.

Although the American colonists brought their dances with them, the play-party game evolved on the shores of the New World. Invented in those areas of the colonies where stern religious practices banned dancing as a form of sinful entertainment, play-party games were dances disguised as games. Those that involved frequent changes of partners had probably been courtship dances in their countries of origin. Some are still danced, or "played," by children—for example, *Skip to My Lou, Shoo Fly,* and *Paw Paw Patch.*

Circle Dances. The oldest form for folk dance is the circle, in which dancers follow one another around a ring. The American Indian hunting, rain, and war dances are circle dances, as are many of the African and Japanese dances. In other countries hands are held in a variety of ways to close up the circle, as in the HORA of Israel and Romania, the *kolo* of Yugoslavia, and the *syrtos* of Greece. Sometimes the circle changes into a long chain dance, with a leader weaving the dancers in patterns around a village or a city street as in the French *bourrée*, which is done in long lines, and the Norwegian *song-dance*. One of the more interesting circle dances is the *sardana*, which is done to many different tunes by the Catalan people of Spain. The famous cellist Pablo Casals has composed may *sardana* melodies. The Ukrainian *arkan* dance—which dates back to pre-Christian times and is danced only by men—honors the sun-god and ends dramatically with the dancers leaping over a roaring fire.

Square Dances. The SQUARE DANCE is usually associated with the United States, but this type of dancing is common to many countries: the Danish *hatter*, the Irish *Sweets of May*, the German *Man in the Hay*, the English *Newcastle*, and the Scottish *eightsome reel* are examples. A square dance called the *beseda* was put together in Czechoslovakia about 1900 as a means of unifying the country through dance. It consists of a potpourri of little dances from many provinces. American square dances developed primarily from dances of England, Scotland, and Ireland.

Contra Dances. Folk dances in which two long lines are formed with dancers facing one another are sometimes called longway, string, or line dances, but they are usually known as contra dances. Contra dances were brought to the United States mainly from the British Isles and have been best preserved in the New England states. They are enjoying a widespread revival throughout the United States and are being done in many other countries. The old English contra called *Childgrove* dates from 1701 and is still done in the United States and England. The most famous contra dance is known in the United States as the Virginia reel, which originated in England, where it was known a *Sir Roger de Coverley*. Because American contra dances date from the colonial period, many of them are named for historical events: *Hull's Victory, Sackett's Harbor,* and *Green Mountain Volunteers.*

Couple Dances. A much later development in folk dance, couple dances are still scarce in many parts of the world. Because they were isolated from the rest of Europe by both mountains and historical events, the Balkan countries were not influenced by other European dances. They have retained the circle dance form and do very few couple dances.

Folk Dance Steps. Many different steps are used in folk dancing, including walking, running, hopping, jumping, skipping, leaping, sliding, and stamping. The way these steps are done depends on the traditional style of the country in which the dance originated, as well as the musical accompaniment, the rhythm of the dance, the costume, the climate, the physical geography, the people, and the history of the country. In

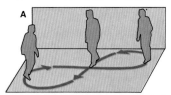

Two forms of the reel, a country dance originating in Great Britain and Ireland, are shown. A Scottish reel of three (A) is a pattern executed within a set, a group of three to four couples. The lead dancer weaves around two other dancers in a figure-8 pattern, alternately passing right and left shoulders. Another country dance is the traveling dance performed by four couples in parallel lines, exemplified here by the "Trip to Helsinki." A running step (B), in which the two lines of dancers skip forward and back twice, commences the dance. The men bow and the women curtsy (C) before beginning the "trip" (D), in which all dancers, placing their hands on the shoulders of the person to their left, cast off to the bottom of the set and circle back to their original positions. When "threading the needle" (E) the lead dancer leads the line under an arch formed by the second and third dancers, then under the arch formed by the third and fourth dancers. When performing the "waves" (F) the first and third couples form an arch under which the second and fourth couples pass. The configuration is repeated until each couple returns to their original position.

addition to the basic steps, there are special steps such as the POLKA, WALTZ, mazurka, schottische, galop, grapevine, and buzz. Steps that are used only in one country or one part of the world include the Swedish *hambo*, the Yogoslav *kolo*, the Yemenite step of Israel and Yemen, the Strathspey step of Scotland, the *jarabe* of Mexico, and the special squat step for Slavic men, called a *prysiadka*. In most countries there are more dances for men than for women. The men's steps are usually livelier and more difficult. For this reason women often do not dance with men, but dance in separate lines.

The use and positioning of the hands are as important as the feet in folk dancing and are often helpful in identifying the nationality of a dance. The hands are held rigidly at the sides of the body in an Irish jig, for example, but they are almost always placed on the hips, in a variety of holds, in Scandinavian dances and in those of Austria, Germany, and Switzerland. In circle dances hands are often placed on shoulders or in a back or front basket hold. Balkan dancers hold each other by the belt, often hanging onto little loops woven into the belts to strengthen their hold. In Hungary men tuck their thumbs into their trouser pockets or belts, and German men tuck their thumbs under their colorful suspenders. Mexican men often dance with hands behind their backs to keep their serapes (blankets) in place. The Ukrainian woman places her hands on her bosom to prevent her beads from crashing into her chin, and the Austrian and German woman holds one hand on her bodice to prevent the many heavy coins of her costume from bumping up and down. In some folk dances the hands are the most important part of the dance because their movements are used to relate a story. The HULA of Hawaii, as well as some of the dances of India and Japan, is especially noted for this. The hands can also be used to express and maintain the mood of the dance, to tease, entice, or flirt with a partner.

Costume. The style of a folk dance is often determined by the costume the dancers wear: in countries where men wear spurs on their boots, there is much heel clicking to emphasize the spur's sound; where women have narrow skirts, there are no high kicks. Hungarian dances feature many spins and twirls to show off the many layers of full petticoats and the ribbons worn by the female dancers. Shoes with heels have to be worn by Spanish FLAMENCO and Mexican zapateado dancers to stamp out the rhythms that are featured in these dances. The Slavic squatting step can be done more easily by men wearing very baggy trousers. The short leather pants, or

lederhosen, which are worn by German and Austrian men, make the *Schuhplattler* thigh-slapping sounds resound. Skirts are worn by men in some countries, such as the kilt worn by the Scottish and the Irish. In Greece men wear a short, white pleated skirt called a *fustanella*. Long embroidered aprons, which influence the movements of their dances, are worn by some Hungarian men.

Folk Dance Accessories. Many different accessories are used in folk dancing. In the Philippines the dancers use coconut shells, long bamboo poles, hats, fans, and kerchiefs. In Hawaii slashed bamboo sticks, called *puili* sticks, are used for striking the floor and the arms and shoulders of the dancers, who are dancing in a squatting position. Almost every country has some sort of sword dance. In addition to castanets, finger cymbals and stones are used to produce the rhythm. Large poles and sticks are used in many men's dances. Masks are frequently used, as in the Mexican *Los Viejitos* ("Old Man's Dance"). In some dances bottles are carried on the head, or lighted candles are held throughout the dance. Ribbons, hoops, garlands or trays of flowers, whips, and bells tied around the ankles or wrists are some other accessories used in folk dancing. The handkerchief is the most common accessory used in folk dancing. Its most exciting use is in English *Morris* dancing, in which six men execute intricate steps while they twirl and fling kerchiefs into the air. The leader of Balkan dances has to be quite expert in keeping his or her steps in time while constantly twirling a handkerchief to set the pace of a dance. In Mexico a man uses his sombrero in the national dance *jarabe tapatío*, or the Mexican hat dance. The man tosses the hat on the floor in front of a woman, and, if she accepts him, she dances on its wide brim. Folk dancers frequently accompany their movements with yells, rhymes, yodels, and other sounds, which vary according to country and type of dance.

In the past, people danced only the dances of their native land, but today, with swifter and easier travel, people visit other countries more often. As a result, the folk dances of each country have spread across international borders, and people enjoy dances of many lands. There are many international folk festivals and folk dance camps and clubs in which people share and learn dances. In the United States there are many monthly folk dance publications and newsletters. Folk dance clothes, rather than costumes, are a big part of the folk dance movement. Folk dance is an extremely popular recreation and is frequently taught in schools and colleges. Many dances would probably have been lost if they had not been perpetuated by folk dance societies.   MARY ANN HERMAN

Bibliography: Allen, R., et al., *Voices of the Americas* (1988); Duggan, A. S., et al., *Folk Dance Library*, 5 vols. (1948; repr. 1978); Hall, J. T., *Dance!* (1963; repr. 1980); Horst, L., *Pre-Classic Dance Forms* (1937; repr. 1987); Lawson, J., *European Folk Dance* (1953; repr. 1980); Leach, M., ed., *Funk and Wagnall's Standard Dictionary of Folklore, Mythology, and Legend*, rev. ed. (1972; repr. 1984); Lidster, M. D., and Tamburini, D. H., *Folk Dance Progressions* (1965); Nivell, R., *A Time to Dance: American Country Dancing from Hornpipes to Hot Hash* (1977); Sachs, Curt, *World History of Dance*, 2d ed. (1963).

folk medicine

Folk medicine encompasses traditional healing beliefs and methods used in past and contemporary cultures mostly by people who are not licensed medical practitioners. As an integral part of a culture's knowledge and values, folk medicine is a system based on traditional modes of conduct, of coping with sickness. Often sanctioned by empirical claims or magico-religious beliefs, these popular practices are used to alleviate the distress of diseases and restore harmony in people who are emotionally or physically ill, or both. Folk medicine's lore is widely known among members of a culture and is usually handed down from generation to generation by word of mouth. In general, the system is flexible, allowing the introduction of new ideas about sickness and healing practices, many of them borrowed from classical and modern medicine.

HEALERS

To implement the various folk curing practices, most social groups have established a hierarchy of healers—beginning with the individuals affected, their immediate families and friends, knowledgeable herbalists, members of the clergy, faith healers, and SHAMANS, or medicine men. Many are consulted because of their empirical knowledge of roots and herbs possessing medicinal properties. Others are considered endowed with healing gifts because of station or accidents of birth. The belief that posthumous children have such talents is widely known in the United States. In the European folk-medicine tradition, seventh sons and daughters are said to possess unusual curing powers; the same applies to twins. Often spouses and children of known healers are automatically considered to have similar gifts. As in primitive medicine, many people affected by ailments that are considered minor and natural treat themselves, with the help of family members. A vast array of easily available herbal preparations known to most members of the culture is used to effect a cure. More difficult cases suspected to be of a magico-religious nature are referred to local healers who are endowed with special powers. These shamans stage a variety of ceremonies and employ many of the techniques used in preliterate social groups.

AMERICAN FOLK MEDICINE

Navajos. Native American folk medicine is popular in the less acculturated Indian tribes. A notable example are the Navajos still living in their homeland. Disease is considered a disruption of harmony caused either by external agents such as lightning and winds, powerful animals and ghosts, and witchcraft, or by the breaking of taboos. Three categories of folk healers are usually consulted: first the herbalists, for symptomatic relief of minor ailments; if no improvement is observed, then the hand trembler, or diviner, is called; finally, the singer, or MEDICINE MAN, will carry out specific healing ceremonies suggested by the hand trembler's diagnosis. Ritual sweatbaths, drinking of herbs, and elaborate sandpainting ceremonies characterize Navajo folk healing.

Hot-Cold Theory. The hot-cold theory of disease ranks among the most popular systems of contemporary folk medicine in the United States. In health, the human body displays a balanced blending of hot and cold qualities. Sickness will ensue if an excess of hot or cold foodstuffs is ingested. The basic scheme was introduced into Latin America by the Spanish during the 16th century. Reinforced by native cultural values, it became firmly embedded in popular Latin healing traditions. The hot-cold scheme is applied to foods, diseases, and remedies. The terms *hot* and *cold* do not necessarily refer to the temperature of foods or remedies. Qualities are as-

signed on the basis of origin, color, nutritional value, physiological effects of the food or remedy, as well as therapeutical action. Among New York Peurto Ricans, for example, bananas, coconuts, and sugarcane are considered cold, whereas chocolate, garlic, alcoholic beverages, and cornmeal are hot. Cold-classified illnesses such as arthritis, colds, and gastric complaints must be treated with hot foods and remedies. Their hot counterparts—constipation, diarrhea, and intestinal cramps—require treatment with cold substances.

Black Americans. The medical folklore of black Americans contains elements derived from popular European and African beliefs, blended with religious elements belonging to Christian Fundamentalism and West Indian voodoo. The world is seen as a dangerous place, prompting individuals to constantly exert caution because of the whims of nature, frequent divine punishment, and the threat of witchcraft practiced by hostile humans. Individuals are urged to look out for themselves, be distrustful, and avoid the wrath of God. Sickness is broadly divided into "natural" and "unnatural." The former comprises bodily conditions caused by environmental forces as well as God's punishment for sin. Unnatural illness represents health problems caused by evil influences and witchcraft after the loss of divine protection; the magical intrusion of "animals" into the body and the placement of a certain hex play prominent roles in the causation of disease.

Mexican-Americans. Folk medicine is still popular among large groups of Mexican-Americans in New Mexico, Colorado, Arizona, California, and especially in West Texas. Their healing system, based on pre-Columbian indigenous lore, reflects a degree of isolation and unwillingness to assimilate Anglo-Saxon culture. Moreover, the inability of scientific medicine to offer relief for various categories of folk illness further enhances the usefulness of these practices. Five types of folk illness are most prominent: *mal de ojo* (evil eye), *empacho* (gastrointestinal blockage due to excessive food intake), *susto* (magically induced fright), *caida de la mollera* (fallen fontanel, or opening in or between bones), and *mal puesto* (sorcery). Prominent among Mexican-American folk healers is the *curandero*, a type of shaman who uses white magic and herbs to effect cures. In the cosmic struggle between good and evil, the *curandero*, using God-given powers, wards against harmful spells and hexes. As in other folk systems, faith in the *curandero's* abilities is the essence of the healer's continued success.

FOLK MEDICINE TODAY

Folk medical systems, especially those functioning in a pluralistic society comprising several distinct ethnic groups (as in the United States), govern domestic healing activities to a great extent. Recently, the increasing complexity, technicality, and cost of modern medicine have spurred renewed attempts at self-medication and the use of herbal preparations, thus reviving folk medical practices.

A number of folk remedies used in the past are now manufactured as pharmaceutical preparations prescribed by physicians. For examle, rauwolfia is an extract of the snakeroot plant, which was used for centuries in the Far East for its calming effect. It is now prescribed by physicians to lower blood pressure. Reserpine, a derivative of rauwolfia, has been used by psychiatrists in treating sever mental disorders. Foxglove was first brewed by Indians to treat dropsy, fluid in the legs caused by heart problems. This practice occurred for hundreds of years before it was discovered that foxglove contributed the active ingredients now known as digitalis. Today digitalis is commonly used to stimulate weakened hearts.
                                                    GUENTER B. RISSE

Bibliography: Hand, Wayland D., *Magical Medicine* (1980); Janos, E., *Country Folk Medicine* (1991); Kiev, Ari, *Curanderismo: Mexican-American Folk Psychiatry* (1968); Kourennoff, Paul, *Russian Folk Medicine* (1970); Maloney, C., ed., *The Evil Eye* (1976); Maple, E., *Magic, Medicine, and Quackery* (1968); Meyer, C., *American Folk Medicine* (1973; repr. 1985); Rinzier, C. A., *The Dictionary of Medical Folklore* (1980); Saunders, Lyle, *Cultural Difference and Medical Care* (1954); Scarborough, John, ed., *Folklore and Folk Medicine* (1987); Steiner, Richard P., *Folk Medicine* (1985).

See also: MEDICINE, HISTORY OF; MEDICINE, TRADITIONAL.

folk music

The American singer Joan Baez became prominent during the early 1960s for her moving interpretations of traditional folk songs. With contemporaries such as Pete Seeger and Bob Dylan, Baez played a major role in the development of the modern urban folk song as a vehicle for social protest. By adapting traditional melodies and supplying new lyrics, modern folk performers have publicized such movements as the civil rights effort and opposition to the Vietnam War.

The concept of folk music, though generally understood by most people, has no simple, widely accepted definition. Narrowly construed, folk music is music that lives in oral tradition and is learned "by ear," without the use of written music, primarily in rural cultures. Because folk music is relatively simple in a technical sense, it can be performed by most members of society and lives in the traditions of families and closely knit social groups. It is frequently associated with the activities that it accompanies, such as ritual, dance, and work. In those societies that have classical music traditions under the patronage of elite institutions, folk music is often thought of as the music of the lower educational and socioeconomic strata. Although folk music is found in all so-called high cultures, the usefulness of the concept is most conveniently used to designate a type of MUSIC in Western culture.

The definition given above applies well to Europe and the Americas before about 1900, when rural populations were isolated from cities, literacy was less widespread, and music was not yet disseminated by radio, records, and television. Such conditions still exist in some parts of eastern and southern Europe and in other isolated areas. But the concept of folk music in most of the Western world today has generally been expanded to include other phenomena, such as, for example, songs of rural origin performed by formally trained singers on the concert stage, or by popular performer in the styles of "country music" and ROCK MUSIC; the SPIRITUALS of rural churches sung in distinctive folk styles; songs cast in the form of folk music but composed for political and social purposes by popular musicians such as Bob DYLAN, Woody GUTHRIE, and Pete SEEGER and consumed through radio and records by urban audiences; authentic folk music forgotten in the villages but preserved by specially trained singers under government auspices, a practice common in eastern Europe; and the establishment of orchestras of folk instruments that perform in formal concerts, a custom widespread in the USSR. In this article, however, the more restricted definition of folk music is used.

The Folk Tradition.   To exist for any length of time, a folk song must be accepted by a community—nation, village, family—and must be known to more than an elite. Another distinguishing feature of the folk song is its tendency to change as it passes from one person to another. Contrary to widespread earlier belief, folk songs are often composed by individuals, but once taught to others, they are changed and often simplified. Each person who sings the song may develop his or her own version. The well-known BALLADS "Barbara Allen" and "Lord Randall," for example, exist in a large number of variations. In the course of this process, called "communal recreation," a tune may be fitted with a completely new set of words, and eventually a text (such as the "Barbara Allen" story) may be sung to a group of completely different tunes. A group of related tunes that seem to have descended from a single parent tune are called a tune family; its original parent tune, which may have been composed and sung centuries ago, cannot normally be identified or reconstructed. A tune family tends to remain within a nation or language group, such as France or the English-speaking world. Researchers have speculated that the vast majority of Anglo-American folk songs belong to about 40—and most of those songs to only 7—dominant tune families. Some tunes that seem to have spread throughout Europe centuries ago have developed nationally distinctive variants in many countries. Tunes sometimes cross national boundaries, especially where there are mixed populations, but usually the words—even in translation—do not travel along. Text types such as ballad stories, however, are more internationally distributed than tunes. The folk ballad "Lady Isabel and the Elf Knight," for example, has been collected in most European nations but is sung to tunes that are not internationally related.

Folk songs may change slightly or radically in the process of oral transmission. In some cases a change of a note here and there or a change from duple to triple rhythm is all that happens. In other cases a song with, for example, four musical lines—perhaps with ABCD construction—may lose its first two lines and become CDCD; later folk singers may add two new lines, giving it the form CDEF.

These changes are part of the folk process and result from the dependence on oral tradition. The function of a song in society may determine how much change is tolerated. Ritual songs are usually permitted less change than are songs sung mainly for entertainment, such as ballads. Folk music is frequently said to be functional because it is an integral part of other activities. In a traditional folk society, music is essential in rituals and festivals. Calendric songs, accompanying various seasonal changes, agricultural activities, and key stages in the life cycle, are particularly common in stable, traditional groups. The words of a folk song may serve as chronicle or newspaper or may provide a way for young people to learn about their culture. In modern industrial nations, folk music is perpetuated by ethnic, occupational, and religious minorities, promoting their self-esteem and social solidarity. Isolated culture enclaves, such as Germans who lived in Czechoslovakia before 1945 or Slovak-Americans who live in Cleveland, often preserve particularly old forms of folk music.

Musical Style.   Each nation or culture has a distinctive style of performing its folk music. Some features, however, are common to all of Western culture. For example, all Western nations have ballads (songs that tell stories), dance songs, and work songs dealing with labor or agriculture. The most common structure of such songs is strophic: a tune, frequently consisting of four separate musical lines, is repeated several times, each time with a different stanza of the text. In contrast, much instrumental folk music consists of a series of short lines, each repeated once.

Polyphonic music (see POLYPHONY), in which two or more tunes are sung at one time by small groups of singers or choirs, played by instrumental ensembles, or even played on a single instrument such as the Yugoslav double flute, is most common in eastern and southern Europe. Variations range from the accompaniment of a single sustained tone (drone) to the very sophisticated choral songs of Russia and isolated parts of the Balkans and Italy. Parallel singing is another prevalent form. Parallel thirds—singing the same tune at the interval of a third—is found in Spain, German, and Italy; parallel fourths and fifths are used in various Slavic countries, and parallel seconds, in Yugoslavia.

Singing style is one of the most characteristic features of folk music. The handling of rhythm differentiates two styles identified by Béla Bartók. In *parlando-rubato* singing, which is probably the older style, the singer stresses the words, embellishes tones, and departs frequently from the basic rhythmic structure. *Tempo giusto* singing follows metric patterns and maintains an even tempo. Both styles are found throughout Europe. Alan Lomax (see Lomax family), using different criteria, found three main singing styles. The Eurasian, mainly in southern Europe and parts of Great Britain and North America—areas where solo singing is prevalent—is tense, ornamented, and rhythmically uneven. The Old European style, found in central and eastern Europe, where group singing is developed, is more relaxed and is sung with full voice in even rhythm, the voices blending well in the choruses. The modern European style, found in more recent music in western Europe, combines elements of the other two.

Instruments. Most folk music is sung, but much of it is also performed on a variety of instruments. The simplest, which are shared by many societies in the world, include rattles, bone whistles, and long wooden trumpets such as the Swiss ALPHORN. A number of instruments now common in the West were adapted from Asian or African cultures; these include BAGPIPES, BANJOS, and XYLOPHONES. Many instruments originated and developed in the folk cultures in which they are used. The *Dolle*, a fiddle made from a wooden shoe and common in western Germany, is a simple example. The more sophisticated bowed LYRE, once widespread in northern Europe, is now restricted to Finland. A final group includes instruments taken over by folk cultures from city, church, or court and often maintained long after they had been discarded and replaced in their place of origin. Examples are the HURDY-GURDY and the Norwegian Hardanger fiddle, a violin with sympathetic strings.

The Modern World. In the 20th century, especially since 1945, folk music has declined in its ritual habitat for a number of reasons, including the spread of industrialization, the fact that villagers now live much like city dwellers, and the ready accessibility of all kinds of music through the mass media. Despite its decline in rural areas, folk music has assumed new roles, including the reinforcement of ethnic identities, the advocacy of social change (as in the U.S. civil rights movement), and the building of national consciousness in heterogeneous nations. Folk music continues to be a vital force in the world's musical life.

BRUNO NETTL

Bibliography: Bohlman, Philip V., *The Study of Folk Music in the Modern World* (1988); Brand, Oscar, *The Ballad Mongers* (1962; repr. 1979); Griffin, Clive D., *Folk Music* (1990); Karpeles, Maud, *An Introduction to English Folk Song* (1973); Lomax, Alan, *The Folk Songs of North America* (1960; repr. 1975) and *Folk Song Style and Culture* (1978); Nettl, B., and Myers, H., *Folk Music in the United States*, 3d rev. and exp. ed. (1976); Nettl, B., et al., *Folk and Traditional Music of the Western Continents*, 3d ed. (1990); Sandberg, L., and Weissman, D., *The Folk Music Sourcebook*, rev. ed. (1989); Sharp, Cecil, *English Folk Song: Some Conclusions*, 4th ed. (1965; repr. 1977).

folk song: see FOLK MUSIC.

folklore

The term *folklore*, literally "folk learning," is generally limited to knowledge that is transmitted from one generation to another by word of mouth or imitation. In societies without writing, all traditional knowledge can be considered folklore; but in literate societies such as our own, folklore refers only to a fraction of the total culture and consists principally of FOLK DANCE, FOLK MEDICINE, FOLK MUSIC, and the various forms of folk literature—FOLKTALES, legends, myths, and proverbs. Music and literature, especially, have been the primary focus of studies by folklorists.

The beginnings of the academic discipline of folklore date from the early 19th century, when the German philologist Jacob GRIMM, with his brother Wilhelm, began gathering German folktales in the field—that is, from the people for whom the tales, heard throughout their lives, formed part of their culture. The collection of folkloric materials and the creation of systems for cataloging them became a preoccupation of folklorists in Europe and the United States—not only for specialists in language and literature, but also for scholars in the fields of religion, psychology, and anthropology. Speculations about the origins of folktales, and the reasons for the similarity of many of them to tales told in other European cultures, were to provide material for the theoretical structure of the study of folklore. The Grimm brothers, for example, thought that the tales were the remnants of old myths long suppressed by Christianity but still surviving among peasant folk.

Interpretations of Folklore. Although much folk literature seems to be told and preserved primarily for entertainment, it also has an important educational function, imparting cultural values and behavioral norms to its audience. Folktales may sometimes provide psychological release or the background for fantasy. Some folk literature allows its audience to imagine behavior that is forbidden or even sinful according to their own ethical codes. The gods in classical Greek mythology, for example, often broke the rules by which their worshipers lived. Certain North American Indian peoples told myths about a trickster called Coyote who committed acts that would have been considered shocking, sinful, or criminal if they had been done by ordinary mortals. Some psychologists, beginning with Sigmund FREUD, have found folktales and myths to be filled with sexual symbolism; Carl JUNG and others have viewed them as expressions of the collective human unconscious.

Folklorist Techniques. The folklore specialist goes to "the field" for the materials that form his or her subject and collects folk literature—tales, aphorisms, riddles, legends—or songs, dances, artifacts. Contemporary folklorists use film and tape to record the precise words, sounds, and look of their material and also collect information about the provenance of the material, the circumstances in which their informants learned it.

Extensive archival systems have been established to classify and catalog folkloric collections. Even more specific are the "type-indexes" that have evolved to classify folk material, particularly folk literature and song lyrics, according to the use that has been made of its common elements. A folktale might be classified according to its broad theme—a lost princess, for example—and, even more narrowly, by such special factors as the presence of a cruel stepmother, a band of brothers, a set of impossible tasks. Folklorist Stith Thompson's great work, *The Motif Index of Folk Literature* (6 vols., 1955–58), classifies over 40,000 entries taken from folktales, ballads, myths, fables, medieval romances, exempla, fabliaux, jest books, and local legends.

Approaches to the material of folklore are drawn from several disparate fields. Some scholars collect and study folklore as a means of revivifying or preserving an old language or a vanishing culture. Others come to folklore through anthropological studies, and view it as another means of learning the history and culture of a people. Literary folklorists, such as poet Robert GRAVES, have searched myths for the origins of poetic inspiration or analyzed folktales for the source of narrative forms. Psychologists see folkloric materials as providing a window into the workings of the human mind.

In most cultures folklore still plays a role in the formation of values and attitudes. Although the explosion of communications technologies in Western societies seems to have eliminated the oral tradition, the maintenance and development of folkloric material continues—as witnessed by the growth of a relatively new study, the folklore of cities.

CHARLES WAGLEY

Bibliography: Bausinger, Hermann, *Folk Culture in a World of Technology* (1990); Brunvand, Jan H., *The Study of American Folklore: An Introduction*, 3d ed. (1986); Dorson, Richard M., et al., eds., *Handbook of American Folklore* (1986); Dundes, Alan, *Cracking Jokes* (1987), *Folklore Matters* (1989), and *Little Red Riding Hood: A Casebook* (1989); Farrar, Claire R., ed., *Women and Folklore: Images and Genres* (1986); Leach, Maria, ed., *Funk & Wagnalls Standard Dictionary of Folklore, Mythology and Legend*, 2 vols. (1949–50; repr. 1984); Newell, Venetia, *An Egg at Easter: A Folklore Study* (1989); Tatar, Maria, *The Hard Facts of the Grimms' Fairy Tales* (1987); Thompson, Stith, *The Folktale* (1946; repr. 1977).

folktale

A folktale may be defined as a traditional oral prose narrative. Like other kinds of FOLKLORE, the folktale circulates by word of mouth in a consistent yet shifting form; since each new teller does not read from or recite a fixed text, the words are constantly being altered to some degree. If a collector records and prints a tale in a book, it becomes merely a printed version of a folktale, lacking the intonation, inflection, gestures, facial expressions, and audience responses that make the narrating of a folktale a living performance. A writer's paraphrase or embellishment of a folktale he or she has heard or has read is a literary version of the folktale, considerably removed from the original and authentic oral version. What makes an oral story a folktale are the variants of the story that can be located over time and space. A story that is told only once is not a folktale because, although oral, it is not traditional.

No precise terminology exists in English to label the folktale and its subcategories. The term *folktale* itself is customarily used in a restricted way to signify oral fictions in which supernatural and magic-making beings, royal and aristocratic characters, and talking animals have the main roles. In popular usage this kind of story is called a FAIRY TALE. Fairy tales do not necessarily deal with fairies, however, and the purportedly truthful accounts Irish storytellers tell of the sightings and powers of these diminutive creatures are more properly called legends, since they are not intended as fictions. A distinction needs to be made between folk legends in oral circulation and popular and literary legends that circulate through print and other media. Stories about Paul Bunyan, for example, appear chiefly in books and newspapers and are very rarely collected in the field by folklorists; they should be called popular legends rather than folk legends. Unlike the fluent form of a literary or popular legend, the folk legend is usually told in a fragmentary and episodic, or anecdotal, manner.

The length, subject matter, and form of folktales vary enormously. A one-minute joke and an adventure-laden romance requiring several nights to narrate can both be characterized as folktales, if they exist in oral variants. Folktales may be set in a mythical past, in historic times, or in the present. Since storytelling is a basic human need, folktales are told even in the midst of technological cultures saturated with electronic media. Modern Americans specialize in snappy jokes with punchline endings and urban horror legends that are told as true. Some folklorists feel that stories of personal experience, based on actual incidents that strike the teller and the listeners as in some way unusual, should also be considered folktales if they are often repeated and acquire formulaic characteristics.

These categories apply primarily to storytelling in the Western world. The folktales produced by tribal societies often include animal tales, in which beasts and birds behave like human beings; dilemma tales, popular throughout black Africa, in which an unresolved ending is left for the audience to decide; and creation myths, which explain the origin of the Earth in ethnocentric terms. Frequently the primitive storyteller draws no clear distinction between fiction and reality. Every society known to humankind tells folktales, which take an endless variety of forms. What unites all these forms is the artistry of a teller and the responsiveness of an audience. A folktale lives in the spoken word and dies on the printed page.

RICHARD M. DORSON

Bibliography: Arne, A., *The Types of the Folktale*, 2d rev. ed., trans. and ed. by S. Thompson (1964); Brunvand, Jan H., *The Mexican Pet: More "New" Urban Legends and Some Old Favorites* (1986); Degh, L., *Folktales and Society* (1969; repr. 1989); Dorson, R. M., ed., *Folklore and Folklife* (1982); Dundes, A., *Interpreting Folklore* (1980); Laubach, D. C., *Introduction to Folklore* (1989); Mieder, W., *Tradition and Innovation in Folk Literature* (1987); Thompson, S., *The Folktale* (1946; repr. 1977) and *Motif-Index of Folk-Literature*, 6 vols., rev. ed. (1955–58).

folkways

Folkways are the routine habits, customs, or patterns of social intercourse shared by members of a social group. Examples include such traditional customs as table manners and wait-ing one's turn in line. When such more or less automatically performed behaviors become well-established by conscious common agreement so that they are proper and indispensable to society, they become mores (Latin for "customs"). Neither folkways nor mores are laws, although they may be incorporated into laws. The term *folkways* was first used by the American sociologist William Graham SUMNER (1840–1910). Sumner considered folkways and mores obstacles to social progress.

CHARLES WAGLEY

follicle stimulating hormone: see
GONADOTROPHIN; HORMONES; PITUITARY GLAND.

Folsom   [fohl'-suhm]

The Folsom stone-tool complex is one of two major tool complexes associated with prehistoric people in North America (the other being Clovis—see CLOVIS CULTURE). Characterized by distinctive fluted projectile points, the artifacts were initially discovered (1926) in association with the remains of extinct giant bison at a site near Folsom, in east central New Mexico. Folsom artifacts have been found at other sites in the western and southwestern United States and in Canada. The Folsom points, which are about 5 cm (2 in) long, with a concave base and a lengthwise groove, or flute, date from c.9000–8000 BC. Other flint implements include end scrapers with steep working edges, small perforators and gravers, side scrapers, and chisels and knives. At the Lindenmeier site in Colorado bone awls and a needle were also found.

The people who used Folsom points were probably organized in small bands and inhabited temporary and more permanent camps located near stone quarries. Although many Folsom sites are bison kill-sites, it is unlikely that the Folsom people depended entirely on big game hunting; they probably also hunted smaller game and collected seeds, berries, and other foods.

JAMES B. GRIFFIN

Fon   [fahn]

The Fon, also known as the Dahomey, are a West African people of Benin, Togo, and Nigeria. They number more than 900,000 and speak a Kwa language of the Niger-Congo family of African languages. Their economy is based on farming and many crafts, including metalwork, weaving, and pottery. A cowrie-shell money exhange was traditionally used in Fon markets. Descent and residence are determined through the male line. Marriage is polygynous, with separate houses for co-wives and their children. Fon religion centers around three pantheons of gods—of the sky, earth, and thunder—as well as personal gods, the ancestral cult, and magic.

The Fon were part of the once-powerful military kingdom of Dahomey, founded in the 17th century and conquered (1894) by the French. It was headed by an absolute ruler whose elaborate court system at Abomey was supported by many officials and a taxation system. Ranked socioeconomic classes existed, including hereditary craft workers and numerous slaves, who worked on the king's plantations and in private households and were sold to European slave traders. Dahomey music, folklore, and dance were highly developed. The rich and varied plastic arts include work in metals and carved wood, graphic arts, appliquéd cloths, sacred wall paintings, and designs incised on calabashes.

PHOEBE MILLER

Bibliography: Herskovits, Melville J., *Dahomey: An Ancient West African Kingdom*, 2 vols. (1938; repr. 1967).

Fonda   (family) [fahn'-duh]

Henry, Jane, and Peter Fonda represent one of the few family acting dynasties in American film. **Henry Fonda**, b. May 16, 1905, d. Aug. 12, 1982, was a versatile actor who began his career as a stage actor. Known for his slow, midwestern drawl and easy mannerisms, Fonda distinguished himself in a wide variety of Hollywood films: social drama (*The Grapes of Wrath*, 1940), light comedy (*The Lady Eve*, 1941), historical drama (*Young Mr. Lincoln*, 1939), westerns (*My Darling Clementine*, 1946), war drama (*Mr. Roberts*, 1955), and political

Henry Fonda, flanked by his children, Jane and Peter, accepts the American Film Institute's Life Achievement Award at a testimonial dinner held (March 1978) in his honor. Henry and Jane Fonda have enjoyed brilliant acting careers, but Peter, also a skilled performer, has shown more interest in directing films.

drama (*The Best Man*, 1964). Fonda, who appeared in 87 films (and 21 plays), won his first Academy Award for best actor for his performance in *On Golden Pond* (1981). His daughter, actress **Jane Fonda**, b. Dec. 21, 1937, once famous for her outspoken stands on political issues, has since been hugely successful as the author of a number of keep-fit books and videotapes. Her best performances have been in *Cat Ballou* (1965), *They Shoot Horses, Don't They?* (1969), *Klute* (1971; Academy Award for best actress); and *Coming Home* (1978; Academy Award for best actress). She has also appeared in *Nine to Five* (1980), *The Morning After* (1986), and *Stanley and Iris* (1990). Her brother, **Peter Fonda**, b. Feb. 23, 1940, scored an unexpected success with *Easy Rider* (1967), a film that he produced independently.   LESLIE HALLIWELL

Bibliography: Anderson, C., *Citizen Jane* (1990); Cole, G., and Farrell, W., *The Fondas* (1985); Roberts, A., and Goldstein, M., *Henry Fonda* (1984).

Fonseca, Manuel Deodoro da   [fun-sek'-uh, mahn-wel' dee-u-dohr'-u dah]

Manuel Deodoro da Fonseca, b. Aug. 5, 1827, d. Aug. 23, 1892, was the first president of the Republic of Brazil. An army officer, he helped depose Emperor PEDRO II in 1889, led the provisional government, and was elected president of the formally established republic in 1891. In November 1891 he was forced out of office and replaced by his vice-president, Floriano PEIXOTO.

font   [fahnt]

A font is a basin, usually of stone, lead, or marble, containing water used in Christian BAPTISM. In Western Europe fonts are commonly situated near the west entrance of the church, or in a separate building, called a BAPTISTERY. The basin, which may be circular or octagonal, is elevated on a pedestal. From the earliest days of church architecture, the sides, pedestals, and covers of fonts have been decorated with religious carving and sculpture executed in the then prevalent style.

Font de Gaume   [fohn duh gohm]

Font de Gaume is considered one of the finest sites of prehistoric cave art in Les Eyzies, a district in the Dordogne, France. On the cave walls are numerous paintings (many in color) and engravings of animals, including friezes of bison, mammoths, horses, woolly rhinoceroses, and a rare scene of a male and female reindeer portrayed together. Most of the cave art is ascribed to the Early and Middle MAGDALENIAN periods (c.15,000 BC). The cave site was discovered in 1901.   LYA DAMS

Fontaine, Jean de La: see LA FONTAINE, JEAN DE.

Fontaine, Pierre François Léonard   [fohn-ten']

Pierre François Léonard Fontaine, b. Sept. 20, 1762, d. Oct. 10, 1853, was a French painter, architect, and architectural historian. He is best known for his collaboration with Charles PERCIER, with whom he initiated the EMPIRE STYLE. On the recommendation of the painter Jacques Louis David, Napoleon appointed Fontaine and Percier his official architects, and their first work for him was the restoration (c.1794) of the palace of La Malmaison in Paris. They later restored parts of the Louvre, including the east facade (1802), and built (1806–07) the Arc de Triomphe du Carrousel, Paris, an outstanding example of the richness and elaboration of the Empire style.
                                        SUZANNE WILSON

Fontainebleau   [fohn-ten-bloh']

Fontainebleau (1982 pop., 15,679) is a municipality in northern France in Seine-et-Marne department. It is 64 km (40 mi) from Paris on the left bank of the Seine. Located in the Forest of Fontainebleau, it is a military center with a military college and an engineering school. By 1169, Fontainebleau was a residence of the French kings who were attracted by the forest's good hunting. The château, southeast of the town, was begun in 1528 by Francis I and served as the royal residence until construction of Versailles. Napoleon I held Pope Pius VII prisoner in the château from 1812 to 1814. It now serves as the summer residence of the president of France.

Fontainebleau, Château de

The Château de Fontainebleau, situated 64 km (40 mi) southeast of Paris in the forest of Fontainebleau, is one of the largest and most magnificent of the royal residences of France. The original building, of which very little remains, was a medieval hunting lodge. The present structure, comprising five separate groups of buildings, was begun in 1528 during the reign of Francis I. Francis gathered a large number of French, Italian, and Flemish architects, painters, and craftspersons to work on the château, thus introducing the styles of the Italian Renaissance into France and forming what has become known as the school of Fontainebleau. Later sovereigns, including Henry II, Francis II, Catherine de Médicis, and Henry IV, enlarged and embellished the building, which was provided with new furnishings by Napoleon I after the French Revolution. The spacious gardens were planned by André de Nôtre, a celebrated 17th-century landscape gardener, during the reign of Louis XIV.

Fontainebleau, school of

The term *school of Fontainebleau* designates two distinct schools of painting and architectural decoration. The first, and more important, school consisted of artists brought to France from Italy and the Netherlands by Francis I during the first half of the 16th century to work on the interior decoration of the newly constructed Château de Fontainebleau. Eminent painters and craftsmen who imported the style of the Italian Renaissance to France included Benvenuto CELLINI, Francesco PRIMATICCIO, ROSSO FIORENTINO, and Niccolo dell'Abate. Their collaboration with French and Flemish artists resulted in the international Mannerist style (see MANNERISM), which intervenes between the Renaissance and the baroque and is characterized by its self-consciously elegant treatment of natural forms. The Francis I Gallery of the château, painted by Rosso and his assistants, is one of the crowning achievements of this style.

A second group of painters who inherited the Mannerist style but implemented it rather less forcefully were employed at the château during the reign of Henry IV at the close of the 16th century. These included Ambroise Dubois, Toussaint Dubreuil, and Martin Fréminet, who, though competent, did not equal the achievements of their predecessors. Their re-

The elaborate decoration of the Gallery of Francis I at Fontainebleau illustrates the style favored by artists of the Fontainebleau school. Designed by Rosso Fiorentino and Francesco Primaticcio, the painting and sculpture exhibit the languid figures and studied refinement of Italian Mannerism. (c.1533–44; Fontainebleau, France.)

fined styles and accomplished technique were, however, important influences on Claude LORRAIN and Nicolas POUSSIN.

Bibliography: David, M., ed., *The School of Fontainebleau* (1965); Lucie-Smith, Edward, *A Concise History of French Painting* (1971).

Fontana, Carlo   [fohn-tah'-nah]

The Roman architect, engineer, and author Carlo Fontana, c.1634–1714, was a prolific and influential architect of the baroque period (see BAROQUE ART AND ARCHITECTURE). Fontana began his career as an assistant to Carlo RAINALDI and Giovanni BERNINI, but he soon emerged as an independent master. He executed numerous chapels, palaces, and altars in Rome after 1680, and in 1690 was appointed to the important Vatican post of surveyor of SAINT PETER'S BASILICA, where he built the Baptismal Chapel (1692–98). His skillful use of polychromy may be seen in the Ginetti Chapel of Sant'Andrea del Valle (1671) and in the Cibo Chapel of Santa Maria del Popolo (1683–87); his finest conception, however, is the facade of San Marcello al Corso (1682–83), in which he overcame limitations of space by using a curving facade. His largest work, a design for the church and college of Loyola, Spain (1681), although not executed under his supervision, reveals Spanish influences.

Fontana was an influential theoretician as well as an able practitioner. His studies were preserved in a book of engravings, *Templum Vaticanus* (1694), and in manuscripts and drawings preserved in the Royal Library at Windsor Castle, in England. Fontana's international fame drew many students to his studio, among them Filippo JUVARRA and James GIBBS.

HOWARD BATCHELOR

Bibliography: Wittkower, Rudolf, *Art and Architecture in Italy: 1600–1750* (1965) and *Studies in the Italian Baroque* (1975).

Fontana, Domenico

The Italian architect Domenico Fontana, 1543–1607, traveled to Rome from his native Lugano in 1563, accompanied by his older brother Giovanni, who later became a celebrated engineer. Fontana was commissioned in 1585 by Cardinal Felice Peretti to design a chapel in the Basilica of Santa Maria Maggiore, and when the cardinal was elected Pope Sixtus V in the same year, Fontana became the architect to the papacy. During the 5-year reign of Sixtus, the city of Rome was extensively rebuilt under Fontana's direction; it took on the baroque form that survives to this day. Fontana's part in this large project included the designs of the Vatican, Lateran, and Quirinal palaces (see VATICAN PALACE), the Vatican Library, and completion of the dome of SAINT PETER'S BASILICA, all of which were executed between 1585 and 1590. In 1586, Fontana removed an ancient Egyptian obelisk from the side of the Vatican to its present position in front of Saint Peter's, where it

distracts from the effect of Giovanni Lorenzo BERNINI's colonnades. For this, as for almost all his other work, Fontana has been denigrated by modern architectural historians, who have characterized his talent as uninspired and mediocre. Fontana was deprived of his post by Pope Clement VIII in 1592. He was obliged to move to Naples, were he built the Palazzo Reale (1600–02).

HOWARD BATCHELOR

Bibliography: Giedion, S., *Space, Time, and Architecture* (1954); Heydenreich, Ludwig, and Lotz, Wolfgang, *Architecture in Italy: 1400–1600* (1967).

Fontana, Lavinia

The Bolognese artist Lavinia Fontana, 1552–1614, was renowned as a painter of portraits and religious subjects. After studying with her father, the Mannerist Painter Prospero Fontana, she became a popular portraitist, recording her aristocratic sitters and their bejeweled clothes with scintillating precision, usually in small oil paintings on metal medallions, a type of MINIATURE PAINTING called *rametti*. She was also known for her altarpieces, especially for those done in Rome, where she lived after 1603.

Bibliography: Tufts, Eleanor, *Our Hidden Heritage: Five Centuries of Women Artists* (1974).

Fontana, Lucio

Lucio Fontana, b. Argentina, Feb. 19, 1899, d. Sept. 7, 1968, was an Italian abstract artist who began his career as a sculptor and pottery designer in Milan in the 1930s. After spending the years of World War II in Argentina, Fontana published his *White Manifesto*, which proposed a theory of "spatialism" in art whereby artists and scientists might collaborate in new forms of expression. His later works united the mediums of painting and sculpture to overcome conventional limitations of space and form.

Bibliography: Billeter, Erika, *Lucio Fontana, 1899–1968* (1977).

Fontane, Theodor   [fohn-tah'-ne]

Theodor Fontane, b. Dec. 30, 1819, d. Sept. 20, 1898, was a German poet and travel writer, and an important novelist. He worked as an apothecary before turning to journalism in 1850. He first became known for the stirring patriotic ballads in *Gedichte* (Poems, 1851) and *Balladen* (Ballads, 1861). His *Wanderungen durch die Mark Brandenburg* (Travels through Brandenburg Province, 4 vols., 1862–82) is a readable historical travelogue. Fontane wrote his first novel, the historical *Vor dem Sturm* (Before the Storm, 1878), when he was nearly 60 years old. He is now best known for his social novels set in or near Berlin of the late 19th century. *Irrungen, Wirrungen* (1887; trans. as *Trials and Tribulations*, 1917), *Frau Jenny Trei-*

The 19th-century German author Theodor Fontane is best known for his realistic social novels. Set in a contemporary framework, the novels explore the rise of the middle class and their ensuing problems of redefining values.

bel (1892), *Effi Briest* (1895; Eng. trans., 1967; film, 1974), and *Der Stechlin* (Lake Stechlin, 1898), are among the best 19th-century German novels. HENRY GARLAND

Bibliography: Bance, A., *Theodor Fontane: The Major Novels* (1982); Garland, Henry, *The Berlin Novels of Theodor Fontane* (1980); Robinson, A. R., *Theodor Fontane* (1976).

Fontanne, Lynn: see LUNT, ALFRED, AND FONTANNE, LYNN.

Fontéchevade man [fohn-tay-she-vahd']

Skull fragments of two individuals, collectively known as Fontéchevade man, were excavated in 1947 at the cave of Fontéchevade, in Charente, France. These fossils were found at a level that dates from the Riss-Würm Interglaciation (about 125,000–75,000 years ago); discovered with them were flaked stone tools of a pre-MOUSTERIAN industry, the Tayacian.

Initially the Fontéchevade fossils received a great deal of attention because they were thought to possess a number of structural features similar to those of modern humans. The fossils were interpreted as possible evidence for the presence in Europe of an early form of modern human before and during the period of the NEANDERTALERS, who first appear in the European fossil record in the Würm Glaciation. Today, however, most researchers dispute the significance of these fossils. The small brow ridge of these frontal fragments and cranial measurements suggest they are from an immature Neandertal rather than an early modern human.
ALAN MANN AND NANCY MINUGH

Bibliography: Andrews, P. J., and Stringer, C. B., *Human Evolution* (1989); Schwartz, J. H., *What the Bones Tell Us* (1993).

Fontenelle, Bernard le Bovier de [fohn-tuh-nel', bair-nahr' luh boh-vee-ay' duh]

The French Enlightenment writer Bernard le Bovier de Fontenelle, b. Feb. 11, 1657, d. Jan. 9, 1757, devoted his long life to science, literature, and philosophy. A nephew of the playwright Pierre Corneille, he first produced literary works, followed later by the *Nouveaux dialogues des morts* (New Dialogues of the Dead, 1683) and the *Histoire des oracles* (History of Oracles, 1687). He earned fame by popularizing new philosophical ideas and the Cartesian method. In the *Entretiens sur la pluralité des mondes* (1686; A Plurality of Worlds, 1688), he supported the Copernican system. He became permanent secretary of the Academy of Sciences in 1697.
MADELEINE ALCOVER

Fonteyn, Dame Margot [fahn-tayn']

Margot Fonteyn, b. Reigate, Surrey, May 18, 1919, d. Feb. 21, 1991, was an English ballet dancer whose career as a prima ballerina spanned several decades. Born Margaret Hookham, she traveled with her parents as a child to North America and China. Returning to London, she attended the Sadler's Wells Ballet School and made her debut as a snowflake in Tchaikovsky's *Nutcracker* at Sadler's Wells in 1934. Ninette de Valois picked her out to succeed Alicia MARKOVA as the company's ballerina, and within five years she had danced *Giselle, Swan Lake,* and *The Sleeping Beauty.* Moreover, she became the chosen interpreter of the ballets of Frederick ASHTON, who joined the Vic-Wells Ballet (later Royal Ballet) in 1935 and began by creating *Le Baiser de la Fée* for her. This first was followed by such ballets as *Apparitions, Nocturne, Horoscope,* and after World War II, *Symphonic Variations, Scènes de ballet, Cinderella, Sylvia,* and *Ondine,* among others. Fonteyn was always notable for exquisite line, infallible musicality, and lyricism rather than virtuosity in elevation and pirouettes. Over the years she became a magisterial interpreter of such classic ballets as Marius PETIPA's *Sleeping Beauty, La Bayadère,* and *Raymonda.*

Fonteyn's partnership with Rudolf NUREYEV, beginning with *Giselle* in 1962, gave her a new lease on her career at an age when most dancers are contemplating retirement. Ashton set

Dame Margot Fonteyn appears with Rudolf Nureyev in the Royal Ballet production of Prokofiev's Romeo and Juliet. Fonteyn's exquisite style and characterization made her one of the world's most admired dancers. In 1956 she was created a Dame of the Order of the British Empire in recognition of her contributions.

the seal on this partnership the following year with his *Marguerite and Armand.* Although she returned from time to time to her parent company, Fonteyn became a jet-age version of the peripatetic ballerinas of earlier times (such as Fanny Elssler and Anna Pavlova), appearing with many partners and companies all over the Western world. In 1979, on her 60th birthday, she was named *prima ballerina assolutta,* a title officially given only three times in the history of the Imperial Russian Ballet and its Soviet successors.

In 1955, Fonteyn married Roberto Arias (d. 1989), a Panamanian politician who became totally paralyzed after an assassination attempt on his life ten years later. She devoted herself to caring for him while continuing to dance. Although she reduced her stage appearances by the late 1970s, she continued to appear on television and wrote several books, including *Margot Fonteyn: Autobiography* (1976), *A Dancer's World* (1979), and *Pavlova* (1984). DAVID VAUGHAN

Bibliography: Money, Keith, *The Art of Margot Fonteyn* (1965) and *Fonteyn: The Making of a Legend* (1973).

Fonvizin, Denis Ivanovich [fahn-vee'-zeen]

Denis Ivanovich Fonvizin, b. Apr. 14 (N.S.), 1744 or 1745, d. Dec. 12 (N.S.), 1792, was a Russian playwright who wrote the first original comedies in Russian. *The Brigadier* (1769) satirizes the mania for things French in 18th-century Russia, whereas *The Minor* (1782) lampoons the ignorance and backwardness that typified the provincial gentry. Other works by Fonvizin addressed the growing repressiveness of Empress Catherine II. Also of interest are Fonvizin's letters from western Europe (1777–78, 1784–85), in which he presents life abroad in a negative light. HAROLD B. SEGEL

Bibliography: Segel, Harold B., *The Literature of Eighteenth-Century Russia,* 2 vols. (1967).

Foochow: see FUZHOU.

food

All living organisms require food for survival, growth, and reproduction. Most broadly, the term *food* can be taken to include any kind of nutrient needed by animals, plants, and simpler forms of LIFE, on down to bacteria. This would include, for example, the inorganic substances that plants draw from air and water. The processes that circulate these basic nutrients in the environment are called NUTRIENT CYCLES, and the processes by which organisms make use of nutrients are collectively known as METABOLISM.

In terms of the energy needs of humans and other animals, food consists of CARBOHYDRATES, FATS, and PROTEINS, along with VITAMINS AND MINERALS (see NUTRITION, HUMAN). Humans may consume a wide range of different food substances, as long as they meet nutrition requirements (see DIET, HUMAN and many separate articles on individual foods). Otherwise NUTRITIONAL-DEFICIENCY DISEASES will develop. See also FAMINE and entries on eating disorders such as ANOREXIA NERVOSA.

Food production and distribution are discussed in AGRICULTURE AND THE FOOD SUPPLY, FOOD INDUSTRY, and FOOD SERVICE SYSTEMS. Food-processing methods are taken up in such entries as CANNING, COOKING, FOOD ADDITIVES, FOOD PRESERVATION, FREEZE-DRYING, FROZEN FOODS, and HEALTH FOODS.

food additives

A food additive is a nonfood substance added to food during its processing to preserve it or improve its color, texture, flavor, or value. (By legal definition the class also includes substances that may become components of food indirectly, as a result of the manufacturing or packaging process. A chemical used to make cereal packaging paper, for instance, is considered a food additive if the packaged cereal absorbs it, even in minute quantities.) Iron, minerals, and vitamins are regularly introduced into foods to compensate for losses during processing or to provide additional nutrient value. Flavoring agents make up the largest single class of additives and include salts, spices, essential oils, and natural and synthetic FLAVORS. Additives that improve texture include emulsifiers, stabilizers, and thickeners. PECTIN and GELATIN thicken jams and jellies. LECITHIN acts as an emulsifier in dressings and chocolates.

The additives used to preserve food are primarily chemical microbial agents, such as the benzoates, PROPIONATES, and sorbates that retard spoilage by bacteria, yeasts, and molds. ANTIOXIDANTS are used to keep fats and oils from spoiling and to prevent discoloration of smoked or canned meats. Ascorbic acid helps to prevent the discoloration of canned fruits.

The wide use of synthetic additives is a 20th-century phenomenon associated with the growth of the food industry. Some of the additives used today are labeled, in the terminology of the U.S. FOOD AND DRUG ADMINISTRATION (FDA), Generally Recognized As Safe (GRAS). A number of these substances had been used before 1958 (when amendments to the Food, Drug, and Cosmetic Act required that new food additives be tested for safety) with no recorded evidence of harmful effects. Others were given GRAS status after 1958. Over recent decades, however, the FDA has reviewed many of the GRAS substances and a few, such as the artificial sweetener CYCLAMATE, have been banned. Others, like the sweetener SACCHARIN, have been removed from the list but may still be used, although foods containing them must carry warning labels. (Certain health questions about the artificial sweetener ASPARTAME have yet to be resolved; it was FDA-approved in 1983 for both foods and soft drinks.) Synthetic food colors have come under FDA scrutiny, and some dyes are now prohibited as food additives. In 1986 the FDA banned SULFITES for use as color preservatives in fresh fruits and vegetables; it had already required labeling of sulfite content in other foods.

In addition to additives that reach food indirectly through packaging materials, concern is growing about chemicals that find their way into foods by way of pesticide residues on fruits and vegetables or through medications and stimulants given to animals. The FDA banned the use of the synthetic hormone diethylstilbestrol in cattle in 1979 because residues were showing up in meat products (see DES). In the 1990s the FDA and other federal agencies responsible for food safety have increased the amount of testing for pesticides they perform.

Bibliography: Goodman, D., and Redclift, M., *Refashioning Nature* (1992); Goodman, R. A., *A Quick Guide to Food Additives* (1990); Lewis, R. J., *Food Additives Handbook* (1989); Nordquist, J., ed., *Food Pollution* (1990); Schwartz, G. R., *In Bad Taste: The MSG Syndrome* (1989).

Food and Agriculture Organization

The Food and Agriculture Organization (FAO), a specialized agency of the United Nations (UN), was established in 1945 as a research and coordinating organization to develop programs in the field of world food supply. Almost every UN member nation and several non-UN nations participate in the FAO, which is headquartered in Rome. The projects it initiates, primarily in the developing nations, are designed to improve

efficiency in the production and distribution of agricultural products and to better the living conditions and nutrition levels of rural populations.

To achieve these aims, the FAO promotes the development of the basic soil and water resources of various countries. It encourages the global exchange of new agricultural techniques and improved plant types, combats epidemics of animal diseases, provides technical assistance, and promotes the development and utilization of the resources of the sea.

On an international level the FAO works to establish a stable international market for agricultural commodities and plans projects in conjunction with other UN agencies, such as the World Health Organization and the International Bank for Reconstruction and Development (World Bank).

Bibliography: Fauriols, George, *The Food and Agriculture Organization: A Flawed Strategy in the War against Hunger* (1984).

Food and Drug Administration

The Food and Drug Administration (FDA) is the agency of the U.S. Department of Health and Human Services that oversees the safety of foods, drugs, cosmetics, and medical devices, and operates the National Center for Toxicological Research. In 1906, in response to complaints about untested chemical additives in food, Congress passed the Pure Food and Drug Act (see PURE FOOD AND DRUG LAWS), which established the agency. Although initially the FDA could act only on FOOD ADDITIVES and drugs already in use and proven harmful, a series of subsequent laws expanded its jurisdiction. The Food, Drug, and Cosmetic Act of 1938 required manufacturers to test their products on both animals and humans before marketing them. In 1957 testing was required for new food additives, while the Delaney Clause (1958) prohibited the use of substances in food if they caused cancer in laboratory animals. In 1962 the FDA ruled that new drugs must be proven effective as well as safe and began a 20-year review to determine the effectiveness of prescription drugs already in use.

In 1962, having averted disaster by delaying approval of THALIDOMIDE, the FDA issued new regulations that made the drug review process far more stringent, and FDA approval for many new drugs now required up to three years of testing. The Orphan Drug Act of 1983 offers tax credits and other inducements to encourage pharmaceutical companies to develop drugs for rare diseases that affect a small population. Controversial "fast-track" approval procedures for these drugs have been instituted in some cases, causing concern about the potential for new drug hazards. The use of antibiotics in animal feed is another unresolved issue. However, regulations to improve the nutritional labeling on foods—an issue that had long been an FDA concern—were finally adopted in 1992 (see FOOD INDUSTRY).

Bibliography: Benson, James S., "FDA Enforcement Activities Protect Public," *FDA Consumer*, Jan.–Feb. 1991; Patrick, Bill, *The Food and Drug Administration* (1988).

food industry

The food industry comprises all business operations that are involved in producing a raw food material, processing it, and distributing it to sales outlets. The entire complex of the industry includes: farms and ranches; producers of raw materials, such as phosphates, for agricultural use; water-supply systems; food-processing plants; manufacturers of packaging materials and food-processing and transportation equipment; transportation systems; and retail stores and food-service operations such as restaurants, institutional feeding commissaries, and vending-machine servicers.

HISTORY OF THE INDUSTRY

The organized trading and transport of salt, spices, grain, olive oil, fermented beverages, and other foods have probably been practiced almost since the time of the first agricultural surpluses. Inventories of livestock and foodstuffs are among the first written records. However, until modern preservation methods were developed, the kinds of foods that could be traded were limited to those which did not spoil quickly.

Most food-processing operations seem to have begun as extensions of kitchen preparation techniques, scaled up to furnish enough surplus product to be bartered or sold outside the household. Enlargement of a business entailed simply building more or larger processing equipment—oil presses, baking ovens, or wine vats. Gradual improvements in design were made to increase yields or improve quality. This was the general pattern until the Industrial Revolution, when major qualitative changes began to be made in food processing and distribution operations. Not only were factories greatly enlarged and much of the manual labor replaced by machinery, but entirely new principles of processing, such as canning and spray drying, were invented. Channels of distribution became much more complex and extended, and special techniques for retaining quality were used, for example, shipping by means of refrigerated railroad cars. The present-day industry slowly took shape as it responded to ever-growing agricultural surpluses, to advances in transportation, and to the enormous changes made possible by the growth in processing technologies.

Distribution Patterns. Farmers, ranchers, other producers of agricultural raw materials, and feedlot operators usually sell their output to collection points, such as grain terminals or stockyards. The terminal or stockyard supplies the processing companies, which select needed raw materials from the available stock and process them either into finished foodstuffs, for example, cuts of meat, or into food ingredients, such as flour.

From the final processor, finished food products are moved by truck or rail to warehouses, usually located near a city. Most modern warehouses have storage areas for frozen and refrigerated food and are equipped to control temperature and humidity within a narrow range. Warehouses can assemble full truckloads of products originating from many different suppliers for shipment to one large retailer or to a number of smaller outlets in a given region, allowing a great reduction in unit transportation costs as compared to shipping a small quantity of one item directly from the producer to the retailer. If the retail outlet is large enough to accept complete truckloads directly from the manufacturer, direct shipments from the factory are sometimes made.

Processors of perishable foods (dairies, ice cream manufacturers, wholesale bread bakeries, and meat-packers) usually maintain their own fleets of trucks for carrying fresh products directly to their retailer customers. Truck drivers from bakeries and dairies may also service retail outlets by rotating stock and picking up stale products and returning them to the factory. Restaurants and institutional commissaries purchase staples and nonperishable foods from the warehouses of specialized distributors, but they also receive direct shipment from dairies, bakeries, and meat-packers.

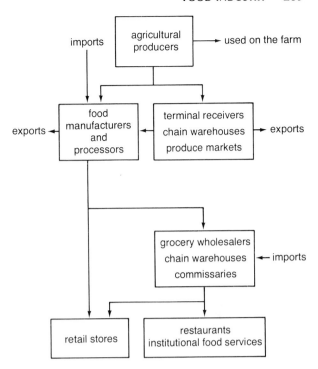

Flow of goods in the food industry

FOOD PROCESSING

Among the largest U.S. industries, food processing comprises all the methods used to transform basic food items—grains, fruits, vegetables, meats, and fish—into food products: bread, for example, canned peaches, frozen peas, bacon, or sardines. The field includes the industries that make products at only one remove from their origins on ranches and farms: meat-packers, who slaughter livestock, ship fresh and frozen meat, and prepare processed meats; poultry and fish processors; and milk processors, who pasteurize and bottle fresh milk and cream, butter, and unripened cheeses. Other processors mill grains into flour, make sugar from cane and sugar beets, produce oils from oilseeds, process herbs and spices from plants and extract flavors from plant oils. Still others use these processed products to make the canned, frozen, dried,

The sale of "natural" foods was once confined to small specialty shops that carried much of their merchandise in bulk (as in the store at left). Growing consumer interest in unprocessed foods, however, opened a new market for the giant food retailers. Today, packages of whole grains, raw nuts, and dried fruits produced without chemical preservatives can be found on the shelves of most supermarkets (right).

and baked items that are packaged and sold to consumers from retail shelves.

Quality Control. Nearly all food processing companies, as well as many food service chains, have a quality-control or quality-assurance department that evaluates raw materials, processes, and finished products. Most quality-control personnel are highly trained in chemistry, food technology, home economics, or microbiology. Their activities include sampling ingredients, packaging materials, and finished goods to determine compliance with specifications and inspecting the plant and transport means (trucks, railroad cars) to assess sanitary conditions.

Tests may be based on physical properties such as dimensions, viscosity, chemical properties (such as vitamin content or pH), sensory attributes (such as appearance, taste, odor, texture), functionality (such as response to consumer cooking procedures), legal requirements, or public health considerations such as the presence of certain microorganisms.

EVOLUTION OF FOOD RETAILING

Prior to World War I most food was sold through small neighborhood groceries. During the 20th century the following major changes in food distribution occurred: the evolution of the chain-store system, the development of retailer-owned cooperatives and wholesaler-sponsored voluntary groups, and the development and expansion of self-service supermarkets.

The first successful food-store chain was the Great Atlantic and Pacific Tea Company (A&P), which was founded in 1859 but began its great expansion after World War I. Because chains could pool the purchases of many stores, coordinate distribution, and standardize management practices, marketing costs were reduced; a chain could undersell the independent store owner while maintaining adequate profit margins. To meet this challenge, independent store owners developed two different approaches: they joined voluntary cooperatives, which, for a licensing fee, provided many of the mass-purchasing and distribution efficiencies of chains; or they affiliated with a wholesaler-distributor network, which gave them some of the same advantages in return for semiexclusive dealing. By the mid-1970s, however, grocery chains had captured well over two-thirds of the consumer market.

In the early 1990s some 60% of U.S. food sales originated in grocery stores (the other 40% was consumed in restaurants and in other FOOD SERVICE establishments). Of this total, over half was bought at supermarkets, stores whose annual volume exceeds $2 million. The number of "convenience" stores—small establishments, usually owned by chains, that sell a limited assortment of foods and achieve their largest volume on sales of milk and bread—multiplied, while small, owner-operated stores had difficulty maintaining sales in competition with the larger units. Nevertheless, the number of all grocery stores increased over the decade of the 1980s. Total food-store sales reached over $350 billion.

In 1928 grocery stores stocked an average of 867 items. Today large supermarkets may stock up to 24,000 items and will feature special departments: lunch counters, salad bars, imported cheese counters, book aisles, and so forth. In addition, the number of new products to be displayed on store shelves increases every year. By the end of the 1980s more than 12,000 products were being introduced annually, although some 80 percent of them failed to sell profitably and were withdrawn.

Computerization. Computers are increasingly used as tools to control inventories, cut operating costs, and assess changing consumer demands. Electronic scanning of Universal Product Code (UPC) symbols is designed to improve efficiency at the checkout counter, reduce errors, and assist inventory control. The UPC symbol is printed on each prepriced item, and it is "read" when the checkout clerk passes it over a scanner. The product identification is relayed by the scanning unit to a computer, which selects the appropriate price and description from its memory bank and causes this information to be printed on the cash register tape. The computer simultaneously deducts the item from the inventory carried in its memory.

Warehouse Stores. Warehouse stores generally have a no-frills decor, do little advertising, eliminate price marking on individual items, display merchandise in its shipping carton or in bulk bins, and require customers to bag their purchases in their own containers. As a result of the cost-savings thus achieved, average prices can be cut 10% or more below those of competing full-service outlets.

INDUSTRY PRICE STRUCTURE

In 1920 a grocery product costing the wholesaler $1.00 would usually be priced to the retailer at $1.13; the consumer would pay $1.40. Today, the product, sold in a supermarket, reaches the retail customer at about $1.20. The gross margin of a chain retailer usually varies from 16% to 20%, which is expected to cover both wholesale and retail functions. An independent store operator who buys from cooperative purchasing operations or from an affiliated wholesaler can usually match chain prices and margins. In the latter case, the wholesaler would have a margin of about 4% to 5%, and the retailer, about 12% to 13%. Expenses of handling produce, frozen foods, health and beauty aids, and meats are greater, and the margins are correspondingly higher.

Food prices have increased almost continually in recent years, mainly because of rises in marketing costs—the prices and quantities of labor, capital, and other factors employed in processing, wholesaling, and retailing food through food stores and public eating places. Costs per unit of food marketed have increased as a result of increases in consumption of prepackaged, ready-to-eat foods; a continuing trend toward away-from-home eating; service operations—delicatessens, bakeries, and so on—in food stores; rising wages and salaries; and higher costs for materials.

Overall, retailing profits expanded and shrank regularly throughout the 1980s, from minus figures in the early years of the decade to 1.12% of total sales in 1989 and 0.86% in 1990.

GOVERNMENT REGULATIONS

The government's influence in the operations of the food industry is all-pervasive. Although the laws relating directly to food—the Pure Food, Drug, and Cosmetic Act and the Fair Packaging and Labeling Act (see PURE FOOD AND DRUG LAWS)—are quite comprehensive, in recent years the number of other statutes affecting the food industry has increased. Among these are the Consumer Product Safety Act; the Occupational Safety and Health Act; the Water Pollution Control Act; the Clean Air Act; the Federal Insecticide, Fungicide, and Rodenticide Act; and the Clean Water Act.

The agencies charged with administering these acts include the Food and Drug Administration (FDA), the Department of Agriculture (DOA), the Environmental Protection Agency (EPA), and the Federal Trade Commission (FTC)—all of whom also issue regulations of their own. In recent years the FDA has approved the use of the artificial sweetener ASPARTAME for use in food and soft drinks and the addition of a new low-calorie fat substitute for use in a variety of foods. The EPA has

COST FACTORS CONTRIBUTING TO RETAIL PRICES OF CERTAIN FOODS IN GROCERY STORES

	Fresh Orange	Canned Tomato Juice	Chocolate Candy Bar	Loaf of Bread
Price to the consumer*	100.0	100.0	100.0	100.0
Price to the retailer, less discounts	64.2	78.5	75.0	81.5
Price to the wholesaler	——	72.4	71.2	——
Processor's costs and profits				
Ingredients and raw materials	20.1	10.9	38.5	18.0
Packaging materials	5.7	26.0	7.6	3.7
Labor and overhead (including utilities)	11.4	18.5	9.5	19.6
Transportation and storage	14.3	2.1	3.0	**
Selling expenses, including advertising and promotion	2.8	6.2	8.0	33.2
Profit before taxes	2.8	2.0	3.1	3.6
Scrap, spoiled, defective, trim, and returns	7.1	6.7	1.5	3.5

* These costs, in cents, are based on the price to the consumer of enough product to equal one dollar, before sales taxes. They are intended to be typical, but not necessarily averages, of data from any group of manufacturers.
** Included in selling expenses.

been concerned, among other issues, with the pesticide residues that may remain on produce when it is bought by consumers.

The various proposals for new standards in food labeling have included the listing of artificial colors under their specific names; naming the actual ingredients in "standardized" foods such as mayonnaise; grouping all sweeteners together, where a food contains more than one; and listing the percentage and type of fruit juice contained in juice drinks. The new regulations announced by the Bush administration in 1992, however, were confined principally to producing food labels with more comprehensive nutritional information. The regulations provide that by May 1994, the label for a packaged food must include, among other facts, its total fat, saturated fat, cholesterol, sodium, sugar, dietary fiber, and protein quantities in grams—as well as the percentage of the recommended daily intake (the Daily Value chart) supplied by each substance. Descriptions such as "low fat" will have to be literally true: that is, 50 grams of the food may not contain more than 3 grams of fat.   SAMUEL MATZ

Bibliography: Birch, G. G., et al., *Food for the Nineties* (1990); Chiba, H., et al., eds., *Food Science and Technology* (1980); Cottrell, Richard, *Food Processing* (1990); Cross, Jennifer, *The Supermarket Trap*, rev. ed. (1979); Ritson, C., et al., *The Food Consumer* (1986); Scola, Roger, *Feeding the Victorian City: The Food Supply of Manchester, 1770–1870* (1992); Walsh, W. I., *The Rise and Decline of the Great Atlantic and Pacific Tea Co.* (1986).

See also: AGRIBUSINESS; FARMS AND FARMING.

Food for Peace: see FOREIGN AID.

food poisoning and infection

Food poisoning, or intoxication, is a group of disorders generally characterized by the symptoms of nausea, vomiting, and loss of appetite (anorexia); fever and abdominal pain or discomfort (gastroenteritis); and diarrhea, in varying degrees. It may result from poisons, or toxins, produced by microorganisms in food; ingestion of heavy metals such as copper and mercury; and ingestion of natural poisons such as those found in some mushrooms and seafood.

Microorganisms. The most common type of food poisoning, accounting for nearly 70 percent of cases, is due to *Salmonella typhimurium*, a bacteria commonly found in meats, eggs, and milk. Symptoms of nausea, vomiting, gastrointestinal discomfort, and fever may appear 12 to 48 hours after eating contaminated food.

The various species of *Staphylococcus* bacteria multiply rapidly at room temperature and may directly infect the gastrointestinal tract. The culprit is usually careless food handling; workers may sneeze or cough on food or may have infected pimples or wounds on the hands or face and transmit the bacteria to the food. Symptoms of nausea, vomiting, and diarrhea develop 1 to 8 hours after exposure to the *Staphylococcus* bacteria. Treatment is usually a combination of fluid and electrolyte replacement; deaths are rare.

If food contaminated by the bacterium *Clostridium botulinum* is improperly canned or bottled, the bacteria are able to produce a toxin, which produces the disease BOTULISM. The botulin toxin is absorbed, and within 8 to 36 hours after ingestion of the contaminated food, acts by paralyzing certain nerves that regulate muscle function. This results in respiratory failure, as the muscles that control breathing weaken. The mortality rate can be as high as 65 percent, with most fatalities occurring between the second and ninth day after ingestion of the toxin. Recovery is slow in survivors. Potent antitoxins, prepared from the plasma of horses, are most effective before the patient shows symptoms.

Diarrhea and vomiting may result from infection by the protozoan *Entamoeba histolytica*, acquired by eating uncooked vegetables or drinking contaminated water (amoebic dysentery). This food-borne infection usually develops within 12 to 48 hours of ingesting the protozoan. The loss of fluids resulting from diarrhea and vomiting can lead to dehydration, which can threaten the life of young or elderly patients. Treat-

ment includes bed rest, fluids, and blood or plasma expanders if shock is impending.

Certain rare strains of the bacteria *Escherichia coli* can cause food poisoning in young children, the elderly, and people with impaired immune systems. *E. coli* 0157: H7, normally found in the intestines and fecal matter of humans and animals, can survive in meat if the meat is not cooked past 155° F. A 1993 U.S. outbreak of this type of food poisoning, which affected over 450 people, was attributed to contaminated hamburgers that were cooked rare.

Metals. Ingestion of heavy metals, such as lead and mercury, can cause acute nausea, vomiting, and diarrhea and may cause respiratory or nervous system damage over the long term. The severity of the symptoms depends on the irritant and the dose, as well as the resistance of the patient. Treatment includes bed rest, fluids, and blood or plasma expanders in severe cases where shock is anticipated.

Natural Poisons. The ingestion of naturally occurring poisons is involved in mushroom, or toadstool, poisoning; fish poisoning; shellfish poisoning; and poisoning from contaminants. Mushroom poisoning, from mushrooms such as *Amanita phalloides* or *muscaria*, can result in the symptoms of sweating, cramps, diarrhea, confusion, and sometimes convulsions. Patients usually recover within 24 hours. If the infecting mushroom is *Amanita phalloides*, however, liver damage is common, leading to jaundice; remissions may occur, but the mortality rate is about 60 percent or higher.

Fish poisoning can result from Pacific types such as sea bass, Caribbean types such as cavallas, Scrombroid types such as mackerel, and Tetraodon types such as puffers. Symptoms include numbness of the limbs, joint aches, chills, and fever. Muscle weakness and paralysis can also occur, and death may result within 24 hours. Mussels and clams may ingest a poisonous dinoflagellate (RED TIDE) from June to October that produces a toxin not destroyed by cooking. Symptoms include nausea, vomiting, and abdominal cramps, and death can occur as a result of respiratory failure.   MILO DON APPLEMAN

Bibliography: Cliver, Dean O., ed., *Foodborne Diseases* (1990); Cody, Mildred M., and Keith, Mary, *Food Safety for Professionals* (1991); Hathcock, John N., ed., *Nutritional Toxicology* (1989); Monahan, John, *Food Poisoning* (1987).

food preservation

The preservation of food is accomplished by controlling and, where possible, destroying the agents of food spoilage. These agents are present in abundance, not only within the food, but in the environments where foods are grown, harvested, processed, stored, and consumed. They include bacteria, molds, yeasts, insects, rodents, enzymes, and a wide variety of other chemical, biochemical, or physical factors.

There are many methods for destroying or inhibiting the growth of spoilage agents. High temperatures, low temperatures, eliminating or reducing the free water in foods, and using acids, chemicals, and ionizing radiation will all retard deterioration or destroy spoilage agents.

Heat Processing. Most preservation processes are aimed at affecting bacteria, molds, and yeasts, and a number of methods are available for controlling or destroying these microorganisms. The food to be preserved can be subjected to temperatures that are high enough to kill most microorganisms. CANNING, the principal form of thermal, or heat, processing, has long been a major method of preservation. It was invented almost 200 years ago by Nicolas APPERT, who heated the food in closed containers. Since Appert's day, and mainly in this century, canning technology has been greatly refined. Much more is known about sterilization temperatures and durations, and much research has been done on the packaging of canned foods and on canning machinery. Foods sterilized in airtight, heat-resistant retort pouches (laminations of plastic and aluminum film) can be preserved indefinitely. Developed for the U.S. space program, these flexible pouches are now widely used in commercial food preservation.

Acids have a preservative effect, and acidic foods—tomatoes, for example—can be sterilized at a lower temperature than bland foods. *Clostridium botulinum,* the organism that causes the deadly food-poisoning disease botulism, cannot grow in oxygen-free foods with a pH value below 4.5, a fairly high acidity.

Dehydration. DEHYDRATION of food is an effective weapon against microbial attack, since the free water in food is essential for the proliferation of bacteria. The preservation of food by drying is an ancient practice, but advances in food science and technology have created wholly new forms, such as compressed, freeze-dried foods that resume their original shape on rehydration.

Chemical Additives. Although a number of chemicals will destroy microorganisms, their use is restricted by the Food Additive Amendment of 1958. At low levels, and only in specified foods, ethyl formate, sodium benzoate, sodium and calcium PROPIONATE, sodium nitrite or nitrate, sorbic acid, and sulfur dioxide are permitted. Salt and sugar are effective preservatives; their action binds the water in a food so that it cannot be used by microorganisms. Smoke has some chemical preservation properties, since it contains guaiacol (2-methoxyphenol), which has limited bactericidal and ANTIOXIDANT action. An antioxidant inhibits oxygen reactions, such as the chemical changes that cause food to become rancid or the bacteriological activity that can take place only in the presence of oxygen. However, the mild smoke treatment usually given meat or fish is insufficient for lengthy preservation, and heat or cold is required to assure keeping quality. The principal purpose of smoking today is to give foods an appealing flavor. Some spices have value as antioxidants, but their primary function is flavor enhancement, as is the use of the additive MONOSODIUM GLUTAMATE.

Refrigeration and Freezing. Preserving food by refrigeration or by frozen storage is a widely used food processing method. Low temperatures do not sterilize foods, but they slow down the growth of microorganisms and decrease the rate of the chemical reactions that deteriorate foods. Quick-frozen foods retain their nutrients almost intact, and the characteristics of their flavor remain virtually undiminished. FROZEN FOODS must be stored and kept at 0° C (32° F) or below, because even partial thawing and refreezing lowers the overall quality of the product.

Preservation in Packaging. The plastic-aluminum retort pouch previously mentioned is only one of a number of innovative ways to preserve food in packages. Fruits and vegetables are wrapped in plastic film, which is then shrunk tightly around the product to keep its freshness longer. Frozen vegetables need never be removed from the plastic bags in which they are packaged until after they are cooked. Bags containing snack foods such as potato chips are charged with nitrogen—which does not have the deteriorating effect of oxygen—before being hermetically sealed.

Preservation by Irradiation. Ionizing radiation, obtained from radioactive isotopes such as cobalt 60, can reduce or eliminate the microorganisms, insects, and parasites that live on food. Low levels of radiation kill some types of infestations. Very high levels can literally sterilize foods.

Some 20 countries, including the United States, have approved irradiation for use on a limited group of foods: fresh fish, shellfish, and spices in Holland, potatoes in almost every country, tropical fruits in South Africa. There is considerable controversy about the ultimate health effects of the process, however, and U.S. consumers are generally wary of irradiated foods. In 1990, the U.S. Food and Drug Administration approved the use of irradiation for poultry, in order to reduce the threat of salmonella, a bacteria that causes food poisoning.   MARTIN SEVERIN PETERSON

Bibliography: Holdsworth, S. D., *The Preservation of Fruit and Vegetable Food Products* (1984); Thorne, S., ed., *Developments in Food Preservation,* 5 vols. (1981–89), and *The History of Food Preservation* (1986); Urbain, W. M., *Food Irradiation* (1986).

food service systems

Food service systems supply prepared food to institutions, such as schools and hospitals, or to large groups of consum-ers, such as air passengers. Fast-food chain restaurants, which use sophisticated techniques of food preparation, packaging, and transportation, are also considered to be food service systems. Although conventional RESTAURANTS also purvey food, sometimes in large quantities, most of them operate as independent units and serve food that is prepared from raw materials to the customer's order.

The growth of modern food service systems was made possible by the development, particularly since the 1960s, of new food technology. Today in the United States, eating and drinking places—where more than 40 percent of every consumer food dollar is spent—earn an annual volume of over $160 billion; fast-food restaurants account for 40 percent of that total. School lunches, many hospital meals, airline food, and even some hotel and restaurant menus are supplied by institutional feeders. They usually prepare whole meals in a central facility, package them in such a way that they remain fresh for the necessary period of time, and distribute them to dining rooms, sometimes at considerable distances from the preparation facility. Packaged meals are prepared much like any other mass-produced item: systems are set up for efficient purchasing, transportation, and storage of raw materials, and for the delivery of the prepared food; recipes are standardized; and the preparation of the food itself takes place in assembly-line fashion, using sophisticated, sometimes computerized, pressure cookers, fryers, grills, cooking vats, and ovens. Preservation techniques include fast freezing, precooking, and dehydrating. Microwave ovens and other machinery in institutional kitchens reheat or reconstitute the meals.

The phenomenal growth of fast-food chains since the 1950s is in large part the result of the same new technologies. Although some of the food in these establishments is cooked to order, all of it is sent from a central shipping point, where it has been processed into a ready-to-cook state: hamburgers and fish are already portioned and shaped, potatoes are ready-cut for frying, portions of pie are packaged in containers that will fit onto the moving belt of special microwave ovens. These hugely successful enterprises rely heavily on highly automated systems of food buying and preparation. Like the institutional feeders, their managements use operations-research techniques and computers to schedule production and forecast consumer demand.

Bibliography: Khan, M. A., *Foodservice Operations* (1987); Paine, F., *Modern Processing, Packaging, and Distribution Systems for Food* (1987); Spears, M. C., *Food Service Organizations* (1990).

Food Stamp Program

The U.S. Food Stamp Program, established in 1964, is designed to enable low-income households to buy quantities and kinds of food that would ordinarily be beyond their budgets. The program is administered by the Food and Nutrition Service of the U.S. Department of Agriculture, principally through welfare and public assistance agencies.

Participants are given stamps that they can use to purchase food. A household is eligible to join the program if it has an income below a specified level and meets certain other qualifications. The stamps cannot be used to buy imported food or nonfood items, including household goods, cigarettes, tobacco, or alcoholic beverages. The federal government reimburses retailers for the difference between the food stamp price and the regular price of items purchased. In 1977 the requirement that recipients pay for food stamps was abolished. In 1978 eligibility requirements were tightened, reducing the number of Americans enrolled—although the numbers began to rise once again during the late 1980s, to more than 20 million people in the early 1990s. Local welfare and public assistance offices accept applications for the Food Stamp Program.

Bibliography: Maney, Ardith L., *Still Hungry after All These Years: Food Assistance Policy from Kennedy to Reagan* (1989).

food technology: see FOOD INDUSTRY; FOOD PRESERVATION.

fool

Fools, or professional jesters, were employed by the wealthy and powerful from ancient Egyptian times until the 18th century. Often an insane or deformed person whose antics were a source of amusement, the fool may also have served as a scapegoat, or bearer of ill fortune. The long and complex tradition of fools in Western literature includes Sebastian Brant's satire *The Ship of Fools* (1494), translated into many languages and popular throughout Europe. Brant's perspective is shared by Desiderius Erasmus's ironic treatise *The Praise of Folly* (1509; Eng. trans., 1549), and finds its most powerful expression in the plays of William Shakespeare, where the fool's madness or innocence, real or feigned, gives him license to mock the pretensions and self-deceptions of his patrons. The motley clothing of the fool on the Elizabethan stage, like the ludicrous appearance of the modern circus clown, parodies the customs of sane society. Shakespeare's fools take advantage of their privileged role to speak unwelcome or comic truth, and provide, especially in *As You Like It* and *King Lear*, perceptive commentary on both tragic and comic events. Modern satiric comedy also relies upon the tradition of the fool. A notable example is the half-humorous, half-sinister figure of Harpo Marx.

Bibliography: Billington, Sandra, *A Social History of the Fool* (1984); Doran, John, *The History of Court Fools* (1858; repr. 1969); Goldsmith, Robert H., *Wise Fools in Shakespeare* (1958); Kaiser, Walter, *Praisers of Folly* (1963); Swain, Barbara, *Fools and Folly* (1932); Welsford, Enid, *The Fool* (1935; repr. 1966).

Fools, Feast of

The Feast of Fools was a mock religious festival held in England and France between the 5th and 16th centuries during the week after Christmas. A self-styled bishop of fools would lead a group of lower clergy in parodying the customs and rituals of the church. Other actors disguised themselves in costume and engaged in obscene dances and songs. The feast was finally suppressed during the Reformation.

fool's gold: see PYRITE.

Foot, Michael

Michael Mackintosh Foot, b. July 23, 1913, was leader of the British Labour party from 1980 to 1983. Foot entered Parliament in 1945 and for 9 years (1948–52, 1955–60) was editor of the left-wing journal *Tribune*. In the Labour government of the 1970s he served as secretary for employment (1974–76) and lord president of the council and leader of the house of Commons (1976–79). He resigned after leading the Labourites to defeat in the general election of June 1983.

foot-and-mouth disease

Foot-and-mouth is a highly contagious viral disease that can affect all cloven-hoofed animals. Although it is not prevalent in North America, it is constantly guarded against because it could easily be introduced through the import of live animals, fresh or frozen beef, or even animal bones used as fertilizer. Symptoms of the disease include fever, watery blisters in the mouth, excessive drooling, blistering between the hoof claws, and lameness. Occasionally, the disease will devastate a herd; more often, it does not kill but causes enormous economic losses through weight loss, quarantine, and poor performance of infected cattle. The protection afforded by vaccination is not permanent. ALVIN L. NEUMANN

foot-binding

Foot-binding was a traditional Chinese custom whereby the feet of young girls were tightly bound with strips of linen in order to prevent further growth. The large toe was bent backward over the top of the foot, and the remaining toes were folded underneath. Girls between the ages of 5 and 12 were selected to undergo foot-binding, especially if they gave

promise of future beauty. The process could not be reversed.

The origin of foot-binding, which is no longer performed, is obscure. At the beginning of the Sung dynasty (AD 960–1279), the practice was confined to court dancers. Later the custom spread throughout all social classes in China. From a mark of beauty and gentility, it came to be a requirement for a bride. The upper classes, in particular, favored foot-binding because it showed that they could support women incapable of physical labor. In 1912 the Chinese government officially banned the custom. DONN V. HART

foot disorders

The human foot is a complex structure that must be able to bear the weight of the entire body, and it is prone to a number of disorders and injuries. Unlike the foot in other primates, it is adapted solely for use in locomotion. It consists of 26 bones together with muscles, tendons, blood vessels, nerves, skin, and nails. The two largest bones are in the ankle, or tarsal, region: the heel bone, or calcaneus; and the talus, a compact bone between the lower leg and the calcaneus, completing the body's weight-bearing axis. The midfoot contains five cylindrical bones, the metatarsals, each forming a movable joint with one of the toes, or phalanges (see HUMAN BODY). Foot disorders are of three main types: those unique to the foot, those found elsewhere in the body but that are distinctly different in the foot, and those which occur similarly throughout the body.

Unique Conditions. The most important congenital foot disorder is CLUBFOOT, or *talipes equinovarus*, in which the foot is twisted inward and downward through shortening of ligaments and tendons. In some cases the condition is inherited, whereas in others it appears to be caused by diseases or other factors. Milder cases may be treated with a progressive series of casts, but more severe ones require surgery.

Other important congenital deformities involve the arch of the foot: flatfoot, or *pes planus;* and a narrow, rigid foot with a high arch, called *pes cavus.* Both cause pain, and both are usually treatable with arch supports. Surgery is required in some cases, however. One form of flatfoot, called pronation, is observed in infants and children and is usually not painful at that age. Ligament laxity allows the heels to roll outward, causing walking deformities and possible painfulness in later life unless corrected.

A bunion, or *hallux valgus,* is most commonly a disorder affecting the joint between the big toe and its metatarsal bone. The bursa, a fluid-filled sac in the joint, becomes inflamed and swells (see BURSITIS), causing pain and often twisting the big toe toward the second toe. The result is deformity and pain. Disabling bunions require surgery. Some cases are congenital, but most result from poorly fitting shoes. Corns are simply skin thickenings that become painful as they taper into the skin and cause pressure on nerve endings.

Distinctive Conditions. Three skin disorders that can also affect other parts of the body have distinct features when they occur on the foot. One, the plantar wart (also called a verruca), is caused by the same virus as that of the common WART elsewhere. On the sole of the foot, however, the firm wart acts like a pebble in a shoe, pushing against deeper skin layers that give way before it and causing great pain. Plantar warts may be treated by such techniques as freezing.

Ingrown toenail involves common bacterial infection but in a specialized site. It occurs on the rim of the nail of the big toe, where shoe pressure causes the flap of skin to be forced over the nail. This carries bacteria beneath the skin surface, and infection results. Surgical removal of part of the nail may be required in severe cases.

A special variety of FUNGUS DISEASE, called athlete's foot, *tinea pedis,* is caused by *Trichophyton nentagrophytes, T. rubrum,* and other fungus species. Most commonly, it occurs when the moist warmth of socks acts as an incubator for fungi picked up from the environment.

General Disorders. Joints of the foot may be affected by the various forms of ARTHRITIS found elsewhere in the body. These include rheumatoid arthritis, OSTEOARTHRITIS, and GOUT. The most common site for an attack of gout is the joint between the big toe and its metatarsal, as in bunions. Treatment of arthritis in the foot is substantially the same as in other parts of the body. Arthritic spurs on the big-toe joint cause rigidity that may make normal walking impossible in severe cases. Sometimes special shoes may be sufficient to alleviate the problem, but in some cases replacement of the joint with a synthetic one is required. Arthritic spurs are most common either on the top of the foot at the joint between the metatarsal and one of the ankle bones, or on the heel bone. Such spurs may require surgical removal.

Inflammations of the back part of the foot are common. The one most frequently seen is TENDONITIS of the Achilles tendon, the large tendon of the back of the heel. The inflammation may be a symptom of gout but is more commonly the result of stress. The posterior tibial tendon, which runs along the inner side of the foot, is a similar cause of pain in persons with flatfoot. The plantar fascia, a thick sheet of fibrous tissue running from the heel bone forward to the joints between the metatarsals and the toes, is a major support of the long arch of the foot, and when it becomes inflamed it can cause great disability. Pain is usually relieved by firm arch supports.

Arterial diseases not uncommonly affect the foot, particularly ATHEROSCLEROSIS. The disease is much more severe in the leg than in the arm, perhaps due to the greater hydrostatic pressure. When artery narrowing caused by the disease is severe, the cells farthest from the heart receive insufficient oxygen and nutrients. Diseases of the arteries anywhere in the leg are likely to be observed first in the foot and especially in the toes, and they may produce extensive GANGRENE, or tissue death. Persons with DIABETES may develop this condition, sometimes necessitating amputation of part or all of the lower extremity.

Injuries. The foot is prone to injury. Twisting of the foot relative to the lower leg results in fractures about the ankle. Toes and metatarsal bones may be crushed by falling objects, and jolts caused by jumping or other actions can fracture the heel bone. Hairline fractures of the second metatarsal bone, once called "march fractures" because they were observed in army recruits after a long march, are now frequently seen in joggers. They cause much pain and are hard to diagnose.

AARON D. FREEDMAN, M.D.

Bibliography: Alexander, I., *The Foot* (1990); Cailliet, R., *Foot and Ankle Pain*, 2d ed. (1982); Gould, J. S., *The Foot Book* (1987); Luces, J. R., *A Color Atlas of Foot Disorders* (1990); Schneider, M. J., and Sussman, M. D., *The Family Foot Care Book* (1986).

football

Football, in its American version, is a physically tough team sport that rivals baseball as the most popular athletic event for spectators in the United States. Millions watch football games on the interscholastic, intercollegiate, and professional levels. Games are often accompanied by halftime shows, with marching bands, and alumni or fan-club gatherings; fierce loyalties develop on the part of some spectators. Much illicit wagering takes place on the point spread in the final score. On the intercollegiate and professional levels, crowds of 50,000 to 100,000 at games are common, and millions more watch games on television.

Football is basically an autumn sport, with teams playing from 8 to 16 games, usually on successive weekends. The best of the teams then enter postseason play-offs. Many states have championships at the interscholastic (high school) level. The best of the college teams play in several bowl games—the most popular being the Rose Bowl, the Sugar Bowl, the Orange Bowl, and the Cotton Bowl. Although there is no one official college championship team, the unofficial intercollegiate champion is selected by a vote. (Coaches, sportswriters, and broadcasters cast ballots.) The professional teams of the National Football League (NFL) culminate their season with the Super Bowl game, between the winners of the American and National conference play-offs.

Despite its tremendous popularity in the United States, foot-ball has remained basically an American sport. Except for Canadians, who play the game with slightly altered rules (for example, 12 players to a side instead of 11 as in the U.S. game), football has failed to take hold elsewhere. This fact has added to the mystique of the sport's popularity in the United States.

RULES OF AMERICAN FOOTBALL

The rules of football have evolved over a long time, partly because American football can be directly traced to rugby and the modifications that Americans made to that sport to develop their own version. The rules are constantly changed to maintain a balance between offense and defense and to lessen the sport's violent nature. A set of football rules is long and sometimes almost unwieldy; high schools, colleges, and professionals play by three different sets of rules, which vary widely. The rules are enforced by a number of officials on the field—ranging from four in high school games to seven in professional football.

A common denominator of all three levels of American football is the size of the field. It is 100 yd (91.4 m) long with two additional 10-yd (9.14-m) areas called end zones. The field is 53⅓ yd (48.8 m) wide. On the field, teams of 11 players line up in offensive and defensive positions. Teams advance the ball by running with it, passing (throwing) it, and kicking it. The lines at each end of the 100 yd are called goal lines, and the object of the game is for a player to cross the other team's goal line with the ball and thus score points.

Scoring. When a player carries the ball over the opponent's goal line or passes the ball to a teammate, who either catches the ball in the end zone or catches it within the playing area and carries it over the goal line, the team is credited with a touchdown, worth six points. A team can also score three points instead of trying for a touchdown by kicking the ball (a field goal) over the uprights above the crossbar (the goalpost) of the end zone that the opponent is defending. The goalposts are stationed on the two end lines in all levels of football. Points can also be scored by stopping an opponent with the ball behind that opponent's own goal line (a safety, worth two points) and on a conversion play following a touchdown. In a conversion attempt, the team that has scored the touchdown is given an opportunity to kick the ball through the uprights or advance it across the goal line again from the opponent's 2-yd line (the 3-yd line in college football). In the National Football League, both types of conversion plays are worth one point; in college play, kicking is worth one point, but advancing over the goal line by a run or a pass is worth two points.

Operation of Play. College and professional games are 60 minutes long; high school games are 48 minutes. Play is divided into two halves, and the halves are divided equally so that in a complete game there are four quarters. The games actually last much longer, however, because the clock is stopped after scores and for penalties, measurements, injuries, out-of-bounds plays, and incomplete passes. Teams are allowed to take a limited number of time-outs; they also leave the field to take a rest break at halftime, at which time they can readjust their strategies.

Play begins with a kickoff, in which a member of one team kicks the ball off the ground (from its own 35-yd line in NFL games; from the 40-yd line in college and high school play). A coin flip just before the start of the game determines which team will perform the kickoff. Subsequent plays are begun with the center hiking the ball (passing it backward through the legs or handing it underneath the legs to a quarterback stationed directly behind) from the point—called the scrimmage line—where the center's team has advanced the ball. A play ends when the ballcarrier—a rusher (runner) or a pass-receiver—is tackled by an opponent, falls to the ground (in professional football, he must be tackled to the ground), or runs out-of-bounds, or when a forward pass is not completed (caught by a teammate).

The offensive team (the team in possession of the ball) lines up in different formations, dictated by strategy, and is allowed four plays, called downs, to advance the ball 10 yd. Each time the team does so, it is credited with a first down and is given four more downs to make 10 yd again. If the offensive

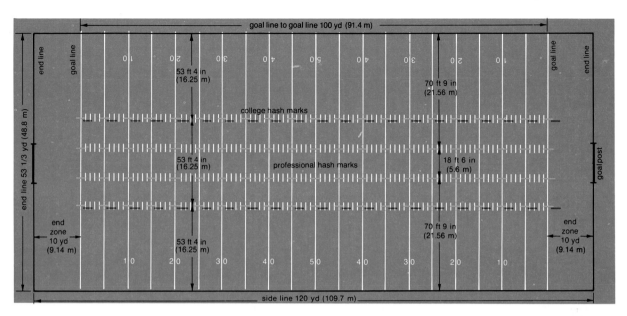

(Above) *The diagram of a modern football field indicates the standard dimensions and the difference between hash marks observed in collegiate and professional play. Rule changes adopted (1912) by college officials established the 100-yard field of play between goal lines.*

figure 1

figure 2

Some fundamental playing situations are demonstrated by the quarterback (A) attempting a pass, a running back (B) eluding a tackle, a lineman (C) blocking a defender, and a kicker (D) just having punted the ball to the opposing team. The contact involved in football requires that players wear padding (Fig. 1) to protect the ribs, hips, and upper torso. The basic gear (Fig. 2) includes: the ball, an inflated, leather-sheathed rubber bladder; a helmet with a protective face guard; and shoes equipped with cleated soles for traction.

team fails to advance 10 yd in any series of four plays, the opposition takes possession of the ball and goes on offense. Often a team that is stopped deep in its own territory with little chance of making the 10 yd will kick, or punt, the ball in order to put the opponent farther back in its own territory. At any point in the game, however, the defense can get the ball by intercepting a pass or recovering a fumble (dropped ball). Generally, football teams have specialists for both offense and defense, and the same players do not participate in both phases of the game, although they are allowed to.

Equipment. The basic equipment for playing the game is a ball in the shape of an oblate spheroid 11-11¼ in (28-28.6 cm) long and 21¼-21½ in (54-54.6 cm) around its longest axis; the ball weighs 14-15 oz (396.9-425.25 g). The goalposts vary in different levels of play. In addition, players are heavily burdened with different types of protective equipment so that they resemble modern-day gladiators.

HISTORY OF FOOTBALL

Any number of theories exist about the evolution of American football, but most historians agree that it is a modification of the English game of RUGBY and of soccer. American football evolved slowly in the 19th century.

19th-Century Development. Football made its first appearance at the intercollegiate level. As a prelude to what would become an American game, collegians played rugby, but the sport was so grueling that it was barred at Harvard in 1860. Nine years later, on Nov. 6, 1869, two New Jersey universities, Rutgers and Princeton, played what is considered the first intercollegiate game in the United States—although it hardly resembled modern-day football, or even the football that was played at the turn of the century. There were 25 players on each side, and the scoring was decided by goals, not touchdowns, conversions, and field goals. Rutgers won that first game, and Princeton won a rematch a week later. Before long, other universities began taking up the game—Columbia in 1870, followed by Yale 2 years later.

Harvard continued to play a game more similar to rugby; but in 1875, when it played Yale, Harvard convinced its opponent to play under new rules, which brought the game into a new era. Touchdowns counted only one point, compared to four for a successful conversion kick. A field goal was worth five points.

Walter CAMP, a freshman at Yale in 1876, became the organizational genius that the college game badly needed to unify and organize the rules. Under his influence the teams were decreased in size from 15 to 11. The field varied from 140 yd (128 m) by 70 yd (64 m) to 110 by 53⅓ yd (100.5 by 48.8 m), and the ball was put in play by having the offensive team's center get the ball from his line of scrimmage to the quarterback. In 1889, another innovation Camp shared in was the selection of the first All-America team, which started the trend toward glamorizing individual stars.

The first significant rules convention was held in 1880. The participants neglected, however, to provide incentives for advancing the line of scrimmage, thus sustaining the dull, 90-minute game. In 1882, Camp successfully campaigned for the rule that made the offensive team give up possession if it moved the ball less than 5 yd forward in three downs.

Camp also standardized the scoring system in 1883, showing a strong prejudice toward the kicking influence of rugby and soccer. Touchdowns scored only two points, whereas the conversion kick scored four and field goals five.

20th-Century Innovations. Because of the violent, physical way in which football games were conducted in the 19th century, many deaths and maiming injuries occurred. As a result of 18 deaths and 159 serious injuries in 1905, President Theodore Roosevelt insisted that the colleges make their game safer or he might ban it. Representatives of 62 colleges met in New York City after the 1905 season, and in early 1906 rules were suggested and approved that would eliminate the negative aspects. The emphasis was shifted from brawn to speed and strategy. The legalization of the forward pass made much of this possible. The game was also shortened from 70 to 60 minutes, and the required yardage for a first down was reset at 10 yd. A neutral zone was set up between teams at the scrimmage line, and the offense had to have at least six men on the line of scrimmage, thus eliminating the dangerous plays in which blockers took running starts before the snap of the ball. A seventh blocker on the line of scrimmage was mandated in 1910 to make the game even safer.

Football rules were changed constantly, however, to maintain the delicate offense-defense balance. After 1912, however, when the number of chances to make a first down was increased to four, the changes were less drastic.

The Passing Game. Modern football differs most from the turn-of-the-century game because of the skills of passers. When the passing rule was instituted in 1906, few took advantage of it. Actually, some rules limited its advancement, including the one that said that no pass could travel more than 20 yd beyond the line of scrimmage and the one that stated that an incomplete pass resulted in a 15-yd loss.

But the passing combination of quarterback Gus Dorais and Knute ROCKNE at Notre Dame in 1913 popularized the pass. This aspect of the game brought fame to Notre Dame and its future coach Rockne, who became a legend. Notre

(Left) Jim Thorpe, an outstanding football player of the early 20th century, became a collegiate star at Carlisle (Pa.) Indian School, where he won All-American honors. As a professional (starting with the Canton Bulldogs in 1915), Thorpe stimulated the growth of the sport.

This early football game pitting Yale against its longtime rival Princeton was played in 1909, 40 years after the first intercollegiate game was contested. Yale, with a perfect 10-0-0 record, was selected as national collegiate champion in 1909, outscoring its opponents 209-0.

(Left) *Each play begins from the line of scrimmage, an imaginary plane spanning the width of the field, passing through the portion of the ball nearest to the defensive team. A minimum of seven offensive players must position themselves within a yard of the line of scrimmage.*

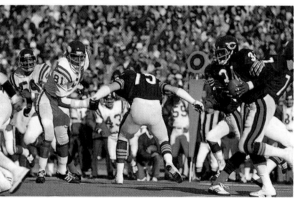

(Left) *Running back Walter Payton of the Chicago Bears gains yardage on the ground during an NFL game. In 1984, Payton became the NFL's all-time leading rusher, passing the legendary Jimmy Brown.*

(Right) *Rafael Septien of the Dallas Cowboys attempts to kick a field goal. The field goal, worth three points, is scored by placekicking the ball between the uprights of the goalpost.*

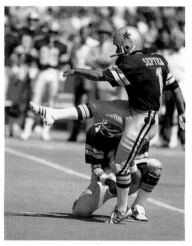

(Below) *Quarterback Joe Montana of the San Francisco 49ers prepares to release a forward pass, one means by which the offense may advance the ball. A legal pass must be thrown from behind the line of scrimmage; only six offensive players may receive or pass the ball.*

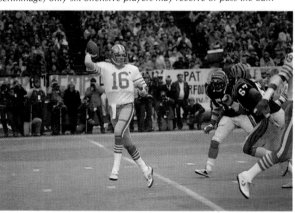

Dame defeated a powerful West Point team that year, with Dorais passing for 243 yd.

The ball was gradually made smaller as passing became more important. It was instrumental in increasing interest in professional football, which lagged well behind college football until the 1950s. The passing skills of such players as Sammy BAUGH, Otto GRAHAM, and Johnny UNITAS helped the professional sport achieve a rapid growth in popularity.

Professional Football. The game was first played with paid players in 1895, when a team from Latrobe, Pa., hosted a game with a team from nearby Jeannette. Except for barnstorming (touring) teams, however, there was little professional football of any significance until 1919, when the founders of what would become the National Football League met in Canton, Ohio, to organize the sport. Jim THORPE was named president of the league to capitalize on his reputation.

Professional football grew slowly, however. There were times of increased interest, such as the period during the 1920s when Red GRANGE signed to play professionally and drew crowds of 36,000 in Chicago and 68,000 in New York City. The college teams, including the Ivy League schools, still captured the attention of the sports public.

A second professional league, the All-America Football Conference, was founded in 1946 to compete with the NFL, but that league was absorbed by its competitor in 1950. The coming of the television age and America's unending thirst for more sports after World War II helped the NFL grow. By the late 1950s the televising of football games, which was held to a minimum by the colleges, was utilized by the professional teams to promote their game. Rising attendance prompted the founding (1960) of a new circuit, the American Football League. The NFL and AFL competed to sign new players and wisely loosened their rules to allow more scoring. Before long they were competing on an equal level with the colleges for the football fan. The AFL was absorbed by the NFL in 1970 as a result of a merger agreement in 1966. From this agreement came a plan for a postseason championship game, which became known as the Super Bowl, consistently the most popular televised sports event. The short-lived World Football League (1974–75) and United States Football League (1983–85) were other challengers to the NFL's supremacy.

Canadian Football. Like U.S. football, Canadian football developed from rugby and soccer during the late 19th century. In 1909, Lord Grey, governor-general of Canada, donated a trophy—subsequently called the Grey Cup—to be awarded annually to Canada's best football team. Although Grey Cup play became predominantly professional during the 1930s,

NATIONAL FOOTBALL LEAGUE CHAMPIONS*

1933	Chicago Bears 23	New York Giants 21	
1934	New York Giants 30	Chicago Bears 13	
1935	Detroit Lions 26	New York Giants 7	
1936	Green Bay Packers 21	Boston Redskins 6	
1937	Washington Redskins 28	Chicago Bears 21	
1938	New York Giants 23	Green Bay Packers 17	
1939	Green Bay Packers 27	New York Giants 0	
1940	Chicago Bears 73	Washington Redskins 0	
1941	Chicago Bears 37	New York Giants 9	
1942	Washington Redskins 14	Chicago Bears 6	
1943	Chicago Bears 41	Washington Redskins 21	
1944	Green Bay Packers 14	New York Giants 7	
1945	Cleveland Rams 15	Washington Redskins 14	
1946	Chicago Bears 24	New York Giants 14	
1947	Chicago Cardinals 28	Philadelphia Eagles 21	
1948	Philadelphia Eagles 7	Chicago Cardinals 0	
1949	Philadelphia Eagles 14	Los Angeles Rams 0	
1950	Cleveland Browns 30	Los Angeles Rams 28	
1951	Los Angeles Rams 24	Cleveland Browns 17	

1952	Detroit Lions 17	Cleveland Browns 7	
1953	Detroit Lions 17	Cleveland Browns 16	
1954	Cleveland Browns 56	Detroit Lions 10	
1955	Cleveland Browns 38	Los Angeles Rams 14	
1956	New York Giants 47	Chicago Bears 7	
1957	Detroit Lions 59	Cleveland Browns 14	
1958	Baltimore Colts 23	New York Giants 17	
1959	Baltimore Colts 31	New York Giants 16	
1960	Philadelphia Eagles 17	Green Bay Packers 13	
1961	Green Bay Packers 37	New York Giants 0	
1962	Green Bay Packers 16	New York Giants 7	
1963	Chicago Bears 14	New York Giants 10	
1964	Cleveland Browns 27	Baltimore Colts 0	
1965	Green Bay Packers 23	Cleveland Browns 12	
1966	Green Bay Packers 34	Dallas Cowboys 27	
1967	Green Bay Packers 21	Dallas Cowboys 17	
1968	Baltimore Colts 34	Cleveland Browns 0	
1969	Minnesota Vikings 27	Cleveland Browns 7	

*League merged with the American Football League before the 1970 season, forming two conferences, the American and the National. Winners of the respective conference championships (listed separately) meet in the Super Bowl to decide the NFL championship.

AMERICAN CONFERENCE (NFL) CHAMPIONS

1970	Baltimore Colts 27	Oakland Raiders 17
1971	Miami Dolphins 21	Baltimore Colts 0
1972	Miami Dolphins 21	Pittsburgh Steelers 17
1973	Miami Dolphins 27	Oakland Raiders 10
1974	Pittsburgh Steelers 24	Oakland Raiders 13
1975	Pittsburgh Steelers 16	Oakland Raiders 10
1976	Oakland Raiders 24	Pittsburgh Steelers 7
1977	Denver Broncos 20	Oakland Raiders 17
1978	Pittsburgh Steelers 34	Houston Oilers 5
1979	Pittsburgh Steelers 27	Houston Oilers 13
1980	Oakland Raiders 34	San Diego Chargers 27
1981	Cincinnati Bengals 27	San Diego Chargers 7
1982	Miami Dolphins 14	New York Jets 0
1983	Oakland Raiders 30	Seattle Seahawks 14
1984	Miami Dolphins 45	Pittsburgh Steelers 28
1985	New England Patriots 31	Miami Dolphins 14
1986	Denver Broncos 23	Cleveland Browns 20
1987	Denver Broncos 38	Cleveland Browns 33
1988	Cincinnati Bengals 21	Buffalo Bills 10
1989	Denver Broncos 37	Cleveland Browns 21
1990	Buffalo Bills 51	Los Angeles Raiders 3
1991	Buffalo Bills 10	Denver Broncos 7
1992	Buffalo Bills 29	Miami Dolphins 10

NATIONAL CONFERENCE (NFL) CHAMPIONS

1970	Dallas Cowboys 17	San Francisco 49ers 10
1971	Dallas Cowboys 14	San Francisco 49ers 3
1972	Washington Redskins 26	Dallas Cowboys 3
1973	Minnesota Vikings 27	Dallas Cowboys 10
1974	Minnesota Vikings 14	Los Angeles Rams 10
1975	Dallas Cowboys 37	Los Angeles Rams 7
1976	Minnesota Vikings 24	Los Angeles Rams 13
1977	Dallas Cowboys 23	Minnesota Vikings 6
1978	Dallas Cowboys 28	Los Angeles Rams 0
1979	Los Angeles Rams 9	Tampa Bay Buccaneers 0
1980	Philadelphia Eagles 20	Dallas Cowboys 7
1981	San Francisco 49ers 28	Dallas Cowboys 27
1982	Washington Redskins 31	Dallas Cowboys 17
1983	Washington Redskins 24	San Francisco 49ers 21
1984	San Francisco 49ers 23	Chicago Bears 0
1985	Chicago Bears 24	Los Angeles Rams 0
1986	New York Giants 17	Washington Redskins 0
1987	Washington Redskins 17	Minnesota Vikings 10
1988	San Francisco 49ers 28	Chicago Bears 3
1989	San Francisco 49ers 30	Los Angeles Rams 3
1990	New York Giants 15	San Francisco 49ers 13
1991	Washington Redskins 41	Detroit Lions 10
1992	Dallas Cowboys 30	San Francisco 49ers 20

SUPER BOWL*

Year	Teams and Scores		Location
1966–67	Green Bay Packers 35	Kansas City Chiefs 10	Los Angeles
1967–68	Green Bay Packers 33	Oakland Raiders 14	Miami
1968–69	New York Jets 16	Baltimore Colts 7	Miami
1969–70	Kansas City Chiefs 23	Minnesota Vikings 7	New Orleans
1970–71	Baltimore Colts 16	Dallas Cowboys 13	Miami
1971–72	Dallas Cowboys 24	Miami Dolphins 3	New Orleans
1972–73	Miami Dolphins 14	Wash. Redskins 7	Los Angeles
1973–74	Miami Dolphins 24	Minnesota Vikings 7	Houston
1974–75	Pittsburgh Steelers 16	Minnesota Vikings 6	New Orleans
1975–76	Pittsburgh Steelers 21	Dallas Cowboys 17	Miami
1976–77	Oakland Raiders 32	Minnesota Vikings 14	Pasadena
1977–78	Dallas Cowboys 27	Denver Broncos 10	New Orleans
1978–79	Pittsburgh Steelers 35	Dallas Cowboys 31	Miami
1979–80	Pittsburgh Steelers 31	Los Angeles Rams 19	Pasadena
1980–81	Oakland Raiders 27	Philadelphia Eagles 10	New Orleans
1981–82	San Francisco 49ers 26	Cincinnati Bengals 21	Pontiac
1982–83	Wash. Redskins 27	Miami Dolphins 17	Pasadena
1983–84	Oakland Raiders 38	Wash. Redskins 9	Tampa
1984–85	San Francisco 49ers 38	Miami Dolphins 16	Palo Alto
1985–86	Chicago Bears 46	New England Patriots 10	New Orleans
1986–87	New York Giants 39	Denver Broncos 20	Pasadena
1987–88	Wash. Redskins 42	Denver Broncos 10	San Diego
1988–89	San Francisco 49ers 20	Cincinnati Bengals 16	Miami
1989–90	San Francisco 49ers 55	Denver Broncos 10	New Orleans
1990–91	New York Giants 20	Buffalo Bills 19	Tampa
1991–92	Wash. Redskins 37	Buffalo Bills 24	Minneapolis
1992–93	Dallas Cowboys 57	Buffalo Bills 17	Pasadena

*AFL-NFL interleague championship 1966–70; NFL championship since 1970–71.

AMERICAN FOOTBALL LEAGUE CHAMPIONS*

1960	Houston Oilers 24	Los Angeles Chargers 16
1961	Houston Oilers 10	San Diego Chargers 3
1962	Dallas Texans 20	Houston Oilers 17
1963	San Diego Chargers 51	Boston Patriots 10
1964	Buffalo Bills 20	San Diego Chargers 7
1965	Buffalo Bills 23	San Diego Chargers 0
1966	Kansas City Chiefs 31	Buffalo Bills 7
1967	Oakland Raiders 40	Houston Oilers 7
1968	New York Jets 27	Oakland Raiders 23
1969	Kansas City Chiefs 17	Oakland Raiders 7

*League merged with NFL in 1970 and became the American Conference.

amateur teams were not banned until 1956, when the current structure of the organization that would become (1960) the Canadian Football League (CFL) was solidified. Canadian football differs from its U.S. professional counterpart in several ways: the field is 110 yd (100.6 m) long and 65 yd (59.4 m) wide, with 25-yd-deep (22.9-m) end zones; there are 12 players per team on the field; the offensive team has 3 downs to gain 10 yd; an untouched punt or unsuccessful field-goal attempt may be recovered by the kicking team; after a touchdown, a team may try for 2 points; a team can score a rouge

(1 point) if their opponents fail to run a kick out of their own end zone.   JIM BENAGH

Bibliography: Hollander, Zander, *The Complete Handbook of Pro Football*, 14th ed. (1988); Neft, D. S., et al., *The Sports Encyclopedia: Pro Football*, 6th ed. (1989).

football, association: see SOCCER.

Foote, Andrew Hull   [fut]

Andrew Hull Foote, b. Sept. 12, 1806, d. June 26, 1863, was a U.S. naval officer. After engaging in suppression of the slave trade along the African coast (1849–51), he commanded (1856–58) the *Portsmouth* off China and led (1856) a raid to capture four barrier forts south of Canton that had fired on his ship. During the U.S. Civil War, Foote was in charge of Union naval operations on the upper Mississippi. In 1862 his gunboats assisted in the capture of FORT HENRY AND FORT DONELSON and Island No. 10. A temperance advocate, Foote brought about abolition (1862) of alcohol on naval ships.

Foote, Horton

The playwright and scriptwriter Horton Foote, b. Wharton, Tex., Mar. 14, 1916, has had remarkable success in mining the history of his family for his many dramas. An actor and theater manager, Foote began writing plays, most of them based in small-town Texas, in the early 1940s. His screenplays include his adaptation of the novel *To Kill a Mockingbird* (1962) and *The Trip to Bountiful* (1985), taken from his own 1953 play and TV script. Both screenplays won academy awards. In recent years, most of his work has appeared on television, notably the three-part miniseries "Story of a Marriage" (1987).

Foote, Robert Bruce

Robert Bruce Foote, 1834–1912, was a British geologist and archaeologist. Considered the father of prehistoric studies in India, he established there a basic chronology from the Paleolithic to the Iron Age. A summary of his work appears in his major writing, *Indian Prehistoric and Protohistoric Artefacts* (1916).   STEPHEN KOWALEWSKI

For Whom the Bell Tolls

For Whom the Bell Tolls (1940; film, 1943), Ernest HEMINGWAY's fifth and most genuinely tragic novel, tells the story of Robert Jordan, an American teacher who has volunteered his services to the Loyalists in their fight against the Fascists in the Spanish Civil War. Charged with dynamiting a strategic bridge, he joins a guerrilla band in the Guadarrama Mountains. His brief love affair with the young woman Maria is partly instigated by the spiritualist Pilar, who foresees Jordan's death. Despite the treason of Pilar's consort Pablo, Jordan destroys the bridge but dies while covering the guerrillas' retreat.   CARLOS BAKER

Bibliography: Grebstein, Sheldon, ed., *The Merrill Studies in "For Whom the Bell Tolls"* (1971).

Forain, Jean Louis   [fohr-an']

Jean Louis Forain, b. Oct. 23, 1852, d. Jan. 11, 1931, was a French painter, graphic artist, and satirist. Forain exhibited at the fourth impressionist exhibition in 1879 and continued painting while supporting himself by satirical graphic contributions to numerous periodicals. His debt to Honoré DAUMIER is apparent in his satires of low life, the legal system, and the horrors of war.   STEFANIE M. WINKELBAUER

foraminifera   [fohr-am-i-nif'-ur-uh]

Foraminifera, often called forams, constitute an order, Foraminifera, of amoeboid PROTOZOA with calcareous shells. Pseudopods protrude through holes in the shells—hence the name Foraminifera, which means "hole bearers." These shells may accumulate in such numbers on the ocean floor that they form the predominant bottom deposits in some areas and may eventually contribute to land-mass formation.

Growth and Reproduction. The single cell of the living foraminiferal animal may have one or more nuclei. As the animal grows, it adds chambers to its shell, or test. The body substance (protoplasm) fills all these chambers, which are connected by openings called foramina. Pseudopods (long, fine extensions of the protoplasm) project through numerous small pores in the test. The pseudopods gather food and construct the new chambers.

Foraminifera reproduce by alternating asexual and sexual generations. Asexually produced organisms originate from the division of a single parental individual. At maturity, asexual individuals produce gametes (reproductive cells). Gametes from two different parents form a new individual, which reproduces asexually to complete the reproductive cycle.

Distribution. Nearly all foraminifera are marine, and the great majority of these are benthic (dwellers on the sea floor). Species of benthic forams that are restricted to particular types of sediment, temperatures, or salinity conditions may be good indicators of environmental factors. Particular species of planktonic (floating) forams, however, are often characteristic of cold-water or warm-water oceanic regions. Shifts in the geographic distribution of planktonic species in Pleistocene deposits are used to map the changing positions of oceanic currents of glacial and interglacial stages.

Importance. Foraminifera are important components of some well-known rock formations. They are abundant and useful for correlation in Cretaceous chalks like those forming the White Cliffs of Dover, on the southeastern coast of England. Large, coin-shaped forams (up to 20 mm in diameter), called nummulitids, were found in the limestone blocks of some of the

The foraminiferan Almaena taurica (1), photographed with an electron diffraction microscope, is known from Upper Eocene deposits in the USSR. Globigerinoides fistulosus (2), known from the Middle Pliocene to recent epochs, has spherical chambers except for the last one or two, which form finger-shaped extensions. Globigerina nepenthes (3), with spherical to ovate chambers, occurs in Miocene and Pliocene strata. Elongation of the last two chambers characterizes Globigerina digitata digitata (4), found in the Quaternary Period. Shells of the species shown measure about 1 mm (0.04 in) in diameter.

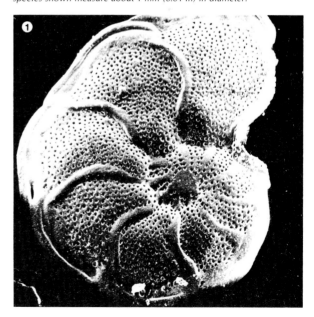

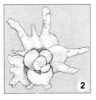

pyramids of Egypt. In the 1920s, paleontologists demonstrated the value of fossil forams in stratigraphic correlation (determining the age of sedimentary formations). Foraminifera are found in sedimentary rocks of all periods from the Cambrian onward, but they are most useful for correlation of Late Paleozoic, Cretaceous, and Cenozoic strata.

Forams are so small (generally less than 1 mm in diameter) that they come up intact in small chips of rock obtained from wells drilled for oil. Thus they have played an important role in the development of the petroleum industry. The rapid evolutionary changes in the form of forams' tests indicate precisely the age of the strata in which these fossils occur and thus the likelihood that the rock contains oil.

Bibliography: Broadhead, T. W., ed., *Foraminifera* (1982); Cushman, Joseph, *Foraminifera*, 4th rev. ed. (1948); Murray, John, *Distribution and Ecology of Living Benthic Foraminiferids* (1973).

Forbes

Published fortnightly since 1917, *Forbes* magazine is a business-oriented publication that profiles leaders in industry, seeking to define the quality and impact of management policies. Founded by Bertie Charles Forbes (1880–1954), the magazine reached a large readership (735,000 in 1990) under the management of Bertie's flamboyant sportsman son Malcolm Stephenson Forbes (1919–90).

Forbes, John

John Forbes, b. Sept. 5, 1707, d. Mar. 11, 1759, was the British general who captured Fort Duquesne (Pittsburgh, Pa.) during the FRENCH AND INDIAN WAR (1755–63). In 1758 he marched from Philadelphia across the Alleghenies with several thousand Americans and British regulars, cutting a road that later became a major emigration route. When his agent Christian Frederick Post was able to secure the defection of the Indians on whom the French depended, Forbes took Fort Duquesne on Nov. 25, 1758, without a struggle. British control of the Ohio Valley was thus assured.

Bibliography: Jennings, Francis, *Empire of Fortune* (1988); Stotz, Charles M., *Drums in the Forest* (1958).

Forbes, Robert Bennet

Robert Bennet Forbes, b. Sept. 18, 1804, d. Nov. 23, 1889, was a Boston sea captain and merchant who made a fortune selling opium to China and importing Chinese silk, earthenware, and teas. He was one of the first to use steamships with screw propellers and iron hulls. During the Civil War he organized a small coast guard and supervised the construction of nine gunboats for the federal navy.

Forbes-Robertson, Sir Johnston

Johnston Forbes-Robertson, b. Jan. 16, 1853, d. Nov. 6, 1937, was a famous 19th-century British stage actor. His career spanned almost 40 years in a variety of Shakespearean and modern roles in England and the United States. Forbes-Robertson was knighted in 1913, two years before his retirement from the theater.

Bibliography: Donaldson, Frances, *The Actor-Managers* (1970); Forbes-Robertson, Johnston, *A Player under Three Reigns* (1925; repr. 1971).

Forbidden City

The Forbidden City usually refers to the group of imperial buildings found within the Inner City of PEKING (Beijing), China. Walls up to 11 m (35 ft) high enclose the Forbidden City, whose buildings consist of palaces, shrines, and halls used by Chinese emperors between 1421 and 1911. T'ai-ho Tien, the Hall of Supreme Harmony, stands in the center of the compound and was used as the emperors' throne room. The white marble terraces, yellow-tiled roofs, and formal gardens attract many tourists to the Forbidden City, which has been open to the public as a museum since 1949.

LHASA, Tibet, is also referred to as the Forbidden City because of its isolation from the rest of the world and because of traditional Tibetan hostility toward visitors.

force

In physics, force is an influence that pushes or pulls matter and in so doing tends to induce motion. Force, which is intimately involved in all natural processes, ranges in magnitude from tiny subatomic forces to the great gravitational forces of planets and stars.

A force is a vector quantity, that is, it is composed of both a magnitude and a specific direction. If either component changes, the force itself is said to change. The analysis of force problems is facilitated by a special branch of mathematics known as VECTOR ANALYSIS, with which forces and their interactions may be framed in mathematical terms.

The study of the interaction of forces, objects, and motion, known as mechanics, is the oldest branch of physical science. Mechanics includes force systems in equilibrium (STATICS), the mathematics of motion (KINEMATICS), and the relationship of force and motion (DYNAMICS).

The effect of force on matter was described three centuries ago by Sir Isaac Newton in what are known today as Newton's LAWS OF MOTION. Using these natural laws, it was established that acceleration is caused by an unbalanced force; that force, mass, and acceleration are simply related; and that all forces in nature occur in opposing pairs. Newton also discovered the universal law of GRAVITATION, which relates the gravitational attraction of two bodies to their masses and to their separation distance. Other natural principles peculiar to specific areas of physics serve to relate the various parameters responsible for electrical, magnetic, frictional, aerodynamic, and other forces.

It is important to distinguish between mass, an inherent characteristic of matter, and the force experienced by that mass in a gravitational field. Specifically, a person's weight is not the same as the person's mass; it is merely the force exerted on the mass by gravity.   GARY S. SETTLES

Bibliography: Davies, P. C. W., *The Forces of Nature,* 2d ed. (1986); Grigoryev, V., and Myakishev, G., *Forces of Nature* (1975); Youmans, Edward L., *The Correlation and Conservation of Forces* (1981).

Ford   (family)

The Ford family has had a major impact on the development of the U.S. AUTOMOTIVE INDUSTRY. **Henry Ford**, b. July 30, 1863, d. Apr. 7, 1947, was the son of William Ford, who had emigrated from Ireland in 1847 and settled on a farm in Dearborn, Mich. Henry disliked farm life and had a natural aptitude for machinery; when he was 15 he went to Detroit and trained as a machinist. In 1888 he married Clara Bryant. They had one child, a son, **Edsel**, b. Nov. 6, 1893, d. May 26, 1943.

Henry Ford began to experiment with a horseless carriage about 1890 and completed his first car, the quadricycle, in 1896. It was the sixth American-built gasoline-powered car. During the following years he tried unsuccessfully to get it into production. During this period he built racing cars and became a well-known racing driver. In 1903 he launched the Ford Motor Company with a capital of $100,000, of which $28,000 was in cash. By this time he had formulated his ideal

The American inventor and industrialist Henry Ford poses in his quadricycle, an automobile powered by a 2-cylinder gasoline engine, which he developed in 1896. Ford introduced modern mass-production techniques to the automotive industry with his amazingly successful Model T, the first car built on a moving assembly line.

of production: "The way to make automobiles is to make one automobile like another automobile, to make them all alike. . . ."

He achieved spectacular success with the MODEL T Ford, introduced in 1908 and eventually produced (1913) on a moving ASSEMBLY LINE. Henry Ford was the major figure in the world's automobile industry for the next 15 years. His production methods were intensively studied; in Germany they were called *Fordismus*. He also startled the world by instituting (1914) the then high base-wage scale of $5 a day. He had gained favorable publicity (1911) by resisting the holders of the Selden patent, which purported to be a basic patent on the gasoline automobile, under conditions that made him appear to be a little man challenging a monopoly.

Ford thus became a figure of legend, the native genius who could work miracles. He had considerable mechanical ability, but his conclusions were reached intuitively rather than logically. He was basically uneducated and given to naive ideas about the world. In 1915 he sent a Peace Ship to Europe, hoping to persuade the belligerents to stop the war. For years he financed anti-Semitic propaganda in his newspaper, the *Dearborn Independent*, which he subsequently had to disavow. Yet he also helped to preserve artifacts of American history by establishing Greenfield Village and the Henry Ford Museum and by restoring the Wayside Inn in Sudbury, Mass., immortalized in a Longfellow poem. Inevitably, he was considered for public office. He ran as a Democratic candidate for the U.S. Senate in 1918 and was narrowly defeated. A few years later he was touted as a presidential candidate but, after some hesitation, withdrew on the advice of his close friends. In 1936 he and his son Edsel established the FORD FOUNDATION, to which they bequeathed much of the company's stock.

Henry Ford became a victim of his own success in that he clung to the Model T too long, refusing to see that its popularity was fading, and consequently lost first place in the industry to General Motors in 1926. He had turned the presidency of the Ford Motor Company over to Edsel in 1919 but never gave Edsel effective authority. The elder Ford remained firmly in control. He showed occasional flashes of his mechanical brilliance, producing the Model A (1928) and the V-8 engine (1932), but he was an aging autocrat, resisting change and becoming increasingly influenced by his security chief, Harry Bennett. Edsel struggled vainly against this situation, and the frustrations of his position undoubtedly contributed to his death at age 50. His father resumed the presidency.

By that time Henry Ford had had two strokes and was incapable of managing the company. **Henry Ford II,** b. Sept. 4, 1917, d. Sept. 29, 1987, Edsel's oldest son, was released from the navy and made executive vice-president. He became president in 1945. Unlike his father, who had not been allowed to go to college, Henry II attended Yale University. When he assumed control of the company at the age of 28, management was in chaos, labor relations were poor, and the financial situation was shaky. He recruited talent from outside the company and effected a sweeping reorganization. The company secured firm control of second place in the American automobile industry. In the 1960s it expanded into electronics and astronautics by purchasing the Philco Corporation, and Henry Ford II was regarded as an industrial statesman. He retired from his top company posts in 1979 and 1980.   JOHN B. RAE

Bibliography: Bryan, F. R., *The Fords of Dearborn* (1989); Collier, P., and Horowitz, D., *The Fords: An American Epic* (1987); Hayes, W., *Henry* (1990); Lacey, R., *Ford: The Men and the Machine* (1986); Nevins, A., and Hill, F., *Ford*, 3 vols. (1951–62; repr. 1976).

Ford, Ford Madox

Ford Madox Ford, originally named Ford Herman Hueffer, b. Dec. 17, 1873, d. June 26, 1939, was an English writer and editor best known for his advocacy of experimental fiction and for his intricate and subtle novel *The Good Soldier* (1915).

Ford was the son of a German émigré and the grandson of the Pre-Raphaelite painter Ford Madox Brown. He began writing at an early age, collaborated with Joseph Conrad on *The Inheritors* (1901) and *Romance* (1903), and in 1908–09

founded and edited the *English Review*. In this short-lived journal he published the works of such young writers as D. H. Lawrence and Ezra Pound. After service in World War I, Ford edited (1923–24) the *Transatlantic Review* in Paris, publishing such writers as James Joyce and Ernest Hemingway.

Although Ford published some 70 different works, he is best remembered today for five of his novels, beginning with *The Good Soldier*. This ironic work is a masterly exploration of life's illusions and realities. His distinguished tetralogy *Parade's End*, consisting of *Some Do Not* (1924), *No More Parades* (1925), *A Man Could Stand Up* (1926), and *The Last Post* (1928), deals with a man whose certain and ordered world is shattered by the events leading up to World War I. An amiable eccentric, Ford also wrote a number of amusing, inaccurate memoirs, including *Thus to Revisit* (1921), *Return to Yesterday* (1931), and *It Was the Nightingale* (1933). His *A History of Our Times* (ed. by S. Beinfeld and S. J. Stang) was not published until 1988.   HARRY T. MOORE

Bibliography: Cassell, R. A., ed., *Critical Essays on Ford Madox Ford* (1987); Hoffman, C. G., *Ford Madox Ford*, rev. ed. (1989); Judd, Alan, *Ford Madox Ford* (1991); Mizener, Arthur, *The Saddest Story* (1971); Stang, S. J., ed., *The Presence of Ford Madox Ford* (1981).

Ford, Gerald R.

Gerald Rudolph Ford, Jr., became the 38th president of the United States on Aug. 9, 1974, after Richard M. NIXON resigned to avoid probable impeachment as a result of the WATERGATE affair. For 25 years a Republican member of Congress without national ambitions, Ford had been appointed vice-president in 1973 by President Nixon to replace Spiro T. AGNEW, who resigned after being accused of bribery and of violations of the income tax laws.

Early Life. The only child of Leslie and Dorothy Gardner King, Ford was born on July 14, 1913, in Omaha, Nebr., and was originally named Leslie Lynch King, Jr. His parents were divorced when he was two years old, and his mother moved to Grand Rapids, Mich., where she met and married a businessman named Gerald R. Ford, who formally adopted the young boy and gave him his name.

In school, young Ford was a good student and an excellent athlete. He became a star center on the University of Michigan football team and graduated from the university in 1935 with a B average. After graduation, he took a job as a football and boxing coach at Yale University. He was soon admitted to the Yale Law School, finishing in the top third of his class. With the outbreak of World War II, his fledgling law practice in Grand Rapids was interrupted. He entered the navy, served aboard an aircraft carrier in the Pacific, and was discharged at the end of the war with the rank of lieutenant commander.

Ford returned to Grand Rapids and resumed his law practice. In 1948 he married Elizabeth ("Betty") Bloomer Warren, a fashion coordinator and former dance student whose first marriage had ended a year earlier in divorce. In the same year he entered the Republican primary in Michigan, upset the incumbent representative from the state's Fifth District, and easily won election to the House of Representatives in November. He won reelection every two years thereafter, until he resigned in 1973 to become vice-president.

In the House, Ford gained a reputation as a moderately conservative, hardworking, and loyally partisan member of the Republican party, who made up for his lack of legislative brilliance by providing effective personal service to his Michigan constituents. In 1965 he was chosen as House Republican leader. Had the Republicans gained a majority of the seats while he was party leader, he would certainly have been named speaker of the House. After Spiro Agnew resigned on Oct. 10, 1973, however, Nixon nominated Ford as vice-president under the provisions of the 25TH AMENDMENT to the U.S. Constitution, the first time that the procedures outlined in the amendment were utilized. Following congressional approval of his appointment, Ford was sworn in on Dec. 6, 1973.

Presidency. A little more than eight months later, Nixon resigned after the House Judiciary Committee voted to recommend his impeachment. Ford automatically succeeded him

GERALD RUDOLPH FORD
38th President of the United States (1974–77)

Nickname: "Jerry"
Born: July 14, 1913, Omaha, Nebr.
Education: University of Michigan (graduated 1935);
   Yale University Law School (LLB 1941)
Profession: Lawyer, Public Official
Religious Affiliation: Episcopalian
Marriage: Oct. 15, 1948, to Elizabeth Bloomer
   (1918–   )
Children: Michael Gerald Ford (1950–   ); John
   Gardner Ford (1952–   ); Steven Meigs Ford
   (1956–   ); Susan Elizabeth Ford (1957–   )
Political Affiliation: Republican
Writings: *Portrait of the Assassin* (1965), with J. R.
   Stiles; *A Time to Heal* (1979); *A Vision for America*
   (1981); *Humor and the Presidency* (1987).
   Vice-President: Nelson A. Rockefeller
   Secretary of State: Henry A. Kissinger
   Secretary of the Treasury: William E. Simon
   Secretary of Defense: James R. Schlesinger (1974–
   75); Donald H. Rumsfeld (1975–77)
   Attorney General: William B. Saxbe (1974–75);
   Edward H. Levi (1975–77)
   Secretary of the Interior: Rogers C. B. Morton
   (1974–75); Stanley K. Hathaway (1975); Thomas
   S. Kleppe (1975–77)
   Secretary of Agriculture: Earl L. Butz (1974–76);
   John A. Knebel (1976–77)
   Secretary of Commerce: Frederick B. Dent (1974–
   75); Rogers C. B. Morton (1975); Elliot L.
   Richardson (1976–77)
   Secretary of Labor: Peter J. Brennan (1974–75);
   John T. Dunlop (1975–76); W. J. Usery (1976–77)
   Secretary of Health, Education, and Welfare:
   Caspar W. Weinberger (1974–75); F. David
   Mathews (1975–77)
   Secretary of Housing and Urban Development:
   James T. Lynn (1974–75); Carla Anderson Hills
   (1975–77)
   Secretary of Transportation: Claude S. Brinegar
   (1974–75); William T. Coleman, Jr. (1975–77)

and thus became the first president in U.S. history who had not been chosen in a national election either as president or as vice-president. Nevertheless, Ford's unaffected personal style and his attempts to bring the presidency closer to the public were well received by the American people.

His political problems began four weeks after he took office, when he issued a full pardon to Nixon for any crimes he might have committed as president. In addition, the Ford administration was faced with a major economic slump, in which inflation was uniquely combined with recession to produce stagflation. Ford engaged, moreover, in a running battle with the Democratic Congress. During his two and a half years as president, he vetoed 61 bills that had been passed by Congress. Only 12 of the vetoes were overridden. The resultant popular impression that the government in Washington was deadlocked probably hurt Ford's reelection chances.

In foreign relations he generally followed his predecessor's policies. Major events during Ford's administration included the collapse of South Vietnam in 1975 and, in the same year, the overthrow of the Lon Nol regime in Cambodia (Kampuchea) by Communist forces. The latter led to the Mayagüez incident in which a small force of U.S. Marines were sent to recapture the U.S. freighter *Mayagüez* and its crew, which had been seized by Cambodian forces.

Ford received the Republican nomination for the presidency in 1976, despite a serious challenge in state presidential primary elections by former California governor Ronald REAGAN. At the beginning of the fall campaign, he trailed the Democratic nominee, Jimmy CARTER of Georgia, by ten points in the Gallup Poll; but after a vigorous campaign in the final weeks, Ford lost to Carter by only 2.1 percent of the popular vote. Although disappointed, he retired from public office with characteristic good grace. He remains active in corporate and charitable affairs.
                                                    STANLEY W. CLOUD

Bibliography: Fitzgerald, C. B., ed., *Gerald R. Ford* (1991); Reeves, Richard, *A Ford, Not a Lincoln* (1975); terHorst, Jerald, *Gerald Ford and the Future of the Presidency* (1984); Thompson, K. W., ed., *The Ford Presidency* (1988); White, Theodore H., *Breach of Faith* (1975).

Ford, Henry: see FORD (family).

Ford, John   (film director)

John Ford was the name adopted by Sean Aloysius O'Feeny, b. Feb. 1, 1895, d. Aug. 31, 1973, an American film director whose works are noted for their sustained creativity, breadth of vision, and pictorial beauty. Ford began directing Westerns in 1917, but his first great success was not until *The Iron Horse* (1924), followed by another, *Three Bad Men* (1926). Thirteen more years passed, however, before Ford, whose name became associated with the Western film, would make another, *Stagecoach* (1939), still regarded as a classic of the genre. In the intervening years he directed such varied works as *Judge Priest* (1934), *The Informer* (1935), *Steamboat Round the Bend* (1935), and *The Hurricane* (1937).

Stagecoach was followed by an outpouring of major works—*Young Mr. Lincoln* (1939), *Drums Along the Mohawk* (1939), *The Grapes of Wrath* (1940), *The Long Voyage Home* (1940), and *How Green Was My Valley* (1941). These films celebrated community life and were imbued with an elegiacal sense of the past.

The war years resulted in the first American war documentary, *The Battle of Midway* (1942), and another of Ford's enduring works, *They Were Expendable* (1945). After the war, Ford returned to the Western with the lyrical *My Darling Clementine* (1946); a loose trilogy of cavalry life—*Fort Apache* (1948), *She Wore a Yellow Ribbon* (1949), and *Rio Grande* (1950); and an innovative blending of song and story in *Wagonmaster* (1950).

During the six years before Ford's next Western, he directed *The Quiet Man* (1952)—a touching and humorous story of an Irish-American's return to his homeland—and several other films. Returning to the Western with *The Searchers* (1956), Ford revealed a new ambiguity in his vision of the American

John Ford was an American filmmaker whose name is most closely associated with Western films. His direction in other movie genres, however, was equally adept. Ford received four Academy Awards for best director, and all four films were non-Westerns: The Informer (1935), The Grapes of Wrath (1940), How Green Was My Valley (1941), and The Quiet Man (1952). The Battle of Midway (1942) and December 7 (1943) were wartime documentaries that earned him two more Oscars. Tobacco Road (still at left), Ford's 1941 adaptation of Erskine Caldwell's best-selling novel, was one of several ventures into social commentary, wherein grittily realistic portrayals of the poor became a Ford hallmark. Even comedy was explored—with Mister Roberts *(1955).*

past. Increasingly, in such later works as *The Man Who Shot Liberty Valance* (1962) and *Cheyenne Autumn* (1964), the exaltation of the civilizing of the West that was seen in his earlier films was darkened by a regret over the loss of freedom brought by civilization. During his career, Ford established and repeatedly used a stock company of actors, including Henry Fonda, James Stewart, John Wayne, Ward Bond, and Victor McLaglen.   WILLIAM S. PECHTER

Bibliography: Bogdanovich, Peter, *John Ford*, exp. rev. ed. (1978); Gallagher, Tag, *John Ford: The Man and His Works* (1988); Place, J. A., *The Non-Western Films of John Ford* (1979) and *The Western Films of John Ford* (1974); Sarris, Andrew, *The John Ford Movie Mystery* (1975); Stowell, Peter, *John Ford* (1986).

Ford, John   (playwright)

John Ford, b. Apr. 17, 1586, d. *c.*1639, was an English playwright, generally considered among the best of the early Stuart dramatists. After writing several nondramatic pieces, Ford collaborated with Thomas Dekker on *The Witch of Edmonton* (1621). Among the seven intense, pessimistic tragedies he wrote on his own are: *The Lovers' Melancholy* (1628), *The Broken Heart* (1633), *'Tis Pity She's a Whore* (1633), and *Perkin Warbeck* (1634). Influenced by Robert Burton and contemporary Neoplatonism, Ford's drama deals with a variety of love relationships. Although sometimes prurient, the plays in general are carefully balanced in their presentation of questionable moral stances.   W. L. GODSHALK

Bibliography: Anderson, D. K., Jr., ed., *Concord in Discord: 1586–1986* (1986); Huebert, Ronald, *John Ford: Baroque English Dramatist* (1978); Neill, M., ed., *John Ford: Critical Revisions* (1988); Robson, Ian, *The Moral World of John Ford's Drama* (1983).

Ford, Paul Leicester

An American historian and bibliographer, Paul Leicester Ford, b. Brooklyn, N.Y., Mar. 23, 1865, d. May 8, 1902, is best known for two novels, *The Honorable Peter Stirling and What People Thought of Him* (1894) and *Janice Meredith: A Story of*

the *American Revolution* (1899). *Winnowings in American History* (15 vols., 1890–91) shows his importance as a bibliographer; *The Many-Sided Franklin* (1899) is among several biographies he wrote.   F. M. PAULSEN

Bibliography: Du Bois, Paul Z., *Paul Leicester Ford* (1977).

Ford, Whitey

Hall of Fame member Edward Charles "Whitey" Ford, b. New York City, Oct. 21, 1928, pitched in more World Series (11) and won (10) and lost (8) more series games than any player in baseball history. Ford spent his entire career (1950, 1953–67) with the American League's New York Yankees, amassing 236 wins against 106 losses for a winning percentage of .690, a major-league record for pitchers with 200 or more career decisions. In 1961, Ford was 25-4 and won the Cy Young award as baseball's best pitcher. Another series record he holds is that for consecutive scoreless innings pitched—33.

Bibliography: Ford, Whitey, and Mantle, Mickey, *Whitey and Mickey: A Joint Autobiography of the Yankee Years* (1977); Ford, Whitey, with Phil Pepe, *Slick: My Life in and around Baseball* (1987).

Ford Foundation

The Ford Foundation is a private foundation established in 1936 by the FORD family, with a broad mandate to serve the general welfare. Later it received large bequests from Henry and Edsel Ford. In 1989 the Ford Foundation's assets exceeded $5.6 billion, which put the foundation in first-rank position among U.S. philanthropies.

Until 1950 the foundation's activities were directed to charitable and educational institutions in Michigan. Currently, policies are set by a board of trustees, but grant evaluation and program development are administered by a staff at the headquarters in New York City. The building, with its 12-story enclosed courtyard, is an architectural landmark.

The foundation focuses its program work in six broad areas—urban poverty, rural poverty and resources, human rights and social justice, governance and public policy, education and culture, and international affairs—and in 1989 approved grants, respectively, of $39.9 million, $27.3 million, $32.4 million, $37.6 million, $46.9 million, and $24.2 million. Total 1989 program approvals were $217.9 million. Cumulative totals for grants and operations in the 1980s reached $2 billion. Two-thirds of the grants are made in the United States, and one-third are for activities overseas. The foundation was headed by McGeorge BUNDY (1966–79), then Franklin A. Thomas.

Bibliography: Macdonald, Dwight, *The Ford Foundation* (1988).

Ford Trimotor

Known universally as the *Tin Goose*, the Ford Trimotor represented one of the most significant advances in air-transport design. A total of 200 of these planes were constructed in

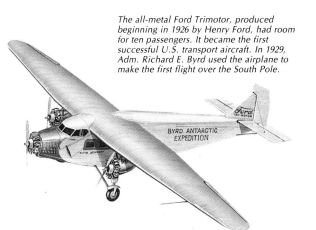

The all-metal Ford Trimotor, produced beginning in 1926 by Henry Ford, had room for ten passengers. It became the first successful U.S. transport aircraft. In 1929, Adm. Richard E. Byrd used the airplane to make the first flight over the South Pole.

seven basic models. The aircraft, a sturdy, high-wing mono-plane of all-metal construction, was equipped with three radial engines (hence the name). Its development, stimulated when the Ford Motor Company purchased (1925) the Stout Metal Airplane Company, led to the Model 4-AT (1926) and the refined Model 5-AT (1928). The 4-AT had a 22.5-m (74-ft) wingspan and 15.2-m (50-ft) length. Variants were also produced for the military. The Trimotor remained an important transport plane through the early 1930s.   PETER M. H. LEWIS

Fordham University   [fohrd'-uhm]

Established in 1841 and conducted by the Jesuits, Fordham University (enrollment: 13,124; library: 1,100,000 volumes) is in the Bronx, N.Y., with a campus at Lincoln Center in New York City and a graduate campus in Tarrytown, N.Y. In 1974, Thomas More College (1964), an undergraduate school for women, merged with Fordham College. Fordham has schools of arts and sciences, law, business, social service, and education and a graduate school of religion.

Ford's Theatre

Ford's Theatre in Washington, D.C., earned notoriety on Apr. 14, 1865, when President Abraham LINCOLN was fatally shot during a performance of *Our American Cousin*. John Thomson Ford (1829–94), the builder of the theater, was imprisoned for more than a month after the assassination until acquitted of complicity. Congress then forced him to sell the theater, and closed it to further productions. Misfortune struck again in 1893 when part of the edifice collapsed, killing 28 people. Since 1968 the building has been maintained by the National Park Service as a Lincoln museum.

foreclosure: see MORTGAGE.

Foreign Affairs

Foreign Affairs, founded in 1922, is a scholarly periodical published five times per year presenting diverse opinions on international politics, foreign policy, business, and government. It has a circulation of 97,457, high for journals of this type, and draws its readership from the international political community. *Foreign Affairs* sometimes publishes influential articles by world leaders.   ROLAND E. WOLSELEY

foreign aid

Foreign aid is assistance in the form of capital, goods, or services given by one country to another. The donor is usually a government or international organization, although assistance provided by private charitable groups is sometimes considered foreign aid as well.
U.S. Aid Programs. The United States began extending foreign aid in large amounts during World War II when it helped its military allies with shipments of war supplies under the LEND-LEASE program. Altogether, it extended assistance totaling $47.9 billion to 38 countries.
Between 1946 and 1990 the U.S. government disbursed over $374 billion in foreign aid; more than $277 billion of this was in the form of grants, and the rest was in loans. About 62% of U.S. aid during this period was designed to facilitate the economic recovery of war-torn industrialized countries, to alleviate the immediate aftereffects of natural disasters, or to stimulate economic growth in less-developed countries. The other 38% was military aid to U.S. allies and other non-Communist countries. The proportion of military aid varied from year to year, averaging 57% in 1970–73, falling to 32% in 1975, 22% in 1980, and rising to 31% in 1990.
Since World War II, foreign aid has been an important element of U.S. foreign policy. In 1947, President Harry S. TRUMAN proposed a $400 million aid program to help Greece and Turkey resist communism. This program, which became known as the Truman Doctrine, was the first U.S. aid policy aimed at containing communism. Later in the same year, Secretary of State George MARSHALL invited European nations to draw up a plan for postwar economic reconstruction to be fi-

nanced by the United States. The MARSHALL PLAN, formally known as the European Recovery Program, disbursed more than $13 billion in economic aid in 1948–52, at least 90% of it in the form of grants. The Marshall Plan had two basic goals: to stimulate the economic recovery of Europe as a trading partner for the United States and to check the advance of communism in Europe by eliminating economic conditions that could be exploited by the Communists.
In his 1949 inaugural address Truman called for "a bold new program for making the benefits of our scientific advances and industrial progress available for the improvement and growth of underdeveloped areas." This proposal, the fourth of a series in the address, resulted in the POINT FOUR PROGRAM of aid to less-developed countries. During the 1950s the United States placed increasing emphasis on such countries in its aid program, disbursing more development aid than all other aid donors combined.
Another important element of U.S. aid was the Food for Peace program, which made surplus agricultural commodities available to foreign countries on easy terms or as a gift. From 1954 to 1990, the program supplied about $43 billion worth of such commodities.
Although the absolute level of U.S. aid rose gradually through 1985 (followed by a decline in 1986 and 1987), the proportion of the U.S. gross national product (GNP) allocated to foreign aid fell from more than 2% in the 1940s to 0.20% in 1989. Several other countries, including Norway, the Netherlands, Denmark, Sweden, and France, allocated larger percentages of their GNP during the 1980s for aid than did the United States.
The emphasis of U.S. aid programs has been redirected from Europe to Asia, including the Middle East. Europe received about 13% of the U.S. aid disbursed in 1945–90, but most of this was given in the years immediately following World War II. South Asia and the Middle East received more than 37% of U.S. aid in this period, Latin America received approximately 8%, and Africa received approximately 6%. Since the end of the Marshall Plan, South Vietnam, Israel, South Korea, India, Egypt, Turkey, Pakistan, and Taiwan have received the largest amounts of U.S. aid. Israel has received more aid than any other country, about $47 billion.
Aid by Other Countries. Foreign economic aid is provided by many countries other than the United States. Since 1960, Canada, Japan, and the Western European nations have emerged as increasingly significant sources of economic aid for the poor areas of the world, providing many billions of dollars for development. The United States regularly provided more economic aid than any other country until 1989, when Japan became the world's largest donor and lender of foreign aid.
Military aid is usually given directly by one country to another, but economic aid is often given indirectly through international organizations. The WORLD BANK Group—which includes the International Bank for Reconstruction and Development, the INTERNATIONAL DEVELOPMENT ASSOCIATION, and the INTERNATIONAL FINANCE CORPORATION—disburses the bulk of such multilateral aid. From 1946 to 1990 the World Bank Group distributed more than $258 billion in loans, most of which went to the less-developed areas of the world.

U.S. FOREIGN AID, 1946–90
(in millions of dollars)

Year	Total Economic and Military Aid	Economic Aid*	Military Aid
1946–52	41,661	31,116	10,545
1953–61	43,355	24,053	19,305
1962–69	50,254	33,392	16,862
1970–79	65,714	26,902	38,812
1980–84	62,295	40,648	21,647
1985–90	93,236	61,942	31,294

SOURCE: U.S. Agency for International Development.

*Economic aid represents total U.S. economic aid, including Food for Peace, Peace Corps, and paid-in subscriptions to international financial institutions such as IBRD and IDB.

Communist countries disbursed most of their aid directly rather than through international organizations. China's relatively small economic aid program disbursed more than $7 billion between 1954 and 1985. In 1983, China's aid totaled $150 million. The USSR was long the largest Communist aid donor; it disbursed about $14 billion to developing nations from 1954 to 1984, during which period Soviet military aid totaled about $75 billion. Soviet aid usually took the form of loans and tended to be concentrated in a few countries, which have included Cuba, Poland, and Vietnam. The severe economic problems facing the Soviet Union have forced dramatic cuts in aid to Cuba, and Poland has turned to the West for aid since the end of Communist rule there in 1989.

Political Influences on Aid Programs. Foreign aid programs in the United States have always been unpopular with voters, who see many domestic uses for the funds, especially in times of lean budgets. Congress has responded by "earmarking" funds for specific countries, severely constraining the ability of an administration to respond to changing circumstances by shifting resources. Congress also responds to powerful lobbying efforts by some foreign governments, mandating, for example, that a specific ratio of aid be maintained between Turkey and Greece. At the same time, aid often continues to be granted on political grounds, such as rewarding a loyal ally, rather than on the basis of demonstrable need. Congress has also sometimes required presidential certification that specified conditions, such as a poor human rights record, have been corrected before a particular country can be authorized to receive assistance payments. Efforts have intensified to tie aid to the purchase of U.S. goods and services by recipient governments.

DAVID A. BALDWIN

Bibliography: Baldwin, D., *Economic Development and American Foreign Policy* (1966); Cassen, R., et al., *Does Aid Work?* (1986); Eberstadt, N., *Foreign Aid and American Purposes* (1988); Mikesell, R. F., and Kilmarx, R. A., *The Economics of Foreign Aid and Self-Sustaining Development* (1983); Mosley, P., *Foreign Aid: Its Defense and Reform* (1987); Wexler, I., *The Marshall Plan Revisited* (1983); Wilhelm, J., and Feinstein, G., eds., *U.S. Foreign Assistance: Investment or Folly?* (1984); Wood, R. E., *From Marshall Plan to Debt Crisis* (1986); Yasutomo, D. T., *The Manner of Giving: Strategic Aid and Japanese Foreign Policy* (1986).

foreign exchange: see EXCHANGE RATE.

foreign languages, teaching of

The study of foreign languages has never ranked high among the fields that attract U.S. students. Educators have attempted to change this characteristic American disinterest in learning other languages by improving teaching techniques and emphasizing the study of modern languages.

Like their European counterparts, 18th- and 19th-century American secondary schools taught Latin; colleges required the study of Latin and, often, Greek. Students learned the rules of the language's grammar by rote, memorized vocabulary, and practiced what they had learned by translating into and out of English. Toward the end of the 19th century, French and German began to grow in popularity in school curricula; by the 1940s, Spanish had become the most widely studied language. In the early 1900s a new technique, the direct method, began to be used in a few schools. The direct method, which requires teachers with great fluency in their subject language, uses no English; all instruction is given in the language being taught. Used to great effect during World War II in the intensive courses set up to teach U.S. troops foreign languages, it is still popular in U.S. schools, particularly for teaching young children. The audiolingual approach, developed in the 1950s and 1960s, emphasizes spoken dialogues supplemented by intensive word exercises to habituate the student to the sounds and the structure of the language.

As students of foreign languages, Americans rank far below Europeans and Asians, many of whom—from an early age—study languages other than their own. The "relevance" of foreign language studies to American students became an issue during the late 1960s and '70s, and some university foreign language course requirements were reduced or eliminated.

High schools, in response, no longer required foreign language study of their college-bound students. The 1980s, however, saw a revival of foreign language study—prompted in large measure, according to educators, by the demands of international trade, as well as campaigns for higher educational standards and greater interest in foreign affairs. As a result, many public school systems instituted language courses, and numerous colleges added or restored language requirements. Many communities also have provided the teaching of English as a second language (ESL) for those whose native tongue is other than English, and college courses have been offered for ESL training. In the 1990s, Spanish was the most widely studied foreign language in the United States, followed by French and German. Enrollments in Russian and Japanese were up.

Bibliography: Bourgoin, Edward, *Foreign Languages and Your Career*, rev. 3d ed. (1984); Brown, H. Douglas, *Principles of Language Learning and Teaching* (1980; repr. 1987); Harley, Birgit, et al., eds., *The Development of Second Language Proficiency* (1990).

foreign legion: see FRENCH FOREIGN LEGION.

foreign policy

Foreign policy is a goal or series of goals (ends) that a country hopes to achieve with respect to other countries and international issues. Countries are not the only actors in international politics, and increasingly a country's foreign policy extends beyond relations with other countries to include interactions with other international actors including international organizations, multinational corporations, alliances, regional organizations, and others. Foreign policy also includes the tools or instruments (means) that a country employs to achieve its international goals. Many scholars also extend the study of foreign policy to the process by which a country decides on which goals it will pursue and which tools it will use to implement those goals. In sum, foreign policy includes how a country decides, what it decides, and how it acts.

FOREIGN POLICY PROCESS

The foreign policy process is how a country decides on policy and its implementation. Some analysts believe that policy choices are influenced by who makes decisions and how decisions are made. Recent scholarship, for example, shows that authoritarian governments are more likely to go to war with other authoritarian governments or with democracies than democracies are likely to go to war with other democracies.

There is also strong evidence that within a particular type of government, such as a democracy, there is no single foreign policy process, but rather a variety of processes. There are several explanations about how and why the policy process varies, but the most common is the idea that different types of issues are processed differently. One distinction is between crisis and noncrisis policy. Crisis policy is normally decided by the political leader (such as the president or prime minister) and a small circle of the leader's close advisors with little general debate or public dissent. Noncrisis policy is subject to wider discussion and dissent and may even be decided by lower levels of the government.

Domestic Impact Considerations. Foreign policy and domestic policy have traditionally been distinguished, but in many cases they overlap. These issues that have both international and domestic aspects are sometimes called "intermestic" policies. Deciding on federal highway funds is an example of pure domestic policy. Making a decision on which of the various political factions to support in a given country is a pure foreign policy, which has little or no domestic impact within say, Canada or the United States. The question of whether or not to have a free-trade treaty between the United States and Canada is intermestic policy because it involves international relations with another country but, at the same time, is a domestic political matter insofar as it affects jobs and industries in both countries. Intermestic issues tend to activate stronger activity by legislatures (Congress or Parliament), interest groups (business, labor unions), and public opinion.

Multiple Branches of Government. People often refer to "the government," but in a system such as that in the United States or Canada, there is a dispersion of powers among various branches of government. This is essential in a democracy, but it is also true that the process can be cumbersome and even produce contradictory results. While the U.S. Constitution reserves to the executive branch the authority to negotiate treaties, for example, they must be ratified by the Senate. Since Congress is more sensitive to a variety of domestic political pressures, the Senate often has different priorities in seeking agreement with foreign governments.

In a democracy, therefore, public opinion plays a role in determining foreign policy because Congress responds to voter and interest group sentiment and because the president is not only a statesman but a political leader who keeps an eye on public and congressional opinion. The freedom to protest foreign policy decisions also can produce direct pressure on decision makers, as happened during the Vietnam War.

Congress has great potential foreign policy power, and presidents must inform and persuade members of Congress who can deny funds for a particular foreign policy initiative or write legislation requiring that funds be spent in specified ways. The growing tendency for Congress to involve itself in the conduct of foreign policy is a trend that frustrates and alarms many in the executive branch who charge Congress is trying to "micromanage" policy.

Models of Foreign Policy Making. There are a number of models of the foreign policy process. One of the most common is the "rational-actor model." This model suggests that policymakers examine their options, define their goals, examine the various alternative ways of achieving their options, and select the most efficacious method to implement the chosen policy. Another widely discussed view is the "bureaucratic model." Here, various parts of the executive branch have differing views of what policy should be. These views are based, in part, on the divergent, self-interested goals of the bureaucratic units. Policy, according to this model, is the result of the struggle among the bureaucratic actors. A third model might be called the "political model," and it holds that policy is the outcome of many elements in the political system struggling with, reacting to, and compromising with one another. In addition to executive leaders and bureaucracies, these elements would include legislatures, interest groups, political opponents of the government, and the public.

FOREIGN POLICY GOALS

The international goals that a country is trying to achieve range from the very specific (resolve a border dispute) to the general (enhance the country's influence). In an international system of sovereign, often competing, countries, foreign policy goals are usually self-interested objectives. Less frequently, goals may be cooperative among several countries (alliance behavior) or, still less often, motivated by idealism (humanitarian foreign aid). When countries pursue self-interested goals, they are said to be following their "national interest." The core element of national interest is national DEFENSE—providing for the physical safety of a country's citizens. A second element is providing for the economic prosperity of the country insofar as it is affected by the supply of resources, trade balances, monetary exchange rates, and other factors of the international political economy. A third element of national interest is providing a favorable political environment. At a minimum this includes the ability of a country's citizens to choose their own form of government, and it may also include promoting values (individual rights) and processes (democracy) in other countries that are compatible with one's own values and processes. A fourth national interest element is ensuring national cohesion. This means avoiding foreign policies or other pressures (separatist movements that threaten civil war), irreconcilable domestic divisions, or other clashes that could fragment the country.

The concept of national interest assumes that at least to some degree the rational-actor model is used to formulate policy. To the degree that other models govern the policy process, then a country's goals may be either in the narrow interest of the prevailing bureaucratic or political actors or a lowest common denominator interest reached through compromise rather than an expression of a more general interest.

FOREIGN POLICY IMPLEMENTATION

Countries have a variety of instruments by which they can attempt to achieve their foreign policy goals. These tools include the military instrument, the penetration and intervention instrument, and the diplomatic instrument. The degree to which a country can use any of these instruments will vary according to the country's power, which is defined as its ability to force or persuade another country to act in a desirable way. A country may be powerful in some ways and not in others. Japan has vast economic power and much less military power. The former Soviet Union had enormous military power and little economic power. The applicability of power will also vary with the situation.

The military instrument relies on the implicit or explicit threat to use force and the actual use of force. The possession of military power is also a tool because it enhances a country's reputation and increases its influence. Despite its staggering economy and political disarray, the Soviet Union remained a superpower because of its military capability. Some scholars contend that military power is becoming a less important and acceptable instrument. Iraq's 1990 invasion of Kuwait was almost unanimously condemned in the United Nations.

Cross-border invasion is now less acceptable behavior, although some still justify the application of limited force, especially within implicitly recognized spheres of influence by a major power (the U.S. incursions into Grenada and Panama, for example). Penetration and intervention involves trying to manipulate another country's domestic political situation and process. This instrument can be accomplished through such methods as propaganda, military support of dissidents, co-opting political leaders, sabotage, and terrorism. The diplomatic instrument involves communicating with another country. Methods include direct, government-to-government negotiations and presenting its case in the arena of an international organization. The United Nations, for example, is the forum for debates and diplomatic maneuvering on a wide variety of issues, and it has rendered decisions (often rejected or ignored) on many international disputes.

Another diplomatic method is signaling. This means doing or saying things publicly or through intermediaries that are meant as messages for another government. Publicly pledging support of an ally in time of crisis is a signal to a possible aggressor. Public diplomacy is a third method of diplomacy. This means trying to create an international impression that will enhance a country's image and influence. Mikhail Gorbachev's projection of himself as a reformer and of his country as increasingly benign significantly changed Western perceptions of the Soviet Union. The economic instrument can be used as either a carrot or a stick. Extending better TARIFF rates or trade credits, sending foreign aid, granting loans, and encouraging mutual investment are some positive economic methods. Imposing economic SANCTIONS by limiting or embargoing trade, withdrawing aid, and barring investments are negative economic tools.   JOHN T. ROURKE

Bibliography: Allison, G. T., *Essence of Decision: Explaining the Cuban Missile Crisis* (1971); Dougherty, J. E., and Pfaltzgraff, R. L., Jr., *Contending Theories of International Relations,* 3d ed. (1990); Hermann, C. F., et al., eds., *New Directions in the Study of Foreign Policy* (1987); Hermann, M. G. and C. F., "Who Makes Foreign Policy Decisions and How," *International Studies Quarterly* (December 1989); Jensen, L., *Explaining Foreign Policy* (1982); Rosenau, J. N., *The Scientific Study of Foreign Policy* (1980); Rourke, J. T., *Making Foreign Policy: United States, Soviet Union, China* (1990); Waltz, K. N., *Man, the State and War* (1959).

foreign service

A foreign service is an organization of trained career officials, called diplomats, who help implement the foreign policy of their government by representing their country in its relations with other countries or with international organizations. A foreign service is typically part of a foreign ministry (the Department of STATE in the United States). Most major foreign services maintain an embassy, consulates, and trade and cultural centers in each country with which they have diplomatic relations.

An embassy is headed by an AMBASSADOR, assisted by a staff of diplomats and attachés who have various functions. The political and economic sections report on developments in the host country. The consular section assists its nationals living or traveling in the host country with commercial and legal matters and issues visas to local residents who wish to travel to its country (see CONSUL, modern government official). The cultural section promotes the culture of its own country.

The history of foreign services can be traced to the intense diplomatic intercourse between Egypt and its neighbors long before 1000 BC. Not until the 12th and 13th centuries AD, however, did diplomacy begin to assume its modern form. Rules were developed by the Italian city-states to govern the appointment and conduct of ambassadors, and in 1455, the duchy of Milan established the first permanent embassy in Genoa. In the 16th century other European states followed the Italian example and appointed permanent ambassadors. Under the influence of 16th- and 17th-century writers, such as Hugo GROTIUS and Alberico Gentili, the privileges of diplomats were more precisely defined and incorporated in international law. The Congress of Vienna in 1815 and the Vienna Convention on Diplomatic Relations in 1961 defined and redefined classes of diplomatic representatives. In the 20th century, consular and diplomatic services, formerly separate, have been merged in many countries, including the United States (1924).

Diplomats stationed in a foreign country enjoy privileges known as diplomatic immunity: they are not subject to local civil and criminal laws; they are free to communicate with their government; and the embassy buildings and grounds are treated as the territory of their state (see EXTRATERRITORIALITY). A country can expel a foreign diplomat whom it considers undesirable by declaring the diplomat persona non grata. Some countries have seized diplomats as hostages (see IRANIAN HOSTAGE CRISIS).

The period since World War II has seen new developments in diplomacy. Heads of state now confer directly in summit conferences. In times of crisis, U.S. and Soviet leaders communicate over a hot line, a direct telephone link between the White House and the Kremlin. Foreign ministers engage in shuttle diplomacy—flying between capitals in continual negotiations. These developments have reduced the importance of foreign-service representatives in direct policy-making.

Bibliography: Barnes, W., and Morgan, J., *The Foreign Service of the United States* (1961; repr. 1978); Barston, R. P., *Modern Diplomacy* (1988); Newsom, David D., *Diplomacy and the American Democracy* (1988); Roy, S. L., *Diplomacy* (1984); Simpson, Smith, ed., *Education in Diplomacy* (1985).

foreign-trade zone: see FREE PORT.

Foreman, George

George Foreman, b. Marshall, Tex., Jan. 22, 1948, is an American boxer and former world heavyweight champion with enormous punching power. Foreman won the 1968 Olympic heavyweight gold medal, then rose quickly professionally. He took the world heavyweight title from Joe FRAZIER with a 2d-round knockout on Jan. 22, 1973, but lost it in a stunning upset to Muhammad ALI on Oct. 30, 1974. After an even more surprising loss to Jimmy Young in 1977, Foreman retired with a record of 45–2. He returned to the ring 10 years later. In 1991, at age 42, he went the full 12 rounds before losing by decision in a bout with world champion Evander Holyfield.

Foreman, Richard

Richard Foreman, b. New York City, June 10, 1937, is a playwright and founder (1968) of the Ontological-Hysteric Theater. As writer, director, designer, and theorist, Foreman has produced a highly imagistic and personal theater, one that, over the years, has become less anarchic, more comedic and humanistic. Foreman won recognition for his staging of *The Threepenny Opera* (1976) and for his long-running hit musical, *Dr. Selavy's Magic Theater* (1972, 1984). His writings include *Plays and Manifestos* (1976) and *Reverberation Machines: The Later Plays and Essays* (1985).   BONNIE MARRANCA

forensic science

Forensic science is the application of science to criminal investigation in order to provide evidence that can be used in the solution of criminal cases. Forensic scientists also play a vital role in criminal trials, where they may testify as expert witnesses. The many fields of knowledge that constitute modern forensic-science practices include pathology, toxicology, anthropology, odontology, psychology, and criminalistics. The forensic pathologist is concerned with determining the cause of sudden or unexpected death and will usually perform an AUTOPSY on the victim to detect any signs of injury or disease that may have contributed to the death (see also PATHOLOGY). The forensic toxicologist provides the pathologist with data relating to the presence of poisons or drugs found in a victim's body. The identification of bones and skeletal remains is the responsibility of the specialty called forensic anthropology, which is derived from the anthropological study of comparative body and bone measurements and morphology. Forensic odontology, or dentistry, utilizes dental evidence to identify human remains and is employed in the characterization of bite-mark impressions. Forensic psychiatrists analyze human behavior and personality in connection with issues pertaining to a criminal act or to criminal conduct. Psychiatric examinations may serve to determine whether the state of mind of the accused at the time of the offense conforms to the definition of insanity in the jurisdiction where the crime occurred and whether the accused is competent to stand trial (see INSANITY, LEGAL).

The term *criminalistics* encompasses those areas of the physical and natural sciences applicable to the analysis of physical evidence—the objects retrieved from the scene of a crime that can aid investigators in determining whether a crime was committed or that can provide a link between a crime and its victims or perpetrators. Such evidence includes a great variety of materials—drugs, hair, fibers, soil, blood, paint chips, firearms, FINGERPRINTS, documents—which must be analyzed to determine content, type, authenticity, and so on. A new technique, DNA "fingerprinting," can be used to identify the source of semen or blood stains (see GENETIC ENGINEERING).

Criminalistic services are provided by forensic chemists and biologists employed in crime laboratories. These facilities, first established in the United States in the early 1930s, operate at the federal, state, county, or municipal levels of government. Most crime laboratories function as elements of police departments or under the direction of a prosecutor's or district attorney's office. The largest crime laboratory in the world is operated by the U.S. Federal Bureau of Investigation.
                                                RICHARD SAFERSTEIN

Bibliography: Joyce, C., and Stover, E., *Witnesses from the Grave* (1991); Saferstein, Richard, *Criminalistics: An Introduction to Forensic Science*, 3d ed. (1987).

Forester, C. S.   [fohr'-es-tur]

Cecil Scott Forester, b. Aug. 27, 1899, d. Apr. 2, 1966, was a prolific English writer of novels, histories, biographies, and travel literature. Educated at Dulwich College, Forester won a wide international audience through his series of 11 historical novels depicting the career of Capt. Horatio Hornblower, a fictional British navy officer during the Napoleonic Wars. The first of these, *A Ship of the Line*, won the James Tait Black Memorial Prize for Literature in 1938. He described the series in *The Hornblower Companion* (1964). His other successful novels include *Payment Deferred* (1926), *The Gun* (1933; film, 1957), and *The African Queen* (1935; film, 1952). In his later life Forester lived in the United States.   PHILIP FLYNN

Bibliography: Forester, C. S., *Long before Forty* (1968).

forests and forestry

A forest is a community of trees, shrubs, herbs, microorganisms, and animals, with trees the most obvious living structures. Trees can survive under a wide range of climatic conditions, but forests generally occupy the moister, less frigid

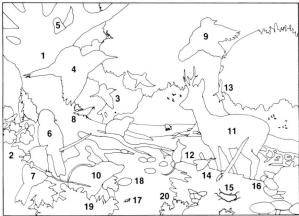

New Forest, located in southern England, typifies the temperate-climate woodland. The most common tree is the English oak, Quercus robur (1); other trees are the hawthorn, Crataegus monogyna (2), and the hazel, Corylus avellena (3). Birds include the great spotted woodpecker, Dendrocopos major (4), which drums by pecking a tree trunk with its beak. The tawny owl, Strix aluco (5), common throughout Britain, roosts by day and hunts for small animals at night. A male European robin, Erithacus rubecula (6), sings to warn other robins away. A blue tit, Parus caeruleus (7), now is commonly seen in gardens. A song thrush, Turdus philomelos (8), has a complex song, which is warbled more than once before changing the melody. The Eurasian jay, Garrulus glandarius (9), collects and buries acorns. The badger, Meles meles (10), the roe deer, Capreolus capreolus (11), and the wood mouse, Apodemus sylvaticus (12), are mammals that inhabit the New Forest. The gray squirrel, Sciurus carolinensis (13), native to North America, was introduced into Britain and spread rapidly. A mottled umber moth, Erannis defolaria (14), and a wood louse, Oniscus asellus (15), rest on an old log eaten away by a fungus, genus Polystictus (16). A ground beetle, genus Carabus (17), walks along the forest floor, which is carpeted with mushrooms (18), primroses, Primula vulgaris (19), and wood anemones, Anemone nemorosa (20).

parts of the terrestrial BIOSPHERE. To different human cultures at different times, forests have been regarded as places of danger, security, economic opportunity, recreation, and aesthetic pleasure. They take part in natural processes of nutrient cycling and water purification, and otherwise help maintain a clean environment. Forests are important sources of many products. Forestry is the science, art, and technology of managing these forest resources.

FORESTS

The large size and slow growth of trees make forests appear stable and permanent, but in fact they are dynamic sites of ongoing processes such as TREE growth and death and SOIL formation. The tree species in a particular area are also constantly changing as species migrate and new trees invade disturbed areas. Climates themselves change, but this generally occurs so slowly—over tens or hundreds of years—that a given forest

area appears to contain a constant group of species.

Ecology.   The inhabitants of forest communities interact in complex ways. Trees compete with each other for sunlight, moisture, and mineral nutrients. These materials are necessary for PHOTOSYNTHESIS, the process by which green plants produce organic compounds for energy to live and grow. As trees photosynthesize, they absorb carbon dioxide from the air and extract moisture from the soil. Trees help to retain water; heavy rains do not run rapidly off forest land. Natural or human activities that destroy forests result in increased run-off and in temporarily higher levels of carbon dioxide in the atmosphere. After this the growing forest increases the oxygen content of the atmosphere. After a forest is mature, it adds less oxygen to the atmosphere. A global research project to measure the overall influence of forests on the Earth's atmosphere is in progress.

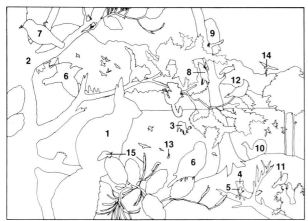

The Siberian taiga, a northern coniferous forest, is characterized by low temperatures and hardy trees and animals. Located west of the Ural Mountains, the taiga has marshy evergreen forests that contain spruce, pine, and fir trees. A Eurasian red squirrel, Sciurus vulgaris (1), and its young balance on branches of a Siberian spruce, Picea obovata (2). Other mammals include a moose, Alces alces (3), which feeds on marsh grass; and a sable (4), Martes zibellina, with a chipmunk, Eutamias sibiricus (5), it has caught. Birds of the taiga include the red crossbill, Loxia curvirostra (6), a finch whose beak is adapted for plucking seeds from spruce cones; the Siberian jay, Perisoreus infaustus (7); the black woodpecker, Dryocopus maritus (8), feeding its young; the great gray owl, Strix nebulosa (9), which sleeps by day and is active at night; the capercaillie, Tetrao urogallus (10), the largest grouse; and the blue throat, Erithacus svecicus (11), a small thrush. Bohemian waxwings, Bombycilla garrulus (12), are so named because of the small, red spots on the wings, which resemble sealing wax. Redshank sandpipers, Tringa totanus (13), breed during the summer in the marshy ground of the taiga. A goshawk, Aoccipiter gentilis (14), flies away with its prey, a squirrel. A nun moth, Lymantria monacha (15), and its caterpillars feed on the spruce tree, causing extensive damage to trees in the forest.

Trees also serve as temporary repositories for mineral nutrients in ecosystems; these nutrients accumulate in tree roots and thus are not easily washed away. Natural or human destruction of forests alters the NUTRIENT CYCLES, especially in the case of the NITROGEN CYCLE, where plants play a substantial role. Regrowth of young forests may increase the nitrogen added to the ecosystem. Trees take up the nutrients they need from the soil and from dead organic matter with the assistance of mycorrhizae (fungi that grow symbiotically on tree roots, obtaining food from the tree).

The process of soil development, aided by SOIL ORGANISMS, occurs in all forests. Microorganisms break down minerals in the soil and create passages for air and water movement, decomposing the remains of plants and animals and extracting and releasing nutrients. Depending on the climate, decomposition occurs at different rates. In cool or dry climates, organic matter will decompose slowly and a thick layer will develop, whereas in warm, moist climates, organic matter will decompose rapidly, releasing minerals that are quickly absorbed by plant roots. Little organic matter will accumulate.

After a forest is destroyed (all or in part) by a disturbance, such as fire or wind or avalanche, trees and other plants reinvade the area, halting erosion and nutrient loss and maintaining water quality. This series of changes in vegetation structure, known as ecological succession, makes the forest more suitable for some animals and plants and less suitable for others.

Depending on environmental conditions, different tree species will be dominant at different successional stages. The characteristic group of tree species in a given area is referred to as a forest type. Within each type, certain species may be found most commonly under specific soil and climate conditions and at certain times after a disturbance; these species are best evolved physiologically to compete under these conditions. In areas of recurrent fire, for example, fire-resistant trees will likely predominate.

Types of Forests. Tree species can be divided into six groups based on their evolutionary origins; Holarctic (originating in the northern hemisphere); Neotropic (originating in central and South America); Paleotropic (originating in Africa and tropical Asia); Capensis (originating in southern Africa); Australian; and Antarctic. A species is found naturally only where it first developed or where it migrated thereafter. Pines are found naturally in the Northern Hemisphere and thus belong to the Holarctic group. Many species have been introduced into other areas with similar climates; for example, pines are planted in many parts of the Southern Hemisphere, and eucalyptus, a tree genus native to Australia, is planted in other places in the world.

Forest communities with different genetic backgrounds that grow under similar soil and climate conditions in different parts of the world have many of the same structural characteristics. Thus forests can be classified as major parts of many BIOMES. Taiga and boreal forests are coniferous forests with few species in areas of cool climates. Temperate deciduous forests are predominantly broadleaf forests in areas of moderate temperature and rainfall with cold winters. Subtropical evergreen forests are a combination of broadleaf and conifer forests in areas of sufficient rainfall and mild winters. Tropical rain forests are lush forests of complex structure with many species in warm, moist regions (see JUNGLE AND RAIN FOREST). CHAPARRAL or sclerophyllous forests are thicketlike forests of shrubs and small trees in areas with mild winters and warm, dry summers. Tropical grasslands and SAVANNAS are grasslands with scattered trees that occur in warm regions with seasonal drought.

FORESTRY

Forestry involves the use and management of forest resources. Forest uses can be divided into two categories: nonconsumptive and consumptive. Nonconsumptive uses, which remove little from the forest, include watershed protection, wildlife and fish habitat, recreation, and aesthetic uses. These specific uses require that the forests be maintained in conditions with which other nonconsumptive and consumptive uses are sometimes incompatible. Consumptive uses involve the extraction of products from forests; this often requires the harvesting of trees. Forest resources are renewable, since new trees can grow after the old ones are cut.

Products. The use of forests to obtain WOOD, chemicals, and other products is consumptive. About half of the wood harvested in the world is used directly for fuel. Wood is the primary fuel source in developing countries; its use fluctuates with the cost of alternative energy sources. Wood has been used for LUMBER for construction purposes for thousands of years. Today, wood for structures primarily comes from straight, strong, conifer trees. PAPER was first made from wood about 150 years ago, and it is still made primarily from wood. The cellulose fibers in wood can also be used to make RAYON, photographic film, artificial sponges, synthetic lacquers, and other plastics. Wood might be more widely used in industry to produce plastics, except that petroleum, an alternative raw material, is cheaper than wood is.

Various chemicals are made from by-products of pulp and paper manufacture and from the independent distillation of wood; these include charcoal, acetic acid, methanol, various oils, and medicinal chemicals. Turpentine and tar may be obtained from destructive distillation or by scarring and scraping the wound of living pine trees. Maple sugar is obtained by taking the sap from the interior of living maple trees, and various trees provide other products.

Management. Forests are managed for a variety of objectives, ranging from carefully tended plantations to relatively natural areas of no cutting and minimal protection from disturbance. The intensity of management depends on the growth potential of the forest and various economic and political objectives. Even the most carefully tended forest plantations, however, are not managed as intensively as most agricultural crops, and

The work of a forester includes taking core samples from trees. Analysis of such a cross section helps trace a tree's life history. The number of annual growth rings indicates the tree's age; the width of each ring shows the rate of growth in a given year.

for a number of reasons. Unlike agricultural crops, forest crops take many years to grow, even on the most productive soils. Often the products in demand change before the forest is suitable for a specific use; forest management needs to be flexible.

The ultimate unit of forest management is the "stand." A stand is a group of trees of uniform age, species, structure, and growth conditions. Stands vary in size from 0.4 to more than 40 ha (1 to 100 acres). The technology of manipulating stands is known as silviculture. Many silvicultural techniques mimic disturbances of some kind, often to remove existing trees or other vegetation in order to allow desired trees to become established and grow. Four methods are used to remove trees from forest stands: clearcutting, or the cutting of all the trees at one time, creating an even-age stand by planting or natural regeneration; seed tree cutting, or the cutting of all the trees except for a few trees for reseeding, creating an even-age stand (except for the seed trees); shelterwood cutting, or the removal of an old stand of trees in a series of cuttings extended over several years, creating an even-age stand; and selection cutting, or the removal of a few mature trees, usually repeatedly, over relatively short intervals, creating an uneven-age stand.

Each system has its advantages and disadvantages; the proper method must be chosen on the basis of management goals and conditions at the stand in question. The system of LOGGING the stand by clearcutting is appropriate where trees can become established and grow without shade. Where the clearcut area will be exposed to public view or to extreme temperatures, the conditions for forest regeneration are poor and the site can be aesthetically displeasing until the trees grow. Seed tree cutting is used in reforestation (discussed below). The shelterwood system is desired where extreme temperatures will inhibit growth of a new forest, and the selection system may be chosen where uneven-age stands are desired for some use and the regenerating species can grow in partial shade.

Inappropriate selection cutting of mixed-species forests in many parts of the world has left stands of diseased trees of lit-

After trees are harvested, the forest soil must be prepared for reforestation. Foresters often use bulldozers to remove stumps and loose roots and to level the soil.

tle value that prevent vigorous trees from growing. The proper logging method should be chosen for a particular stand, or the stand may lose its usefulness or even become an erosion or fire hazard.

Silvicultural techniques constantly change with technological advances. They involve the use of fire, machinery, and chemicals for preparing stands for regeneration and for removing competing plants; nurseries for growing seedlings; genetic improvements resulting in more efficiently growing trees; fertilizers for increasing growth; and remote-control machines for pruning unwanted limbs.

It might seem odd to mention fire as one means of forest management, because the enormous destructiveness of great forest fires is well known. Controlled fires, however, are useful in preparing ground for planting and in clearing the ground of weeds or fungal diseases that would harm seedlings. Controlled fires may also be used in attempting to block the course of great disaster fires. The majority of forest fires are caused by human carelessness, although many of the largest that sweep vast remote areas are produced by lightning. However damaging such natural fires are to human interests, they play a contributing role in forest evolution.

Conservation. CONSERVATION is the planned management of natural resources to prevent their neglect, exploitation, and destruction. Forests provide each of the uses described earlier, but only under certain conditions. Forests have changed and will continue to change as trees grow and die, species migrate, and climates change. Often a forest is stressed by these changes, and the trees can become weakened and infected by insects or diseases, resulting in their death. Air pollution and water pollution created by human or natural activity can further damage trees. In northern Europe, many hectares of forests have been affected by ACID RAIN.

One objective of conservation is the prevention of unintentional destruction of forests by disease, insects, and other agents. The other objective is the determination of management goals for each area of forest. Once the objectives of each stand are determined, the actual management requires the understanding of the natural sciences, long-term processes and history, and modern technologies. Deciding what values to conserve is a scientific, technological, and political subject. The decision requires the understanding of what natural and human activities will most readily destroy the stand and the knowledge of the most realistic uses, which entail both the private rights of the individual landowner and the public.

The objectives of conservation have changed along with changes in such related areas as the understanding of forest process, human values themselves, demands on the forest, availabilities of various resources, and technologies. Early forest conservation in North America was aimed at protecting forested areas from clearing for agricultural lands. Pine trees were conserved and harvested for making sailing ships. In the late 1800s and early 1900s forests were protected from fire, overharvesting, and overgrazing by the establishment of grazing laws, fire control practices, and harvesting regulations. Aesthetically unique areas and high-quality watersheds were set aside as national parks and forests. In the mid-20th century, unproductive farmland was converted to forests through the subsidizing of reforestation, thus halting erosion and providing for future forests. In the 1930s, southern U.S. forest industries began to grow seedlings on a large scale in forest tree nurseries and to replant large deforested areas.

In the past few decades, increases in mobility, leisure time, and disposable income have led to more interest in conserving forests for nonconsumptive purposes. In the United States, management objectives for national forests have shifted from timber production to multiple uses. More areas of public lands are mandated for nonconsumptive uses such as watershed and wildlife management and recreation. Various U.S. states have established or revised Forest Practices Acts to ensure that some uses of privately held lands are conserved.

Forests have been used for consumptive purposes throughout the world; in tropical regions, where forest soils grow rapidly, forest harvesting is occurring at a rapid rate. In parts of Africa, where the soils are easily eroded and the climate is un-

Selection cutting (1), which leaves small openings in the forest canopy, is used for such shade-tolerant trees as spruce. Clearcutting (2) removes all trees within a given area; such shade-intolerant species as black cherry and southern pine are planted, or regenerate naturally, in the large clearing. Seed tree cutting (3) leaves a few scattered seed-bearing trees to reforest the area. Shelterwood cutting (4) harvests trees in stages and is used for white pine and other species that require shade to develop.

predictable, forests and woodlands are being diminished. Agricultural practices may lead to deforestation under pressures of increasing population.

Three solutions to the deforestation problem have met with some success: the first involves the use of local people in forest management; the second involves "agroforestry," or the planting of trees in croplands and pastures; and the third involves the use of the financial resources of developed countries. The Food and Agriculture Organization of the United Nations has gained support for the protection of the world's forests and their role in rural development.

In the United States less than 5 percent of the virgin forests that used to blanket the country remain. In the face of population increases and continued industrialization, environmental activists in the United States have undertaken a constant watch to ensure that the remaining forests are conserved as humans increasingly alter the environment. As scientific knowledge of forest growth expands and a better understanding of detrimental effects of human activity develops, conservation efforts are working to turn the tide and prevent the demise of forests as sources of consumptive products, clean water, wildlife and fish habitats, and recreational areas. These efforts are being applied globally to prevent the neglect, exploitation, and destruction of forests.   CHADWICK D. OLIVER

Bibliography: Attiwell, P. M., and Leeper, G. W., *Forest Soils and Nutrient Cycles* (1987); Bormann, F. H., and Likens, G. E., *Pattern and Process in a Forested Ecosystem* (1984); Graewohl, J., and Greenberg, R., *Saving the Tropical Forests* (1988); Hecht, S., and Cockburn, A., *The Fate of the Forest* (1989); Hutchinson, B. A., and Hicks, B. B., eds., *The Forest-Atmosphere Interaction* (1985); Jordan, C. F., *Nutrient Cycling in Tropical Forest Ecosystems* (1985); Puri, G. S., et al., *Forest Ecology*, 2 vols. (1985, 1988); Sharpe, G. W., and Hendes, C., *Introduction to Forestry*, 5th ed. (1986); Smith, D. M., *The Practice of Silviculture*, 8th ed. (1986); Smith, W. H., *Air Pollution and Forests*, 2d ed. (1989); Tompkins, S., *Forestry in Crisis* (1990).

See also: FIRE PREVENTION AND CONTROL; HYDROLOGIC CYCLE.

forfeiture   [fohr'-fi-chur]

Forfeiture is confiscation of specific property or deprivation of rights as punishment for a breach of contract or a crime. Forfeiture of an estate as punishment for a crime was common during the Middle Ages under FEUDALISM, but is generally prohibited today. Under U.S. law, there remain specific forfeitures for certain violations of the law, such as forfeiture (following DUE PROCESS of law) of illegal gambling houses or of drivers' licenses following serious moving violations.

forge

A forge is an establishment where metal is shaped into useful configurations, usually by heating and hammering. Both ferrous and nonferrous metals can be forged, including low-carbon steel, copper, aluminum, magnesium, and titanium. A forge may be distinguished from a FOUNDRY, where metal is melted by furnaces and cast from molds. WROUGHT IRON may also be produced from pig iron or iron ore in a forge.

Forging is accomplished by the use of hammers, dies, and mechanical presses, and by the method known as roll forging. All of these methods work by applying pressure to a properly selected size of metal block, known as a billet, which is heated to the proper temperature. Hammering, the oldest forging technique, has evolved from the simple hammer and anvil of the familiar BLACKSMITH to large drop hammers, which may employ air, steam, or hydraulic pressure to increase the applied force. The blocks of metal may also be shaped by the use of dies, molds into which the metal is pressed to produce shaped pieces. Upper and lower die parts are attached to the hammers, and the upper hammer is dropped or forced down upon the metal and the lower, stationary hammer. Several different dies may be used before a finished shape is produced.

Roll forging is used to shape metal into long, thin sections. The rolls are semicylindrical and have several grooves machined into them through which the unshaped billets pass from one size groove to the next. The metal is forced to conform to the size and shape of the grooves, resulting in a variety of desired shapes.

Forging is widely used because it is a MASS PRODUCTION technique. A large number of precisely similar parts can be

A well-equipped 19th-century blacksmith shop contained a furnace and tools that the smith and his helpers used in forging various iron articles. A bellows (1) blew in air to increase the furnace temperature. An anvil, which was used for hammering hot iron into shape, comprised a tool hole (2), a punch hole (3), a face (4), and a pointed beak (5). The anvil body (6) was set on an elm block (7). A hot-coal rake (8) lay with other tools on a tool rail (9). After the red-hot iron was shaped by the smith (10) and the striker (11), it was cooled in the water trough (12). A floor mandrel (13) held other tools in use near the furnace (14).

made quickly over a long period of time. Forged products are used in virtually all aspects of technology, from automobile engines to rocket components.   MERLE C. NUTT

Bibliography: Hrisoulas, J., *The Complete Blacksmith* (1987); Nisbett, E. G., and Melilli, A. S., eds., *Steel Forgings* (1986).

See also: METALLURGY; TOOL AND DIE MAKING.

forgery

Forgery is the fraudulent alteration of a written document with the intent to defraud, or the falsification of any instrument (such as a deed, bond, or stock certificate) for the purpose of deception or FRAUD. A person who signs another's name on a check is guilty of a forgery. When the forger presents the check to the bank and the bank cashes it, he or she commits the companion crime called uttering a forged document. In some states, the two crimes of forgery and uttering have been combined into the crime of forgery. The forgery of government obligations such as money or bonds is called COUNTERFEITING.

forgery in art

Forgery in art, the fabrication of an art object with intent to deceive a purchaser as to its true origin, is as ancient as the practice of collecting. Forgery, or deliberate fraud, must be distinguished from innocent imitation without deceitful motive. Every kind of art has inspired spurious reproductions, and the history of forgery reflects changes in taste, since the forger supplies a demand for coveted objects and follows the preferences of the time. The techniques of the forger include direct copying of famous works, imitating the style of a particular painter or period, piecing together old fragments to simulate antiquity, and the false attribution of minor works to major artists.

Techniques of Forgery. The earliest records of forgery date from classical Rome, where a demand for early Greek art became prevalent and sculptors signed their statues with the names of the celebrated Greek artists Phidias and Praxiteles in order to dupe collectors. During the Renaissance, which witnessed the beginnings of the modern interest in artistic personality, copying of both antique and contemporary art became commonplace. Lorenzo GHIBERTI was one among many artists who increased their knowledge of classical art by reproducing its styles and techniques.

One of the most notable forgeries of all time was perpetrated by the young MICHELANGELO who, according to Giorgio Vasari, gave his statue of Cupid, executed in the ancient Greek manner, an antique appearance by burying it in earth for several months. After selling the statue to a collector, he claimed it as his work, thus calling attention to his skill. Some deceptions are practiced not by artists but by unscrupulous dealers. The sculptor Giovanni Bastianini (1830–68), a skillful imitator of Renaissance art, originally sold his work with correct attribution and for modest sums of money. His versions of Italian 15th-century sculpture were so convincing, however, that they were later sold as originals at high prices. One work was even purchased by the Louvre before Bastianini discovered what had occurred and revealed the origin of the works.

The less scrupulous Alceo Dossena (1878–1936) began his career as a restorer of marble statues in his native Cremona, Italy. His work, which reproduced both antique and Renaissance styles with astonishing skill, was never an imitation of a single original but recreated the style of a particular artist or school. Works by Dossena were acclaimed as period masterpieces, and many of them were purchased by well-known collectors.

Forgeries of celebrated works are relatively easy to reveal by comparison with the original. The most successful forgers, like Dossena, have adopted more subtle techniques. Hans van Meegeren (1884–1947), one of the most notorious forgers of this century, was aware of scholarly conjecture that Jan Vermeer had painted religious works prior to his concentration on secular subjects. Van Meegeren supported this notion by producing a group of "early" religious Vermeers, which he sold to members of the German Nazi government during World War II. Accused after the war of selling Dutch national treasures, he proved his innocence by painting another "Vermeer" in his prison cell.

Oriental and Pre-Columbian art is also forged frequently. In China, the making of deceptive copies of paintings dates from the T'ang dynasty (AD 618–906) and has continued to modern times. Pre-Columbian art has been forged only since the 19th century, when it became sought after by collectors, but the production of fake South American art has now assumed vast proportions.

Detection of Forgeries. An array of modern technical devices such as microscopic and chemical analysis and X-ray, infrared, and ultraviolet photography can now be used to detect forgeries. These devices are useful in revealing what is not immediately apparent to the naked eye. An X ray may reveal a figure in 18th-century clothes under what is purported to be a 17th-century Rembrandt. Infrared radiation can reveal a signature that was painted over when the forger substituted the name of a more famous artist. Chemical analysis of a small piece of paint will determine whether pigments invented after the supposed date of the painting have been used.

Art objects other than paintings require different methods of detection: an object consisting of an organic material such as wood can be dated fairly accurately by the radio-carbon technique, providing the object was made between 1,000 and

(Below) Hans van Meegeren paints an "early Vermeer," The Young Christ, in his cell to prove to Dutch authorities that he forged the "masterpieces" he sold to Nazi officials. Both Van Meegeren and Alceo Dossena, who created the "Renaissance" Madonna and Child (right), worked only in the style of a particular artist or period and copied no specific work.

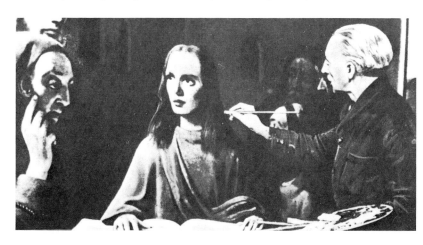

50,000 years ago. Papers and inks can be dated on the basis of the material content and methods of manufacture. Ultraviolet radiation can be used to discover alterations and restorations of paintings and pottery.

With the development of technical procedures and the expansion of interest in art of all periods, there has been a tremendous growth both in the production of forgeries and in the methods of detecting them. In spite of this, the most effective safeguard against deception is the judgment of a trained observer whose intuition can reject the false after long acquaintance with the values of genuine works.

REVIEWED BY JOHN TANCOCK

Bibliography: Asmole, B., *Forgeries of Ancient Sculpture: Creation and Detection* (1961); Dutton, D., *The Forger's Art* (1983); Feder, K. L., *Frauds, Myths, and Mysteries* (1990); Fleming, S., *Authenticity in Art* (1976); Kurtz, O., *Fakes* (1967); Marinjinssen, R. H., *Paintings—Genuine, Fraud, Fake: Modern Methods of Examining Paintings* (1987); Princeton University Art Museum, *Problems of Authenticity in 19th- and 20th-Century Art* (1973); Savage, G., *Forgeries, Fakes and Reproductions* (1963); Schmitt, H., *3,000 Years of Deception in Art and Antiques*, trans. by J. M. Brownjohn (1961).

forget-me-not

The forget-me-not M. sylvatica *bears tiny, delicate blossoms on thin stalks. It grows abundantly along shady streams and is cultivated as a border plant and under trees in gardens.*

Forget-me-nots, *Myosotis*, are a genus of annual, biennial, or perennial herbaceous plants belonging to the borage family, Boraginaceae. They produce blue, white, or pink flowers and thrive in cool, partially shaded, and moist locations. Dwarf varieties make excellent edging plants; one of the most attractive spring-blooming species is *M. dissitiflora*, the flowers of which are a delicate shade of blue. The forget-me-not blooms from April until well into June. It is the state flower of Alaska.

forgetting: see MEMORY.

Forlì   [fohr-lee']

Forlì (1984 est. pop., 110,943), a city in northern Italy, is situated on the Montane River about 30 km (20 mi) from the Adriatic Sea. Forlì is the commercial and industrial center for the surrounding agricultural region. Its manufactures include textiles, furniture, light machinery, chemicals, and shoes.

Called Forum Livii by the Romans, it was a market town on the Via Aemilia. In the 11th century, Forlì became independent. It was ruled by the Ordelaffi family from 1315 to 1500, and it joined the Papal States in 1504. In 1860, Forlì became part of unified Italy.

formaldehyde   [fohr-mal'-duh-hyd]

Formaldehyde, HCHO, is the simplest member of the class of organic compounds known as ALDEHYDES. At room temperature formaldehyde is an extremely reactive colorless gas with a suffocating odor. It is commonly sold as an aqueous solu-

tion (formalin) or in solid polymeric forms (paraformaldehyde and trioxane). Formaldehyde is used in the manufacture of dyes, in the production of synthetic resins, and as a preservative for biological specimens.

formalism

In literature, formalism is a school of thought that evolved in Russia during World War I, had its heyday in the early 1920s, and was suppressed as a heresy in 1930. It was championed by such unorthodox philologists and students of literature as Roman JAKOBSON, B. Eichenbaum, Victor Shklovsky, Boris Tomashevsky, and Y. Tynyanov.

According to the formalists' doctrine, literature is a unique form of discourse characterized by the "emphasis on the medium" or "perceptibility of the mode of expression." In literary art, it was argued, language is not simply a vehicle of communication. From a mere proxy for an object, the word becomes an object in its own right, and source of pleasure, as multiple devices at the writer's disposal converge upon the verbal sign in order to dramatize its complex texture.

The formalists caused these methodological assumptions to be brought to bear on general problems of versification and prose theory and on Russian literary history. Formalist research into such masters of Russian literature as Pushkin, Gogol, Dostoevsky, and Tolstoi resulted in drastic reexaminations of these authors' works, often one-sided but invariably illuminating. Viewed in a broader perspective, Russian formalism was one of the earliest manifestations of the 20th-century trend toward structural analysis (see STRUCTURALISM) of literature and art.

VICTOR ERLICH

Bibliography: Bakhtin, M. M., and Medvedev, P. N., *The Formal Method in Literary Scholarship,* trans. by A. J. Wehrle (1985); Erlich, V., *Russian Formalism,* 2d rev. ed. (1965); Jackson, R., and Rudy, S., eds., *Russian Formalism* (1985).

Forman, Milos

The Czech-born film director Milos Forman, b. Feb. 18, 1932, is noted for his powers of observation and his subtle, ironic humor. He began writing screenplays and directing in the 1950s and participated in the early Laterna Magika mixed media presentations. His Czech films include *Peter and Pavla* (1964), *Loves of a Blonde* (1965), and *The Firemen's Ball* (1967). After coming to the United States he directed *Taking Off* (1971); *One Flew Over the Cuckoo's Nest* (1975), for which he won an Academy Award for direction; *Hair* (1979); *Ragtime* (1981); *Amadeus* (1984), for which he received a second Academy Award; and *Valmont* (1989).   ROY ARMES

Bibliography: Slater, T. J., *Milos Forman: A Bio-bibliography* (1987).

formic acid

Formic acid, HCOOH, the simplest CARBOXYLIC ACID, is a strong reducing agent that exists as a colorless liquid. It is contained in the poison of stinging ants (Latin *formica,* "ant"), stinging caterpillars, and stinging nettles. Formic acid forms salts with alkali metals and forms esters with alcohols. It is widely used in electroplating, dyeing, tanning, and the manufacture of chemicals and medicines.

Formosa: see TAIWAN.

Forrest, Edwin

Edwin Forrest, b. Philadelphia, Mar. 9, 1806, d. Dec. 12, 1872, was the most popular and perhaps the greatest American tragedian of the 19th century. He made his debut at the age of 14 and acted in many Shakespearean roles, particularly Othello. Forrest also had parts created for him by offering prizes to encourage American playwriting. His booming voice and fierce looks, coupled with his arrogance and short temper, suited contemporary histrionic fashion. His feud with the English actor William Charles MACREADY caused the 1849 ASTOR PLACE RIOT.   MYRON MATLAW

Bibliography: Alger, William R., *Life of Edwin Forrest,* 2 vols. (1877); Moody, Richard, *Edwin Forrest* (1960).

Forrest, John, 1st Baron Forrest

John Forrest, b. Aug. 22, 1847, d. Sept. 3, 1918, was Western Australia's most notable explorer and political leader. In 1869, while a surveyor, he led an unsuccessful search for traces of the explorer Ludwig Leichhardt, who had disappeared in central Australia in 1848. Forrest then made two successful overland journeys, from Perth to Adelaide by the south coast (1870) and from Champion Bay to the telegraph post near modern Oodnadatta in central Australia (1874). As the first premier of Western Australia from 1890 to 1901, he initiated a water pipeline from Perth to the Coolgardie gold fields. A member of the Federal Parliament from 1901, he promoted a railroad from Port Augusta to Kalgoorlie. He held several federal cabinet posts between 1901 and 1918, when he was created Baron Forrest of Bunbury. He was the first Australian to become a British peer.   E. J. TAPP

Bibliography: Crowley, F. K., *Forrest 1847–1918* (1971); Rawson, Geoffrey, *Desert Journeys* (1948).

Forrest, Nathan Bedford

Nathan Bedford Forrest, b. July 13, 1821, d. Oct. 29, 1877, was a Confederate general in the U.S. Civil War especially known for his brilliant cavalry tactics. A wealthy businessman in his native Tennessee, he joined the Confederate Army in 1861 and became commander of a cavalry battalion raised and equipped at his own expense. At the surrender of Fort Donelson (1862), Forrest escaped capture by leading his entire force through a gap in the Northern lines. He later won fame for his daring and successful raids against Union armies and for his repeated victories over opponents that outnumbered him. The most celebrated of the latter was his defeat of an expedition under Gen. S. D. Sturgis at Brice's Cross Roads, Miss. (June 10, 1864). Forrest was charged with responsibility for a massacre of Black Union soldiers at Fort Pillow, Tenn. (April 1864). After the war he was a leader of the Ku Klux Klan.
                                             RICHARD M. McMURRY

Bibliography: Wyeth, J. A., *That Devil Forrest* (1989).

Forrestal, James V.   [fohr-'es-tul]

James Vincent Forrestal, b. Beacon, N.Y., Feb. 15, 1892, d. May 22, 1949, was an American investment banker and public official who served as the first U.S. secretary of defense. A successful Wall Street financier, Forrestal became an administrative assistant to President Franklin D. Roosevelt in 1940. He was undersecretary of the navy from 1940 to 1944 and secretary of the navy from 1944 to 1947. When the War Department and Navy Department were unified in 1947, President Harry S. Truman named Forrestal to be secretary of defense. He served until March 1949, when policy differences with Truman led to his resignation. Hospitalized for acute depression, he committed suicide.

Bibliography: Forrestal, James, *Forrestal Diaries*, ed. by Walter Millis (1951); Rogow, Arnold A., *James Forrestal: A Study of Personality, Politics and Policy* (1963).

Forrester, Jay Wright   [fohr'-es-tur]

The electrical engineer Jay Wright Forrester, b. Anselmo, Nebr., July 14, 1918, made basic contributions to the development of computers. From 1944 to 1951 he designed and supervised construction of the Whirlwind I computer at the Massachusetts Institute of Technology. The largest, fastest, and most powerful of the early electronic computers, Whirlwind incorporated innovations in software, including a comprehensive system for translating symbolic instructions into machine operations. Forrester directed (1951–56) the MIT Digital Computer Laboratory, which he had founded in 1945 and where he invented magnetic core memory (see COMPUTER MEMORY; INFORMATION STORAGE AND RETRIEVAL). Forrester also worked (1952–56) at MIT's Lincoln Laboratory, adapting the technology of Whirlwind for use in an early warning air defense system. Since 1956 he has been a professor of industrial management at MIT.   KENNETH THIBODEAU

E. M. Forster, a major 20th-century British writer, infused his fiction with humanitarian ideals. His last novel, A Passage to India (1924), examines the cultural difficulties brought about by British colonialism in India. (Portrait, 1920, by Dora Carrington, National Portrait Gallery, London.)

Forster, E. M.   [fohrs'-tur]

Edward Morgan Forster, b. Jan. 1, 1879, d. June 7, 1970, was a prominent English novelist, essayist, and short-story writer. Educated at Cambridge, and an important member of the BLOOMSBURY GROUP, he began his literary career in 1903 as a writer for *The Independent Review*, a periodical of liberal, antiimperialist sympathies. *Where Angels Fear to Tread* (1905), his first novel, was followed by three increasingly impressive novels, *The Longest Journey* (1907), *A Room with a View* (1908), and *Howard's End* (1910). After publication of his volume of short stories, *The Celestial Omnibus* (1911), he visited India, where he closely observed British colonial attitudes toward the native peoples. During World War I he worked for the International Red Cross in Egypt, returning to London at war's end to pursue a career in literary journalism. In 1922 he made a second visit to India; he channeled his observations on both visits into his most enduring novel, *A Passage to India* (1924). He was made an honorary fellow of Kings College, Cambridge, where he delivered the Clark Lectures in literature, later published as *Aspects of the Novel* (1927). His work in later life included short stories (many published posthumously), essays, and biography. An early novel, *Maurice*, completed in 1914, was not published until 1971, partly because of its frank portrayal of homosexuality.

Forster's finest achievements were his novels, in which character and the clash of ideas overshadow plot. His narrative point of view was normally that of an outsider, and his novels, especially *A Passage to India* and *Howard's End*, are sad examinations of the social codes and barriers that thwart communication and frustrate human feeling.   PHILIP FLYNN

Bibliography: Beer, J. D., ed., *A Passage to India* (1985); Furbank, P. N., *E. M. Forster* (1978; repr. 1981); Lago, M., and Furbank, P. N., eds., *Selected Letters of E. M. Forster*, 2 vols. (1983, 1984); McDowell, F., *E. M. Forster*, rev. ed. (1982); Page, N., *E. M. Forster* (1988); Summers, C., *E. M. Forster* (1987); Trilling, L. M., *E. M. Forster*, 2d ed. (1965); Wilde, A., *Critical Essays on E. M. Forster* (1985).

Forsyte Saga, The   [fohr'-syt]

The Forsyte Saga, by the English novelist John GALSWORTHY, is primarily composed of three novels: *The Man of Property* (1906), *In Chancery* (1920), and *To Let* (1921). A second trilogy—*The White Monkey* (1924), *The Silver Spoon* (1926), and *Swan Song* (1928)—is often included. Money, power, and family intrigue dominate the interests of most of the late-Victorian upper–middle-class Forsytes and their mates. The second trilogy deals principally with the younger Forsytes as they cope with postwar disillusionment in the 1920s. Soames Forsyte, "the man of property," plays a central role in both trilogies. *The Forsyte Saga* was adapted (1967–70) into a popular television series.   DONALD SMALLEY

Forsyth, John   [fohr'-syth]

John Forsyth, b. Oct. 22, 1780, d. Oct. 21, 1841, was a Georgia senator and supporter of President Andrew Jackson. He was a U.S. congressman (1813–18), ambassador to Spain (1819–23), and again a congressman (1823–27) before his term in the

Senate (1829–34). In the NULLIFICATION crisis of 1832, he was largely responsible for preventing Georgia from following South Carolina's example in defying the federal government. In return for his loyalty, Jackson appointed (1834) him secretary of state, a post he held until 1841.

forsythia [fohr-sith'-ee-uh]

Forsythia intermedia, *one forsythia species, is a flowering deciduous shrub with arching branches that grow as high as 3 m (10 ft). Among the first shrubs to bloom in cool climates, forsythias produce bright yellow flowers, each with four oblong petals, in early spring.*

Forsythia, genus *Forsythia*, is any of several species of hardy, deciduous shrubs belonging to the olive family, Oleaceae. Forsythias are among the showiest of spring-flowering shrubs, producing brilliant yellow flowers in early spring before the leaves unfold. They are very adaptable plants and can grow in a variety of soils. The principal species are *F. suspensa*, which reaches heights of 2.4 m (8 ft) or more; *F. intermedia*, which has several varieties, including *spectabilis*, showy-border forsythia; *F. viridissima*, with bright-green stems; and *F. ovata*, a Korean species that is the hardiest and earliest to bloom.

Fort, Paul

Paul Fort, b. Feb. 1, 1872, d. Apr. 20, 1960, was a French symbolist poet and dramatist. At the age of 18, he founded the experimental Théâtre d'Art, where from 1890 to 1893 he presented such symbolist dramas as Maeterlinck's *The Intruder* and *The Blind* (both 1891); readings of poetry by Mallarmé, Poe, and Rimbaud; and settings by such painters as Vuillard, Denis, and Sérusier. Fort's own writings include 40 volumes of *Ballades françaises* and *Chroniques de France* (1897–1951), which commemorate France's history and culture.

BETTINA KNAPP

Fort Benning

Fort Benning, site of the U.S. Army Infantry Center, is a 765-km² (295-mi²) base located 14 km (9 mi) south of Columbus, Ga., on the Chattahoochee River. The number of personnel assigned there as of 1992 was about 26,200. Besides infantry classes, airborne and ranger training courses are offered. Fort Benning contributes greatly to the economy of the Columbus area. Founded as Camp Benning in 1918, the base was named in honor of the Confederate army officer Henry L. Benning.

Fort Bragg

Fort Bragg is a 932-km² (360-mi²) U.S. Army base located 16 km (10 mi) northwest of Fayetteville, N.C. The Special Warfare Center trains troops in psychological and guerrilla warfare. Since World War II the 82d Airborne Division has been housed there. The base was established in 1918 and named for Gen. Braxton Bragg of the Confederate Army.

Fort-de-France [fohr-duh-frahns]

Fort-de-France (1990 pop., 101,540) is the capital of Martinique, a French overseas department in the Lesser Antilles. Located on the west coast, it is the largest city in the French West Indies. A commercial and shipping center on Fort-de-France Bay, the city exports sugarcane, rum, and bananas. The French fleet in the Caribbean is stationed there. Its climate is tropical, with a hurricane season lasting from July to November. Founded in 1672, the city was made the capital in 1680. It was severely damaged by an earthquake in 1839 and by fire in 1890. After the destruction of Saint-Pierre by the eruption of Mount Pelée in 1902, Fort-de-France became the island's commercial center.

Fort Dearborn

Fort Dearborn was a frontier military post established in 1803 on the site of present-day Chicago and named for the then secretary of war, Henry Dearborn. Its garrison was massacred by Indians in 1812, but the fort was reoccupied in 1816 and continued to be used until 1836.

Fort Dix

Fort Dix is a U.S. Army training center located 27 km (17 mi) southeast of Trenton, N.J. It covers about 130 km² (50 mi²). Formerly an infantry basic-training center, Fort Dix became a training center for reserve component units in 1992. It was founded in 1917 and named for John A. Dix, a Civil War major general. During World War II, five corps, ten divisions, and an air force were trained for overseas duty there, and about 1,200,000 soldiers were discharged from there after the war. McGuire Air Force Base borders the fort.

Fort Donelson: see FORT HENRY AND FORT DONELSON.

Fort Duquesne [due-kayn']

Fort Duquesne, a wilderness fortification at the confluence of the Allegheny and Monongahela rivers on the site of present-day Pittsburgh, Pa., was a key position in the French line of defense against the British in the FRENCH AND INDIAN WAR (1754–63). Construction began in 1754, after which the fort served as a base for French and Indian raiding activity against the Virginia frontier. Although the French managed to rout Gen. Edward BRADDOCK's advancing army in July 1755, the approach of Gen. John FORBES's army in November 1758 caused them to abandon Fort Duquesne.   DOUGLAS EDWARD LEACH

Fort Henry and Fort Donelson

Fort Henry, on the Tennessee River, and Fort Donelson, on the Cumberland River, were strategic Confederate fortifications in the U.S. Civil War. Built by Confederate authorities in midsummer 1861, they were designed to repel invasion of Tennessee and the Deep South. They were not well sited but their very existence brought Union attention. A coordinated land and water offensive led by Gen. Ulysses GRANT and Flag Officer Andrew FOOTE captured first Henry (Feb. 6, 1862) and then Donelson (Feb. 16, 1862). The Donelson fight was fierce and might have gone either way, save for incompetence in the Confederate high command. The loss of these two strategic forts turned the flank of Confederate defenses at Columbus, Ky., and forced Gen. Albert S. JOHNSTON's withdrawal to the middle South. Confederate losses, including prisoners, at the two forts were more than 12,000 men, and these, combined with the psychological effect of twin defeats, cast gloom over the Confederacy.   FRANK E. VANDIVER

Bibliography: Catton, Bruce, *Grant Moves South* (1960; repr. 1990); Horn, Stanley F., *The Army of Tennessee* (1953; repr. 1968).

Fort Hood

Fort Hood is a U.S. Army base covering 878 km² (339 mi²), located 3 km (2 mi) west of Killeen, Texas. It houses armored and mechanized units. Founded in 1942 as Camp Hood, it was named for Confederate general John B. Hood; in 1950 it became Fort Hood.

Fort Knox

Fort Knox is a U.S. Army military post located approximately 50 km (30 mi) southwest of Louisville in Hardin and Meade counties, Ky. Established in 1918 as a training camp, it became a permanent military base in 1932. Since 1936, Fort Knox has been the site of the U.S. Gold Bullion Depository. The gold is stored in concrete and steel vaults inside a bomb-proof building (exterior dimensions: 37 × 32 m/121 × 105 ft), protected by guards armed with machine guns. The vaults are guarded by electronic devices, and the interiors are constantly visible to security personnel.

Fort-Lamy: see N'DJAMENA.

Fort Lauderdale

Fort Lauderdale, Fla., located 40 km (25 mi) north of Miami, has a population of 149,377 (1990) and is the seat of heavily urbanized Broward County, which has 1,255,488 residents. With temperatures averaging 20° C (69° F) in January and 28° C (82° F) in July, Fort Lauderdale is best known as a vacation and retirement center. The city has a large boat basin, and about 10% of its 78-km² (30-mi²) area is composed of a network of inland waterways that create small islands. The famous beach is one of the largest public beaches in the state. Electronics and concrete are produced, and dairy and citrus farming takes place in the surrounding area. Port Everglades is a major deepwater facility.

A military post was established on the site in 1838. A settlement grew up around the fort and experienced its most rapid growth during the Florida land boom of the 1920s and again after World War II.

Fort McHenry

Fort McHenry was an American military installation built on a peninsula in Baltimore harbor in 1799. During the War of 1812 it was bombarded (Sept. 13–14, 1814) by a British fleet, an attack that inspired Francis Scott KEY, a prisoner aboard a British ship, to write the STAR-SPANGLED BANNER. Later used as a storage depot and military prison, Fort McHenry was established as a national park in 1925. It was redesignated a national monument and historic shrine in 1939.

Fort Moultrie

Fort Moultrie was a fortification on Sullivan Island at the entrance to the harbor of Charleston, S.C. Originally named Fort Sullivan, it was held by a garrison of American troops under Col. William Moultrie (1730–1805) against a 10-ship attack on June 28, 1776, in the American Revolution. The fort was renamed to honor Moultrie. A new structure built on the site (1807–11) was the Confederate headquarters for the bombardment of FORT SUMTER in April 1861, at the beginning of the U.S. Civil War. Now included in the the Fort Sumter National Monument, Fort Moultrie contains the tomb of the Seminole chief OSCEOLA, imprisoned there during the Seminole Wars.

Fort Niagara

Fort Niagara, a post on the Niagara River at Lake Ontario, guarded the passageway to the rich western fur-trapping lands. In the 1670s the French erected a stockade on the site, and in 1726 they completed a stone fort. The British captured the fort in 1759 during the French and Indian War, and they used it to launch frontier raids during the American Revolution. Fort Niagara was relinquished to American troops in 1796 as provided by Jay's Treaty (1794), but the British seized it again during the War of 1812. Returned to the United States

in 1815, the fort served as a military post until 1946; it then became part of a New York state park.

Fort Smith

Fort Smith is one of the two seats of Sebastian County, in western Arkansas. It is located on the Arkansas River, near the Oklahoma border. It had a population of 72,798 in 1990. The city grew up around a U.S. Army fort established in 1817 to control Indian tribes settled in the area. The discovery of gold in California in 1848 transformed Fort Smith into a bustling supply depot for prospectors taking the southern route across the Great Plains. Today its economy is based on the deposits of coal and natural gas, timber, and the fertile farmlands of the surrounding region. Its diversified industries manufacture furniture, automobiles, electrical appliances, and metal, glass, paper, and plastic products. The Fort Smith National Historic Site is located there.

Fort Sumter

Confederate troops open fire on Fort Sumter in this engraving from Harper's Weekly. Although the federal garrison in Charleston harbor was forced to capitulate after two days of shelling (Apr. 12-13, 1861), this first engagement of the Civil War claimed but one life, that of a soldier killed by a misfiring gun during the surrender ceremonies.

Fort Sumter, construction of which was begun in 1829 at the entrance to the harbor of Charleston, S.C., was the site of the CIVIL WAR's first shot on Apr. 12, 1861. Unimportant militarily, the fort became a vital symbol to both North and South.

Confederate authorities sought throughout March 1861 to negotiate the peaceful evacuation of the Union garrison at Fort Sumter under Maj. Robert Anderson. Once convinced that Abraham Lincoln's administration would not give up the fort, President Jefferson Davis faced a crisis in diplomacy. If Sumter were not taken, the Confederate States could not boast independence; if action against it were delayed, South Carolina threatened unilateral seizure; and any action might trigger war with the United States. Davis and his cabinet, fearing Union reinforcement of the garrison, decided that domestic politics and international posture demanded Sumter's capture and ordered Gen. P. G. T. BEAUREGARD to take it. He opened fire at 4:30 AM on April 12. Anderson surrendered the next day, and his forces left the fort on April 14. War was on, and the U.S. flag was not raised again over the fort until Feb. 18, 1865.

FRANK E. VANDIVER

Bibliography: Current, Richard, *Lincoln and the First Shot* (1963; repr. 1990); Hendrickson, Robert, *Sumter: The First Day of the Civil War* (1990); Swanberg, W. A., *First Blood* (1958).

Fort Ticonderoga: see TICONDEROGA.

Fort Wayne

Located in northeastern Indiana where the Saint Joseph and Saint Marys rivers meet to form the Maumee, Fort Wayne is the seat of Allen County and the state's second largest city, with a population of 173,072 persons within the city and 363,811 in the metropolitan area (1990). It is a commercial and transportation center with diversified industries, including electronics and automotive parts. Within the city is the gravesite of Johnny Appleseed (John Chapman).

Fort Wayne was the chief village of the Miami Indians before the French established Fort Miami as a trading post there in the 1680s. The British captured the fort in 1760 but were driven out by Indians during Pontiac's Rebellion in 1763. The present city traces its origin to a fort built by Gen. Anthony Wayne in 1794.

Fort Worth

Fort Worth, a city in north central Texas, lies 48 km (30 mi) west of DALLAS near the headwaters of the Trinity River. It is the seat of Tarrant County and has a population of 447,619 (1990), with 3,885,415 persons in the Dallas–Fort Worth metropolitan area. First a frontier outpost maintained (1849–53) by the U.S. Army, Fort Worth flourished in the early 1870s as a watering place on the Chisholm Trail. The arrival of the Texas and Pacific Railway in 1876 turned it into a cattle-shipping and meat-packing center and an important point for grain milling and distribution. The discovery of oil in 1917 only 145 km (90 mi) west transformed the city again into a booming center of refining operations. Today many other industries spur its economy, particularly the aerospace industry.The huge Dallas–Fort Worth airport and Carswell Air Force Base are nearby. The city's cultural institutions include the Amon Carter Museum of Western Art, Kimbell Art Museum, and the Fort Worth Museum of Science and History. Texas Wesleyan University, Texas Christian University, and Southwestern Baptist Theological Seminary are located there.

Fortaleza   [fohrt-uhl-ay'-zuh]

Fortaleza is located on the Paejú River along the northeast coast of Brazil. It is the capital of the state of Ceará, and the population is 1,582,414 (1985 est.) The city is a regional commercial center, fishing port, and beach resort. Textiles, soap, and refined sugar are its major products, and it ships raw materials such as carnauba wax and hides. Fortaleza is the site of the Federal University of Ceará (1955). Founded by the Portuguese in 1609, Fortaleza is today the focus of a large Brazilian regional development plan.   JAMES N. SNADEN

Fortas, Abe   [fohrt'-uhs]

Abe Fortas, b. Memphis, Tenn., June 19, 1910, d. Apr. 5, 1982, was a prominent Washington, D.C., attorney and presidential advisor when President Lyndon B. Johnson appointed him to the U.S. Supreme Court in 1965. Johnson's subsequent nomination of Fortas as chief justice was blocked by Senate foes of his activist stand on civil liberties. In 1969, following charges of conflict of interest, Fortas resigned from the Court. His arguments in GIDEON V. WAINWRIGHT (1962) established the right of the poor to legal counsel.

Bibliography: Kalman, Laura, *Abe Fortas* (1990).

Fortes, Meyer

Meyer Fortes, b. Apr. 25, 1906, d. Jan. 27, 1983, a British social anthropologist, was best known for his comparative studies of kinship and religion among nonindustrial societies. Along with Alfred R. Radcliffe-Brown, Fortes was a leading authority on the political systems of African societies. His writings include *Kinship and the Social Order* (1969) and *Time and Social Structure* (1970). He was professor of social anthropology at Cambridge University (1950–73).

FORTH

FORTH is a medium-level computer language that combines the speed of low-level, or machine-level, language and the readability of higher-level languages such as BASIC and FORTRAN. FORTH was created by programmer Charles H. Moore and was first used to control the telescope at the Kitt Peak Observatory. It has since developed a small but enthusiastic following of users who enjoy the independence allowed by its adaptability and its user-oriented programming logic. Users of FORTH write their own word commands, or functions, which are then used repeatedly in writing new programs. FORTH is economical in that it employs a small number of subroutines to build an entire program.

Forth, River

The River Forth originates in the highlands of south central Scotland. Flowing eastward, it widens to an estuary, the Firth of Forth, at Alloa, near Stirling. The combined length of the river and firth is 187 km (116 mi); the firth, which extends 89 km (55 mi) to the North Sea, is 31 km (19 mi) across at its widest point. Edinburgh's port, Leith, and Grangemouth are the principal ports. A naval base is located at Rosyth. The firth is spanned by three bridges, including the Forth Railway Bridge, one of the first cantilever bridges ever built (1890), and the Forth Road Bridge (1964; 1,006 m/3,300 ft), one of the longest suspension bridges in Europe.

fortification

Fortification is the military science of strengthening terrain to protect armed defenders. Fortifications may be categorized according to intended duration of occupation. Temporary field fortifications—foxholes, trenches, breastworks, and fire bases—secure battlefield positions and are relatively simple. Permanent fixed fortifications, including citadels, castles, walls, and casemates, dominate key locations of lasting military value and are much more elaborate, usually consisting of stone or concrete constructions. Geographic extent offers a second way to distinguish defensive works. Fortresses protect a single point, such as a city. Lines shield an entire region. Fortifications often feature combinations of these basic types. Whatever the category, these military engineering projects are designed by combat engineers, built by available military and civilian labor, and defended by a garrison. Combat engineers also use their knowledge of fortification to direct siege operations aimed at the capture of enemy defensive systems.

Early Fortifications. Since prehistoric times, outnumbered settled peoples have created defenses to hold mobile nomadic marauders at bay. Ancient and classical civilizations recognized the military utility and manpower economy inherent in prepared defenses. Excellent examples of all four major types of fortifications abounded in ancient times. The Roman legions' stout nightly camps set the standards for field works. Important fixed positions included the long walls that connected Athens to its port, Piraeus; these walls allowed Athenians to resist a lengthy Spartan siege during the Peloponnesian War (431–404 BC). Jerusalem, Tyre, and Loyang, China, were particularly formidable fortress cities.

Defensive lines, from the relatively modest 121-km-long (75-mi) HADRIAN'S WALL in Roman Britain to the massive 3,200-km (2,000-mi) GREAT WALL OF CHINA, separated barbarians from the civilized peoples of the ancient world. Still, any of these fortifications could be penetrated by determined and skilled attackers employing siegecraft. In the end, the structures were only as good as their garrisons and the mobile reserves that supported them. When the soldiers in and behind the forts and walls faltered, the fortifications themselves could not prevent outsiders from coming through.

After the fall of the Roman Empire in the 5th century AD, fortifications in the West became more rudimentary. In their lengthy struggle with invaders such as the Vikings and the Magyars, settled peoples in western Europe developed a feudal military system of local defense. In each area, a few knights defended a large mass of serfs, who farmed for their

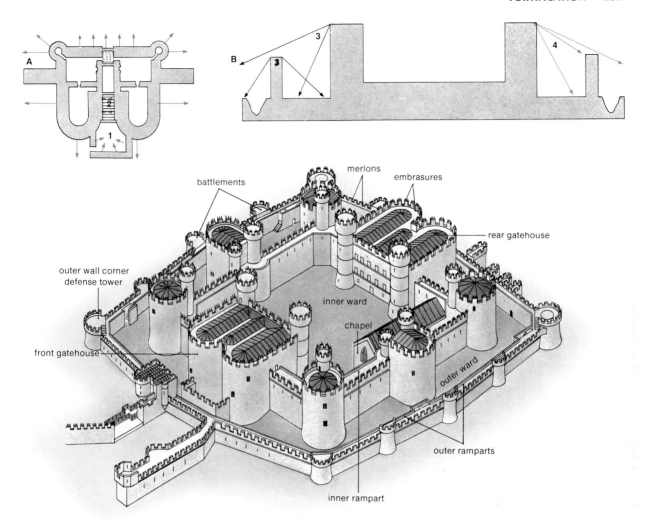

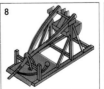

The concentric castle of the 13th century, protected by two (occasionally three) turreted outer walls and a complex system of inner defenses, was designed as an impregnable fortress. Shown in the detail (A) is the high gatehouse overlooking the gateway in the outer wall. Attackers who breached the first wall (1) faced a narrow passage into the gatehouse (2), where they were exposed to arrows from bowmen stationed above them. A cross section of the walls (B) shows the defensive firing lines (3, 4). The attackers used a variety of battering and bolt-hurling weapons: siege tower (5); ballista (6); mangonel (7); trebuchet (8); battering ram (9); and bore (10).

overlords. In return for surrendering their freedom, in times of danger, the serfs could seek refuge in a central hilltop tower known as a keep. By AD 1000, keeps had begun to evolve into the familiar medieval CASTLE. Behind and atop the multiple concentric rings of tall stone walls bolstered by corner towers and fronted by a wide moat, knights could draw on stored food to hold out against besieging enemies. The successive walls and bastions allowed defenders to withdraw if outer works fell, making a siege assault laborious and bloody. When trading towns arose, they too were fortified with walls and turrets. In time, from these towns came developments that made castles obsolete: the invention of gunpowder and the rebirth of interest in classical military engineering.

The Early Modern Period. Assailed by the consistent bombardment of newly cast guns and undermined by the persistent burrowing of Renaissance engineers, the high walls of medieval castles gave way. Enthusiasm for fortifications waned. The same mathematics that allowed precision gunlaying, however, permitted engineers to create new varieties of prepared defenses. King Louis XIV of France employed Sebastien Le Prestre de VAUBAN (1633–1707) to design a series of low-lying, angular stone works called star forts because of their shape when viewed from above. Vauban's geometric fixed fortifications were hard to see from ground level and even harder to breach. Their low, thick, gently sloping walls, often reinforced with soft earth, deflected artillery fires. At-

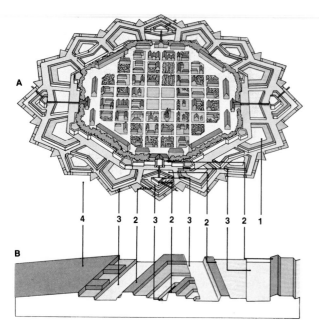

The Neuf Brisach fortress in Alsace, France, is an example of the star fort developed by the French military engineer Vauban late in the 17th century. Used for more than 200 years, the star fort provided protection in depth in particularly vulnerable areas. Plan view (A) reveals a complex of large, arrowhead-shaped bastions (1) that surrounded the inner fort and enabled the defenders stationed there to fire at attackers from any angle. A series of earthen ramparts (2) and moats (3), shown in cross section (B), slowed attacking forces and exposed them to defensive fire. A high, sloping, earthen rampart, or glacis (4), protected the inner defenses from direct artillery fire.

The Martello Tower was a peculiar kind of fortification used by the British in the early 19th century, when 74 of them were built on the south coast of England to protect it from an expected invasion by Napoleon. The towers were cylindrical in shape and constructed with thick stone walls. The only doorway (1) was placed 6 m (20 ft) above ground to make it difficult for attackers to gain entrance. A slide was extended through the door when supplies had to be brought in. Munitions and other supplies were stored in the cellar (2) and ground floor (3). A single long gun (4) was mounted on a pivoted platform on the roof for defense against attacking ships.

tackers scrambling up to the wide walls stumbled into hidden moats and open killing grounds, ran afoul of camouflaged outworks and surprise ambush sites, and faced a steady, murderous gauntlet of carefully placed defensive cannon and musket crossfires. Fort Ticonderoga, N.Y., and Neuf Brisach in Alsace are examples of the Vauban star fort. Interestingly enough, Vauban also developed a painstaking siege process to counter his new fortresses. Vauban's siegecraft used three parallel rings of entrenchments and other field fortifications, emplaced gun batteries, and zigzagging approach trenches known as saps, plus tunneling and subterranean demolitions. Vauban's elite engineers spearheaded the assault, and became known as sappers for their trench-digging efforts. Although in theory Vauban's system permitted both attack and defense of the new fortifications, in practice, fortress garrisons again enjoyed a measure of superiority. Only the excessive costs of the new defensive systems restricted their wide adoptions.

Throughout the wars of the 18th century and the Napoleonic period that followed, complicated army maneuvers often pivoted on such seemingly impregnable fortress complexes as Metz, Berlin, Vienna, and Verdun. The duke of Wellington created a similar stronghold using field fortifications outside Lisbon in 1810; his Lines of Torres Vedras held firm under an aggressive French siege. Such tough positions were more often taken by guile or luck than Vauban-style sieges and assaults.

The 19th Century. The introduction of rifled weapons in the 19th century altered the situation that had prevailed since Vauban's time. The perfection of rifled artillery in the U.S. Civil War (1861–65) restored potency to the siege forces. The Union Army's rapid capture of Fort Pulaski, Ga., in 1862 signaled the end of fixed masonry fortifications. On the defenders' side, rifled shoulder arms allowed garrisons to deliver deadly volumes of accurate fire against attackers; such fire was just as effective from piled wood and stone breastworks as from expensive, vulnerable masonry fortresses. The squalid Petersburg trenches and the ramshackle rubble and earthen bastions of the Charleston, S.C., harbor defenses characterized the new trend in fortifications, which were usually built in conformity with local terrain rather than geometric formulas.

This pattern prevailed in the siege of Paris during the Franco-Prussian War (1870–71), the struggle for Plevna during the Russo–Turkish War of 1877–78, and in the battle for Port Arthur during the Russo-Japanese War (1904–05). With the help of relatively rudimentary preparations, any competent rifle-armed defender could bludgeon an attacker to a bloody standoff. Unfortunately for most soldiers in Europe, these lessons were largely lost upon conservative generals still steeped in the Napoleonic traditions of few fortresses and wide maneuvers.

Contemporary Fortifications. Trends first seen in the U.S. Civil War reached their fruition in World War I. Continuous, opposing lines of field fortifications spanned both western and, to a lesser extent, eastern Europe. Layers of trenches, rimmed with sharp barbed wire and guarded by chattering machine guns and quick-firing rifled artillery, gave the entire war the characteristics of a ghastly, endless siege. Massed infantry assaults into the "no man's land" between the trenches invariably miscarried with horrific losses. Poison gas, flame-throwers, air bombardment, and even experimental use of tanks failed to break the deadlock. Only the German adoption of infantry infiltration tactics in 1918 restored fluidity to the battlefield. Elite stormtroopers snaked through enemy weak spots, just as Vauban's sappers had exploited weakened walls centuries before. Once through the crust of trenches, the stormtroops ravaged the enemy's unprotected rear-area supplies and headquarters. While they did break the trench stalemate, the German infiltrators took terrible casualties after the more numerous British, French, and U.S. forces reestablished solid defenses. By the war's end, the absolutely dominant value of defensive works seemed to be the chief military lesson.

Fearful of a German resurgence, the wary French took this presumed lesson to heart. Despite the fearful financial burden, France constructed the MAGINOT LINE, a nearly 322-km (200-mi) steel and concrete trench system along their border with Germany. Although it bristled with gun turrets and extended many stories underground, it did not shield the section of France bordering Belgium; such an extension was judged to be too expensive. The French hoped that their mobile field armies could use the incomplete Maginot Line as a pivot, much as Napoleon had done with earlier fortresses. The Germans did not oblige, however. By 1940 the German military had wedded tanks and aircraft to their World War I infiltration tactics to create *blitzkrieg*—lightning war. In 1940, German mechanized units, striking through Belgium, speedily outflanked the French line, thereby turning the pivot point against its owners.

Throughout World War II, all combatants employed both fixed and field fortifications in both point and linear configurations, although advances in mobility ruled out a repetition of the continuous entrenched fronts of World War I. Significant fortification efforts included the British fixed defenses around Singapore, the U.S. fortress island of Corregidor, Russian antitank webs around Kursk, the German Atlantic Wall pillboxes and minefields in Normandy, and deep Japanese cave bunkers on Iwo Jima. Defenders might exact heavy tolls, but skilled attackers could seize these fortifications by concentrated use of artillery, airpower, and close cooperation among tanks, infantry, and engineers armed with flamethrowers and demolition charges. U.S. Marines gave these torturous siege tactics the caustically apt name "corkscrew and blowtorch."

Since World War II, all sorts of fortifications remain in use. Field fortifications predominated on conventional battlefields. Lines of traditional fieldworks, such as the U.S. Kansas Line in 1951 Korea, and temporary fortresses, such as the U.S. Khe Sanh Combat Base in 1967–68 Vietnam, continued to serve a purpose in limited conflicts worldwide. Fixed fortifications enjoy a small but potentially critical role in nuclear defenses. The United States, Soviet Union, People's Republic of China, and France all employ hardened concrete and steel missile silos and deeply buried command bunkers. Not surprisingly, nuclear "besiegers" have recently experimented with earth penetrators, larger explosive yields, and neutron radiation enhancement to cope with the latest defensive techniques. Thus far, the efficacy of nuclear fortifications and potential countermeasures remain untested by combat.　　　DANIEL P. BOLGER

Bibliography: Grant, B., *American Forts* (1965); Johnson, A., *Roman Forts* (1984); Pepper, S., and Adams, N., *Firearms and Fortifications* (1986); Roberts, R. B., ed., *Encyclopedia of Historic Forts* (1986); Toy, S., *A History of Fortification from 3000 B.C. to 1700 A.D.* (1955).

See also: CASTLE.

FORTRAN　[fohr'-tran]

FORTRAN, an acronym meaning FORmula TRANslation language, was one of the first COMPUTER LANGUAGES intended to be machine-independent. It was developed in the 1950s as a tool for simplifying scientific PROGRAMMING and allows the programmer to write in a form that resembles algebraic notation. Early versions of FORTRAN were somewhat primitive, but the language has been modified and extended to include many useful features of subsequent languages. FORTRAN was defined to reflect the structure of a conventional COMPUTER. As a result, FORTRAN programs require relatively little computer time. This is important in lengthy scientific computations, for example, weather forecasting or the analysis of stress in a pipe.　　　SUSAN OWICKI AND ELLIOTT ORGANICK

Fortuna　[fohr-toon'-uh]

Fortuna, the Roman goddess of luck, fortune, and chance, had the power to lift up lowly mortals and cast down the mighty. She was worshipped under a number of forms; in Rome, altars were raised to Good Fortune, Public Fortune,

and Private Fortune. Like her Greek counterpart Tyche, Fortuna's symbols in art were a ship's rudder and a cornucopia.

fortune-telling

A fortune-teller predicts the future by reading and interpreting the symbolic pictures on tarot cards. Pictures on the cards represent both the forces of nature and human vices and virtues. Introduced in Europe during the 14th century, tarot cards may be of ancient origin.

Fortune-telling is the predicting of a person's destiny. Innumerable kinds of fortune-telling, or DIVINATION, were known to the people of ancient civilizations who believed that the future was determined by the gods and revealed to humans through omens, portents, and signs.

Most methods of fortune-telling involve the interpretative observation of objects, and they take their respective names from the specific objects that are "read." These objects can be those that naturally exist without human intervention, such as the stars (ASTROLOGY), the lines of the palm (palmistry), the proportions of the head (PHRENOLOGY), and the leaves of plants (botomancy); or they can be man-made objects, such as TAROT or playing cards (cartomancy) and crystal balls (crystallomancy). Fortune-telling can also be performed by manipulating objects, either natural or man-made. Included in this category are bibliomancy, divination by the opening of books (particularly the Bible) at random; sortilege, performed by the casting of lots or throwing of dice; rhabdomancy, accomplished by observing the movement of a rod or stick held in the hands, as in water-divining; and lithomancy, the interpretation of the pattern made by pebbles tossed on the ground.

Many fortune-telling techniques have long histories in both Eastern and Western cultures. Astrology was practiced in ancient Egypt, Greece, India, China, and the Islamic world. The I CHING has been used by the Chinese for fortune-telling since the 2d millennium BC. Onomancy is the interpretation of the letters of one's name. It derives from the mystic belief found in the history of many world religions that the act of naming is the act of creation itself, and that a name contains all that an object or person is (see KABBALAH; GNOSTICISM.). Numerology, which may be considered a correlate of onomancy, assigns numbers to the letters of names; it also assigns numerological significance to every other aspect of a person's life. Like onomancy, it is found in many ancient cultures. Oneiromancy, the interpretation of dreams, predates the Greeks, who gave it its name.　　　BENJAMIN WALKER

Bibliography: Bunker, D., *Numerology, Astrology, and Dreams* (1987); Kennedy, C., *The Divination Handbook* (1990); Leek, Sybil, *The Sybil Leek Book of Fortune Telling* (1969); Loewe, Michael, and Blacker, Carmen, eds., *Oracles and Divination* (1981); Manas, J. H., *Divination Ancient and Modern* (1947); Shimano, Jimmei, *Oriental Fortune Telling* (1965); Wehmeyer, L. B., *Futuristics* (1986).

Fortune Theatre

The Fortune Theatre was built just outside Cripplegate, London, in 1600 and for many years served as the home of the ADMIRAL'S MEN. Its building contract survives and provides unique information about the structure of the Elizabethan playhouse. The square structure measured 26.6 m (80 ft) on each side, with three superimposed galleries surrounding an open yard measuring 17.6 by 18.3 m (53 by 55 ft). The stage measured 14.3 by 9 m (43 by 27.5 ft).   C. WALTER HODGES

Bibliography: Adams, Joseph Q., *Shakespearean Playhouses* (1917; repr. 1959).

Fortune 500

The fortnightly U.S. business magazine *Fortune* is particularly noted for its annual compilation of the "Fortune 500" list of the 500 largest publicly held industrial corporations in the United States in terms of sales. *Fortune* was founded in 1930 by Henry Robinson LUCE, the publisher of Time, Inc.

Fortune also ranks the 500 largest companies globally and the 500 largest U.S. service corporations (in terms of sales, revenues, or assets), including the 100 largest diversified service companies and commercial banks; and the 50 largest savings institutions; utilities; and life insurance, retail, transportation, and diversified financial companies. The U.S. lists include information on each company's assets, number of employees, profits, earnings per share of stock, and return on investment. The performance of the ten top-ranking and the five bottom-ranking companies is treated in detail.

forty-niners: see GOLD RUSH.

forum

The word *forum*, a Latin word meaning "open space" or "marketplace," refers generically to the open space in any Roman town or city where business, judicial, and municipal affairs and even, at times, religious activities were conducted. In many ways a forum was like the Greek AGORA, except that in a forum the space was more clearly defined, with buildings set closely together, often aligned on predetermined axes. In the later imperial forums in Rome open spaces were enclosed by parallel colonnades and dominated by temples often dedicated to Jupiter or Mars.

Ancient Rome's forum contains: Temple of Trajan (1); Trajan's Basilica Ulpia (2); Forum of Trajan (3); Forum of Augustus (4); Forum of Caesar (5); Curia (6); Temple of Juno Moneta (7); Temple of Jupiter (8); Temple of Concord (9); Forum Romanum (10); Basilica Julia (11); Forum of Nerva (12); Basilica Aemilia (13); Temple of Divus Julius (14); Arch of Augustus (15); Temple of Castor and Pollux (16); Temple of Minerva (17); Forum of Vespasian (18); Temple of Antoninus and Faustina (19); Regia (20); House of the Vestal Virgins (21); Temple of Sacrae Urbis (22); Temple of Romulus (23); Porticus Neronis (24); Basilica of Constantine (25); Temple of Venus and Rome (26); Vicus Jugularius (27); Via Sacra (28).

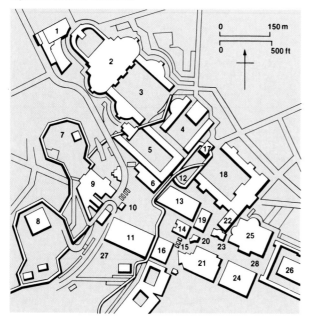

A typical forum was surrounded by market buildings, temples, and basilicas (spacious, roofed structures for conducting business or legal proceedings). Often, in planned towns that had begun as military camps, the forum lay at the meeting of the principal north-south street, the *cardo*, and the principal east-west street, the *decumanus*. The Roman architect Vitruvius (active 46–30 BC) suggested that a forum should be large enough to contain a crowd but not so large as to dwarf it, and that its proportions be 3:2 (length to width).

In ancient Rome, *Forum* was virtually a proper name for the ancient forum east of the Capitoline Hill and west of the Palatine Hill. Flanked by the Tabularium and the temples of Concord, Vespasian, and Saturn to the west, the House of the Vestal Virgins to the east, and the Curia and Basilica Aemilia to the north, the Forum contained the large Basilica Julia, the temple of Castor and Pollux, the temple of Divus Julius, the Arch of Augustus, the Arch of Septimius Severus, and the Rostrum, a speaker's platform decorated with the prows of captured enemy ships. The Forum was the administrative and corporate heart of Rome. Large, imposing forums were built in Rome by successive emperors, among them Augustus, Nerva, Vespasian, and Trajan, who built the largest. Trajan's Forum has the Vitruvian proportions, 3:2; designed by APOLLODORUS OF DAMASCUS, it measures 280 × 190 m (920 × 620 ft) and covers an area of 10 ha (25 acres).   LELAND M. ROTH

Bibliography: MacDonald, W. L., *The Architecture of the Roman Empire* (1982); Ward-Perkins, J. B., *Roman Architecture* (1988).

Foscolo, Ugo   [fohs'-koh-loh, oo'-goh]

Ugo Foscolo, b. Feb. 6, 1778, d. Sept. 10, 1827, an Italian novelist and poet, was the author of *Le ultime lettere di Jacopo Ortis* (The Last Letters of Jacob Ortis, 1802), often called the first modern Italian novel. In epistolary form, the story is of unrequited love and futile patriotism, which eventually cause the protagonist's suicide. Foscolo's lyrics, among them *Dei sepolcri* (From the Tombs, 1807), a poem inspired by humanism and patriotism, influenced later Italian writers.

Bibliography: Cambon, G., *Ugo Foscolo* (1980).

Fosdick, Harry Emerson   [fahz'-dik]

Harry Emerson Fosdick, b. Buffalo, N.Y., May 24, 1878, d. Oct. 5, 1969, was a controversial American clergyman. He became a Baptist minister (1903) after studying at Colgate University and Union Theological Seminary. A reputation for pulpit eloquence led New York's First Presbyterian Church to offer him the post of associate minister. Fosdick's controversial 1922 sermon "Shall the Fundamentalists Win?" challenged religious conservatives with his position that social reform is the best expression of Christian principles.

In 1926, Fosdick transferred his ministry back to a Baptist congregation, which became New York's Riverside Church in 1930. He made that church an outstanding example of liberal ideals and social service. The church's programs were deliberately interdenominational and interracial. Fosdick retired in 1946. He wrote many books, including *The Living of These Days: An Autobiography* (1956).   HENRY WARNER BOWDEN

Bibliography: Miller, R. M., *Harry Emerson Fosdick* (1985).

Foss, Lukas   [faws]

Lukas Foss, b. Aug. 15, 1922, is a Berlin-born American composer, conductor, and pianist who received his early training in Berlin and Paris. In 1937 he went to the United States and studied at the Curtis Institute in Philadelphia; he also attended Serge Koussevitzky's conducting classes at the Berkshire Music Center, where he later taught. He was conductor of the Buffalo Philharmonic Orchestra (1963–70), the Brooklyn Philharmonic (1971–90), and the Milwaukee Symphony (1981–86), serving the latter two thereafter as conductor laureate. His works include ballets, cantatas, chamber music, concertos, operas, and orchestral pieces.   CAROLYN BAILLEY

Bibliography: Salzman, E., *Twentieth-Century Music*, 3d ed. (1988).

fossa [fahs'-uh]

The physical characteristics of the fossa, Cryptoprocta ferox, are a mixture of those found in the cat, civet, and mongoose.

The fossa, *Cryptoprocta ferox*, the largest carnivore of Madagascar, is a member of the civet family, Viverridae. It grows to a length of about 140 cm (55 in) including a tail of approximately 66 cm (26 in). Its coat is dense, soft, and reddish brown. When annoyed, the fossa discharges an odorous scent from its anal glands. The fossa is nocturnal and preys on lemurs and small domestic animals.   EVERETT SENTMAN

Fosse, Bob

American director and choreographer Robert Louis Fosse, b. Chicago, June 23, 1927, d. Sept. 23, 1987, performed in vaudeville and as a professional dancer before making his Broadway debut in 1950. He choreographed or staged such shows and films as *Pajama Game* (1954; film, 1957), *Damn Yankees* (1955; film, 1958), and his own *Sweet Charity* (1966; film, 1969, which he directed); performed in such films as *Kiss Me, Kate* (1953); and twice took the title role in revivals of *Pal Joey* in the 1960s. Fosse first directed *Redhead* (1959) and thereafter directed and choreographed *Pippin* (1972), his own *Chicago* (1975), and *Dancin'* (1978), among others, also directing the films *Cabaret* (1972), *Lenny* (1975), and the semiautobiographical *All That Jazz* (1979). Noted for his angular, jazzy choreography, he was the recipient of many awards.

Bibliography: Grubb, K. B., *Razzle Dazzle* (1989).

Fossey, Dian

Dian Fossey, b. San Francisco, Jan. 16, 1932, d. 1985, was a zoologist known for her field studies of the rare mountain gorilla in east central Africa. From 1963 until her death, she carefully observed the gorillas in their native habitat with little outside assistance. Fossey's book *Gorillas in the Mist* (1983) chronicles her observations of three generations of mountain gorillas and urges the preservation of this endangered species. Fossey was found murdered on Dec. 27, 1985 at the Karisoke Research Center in Rwanda, which she established in 1967.

Bibliography: Hayes, H. T. P., *The Dark Romance of Dian Fossey* (1990).

fossil fuels: see COAL AND COAL MINING; ENERGY SOURCES; NATURAL GAS; PETROLEUM.

fossil record

Fossils are remains of prehistoric organisms. Preserved by burial under countless layers of sedimentary material, they are a record of the history of life beginning approximately 3.5 billion years ago, the study of which is called PALEONTOLOGY.

Some fossils are abundant in the strata of the Earth's crust. The chalk cliffs of Dover, England, and the Niobrara Chalk of Kansas are composed of complex platelets of algae, so small that millions fill a cubic millimeter. Shells of invertebrate marine animals, such as brachiopods, bryozoans, clams, snails, corals, and echinoderms, are preserved in many beds of lime-

stone, and the bones and teeth of vertebrates are sometimes so numerous that they form deposits called "bone beds." In other SEDIMENTARY ROCKS, such as the majority of the world's RED BEDS, shells and bones are rarely found, although tracks and burrows may be abundant. Fossils are uncommon in sedimentary rocks of PRECAMBRIAN TIME, although some rocks of the latter part of that era have yielded a moderately diverse assemblage known as the EDIACARAN FAUNA.

KINDS OF FOSSILS

Entire or partial bodies of organisms are called body fossils. In contrast, marks left in rock by the activities of organisms are called trace fossils. These include artifacts, burrows, feces, tracks, and trails. Microfossils are studied in the field of MICROPALEONTOLOGY. A related study of microscopic spores, pollen grains, and cysts extracted from sediment by hydrofluoric-acid treatment is called palynology (see PALEOBOTANY). Chemical paleontologists study the record of organic macromolecules, the presence of which in rocks may reveal the existence of certain groups of organisms in the distant past.

HOW AND WHERE FOSSILS FORM

The Earth is teeming with life, all of it searching for food. As a result, very little digestible organic matter escapes destruction, and indigestible skeletal material, such as shells, bones, and teeth, has a much better chance of burial and preservation. Shell material is typically composed of calcium carbonate, as are mollusk shells; teeth and bones are composed of calcium phosphate; sponge spicules, diatom frustules, and radiolarian skeletons are composed of opaline silica. The highly indigestible organic jackets of spores and pollen grains also commonly escape destruction. Such materials form most of the body fossils common in layered rocks.

Much rarer are accumulations of sediment in settings from which scavengers are excluded and in which the bodies of plants and animals, carried in from outside, may retain their general form. These are of greatest value to the paleontologist because they give the most comprehensive view of past life. Certain rock formations are well known for this reason. One is the Precambrian Gunflint Chert on the north shore of Lake Superior. It contains well-preserved bacteria and blue-green algae approximately 2 billion years old. Another, the Burgess Shale of British Columbia, contains carbonaceous films of soft-bodied marine worms and crustaceans of the Cambrian Period. At the Carboniferous Mazon Creek locality in Illinois, both land plants and marine invertebrates are preserved. The Holzmaden oil shale (see SHALE, OIL) of southern Germany, of Early Jurassic age, is well known for its many fish and CRINOIDS, as well as for the ichthyosaurs and other marine reptiles that have been found there. Even better known is the

When this fish died, its body settled to the ocean bottom and became covered by calcareous sediments. The organic material of the fish decayed; because the bones contain large amounts of calcium phosphate, which resists decay, the skeleton was well preserved.

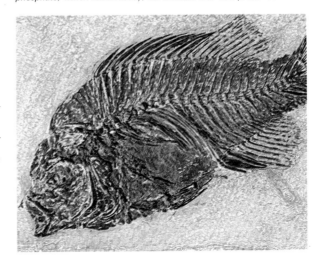

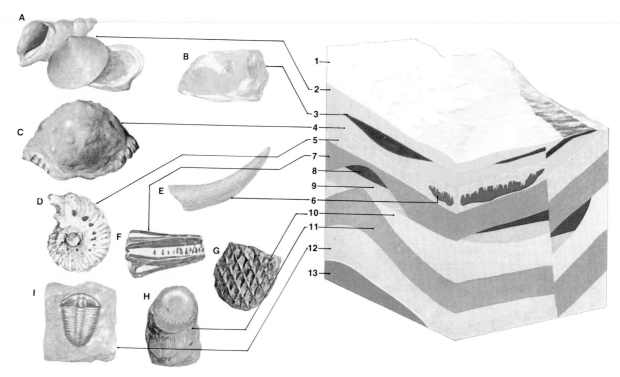

A theoretical section through the Earth's surface shows strata containing fossils. A glacier (1) may contain bodies of mammoths and other recently extinct animals. Quaternary limestone (2) contains shells of mollusks (A), such as Glycimeris *(center). Entire insect bodies (B) are preserved in amber, which occurs with lignite (3). Tertiary sandstone (4) contains shells of the crab* Xanthopsis *(C). Such ammonites as* Euhoplites *(D) occur in Cretaceous limestone (5). Deer antlers (E) may be found in caves (6). Jurassic rocks (7) contain such remains as a jaw of* Ichthyosaurus *(F), a marine reptile. A bark impression of the treelike club moss* Lepidodendron *(G) may be found in Upper Carboniferous limestone (10). Fossils of such corals as* Aulophyllum *(H) occur in Lower Carboniferous rock (11). Cambrian rocks (12) contain fossils of such trilobites as* Conocoryphe *(I). Oil (8) and water (9) deposits and volcanic rock (13) are also shown.*

Late Jurassic Solnhofen limestone of southern Germany, where the quarries, worked for lithographic stone, have yielded not only large numbers of well-preserved jellyfish and horseshoe crabs, but also flying reptiles (pterodactyls) and the world's earliest known bird, ARCHAEOPTERYX.

Some of the most spectacular fossils of the Cretaceous Period, including fish, marine reptiles, pterodactyls, and birds, have come from the Smoky Hill Chalk, near Hays, Kans. A remarkable Eocene lake fauna has been uncovered in the Green River Formation, near the town of Fossil, Wyo. Along the shore of the Baltic Sea, insects, spiders, and the like are found preserved in AMBER, fossilized resin exuded from trees.

The most information on Pleistocene faunas, from vultures to bisons, wolves to saber-toothed cats to beetles, has come from tar seeps, such as the LA BREA TAR PIT in Los Angeles, Calif., where prehistoric animals got mired and embalmed in the tar, as they do in modern tar pits. Most extraordinary are the few finds, in Alaska and Siberia, of prehistoric but presumably post-Pleistocene MAMMOTHS, frozen into the arctic PERMAFROST and preserved by natural refrigeration.

Important as these unusual localities are, most of the fossil record is composed of skeletons that can be recovered from ordinary sediment, in a cliff or quarry or roadcut, or from wells drilled deep into the ground. These skeletons and skeletal fragments may be preserved as the original material, as hollows (molds) formed by dissolving the original matter to leave only an imprint, or as replacement material, with a mineral such as quartz or pyrite having replaced the original bone or shell.

FOSSILS AND EARTH HISTORY

Toward the end of the 17th century, the naturalist Robert HOOKE turned his attention to spectacular marine fossils found in his native England. Determining that these must be the remains of once-living animals, he noted that they did not resemble any living species then known, causing him to believe that life might have changed at some time in the past

and that fossils might be a chronological guide to geologic history. Hooke also noted that these fossils looked more like tropical shells than species then living on British shores and wondered whether Britain's geographic latitude had also changed since the time these animals lived. The first suggestion was verified a century later, and the second three centuries later with the discovery of CONTINENTAL DRIFT.

The Earth's sedimentary strata are initially layers of muds and sands, each covering an older stratum and being covered, in turn, by a younger one (see STRATIGRAPHY). They form, in this manner, a historical sequence, and the fossils that they contain can be arranged in time, by what has come to be known as the law of superposition. Early in the 1800s, William SMITH, in England, noted that fossils were distinctive of individual beds or groups of beds in such sequences of strata, and that distinctive assemblages of fossils could be traced cross-country. Geologists soon discovered that the sequences of fossils in England could be matched with similar sequences elsewhere in the world.

Any given area contains a stratigraphic record of only some part of Earth history. By combining information from many different areas, geologists can determine global Earth history. Nearly two centuries of such efforts, including the description of fossils in monographs and journals, have resulted in ever more detailed classification of the more fossiliferous part of Earth history—the last 600 million years.

The smallest units of this classification, generally characterized by certain species or combinations of species, are called zones. These may be recognizable only locally, but many have been traced worldwide. Combinations of zones are the chief criteria for the recognition of worldwide units of geologic time, called stages, generally having a duration of approximately 10 million years. These in turn include the larger time periods, called systems and eras.

In terms of time, the fossil record yields a relative chronology rather than an absolute one (see GEOLOGIC TIME), but the development of RADIOMETRIC AGE-DATING methods has enabled scientists to calibrate Earth history in actual years.

THE PROGRESSION OF PREHISTORIC LIFE

The first chemical traces of life processes found thus far occur in sediments 3.77 billion years old. The earliest megafossils, some 1 to 3.5 billion years old, are STROMATOLITES, calcareous masses formed in shallow water by blue-green algae. Microfossils from CHERTS this old include a variety of blue-green algal and bacterial forms. Approximately 1 billion years ago, a wider variety of microscopic cells had appeared, including some that may have had nuclei. In deposits approximately 600 million years old, imprints of soft-bodied invertebrates are found. In sediments 570 million years old (the beginning of the CAMBRIAN PERIOD), the first skeletal invertebrates appeared—mollusks, brachiopods, and trilobites. The appearance of these invertebrates, in rocks deposited at the beginning of the PALEOZOIC ERA, coincided with the first widespread signs of burrowing. In rocks of the ORDOVICIAN PERIOD (500–425 million years ago), researchers have found fossil animal burrows that are evidence of the earliest known land animals. These trace fossils indicate that terrestrial ecosystems may have evolved sooner than was once thought. Most of the modern classes of invertebrates, as well as the OSTRACODERMS (the fishlike organisms), were represented by this time, and marine faunas had become much more diverse. In the SILURIAN PERIOD (425–400 million years ago) landmasses were colonized by rapidly evolving higher plants, whose supporting structures and water-conducting vessels now made life on dry land possible. In the DEVONIAN PERIOD (400–345 million years ago) the main groups of FISH—COELACANTHS, LUNG-FISH, SHARKS, bony fish, and the extinct ARTHRODIRES—were differentiated. Forests and the first primitive INSECTS appeared on land, as did AMPHIBIANS. The CARBONIFEROUS PERIOD (345–280 million years ago), known for its great coal deposits, witnessed the development

of REPTILES, the first animals having an amniote egg, which enables the embryo to develop on dry land.

The MESOZOIC ERA (225–65 million years ago), which includes the TRIASSIC, Jurassic, and Cretaceous periods, is known particularly for the evolution of gigantic reptiles, both in the sea (ICHTHYOSAURS, PLESIOSAURS, and MOSASAURS) and on land (DINOSAURS). Flying reptiles (PTERODACTYLS) and BIRDS, as well as MAMMALS, appeared during the JURASSIC PERIOD (190–135 million years ago). On land, forests of CONIFERS and CYCADS had largely replaced the lycopod- and seed-fern-dominated forests of the Paleozoic Era. In the sea tiny calcite-armored, photosynthetic unicells called coccolithophorids appeared, and massive calcium carbonate (chalk) deposition began in the deeper oceans (see OOZE, DEEP-SEA). The CRETACEOUS PERIOD (135–65 million years ago) is the time of origin of two great groups of plants—the flowering plants (ANGIOSPERMS) on land and the water plants (DIATOMS) in water. Flowering plants changed the face of the Earth in many ways and triggered a great wave of evolution among the insects. At the end of Cretaceous time, the extinction of dinosaurs resulted in the spectacular evolution of terrestrial mammals, and giant sharks and marine mammals replaced large reptiles in the sea.

The group of mammals known as the PRIMATES—now represented by lemurs, monkeys, apes, and humans—dates back to the beginning of the CENOZOIC ERA (65 million years ago to the present), but humanlike creatures (see PREHISTORIC HUMANS) are known only from the last few million years, the Pliocene and PLEISTOCENE epochs. *Homo sapiens*, modern humans, appeared in the Old World during the Pleistocene but did not reach the Americas until its latter part.

Fossils record the progressive evolutionary diversification of living things, the progressive colonization of habitats, and the development of increasingly complex organic communities. The development of new species and such larger groups of

Rarely, an entire organism may be preserved, as are some insects in amber (A). Only hard parts may be preserved, as with mammal bones in asphalt (B). In the case of a carbonized leaf (C), a carbon residue remains after the organic material decays. Silica may replace the organic material of wood (D) molecule by molecule. Molds (E) and casts (F) may remain after the original material of the organism has dissolved. Dinosaur footprints (G) are an example of trace fossils.

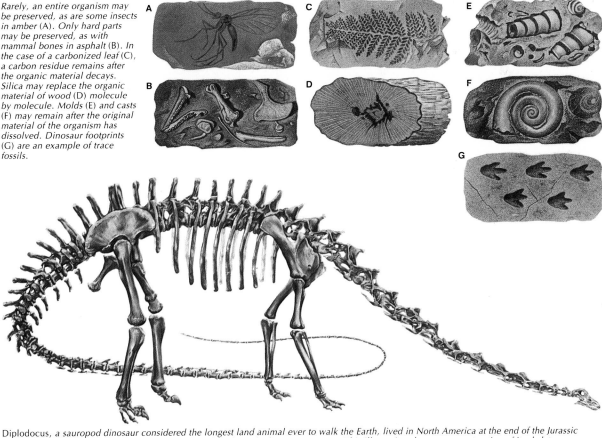

Diplodocus, a sauropod dinosaur considered the longest land animal ever to walk the Earth, lived in North America at the end of the Jurassic Period. It measured more than 25 m (82 ft) in length and weighed 20 tons or more. This illustration shows a reconstruction of its skeleton, which became fossilized as the minerals in groundwater slowly permeated the bones, making them as durable as stone.

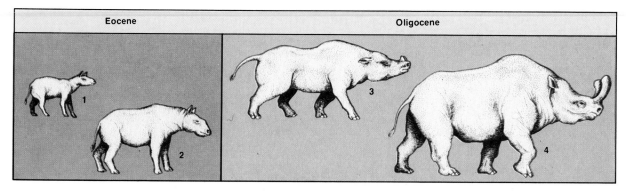

| Eocene | Oligocene |

Titanotheres, browsing mammals related to horses, lived from the Lower Eocene to the Middle Oligocene. Their evolutionary history in North America can be traced from the hornless Eotitanops (1), about 50 cm (20 in) tall, through Manteoceras (2), about 1.2 m (4 ft) tall, with small knobs on the head; the horned Brontotherium leidyi (3); and the elephant-sized B. platyceras (4), which bore much larger horns.

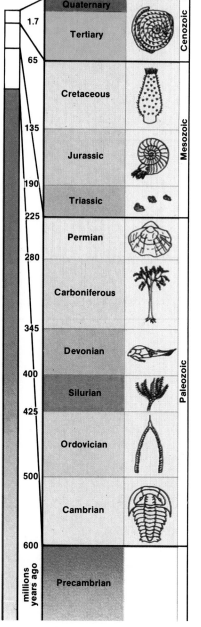

1.7	Quaternary
	Tertiary (Cenozoic)
65	
	Cretaceous (Mesozoic)
135	
	Jurassic
190	
	Triassic
225	
	Permian
280	
	Carboniferous
345	
	Devonian (Paleozoic)
400	
	Silurian
425	
	Ordovician
500	
	Cambrian
600	
millions years ago	Precambrian

Fossils that characterize particular geologic strata are known as index fossils; ideally, they are abundant and have a wide geographic distribution within a limited geologic time. Although evidence of bacterialike life exists in rocks up to 3.5 billion years old, multicellular organisms do not become numerous in the fossil record until the Paleozoic Era. Index fossils of the Paleozoic include trilobites in the Cambrian Period, graptolites in the Ordovician, crinoids in the Silurian, fishes in the Devonian, land plants in the Carboniferous, and certain brachiopods in the Permian. Mesozoic Era strata contain reptile footprints in the Triassic Period, ammonites in the Jurassic, and sea urchins and sand dollars in the Cretaceous. Shells of foraminifera are common in Cenozoic marine deposits. Dating rocks by means of index fossils can be difficult: species do not always span the same time ranges in different locations, and the appearance of index fossils may change from place to place. Greatly refined tools and techniques have expanded the list of index fossils.

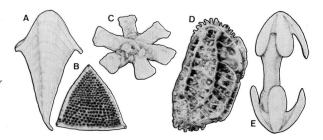

Pelagic microfossils, remains of open-sea microorganisms, are found in ocean-floor deposits. Pteropods (A), small snails with calcite shells, often occur in Atlantic and Mediterranean sediments. Diatoms (B), single-celled algae with siliceous shells, are abundant in cool seas. Coccolithophorids (C) are photosynthetic plankton, covered by calcite plates, which accumulate in deep-sea sediments. Ostracods (D) are minute, bivalved crustaceans with calcite shells. Siliceous spicules (E) remain from skeletons of certain glass sponges.

species as genera and families has gone on throughout time, but so also has the loss of species by EXTINCTION. The rate of extinction at some times in Earth history greatly exceeded the rate of speciation, and the faunas and floras of the world became reduced. Notable biotic crises occurred in Cambrian time, near the end of the Devonian time, at the close (PERMIAN PERIOD) of the Paleozoic Era, and at the end of the Cretaceous Period. Various theories have been advanced to explain the cause of these extinctions.

FOSSILS AND EVOLUTION

The fossil record corresponds to the general theory of organic evolution, and any group of plants or animals can be seen to change through the record of strata. The smallest general unit of classification is the species, recognized in the fossil record by great similarity of form. Most species are seen to have an existence that is short in terms of Earth history—usually one to several million years, more rarely tens of million years, and very rarely hundreds of million years. Most genera (groups of related species) can be traced through time spans of tens of millions of years; larger units of this classification system, or taxonomy, tend to persist through longer time spans. The majority of the classes and phyla of invertebrate animals, for example, have records beginning in the Early Paleozoic Era.

All of the larger groups of animals are seen to have evolved a wide range of life forms. Reptiles, for example, having evolved in late Paleozoic time out of small or medium-sized predatory amphibians, developed into a great diversity of animals that included herbivores and carnivores, dwarves and giants, creepers, runners, climbers, burrowers, swimmers, and flyers, all in competition with other groups of animals living in the same ways. They have continued to occupy some of these functions (niches, in ECOLOGY) throughout their history and have vacated others. Reptiles are still among the more effective small creeping and running predators on land (lizards, the tuatara), replaced by birds as aerial dwellers and by mammals as large terrestrial herbivores and predators. A succession of animals have been marine "superpredators." In the Triassic and early Jurassic periods, this was the domain of ichthyosaurs; in late Jurassic and early Cretaceous time, these were replaced by plesiosaurs; in the Cretaceous, by mosasaurs; in the Eocene, by the zeuglodont whales (mammals); and since the Miocene, by the great carcharodont sharks. The fossil record suggests that evolution has resulted mainly from the tendency of all species to experiment with new ways of living, to thereby exploit new opportunities as they arose in an ever-changing world, gaining a new foothold in one place and losing one in another.

With Charles DARWIN's theory of evolution in the mid-1800s came the expectation that the fossil record would provide unbroken evolutionary sequences, in which species after species would be seen to emerge gradually from their ancestors and pass, equally gradually, into their descendants. Most species, however, are seen to appear abruptly, to maintain their typical form for most of their history, and to vanish as suddenly as they appeared. This failure to trace coherent lineages of ancestors and descendants does not prevent recognition of changes in larger groups of animals: horses are seen to have developed through Cenozoic time from small to large, from five-toed to one-toed, and from short- to long-toothed, but complete records of the transition from one species to another have not been found. This caused some paleontologists to doubt Darwin's belief that evolution proceeds by the gradual accumulation of small changes. It has now been determined that evolution does not proceed steadily, in response to some mysterious internal force, but in response to new opportunities. In a stable, unchanging environment, a well-adapted species is not likely to change, whereas in a changing one it may find better opportunities by changing its way of life. In addition, evolution does not normally occur throughout a species but in interbreeding populations, occupying some small part of the geographic range of the species as a whole. It is such populations and adjacent populations, linked by exchange of genes, that deviate from the ancestors and from the species as a whole, to form races or subspecies, and, eventually, species. At any one time, a species is a combination of such groups, diverging episodically from one another. As geography and habitat change, these groups shift about, either blending when they meet, abruptly displacing one another, or coexisting side by side in different ways of life.

One of the most difficult problems in evolutionary paleontology has been the almost abrupt appearance of the major animal groups—classes and phyla—in full-fledged form, in the Cambrian and Ordovician periods. This must reflect a sudden acquisition of skeletons by the various groups, in itself a problem. Paleontologists are not certain whether the soft-bodied forms of the Precambrian Ediacaran fauna are in fact ancestral to modern groups. In any case, the lack of well-documented animal remains in older rocks indicates that differentiation of the major groups occurred more rapidly than did their subsequent evolution.

FOSSILS AND ANCIENT LANDSCAPES

The fossil record contains a history of the evolution of life on Earth and provides geologists with a chronology far more detailed and widely applicable than that of GEOCHEMISTRY. It also contains much information about the geographical-ecological changes that have occurred in the course of geologic time. This interpretation of the fossil record predates the other, in that some of the early Greek philosophers and Renaissance naturalists recognized certain strata as marine and as evidence of former higher sea levels, on the basis of the enclosed fossils, long before the evolutionary nature of fossils was known.

The best example of this is the recognition of ancient seas and landmasses. The deposit of LOESS containing grass seeds and land-snail shells can be quite easily recognized as the windblown accumulation of dust in an ancient grassland or prairie. The accumulation of PEAT or coal, containing abundant woody material along with spores or pollen, and possibly skeletons of land animals, is evidence of an ancient peat bog or swamp. A bed of limestone containing a wide variety of clams and snails belonging to marine families, as well as

the remains of sea urchins or other ECHINODERMS (a phylum that seems always to have been restricted to the sea), is evidently of marine derivation.

The fossil record can be used to reconstruct ancient environments. For example, strata of TERTIARY age in the oil-bearing "transverse basins" of California, such as the Los Angeles and Ventura basins, contain many microfossils of the protozoan group called FORAMINIFERA. These were studied because they provided a means of tracing strata from one oil well to another, in accumulations of sediment thousands of meters thick. This sedimentary sequence began with stream deposits in the Oligocene epoch, passed through a long marine phase in the Miocene and Pliocene, and reverted to mammal-bearing alluvial deposits in the PLEISTOCENE EPOCH (see also QUATERNARY PERIOD). In order to learn something about the conditions under which the oil-bearing marine portion was deposited, paleontologists compared the fossil assemblages with the depth range of the same species or the most closely related species living today off the California coast. Interpreted in this manner, environmental change from continental, through shallow near-shore, into deep-water (more than 1,500 m/5,000 ft), back through the shallow water, and into alluvial was revealed. This history has been confirmed by the study of fossil fish scales. Although sardine scales are found throughout the marine parts, angler fish and other species of the BATHYAL ZONE are found only in association with deep-water foraminifera.

This is one example of the field of study that is called PALEOECOLOGY. Palynologists studying pollen grain assemblages from lake beds and peat bogs have determined the shifting of forests and grasslands that occurred in the later stages of the Pleistocene ICE AGE and in the interval since then and are establishing a much-needed history of climates, which can be related directly to the historical record (see POLLEN STRATIGRAPHY). Study of the foraminifera in marine cores enables scientists to chart the distribution of OCEAN CURRENTS and water masses during the height of the last glaciation, 18,000 years ago, in an effort to understand the Ice Age and its cause.

Fossil chemistry is another area of research for paleoecologists. Many elements occur in two or more atomic forms that differ from each other in weight—isotopes. Thus, oxygen occurs as O^{16} and O^{18}, O^{16} being by far the most abundant. When an organism such as a foraminifera builds a skeleton of calcium carbonate ($CaCO_3$), it incorporates O^{16} and O^{18} in a proportion that depends on the ratio in which they occur in the ambient water, and on the temperature of the water. The higher the temperature, the less O^{18} is put into the skeleton. If the ratio of the isotopes has remained constant in the oceans, then the ratios of such isotopes in a foraminiferal shell are a

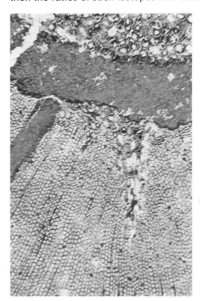

This microphotograph of fossil wood (artificially stained) shows the preservation of structural detail. The original wood material was replaced molecule by molecule, in this case by the mineral francolite. This fossil was found in Lower Cretaceous rocks of the eastern Netherlands.

direct indication of temperature. The isotopic composition of the seas, however, has not remained constant, and the ratios in the shells can be disturbed by chemical changes after burial, but paleoecologists have demonstrated, for example, that the thermal structure of the oceans in Cretaceous times was much different from what it is today, with much warmer midwater masses.

FOSSILS AND PALEOGEOGRAPHY

The distribution of plant and animal species in the world today reflects the interplay between the physical environment, which, for example, restricts polar bears to the high latitudes, and geographical barriers to migration, which, for example, have kept polar bears from invading the Antarctic and keep the marine snakes of the Pacific side of Panama from invading the Caribbean Sea. Such barriers divide the world into biogeographic provinces. The fossil record enables paleontologists to reconstruct such provinces for the past and to study their history. South America, for example, was joined to Africa during most of the Mesozoic Era, as its Triassic and Jurassic reptile faunas demonstrate. When it broke away, in mid-Cretaceous time, with the opening of the South Atlantic Ocean, the dinosaurs of South America succumbed to the Cretaceous crisis and the mammals took their place as the dominant land animals, forming a very different kind of mammalian fauna that evolved independently of the Eurasian-American fauna. Australia underwent similar changes except that it remained isolated, and its indigenous mammalian fauna (a marsupial one) has evolved to its modern state. South America became linked with North America during the Pliocene Epoch, and the two very different mammalian faunas invaded each other's territories, pitting species against species for existence. Eventually, North America assimilated some South American mammals (ground sloths, armadillos, opossums, and porcupines), but the majority of South American species became extinct.

The fossil record also shows that the Caribbean and eastern Pacific marine faunas were essentially identical in Miocene times, diverging only since the Panamanian land bridge closed in Pliocene time. The question of whether to build a Panamanian sea-level canal has focused attention on what would happen to present faunas if communications were to be reestablished. Would the Pacific sea snakes, for example, invade the Caribbean to the detriment of fisheries there?

OVERVIEW

The fossil record spans three-quarters of Earth history but forms a coherent whole only since the time that animals with skeletons appeared at the beginning of the Cambrian period. Both the origin of life and the origin of the major groups of animals remain unknown. The seafloor became heavily populated with animals in Cambrian time, and the lands were colonized in the Silurian Period. Organic communities have become more complex through geologic time, but not in a linear fashion. Extinction of species is normally counterbalanced by speciation, but at times it has prevailed, and during the great biotic crises some communities were reduced to low levels throughout the world, and major groups of organisms, such as the dinosaurs and AMMONITES, were lost. That part of the record is a reminder that organisms exist at the tolerance of the environment, and that this environment, throughout geologic time, has exhibited variations of a nature and magnitude outside the realm of human experience.

ALFRED G. FISCHER

Bibliography: Bromley, Richard, *Trace Fossils: Biology and Taxonomy* (1990); Cloud, Preston, *Oasis in Space: Earth History from the Beginning* (1989); Colbert, Edwin H., *Evolution of the Vertebrates,* 3d ed. (1980), and *The Great Dinosaur Hunters and Their Discoveries* (1984); Eldredge, Niles, *Life Pulse: Episodes from the Story of the Fossil Record* (1987); Lewin, Roger, *Bones of Contention: Controversies in the Search for Human Origins* (1987); Paul, Chris, *The Natural History of Fossils* (1980); Raup, David M., and Stanley, Steven M., *Principles of Paleontology,* 2d ed. (1978); Simpson, George G., *Fossils and the History of Life* (1983) and *Discoverers of the Lost World* (1984); Taylor, Thomas N., *Paleobotany* (1981); Tschudy, R. H., and Scott, R., eds., *Aspects of Palynology* (1969; repr. 1990); Valentine, J. W., *Evolutionary Paleoecology of the Marine Biosphere* (1973).2

See also: EARTH, GEOLOGICAL HISTORY OF.

Foster, Abigail

Abigail Kelley Foster, b. near Amherst, Mass., Jan. 15, 1810, d. Jan. 14, 1887, was an American crusader for the abolition of slavery and for women's suffrage. A teacher in Quaker schools, she married (1845) a radical abolitionist, Stephen S. Foster (1809–81). Foster was one of the first women to deliver speeches before sexually mixed audiences.

Foster, Stephen

Stephen Collins Foster, b. Lawrenceville, Pa., July 4, 1826, d. Jan. 13, 1864, was an American composer of songs whose words and music have become associated with the American South. Among his best-known songs are "Camptown Races" (1850), "Old Folks at Home" ("Swanee River") (1851), "My Old Kentucky Home" (1853), "Jeanie with the Light Brown Hair" (1854), and "Old Black Joe" (1860).

Foster never lived in the South and was reluctant to have his name associated with songs of his that were written in a stage Negro dialect. (These were sometimes referred to by his contemporaries as Ethiopian melodies.) Such music was popularized by minstrel shows, especially that of Edwin P. CHRISTY, for whom Foster wrote many songs. The greater number of Foster's more than 200 songs, however, were written for family singing at home.

Although his music was immensely popular, Foster never gained great financial reward from its sale because he usually accepted a flat sum from his publisher for each song. For example, Foster compiled an anthology of instrumental music, including many of his own works, called *The Social Orchestra* (1854), which sold at $1 a copy with considerable success. Foster received the fee of $150 for his efforts.

Toward the end of his life, Foster drank heavily and lived in virtual poverty. He died in New York City.

Bibliography: Austin, W. W., "Susannah," "Jeanie," and the "Old Folks at Home," 2d ed. (1989); Foster, Stephen, *The Stephen Foster Songbook* (1974); Howard, J. T., *Stephen Foster,* rev. ed. (1962); Morneweck, E. F., *The Chronicles of Stephen Foster's Family,* 2 vols. (1944; repr. 1973); Saunders, S., and Root, D. L., *The Music of Stephen C. Foster,* 2 vols. (1990).

Foster, William Z.

William Zebulon Foster, b. Taunton, Mass., Feb. 25, 1881, d. Sept. 1, 1961, was a leader of the U.S. Communist party. From an Irish working-class background, Foster achieved prominence as a union organizer for the AFL during World War I. He joined the Communist party in 1921 and was its candidate for the presidency in 1924, 1928, and 1932. Eclipsed by Earl BROWDER for the next decade, he reemerged as party chairman from 1945 to 1957. In 1948, Foster was indicted under the Smith Act with 11 other top American Communists but escaped trial because of poor health. He died in the USSR, where he was given a state funeral.

foster care: see ADOPTION AND FOSTER CARE.

Fothergill, John   [fah'-thur-gil]

John Fothergill, b. Mar. 8, 1712, d. Dec. 26, 1780, an English physician, was the first to describe symptoms and treatment of diphtheria; he also first described true facial neuralgia (tic douloureux) and coronary arteriosclerosis. As a friend of Benjamin Franklin, he helped found the Pennsylvania Hospital and University of Pennsylvania Medical School.

Bibliography: Fox, Richard, *Dr. John Fothergill and His Friends* (1919).

Foucauld, Charles de   [foo-koh']

Charles Eugène de Foucauld, b. Sept. 15, 1858, d. Dec. 1, 1916, was a French missionary and ascetic. After serving in the French army, he became a Trappist monk in 1890. Ordained a Roman Catholic priest in 1901, he was sent to the missions of the Sahara. He finally settled (1905) in Algeria, where he lived a life of prayer and penance among the Muslim Tuaregs. He was killed by the Tuaregs during their revolt against France.

Foucauld's writings inspired the establishment of communities of hermits around the world. The groups are known as the Little Brothers of Jesus and the Little Sisters of Jesus. Foucauld's autobiography was translated (1964) as the *Spiritual Autobiography of Charles de Foucauld.*   JOAN A. RANGE

Bibliography: Lepetit, Charles, *Two Dancers in the Desert*, trans. by John Griffiths (1984); Lorit, Sergius C., *Charles De Foucauld: The Silent Witness*, 3d ed. (1983).

Foucault, Jean   [foo-koh']

Jean Bernard Léon Foucault, b. Sept. 19, 1819, d. Feb. 11, 1868, a French physicist, took the first photograph of the Sun in 1845, measured the velocity of light in the laboratory using a rapidly rotating mirror, and showed that the brain combines separate color images from the two eyes into a single image. His name is also associated with important developments in telescope mirrors, lenses, prisms, and arc lamps, but most of all with the gyroscope and the FOUCAULT PENDULUM, with which he demonstated, rather than deduced, the rotation of the Earth for the first time.   CARL ZAPFFE

Foucault, Michel

The French cultural historian Michel Foucault, b. Oct. 15, 1926, d. June 25, 1984, was a professor at the Collège de France from 1970; earlier, he had taught in Sweden and West Germany. Foucault examined the codes and theories of order by which societies operate and the "principles of exclusion" through which they define themselves: for example, the sane and the insane, the innocent and the criminal, the insider and the outsider. His thoughts on history and the self have interested contemporary philosophers and literary critics. His works include *Madness and Civilization* (1961; Eng. trans., 1965), *The Order of Things* (1966; Eng. trans., 1971), *Death and the Labyrinth* (1963; Eng. trans., 1987), and *The History of Sexuality*, 3 vols. (1976–84; Eng. trans., 1978–86).

Bibliography: Hoy, D., *Foucault: A Critical Reader* (1986); Merquior, J. G., *Foucault* (1987); Shumway, D., *Michel Foucault* (1989).

Foucault pendulum

A Foucault pendulum, named for its inventor Jean FOUCAULT, who first demonstrated it in 1851, is a long, simple pendulum that is mounted so that it can be driven to maintain constant amplitude without influencing its direction of swing. Such a pendulum maintains a fixed plane of oscillation with respect to the stars. Consequently, if one were mounted at the North Pole, the Earth would rotate under it, and the plane of the pendulum would appear to rotate through 360° in 24 hours. At a latitude of θ, the plane rotates through $360° \sin\theta$ in 24 hours. The Foucault pendulum furnishes proof of the Earth's rotation.   C. E. SWARTZ

Fouché, Joseph   [foo-shay']

Joseph Fouché was a Jacobin leader during the French Revolution and minister of police under Napoleon I. Born at Nantes, probably on May 21, 1760, he was educated by the Oratorians and taught in Nantes until the outbreak of the revolution. He was elected (1792) to the National Convention and voted to execute King Louis XVI. A spokesman for the radical Jacobins, Fouché served as a convention representative in the Vendée but is better known for his ruthless suppression (1793) of counterrevolutionaries in Lyon. For supporting the atheistic movement, Fouché was expelled from the Jacobin club by Maximilien Robespierre, but he worked with other malcontents to overthrow Robespierre on July 27, 1794.

Under the Directory, Fouché served as ambassador in Milan (1798) and The Hague (1799) but was recalled by Emmanuel Sièyes to become minister of police. He supported the coup by Napoléon Bonaparte (later Napoleon I) against the Directory and was retained as minister of police under the newly established Consulate. Fouché's elaborate police system was well organized and highly efficient, especially at internal spying. Nevertheless, his involvement in political maneuvering against Bonaparte led to his dismissal (1802). Reinstated in

1804, he was created duc d'Otrante (1809) but was again ousted in 1810 after intriguing with the British. He was appointed governor of Rome and, in 1813, administrator of Illyria.

After Napoleon's first abdication (1814) Fouché's services were rejected by the restored Bourbons. When Napoleon returned in 1815, the opportunistic Fouché was reappointed minister of police, but he secretly corresponded with the Allies to assure his future. He thus became president of the provisional government established after Napoleon's defeat at Waterloo and continued for a time to serve Louis XVIII. The law proscribing those responsible for the death of Louis XVI forced Fouché into exile in 1816, and he died in obscurity.   DONALD D. HORWARD

Bibliography: Cole, Hubert, *Fouché, the Unprincipled Patriot* (1971); Forssell, Nils, *Fouché, the Man Napoleon Feared* (1928; repr. 1970); Zweig, Stefan, *Joseph Fouché: The Portrait of a Politician* (1930).

foulard   [foo-lahrd']

Foulard is a soft, lustrous, lightweight fabric made of plain-woven or twilled silk and usually printed with small designs on a solid-colored ground. Imitation foulards are now made of rayon and other synthetic fibers. Foulards are used for neckties, scarves, robes, and dresses. The first foulards were imported from India, and the word has come to mean a scarf as well as the material it is made of.   ISABEL B. WINGATE

found poem

A found poem is one that is purported to be "given" to the poet or, in a manner of speaking, one the poet "finds" already created. Samuel Taylor Coleridge made this claim for "Kubla Kahn." Paul Valéry spoke of the *ligne donée*, a line of verse that is given by God, a Muse, or some other outside power; the other lines had to be furnished by the poet.   J. A. CUDDON

foundation, building

A foundation supplies the base for a structure such as a building, bridge, dam, or breakwater, transmitting the load of the superstructure to the supporting soil or rock in such a way as to prevent the settling or slippage of the structure.

The construction of a foundation is preceded by a study of the material on which the structure is to be built, including test pits and borings to determine the type of soil and the depths at which rock or water are encountered.

Foundations fall into two general classifications, spread and deep. A common type of spread foundation is the footing, a slab, block, or pedestal that forms an enlargement of the bottom of an individual pier or bearing wall and distributes the load to a broader area of the underlying material. Another type, the mat or raft foundation, is used for heavier, more widely distributed loads. It consists of a number of footings combined into a single, thick reinforced concrete slab beneath the entire structure. A third kind of spread foundation, which is used in soils that may settle or slide, is the floating foundation, a boxlike underground construction with a weight equal to or slightly exceeding that of the excavated soil.

There are two principal types of deep foundations, piles and CAISSONS. Piles, which can be made of timber, concrete, or steel, are driven by hammers into the ground. End-bearing piles are sunk to the bearing stratum (the depth at which soil resistance can support the weight of the structure) or sometimes bedrock. Friction piles, which are rough-surfaced and tapered, transfer their load to the adjacent soil along the length of the pile through friction and adhesion. Caissons, which are hollow boxlike or cylindrical structures, are used in excavating down to the bearing stratum and ultimately become part of the completed foundation.

Existing foundations may be given added support by underpinning, or excavating section by section under the old wall and replacing the earth with footings, piles, piers, or caissons.

BRIDGE foundations were once constructed by using a COFFERDAM, an enclosure to exclude water. The invention in the

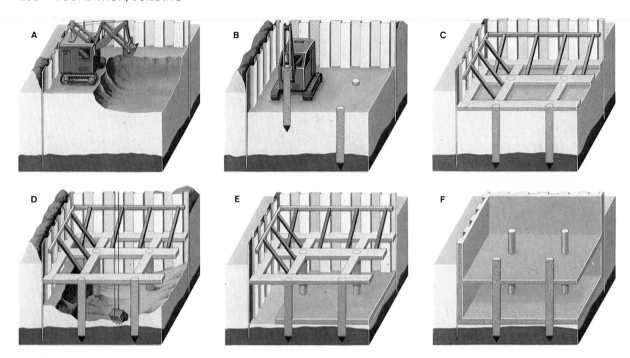

In constructing buildings in areas of soft, waterlogged clay and gravel, support foundations are often of piles sunk in solid bedrock and strengthened with a hollow concrete box structure. Such foundations transmit the weight of the building directly to the bedrock. Interlocking sections of steel sheeting are first driven into the bedrock to form a watertight casing; then part of the ground is excavated (A). Precast, steel-tipped, concrete piles are driven into the bedrock (B) to a predetermined level. Concrete crossbeams are cast on top of the piles to keep the casing upright (C), and the remainder of the earth is removed down to the bedrock (D). A concrete base is cast on the bedrock (E), a concrete platform is laid over the crossbeams, and the box structure is completed with concrete (F).

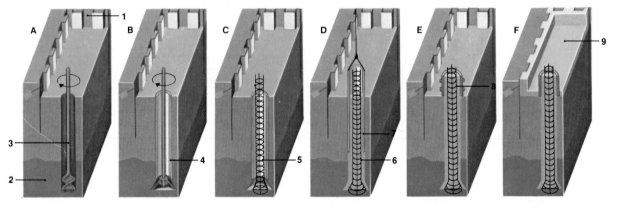

A modern method of sinking deep foundations for high-rise buildings involves casting concrete piles in place. After excavation of the ground to the desired level, interlocking steel sheets are driven around the site perimeter (1), and a hole is driven through the soft clay into hard rock (2). The base of the hole is widened with a special tool (3), and a cylindrical steel liner (4) is sunk into the hole, along with a reinforcing steel grid (5). Concrete (6) is poured into the hole and allowed to set; the steel liner (7) is then withdrawn. The concrete pile (8) is continued up into the building, and the floor (9) and sheet-steel walls are concreted in. The number of such deep-set concrete piles that are used in a foundation will depend on the condition of the ground, the depth of the rock layer, and the planned height of the building.

1850s of the pneumatic caisson, which uses compressed air to keep soil and water from entering the excavation, made possible much deeper foundations. Deep water and swift currents often create special problems, which are solved by specially adapted caissons. Modern bridge foundation technique sometimes replaces the caisson with clusters of large-diameter piles or hollow cylinders filled with concrete.

In DAM foundations, poor soil characteristics are countered by measures such as grouting (piping in a cement curtain), building cutoff trenches, excavating drainage wells, or building a concrete drainage blanket under the dam on the upstream side. Harbor installations such as breakwaters and docks are built on caissons or piles. In addition to conventional timber, reinforced concrete, and steel piles, modern quay design often calls for steel sheet-piling, consisting of flat sections with interlocking grooves.

Bibliography: Kerisel, J., *Down to Earth: Foundations Past and Present* (1987); Peck, R., et al., *Foundation Engineering*, 3d ed. (1988); Ramsey, D., *The Complete Foundation and Floor Framing Book* (1987).

foundations and endowments

Foundations are organizations that distribute private wealth for the public good, usually by making grants to other nonprofit organizations and individuals engaged in social welfare, educational, charitable, or religious activities. Some private foundations use the words *fund, trust,* or *endowment* in their names, but this implies no difference in function or law.

There are several kinds of foundations. Independent foundations usually derive their funding from a single source, such as an individual or family. Operating foundations make few if any grants; they plan and carry through programs managed by their own staffs. Community foundations derive their principal funds from many donors, generally make grants only in their own metropolitan areas, and are governed by boards broadly representative of the community. Company-sponsored foundations derive their funds from profit-making companies but are legally independent. Federal government foundations usually make grants from tax money appropriated by Congress.

A wide variety of other organizations use the word *foundation* in their names; they may have endowments, but seldom, if ever, do they engage in broad-purpose, discretionary grant making. They generally seek funds through public solicitation and use their resources to further a particular point of view or cause or to aid only a specified institution.

HISTORY

The modern foundation is derived from the fixed-purpose charitable trusts that have existed at least since ancient Egypt and Greece. The concept was given legal definition in the English Statute of Charitable Uses (1601), which granted certain privileges to private citizens or groups of citizens willing to serve the public good by performing or supporting acts of charity. In general, legal doctrines in the common-law countries since then have confirmed this definition for all types of charitable organizations, such as foundations, churches, hospitals, and colleges, and have ensured their right to tax exemption and existence in perpetuity as long as they meet the test of being charitable.

The general-purpose foundation, whose broad charter enables its trustees to address any problem affecting the general welfare worldwide, is an American innovation originating between the end of the 19th century and the beginning of World War I. Notable examples are the Carnegie Corporation of New York (1911) and the ROCKEFELLER FOUNDATION (1913). In practice, general-purpose foundations have limited their programs to a few broad fields of interest but retain the power to move into new fields as social conditions change.

REGULATION OF FOUNDATIONS

Foundations in the United States have come under three waves of attack in recent decades. In the 1950s charges were made of Communist penetration and subversion, but two successive congressional investigations failed to substantiate the charges. In the 1960s, the disclosure of irregular fiscal and administrative practices led to the passage of new tax law provisions. And in the 1970s, critics, mainly outside Congress, raised questions about foundation decision making, the composition of boards, and accountability to the public.

Private foundations are now defined and regulated principally by provisions of the Tax Reform Act of 1969, with some modifications enacted in subsequent years. The crucial distinction between the status of a private foundation and that of other charitable organizations is the amount of private financing received from a single source. Congress assumed that although publicly supported organizations are subject to the discipline of public opinion, institutions drawing their funds from one source are not subject to this corrective influence and should be regulated in some other way. Therefore, special rules for private foundations, which are not applicable to most community foundations or to other charities, were added to the Internal Revenue Code in 1969. These regulate the relations between wealthy persons and the foundations with which they are involved, minimum expenditures to charities by foundations and maximum administrative costs, foundation ownership and control of private business, foundation investments, and the use of foundation money for noncharitable purposes. An annual 2 percent (originally 4 percent) excise tax on net investment income is levied on private foundations to support auditing and other administrative expenses incurred by the Internal Revenue Service. The tax can be reduced to 1 percent under certain circumstances.

Critics of these laws concede that the 1969 legislation was necessary to correct abuses by a relatively small number of foundations. However, they point out that the excise tax

breaks a 50-year-old U.S. tradition of exempting charitable organizations of this type from federal taxation and that the tax has consistently yielded far more in revenues than is used for administrative costs, reducing funds that would otherwise be available for grant making. Other special provisions affecting foundations and inflation, which affects the budgets of grantees, tend to diminish the impact of foundation grants and, in the long run, may threaten the existence of foundations.

Proponents of a limited life for foundations seem to fear most of all that the dead hand of a wealthy donor may perpetually bind funds to be used for whatever purposes the donor chooses, even when those purposes are or become of little or no value. They see foundations as elitist institutions existing uneasily in a democratic society. Counterarguments cite the remedy of *cy pres*, legal proceedings by which the courts may alter a will or trust outmoded by changing social needs. Professional staffing and independent boards also serve as insurance against donor control.

EXTENT OF FOUNDATION ACTIVITY

The more than 27,000 U.S. foundations are spread throughout the country, many of them concentrated in the northeast. Most U.S. foundations are funds of between $1 million and $5 million, but the combined assets of all U.S. foundations exceed $100 billion, and together they give away more than $6 billion each year. Education has always ranked highest in grants received, followed by health, science, welfare, humanities, international activities, and religion. Among the largest foundations are the CARNEGIE FOUNDATIONS, FORD FOUNDATION, J. Paul Getty Trust, ROBERT WOOD JOHNSON FOUNDATION, Kellogg Foundation, KRESGE FOUNDATION, Lilly Endowment, MACARTHUR FOUNDATION, MELLON FOUNDATION, Pew Charitable Trusts, and the Rockefeller Foundation. Foundations in many communities make grants for local projects and services.

The Council on Foundations in Washington, D.C., is a membership organization of grant makers promoting responsible and effective grant making and fostering the growth of the field. The Foundation Center in New York compiles and makes available current information about foundations to all segments of the general public including those seeking foundation grants.

Outside the United States the largest concentration of foundations are in Canada, Western Europe, and Japan. Among these are the NUFFIELD FOUNDATION (England), Donner Canadien, Volkswagenwerk (Germany), Gulbenkian (Portugal), Agnelli (Italy), and the Toyota Foundations (Japan).

THOMAS R. BUCKMAN

Bibliography: Europa Publications, *International Foundation Directory*, 4th ed. (1986); Freeman, D. F., *The Handbook on Private Foundations* (1981); Odendahl, T., ed., *America's Wealthy and the Future of Foundations* (1987); Olson, S., ed., *The Foundation Directory*, 12th ed. (1989); Read, P., *Foundation Fundamentals*, 3d ed. (1986); Renz, L., ed., *Foundations Today*, 6th ed. (1989).

foundry

A foundry is an establishment where iron, steel, and other metal CASTINGS are produced. Most foundries melt down metal scrap in an ELECTRIC FURNACE; older foundries may use cupolas, furnaces that are similar in design but smaller than the BLAST FURNACE. Different types of cast iron are defined by their silicon and carbon content. Gray cast iron is the most easily cast and machined, and is used for casting automobile engine blocks and machine tools. Other grades of cast iron are derived from gray iron by remelting it or by controlling the rate at which it is cooled after casting. Foundries produce the pig iron for the IRON AND STEEL INDUSTRY as well as dies, machine parts, and other finished castings. MERLE C. NUTT

See also: FORGE; METALLURGY; TOOL AND DIE MAKING.

fountains

Fountains, which are channels or spouts through which water is directed under pressure for decorative or cooling effects, have been an important feature of cities, GARDENS, and private houses throughout history. The earliest fountains were natural springs, but the artificial harnessing of water power dates back to the first Egyptian and Babylonian civilizations. The ancient Greek custom of regarding springs as sacred sources of life was perpetuated by the Romans, who devised the *nymphaeum*, a structure enclosing a pool. Fountains decorated the villas and gardens of wealthy Romans but also served a practical function in cities as sources of public water supply. The most elaborate waterwork of this period was constructed (AD 118–34) by the Emperor Hadrian in the gardens of his palace at Tivoli (see HADRIAN'S VILLA).

Water was put to still more ingenious uses in Western Europe during the Middle Ages, when the *Fontana Maggiore* (1278), in Perugia, Italy, was built by Nicola and Giovanni PISANO. The *Fontana Maggiore* was the first to exploit the now-familiar decorative effect of water cascading from a central spout. Italian architects and sculptors of the RENAISSANCE exploited the movement and sound of water in such works as Giovanni da BOLOGNA's *Neptune Fountain* (1563–67), in Bologna, or even imposed sculptural form upon the water itself, as in the immense series of cascades constructed at the Villa d'Este near Rome by Pirro Ligorio (c.1510–1583). Fountains became a crucial element in Italian LANDSCAPE ARCHITECTURE, whose practitioners often exploited natural undulations in the land to create water pressure, as in the Boboli Gardens (begun 1560) of the PITTI PALACE in Florence, or Giacomo Barozzi da VIGNOLA's Villa Farnese (begun 1559) at Caprarola.

Unlike their Oriental and Indian counterparts, who have used water to induce calm contemplation, European architects and sculptors have generally been attracted by the theatrical effects of jets and cascades. This is especially true of Giovanni Lorenzo BERNINI's *Fountain of the Four Rivers* (1648–51) and Nicola SALVI's TREVI FOUNTAIN (1732–62), both in Rome. The Italian formal garden, where fountains formed the focal points of radiating avenues, was emulated in France, where Marie de Médicis ordered the building of the Jardins de Luxembourg, Paris (1611–20), and André LE NÔTRE planned (c.1660) the vast gardens of Versailles, where soaring jets of water proclaimed the affluence of Louis XIV.

Fountains have continued to fascinate 20th-century garden and city designers, who have made use of modern materials and engineering techniques unavailable to their predecessors. Alexander CALDER's *Water Ballet* at the General Motors company building in Detroit, Mich. (1954) consists of 21 jets that rise 40 feet into the air and are illuminated at night in red, blue, and green. At the IBM headquarters in Armonk, N.Y., (1964), Isamu NOGUCHI has used an electronically controlled fountain to celebrate the spirit of scientific inquiry. Local topography and history constitute the symbolic theme of Carl MILLES's fountain *The Meeting of the Waters* (1940), in Saint Louis, Mo.; the fountain represents the confluence of the Missouri and Mississippi rivers. In smaller projects, such as Paley Park in New York City, designed by Zion and Breen Associates, moving water is valued for its cooling, as much as for its decorative, qualities. The perennial fascination of water as an architectural element is reaffirmed by Charles MOORE's *St. Joseph's Fountain* in the Piazza d'Italia (1978), an urban renewal project in New Orleans. Moore's fountain, which pays tribute to the Italian population of the city, brings that tradition of fountain building full circle by reinterpreting the ancient Roman and baroque traditions of fountain architecture.

HOWARD BATCHELOR

Bibliography: Comito, Terry, *The Idea of the Garden in the Renaissance* (1978); Gurevich, Ilya, *The Fountains of Petrodvonets Near Leningrad* (1980); Jellicoe, Susan and Geoffrey, *Water: The Use of Water in Landscape Architecture* (1971); MacDougall, Elizabeth B., ed., *Fons Sapientiae: Renaissance Garden Fountains* (1978); Miller, Naomi, *French Renaissance Fountains* (1977); Newton, Norman T., *Design on the Land: The Development of Landscape Architecture* (1971).

Fouquet, Jean   [foo-kay']

Jean, or Jehan, Fouquet, c.1420–1481, was the most important French painter of the 15th century. As a result of a trip to Italy about 1443–47, he assimilated characteristics of Italian Renaissance art with his native French style. He is known to have been in Rome before 1447 because he was asked to paint a portrait of Pope Eugene IV (now lost). By 1448, Fouquet was working in his native Tours for King Charles VII; he was appointed court painter by Louis XI in 1475. His most famous work is a manuscript he illustrated for Étienne Chevalier about 1452, of which only fragments survive (Musée Condé at Chantilly). Another widely known work is *Virgin and Child Surrounded by Angels* (c.1450; Antwerp Museum). Several panel paintings have been attributed to Fouquet, among which are portraits of Charles VII (c.1445) and of Juvenal des Ursins (c.1455), both in the Louvre Museum in Paris.

ROBERT G. CALKINS

Bibliography: Melet-Sanson, J., *Fouquet* (1978); Wescher, Paul, *Jean Fouquet and His Time* (1947).

Fouquet, Nicolas   [foo-kay']

Nicolas Fouquet, b. January 1615, d. Mar. 23, 1680, was an adept French judge-administrator and lavish patron of the arts, whose apparent desire to succeed Cardinal MAZARIN as chief minister caused his disgrace when LOUIS XIV assumed personal rule in 1661. An army and provincial intendant, Fouquet became Mazarin's trusted agent during the FRONDE. He attained the high post of *procureur general* in the parlement of Paris in 1650 and the superintendancy of finance in 1653.

Irregular financial methods, including personal loans, kept the treasury afloat and made him fabulously wealthy; they also allowed his rival Jean Baptiste COLBERT to discredit him with Louis XIV. The king, already determined to be his own prime minister, was wary of Fouquet's independent power and probably jealous of his Vaux-le-Vicomte château. He had Fouquet arrested in 1661, subjected him to an irregular trial that lasted three years, then changed the sentence from banishment to perpetual imprisonment.   A. LLOYD MOOTE

four-color theorem

The four-color theorem, first proposed around 1850 by Francis Guthrie, states that four colors suffice to color any map, given the requirement that any two countries with a contiguous boundary should have different colors. In 1879, A. B. Kempe published a proof of this conjecture, but some years later the proof was found to be incomplete. Only in 1976 did Kenneth Appel and Wolfgang Haken of the University of Illinois prove this conjecture with the aid of a modern large-scale computer. They proved that instead of considering infinitely many maps, one could reduce the problem to considering only a finite number of maps. Using a computer they developed a catalog of 1,936 "unavoidable configurations," of which any map must contain at least one, and showed that each of these could be reduced to four colors. Thus, the assumption that there exists a map that cannot be colored by four colors leads to an absurdity.   MORTON L. CURTIS

Bibliography: Barnette, D. W., *Map Coloring, Plyhedra, and the Four-Color Problem* (1984); Saaty, T. L., and Kainem, P. G., *The Four-Color Problem* (1986).

four-eyed fish

The four-eyed fish, *Anableps anableps*, is found in muddy streams in southern Mexico, Central America, and northern South America. It seldom exceeds 30 cm (12 in) in length. Because each of its two eyes is divided horizontally by a band of tissue, the fish appears to have four eyes. The upper half of

The four-eyed fish, A. anableps, a freshwater fish of Central America and parts of South America, has eyes that divide at the waterline, enabling it to see above and below the surface simultaneously.

each eye is adapted for seeing above the water and the lower half for seeing below, the fish cruising just below the surface with the upper half of its eyes protruding. Light passes through the oval-shaped lens of each eye at different angles in the upper and lower halves, giving each half the required different focal lengths for vision in air and water.

Each male has a sex organ that can be moved only to the right or only to the left. Each female's genital aperture opens either only to the right or only to the left. Consequently, a "right-handed" male can mate only with a "left-handed" female, and vice versa.　　　　　　　　　　　A. R. EMERY

Four Freedoms

The Four Freedoms was a list of basic human rights formulated by President Franklin D. Roosevelt on Jan. 6, 1941. In his State of the Union message to Congress, Roosevelt identified them as freedom of speech and expression, freedom of worship, freedom from want, and freedom from fear. Later that year they were in large part incorporated into the ATLANTIC CHARTER, a joint British and U.S. statement of aims for a peaceful world. The Four Freedoms were criticized by some as being too vague to serve as a practical guide.

4-H program

The 4-H program was founded in 1900 to provide local educational clubs for rural youth from age 9 to 19. Designed to teach better home economics and agricultural techniques and to foster character development and good citizenship, the program, administered by the Cooperative Extension Service of the U.S. Department of Agriculture, state land grant universities, and county governments, emphasizes projects that improve the four H's: head, heart, hands, and health. The 4-H pledge reflects these concerns: "I pledge my Head to clearer thinking, my Heart to greater loyalty, my Hands to larger service, and my Health to better living, for my club, my community, my country, and my world."

The 4-H program, expanded to include urban and suburban youth, has nearly 5 million members in the United States, and about 80 other countries also have some type of 4-H club program. Each year a national meeting of the clubs is held in Chicago to demonstrate improvements in such fields as livestock breeding, food cultivation, canning, and handicrafts.

Bibliography: Erickson, Theodore A., *My Sixty Years with Rural Youth* (1956); Garaventa, John, "American 4-H Adventure," *National Geographic*, June 1979; Reck, F. M., *The 4-H Club Story* (1951).

Four Horsemen of the Apocalypse

In the New Testament, the Four Horsemen of the Apocalypse are the allegorical figures of the sixth chapter of the Book of REVELATION (sometimes called the Apocalypse). Riding a white, a red, a black, and a pale horse, the horsemen are generally understood to symbolize power or conquest, violence or war, poverty or famine, and death. The rider on the white horse is sometimes interpreted as representing Jesus Christ. The four horsemen are frequent symbols in works of art and literature. Albrecht Dürer's *Apocalypse* (1498) is a series of woodcuts representing them. Vicente BLASCO-IBÁÑEZ became famous through his war novel *The Four Horsemen of the Apocalypse* (1916; Eng. trans., 1918).　　　DOUGLAS EZELL

four-o'clock

Four-o'clock, *Mirabilis jalapa*, family Nyctaginaceae, is a nonhardy, rapid-growing, tuberous-rooted flowering perennial plant. Its tubers must be dug, and the plants are treated as annuals in colder climates. Its various-colored flowers open in late afternoon, hence the plant's name.

Four Quartets

Four Quartets, a suite of meditative poems written by T. S. ELIOT, concerns the interaction of time and timelessness. Each poem is named for a place—"Burnt Norton" (1936), "East Coker" (1940), "The Dry Salvages" (1941), and "Little Gidding" (1942). Each is centered on one of the medieval elements—

air, earth, water, and fire. "Little Gidding," for example, describes wartime bombings and focuses on fire. *Four Quartets* employs Eliot's idiosyncratic style of musical free verse, the form of a quartet, and personal allusions mixed with allusions to previous literature.　　　　　　　JANE COLVILLE BETTS

Bibliography: Blamires, Harry, *Word Unheard* (1969); Gardner, Helen, *The Composition of "Four Quartets"* (1978).

Fourcroy, Antoine François, Comte de
[foor-kwah']

Antoine François de Fourcroy, b. June 15, 1755, d. Dec. 16, 1809, a French chemist, was one of the first supporters of the new antiphlogistic theory of Antoine Laurent LAVOISIER. He collaborated in 1787 with Lavoisier and others in revising chemical nomenclature. In addition to his work on inorganic and animal chemistry, mostly in collaboration with Nicolas Louis Vauquelin, he held a number of political positions. The two played a significant role in the discovery of the element iridium (1803) and gave the first satisfactory account of urea, which they named in 1799.　　　　　GEORGE B. KAUFFMAN

Bibliography: Smeaton, W. A., *Fourcroy* (1962).

Fourier, Charles　　[foor-yay', sharl]

François Marie Charles Fourier, b. Apr. 7, 1772, d. Oct. 10, 1837, was a French social theorist whose vision of the ideal society centered on the phalanstery, a small cooperative agricultural community. After inheriting an income, Fourier devoted himself to writing. He first set forth his ideas in *Théorie des quatre mouvements et des destinées générales* (1808; *The Social Destiny of Man; or, Theory of the Four Movements*, 1857). The basis of the phalanstery would be mutual cooperation and personal fulfillment, with all members, including women and children, sharing both the work and the profits. Communities based on Fourier's ideas were founded in Red Bank, N.J., and at BROOK FARM in Massachusetts (1841–46). After his death his work was continued by his disciple, Victor CONSIDÉRANT.

Bibliography: Barthes, Roland, *Sade-Fourier-Loyola*, trans. by Richard Miller (1976); Beecher, J. F., *Charles Fourier* (1987); Riasanovsky, N. V., *The Teaching of Charles Fourier* (1969).

Fourier, Joseph　　[foor-yay', zhoh-zef']

Jean Baptiste Joseph Fourier, b. Mar. 21, 1768, d. May 16, 1830, was a French mathematician known chiefly for his contribution to the mathematical analysis of heat flow. Trained for the priesthood, Fourier did not take his vows but instead turned toward mathematics. He first studied (1794) and later taught mathematics at the newly created École Normale. He joined (1798) Napoleon's army in its invasion of Egypt as scientific advisor, to help establish educational facilities there and to carry out archaeological explorations. In 1801 he was appointed prefect of the department of Isère.

Throughout his life Fourier pursued his interest in mathematics and mathematical physics. He became famous for his *Theorie analytique de la chaleur* (1822), a mathematical treatment of the theory of heat. He established the partial differential equation governing heat diffusion and solved it by using infinite series of trigonometric functions. Although these series had been used before, Fourier investigated them in much greater detail. His research, initially criticized for its lack of rigor, was later shown to be valid. It provided the impetus for later work on trigonometric series and the theory of functions of a real variable.　　　　　　　ARTHUR SCHLISSEL

Bibliography: Bell, Eric T., *Men of Mathematics* (1937; repr. 1986); Grattan-Guinness, Ivor, *Joseph Fourier* (1972); Herivel, John, *Joseph Fourier: The Man and the Physicist* (1975).

Fourier analysis　　[foor-yay]

Fourier analysis is a branch of mathematics that is used to analyze repeating, or periodic, phenomena. Many natural and artificial phenomena occur in cycles that repeat constantly. These phenomena—such as alternating currents, business cycles, high and low tides, the orbits of planets and artificial satellites, and the vibrations of electromagnetic waves—can be described by a mathematical concept called a function. Since these phenomena are periodic, their functions are called PERIODIC FUNCTIONS. In general, a function is said to be periodic if its graph is a repeating pattern.

The basic goal of Fourier analysis is to represent periodic functions in terms of series of particular, and generally simpler, periodic functions. Most of the simpler functions occur in TRIGONOMETRY and are therefore called trigonometric functions. They are often used in Fourier analysis to expand a given function. If the function does possess a Fourier series, the coefficients can be calculated by means of integral calculus. Fourier analysis was first developed by Joseph Fourier in the 1820s and has been highly elaborated. An analogous method making use of a small mathematical fluctuation called a "wavelet" was developed in the late 1980s. Wavelet analysis offer advantages in analyzing rapidly changing signals and in handling gaps in a body of data.

Bibliography: Korner, T. W., Fourier Analysis (1988); Rees, C., et al., Theory and Applications of Fourier Analysis (1980); Wallich, Paul, "Wavelet Theory," Scientific American, January 1991.

Fourteen Points

The Fourteen Points were a program announced by U.S. President Woodrow WILSON before a joint session of Congress on Jan. 8, 1918, as the basis for a just peace settlement following World War I. Wilson hoped to rally liberal opinion throughout the world with his address, but his opening remarks were also designed as a sympathetic response to the new Bolshevik leaders in Russia, who had called upon Russia's western Allies to begin peace negotiations on a program of no annexations, no indemnities. Although many of Wilson's suggestions had been made before, the speech represented a radical departure from the old diplomacy and called upon future victors and vanquished to liberalize their diplomacy and ideology.

The first 5 points included the following: open covenants, openly arrived at; freedom of the seas; removal of economic barriers in international trade; reduction of national armaments to the lowest point consistent with domestic safety; and adjustment of all colonial claims on the basis of the self-determination of peoples. Points 6 through 13 dealt with specific territorial settlements. The 14th point became most important to Wilson: a general association of nations for the purpose of providing mutual guarantees of political independence and territorial integrity for all nations.

Widely publicized and acclaimed in the belligerent countries on both sides, the address at once gave Wilson moral leadership of the Allies and became a powerful diplomatic and propagandist weapon. The Allies generally accepted it as a statement of war aims, and when Germany sued for peace it was on the basis of the Fourteen Points.

At the PARIS PEACE CONFERENCE (1919–20) the second point was quickly repudiated by Britain, and several others were modified or compromised in spirit by territorial agreements. On the whole, however, the final settlement was nearer the Fourteen Points than Wilson and his major advisors had at first thought possible. Out of the 14th point came the LEAGUE OF NATIONS.   DAVID W. HIRST

Bibliography: Baker, Ray Stannard, Woodrow Wilson and World Settlement, 3 vols. (1922; repr. 1958); Mayer, Arno, The Political Origins of the New Diplomacy, 1917–1918 (1959).

14th Amendment

Although the 14th Amendment to the CONSTITUTION OF THE UNITED STATES, ratified in 1868, was designed to restrain state governments from abridging the rights of former slaves after the Civil War, it has been used to extend virtually all of the personal liberties and rights granted in the BILL OF RIGHTS to protection against infringement by state governments. The amendment itself defines citizenship and restrains states from abridging the privileges or immunities of a citizen, requires DUE PROCESS of law and EQUAL PROTECTION OF THE LAWS for persons under its jurisdiction, reduces representation in Congress for states that deny voting rights, disqualifies for office certain

officials of the Confederacy, and invalidates any war debts of the confederate states.

The amendment was first construed by the U.S. Supreme Court in the SLAUGHTERHOUSE CASES (1873) and then in HURTADO V. CALIFORNIA (1884) to afford no protection of the personal rights and liberties extended by the Bill of Rights from impairment by a state. In cases like these the basis was laid for GOVERNMENT REGULATION. In LOCHNER V. NEW YORK (1905), however, and in other decisions through the 1930s, the Court interpreted the due process clause of the 14th Amendment to invalidate state legislation regulating working conditions, hours, and minimum wage laws. Many of the notable dissenting opinions of Justices Oliver Wendell HOLMES, Jr., Louis BRANDEIS, and Benjamin CARDOZO, which later became law, can be found in decisions of this era relating to issues arising under the 14th Amendment.

It was not until 1925 in GITLOW V. NEW YORK that the Court used the due process clause of this amendment to incorporate a provision of the Bill of Rights by extending the 1ST AMENDMENT protection of freedom of speech to persons against abridgment by state action. By 1937 (Palko v. Connecticut), all of the 1st Amendment protections were binding on the states under the theory that provisions of the Bill of Rights "implicit in the concept of ordered liberty" were included in the due process guarantee of the 14th Amendment. The Court has gradually included all amendments of the Bill of Rights except the 2d, 3d, 7th, 10th, and the requirement of grand jury indictment in the 5th Amendment in its "selective incorporation doctrine," protecting individual rights from state encroachment. The due process clause has also been used to acknowledge the right to privacy (ROE V. WADE, 1971).

The equal protection clause has been used to limit racial discrimination (BROWN V. BOARD OF EDUCATION OF TOPEKA, KANSAS, 1954), maintain fair legislative apportionment (BAKER V. CARR, 1962), and to forbid the use of rigid quotas in public EQUAL OPPORTUNITY programs (UNIVERSITY OF CALIFORNIA V. BAKKE, 1978). The 14th Amendment has been both praised and vilified over the years. While proponents point to advancement in standards of justice and civil liberties, critics assert that the Supreme Court interpretations of the due process and equal protection clauses have broadened the scope of judicial review to the examination of the substance of much state and federal law, a responsibility that these critics assert is properly the responsibility of legislative bodies.

Bibliography: Collins, C. W., The Fourteenth Amendment and the States (1912; repr. 1974); Corwin, E. S., Edward S. Corwin's The Constitution and What It Means Today, ed. by H. Chase and C. Dued, rev. 14th ed. (1978); Fairman, Charles, and Morrison, Stanley, The Fourteenth Amendment and the Bill of Rights (1949; repr. 1970); Levy, Leonard W., et al., Encyclopedia of the American Constitution (1986); Lockhart, William, et al., Constitutional Rights and Liberties, 6th ed. (1986); Schwartz, Bernard, ed., The Fourteenth Amendment (1970).

See also: CIVIL RIGHTS; FREEDOM OF THE PRESS; FREEDOM OF SPEECH; GRISWOLD V. CONNECTICUT; MAPP V. OHIO; PLESSY V. FERGUSON; GIDEON V. WAINWRIGHT.

4th Amendment

Among the rights protected by the 4th Amendment to the CONSTITUTION OF THE UNITED STATES are freedom from unreasonable search and seizure and certain other arrest and prearrest activities of law enforcement officials. Any search of the person, home, or automobile, for example, without "probable cause" or a valid SEARCH WARRANT is an invasion of privacy protected generally under the 4th Amendment. Moreover, since the Supreme Court decision in MAPP V. OHIO (1961), which used the 14th AMENDMENT to extend earlier decisions to the state level, courts have excluded any evidence obtained through an illegal search as a violation of the 5th AMENDMENT protection against SELF-INCRIMINATION. This rule has been the source of much controversy, but courts have increasingly insisted that only exclusion of such illegally obtained, although valid, evidence will cause law enforcement officials to operate constitutionally. In 1967 the Supreme Court broadened the prohibition against electronic eavesdropping and WIRETAPPING, which is now illegal without a valid warrant, whereas previous courts had only ruled that evidence so obtained was inadmissible.

The 4th Amendment, a part of the BILL OF RIGHTS, grew out of strong colonial objections to WRITS OF ASSISTANCE, or general warrants, which gave crown officials the right to enter any home and search and seize belongings without probable cause. The right to privacy, although not specifically mentioned anywhere in the Constitution, falls under the "penumbra" of the 1st, 3d, 4th, 5th, 9th, and 14th amendments.

Bibliography: Lasson, N. B., *History and Development of the Fourth Amendment to the U.S. Constitution* (1937; repr. 1970).

See also: GRISWOLD V. CONNECTICUT; PRIVACY, INVASION OF.

fourth dimension: see RELATIVITY.

Fourth Estate

Fourth Estate is a term used to describe the press—the journalistic profession or its members. Thomas Carlyle wrote that the British statesman Edmund Burke called the reporters' gallery in Parliament "a Fourth Estate more important by far" than the other three estates of Parliament—the peers, bishops, and commons. This exaggerated acknowledgment of the power of the press was echoed by Thomas Babington Macaulay, whose essay *On Hallam's Constitutional History* (1828) refers to the reporters' gallery as a "fourth estate of the realm."

CHRISTOPHER G. TRUMP

Fourth Republic: see FRANCE, HISTORY OF.

Fowler, H. W. [fow'-lur]

Henry Watson Fowler, b. Mar. 10, 1858, d. Dec. 26, 1933, was an English lexicographer who is best known for *A Dictionary of Modern English Usage* (1926). This commentary on English style and usage was conceived with his brother, Francis George Fowler (1870–1918), and completed by H. W. Fowler after Frank's death. The two brothers also collaborated on *The King's English* (1906) and *The Concise Oxford Dictionary of Current English* (1911). Fowler's books, esteemed and authoritative, have gone through many editions and reprintings.

F. P. DINEEN, S.J.

Bibliography: Gowers, Ernest, *H. W. Fowler* (1957).

Fowles, John [fowlz]

John Fowles, b. Mar. 31, 1926, is an English writer whose first two novels, *The Collector* (1963; film, 1965)—a thriller—and *The Magus* (1966; film, 1968), explored unusual psychological states and philosophical themes. In *The French Lieutenant's Woman* (1969; film, 1981), Fowles used an experimental framework to contrast contemporary and Victorian attitudes toward sex. In *Daniel Martin* (1977), considered his finest novel to date, Fowles emphasized a theme common to all his work: the search for where individuals—and, by extension, Western civilization as a whole—went astray and how the future can be salvaged. His other books include *The Aristos* (1965), a "self portrait in ideas"; *The Ebony Tower* (1974); a revised version of *The Magus* (1978); *Mantissa* (1982); and *A Maggot* (1985).

Bibliography: Conradi, P. J., *John Fowles* (1982); Fawkner, H. W., *Timescapes of John Fowles* (1984); Pfifer, E., ed., *Critical Essays on John Fowles* (1986); Tarbox, K., *The Art of John Fowles* (1989).

Fox

Members of this Algonquian-speaking North American Indian tribe call themselves *Meskwakihuk* or *Mesquakie* ("Red Earth People"), but they have become generally known by the name Fox, derived from the name of the first Mesquakie clan that French explorers encountered, the *Wagosh* ("Red Fox"). Originally from central Michigan, the Fox migrated to Wisconsin sometime before 1670. They settled along the Fox and Wisconsin rivers where they attempted to disrupt trade between the French and their enemies the Sioux. Extremely individualistic and warlike, the Fox precipitated a series of wars in the Great Lakes area in the first half of the 18th century.

Their power was eventually broken by an alliance of French, Ottawa, Potawatomi, Sioux, and Menominee. Their population had been greatly reduced when they amalgamated with the SAUK tribe and moved into Illinois and Iowa. Assigned (1842) to a reservation in Kansas, the tribe later returned (1859) to Iowa. There they sold their pony herds and purchased lands near Tama, on the Iowa River. They have since enlarged their land holdings; today tribal enrollment is about 1,050.

JAMES A. CLIFTON

Bibliography: Gearing, Frederick O., *The Face of the Fox* (1970; repr. 1988); Hagan, W. T., *The Sac and Fox Indians* (1958).

fox

The red fox, V. vulpes, *has been widely represented in fables and stories since ancient times as a clever and sly creature. This fox ranges throughout temperate and warm regions of the Northern Hemisphere.*

The fox is the smallest member of the dog family, Canidae. Foxes are agile predators that usually weigh under 7 kg (15 lb). They scavenge carrion and wild fruits and hunt small rodents, rabbits, birds, and invertebrates. Because they hunt small prey sufficient to feed only one animal, foxes are solitary predators and do not hunt in packs.

Foxes are a diverse group of canids containing 14 species and occupying almost all continents. The best-known foxes are the forest, chaparral, and farmland species. This group contains the gray fox, *Urocyon cinereoargenteus,* of North America, and the red fox, *Vulpes vulpes,* of North America, Europe, Asia, and North Africa. The red fox is the most widely distributed and the most common fox species.

A pair of red foxes normally occupies a territory of 2.6 to 7.8 km² (1 to 3 mi²), which they defend against other foxes. The male and female mate during midwinter, and four to seven young are born after an average gestation period of 51 days. The dog fox brings food to the vixen while she is nursing; later both parents feed the pups. By midsummer the young foxes begin to hunt on their own and are self-sufficient by autumn. During early winter the family group breaks up, and the young leave the territory.

Scavenging red foxes leave urine to convey messages to one another. A urine mark left at a site by one fox tells another fox that no food is left nearby; unless the remaining food odor is very strong, the second fox will search for food elsewhere without investigating this urine-marked location.

Some fox species show clear adaptations to the special environments they inhabit. The sand foxes include the small fennec, *Fennecus zerda;* Ruppell's sand fox, *V. ruppelli,* of the Sahara Desert; the Cape fox, *V. chama,* of South Africa; and the kit fox, *V. macrotis,* of the southwestern United States. These species all have evolved a sandy-colored coat, dense fur, dark eyes as protection against the Sun, and the ability to go without water for long periods. Their most striking feature is their large ears, which disperse body heat without water being lost through panting or sweating.

The arctic fox, *Alopex lagopus,* on the other hand, is superbly adapted to the tundra and polar ice of the far north. Its thick coat, short muzzle, hairy footpads, and short, well-furred ears minimize heat loss; it does not burn additional calories to maintain body warmth until the temperature falls below −34° C (−30° F).   J. DAVID HENRY

Bibliography: Burrows, Roger, *Wild Fox* (1968; repr. 1989); Fox, M. W., *The Wild Canids* (1975); Henry, J. David, *Red Fox* (1986).

Fox, Charles James

The English Whig statesman Charles James Fox spent most of his political career in opposition, detested by King George III. Challenging the policies of William Pitt the Younger, Fox became known as a champion of individual liberties. He was instrumental in securing abolition of the slave trade.

Charles James Fox, b. Jan. 24, 1749, was perhaps the ablest though most wayward leader in the history of the British WHIG PARTY. A son of the influential 1st Baron Holland, he could easily have ascended the conventional ladder of Whig political preferment after entering Parliament in 1768. Instead, Fox openly opposed George III during the American Revolution. He served (1782) in Lord ROCKINGHAM's brief ministry, and in 1783 he further alienated the king by allying with his old enemy Lord NORTH to lead a coalition ministry. George himself brought the ministry down, in December 1783, by securing parliamentary defeat of its bill to reform the government of India.

Except during the last months of his life, when he was a member (1806) of the wartime "ministry of all the talents," Fox spent the rest of his career in opposition. He espoused many liberal causes, including parliamentary reform, the repeal of the laws restricting Roman Catholics and dissenters, and the abolition of slavery. He was the only major British politician to approve the French Revolution, and when many of his friends, led by Edmund BURKE, went over to the government's side in 1794, he preferred to see his party split rather than to abandon his reforming principles.

Fox died on Sept. 13, 1806, a few months after the death of his great rival, William PITT the Younger, and a few months before the slave trade, against which he had led the fight, was abolished. Though often reviled in his lifetime for his political opportunism and his supposedly scandalous private life, Fox kept alive a spirit of reform that was later to determine the direction the Whig party would take in the 19th century.

PAUL LANGFORD

Bibliography: Derry, John, *Charles James Fox* (1972).

Fox, George

George Fox, b. July 1624, d. Jan. 13, 1691, was an English preacher who founded the Society of Friends (Quakers; see FRIENDS, SOCIETY OF). The son of a Puritan weaver, he learned to read and write, although there is no record that he had any formal education. He was apprenticed to a shoemaker. In 1643, Fox underwent a religious crisis and left home. His religious experience led him to conclude that Christianity should stress the inner life of the soul illumined by Christ, rather than the externals of religion. He began to preach in 1647, making converts mostly in the north of England. The Friends spread rapidly, with major concentrations in London and Bristol by 1654. By 1660 there were Quakers in America, Ireland, and the West Indies. The organizational center became Swarthmoor Hall, and Fox and Margaret Fell, whom he married in 1669, coordinated the missionary activity.

Persecution of the Friends was sporadic during the Puritan Commonwealth and Protectorate (1649–60), but after the restoration of the monarchy a determined effort was made to suppress all nonconformists. Fox was imprisoned many times. Reacting to internal divisions and to the arrest of the movement's leaders, Fox established procedural guidelines and a structural framework of monthly, quarterly, and yearly meetings. He proclaimed the right of women to full spiritual equality and, in 1660, insisted that Friends should not participate in war.

In 1671–72, Fox journeyed to North America, visiting Quaker meetings. By the time of Fox's death in 1691, the Quakers in England had shed much of their missionary zeal and had become a respectable denomination.   J. WILLIAM FROST

Bibliography: Barbour, Hugh, *Quakers in Puritan England* (1964); Fox, George, *An Autobiography,* ed. by R. M. Jones (1903–04), and *Journal,* ed. by John L. Nickalls (1952); Gwyn, Douglas, *Apocalypse of the Word* (1986); King, Rachel, *George Fox and the Light Within* (1940); Yolen, Jane, *Friend: The Story of George Fox and the Quakers* (1972).

Fox, Margaret

An American spiritualist, Margaret Fox, b. Oct. 7, 1833, d. Mar. 8, 1893, and her younger sister Kate claimed to communicate with the spirit world through a system of "rappings" that they created in their old, supposedly haunted farmhouse near Hydesville, N.Y. Many believed in their claims. The sisters held séances, toured with P. T. Barnum, and soon became celebrities. After her conversion to Roman Catholicism in 1888, Margaret declared that the rappings had been a hoax. Spiritualists insisted that her confession was made for money, and later Margaret did return to SPIRITUALISM for a living.

Fox, Virgil

Virgil Keen Fox, b. Princeton, Ill., May 3, 1912, d. Oct. 25, 1980, established the modern organ as a concert instrument and was renowned for his blazingly fast and impeccable organ pedal technique. Fox studied at Peabody Conservatory and with Marcel Dupré in Paris, and he first performed in London and New York in 1933. He was head (1938–42) of the organ department at Peabody Conservatory and organist (1946–65) of Riverside Church in New York City. Fox was named (1952) Most Popular Organist by *Choral and Organ Guide.*

RAYMOND GRAUNKE

fox terrier

The fox terrier is one of the oldest English working terriers, known before 1800 for its use in flushing fox and other animals both above and below ground. There are two varieties of fox terrier, smooth and wirehaired, distinguished by coat, but identical in all other respects. The wirehaired has been at times one of the most popular breeds, being first in popular-

The wirehaired fox terrier was originally bred as a hunting dog in England. Quick intelligence, an energetic disposition, and a smart appearance have earned the wirehaired terrier top honors in competition.

ity in England after World War I. Fox terriers are small dogs with V-shaped drop ears and an erect, docked tail. Males stand up to 40 cm (15½ in) high at the shoulder and weigh 8 kg (18 lbs). Females are slightly smaller. Fox terriers should be predominantly white in color, although they frequently have brindle, red, fawn, or liver markings.   JOHN MANDEVILLE

Bibliography: Nedell, H., *The New Fox Terrier* (1987); Nicholas, A. K., and Foy, M., *The Fox Terrier* (1990); Williams, E., *The Fox Terrier* (1988).

Foxe, John

John Foxe, b. 1516, d. Apr. 18, 1587, was an English clergyman who wrote the famous Protestant martyrology. He was educated at Oxford and became a fellow of Magdalen College. When Mary I became queen in 1553, he fled to Strasbourg, Frankfurt, and then to Basel, where he stayed until 1559. There he began to write a history of the persecutions of Christians, which was later expanded and published (1563) as the *Acts and Monuments of These Latter and Perillous Dayes.*

The work, known almost immediately as the *Book of Martyrs,* extolled the heroism of the Protestant martyrs of the Reformation. Foxe described their sufferings in vivid terms, but the value of his work is limited by an uncritical use of sources and his strong prejudices. Although the book has gone through many editions, its popularity declined during the 19th century. More recently, however, the enduring worth of Foxe's book has been recognized. It contains much information about 16th-century England unobtainable elsewhere.
                                        FREDERICK A. NORWOOD

Bibliography: Mozley, J. F., *John Foxe and His Book* (1940; repr. 1970).

foxglove

The common foxglove, D. purpurea, bears spikes of bell-shaped, speckled flowers. The dried leaves are used to produce digitalis, a drug that stimulates the heart. A single hectare of land yields hundreds of kilograms of dried leaves, so only a few hundred hectares are needed to meet the worldwide demand for digitalis in medicine.

Foxglove is the common name for about 20 to 30 species of summer-flowering biennial or short-lived perennial herbs in the genus *Digitalis,* family Scrophulariaceae. They are native to Europe and northwest Africa to Central Asia. The common foxglove, *D. purpurea,* grows to a height of 150 cm (5 ft). Its leaves are alternate, lance-shaped, up to 30 cm (1 ft) long, and hairy above with soft white hairs below. Leaves are tapered at the base to form winged stalks. The flowers droop on erect racemes, and the fruit are capsules with numerous seeds.

Common foxglove is found in clearings, in burned areas, and in hilly dry pastures, and it is often grown as an ornamental. Many varieties have been originated through breeding, with flowers varying from white to a deep rose color. The dried leaves, the source of the drug DIGITALIS used for heart trouble, have been used medicinally since as early as the 13th century.   K. B. PAUL

foxhound: see AMERICAN FOXHOUND; ENGLISH FOXHOUND.

foxtail

Foxtail is a common name for several perennial or annual grass species of temperate northern regions, particularly *Setaria italica* and the 30 species of genus *Alopecurus.* They are named for their brushy seed spikes. Meadow foxtail, *A. pratensis,* a perennial, has a creeping base from which stems rise to 90 cm (3 ft) in height.   K. B. PAUL

fox-trot

The fox-trot is a syncopated ballroom dance in 4/4 time consisting of an ordinary walk, quarter turns, sideward slides of the feet, and alternating fast and slow steps. By adding rapid trotting steps to the one-step for his act in the Ziegfeld Follies in 1913, Harry Fox created Fox's Trot. After Oscar Duryea standardized a less strenuous form of the dance, the fox-trot's simple execution and many, uncomplicated variations assured its lasting success.   BARBARA NEWMAN

Foxx, Jimmie   [fahx]

Baseball Hall of Fame member James Emory Foxx, b. Sudlersville, Md., Oct. 22, 1907, d. July 21, 1967, known as "Double X," was a power-hitting first and third baseman during the Babe Ruth era. He hit 58 home runs in 1932, only 2 short of Ruth's best seasonal total. Foxx spent 11 years with the Philadelphia Athletics (1925–35), then went to the Red Sox, Cubs, and Phillies before retiring (1945). He hit at least 30 home runs in 12 straight seasons and accumulated 100 or more runs batted in for 13 straight seasons. American League Most Valuable Player 3 times (1932–33, 1938), Foxx had a lifetime batting average of .325 with 534 home runs.

Foy, Eddie

Edwin Fitzgerald Foy, b. New York City, Mar. 9, 1856, d. Feb. 16, 1928, an American comedian and dancer, established his reputation in vaudeville during the 1870s. He later performed in such musical comedies as *Hotel Topsy Turvy* (1898) and *Mr. Hamlet of Broadway* (1908). His children appeared with him from 1913 as "The Seven Little Foys."

Foyt, A. J.   [foyt]

Anthony Joseph Foyt, Jr., b. Houston, Tex., Jan. 16, 1935, is one of American auto racing's most versatile drivers, having won major championships on the stock-car circuit, the USAC (U.S. Auto Club) tour, the Indianapolis 500, and Le Mans. Foyt won the USAC driving title seven times and the Indy 500 a record four times (1961, '64, '67, '77). Less than two weeks after winning the 1967 Indy 500, he teamed with Dan Gurney to win at Le Mans, France, for one of the greatest double victories ever achieved in the sport. He became the first and only driver to win 100 USAC-sponsored races—in sprint, stock, midget, and championship classes.

Bibliography: Libby, Bill, *Foyt* (1974).

Fracastoro, Girolamo   [frah-kah-stor'-oh, jee-roh-lah'-moh]

The Italian physician Girolamo Fracastoro, b. c.1478, d. Aug. 6, 1553, described and named the disease SYPHILIS in 1530. Sixteen years later, in his work *De contagione et contagiosis morbis,* he discussed the nature and the spread of INFECTIOUS DISEASES, foretelling in many ways the germ theory of disease.
                                        BARBARA TCHABOVSKY

Fracci, Carla   [fraht'-chee, kar'-lah]

Carla Fracci, b. Aug. 20, 1936, was the first Italian ballerina of the 20th century to achieve international stardom. She began her training at the La Scala Opera House in 1946, graduated into its ballet company in 1954, and became prima ballerina in 1958. Although not a formidable technician, Fracci is an exquisite stylist, specializing in the great romantic ballets of the 19th century, notably *Giselle* and *La Sylphide.* Her performances are enhanced by her dramatic flair and her personal beauty and charm. In 1967 she became associated with the American Ballet Theatre, dancing with Erik Bruhn. She starred in a touring group directed by her husband, Beppe Menegatti, and in 1984 appeared in a television movie, *The Ballerinas*.

Bibliography: Gruen, J., *Private World of Ballet* (1976); Migel, P., "A Romantic Ballerina in Our Times," *Dance Magazine*, December 1984.

fractal: see GEOMETRY, FRACTAL.

fraction

A fraction is the quotient of two integers: one integer, called the numerator, divided by another, nonzero integer, called the denominator. Where a represents the numerator and b the denominator, a fraction can be written $\frac{a}{b}$, a/b, or $a \div b$.

Often different symbols are used to represent the same ratio. For example, 1/2, 2/4, and 3/6 all represent the same ratio, so they are called equivalent fractions. Two fractions a/b and c/d are equivalent if $a \cdot d = b \cdot c$. For any two fractions a/b and c/d with positive denominators, a/b is less than c/d (denoted $a/b < c/d$) if $a \cdot d < b \cdot c$.

Since for any fraction there are infinitely many equivalent fractions, there is a need for a preferred form of a fraction to represent a given ratio. This form, called a reduced fraction, is the fraction that results when all common factors have been divided out of the numerator and denominator.

Addition and subtraction of any fractions a/b and c/d are defined by

$$\frac{a}{b} + \frac{c}{d} = \frac{ad + bc}{bd} \text{ and } \frac{a}{b} - \frac{c}{d} = \frac{ad - bc}{bd}.$$

When fractions have a common denominator, addition and subtraction can be accomplished by adding or subtracting the numerators and retaining the same denominator.

Multiplication is the easiest operation to perform on two fractions: the numerator is multiplied by the numerator and the denominator is multiplied by the denominator. For any fractions a/b and c/d,

$$\frac{a}{b} \cdot \frac{c}{d} = \frac{a \cdot c}{b \cdot d} = \frac{ac}{bd}.$$

Division by zero is undefined in any number system. For any fractions a/b and c/d with c not equal to zero,

$$\frac{a}{b} \div \frac{c}{d} = \frac{a}{b} \cdot \frac{d}{c} = \frac{ad}{bc}.$$

Fractions are classified as (1) proper fractions, in which the numerator is less than the denominator; (2) improper fractions, in which the numerator is greater; or (3) mixed numbers, in which the number is expressed as a whole number and a proper fraction.   JOHN M. PETERSON

Bibliography: Burke, J. M., *Focus on Fractions* (1988).

fractionation   [frak-shun-ay'-shuhn]

Fractionation is a process that separates a mixture of chemical substances into its individual fractions, or components. The term most often refers to fractional distillation, which involves the volatilization, or boiling, and subsequent condensation and collection of volatile liquids with different boiling points. This process is known as "cracking" in the PETROLEUM industry. Other methods of fractionation include fractional crystallization, ION EXCHANGE, CHROMATOGRAPHY and solvent EXTRACTION, and field-flow fractionation.

Each method takes advantage of differences in properties of the components involved. The effectiveness of fractional crystallization, for example, depends on slight differences in the solubility of the different compounds. The least soluble solutes crystallize first and are removed in sequence from the remaining solution, or mother liquid. Ion exchange is based on the selective absorption of anions or cations from solution by passage through certain finely divided solid materials that are capable of exchanging their component ions for other ions. In chromatography, differential absorption of substances occurs at different positions along materials held in a column or tube. The fractions can then be withdrawn from the column by selective use of solvents. Field-flow fractionation is used in separating materials in the macromolecular and colloidal size range. It resembles the technique of chromatography except that separation of components is induced by an electrical, magnetic, thermal, or other field applied to the flow of materials.   A. J. CACELLA

fracture   (geology):   see FAULT; JOINT.

fracture   (medicine)

In medicine, a fracture is a break in a BONE. In normal bones, fracture results from injury or from violent stress. In bones weakened by disease, fractures can occur spontaneously under ordinary stresses, a condition called pathological fracture. The susceptibility of a bone to fracture under stress depends on its brittleness, which in turn is determined by its degree of calcification. The bones of infants and young children have low calcification and are therefore softer and more flexible than those of older persons, whose bones are highly calcified. Fractures in infants and young children are commonly incomplete fractures, called greenstick fractures, because the bone cracks on one side and bends on the other. In contrast, brittle bones of older persons can shatter (see OSTEOPOROSIS).

When bone fragments protrude through skin, the fracture is called open, or compound; if the skin is not broken, it is called a closed, or simple, fracture. Although fractures of the extremities are painful and partially disabling, they are not as dangerous as fractures of the skull or spinal column, which can result in permanent damage if bone fragments penetrate nerve tissue. Only a trained professional should move an individual who might have a broken neck or back.

Signs of a limb fracture may include pain and swelling in the overlying tissues, skin discoloration, distortion, impaired or complete loss of function, and a grinding sensation in the limb during movement. The injured person should not be moved unless the limb has been immobilized with splints.

Fractures are treated by aligning the ends of broken bones by traction or surgery and holding them in place for several weeks in plaster casts or splints; metal wires or screws may be needed for smaller bone fragments. Healing begins with formation of special tissue called callus. This grows in excess of need, so that a bone is permanently thicker in the vicinity of a healed fracture. A polymer has also been developed that is absorbed by the body as it holds bones in place without metal fixtures, and specially treated coral is being used in the same manner. Other methods to speed bone healing are also being researched. Treatment of a fracture is usually followed by physical therapy.   PETER L. PETRAKIS

Bibliography: American College of Surgeons, *Early Care of the Injured Patient*, 3d ed. (1982); Connally, J. F., *Fracture Treatment* (1988).

fracture zones, oceanic: see OCEANIC FRACTURE ZONES.

Fraenkel-Conrat, Heinz

German-American biochemist Heinz Ludwig Fraenkel-Conrat, b. July 29, 1910, is noted for his studies of viral proteins. He obtained a medical degree from the University of Breslau in 1933 and a doctorate in biochemistry from the University of Edinburgh in 1936. He went to the United States in 1938 and became a citizen in 1941. There he studied the protein constituents of many substances, including snake venoms, and conducted research on the effects of chemically altering the proteins. At the University of California at Berkeley, beginning in 1958, he and his colleagues took apart the tobacco mosaic virus. They showed that the virus's ability to infect plants resided in its core of ribonucleic acid (RNA) and restored this ability by recombining the components of the virus.

fragile X syndrome

Fragile X syndrome is the general term for cases of MENTAL RE-TARDATION that are linked with a genetic defect called "fragile X." Infants with the syndrome sometimes have minor structural abnormalities and may later exhibit such behaviors as hyperactivity and failure to make eye contact, as well as a range of learning disabilities. Males with the defect are about three times more likely than females to display symptoms, and they may also show AUTISM. The fragile X defect exists at the tip of the X chromosome (see GENETIC CODE), where a small portion tends to break fairly readily. Other such fragile sites occur, but this is the only one identified with a specific disorder. In fact, except for Down syndrome, fragile X syndrome is the most common chromosomal defect to be linked with mental retardation. Perhaps 1 out of every 1,500 persons in the general population is affected to some degree. The pattern of inheritance of the syndrome is not yet well understood.

Fragonard, Jean Honoré   [frah-goh-nar']

Jean Honoré Fragonard, b. Apr. 5, 1732, d. Apr. 22, 1806, was the last great French painter of the rococo period (see ROCOCO STYLE). "Frago," as he was known, was born in Grasse and moved with his family to Paris in 1738. About 1748, Fragonard was apprenticed to the painter J. B. S. CHARDIN; after only six months, however, he joined the studio of François BOUCHER, where he remained for four years. From 1756 to 1761, Fragonard was a student at the French Academy in Rome. While in Italy he developed an interest in landscape drawing and produced some of the most luminous and majestic nature studies ever made. His primary style, however, remained rococo, as he had learned it from Boucher. Although some of Fragonard's later works foreshadow 19th-century romanticism, for the most part he adhered to the subjects and style of the rococo even after they had become outmoded.

The character of the society in which Fragonard's art flourished is epitomized in such works as *The Swing* (c.1767; Wallace Collection, London) and the four paintings originally constituting the *Progress of Love* suite (1771; Frick Collection, New York). *The Swing* was commissioned by the Baron de Saint-Julien, who directed Fragonard to depict his mistress on a swing and the baron himself in a position to glimpse her legs beneath her skirts as she swings above him. The Frick canvases, created for Madame du Barry, are a playful narration of the theme of pursuit and conquest. All four scenes are embroidered with ornamental patterns of branches, leaves, and flowers. These paintings celebrate a life-style that encouraged a joyous abandonment to the pleasures of the senses and to the delights of gaiety and wit. Fragonard's facile and confi-

The voluptuous nudes of the Bathers, *by the French rococo artist Jean Honoré Fragonard, are painted in a luminous, fluid, and spontaneous style; sensuality is balanced by innocence and grace, as the frivolity is balanced by consummate brushwork. (Louvre, Paris.)*

dent brushwork is particularly evident in these works. Other paintings are still freer and bolder in handling. The *Bathers* (c.1765; Louvre, Paris) is almost a sketch, brushed in rapidly with broad strokes. The speed and dazzling bravura of which Fragonard was capable are also revealed in his fantasy portraits, for example, *Portrait of a Man,* or *The Warrior* (c.1769; Clark Art Institute, Williamstown, Mass.), which he is said to have painted in only one hour. His fiery palette and flashing technique could well have inspired the Goncourt brothers' pronouncement that Fragonard was "the final bonfire of the 18th century."   DONALD POSNER

Bibliography: Ashton, D., *Fragonard in the Universe of Painting* (1988); Cuzin, Jean-Pierre, *Fragonard: Life and Work* (1988); Rosenberg, Pierre, *Fragonard* (1988); Sheriff, Mary, *Fragonard: Art and Eroticism* (1990).

France

France is an independent nation in Western Europe and the center of a large but diminishing overseas administration. It is the largest Western European country. France is shaped roughly like a hexagon, and three of its six sides are bounded by water—the English Channel on the northwest, the Atlantic Ocean and Bay of Biscay on the west, and the Mediterranean Sea on the southeast. The remaining sides are mostly mountainous and are shared by seven European neighbors—Belgium and Luxembourg on the northeast; Germany, Switzerland, and Italy on the east; and Spain and tiny Andorra on

FRENCH REPUBLIC

LAND. Area: 543,965 km² (210,026 mi²). Capital and largest city: Paris (1990 pop., 2,152,423).
PEOPLE. Population (1991 est.): 56,942,000; density: 104.7 persons per km² (271 per mi²). Distribution (1990): 74% urban, 26% rural. Average annual growth (1990): 0.5%. Official language: French. Major religion: Roman Catholicism.
EDUCATION AND HEALTH. Literacy (1990): 99% of adult population. Universities (1989): 72. Hospital beds (1988): 686,854. Physicians (1988): 177,746. Life expectancy (1990): 77. Infant mortality (1990): 7.5 per 1,000 live births.
ECONOMY. GNP (1990): $1,191 billion; $21,080 per capita. Labor distribution (1989): services—63.7%; industry—22.6%; agriculture—6.5%; construction—7.2%. Foreign trade (1990): imports—$232 billion; exports—$210 billion; principal trade partners—Germany, Italy, Belgium-Luxembourg, United Kingdom, United States. Currency: 1 franc = 100 centimes.
GOVERNMENT. Type: republic. Legislature: Parliament—National Assembly and Senate. Political subdivisions: 22 regions, 96 metropolitan departments, 4 overseas departments, 4 overseas territories, 2 collective territories.
COMMUNICATIONS. Railroads (1989): 36,680 km (22,792 mi) total. Roads (1989): motorways and national roads—35,300 km (21,934 mi); other roads—1,500,000 km (932,056 mi). Major ports: 6. Major airfields: 10.

the south. France's eighth neighbor is Monaco, located on the Mediterranean coast near Nice and entirely surrounded by French territory. The diameter of the hexagon measures close to 1,000 km (620 mi) from each of its six corners to the opposite corner.

In ancient times France was part of the Celtic territory known as Gaul or Gallia. Its present name is derived from the Latin *Francia,* meaning "country of the Franks," a Germanic people who conquered the area during the 5th century, at the time of the fall of the Western Roman Empire. It became a separate country in the 9th century.

Since the 17th century France has played a major role in European and world events. In the 20th century it has experienced numerous crises, including the devastation of two world wars, political and social upheavals, and the loss of a large empire in Indochina, Algeria, and West and Equatorial Africa. It has, however, survived and emerged from the ruins of World War II to become an important world supplier of agricultural and industrial products and a major partner in the EUROPEAN COMMUNITY (EC).

Today, the term *metropolitan France* refers to the mainland departments and CORSICA, a large island located in the Medi-

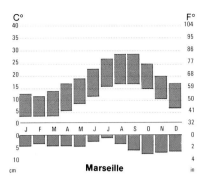

Marseille

Annual climate charts for two cities in France illustrate distinct climate zones in that country. Bars indicate the monthly ranges of temperatures (red) and precipitation (blue). Marseille, France's principal seaport, has a typically Mediterranean climate characterized by warm, dry summers and cool, wet winters. Paris, the nation's largest city, is located far inland on the banks of the Seine River in a low-lying plain called the Paris Basin. With its marine west-coast climate, Paris has precipitation year-round and a wide annual temperature range.

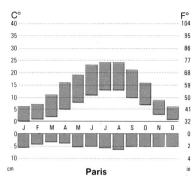

Paris

terranean Sea off the coast of Italy that has been a part of France since 1768. France has six overseas departments— FRENCH GUIANA in South America; GUADELOUPE and MARTINIQUE in the West Indies; MAYOTTE, an island formerly part of the Comoros, located in the Indian Ocean; RÉUNION, an island in the Indian Ocean; and SAINT PIERRE AND MIQUELON, islands off the east coast of Canada. In addition, France has numerous small possessions called overseas territories. These include a group of widely scattered islands in the South Pacific, which are administered from Tahiti and are known collectively as FRENCH POLYNESIA; FRENCH SOUTHERN AND ANTARCTIC TERRITORIES; NEW CALEDONIA and WALLIS AND FUTUNA ISLANDS; and many small islands in the southern oceans, including the Kerguelen and Crozet archipelagos, and the islands of St. Paul and Amsterdam (Indian Ocean). The overseas departments and territories are represented in the French National Assembly.

LAND AND RESOURCES

France may be divided into two regions by an imaginary line joining BIARRITZ in the southwest and Luxembourg in the northeast. Broad plains, low hills, and low plateaus predominate north and west of this line, and elevated plateaus and high mountains, including Mont BLANC (4,807 m/15,771 ft), the highest point in France and in Europe (outside of the USSR), are found south and east of the line. Linking the two types of terrain, as well as providing easy communication with other parts of Europe, are several wide valleys and gaps, including the BELFORT GAP, the Saône valley, the upper Rhône valley, the combined Rhône-Saône corridor south of LYON, and the gaps at CARCASSONNE and TOULOUSE.

France is sometimes described as a microcosm of Europe because the three major types of European landforms—sedimentary basins and lowlands, worn-down Hercynian mountain blocks, and younger, folded mountain belts—are all well represented in France. The principal sedimentary basin is the Paris Basin, which forms a vast, saucer-shaped lowland, covering about 100,000 km² (39,000 mi²) and composed of alternating layers of hard and soft rocks that afford a varied relief. The smaller Aquitaine Basin, also sedimentary, lies southwest of the Paris Basin. Other lowlands include several long, narrow plains that run north-south, including the Alsace Plain west of the Rhine and the Rhône-Saône corridor, and coastal plains, including the Languedoc Plain, along the Mediterranean coast. The basins and plains have fertile soils, notably loam and alluvial deposits, and are excellent for farming.

The Hercynian mountain blocks are remnants of ancient mountains formed during the Hercynian orogeny (a mountain-building period during the Carboniferous and Permian periods, 340 to 230 million years ago) and subsequently worn down before being uplifted during the Tertiary Period (65 to 2 million years ago). The principal uplands are the Armorican Massif, the MASSIF CENTRAL, the VOSGES, and the ARDENNES. The Armorican Massif, located in northwestern France, is composed mainly of low plateaus. The Massif Central is located in south-central France between the Rhône-Saône corridor and the Aquitaine Basin, and consists of plateaus that rise to more than 1,000 m (3,300 ft). The Auvergne Mountains, of volcanic origin, rise from the plateaus. The Vosges are located in eastern France between the Paris Basin and the Alsace Plain, and reach more than 1,200 m (4,000 ft) in the Ballons d'Alsace. A

small portion of the Ardennes, which lie mostly in Belgium and Luxembourg, extends into France. The soils in all the Hercynian uplands are usually thin and developed on underlying granite and crystalline rocks.

The two principal mountain chains in France are the PYRENEES, which form the border with Spain, and the ALPS, which form most of the border with Switzerland and Italy. The Pyrenees are difficult to cross because of their high altitude—several summits exceed 3,000 m (10,000 ft)—and the absence of low passes. The French Alps, the western end of the European Alpine chain, are also high and rugged, with elevations of 3,500 m (11,500 ft). Unlike the Pyrenees, however, the Alps are broken by several important river valleys, including the Rhône, Isère, and Durance, providing access to Switzerland and Italy. The JURA, a mountain range on the Swiss border, are lower and less rugged components of the Alpine chain.

France's coastline is 3,427 km (2,129 mi) long, including 644 km (400 mi) on Corsica. The character of the coastline ranges from sandy and straight, as in LANGUEDOC on the Mediterranean, to deeply indented capes and bays, as in BRITTANY, the CÔTE D'AZUR, and Corsica.

Climate. Four climatic types prevail in France. A true temperate maritime climate is found in the west, near the coasts, and is exemplified at BREST, where winters are mild (7° C/45° F in January), summers are cool (16° C/61° F in July), and rainfall is frequent (800 mm/32 in) during 180 days of the year. A midlatitude continental climate prevails in the interior of the country, with hotter summers (average July temperature of 18° C/64° F in PARIS) and more rigorous winters (average January temperature of 2° C/36° F in Paris), and rain falls on fewer days of the year.

A mountain climate prevails at high elevations, where temperatures are influenced mainly by altitude, and winters are generally bitterly cold and prolonged. Precipitation increases with elevation and occurs in the form of snow in winter, many villages in the high valleys receiving more than 50 days of snow each year. Briançon, in the Alps, has a mean temperature of −2° C (28° F) in January, and 17° C (63° F) in July; annual precipitation there averages 587 mm (23 in). A Mediterranean type of climate is found in a zone about 20 to 60 km (12 to 35 mi) wide along the Mediterranean coast. It is characterized by hot, dry summers, mild and humid winters, and a small number of rainy days during the year. In MARSEILLE, 550 mm (22 in) of rain falls during 60 days of the year, and the sun shines for over 3,000 hours yearly. The average temperature is 7° C (45° F) in January and 23° C (73° F) in July.

Drainage. The SEINE, the best-known river in France, passes through Paris and drains the Paris Basin. It is 776 km (482 mi) long. The major tributaries are the MARNE, Oise, and Yonne rivers. The LOIRE, with a length slightly more than 1,000 km (620 mi), is France's largest river. Its major tributaries are the Sarthe, Loir, Vienne, Cher, and Allier. The RHÔNE—the deepest river, with the largest volume of flow—has a length of only 523 km (325 mi) in France (the upper reaches are in Switzerland) and receives, among its major tributaries, the SAÔNE and ISÈRE rivers. The Garonne and Dordogne rivers, also important, join below BORDEAUX to form the Gironde.

Vegetation and Animal Life. France was entirely wooded before the Neolithic Period, when deciduous forests, principally beeches and oaks, covered the country except for temperate

This view of Paris, capital of France and the country's economic and cultural center, is taken from the Eiffel Tower, the landmark that was built for the International Exposition of 1889. The 300-m (984-ft) tower directly overlooks the Champ-de-Mars, and the view from its topmost platform can extend for 80 km (50 mi).

mountain forests composed of firs and piceas, and Mediterranean forests of pines and oaks in the southeast. Because of centuries of intensive agricultural and pastoral activity, the forests have been largely destroyed. Extensive forests now exist only in the mountains, on soils that are unsuitable for agriculture, and in protected forest preserves.

The original fauna, comprised mostly of deer, roebucks, and wild boars, has been virtually eliminated. Since the end of the 19th century, however, programs to protect the natural environment have been implemented, particularly in the national and regional parks. Conifers have been planted in reforestation programs in all parts of the country, and forests now cover 25% of France's land area.

Resources. Although diverse, the natural resources of France are relatively limited in quantity. France has some coal, iron ores, bauxite, and uranium; but the coal veins are deep and difficult to work and are unsuitable for use in the manufacture of steel. Iron ores are of a low grade, and the uranium ore is found only in small quantities. Deposits of petroleum are almost nonexistent, and natural gas reserves discovered (1951) at Lacq in the Pyrenees are now nearly exhausted. Hydroelectric production, although well developed, does not meet France's needs. On the other hand, high-quality soils cover almost half the country's surface, giving France an agricultural surplus that makes it an exporter of food.

PEOPLE

The modern French population is largely native-born and represents a fusion of many peoples of Celtic, Germanic, Latin, and Slavic origins. Contrary to what has happened in many other countries, the immigrants have blended so well into existing French society that today it is difficult to determine the ethnic origins of most French citizens. More ethnically prominent are the 20th-century immigrants, including an estimated 4 million foreigners—mainly Portuguese, Spanish, and Italians—and many French citizens, a large number of them Arabs, who have recently entered France from former French colonies in Algeria and sub-Saharan Africa. In 1990 an estimated 2.5 million North Africans lived in France.

The French language is understood and spoken by virtually the entire population, although other languages and dialects persist alongside French in peripheral areas; they include BASQUE, Alsatian, Corsican, Breton, Provençal, Catalan, and Flemish. About 80% of the population nominally belongs to the Roman Catholic church, although only a minority participates regularly in church activities. Protestants constitute less than 2% of the population; Jews, about 1%; Muslims, who have entered France recently from former North African colonies, about 4%.

Demography. In 1801, France, with a population of 28 million, was the most populous country in Europe; by 1850, the population had grown to 36 million. During the late 19th and early 20th centuries, however, the French birthrate dropped to

(Right) An agricultural laborer unloads his burden of freshly harvested wine grapes. France and its neighbor Italy are the world's largest producers of wine. France, however, is distinguished for its prestigious specialty wines—including champagne, Bordeaux, and Burgundy—which are named for their regions of origin.

levels lower than those in the rest of Europe, and France experienced a much slower rate of population growth than the rest of the continent. At the end of World War II the population was only 40 million. After 1946, however, the birthrate rose to 21 per 1,000, a higher rate than had existed for more than a century. Although the rate fell to 18 per 1,000 in 1963 and to 13.6 per 1,000 in 1989, the last few decades have witnessed an unprecedented expansion of the population that added millions of people to France's schools and, later, to the labor force and consumer markets.

This unusual demographic evolution explains why population densities in France today are only one-half to one-third that of other Western European nations. Within France, the population distribution is uneven and closely reflects levels of economic development. Regions without industry or with poor soils are only sparsely populated. On the other hand, the regions with the largest populations are the great centers of economic activity: the industrial north; Lyon, where industry is important; along the Côte d'Azur, which depends on tourism; and especially Paris, where diverse economic activities are concentrated.

Since 1950, France has experienced rapid urbanization. Almost all cities have increased in size, at the expense of the rural population. In the early 1990s more than three-quarters of the country's population lived in cities, and the figure is even higher when commuters are included. France has, therefore, now largely caught up with the rest of Europe in its urbanization. The country is unusual in its urban structure. Metropolitan Paris is the home of one-sixth of France's population and is the largest urban agglomeration in Europe outside the USSR. Other French cities are small by comparison, the largest being the metropolitan areas of Lyon (1.2 million) and Marseille (1.1 million); next in size is LILLE, which has a metropolitan area of 1,020,000; after that comes Bordeaux, which has 640,000, Toulouse (541,000), NANTES (465,000), NICE (450,000), and STRASBOURG (400,000).

Education and Health. Education is compulsory for all children between the ages of 6 and 16, who may attend either free public schools or fee-charging private schools run mostly by the Roman Catholic church. About one-sixth of schoolchildren attend the private schools. Preschool education for children between the ages of 2 and 6 is optional but is now widely accepted; more than 2.3 million children are enrolled in preschool programs. Children between the ages of 6 and 11 attend primary schools, and all proceed at age 12 to secondary schools, called *lycées* and *collèges*. Work in the secondary schools is divided into a compulsory first cycle for ages 12 to 16, after which a student may leave school or take an optional second cycle of courses; students who wish to pursue higher education take the long course of the second cycle and are prepared for the difficult *baccalauréat* exam, which is the minimum university entrance requirement. Students who will pursue a technical career take a short course that offers practical training.

Beginning in 1980 the Mitterrand government introduced greater local control and a more flexible curriculum into the formerly highly centralized school system. A plan to extend state control over private schools was abandoned because of widespread public opposition.

Higher education is free to qualified students. Nearly one million students, or five times as many as a generation ago, now continue their studies after secondary school in 72 universities, and in technological institutes and *grandes écoles* (prestigious schools that prepare students for high-ranking careers in business and government).

France's state-subsidized medical system is considered lib-

Lyon, the capital of Rhône department, is the third-largest city and the second-largest metropolitan area in France. The city became a major commercial center at the beginning of the Christian era because of its location at the confluence of the Rhône and Saône rivers. Since the 15th century Lyon has been famous for the production of silk fabrics.

eral because doctors and dentists establish private practices, and patients, who are free to choose their own doctors and dentists, are reimbursed by the state for up to 85% of medical costs. Hospital facilities, although greatly expanded since World War II, are still considered inadequate. Doctors tend to be concentrated in the cities and are in short supply in some rural areas. The death rate, life expectancy, and infant mortality rate are similar to those of other industrialized nations. As is true of most developed countries, the principal causes of death are cancer and cardiovascular diseases.

The Arts. French literature includes a roster of world-famous novelists, poets, playwrights, and philosophers. Many of the new art movements of the 19th and 20th centuries, including IMPRESSIONISM and CUBISM, began in France. A ministry of culture was established in 1959 to preserve this rich cultural heritage and to make it more widely available outside of Paris. Cultural institutions have now been established throughout the country, and numerous expositions and festivals are held during the summer. (See FRENCH ART AND ARCHITECTURE; FRENCH LITERATURE; and FRENCH MUSIC.)

ECONOMIC ACTIVITY

By the 18th century France was one of the world's richest nations. Industrialization began promisingly at the end of the 18th century, as it did in England. Unlike England and the rest of Europe, however, France failed to maintain the momentum of its early industrial start and was still primarily an agricultural nation at the end of the 19th century. Industry expanded behind protective trade barriers in the early 20th century, but most growth has occurred since the end of World War II. France now ranks among the world's most economically advanced nations.

A distinctive feature of the postwar French economy has been national economic development plans. The first, the Monnet Plan (named for Jean MONNET, who conceived it), ran from 1947 to 1953. Railways were nationalized in 1937, and many other sectors of the economy, including the coal, natural gas, electricity, banking, and transportation (Renault and Air France), came under state control shortly after World War II. Other major industries were nationalized in the early 1980s. The increasing state control of production has been matched by a partial removal of protective trade tariffs and membership in the European Community.

Manufacturing. In the early 1990s manufacturing employed between 20% and 25% of the labor force. The principal industrial concentrations are around Paris, in the Nord-Pas de Calais and Lorraine coalfields, in the Lyon and SAINT-ÉTIENNE complex of the Rhône valley, and in the new industrial centers that have emerged in the English Channel ports of DUNKERQUE and LE HAVRE and the Mediterranean industrial complex at Fos (west of Marseille) because of the use of imported raw materials. Many French business enterprises are small to moderate in size, although the competitive business climate created by membership in the EC has forced many companies to be restructured and combined to form powerful corporations.

The leading manufacturing industries are metallurgy, mechanical and electrical engineering, chemicals, and textiles. In 1986, France ranked third in Europe (excluding the USSR) in steel production (after West Germany and Italy), with an output of 14.8 million metric tons (16.3 million U.S. tons), and second (after West Germany) in aluminum output. These and imported metals are fabricated into a wide range of mechanical and electrical equipment marketed throughout the world. French locomotives, turbines, electronics equipment, nuclear power plants and submarines, and television systems are famous for their innovative design, as are French automobiles, such as Citroën, Peugeot, Simca, and Renault, and French aircraft, such as Mirage, Concorde, and Airbus. In 1985, France ranked fourth in the world (after Japan, the United States, and West Germany) in production of passenger cars and third (after Japan and the United States) in output of commercial vehicles. A wide range of chemicals, including perfumes, pharmaceuticals, nitric acid, sulfuric acid, and fertilizers, are also produced. The French textile and garment industry has long been known for its high fashion, although in re-

Hayange, an industrial community in Moselle department, is the oldest iron-working center in the Lorraine region of northeastern France. Lorraine, where much of the nation's heavy industry is concentrated, contains sizable deposits of coal, iron ore, and potash.

cent years the industry has lost many former markets to lower-priced imports from countries with lower labor costs.

Mining. Less than 1% of the labor force is engaged in mining. In 1988 coal production was 14.5 million metric tons (16 million U.S. tons), most of it from two principal coalfields—the Lorraine coalfield near METZ, which is an extension into France of the Saar coalfield; and the Nord-Pas de Calais coalfield around Lille, which is an extension into France of Belgium's Sambre-Meuse coalfields and is similarly thin-seamed, faulted, and difficult to work. Since the 1950s many inefficient mines in the north and in the Massif Central have been closed, and coal output has declined by about 75%. The Lorraine basin will probably be the only producing area left by the end of the century.

Lorraine has the largest iron ore deposits in Europe outside the Soviet Union, but the deposits have a low iron content and are in less demand than higher-grade imported ores. Large bauxite deposits (from which aluminum is produced) are mined in the south; France is one of Europe's leading producers of bauxite. Potash deposits, used in the chemical industry, are extensive in the vicinity of MULHOUSE. Natural gas deposits have been worked since 1951 near PAU, close to the Spanish border. The natural gas has a high sulfur content, and France is a major European supplier of this mineral, which is extracted at Lacq. Small amounts of petroleum are produced at the Parentis oilfield in the southwest, and the search for petroleum deposits continues off the coast of Brittany and in the Bay of BISCAY.

Power. France's fuel resources are inadequate. The country has to import about three-quarters of the fuel, mainly petroleum, needed to meet its requirements. However, production of electrical energy is significant. In 1988 output reached 372 billion kW h, with nuclear energy representing 70% of the total. France is the world's second-largest supplier of nuclear power (after the United States). Hydroelectric plants operate on the Isere, Durance, Rhine, Rhône, and Dordogne rivers. A tidal power plant is located on the Rance River in Brittany.

Agriculture and Fishing. France is the leading agricultural nation in Europe (excluding the USSR), and about 7% of the labor force is engaged in agriculture, forestry, and fishing. Three-fifths of the land area is used for agriculture; about 31% is cultivated, 3% is in vineyards and orchards, and 24% is used as meadow and pasture. Since the end of World War II, agricultural policy has been directed toward modernization of agriculture, including mechanization of farms, raising productivity per hectare, and consolidating numerous small holdings into larger, more efficient, farms.

In 1988, 47.6% of France's farm income came from livestock raising. Cattle are raised mainly in the north and west; sheep and goats are raised primarily in the drier, more mountainous south and east, and pigs and chickens are raised throughout the country. France is Europe's (excluding the USSR) leading producer of beef, veal, poultry, and cheese and a leading producer of milk and eggs.

Crops contribute about 52% of farm income, with cereals and sugar beets the most important products. Wheat is widely grown in the Paris Basin, and France ranks fifth in world wheat production. Other grains grown are barley, corn, and oats, which, with sugar beet factory residues, are used primarily for livestock feed; some rice is grown under irrigation in the Rhône delta. Wine is a major crop throughout the country, both the *vin ordinaire,* or everyday wine, of the region and the *appellation contrôlée,* or quality-controlled, wines of such regions as BURGUNDY, CHAMPAGNE, Bordeaux, and Alsace (see ALSACE-LORRAINE). In recent years the government has tried to discourage overproduction of wine. Flowers are grown for perfume at Grasse, and a wide variety of fruits and vegetables are raised in the warm Mediterranean region for shipment to northern and central Europe.

Fishing, unlike agriculture, occupies only a modest place in the economy, but France ranks 20th among the nations of the world in total fish production. Fishing is locally important in the coastal areas of Normandy and Brittany, the southern Atlantic coast, and the Mediterranean. Concarneau, BOULOGNE-SUR-MER, Lorient, and LA ROCHELLE are leading fishing ports.

Transportation. Major efforts have been made since World War II to improve and modernize the extensive French transportation system and to lessen its historical focus on the Paris metropolitan area. Train service, provided by the state, is fast and efficient, especially on the more than 12,000 km (7,456 mi) of electrified track. The French National Railways' Trains à Grande Vitesse (TGV, "high speed trains") are world famous. In 1988 a consortium of French and British construction companies began work on the English Channel Tunnel or "Chunnel," scheduled for completion in 1993, which will establish the first direct rail link between France and Britain. Airlines are also state run; Air France is one of the world's largest airline companies.

France's road system provides access to all parts of the nation. The network of expressways (7,000 km or 4,350 mi) is in the process of being expanded. In 1990 there were 23 million passenger cars and more than 5 million trucks and buses. Waterways carry much of the nation's bulk freight; the three principal waterways deep enough to accommodate the 1,500-ton barges common in Europe are the Rhine River, the Seine between Le Havre and Paris, and the canalized section of the Moselle below Metz.

Trade and Tourism. France is the fourth-largest exporter and the fifth-largest importer on the foreign trade market. The two principal ports are Marseille and its annexes on the Mediterranean, and Le Havre at the mouth of the Seine on the English Channel. In 1989 major imports broke down as follows: machinery (26.6%); chemicals and chemical products (15.7%); agricultural products (11.6%); automobiles (5.8%); petroleum and petroleum products (4.5%); other fuels (4.3%). Major exports were machinery (27.7%), agricultural products (17.5%), chemicals (15.1%), and transportation equipment (12.7%). Most trade is conducted with other members of the European Community. In 1989 more than 42 million foreign tourists visited France, which ranked third among the nations of the world in numbers of tourists (after Spain and the United States).

GOVERNMENT

France's political institutions have undergone several changes since the 1789 revolution. The present constitution, adopted in 1958 and revised in 1962, established the Fifth Republic and provided for a powerful president, originally Charles DE GAULLE, and a bicameral legislature with less power than it had in the past. The president is elected by direct popular vote for a 7-year term. He appoints the prime minister and may dissolve the National Assembly.

The legislature consists of a 318-member Senate elected indirectly by an electoral college, and a politically more important 577-member, directly elected National Assembly. The five overseas departments of French Guiana, Guadeloupe, Martinique, Réunion, and St. Pierre and Miquelon are represented in the National Assembly, as are New Caledonia, Mayotte, Wallis and Futuna Islands, and French Polynesia. Senate members serve 9-year terms, with one-third of the seats falling due for election every three years. The National Assembly is elected every five years. The minimum voting age is 18 years.

The four leading French political parties are the Socialist party; the conservative Rassemblement pour la republique (RPR), founded by Charles de Gaulle and now led by Jacques CHIRAC; the Union pour la démocratie française (UDF); and the French Communist party. François MITTERRAND, leader of the Socialist party, was elected president in May 1981, giving the Fifth Republic its first socialist government. When a UDF-RPR coalition won a majority of seats in the parliamentary election of 1986, Mitterrand had to call on opposition leader Chirac to form a government, marking another first for the Fifth Republic—a "cohabitation" arrangement in which the president and the prime minister were of different parties. The Chirac government modified many of the socialist reforms introduced earlier by Mitterrand. When Mitterrand was elected to a second term in 1988, he was able to replace Chirac with a succession of Socialist premiers. A second period of cohabition under Prime Minister Edouard Balladur began after a Socialist defeat at the polls in March 1993.

Local administration of France is organized around 22 admin-

Pastoral communities occupy the fertile valleys of the Pyrenees, a mountain range that forms the boundary between France and Spain. Although tourism and industry are of growing importance in the mountains, livestock raising remains the major occupation.

Terraced farmland surrounds an alpine village in northern Provence, a historic region in southeastern France adjacent to Italy. The southern portion of Provence, which extends to the Mediterranean Sea, is notable for its groves of citrus fruit and olives.

istrative regions and 96 metropolitan departments, and the Mitterrand government implemented (1982) a devolution plan, giving more authority to regions and departments. Each department covers about 5,000 km² (1,930 mi²) and is administered by an elected departmental council. Within the departments are about 36,000 communes, corresponding to the parishes of prerevolutionary France, which are small and are headed by elected mayors.   DANIEL NOIN
Reviewed by ANNE DEPIGNY AND AGNES JOLIVET

Bibliography:
GENERAL: Ardagh, John, *A Cultural Atlas of France* (1991); Bernstein, Richard, *Fragile Glory: A Portrait of France and the French* (1990); Braudel, Fernand, *The Identity of France*, vol. I, trans. by S. Reynolds (1989).
GEOGRAPHY: Clout, Hugh, *The Geography of Post-War France* (1972); Pinchemel, Philippe, *France: A Geographical, Social, and Economic Survey*, trans. by Dorothy and T. H. Elkins (1987); Tuppin, J., *The Economic Geography of France* (1983).
ECONOMY: Hough, Jean, *The French Economy* (1982); Keating, Michael, and Hainsworth, Paul, *Decentralization and Change in Contemporary France* (1986); Price, Roger, *An Economic History of Modern France* (1981).
POLITICS AND GOVERNMENT: Harrison, Martin, et al., *De Gaulle to Mitterrand: Presidential Power in France* (1993); McCarthy, Patrick, ed., *The French Socialists in Power* (1987); Pickles, Dorothy, *Problems of Contemporary French Politics* (1982); Safran, William, *French Polity*, 3d ed. (1991); Wright, Vincent, *The Government and Politics of France*, 3d ed. (1989).

France, history of

Modern French institutions and people are derived from 2,000 years of contacts with diverse cultures and peoples. Into the area now defined as France came the Celts, Romans, Franks, and other peoples, producing a mixture of practices and races. Since 1500 the French have formed a relatively unified territorial state in which diversity nevertheless persists.

ANCIENT GAUL

When Julius CAESAR invaded GAUL in 58 BC, he found a territory reaching from the Mediterranean to the North Sea, from

The conquest of France (ancient Gaul) by Julius Caesar during the Gallic Wars (58–51 BC) marked the beginning of 500 years of Roman rule. The Pont du Gard, a Roman aqueduct spanning the Gard River, is a product of the distinctive Gallo-Roman culture.

the Pyrenees and the Atlantic to the Rhine and the Alps. The population of possibly 10 million possessed neither homogeneous roots nor unified rule. Several centuries earlier, the CELTS had surged from their Danubian homeland into the valleys of the Rhine and Rhône and as far as today's Belgium, England, and Ireland. The newcomers mingled with the native Ligurians of the Alps, Iberians of the Pyrenees, and numerous folk elsewhere who were often of Phoenician, Greek, or Roman stock.

The Celts. Celtic rule in Gaul was decentralized. The Gauls (Latin for Celts) were basically grouped as members of clans that sometimes functioned separately and sometimes formed into one of over 400 tribes, which in turn often joined into one of the 70 or so nations. Thus the Gauls had no single leader or authority, and except for Marseille and Nice, they had no cities or towns either. Most lived in scattered mud huts generally surrounded by a stockade. Hunting, fishing, and pastoral pursuits supplied basic needs. Some surpluses and craftwork in wood and leather found their way to local markets for sale or exchange. Gallic religious life too was localized and pluralistic, with pantheistic worship of rivers, woods, and other elements of nature. The most widespread but not universal cult was that of the DRUIDS, centered in Brittany.

Roman Conquest. Roman legions marched into Gaul in 58 BC not only to protect the Roman republic's Mediterranean holdings but also to promote Julius Caesar's personal ambitions beyond his proconsulship of Cisalpine and Transalpine Gaul. The Gauls contributed to their own subjugation by their tribal rivalries and inability to resist the infiltration of trans-Rhenish barbarians and the Swiss (Helvetii). Caesar's speedy success in stopping the barbarians was followed by the conquest of all Gaul. The Roman victory was not due to superior numbers of troops but to their training, discipline, and weaponry and to Gallic disunity. Even the heroism of the Gallic prince VERCINGETORIX failed to halt or reverse the Roman conquest.

Five hundred years of Roman rule produced striking consequences for Gaul. Politically, the idea was planted of citizenship of a common state with a single set of laws and administrators and a more or less unified tax system. In practice, much localism remained, and the direct and indirect taxes were assessed and collected inequitably. If imperial Rome benefitted by holding provincial Gaul (from financial exactions, manpower, and cheap grain), the Gauls also derived economic advantage from their connection. Security against barbarians and bands of brigands encouraged the Gauls to clear more forests and farm more lands. Better roads, bridges, and communications fostered greater trade. Towns and vil-

lages began to appear in place of the mud-hut habitations.

Culturally, a taste for learning Latin and Greek was cultivated in rudimentary educational institutions in cities like Marseille, Bordeaux, and Lyons. Frequently, the interest was superficial, and outlying regions remained untutored in Latin. They also continued to practice old Celtic paganism and Druidism despite the spread of Christianity. As missionaries crisscrossed Gaul to convert the pagans and to organize the church, other Christians clustered in monasteries to pray and to establish islands of learning. When the Roman Empire collapsed, the surviving Roman church would be crucial for the retention of Gallic-Roman forms and practices.

FRANKISH KINGDOM

The 5th-century decline of Rome was disastrous for Gaul's political unity, economic development, and cultural life. An accelerated flow of barbarians—invading in variously sized groups of FRANKS, GOTHS, and Burgundians, rather than in a single coordinated force—began the process of splintering Gaul. However, as the Romans and Gauls had become assimilated, so too did the Gallo-Romans and the barbarians adopt each other's ways. The France that emerged by the year 1000 was thus a combination of Celts (Gauls), Romans, and barbarians (Franks, Teutons, Visigoths, Burgundians, Vandals, Vikings, and others).

Merovingians. Out of the welter of political and territorial shifts from the 5th to the 11th century, the church and the successive dynasties of the MEROVINGIANS (431–751) and the CAROLINGIANS (c.747–987) supplied links of continuity. The founder of the Frankish kingdom was CLOVIS (r. 481–511), a Merovingian. He completed work of his grandfather, the Salian Frankish chieftain Merowen, by first overwhelming the Gallo-Roman forces at Soissons in 486. Thereafter he extended Frankish rule over Burgundy and the whole southern region to the Pyrenees by defeating the Visigoths. A convert to Christianity in 496, Clovis found that his services to the church helped his own status in and beyond his new capital, PARIS.

Upon Clovis's death in 511, the Frankish kingdom was parcelled out among his four sons, whose heirs subdivided their holdings and waged bitter wars against one another and outsiders. In the last century of their rule, the Merovingians exhibited their declining authority even in their particular kingdoms. Aristocratic landowners whittled away at royal power in administrative, legal, military, and tax matters. Agriculture and trade were in disarray with the countryside ravaged by feuding chiefs and barbarian bands. Towns and villages, although still furnishing some shelter for occupants and rural refugees, dwindled as commerce ebbed. The strong influence of the church continued, with bishops protecting townsmen and monastic orders maintaining some semblance of culture, but even the church could not prevail against Merovingian rot. Finally, at the beginning of the 8th century, after decades of incompetent Merovingian rule over the remnants of the Frankish kingdom, the Carolingians, who had served as palace mayors (or advisors), secured the reins of power.

Carolingians. Even before a Carolingian, CHARLEMAGNE, became king of the Franks in 768 and emperor in 800, his grand-

The Carolingian king Charlemagne, who was crowned emperor of the West by Pope Leo III in 800, is depicted on this silver coin. During his reign trade routes were expanded, and coins bearing his image have been found throughout Europe. Carolingian currency was based on silver because of the scarcity of gold.

father CHARLES MARTEL had amassed sufficient power to "save" Europe from the Moors at Tours in 732. Martel's talents and military forces were passed on to Charlemagne's father, PEPIN THE SHORT, whose aid to the missionary Saint BONIFACE was compensated by the pope's endorsement of Pepin and his sons as the legitimate dynasty of the Frankish kingdom. Upon these foundations, Charlemagne waged innumerable wars and gained all Europe from the Pyrenees to the Vistula. His rule encompassed more than Gaul or the Frankish kingdom, but it left a strong imprint upon France nevertheless. It also foreshadowed the feudal system, which was already being born.

Within the Frankish state, the vigorous and attractive Charlemagne extended royal power and financial resources. In exchange for extensive but nonhereditary land grants and the right to levy local taxes, lords of manors furnished military and judicial services to the king, and the lower classes provided labor on road and other public works. As a check on the local notables, Charlemagne sent out teams of *missi dominici* (usually a bishop and a count) to inspect the districts and report on any irregularities. Two assemblies were held each year, possible forerunners of the States-General (parliament). In the spring session noblemen had opportunity to discuss their problems, and the king could present his program or impressions of the realm.

In his capital at AACHEN (Aix-la-Chapelle) and in other towns, Charlemagne rekindled intellectual life by gathering holy men, scholars, and literary figures like ALCUIN. Works of Greek and particularly Latin were copied and analyzed in new schools founded by favored churchmen. Charlemagne's encouragement of learning had perhaps more long-range significance for French and Western civilization than his sensational military and political ventures.

The Carolingian decline after Charlemagne followed the same pattern as the Merovingians' after Clovis. The same type of partition of lands, notably formalized in the Treaty of Verdun in 843 (see VERDUN, TREATY OF), resulted in the area roughly equivalent to medieval France being assigned to the Frankish emperor CHARLES II. He and his descendants held an ever-weakening grip over the kingdom against invading Vikings—who, as NORMANS, established the duchy of Normandy—and predatory lords. Over the shrunken French state the Capetian dynasty would achieve kingship by 987, and within that state the feudal system would flower.

CAPETIAN KINGDOM (987-1328)

For nearly 1,000 years, the house of Capet furnished France with kings, first as direct-line CAPETIANS and later through the branch families of Valois and Bourbon. The line was literally cut by the guillotining of Louis XVI in 1792, although his brothers Louis XVIII and Charles X and his distant cousin Louis-Philippe served as monarchs after Napoleon I.

Between Hugh Capet's coronation in 987 and the succession of the Valois in 1328 or the inception of the Hundred Years' War in 1338, the feudal system became crystallized along with the concept of French kingships. Cities and towns revived, peopled by bourgeois citizens engaged in a resurgent trade of agricultural and craft products. A cathedral-building boom satisfied the religious spirit and supplied jobs. The Crusades absorbed the energies of kings, counts, clergy, and commoners. And the Norman conquest of England established the centuries-long connection and rivalry with that island kingdom.

FEUDALISM, rooted in land grants of Charlemagne and the subsequent breakdown of his empire, became almost inevitable when weak kings failed to check the Viking incursions of the 9th and 10th centuries. Surely but haphazardly, feudalism developed as a contractual arrangement between lord and king, and MANORIALISM came to determine the relationship between lord and peasant. As warriors for the king, the lords were bound to render military service at their own cost. In return, not only did they receive hereditary title to tracts as large as provinces but also the right to tax, oversee, and judge their inhabitants. Toward their subjects, the lords owed protection and the preservation of order; from them, they were due loyalty, rents, fees, and obligations of a military and economic nature.

KINGDOM OF ENGLAND

English Channel

KINGDOM OF ARLES

HOLY ROMAN EMPIRE

C. OF FLANDERS
D. OF BRABANT
HAINAUT
C. OF AMIENS
C. OF VERMANDOIS
DUCHY OF NORMANDY
Strasbourg
C. OF MAINE
ÎLE OF FRANCE
Paris
DUCHY OF BRITTANY
C. OF ANJOU
Orléans
DUCHY OF BURGUNDY
C. OF POITOU
BAY OF BISCAY
DUCHY OF AQUITAINE
Bordeaux
COUNTY OF TOULOUSE
C. OF VIVIERS
DUCHY OF GASCONY
C. OF PROVENCE
SPANISH KINGDOMS
MEDITERRANEAN SEA

km 300
mi 200

FRANCE 1154-80

☐ French domains   ☐ English domains
☐ Fiefs of French crown   ☐ English possessions

Cartographic Production by Lothar Roth & Associates

This map shows the extensive English land holdings in France during the 12th century. With the marriage of Eleanor of Aquitaine and Henry II of England, the area of France under English control was greater than that under the royal domain of the French king Louis VII.

(Left) Louis IX (r. 1226-70) of France, who was canonized in 1297, is portrayed instructing his son, the future King Philip III, in this 14th-century miniature from the Recueil de traités de dévotion. The generally peaceful reign of Saint Louis was characterized by his religious concerns and the establishment of a French judicial system.

The relative strength of lords and kings often depended not upon title but upon personal traits and capabilities, extent of landholdings, resources available, alliances possible, and church support. The local lords' power was demonstrated in the election of HUGH CAPET to the kingship in 987. His predecessors were mere counts of Anjou and Blois, and his supporters included the duke of Normandy. As kings, the Capetians were in actual possession of only their family lands of central France—the Île de France—situated around Paris and

Orléans. It was long a question how much authority would be allowed the kings of France in the lands of the dukes or counts of NORMANDY, AQUITAINE, BURGUNDY, and FLANDERS. An outstanding example was the case of the dukes of Normandy. Duke William's conquest of England in 1066 and his ascent to the English throne, as WILLIAM I, obviously made the subsequent dukes of Normandy/kings of England awesome competitors to their feudal overlords, the kings of France. The English kings extended their French holdings even further when ELEANOR OF AQUITAINE, after the annulment of her marriage to the pious Capetian LOUIS VII, married (1152) the future HENRY II of England.

To tip the precarious balance in their favor, shrewd Capetian kings frequently encouraged and linked up with the new middle class, whose urban and commercial interests often clashed with the warrior and rural concerns of the feudal lords. Royal charters granted special privileges and wider markets to the bourgeoisie, and the bourgeois could pay. Churchmen too could be wooed to the king's side with his patronage for cathedrals, schools, and crusades. With glaring exceptions and tragic consequences, French participation in the CRUSADES stimulated a spirit of national rather than local pride, tied the church more closely to the monarchy, and created contacts with Italy and the Middle East for French merchants and scholars.

Of unquestionable vitality in this medieval era was the cultural expression. In monasteries and universities, churchmen and laymen studied, discussed, and debated theological tracts, Greek and Latin works, and a spate of literature beginning to appear in the vernacular French language.

CONSOLIDATION OF ROYAL POWER (1328-1715)

Such Capetians as Hugh Capet, PHILIP II, LOUIS IX, and PHILIP IV succeeded in upholding and enlarging the royal prerogative beyond their family lands; other Capetians failed. The VALOIS branch (1328–1589), after a dreary start and before a whimpering end, drove the English out of France, consolidated the kingdom, asserted royal authority, launched expeditions into Italy, and ushered in a cultural Renaissance. What the Valois left undone was completed by the BOURBONS.

From the Hundred Years' War to the Wars of Religion. The expulsion of the English involved the French in the HUNDRED YEARS' WAR (1338–1453), a conflict of intermittent intensity. Mixed into the origins of the war were the quest for commer-

The chronicles of Jean Froissart recorded the history of western Europe from the early 1300s to 1400, a period that covered the first half of the Hundred Years' War. This miniature shows the attack (1373) on Brest by the English. The long conflict between France and England finally ended when Castillon fell to Charles VII in 1453 and the English were expelled from France (except Calais).

Huguenots (French Protestants) are shown under attack by French soldiers after the revocation of the Edict of Nantes in 1685. The edict, which granted toleration to the Huguenots, had been promulgated (1598) by King Henry IV to bring to an end the prolonged Wars of Religion of the 16th century. Government persecution against Protestants was resumed in 1685, however, when Louis XIV revoked it.

cial and political prizes in Flanders and the duel between the English and French kings for Normandy, Aquitaine, and other provinces. One highlight of the war was the contribution of Saint JOAN OF ARC. Inspired by visions instructing her to present herself to the Dauphin (later CHARLES VII) and free Orléans from the English, she in turn inspired the Dauphin, his advisors, and the public. Although she was burned at the stake in 1431, her mission was accomplished within a generation. Relieved of the English presence, the French monarchs, notably LOUIS XI (r. 1461–83), finished the task of consolidating the kingdom. They then began to seek extension of their power beyond the boundaries of France. CHARLES VIII invaded Italy in 1494, launching the ITALIAN WARS and a long dynastic rivalry with the Habsburgs of Austria and Spain.

Sixteenth-century France was blessed by two strong kings, FRANCIS I and HENRY II, and cursed by three weak ones, the sons of Henry II by CATHERINE DE MÉDICIS. French prosperity and solidarity were spoiled not only by the weak monarchs but by the Wars of Religion (see RELIGION, WARS OF) after 1560. Catholics battled Calvinist HUGUENOTS, each faction aspiring to control the monarchy. Catherine de Médicis steered a Machiavellian course to maintain her children's status. However, she was barely outlived by her last son, HENRY III, who was assassinated in 1589. This paved the way for the first Bourbon, HENRY IV, leader of the Huguenots, to fight and compromise his road to the throne by 1598. He satisfied Huguenots by the tolerant Edict of Nantes in 1598 (see NANTES, EDICT OF) and mollified Catholics by his own conversion so as to enter the Paris he considered "worth a Mass."

Bourbon Reconstruction. By tact, persuasion, and force, Henry IV reduced religious tensions, stimulated commerce and manufacturing, and curbed the nobility. The last process was vigorously pursued by cardinals RICHELIEU and MAZARIN, the de facto rulers of France under Henry's weak son LOUIS XIII.

It was LOUIS XIV, however, who truly tamed the aristocracy, at least until the end (1715) of his own absolutist reign. Already deprived by Richelieu of their fortresses in the countryside, prohibited from dueling, and subjected to royal edicts and administrators, the nobles were turned by Louis into powerless courtiers, forced to attend him in the new Palace of Versailles (see VERSAILLES, PALACE OF). The grandeur of Versailles, imitated by so many European monarchs, was not merely architectural and social in value. It was also a focal point from which emanated favors and patronage for artists, writers, and scientists.

In this period the bourgeoisie was the beneficiary of mercantilist policies (see MERCANTILISM) developed most notably by Jean Baptiste COLBERT. The interests of the royal treasury

The grandiose temperament of Louis XIV is captured in this portrait (1694) by the French artist Hyacinthe Rigaud. Known as "Le Roi Soleil" (The Sun King), Louis established an absolute monarchy and expanded French territorial holdings. His Palace at Versailles is a lasting testimony to the grandeur of his long reign (1643–1715). (Prado, Madrid.)

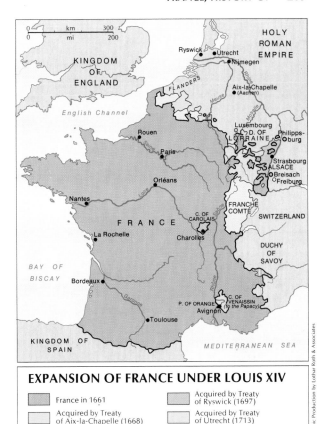

EXPANSION OF FRANCE UNDER LOUIS XIV

- France in 1661
- Acquired by Treaty of Aix-la-Chapelle (1668)
- Acquired by Treaty of Nijmegen (1678)
- Acquired by Treaty of Ryswick (1697)
- Acquired by Treaty of Utrecht (1713)
- Ceded to Savoy (1696–1713)

Cartographic Production by Lothar Roth & Associates

(Above) The military campaigns of King Louis XIV expanded French territorial control, with the goal of European supremacy. Shaded areas of the map indicate France as it was in 1661 and its substantial territorial gains in subsequent years. (Below) The provinces of France as they were during the ancien régime before the Revolution.

PROVINCES OF FRANCE BEFORE THE FRENCH REVOLUTION

often coincided with subsidies for manufacturing and for expanded internal, colonial, and foreign trade. The middle class and the peasantry paid, however, by a heavy tax burden to finance Louis XIV's wars and other enterprises.

French influence abroad rose as the secular-minded Cardinal Richelieu engaged Catholic Frenchmen as allies with Protestant princes against the Holy Roman emperors, the German Catholic princes, and Spain in the THIRTY YEARS' WAR, after which France gained Alsace by the Peace of Westphalia (1648). Louis XIV further expanded French territory in Europe and overseas and placed his grandson on the Spanish throne as PHILIP V—all through wars, diplomacy, and marriage.

THE OLD REGIME AND THE ENLIGHTENMENT (1715–89)

After Louis XIV's death, the kingdom remained unified, powerful, and prosperous, despite some distressing signs. As Europe's most populous, single unified state, endowed with the greatest military and economic resources, France did not cease to be a great power. It even extended its boundaries by the acquisition (1766) of Lorraine. Colonially, however, the story was different. The FRENCH EMPIRE that had come into being in the 17th century was largely lost to Britain as a result of the SEVEN YEARS' WAR (1756–63).

Revival of the Nobility. LOUIS XV and LOUIS XVI retained, in principle, divine right and absolute sovereignty—legislative, executive, judicial, administrative, and military. In practice, however, these kings failed to exercise that power, whether through lack of interest, lack of capacity, or lack of ruthlessness. Consequently the nobility of old feudal blood (nobility of the sword) and of the purchased variety (nobility of the robe) moved to displace the bourgeoisie and fill the functions of state at Versailles, in the provinces, army, and church. The first two estates—clergy and nobility—aimed to dominate France and keep their many privileges. This "reinfeudation" displeased the third estate—the rest of the population. Although increasingly prominent in the economic advances of the period, the bourgeoisie found itself excluded from political posts and unfairly shouldering the tax burden along with the lower classes.

Enlightenment. The most illustrious aspect of the Old Regime was the work and influence of its philosophers of the ENLIGHTENMENT. From the essays, tracts, encyclopedias, novels, plays, and letters of such intellectual giants as Denis DIDEROT, MONTESQUIEU, VOLTAIRE, Caron de BEAUMARCHAIS, and Jean Jacques ROUSSEAU, there flowed a penetrating critique of man and society. Often corrosive of the principles and practices of the Old Regime, the philosophers advocated natural instead of divine law, reason against superstition, anticlericalism versus church domination, and justice as opposed to privilege.

RULERS OF FRANCE

Carolingians		Valois		Third Republic (presidents)	
Pepin (the Short)	751–68	Philip VI	1328–50	Louis Jules Trochu (provisional)	1870–71
Carloman	768–71	John II (the Good)	1350–64	Adolphe Thiers	1871–73
Charlemagne	768–814	Charles V (the Wise)	1364–80	Patrice de MacMahon	1873–79
Louis I (the Pious)	813–40	Charles VI (the Mad or Well-Beloved)	1380–1422	Jules Grévy	1879–87
Charles II (the Bald)	843–77	Charles VII (the Well-Served)	1422–61	Sadi Carnot	1887–94
Louis II (the Stammerer)	877–79	Louis XI	1461–83	Jean Casimir-Périer	1894–95
Louis III	879–82	Charles VIII	1483–98	Félix Faure	1895–99
Carloman	879–84	Louis XII	1498–1515	Émile Loubet	1899–1906
Charles the Fat	884–87	Francis I	1515–47	Armand Fallières	1906–13
Odo, or Eudes (non-Carolingian)	887–98	Henry II	1547–59	Raymond Poincaré	1913–20
Charles III (the Simple)	898–922	Francis II	1559–60	Paul Deschanel	1920
Robert I (non-Carolingian)	922–23	Charles IX	1560–74	Alexandre Millerand	1920–24
Rudolf (of Burgundy; non-Carolingian)	923–36	Henry III	1574–89	Gaston Doumergue	1924–31
		Bourbons		Paul Doumer	1931–32
Louis IV (d'Outremer)	936–54	Henry IV	1589–1610	Albert Lebrun	1932–40
Lothair	954–86	Louis XIII	1610–43	**Vichy Government**	
Louis V	986–87	Louis XIV	1643–1715	Henri Philippe Pétain,	1940–44
Capetians		Louis XV	1715–74	chief of state	
Hugh Capet	987–96	Louis XVI	1774–92	**Provisional Government**	
Robert II (the Pious)	996–1031	**First Republic**		(presidents)	
Henry I	1031–60	National Convention	1792–95	Charles de Gaulle	1944–46
Philip I	1060–1108	Directory	1795–99	Félix Gouin	1946
Louis VI (the Fat)	1108–37	Consulate	1799–1804	Georges Bidault	1946
Louis VII (the Young)	1137–80	**First Empire**		Léon Blum	1946
Philip II Augustus	1180–1223	Napoleon I	1804–15	**Fourth Republic** (presidents)	
Louis VIII	1223–26	**Bourbons** (restored)		Vincent Auriol	1947–54
Louis IX (St. Louis)	1226–70	Louis XVIII	1814–24	René Coty	1954–59
Philip III (the Bold)	1270–85	Charles X	1824–30	**Fifth Republic** (presidents)	
Philip IV (the Fair)	1285–1314	**House of Orléans**		Charles de Gaulle	1959–69
Louis X (the Stubborn)	1314–16	Louis Philippe	1830–48	Georges Pompidou	1969–74
John I	1316	**Second Republic**		Valéry Giscard d'Estaing	1974–81
Philip V (the Tall)	1316–22	Louis Napoléon, president	1848–52	François Mitterrand	1981–
Charles IV (the Fair)	1322–28	**Second Empire**			
		Napoleon III	1852–70		

REVOLUTIONARY AND NAPOLEONIC ERA (1789–1814)

The coming of the FRENCH REVOLUTION has been attributed to many causes. The challenging ideas of the philosophers subverted the Old Regime and demanded new solutions to governmental and societal problems. Material conditions—agricultural disaster and depression in commerce, finance, and manufacturing—sharpened class tensions and provoked cries for reform. Conflicting political aims separated aristocratic, bourgeois, and popular elements; and presiding over the nation in this troubled state was the inept Louis XVI.

The Revolution. All of these and other factors contributed to the drama unfolded in 1788 and 1789. Inflated by aid to the American Revolution, the French public debt reached crushing proportions. The king and his ministers pondered the alternative approaches to resolve the fiscal crisis. Aristocrats, fearful of losing their privileges and desirous of an even larger share in national policymaking, boldly forced the king to call the STATES-GENERAL in 1789. In disuse since 1614, the States-General was expected to sit and vote by estate, by order. However, the deputies of the third estate were incensed at the prospect of being outvoted by the first two estates. Their forcing of the king to accept voting by head resulted in the transformation of the States-General into a National Assembly by June 1789. Workers and peasants soon entered the fray by storming the hated BASTILLE in Paris on July 14, 1789, and by pillaging and burning in the countryside.

Between 1789 and 1792, a new France was born, characterized by a declaration of rights, the end of the feudal system, the drafting of a constitution, reform of the church, and reorganization of local government. On paper, the Old Regime was dead—hereditary privilege was terminated as was the absolutism of the king and the hold of the church.

The Revolution became more radical after 1792 with the guillotining of the "treasonable" king, the outbreak of civil war at home, the FRENCH REVOLUTIONARY WARS abroad, and the lower classes' militancy for political and other advantages. The Reign of Terror (1793–94), a period of brutal dictatorship under the leadership of Maximilien ROBESPIERRE, was ended by the Thermidorean Reaction of July 1794. Thereafter, France was ruled by a DIRECTORY until the victorious general

REVOLUTIONARY FRANCE 1789–1801

▨ Areas of open civil war	▨ French annexations 1789–1801	—— French boundary 1789
▨ Areas of minor insurrection	▤ French occupation 1796	◂— Anti-revolutionary forces

This map illustrates the turbulent conditions in France during the years 1789-1801. The country was beset internally by civil unrest and insurrection while undergoing antirevolutionary attacks from foreign powers during the French Revolutionary Wars.

Cartographic Production by Lothar Roth & Associates

Louis XVI, the last king of France before the Revolution, is portrayed with the French explorer Jean François La Pérouse, who navigated the South Pacific. Louis, who was condemned by the Convention and guillotined in 1793, was incapable of resolving the social and political upheavals that led to the Revolution and ended the absolute monarchy.

Napoléon Bonaparte established the CONSULATE in 1799. He crowned himself emperor as NAPOLEON I in 1804.

Napoleon I. Napoleon's initial reforms incorporated much of the revolutionary decade's intentions and helped pacify France internally. Internationally, his conquests had already created an extended French empire in Europe by 1802. But after a brief respite in warfare, Napoleon renewed his expansionist drive. Setbacks in Spain and defeat in Russia in 1812 turned the tide against him. After defeat in 1814 he was forced to abdicate, and the Bourbon dynasty was restored in the person of LOUIS XVIII. Although Napoleon briefly seized power again in 1815, the NAPOLEONIC WARS were concluded by his defeat in the Battle of WATERLOO (June 1815).

A SUCCESSION OF REGIMES (1814–70)

The search for permanent political forms hypnotized the French from 1814 to 1870. The conservative CHARLES X, Louis XVIII's brother and successor, became increasingly despotic. He curtailed the powers of even the elite deputies in the parliament and threatened the civil rights and freedoms of the middle class. The Restoration regime was supplanted by the constitutional Orleanist monarchy of LOUIS PHILIPPE in the JULY REVOLUTION OF 1830. Initially welcomed by the business interests and professional classes, the new ruler eventually lost their favor as his government slid into corruption, subversion of parliamentary power, suppression of civil liberties, economic mismanagement, and a lackadaisical foreign policy. The February REVOLUTION of 1848 dislodged Louis Philippe and established the Second Republic.

After some months of flawed attempts at handling the economic and social crisis, the Second Republic elected Louis Napoléon (subsequently NAPOLEON III), nephew to Napoleon I, as president. He transformed the republic into the Second Empire in 1852 and ruled in an authoritarian fashion with efforts at mass appeal through plebiscites and later liberalization of the empire. Napoleon III's participation in the CRIMEAN WAR and the Italian wars of unification brought only faint luster to France. Moreover, the emperor was no match for the Prussian chancellor Otto von BISMARCK's diplomatic and military maneuvers of the 1860s. The defeat of Napoleon III in the FRANCO-PRUSSIAN WAR (1870–71) led to the proclamation of the Third Republic.

This plethora of regimes was produced by many elements. Political issues of restrictive suffrage and office-holding not only alienated the lower social classes from the monarchical form but aggravated the relations of the monarchs with many middle-class citizens. This was especially the case when the Bourbons and Napoleon III gave favors to aristocrats and clergy. On the other hand, the wealthy bourgeois joined church and nobility in abhorring the anticlericalism of republicans. Similarly, although the bourgeois, peasants, and work-

Recognized throughout Europe for his military acumen and leadership as general of the French forces, Napoléon Bonaparte was crowned emperor in 1804. The legendary spirit of his romantic heroism is preserved in this portrait (1800) by Jacques Louis David, which depicts Napoléon pointing the way for his troops to cross the Alps.

ers were linked by the desire for broader suffrage, neither the peasants nor the middle class looked with relish upon republican inclinations toward costly efforts to ameliorate the industrial woes of the urban workers. Political divisions were multiplied, too, by the social tensions stemming from industrialization, socialist movements, and trade unionism.

Nationalist fervor contributed to the lack of consensus for monarchy, empire, or republic. Orleanist feebleness in foreign affairs was viewed poorly by patriotic bourgeois who became attracted to the glorious aspects of the Napoleonic legend. For the Second Empire to survive, it required prestige in international affairs, which it lost when Napoleon III first bungled the endeavor of placing Archduke Maximilian (see

MAXIMILIAN, EMPEROR OF MEXICO) on the Mexican throne and then was defeated by the Prussians at Sedan in 1870.

Despite its poor political record, France did move ahead economically, building railroads and factories, opening mines, actively trading at home and abroad, and modernizing the city of Paris. Intellectual and cultural life too was at a peak as painters, sculptors, and writers displayed their talents in the ages of romanticism and realism.

THE REPUBLICS SINCE 1870

Since 1870 the French have experienced the survival of republican forms, the traumas of two world wars and several colonial ones, modernization of the economy, transformation of societal structure and mores, and more than lingering attention to intellectual and cultural questions.

Third Republic. The Third Republic of 1870 required much maneuvering and luck before its organic laws were formulated by 1875. Repression of the COMMUNE OF PARIS in 1871 and facing down the monarchists gave the republic respectability by 1880. The popularly elected deputies of parliament had also gained ascendancy over the executive branch of president and cabinet. Republican forces succeeded in wresting control over the educational system away from the church in the 1880s and finally separated the church from the state in 1905. The republic was shaken by scandals over presidential abuses, parliamentary bribery in the projected building of the Panama Canal, and the court-martial of the Jewish army captain Alfred Dreyfus as an alleged spy. The ultimate effect of the long-drawn-out DREYFUS AFFAIR, however, was to discredit further the remnants of antirepublican aristocrats, army officers, and clergy and to solidify the republic.

Industrialization proceeded rapidly, although at a slower pace than in Germany or Britain. Along with other major European powers and often in competitive rivalry with them, France engaged in a burst of imperialism, adding substantial holdings in Africa and Asia by 1914. Diplomatically, it escaped from the isolation imposed upon it until 1890 by the shrewd statesmanship of Bismarck. By 1914, French diplomats had forged a system of alliances including a defensive military pact with Russia (1894) and an Entente Cordiale with Britain (1904; see TRIPLE ENTENTE). Paris in the pre-1914 era—indeed until 1940—was the center for French and foreign artistic and literary figures.

World Wars. When WORLD WAR I began in August 1914, the French anticipated a brief conflict in which they could recover both the territory (Alsace-Lorraine) and prestige lost in 1871. In fact, French troops marched into a long war of attrition and emerged shaken by losses and casualties on a greater scale than other belligerents. The Treaty of Versailles temporarily restored French ascendancy, but the Great Depression of the 1930s, with its consequences of domestic political-social polarization, and the challenge of Nazi Germany spelled disaster for France by 1940.

At home, Socialist premier Léon BLUM's Popular Front of Socialists, Communists, and Radical-Socialists in 1936–37 preserved the republic against the threat of fascist groups, such as the ACTION FRANÇAISE, and enacted a wide range of social and economic reforms. A foreign policy of appeasement of Adolf Hitler throughout the 1930s was adopted because of the painful memories of World War I, internal dissension, and uninspired leadership. Appeasement, however, failed to maintain international peace, and WORLD WAR II finally began in September 1939.

Guided by an antiquated military strategy, the French armies suffered blitzkrieg defeat by Hitler's panzers in May 1940. From the rubble rose the collaborationist VICHY GOVERNMENT under Marshal Henri Philippe PÉTAIN, the Free French movement of Charles DE GAULLE, and the resistance movement within France. De Gaulle managed by 1943 to coordinate the anti-German activities of his Free French forces in London and then Algiers with the resistance groups in occupied France. Allied victory brought liberation in 1944 and had ushered in the Fourth Republic by 1946.

Fourth Republic. The Fourth Republic strongly resembled the Third in political form and practice. Until 1947 the Communist, Socialist, and liberal Catholic parties worked together to

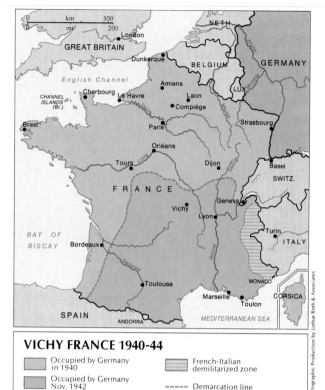

VICHY FRANCE 1940-44

- ▨ Occupied by Germany in 1940
- ▨ Occupied by Germany Nov. 1942
- ▨ French-Italian demilitarized zone
- ----- Demarcation line

This map illustrates the division of France between the Vichy Government and the German occupying forces in World War II. In July 1940, Marshal Henri Philippe Pétain set up Vichy as an autonomous regime. The Germans occupied all of France in 1942.

Paris was liberated from the Germans by the Free French troops of General Charles de Gaulle and by other Allied forces on Aug. 15, 1944. De Gaulle served as head of the provisional government until the Fourth Republic was established by 1946.

deal with the reconstruction of the country. In 1947, however, the Communists moved into the opposition, and the rise of the Gaullist right in the form of the *Rassemblement du peuple français* placed the Socialists and center parties in the quandary of forming fragile coalitions to preserve the republic against the left and right challengers.

The Fourth Republic legislated many economic and social reforms, nationalizing several large banks, insurance companies, and war-related industries; finally enfranchising French women; and expanding the previously feeble warfare benefits of French men, women, and children. Under Jean MONNET's plan, and with U.S. aid, the republic also built the substructure for a modern economy, tied in with the EUROPEAN COMMUNITY. To meet the Soviet threat in the cold war, France joined (1949) the NORTH ATLANTIC TREATY ORGANIZATION (NATO) but began to develop its own nuclear arsenal. Hostility from the Communist left and the Gaullist right weakened the republic and its ability to cope with the colonial wars in Indochina and Algeria (see VIETNAM WAR; ALGERIAN WAR).

Fifth Republic. On the verge of civil war over the Algerian question in 1958, the French called de Gaulle out of retirement to resolve the situation. His price was the right to draft a new constitution to be submitted to a referendum. The price was paid and the Fifth Republic was born, with the election (December 1958) of de Gaulle as president. The new republic gave more power to the executive than to the previously dominant parliament. Having liquidated the Algerian War in 1962 and introduced prosperity and stability, de Gaulle nonetheless faced a large-scale student-worker revolt in 1968. He weathered this crisis but left office the following year. The Gaullist party and its moderate partners continued to dominate politics through the 1970s under de Gaulle's successors, Georges POMPIDOU and Valéry GISCARD D'ESTAING. An energy crisis contributed to rising inflation and unemployment in the 1970s.

The general elections of 1981 produced a dramatic change of direction. Socialist François MITTERRAND edged the incumbent Giscard out of the presidency, and Socialists gained a solid majority in the parliament. Mitterrand immediately proposed measures to create new jobs, shorten working hours, and extend welfare benefits. He also took steps to nationalize several large banks and selected industries while decentralizing administrative authority. In foreign affairs the new president reaffirmed France's commitment to NATO and took a more critical stance toward the USSR than had his predecessor. When the Socialists lost their parliamentary majority in 1986, he had to appoint Gaullist leader Jacques CHIRAC as premier. This marked the beginning of a ''cohabitation'' system in which the president shared power with his prime minister. Over Mitterrand's opposition, Chirac lowered taxes and pushed through a privatization plan, selling off many of the banks and industries previously nationalized by the Socialists. When Mitterrand was reelected to the presidency in 1988, he was able to abandon cohabitation, working with Socialist governments under Michel ROCARD, Edith CRESSON, and Pierre Bérégovoy. After a major electoral defeat for the Socialists in March 1993, another conservative coalition took office under Edouard Balladur.   DONALD J. HARVEY

Bibliography: Agulhon, Maurice, *The French Republic, 1879–1992*, trans. by A. Neville (1993); Briggs, Robin, *Early Modern France* (1977); Brogan, D. W., *The French Nation: From Napoleon to Pétain, 1814–1940* (1958); Brogan, Olwen, *Roman Gaul* (1973); Dunbabin, Jean, *France in the Making: 843–1180* (1985); Duby, Georges, *France in the Middle Ages*, trans. by Juliet Vale (1991); Funck-Brentano, Frantz, ed., *National History of France*, 10 vols. (1923–38; repr. 1974); Jenkins, Brian, *Nationalism in France* (1990); Wright, Gordon, *France in Modern Times*, 4th ed. (1987).

France, Anatole   [frahns, ah-nah-tohl']

Anatole France, the pseudonym of Jacques Anatole François Thibault, b. Apr. 16, 1844, d. Oct. 12, 1924, was a French novelist, poet, critic, and man of letters. An erudite man who wore his learning lightly and wrote in a melodious style, France was the most respected writer of his age by the time of his election to the Académie Française in 1896. He was awarded the Nobel Prize for literature in 1921. France wrote numerous books, including an early volume of poems in the Parnassian manner (see PARNASSIANS), *Poèmes Dorés* (Golden Verses, 1872); the successful novels *The Crime of Sylvestre Bonnard* (1881; Eng. trans., 1906) and *At the Sign of the Reine Pédauque* (1893; Eng. trans., 1913); and an exquisite collection of short stories, *The Mother-of-Pearl Box* (1892).

After the turmoil of the DREYFUS AFFAIR, France wrote his satiric allegory of civilization, *Penguin Island* (1908; Eng. trans., 1909), but his historical novel of the French Revolution, *The Gods Are Athirst* (1912; Eng. trans., 1913), preserves a skeptical balance between political extremes.

France's literary achievement was founded on his penetrating irony and his appreciation of classical art and 18th-century French literature. He held sway over the writers of his time through his weekly critical essays, published in the Paris newspaper *Le Temps* between 1887 and 1893.

Bibliography: Segur, N., *Conversations with Anatole France* (1977); Shanks, L. P., *Anatole France* (1987).

Franche-Comté   [frahnsh kohn-tay']

The Franche-Comté (Free County of Burgundy) is a historic province in eastern France that constitutes one of the country's 21 administrative regions. BESANÇON is its capital. The region was occupied (4th century BC) by the Celtic Sequani tribe and was taken (52 BC) by Julius Caesar. The Burgundians had settled there by the 5th century AD. During the 9th century the area was unified with Transjurane BURGUNDY, which in turn became (933) part of the united Kingdom of Burgundy. All of Burgundy was integrated into the Holy Roman Empire in 1032. The name *free county* was acquired during the 12th century when the local count refused to pay homage to the German king. In 1556, the Franche-Comté passed to the Spanish Habsburgs. France annexed the province in 1678 by the Peace of Nijmegen. In 1790, during the administrative reorganization of France, the Franche-Comté was divided into the departments of Doubs, Haute-Saône, and Jura. Farming, particularly dairying and viticulture, remains the chief economic activity.   TIMOTHY J. RICKARD

franchise   (business)   [fran'-chyz]

A franchise, in law and business, is a privilege or right, granted by a government entity or sold by a business, that allows the recipient to carry on commercial activity under protected, or monopoly, conditions. The legal concept dates from the Middle Ages, when a lord could grant a knight or abbot the right, or franchise, to govern part of his domain. Markets, fairs, and certain other commercial activities were also conducted under franchise.

In the United States since the mid-19th century, municipalities and states have granted monopoly franchises to utility and public transportation companies in return for the right to regulate the firms' activities. The franchisees undertake to provide certain services (electric power throughout a town, for example), and the rates charged for the services are controlled by the government, usually through expert commissions.

The term *franchise* today, however, is most closely associated with the business arrangement that allows a distributor or retailer exclusive rights to sell a product or service within a specified area. The benefits of this arrangement were widely demonstrated in the period after World War II in the restaurant, hotel, and motel industries, where the franchising company granted its franchisees the use of a well-known, nationally advertised name, standardized designs for buildings and furnishings, financial assistance, and other business aids. In recent years the largest franchising growth has occurred in the service industries, in areas as diverse as printing, direct mail, home cleaning, and child care. Some dental and optometry clinics, emergency medical organizations, and legal-service firms now operate as franchises.

By the mid-1990s business franchises were earning about one-third of every dollar spent in the U.S. retail sector.

Bibliography: Dicke, T. S., *Franchising in America* (1992).

franchise   (political):   see SUFFRAGE.

Francia, José Gaspar Rodríguez de   [frahn'-syah, hoh-say' gahs-par' roh-dree'-gays day]

José Gaspar Rodríguez de Francia, b. Jan. 6, 1766, d. Sept. 20, 1840, was a dictator of Paraguay who established that country's independence. Francia participated in the bloodless revolution against Spain in 1811 and was a member of the junta that took control of the government. In 1814, however, he established himself as the sole ruler. Thereafter, Francia, who became known as El Supremo, ruled as undisputed dictator until his death. Assuming direction of the church, he broke the power of the clergy and upper classes. He also promoted agricultural and industrial development, though his attempt to make the country self-sufficient by cutting off virtually all foreign commerce was only marginally successful.

Francis, Sam

Composition (1960) by Sam Francis, an American abstract expressionist, combines vivid patches of color, dripped and splattered paint, and large areas of bare canvas. (Galérie Jacques Dubourt, Paris.)

Samuel Lewis Francis, b. San Mateo, Calif., June 25, 1923, is an abstract expressionist painter who, by 1947, was creating works influenced by Jackson POLLOCK, Mark ROTHKO, and Clyfford STILL. Francis spent much time from 1950 to 1957 in Paris at the studio of the cubist master Fernand LÉGER. During the 1950s, crucial years in the development of contemporary art, he made prolonged sojourns in Europe and the Orient that resulted in his gaining more fame abroad than at home. Ebullient color, smooth weightless shapes, and infinite space characterize his major commission, *Basel Triptych* (1956–58; a portion of which is *Basel Mural II*, Stedelijk Museum, Amsterdam).   HARRY RAND

Bibliography: Selz, Peter, *Sam Francis* (1975).

See also: ABSTRACT EXPRESSIONISM.

Francis of Assisi, Saint   [uh-see'-zee]

Saint Francis, b. Assisi, Italy, c.1182, was the founder of the FRANCISCANS. The son of a rich merchant named Pietro di Bernardone, he was very worldly in his early years and was recognized as a leader in the escapades of the town's youth. He was held prisoner for several months in 1202 during a dispute between Assisi and Perugia. This was followed by a period of illness. Dissatisfied with his life, he turned to prayer and service to the poor, and in 1206 he publicly renounced his father's wealth.

Francis began to live as a hermit and soon attracted followers. He preached the necessity of a poor, simple life-style based on the ideals of the Gospels. Pope Innocent III approved his way of life, gave him and his disciples permission to preach on moral topics, and had Francis ordained a deacon. The followers increased and were called friars minor by Francis, that is, the lesser brethren. With the collaboration of Saint CLARE, Francis founded (1212) a branch of his order for women, called the Poor Clares. Later, he established (1221) another branch for lay men and women, called the Third Order. In 1219, during the Fifth Crusade, Francis made his famous but fruitless attempt to convert the sultan al-Kamil while the crusaders laid siege to Damietta in Egypt.

A detail from Giotto's panel painting (c.1300) of the life of Saint Francis of Assisi portrays the saint preaching to the birds. The story of Saint Francis preaching to the sparrows at Alviano was one of the many legends about this popular saint in the hagiographical anthology Little Flowers of Saint Francis.

Francis was not adept at day-to-day organization. Under the influence of more practical men, such as Cardinal Ugolino, the future pope GREGORY IX, and Brother Elias, Francis retired from the government of the order to a life of contemplation, during which he received the STIGMATA, the imprint of the wounds of Christ in his own body, and composed his famous poem, the *Canticle of Brother Sun*. He died Oct. 3, 1226, and was canonized in 1228. Feast day: Oct. 4.

During the Middle Ages, a number of movements were based on the ideal of poverty. What made the movement led by Saint Francis different was his attractive personality and passionate dedication to the message he preached. One of the most popular of saints, he combined austerity with poetic gentleness. Francis popularized the custom of the Christmas crib. Besides the three branches of the order that he established, many other religious societies bear his name.

CYPRIAN DAVIS, O.S.B.

Bibliography: Armstrong, E. A., *St. Francis, Nature Mystic* (1963); Chesterton, G. K., *Saint Francis of Assisi* (1957; repr. 1987); Cunningham, L. S., *Saint Francis of Assisi* (1976; repr. 1981); Green, J., *God's Fool: The Life and Times of Francis of Assisi* (1985); Habig, M. A., ed., *English Omnibus of Sources: St. Francis of Assisi*, new ed. (1977); Sorrell, R. D., *Saint Francis of Assisi and Nature* (1988).

Francis de Sales, Saint   [duh-sahl']

Francis de Sales, b. Aug. 21, 1567, d. Dec. 28, 1622, was a French bishop and one of the Doctors of the Church. After studying law at Paris and Lyon, he decided to enter the priesthood, despite his father's opposition. His early years as a priest were spent preaching in the countryside of the Chablais area of Savoy. In 1602 he was consecrated bishop of Geneva. As bishop he promoted the measures for reform that were part of the COUNTER-REFORMATION initiated by the Council of Trent (1545–63). He is remembered today for his writings, especially the spiritual classic *Introduction to a Devout Life,* and for the various orders and congregations founded under his patronage. He was canonized in 1665 and was designated the patron saint of writers by Pius XI in 1923. Feast day: Jan. 24 (formerly Jan. 29).   JOHN W. O'MALLEY

Bibliography: Marceau, W. C., *Optimism in the Works of St. Francis De Sales* (1989); Palmer, C. H., *The Prince Bishop* (1974).

Francis Joseph, Emperor of Austria

Francis Joseph's long reign as emperor of Austria began in the revolutionary turmoil of 1848 and ended in the midst of World War I, which was to destroy the Austrian Empire. He

Francis Joseph is portrayed here at the beginning of his long reign (1848-1916) as Austrian emperor. Despite economic and cultural progress, his reign was marked by increasing conflict among the empire's many nationalities. Francis Joseph died two years before the final breakup of the empire at the end of World War I. (Castle Schönbrunn, Vienna.)

Saint Francis Xavier, one of the original seven members of the Society of Jesus, or Jesuits, was ordained a priest in 1537 and began missionary journeys to the Far East in 1541. His extremely successful ministry incorporated efforts to adopt native languages and customs and to train a native clergy. His work in India, the East Indies, and Japan resulted in his canonization in 1662.

was born on Aug. 18, 1830, the son of Archduke Franz Karl. He succeeded his feebleminded uncle FERDINAND I to the throne, mainly on the advice of Minister-President Felix Schwarzenberg (see SCHWARZENBERG family), who wished to refurbish the image of the HABSBURG dynasty.

The new emperor and Schwarzenberg called in a Russian army to suppress the REVOLUTION OF 1848 in Hungary and thus free Austria to attempt to thwart Prussia's drive to dominate Germany. In 1851 they inaugurated a program of centralized absolutism designed to modernize the empire along German lines. This regime, called the Bach System, antagonized the other nationalities of the empire, and after the Austrian defeat by Sardinia and France in 1859, it gave way to the February Patent of 1861, which provided a moderately liberal constitution. After the defeat by Prussia in the SEVEN WEEKS' WAR of 1866, Francis Joseph was compelled to grant Hungary autonomy and full parity with Austria in the Compromise of 1867. Henceforth the empire was known as AUSTRIA-HUNGARY, with Francis Joseph as emperor of the first and king of the second, the only common ministries being those of war, finance, and foreign affairs. In both parts he ruled constitutionally with parliaments elected by the propertied classes and dominated by the Germans and the Magyars.

Francis Joseph's reign saw remarkable economic and cultural progress, notably in education, medicine, literature, and music. However, the clashes of nationalities and economic classes generated such turmoil that after 1900 parliamentary majorities were increasingly rare and rule by imperial decree common. Universal manhood suffrage, granted in Austria in 1907, did not solve the problem.

The emperor suffered much personal tragedy: the execution of his brother MAXIMILIAN in Mexico in 1867; the suicide of his son RUDOLF at Mayerling in 1889; the assassination of his wife, Empress ELIZABETH, in 1898; and in 1914 the assassination of his heir apparent, FRANZ FERDINAND, which precipitated World War I. Through all vicissitudes he maintained an austere personal life, a lofty concept of duty, and a sober, realistic view of statecraft—qualities that elicited personal loyalty from all nationalities and helped the empire to survive two years beyond his death, which occurred on Nov. 21, 1916.

ENNO E. KRAEHE

Bibliography: Clark, Chester W., *Franz Joseph and Bismarck* (1934; repr. 1968); Marek, G. B., *The Eagles Die* (1974); Redlich, Joseph, *Emperor Francis Joseph of Austria* (1929; repr. 1963).

Francis Xavier, Saint [zay'-vee-ur]

Francis Xavier, b. Apr. 7, 1506, d. Dec. 3, 1552, was a Spanish-Basque Jesuit missionary called the Apostle of the Indies and of Japan. The son of an aristocratic family, he studied at Paris, where he met IGNATIUS LOYOLA. At Montmartre in 1534, Loyola, Xavier, and five others bound themselves by vow to the

work of preaching the gospel in non-Christian areas of the world. After his ordination to the priesthood, Xavier worked with Loyola in Italy, where they drew up the rules for the new order, called the Society of Jesus (see JESUITS).

In 1541, Xavier left for India. After a long and dangerous voyage, he reached (1542) Goa, his headquarters for the next ten years. After working for seven years in Goa, Travancore, Malacca, the Molucca Islands, and Ceylon, he went (1549) to Japan. After he had learned the local language, he spent the next two years setting up missions. During this time, he also translated a catechism. Xavier returned (1552) to Malacca and then to Goa, but he was there only a few months before departing for China. He arrived at Sancian (Shang-ch'uan), an island not far from Canton, but died there. His body, found to be undecayed after two months of burial, was later taken to Malacca and then to Goa, where it now rests. Because of his zeal and success as a missionary, he is considered the patron saint of the Orient and of missionaries. He was canonized in 1662. Feast day: Dec. 3.

THOMAS E. MORRISSEY

Bibliography: Brodrick, James, *Saint Francis Xavier 1506-1552* (1952); Kelly, Hugh, *St. Francis Xavier S. J. 1506-1552* (1964); Nevins, Albert, *St. Francis of the Seven Seas* (1955).

See also: MISSIONS, CHRISTIAN.

Francis I, Emperor of Austria: see FRANCIS II, HOLY ROMAN EMPEROR.

Francis I, King of France

Francis I, the autocratic king who ruled France from 1515 to 1547, personified the splendors of the Renaissance. He was born at Cognac on Sept. 12, 1494, the son of Charles of Angoulême and Louise of Savoy. His marriage (1514) with Claude, daughter of ANNE OF BRITTANY and his predecessor, LOUIS XII, continued the association of Brittany with the crown.

In July 1515, seven months after his accession, Francis led an army across the Alps and conquered Milan with his victory at Marignano. Four years later his rivalry with the house of HABSBURG intensified when he became a candidate for the imperial crown in Germany. The election was won by the Habsburg king of Spain, who became Holy Roman emperor as CHARLES V. Francis's subsequent war against Charles ended in total defeat at the Battle of PAVIA (1525), in which Francis himself was captured. Released in 1526, he disavowed his promise to cede Burgundy and began a new war, which lasted until the Peace of Cambrai in 1529. Francis sought alliances with the German Protestant princes and the Turkish sultan, and he fought further wars against Charles V in 1536-38 and 1542-44.

Like his elder sister, Margaret of Angoulême, the king be-

Francis I of France began his reign with the conquest of Milan in 1515 and was at war with his Habsburg rival, Emperor Charles V, for much of the ensuing 32 years. A patron of the arts as well as an athlete and warrior, Francis enjoyed great popularity among his subjects.

came a patron of the arts and humanist learning. He founded (1529) the Collège de France, brought Leonardo da Vinci to Amboise, and built magnificent châteaus, such as CHAMBORD and FONTAINEBLEAU.

Francis's concordat with the papacy at Bologna in 1516 gave him control of church appointments, but the church became increasingly corrupt under the government of his chancellor, Cardinal Duprat, himself a great pluralist. Until 1534, the king was tolerant of Protestantism, but in that year a series of extremist Protestant placards gave him personal offense. Persecution increased toward the end of his reign.

At the same time, the royal court was divided into factions under the influence of Francis's favorites and his mistress, the duchesse d'Étampes. War and patronage so strained the royal resources that Francis had to adopt devices such as the sale of government offices and the prosecution of his own financiers. By the time of the king's death at Rambouillet on Mar. 31, 1547, the early glamour of his reign had become tarnished.

J. H. M. SALMON

Bibliography: Hackett, Francis, *Francis the First* (1935; repr. 1968); Seward, Desmond, *Prince of the Renaissance: The Golden Life of François I* (1973).

Francis II, King of France

Francis II, b. Jan. 19, 1544, d. Dec. 5, 1560, king of France, was the oldest son of HENRY II and CATHERINE DE MÉDICIS. Francis married MARY, QUEEN OF SCOTS, in April 1558. After succeeding to the throne in 1559, Francis came under the influence of Mary's powerful GUISE relatives, who sought to destroy the French Protestants, or HUGUENOTS. The ensuing persecution provoked the Huguenot Conspiracy of Amboise (1560), a plot to abduct Francis and arrest his Guise mentors. The plan was discovered and the incipient rebellion bloodily crushed, but Francis's death curtailed Guise influence.

See also: RELIGION, WARS OF.

Francis I, Holy Roman Emperor

Francis I, b. Dec. 8, 1708, served as Holy Roman emperor from Sept. 13, 1745, until his death on Aug. 18, 1765. The second son of Leopold, duke of Lorraine, he ruled over his native duchy from 1729 to 1736. However, on Feb. 12, 1736, he married the Habsburg heiress, MARIA THERESA, and as part of a diplomatic compromise that ended the War of the POLISH SUCCESSION (1733-35) Francis transferred Lorraine to STANISŁAW I, the deposed king of Poland, in return for the Italian state of Tuscany, whose last Medici grand duke died in 1737. When Maria Theresa inherited the Habsburgs' central European domains in October 1740, a coalition of powers contested the succession in the War of the AUSTRIAN SUCCESSION, and the imperial election went to the Bavarian candidate, CHARLES VII rather than Francis. Only on Charles's death in 1745 did Maria Theresa secure the crown for her husband. Francis exercised little political influence, leaving government in the hands of his wife.

JOHN A. MEARS

Francis II, Holy Roman Emperor

Francis II, b. Feb. 12, 1768, was the last Holy Roman emperor (1792-1806) and, as Francis I, the first emperor of Austria (1804-35). Succeeding his father, LEOPOLD II, in 1792, he was confronted with the war declared by Revolutionary France in the west and by a Polish crisis in the east; his entire reign was dominated by the dangers coming from both directions. Successive defeats by France in the FRENCH REVOLUTIONARY WARS and NAPOLEONIC WARS compelled him to accept a series of treaties, from Campo Formio in 1797 to Schönbrunn in 1809, that destroyed the Holy Roman Empire and shrank the new Austrian Empire to its core lands lacking even a seacoast.

Francis's greatest achievement, possible only through perseverance and self-sacrifice, was Austria's recovery. This was accomplished first by allying with NAPOLEON I, who married Francis's daughter, Marie Louise, in 1810, and then by joining (1813) the coalition that defeated him. Francis's reward was serving as host to the Congress of Vienna (1814-15; see VIENNA, CONGRESS OF), where his brilliant minister, METTERNICH, by skillful manipulation recovered Austria's territorial position and its old preeminence in central Europe.

In domestic policy Francis favored his uncle JOSEPH II's centralized bureaucratic administration but lacked the latter's enlightened ideals. His rule, like his personal life, was austere, disciplined, and aimed at stability. At his death on Mar. 2, 1835, Austria was allied to Prussia and Russia in a common cause to suppress change. Francis was succeeded by his son FERDINAND I.

ENNO E. KRAEHE

Bibliography: Langsam, Walter C., *Francis the Good: The Education of an Emperor, 1768-1792* (1949).

Franciscans   [fran-sis'-kuhnz]

The Franciscans are members of a religious order that follows the rule of Saint FRANCIS OF ASSISI. The first Franciscans, called the Order of Friars Minor, followed an ideal of total poverty; they possessed nothing in common or individually. Forbidden to accept money, they lived from day to day by working and begging. When they began studying and living at universities, however, they had to modify their strict ideal of poverty. By the time Saint Francis died (1226), the order had spread from Italy to England, the Holy Land, and all of Europe. The friars were known as the people's preachers. They wore a gray tunic with a white cord at the waist; hence, their English name Grey Friars.

From the beginning, there were disagreements about the direction the order would take. The Franciscan minister general, Saint BONAVENTURE, sought a balance between the Conventuals, who wanted to adapt their poverty to the needs of the time, and the Spirituals, who wanted a strict poverty. The quarrel intensified during the 14th century when some of the Spiritual Franciscans, known as the Fraticelli, were condemned (1317-18) by Pope JOHN XXII. Disagreements about the ideal of poverty brought a permanent division in the 15th century between the Friars Minor Conventual (O.F.M. Conv.)

and the Order of Friars Minor (O.F.M.). In the 16th century, the Order of Friars Minor Capuchin (O.F.M. Cap.) established a stricter independent branch of Franciscans.

Preaching, teaching, foreign missions, and parish work remain the work of the Franciscans today. The Poor Clares, Franciscan nuns, are the second order. The Third Order comprises lay men and women who combine prayer and penance with everyday activity. Many sisters, brothers, and priests follow the Franciscan ideal in communities affiliated with the Third Order. There are Franciscan communities in the Roman Catholic church and the Anglican (or Episcopalian) churches.

The English philosopher and scientist Roger BACON was a Franciscan, as were the philosopher-theologians DUNS SCOTUS and WILLIAM OF OCCAM. Other famous Franciscans include Saint ANTHONY OF PADUA; two Renaissance popes, SIXTUS IV and SIXTUS V; and JUNIPERO SERRA, the founder of the California missions.   CYPRIAN DAVIS, O.S.B

Bibliography: Lambert, M. D., *Franciscan Poverty* (1961); Moorman, John R., *A History of the Franciscan Order From Its Origins to the Year 1517* (1968; repr. 1988); Short, W., *The Franciscans* (1989).

francium   [fran'-see-uhm]

Francium is a radioactive chemical element, one of the alkali metals in Group 1A of the periodic table. Its symbol is Fr and its atomic number 87. The atomic weights of Fr isotopes range widely; the stablest isotope is ^{223}Fr, also called actinium-K, with a half-life of about 21 minutes. Mendeleyev postulated the existence of element 87, calling it eka-cesium, but francium was not identified until 1939, when a French scientist, Marguerite Perey, discovered it as a product of actinium decay. Francium occurs in such minute amounts in nature that it cannot be isolated. Many francium isotopes, all radioactive, are artificially produced.

Franck, César   [frahnk, say-zar']

César Auguste Franck, b. Dec. 10, 1822, d. Nov. 8, 1890, was a Belgian composer, organist, and teacher. He studied (1830–35) at the Royal Conservatory in Liège and at the age of 11 made a concert tour through Belgium. As a student at the Paris Conservatory from 1837 to 1842, Franck won prizes for his playing and for his compositions; in 1844 he settled permanently in Paris. From 1858 until his death he was organist at the Church of Sainte-Clotilde, where his pupils, friends, and admirers gathered to hear him improvise on the organ. As professor of organ at the conservatory from 1872, Franck had a great influence on the younger generation of French musicians. A kind man, he was much loved by his pupils.

As a composer, however, Franck suffered long years of neglect. In 1879 he completed his oratorio, *The Beatitudes*, although it was not publicly performed until 3 years after his death. He composed his only symphony (in D minor) at age 66; unappreciated at its first performance in 1889, it has become a standard work in the orchestral repertoire. In his last year, Franck wrote his *Three Chorales* for organ, which are considered among the most important organ works of the 19th century. In addition to his popular symphony, he is best known for the *Violin Sonata in A* (1886), the *Symphonic Variations* (1885) for piano and orchestra, and the *Prelude, Chorale, and Fugue* (1884) for piano solo. He also wrote chamber music, operas, songs, symphonic poems, and much organ, piano, and religious music. Franck was fond of cyclic form (the appearance of the same theme in more than one movement of a composition).

Bibliography: Davies, Laurence, *César Franck and His Circle* (1970; repr. 1977) and *Franck* (1973); d'Indy, Vincent, *César Franck*, trans. by Rosa Newmarch (1910; repr. 1965); Vallas, Léon, *César Franck*, trans. by Hubert Foss (1951; repr. 1973).

Franck, James   [frahnk]

The German physicist James Franck, b. Aug. 26, 1882, d. May 21, 1964, is known for his contributions to quantum mechanics. In 1911, Franck and Gustav HERTZ began experiments on the collisions of electrons with atoms, for which they shared

the Nobel Prize for physics in 1925. When Adolf Hitler came to power, Franck moved to the United States, where he became a professor at the Johns Hopkins University and later at the University of Chicago. During World War II he worked on the Manhattan Project and prepared the "Franck Report," which urged President Harry Truman to demonstrate the bomb before authorizing its use.   JOHN G. MAY

Franco, Francisco   [frahn'-koh, frahn-sees'-koh]

General Francisco Franco of Spain established his authoritarian regime in 1939, after leading the Nationalist forces to victory in the Spanish Civil War. Impervious to criticism, Franco neither sought nor received popular acclaim once in office. His rule, somewhat liberalized during the 1950s and '60s, saw increased industrial and economic development.

Generalissimo Francisco Franco led the Nationalist forces in the SPANISH CIVIL WAR (1936–39) and ruled Spain as dictator until his death in 1975. Born on Dec. 4, 1892, he entered the Infantry Academy at Toledo in 1907 and became a second lieutenant in 1910. In 1912 he volunteered for the Moroccan war and quickly distinguished himself as a courageous and intelligent officer. He was personally sober, quiet, serious, and aloof, qualities that gained him much respect but few friends. In 1923 he became commander of the Spanish Foreign Legion, and in 1925 he led the attack on Alhucemas Bay that brought victory over the Moroccan leader ABD EL-KRIM. In 1926 he became Spain's youngest general, and two years later he was named director of the General Military Academy in Saragossa.

From 1931 to 1935, Franco stayed out of the many military conspiracies against the new Spanish Republic. He gained the admiration of conservatives and the hatred of the left by his repression of a miners' revolt in Asturias in 1934. In 1935 a conservative government appointed him chief of the general staff. In 1936 the Popular Front government exiled him by making him military commander of the Canary Islands, but there he joined the growing military and conservative conspiracy.

On July 18, 1936, when the Nationalist rebellion broke out, Franco flew to Morocco, where he took over the Spanish garrison. During the summer and fall of 1936 his forces invaded southern Spain and advanced on Madrid. By September Spain was divided between government and Nationalist territories, and the Nationalists established a government of their own. On Oct. 1, 1936, they appointed Franco head of state and commander in chief. In the slow conquest of Loyalist Spain that followed he showed himself cautious in strategy, cunning in diplomacy, reactionary in politics, and heartless toward his enemies. The war ended on Apr. 1, 1939, and was followed by the execution or imprisonment of hundreds of thousands of Loyalists.

During World War II Franco kept Spain neutral, although his fascist regime was pro-Axis. By a referendum in 1947 the regime turned itself into a monarchy, with Franco as regent, given the power to choose the next king. In the aftermath of the civil war, Spain had to endure a shattered economy, international ostracism, and much government corruption.

In the 1950s, Franco modified his fascist image into a more moderate anti-Communist one, thereby gaining the approval of the United States, with which he concluded a military bases agreement in 1953. An improving economy and increasing contacts with Western nations led to a gradual liberalization of the regime. In 1955 Spain joined the United Nations and the following year pulled out of northern Morocco. In the last decade of his life, Franco allowed further mild liberalization and delegated greater powers to his ministers. Yet he never faltered in his conviction that he alone had saved Spain from anarchy and revolution. In 1969 he chose JUAN CARLOS, grandson of Alfonso XIII, as his successor. Franco died on Nov. 20, 1975.

DANIEL B. HEADRICK

Bibliography: Beaulac, W. L., *Franco* (1986); Fusi, J., *Franco: A Biography*, trans. by F. F. Armestro (1988); Hills, G., *Franco: The Man and His Nation* (1967); Payne, S. G., *The Franco Regime, 1936–1975* (1987); Yglesias, J., *The Franco Years* (1977).

Franco-Prussian War

The Franco-Prussian War of 1870–71 brought on the fall of the Second French Empire and created the situation that enabled Otto von BISMARCK to establish the German Empire. It was the first European war in which both principal adversaries used railroads, the electrical telegraph, rifles, and rifled and breech-loading artillery—technological innovations that revolutionized warfare in the 19th century.

Causes. The two nations went to war nominally over the candidacy of a HOHENZOLLERN prince for the Spanish throne but actually over Prussia's growing power in Germany, which NAPOLEON III saw as a threat to French security. In 1870, Bismarck, anxious to complete the unification of Germany begun in 1866, undertook to use the issue of the Spanish succession to provoke France into an act of war that would frighten the south German states—which had not yet joined the North German Confederation organized in 1867—into alliance with Prussia. On July 13 the Prussian king (later Emperor WILLIAM I) sent a message to Napoleon III reporting a fairly innocuous meeting with the French ambassador. Bismarck, however, edited this Ems Telegram to suggest that the meeting consisted of an exchange of insults. He thus maneuvered the French government into a position where it had either to accept a diplomatic defeat or go to war. Napoleon III's government,

A grenadier of the French imperial guard (left) shares a drink with a franc-tireur (right), one of the guerrilla, or partisan, soldiers who aided in the defense of France during the Franco-Prussian War. Because the francs-tireurs were not affiliated with the national army of France, they were considered spies and were executed when captured by the Prussians. The franc-tireur carries an 11-mm chassepot rifle, a weapon adopted by the armed forces of France in 1866.

judging the former course to be politically dangerous at home, declared war on Prussia on July 19, 1870.

Course of the War. When hostilities began, the French armies, outnumbered and outgeneraled, fell back from the frontier—one army to Metz, where it was besieged, the other to Sedan, where it was surrounded in an untenable position. The emperor, judging further resistance there to be futile, surrendered the army of Sedan and himself to Bismarck on Sept. 2, 1870.

When news of Sedan reached Paris on September 4, republicans proclaimed the Third Republic and established the Government of National Defense to carry on the war. The government remained in Paris but established a delegation in Tours, under Léon GAMBETTA, to direct the war effort in the provinces.

The map indicates major battle sites and the routes of German invasion during the Franco-Prussian War of 1870–71. This conflict resulted in the ignominious defeat of France, which was forced to relinquish Alsace and Lorraine, and led directly to the creation of the German Empire.

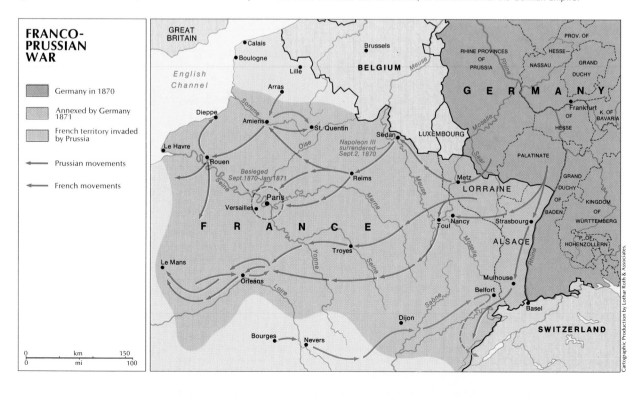

FRANCO-PRUSSIAN WAR

Germany in 1870
Annexed by Germany 1871
French territory invaded by Prussia
→ Prussian movements
→ French movements

GREAT BRITAIN

English Channel

BELGIUM

Calais
Boulogne
Lille
Arras
Dieppe
Amiens
St. Quentin
Le Havre
Rouen
Reims
Paris
Versailles
Le Mans
Troyes
Orleans
Bourges
Nevers
Dijon

Brussels
Sedan
LUXEMBOURG
Napoleon III surrendered Sept. 2, 1870
Besieged Sept. 1870–Jan. 1871
Metz
LORRAINE
Nancy
Toul
Strasbourg
ALSACE
Mulhouse
Belfort
Basel

RHINE PROVINCES OF PRUSSIA
PROV. OF HESSE
NASSAU
GRAND DUCHY
GERMANY
Frankfurt
OF HESSE
K. OF BAVARIA
PALATINATE
GRAND DUCHY OF BADEN
KINGDOM OF WÜRTTEMBERG
P. OF HOHENZOLLERN

FRANCE

SWITZERLAND

0 km 150
0 mi 100

Cartographic Production by Lothar Roth & Associates.

Although the Prussian-led army that invaded France in 1870 was composed of units from more than a dozen German states, most of the troops from different states wore similar uniforms with the colors of blue and red. Infantrymen from Württemberg (left), Prussia (center), and Bavaria (right) are distinguished from the other troops chiefly by their headgear and regimental insignia.

From September 23 to January 28, Paris was beseiged and for the last 23 days was bombarded by German artillery. In the Loire Valley, Gambetta organized and equipped new armies and carried on the war for five months, but he failed to relieve Paris. On January 28 the government concluded an armistice with Bismarck. This gave the French three weeks in which to elect a national assembly that would reflect the public's choice between war and peace and have authority to negotiate a peace in the name of France. The elections in early February returned a large majority in favor of ending the war, and a peace was quickly concluded. By the Treaty of Frankfurt (May 10, 1871), France was required to cede Alsace and part of Lorraine to Germany and to pay an indemnity of unprecedented size—5 billion francs.

Results. At the outbreak of war the south German states joined their forces with those of Prussia. Aided by the impressive military victories of August and September 1870, Bismarck persuaded all the German rulers to join together in forming the new German Empire with the king of Prussia as the German emperor. The empire was formally proclaimed in the Hall of Mirrors of the Palace of Versailles on Jan. 18, 1871. It was to survive only until Germany's defeat in World War I, when Germany became a republic and France recovered its lost territories. DAVID H. PINKNEY

Bibliography: Bury, J. P. T., *Gambetta and the National Defense* (1936; repr. 1970); Howard, Michael, *The Franco-Prussian War: The German Invasion of France, 1870–71* (1961; repr. 1981); Steefel, Lawrence D., *Bismarck, the Hohenzollern Candidacy, and the Origins of the Franco-German War of 1870* (1962).

Franconi   (family)   [frahn-koh'-nee]

The Franconis are the oldest and most illustrious family in the history of the French circus. The founder of the dynasty, **Antonio**, 1737–1836, took over the Parisian amphitheater of Philip ASTLEY at the time of the French Revolution. Assisted by his sons **Laurent** and **Henri**—the former a celebrated rider in advanced horse exercises, the latter an author and director of circus pantomimes—he later established the famous Cirque Olympique.

In 1827 they were succeeded by Henri's son **Adolphe**, who in 1836 joined Louis Dejean to found a new circus in Paris, the Cirque des Champs-Elysées, or Cirque d'Eté. Laurent Franconi, in association with his son **Victor**, established the first Paris hippodrome in 1845; and a son of Henri, **Henri Narcisse**

Franconi, brought this type of entertainment to America in 1853. **Charles Franconi**, son of Victor and the equestrienne Virginie Kenebel, later managed both the Cirque d'Eté and the still extant Cirque d'Hiver. The male line of the family became extinct on Charles's death in 1910, but a number of descendants through the female line are still active in the circus. A. H. SAXON

Franconia   [frang-kohn'-ee-uh]

Franconia consists of the central German lands in the Main River valley and forms the northern segment of the state of BAVARIA in Germany. Its strategic importance lies in its being the geographical connection between north and south Germany.

It derived its name from the FRANKS who settled there early in the Middle Ages. After the Carolingian collapse, Franconia became one of the five tribal duchies of Germany, and one duke became German king as CONRAD I (r. 911–18). Emperor OTTO I suppressed and partitioned the duchy in 939. The nominal duchies of Eastern and Western Franconia emerged, but ecclesiastical princes—notably the archbishops of Mainz and the bishops of Würzburg, Bamberg, and Speyer—later dominated the area. The city of Nuremberg was also important. From Western, or Rhenish, Franconia came the Salian, or Franconian, dynasty of the HOLY ROMAN EMPIRE. In the 16th century the empire was divided into administrative areas called *Kreis* ("circles") one of which was the Franconian Circle, including most of the territories of Eastern Franconia. Most of this area passed to Bavaria on the dissolution of the empire in 1803–06. RAYMOND H. SCHMANDT

Frank, Anne

Anne Frank, b. June 12, 1929, d. March 1945, was a young Jewish girl who kept a diary while hiding from Nazi persecution in the Netherlands during World War II. She and her family lived in a secret apartment in Amsterdam for two years before being discovered. Anne died in a German concentration camp. Her poignant diary was published in 1947, and an annotated edition was brought out by the Dutch in 1989.

Bibliography: Gies, Miep, *Anne Frank Remembered* (1987); Schnabel, Ernst, *Anne Frank: A Portrait in Courage* (1958).

Frank, Ilya Mikhailovich

The Soviet physicist Ilya Mikhailovich Frank, b. Oct. 23, 1908, d. June 22, 1990, received the 1958 Nobel Prize for physics, with P. A. CHERENKOV and I. Y. TAMM, for his interpretation of CHERENKOV RADIATION. A graduate of the University of Moscow (1930, 1944), he was a member of the USSR Academy of Sciences and received the Stalin Prize in 1946. Frank also investigated the photoluminescence of solutions and other areas of photochemistry. RAYMOND J. SEEGER

Frank, Jacob

Jacob Frank, b. Galicia, 1726, d. Dec. 10, 1791, was the Polish-Jewish founder of a messianic sect called the Frankists. He claimed to be a reincarnation of SABBATAI ZEVI, founder of the Sabbateans. The followers of Frank rejected the Torah, claiming exemption from the moral law, and practiced sexually promiscuous rites.

Frank became deeply involved with extremist Sabbateans during a visit to Salonika in 1753. After his return to Poland, he and his followers had difficulties with the Jewish communal authorities, and Frank was deported to Turkey.

In 1756 he returned to Poland, but he was arrested and again deported to Turkey, where, in 1757, he became a Muslim. Frank and his followers returned to Poland in 1759 and accepted Christian baptism en masse. But their clannish behavior led to prosecution by the Inquisition, and Frank was imprisoned from 1760 to 1773. Released, he lived in Brno until 1786 and then in Offenbach, where he died. His daughter inherited leadership of the sect but was unable to hold it together, and the sect eventually disappeared. JOSEPH L. BLAU

Frank, Robert

Robert Frank, b. Switzerland, Nov. 9, 1924, a photographer and filmmaker, is best known for his book of photographs, *The Americans* (1959), with text by Jack Kerouac. Kerouac wrote about Frank's work: "After seeing these pictures you end up . . . not knowing . . . whether a jukebox is sadder than a coffin." In the United States from 1947, Frank worked as a fashion photographer for *Harper's Bazaar* and, from 1948, also photographed in South America and Europe. On a 1955–56 Guggenheim fellowship, Frank traveled America, producing the ironic pictures that make up his famous work. He subsequently made a series of films, of which *Pull My Daisy* (1959), a short classic on the authors of the Beat Generation with a screenplay by Kerouac, is the most successful.   KEITH F. DAVIS

Frankel, Zacharias   [frahng′-kul, zak-uh-ry′-uhs]

Zacharias Frankel, b. Sept. 30, 1801, d. Feb. 13, 1875, was a German-Jewish rabbi and scholar. He formulated a position that accepted accurate scholarly ("positive") investigation of Judaism while retaining the ritual and spirit of traditional ("historical") Judaism. Frankel's "positive-historical Judaism" became the central thrust of the Conservative Jewish seminary at Breslau, created at his urging. He was named director at its foundation in 1854.

Frankel was a major force in differentiating this position from that of the extreme Reform party. Unlike the reformists, he opposed rejection of messianic belief and elimination of Hebrew from Jewish services, because he considered both of them important for Jewish survival. Mainly because of these issues, Frankel left the Frankfurt rabbinical conference in 1845. Yet he was not acceptable to the Orthodox party, because he favored consideration of modern and advanced positions. His influence on later scholarship persists, and he is claimed as an ancestor by the Conservative movement in American Judaism.   JOSEPH L. BLAU

Bibliography: Blau, Joseph L., *Modern Varieties of Judaism* (1966).

Frankenstein   [frank′-en-stine]

Frankenstein; or, The Modern Prometheus (1818), one of the most famous horror stories ever composed, was the first novel of Mary Wollstonecroft SHELLEY. It was written in 1816 as a result of a contest among Mary Shelley; her husband, Percy; Lord Byron; and Byron's physician, Polidori; to write a ghost story. The tale concerns Frankenstein, a German student scientist who learns how to breathe life into dead flesh and who thus creates a nameless monster. Physically ugly but innately good, the monster turns evil when Frankenstein refuses to accept and nurture him. After the monster kills Frankenstein's wife and brother, the scientist pursues him to the North Pole, where they both perish. In his "Preface," Shelley warned against interpreting his wife's book as an attack on romantic philosophy; rather, it attacks romantic isolation. Numerous films were based on the story, including a popular 1931 version with Boris KARLOFF as the monster.   JANET M. TODD

Bibliography: Florescu, Radu, *In Search of Frankenstein* (1975); Small, Christopher, *Mary Shelley's Frankenstein: Tracing the Myth* (1973).

Frankenthaler, Helen   [frank′-en-thahl-ur]

The American painter Helen Frankenthaler, b. Dec. 12, 1928, is one of the inventors of a style of abstract art termed COLOR-FIELD PAINTING. After studying at Bennington College in Vermont, she returned to her native New York and through her relationship with art critic Clement GREENBERG, was exposed to ABSTRACT EXPRESSIONISM in the 1950s. She was influenced by the work of Arshile Gorky, Willem de Kooning, Jackson Pollock, and the cubist painters.

Frankenthaler developed an innovative staining technique in which acrylic pigment is poured directly onto unsized canvas. The result is both an expressive, personal image and a sumptuous surface of vivid color. Her *Mountains and Sea* (1952; Metropolitan Museum, New York City) influenced the mature styles of the artists Morris Louis and Kenneth Noland. Since 1961, Frankenthaler's works have tended to become larger, simpler, and more geometric in form. *Guiding Red* (1967), one of her largest works, measures 9.1 × 4.9 m (30 × 16 ft).   HARRY RAND

Bibliography: Carmean, E. A., Jr., *Helen Frankenthaler: A Painting Retrospective* (1989); Elderfield, John, *Frankenthaler* (1989); Rose, Barbara, *Frankenthaler* (1971).

Helen Frankenthaler's Blue Territory (1955) is typical of the vivid colors and lyrical moods of her work during the 1950s. With her invention of the "soak-stain" technique, Frankenthaler became an innovator among American abstract color-field painters. (Whitney Museum, New York City.)

Frankfort   [frank′-furt]

Frankfort (1990 pop., 25,968) is the capital of Kentucky and the seat of Franklin County. It is located in the north central part of the state on the Kentucky River near a picturesque gorge. It is in the center of the famous bluegrass region noted for Thoroughbred horses. Surrounded by fertile farmland, the city is a trade and distribution center for corn and burley tobacco. Its industries include a bourbon distillery and manufacturing plants for electronic equipment, furniture, and shoes.

Frankfort was founded in 1786, becoming the capital in 1792 when Kentucky entered the Union. Many of Frankfort's stately homes date from its early period, notably Liberty Hall (1796) and the Orlando Brown House (1835). The Old Capitol, built (1827–29) of native limestone, now houses a historical museum.

Frankfurt am Main   [frahnk′-foort ahm mine′]

Frankfurt am Main, the largest city of the German state of Hesse, is located on the Main River about 32 km (20 mi) east of its confluence with the Rhine. Its name is derived from *Frankonovurt* ("the ford of the Franks"). The city has an area of 222 km² (86 mi²) and a predominantly Protestant population of 618,500 (1987 est.). Lying in a protected valley 88 to 212 m (290 to 695 ft) above sea level, Frankfurt has a comparatively temperate climate.

Mentioned as early as AD 793, Frankfurt is one of Germany's oldest cities. Recent archaeological findings indicate that a Roman post occupied the site as early as the 1st century. The original "Old Town" was built on the right bank of the river and was enclosed by walls in the 12th century. The "New Town" was added in the 14th century and was ringed by still

Frankfurt am Main, a major German manufacturing city and river port, is one of Germany's oldest commercial centers. Founded by the Romans during the 1st century AD, Frankfurt has hosted annual trade fairs since 1240 and is today a leading financial city.

more fortifications. Most of these walls, however, were razed as the city expanded. The most conspicuous remnant is the Eschenheimer Tor, a 47-m (155-ft) tower dating from the 15th century. The historic center of Frankfurt is the Römerberg, a square surrounded by medieval houses. The most outstanding of these is the Römer, a complex of several gabled buildings housing the city government.

Situated at a convenient crossroad between south and north Germany, Frankfurt developed into one of Germany's most important commercial, industrial, and transportation centers. Manufactures include chemicals, pharmaceuticals, leather goods, and electrical equipment, and the city is also noted for banking. It annually holds two great trade fairs, one in the spring (initiated in 1330) and one in the fall (held since 1240). It is a major railroad junction as well as an important river port. Its airport is one of the busiest in Europe.

Charlemagne held his imperial assembly in Frankfurt in 794. Emperor Louis I chose the city as his headquarters and had a large palace erected here in 822. In 843, Frankfurt became the capital of the East Frankish kingdom. The Golden Bull of 1356 designated Frankfurt as the seat for the election of the Holy Roman emperors, and beginning in 1562 they were crowned in the city's Gothic cathedral. Johann Wolfgang von Goethe, Germany's most celebrated poet, was born in Frankfurt in 1749. In 1815 the city became the capital of the German Confederation. During the Revolutions of 1848 it hosted the Frankfurt Parliament, which met in the city's St. Paul Church to draft a liberal German constitution. In 1866, however, Frankfurt was occupied by the Prussian army and incorporated into Prussia, thus losing its cherished free-city status. In 1871 the peace treaty ending the Franco-Prussian War was signed there and came to be known as the Treaty of Frankfurt.

EDWARD TABORSKY

Frankfurt Parliament

The Frankfurt Parliament was the popularly elected German national assembly that convened during the REVOLUTIONS OF 1848 with the purpose of creating a unified Germany. On Mar. 31, 1848, liberal leaders met in Frankfurt am Main and called on all the German states to elect delegates by universal male suffrage to a national assembly. On May 18 about 600 duly elected delegates gathered at Frankfurt; after lengthy debates, they adopted a constitution in March 1849. It provided for the union of the German states (excluding Austria) under a federal government, with a popularly elected parliament and a hereditary emperor. The crown was offered to FREDERICK WILLIAM IV of Prussia, but he refused it (April 1849), asserting that he would accept only a crown offered by the German princes. The Frankfurt Parliament soon dispersed. Its constitution, although never implemented, formed the basis for Otto von BISMARCK's constitution for the North German Confederation in 1867.

Bibliography: Eyck, Frank, *Frankfurt Parliament: 1848–49* (1968).

Frankfurter, Felix   [frank'-furt-ur, fee'-liks]

Felix Frankfurter, b. Vienna, Austria, Nov. 15, 1882, d. Feb. 22, 1965, was a justice of the U.S. Supreme Court known for his scholarship and his belief in judicial restraint. He came to the United States from Austria in 1894, studied at the College of the City of New York, and in 1906 received a law degree from Harvard. Frankfurter's first position was assistant U.S. attorney in New York, then from 1911 to 1914 he was a legal officer in the Bureau of Insular Affairs, but in 1914 Frankfurter returned to Harvard, where he taught law until 1939. During World War I he was legal advisor to Newton D. Baker, secretary of war and chairman of the War Labor Policies Board. He was an advisor to President Woodrow Wilson at the Paris Peace Conference in 1919. A liberal and a Zionist, Frankfurter helped found (1920) the American Civil Liberties Union. In 1927 he gained public attention by publishing a critique of the SACCO AND VANZETTI trial. During the 1930s, Frankfurter became influential in the New Deal. President Franklin Roosevelt appointed him to the Supreme Court in 1939, where, despite his reputation as a liberal, Frankfurter turned against some liberal positions, notably in his narrow interpretation of rights under the 1st Amendment. He also believed that in a complex society the courts should be slow to interfere with acts of legislatures.

Bibliography: Jacobs, Clyde, *Justice Frankfurter and Civil Liberties* (1974); Kurland, Philip B., *Mr. Justice Frankfurter and the Constitution* (1971); Mendelson, Wallace, *Justices Black and Frankfurter*, 2d ed. (1966); Simon, James F., *The Antagonists* (1989); Stevens, Richard G., *Frankfurter and Due Process* (1987).

Felix Frankfurter, an American jurist, was active in several liberal causes, including the founding of the American Civil Liberties Union, before his appointment to the Supreme Court in 1939. As an associate justice, Frankfurter advocated judicial restraint, a reluctance to interfere with decisions made by state legislatures or the U.S. Congress.

frankincense   [frank'-in-sens]

Frankincense is an aromatic gum resin from trees of the genus *Boswellia,* in the family Burseraceae, which grow in Somalia and in the southern Arabian peninsula. It was used in the ancient world for religious and medicinal purposes; today it is an ingredient of incense, fumigants, and perfumes. Frankincense is obtained by making a deep incision in the trunk of the tree, which exudes a milky juice that on exposure to air hardens into semiopaque lumps. From ancient times through the Middle Ages, frankincense was a principal Arabian trading commodity.   FRANCES GIES

See also: MYRRH; RESIN.

Frankl, Paul   [frahnk'-ul]

Paul Frankl, b. Prague, 1878, d. Jan. 30, 1962, was one of the most respected art historians and teachers of the 20th century. After studying architecture, Frankl received (1910) a doctorate from the University of Munich, where he began teaching art history under Heinrich WÖLFFLIN in 1913. He taught at the University of Halle-Wittenberg from 1921 to 1934 when he was ousted in the anti-Semitic Nazi purge. Frankl emigrated (1939) to the United States and worked at the Institute for Advanced Study in Princeton, N.J., for the rest of his life. Frankl published many books, both on principles of art—*Die Entwicklungsphasen der neueren Baukunst* (Stages in the Development of the New Architecture, 1914), *Das System der Kunstwissenschaft* (A System of Art History, 1938), and *The Gothic* (1960)—and on analyses of individual works of art.
                              BARBARA CAVALIERE

Bibliography: Frankl, Paul, *Gothic Architecture,* trans. by Dieter Pevsner (1962) and *Principles of Architectural History: The Four Phases of Architectural Style, 1420–1900,* trans. and ed. by James F. Gorman, foreword by James Ackerman (1968).

Frankl, Viktor

Viktor E. Frankl, b. 1905 in Vienna, is the originator of the psychotherapeutic school of logotherapy. Frankl attended the University of Vienna, where he earned doctorates in medicine and philosophy; he was appointed professor of neurology and psychiatry there in 1947. Frankl was imprisoned for several years during World War II in the concentration camps at Auschwitz and Dachau, and partly through that experience came to the central premise of logotherapy: that human's most fundamental motive is to find meaning in life. Logotherapy has been called the third Viennese school of psychotherapy, succeeding those of Sigmund FREUD and Alfred ADLER.
                              GEORGE E. ATWOOD

Bibliography: Fabry, J. B., *The Pursuit of Meaning,* rev. ed. (1987); Frankl, V., *The Doctor and the Soul* (1955) and *Man's Search for Meaning: An Introduction to Logotherapy* (1959).

Frankland, Sir Edward   [frank'-luhnd]

The British chemist Sir Edward Frankland, b. Jan. 18, 1825, d. Aug. 9, 1899, proposed (1852) the "doctrine of atomicity [valence] or equivalents of elements." From his work on zinc methyl, zinc ethyl, and organic compounds of tin, antimony, and mercury, he found that the combining powers of metals are satisfied by a definite number of atoms that combine with them. The present ideas of VALENCE have developed from these researches. Frankland also tacitly assumed that the valence of an element may vary, and in 1866 he pointed out that elements assume valences according to definite laws. In 1863, Frankland discovered the important synthetic reagent acetoacetic ester, independently of Anton Geuther in Göttingen.
                              VIRGINIA F. MCCONNELL

Franklin, Aretha

The leading SOUL singer of the 1960s and early '70s, Aretha Franklin, b. Detroit, Mich., Mar. 25, 1942, is the daughter of a prominent black minister. Her earliest musical training was in GOSPEL singing, and at age 14, she was a soloist in her father's choir. At age 18 she began singing professionally, and by the mid-1960s her records—including many songs that she wrote and produced herself—had sales in the millions. Franklin's gospel training was well suited to the highly ornamented soul music she sang. Her intensity, flawless technique, four-octave range, and deep conviction place her, along with Sarah Vaughan and Ella Fitzgerald, among the greatest singers of the era.   JONATHAN KAMIN

Bibliography: Bego, Mark, *Aretha Franklin: The Queen of Soul* (1989).

Franklin, Benjamin

In his many careers as printer, moralist, essayist, civic leader, scientist, inventor, statesman, diplomat, and philosopher, Benjamin Franklin became for later generations of Americans both a spokesman and a model for the national character.

He was born in Boston on Jan. 17, 1706, into a pious Puritan household. His father, Josiah, was a candlemaker and a skillful mechanic, but Benjamin said that his father's "great Excellence lay in a sound understanding, and solid Judgment." He described his mother, originally named Abiah Folger and born on the island of Nantucket, as "a discreet and virtuous Woman." His parents raised a family of 13 children. In honoring them and in a lifelong affection for New England ways, Franklin demonstrated the lasting impact of his Puritan heritage.

The Bookman. After less than two years of formal schooling, Franklin was pressed into his father's trade, but his more profound talents proved to be intellectual. He devoured books by John Bunyan, Plutarch, Daniel Defoe, and Cotton Mather at home, and, after being apprenticed to his brother James, printer of *The New England Courant,* he read virtually every book that came to the shop. He generally absorbed the values and philosophy of the English Enlightenment. Like his favorite author, Joseph ADDISON, whose essays in the *Spectator* he virtually memorized, Franklin added the good sense, tolerance, and urbanity of the neoclassic age to his family's Puritan earnestness. He rejected his father's Calvinist theology, however, and soon espoused what became a lifelong belief in rational Christianity.

At the age of 16, Franklin wrote some pieces for the *Courant* signed "Silence Dogood," in which he satirized the Boston authorities and society. In one essay he argued that "hypocritical Pretenders to Religion" more injured the commonwealth than those "openly Profane." At one point James Franklin was imprisoned for similar statements, and Benjamin

Benjamin Franklin, an 18th-century American statesman, inventor, and writer, figured prominently in the governmental organization of the emerging American nation. He made invaluable contributions to the Declaration of Independence and the U.S. Constitution.

Poor Richard, 1733.

AN

Almanack

For the Year of Chrift

1733,

Being the Firft after LEAP YEAR:

And makes fince the Creation	Years
By the Account of the Eastern *Greeks*	7241
By the Latin Church, when ☉ ent. ♈	6932
By the Computation of *W. W.*	5742
By the *Roman* Chronology	5682
By the *Jewish* Rabbies	5494

Wherein is contained

The Lunations, Eclipfes, Judgment of the Weather, Spring Tides, Planets Motions & mutual Afpects, Sun and Moon's Rifing and Setting, Length of Days, Time of High Water, Fairs, Courts, and obfervable Days.

Fitted to the Latitude of Forty Degrees, and a Meridian of Five Hours Weft from *London*, but may without fenfible Error, ferve all the adjacent Places, even from *Newfoundland* to *South-Carolina*.

By *RICHARD SAUNDERS*, Philom.

PHILADELPHIA:
Printed and fold by *B. FRANKLIN*, at the New Printing-Office near the Market.

The frontispiece to Benjamin Franklin's Poor Richard's Almanack (1732–57) indicates that the almanac contained all the meteorological and astronomical information common to the genre. In addition, Franklin's compendium was peppered with the original aphorisms that made his work enormously popular.

carried on the paper himself. Having thus learned to resist oppression, Benjamin refused to suffer his brother's own domineering qualities and in 1723 ran away to Philadelphia.

Though penniless and unknown, Franklin soon found a job as a printer. After a year he went to England, where he became a master printer, sowed some wild oats, astonished Londoners with his swimming feats, and lived among the aspiring writers of London. Returning to Philadelphia in 1726, he soon owned his own newspaper, the *Pennsylvania Gazette,* and began to print *Poor Richard's Almanack* (1732). His business expanded further when he contracted to do the public printing of the province, and established partnerships with printers in other colonies. He also operated a book shop and became clerk of the Pennsylvania Assembly and postmaster of Philadelphia. In 1748, Franklin, aged 42, retired to live comfortably off the income from his business, managed by others, for 20 years.

In the sayings of "Poor Richard" like "Early to bed and early to rise make a man healthy, wealthy, and wise" and in his scheme for moral virtue later set out in his famous *Autobiography,* Franklin summarized his view of how the poor man may improve himself by hard work, thrift, and honesty. *Poor Richard's Almanack* sold widely in North America, and a summarized version known as *The Way to Wealth* was translated into many languages.

The Civic Leader and Scientist. In 1727, Franklin began his career as a civic leader by organizing a club of aspiring tradesmen called the Junto, which met each week for discussion and planning. They aspired to build their own businesses, insure the growth of Philadelphia, and improve the quality of its life. Franklin thus led the Junto in founding a library (1731), a fire company (1736), a learned society (1743), a college (later the University of Pennsylvania, 1749), and an insurance company and a hospital (1751). The group also carried out plans for paving, cleaning, and lighting the streets and for making them safe by organizing an efficient nightwatch. They even formed a voluntary militia.

Franklin began yet another career when in 1740 he invented the Pennsylvania fireplace, later called the Franklin stove, which soon heated buildings all over Europe and North America. He also read treaties on electricity and began a series of experiments with his friends in Philadelphia. Experiments he proposed, first tried in France in 1752, showed that

lightning was in fact a form of electricity. Later that year his famous kite experiment, in which he flew a kite with the wire attached to a key during a thunderstorm, further established that laboratory-produced static electricity was akin to a previously mysterious and terrifying natural phenomenon. When the Royal Society in London published these discoveries, and the lightning rods he soon invented appeared on buildings all over America and Europe, Franklin became world famous. He was elected to the Royal Society in 1756 and to the French Academy of Sciences in 1772. His later achievements included formulating a theory of heat absorption, measuring the Gulf Stream, designing ships, tracking storm paths, and inventing bifocal lenses.

The Politician and Provincial Agent. In 1751, Franklin was elected to the Pennsylvania Assembly, thus beginning nearly 40 years as a public official. He intended at first merely to enlist political support for his various civic enterprises, but partisan politics soon engulfed him. He opposed the Proprietary party that sought to preserve the power of the Penn family in Pennsylvania affairs, and as the legislative strategist and penman for the so-called Quaker party, he defended the powers of the elected representatives of the people. Franklin thus knew the virtues of self-government a generation before the Declaration of Independence.

Franklin did not at first, however, contemplate separation from Britain, which he regarded as having the freest, best government in the world. In the Plan of Union, which he presented (1754) to the ALBANY CONGRESS, he proposed partial self-government for the American colonies. A year later Franklin supported the ill-fated expedition of Gen. Edward BRADDOCK to recapture Fort Duquesne, and he persuaded the Quaker-dominated Pennsylvania Assembly to pass the colony's first militia law. He himself led a military expedition to the Lehigh Valley, where he established forts to protect frontiersmen from French and Indian raiders. As Franklin helped the empire fight for its life, however, he saw that colonial and ministerial ideas of governing the colonies were far apart. When he went to England in 1757 as agent of the Pennsylvania Assembly, he was alarmed to hear Lord Granville, president of the Privy Council, declare that for the colonies, the king's instructions were "the *Law of the Land:* for the King is the Legislator of the Colonies."

In England from 1757 to 1762, Franklin worked to persuade British officials to limit proprietary power in Pennsylvania. He also immensely enjoyed English social and intellectual life. He attended meetings of the Royal Society, visited David Hume in Scotland, heard great orchestras play the works of Handel, made grand tours of the continent, and received honorary doctor's degrees from the universities of St. Andrews (1759) and Oxford (1762).

He created a pleasant family-style life at his Craven Street boarding house in London, and began a long friendship and scientific-humorous correspondence with his landlady's daughter, Mary Stevenson. Their letters reveal his gifts for lively friendship, for brilliant letter writing, and for humane understanding.

At home from 1762 to 1764, Franklin traveled throughout the colonies, reorganizing the American postal system. He also built a new house on Market Street in Philadelphia—now reconstructed and open to visitors—and otherwise provided for his family, which included the former Deborah Read, his wife since 1730; their daughter Sally, who married Richard Bache and had a large family of her own; and his illegitimate son, William. Though he was appointed governor of New Jersey in 1762, William became a Loyalist during the American Revolution, completely estranged from his father.

As an influential politician, Franklin opposed the bloody revenges of frontier people against innocent Indians after PONTIAC'S REBELLION (1763) and helped to defend Philadelphia when the angry pioneers threatened its peace. In 1764 he lost his seat in the assembly in an especially scurrilous campaign. However, his party sent him to England in 1764 to petition that Pennsylvania be taken over as a royal colony.

The Defender of American Rights. The crisis precipitated by the STAMP ACT (1765) pushed that effort into the background and propelled Franklin into a new role as chief defender of American rights in Britain. At first he advised obedience to the act until it could be repealed, but news of violent protest against it in America stiffened his own opposition. After repeal of the Stamp Act, Franklin reaffirmed his love for the British Empire and his desire to see the union of mother country and colonies "secured and established," but he also warned that "the seeds of liberty are universally found and nothing can eradicate them." He opposed the TOWNSHEND ACTS (1767) because such "acts of oppression" would "sour American tempers" and perhaps even "hasten their final revolt." When the British Parliament passed the Tea Act (1773), which hurt the colonial merchants, Franklin protested in a series of finely honed political essays, including "An Edict by the King of Prussia" and "Rules by Which a Great Empire May Be Reduced to a Small One." As these satires circulated in England, Franklin wrote his sister: "I have held up a Looking-Glass in which some of the Ministers may see their ugly faces, and the Nation its Injustice."

In 1773, Franklin's friends in Massachusetts, against his instructions, published letters by Gov. Thomas HUTCHINSON that Franklin had obtained in confidence. Apparently exposed as a dishonest schemer, Franklin was denounced before the Privy Council in January 1774 and stripped of his postmaster general's office. Although he continued to work for conciliation, the Boston Tea Party and Britain's oppressive response to it soon doomed such efforts. In March 1775, Franklin sailed for home, sure "the extream corruption in this old rotten State" would ensure "more Mischief than Benefit from a closer Union" between Britain and its colonies.

From April 1775 to October 1776, Franklin served on the Pennsylvania Committee of Safety and in the Continental Congress, submitted articles of confederation for the united colonies, proposed a new constitution for Pennsylvania, and helped draft the Declaration of Independence. He readily signed the declaration, thus becoming a revolutionist at the age of 70.

The Diplomat. In October 1776, Franklin and his two grandsons sailed for France, where he achieved an amazing personal triumph and gained critical aid for the Revolutionary War. Parisian literary and scientific circles hailed him as a living embodiment of Enlightenment virtues. Wigless and dressed in plain brown clothes, he was called *le Bonhomme Richard.* Franklin was at his best creating the legend of his life among the ladies of Paris, writing witty letters, printing bagatelles, and telling anecdotes.

He moved slowly at first in his diplomacy. France wanted to injure Britain but could not afford to help the American rebels unless eventual success seemed assured. Franklin thus worked behind the scenes to send war supplies across the Atlantic, thwart British diplomacy, and make friends with influential French officials. He overcame his own doubts about the possibly dishonest dealings of his fellow commissioner Silas DEANE in channeling war materials to American armies, but the third commissioner, Arthur Lee (1740–92), bitterly condemned both Deane and Franklin. Despite these quarrels, in February 1778, following news of the American victory at Saratoga, the three commissioners were able to sign the vital French alliance.

Franklin then became the first American minister to France. For seven years he acted as diplomat, purchasing agent, recruiting officer, loan negotiator, admiralty court, and intelligence chief and was generally the main representative of the new United States in Europe. Though nearly 80 years old, he oversaw the dispatch of French armies and navies to North America, supplied American armies with French munitions, outfitted John Paul JONES—whose famous ship the *Bonhomme Richard* was named in Franklin's honor—and secured a succession of loans from the nearly bankrupt French treasury.

After the loss at Yorktown (1781) finally persuaded British leaders that they could not win the war, Franklin made secret contact with peace negotiators sent from London. In these delicate negotiations he proposed treaty articles close to those finally agreed to: complete American independence, access to the Newfoundland fishing grounds, evacuation of British forces from all occupied areas, and a western boundary on the Mississippi. Together with John Jay, Franklin represented the United States in signing the Treaty of Paris (Sept. 3, 1783), by which the world's foremost military power recognized the independence of the new nation.

Franklin traveled home in 1785. Though in his 80th year and suffering from painful bladder stones, he nonetheless accepted election for three years as president of Pennsylvania and resumed active roles in the Pennsylvania Society for Promoting the Abolition of Slavery, the American Philosophical Society, and the University of Pennsylvania. At the Constitutional Convention of 1787, although he was too weak to stand, Franklin's good humor and gift for compromise often helped to prevent bitter disputes.

Franklin's final public pronouncements urged ratification of the Constitution and approved the inauguration of the new federal government under his admired friend George Washington. He wrote friends in France that "we are making Experiments in Politicks," but that American "affairs mend daily and are getting into good order very fast." Thus, cheerful and optimistic as always, Benjamin Franklin died in Philadelphia on Apr. 17, 1790.   RALPH KETCHAM

Bibliography: Buxbaum, M. H., *Critical Essays on Benjamin Franklin* (1987); Crane, V. W., *Benjamin Franklin and a Rising People* (1954; repr. 1962); Ketchum, R. L., *Benjamin Franklin* (1965); Labaree, L. W., et al., eds., *The Papers of Benjamin Franklin,* 27 vols. to date (1959–1988); Wright, E., *Franklin of Philadelphia* (1986) and *Benjamin Franklin: His Life As He Wrote It* (1990).

Franklin, Frederic

Frederic Franklin, b. Liverpool, June 13, 1914, one of the most versatile dancers in modern ballet, appeared in cabaret and musical comedy in Paris and London, then became a leading dancer in the Markova-Dolin Ballet (1935–37) and Ballet Russe de Monte Carlo (1938–51 and 1954–56). He was director of the National Ballet, Washington, D.C., from 1962 to 1974, and since then has worked with various ballet companies, including the Dance Theatre of Harlem, for which in 1984 he staged an award-winning *Giselle.*   DAVID VAUGHAN

Franklin, Sir John

British Rear Admiral Sir John Franklin, b. Apr. 16, 1786, discovered the NORTHWEST PASSAGE but disappeared in the course of the exploration. Entering the Royal Navy in 1800, he saw service in the battles of Copenhagen, Trafalgar, and New Orleans. His seamanship, courage, and resourcefulness led to his appointment to command an overland exploring expedition from York Factory on Hudson Bay to the Arctic. Between 1819 and 1822, Franklin followed the Coppermine River and traced the shoreline east of Coronation Gulf, covering about 8,930 km (5,550 mi). In a second expedition (1825–27) he descended the Mackenzie River and explored the region west of the river's mouth. In recognition of these services, he was knighted in 1829.

After two overland expeditions in northern Canada, British Rear Adm. Sir John Franklin set out in 1845 to find the Northwest Passage. After the entire party had disappeared, searchers uncovered evidence that he had found the passage but that he and all his crew were dead.

After serving (1836–43) as governor of Van Diemen's Land (Tasmania), Franklin was sent in search of the Northwest Passage in 1845. His ships, *Erebus* and *Terror,* were last seen in Baffin Bay on July 25 or 26, 1845. When nothing was heard from the party, no fewer than 40 expeditions were sent to find him. In 1854, Dr. John Rae of the Hudson's Bay Company found the first proof that Franklin's vessels had sunk. In 1859, Leopold McClintock, commanding *Fox,* a search vessel outfitted by Lady Franklin, discovered a cairn that revealed Sir John had died on June 11, 1847, in King William's Land and had, in fact, found the Northwest Passage. Further expeditions were sent to the Arctic, but they simply confirmed the earlier discoveries.   GEORGE F. G. STANLEY

Bibliography: Franklin, Sir John, *Narrative of a Journey to the Shores of the Polar Sea in the Years 1819–22* (1823); Neatby, L. H., *In Quest of the North West Passage* (1958) and *The Search for Franklin* (1970).

Franklin, John Hope

John Hope Franklin, b. Rentiesville, Okla., Jan. 2, 1915, an American historian, taught at the University of Chicago from 1964 to 1982, when he went to Duke University. He earned his doctorate from Harvard in 1941 and has written extensively on blacks in the United States. His books include *From Slavery to Freedom* (1947; 6th ed., 1987); *Racial Equality in America* (1976); and *Race and History* (1990).

Franklin, Miles

Australian novelist Stella Maria Sarah Miles Franklin, b. Oct. 14, 1879, d. Sept. 19, 1954, wrote her first novel, the popular *My Brilliant Career* (1901; film, 1979), at the age of 20. Later works—some of them written during her 30-year residence in the United States and Great Britain—were not successful. Six novels about Australian settlers in the 19th and early 20th centuries were published under the pseudonym "Brent of Bin Bin" and were not recognized as hers until after her death.

Bibliography: Franklin, Miles, *Childhood at Brindabella* (1963); Barnard, Marjorie, *Miles Franklin* (1967).

Franklin, Rosalind

Rosalind (Elsie) Franklin, b. July 25, 1920, d. Apr. 16, 1958, a British biophysicist, used X-ray diffraction to provide two important facts concerning the structure of the DNA: that the phosphate groups lie on the outside of the molecule, and that the DNA chain has a helical conformation. This information helped James D. Watson and Francis Crick at Cambridge University to understand DNA structure; Franklin and Maurice Wilkins at King's College, as well as Linus Pauling in California, were also researching DNA structure. Franklin's publications included pioneering work with tobacco mosaic virus and X-ray diffraction studies of carbon structure.

Bibliography: Sayre, Anne, *Rosalind Franklin and DNA* (1978); Watson, James Dewey, *The Double Helix* (1980).

Franklin, State of

Franklin was a short-lived state established after the Revolutionary War in what is now eastern Tennessee. North Carolina claimed jurisdiction over the area and offered to cede it to the federal government in 1784. Its inhabitants retaliated by forming their own state, with land speculator John SEVIER as governor. The United States refused to recognize Franklin, and when Sevier's term expired in 1788 and no successor was chosen, North Carolina resumed control.

Bibliography: Gerson, Noel B., *Franklin, America's "Lost State"* (1968); Williams, Samuel C., *History of the Lost State of Franklin*, rev. ed. (1933; repr. 1974).

Franklin Institute

The Franklin Institute is a private, nonprofit educational organization located in Philadelphia, Pa. Founded in 1824, the institute received the first government grant for scientific research for its early investigations of steam-boiler explosions. Other areas in which the institute was active during the 19th century included technical education and industrial exhibi-

tions. Success in the latter area led to the establishment in 1934 of the popular Franklin Institute Science Museum, which includes the Fels Planetarium. Along with its programs designed to increase public understanding of science and technology, the Franklin Institute maintains an extensive technical library and through its press publishes journals, monographs, and books.   JEFFREY L. STURCHIO

Franklin and Marshall College

In 1853, Franklin College (1787) merged with Marshall College (1834) to form Franklin and Marshall College (enrollment: 1,922; library: 270,000 volumes). Located in Lancaster, Pa., the private 4-year liberal-arts school for men and women was formerly affiliated with the United Church of Christ.

franklinite

Franklinite is a zinc and iron-manganese OXIDE MINERAL, $Zn(FeMn)_2O_4$, that occurs abundantly only at Franklin, N.J., where, associated with zincite and willemite, it has been mined as an ore of zinc and manganese. A member of the SPINEL group, franklinite forms brilliantly metallic, iron-black octahedral crystals (isometric system), rounded grains, and granular masses in strongly altered limestone. Hardness is $5\frac{1}{2}$–$6\frac{1}{2}$, streak is reddish brown, and specific gravity is 5.1–5.2.

Franks

The Franks were a group of GERMANIC PEOPLES inhabiting the lower and middle Rhine Valley by the 3d century AD, when they are first mentioned by classical authors. Identified by these writers as the Salians, Ripuarians, and Chatti, they are said to have shared the same language and to have had many similar laws.

Toward the middle of the 3d century the Franks began

This map illustrates the expansion of the Frankish kingdom from its founding by Clovis (r. 481–511) through the reign of Charlemagne. It was under the Carolingian Charlemagne, who was crowned emperor by the pope in 800, that the Frankish empire reached its height.

EXPANSION OF FRANKISH POWER, 481-814

■ Territory in 481	■ Conquests, 531-768
■ Conquests of Clovis, 486-511	■ Conquests of Charlemagne, 768-814

This 14th-century miniature portrays the coronation of the Merovingian ruler Clovis, founder of the Frankish kingdom during the early Middle Ages. After ending Roman domination in Gaul (486), Clovis gained control and unified most of Gaul, establishing the foundation of the future French monarchy.

penetrating the Roman frontier around Mainz. They were driven back by Emperor Probus. In 358, JULIAN THE APOSTATE handed over Toxandria, the region between the Meuse and the Scheldt rivers, to the Salian Franks, who became Roman allies and provided troops for the imperial army.

The Salian Franks were divided into several groups led by chiefs (*reguli*). One of these groups, the MEROVINGIANS, which took its name from the chief Merovech (Merowen), was particularly successful. Merovech and his successor, Childeric (d. 481), extended Salian domination to the south, perhaps as far as the Somme River. Childeric aided the Romans, but after the death (461) of Emperor Majorian he sought to overthrow Aegidius, the imperial governor in northern Gaul. Aegidius forced Childeric into exile among the Thuringians, but he returned after a few years and, in alliance with some Saxons, defeated the Romans.

Syagrius, Aegidius's son and successor, was able to keep Childeric from moving his people south of the Somme, but another *regulus* took control of Le Mans. Cambrai and Thérouanne were also held by Salian *reguli*. CLOVIS, Childeric's son, conquered most of Gaul and unified the Franks under the Merovingian dynasty. Clovis also converted to Christianity.

The Ripuarian Franks and the Chatti raided across the middle Rhine frontier during the first quarter of the 5th century. In the wake of the Hunnic invasion of Gaul, a band of Ripuarians gained control of Cologne. By c.470, Trier was in Ripuarian hands, and thereafter Metz, Toul, and Verdun fell to the Franks. The CAROLINGIAN dynasty, which succeeded the Merovingians, is considered to have been of Ripuarian origin.

Under the Carolingians, the Franks formed a vast empire that reached its pinnacle in the reign (768–814) of CHARLEMAGNE. This empire was divided in the mid-9th century, from it emerging the West Frankish kingdom (France) and the East Frankish kingdom (Germany).

Much is known about the material civilization of the Franks during the period before they became Christians. Thousands of graves have been discovered in which have been found not only skeletons but various kinds of weapons, jewelry, and even bits of cloth and leather. The most celebrated find was the grave of Childeric, discovered at Tournai in 1653. A great wealth in gold, including a signet ring with his portrait on it, and the severed head of his horse were among its contents.

BERNARD S. BACHRACH

Bibliography: James, E., *The Franks* (1988; repr. 1991); Lasko, Peter, *Kingdom of the Franks* (1971); Thorpe, Lewis, trans., *The History of the Franks: Gregory of Tours* (1976); Wallace-Hadrill, J. M., *The Long-Haired Kings and Other Studies in Frankish History* (1961).

Franny and Zooey

Franny and Zooey (1961), by J. D. SALINGER, first appeared as two separate stories in *The New Yorker* magazine (1955; 1957). Zen Buddhism is central to the story of the Glass family. Discerning the inner workings of their own beings is the obsession of both Franny Glass, a college student dissatisfied with life around her and seeking deliverance from her own ego, and her older brother Zooey, an actor and intellectual who feels alienated from his family and from society. *Franny*

and Zooey appealed strongly to the college generation of the 1950s and '60s and contributed to Salinger's status as a cult author.

JEROME KLINKOWITZ

Bibliography: Gwynn, F., and Blotner, J., *The Fiction of J. D. Salinger* (1958); Wenke, J., *J. D. Salinger: A Study of the Short Fiction* (1991).

Franz Ferdinand, Austrian Archduke   [frahnts fair'-dee-nahnt]

Archduke Franz Ferdinand, heir presumptive to the Austro-Hungarian thrones, and his wife, Sophie Chotek, were assassinated by a Serbian nationalist while visiting the Bosnian city of Sarajevo in 1914. Their deaths resulted in Austria's declaration of war against Serbia, marking the opening hostilities of World War I.

Franz Ferdinand, b. Dec. 18, 1863, was the Austrian archduke whose assassination by a Serbian nationalist at Sarajevo on June 28, 1914, sparked WORLD WAR I. A nephew of Emperor FRANCIS JOSEPH, he became heir apparent after the suicide (1889) of Archduke RUDOLF. The Emperor, however, disapproved of his marriage (1900) to a Czech commoner, Sophie Chotek, and their children were barred from the succession. Although reactionary, Franz Ferdinand for a time favored the reorganization of AUSTRIA-HUNGARY to create a third kingdom of Croatia. This was one reason for his assassination by the Serbian nationalist Gavrilo Princip.

ROBIN BUSS

Franz Joseph: see FRANCIS JOSEPH, EMPEROR OF AUSTRIA.

Franz Josef Land   [frans joh'-zef]

Franz Josef Land, an archipelago of about 187 islands in the northern part of the Barents Sea, is the northernmost possession of Russia. The land area is about 20,700 km² (8,000 mi²) and is divided into three main island groups. Most of the terrain includes elevated plateaus that are covered by ice. The area was discovered by an Austro-Hungarian expedition in 1873 and was named after the Austrian emperor; in 1928 the USSR claimed the region.

Frascati National Laboratory   [frah-skah'-tee]

The Frascati National Laboratory, a research center for high-energy physics and fusion energy, was founded (1953) near Rome, Italy. Operated by the Comitato Nazionale per Energia Nucleare and the Istituto Nazionale di Fisica Nucleare, it held the world's first electron-positron storage ring, called AdA. Present major installations are tokamak fusion devices, a 450-MeV linear accelerator, and a 1.5-GeV electron-positron storage ring, called Adone.

BRIAN SOUTHWORTH

Frasch, Herman   [frahsh]

A German-born chemist who immigrated (1868) to the United States, Herman Frasch, b. Dec. 25, 1851, d. May 1, 1914, invented a process that made possible the economical mining of SULFUR. Frasch obtained his first patent for an oil-refining process and, in 1885, organized the Empire Oil Company, later part of Standard Oil; he obtained for the firm 21 patents for processes to remove sulfur from crude oil. In 1891 he patented the Frasch sulfur-mining process in which boiling water is forced into the deposit to melt the sulfur, which is then pumped to the surface in an almost pure form. In 1895, Frasch organized and became president of the Union Sulphur Company, the world's largest sulfur-mining firm.

Fraser, Dawn

The Australian Dawn Fraser, b. Sept. 4, 1937, became the first swimmer to win the same event in the Olympic Games three different times. She was the greatest sprinter in women's history, winning the 100-meter freestyle event in the 1956, 1960, and 1964 Olympics; she held the record in that event for 16 years. She was the first woman to break 1 minute for 100 meters, a record she broke 9 successive times. She set 27 individual records plus many relay records before her suspension for a prank at the 1964 Olympics.

Fraser, J. Malcolm

J. Malcolm Fraser was prime minister of Australia from 1975 to 1983. Although he was able to curb inflation and attract foreign investment to develop Australia's natural resources, his conservative economic policies and the lifting of the ban on the mining and exporting of uranium aroused widespread opposition. After the defeat of his Liberal-Country party coalition in the general elections of March 1983, Fraser resigned as leader of the Liberal party and gave up his seat in Parliament.

John Malcolm Fraser, b. May 21, 1930, became prime minister of Australia on Nov. 11, 1975. He was appointed to that post by Gov.-Gen. Sir John KERR after Kerr had dismissed the incumbent prime minister, Gough WHITLAM. Whitlam, leader of the Australian Labor party, had been unable to get the upper house of Parliament, where Fraser's Liberal party had a majority, to pass vital bills funding the civil service. As soon as Fraser became prime minister, he allowed the money bills to pass and called a general election in December 1975, which his party won with ease.

Fraser was born into a landed family in Melbourne and attended private schools and Magdalen College, Oxford. He became a prosperous cattle rancher in western Victoria, where a rural constituency elected him to Parliament in 1955. Fraser was minister for the army (1966–68), for education and science (1968–69, 1971–72), and for defense (1969–71) before being elected leader of the Liberal party in March 1975.

Fraser's program as prime minister was strongly conservative. He reduced government expenditures wherever possible, cut back public services, and reorganized the health administration to reduce the government's role. Although he failed to reduce the country's high unemployment, he managed to reduce inflation while cutting the income tax. His austere strategies were not popular, however. His Liberal-Country party coalition, which won a huge majority in the general election of December 1977, was returned with a much-reduced majority in October 1980 and was decisively defeated by the Labor party, led by Robert HAWKE, in March 1983.

Fraser, James Earle

James Earle Fraser, b. Winona, Minn., Nov. 4, 1876, d. Oct. 11, 1953, created some of the best-known sculpture in the United States. Fraser modeled the reliefs of a buffalo and an Indian's head for the nickel issued in 1913. His famous *The End of the Trail* (Cowboy Hall of Fame, Oklahoma City, Okla.), made for the 1915 Pacific Panama Exposition in San Francisco from a smaller version done in 1894, portrays a beaten warrior on a broken pony and symbolizes the fate of the Plains Indians. Fraser's bronze equestrian statue (1923–40) of Theodore Roosevelt stands in front of New York City's Museum of Natural History.   JOAN C. SIEGFRIED

Bibliography: Krakel, Dean, *End of the Trail: The Odyssey of a Statue* (1973); Morris, Joseph, ed., *James Earle Fraser* (1955).

Fraser, Peter

Peter Fraser, b. Aug. 28, 1884, d. Dec. 12, 1950, was prime minister of New Zealand from 1940 to 1949. In 1910 he emigrated from Scotland to New Zealand, where he became a union organizer and helped establish the Labour party in 1916. He served in Parliament from 1918 until his death.

When the Labour party came to power in 1935, Fraser was named minister of education and health. He became prime minister upon the death of Michael Joseph SAVAGE in 1940. During World War II he secured an independent voice for New Zealand in the Allied war councils and was a spokesperson for small countries in the discussions that led to the founding of the United Nations.

Bibliography: Thorn, James, *Peter Fraser* (1952).

Fraser, Simon

Simon Fraser, b. 1776, d. Apr. 18, 1862, was a Canadian fur trader and explorer. The Fraser River is named for him. He was born in Bennington, Vt. (then N.Y.), but his mother took him to Canada after his father, a Loyalist, died in prison during the American Revolution. In 1792 he joined the NORTH WEST COMPANY, and in 1805 he took charge of the company's expansion west of the Rockies. In 1808, believing it to be the Columbia, he explored to its mouth the dangerous river that today bears his name. Fraser's epic journey proved that the river was unsuitable for transporting goods and furs.

Later taking charge of his company's Red River department, Fraser was one of the Nor'westers charged by the Earl of SELKIRK with complicity in the massacre of Seven Oaks, when an armed band attacked Selkirk's RED RIVER SETTLEMENT in 1816. Fraser retired soon after and settled in St. Andrews, Upper Canada (now Ontario), where he died in poverty.   GEORGE F. G. STANLEY

Bibliography: Fraser, Simon, *The Letters and Journals of Simon Fraser, 1806–1808*, ed. by W. Kaye Lamb (1960); Spargo, John, *Two Bennington-Born Explorers* (1950).

Fraser River

The Fraser, a major river in British Columbia, Canada, rises at Yellowhead Pass, Alberta, on the western slopes of the Rocky Mountains. It flows northwest in the Rocky Mountain Trench to Prince George, British Columbia, then south to the Strait of Georgia near Vancouver. The river drains a huge, scenic area of 217,800 km² (84,100 mi²), receiving the Nechako, Quesnel, Thompson, and Chilcotin rivers as well as numerous smaller streams along its 1,369-km (850-mi) course.

Fur traders and gold miners established the early settlements along the river in the first half of the 19th century. Today logging is the most important commercial activity, especially on the upper Fraser. Hydroelectric development is prohibited to protect the river's valuable salmon spawning runs. The Fraser is navigable to Yale, approximately 145 km (90 mi) from its mouth, through the cliffs of Fraser Canyon.

fraternal societies

Fraternal societies are private, voluntary associations of persons with shared interests. Nonprofit organizations, they serve a social function but also often have civic or benevolent purposes—in the tradition of their 16th-century forerunners, the English "friendly societies," which provided members with sickness and death benefits. Many are SECRET SOCIETIES, like the components of the largest organization, FREEMASONRY. Some, such as B'NAI BRITH and the KNIGHTS OF COLUMBUS, have religious backgrounds. Fraternal groups may also be esoteric (the ROSICRUCIANS) or political (TAMMANY HALL).

An early U.S. group, the Independent Order of Odd Fellows, formed in 1819, declared its independence from its English parent in 1842. Other notable U.S. fraternal benevolent life insurance groups began during and after the Civil War, including the Knights of Pythias (1864), the Benevolent and Protective Order of Elks (1868), the Loyal Order of Moose (1888), and the Fraternal Order of Eagles (1898).

Bibliography: Schmidt, A. A., *Fraternal Organizations* (1980).

fraternities and sororities

Fraternities and sororities are organizations that bring together men and women, respectively, for social, honor, service, or recognition purposes. Social fraternities and sororities, usually known by their Greek letters, are commonly found on American college campuses and may be national, with branches at many colleges, or may be on only one campus. PHI BETA KAPPA, the first honor society, or fraternity, was established in 1776.

History. Most social fraternities began in semisecrecy, possibly in imitation of FREEMASONRY, and bore the initials of Greek letters. Kappa Alpha at Union College was the first (1825). Adelphean at Wesleyan College, Georgia, was the first sorority, established in 1851. Fraternities grew rapidly after 1840. Divisiveness and controversy existed from the beginning, and animosity resulted from the fraternities' and sororities' choosing only the more socially favored as members and then encouraging an intensely conformist style of thought and behavior among those selected. In time the fraternities' influence on students rivaled the faculty's. Sensing this, many colleges in the 1870s tried unsuccessfully to abolish them. By 1898 a large minority of male American college students were fraternity members. Fraternities and sororities had developed into established national organizations, run by their alumni, and operating local chapters on many campuses. Separate fraternities and sororities were formed by black students who were excluded from white societies. Their social patterns were similar to those of the white organizations. Fraternities and sororities for people of various ethnic groups and in certain academic disciplines have been established.

Members of fraternities maintained that the experience of living in a fraternity house while in college was the most valuable part of their education, teaching fellowship, mutual sacrifice, and group solidarity. Their critics said that fraternities and sororities divided colleges into factions, promoting envy, and that these organizations encouraged moral laxity, dissipation, contempt for scholarship, and rowdyism.

Recent Trends. During the late 1960s, as college students became involved in serious political activities and in a search for alternative life-styles, fraternities and sororities suddenly lost favor. White societies had already been under attack (and in a few cases locally outlawed) for discriminating against nonwhite students. Some chapters actually closed, and many had trouble filling their available spaces. It seemed that fraternities might be losing their grip on the social scene at many campuses, after more than a century of dominance. Between 1965 and 1972 fraternities nationally lost 20 percent of their undergraduate members. More significantly, as college enrollments boomed and more college students commuted from home, the number of students who became fraternity members dropped dramatically. In 1972 it was less than 4 percent of American male college students.

Yet at the low point in 1972 there remained 4,407 national fraternity chapters, with an average of 34 undergraduates in each chapter. Thereafter fraternities experienced a mild but steady revival. By 1990, despite such resistance as Amherst College's abolition of its fraternities in 1984, there were about 400,000 undergraduate-male and more than 140,000 undergraduate-female members.   LAURENCE VEYSEY

Bibliography: *Baird's Manual of American College Fraternities* (1977); Leemon, Thomas A., *The Rites of Passage in a Student Culture* (1972); Scott, William A., *Values and Organizations: A Study of Fraternities and Sororities* (1965); Sheldon, Henry D., *Student Life and Customs* (1901; repr. 1969); Winston, R. B., Jr., et al., eds., *Fraternities and Sororities on the Contemporary Campus* (1987).

fraud

Courts have distinguished two types of fraud, actual fraud and constructive fraud. Actual fraud is intentional criminal deception for the purpose of inducing another to part with something of value, to acquire something of less than apparent value, or to surrender a legal right. Schemes specifically intended to cheat someone, such as selling shares in nonexistent plots of land, are actual frauds. Constructive frauds are words, acts, or omissions that tend to mislead or deceive someone or violate a confidence but that are not necessarily of malicious intent. Selling a house while forgetting to mention a chronically malfunctioning heating system is an example of constructive fraud. In civil law, fraud is an element in the TORT of deceit (fraudulent representation). To collect DAMAGES or to void a fraudulent contract, the plaintiff must usually show that the defendant knowingly made false statements and deliberately tricked the plaintiff into doing something the plaintiff would not have done if in possession of the facts.

Some examples of fraud include CONFIDENCE GAMES, EMBEZZLEMENT, FORGERY, using stolen credit cards, and impersonation. Other common practices are investment frauds in which swindlers sell worthless securities and consumer frauds where bargain hunters succumb to "bait and switch" schemes or fraudulent "going out of business" sales. Government attempts to prevent fraud led to the creation (1934) of the Securities and Exchange Commission, disclosure laws such as the Truth in Lending Act (1968), and other forms of consumer protection.

Bibliography: Kwitney, Jonathan, *The Fountain Pen Conspiracy* (1973); Oughton, Frederick, *Fraud and White Collar Crime* (1971).

Fraunhofer, Joseph von   [frown'-hoh-fur]

The German optical craftsman Joseph von Fraunhofer, b. Mar. 6, 1787, d. June 7, 1826, was the first to designate and map (1814) the dark lines, first observed by W. H. Wollaston, that cross the solar spectrum. These FRAUNHOFER LINES eventually provided data on the composition of the Sun and other stars.

Fraunhofer diffraction: see DIFFRACTION.

Fraunhofer lines   [frown'-hoh-fur]

In astronomy, Fraunhofer lines are the numerous dark lines that appear in the SPECTRUM of the Sun and other stars. Although they were first observed and mentioned by the British physicist William H. Wollaston in 1802, the lines are named after Joseph von FRAUNHOFER, who made the first detailed

THE MOST INTENSE FRAUNHOFER LINES

Notation	Origin	Wavelength, Å	Notation	Origin	Wavelength, Å
A	O^2	7594–7621*	b_4	Mg	5167.343
B	O^2	6867–6884*	c	Fe	4957.609
C	H	6562.816	F	H	4861.327
α	O^2	6267–6287*	d	Fe	4668.140
D_1	Na	5895.923	e	Fe	4383.547
D_2	Na	5889.953	f	H	4340.465
D_3	He	5875.618	G	Fe	4307.906
E_2	Fe	5269.541	G	Ca	4307.741
b_1	Mg	5183.618	g	Ca	4226.728
b_2	Mg	5172.699	h	H	4101.735
b_3	Fe	5168.901	H	Ca^+	3968.468
b_4	Fe	5167.491	K	Ca^+	3933.666

*Band, due to absorption by Earth's atmosphere.

study of them, starting in about 1814. Some 25,000 Fraunhofer lines have been mapped in the Sun's spectrum. The lines are due to atoms (not molecules) in the star's lower atmosphere that selectively absorb light at the same wavelengths that, under different conditions, they would emit. Thus, the presence of a given element in the star may be proved by demonstrating the existence of Fraunhofer lines in the same positions as in that element's emission spectrum. Fraunhofer designated the more prominent lines by letters, a system still in use.

See also: STELLAR SPECTRUM.

Frazer, Sir James

The Scottish anthropologist and classicist Sir James George Frazer, b. Glasgow, Jan. 1, 1854, d. May 7, 1941, is best known for his masterpiece, The GOLDEN BOUGH (2 vols., 1890; 3d ed., 13 vols. 1911–15; abr. 1 vol. ed., 1922), a monumental study in comparative myth and religion. Written in an eloquent style, the influential work is especially important for its insight into the nature of MAGIC and its examination of Europe's pagan past. Frazer was educated at the universities of Glasgow and Cambridge and was a fellow of Trinity College, Cambridge. His other writings include Totemism and Exogamy (1910) and Folk-lore in the Old Testament (1918).

STEPHEN KOWALEWSKI

Bibliography: Ackerman, Robert, J. G. Frazer: His Life and Work (1988; repr. 1991); Downie, Robert Angus, James George Frazer (1940) and Frazer and the Golden Bough (1970).

Frazier, Edward Franklin

Edward Franklin Frazier, b. Baltimore, Md., Sept. 24, 1894, d. May 17, 1962, was a black American sociologist whose overall concern was the progress, organization, and function of the black family. He wrote The Negro Family in the United States (1939), in which he analyzed the destructive effects of slavery and prejudice on the black family, and Black Bourgeoisie (1957). Frazier was chairman of Howard University's sociology department (1934–59).

Bibliography: Odum, Howard W., American Sociology: The Story of Sociology in the United States through 1950 (1951).

Frazier, Joe

Joseph Frazier, b. Beaufort, S.C., Jan. 12, 1944, an American boxer who became heavyweight champion, is best known for his bouts with Muhammad Ali, which were enormous competitive and financial successes. Frazier turned professional after winning the 1964 Olympic heavyweight title, then emerged with the world title after Ali was stripped of it in 1967. Frazier continued undefeated and eventually defeated Ali in 1971. He lost the title to George Foreman in 1973 but fought and lost to Ali two more times and to Foreman once more before retiring with a 32-4 record in 1976.

Bibliography: Pepe, Phil, Come Out Smokin': Joe Frazier, the Champ Nobody Knew (1972).

Freake limner   [freek]

One of the most skillful "limners," as portrait painters were called in 17th-century America, was the unidentified painter of the portraits of John Freake and of his wife and daughter, Mrs. Elizabeth Freake and Baby Mary (both c.1674; Worcester Art Museum, Mass.). Known to have worked in Boston between 1670 and 1674, the Freake limner painted in a linear style derived from the English Tudor tradition, which had long been outmoded in England. Nonetheless, his work, which may include The Gibbs Children (Worcester Art Museum), conveys a powerful sense of the humanity of his subjects and a fine grasp of detail.   DAVID TATHAM

Bibliography: Barker, Virgil, American Painting (1960).

Fréchet, Maurice René   [fray-shay']

The French mathematician Maurice René Fréchet, b. Sept. 2, 1878, d. June 4, 1973, made major contributions to the topology of point sets and defined and founded the theory of abstract spaces. A versatile mathematician, he served as profes-

sor of mechanics at the University of Poitiers (1910–19) and professor of higher calculus at the University of Strasbourg (1920–27) and held several different positions in the field of mathematics at the University of Paris (1928–48). Fréchet also made important contributions to statistics and calculus.

H. HOWARD FRISINGER

Fréchette, Louis Honoré   [fray-shet']

Louis Honoré Fréchette, b. Nov. 16, 1839, d. May 31, 1908, was a French-Canadian poet whose poems were also acclaimed in France. In 1880 his Les Fleurs boréales (Northern Flowers, 1879) and Les Oiseaux de neige (Snowbirds, 1879) were awarded the Prix Montyon by the Académie Française. Inspired by Victor Hugo's La Légende des siècles (1859–83), he wrote an epic of French Canada, La Légende d'un peuple (The Story of a People, 1887).

Bibliography: McDougall, R., Canada's Past and Present (1965).

freckle

Freckles are small, yellowish or brownish spots on the skin caused by an accumulation of the skin pigment melanin. The pigment cells respond unevenly to sunlight. Freckles appear in susceptible, usually fair-skinned persons as a result of exposure to sunlight and may become permanent. Freckles can sometimes be minimized by the use of sunscreen lotions containing para-aminobenzoic acid (PABA).

Frederick

Frederick is an agricultural center in the fertile Monocacy Valley of north central Maryland. The seat of Frederick County, it was settled in 1745 and has a population of 40,148 (1990). The city is the site of Hood College, a state school for the deaf, and Fort Detrick Army Research Laboratory. Frederick's historical attractions include the grave of Francis Scott Key and the homes of Chief Justice Roger B. Taney and Barbara Fritchie, a legendary Civil War heroine.

Frederick I, Elector of Brandenburg

Frederick I, elector of Brandenburg, b. 1371?, d. Sept. 20, 1440, was the first HOHENZOLLERN ruler in Berlin, where his descendants reigned until 1918. By his many services as Burggraf (count) of Nuremberg, Frederick won the gratitude of the German king Sigismund, who rewarded him with the office of administrator of Brandenburg (1411) and then elector (1417). Frederick's chief tasks were to curb the fractious nobility, restore order, repel external foes, and recover alienated properties. He unsuccessfully schemed (1421–24) to acquire the Polish crown and feuded with the Teutonic Knights. Because he always remained active in other German affairs and retained his Franconian estates, Frederick himself spent less than 6 years in Brandenburg, but he left his sons firmly in control.

RAYMOND H. SCHMANDT

Frederick III, King of Denmark

Frederick III, b. Mar. 18, 1609, d. Feb. 9, 1670, king of Denmark and Norway, established the most thoroughly absolute monarchy in Europe. A younger son of Christian IV, he grew up in Germany as administrator of Bremen and Verden. In 1644 these territories were conquered by Sweden.

Frederick succeeded his father to the throne in 1648, his older brother having died in 1647. At first his power was severely restricted by the aristocracy, and he devoted much time to cultural interests. War with Sweden in 1657–60 made him popular for his defense of Copenhagen. It also gave him control of an army, which he used in 1660 to establish a completely absolute royal regime that survived for 200 years. His son, Christian V, succeeded him.   J. R. CHRISTIANSON

Frederick IV, King of Denmark

Frederick IV, b. Oct. 11, 1671, d. Oct. 12, 1730, was king of Denmark and Norway during the Great NORTHERN WAR. Intelligent but poorly educated, sensual but religious, he succeeded his father, Christian V, in 1699. The wars against Sweden in 1700 and 1709-20 gave him control of the dangerous Swedish satellite, Holstein-Gottorp (also called ducal Schleswig), on Denmark's southern border. Frederick reformed Danish education, the national militia, and the status of peasants. He sponsored one of the earliest foreign missions from Protestant Europe—to India. Unhappily married, he twice became a bigamist. He was succeeded by his son, Christian VI.

J. R. CHRISTIANSON

Frederick VI, King of Denmark

Frederick VI, b. Jan. 28, 1768, d. Dec. 3, 1839, was the last Danish king to rule Norway as well as Denmark. In 1784 he led a bloodless coup that made him the actual ruler, though his insane father, Christian VII, remained king until 1808. Frederick and his advisors carried through reforms to establish an independent landowning peasantry and universal education in Denmark. Allying with France in 1807, he lost Norway when Napoleon I was defeated in 1814. The rest of Frederick's reign was a time of economic depression but intellectual flowering. Dignified and immensely popular, Frederick was succeeded by his cousin's son, Christian VIII.

J. R. CHRISTIANSON

Frederick VII, King of Denmark

Frederick VII, b. Oct. 6, 1808, d. Nov. 15, 1863, king of Denmark, ended absolute monarchy in his country. Neglected by his divorced parents, he was poorly educated, indolent, and eccentric; he was twice divorced before becoming happily married to a ballerina. Frederick became king in 1848 when his father, Christian VIII, died. Facing disturbances, he gave up his absolute rights and signed the constitution of 1849, establishing parliamentary government. This act and his congeniality made him tremendously popular. He recognized CHRISTIAN IX as his successor but left his kingdom on the verge of war with Prussia and Austria over SCHLESWIG-HOLSTEIN.

J. R. CHRISTIANSON

Frederick I, King of Germany and Holy Roman Emperor   (Frederick Barbarossa)

Frederick I, or Frederick Barbarossa, German king and Holy Roman emperor, was one of the outstanding medieval German emperors. An intelligent statesman of imagination and determination, he was also an ideally chivalric personality. He entertained an exalted concept of his dignity as Roman emperor and introduced the use of the word *Holy* in the title. This was intended to reflect a mystical association between himself and the destiny of Christianity as well as his ties with

Frederick I (Barbarossa), German king (1152-90) and Holy Roman emperor (1155-90), is shown flanked by his sons the future emperor Henry VI (left) and Frederick, duke of Swabia. Barbarossa was a powerful statesman and believer in his mystical destiny as emperor.

Charlemagne and the ancient caesars.

Born probably in 1122, Frederick was the nephew of the German king CONRAD III, whom he was elected to succeed in 1152. His HOHENSTAUFEN dynasty had its base in Swabia and Franconia, and he added to his patrimony and developed its resources by encouraging urban expansion. Burgundy came into his hands by his marriage (1156) to its heiress, Beatrix.

Frederick's concept of government was feudal and hierarchical. He created the rank of *Reichsfürst,* prince of the empire, for his chief vassals; in return for their support he aided them against rivals within their domains. His own chief rival was the Welf, or Guelph, HENRY THE LION. To placate Henry, Frederick in 1154 confirmed his rights as duke of both Saxony and Bavaria. When Henry later refused military service, Frederick in 1180 broke his power and seized his duchies. Frederick also dominated the church in Germany.

Anxious to assert his imperial power in Italy, Frederick undertook six expeditions across the Alps. On his first expedition (1154-55) he overthrew the republican ARNOLD OF BRESCIA in Rome and was crowned (1155) by the pope. Later his chief foe was the Lombard towns, who formed the Lombard League against him. Because Frederick fomented a schism by promoting an antipope, Pope ALEXANDER III cooperated with the Lombards. The Lombards finally defeated Frederick at Legnano in 1176. The emperor made his peace with the pope in the Treaty of Anagni (1176), and the subsequent Treaty of Constance (1183) acknowledged his sovereignty over Lombardy but reduced his actual control.

In 1186, Frederick arranged the marriage of his son, the future HENRY VI, to Constance, heiress of Sicily; this soon brought the Norman kingdom of Sicily into Hohenstaufen hands. Joining the Third CRUSADE, Frederick led his army across Europe into Anatolia, where he drowned on June 10, 1190.

RAYMOND H. SCHMANDT

Bibliography: Barraclough, Geoffrey, *The Origins of Modern Germany,* 2d ed. (1957); Hampe, Karl, *Germany under the Salian and Hohenstaufen Emperors,* trans. by Ralph Bennett (1973); Munz, Peter, *Frederick Barbarossa* (1969); Pacaut, Marcel, *Frederick Barbarossa* (1970).

Frederick II, King of Germany and Holy Roman Emperor

Frederick II, German king (1212-20), king of Sicily (1197-1250), and Holy Roman emperor (1220-50), was a fascinating personality. He was a Renaissance man in his philosophy and politics, with a broad cultural outlook and intellectual gifts. However, his policies led to conflict and irrevocably weakened the German monarchy.

The son of Emperor HENRY VI and Constance of Sicily, Frederick was born on Dec. 26, 1194, and grew up in Sicily as the ward and vassal of Pope INNOCENT III. When Henry VI died (1197), his son was recognized as king of Sicily, but in Germany PHILIP OF SWABIA and OTTO IV were elected rival kings. Finally, in 1212, Pope Innocent, disillusioned by Otto, persuaded Frederick to go north to assert his hereditary rights. First, however, Frederick promised to resign his Sicilian kingdom, for the pope feared the loss of his own freedom should both kingdoms be held by the same man.

The Battle of BOUVINES (1214) made Frederick master of Germany, where he stayed until 1220. With the permission of Pope Honorius III, he then exchanged Germany for Sicily as the kingdom he could retain, assigning Germany to his infant son Henry. A short visit (1235-37) was the only other time Frederick resided in the north. His policy toward Germany was to make any concession necessary to avoid controversy. He gave away one royal prerogative after another and compelled his unwilling sons, Henry and CONRAD IV, to acquiesce. At Frederick's death Conrad and then his son, Conradin, could not recover the authority Frederick had dissipated.

Frederick preferred the greater freedom of the Norman kingdom of Sicily, whose government he organized into unparalleled centralized efficiency. The Constitutions of Melfi (1231) are his outstanding pieces of legislation. In northern Italy he revived old imperial claims with the result that the Lombard towns fought him constantly.

Frederick also quarreled with the popes, his feudal over-lords. Honorius III excommunicated him in 1227 for violating his vow to go on crusade. Setting out the next year, Frederick recovered Jerusalem from the Muslims by diplomacy. Already married (1225) to Isabel of Brienne, queen of Jerusalem, he crowned himself king of Jerusalem in 1229. In 1239, Pope GREGORY IX excommunicated Frederick on charges of heresy, and INNOCENT IV induced the Council of Lyon (1245) to declare him deposed. Frederick continued to fight both the popes and Lombards with mixed success until his death on Dec. 13, 1250.   RAYMOND H. SCHMANDT

Bibliography: Einstein, David, *Emperor Frederick II* (1949); Kantoro-wicz, Ernst H., *Frederick the Second, 1194–1250,* trans. by E. O. Lorimer (1957); Powell, James M., *The Liber Augustalis; or Constitutions of Melfi* (1971); Van Cleve, Thomas Curtis, *The Emperor Frederick II of Hohenstaufen* (1972).

Frederick III, King of Germany and Holy Roman Emperor

Frederick III, b. Sept. 9, 1415, d. Aug. 19, 1493, German king from 1440, was the first HABSBURG to be crowned Holy Roman emperor by the pope and the last emperor to be crowned in Rome (1452). Aware of the limitations of his authority within Germany and always short of funds, he concentrated his energies on family matters. Early in his reign he lost control of both Bohemia and Hungary, which his cousin and predecessor, ALBERT II, had acquired.

By the Concordat of Vienna (1448) Frederick regulated control of church offices and helped force dissolution of the Council of Basel, which was asserting conciliar (see CONCILIARISM) supremacy over the popes. He hired as a secretary Aeneas Sylvius Piccolomini (later Pope PIUS II), who first brought Renaissance influences to Germany. Frederick's greatest dynastic achievement was to arrange the marriage (1477) of MARY OF BURGUNDY to his son Maximilian (later Emperor MAXIMILIAN I), thus setting the stage for the Habsburg domination of Europe in the 16th century.   RAYMOND H. SCHMANDT

Bibliography: Barraclough, Geoffrey, *The Origins of Modern Germany* (1947).

Frederick I, King of Prussia

Frederick I, b. July 11, 1657, d. Feb. 25, 1713, the first king of PRUSSIA, was the son of FREDERICK WILLIAM, the Great Elector, whom he succeeded as elector of Brandenburg on May 9, 1688. As Elector Frederick III, he demonstrated more interest in cultural affairs and court life than in his government, which he allowed to fall into the hands of corrupt favorites.

The one substantial political achievement of his largely undistinguished reign came at the outset of the War of the SPANISH SUCCESSION. By agreeing to support the claims of the Austrian Habsburgs to the territorial possessions of their dynasty's extinct Spanish line, Frederick received approval from Emperor LEOPOLD I to assume a royal title. In an elaborate public ceremony at Königsberg on Jan. 18, 1701, Frederick proclaimed himself "king in Prussia." His new crown was an immediate source of prestige for the HOHENZOLLERN dynasty and served as a symbol of unity for the rising state of Brandenburg-Prussia.   JOHN A. MEARS

Frederick II, King of Prussia   (Frederick the Great)

Frederick II, known to posterity as Frederick the Great, ruled the kingdom of PRUSSIA from 1740 to 1786. He was born in Berlin on Jan. 24, 1712, and showed an early interest in literature and music that brought him into conflict with his authoritarian father, FREDERICK WILLIAM I. Frederick William did not understand the cultural pursuits of the young crown prince and imposed a rigidly structured military upbringing upon him. In 1730, Frederick tried to escape his father's tyranny by fleeing the court. He was soon captured, however, and imprisoned in the fortress of Küstrin, where his father forced him to witness the execution of his close friend Lieutenant Katte.

Frederick II, King of Prussia (1740–86), called Frederick the Great, successfully pursued a course destined to aggrandize Prussia culturally, militarily, and commercially. A brilliant general whose wars secured Silesia for Prussia, "Old Fritz" also instituted important legal and administrative reforms.

Thoroughly subdued by a year of confinement, he was determined to regain his father's trust. He took command of an army regiment and immersed himself in administrative duties, learning everything he could about politics and war. As a reward Frederick William allowed him to spend his leisure hours studying philosophy, playing the flute, writing poetry, and corresponding with famous intellectuals, most notably Voltaire. When Frederick finally succeeded his father on May 31, 1740, he was well prepared to assume the responsibilities of kingship.

Frederick began his reign by invading SILESIA, a possession of the Austrian Habsburgs. Having claimed the province as his own, he spent the next 23 years defending this valuable conquest. Illustrious campaigns in the War of the AUSTRIAN SUCCESSION (1740–48) and the SEVEN YEARS' WAR (1756–63) demonstrated his extraordinary military talents and enabled him to consolidate Prussia's position as a leading power in the European state system.

To preserve his gains, Frederick followed a peaceful course after 1763. Without disrupting the continental equilibrium, he negotiated the first partition of Poland with Austria and Russia in 1772 (see POLAND, PARTITIONS OF). Through skillful diplomacy he acquired all of West Prussia except the cities of Danzig (Gdánsk) and Thorn (Torún), thereby bridging the gap between East Prussia and Brandenburg. His major preoccupation, however, was with the rehabilitation of his war-ravaged domains rather than territorial expansion. During the last 23 years of his life, "Old Fritz," as his subjects had come to call him, implemented a series of far-reaching reforms that made his regime a model of 18th-century enlightened despotism.

One of Frederick's first official acts had been the abolition of torture, except for crimes such as murder and treason. He permitted some freedom of speech and press and decreed broad religious toleration, welcoming even Jesuits into his predominantly Protestant country. Only Jews, whom he viewed as "useless to the state," were excluded from this policy. Frederick gradually improved Prussia's judicial system. He established impartial and efficient court procedures and reorganized existing laws into a single code.

When it came to social reform, Frederick was less progressive. He defended traditional distinctions of rank and privilege, in part because he relied on the nobility to staff his bureaucracy and officer corps. He relieved the burdens of peasants who lived on his own lands but did little to ameliorate the lot of serfs tied to the private estates of the aristocracy, or Junkers.

Frederick shaped his economic policies in accordance with the mercantilist principles of the age (see MERCANTILISM). Hoping to turn Prussia into a self-sufficient state, he limited the export of raw materials, erected tariff barriers against foreign goods, and removed many internal tolls. He subsidized the metallurgy and textile industries to meet the requirements of his army and encouraged new enterprises by granting monopolies for products such as porcelain, silk, and tobacco. He also sought to improve agriculture by introducing scientific methods of cattle breeding and crop rotation from western Europe. He fostered the planting of soil-enriching clover and fodder crops as well as inexpensive foods such as turnips and potatoes. He also drained swamps in the Oder and Vistula river valleys, initiated reforestation projects, and settled approximately 300,000 immigrant farmers in sparsely populated areas.

No monarch ever worked harder than Frederick the Great. He maintained a vigorous schedule that customarily started at six in the morning. Unwilling to delegate authority, he wanted all important governmental business to pass across his desk at the palace of Sans Souci near Potsdam. He depended upon written reports from his ministers and personal inspection tours to provide the information he needed to supervise every branch of his administrative machine. Although he stifled initiative and independence, Frederick raised professional standards in his civil service by treating corruption and mismanagement with the utmost severity.

The ceaseless labors of "Old Fritz" did not go unrewarded. By the time of his death on Aug. 17, 1786, Prussia's population was approaching 6,000,000 and its army numbered 200,000 men. He left his successor, FREDERICK WILLIAM II, a full treasury and a smoothly operating, disciplined bureaucracy. Unfortunately, his highly centralized system of government required able leadership at the top, and those who followed him on the Prussian throne lacked his energy, intelligence, and dedication.   JOHN A. MEARS

Bibliography: Asprey, R. B., *Frederick the Great* (1988); Duffy, C., *The Military Life of Frederick the Great* (1986); Ingrao, C. W., *The Hessian Mercenary State* (1986); Johnson, H. C., *Frederick the Great and His Officials* (1975); Kittredge, M., *Frederick the Great* (1987); Mitford, N., *Frederick the Great* (1970); Paret, P., comp., *Frederick the Great: A Profile* (1972); Reddaway, W., *Frederick the Great and the Rise of Prussia* (1904; repr. 1969).

Frederick III, Emperor of Germany

Frederick III, b. Oct. 18, 1831, d. June 15, 1888, emperor of Germany, reigned for only 99 days in 1888. The son of WILLIAM I, king of Prussia and emperor of Germany, Frederick married (1858) Victoria, eldest daughter of Queen Victoria of Britain. As crown prince, he served in the Franco-Prussian War (1870–71) and was a patron of the arts. Frederick was considered a liberal, and his death, from cancer, disappointed many who had looked forward to his rule. He was succeeded by his son WILLIAM II.   ROBIN BUSS

Frederick III, Elector of Saxony   (Frederick the Wise)

The Saxon ruler Frederick III, b. Jan. 17, 1463, d. May 5, 1525, sheltered Martin LUTHER when that religious leader and his doctrines were under attack by the pope and Holy Roman Emperor CHARLES V. A member of the Ernestine branch of the Wettin family, Frederick succeeded as elector of Saxony in 1486. Called "the Wise" because of his reputation for good advice among the German princes, he founded (1502) the university at Wittenberg where Luther and Philipp Melanchthon taught. After the Diet of Worms (1521) placed Luther under an imperial ban, Frederick took him into custody and won an exemption for Saxony from the Edict of Worms's outlawing of Lutheran teachings.

Frederick V, Elector Palatine   (the Winter King)

Frederick V, b. Aug. 26, 1596, d. Nov. 29, 1632, elector palatine (1610–20) and king of Bohemia (1619–20), called the Winter King, was largely responsible for the outbreak of the THIRTY YEARS' WAR.

A member of the Calvinist Palatine branch of the house of WITTELSBACH, Frederick V was the nephew of MAURICE OF NASSAU, virtual ruler of the Netherlands. In 1613 he married Elizabeth, daughter of JAMES I of England. The couple shared religion, personal charm, ambition, and political incompetence. In 1619 the rebellious Bohemians elected Frederick king. Failing to receive support from his powerful relatives, Frederick

was defeated in 1620 by the armies of the Holy Roman emperor and the Catholic League and fled. His generals and other allies continued the war, but the emperor bestowed the Upper Palatinate and the electorate on Frederick's distant relative, MAXIMILIAN, duke of Bavaria.   H. G. KOENIGSBERGER

Bibliography: Wedgwood, Cecelia V., *The Thirty Years' War* (1969).

Frederick Henry, Prince of Orange

Frederick Henry, b. Jan. 29, 1584, d. Mar. 14, 1647, prince of Orange and count of Nassau, established by his military victories the general territorial limits of United Provinces of the Netherlands. The youngest son of WILLIAM I (William the Silent), founder of the Dutch republic, he followed his half-brother MAURICE OF NASSAU as stadholder (governor) of the five principal provinces in 1625 and also of Groningen in 1640. As captain- and admiral-general, Frederick Henry halted the renewed Spanish offensives against the republic and captured numerous cities from Spain between 1627 and 1645. During his reign the golden age of Dutch art flourished.
                                               HERBERT H. ROWEN

Frederick William, Elector of Brandenburg
(the Great Elector)

Frederick William, elector of BRANDENBURG and duke of PRUSSIA, is known as the Great Elector because of his critical contributions to the early development of the HOHENZOLLERN state. Born on Feb. 16, 1620, Frederick William succeeded his father, George William, in 1640, inheriting small and widely dispersed northern German territories that had been ravaged in the fighting of the THIRTY YEARS' WAR (1618–48).

By the time of his death on May 9, 1688, the Great Elector had built a standing professional army of 30,000 men to defend his poverty-stricken lands against outside invasion and a unified administration capable of levying taxes without approval from the local estates (provincial assemblies representing the landed nobility and towns). In asserting his authority over the estates, Frederick William diminished the independence of the JUNKER aristocracy and enlisted their service as army officers. He sought to increase the wealth and prosperity of Brandenburg-Prussia by promoting the growth of agriculture, industry, and commerce and by encouraging Polish Jews, French Huguenots, and other religious refugees to settle within his domains.

In foreign affairs the Great Elector pursued a shifting course between the larger European powers. By the Peace of Westphalia, which ended the Thirty Years' War in 1648, he received Eastern Pomerania and other territories. In the Little Northern War (1655–60) he fought against Poland in alliance with Sweden until 1657 and then allied with Poland against Sweden. By the Peace of Oliva (May 3, 1660) he won formal recognition of his sovereignty over ducal Prussia, formerly held as a fief of the Polish crown. Both in that war and in the second stage (1674–78) of the Third Dutch War (known as the

Frederick William, elector of Brandenburg (1640–88), known as the Great Elector, laid the foundations of the Prussian state. A man of superb organizational ability, he created a centralized administration for his scattered lands, built up the army, and fostered commerce and industry.

Third ANGLO-DUTCH WAR before the English withdrawal in 1674), Frederick William conquered Western, or Swedish, Pomerania but was compelled to surrender it by the peace settlements. His victory over the Swedes at Fehrbellin (June 18, 1675) was the first demonstration of the superiority of the new Prussian army.   JOHN A. MEARS

Bibliography: Schevill, Ferdinand, *The Great Elector* (1947).

Frederick William I, King of Prussia

Frederick William I, b. Aug. 15, 1688, d. May 31, 1740, succeeded his father, FREDERICK I, as king of Prussia in 1713. He devoted his reign to the task of building the military power of his small and impoverished state. He began by centralizing governmental administration in a single board known as the general directory and organizing an efficient bureaucracy that cut royal expenditures while more than doubling annual income. The king utilized this additional revenue to expand his peacetime army to 83,000 men, transforming it into one of the best-trained and best-disciplined military establishments in Europe. To strengthen the economy, he nurtured industry and agriculture through mercantilistic policies, and by avoiding costly wars, he freed himself from dependence on foreign subsidies. Frederick William left to his son, FREDERICK II, whom he treated brutally, a treasury of 7,000,000 thalers.
                                                          JOHN A. MEARS

Bibliography: Ergang, R. R., *The Potsdam Fuehrer* (1941; repr. 1973).

Frederick William II, King of Prussia

Frederick William II, b. Sept. 25, 1744, d. Nov. 16, 1797, king of Prussia, succeeded his uncle FREDERICK II in 1786. From the outset of his reign the new king revealed an incompetence that threatened the political achievements of the Hohenzollern dynasty. Mistresses and favorites dominated his extravagant court. The once-efficient Prussian bureaucracy grew lax, while its highly respected army deteriorated in quality.

From the Polish partitions of 1793 and 1795, Prussia acquired Danzig (Gdánsk) and extensive territories running from Posen through Warsaw to the Niemen River. But Frederick William's mismanaged involvement in the War of the First Coalition (1792–97) against Revolutionary France drained his treasury and foreshadowed Prussia's disastrous defeat by Napoleon I at the Battle of Jena in 1806.   JOHN A. MEARS

See also: FRENCH REVOLUTIONARY WARS; POLAND, PARTITIONS OF.

Frederick William III, King of Prussia

Frederick William III, b. Aug. 3, 1770, d. June 7, 1840, king of Prussia (1797–1840), lived through more turbulence than almost any other member of the Hohenzollern dynasty. The son of Frederick William II, he lacked heroism and imagination, but he had nonetheless an appealing middle-class simplicity and dedication. He desired reform but lacked the drive to accomplish it. His main personal achievement was the emancipation of peasants on the royal estates. After 1806, Frederick William put through the administrative reforms proposed by K. A. HARDENBERG and H. F. K. STEIN. A constitution was promised but never granted by the king, who became increasingly conservative after 1819. The ZOLLVEREIN, or customs union, of 1834 was the major accomplishment of his later years, which were otherwise marred by repression.

The king's foreign policy was marked by caution. Prussia remained neutral in the NAPOLEONIC WARS until 1806, when it allied with Russia and Austria. Immediately defeated by the French in the Battle of Jena, it signed the humiliating Treaty of Tilsit (1807; see TILSIT, TREATIES OF) and thereafter remained out of the war until 1813, when its reorganized army played a major role in the final defeat of Napoleon I. As a result Prussia gained much territory at the Congress of Vienna (1814–15; see VIENNA, CONGRESS OF). Frederick William was an original signatory of the HOLY ALLIANCE (1815), which later became a symbol of reactionary policies.   ENNO E. KRAEHE

Bibliography: Holborn, Hajo, *A History of Modern Germany, 1648–1840* (1964).

Frederick William IV, King of Prussia

Frederick William IV, king of Prussia (1840–61), refused the crown of a united Germany offered (1849) by the Frankfurt Parliament because it came from an elected assembly. His own plan for German unification under Prussian domination was abandoned in the face of Austrian opposition.

Frederick William IV, the king who gave Prussia its first constitution, was artistically and intellectually gifted but lacked the simple realism of his father, Frederick William III. Born on Oct. 15, 1795, he developed a romantic outlook opposed equally to existing bureaucratic absolutism and to modern liberalism. On succeeding to the throne in 1840, he recalled many professors dismissed by his father. In 1847 he summoned an all-Prussian diet, and, initially acceding to the demands made in the REVOLUTIONS OF 1848, he granted a constitution in 1848.

Bold change, however, was not in him. In 1849 he refused the German imperial crown proffered by the FRANKFURT PARLIAMENT, and he withdrew his own plan for union (Olmütz, 1850) when threatened by Austria. He also amended (1850) the Prussian constitution to favor the rich by introducing a three-class voting system and increasingly relied on conservative cronies instead of ministers. Ironically, the reign of this backward-looking romantic also saw extensive railroad construction, industrial development, and legislation favorable to peasants and artisans. In 1857 the king's mental disability necessitated a regency under his brother, William (later German emperor as WILLIAM I), which lasted until Frederick William died on Jan. 2, 1861.   ENNO E. KRAEHE

Bibliography: Holborn, Hajo, *A History of Modern Germany, 1840–1945* (1969).

Fredericksburg   [fred'-riks-burg]

Fredericksburg (1990 pop., 19,027) is a politically independent city in northeastern Virginia. It is located about 64 km (40 mi) southwest of Alexandria on the Rappahannock River, at the fall line, and is a commercial center for the surrounding agricultural area. Fredericksburg was founded in the 1720s and named for Prince Frederick Louis, the father of George III. During the Civil War several important battles were fought at or near Fredericksburg, because of its situation on the land route from Washington to Richmond.

Fredericksburg, Battle of

The Battle of Fredericksburg, an engagement of the U.S. Civil War, was fought at Fredericksburg, Va., on Dec. 13, 1862. Gen. Ambrose E. BURNSIDE, who had just replaced Gen. George B. McClellan in command of the Union Army of the Potomac, attacked the heavily fortified lines of Robert E. LEE preparatory to a drive on Richmond, Va. All through a bloody day federal ranks surged against Lee's lines, melted away, reformed, surged, and melted again. Burnside lost 12,500 men, and his defeat ended federal activity in Virginia until the spring of 1863. FRANK E. VANDIVER

Bibliography: Luvaas, J., and Nelson, H. W., *The U.S. Army Guide to the Battles of Chancellorsville and Fredericksburg* (1989).

Fredericton [fred'-rik-tuhn]

Fredericton, a Canadian city of 44,352 (1986), is the capital of New Brunswick and seat of York County. Located on the Saint John River, it was the site of the French Fort Nachouac (1692) and the Acadian settlement of Saint Anne's Point (1731). Between 1783 and 1785, United Empire Loyalists settled the area, naming it for Frederick, the son of King George III. The city manufactures canoes, footwear, lumber products, and handicrafts and is the provincial headquarters for the Royal Canadian Mounted Police. The University of New Brunswick (founded 1785, reorganized 1859) and St. Thomas University (1910), which shares the University of New Brunswick campus, are in the city. Fredericton has several art museums and buildings of historical interest; the poets Bliss Carman, Sir Charles Roberts, and Francis Sherman were born there.

Fredholm, Erik Ivar [frayd'-hawlm, ay'-rik ee'-var]

Erik Ivar Fredholm, b. Apr. 7, 1866, d. Aug. 17, 1927, was one of Sweden's greatest applied mathematicians. He is especially noted for his work in differential equations and integral equations, and for having given the general solution to an important integral equation that now bears his name. David HILBERT's continuation of Fredholm's work led to the discovery of what are known as Hilbert spaces. J. W. DAUBEN

Fredonian Rebellion [free-dohn'-yuhn]

The Fredonian Rebellion, in December 1826, was an early and abortive attempt by American settlers in Texas to gain independence from Mexico. A gang of 30 men captured the town of Nacogdoches, declared the independence of the Republic of Fredonia, imprisoned the *alcalde* (mayor), and signed a pact with representatives of the Cherokees promising the Indians half of Texas in return for their support. The uprising was short-lived: most settlers, Americans as well as Mexicans, scorned participation with the renegade Fredonians and Cherokees, and more responsible Indian leaders rejected the pact. When Mexican troops and militia from Stephen AUSTIN's colony arrived to suppress the rebellion, the Fredonian leaders fled. SEYMOUR V. CONNOR

Bibliography: Connor, Seymour V., *Texas: A History* (1971).

Fredro, Alexander, Count [fred'-roh]

Count Alexander Fredro, b. July 20, 1793, d. July 15, 1876, is generally regarded as Poland's greatest comic dramatist. As a young man, Fredro joined the Polish army allied with Napoleon and saw action in nearly every major campaign in central and eastern Europe, including the invasion of Russia. Years later he expressed his disenchantment with the Polish-Napoleonic alliance in a posthumously published book of memoirs entitled *Trzy po trzy* (Topsy Turvy Talk, 1877).

Fredro is best remembered, however, for his plays. His most popular comedies are *Maz i zona* (Husband and Wife, 1822), *Ladies and Hussars* (1825; Eng. trans., 1925), *Maidens' Vows; or, The Magnetism of the Heart* (1834; Eng. trans., 1940), *Pan Jowialski* (Mister Joviality, 1832), *Zemsta* (The Vengeance, 1834), and *Dozywocie* (The Life Annuity, 1835). Criticism by younger, radical critics resentful of his conservatism caused Fredro to stop writing plays between 1835 and 1854. When he resumed playwriting, he would not permit his new plays to be staged during his lifetime. Virtually all have now been staged, but they have not had the impact of his earlier comedies. HAROLD B. SEGEL

Bibliography: Fredro, Alexander, *The Major Comedies of Alexander Fredro*, trans. by Harold B. Segel (1969).

free on board: see FOB.

free enterprise system: see CAPITALISM.

free fall

Free fall is motion determined solely by gravitational forces. For example, an object dropped or thrown into the air is in free fall at every point in its trajectory. An object in space, although influenced by the gravitational fields of many celestial bodies, is always in free fall, despite the fact that it may not actually be "falling" toward any of them.

A person inside a vessel that is falling freely is also in free fall and experiences the phenomenon of WEIGHTLESSNESS. Because gravitational effects are the same on both the person and the vessel, no acceleration is felt relative to the vessel.

A parachutist experiences free fall for a brief period before the parachute opens, but the force of air resistance against the person's body soon becomes significant and he or she no longer falls freely. In fact a terminal velocity (maximum speed) is reached of about 180 to 250 km/h (110 to 155 mph). An aircraft can simulate free fall conditions for about a minute by flying a particular parabolic trajectory, thereby subjecting its occupants to temporary weightlessness.

Bibliography: Benedikt, E. T., ed., *Weightlessness* (1960).

free port

A free port or a free zone within a port (also called a foreign-trade zone) is an area where foreign goods may be landed, processed, or manufactured and then reshipped without payment of customs duties. If, however, the goods are sold within the country in which the free port or zone is located, customs duties must be paid.

Free ports flourished in medieval Europe during the time of the HANSEATIC LEAGUE, when German towns such as Hamburg and Bremen became famous as ports for the transshipment of goods. The first free port in the United States was established in 1939 in New York City harbor and was followed by the creation of free ports in New Orleans (1947), San Francisco (1948), and Seattle (1949). Other ports that have free zones include Salina Cruz, Mexico; Colón, Panama; Hong Kong; Singapore; and Macao. Major international airports also have zones where duty-free goods can be bought and sold.

Bibliography: Thoman, R. S., *Free Ports and Foreign Trade Zones* (1956).

free radical

In chemistry, a free radical is an uncharged atom or molecule that has an odd number of electrons; that is, one electron is unpaired. Free radicals are highly reactive and thus have only a temporary existence. They may be formed by cleavage of a covalent bond when both new products retain one electron of the original shared pair. Cleavage of the chlorine molecule Cl_2 yields two chlorine free radicals (chlorine atoms). Free radicals react to yield other free radicals, which can similarly react, causing a chemical chain reaction. Fire is propagated by this mechanism, as are many polymerization reactions. In biology, superoxides—free radicals that contain the O_2^- molecule—are the main cause of the lethal effect that oxygen has on obligate ANAEROBES. The product of many biochemical reactions in the human body, superoxides can injure or kill cells and may contribute to the effects of cancer, heart attacks, strokes, and emphysema.

Bibliography: Halliwell, Barry, and Gutteridge, John M., *Free Radicals in Biology and Medicine*, 2d ed. (1990).

free schools

Free schools are designed to foster noncompetitive, nonauthoritarian attitudes in pupils. Often informal and antibureaucratic, they use OPEN CLASSROOMS and emphasize individualized instruction. Some free schools try to develop political awareness, sensitivity to the feelings of others, and antiracist sentiments. Although free schools such as SUMMERHILL are half a century old, the American movement began to grow in the mid-1960s. Private free schools were formed both in poor neighborhoods and in middle-class communities. Some were established in public school systems as ALTERNATIVE SCHOOLS.

Bibliography: Korn, Claire V., *Alternative American Schools* (1991); Swidler, Anne, *Organization without Authority* (1980).

free silver

In this late-19th-century political cartoon, Uncle Sam is "blind" to the silver controversy. Free-silver advocates—mainly representatives of farming, labor, and silver-mining interests—were unable to convince the federal government to mint unlimited quantities of silver coins.

Free silver was the battle cry used in late-19th-century America by advocates of unlimited coinage of silver. The cause won a large following and was especially popular among silver miners, farmers, and debtors. Until the post–Civil War era the United States had been a bimetallist nation—that is, the value of its currency was based on both gold and silver—but the silver standard was abandoned in 1873, because the metal's relative rarity had driven silver coins from circulation.

A severe depression in the mid-'70s and the sudden decline in silver's market price, which followed expanded production in the western United States, made the concept of free silver increasingly popular. Silverites believed that free coinage of silver would produce inflation and alleviate their financial woes. Although this never became national policy, both the BLAND-ALLISON ACT of 1878 and the Sherman Silver Purchase Act of 1890 included concessions to silverites.

In 1893, in the midst of another national depression and with discontented farmers mobilizing through the POPULIST PARTY, President Cleveland successfully brought about repeal of the Sherman Silver Purchase Act. Repeal strengthened the conviction of many that opposition to free silver was part of a class war by bankers and industrialists on the common people, a conviction exemplified by William Jennings BRYAN's oratorical cry: "You shall not crucify mankind upon a cross of gold!" But Bryan, the Democratic presidential candidate in 1896 and 1900, was twice defeated, and his defeats, plus the return of prosperity and passage of the Gold Standard Act (1900), dealt the free silver crusade blows from which it did not recover.   GERALD W. MCFARLAND

Bibliography: Laughlin, James Laurence, *History of Bimetallism in the United States*, 4th ed. (1897; repr. 1968); Nugent, Walter T. K., *Money and American Society, 1865–1880* (1968); Weinstein, Allan, *Prelude to Populism: Origins of the Silver Issue, 1867–1878* (1970).

Free-Soil party

The Free-Soil party was organized in 1848 to oppose the extension of slavery into the territories newly acquired by the United States from Mexico. Among its leaders was Salmon P. CHASE. The Free-Soil forces, composed of former Liberty party members, antislavery Whigs, and certain New York Democrats known as Barnburners, chose former president Martin VAN BUREN as their presidential candidate in 1848. Although they failed to carry a single state, the substantial Free-Soil vote in New York helped the Whigs defeat the Democrats in that state and thereby win the presidency for Zachary Taylor. They did, however, elect a number of congressmen. The party weakened in the 1852 election; most of its members later joined the new Republican party.   DOUGLAS T. MILLER

Bibliography: Blue, Frederick J., *The Free Soilers* (1973).

free trade

Free trade refers to commerce that is relatively unrestricted and unaided by government regulations, such as TARIFFS, quotas, and subsidies. The concept of free trade was first delineated in reaction against MERCANTILISM by the French PHYSIOCRATS of the 18th century and, later, by the classical economists, especially Adam SMITH and David RICARDO. Extending LAISSEZ-FAIRE principles to international trade, they asserted that nations should specialize in producing and exporting goods that they were most efficient at manufacturing and import goods that they were less efficient in producing. All nations would benefit by this economic law of comparative advantage if there were no barriers to the exchange of goods.

The practice of free trade received its initial impetus in Great Britain with the repeal (1846) of the CORN LAWS and the subsequent sweeping tariff reductions under William GLADSTONE. In order to promote free trade among the fragmented German states, the ZOLLVEREIN, a customs union, had already been formed (1834). The Anglo-French Treaty of 1860 and later free trade treaties introduced the concept of MOST-FAVORED-NATION STATUS, which greatly expanded international trade. Developing nations, however, such as the United States and many European countries, tended to favor high-tariff policies to protect young industries from foreign competition. The United States remained protectionist until the 1930s, when the Reciprocal Trade Agreements Act of 1934 and other initiatives by U.S. Secretary of State Cordell Hull revived interest in free trade. An increased desire for free trade was reflected in the BRETTON WOODS CONFERENCE (1944); the GENERAL AGREEMENT ON TARIFFS AND TRADE (GATT), after World War II; and organizations like the EUROPEAN FREE TRADE ASSOCIATION and the European Economic Community. The EUROPEAN COMMUNITY's effort to create a single European economy, plans for a greater North American free trade zone, and GATT's limited acceptance of noncapitalist members all illustrate the continuing shift toward universal free trade—although some economies, such as Japan's, remain highly protectionist (see PROTECTIONISM).

Bibliography: Corden, W. M., *Protection, Growth, and Trade* (1985); Dell, E., *The Politics of Economic Interdependence* (1987); McCord, N., *Free Trade* (1970); Travis, W. P., *The Theory of Trade and Protection* (1964); Volker, E. L., ed., *Protectionism and the European Community* (1983); Vousden, N., *The Economics of Trade Protection* (1990).

free verse: see VERSIFICATION.

free will: see WILL (philosophy).

Freedmen's Bureau

The Freedmen's Bureau was a U.S. government agency set up at the end of the U.S. Civil War to aid refugees and ex-slaves. Formally titled the Bureau of Refugees, Freedmen, and Abandoned Lands, it was created by Congress on Mar. 3, 1865, and modified by another law passed over a presidential veto on July 16, 1866.

A branch of the armed forces, the bureau was headed by a commissioner—Gen. Oliver Otis HOWARD—and military officers. Its purpose was to provide food, shelter, seeds, and agricultural equipment to white Civil War refugees and the thousands of newly freed blacks who had flocked to Union lines during the Civil War, to superintend the camps in which the freedmen had gathered, and to administer lands abandoned by Confederate sympathizers in such a way as to provide employment to ex-slaves. As the war ended, the bureau also supervised the transition from slavery to freedom in the South, helping employers and employees draw up labor contracts and settle disputes. So long as state courts enforced BLACK CODES or did not adequately protect freedmen's rights, the commissioner set up courts to hear civil and criminal cases in which blacks were parties.

Bureau officials often came into conflict with Southern whites, who felt the bureau was too sympathetic to blacks and encouraged labor unrest. Most bureau activities were discontinued in 1869, after new state constitutions had been adopted in the South in accordance with the congressional RECONSTRUCTION plan.   MICHAEL LES BENEDICT

Bibliography: Bentley, George R., *A History of the Freedmen's Bureau* (1955; repr. 1970); McFeely, William S., *Yankee Stepfather: General O. O. Howard and the Freedmen* (1968; repr. 1983).

freedom, academic: see ACADEMIC FREEDOM.

Freedom of Information Act

The Freedom of Information Act of 1966 requires that the records of U.S. government agencies be made available to the public. Records include all books, papers, maps, photographs, or other documentary material. Information must be made available promptly—within ten working days as a rule—to the person requesting it. The law exempts, however, nine classes of information related to national security or involving trade secrets, investigatory files, material exempted from disclosure by statute, reports prepared for use in regulating financial institutions, and other matters considered to be confidential. In 1982, President Ronald Reagan signed an executive order increasing the amount of security-classified material.

The Freedom of Information Act is supplemented by the Privacy Act of 1974, which requires federal agencies to provide individuals with any information in their files relating to them and to amend incorrect records. Each agency handles requests for information in its own way; some charge fees for searches and making copies of records. An agency withholding information may be sued to show cause why the information should not be disclosed.

Bibliography: American Civil Liberties Union, *Using the Freedom of Information Act* (1980); Casper, D. E., *The Freedom of Information Act* (1989).

freedom of the press

Freedom of the press is the right to gather and publish information or opinions without governmental control or fear of punishment. It applies to all types of printed and broadcast material, including books, newspapers, magazines, pamphlets, films, and radio and television programs.

Historically, freedom of the press has been bound up with the general questions of CENSORSHIP. In countries where censorship is extensive, the right to publish news, information, and opinions is usually tightly restricted. But even in the United States, where censorship is light, the right to publish is not absolute. The constraints on freedom of the press in a free society are controversial and are constantly being redefined by the judiciary.

Types of Restrictions. Governments have restricted the right to publish in two ways: by restraining the press from publishing certain materials and by punishing those who publish matter considered seditious, libelous, or obscene. The first kind of restriction, often called prior restraint, is rare in the United States and in most other democratic countries. One of the first attacks on prior restraint can be found in John Milton's essay AREOPAGITICA (1644), which was directed against the English licensing and censorship laws enacted in 1534 under Henry VIII. These laws were abolished in England in 1695, but the government was still able to take action on grounds of "seditious libel" against those who published material—whether true or false—that criticized government policies.

In the American colonies prosecutions of this kind were made more difficult by a jury's decision in the Zenger case of 1735. John Peter ZENGER, a New York newspaper publisher, had been charged with libel because he had published articles criticizing the policies of the colonial governor. The jury acquitted Zenger on the ground that his charges were true and could therefore not be considered libelous. Not until 1868 did the truth of the published material become an accepted defense in England.

Freedom of the press was protected in the Constitution of the United States by the adoption (1791) of the 1st AMEND-MENT, which states: "Congress shall make no law . . . abridging freedom of speech or of the press." This restraint on the federal government was later made binding on state governments in *Near* v. *Minnesota* (1931) by the Supreme Court's interpretation of the DUE PROCESS clause of the 14th AMENDMENT. In that case the Court ruled that no newspaper or magazine could be banned because of its contents regardless of how scandalous they might be. Still, freedom of the press has frequently been limited in the areas of obscenity and pornography, although the courts have had some difficulty delineating appropriate standards of censorship (see ROTH V. UNITED STATES and MILLER V. CALIFORNIA).

National Security. Restrictions on the press have always occurred during times of national emergency. The extensive censorship during World War I led to the first clear articulation of the limits to FREEDOM OF SPEECH, with which free press issues are closely tied. Justice Oliver Wendell HOLMES, Jr., enunciated (in SCHENCK V. UNITED STATES, 1919) the concept that abridgment of free speech was justified only if the words used constituted a "clear and present danger." This test was used to strike down contempt citations levied on members of the press for being critical of certain judges (BRIDGES V. CALIFORNIA, 1941). During World War II, freedom of the press was greatly curtailed, but the press proved eager to comply with censorship restrictions.

Other than in time of war, censorship for national security reasons has been carefully limited. In 1971 the U.S. government attempted to halt publication of the PENTAGON PAPERS on the grounds that their publication could endanger national security. The Supreme Court ruled (NEW YORK TIMES COMPANY V. UNITED STATES) that this case of prior restraint was unconstitutional. Other cases involving national security have concerned attempts to censor or halt publication of books about the Central Intelligence Agency. In 1983, when U.S. troops invaded the Caribbean island of Grenada, the press was initially barred from the island. The restrictions later imposed were thought to be unprecedented in U.S. practice and generated much controversy.

Control of the press during the Persian Gulf War (1991) was close to 100 percent. Criticisms of the press for accepting conditions that made complete reporting impossible were numerous. After the war ended, questions arose concerning the accuracy of some reports disseminated by the press.

Confidentiality. Constraints upon the press are always controversial. The future of a free press in the United States depends upon public opinion, the legislative agencies, and the courts, especially the United States Supreme Court.

In Minnesota reporters promised anonymity to a political campaign worker who gave them information. Later the editors of the papers revealed his name and he sued them. The Supreme Court ruled (*Cohen* v. *Cowles Media Co.,* 1991) that the 1st Amendment does not confer on the press a constitutional right to disregard promises that otherwise would be enforced under state law, and returned the case to the Minnesota Supreme Court. Further complicating the issue, several previous decisions appeared to narrow the right of newspaper reporters to withhold information given them in confidence. In April 1991, a *Washington Post* reporter was held in contempt of court and jailed for refusing to identify a source.

Defamatory Libel and Public Figures. The Zenger case had established the precedent that truthful statements were not to be considered libelous; the obvious corollary was that damages could be collected for false statements. In NEW YORK TIMES COMPANY V. SULLIVAN (1964), however, the Supreme Court held that public officials are entitled to win damages only if they can show that a statement defaming them was made with "actual malice"—that is, with knowledge that it was false or with reckless disregard of whether it was false or not. Other court rulings have extended the principle to include public figures who are not in government office but who are involved in public controversy. In 1979 the Supreme Court held (*Hutchinson* v. *Proxmire* and *Wolston* v. *Readers' Digest*) that a person who has involuntarily received publicity is not necessarily a public figure and therefore need not prove that statements by the press were made with "actual malice" in order to obtain libel damages.

Privileges of the Press. The privileges of the press have had to be constantly weighed against other considerations. In 1976, for example, the Supreme Court ruled that so-called gag orders by trial courts forbidding the publication of certain information about a defendant were unconstitutional. The Supreme Court has also held (*Zurcher* v. *Stanford Daily,* 1978) that newspapers enjoy no special immunity from searches of their premises by police with warrants. In 1980, however, Congress passed a Privacy Protection Act that required the police in most cases to obtain subpoenas for such searches. In 1979, in a controversial effort to curb prejudicial pretrial publicity, the Court ruled (*Gannett* v. *DePasquale*) that judges have the authority to bar the press and the public from criminal proceedings. In other cases, however, courts have allowed televised proceedings.

Global Status. Perhaps the most significant trend related to freedom of the press is the worldwide movement toward democratic self-government. Although freedom of the press has generally been limited to the United States, Great Britain, and the Commonwealth nations, Western Europe, parts of Latin America, and Japan, it is gaining ground around the world. Still, even in Great Britain and Canada, Official Secrets Acts make it a crime to disclose government documents without permission. Freedom of the press in Communist countries was almost nonexistent. Government ownership and control of all media effectively limited the role of the press to that of an instrument of propaganda. In other dictatorial governments various types of control by government ministries, licensing agencies, censorship boards, or simple violence restrict what the press can print. Many Third World governments contend that Western journalists present distorted views of their countries and, with Soviet bloc support, secured (1980) a UNESCO resolution calling for a new world information order that would, while affirming the principle of freedom of the press, give UNESCO the right to regulate news organizations. The proposal provoked strong protest from Western nations, including the withdrawal from UNESCO of the United States (1983) and Britain (1984) at least in part over the issue of the proposed "new world information order."   DAVID K. BERNINGHAUSEN

Bibliography: Altschull, J. H., *From Milton to McLuhan: The Ideas behind American Journalism* (1990); Anastapl, George, *The Constitutionalist* (1971); Chafee, Zechariah, Jr., *Freedom of Speech and Press* (1955); Chanin, A. S., *The Flames of Freedom* (1990); Emerson, T. I., *The System of Freedom of Expression* (1970); Levy, Leonard, ed., *Freedom of the Press from Zenger to Jefferson* (1966); Lichtenberg, Judith, ed., *Democracy and the Mass Media* (1990); Ruckelshaus, William, et al., *Freedom of the Press* (1976).

freedom of religion

Freedom of religion is a political principle that forbids government constraint on people in their choice of beliefs. Religious freedom requires also that one be free to act upon those beliefs. It therefore includes the freedom to worship, to print instructional material, to train teachers, and to organize societies for their employment. Thus, freedom of religion is closely conjoined with other freedoms, such as freedom of speech, freedom of the press, and freedom of assembly. It is recognized (as are the other freedoms) in a provision of the 1ST AMENDMENT to the Constitution of the United States:

> Congress shall make no law respecting an establishment of religion, or prohibiting the free exercise thereof. . . .

In Western Europe and North America, freedom of religion is almost universally enjoyed, although its legal and institutional nature may differ from country to country. In some other parts of the world, freedom of religion is either severely circumscribed by state action or limited by social pressure.

HISTORY OF RELIGIOUS FREEDOM

For centuries people have been persecuted for their religious beliefs because of the political dangers posed by a new religion, or on the basis of religious principles, or for the sake of expedience. Tolerance for Christians and Jews under the early Roman Empire depended on the attitudes of emperors and local governors; in Christian Europe Jews, Muslims, and heretics were generally persecuted during the Middle Ages. During the Reformation pitched battles occurred between Catholics and Protestants; later, nonconforming Protestant sects were harassed by established Protestant churches. Persecution of Jews, atheists, and agnostics continued into the 20th century, while Protestant-Catholic conflict has persisted to this day in Northern Ireland. Communist countries are mostly officially atheistic and make religious practice difficult.

Before the 18th century, instances of religious toleration were rare. Proliferating Hindu and Buddhist sects created a form of religious freedom in India, Japan, and China, and limited religious liberty was permitted under the Islamic caliphate. In Europe the Roman emperor Constantine issued (AD 313) the Edict of Milan granting freedom to practice the religion of one's choice; within a few years, however, Christianity had become the only legal religion. In 1598 the promulgation of the Edict of Nantes by Henry IV of France enabled the Huguenots to obtain a certain degree of religious freedom.

Religious freedom has become a matter of principle in the U.S. constitutional system, but it developed in the English-speaking world mainly for pragmatic reasons. In the 16th and 17th centuries efforts were made by the state to regulate totally the Church of England and to stamp out or severely constrain Catholics and Protestant sects that did not conform to the Church of England. Licensing laws, for example, were enacted in order to halt the publication of Puritan books and pamphlets—the Puritan John Milton published (1644) his AREOPAGITICA in protest against such laws. The Puritans came to power after the English Civil War (1642–48). They in turn suppressed Catholics. Oliver Cromwell's New Model army was hostile to Presbyterians, who hoped to dominate both England and Scotland, and his victory favored toleration. The Restoration of Charles II in 1660 led to the reestablishment of the Church of England and the CLARENDON CODE (1661–65), which persecuted non-Anglicans. There was, however, an increasing realization that religious oppression in a society of sectarians was deleterious not only to domestic tranquillity but to commerce and trade as well. The Act of Toleration (1689), after the Glorious Revolution and the accession of William III and Mary II, opened the way to fuller development of religious freedom.

Escape from religious persecution was one reason for emigration to the New World, but early settlers were themselves generally unwilling to grant religious liberty for differing beliefs. In Virginia colonial authorities favored the Church of England (Anglican) as far as the English law would allow, and by 1758 a conflict had developed with Presbyterians, Baptists, and other denominations that claimed the liberty to preach and establish congregations. In 1779 the Anglican church was disestablished or separated from the state, and by 1786, Thomas Jefferson, James Madison, and George Mason had produced the Virginia Statute of Religious Liberty, which firmly set forth principles that separated state power from church affairs, a position that reflected the one taken almost a century before by John Locke in his *Letter Concerning Toleration* (1689). Madison drew heavily on this experience in fashioning the Bill of Rights, proposed in 1789.

RELIGIOUS FREEDOM IN THE UNITED STATES

The concept of separation of CHURCH AND STATE is widely used to describe the legal and institutional nature of freedom of religion in the United States. It is not a widespread concept, nor does it necessarily indicate the presence or absence of religious freedom. England, Scotland, and Sweden, for example, have officially established churches but enjoy religious freedom.

It has been difficult literally to separate church and state in the United States. Churches are required to conform to building codes, fire regulations, and sanitation laws. Government is expected to decide whether a group claiming to be religious should be exempt from property taxes or whether the claim is fraudulent. The 1st Amendment pledges the federal government neither to favor nor to be hostile, but to be "neutral." (In the case of *Cantwell* v. *Connecticut,* 1940, the amendment's provision for freedom of religion was made binding on the states through the DUE PROCESS clause of the 14TH AMENDMENT.) The struggle of the courts to be truly neutral in judging the disputes that come before them has long been the hinge of religious freedom in the United States. Courts have had to weigh the requirements of the "free exercise" and "establishment" clauses of the 1st Amendment against certain legal, social, and religious needs of society. Laws against polygamy, for example, were declared constitutional (*Reynolds* v. *United States*, 1878) despite Mormon religious claims based on the "free exercise" clause. The same clause, however, has protected prisoners' freedom of worship (*Cruz* v. *Beto*, 1972) and has struck down compulsory salutes to the flag in public school (*West Virginia Board of Education* v. *Barnette*, 1943). The Court has upheld a city's right to include a Nativity scene in a public Christmas display (*Lynch* v. *Donnelly*, 1984). The "establishment" clause has been interpreted at various times to mean either that government cannot show preference to any particular religion or that there must be complete separation of church and state.

Large areas of dispute exist, and litigation is constantly in progress over such issues as government assistance to religiously sponsored schools, devotional practices in public schools, and the treatment of sectarians whose religious convictions are not easily accommodated by local law.

In education the Supreme Court has held that state reimbursement to parents for money spent to transport their children to parochial schools on the public bus system does not constitute an establishment of religion (*Everson* v. *Board of Education*, 1947). Public school boards may furnish secular textbooks for the use of children in religious schools (*Cochran* v. *Louisiana State Board of Education*, 1930). Public schools may cooperate administratively with churches concerned for the religious education of children, but public property may not be used, public funds may not be directly appropriated, and religion itself may not be promoted (*McCollum* v. *Board of Education*, 1948, and *Zorach* v. *Clauson*, 1952). In public schools a period of silence may be observed in which children may pray if they wish, but the schools may not conduct devotional exercises, compose prayers, read the Bible, or otherwise enter the field of religious instruction (ENGEL V. VITALE, 1962). In 1980, for example, the Court struck down a Kentucky law requiring the posting of the Ten Commandments in all classrooms (*Stone* v. *Graham*). The "equal access" law of 1984, however, gives students the right to hold religious meetings in public high schools outside of class hours.

In 1970 the Supreme Court reaffirmed the traditional exclusion of religious property from taxation (*Walz* v. *Tax Commission*, 1970). In other rulings it has held that government may extend the benefit of public loans to religious schools, provided these buildings have secular purposes.   ELWYN A. SMITH

Bibliography: Hammann, Louis, and Buck, Harry M., eds., *Religious Traditions and the Limits of Tolerance* (1987); Levy, Leonard W., *The Establishment Clause: Religion and the First Amendment* (1986); Murphy, Paul L., ed., *Religious Freedom*, 2 vols. (1990); Swomley, John M., *Religious Liberty and the Secular State* (1987).

freedom of the seas: see SEAS, FREEDOM OF THE.

freedom of speech

Freedom of speech is the liberty to speak and write without fear of government restraint. It is closely linked to FREEDOM OF THE PRESS. In the United States both freedoms—commonly called freedom of expression—are protected by the 1ST AMENDMENT to the Constitution, which provides that "Congress shall make no law abridging the freedom of speech, or of the press."

Most other Western countries guarantee freedom of speech, either in their constitutions or by legislative enactment. All countries, however, limit manifestations of free speech that are regarded as threatening the civil order or as obscene or slanderous. The extent to which speech is regarded as threatening or slanderous and the way in which limits are imposed are critical factors in determining the degree of free speech in a society.

HISTORY OF FREEDOM OF SPEECH
The quest for free speech has a long, turbulent history; it has been one fundamental aspect of the individual's developing relationship both to the state and to society. Until the 17th century various forms of CENSORSHIP of free speech were common and contested principally within the framework of larger issues of political and religious conflict. In England in the 17th century, however, freedom of speech began to assume its own importance. John Milton wrote in his AREOPAGITICA (1644): "Give me the liberty to know, to utter, and to argue freely according to conscience, above all liberties." Other philosophers such as John LOCKE, VOLTAIRE, and, later, John Stuart MILL took up the cry. Beginning with the British Bill of Rights (1689) and the adoption of the French Declaration of the Rights of Man (1789) and the U.S. BILL OF RIGHTS (1791), freedom of speech became an integral part of constitutional law even in countries that do not in reality permit free speech. Freedom of speech gained international recognition in this century with the United Nations proclamation of the Universal Declaration of Human Rights (1948).

FREE SPEECH IN THE UNITED STATES
In the United States freedom of speech and the constitutional limits to it have been defined, in practice, by rulings of the Supreme Court. Originally the free-speech guarantee of the 1st Amendment applied only to acts of Congress. In the 20th century, however, the Supreme Court began to interpret the DUE PROCESS clause of the 14TH AMENDMENT to mean that the states as well as the federal government are bound by the provisions of the 1st Amendment (see GITLOW V. NEW YORK).

Restrictions on freedom of speech have occurred most often in time of war or national emergency. The ALIEN AND SEDITION ACTS of 1798 were the first incursions by Congress on this freedom. These laws were never tested in the courts and were allowed to expire after several years.

Clear and Present Danger. The first clear-cut test came over the Espionage Act (1917) passed by Congress during World War I; this act made it illegal to interfere with the recruitment or drafting of soldiers or to do anything adversely affecting military morale. In SCHENCK V. UNITED STATES the Court upheld the conviction of a socialist indicted under the act on the ground that freedom of speech is not absolute. Justice Oliver Wendell HOLMES, Jr., delivering the Court's unanimous opinion, argued: "The most stringent protection of free speech would not protect a man in falsely shouting fire in a theatre and causing a panic. . . .The question in every case is whether the words used are used in such circumstances and are of such a nature as to create a clear and present danger that they will bring about the substantive evils that Congress has a right to prevent."

Bad Tendency. The "clear and present danger" doctrine became one of the tests the Court applied to subsequent cases involving freedom of speech. Another test, which placed more restrictions on individual expression, was whether an expression had a tendency to lead to results that were bad for the public. In *Gitlow* v. *New York* (1925) the Court held that "a State in the exercise of its police power may punish those who abuse this freedom by utterances inimical to the public welfare, tending to corrupt public morals, incite to crime, or disturb the public peace. . . ." Gitlow had been indicted under a New York State law prohibiting the advocacy of the overthrow of the government by force or violence.

Society's Interests. In 1940, Congress enacted the SMITH ACT, which declared it unlawful to advocate overthrowing the government by force or violence. Eleven leaders of the Communist party were convicted under the act and appealed on the ground that it was unconstitutional. The Court upheld the act's constitutionality in DENNIS V. UNITED STATES (1951) but not on the ground of "clear and present danger." Instead, the majority adopted a standard put forward by Judge Learned HAND: ". . .whether the gravity of the 'evil,' discounted by its improbability, justifies such invasion of free speech as is necessary to avoid the danger." This standard has been called the "clear and probable danger" test. This approach, modified by other cases, has been termed the "balancing" test. When applying the balancing approach, the Supreme Court strives to strike a balance between the value of liberty of expression and the demands of order in a free society. Many critics of the balancing approach have contended that a balance is rarely struck—that in most cases in which it is involved, society prevails over the individual.

Preferred Freedoms and the Absolute Approach. The preferred freedoms approach, a position originally set forth by Justice Harlan F. STONE, has been important in constitutional law since World War II. This approach stresses that the civil liberties have a preferred position among other constitutional values since they are requisite to a democracy. Under this concept the burden lies largely with the government to prove that clear and present danger exists when a freedom is exercised.

Some justices, notably Hugo BLACK and William DOUGLAS, have tended to see freedom of speech as nearly an absolute right. The difficulty of the absolute approach to free speech issues was shown (1977–78) when a group of American Nazis sought to hold a rally in Skokie, Ill. They were denied a permit by the municipality on the ground that a Nazi rally would incite hostility in the largely Jewish population, which included many survivors of Nazi concentration camps. Lawyers for the AMERICAN CIVIL LIBERTIES UNION (ACLU) represented the Nazis, arguing that the Skokie laws limiting public demonstrations were unconstitutional. A U.S. court of appeals agreed with the ACLU, but many Americans were outraged at the defense of those they considered the enemies of free speech.

The judicial interpretation of the right of free speech has yet to produce a clear definition of what is permissible. Insofar as seditious speech is concerned, the courts have held language permissible so long as it does not tend to incite the violent overthrow of the government. In other free-speech areas, such as in obscenity and PORNOGRAPHY, "fighting words," picketing or demonstrating, symbolic speech (for example, wearing armbands or burning the flag), and loyalty oaths, the courts have also had to consider the various interests of society and the requirements of the Constitution.

GLOBAL STATUS OF FREEDOM OF SPEECH

In several treaties and conventions, European, Latin American, and international organizations have pledged respect for fundamental freedoms and HUMAN RIGHTS. The practice of free speech, however, is consistent only in the democracies of Western Europe, English-speaking countries, and Japan. Authoritarian, theocratic, totalitarian, and dictatorial governments such as those in the Communist countries, most of the Arab world, much of Africa and Asia and, until recently, in most of Latin America and Eastern Europe commonly suppress freedom of speech. Many developing countries cite the task of economic progress as reason for denying this liberty.

The 1980s witnessed a strong trend toward greater free speech in the world. In 1985, Mikhail GORBACHEV introduced an unprecedented level of free discourse in the Soviet Union with his program of GLASNOST, meaning "openness." Most of Latin America's military regimes and the Communist governments of Eastern Europe have been replaced by fledgling democracies. This trend, however, has frequently resulted in political instability and renewed repression. China's pro-democracy movement, for example, was militarily crushed in 1989, marking the return of full dictatorial rule.

DAVID K. BERNINGHAUSEN

Bibliography: Barendt, Eric, *Freedom of Speech* (1987); Bosmajian, Haig A., *The Principles and Practices of Freedom of Speech,* 2d ed. (1983); Mill, John Stuart, *On Liberty: Freedom of Speech* (1859; repr. 1990); O'Neil, Robert M., *Free Speech: Responsible Communications under Law,* 2d ed. (1972); Schauer, Frederick, *Free Speech: A Philosophical Enquiry* (1982).

freeholder

Freeholder, a term derived from feudal law, refers to a landowner with an inheritable life title to his or her land. In some American colonies only freeholders had the right to vote and hold office. In contemporary New Jersey, a freeholder is an elected county official.

Freeling, Nicolas

English author Nicolas Freeling, b. Mar. 3, 1927, has written both cookbooks and detective novels. Works featuring the Dutch inspector Van der Valk include *The King of the Rainy Country* (1966; Edgar Allan Poe Award, 1967) and *Après de ma blonde* (1971), in which Van der Valk dies. In *Arlette* (1981), Van der Valk's wife acts as detective. Among later Freeling works are *Cold Iron* (1986) and *Those in Peril* (1991).

Freeman, Douglas Southall

A newspaper editor and historian, Douglas Southall Freeman, b. Lynchburg, Va., May 16, 1886, d. June 13, 1953, is best known for his books on the U.S. Civil War. *Lee's Lieutenants* (3 vols., 1942–44) is a classic study of Confederate commanders. Freeman won two Pulitzer Prizes—the first (1935) for *R. E. Lee* (4 vols., 1934–35) and the second (posthumously, 1958) for *George Washington* (7 vols., 1948–57), which was completed by J. A. Carroll and M. W. Ashworth.

Freeman, Mary E. Wilkins

Mary Eleanor Wilkins Freeman, b. Randolph, Mass., Oct. 31, 1852, d. Mar. 13, 1930, was an American short-story writer best known for *A Humble Romance and Other Stories* (1887) and *A New England Nun and Other Stories* (1891). Both contain grimly realistic and frequently ironic portraits of rural New England residents.   F. M. PAULSEN

freemasonry   [free'-may-suhn-ree]

Freemasonry refers to the principles, institutions, and practices of the fraternal order of the Free and Accepted Masons. The largest worldwide society, freemasonry is an organization of men based on the fatherhood of God and the brotherhood of man, using builders' tools as symbols to teach basic moral truths generally accepted by persons of goodwill. It is religious in that a belief in God is the prime requirement for membership, but it is nonsectarian in that no religious test is used. The purpose of freemasonry is to enable men to meet in harmony, to promote friendship, and to be charitable. Its basic ideals are that all persons are the children of one God, that all persons are related to each other, and that the best way to worship God is to be of service to people.

This 19th-century lithographic print shows the initiation ceremony of a Mason. Freemasonry places its emphasis on the brother- and sisterhood of humankind, and the principal activities of its lodges are related to social and charitable works.

The basic unit of freemasonry is the lodge, which exists under a charter issued by a grand lodge exercising administrative powers. The lodges are linked together informally by a system of mutual recognition between lodges that meet the Masonic requirements. The lodge confers three degrees: Entered Apprentice, Fellow Craft, and Master Mason. Additional degrees are conferred by two groups of advanced freemasonry: the York Rite, which awards 12 degrees, and the Scottish Rite, which awards 30 higher degrees. In the United States and Canada members have formed a large number of groups to enable them to expand their social and charitable activities. The best known of these groups is the Shriners, who hold festive parades and support hospitals for crippled and burned children. There are also the Order of the Eastern Star for Master Masons and their wives; the Order of De Molay for boys; and the Order of Job's Daughters and the Order of Rainbow for girls.

Many legendary theories exist concerning the origin of freemasonry, but it is generally believed that it evolved from the medieval guilds of the stonemasons. Its present organizational form began on June 24, 1717, when a grand lodge was formed in London. Since that time lodges have spread all over the world with local grand lodges formed whenever enough lodges exist in an area. Lodges first appeared in America in Philadelphia (1730) and Boston (1733).

At various times and places freemasonry has met religious and political opposition. Religious opponents, especially the Roman Catholic and Eastern Orthodox churches, have traditionally claimed that freemasonry is a religion and is a secret organization. A papal ban on Roman Catholic membership in Masonic lodges was rescinded in 1983.

Freemasons hold that the organization is religious but not a religion, and that it is not a secret organization since it works openly in the community. Freemasonry has always been suppressed in totalitarian states.

There are approximately 4.8 million Freemasons in regular lodges scattered around the world. Of this number, more than 3 million are to be found in the United States, where there are numerous distinct Masonic groups. Many notable men in history have been Freemasons, including Benjamin Franklin, Mozart, Henry Ford, Rudyard Kipling, Douglas MacArthur, Will Rogers, and George Washington and a number of other presidents of the United States.   ALPHONSE CERZA

Bibliography: Coil, Henry, *Masonic Encyclopedia* (1962) and *A Comprehensive View of Freemasonry* (1954; repr. 1985); Denslow, William R., *10,000 Famous Freemasons*, 4 vols. (1957–60); Macoy, Robert, *Dictionary of Freemasonry* (1989); Robinson, John J., *Born in Blood: The Lost Secrets of Freemasonry* (1990).

Freer, Charles Lang   [freer]

Charles Lang Freer, b. Feb. 25, 1856, d. Sept. 25, 1919, was the Detroit industrialist whose important Oriental art collection forms the nucleus of the Freer Gallery of Art, which is part of the Smithsonian Institution in Washington, D.C. Initially a collector of contemporary American painting, Freer became interested in Oriental fine arts while on a trip to the Far East around the turn of the century. From that time he avidly collected Asian works of art and traveled many times to China, Japan, India, Southeast Asia, and the Near East. He bequeathed his entire collection to the U.S. government in 1906, along with funds for constructing a museum and endowing future acquisitions and study of Far Eastern art.

The Freer gallery, designed in Renaissance style according to Freer's plan, was completed in 1921. The Asian collections consist of paintings, sculptures, ceramics, and decorative objects, including some of the nation's finest examples of Chinese and Japanese art.

The museum also houses Freer's extensive collection of paintings by such artists as Winslow Homer, John Singer Sargent, and James McNeill Whistler. The collection includes Whistler's famous Peacock Room (from the London home of Frederick Leyland), which is orientalized with exotic decorations in blue, green, and gold hues.

Bibliography: Saarinen, Aline B., *The Proud Possessors* (1958).

freesia   [free'-zhuh]

Freesia F. refracta, an elegant greenhouse plant, produces arched rows of exquisitely scented flowers. It is becoming increasingly popular for cut floral arrangements.

Freesia is a genus of about 19 species of South African bulbous plants in the iris family, Iridaceae. They are usually grown for cut flowers. The flowers are very fragrant, typically white or yellow, and are borne in spikelike racemes.

K. B. PAUL

freethinker: see DEISM.

Freetown

Freetown is the capital and largest city of Sierra Leone in West Africa. It has a population of 469,776 (1985). A busy Atlantic port, it is located on the shore of a rugged peninsula that shelters a large natural harbor; mountains on the peninsula rise almost 275 m (900 ft) above sea level. Freetown is the shipping, commercial, and industrial heart of Sierra Leone. Its various industries include diamond cutting, food processing, and petroleum refining.

The city was settled in the late 1780s under British auspices by freed slaves from England and the New World; they mingled with the indigenous population to produce a new language, Krio, and a society known as Sierra Leone Creole. Today the city is a blend of Western and African in which Muslims now outnumber Christians. The city's university incorporates colleges founded as early as 1827.

freeze-drying

Freeze-drying is a FOOD PRESERVATION technique in which food is first frozen into a solid state; then, with the application of heat, the frozen moisture content is vaporized—a phenomenon known as sublimation (see SUBLIMATION, chemistry). Freeze-dried foods, most often liquids or small foods such as bamboo sprouts, lose at least 90 percent of their water content through this process. They regain a very close approximation of their original shape, texture, and flavor when reconstituted with the addition of water. The process is rather costly and is therefore restricted in use to such luxury products as coffee and seafoods.   MARTIN SEVERIN PETERSON

freezing point

The freezing point (also called fusion point or melting point) is the temperature at which a substance's solid and liquid forms can coexist indefinitely.

At a pressure of one atmosphere, the freezing (or melting) point of water is 0° C (32° F) and of hydrogen is −259.2° C. Among high-melting substances, tungsten (used in light-bulb filaments) melts at 3,370° C, and diamonds, above 3,500° C.

Impurities always lower freezing points. Salt water freezes at a lower temperature than pure water, which is why salt is often spread on icy streets. Certain metals can be mixed to produce low-melting alloys, such as solder and type metal.

Freezing and melting points can be used to test a substance's purity. Every mole (6.022×10^{23} particles) of impurity in 1,000 grams of water lowers water's freezing point 1.86° C. Conversely, freezing points can be used to determine molecular weights and degrees of dissociation of substances in solution.

Increasing the pressure on a substance that expands on melting raises its melting point. Conversely, for substances such as water that expand on freezing, increasing the pressure lowers the freezing point. Under a pressure of 2,000 atmospheres, liquid water (density 1 g/cm^3) freezes to ordinary ice (density 0.92 g/cm^3) at $-22°$ C. Under a pressure of 20,000 atmospheres, however, liquid water freezes to compact ice VIII (density 1.7 g/cm^3) at about 81° C.   HENRY A. BENT

Frege, Gottlob   [fray'-geh, gawt'-lohp]

Gottlob Frege, b. Nov. 8, 1848, d. July 26, 1925, a German philosopher and mathematician, was one of the founders of modern symbolic LOGIC. He received his education at the universities of Göttingen and Jena and then taught at Jena in the department of mathematics.

Frege's writings on the philosophy of logic, philosophy of mathematics, and philosophy of language are of seminal importance. He was the first to fully develop the main thesis of logicism, that mathematics is reducible to logic. His works *The Foundations of Arithmetic* (1884; Eng. trans., 1950) and *The Basic Laws of Arithmetic* (1893; Eng. trans., 1964) are devoted to this project. He was a major influence on Bertrand RUSSELL.   E. D. KLEMKE

Bibliography: Dummet, Michael, *Frege: Philosophy of Language*, rev. ed. (1981); Klemke, E. D., ed., *Essays on Frege* (1968); Resnik, Michael, *Frege and the Philosophy of Mathematics* (1980); Wright, C., ed., *Frege* (1985).

Frei Montalva, Eduardo   [fray mohn-tahl'-vah, ay-dwar'-doh]

Eduardo Frei Montalva, b. Jan. 16, 1911, d. Jan. 22, 1982, was president of Chile from 1964 to 1970. He graduated from the faculty of law of the Catholic University of Chile in 1933. Political interests led him in 1938 to help form the reformist-conservative National Falange party, which became (1957) the Christian Democratic party. He was minister of roads and public works from 1945 to 1949. Elected president in 1964, Frei instituted a program that included nationalization of the copper industry, land reform, and expenditures on public health and education. When his party was defeated in 1970 by Salvador ALLENDE, he became an opposition spokesman.

Bibliography: Gross, Leonard, *The Last, Best Hope: Eduardo Frei and Chilean Democracy* (1967).

Freiburg im Breisgau   [fry'-boork im brys'-gow]

Freiburg im Breisgau is a cultural and commercial center in Baden-Württemberg, southwestern Germany, located on the Dreisam River at the western edge of the BLACK FOREST, about 150 km (95 mi) southwest of Stuttgart. It has a population of 182,200 (1987 est.). The city's industries produce wood and paper products, chemicals, glass, textiles, and precision instruments. Tourism is also important, and wine making is extensive in the vicinity.

Freiburg was established in 1120 by the duke of Zähringen as the capital and free-market town of the Breisgau area. It passed to the Habsburgs in 1368 and was the scene of a major victory (1644) by the French over the Austrians and Bavarians in the THIRTY YEARS' WAR. Captured by the French in 1677 and again in 1744, Freiburg became part of Baden in 1805.

During World War II many of the city's older buildings were destroyed, but the Gothic cathedral (begun *c.*1200)—with its lacework steeple, magnificent stained-glass windows, and altar paintings by Hans BALDUNG-GRIEN, Lucas CRANACH the Elder, and Hans HOLBEIN the Younger—was unharmed. Other buildings of note are the 13th-century Church of St. Martin and the 16th-century Kaufhaus and Old Town Hall. Freiburg im Breisgau is also noted for the Albert Ludwig University (1457).

Freie Bühne, Die   [fry'-eh byoo'-neh, dee]

The Freie Bühne, a Berlin theater modeled after André ANTOINE's Théâtre Libre in Paris, was the first German theater to perform modern naturalist drama. Organized as a private society in 1889 by Otto BRAHM and Paul Schlenther, the theater presented such controversial works as Ibsen's *Ghosts* and Strindberg's *Miss Julie*. Although officially disbanded in 1892, it sponsored occasional performances until 1894, most notably *The Weavers* (1893) by Gerhart HAUPTMANN, a playwright discovered by the Freie Bühne.   MARVIN CARLSON

Bibliography: Miller, Anne Irene, *The Independent Theatre in Europe, 1887 to the Present* (1931).

freighter

A freighter is a cargo vessel that is primarily engaged in carrying general merchandise. Of the two basic types, cargo liners have a regular schedule and tramp ships do not. Freighters generally have large, unobstructed cargo holds with overall capacities of 10,000 deadweight tons and top speeds of about 26 km/h (16 mph). Following the era of the Liberty ship, the mass-produced World War II freighters whose simple design made them quick and easy to build, the number of decks on freighters gradually increased to augment the speed and flexibility of loading. Today, freighters may have capacities of up to 14,000 deadweight tons, and some may be adapted to carry containers.

Cargo liners usually carry diverse cargo from many companies. Handling is, therefore, slow and expensive, but the liners provide a useful service for the small shipper. A tramp usually carries bulk cargo, such as coal, ore, grain, or timber, with each voyage being negotiated separately. Recently, the number of tramp vessels has dropped because more manufacturers are operating their own vessels of specialized design to satisfy their own shipping needs.   ALAN E. BRANCH

Bibliography: Cufley, C. F., *Ocean Freights and Chartering* (1964; repr. 1980); Robin, Craig, *Steam Tramps and Cargo Liners* (1980).

See also: CONTAINERIZATION; SHIP; SHIPPING.

Freiligrath, Ferdinand   [fry'-lik-raht]

The German poet and translator Hermann Ferdinand Freiligrath, b. June 7, 1810, d. Mar. 18, 1876, championed the radical political views that culminated in the REVOLUTIONS OF 1848. *Ein Glaubensbekenntnis* (My Credo, 1842) was an expression of these ideas. *Neuere Politische und Soziale Gedichte* (New Political and Social Poetry, 2 vols., 1849, 1851) contains some of his best revolutionary poems.

Fréjus   [fray-zhoos']

Fréjus (1982 pop., 31,662) is a French resort and manufacturing center located on the Riviera. The town was the scene of a tragic devastation when, on Dec. 2, 1959, the Malpasset Dam, a thin-arch concrete structure that had been completed 5 years previously, was swept away during a flood, releasing a wave that inundated Fréjus and drowned more than 400 people. The failure was traced to weak foundation rock, which caused a hydraulic uplift that raised the dam off its foundations.   F. EUGENE MCJUNKIN

Bibliography: International Commission on Large Dams, *Lessons from Dam Incidents* (1973); Jaeger, C., "The Malpasset Report," *Water Power*, vol. 15 (1963).

Frelinghuysen, Frederick Theodore   [free'-ling-hy-zen]

Frederick Theodore Frelinghuysen, b. Millstone, N.J., Aug. 4, 1817, d. May 20, 1885, was a U.S. senator and secretary of state. He served in the Senate from 1866 to 1869, and again from 1871 to 1877, and in 1881 was appointed by President Chester A. Arthur to succeed James G. Blaine as secretary of state. Frelinghuysen reversed Blaine's policies, withdrawing from a modest diplomatic intervention in the War of the Pacific; urging abrogation of the Clayton-Bulwer Treaty with Great Britain, rather than modification; and, also, taking back invitations Blaine had extended to the Latin American nations to attend a Pan-American Conference in Washington.

ROBERT H. FERRELL

Bibliography: Bemis, Samuel Flagg, ed., *American Secretaries of State and Their Diplomacy,* vol. 8 (1928).

Frémont, John C.   [free'-mahnt]

John C. Frémont, an American military leader and explorer, led several expeditions into the Far West, eventually participating in the conquest of California during the Mexican War. Frémont won nomination in 1856 as the Republican party's first presidential candidate.

John Charles Frémont, b. Savannah, Ga., Jan. 21, 1813, d. July 13, 1890, was an American explorer, soldier, and politician, best known as "the Pathfinder" for his western explorations of 1842–44. Following military training, he married (1841) Jessie Benton, daughter of the influential Senator Thomas Hart BEN-TON. Frémont's prominence as an explorer began in 1842 when, with Benton's sponsorship, he was given the assignment of surveying the OREGON TRAIL up the Platte River to South Pass.

It was during his second expedition in 1843–44 that Frémont made the contributions to knowledge that were to secure his fame. On this expedition he made a massive circle of the least-known parts of the West: from the Colorado Rockies north to the South Pass, northwest to the Columbia, south along the Cascade and Sierra Nevada ranges into California, and southward before turning east across the desert to the vicinity of Salt Lake and thence east across the Colorado Rockies. He returned to St. Louis in August 1844, after proving the existence of Salt Lake and a vast region of interior drainage (the Great Basin), dispelling the myth of the San Buenaventura River (supposed to flow from the Rockies to California), and demonstrating that the South Pass was the best route across the mountains.

In 1845, Frémont returned to California, where he encouraged the American settlers to revolt against Mexican rule and establish (June 1845) the BEAR FLAG REPUBLIC. In the ensuing dispute over command between Commodore Robert STOCKTON and Gen. Stephen KEARNY, Frémont supported the former and was consequently courtmartialed for insubordination.

Frémont resigned from the army in 1847, but he continued his explorations with private backing. In 1850–51 he served as U.S. senator from the new state of California, and in 1856 he was defeated in the presidential election as the first candidate of the Republican party. At the start of the Civil War he was made commander of the Western Department, but he was removed after ordering emancipation of the slaves in Missouri on his own authority. He was then given command of the Mountain Division (1862) but resigned when subordinated to John POPE. Business failures, including a disastrous transcontinental railroad project, made Frémont a near-pauper. Congress finally granted him a pension for his explorations only three months before his death.   JOHN L. ALLEN

Bibliography: Egan, F., *Frémont, Explorer for a Restless Nation* (1930; repr. 1985); Jackson, D., and Spence, M. L., eds., *The Expeditions of John Charles Frémont,* vol. I (1970); Nevins, A., *Frémont* (1955).

Fremstad, Olive   [frem'-stahd]

Olive Fremstad, b. Stockholm, Mar. 14, 1871, d. Apr. 21, 1951, was a Swedish-American dramatic soprano. In 1893 she went to Berlin to study with Lilli Lehmann, making her operatic debut (1895) in Cologne. She made her Metropolitan Opera de-

but in 1903, specializing in Wagnerian roles but also singing *Carmen* with Enrico Caruso and with the Boston and Chicago operas. She gave her farewell concert in New York in 1920.

ELLA A. MALIN

French, Daniel Chester

Daniel Chester French's Minute Man (1873–75), a bronze created to commemorate the Battle of Concord in 1775, is a naturalistic representation of an idealized American patriot. French's work characteristically expressed heroic or allegorical sentiment in a moving, realistic manner.

Daniel Chester French, b. Exeter, N.H., Apr. 20, 1850, d. Oct. 7, 1931, was America's unsurpassed sculptor of public monuments. He studied modeling with Abigail Alcott, anatomy with William Rimmer, and drawing with William Morris Hunt in Boston. For his first commission, the rugged *Minute Man* (1873–75; Concord, Mass.), which commemorates the first New Englanders to fall in the American Revolution, French used the pose of the Apollo Belvedere, invigorating the surfaces with the details of the colonial garments.

After a sojourn (1886–88) in France, where he mastered the lively Parisian treatment of surfaces in Jean Antonin Mercié's studio, French rapidly gained a reputation as a creator of monumental personifications of national sentiments and ideals. His *Mourning Victory* (1906–08; Sleepy Hollow Cemetery, Concord, Mass.), a half-bared, full female figure is a memorial to the North's Civil War dead. Recalling Auguste Rodin's adaptations of Michelangelo's unfinished figures, the figure emerges from the marble block past a shrouding flag that surrounds her with flowing Art Nouveau curves.

The gigantic seated *Abraham Lincoln* (1911–22) for the Lincoln Memorial in Washington, D.C., climaxed French's career. The seated pose, reflecting the classically balanced proportions of the Doric temple, conveys the president's firmness of purpose as does the bony frame and especially the steady hands.   JOAN C. SIEGFRIED

Bibliography: Adams, Adeline, *Daniel Chester French, Sculptor* (1932); Craven, Wayne, *Sculpture in America* (1968); Cresson, Margaret, *Journey into Fame: The Life of Daniel Chester French* (1947); Richmond, Michael, *Daniel Chester French: An American Sculptor* (1976).

French, John, 1st Earl of Ypres

John French, b. Sept. 28, 1852, d. May 22, 1925, was a British field marshal who commanded the British forces in Belgium and France in the early stages of World War I. He served in the South African War (1899–1902) and was chief of the imperial general staff (1912–14). Given command of the British Expeditionary Force (BEF) in August 1914, he failed to coordinate with the French armies, and the BEF suffered huge casualties at the first and second battles of Ypres and at Loos. In December 1915 he was replaced by Gen. Douglas Haig.

French Academy: see ACADÉMIE FRANÇAISE.

French art and architecture

The earliest artistic remains in France date from Paleolithic times (see PREHISTORIC ART). The periods of Celtic culture from the late 5th century BC to the 1st century AD and of Roman occupation from the 1st century to the 5th century AD saw the building of towns and the creation of artifacts (see CELTIC ART; ROMAN ARCHITECTURE). It is not possible, however, to speak of a nationally distinct French art before the mid-5th century AD, when the Merovingian and Carolingian dynasties established authority over this region.

MEROVINGIAN AND CAROLINGIAN PERIOD

After the decline of the Roman Empire, France was left as it had been before the Roman conquest, divided among many small regional tribes. These became small kingdoms and duchies between the 2d and the 5th century AD. Christianity spread during this period, leading to the foundation of many abbeys and monastic communities in the 5th to the 7th century. Few artifacts survive from the Merovingian period (see MEROVINGIAN ART AND ARCHITECTURE), named for the dynasty of Frankish kings that began with Clovis (c.481). The most notable Merovingian survival is the baptistery of Saint Jean at Poitiers, dating from the 7th century. Merovingian churches, with floor plans based on the Roman BASILICA, had stone walls, timber roofs, prominent bell towers, and echoed classical motifs in their ornamentation.

Charlemagne's Palace Chapel at Aachen, West Germany, or Aix-la-Chapelle (top), was designed by Odo of Metz and dedicated in 805. Based on the design of the church of San Vitale at Ravenna, the chapel plan is essentially octagonal, with a 16-sided structure forming aisles (1) and galleries (2) and the alternating sides of the polygon converging on eight massive stone piers (3). Unlike the expansive interior of San Vitale, the interior space of the chapel is clearly defined by its heavy stone masonry with superimposed arches (4) and its Roman columnar supports (5). The clerestory (6) illumines the mosaics of the central vault. Turreted stairwells (7) flanking the entrance later developed into the elaborate western facade. The entire palace complex (bottom), of which only the chapel remains, consisted of the royal hall (8), gatehouse (9), and chapel flanked by annexes (10, 11). The whole was linked by an enclosed corridor (12).

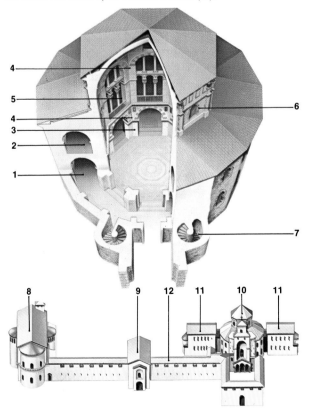

In the 8th century, under the authority of Charlemagne—the first king to create a unified realm—a great building campaign began. Carolingian churches were intricately decorated with pictorial murals, mosaics, goldwork, and tapestries. The richness of Carolingian church interiors was equaled by the ILLUMINATED MANUSCRIPTS created at the monasteries of Reims, Tours, Metz, and Paris. The best preserved of Carolingian churches is the Chapel of Charlemagne (796–804) at Aachen (Aix-la-Chapelle), whose octagonal sanctuary reflects the influence on Carolingian art of the Early Christian, Byzantine, and Greco-Roman traditions. The Aachen chapel is modeled on the octagonal Byzantine church of SAN VITALE (526–47) in Ravenna.

In larger Carolingian churches, built from the 8th to the 10th century, several important innovations were made, including the construction of an elaborate westwork, or entrance FACADE flanked by towers; an ambulatory, or semicircular aisle around the ALTAR, allowing worshipers to circulate without disturbing services; and the use of the composite PIER instead of a simple, massive COLUMN to support the upper walls and roof above the NAVE.

ROMANESQUE PERIOD

Architecture. Two forces affected the development of church architecture in France from the 10th to the 12th century. One was the growth of large, wealthy monastic orders, and the other was a rapid increase in the number of religious pilgrimages to holy shrines.

The Romanesque style in architecture (see ROMANESQUE ART AND ARCHITECTURE) can be thought of as a product of the architectural experiments of the Carolingian period and as a response to the needs of monasteries and pilgrimage churches. Romanesque style varied from region to region, reflecting local traditions and requirements. The largest and most important Romanesque structure was the Benedictine monastery church at CLUNY in Burgundy (begun in 1088 and destroyed in the 19th century). Cluny was the center of the Benedictine order in France. The massive monastery church, crowned with a stone vault (see ARCH AND VAULT), contained five aisles, two TRANSEPTS, a chevet (an ambulatory with chapels radiating from the APSE), an imposing westwork, and a NARTHEX. The pattern established at Cluny was imitated by Benedictine churches throughout France.

The ability to surpass the limitations of a wooden beam ceiling by constructing a stone barrel vault allowed the builders of Cluny to make the body of the nave unusually broad. Although the use of wooden roofs continued in northern France, the stone vault was one of the most successful Romanesque innovations. The stone roof took several forms: a barrel vault, pointed as at Autun Cathedral (1120–1132), or a groin vault, as at Vézelay (1089–1206). Although the walls were made extremely thick to support the stone vaults and give an impression of enormous weight, the interiors were well lit through CLERESTORY windows set high in the walls of the nave above the lower roofs covering the side aisles.

Sculpture. The principal fulfillment of the devout medieval Christian was a pilgrimage to Rome, or to one of the many European shrines that contained holy relics. Pilgrimage routes crossed national boundaries to shrines as distant as Santiago de Compostela in Spain, and churches were built along these well-traveled routes, many of which traversed France. Romanesque sculpture developed as decorations in these pilgrimage churches and is characterized by its highly stylized depictions of natural forms. The most prominent location for religious sculpture was in the TYMPANUM over the main west door leading to the center aisle of the church. Here artists depicted scenes from the life of Christ or other subjects familiar to pilgrims and suitable for their contemplation. A fine example of such a carved tympanum survives at the church of Saint Pierre in Moissac. Sculpture also adorned columns, CAPITALS, wells in CLOISTERS, and CRYPTS.

Enamelwork. The ancient art of enamelwork (see ENAMEL), which had continued to develop in France throughout the Merovingian and Carolingian periods, reached unprecedented heights in the 11th and 12th centuries, when the technique of *champlevé* came into general use. LIMOGES was a center of

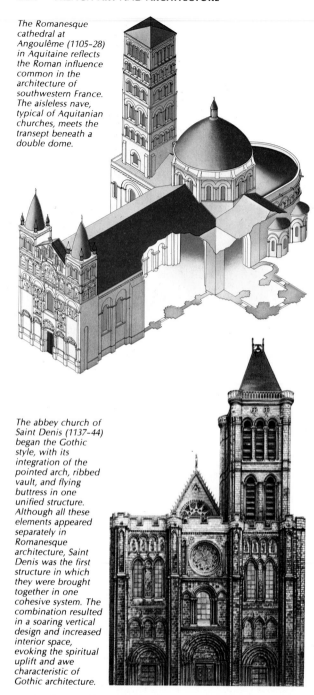

The Romanesque cathedral at Angoulême (1105–28) in Aquitaine reflects the Roman influence common in the architecture of southwestern France. The aisleless nave, typical of Aquitanian churches, meets the transept beneath a double dome.

The abbey church of Saint Denis (1137–44) began the Gothic style, with its integration of the pointed arch, ribbed vault, and flying buttress in one unified structure. Although all these elements appeared separately in Romanesque architecture, Saint Denis was the first structure in which they were brought together in one cohesive system. The combination resulted in a soaring vertical design and increased interior space, evoking the spiritual uplift and awe characteristic of Gothic architecture.

production, and its enamelwork was prized throughout Europe.

GOTHIC PERIOD

The Gothic style grew out of the Romanesque in a surge of activity that began in the mid-12th century (see GOTHIC ART AND ARCHITECTURE). The increasing affluence of that period brought new commercial centers into prominence. Mercantile interests sponsored the construction of great cathedrals, thus giving the cities the initiative in artistic innovation over the rural monastic and pilgrimage churches that had dominated the preceding centuries. Gothic art evolved in Northern France and spread throughout Europe, becoming the universal style from the 13th through the 16th century. Although the influence of Romanesque architecture had spread beyond France, Gothic was the first French style to dominate Europe.

This relief from the Romanesque Cathedral of Saint Lazare, Autun (1120–32), originally formed the lintel of the north portal. It shows a bemused Eve at the moment of plucking the apple. (Musée Rolin, Autun.)

Architecture. Gothic architecture began with the construction of cathedrals in Noyon (begun c.1150–70) and Laon (begun c.1160) and of the abbey church of SAINT-DENIS near Paris. It continued to develop in churches close to Paris, at Senlis (1153–84) and Sens (begun c.1140), and in the cathedrals of REIMS (begun 1210) and Rouen (begun after 1200). Saint-Denis, the most important achievement of early Gothic architecture, was built on the foundations of an earlier church between 1137 and 1144. The Abbott SUGER intended to make Saint-Denis a splendid showplace in keeping with its function as the royal abbey church of France and burial place of French kings.

In order to make these Gothic churches larger, the ribbed vault, capable of spanning large areas, was devised. Ribbed vaults were made loftier by enlarging the clerestory zone and its windows to enormous size, inserting a new zone, the TRIFORIUM, below it, and supporting them on an ARCADE of high piers lining the nave. To bear the greater stress of these taller, broader interiors, and to create larger window areas, a system of external supports or flying buttresses (see BUTTRESS) was developed. This created a greater sense of unity between the spaces of the nave and the adjacent aisles and ambulatory chapels. As the builders became more sophisticated, they were able to achieve ever grander effects at NOTRE DAME DE PARIS (begun 1163), CHARTRES CATHEDRAL (1145; rebuilt after a fire begun 1194), AMIENS CATHEDRAL (begun 1220), the SAINTE-CHAPELLE in Paris (begun after 1243, completed 1248), and Reims. The windows were enlarged, not to lighten the interiors, but rather for extensive use of STAINED GLASS, which attained the height of its development in the late 12th and 13th centuries at Chartres and the Sainte-Chapelle.

Sculpture. Both the exteriors of these churches and certain interior elements were decorated with elaborate sculpture. Facades were populated with large figures of kings; portals were flanked by pillar-statues, called jamb figures, of saints, angels, and apostles; and other parts of the building were encrusted with decorative cusps, finials, and grotesque GARGOYLES. Gothic sculptors took a revolutionary step beyond their Ro-

The upper chapel of the Sainte-Chapelle, Paris, one of the finest achievements of High Gothic, was built by Louis IX between 1243 and 1248 as a shrine for sacred relics. The chapel wall, relieved of its support function by the system of ribbed vaults and buttresses, was filled with large stained-glass windows rivaling in beauty those of Chartres.

manesque predecessors in their conception of the figures as independent, almost free-standing statues rather than as reliefs. From the columnar verticality of the jamb statues at Chartres, Gothic sculpture evolved quickly toward the sympathetic depiction of character in the figures at Reims (c.1224–45). Gothic sculpture became more sophisticated in the ensuing centuries. One of the finest 14th-century creations is the refined and mannered figure of the Virgin that stands in the south transept of Notre Dame de Paris.

RENAISSANCE PERIOD

The Italian RENAISSANCE began to influence French art in the last decade of the 15th century, when Charles VIII returned (1496) from his conquest of Naples accompanied by several Italian artists. Italian styles first appeared in the chateaux of the Loire Valley and became predominant during the reign (1515–47) of Francis I. Initially, however, Italian decorative elements were superimposed on Gothic principles. The earliest example is the Château d'Amboise (c.1495), where LEONARDO DA VINCI spent his last years. The Château de CHAMBORD (1519–36) is a more elaborate marriage of Gothic structure and Italianate ornament. This style progressed in the work of Italian architects such as Sebastiano SERLIO, who was engaged after 1540 in much of the work at the Château de FONTAINEBLEAU.

At Fontainebleau grand interior galleries and ballrooms were decorated by Italian artists who formed the first school of Fontainebleau. The principal figures of this school were ROSSO FIORENTINO, Francesco PRIMATICCIO, and Niccolò dell' Abbate (1512–c.1570). The art of engraving was also developed in France by foreign artists who helped disseminate the Italianate style.

The climate of active royal and aristocratic patronage encouraged many talented artists and architects, including Jacques Androuet du Cerceau (c.1520–1585), Philibert DELORME, (c.1510–70), Giacomo VIGNOLA, and Pierre LESCOT. One of the finest surviving monuments of the French Renaissance is the southwest interior facade of the Cour Carrée of the Palais du LOUVRE in Paris, designed by Lescot and covered with exterior carvings by Jean GOUJON. Strong regional schools appeared in Lorraine as the arts continued to flourish under the reigns of Henry II and Henry III.

BAROQUE PERIOD

The reign of Henry IV (1589–1610) was a period of competent and enlightened government. The king's marriage to Marie de' Medici of the ruling house of Florence helped to ensure high esteem for Italian artistic accomplishments. The Place des Vosges (1605), then called the Place Royale, and the Place Dauphine (1607) were planned and built. In Paris a second generation of artists—called the second school of Fontainebleau—were trained or inspired by Italian painters to perpetuate the Italianate tradition under the patronage of Henry IV.
Architecture. In the second and third quarters of the century, during the ministries of Cardinal Richelieu to Louis XIII and of Cardinal Mazarin to the child-king Louis XIV, France became a great European power. These sage men required prestigious dwellings suited to their station. The architects Jacques LEMERCIER—builder of Richelieu's Palais Cardinal (begun 1633), now site of the the Palais Royale, and of the Church of the Sorbonne (begun 1635)—François MANSART and Louis LE VAU adapted the Italian baroque style to French needs (see BAROQUE ART AND ARCHITECTURE).

During the personal reign of Louis XIV (1661–1715) the arts served the state under the direction of the powerful minister of commerce and of royal works, Jean Baptiste COLBERT. The Louvre was enlarged, and the magnificent palace of VERSAILLES (c.1669–90) was built as a fitting residence for the powerful king of France. The leading architect of the latter half of the 17th century was Jules HARDOUIN-MANSART, who designed parts of the palace of Versailles, the Orangerie, and numerous squares and public buildings in Paris.
Painting. Italy played a fundamental role in the redirection of French painting in the 17th century. Some French artists, notably Nicolas POUSSIN and Claude LORRAIN, created new modes of painting while living in Italy. Other artists, such as Simon VOUET, fostered a native French baroque style. Colbert

Nicolas Poussin's The Childhood of Bacchus (c.1629), with its warm palette, free brushwork, and spontaneous drama, reflects the influence of Titian on the artist's early work. Poussin's later painting became increasingly sculptural and classical in style. (Louvre, Paris.)

founded the Royal Academy of Painting and Sculpture (1663) to protect this group of artists and enlist their services for the state. Charles LE BRUN was named first painter to the king and guided the academy. Under his leadership, artists celebrated the triumphs of the Sun King. Their work included MURAL PAINTINGS, altarpieces, tapestry CARTOONS, and other large-scale narrative works associating Louis XIV and his reign with great men and events from classical literature. The same was true in sculpture—monumental figures of the king or large-scale structures were needed to ornament public squares and formal gardens.

Recognizing that Italy was the great school of both classical and Renaissance art, Colbert founded the French Academy in Rome in 1666, to which gifted French artists and architects were sent at the expense of the crown.

THE 18TH CENTURY

On the death of Louis XIV in 1715, his 5-year-old great-grandson, Louis XV, became king. The realm was guided until 1723 by a regent, Louis XIV's nephew Philippe d'Orléans. During the regency, the single-minded direction given the arts by Louis XIV was relaxed in favor of individualism and personal indulgence.
Painting and Sculpture. During the last years of the reign of Louis XIV and the first half of the 18th century, the French became enamored of the small genre subjects of 17th-century Holland and of the more lighthearted, mythological scenes of the Italian baroque. In French hands, these subjects gave new definition to social refinement and luxury. Decorative arts and interior design were transformed by the growing popularity of the ROCOCO STYLE, a light-hearted and elegant style based on asymmetrical natural forms.

While the academies continued to pay lip service to the granduer of the age of Louis XIV, public attention shifted from the courtly taste set at Versailles to the fashion set by the nobility and wealthy bourgeoisie in their private Parisian residences, called hôtels. Here literate free-thinking tastes led to a delightful style of painting and sculpture rich in decorative effect and expressive of human sentiment. This new spirit received its finest expression in the brilliant work of the Flemish painter Antoine WATTEAU, whose scenes of revelers in contemporary dress, inhabiting a mythological realm of pleasure, changed the direction of private patronage in France. Artists such as François BOUCHER were inspired by the subject matter and technical brilliance of Watteau to create ravishing combinations of color and graceful forms. This development was encouraged by the court of Louis XV, who adopted the taste of Paris as his courtly style in the second quarter of the 18th century.

In the third quarter of the 18th century, an effort was made by members of the Royal Academy and Arts administration, notably the Marquis de Marigny (1727–81), director of Royal

Jacques Louis David's portrait Madame Recamier *(1800) exhibits the typically cool, crisp line of French neoclassicism. Like Poussin, David was inspired by his study of Roman sculpture to re-create the simplicity and clarity of classical forms. (Louvre, Paris.)*

Works, to revive the disciplined and elevated goals of art established in the 17th century by Louis XIV and his minister Colbert. The demand for a didactic, grand style led to the emergence in the last quarter of the century of a generation of artists devoted to high principles of art and the service of the state. Most famous of these was the painter Jacques Louis DAVID, pioneer of a pure classicizing style based on that of Poussin. A wide divergence existed between the didactic art of David and the courtly taste of Louis XV and his grandson, Louis XVI, who preferred artists such as Jean Honoré FRAGO-NARD and Hubert ROBERT. Consequently, a healthy variety characterized the art of late-18th-century France. With the radical change of political and social structure that came with the French Revolution and the rise of Napoleon I, the didactic art of David found a new outlet never anticipated by his royal sponsors.

Architecture. French architecture of the 18th century continued the classicizing tendencies of the 17th century in France with greater reserve and refinement, using classical motifs in a late baroque style. Restrained ornament, delicate carved limestone details, and the sophisticated play of volume and lighting give the domestic and public architecture of the period a sense of calm grandeur. Among the architectural gems of the reign of Louis XV is the PETIT TRIANON (1762) by Ange Jacques Gabriel, a leisure retreat in the park at Versailles. The regular and sedate proportions of the nearly cubic Petit Trianon never become ponderous or dull, so refined are the rhythms of the surface ornamentation, arrangement of windows, and crowning balustrade.

Late-18th-century architecture was affected by a neoclassical revival comparable to that in painting, and quoted architectural usages of the past with archaeological correctness. NEOCLASSICISM was particularly well suited to monumental buildings, such as Jacques Germain SOUFFLOT's Saint-Geneviève, now called the Panthéon, in Paris.

THE 19TH CENTURY
The 18th century interest in sentiment and emotion led to an interest in extremes of sensibility in the romantic art of the following century (see ROMANTICISM, art).

Painting. The greatest practitioners of romantic painting in France were Théodore GÉRICAULT, Eugène DELACROIX, and Jean Auguste Dominique INGRES. Géricault's *Raft of the Medusa* (1818–19; Louvre, Paris), a depiction of the victims of a shipwreck, exposed the full range of human emotions from despair to exhilaration. Delacroix's *Death of Sardanapalus* (1827; Louvre) explored the potential of color and vibrant brushwork as a means of heightening the sensations aroused by a dramatic narrative episode. In harem scenes such as *The Great Odalisque* (1814; Louvre) Ingres reflects 19th-century European fascination with the life of the senses and exotic foreign cultures.

By the mid-19th century the self-indulgence of romanticism was tempered by the changing relationship of the artist to the subject matter. Gustave COURBET insisted that his painting owed no debt to any school or style and that art should offer detached observations of unidealized reality. Courbet's paintings of peasants, such as *Funeral at Ornans* (1850; Louvre), caused a scandal at that time, but his powerful depiction of nature found other exponents in Jean François MILLET and Honoré DAUMIER (see REALISM, art).

An outgrowth of realism was a new conception of art as an activity that was worthwhile for its own sake regardless of its subject matter or allegiance to institutional values. This attitude was a necessary precondition for the emergence of IMPRESSIONISM, a movement in painting that concentrated on the effects of light and color. The favored subjects of Claude MO-

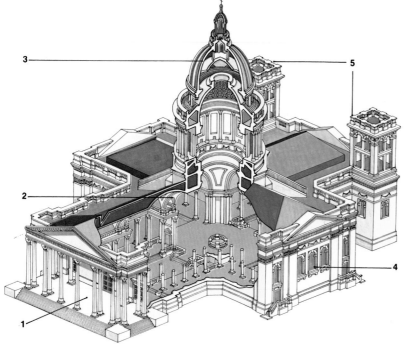

The Panthéon (c.1755–90) in Paris, originally the church of Sainte Geneviève, was designed by Jacques Germain Soufflot, one of the leading neoclassical architects of France. Neoclassical architecture reacted against baroque and rococo ornateness and emulated the massive form and restrained line of antique architecture. Soufflot integrated many Gothic elements into the structure of the Panthéon: the vaulting, for example, increased strength and interior lightness while preserving classical form. Corinthian columns support both the portico (1), based on the Roman Pantheon, as well as the saucer domes (2) within the roof of each arm of the building, which is constructed in the form of a Greek cross. The central dome (3), whose three shells resemble the triple-constructed dome of Wren's Saint Paul's Cathedral, is supported by four slender piers, later thickened and strengthened by Rondelet. The windows (4) were eventually eliminated and the towers (5) removed to emphasize the austere, rigid classicism popular at the beginning of the 19th century. During the French Revolution the building was renamed the Panthéon and secularized as a memorial to French heroes.

(Left) *Théodore Géricault's* Officer of the Imperial Guard *(1812), painted when the artist was 21, was one of only three works exhibited during his lifetime. The officer's struggle against a turbulent nature epitomizes an ideal of romantic heroism that Géricault's paintings helped establish. (Louvre, Paris.)*

Edgar Degas's luminous pastel Blue Dancers *(1890) shows the busy preparations of ballet dancers waiting in the wings. Degas shared a concern for immediacy with the other impressionists, but his compositional use of space foreshadows post-impressionism. (Louvre, Paris.)*

(Right) *Jean Auguste Dominique Ingres's* Turkish Bath *(1863), one of the artist's late nude scenes, shows his sensitive modeling of delicate bodily contours. Although he often appealed to the exotic romanticisim of his day, Ingres perfected the clear linear style and polished surface of the neoclassical ideal. (Louvre, Paris.)*

NET, Pierre Auguste RENOIR, and Camille PISSARRO, were coastal and river scenes in which light dissolves form and softens focus. The loosely associated impressionist group also included Edgar DEGAS, whose interior scenes challenged conventional theories of formal composition and subject matter.

POSTIMPRESSIONISM, a general term for the work of such painters as Paul CÉZANNE, Paul GAUGUIN, Vincent VAN GOGH, Georges SEURAT, and Pierre BONNARD, evolved in reaction to the neutrality of subject matter and dissolution of form inherent in impressionism. These artists had few qualities in common, but their individual styles did much to determine the directions that painting would take in the 20th century.

Sculpture. In sculpture, the 19th century tended to be conservative. The romantic sculpture of François Rudé, Jean Baptiste CARPEAUX, and Antoine Louis BARYE stands out. Auguste RODIN revitalized sculpture by returning to the direct study of the human form. Rodin's portrayal of physical and emotional stress led to a fresh appreciation of the Renaissance masters Michelangelo and Donatello and exercised a profound influence on 20th-century sculpture.

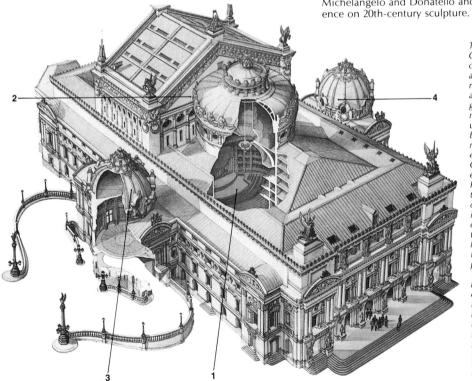

The Paris Opéra, designed by Charles Garnier in 1861 and completed in 1875, was initiated as part of Napoleon III's replanning of Paris between 1853 and 1868 and was designed to glorify the Second Empire. The monumental structure, based upon precepts of the École des Beaux-Arts, broke with neoclassical restraint in an exuberant revival of the baroque. Garnier's eclectic facade, employing elements from Renaissance architectural tradition, is elaborately ornamental. The sumptuous interior focuses upon a central domed auditorium (1) with tiered balconies and a large stage house (2). Private entrance wings for the emperor (3) and house patrons (4) flank the auditorium. The showpieces of the Opéra, however, are the frankly ostentatious gilt foyers and the immense staircase of multicolored marble. Although the Opéra's splendor appealed to the new industrial bourgeoisie, such ornamental profusion influenced the development of the unadorned aesthetic of 20th-century architecture.

(Above) *Paul Cézanne's mature work* The Card Players *(c.1892), with its distortion of figures and table space and its unifying color motifs, illustrates the artist's transition from representational impressionism to abstract art. (Courtauld Institute Galleries, London.)*

Henri Matisse's Dance *(1910) conveys a delight in pure color and a love of rhythmic, undulating line. Throughout his career Matisse sought a lively simplicity of expression. (Hermitage, Leningrad.)*

Architecture. In architecture, the neoclassicism of the late 18th century was perpetuated by monumental forms serving the political ambitions of the Second Empire (1852–70) of Napoleon III. Later, an eclectic style based on both classical and baroque architecture emerged in the work of architects trained at the ÉCOLE DES BEAUX-ARTS. Beaux-Arts buildings such as Jean Louis Charles GARNIER's spectacular PARIS OPÉRA (1861–75) played an important role in Baron HAUSSMANN's modernization of the city during the Second Empire. Properties of new industrial materials and construction techniques were investigated by such pioneers as Henri LABROUSTE and Alexandre Gustave EIFFEL, whose EIFFEL TOWER (1889) has become a symbol of Paris.

THE 20TH CENTURY
Painting and Sculpture. In the early 20th century Paris was the center of the art world, but art in France—not French art—must be considered when describing the international influence of the Parisian avant-garde, because many expatriate artists worked in the city. The course of 20th-century art was shaped from Paris by the Spaniard Pablo PICASSO, the Russian Wassily KANDINSKY, the Romanian Constantin BRANCUSI, and many lesser figures.

The history of 20th-century expressionist art (see EXPRESSIONISM, art) descends from van Gogh and other postimpressionists through the Fauve group (see FAUVISM) that formed around Henri MATISSE, one of the most influential French artists of the 20th century. Picasso and Georges BRAQUE changed the direction of painting through their cubist experiments with the pictorial values of composition, color, and form (see CUBISM). The last influential Parisian artistic movement was SURREALISM, a literary and artistic movement devoted to the exploration of irrational and subconscious states of mind.

Architecture. In architecture, France was at the forefront of the creation of a new 20th-century aesthetic. At the turn of the century, the experiments of ART NOUVEAU led to the creation of graceful decorative motifs based on natural forms. The Swiss architect Charles Édouard Jeanneret, called LE CORBUSIER, in France, pioneered a philosophy of functionalism in architecture that can be summarized by this famous dictum: "buildings are machines to live in." The theory and practices of Le Corbusier, reinforced by those of the BAUHAUS, in Germany, became the fundamental principles of the International Style (see INTERNATIONAL STYLE, architecture) typified by Le Corbusier's Villa Savoire (1929–31; Poissy-sur-Seine). Major achievements of French art since World War II include the paintings of Jean DUBUFFET, the brilliantly colored paper cut-outs of Matisse, and Le Corbusier's Pilgrim Church of Notre Dame at Ronchamp (1950–55). ALDEN RAND GORDON

Georges Braque's Still Life with Playing Cards (1913) isolates specific aspects of form, color, and texture from its constituent objects and re-creates the table, grapes, apple, and cards through superimposed patches. Braque's fruitful collaboration with Picasso brought about the full development of cubism. (Musée National d'Art Moderne, Paris.)

Bibliography: Blunt, Anthony, *Art and Architecture in France, 1500–1700*, 3d ed. (1970); Boime, Albert, *The Academy and French Painting in the 19th Century* (1971; repr. 1986); Bouret, Jean, *The Barbizon School: 19th-Century French Landscape Painting* (1973); Bretell, Richard R., et al., *A Day in the Country: Impressionism and the French Landscape* (1984); Bryson, Norman, ed., *Word and Image: French Painting of the Ancient Regime* (1983); Cleveland Museum of Art, *Japonisme: Japanese Influence on French Art 1854–1910* (1975); Dennison, Lisa, *Angles of Vision: French Art Today* (1986); Evans, Joan, *Art in Medieval France, 987–1498* (1969); Freeman, Judi, et al., *The Fauve Landscape* (1990); Friedlaender, Walter, *David to Delacroix*, trans. by Robert Goldwater (1952); von Kalnein, Wend, and Levey, Michael, *Art and Architecture of the 18th Century in France* (1972); Mâle, Émile, *Art and Artists of the Middle Ages* (1986) and *Religious Art from the 12th to the 18th Century* (1982); Muehsam, Gerd, comp. and ed., *French Painters and Paintings from the 14th Century to Post-Impressionism* (1970); Orpen, William, *The Conflict Between Realism and Impressionism in France* (1990) and *The French Revolution and the Romantic Movement: Their Influence on Art* (1985); Perl, Jed, *Paris Without End: On French Art Since World War I* (1988); Rewald, John, *The History of Impressionism*, 4th ed. (1973), and *Post-Impressionism from Van Gogh to Gauguin* (1956; repr. 1986); Stoddard, W. S., *Art and Architecture in Medieval France* (1972); Wakefield, D., *French 18th Century Painting* (1983).

French bulldog

The French bulldog is a small but massive breed, reaching only 30 cm (12 in) high at the shoulders but weighing up to 13 kg (25 lb). It is low-set and smooth-coated, with a blunt,

The French bulldog, smaller than the English bulldog, is distinguished by its batlike ears. This nonsporting breed reached its greatest popularity in the early 1900s.

heavy head and relatively high, batlike ears. The tail is naturally short, not docked. Coat colors are brindle, fawn, white with brindle patches, or solid white. The breed's exact origin is uncertain. The English claim that it originated from miniature English bulldogs brought to France about the middle of the 19th century. The French claim the breed is an old native one. Although the breed probably did originate from small English bulldogs, its development was French and its preservation the result of efforts by American breeders. The French Bulldog Club of America was founded in 1898.

JOHN MANDEVILLE

Bibliography: Eltinge, S., *The French Bulldog* (1988); Nicholas, A. K., *French Bulldogs* (1990).

French colonial empire

From its beginnings in the early 1600s through the great expansion of the late 19th century, the French overseas empire was formed more by the agencies and stimulation of the state, church, and armed forces than by the initiation of the business community. Merchants, financiers, and manufacturers did engage in and profit from French imperial ventures, but generally they had to be prodded into participation by monarchical or republican officials. In this the French colonial empire differed from its chief rival, the BRITISH EMPIRE.

Before the French Revolution, Henry IV, Louis XIV, and the latter's minister Jean Baptiste COLBERT, who founded the French East India Company, and many missionaries, explorers, and merchants helped acquire Canada, Louisiana, several West Indian islands, and parts of India for France. In 1763, at the end of the SEVEN YEARS' WAR, the French lost Canada and India to the British, and in 1803, Napoleon I sold the Louisiana Territory to the United States. By 1815 only the West Indian sugar islands and some scattered African and Asian posts remained French.

The foundations of a second French colonial empire were laid between 1830 and 1870, when Louis-Philippe's forces penetrated Algeria and Napoleon III's seized Cochin China in southeastern Asia. Along with other European powers, France rode the post-1870 wave of new imperialism. By 1914, France had amassed an empire incorporating over 10,000,000 km^2 (4,000,000 mi^2) and 60 million people. In Southeast Asia the French pieced together the colony of INDOCHINA by 1893, adding Laos, Cambodia (now Kampuchea), Annam, and Tonkin to Cochin China. Tunisia and Morocco became protectorates. France's vast African empire also included FRENCH EQUATORIAL AFRICA, FRENCH WEST AFRICA, French Somaliland (now Djibouti), and the islands of Madagascar and the Comoros.

The motives for this overseas penetration varied from the search for markets, raw materials, investments, and cheap labor to the drive for glory, prestige, strategic advantage, and manpower. Prominent, too, was the *mission civilisatrice*, the urge to implant Roman Catholicism and French culture.

The governance of the empire followed two patterns, sometimes intertwined: assimilation and association. Where there prevailed long traditions of organized political life and a common culture, the French tended to rule indirectly through existing local authorities, as in Tunisia and Morocco. In less structured societies like those of West Africa, the French imposed direct rule and attempted to assimilate the populace. More than the British, the French intermixed with the indigenous population. The British, on the other hand, were more wont to prepare some colonies for autonomy or independence.

The French colonial empire survived World War I, but World War II led to its reorganization as the FRENCH UNION

A global map shows France and its overseas colonial possessions in 1900. During the period between the end (1871) of the Franco-Prussian War and the onset (1914) of World War I, the French colonial empire expanded greatly, notably in Africa and the Far East.

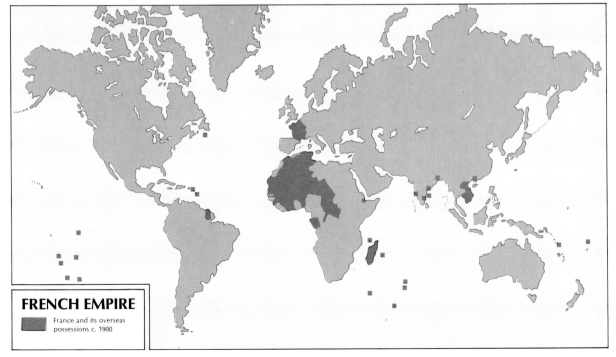

FRENCH EMPIRE

France and its overseas possessions c. 1900

and finally to its dissolution, primarily as the result of the wars in Indochina and Algeria.   DONALD J. HARVEY

Bibliography: Baumgart, W., *Imperialism: The Idea and Reality in British and French Colonial Expansion* (1982); Brunschwig, H., *French Colonialism* (1966); Harrison, C., *France and Islam in West Africa* (1988); Johnson, G. W., ed., *Double Impact: France and Africa in the Age of Imperialism* (1985); Kahler, M., *Decolonization in Britain and France* (1984); McNeill, J. R., *Atlantic Empires of France and Spain* (1985); Roberts, S. H., *The History of French Colonial Policy* (1963); Shorrock, W. I., *French Imperialism in the Middle East* (1975).

See also: ALGERIAN WAR; COLONIALISM; EAST INDIA COMPANY, FRENCH; FRANCE, HISTORY OF; VIETNAM WAR.

French Community

The French Community, established under the constitution of the Fifth Republic in 1958, replaced the FRENCH UNION as the formal organization of France and its former colonies, territories, and overseas departments. Member states, which under the union had been represented in the French national assembly and governed by the president of the French Republic, became self-governing and were linked through the community's institutions set up to handle foreign policy, defense, economic policy, education, and other matters of common interest. The community began to fragment in the early 1960s, when many African member states chose to become fully independent. France still maintains close economic and cultural ties with most of its former colonies, however.

French East India Company: see EAST INDIA COMPANY, FRENCH.

French Equatorial Africa

French Equatorial Africa was a former (1910–59) administrative grouping of four French territories in west central Africa. It comprised Chad, Ubangi-Shari (Central African Republic), Gabon, and the Middle Congo (Congo). Brazzaville, Congo, served as the capital.

French foreign legion

The *Légion Étrangère* ("foreign legion") is a French military corps founded originally to serve in the French colonies. It is now an elite corps in the French army. The legion was first raised by King Louis Philippe in 1831. Garrisoned in Algeria until that country achieved independence in 1962, the legion was not permitted in France during peacetime. Since 1962, however, it has been headquartered at Aubagne, near Marseille. Although the majority of its officers are French, about 60% of its members are foreign volunteers who, upon joining, swear an oath of allegiance to the legion but not to France. They can, however, become French citizens after completing one enlistment (five years).

Because of its reticence about the backgrounds of its enlistees, the French foreign legion acquired a reputation for attracting fugitives from justice. It has captured the popular imagination as a subject of romance, epitomized in the classic American film *Beau Geste* (1939; based on the novel by P. C. Wren). During World War I its *régiment de marche* was France's most decorated army unit. After World War II the legion fought in Indochina, in Algeria, in Zaire, and in Chad. Now primarily a rapid deployment force with a strength of 8,000 men, it was involved in the 1991 GULF WAR. The Spanish army has a similar corps, the *Legión Extranjera,* formerly stationed in Spanish Morocco, and now in the Canary Islands.

Bibliography: Young, J., *The French Foreign Legion,* 2d ed. (1985).

French Guiana   [gee-ah'-nuh]

French Guiana is an overseas department of France—an administrative status that renders it an integral part of the French Republic. It is located on the northern coast of South America and is bordered on the west by Suriname, on the south and east by Brazil, and on the north by the Atlantic Ocean. Its capital is CAYENNE, a port on the north coast and the country's

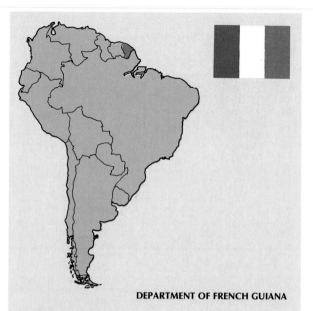

DEPARTMENT OF FRENCH GUIANA

LAND. Area: 91,000 km² (35,135 mi²). Capital and largest city: Cayenne (1982 pop., 38,135).

PEOPLE. Population (1990 est.): 97,781; density: 1.1 persons per km² (2.8 per mi²). Distribution (1982): 73% urban, 27% rural. Annual growth (1988): 2.6%. Official language: French. Major religion: Roman Catholicism.

EDUCATION AND HEALTH. Literacy (1982): 82% of adult population. Universities (1991): 1. Hospital beds (1987): 861. Physicians (1987): 237. Life expectancy (1990): women—76; men—68. Infant mortality (1990): 19 per 1,000 live births.

ECONOMY. GDP (1982): $210 million; $3,230 per capita. Labor distribution (1982): agriculture and mining—12%; manufacturing—4%; construction, finance, transport and communications, utilities—20%; public administration and services—31%. Foreign trade (1987): imports—$394.4 million; exports—$53.8 million; principal trade partners—France, Germany, Japan, Italy. Currency: 1 French franc = 100 centimes.

GOVERNMENT. Type: overseas department of France. Legislature: General Council; Regional Council. Political subdivisions: 2 arrondissements.

COMMUNICATIONS. Railroads (1991): none. Roads (1988): 1,137 km (706 mi) total. Major ports: 1. Major airfields: 1.

only important urban center. There are a number of small, rocky islands along the coast, the most famous of which is DEVIL'S ISLAND, long a French penal colony.

LAND AND ECONOMY

The coastal strip of French Guiana was once the center of a prosperous sugar industry and still grows small quantities of sugarcane as well as rice and corn. The densely forested interior, almost totally undeveloped, rises gradually to the mountains along the Brazilian border in the south. Mount Saint Marcel (635 m/2,083 ft), the highest point, is there.

The climate is tropical, with an annual average temperature of 27° C (80° F); rainfall is heavy, averaging 3,200 mm (126 in) a year at Cayenne. A dry season, however, lasts from August to November. Agricultural activities along the coast have been in decline since the abolition of slavery in 1848 made plantation agriculture uneconomic. For many years the principal economic activity centered on the penal colony on Devil's Island. With the closing of the prison in 1945, however, this source of income disappeared. The French government provides many jobs at French-scale wages and substantial aid. Fisheries are being developed, especially for shrimp.

Extensive mineral resources are known to exist, including iron ore, copper, silver, lead, platinum, diamonds, and gold, but they remain unexploited. The rain forests that cover nearly 90% of the country are an abundant resource of tropical hardwoods. In the 1960s the de Gaulle government established the Guianan Space Center there, primarily because its

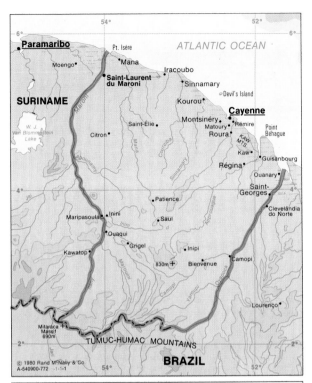

FRENCH GUIANA

+ Spot Elevation
National capitals are underlined

Scale 1:5,280,000

Meters	Feet	Meters	Feet
1000	3281	0	0
500	1640	200	656
200	656	Below 2000	Below 6562
0	0		

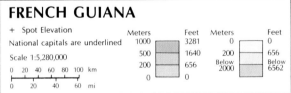

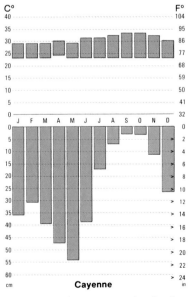

Bars indicate monthly ranges of temperature (red) and precipitation (blue) in Cayenne, the capital of French Guiana. Cayenne has a tropical wet-dry climate.

Cayenne

proximity to the equator makes it a favorable site for the launching of space vehicles. The European Space Agency's rocket Ariane is launched from the center, at Kourou. Overall French investment has declined, however, and the economy has tended to stagnate since the 1970s.

PEOPLE
Most of the people of French Guiana are Creoles—people of mixed European and African descent. There are small minorities of Europeans (mostly French), American Indians, Chinese, and Laotians. In recent decades there has been some migration of people of mixed African-European ancestry from Haiti, Martinique, and Guadeloupe. In the interior are a group of blacks who are descended from escaped slaves and have reverted to an African tribal form of life.

HISTORY
The first permanent French settlement was effected in 1604. Cayenne was taken by the Dutch in 1676 and held for a year. The Portuguese occupied the town from 1808 to 1817. The region was long neglected, and development was hindered by the establishment of the penal colony. In 1946, when most of the penal colonies had been closed, French Guiana was made an overseas French department with representation in the French national assembly and senate.   ROBERT J. ALEXANDER

French horn

The modern French horn evolved from the hunting horn developed during the 17th century. The "double horn" shown here, a late-19th-century invention, is a combination F horn and B-flat horn; a valve operated by the thumb allows the player to switch from one key to the other. Three other valves provide a full chromatic range. The player's right hand is inserted in the bell to modulate the open tone.

The French horn (so called to distinguish it from the ENGLISH HORN, a member of the OBOE family) is the developed European orchestral member of the true horn family. The instrument is classified technically as a lip-vibrated aerophone (see MUSICAL INSTRUMENTS), characterized by a conical bore and funnel-shaped mouthpiece, as opposed to the cylindrical bore and cup-shaped mouthpiece of the TRUMPET family.

Descended from primitive animal-horn prototypes (for example, the biblical SHOFAR), short, curved horns were used in medieval Europe primarily as signal instruments, especially for the hunt; they could usually be relied on only for the rhythmic sounding of a single pitch. In the late 16th and 17th centuries the horn, from this time usually made of brass, was lengthened and coiled—first in a small, spiral coil, later in a wider, open loop. By the late 17th century in France the *cor de chasse* ("hunting horn") emerged with a wide, flaring bell and a tube length of up to 4.37 m (14 ft), the obvious prototype of the modern instrument. Responsive to a greatly increased number of its natural overtones, the *cor de chasse* possessed a wide enough range of pitches for use in the orchestra of the early 18th century.

The addition of "crooks" (curved extensions to the tubing of various lengths) and the technique—attributed to the Dresden virtuoso Anton Joseph Hampel—of altering the pitch by stopping the bell with the hand made the horn still more complete melodically in its middle ranges, thus greatly increasing its versatility in the orchestra of the classical period of Haydn and Mozart. Also at this time (the late 18th century) the cup-shaped, trumpetlike mouthpiece was abandoned for the funnel-shaped mouthpiece of the modern horn, resulting in a smoother, less raucous sound.

During the early 19th century valves were added (patented in 1818 by Heinrich Stölzel and Friedrich Blühmel in Berlin) to vary the playing length of the tube, yielding an instrument virtually chromatic (proceeding by semitones) throughout its range. Although it was slow to be accepted, the valve horn prevailed by the end of the 19th century. The modern French horn is usually pitched in F, and has three valves and a tube length of about 3.75 m (12 ft). The great demands on the resources of the horn have led to the widespread adoption of the "double horn," in which a separate set of coils for a horn in B-flat is added to a horn in F, a fourth valve acting as a switch between the two sets of coils.   NICHOLAS RENOUF

Bibliography: Baines, Anthony, *Brass Instruments: Their History and Development* (1976); Carse, Adam, *Musical Wind Instruments* (1939; repr. 1965); Fitzpatrick, Horace, *The Horn and Horn Playing and the Austro-Bohemian Tradition from 1680 to 1830* (1970); Gregory, Robin, *The Horn: A Comprehensive Guide to the Modern Instrument and Its Music*, 2d ed. (1969); Morley-Pegge, R., *The French Horn*, 2d ed. (1973).

French and Indian Wars

The French and Indian Wars were a series of armed conflicts between England's colonies in North America on the one side and rival European colonies on the other during the period 1689–1763. Each conflict was part of a larger war in Europe and on the high seas.

By the 1680s, Spain held Florida, France occupied Canada (NEW FRANCE), and England possessed a chain of colonies along the Atlantic seaboard from New England to the Carolinas. West of the Appalachians lay a vast extent of territory open to international competition and strife. Inevitably involved on both sides were the various tribes of Indians, whose own deep-seated rivalries meshed with the rivalries of the Europeans. The IROQUOIS LEAGUE, often known as the Five (later Six) Nations, was a particularly influential and powerful group of Indians occupying the area south and east of Lake Ontario, thereby dominating the fur-trading routes leading both to French Montreal and English Albany, N.Y. In general, the Iroquois tended to support the English against the French, but increasingly they found advantage in playing one side off against the other.

The wars in North America were long and bloody, causing immense suffering for the Indians, blacks, and whites involved. Among those who suffered most were frontier settlers exposed to sudden enemy raids, as a result of which many lost their homes, not a few lost their lives, and some underwent the dreaded experience of captivity. One profitable form of wartime activity in which colonists engaged was privateering—legalized piracy against enemy merchant vessels. Another was hunting enemy Indians for the purpose of scalping them and claiming the cash bounty offered by colonial governments.

During these wars the French and Spaniards had the advantage of authoritarian government, while the English colonies often quarreled among themselves and seldom achieved full cooperation for common gain. But the English always enjoyed a tremendous preponderance of population. For example, in 1689, New France had only about 12,000 inhabitants, while the English colonists numbered over 200,000. By 1760 the population of New France may have reached 60,000, but at the same time the British colonies swarmed with nearly 1.6 million people. (These figures do not include unassimilated Indians.)

KING WILLIAM'S WAR

In May 1689, England, under its new Dutch king, WILLIAM III, entered the War of the GRAND ALLIANCE against France. That summer in America an Iroquois raiding party struck hard at the French settlement of Lachine near Montreal. Soon a new French governor, the comte de FRONTENAC, arrived in New France and initiated a counteroffensive against the English frontier, carried out in 1690 by mixed parties of French and Indians. Their ferocity and destructiveness did much to establish a pattern of savagery in border warfare for the next century. Serious losses were suffered by the English at Schenectady, Salmon Falls, and Falmouth (now Portland, Maine).

Recognizing that Quebec on the Saint Lawrence River was the heart of New France, English colonial leaders decided to attempt its capture. A land army was to advance down the Champlain Valley toward Montreal, while a fleet commanded by Sir William PHIPS was to proceed from Boston to the Saint Lawrence and up to Quebec. The failure of the land army to get within a hundred miles of Montreal enabled Frontenac to shift troops from that town to Quebec. Phips took Port Royal (now Annapolis Royal, Nova Scotia), but by the time he reached Quebec in October 1690, that city was too strongly defended to be taken. The New Englanders had to withdraw in humiliation, losing Port Royal to the French again in 1691.

Thereafter, the war was characterized by sporadic, small-scale raiding activity against isolated frontier settlements. For example, the sieur d' IBERVILLE led a series of attacks on English fur-trading posts on Hudson Bay and on settlements in Maine and Newfoundland, capturing Saint John's in 1696. Such raids terrorized the inhabitants but contributed little toward a decisive victory by either side. In Europe both sides were growing weary of the struggle, and a peace was arranged at Ryswick in September 1697, ending the war indecisively.

QUEEN ANNE'S WAR

The French then resumed their expansion into the region of the Great Lakes and the Mississippi Valley, causing the English to fear that the whole trans-Appalachian West would come under the French flag. When Louis XIV of France secured the Spanish throne for his grandson, Philip V of Spain, the War of the SPANISH SUCCESSION broke out in Europe in 1701. England entered the conflict in May 1702, this time declaring war on both France and Spain. Thus in the American theater, where the war was named for the English monarch Queen Anne, the English colonies now faced enemies to the south as well as to the north.

In 1702 the Carolinas sent an expedition against the Spanish settlement of Saint Augustine. After an unsuccessful siege the Carolinians returned home, but Florida was too weak to retaliate, and in subsequent years the Carolinians ravaged the Apalachee region with impunity. In the meantime, New England again was struggling to cope with French and Indian raiders along its lengthy and ill-defended frontier. Various settlements in Maine were attacked, and early in 1704 a party of French and Indians surprised Deerfield, Mass., killing many of the inhabitants and taking others into captivity.

England sent military and naval assistance to New England in 1710, with the result that Port Royal, and with it ACADIA, was seized by the British in that year. In 1711 a powerful British naval expedition sailed into the Saint Lawrence to complete what Phips had failed to do in 1690; but some of the ships were wrecked on a rocky shore 400 km (250 mi) short of their objective, putting an end to the venture. During that same year the Tuscarora Indians of North Carolina rose up against the English, beginning an Indian war that ended two

Dates	American Name	European Name	Peace Treaty
1689–97	King William's War	War of the Grand Alliance	Ryswick
1702–13	Queen Anne's War	War of the Spanish Succession	Utrecht
1739	War of Jenkins's Ear		
1744–48	King George's War	War of the Austrian Succession	Aix-la-Chapelle
1754–63	French and Indian War	Seven Years' War	Paris

years later with the defeat of the Tuscaroras. That tribe then migrated northward and became the sixth nation of the Iroquois League.

France and Spain were much weakened by their widespread exertions against Britain and its allies, and by 1712 they were eager for peace. After lengthy negotiations, an international agreement was reached at Utrecht in the spring of 1713. Spain retained Florida, but France was forced to relinquish Acadia to the British, and it became the new British colony of Nova Scotia. Britain also secured Newfoundland.

The Treaty of Utrecht (see UTRECHT, PEACE OF) introduced a period of uneasy peace that lasted just 26 years in North America. During this period both the British and the French resumed their competitive expansion into the trans-Appalachian West. At the same time, the Indians were showing their resentment at what the English traders and pioneers were doing to the Indian way of life. The Yamassee War (1715-28) in South Carolina and Dummer's War (1722-25) in New England illustrate the problem. Britain sought to strengthen the southern flank of its colonies by founding the new colony of Georgia in 1733 under the leadership of James OGLETHORPE.

WAR OF THE 1740s
Commercial rivalry between Britain and Spain produced the War of Jenkins' Ear—named for the alleged mutilation of an English sea captain by the Spanish—in 1739. This gave Oglethorpe an opportunity to lead Carolinians and Georgians against Saint Augustine in 1740, but he had to abandon the siege after several weeks. In 1742 he thwarted a Spanish invasion of Georgia, making the war in the south a standoff.

New England's relative security ended in 1744 when France entered the war as an ally of Spain in what was to become known as King George's War. After their loss of Nova Scotia in 1713, the French had constructed the large fortress of LOUISBOURG on Cape Breton Island at the southern entrance to the Gulf of Saint Lawrence. From Louisbourg, French sea raiders could prey upon New England shipping. In 1745, Gov. William SHIRLEY of Massachusetts decided to capture Louisbourg; he appointed William PEPPERRELL of Maine to command a New England army in that venture. Pepperrell also gained the invaluable assistance of a squadron from the Royal Navy. Cooperation between these ships and Pepperrell's army of relatively inexperienced New Englanders resulted in the surrender of Louisbourg in June 1745 after a 7-week siege.

Since 1731 the French had also had an advance base at CROWN POINT on Lake Champlain whence they could send parties of French and Indian raiders south to attack the frontiers of New England and New York. During the War of the 1740s, such raids did considerable damage and discouraged the British colonists in the area, who lacked the means and the will to attempt the capture of Crown Point.

With neither side close to a decisive victory either in North America or in the wider War of the AUSTRIAN SUCCESSION, the European powers again needed peace. In 1748 an international agreement was reached whose terms required that Louisbourg be given back to France, to the disgruntlement of many New Englanders. The Treaty of Aix-la-Chapelle was not decisive—certainly not in North America, where the question of which European nation would predominate remained unsettled.

The map indicates major troop movements of the French and the British, forts, and significant battle sites of the French and Indian War (1754-63). During this conflict both colonial powers competed for the loyalties of powerful Indian tribes, whose affiliations are also shown on the map. The fighting in North America became part of the larger conflict among the European powers known as the Seven Years' War (1756-63).

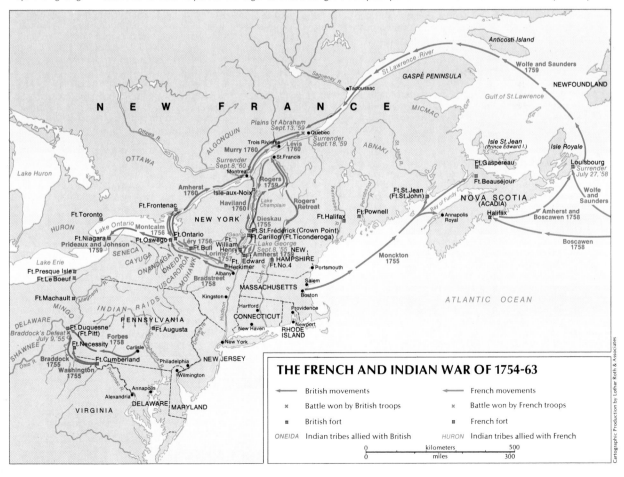

THE FRENCH AND INDIAN WAR OF 1754-63

←	British movements	←	French movements
×	Battle won by British troops	×	Battle won by French troops
■	British fort	■	French fort
ONEIDA	Indian tribes allied with British	*HURON*	Indian tribes allied with French

kilometers 0 — 500
miles 0 — 300

Cartographic Production by Lothar Roth & Associates

Gen. James Wolfe, the commander of the victorious British army that captured the French city of Quebec in 1759, lies dying from the wounds he received in battle. The painting (1770) is by the artist Benjamin West. (National Gallery of Canada, Ottawa.)

FRENCH AND INDIAN WAR

In the continuing colonial rivalry, attention soon focused on the Forks of the Ohio River, a strategically crucial area claimed by both the British and the French but effectively occupied by neither. In 1754 the OHIO COMPANY of Virginia, a group of land speculators, began building a fort at the Forks only to have the workers ejected by a strong French expedition, which then proceeded to construct FORT DUQUESNE on the site. Virginia militia commanded by young George WASHINGTON proved no match for the French and Indians from Fort Duquesne. Defeated at Fort Necessity (July 1754), they were forced to withdraw east of the mountains.

The British government in London, realizing that the colonies by themselves were unable to prevent the French advance into the Ohio Valley, sent a force of regulars under Gen. Edward BRADDOCK to uphold the British territorial claims. In July 1755, to the consternation of all the English colonies, Braddock's army was disastrously defeated as it approached Fort Duquesne.

Again the British looked to the Iroquois League for assistance, working through William JOHNSON, the superintendent of Indian affairs in the north. As usual, the Iroquois responded but without much enthusiasm. Other tribes, impressed with French power, either shifted allegiance to the French or took shelter in an uneasy neutrality. In 1755 the British forcibly deported virtually the entire French peasant population of Nova Scotia (Acadia) to increase the security of that province. But it was not until May 1756, nearly two years after the outbreak of hostilities on the Virginia frontier, that Britain declared war on France. For the time being Spain remained uncommitted in the conflict, which was part of the larger SEVEN YEARS' WAR.

Under the effective generalship of the marquis de MONTCALM, New France enjoyed victory after victory. In 1756, Montcalm forced the surrender of the British fort at Oswego on Lake Ontario, thereby breaking the British fingerhold on the Great Lakes. A year later he destroyed Fort William Henry at the south end of Lake George, dashing British hopes for an advance through the Champlain Valley to Crown Point. The northern frontier seemed to be collapsing in upon the British colonies.

William PITT (the Elder), Britain's new prime minister, had adopted a policy of drastically increasing aid to the American colonies, and he was able to do so because the Royal Navy kept the sea-lanes open. France, in contrast, found itself unable to maintain large-scale support of its colonies. As a result, by 1758 the period of French ascendancy was coming to an end. The British, employing increasing numbers of regulars, sometimes in conjunction with provincial troops, began gaining important victories under the military leadership of Jeffrey, Lord AMHERST.

In 1758 a British expedition forced the surrender of Louisbourg, and another expedition advancing west from Philadel-phia caused the French to abandon the Forks of the Ohio. This latter victory, in turn, convinced many Indians that Britain would prevail after all, accelerating a shift of tribal support away from the French. Only at TICONDEROGA, south of Crown Point, did British arms suffer a major defeat.

For the British, 1759 proved to be a year of stunning successes in America. One British expedition took Niagara. Another, led by Amherst himself, seized both Ticonderoga and Crown Point, thereby opening the way to Montreal. A third, commanded by young Gen. James WOLFE, sailed up the Saint Lawrence and, after much difficulty, defeated Montcalm on the Plains of Abraham just outside Quebec. The surrender of Quebec itself soon followed. In 1760, Amherst completed the conquest of Canada with a successful three-pronged offensive against Montreal.

By the end of 1760, French resistance in North America had virtually ceased. The only fighting still going on was between the British and the Cherokee Indians in the south, and that ended in a British victory in 1761. The Seven Years' War did continue elsewhere, with Spain becoming involved against Britain early in 1762. The overwhelming strength of British sea power, however, rapidly eroded French hopes of success. Britain, too, needed peace, primarily for financial reasons.

The war-weary nations began negotiations that in February 1763 produced the decisive Treaty of Paris. Britain gained all of North America east of the Mississippi River, including Canada and Florida, so that a bright future for its colonists seemed assured. With the French and Spanish menace now removed from their frontiers and the Indians deprived of foreign support in their resistance to British expansion, the inhabitants of the coastal colonies could feel less dependent on Britain and better able to fend for themselves. Their experience with British regular forces during the war, moreover, had generated mutual dislike, which was not softened by the American habit of trading with the enemy in the Caribbean. At the same time, Britain's costly struggle with France had depleted the British treasury, a fact that soon would lead Parliament to seek additional revenue by taxing the American colonies. Clearly, then, conditions arising from the French and Indian Wars helped set the stage for the AMERICAN REVOLUTION.

DOUGLAS EDWARD LEACH

Bibliography: Hamilton, Edward, *The French and Indian Wars* (1962); Jennings, Francis, *Empire of Fortune* (1988; repr. 1990); Leach, Douglas, *Arms for Empire* (1973); Parkman, Francis, *France and England in North America*, 9 vols. (1865–92).

French language: see ROMANCE LANGUAGES.

French literature

French literature, one of the world's most brilliant, has been for centuries an impressive facet of French civilization, an object of national pride, and a principal focus for feelings of national identity. Because the French are a literate people, passionately interested in questions of language and in the exploration of ideas, the influence of French intellectuals on the course of French history during the last three centuries has been great and remains so today. A high proportion of European literary trends have originated in France. The continuing prestige of literature in France is evidenced today by the innumerable private societies devoted to individual authors and by the large number of literary prizes awarded each year. A knowledge of French literature, in short, is the key to an understanding of the French people.

THE MIDDLE AGES

French literature began when writers started using the dialects that had evolved from the Latin spoken in the parts of the Roman Empire that would become France. Eventually, the dialect in popular use around Paris gained supremacy over the others and by the 10th century was vying with Latin for prestige. The 11th century witnessed the emergence of a literature in the French language in the form of numerous epic poems, called CHANSONS DE GESTE. These poems told of the heroic deeds of the knights fighting with or against Charlemagne. Of the more than 80 *chansons* remaining, the masterpiece is the CHANSON DE ROLAND (12th century), which narrates the death of Charlemagne's nephew, Roland, in a rearguard action against the Saracens at Roncesvalles in the Pyrenees. Exhibiting great skill in the differentiation of characters, this poem contributed to the awakening of a French national consciousness.

The *chansons* were followed in the second half of the 12th century by the *romans courtois,* or tales of COURTLY LOVE, which were written in verse in the Romance tongue and were intended to be read aloud before aristocratic audiences. Celebrating the heroism of knights fighting in honor of their ladies, many of these poems are set at King Arthur's court and are steeped in the Celtic mythology of Brittany, Cornwall, and Wales. Of particular importance was the Tristan and Iseult cycle, which, in its powerful, semimystical evocation of a love as strong as death, inspired poets in every part of Europe. Eventually, it served as the basis for Richard Wagner's great opera *Tristan und Isolde* (1865). The greatest poet in this tradition was CHRÉTIEN DE TROYES, author of *Erec, Lancelot,* and *Perceval.* The *lais* were very short *romans courtois,* a genre to which MARIE DE FRANCE contributed many delightful examples. The single most significant medieval poem was the ROMAN DE LA ROSE, whose first 4,000 lines were written about 1230 by GUILLAUME DE LORRIS in the courtly tradition; about 40 years later, Jean de Meung added 18,000 lines in a realistic, satirical vein. The allegorical quest of the Rose (the Lady) was to remain influential until the 17th century.

Outside aristocratic circles a very different type of literature flourished. The FABLIAUX were short narratives in verse, simple, earthy, and bantering in tone, sparing no one, least of all women or clergy. FABLES, allegorical stories in which animals were used to satirize human characteristics or to point to a moral, were equally popular, the most celebrated of this type being REYNARD THE FOX.

The greatest French poet of the late medieval period was François VILLON—thief, murderer, and prison inmate—whose alternately bitter, amusing, and deeply moving *Testament* (1461; Eng. trans., 1924) sounds a strangely modern note. In it are many examples of the BALLADE and the RONDEAU, forms in which Villon demonstrated his mastery.

The Middle Ages also saw the development of history as a prose genre. Geoffroi de VILLEHARDOUIN, in his *Conquest of Constantinople* (c.1207; Eng. trans., 1829), gave an eyewitness account of the sacking of the Byzantine capital in 1204 by western crusaders en route to the Holy Land. Jean Sire de JOINVILLE acted as memorialist of Louis IX's disastrous crusade (1248-52) in Egypt, completing his entertaining *Histoire de Saint Louis* in 1309 (Eng. trans., 1807). Jean FROISSART's *Chronicles* (Eng. trans., 1523-25) vividly evoke the barbarities of the Hundred Years' War as it was fought between 1325 and 1400. The *Memoirs* (1489-90, 1497-98; Eng. trans., 1596) of Philippe de COMMYNES, dealing with the reigns of Louis XI and Charles VIII, reveal a truer historian, one more concerned with the hidden causes of events than with mere chronicling.

THE FRENCH RENAISSANCE
A third of the way into the 16th century, François RABELAIS, in one of the great comic works of world literature, gave pointed expression to the feeling of rebirth then being experienced by the European intellectual community. In *Gargantua* (1534) his giant hero reports to his son Pantagruel on the amazing intellectual progress that has occurred in the course of just one generation thanks to the revival of the literature and thought of antiquity. This was primarily due to the popularization of printed books, which encouraged the translation of ancient texts and the development of precise critical methods. Behind the rollicking carnivallike story, the incoherence, the coarse humor, and the symbolic exaggerations of *Gargantua* and the associated *Pantagruel* volumes (1532, 1556; Eng. trans. of Rabelais's *Works,* 1653-94) hid an immense learning and understanding of the problems faced by Rabelais's contemporaries (see GARGANTUA AND PANTAGRUEL).

Out of such sources, likely and unlikely, a new ideal of humankind in relation to God and life, known as humanism, was being forged. In religion this found expression in Protestantism, whose chief voice in France, during the years it competed with Catholicism, was the great Genevan reformer John CALVIN. Calvin explained his complex doctrines in a simple style in *The Institutes of the Christian Religion* (1541; Eng. trans., 1813), which conquered for the French language the ability to discuss religious subjects that had previously been reserved for Latin.

Humanism was perhaps best exemplified by Michel de MONTAIGNE, who in the second half of the 16th century invented a genre, the familiar ESSAY, that proved ideally suited both as a showcase for his learning and urbanity and as a forum for the critical exploration of personality and ideas. Although inspired by an enormous number of quotations, his *Essays* (1580, 1588; Eng. trans., 1603) are nevertheless profoundly original and together constitute one of the most honest and ingratiating self-examinations ever conducted in a literary work. With them Montaigne found a mode of expression that would be imitated, if not surpassed, by scores of writers in innumerable countries from the 17th to the 20th century.

French prose was not alone in feeling the winds of change. The break with the past was even more pronounced in poetry. New forms like the sonnet imported from Italy, as well as Greek and Latin odes, all enjoyed popularity. But French poets were also interested in making of their native language a more supple instrument. In 1549, Joachim DU BELLAY wrote a nationalistic manifesto calling for the enrichment of the French language to insure its parity with ancient tongues. His poetic works are delicate, melancholy, and sensitive. The prince of Renaissance poets, however, was Pierre de RONSARD, the uncontested leader of the constellation of poets called the PLÉIADE. With the lyric sonnets, light odes, and political verse of his later career, he helped to free French poetry from the pedantry of the past.

THE TRIUMPH OF CLASSICISM
France's political position as the most powerful nation in Europe during the reign of Louis XIV was reflected in the preeminence French literature attained in the 17th century. This Golden Age literature still forms the foundation of French liberal education. The period showed a continuing trend toward the reinforcement of royal authority and, except at the end, of Catholic influence. In 1635, Cardinal Richelieu created the ACADÉMIE FRANÇAISE with the aim of regulating language and literary expression. The conflict between two literary tendencies—one toward greater creative freedom, which modern critics call baroque, and the other toward an acceptance of literary rules—had been virtually resolved in favor of CLASSICISM by 1660. The components of this creed would be codified by Nicolas BOILEAU-DESPRÉAUX, the founder of French literary criticism, in his *Art of Poetry* (1674; Eng. trans., 1683), in which reason, proportion, and harmony were defined as the outstanding literary values.

France's two greatest dramatists emerged during this period. Pierre CORNEILLE, whose tragic masterpiece *The Cid* (1637), dramatizing the conflict between duty and passion, remains unequaled in the grandeur of its conception, wrote over 30 plays, most of them, after 1634, in accordance with the Aristotelian unities of time, place, and action. He was surpassed in popularity and critical esteem only by Jean RACINE, whose simpler style and more realistic characters and plot structures, as in *Andromache* (1667; Eng. trans., 1675) and *Phaedra* (1677; Eng. trans., 1776), reveal a world of ferocious passions beneath a veneer of elegant poetry. In the comic arena, MOLIÈRE, ranging from the farcical to the sharpest explorations of social, psychological, and metaphysical questions, created a body of plays that seem as fresh and pointed today as they were when first produced. His masterpieces were *Tartuffe* (1664; Eng. trans., 1670) and *The Misanthrope* (1666; Eng. trans., 1709).

The French novel, which in the first part of the 17th century was long, diffuse, and full of improbable adventures (*L'Astrée,* 1607-28, for instance), also came of age. In *The Princess of Clèves* (1678; Eng. trans., 1925), a concise psychological analysis of a moral problem in married life, the Comtesse de LA FAYETTE fashioned a perfect model of the novel of character as the genre would develop in France.

Pierre Corneille (1606-84)

Jean Racine (1639-99)

Molière (1622-73)

Minor literary forms were ennobled by such brilliant practitioners as Madame de SÉVIGNÉ, who in her correspondence created definitive models of letter writing; the Duc de LA ROCHEFOUCAULD, whose *Maxims* (1665; Eng. trans., 1694) wittily analyzed human motives in terms of self-interest; and Jean de LA BRUYÈRE, whose wide-ranging and insightful study of social conditions and types in his *Characters* (1688; Eng. trans., 1699) anticipated the liberal, scientifically oriented tendencies of the 18th century. The poet Jean de LA FONTAINE achieved lasting fame with his successive volumes of *Fables* (1668, 1678, 1694; Eng. trans., 1734), a genre he made indelibly his own by combining sophisticated "morals" with a deliberately archaic and deceptively simple style. The art of memoir writing assumed a new power and subtlety when composed by such participants in historical events as the Duc de SAINT-SIMON, La Rochefoucauld, and Cardinal de Retz.

The enormously influential DISCOURSE ON METHOD (1637) not only established its author, René DESCARTES, as the first modern philosopher but set the precedent for that clarity, precision, and rationalism with which French thinking and writing would subsequently be associated. Another philosopher admired as much for the perfection of his prose as for the character of his thought was Blaise PASCAL. His *Lettres provinciales* (1656-57; Eng. trans., 1816) demonstrated the devastating effectiveness of a simplicity informed by intelligence and wit, whereas the *Pensées* (1670; Eng. trans., 1688) directed the reader to faith in the Christian God through an eloquent combination of reason, passion, and insight into the human condition. More grandiloquent, and certainly better representative of 17th-century religious orthodoxy, were the sermons and funeral orations of the great preacher and theological polemicist Jacques BOSSUET. His Quietist opponent, François FÉNELON, combined the interests of a classicist with the critical spirit of the 18th century in his didactic novel *Télémaque* (1699; Eng. trans., 1743).

THE FRENCH ENLIGHTENMENT

If reason, understood as harmony and balance, stamped the "splendid century," it was above all the spirit of scientific inquiry that gave to the 18th century its special character. With the decline in the authority of the French monarchy, all social and political institutions came under question and, eventually, attack. Ideas assumed sovereign power as, one by one, traditional bastions were subjected to the scrutiny of the PHILOSOPHES. Probably no other country or century has witnessed such a concentration of intellectual talent as that represented by the French ENLIGHTENMENT.

Pierre BAYLE, a Protestant philosopher turned freethinker who advocated religious toleration, set the tone of the century with his *Dictionnaire historique et critique* (1697; rev. 1704-06; Eng. trans., 1709). In this work he foreshadowed the aggressive strategy of religious and social criticism that would later be used by VOLTAIRE in his malicious but amusing *Dic-*

tionnaire philosophique (1764; Eng. trans., 1765). Voltaire wrote tragedies in the classical mode, works of history, deistic poetry, and light verse. He is chiefly remembered, however, for his philosophical tales, such as *Zadig* (1747; Eng. trans., 1749) and *Candide* (1759; Eng. trans., 1759); his *Letters concerning the English Nation* (1733), comparing English and French institutions (to the latter's disadvantage); and his *Essai sur les moeurs et l'esprit des nations* (1769; partially trans. as *The General History and State of Europe*, 1754), an anthropologically organized comparative history of national characteristics. These works were the centerpiece of his lifelong battle against intolerance, injustice, and obscurantism.

MONTESQUIEU also adopted the method of comparative analysis, producing in his masterpiece, *The Spirit of the Laws* (1748; Eng. trans., 1750), a profound study of the different types of government. In this treatise he expounded the doctrine of the separation of powers. This contributed to the 18th-century French admiration for British political institutions and helped mold the U.S. Constitution.

The biggest weapon leveled against prejudice and traditional authorities was the *Encyclopédie,* published in 35 volumes between 1751 and 1780 and incorporating most of the materialist, skeptical, and antireligious ideas of the day. This was a collective enterprise directed by Denis DIDEROT to which the best minds of the age contributed: Jean d'ALEMBERT, Baron d'HOLBACH, Étienne de CONDILLAC, Anne Robert Jacques TURGOT, Montesquieu, Voltaire, and Rousseau.

Jean Jacques ROUSSEAU, whose political and social ideas enjoyed an even wider vogue in the 19th and 20th centuries than in the 18th, asserted the principle of the collective sovereignty of the people in *The Social Contract* (1762; Eng. trans., 1764); in *Émile* (1762) he expressed pedagogical theories that formed the basis of later experiments in progressive education. His novel *La Nouvelle Héloïse* (1761), a compendium of the major intellectual questions discussed at the time, was a forerunner of ROMANTICISM through which Rousseau popularized the "return to nature" and the natural morality he believed would flow from such a state. Rousseau's *Confessions* (1781, 1788) and *Rêveries* (1782; Eng. trans. for both, 1783) were daring autobiographical works that helped to develop the romantic taste for the public display of the inner self.

The development of the novel and the drama contributed to the explosion of the new sensibility. Alain René LESAGE's (1668-1747) picaresque romance *Gil Blas* (1715, 1724, 1735; Eng. trans., 1749) opened the way to the novels of "sentimental education," especially as produced in England by Tobias SMOLLETT and Henry FIELDING. In *Manon Lescaut* (1731; Eng. trans., 1738), the Abbé PRÉVOST presented a tale of passion triumphing over every obstacle but death, while in *Les Liaisons dangereuses* (1782), Pierre Choderlos de Laclos (1741-1803) analyzed the perverse psychology of a cynical seducer. From the lively plays of Pierre de MARIVAUX came the term *mari-*

Charles de Montesquieu (1689–1755)

Denis Diderot (1713–84)

Victor Hugo (1802–85)

vaudage, meaning the style in which the subtle psychological components of love and dalliance were portrayed by the playwright. Toward the end of the century BEAUMARCHAIS held the stage with his popular comedies *The Barber of Seville* (1775; Eng. trans., 1776) and *The Marriage of Figaro* (1784; Eng. trans., 1785), which also conveyed a subtly rebellious political message.

Poetry in the 18th century suffered from the desiccating influence of rational analysis, but one great poet emerged. André CHÉNIER, whose verse was inspired by the harmonies of classical Greek models and by a love of liberty, became after his execution during the Terror an important influence on the early romantic school.

THE 19TH CENTURY
The romantic tendencies implicit in the 18th century had by 1830 become a full-fledged and triumphant movement affecting every area of French letters—poetry, drama, the novel, history, and criticism. Poetry completely recovered its élan, while the novel, as the most suitable genre for registering the social upheavals brought first by the French Revolution and Napoleonic wars and then by the expansion of capitalism and the industrial revolution, ultimately became the dominant mode of expression. The century-long conflicts between reactionaries and liberals, the church and the anticlericals, and the bourgeoisie and the proletariat provided ample scope for the literary giants of the age—Hugo, Balzac, Michelet, and Zola, each endowed with a prodigious productivity.

The aristocratic Vicomte de CHATEAUBRIAND ushered in the century with an aggressive defense of Catholicism, *Le Génie du christianisme* (1802; trans. as *The Beauties of Christianity,* 1815), and two novels set among the American Indians. His

Mémoires d'outre-tombe (Eng. trans., 1902), composed between 1811 and 1841 in a romantic vein, is considered a classic of French autobiographical writing. Madame de STAËL, notable chiefly as a literary critic, became the champion of German romantic literature in her *De L'Allemagne* (1813; trans. as *Germany,* 1913). Her influence can be seen in Benjamin CONSTANT's novel *Adolphe* (1816; Eng. trans., 1817), analyzing the waning passion of a young man for an older woman, which suggests many parallels with Constant and de Staël's own tortuous relationship.

Alphonse de LAMARTINE, with his *Méditations poétiques* (1820; Eng. trans., 1839), brought French poetry back to its lyric roots. He was the first in a line of great French romantic poets that included Alfred de VIGNY, who came to prominence with his *Poèmes antiques et modernes* (1826); Alfred de MUSSET, known alike for his Byronic poetry—alternately impish and moving—and his affair with George SAND, herself a romantic novelist and early feminist; and the giant among them, Victor HUGO, who for 65 years would magnificently amplify every possible poetic theme and reign as chief spokesman and practitioner of the romantic credo.

The first break with romanticism was made by Théophile GAUTIER, a onetime enthusiast whose art-for-art's-sake credo announced the arrival of the PARNASSIANS, a group of poets infatuated with formal perfection and objectivity and hostile to the romantics' subjective effusions. Led by Charles Marie LECONTE DE LISLE in the 1860s, the Parnassians saw their ideals best realized in the sonnet collection *Les Trophées* (1893; Eng. trans., 1897) of José Maria de HEREDIA.

Influenced by the Parnassians but determined to create beauty even out of the horrors of life, Charles BAUDELAIRE in

Voltaire (1694–1778)

Jean Jacques Rousseau (1712–78)

Honoré de Balzac (1799–1850)

Charles Baudelaire (1821-67)

Émile Zola (1840-1902)

Marcel Proust (1871-1922)

The Flowers of Evil (1857; Eng. trans., 1909) sounded a new note—obsessive, morbid, presenting the poet as an accursed being—that would significantly influence all subsequent French poetry. Arthur RIMBAUD, in *A Season in Hell* (1873; Eng. trans., 1932) and *Illuminations* (1886; Eng. trans., 1932), reached an absolute of revolt, experimenting with mixtures of verse and prose, with rhythms, and with the juxtaposition of unrelated words. His older friend and lover Paul VERLAINE brought to French poetry a musical, melodic quality it had not previously attained, seen especially in his collection *Jadis et naguère* (Once Upon a Time and Not Long Ago, 1884). Stéphane MALLARMÉ, whose most celebrated poem was *Afternoon of a Faun* (1876; Eng. trans., 1951), which Debussy later set to music, guided poetry toward even more abstruse paths and, as the leader of the symbolists (see SYMBOLISM, literature) in the 1880s and 1890s, exercised an enormous influence over his contemporaries that is still lively today.

The 50 years between 1830 and 1880 witnessed enormous changes in the shape of the novel as it was molded by a succession of innovators. Madame George Sand, exemplifying romanticism in its most individualistic form, in *Lélia* (1833; Eng. trans., 1978) championed the ultimate moral claim of passion over convention, though her novels of country life, such as *The Country Waif* (1847; Eng. trans., 1976) and *Fanchon the Cricket* (1848; Eng. trans., 1977), have endured better. STENDHAL, who also portrayed the dominant role of passion as a motivating force in life, nevertheless injected into his two great novels, *The Red and the Black* (1830; Eng. trans., 1916) and *The Charterhouse of Parma* (1839; Eng. trans., 1901), an ironic tone and analytical power that foreshadowed the 20th-century psychological novel. Victor Hugo, in his evocation of medieval Parisian life, *The Hunchback of Notre Dame* (1831; Eng. trans., 1833), and Alexandre DUMAS père, in a whole series of adventures covering high points of the 16th, 17th, and 18th centuries in France, made the historical novel a genre to be reckoned with. Hugo's later work, *Les Misérables* (1862; Eng. trans., 1862), recounting the redemption of a convict emerging from the lower depths, successfully merged high drama with questions of social morality.

The colossus of 19th-century French novelists, however, was Honoré de BALZAC, whose prodigious, multivolume *Human Comedy* (1842-48; Eng. trans., 1895-98), encompassing more than 2,000 characters drawn from every rank and walk of life and sweeping imaginatively over 40 years of French history, brilliantly delineated a major society in flux. His genius for realistic detail, together with his emphasis on material gain as the engine of human behavior, directly links Balzac with the novelistic REALISM that won the day in the second half of the century.

This was most triumphantly realized in Gustave FLAUBERT's *Madame Bovary* (1857; Eng. trans., 1886), the story of a provincial adulteress whose bleak life ends in tragedy—a novel as notable for its perfection of style as for its unerring observation. A disciple of Flaubert, Guy de MAUPASSANT, excelled in the sparely told, realistic, often ironic short story, as in such collections as *La Maison Tellier* (1881; Eng. trans., 1910) and *Mademoiselle Fifi* (1882; Eng. trans., 1917). Influenced by contemporary determinist thought, Émile ZOLA sought to make the novel a more scientific reflection of reality. His 20-volume fictional examination of every level of social life during the Second Empire, *Les Rougon-Macquart* (1871-93), with its emphasis on the sordid and the depressing, remains the outstanding exemplar of NATURALISM whose influence as a movement it spanned.

History and criticism also came to maturity during the 19th century. Jules MICHELET, whose immense 17-volume *History of France* (1833-43, 1855-67; Eng. trans., 1882-87) vibrantly resurrected the past, exemplified the romantic narrative tradition at its best. Alexis de TOCQUEVILLE, in his probing *Democracy in America* (1835, 1840; both trans. the same years), offered analyses of American politics and character in large part still valid today. Charles Augustin SAINTE-BEUVE, in his astute study *Port-Royal* (1840-59) and in his in-depth analyses of French literary figures, gave to literary criticism the importance it has retained since. In applying his erudition as Hebrew scholar and philologist to religion in *The Origins of Christianity* (7 vols., 1863-83; Eng. trans., 1888-89), Ernest RENAN established modern critical methods in France. Simultaneously, the philosopher and historian Hippolyte TAINE, seeking a scientific explanation for historical and cultural phenomena, professed to discover in the interplay of physical and psychological factors the cause of national and individual variations. Zola's naturalistic oeuvre was the application of this hypothesis to literature.

The French theater was at first dominated by the romantic dramas of Hugo, whose *Hernani* (1830; Eng. trans., 1830) liberated playwrights from the confining traditions of the past, and by those of Dumas père. These were followed in popularity by the WELL-MADE PLAYS of Eugène SCRIBE, Victorien SARDOU, and Alexandre DUMAS fils, who also defended social theses.

THE 20TH CENTURY

The 20th century in France has been characterized by a tremendous expansion in literary output and the ever-faster pace of experimentation with new means of expression. Both Marxism and Freudianism have left a deep imprint on literature, as on all the arts. Two world wars have tried France sorely, while the technological revolution confronts the current generation with an altogether new world. The result of such profound socioeconomic and political change has been a continuous questioning of all moral, intellectual, and artistic traditions.

In poetry, symbolism continued to serve as an inspiration without stifling new departures. Paul CLAUDEL, notable as both

Colette (1873–1954)

Jean Paul Sartre (1905–80)

Albert Camus (1913–60)

dramatist and poet, injected a mystical Catholicism into his masterpiece, *Five Great Odes* (1904–10; Eng. trans., 1967). Paul VALÉRY became famous for delicate poems that were at once meditative, musical, and rich in imagery. Guillaume APOLLINAIRE deliberately aimed for modernity in his poetry, which was full of whimsical surprises. He not only coined the term *surrealist* but in *The Breasts of Tiresias* (1918; Eng. trans., 1961) produced the first surrealist play. Under the leadership of André BRETON, the movement's theorist, SURREALISM aimed for a complete revolution in poetry and the visual arts to be achieved through an exploration of the subconscious, considered as poetry's deepest source. A rejuvenator of poetic imagination, surrealism launched, among others, the poet and novelist Louis ARAGON, although Aragon after 1930 found inspiration in his Marxist beliefs.

The novel thrived especially during the first half of the century. Anatole FRANCE kept the tradition of political satire alive with his allegorical spoof, *Penguin Island* (1908; Eng. trans., 1909). Romain ROLLAND, with his 10-volume *Jean-Christophe* (1904–12; Eng. trans., 1910–13), followed later by Jules ROMAINS with his even larger *Men of Good Will* series (27 vols., 1932–47; Eng. trans. in 14 vols., 1933–46), demonstrated the continuing popularity of the *roman-fleuve,* or cyclical novel, in France. André GIDE, from *The Immoralist* (1902; Eng. trans., 1930) through *The Counterfeiters* (1926; Eng. trans., 1927), novels that are still compelling, championed the individual at war with conventional morality. France's greatest 20th-century novelist, however, was Marcel PROUST, the extent of whose contributions to the genre can be compared only with those of James Joyce. In the multivolume, multilevel *Remembrance of Things Past* (1913–27; Eng. trans., 1922–31), Proust sought to recapture the essence of lost time, for him a spiritual reality, through reconstructing the external shape or sensations of the past; the whole was narrated chiefly by means of an interior monologue.

Working on a smaller canvas, COLETTE produced short novels that shrewdly analyzed the complexities of intimate relations, while François MAURIAC took as his special preserve, in a series of novels influenced by his Catholicism, the eternal battle between spirit and flesh. Two of the freshest voices in the decade before World War II belonged to Louis Ferdinand CÉLINE, whose cynical, often scurrilous *Journey to the End of Night* (1932; Eng. trans., 1934) and *Death on the Installment Plan* (1936; Eng. trans., 1938) spoke for the fascism to come, and to the then politically radical adventurer-writer André MALRAUX in *Man's Fate* (1933; Eng. trans., 1934) and *Man's Hope* (1937; Eng. trans., 1938).

Philosophical EXISTENTIALISM dominated literature in postwar France, spilling over into the novel as onto the stage. Jean Paul SARTRE, leader of the movement, had previously explained its tenets (namely, the human freedom to choose and to forge one's own values) in the novel *Nausea* (1938; Eng.

trans., 1949), the play *No Exit* (1944; Eng. trans., 1946), and a trilogy of novels dealing with World War II. Its themes would be echoed by others, most notably by Albert CAMUS in *The Stranger* (1942; Eng. trans., 1946) and *The Plague* (1947; Eng. trans., 1948), in which the absurdity, or meaninglessness, of life is stressed. Simone de BEAUVOIR, Sartre's lifelong friend and disciple, also dealt with existentialist problems in her novels but is probably best known for her massive treatise on the status of women, *The Second Sex* (1949; Eng. trans., 1952), and a series of distinguished memoirs.

From the 1950s, the dominant trend was the NEW NOVEL, or antinovel, as represented by Nathalie SARRAUTE, Michel BUTOR, and Alain ROBBE-GRILLET. Although these authors have no common doctrine, all reject plot and verisimilitude as traditionally understood. Their work, allied with new insights provided initially by the adherents of STRUCTURALISM, has had a marked effect on literary expression, analysis, and criticism (as in the work of Roland BARTHES and Jacques DERRIDA).

The French theater, perhaps more than any other form, illustrates the profound literary revolution that has swept France since the days of Edmond ROSTAND's flamboyant *Cyrano de Bergerac* (1897; Eng. trans., 1937). The poetical plays of Jean GIRAUDOUX, especially the astringent *Madwoman of Chaillot* (1945; Eng. trans., 1947), continued to appeal to postwar audiences, as did the productions of Jean ANOUILH, some smiling, some ferocious. But with Eugéne IONESCO's *The Bald Soprano* (1950; Eng. trans., 1958), an altogether new drama, called the THEATER OF THE ABSURD, came into being, marking a sharp break with the past. Samuel BECKETT best exemplified both the strengths and limits of this theater in *Waiting for Godot* (1953; Eng. trans., 1954) and *Endgame* (1957; Eng. trans., 1958). In these two plays the sets, the characters, and language itself disintegrate into an awesome void. The plays of Jean GENET, such as *The Balcony* (1956; Eng. trans., 1958) and *The Blacks* (1958; Eng. trans., 1960), also aim at destruction, but in a fuller, more theatrical, sacramental way. Yet however baffling and depressing these productions are, there can be no doubt that they powerfully illuminate the underlying somber concerns of the present era. Above all, they testify to the ever-present originality and vitality of French literature and confirm its enviable avant-garde role.   JEAN BOORSCH

Bibliography: Atkinson, Geoffrey, *The Sentimental Revolution: French Writers of 1690–1740* (1966); Balakian, Anna, *Surrealism: The Road to the Absolute* (1959; rev. ed. 1970); Becker, Lucille F., *20th Century French Women Novelists* (1989); Birkett, Jennifer, *Sins of the Fathers: Decadence in France, 1870–1914* (1987); Bree, Germaine, *20th Century French Literature, 1920–70* (1983); Brereton, Geoffrey, *A Short History of French Literature,* 2d ed. (1976); Brombert, Victor: *The Hidden Reader: Stendhal, Balzac, Hugo, Baudelaire, Flaubert* (1988); Broome, Peter, and Chesters, Graham, *The Appreciation of Modern French Poetry, 1850–1950* (1976); Crocker, Lester G., ed., *The Age of Enlightenment* (1969); Cruickshank, John, *Albert Camus and the Literature of Revolt* (1959); Esslin, Martin, *The Theater of the Absurd* (1961; rev. ed. 1973);

Fowlie, Wallace, *French Literature: Its History and Meaning* (1973) and *Poem and Symbol: A Brief History of French Symbolism* (1990); Frank, Grace, *The Medieval French Drama* (1972); Gay, Peter, *The Enlightenment: An Interpretation*, 2 vols. (1966–69); Guicharnaud, Jacques and June, *Modern French Theater* (1967); Hollier, Denis, ed., *A New History of French Literature* (1989); LeGoff, Jacques, *The Medieval Imagination* (1988); Picon, Gaetan, *Contemporary French Literature: 1945 and After* (1974); Robinson, Christopher, *French Literature in the 20th Century* (1980); Peyre, Henri, *What is Romanticism?* (1977); Waelti-Walters, Jennifer, *Feminist Novelists of the Belle Epoque* (1990).

French music

The term *French* is used here in its broadest cultural sense to include all geographical areas within the influence of the French language and some composers of non-French origin who worked in France.

The earliest French influence on Western music is found in the plainsong of the Christian Church. It is believed that Gregorian chant as it is known today is an 8th- or 9th-century Gallican interpretation of Roman chant, but it is difficult to distinguish the Gallican ornamentation from its Roman basis. It has been suggested that the basic idea of the trope (an interpolation in a preexistent chant) is Gallican and that the surviving body of medieval tropes and sequences had a French influence.

During the later Middle Ages France led in the development of European music in all its forms. Some of the earliest manuscripts containing organum (the earliest form of polyphony) are found from the 10th century in Chartres, Montpellier, Fleury, Tours, and other French cities. Especially important was the group of musicians active during the 10th and 11th centuries at the Abbey of St. Martial in Limoges. In the late 12th century a brilliant group of composers emerged who were associated with the cathedral of Notre Dame in Paris. The most notable of these were Léonin and Pérotin. From this group came some of the earliest motets as well as a number of theoretical treatises on music.

Medieval secular music in France consisted almost entirely of the songs of the troubadours and trouvères, poet-musicians who flourished from the late 11th until the 13th century. Among them was the famous ADAM DE LA HALLE. They created such musical forms as the *lai* and the *ballade* (setting of a poem with the refrain at the end of each stanza). Active during the same period were the jongleurs, roving minstrels who performed the courtly love lyrics of the troubadours.

The music of the 14th century took its name, *Ars Nova,* from a treatise by Philippe de VITRY (1291–1361), who codified an improved system of musical notation. Vitry is credited by some scholars with the invention of the isorhythmic motet, one of the most important musical forms of the century. Guillaume de MACHAUT (c.1300–1377), master of all 14th-century forms and the leading poet of his time, brought the medieval motet to its highest peak.

With the beginning of the Renaissance style in the 15th century, the center of musical activity shifted from Paris to Burgundy, then a separate state. Active there were Guillaume DuFAY, Gilles BINCHOIS, and the Englishman John DUNSTABLE; all

wrote in a new, expressive style. The chief musical forms of this period were the motet—now little resembling its medieval ancestor—and the cyclic mass.

By the late 15th century musical supremacy was taken over by Flemish musicians; never again was French music to dominate as it had during the Middle Ages. Nevertheless, many French composers were active during the Renaissance—for example, Jean Mouton (c.1475–1522) and Pierre Certon (c.1510–72)—but their music was overshadowed by that of the Flemish and Italians. The most important French contribution to the Renaissance was the CHANSON, a secular, polyphonic song, usually light in style. It was later adapted by the Italians into the keyboard canzona.

The Reformation in France took the form of Calvinism, which allowed only the singing in unison of metrical French translations of the Psalms. The tunes composed by Louis Bourgeois (c.1510–c.1561) and others went with the Calvinist Psalter to Scotland and found their way into English hymnody where several still exist. Polyphonic settings of the Psalter tunes were composed for nonliturgical use by Claude Goudimel (c.1505–72) and Claude Le Jeune (1528–1600), but they had little impact on church music in general.

The 17th, 18th, and 19th centuries were a time of Italian and German dominance in music. Opera was the ruling 17th-century form, and French composers wrote operas of a uniquely French type. Beginning with Balthasar de Beaujoyeaux's *Ballet comique de la reine* (1580), French composers combined elements of opera, ballet, and spoken drama in a form sometimes called opera-ballet. The arias were simple and songlike, in contrast to the long, florid arias of Italian music, and the influence of Italian recitative is slight. The foremost French operas in the 17th century were those of Jean Baptiste LULLY and in the 18th century those of Jean Philippe RAMEAU. Ballet, spoken dialogue, and the absence of the Italian-style recitative-aria remained characteristic of French *opéra comique* through the 19th century.

French harpsichord music of the baroque period was of high quality. It consisted mostly of suites of dance movements and short character pieces (often with descriptive titles) rather than the longer preludes and fugues, toccatas, and fantasias

This French miniature portrays Guillaume Dufay and Giles Binchois, two of the most influential European composers of the 15th century. Associated with the development of French music at the Burgundian court, Dufay and Binchois composed chiefly motets, chansons, and cyclic masses.

This 19th-century caricature depicts the French romantic composer Hector Berlioz conducting a giant orchestra. Berlioz was criticized by many of his contemporaries for unconventional orchestrations calling for large numbers of instruments.

cultivated by the Germans. Representative composers were Jacques Champion de Chambonnières, Louis Couperin, François Couperin, and Rameau. All influenced the development of keyboard technique. Rameau wrote theoretical treatises, and his theory of harmony has influenced the teaching of the subject to the present day. He was the first to introduce the clarinet into the orchestra. François Joseph Gossec became the pioneer composer of symphonies in France.

The turmoil of the Revolution and the Napoleonic wars did not encourage artistic activity. Nevertheless, during this time the Paris Conservatory and the national opera were established. In the early 19th century, Paris was a center for musicians from other countries, such as Frédéric Chopin and Franz Liszt. Music by French composers consisted mostly of inferior operas or empty, virtuosic salon pieces. A notable exception were the works of Hector Berlioz, the greatest of the French romantics, who expanded the orchestra and whose grand style influenced Richard Wagner.

The late 19th century saw an increase of quality in French music. Camille Saint-Saëns worked for the establishment of a

Pierre Boulez, a 20th-century French composer, pianist, and conductor, emerged at the forefront of the post–World War II avant-garde in European music. After founding and directing several French musical organizations, he became (1971) musical director of the New York Philharmonic. Boulez returned to Paris in 1979 to head the Beaubourg's experimental music laboratory.

At the close of the 19th century, musical impressionism found its fullest expression in the compositions of Claude Debussy. Reacting to the romantics and to set traditional forms, Debussy developed an improvisatory style, evoking subtle ranges of mood and color in his music.

French instrumental style based on the classical tradition, and César Franck helped restore the quality of French organ and church music. The works of Georges Bizet, Charles Gounod, and Jules Massenet brought a new spontaneity and color to French opera. IMPRESSIONISM, exemplified in the music of Claude Debussy and the early works of Maurice Ravel, blossomed toward the end of the century. The movement, inspired by the work of French impressionist painters and poets, attempted to give music a more improvisatory character with subtle and understated coloristic effects. An outstanding body of "art songs" was produced by Debussy, Ravel, Gabriel Fauré, and Henri Duparc.

Between the two world wars, French music—such as the later work of Albert Roussel—was often written in "neoclassical" style: it was direct, simple, and accessible. Erik Satie

was a major composer of the time, as were several of the group of young musicians who gathered around him and were known as "Les Six": Arthur Honegger, Darius Milhaud, Francis Poulenc, Georges Auric, Germaine Tailleferre, and Louis Durey.

The eclectic aspect of contemporary French music, which uses serialism, electronic music, and aleatory techniques, as well as Oriental and other non-Western modes, is largely due to the influence of composer Olivier Messiaen, who taught many of the major postwar composers, most notably, Pierre Boulez.   WILLIAM HAYS

Bibliography: Anthony, James R., *French Baroque Music* (1974; repr. 1981); Barzun, Jacques, *Berlioz and His Century: An Introduction to the Age of Romanticism* (1962; repr. 1982); Cazeaux, Isabelle, *French Music in the 15th and 16th Centuries* (1975); Cooper, Martin, *French Music from the Death of Berlioz to the Death of Fauré* (1970); Cowart, Georgia, and Buelow, George J., eds., *French Musical Thought, 1600–1800* (1989); Harding, James, *The Ox on the Roof: Scenes from Musical Life in Paris in the 20s* (1972); Myers, Rollo, *Modern French Music from Fauré to Boulez* (1971; repr. 1984); Rosenberg, S., and Tischler, H., eds., *Chanter M'estuet: Songs of the Trouvères* (1981); Rostand, Claude, *French Music Today* (1955; repr. 1973).

French Polynesia

French Polynesia is an overseas territory of France. It comprises some 130 islands, with a total land area of 3,885 km^2 (1,500 mi^2), in the south central Pacific Ocean. Over half the total population of 188,814 (1988) live on the island of TAHITI. The capital is PAPEETE, Tahiti.

Land, People, and Economy. There are five major island groups: the SOCIETY ISLANDS; Tuamotu Archipelago; Tubuai (Austral) Islands; MARQUESAS ISLANDS; and Gambier Islands. The French government conducts nuclear tests on Mururoa Atoll, in the Tuamotu Archipelago. The islands are mainly mountainous and generally of volcanic origin, except for the coral atolls of the Tuamotu islands. The high islands (those with volcanic peaks) are heavily eroded and frequently marked by deep valleys. Mount Oroheno on Tahiti rises to a height of 2,237 m (7,339 ft). The high islands are forested, with areas of dry grassland. Coconut and pandanus trees abound on the flat atolls and the coastal plains of the high islands.

Southeast trade winds create equable temperatures (an annual average of about 24° C/76° F) and bring higher rainfall to the windward sides of the islands. Average annual rainfall at Papeete is 1,905 mm (75 in), but on the windward coasts it can reach as much as 3,050 mm (120 in). Although the atolls lack natural streams, the high islands frequently have drainage systems of short, rapid-flowing streams.

The population, which is concentrated along the coast, consists mainly of indigenous Polynesians or part Polynesians (called Demis), with Asian, European, and American minorities. The official language is French, but eastern Polynesian languages are widely spoken. The predominant religions are Protestantism and Roman Catholicism. Education is primarily

Maurice Ravel, an important French composer of the first half of the 20th century, became a leading exponent of musical impressionism. Ravel's most famous works include the ballet Daphnis et Chloë (1909–11), which was performed by Serge Diaghilev's Ballets Russes, and his orchestral masterpiece, Boléro (1928).

in government-aided mission schools; the population is 95% literate.

Village agriculture is at a subsistence level and is based on root crops, fruits, and coconut. A decline in the production of traditional commercial crops (copra, vanilla, and coffee) and mother-of-pearl has been offset by a rapid rise in tourism; economic ties with France remain strong.

History and Government. Some islands were inhabited as early as AD 300; European exploration took place from the 16th to the early 19th century. Tahiti became a French protectorate in 1844, and the other islands were gradually annexed. In 1946, French Polynesia became a French overseas territory with representation in the French assembly—a status confirmed in 1958 by vote of the islanders. A directly elected legislature has control over local affairs. French nuclear weapons testing, conducted at Mururoa Atoll in the Tuamoto Archipelago since 1966, is opposed by many Pacific nations and has fueled local demands for greater autonomy.   GARY A. KLEE

Bibliography: Ridgell, R., *Pacific Nations and Territories,* 2d ed. (1988).

French Revolution

Two figures representing the French clergy and nobility blithely crush the life out of a peasant in a drawing symbolizing the social injustice and feudal institutions tolerated by the French monarchy under the ancien régime. These conditions helped precipitate the great upheaval of the French Revolution.

The French Revolution (1789–99) violently transformed France from a monarchical state with a rigid social hierarchy into a modern nation in which the social structure was loosened and power passed increasingly to the middle classes.

CAUSES

There is considerable controversy over the causes of the Revolution. Marxist scholars emphasize material factors: as the population increased, food supplies grew short; land had become divided into such small parcels that most Frenchmen lived close to the subsistence level; and after 1776 agricultural recession forced property owners to exploit their sources of revenue. Marxists also maintain that commercial prosperity had stimulated the growth of a monied middle class that threatened the position of the established landed aristocracy. Other social historians emphasize the importance of the growing discrepancy between reality and the legally defined social structure, which distinguished men by hereditary or acquired rank and recognized corporate rather than individual rights. They also emphasize, however, the complexity of French society and question the importance of capitalism.

Political historians usually regard the weakness of the monarchy as a crucial factor. Nominally, the benevolent LOUIS XVI (r. 1774–92) was the absolute ruler of a united country. Actually, so many rights, or privileges, were retained by provinces, towns, corporate bodies, the clergy, and the nobility that the king had little freedom of action. Moreover, since of-fices in the legal and administrative system—and the noble rank that went with them—could be purchased and bequeathed as property, a new aristocracy of ennobled officials had developed. These men were able to monopolize profitable employment, to frustrate royal reforms, and to prevent the monarchy from raising taxes to meet the ever-increasing costs of government and of war. Some writers contrast the arbitrariness of the old regime with the desire, stimulated by the ENLIGHTENMENT and the example of America, for reforms and more participation in government; curiously, few historians have attached much importance to the gradual growth of national consciousness.

The expense of the French participation in the AMERICAN REVOLUTION made fiscal reform or increased taxation imperative after 1783. Since no further revenue could be raised from a peasantry already overburdened by taxes and manorial dues, the royal ministers—particularly Charles Alexandre de CALONNE—attempted to tax all landowners regardless of privileges. When this plan met with resistance in the law courts and provincial assemblies, the ministers tried to replace those bodies with more representative ones. In 1788 this led to the Aristocratic Revolt, a wave of defiance of "despotism" that compelled the ministers to agree to convene the STATES-GENERAL for the first time since 1614.

THE COURSE OF THE REVOLUTION

The Revolution of 1789. The first phase of the Revolution was marked by moral and physical violence. The States-General met in 1789 in Versailles but were paralyzed by the refusal of the Third Estate (the Commons) to meet separately as a distinct, inferior body. On June 17 the Commons took the crucial revolutionary step of declaring their assembly to be the National Assembly, thereby destroying the States-General. This first assertion of the sovereign authority of the nation soon inspired a popular rising in Paris, marked by the storming of the BASTILLE on July 14. Concurrently, urban and rural revolts occurred throughout France. Suspicions generated by the political crisis had aggravated the discontent aroused by the failure of the 1788 harvest and an exceptionally severe winter. The peasants pillaged and burned the châteaux of the aristocracy—an episode known as the *Grande Peur* ("Great Fear")—destroying the records of their manorial dues.

The National Assembly established a new legal structure by abolishing privileges, venality, and "feudal" obligations (August 4); formulating a Declaration of Rights (August 26); and specifying basic constitutional principles that left the king as the chief executive but deprived him of any legislative power except a suspensive veto. Louis's reluctance to sanction these decrees led to a second Parisian uprising, the so-called

Louis XVI dutifully accepts the laws of the people in an allegorical painting produced during the early phase of the Revolution. From 1789 to 1791 France was governed by the National Assembly, which issued the Declaration of Rights and drafted the Constitution of 1791, establishing a constitutional monarchy. Within a year the constitution had collapsed. A republic was proclaimed on Sept. 22, 1792, and Louis XVI and his queen, Marie Antoinette, were executed in 1793.

March of the Women. On October 5 a mob marched to Versailles and forced the king, who had to be protected by the revolutionary national guard under the marquis de LAFAYETTE, to capitulate. Louis and his queen, MARIE ANTOINETTE, were moved immediately to Paris, followed by the Assembly. France thus became a constitutional monarchy, and legal distinctions between Frenchmen disappeared; but the king was practically a prisoner, and many people were permanently alienated by the pretensions of the Assembly and the prevailing disorder.

The Reconstruction of France. In 1789–91, a comparatively peaceful period, the National Assembly did much to modernize France. Despite the Declaration of Rights, the reformed franchise still excluded the poor; but the public maintained its faith in freedom and unity, as shown in the first Festival of Federation, a celebration of national unity on July 14, 1790. Bankruptcy was averted by the confiscation of ecclesiastical land, and the church and law courts were reconstructed to conform with a rational and uniform system of local government by elected councils. Dissension nevertheless developed as several drastic changes, such as the reorganization of the church by the Civil Constitution of the Clergy (1790), followed in rapid succession. In 1791 the call for a clerical oath of loyalty crystallized the conflict between the new sovereignty and traditional loyalties and split the whole country.

When King Louis tried to escape from Paris (the flight to Varennes, June 20, 1791), civil war seemed imminent. The Assembly, however, retained control. A Parisian crowd, which had assembled to demand a republic, was dispersed by force on July 17, and Louis was reinstated after he had accepted the completed Constitution of 1791. The Revolution was then believed to be over, and the National Assembly was dissolved on September 30. In reality, however, religious and social strife had shattered the unity of the Third Estate.

The Revolution of 1792. In 1791–92 the hard-won constitution collapsed. On Apr. 20, 1792, the new Legislative Assembly declared war on Austria, which it believed to be instigating counterrevolutionary agitation and thus launched the FRENCH REVOLUTIONARY WARS. Louis, who looked to Austria for succor, vetoed emergency measures, and Austrian and Prussian forces invaded France. Insurrection broke out in Paris. On August 10 the palace was stormed, and Louis was imprisoned by a new revolutionary Commune of Paris. The Legislative Assembly, reduced to a "patriotic" rump, could only dispute the Commune's pretensions and order the election by manhood suffrage of a National Convention. Meanwhile, the invaders took Verdun, and alleged counterrevolutionaries were massacred in the prisons of Paris.

Foundation of the Republic. Born of this second revolution and briefly favored by military victory, the National Convention horrified Europe by establishing a republic (Sept. 22, 1792), inaugurating a policy of revolutionary war, and sending the king to the guillotine on Jan. 21, 1793. It also appalled France by its own furious disputes. A militant minority, the Montagnards, who spoke for Paris and the left-wing club called the JACOBINS, demanded vigorous revolutionary measures. Their opponents, the GIRONDIST leaders of the amorphous majority, looked to the provinces and hoped to consolidate the Revolution. In the spring of 1793, as the military and economic situation deteriorated and a savage royalist rising began in the Vendée region of western France, the Montagnards gained ground. Emergency bodies such as the Committee of Public Safety and the Revolutionary Tribunal were then established, but unified leadership was lacking until the Parisian insurrection of June 2 compelled the Convention to expel the Girondists and accept Montagnard control.

The Reign of Terror, 1793–94. The Montagnard Convention then had to contend with invasion, royalist civil war, and widespread provincial revolts against "the dictatorship of Paris." Initially, Georges DANTON tried to placate the provinces, and the democratic Constitution of 1793 was approved by plebiscite and celebrated at a Festival of Unity (August 10). After July, however, Maximilien ROBESPIERRE's influence prevailed, and armies were sent to subdue rebellious cities. When the city of Toulon voluntarily surrendered to the Brit-

Georges Danton, who became minister of justice in France's revolutionary government in 1792, was instrumental in organizing resistance against the invading Prussian and Austrian armies. He dominated the first Committee of Public Safety (April–July 1793), but his popularity antagonized the more radical revolutionary leaders, and in 1794 he was denounced and executed.

ish, a demonstration in Paris compelled the National Convention to establish (September 5) the repressive regime known as the Terror. A fearful time ensued: the Committee of Public Safety strove to organize the economy and the war effort; the Revolutionary Tribunal sent state prisoners, including the Girondists, to the guillotine; and agents of the Convention known as Representatives of the People enforced bloody repression throughout France. A campaign of dechristianization, marked by a new Revolutionary Calendar computed from Sept. 22, 1792 (1 Vendémiaire, Year I), led to the closing of all churches on 3 Frimaire, Year II (Nov. 23, 1793).

From December 1793, when republican armies began to prevail, both at home and abroad, the Terror became identified with ruthless but centralized revolutionary government. Because dissidence was now classified as counterrevolutionary, moderate Montagnards such as Danton and extremists such as Jacques René HÉBERT, a leader of dechristianization, were guillotined early in 1794. The centralization of repression also brought innumerable victims before the Revolutionary Tribunal, whose work was expedited by the draconian Law of 22 Prairial (June 10). As a result of Robespierre's insistence on associating Terror with Virtue, his efforts to make the republic a morally united patriotic community became equated with the endless bloodshed. Finally, after a decisive military victory over the Austrians at Fleurus (June 26), Robespierre was overthrown by a conspiracy of certain members of the National Convention on 9 Thermidor (July 27, 1794). After trying in vain to raise Paris, the Robespierrist deputies and most members of the Commune were guillotined the next day, July 28.

The Thermidorian Reaction. During the ensuing period (1794–95) of the Thermidorian Reaction, government was so weakened that anarchy and runaway inflation almost overwhelmed the republic. In the southeast the royalists conducted a "white terror," and in Paris gangs of draft-dodgers,

Maximilien Robespierre separates money from his fellow citizens in this satirical cartoon. As the dominant figure of the Committee of Public Safety from July 1793, Robespierre was largely responsible for the repressive measures imposed during the Reign of Terror.

(Above left) *The National Convention, fearful of further purges of its ranks, arrested the radical leader Maximilien Robespierre on the evening of 9 Thermidor (July 27, 1794) and ordered his execution the following day. Robespierre's fall marked the end of the Terror and the beginning of the Thermidorian Reaction, a period in which the most repressive manifestations of the Revolution were discarded.* (Above right) *In this allegorical painting, a figure representing the victorious forces of Reason pays homage to various symbols of the French Revolution.*

called *la jeunesse dorée* ("gilded youth"), persecuted the patriots. Twice, in Germinal and Prairial (April and May, 1795), there were desperate risings demanding "Bread and the Constitution of 1793." Without the Montagnards and Jacobins, however, whose club was closed in November 1794, the *sans-culottes* ("those without kneebreeches," the name given to extreme republicans) could achieve nothing, and the Convention broke the popular movement permanently with the aid of the army. The death (1795) of the imprisoned dauphin (titular King Louis XVII) and an unsuccessful royalist landing in Brittany also checked the reaction toward monarchy, enabling the Convention to complete the Constitution of 1795. This liberal settlement was approved by plebiscite, and it took effect after a reactionary rising in Vendémiaire (Oct. 5, 1795) had been suppressed by General Napoléon Bonaparte (the future Emperor NAPOLEON I) with what he described as "a whiff of grapeshot."

The Directory, 1795–99. The Constitution of 1795 established an executive DIRECTORY, two assemblies, and a property owners' franchise. Many provisions, including the initial derivation of two-thirds of the deputies from the Convention, guarded the republic against any reversion to either democratic Terror or monarchy. The only attempt to renew violent revolution, François BABEUF's communistic Conspiracy of Equals (May 1796), was easily thwarted; but executive weakness and the annual election of one-third of the deputies made stability unattainable.

In 1797 the directors purged the parliament ruthlessly, branding many deputies as royalists and sentencing them to the penal colony of French Guiana (called "the dry guillotine"). This coup d'état of Fructidor (September 1797) was a devastating blow to all moderates. Thereafter, although administration improved and French power increased in Europe, coups against conservative or radical revivals occurred annually until 1799, when the Abbé SIEYÈS, determined to strengthen central authority, enlisted the aid of Bonaparte to effect the coup d'état of Brumaire (November 9–10).

The Consulate, 1799–1804. The Constitution of 1799 established the CONSULATE with Bonaparte as First Consul. He used his power to effect a remarkable reorganization of France, most notably reestablishing centralized control and restoring Catholicism by the Concordat of 1801. Constitutional controls and republican institutions were nonetheless steadily eroded until the creation of the First Empire (1804–15) ended the revolutionary period.

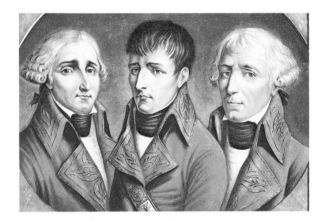

In 1799 a three-man governing body, the Consulate, was established in place of the weak Directory. The first consul, Napoléon Bonaparte, is shown here flanked by his nominal colleagues, Jean Jacques Régis de Cambacérès (left) and Charles François Lebrun (right).

CONSEQUENCES

The most concrete results of the French Revolution were probably achieved in 1789–91, when land was freed from customary burdens and the old corporate society was destroyed. This "abolition of feudalism" promoted individualism and egalitarianism but probably retarded the growth of a capitalist economy. Although only prosperous peasants were able to purchase land confiscated from the church and the emigrant nobility, France became increasingly a land of peasant proprietors. The bourgeoisie that acquired social predominance during the Directory and the Consulate was primarily composed of officials and landed proprietors, and although the war enabled some speculators and contractors to make fortunes, it delayed economic development. The great reforms of 1789–91 nevertheless established an enduring administrative and legal system, and much of the revolutionaries' work in humanizing the law itself was subsequently incorporated in the NAPOLEONIC CODE.

Politically, the revolution was more significant than successful. Since 1789 the French government has been either parliamentary and constitutional or based on the plebiscitary system that Napoleon inherited and developed. Between 1789 and 1799, however, democracy failed. Frequent elections bred apathy, and filling offices by nomination became commonplace even before Napoleon made it systematic. The Jacobins' fraternal—and Jacobin-controlled—community expired in 1794, the direct democracy of the *sansculottes* was crushed in 1795, and the republic perished in 1804; as ideals, however, they continued to inspire and embitter French politics and keep right and left, church and state, far apart.

The Revolution nevertheless freed the state from the trammels of its medieval past, releasing such unprecedented power that the revolutionaries could defy, and Napoleon conquer, the rest of Europe. Moreover, that power acknowledged no restraint: in 1793 unity was imposed on the nation by the Terror. Europe and the world have ever since been learning what infringements of liberty can issue from the concepts of national sovereignty and the will of the people.   M. J. SYDENHAM

Bibliography: Bosher, J. F., *The French Revolution* (1988); Cobb, Richard, and Jones, Colin, eds., *Voices of the French Revolution* (1988); Lefebvre, Georges, *The French Revolution,* 2 vols., trans. by E. M. Evanson and J. Frigulietti (1962–64); Manceron, Claude, *The French Revolution,* 8 vols. projected (1977–   ); Rude, George, *The French Revolution* (1989); Schama, Simon, *Citizens: A Chronicle of the French Revolution* (1989); Soboul, Albert, *A Short History of the French Revolution,* trans. by G. Symcox (1977); Sydenham, M. J., *The French Revolution* (1965) and *The First French Republic* (1974); Tocqueville, Alexis de, *The Old Regime and the French Revolution,* trans. by S. Gilbert (1973).

See also: FRANCE, HISTORY OF; NAPOLEONIC WARS.

French Revolutionary Wars

The ''French Revolutionary Wars'' is the name usually given to the campaigns fought between France and the other Euro-

pean powers from 1792 to 1802, the first decade of conflicts that followed the FRENCH REVOLUTION. In their subsequent phase, from 1803 to 1815, these conflicts are known as the NAPOLEONIC WARS. The French Revolutionary Wars were fought from the Caribbean to the Indian Ocean, but the principal encounters occurred in the Low Countries, the Rhineland, and Lombardy.

Between 1789 and 1792 traditional antagonisms between France and its neighbors, particularly Austria, were greatly aggravated by ideological differences. Every conflict of interest became a confrontation with French democrats and their belief that the will of the sovereign people transcended treaties. Exaggerated fear of Austrian support for an armed assembly of emigrant French nobles at Coblentz consequently led France to declare war on Austria and Prussia in April 1792.

Initially, France was almost overwhelmed. Disorganized advances ended in mutinous retreats, and soon the Prussian army threatened Paris. Halted at Valmy (Sept. 20, 1792), a decisive encounter, the Prussians retired, and the French defeated the Austrians at Jemappes (Nov. 6, 1792) and overran the Austrian Netherlands (Belgium). Britain, Holland, Sardinia, and Spain soon aligned themselves against France, and when in 1793 a French invasion of Holland was repelled at Neerwinden (March 18), this First Coalition attacked France on every frontier. Suppressing civil war at home by the Reign of Terror, the revolutionary republic raised the first national conscript army, and in 1794 its forces were successful everywhere. After the Battle of Fleurus (June 26, 1794), the Low Countries were conquered. In 1795, Prussia became neutral, and Holland and Spain accepted treaties making them virtual French satellites. Austria, too, was compelled to make peace at Campo-Formio (October 1797; see CAMPO-FORMIO, TREATY OF), af-

Nations allied against France during the French Revolutionary Wars, as well as the major areas of conflict, are identified. France, aided by the leveé en masse *of 1793, which created the first national army raised by universal conscription, faced successive coalitions.*

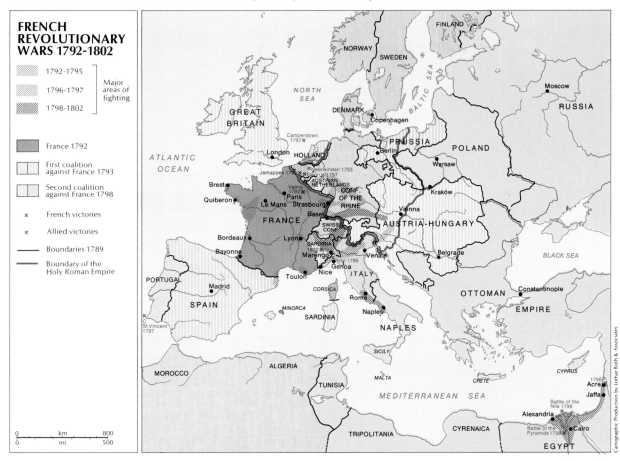

FRENCH REVOLUTIONARY WARS 1792-1802

1792-1795
1796-1797   Major areas of fighting
1798-1802

France 1792

First coalition against France 1793

Second coalition against France 1798

×   French victories

×   Allied victories

———   Boundaries 1789

———   Boundary of the Holy Roman Empire

Cartographic Production by Lothar Roth & Associates

ter the brilliant Italian campaign (1796–97) of Napoléon Bonaparte (later NAPOLEON I).

Britain, paymaster of the anti-French alliances, was now isolated and exposed to invasion. The French fleet, however, had been greatly weakened by the British victory called the Glorious First of June (1794), and in 1797 the Royal Navy defeated the Spanish fleet off Cape St. Vincent (February 14) and the Dutch at Camperdown (October 11), thus ending the threat of a naval combination. In 1798 the French DIRECTORY approved Bonaparte's plan to conquer Egypt. His victories there, however, were nullified by Horatio NELSON's destruction of his fleet in the Battle of the Nile (Aug. 1, 1798) and by the Turks' defense of Acre.

In Bonaparte's absence, a Second Coalition, consisting of Britain, Austria, Russia, and Turkey, was created. Once again, however, the French Republic triumphed. In 1799, Russian armies under Aleksandr SUVOROV swept across Lombardy only to be held at Zurich (September 25) and forced to retreat through the Alps in midwinter. Exposed, the Austrians retired from the Rhine, and an Anglo-Russian landing in Holland then had to be withdrawn. Returning from Egypt, Bonaparte, as first consul, defeated the Austrians at Marengo (June 14, 1800). A further defeat by Jean Victor MOREAU at Hohenlinden (Dec. 3, 1800) forced the Austrians to make peace at Lunéville on Feb. 9, 1801. Isolated for a second time, Britain disrupted a new maritime combination by bombarding the Danish fleet at Copenhagen (April 2, 1801) and destroyed Bonaparte's Egyptian army at Alexandria (August 1801). In March 1802, Britain sought an experimental peace by the Treaty of AMIENS.

Strikingly illustrative of the power of one militant nation in arms, these wars were nonetheless inconclusive: revolutionary republicanism had not dominated Europe, but Napoleonic imperialism had still to be encountered.   M. J. SYDENHAM

Bibliography: Blanning, T. C., *Origins of the French Revolutionary Wars* (1986); Bryant, Sir Arthur, *The Years of Endurance, 1793–1802* (1942); Dickson, H. T., ed., *Britain and the French Revolution, 1789–1815* (1989); Rodger, A. B., *The War of the Second Coalition* (1964); Wilkinson, Spenser, *The Rise of General Bonaparte* (1930).

French Southern and Antarctic Territories

The French Southern and Antarctic Territories form an overseas territory of France, established in 1955, that consists of several groups of islands in the southern Indian Ocean and a sector of Antarctica that is claimed by France. The Antarctic territory is called Adélie Coast (Terre Adélie). It includes the area between 136° and 143° east longitude south of the Antarctic Circle and is about 389,000 km² (150,200 mi²) in area. A staffed research station is located at Base Dumont d'Urville. The island components include the Kerguelen Islands, a group of one large and some 300 small islands, with a total area of about 7,000 km² (2,700 mi²); the Crozet Islands, consisting of 5 large and 15 tiny islands, with a combined area of about 300 km² (116 mi²); St. Paul Island, which is about 7 km² (2.7 mi²); and Amsterdam Island (Nouvelle-Amsterdam), with an area of 60 km² (23 mi²). All are rugged volcanic islands, uninhabited except for the various research stations.

French Union

The French Union was a political entity created in 1946 as a reorganization of the FRENCH EMPIRE. It comprised metropolitan France, Algeria, and the overseas departments; the associated states; and the remaining overseas territories of France. The new arrangement was designed to extend citizenship rights to natives of the French dependencies; create closer ties with protectorates, or associated states; and offer limited autonomy to colonies previously under direct rule. The high council and the assembly of the French Union, an advisory body headed by the French president, soon fell into disuse. The union was replaced by the FRENCH COMMUNITY in 1958.

DONALD J. HARVEY

French West Africa

French West Africa was a federation of French territories in West Africa established in 1895 and dissolved in 1958. The constituent territories were Dahomey (Benin), Ivory Coast, French Guinea (Guinea), Senegal, French Sudan (Mali), Mauritania, Niger, and Upper Volta (Burkina Faso). Dakar, in Senegal, was its capital.

French West Indies

The French West Indies are the several groups of islands in the Lesser Antilles that constitute all the French possessions in the Caribbean Sea. They form two overseas departments of France—MARTINIQUE and GUADELOUPE.

Freneau, Philip   [freh-noh']

Philip Morin Freneau, b. New York City, Jan. 2, 1752, d. Dec. 18, 1832, was one of the most significant early American poets. His early poem "The Power of Fancy" (1770), although neoclassical in style, anticipates the romantics in its awareness of nature.

Freneau's talent was both tested and limited by the times in which he lived. His topical poetry, both patriotic and critical of the British, as in "The British Prison Ship" (1781), earned him the sobriquet "Poet of the American Revolution." In the early 1790s, before the Federalists swept to power, Freneau, in his *National Gazette,* was one of the first political journalists to actively support Jefferson. While he continued to write poetry, usually treating native subjects as in "To a Caty-Did" (1815), his constant struggle for survival finally forced him to become a farmer, a seaman, and then a tinker.   PAULA HART

Bibliography: Axelrad, Jacob, *Philip Freneau: Champion of Democracy* (1967); Bowden, Mary W., *Philip Freneau* (1976).

Freon   [free'-ahn]

Freon is a trademark of E. I. du Pont for a series of chlorinated and fluorinated hydrocarbons. The parent compounds are methane, CH_4, and ethane, C_2H_6; a few Freons contain a bromine atom. The methane-based Freons are designated by du Pont with numbers below 100; those based on ethane are numbered between 100 and 200. The most frequently used Freons are F–11 and F–12, the formulas of which are CCl_3F and CCl_2F_2, respectively.

The Freons are chemically stable, nontoxic, and nonflammable. Other useful properties are high density, low boiling point, and low viscosity. These characteristics make the Freons especially suited for use as refrigerants, as well as AEROSOL propellants, solvents, and expansion agents in polyurethane foams. Freons are FLUOROCARBONS, substances implicated in the depletion of the OZONE LAYER. In 1988 the du Pont company pledged to phase out production of fluorocarbons—or chlorofluorocarbons (CFCs), as they are now called—and to seek substitutes.   WILLIAM J. PATTON

frequency

Frequency is one of the primary characteristics of a wave (see WAVES AND WAVE MOTION). It refers to all kinds of waves and is the number of times the wave varies through a complete cycle in a given unit of time. Frequency is denoted by either the symbol f or the Greek letter nu (ν) and is commonly expressed in hertz (Hz); 1 Hz equals 1 cycle per second. The frequency of a sound wave determines its pitch; that of a light wave determines its color.

frequency allocation

Telecommunications makes use of a limited frequency range in the electromagnetic spectrum (see ELECTROMAGNETIC RADIATION). The available frequencies must be assigned, or allocated, in a way that minimizes interference between the transmitted signals. In the United States, frequencies are allocated by the FEDERAL COMMUNICATIONS COMMISSION. Each type of transmission occupies a certain band, or range of frequencies. For example, the standard band for AM radio broadcasting is 535 to 1,605 kHz. Other forms of radio—FM, citizen's band (CB), CELLULAR RADIO, and maritime and aviation communications, are also allocated bands, as are radar and television. (See also TELEVISION TRANSMISSION.)

Frequencies are classified as follows:

Very low frequency(VLF)	10–30	kHz
Low frequency(LF)	30–300	kHz
Medium frequency (MF)	300–3,000	kHz
High frequency (HF)	3–30	MHz
Very high frequency(VHF)	30–300	MHz
Ultrahigh frequency (UHF)	300–3,000	MHz
Superhigh frequency (SHF)	3,000–30,000	MHz

frequency modulation

Frequency modulation (FM) is a method of MODULATION in which the frequency of a wave is varied in response to a modulating wave. The method was developed (1925–33) by Edwin Howard ARMSTRONG. The wave in which frequency is varied is called the carrier and the modulating wave, the signal. Frequency modulation requires a higher-frequency carrier wave and a more complex method for transmitting information than does AMPLITUDE MODULATION (AM), although FM has an important advantage: Because a frequency-modulated electromagnetic wave has constant amplitude, it is much less susceptible to interference from both natural and artificial sources of ELECTROMAGNETIC RADIATION. Such sources cause STATIC in an amplitude-modulated radio or a telephone receiver. Both types of modulation, however, are used in radio broadcasting, whereas only FM is used for television. FM radio is a popular source of high fidelity music.   FORREST M. MIMS, III

Bibliography: Taub, Herbert, and Schilling, Donald, *Principles of Communication Systems*, 2d ed. (1986).

Frere, Sir John   [freer]

Sir John Frere, b. Aug. 10, 1740, d. July 12, 1807, was an English antiquarian whose ideas about the antiquity of flint artifacts anticipated principles later confirmed by prehistoric archaeology. He was an active member of the Royal Society of Antiquaries from 1771. In 1790 he discovered Paleolithic hand axes at Hoxne, England. In *Account of Flint Weapons Discovered at Hoxne in Suffolk* (1800), he suggested that, contrary to the then-popular belief that the date of the creation was 4004 BC, the finds dated from a much more remote period. His conclusions were only recognized about half a century later.

Bibliography: Eichler, Albert, *John Hookham Frere* (1905; repr. 1965).

fresco painting   [fres'-koh]

Fresco (an Italian word meaning "fresh") is a technique of durable wall painting used extensively for murals (see MURAL PAINTING). In pure, or *buon*, fresco, a fresh wet layer of plaster is applied to a prepared wall surface and painted with pigments mixed with water. The pigments soak into the plaster, which, when dry, forms a permanent chemical bond fusing

This detail from The Defeat of Khusrau *was created by the Italian artist Piero della Francesca as part of his fresco cycle (1452–66) in the choir of the Church of San Francesco in Arezzo, Italy. Fresco painting proliferated in Italy during the Renaissance and culminated during the 15th century.*

paint and wall surface. Another type of fresco, painting on a dry *(secco)* surface with adhesive binder flakes, is not permanent. Because all fresco is susceptible to humidity and weathering, its use is limited.

Although not universally used for wall painting, fresco has a long history. Magnificent examples of this technique survive from the MINOAN ART of Crete in the second millennium BC. Whereas few Greek frescoes survive, examples of Roman frescoes (prior to AD 79) from HERCULANEUM and POMPEII are preserved. The early Christians (AD 250–400) decorated the Roman CATACOMBS with simple frescoes. The Byzantine era (AD c.500–1300) produced both frescoes and mosaics; the former are now found in the USSR, Yugoslavia, and Crete (see BYZANTINE ART AND ARCHITECTURE). Knowledge of the technique was not restricted to Europe: AJANTA, India (200 BC–AD 700), and TUN-HUANG, China (AD 400–800), have vast wall frescoes.

The origins and development of fresco are unclear, as only pieces of early monuments survive. The most sustained use of fresco, however, occurred in Italy between 1300 and 1800. Generations of gifted Italian painters executed frescoes on walls and ceilings of public buildings, churches, and private residences—hence the Italian terminology for fresco techniques.

Most frescoes painted between 1250 and 1400 were *buon*. Because this type of fresco requires wet plaster, plaster was applied only to an area that could be finished in one work session. For the next session fresh plaster was applied to new areas. Hence, the juncture between one "patch" and another is called *giornata*, or "one day's work." Because quick execution was necessary, compositions were planned well in advance. Most early frescoes were first sketched in red chalk or ocher wash called *sinopia* (see CARTOON, art). As the artists worked, they covered the section of the *sinopia* about to be painted with a second layer of plaster called *intonaco*. New techniques for restoring frescoes permit *intonaco* to be peeled off so that the *sinopia* can be studied.

Much has been learned about the procedures of extensive mural projects from these underdrawings. Frescoes were a collective shop effort painted under a master's supervision. Assistants ground and mixed colors, prepared surfaces, and painted parts of the wall based on the master's design. If the wall to be painted was large, artists worked on scaffolding, beginning at the top and working down.

In the early 15th century, painters began to experiment with new techniques to shorten work time and allow greater flexibility. Longevity was often sacrificed in the experiments; for example, LEONARDO DA VINCI's *Last Supper* (1495–c.1497), in Milan, is now all but lost. Artists began to eliminate the *sinopia* by working out their ideas in large-scale cartoons that could be transferred onto the wet *intonaco* by tracing or *pouncing* (dusting through perforations).

Innumerable treasures in Italian fresco survive. Notable examples from the late 13th through the early 14th century include CIMABUE's work in Assisi, Pietro CAVALLINI's in Rome, GIOTTO DI BONDONE's unparalleled cycles in Padua and Florence; and Pietro and Ambrogio Lorenzetti's (see LORENZETTI brothers) and Simone MARTINI's work in Assisi. The later 14th century saw frescoes by Taddeo Gaddi (see GADDI family) and Maso di Banco in Florence. The so-called Black Death Style characterized works by Nardo di Cione, Giovanni da Milano, and Andrew Orcagna in Florence; Francesco TRAINI in Pisa; and Barna da Siena in San Gimignano. Later in the century Antonio Veneziano painted frescoes in Pisa, and Spinello Aretino, Agnolo Gaddi, and Niccolò di Pietro Gerini executed frescoes throughout Tuscany. Altichiero and Vitale da Bologna rank among important non-Tuscan fresco masters.

The early 15th century witnessed important contributions by the revolutionary painters MASACCIO and Paolo UCCELLO as well as more traditional paintings by Lorenzo Monaco. Fra Filippo LIPPI, Fra ANGELICO, Benozzo GOZZOLI, and Andrea del Castagno furnished Florence with highly decorative frescoes while PIERO DELLA FRANCESCA created astonishingly powerful cycles in Arezzo and Rimini. Later in the century Andrea MANTEGNA worked in Mantua while Alesso BALDOVINETTI, Domenico GHIRLANDAIO, Sandro BOTTICELLI, and Luca SIGNORELLI painted major frescoes in Florence, Rome, and Orvieto.

The 16th century saw the great achievements of RAPHAEL's Stanze frescoes and MICHELANGELO's ceiling and *Last Judgment* for the SISTINE CHAPEL in Rome, perhaps the most famous frescoes ever painted. These achievements provided the impetus for ROSSO FIORENTINO, ANDREA DEL SARTO, Jacopo PONTORMO, Giorgio VASARI, and BRONZINO working primarily in Florence, and for Domenico BECCAFUMI working in Siena, Giulio Romano in Mantua, and CORREGGIO in Parma, as well as Perino del Vaga in Rome. Toward the end of the century Paolo VERONESE established a new fresco tradition in Venice.

Rome, the major center of patronage involving frescoes in the 17th century, is the site of commissioned frescoes by Annibale Carracci (see CARRACCI family), Pietro da CORTONA, Guido RENI, Giovanni Lanfranco, and Giovanni Battista GAULLI. The tradition for fresco painting continued in the 18th century with the Neapolitans Luca GIORDANO and Francesco Solimena, culminating in the achievements of the Venetian Giovanni Battista Tiepolo (see TIEPOLO family), whose fame won him commissions in Italy, Germany, and Spain.

During the 19th century fresco fell into disuse; it was revived in the 20th century, however. Inspired by the Italian tradition, the Mexican painters Diego RIVERA, José OROZCO, and David SIQUEIROS used fresco for their murals. During the Depression of the 1930s many American artists, such as Thomas Hart BENTON and others, produced fresco murals under the auspices of the Works Progress Administration.

ADELHEID M. GEALT

Bibliography: Borsook, Eve, *The Mural Painters of Tuscany*, rev. ed. (1981); Freedberg, S. J., *Painting in Italy, 1500–1600* (1971); Hale, Gardner, *Fresco Painting* (1933); Hurlburt, L. P., *Mexican Muralists in the United States* (1989); Immerwahr, S. A., *Aegean Painting in the Bronze Age* (1990); Meiss, M., *The Great Age of Fresco* (1970); Nordmark, O. E., *Fresco Painting* (1947).

Frescobaldi, Girolamo [fres-koh-bahl'-dee, jee-roh'-lah-moh]

Girolamo Frescobaldi, b. Sept. 1583, d. Mar. 1, 1643, was the most important composer for the harpsichord and the organ of the early Baroque period. He began his musical studies in his native Ferrara with the well-known madrigal composer Luzzasco Luzzaschi. Soon after the rule of the Este family in Ferrara ended in 1597, Frescobaldi moved to Rome, where he held several posts as church organist, culminating in positions at Saint Peter's Basilica and at the pope's Julian Chapel, which he held beginning in 1608. He remained in Rome, except for a sojourn in Florence from 1628 to about 1634, during which time he served the Médici grand duke Ferdinando II. His numerous Italian students spread his influence throughout the peninsula, and Johann Jakob Froberger and Johann Kaspar Kerll passed on Frescobaldi's influence to succeeding generations of northern Europeans.

Frescobaldi's works for the keyboard include dance suites; variations; improvisational, often sectional, toccatas; and strictly composed, contrapuntal ricercares and canzonas. His best-known collection, the *Fiori musicali* (1635), consists of toccatas, ricercares, and capriccios intended to be played during the Mass; these pieces often incorporated the melodies of Gregorian chants. As a youth, J. S. Bach copied compositions from the *Fiori musicali* in his own hand to study them.

Bibliography: Palisca, Claude V., *Baroque Music,* 2d ed. (1980).

fresh water

Fresh water is water that contains a relatively low concentration of dissolved mineral solids. The quantity of total dissolved solids varies considerably and depends on a number of factors, including: the total dissolved-solids content of the PRECIPITATION contributing to the water body; the nature of the soil and rock through which the water must pass to reach the water body; and human activities (such as the use of sodium chloride or calcium chloride for snow and ice removal) in adjacent areas. Soil and rock are generally the most important influences; in urbanized areas, however, human activities may be equally significant.

Fresh water usually has a maximum total dissolved-solids content of a few hundred milligrams per liter. In contrast, rainwater generally has less than 50 mg/l (1 mg/l = 1 part per million), and SEAWATER in the open ocean generally contains 35,000 mg/l of total dissolved solids. Brackish waters (those found in ESTUARIES, where rivers mix with the ocean) have total dissolved-solids concentrations ranging from 1,000 to 5,000 mg/l. Inland waters having concentration ranges of 2,000 to 10,000 and 10,000 to 30,000 mg/l may be classified as moderately and severely saline waters. The major dissolved substances in fresh water are the cations sodium (Na^+), calcium (Ca^{2+}), magnesium (Mg^{2+}), potassium (K^+), and ferrous iron (Fe^{2+}); and the anions chloride (Cl^-), bicarbonate (HCO_3^-), carbonate (CO_3^{2-}), and sulfate (SO_4^{2-}). Small quantities of nutrients (nitrates and phosphates) also are generally present, along with trace amounts of other elements.

Bibliography: Viessmann, Warren, et al., *Introduction to Hydrology,* 3d ed. (1988).

See also: GROUNDWATER; LAKE (body of water); RIVER AND STREAM; WATER QUALITY; WATER RESOURCES.

Fresnel, Augustin Jean [fray-nel', oh-goo-stan' zhawn]

The French physicist Augustin Jean Fresnel, b. May 10, 1788, d. July 14, 1827, made fundamental contributions to theoretical and applied optics. Partially anticipated by Thomas YOUNG, Fresnel rejected the view derived from Newton that light consists of material particles and established the wave theory on a firm mathematical-experimental basis. He devised a new lens and other improvements in lighthouse illumination.

ROBERT SILLIMAN

Fresnel diffraction: see DIFFRACTION.

Fresno [frez'-noh]

Fresno, a city in central California, is the seat of Fresno County and the principal commercial center of the agriculturally rich San Joaquin Valley. In 1990 there were 354,202 residents within the city and 667,490 in the metropolitan area. Grapes for wine and raisins, figs, cotton, and vegetables are grown, processed, and marketed. Local industries manufacture paper containers, sheet and optical glass, vending machines, agricultural machinery, fertilizers, and plastics.

Educational institutions include California State University at Fresno and Fresno City College. Founded in 1872 as a station on the Central (later Southern) Pacific Railroad, Fresno (Spanish: ''ashtree'') became an agricultural center when irrigation was introduced in the 1880s.

Freud, Anna [froyd]

Anna Freud, b. Dec. 3, 1895, d. Oct. 10, 1982, was an internationally renowned Austrian-English psychoanalyst and the daughter of Sigmund Freud. When she became a teacher in Vienna her interests in education and psychoanalysis led to the publication of *Introduction to Psychoanalysis for Teachers* (1930; Eng. trans., 1931). She was a pioneer in, and a substantial contributor to, the development of psychoanalysis of the child and is especially noted for her *Introduction to the Technique of Child Psychoanalysis* (1927; Eng. trans., 1928). Other writings include *Normality and Pathology in Childhood* (1965), *The Ego and the Mechanisms of Defence* (1936; Eng. trans., 1937), a psychoanalytic classic, and her collected papers in seven volumes, *The Writings of Anna Freud.*

Anna Freud stressed the function of the ego in coping with the outside world and setting up defenses and in so doing added new directions to her father's emphasis on the id and sexual influences. She devoted considerable effort to the welfare of children. After leaving Vienna for London with her family in 1938, she founded the Hampstead War Nurseries, and after World War II she established the renowned Hampstead Child Therapy Course and Clinic.

HUMBERTO NAGERA

Bibliography: Peters, U. H., *Anna Freud* (1985); Young-Bruehl, E., *Anna Freud: A Biography* (1988).

The Austrian physician Sigmund Freud founded psychoanalysis. Freud used the term to describe both his theories of personality and his method of treating mental illness. Studying the dynamics of the psyche, Freud was the first to recognize the influence of unconscious drives in shaping behavior. Freud's work revolutionized modern psychiatry and strongly influenced 20th century Western theories of child rearing and education, art, literature, and culture. Shown at the right is the study in his London home, where he lived during the last year of his life.

Freud, Sigmund

Sigmund Freud, b. May 6, 1856, d. Sept. 23, 1939, the creator of PSYCHOANALYSIS, was the first person to scientifically explore the human unconscious mind; his ideas profoundly influenced the shape of modern culture by altering man's view of himself. Freud was born in Freiberg, Moravia (now Příbor, Czechoslovakia), the oldest child of his father's second wife. Before Freud was 4 years of age, the family moved first to Leipzig, Germany, and then to Vienna, where Freud remained for most of his life. Freud's father, Jakob, a struggling Jewish merchant, encouraged his intellectually precocious son and passed on to him a tradition of skeptical and independent thinking. Jakob's passive acceptance of anti-Semitic insults, however, troubled the young Freud: his feelings toward his father were ambivalent. Freud shared his mother's attention with seven younger brothers and sisters, but he nevertheless maintained a close attachment to her. Amalie Freud had high hopes for her oldest son—and they were eventually realized.

At 8 years of age Freud was reading Shakespeare and, despite the recognizable influence of an education in Greek, Latin, French, and German classics, he later spoke of "the works of the men who were my real teachers—all of them English or Scotch," referring to their "sober industriousness" and "stubborn feeling for justice." Freud's literary gifts and insights into human motives and emotions were first apparent in letters he wrote during adolescence. He considered studying law but decided instead on a career in medical research in response to an essay on nature attributed to Goethe. Guided by contemporaries such as Ernst von Brücke and Theodor Meynert, Freud began on a promising research career; his later monographs on aphasia and on infantile cerebral paralysis were both the culmination of his neurological research and a harbinger of his burgeoning psychological insight.

In 1886 he married Martha Bernays. In order to support a wife he turned from research to the clinical practice of neurology. By that time Freud's interest in hysteria had been stimulated by Josef Breuer's successful use of therapeutic hypnosis and by Freud's studying with the famous neurologist Jean Martin CHARCOT in Paris. Freud took up Breuer's "cathartic method," and they published their findings in *Studies in Hysteria* (1895), which outlined their "talking cure" and is generally regarded as the beginning of psychoanalysis. Breuer lost interest when sexuality emerged as central to Freud's view of neurosis.

Freud, devoting himself to the new science, discarded authoritarian and cumbersome hypnosis by enlisting his patients' cooperation in "free association." This enabled him to notice the unconsciously motivated resistance of a patient to revealing repressed thoughts and memories, especially sexual ideas. The central discovery of this approach was transference, or the unconscious shift of feelings associated with persons in the patient's past to the therapist. Breuer's defection and the death (1896) of Freud's father precipitated a crisis for Freud to which he reacted by entering a period of self-analysis. Leaning for emotional support on his friend Wilhelm Fliess, Freud explored his dreams and fantasies for clues to his childhood sexual passions—his Oedipus complex.

A comprehensive exposition of the new science of psychoanalysis, *The Interpretation of Dreams* (1900), was regarded by Freud as his greatest book. At first the book was all but ignored; gradually, however, a number of interested persons gathered around Freud to study and apply his revolutionary discoveries. Of his early followers, Alfred ADLER and C. G. JUNG defected to form their own schools of psychology, largely because they could not accept infantile sexuality as pivotal.

Freud's creativity continued undiminished for almost four more decades, during which he developed the technique for psychoanalytic treatment of neuroses and established the guiding principles of psychoanalysis. Indeed, Freud created a wholly new field of scientific inquiry which investigates a human's internal world through controlled methods of introspection and empathy. Freud's ideas aroused considerable hostility during his time, particularly among his medical colleagues. A regular weekly meeting of friends at Freud's home for the purpose of discussing his discoveries grew into the Vienna Psychoanalytic Society and eventually into the International Psycho-Analytical Association. In 1909, Freud was invited by Clark University in Worcester, Mass., to deliver a series of lectures; this was his only visit to the United States.

Shortly after World War I, Freud learned that he had cancer of the jaw, to which he would succumb after nearly 17 years of chronic pain and disability and 33 surgical operations. Throughout this period, however, he remained productive. Although recognition from the scientific community had not yet come, he was honored in 1930 with the Goethe Prize for Literature, and in 1936 he was elected to the Royal Society. When the Nazi occupation of Austria threatened his life and work, he moved to England. He died there on Sept. 23, 1939.

With psychoanalysis, Freud added psychological treatment methods to the biological basis of PSYCHIATRY. Beyond that, Freudian concepts—such as the powerful influence of the unconscious mind on conscious thought and behavior and the equally powerful influence of the apparently forgotten past on the present—have become part of our culture, used unwittingly by even the most vehement anti-Freudians. Freud's lasting impact on the modern world, like that of Marx, Einstein, and Picasso, cannot be denied.   ERNEST S. WOLF

Bibliography: Abramson, J. A., *Liberation and Its Limits: The Moral and Political Thought of Freud* (1984); Decker, H. S., *Freud, Dora and Vienna 1900* (1990); Erdelyi, M. H., *Psychoanalysis: Freud's Cognitive Psychology* (1985); Fancher, R. E., *Psychoanalytic Psychology: The Development of Freud's Thoughts* (1973); Fisher, Seymour, and Greenberg, Roger, eds., *The Scientific Evaluation of Freud's Theories and Therapy: A Book of Readings* (1978; repr. 1985); Freud, Sigmund, *Complete Psychological Works, Standard Edition*, 24 vols. trans. under editorship of James Strachey (1964); Fromm, Erich, *Greatness and Limitations of Freud's Thought* (1980); Gay, Peter, *A Godless Jew: Freud, Atheism, and the Making of Psychoanalysis* (1987), *Reading Freud* (1990), and *Freud: A Life for Our Time* (1988); Jones, Ernest, *The Life and Works of Sigmund Freud*, 3 vols. (1953–57; repr. 1974); Krull, Marianne, *Freud and His Father*, trans. by A. J. Pomerans (1990); Lewis, H. B., *Freud and Modern Psychology*, 2 vols. (1981–83); McGrath, W. J., *Freud's Discovery of Psychoanalysis* (1986); Roazen, Paul, *Encountering Freud* (1989) and, as ed., *Sigmund Freud* (1987); Schur, Max, *Freud: Living and Dying* (1972); Sulloway, F. J., *Freud, Biologist of the Mind* (1983); Wolheim, Richard, *Sigmund Freud* (1981).

Frey   [fray]

In Norse mythology, Frey (or Freyr) was the god of fertility, peace, and prosperity. He was one of the Vanir gods, who were responsible for wealth, and the brother of Freya. Among his magical possessions was a sword that he gave to Skirnir, who in return obtained him Gerda, the most beautiful woman in the world, as his wife.

Freya   [fray'-ah]

In Norse mythology, Freya, or Freyja, was the goddess of beauty and love. A beautiful, blonde, blue-eyed young woman, she was the sister of Frey and in later traditions the wife of ODIN. Freya claimed half of the heroes slain in battle, carrying them to her realm of Folkvang in ASGARD. Most of her myths concern attempts by the giants to abduct her. In Teutonic mythology, she was fused with the goddess FRIGG. Friday is named for her.

Freyre, Gilberto   [fray'-ruh, jeel-bair'-too]

Gilberto Freyre, b. Mar. 15, 1900, d. July 18, 1987, pioneered sociological studies in his native Brazil. His most famous work, *The Masters and the Slaves* (1933; Eng. trans., 1946), examined the relationships of Brazil's Portuguese colonizers and their African slaves. It inspired other studies of African contributions to Brazilian society. Also well known among his 120 books is *The Mansions and the Shanties* (1936; Eng. trans. 1963), which examines the rise of urbanization in 19th-century Brazil and the decline of the rural social structure.

Freytag, Gustav   [fry'-tahk, goo'-stahf]

Gustav Freytag, b. July 13, 1816, d. Apr. 30, 1895, was a German novelist and dramatist who praised the ability of the German bourgeoisie to educate and civilize the German people. He believed that Germany needed unification and played a significant role in that movement. A realist and champion of the well-made play, he had little sympathy with romanticism. Freytag was influenced by Dickens, and realism became a chief characteristic of his own novels, in particular *Debit and Credit* (1855; Eng. trans., 1857). He wrote one of the most famous German comedies, *The Journalists* (1854; Eng. trans., 1913), as well as the extremely influential study *Technique of the Drama* (1863; Eng. trans., 1968).   CARL R. MUELLER

Frick, Ford

Although Ford Christopher Frick, b. Wawaka, Ind., Dec. 19, 1894, d. Apr. 8, 1978, was a sportswriter who never played professional baseball, he served as president of the National League for 17 years and as commissioner of baseball from 1951 to 1965. As president of the league he vigorously supported Jackie Robinson's entrance (1947) as the first black player in the major leagues and was instrumental in the formation (1936) of the Baseball Hall of Fame. As commissioner, Frick aided in the inception of national television coverage.

Frick, Henry Clay

Henry Clay Frick, an American industrialist and philanthropist, managed (1889–1900) and expanded the Carnegie Steel Company and served as director of the U.S. Steel Corporation. Under his guidance, the Carnegie company developed into the world's largest producer of steel at the time. His art collection, bequeathed to the public, is housed in his New York residence.

Henry Clay Frick, b. West Overton, Pa., Dec. 18, 1849, d. Dec. 2, 1919, was an industrialist and philanthropist. As head of a company that supplied coke to the steel mills of Pittsburgh, Pa., he became a millionaire at the age of 30. In 1889, Andrew Carnegie made him chairman of his steel company. While attempting to break the 1892 HOMESTEAD STRIKE at Carnegie's Homestead, Pa., plant, Frick was shot and stabbed by Alexander Berkman, an anarchist. Frick participated in the formation (1901) of J. P. Morgan's U.S. Steel Corporation, of which he became a director. Over the years he amassed a valuable art collection (later known as the Frick Collection) that he bequeathed to New York City. He also gave sums to hospitals, educational institutions, and the city of Pittsburgh.

Bibliography: Harvey, G. B. M., *Henry Clay Frick, the Man* (1928).

Frick Collection

The Frick Collection is an art museum housed in the New York City residence of the industrialist Henry Clay Frick. In 1919, Frick placed the house and works of art in the care of a board of trustees, who have since added to the original holdings through an endowment provided by the founder. The building, designed by Thomas Hastings of the firm of Carrère and Hastings, was erected in 1913–14 and opened as a museum in 1935. The collection is celebrated for the extremely high quality of its holdings, for their fine state of preservation, and for their integrated display in a residential setting.

Among the most celebrated treasures of the collection, which spans the history of Western art from the 14th to the 19th century, are François Boucher's two groups of paintings executed for Madame de Pompadour, *The Arts and Sciences* and *The Seasons*. These masterpieces of French 18th-century painting are complemented by Jean Honoré Fragonard's four large canvases *The Progress of Love* (1773), commissioned by Madame du Barry. The collection also contains fine examples of 17th-century Dutch paintings including several works by Jan Vermeer and Rembrandt.   ALDEN R. GORDON

Bibliography: *The Frick Collection: An Illustrated Catalogue*, 9 vols. (1968–); Munhall, Edgar, *Masterpieces of the Frick Collection* (1970).

friction

Friction is the universal force between surfaces that opposes sliding motion. When surfaces of two bodies are in contact, the interactive force at the surface may have components both perpendicular and tangent to the surface. The perpendicular component is called the normal force, and the tangential component is called the friction force. If there is relative sliding at the surface, the friction force always acts in the opposite direction of this motion.

Most dry surfaces behave approximately according to Coulomb's friction law, which states that when the surfaces slide relative to one another, the friction force is proportional to the normal force and is independent of both the contact area and the speed of sliding. The ratio of the tangential force to the normal force during sliding is called the coefficient of friction and depends on the nature of the two surfaces.

In order to initiate sliding against friction, it is necessary to apply a tangential force at least as great as the product of the coefficient of friction and the normal force. Before the onset of motion, the force is resisted by the equal and opposite force of static friction. The force required to overcome static friction is usually greater than the force needed to sustain uniform sliding motion.

Friction is essential for the success of many operations, such as tires gripping roadways, the driving of pulleys and belts, and even walking. It is the lack of significant friction that makes walking on ice difficult. In many machine parts friction is undesirable, causing wear and unwanted heat and requiring additional power.   CHARLES E. SMITH

Bibliography: Resnick, Robert, and Halliday, David, *Fundamentals of Physics,* 2d rev. ed. (1988).

Friday: see CALENDAR.

Friedan, Betty   [free-dan']

Betty Friedan's best-selling book, The Feminine Mystique (1963), was instrumental in reviving the women's movement in the United States. Friedan, a psychologist and political activist, helped found (1966) the National Organization for Women and in 1970 was an organizer of the Women's Strike for Equality.

Photo Jill Krementz © 1976

Betty Friedan, b. Feb. 4, 1921, an American writer who was trained as a psychologist, became the "founding mother" of contemporary feminism in the United States after publishing The FEMININE MYSTIQUE (1963). In this influential work, she isolated the "housewife syndrome" and stated that—contrary to what psychiatrists, sociologists, and advertisers maintained—women must have opportunities for fulfillment beyond those provided by marriage and motherhood. She has campaigned for reforms that would end both subtle and overt discrimination against women. In 1966, Friedan helped found the National Organization for Women (NOW) and since then has been active in the formation of other feminist groups. Her book *It Changed My Life* (1976) is an account of her years in the women's movement. *Second Stage* (1981; rev. ed., 1986) represents a major shift in Friedan's thinking. She now emphasizes the importance of the family and the necessity for male participation in feminist movements.

Friedel, Georges   [free-del']

Georges Friedel, b. July 19, 1865, d. Dec. 11, 1933, was a French crystallographer and mineralogist. He was the son of chemist Charles Friedel (1832–99) and the grandson of Georges Duvernoy, a coworker of Baron Cuvier. His work

dealt not only with crystallography and mineralogy but also with petrology, geology, engineering, and pedagogy. He synthesized minerals, established through observation Auguste Bravais's theory that the external appearance of crystals was a reflection of their internal atomic structure and proposed that 11 types of crystal symmetry could be distinguished. He also studied liquid crystals (1907–31) and proposed a theory of crystal growth (1924–27).   GEORGE B. KAUFFMAN

Friedlaender, Walter   [freed'-len-dur]

Educator and art historian Walter Ferdinand Friedlaender, b. Mar. 10, 1873, d. Sept. 6, 1966, studied art history in Germany, where he taught at the University of Freiburg from 1914 until his retirement in 1933. In 1935, after his expulsion from Germany, he was appointed professor at New York University, where he remained until his death. He wrote about many aspects of the history of art, including early 19th-century French painting. He is best remembered for his pioneering work on Italian Mannerism and for his studies and catalog of the work of Nicolas Poussin.   JACQUELINE V. FALKENHEIM

Friedländer, Max J.   [freet'-len-dur]

German art historian Max Julius Friedländer, b. June 5, 1867, d. Oct. 11, 1958, was director of the Kaiser-Friedrich Museum in Berlin from 1924 to 1933. In 1938 he fled Germany and settled in Amsterdam, where he remained until his death. His main field of study was German and Netherlandish painting, and as a connoisseur he invoked a keen sensibility and strong powers of observation to bring a new order and accessibility to this art. His writings, including *On Art and Connoisseurship* (Eng. trans., 1942) and *Reminiscences and Reflections* (Eng. trans., 1969), demonstrate his interest both in historical documentation and in the more subjective aspects of critical judgment about art.   JACQUELINE V. FALKENHEIM

Friedman, Bruce Jay   [freed'-muhn]

The many black-humorous works of author Bruce Jay Friedman, b. the Bronx, N.Y., Apr. 26, 1930, often feature guilt-ridden Jewish characters searching for anxiety-free havens in the American mainstream. From his first novel (*Stern*, 1962) Friedman has consistently found readers for his books, as well as audiences for his plays—notably, *Scuba Duba* (1967)—and for screenplays such as *Splash!* (1984).   MELVIN J. FRIEDMAN

Bibliography: Schulz, Max F., *Bruce Jay Friedman* (1974).

Friedman, Herbert

The American astrophysicist Herbert Friedman, b. New York City, June 21, 1916, pioneered in the field of X-RAY ASTRONOMY at the Naval Research Laboratory in Washington, D.C. Using instruments carried by a V-2 rocket, Friedman demonstrated in 1949 that the Sun is a source of X rays. He headed (1960) the team that took the first X-ray photograph of the Sun from an Aerobee rocket, and also supervised (1961) a study of the Sun's ultraviolet spectrum. In 1969, Friedman and his colleagues discovered that the Crab Nebula is also an X-ray pulsar. His autobiography, *Astronomer's Universe,* was published in 1990.   STEVEN J. DICK

Friedman, Milton

The economist Milton Friedman, b. Brooklyn, N.Y., July 31, 1912, is the leading exponent of the conservative, free-enterprise point of view in modern economics identified with the University of Chicago. His practical proposals are often radical in their implications. Friedman's MONETARY POLICY approach to economics offers a major alternative to the FISCAL POLICY of the Keynesians. Friedman's ideas have had a profound impact on economic policy in the United States and elsewhere; they won him the 1976 Nobel Prize for economics.

In *A Monetary History of the United States, 1867–1960* (1963), written with Anna J. Schwartz, and in other works, Friedman argues that John Maynard KEYNES incorrectly mini-

Milton Friedman is America's foremost conservative economist. An opponent of Keynesian economics, he has argued for limiting federal manipulation of the money supply and has advocated the elimination of price supports and protective tariffs. Friedman, a professor of economics at the University of Chicago, won the Nobel Prize for economic science in 1976. Among his recent books is Monetarist Economics (1990).

In The Polar Sea (1824), the 19th-century German romantic landscape painter Caspar David Friedrich reconstructed an actual episode in an Arctic expedition: a wrecked ship crushed by mountainous slabs of ice, trapped forever in a grim, frozen world. (Kunsthalle, Hamburg.)

mized the role of money and greatly exaggerated the efficacy of government taxing and spending policies in determining the level of national income (see INCOME, NATIONAL) and EMPLOYMENT. According to monetarist theory, the level of economic activity is largely determined by the quantity of money in the system. The best general policy for the central bank is to promote a gradual, regular increase in the money supply; sudden, discretionary changes in policy are to be avoided.

Another of Friedman's important contributions is his argument for a negative income tax in *Capitalism and Freedom* (1962). The negative income tax plan would limit the administrative role of government. Payments to the poor would be made automatically when their incomes fell below a certain level.

Friedman served as a professor of economics at the University of Chicago from 1946 to 1982. He is a fellow at Stanford University's Hoover Institution.   RICHARD T. GILL

Bibliography: Butler, E., *Milton Friedman* (1985); Frazer, W., *Power and Ideas*, 2 vols. (1988); Leube, K. R., ed., *The Essence of Friedman* (1987); Silk, Leonard, *Economists* (1976).

Friedrich, Carl J.   [freed'-rik]

The German-American political scientist Carl Joachim Friedrich, b. Leipzig, Germany, June 5, 1901, d. Sept. 19, 1984, taught political science and government at Harvard University from 1926 to 1971 and became well known for his work in the fields of constitutional government, federalism, and totalitarianism. From 1946 to 1949, Friedrich was governmental affairs advisor to the Allied Military Government in Germany. In that capacity he helped frame West Germany's constitution of 1949.

In 1937, Friedrich published his pioneering study of the development and functioning of modern constitutional government, *Constitutional Government and Politics*, which served as a textbook for a generation of political scientists. His other works include *Totalitarian Dictatorship and Autocracy* (1956, with Zbigniew Brzezinski), *The Philosophy of Law in Historical Perspective* (1958), *Man and His Government* (1963), *An Introduction to Political Theory; Twelve Lectures at Harvard* (1967), *Trends of Federalism: Theory and Practice* (1968), *Totalitarianism in Perspective: Three Views* (1969, with Michael Curtis and Benjamin R. Barber), and *Limited Government: A Comparison* (1974).

Friedrich, Caspar David

The German romantic painter Caspar David Friedrich, b. Sept. 5, 1774, d. May 7, 1840, was one of the greatest exponents in European art of the symbolic landscape. He studied at the Academy in Copenhagen (1794–98) and subsequently settled in Dresden, often traveling to other parts of Germany. Friedrich's landscapes are based entirely on those of northern Germany and are beautiful renderings of trees, hills, harbors,

morning mists, and other light effects based on a close observation of nature.

Some of Friedrich's best-known paintings are expressions of a religious mysticism. In 1808 he exhibited one of his most controversial paintings, *The Cross in the Mountains* (Gemäldegalerie, Dresden), in which—for the first time in Christian art—an altarpiece was conceived in terms of a pure landscape. The cross, viewed obliquely from behind, is an insignificant element in the composition. More important are the dominant rays of the evening sun, which the artist said depicted the setting of the old, pre-Christian world. The mountain symbolizes an immovable faith, while the fir trees are an allegory of hope. Friedrich painted several other important compositions in which crosses dominate a landscape.

Even some of Friedrich's apparently nonsymbolic paintings contain inner meanings, clues to which are provided either by the artist's writings or those of his literary friends. For example, a landscape showing a ruined abbey in the snow, *Abbey with Oak Trees* (1810; Schloss Charlottenburg, Berlin), can be appreciated on one level as a bleak, winter scene, but the painter also intended the composition to represent both the church shaken by the Reformation and the transitoriness of earthly things.   DAVID IRWIN

Bibliography: Borsch-Supan, H., *Caspar David Friedrich*, rev. ed. (1987); Guilland, J. and M., *Caspar David Friedrich* (1989).

Friel, Brian

Bernard Patrick "Brian" Friel, b. Northern Ireland, Jan. 9, 1929, is a prominent Irish dramatist whose most successful plays—pungent and evocative portrayals of Irish life and Irish history—include *Philadelphia, Here I Come!* (1964), *The Freedom of the City* (1972), and *Dancing at Lughnasa* (1990). Friel is also a noted short-story writer whose work can be sampled in such collections as *The Diviner* (1983).

Friends, Society of

The Society of Friends, commonly called Quakers, is a body of Christians that originated in 17th-century England under George Fox. In 1988 the society had 200,260 members, with heavy concentrations in the United States (about 109,000), East Africa (45,000), and Great Britain (18,000). Quakers unite in affirming the immediacy of Christ's teaching; they hold that believers receive divine guidance from an inward light, without the aid of intermediaries or external rites. Meetings for worship can be silent, without ritual or professional clergy, or programmed, in which a minister officiates.

Although their antecedents lie in English PURITANISM and in the ANABAPTIST movement, the Society of Friends was formed during the English Civil War. Around 1652, George Fox began preaching that since there was "that of God in every man," a formal church structure and educated ministry were unnecessary. His first converts spread their faith throughout England, denouncing what they saw as social and spiritual compromises and calling individuals to an inward experience of God. In spite of schism and persecution, the new movement expanded during the Puritan Commonwealth (1649–60) and after the restoration of the monarchy (1660). By openly defying restrictive legislation, Friends helped achieve passage of the Toleration Act of 1689.

In colonial America, enclaves of Quakers existed in Rhode Island, North Carolina, Pennsylvania, and western New Jersey. In Pennsylvania, founded by William PENN as a refuge for Quakers and as a ''holy experiment'' in religious toleration, Friends maintained an absolute majority in the assembly until 1755 and remained a potent force until the American Revolution. Between 1754 and 1776, Friends throughout America strengthened their commitment to pacifism and began to denounce slavery. After the Revolution, Friends concentrated on a wide variety of reform activities: Indian rights, prison reform, temperance, abolition, freedmen's rights, education, and the women's movement.

In a conflict over theology that was complicated by social tensions, the Society underwent a series of schisms beginning in 1827 and ending with the formation of three major subgroups: Hicksites (liberal), Orthodox (evangelical), and Conservative (quietist). During the 20th century, however, Friends have attempted to heal their differences. Many yearly meetings have merged, and most Friends cooperate in organizations such as the Friends World Committee for Consultation and the Friends World Conferences. The rapid growth of pastoral Quakerism in Africa and of silent meetings in Europe makes the Society of Friends an international organization.

The AMERICAN FRIENDS SERVICE COMMITTEE (AFSC) is an independent service organization founded in 1917 to aid conscientious objectors. Today it also provides help to the needy in the United States and a number of Third World countries.

J. WILLIAM FROST

Bibliography: Barbour, H., and Frost, J. W., *The Quakers* (1988); Hamm, T. D., *The Transformation of American Quakerism: Orthodox Friends, 1800–1907* (1988); Russell, E., *The History of Quakerism* (1942; repr. 1980).

Friese-Greene, William   [frees'-green]

William Friese-Greene, b. Bristol, England, Sept. 7, 1855, d. May 5, 1921, a British photographer and inventor, was a pioneer in cinematography. With the civil engineer Mortimer Evans, he designed and patented (1890) an ''improved apparatus for taking photographs in rapid series,'' which some authorities consider the first motion-picture camera. Friese-Greene also designed nonphotographic devices and in 1905 patented a two-color method of cinematography. His work was the subject of the film *The Magic Box* (1952).

Bibliography: Allister, Ray, *Friese-Greene: Close-Up of an Inventor* (1948; repr. 1972).

frieze   [freez]

The frieze is the center section of the ENTABLATURE, the structure supported by the COLONNADE of a classically styled building. The three sections that compose the entablature are the CORNICE, frieze, and architrave. The style of the frieze is determined by the style of the entablature (Ionic, Doric, Corinthian or other), and it often contains a decorative relief (see BAS-RELIEF). Interior architectural spaces may contain a different type of frieze. For example, the space between the ceiling or cornice and the paneling in a paneled room is called a frieze, and so is the space below the ceiling or cornice and above the picture railing in a painted or wallpapered room.

frigate   [frig'-uht]

The ultimate derivation of the word *frigate* is unknown, but in 16th-century usage the equivalent term in the major Mediterranean languages indicated a small, fast, oared warship with sails for extended cruising. The generic meaning, a swift warship used for reconnaissance and for raiding, survived and was applied to a specific class of warship in the 18th and ear-

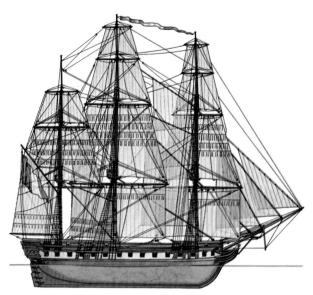

Frigates, such as this French man-of-war (c.1800), were fast, three-masted warships second in size only to ships of the line. Their speed, maneuverability, and relatively heavy armament made them ideal for conducting raids and escorting vulnerable merchant fleets.

ly 19th centuries: the largest class of warship below the ship of the line. It was a three-masted, square-rigged vessel with 24 to 50 guns on two decks (one covered). Frigates could usually outrun whatever ships they could not outfight and outfight the ships they could not outrun. During World War II the term *frigate* was extended to mean an antisubmarine escort vessel intermediate in size between a destroyer and a corvette. The term is used in this sense today, although no clear-cut criteria of size apply.

JOHN F. GUILMARTIN

See also: NAVAL VESSELS; SHIP.

frigate bird

Frigate bird is the common name for birds of the family Fregatidae, which reside in the tropics and subtropics. Their long, pointed wings, which have more surface area per unit

The frigate bird, F. magnificens, the largest species of the family, lives along the coasts of tropical America. The female (left) is white breasted and is usually larger than the male. During courtship, the male inflates a brilliant red throat patch.

of body weight than those of any other bird, give them a unique lightness and grace in flight. Although they are water birds, they seem never voluntarily to enter water, swooping or hovering to take food from the surface of the sea and sometimes robbing other birds. Frigate birds are large (79–104 cm/ 31–41 in) and mostly dark colored and have long, hook-tipped bills and deeply forked tails. In the male, the bare throat becomes greatly inflated during the breeding-season display. The magnificent frigate bird, *Fregata magnificens,* breeds in the American tropics, but it regularly wanders north to Florida and the Gulf Coast and, on occasion, strays far to the north of its normal range.   WILLIAM F. SANDFORD

Frigg

In Scandinavian mythology, Frigg was the supreme goddess and the principal wife of ODIN. She was goddess of the sky and, like the Greek Hera and the Roman Juno, presided over marriage. The myths portray her as very wise and very silent. In Teutonic mythology she was fused with the goddess FREYA.

frigidity

Frigidity is an obsolete term for several forms of sexual dysfunction in women that preclude sexual gratification through intercourse. An imprecise term, it has been used to refer both to a total absence of sexual desire and to difficulties in experiencing orgasm during sex. Mental health professionals stopped using the term because of its imprecision and because it was felt to be derogatory to women.

Preferred alternatives to the term *frigidity* include: hypoactive sexual disorder—a lack of desire for sex; female sexual arousal disorder—a lack of physical arousal during sex; and inhibited female orgasm—persistent delay or lack of orgasm during sex.

See also: IMPOTENCE.

Friml, Rudolf   [frim-ul]

Rudolf Friml, b. Prague, Dec. 7, 1879, d. Nov. 12, 1972, was an American composer of operettas. He was best known for *The Firefly, Rose Marie, The Vagabond King,* and *The Three Musketeers.* From these came such songs as "Indian Love Call." His success on the musical stage was repeated on a greater scale with the advent of sound movies and with the performances of Jeanette MacDonald and Nelson Eddy in film versions of his operettas.   DAVID EWEN

fringe tree

The fringe tree is a deciduous tree or large shrub 6–9 m (20–30 ft) tall that belongs to the olive family, *Oleaceae.* Found in sunny locations along stream banks and borders of swamps, it is also cultivated as an ornamental for its drooping clusters of white, fragrant flowers. *Chionanthus virginica* grows from New Jersey to Florida and westward throughout the Southern Ohio River valley to Missouri, Oklahoma, and eastern Texas. *C. retusus* is a smaller species that grows in parts of China.

Frisbee

A Frisbee (trademark of the Wham-O Corp.) is a circular plastic disk used for a variety of athletic, usually informal recreational activities involving tossing and catching. Emerging during the mid-1950s in the United States, the pastime is now one of the most popular forms of U.S. athletic activity: it is estimated that more Frisbees are sold each year than baseballs, basketballs, and footballs combined. There are local, state, national, and international competitions.

Frisch, Karl von   [frish]

The Austrian zoologist Karl von Frisch, b. Nov. 20, 1886, d. June 12, 1982, contributed greatly to early studies of ANIMAL BEHAVIOR with his research on direction finding and communication among bees. He found that bees can infer the position of the Sun from polarized light and that they use special "waggle" dances to inform other members of the hive of the direc-

tion and distance of a food source. He also found, in earlier work, that fish can discriminate colors. He and two other pioneer researchers in animal behavior, Konrad Lorenz and Nikolaas Tinbergen, shared the 1973 Nobel Prize for physiology or medicine. His writings included *The Dancing Bees* (Eng. trans., 1955) and the autobiographical *A Biologist Remembers* (Eng. trans., 1967).   BARBARA TCHABOVSKY

Frisch, Max

The Swiss dramatist and novelist Max Rudolf Frisch, b. May 15, 1911, d. Apr. 4, 1991, was noted for plays that offer a grimly pessimistic view of modern society. In 1933, Frisch withdrew from the University of Zurich to become a journalist. After traveling in Europe he returned to Zurich in 1936, becoming an architect in 1941. Frisch began to write journals, semiautobiographical novels, and plays while employed as a journalist. His first successful play, *Santa Cruz* (1944), took up a theme that was to prove central to his work: the shaping of individual destiny and behavior by social pressures. In Frisch's work people are controlled by the course of history, of which they are merely an inconsequential fragment. Frisch's friendship with Bertolt Brecht profoundly influenced his dramatic technique of surrealistic fable, effectively used in his play *The Chinese Wall* (1946; Eng. trans., 1961).

Frisch's disturbing conception of Western society was fully realized in his two best-known plays, *The Firebugs* (1958; Eng. trans., 1963) and *Andorra* (1961; Eng. trans., 1962). In *The Firebugs,* the respectable but unknowing Biedermann offers shelter to two arsonists; he is prevented by cowardice from acting on his convictions and gives his guests the matches with which they destroy him and his society. The play points to the failure of European society to prevent the rise of Nazism and other totalitarian creeds but suggests that the basis of political failure is individual weakness. Frisch's moral concerns continued in such novels as *Montauk* (1975; Eng. trans., 1976) and *Man in Holocene* (1979; Eng. trans, 1980). A trio of one-act plays, *Triptych* (1981; Eng. trans., 1981) is an examination of death as it relates to the living.   JACK ZIPES

Bibliography: Butler, M., *The Novels of Max Frisch* (1976) and *The Plays of Max Frisch* (1985); Kieser, R., ed., *Max Frisch: Novels, Plays, and Essays* (1989); Peterson, Carol, *Max Frisch* (1972); Probst, G., and Bodine, J., eds., *Perspectives on Max Frisch* (1982).

Frisch, Ragnar

Ragnar Frisch, b. Mar. 3, 1895, d. Jan. 31, 1973, was a Norwegian economist who, in 1969, shared the first Nobel Prize for economics with Jan Tinbergen of the Netherlands. Frisch used mathematics and statistics to construct economic models that could predict changes in the economy, a study known as ECONOMETRICS. A prolific writer, he served as an advisor to developing countries such as Egypt and India.

Frisian Islands   [frizh'-uhn]

The Frisian Islands are a chain of low-lying islands off the coasts of the Netherlands, Germany, and Denmark, in the North Sea. They are separated from the European mainland by a narrow, shallow channel ranging from 5 to 32 km (3 to 20 mi) in width. The islands are divided into the West Frisians, belonging to the Netherlands and consisting of five main, inhabited islands and other uninhabited ones; the East Frisians, belonging to Germany; and the North Frisians, which are divided between Germany and Denmark.

The parent countries have carried out extensive land reclamation programs to increase the potential farming areas of the islands. In addition to the growing of rye, oats, and potatoes, fishing and the raising of sheep and cattle are the main industries. The islands' beaches attract tourists in the summer.

Frisian language: see GERMANIC LANGUAGES.

Frith, Francis

The British photographer and publisher Francis Frith, 1822–98, was known for his views of the Near East and Europe. In

1856–60 he made three trips to the Holy Land, using photographic plates up to 16 × 20 in. (40.64 × 50.80 cm) in size. The photographs were published in such volumes as *Sinai, Palestine, Egypt, and Ethiopia* (1862). F. Frith and Co. later became famous for its photographs of British and European scenes mass-produced for popular sale.   KEITH F. DAVIS

Bibliography: Gernsheim, Helmut, *A Concise History of Photography,* 3d rev. ed. (1986).

Frith, William

The English painter William Powell Frith, b. Jan. 9, 1819, d. Nov. 2, 1909, became famous for his scenes of Victorian life. He studied at Sass's Academy and the Royal Academy schools and began painting sentimental scenes from history and literature, which were well received. He was made an associate of the Royal Academy in 1845 and a full academician in 1852. Because of his "appreciation of the infinite variety of everyday life," he turned to realistic scenes of modern life on a large scale. His *Ramsgate Sands* (Royal Collection) was exhibited at the Royal Academy in 1854 and was bought by Queen Victoria. He continued in this successful vein with *Derby Day* (1858; Tate Gallery, London), *The Railway Station* (1862; Royal Holloway College, Egham), and *Private View Day at the Royal Academy* (1883). All are marked by a careful attention to detail, for which he used photographs, and a multiplicity of incident, humorous and moralizing. They also provided a popular and immensely successful mirror image for a self-confident Victorian era.   MALCOLM CORMACK

Bibliography: Frith, William P., *My Autobiography and Reminiscences,* 3 vols., 3d ed. (1887); Staley, A., *A Victorian Canvas* (1957); Wood, Christopher, *Dictionary of Victorian Painters,* 2d ed. (1978).

fritillary   [frit-i-lair'-ee]

Fritillary is the common name of any member of the genus *Fritillaria,* comprising close to 100 species of bulbous perennial herbs in the lily family, Liliaceae. Checkered lily, *F. meleagris,* is strikingly beautiful. Its leaves are few and alternate, and the flowers, usually solitary, are bell-shaped and nodding; perianth segments are checkered with reddish purple squares. Fritillaries are found in damp meadows. Their bulbs are poisonous.   K. B. PAUL

Friuli-Venezia Giulia   [free-oo'-lee-vay-net'-see-uh jool'-yah]

Friuli-Venezia Giulia is a region in northeastern Italy, bordered by the Austrian Alps on the north, Yugoslavia on the east, and the Adriatic Sea on the south. It has a population of 1,210,242 (1988 est.) and an area of 7,846 km² (3,029 mi²). TRIESTE is the capital city, principal port, and commercial center. Grain is grown on the coastal plain and in the Tagliamento River valley. Forestry and stock raising are the major occupations in the north, where the land rises to elevations of more than 2,700 m (9,000 ft). Undine, Gorizia, Monfalcone, and Pordenone are industrial centers.

Once part of the Roman Julian region, Friuli-Venezia Giulia was subsequently controlled by the Byzantines. Venice and Austria shared control of the area from the 15th century to 1815, when the entire region came under Austria. Italy took most of the area in 1866, although after World War II Trieste passed to Yugoslavia. In 1954 the city was returned to Italy, and in 1963 the region was given limited autonomy.

Frobenius, Ferdinand Georg   [froh-bay'-nee-us]

Ferdinand Georg Frobenius, b. Oct. 26, 1849, d. Aug. 3, 1917, was a German mathematician best known for his work in group theory. He received his doctorate from the University of Berlin in 1870. In 1892, after having taught elsewhere, he returned to Berlin to become professor of mathematics. In his work in group theory, Frobenius combined results from the theory of algebraic equations, geometry, and number theory, which led him to the study of abstract groups. His representation theory for finite groups later found important applications in quantum mechanics.   J. W. DAUBEN

Froberger, Johann Jacob   [froh'-bur-gur]

Johann Jacob Froberger, b. May 19, 1616, d. May 6 or 7, 1667, was a composer for the keyboard who was influential in the development of middle and late Baroque music. Little is known about his training except that he was a student of Frescobaldi in Rome from 1637 to 1641. Through extensive travel, Froberger came in contact with all the musical styles of Europe. He fused these styles, especially the French, Italian, and German ones, into a more modern, pan-European style that influenced later composers such as Buxtehude and J. S. Bach. Froberger's dance suites in particular foreshadow the suites of Bach. Other than two vocal works, his compositions consist of fantasias, toccatas, canzonas, capriccios, ricercares, partitas, and suites—all of them for the keyboard.   WILLIAM HAYS

Bibliography: Bukofzer, Manfred, *Music in the Baroque Era* (1947).

Frobisher, Sir Martin   [froh'-bish-ur]

Martin Frobisher, b. *c.*1539, was a well-known Elizabethan navigator and explorer. Raised in London by his mother's brother, Sir John York, he made two voyages to Africa as a youth. At one point he was captured by the Portuguese, and he later spent some years as a pirate. Becoming convinced of the existence of a NORTHWEST PASSAGE, he secured substantial support for three voyages in search of it.

On the first voyage in 1576, Frobisher found an inlet in Baffin Island, now known as Frobisher Bay, that he believed to be the Northwest Passage. He returned with an Eskimo and also brought back ore that was mistakenly identified as gold. The latter attracted many investors to the Company of Cathay, organized by Frobisher's partner, Michael Lok. A second voyage in 1577 and a third in 1578 found no gold, but in July 1578, Frobisher sailed up what he called the "Mistaken Strait," later named Hudson Strait.

After the collapse of Lok's company Frobisher had various commands, including that of vice-admiral in Sir Francis Drake's 1585–86 expedition to the West Indies. He served honorably in the defense against the Spanish Armada in 1588 and was knighted. Wounded fighting the Spanish on the coast of France, he died on Nov. 22, 1594.   BRUCE B. SOLNICK

Bibliography: Best, George, *The Three Voyages of Martin Frobisher,* ed. by Vilhjalmur Stefansson, 2 vols. (1938); Kenyon, W. A., *Tokens of Possession: The Northern Voyages of Martin Frobisher* (1975); McFee, William, *Life of Sir Martin Frobisher* (1928).

Fröding, Gustaf   [frur'-ding, gus'-tahf]

Gustaf Fröding, b. Aug. 22, 1860, d. Feb. 8, 1911, was a Swedish poet and journalist who displayed a mastery of the Swedish language in his lyrical and religious verse. He worked as a journalist before publishing the poetry collection *Guitar and Concertina* (1891; Eng. trans., 1925), which comprised nature poems and meditations. *New Poems* (1894; Eng. trans., 1896) and *Stänk och flikar* (Shreds and Patches, 1896) followed. Later works reflect the increasingly serious mental instability from which Fröding suffered most of his life.

Froebel, Friedrich Wilhelm August   [frur'-bul, freed'-rik vil'-helm ow'-gust]

Friedrich Wilhelm August Froebel, b. Apr. 21, 1782, d. June 21, 1852, was a German educator who created and developed the kindergarten. Froebel's educational philosophy and practice was based on his belief in the unity of the universe. Influenced by the Swiss educator Johann Pestalozzi, he viewed infant education as the basis of educational reform. He opened his first kindergarten (1841) and attracted ardent disciples, who helped spread his idea. His major educational work, *The Education of Man* (1826), outlined his philosophy. The purpose of education, he believed, is to help children understand the universal law of divine unity that permeates all life. Froebel's notion of the oneness of life led him to advocate the development of cooperation rather than competition in education, manual training to unite hand and brain, a thorough study of nature, and the use of play as an aid to the harmonious expression of all human faculties. His work was a major inspiration for child-centered PROGRESSIVE EDUCATION.

PAUL NASH

Bibliography: Lawrence, Evelyn, ed., *Friedrich Froebel and English Education* (1953); Lilley, Irene, ed., *Friedrich Froebel: A Selection from His Writings* (1967); Shapiro, Michael S., *Child's Garden: The Kindergarten Movement from Froebel to Dewey* (1983).

See also: EDUCATION; PRESCHOOL EDUCATION.

frog

The typical frog has long hind legs, a large head, a short body, and no tail; it may live entirely in water or may spend much of its life on land. Frogs are found on every continent except Antarctica. They are thought to have evolved from a tailed, four-limbed, amphibious ancestor; their means of locomotion has changed since the time of that ancestor as a result of the loss of the tail, reduction in the number of trunk vertebrae, and lengthening of the hind legs and feet. Their feeding system has also altered, either because the use of the tongue was virtually abandoned or, conversely, because its prey-catching use was stressed. Frogs have adapted to a great variety of ecological situations.

CLASSIFICATION

The classification of frogs above the family level is currently debated. It is usually determined by characteristics of skeletal and muscular structures in larvae and adults, features of the frogs' life histories, and certain genetic and biochemical components. One current theory states that the Leiopelmatidae of New Zealand and the Ascaphidae of the Pacific Northwest are the most primitive living frogs. The Discoglossidae of Europe, Asia Minor, China, northwestern Africa, and the Philippines are also considered primitive.

The family Pipidae of South America and of Africa south of the Sahara is a highly specialized group; the African clawed toad, *Xenopus laevis*, is a member of this family. The southern Mexican Rhinophrynidae, with its single species, may be related to pipids. The Microhylidae of the Americas, Southeast Asia, and Africa constitute a separate group.

The Pelobatidae, spadefoot toads of Europe, North America, and Southeast Asia, are part of a large group of related families that includes the successful family Ranidae—the true frogs, such as the leopard frog and bullfrog. Ranids occur in North and South America, Europe, Asia, and northern Australia. Ranid relatives include the following: the Sooglossidae, two genera on the Seychelles Islands and Madagascar; the Hyperoliidae of Africa, Madagascar, and the Seychelles; and the Rhacophoridae of Africa and Southeast Asia.

The Bufonidae, or true toads, inhabit all landmasses except Australia, New Zealand, New Guinea, and Greenland. The Atelopodidae, Allophrynidae, and Brachycephalidae of Central and South America are closely related to bufonids. The Heleophrynidae of South America and the Myobatrachidae of Australia and New Guinea have affinities with the Leptodactylidae of the New World. Also related are the Hylidae, widespread only in the Americas but with one genus, *Hyla*, occurring nearly worldwide; the Pelodryadidae of Australia; the arrow poison frog, Dendrobatidae, and the green-boned frogs, Centrolenidae, of Central and South America; and the Pseudidae of South America. The status of the Rhinodermatidae of Chile is undecided.

HABITAT

Frogs live in diverse habitats. Pipid frogs and many other types spend their entire lives in ponds and streams in the tropics. Other species require only the moisture found on leaves or under rocks or logs to survive. Desert-dwelling spadefoot toads live buried in sand much of the year and emerge to breed only when it rains. They lay their eggs in puddles, and tadpole metamorphosis must be completed before the puddle dries up. Frogs are widely distributed from lowland tropics to high mountains and high latitudes and from very wet to seasonally dry habitats. Most frogs practice external fertilization in water—the female lays eggs and the male sheds sperm over them. After hatching, the tadpole lives in water, at least until it metamorphoses into adulthood. Only a few species lack the tadpole stage.

STRUCTURE AND FUNCTION

Frogs may be easily identified and classified into species by various external characteristics. These include the proportions of the head, body, and limbs; color patterns; placement of the tympanum, or eardrum; toe webbing and shape; and such ornamentation as cranial crests, the so-called claws, and skin structures. Features unique to frogs include their skeletal structure, their hearing systems (used to perceive the species-specific mating calls), tongue feeding, and modifications of the larynx and vocal sacs that serve to produce sound. Unlike adults, frog tadpoles have tails, respire through internal gills, have cartilaginous skeletons, lack teeth but have horny mouthparts, are limbless until late in development, are usually herbivorous, and have long, coiled intestines.

Frogs, like other amphibians, are cold-blooded (poikilothermic). Scientists formerly believed that these animals had to avoid excessive heat or cold to survive. Recent studies, however, have found that some frogs, like the wood frog *(Rana sylvatica)* and the spring peeper *(Hyla crucifer)* have a natural ability to survive cold temperatures for weeks with as much as 65 percent of their total body water as ice. When ice forms on the frog's skin, it triggers enzymes to convert glycogen to glucose in the liver. The glucose travels in the blood to the major organs where it protects them from freezing while ice fills up the frog's body cavities.

NATURAL HISTORY

The frog's life cycle is complex. Courtship in many species is highly stylized, involving specific calls or prescribed turns and positions before mating occurs. At one point in the ritual, the male clasps the female, and she extrudes her eggs; given this stimulus, he releases his sperm, shedding them over the eggs.

Some females lay several hundred eggs and abandon them. Other frog species lay fewer eggs and protect the developing young in a variety of ways. In the case of the marsupial frog, *Gastrotheca*, the young develop in a pouch in the skin of the back. Males of the species *Rhinoderma darwini* brood the young in their vocal sacs. Other means of reducing the number of young include direct development—laying eggs on land, which then develop through METAMORPHOSIS without the larval stage—and maternal retention of developing young. Direct development occurs among most species of the genus *Eleutherodactylus*. Frequently, only one parent protects the clutch while it develops. A few species retain developing young in their oviducts and give birth to metamorphosed froglets. The Australian *Rheobatrachus silus* broods its eggs in its stomach and coughs up metamorphosed froglets at birth.

In aquatic development, the tadpole's mouthparts develop at hatching, gills are covered by the operculum, and the tail structure is finned. Tadpoles are of different body shapes, depending on their habitat, and their mouthparts also vary. At metamorphosis, limbs develop, hindlegs first, the tail begins to resorb, the shape of the head changes, jaws modify, the intestine shortens, and a host of biochemical changes takes place. During metamorphosis the tadpole is vulnerable to predators, and it cannot feed while its body is reorganizing.

Vocalization in frogs occurs as inspired air is directed into the vocal sacs (pockets in the floor of the mouth) and forced through the larynx at various rates and frequencies. The inner ear of a frog that vocalizes has sensory cells that are specialized to perceive sound at specific frequencies.

The adaptation of long hind limbs has resulted in various locomotor patterns. Temperature, body weight, body proportions, and resistance of the medium all affect the method and rate of locomotion.

There are two types of feeding: tongueless and tongued. Tongueless aquatic species feed by gulping prey into their mouths; tongued forms extend the tongues to capture prey. The end of the tongue has glands that secrete a viscous material that holds the prey on contact. The tongue and prey are then withdrawn into the mouth.

IMPORTANCE OF FROGS

Frogs are significant predators in their ecosystems. Human actions have caused a reduction of numbers of some frogs, and

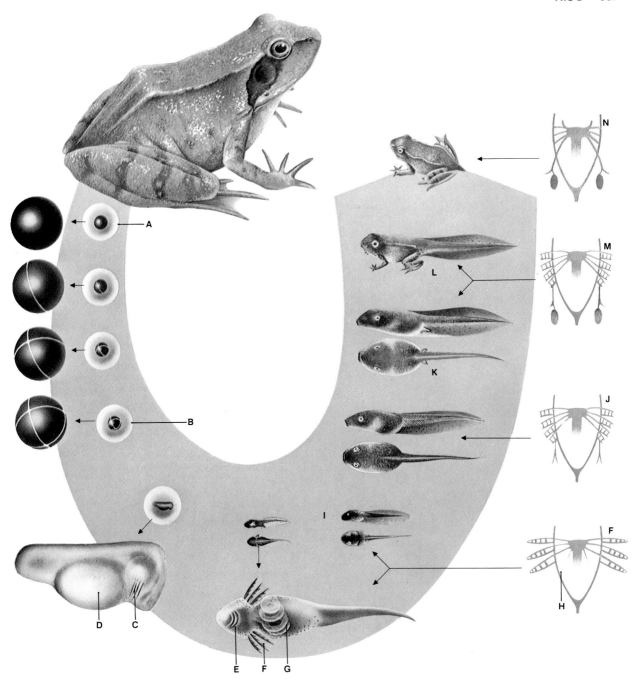

The common European frog, Rana temporaria, lays a mass of black eggs at the end of winter. They become surrounded by a protective jellylike material (A). Each egg cleaves into 2, 4, and 8 cells (B) and so on until a ball of cells forms as the embryo. At the tail-bud stage organs and gill arches (C) are present, and internal yolk (D) supplies nutrient. After 21 days the embryo wriggles out of its jelly capsule and attaches to a weed by its cement gland (E). External gills (F) with branches to (blue) and from (red) the circulatory system (H) supply the body with oxygen. After 4 days horny jaws (I) and a long-coiled intestine (G) equip the larvae for its diet of weeds. External gills are replaced by internal gills (J). Five weeks after hatching the hind limbs develop (K), followed by the forelimbs (L). The mouth widens, horny jaws disappear, lungs begin to develop (M), and about 11 weeks after spawning, the adult frog with fully developed lungs (N) leaves the water.

this has had a detrimental effect in many areas of North America and Europe. Nevertheless, frogs have continued to be in great demand as test animals for studies in biology. As certain frog populations of the United States have been depleted, African clawed frogs have been imported in increasing numbers. This has led to a further problem: when released in nature for breeding purposes, the African clawed frog competes with, and eclipses, the native fauna. This situation is currently un-der control, but the problem of supply of biological experimental material is not yet solved.   MARVALEE H. WAKE

Bibliography: Dickerson, Mary, The Frog Book (1969); Mattison, Chris, Frogs and Toads of the World (1987); Pyron, Jay, Complete Introduction to Frogs and Toads (1987); Storey, Kenneth B. and Janet M., "Frozen and Alive," Scientific American, December 1990; Underhill, Raymond A., Laboratory Anatomy of the Frog, 5th ed. (1988).

See also: AMPHIBIANS; FOSSIL RECORD.

frogfish

Frogfishes comprise about 9 genera and 60 species in the family Antennariidae, order Lophiiformes (see ANGLERFISH). They inhabit shallow tropical waters; some are found in drifting seaweed. Gaudily colored, frogfishes have elongate pectoral lobes, which cause them to crawl on the seafloor like a ponderous duck. The first dorsal fin spine is modified into a rod with a lure on the end for attracting prey.   CAMM SWIFT

frogman

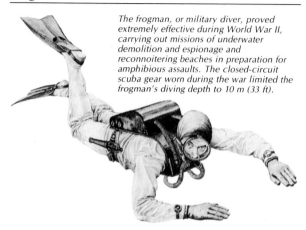

The frogman, or military diver, proved extremely effective during World War II, carrying out missions of underwater demolition and espionage and reconnoitering beaches in preparation for amphibious assaults. The closed-circuit scuba gear worn during the war limited the frogman's diving depth to 10 m (33 ft).

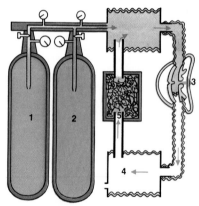

A frogman's scuba unit consists of oxygen (1) and nitrogen (2), mixed and inhaled at the mouthpiece (3). Exhaled gas is vented from an exhaust port (4). The telltale trail of air bubbles is eliminated by "gagging" the exhaust port. When this is done, exhaled gas circulates through a scrubber (5), which purifies the gas for rebreathing.

Frogmen are swimmers equipped for lengthy underwater activities. In the military they may be trained to penetrate hostile defenses underwater—typically for the purpose of gathering intelligence or covertly planting explosives.

The frogman's trademarks are a soft rubber mask with a large faceplate, a soft rubber diving suit for protection from cold, and long, flexible, swimming flippers for the feet. These, with SCUBA DIVING gear and its tanks of compressed breathing gases, waterproof watch, wrist compass, and diver's knife, constitute the essential equipment. The frogman may also carry a wide variety of specialized gear, such as magnetic limpet mines, mine detectors, covert signal lights, and radar or radio beacons.   JOHN F. GUILMARTIN, JR.

frogmouth

Frogmouths are short-legged, wide-mouthed, nocturnal birds constituting the family Podargidae. The 12 or 13 species grow to lengths of about 53 cm (21 in) and inhabit savanna, open woodland, or forest, from India and southeastern Asia into Indonesia and the Philippines. Frogmouths feed primarily on ground-dwelling insects. All species have soft, silky plumage in shades of brown, gray, and black. When disturbed by day,

the frogmouth assumes a position mimicking a broken branch. Frogmouths lay 1 to 2 eggs at a time.   JOSEPH R. JEHL

Frohman, Charles and Daniel   [froh'-muhn]

The theatrical manager Charles Frohman, b. Sandusky, Ohio, June 17, 1860, d. May 7, 1915, dominated the American theater of his time. After becoming an independent manager in 1883, he achieved his first real success in 1889 with the production of Bronson Howard's *Shenandoah,* which made his fortune. About the same time, Frohman, together with a number of others, launched a booking agency and formed the Theatrical Syndicate in 1896, which for years held a near monopoly over American theatrical bookings and tours. Frohman controlled many theaters, and his Empire theater productions, in particular, were among the best in the United States. He also managed successful productions in England. Frohman died at sea when the *Lusitania* was sunk.

His empire, valued at $5 million, was subsequently administered by his brother, Daniel Frohman, b. Sandusky, Ohio, Aug. 22, 1851, d. Dec. 26, 1940. Daniel became a theater manager in 1885 and organized a stock company. He also worked in films and was a founder and later managing director of the Famous Players-Lasky Film Company. He wrote two autobiographies, *Memories of a Manager* (1911) and *Daniel Frohman Presents* (1935).   MYRON MATLAW

Froissart, Jean   [fwah-sahr']

Jean Froissart, c.1337–c.1405, was a French historian and poet whose *Chronicles* provides a lively, if often biased, account of European affairs during the Hundred Years' War. He traveled widely in Europe and enjoyed the patronage of Queen Philippa of England, wife of Edward III, and several European noblemen. In his *Chronicles* (c.1369–1400), which covers events from 1325 to 1400, Froissart borrowed from the work of Jean Le Bel (c.1290–c.1370) for the period up to 1356; his account of subsequent events is based on eyewitness reports. Despite its many inaccuracies, the *Chronicles* remains a major source for the period and its concepts of chivalry. Froissart also wrote *Méliador,* a verse romance, and lyric poetry.

Bibliography: Coulton, George G., *The Chronicler of European Chivalry* (1930; repr. 1977); McGregor, Rob R., *The Lyric Poems of Jean Froissart* (1976); Palmer, J. J. N., et al., *Froissart* (1981).

Froment, Nicolas   [froh-mahn']

Nicolas Froment, c.1430–c.1485, a gifted French painter of the 15th-century school of Avignon, is known for two major altarpieces, *The Raising of Lazarus* (1461; Uffizi, Florence) and *The Burning Bush* (1476; Cathedral of Saint Sauveur, Aix-en-Provence, France). Froment's works reveal an awareness of the innovations of both the Italian Renaissance and the new Flemish realism. His concept of space, initially northern European in his detailed landscapes, seems later to have become more Tuscan, using an Italian style of perspective.

Bibliography: Chatelet, Albert, and Thuillier, Jacques, *French Painting from Fouquet to Poussin,* trans. by Stuart Gilbert (1963); Ring, Grete, *A Century of French Painting: 1400–1500* (1949).

Fromm, Erich   [frawm]

Erich Fromm, b. Frankfurt am Main, Germany, Mar. 23, 1900, d. Mar. 18, 1980, was a psychoanalyst, philosopher, and anthropologist. Fromm stressed the role of culture in the formation of personality; in this he parted company with traditional psychoanalysis. In industrial society, Fromm maintained, people have become estranged from themselves, and he proposed that society should fulfill human needs.

Fromm received his Ph.D. from the University of Heidelberg in 1922 and trained as a psychoanalyst at the Berlin Psychoanalytic Institute. In 1934 he moved from Nazi Germany to the United States, teaching at several schools before becoming (1951) professor of psychoanalysis at the National University of Mexico and later (1961) professor of psychiatry at New York University. Fromm's description of the authoritarian personality has become an important concept in the psychological study of personality. His wide range of works includes *Escape from Freedom* (1941), *Man for Himself* (1947), *Psychoanalysis and Religion* (1950), *The Sane Society* (1955), *The Art of Loving* (1956), *Social Character in a Mexican Village* (1970), and *The Anatomy of Human Destructiveness* (1973).

Bibliography: Evans, Richard I., *Dialogue with Erich Fromm* (1966; repr. 1981); Hausdorff, Don, *Erich Fromm* (1972); Knapp, Gerhard P., *The Art of Living: Erich Fromm's Life and Works* (1989).

Fronde [frohnd]

The Fronde (1648–53) was a series of major revolts in France during the minority of LOUIS XIV. They temporarily blocked the continuation by the regent ANNE OF AUSTRIA and her able but hated advisor, Cardinal MAZARIN, of the harsh policies of Louis XIII and Cardinal Richelieu. Merchants, artisans, and peasants disliked the spiraling taxation caused by the Thirty Years' War, the PARLEMENTS and taxing bureaus resented loss of their functions to the intendants (financial administrators), and nobles were frustrated by erosion of their powers.

During the first, or parlementary, Fronde (1648–49) the Parlement of Paris, joined by more specialized Parisian tribunals and backed by street rioting (Days of Barricades, August 1648), forced the regent to abolish most intendancies, many taxes not registered with parlements, and arbitrary detention. A brief winter siege of Paris by the royal army of Louis II, prince de Condé (see CONDÉ family), ended inconclusively.

The second, or princely, Fronde (1650–53) began as an unsuccessful military uprising in Normandy and Guienne by noble followers of Condé; Condé himself had been imprisoned for seeking to assume Mazarin's powers. In 1651 a coalition of Condé's party, the Parlement of Paris, and a rival noble faction under Cardinal de Retz (1613–79) obtained Condé's release and Mazarin's exile abroad. Rivalry between Condé and Retz, however, as well as basic political differences between the cautious, legalistic judges of the Parlement and the bolder warrior-nobles, allowed Mazarin to return. Condé, although defeated by the vicomte de TURENNE in July 1652, established a brief dictatorship over Paris, but he abandoned the city in October to join the Spanish troops that he had invited into the country. The rebellion soon collapsed, and Mazarin overturned most of the reforms of 1648.

Louis XIV, reacting to the rebellion and his subjects' yearning for order, made his long personal reign the high point of royal absolutism. He took into account the Frondeurs' grievances, however, by making his financial administrative machinery more efficient and less burdensome than Louis XIII's.

A. LLOYD MOOTE

Bibliography: Doolin, Paul, *The Fronde* (1935); Moote, A. Lloyd, *The Revolt of the Judges: The Parlement of Paris and the Fronde, 1643–1652* (1971); Westrich, Sal, *The Ormée of Bordeaux* (1972).

Frondizi, Arturo [frohn-dee'-see]

Arturo Frondizi, b. Oct. 28, 1908, was president of Argentina from 1958 to 1962. He was elected to the lower house of the Congress in 1946 and became an opponent of the president and popular hero Juan Perón, who was ousted in 1955. As president, Frondizi encouraged development of Argentine oil by foreign companies and instituted a number of unpopular policies in an attempt to solve his nation's economic problems. He allowed the *peronistas* to enter the 1962 elections in order to gain their support, but their impressive victories led conservative elements in the military to arrest Frondizi and nullify the elections. He was released in 1963.

Bibliography: Barrera, Mario, *Information and Ideology* (1973).

front

Looking northward at a low-pressure system moving to the east (right) an observer would see high, thin cirrus clouds (1) extending over both the warm (2) and cold (3) fronts. Along the cold front would be fast-rising anvil-topped cumulonimbus clouds (4) with their accompanying violent thunderstorms, high winds, and heavy rains. Low-lying fair-weather cumulus clouds (5) would follow behind the cold front. Above the slowly rising warm front would be altocumulus (6), thick, steadily raining nimbostratus (7), stratus (8), and altostratus (9) clouds.

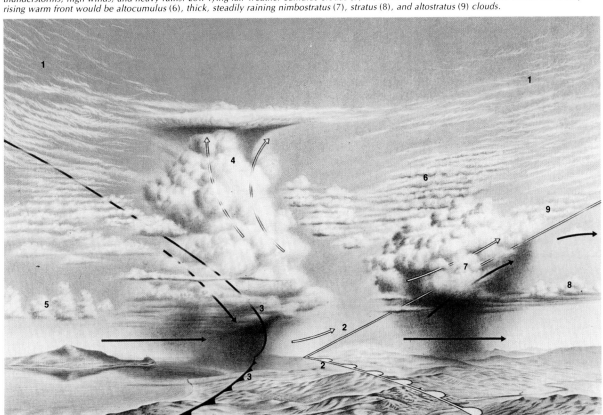

A front is a boundary between air masses having different temperature and humidity. Fronts move in the same direction as the denser, colder air. Thus the leading edge of an advancing cold-air mass demarcates a cold front, whereas the retreat of cold air from the air-mass boundary is a warm front. In a stationary front the winds in the cold air blow parallel to the division. Occluded fronts occur when a cold front catches up to a warm front and forces the intermediate and less dense (warm) air aloft. At the surface, a number of weather indicators determine frontal location: a wind-shift line, a pressure trough, and temperature and dew-point temperature discontinuities, as well as changes in pressure (falling or rising, and how quickly), visibility, precipitation type, and cloud amount across the frontal zone.

Clouds and precipitation result when warmer air associated with these fronts is forced to rise over the colder air. Such active fronts are usually associated with well-developed extratropical cyclones (see CYCLONE AND ANTICYCLONE). On the other hand, if the winds in the warmer air mass slide down and push ahead of the frontal boundary, subsidence and therefore clear skies result, and the front is said to be inactive. Most of the inclement weather in the middle and northern latitudes is a result of active frontal zones. Because of frictional drag on the moving air mass, active cold fronts tend to be steeper (and have a narrower region of inclement weather) than an active warm front with the same magnitude of horizontal temperature contrast.　　　　　　　　　　　ROGER A. PIELKE

Bibliography: Anthes, R. A., et al., *The Atmosphere*, 3d ed. (1981); Longley, Richmond W., *Elements of Meteorology* (1970); Miller, A., and Anthes, R., *Meteorology*, 5th rev. ed. (1985).

See also: ATMOSPHERE; WEATHER FORECASTING.

Frontenac, Louis de Buade, Comte de [frohn-tuh-nak', lwee duh boo-ahd']

Louis de Buade, comte de Frontenac et de Palluau, twice governor-general of New France, is known as French Canada's foremost 17th-century military defender as well as the architect of French expansion into the North American interior. Born at St. Germain-en-Laye near Paris on May 22, 1622, of parents very closely connected with the court, Frontenac spent more than 30 years as an active soldier in Europe and as an extravagant, irascible, and pretentious courtier.

His appointment (1672) as governor-general enabled him to defer repayment of enormous debts in France, to profit personally from the fur trade, and to indulge his vanity by holding vice-regal court at Quebec. This first term (1672–82) was marked by Frontenac's incessant quarrels both with subordinate officials over jurisdiction and precedence and with the Jesuits over moral questions. However, he promoted the western fur trade by sponsoring the endeavors of the sieurs de LA SALLE and DULUTH, Nicolas PERROT, and Henri de TONTY and by the carefully disguised appeasement of English and Iroquois rivals.

War with the Anglo-American colonies and their Iroquois allies dominated his second term (1689–98). Following his haughty rejection of Sir William PHIPS's demand for the surrender of Quebec in 1690, Frontenac successfully defended New France by means of a guerrilla war of attrition. By building many new fortified posts in the west and southwest, albeit for personal gain, he not only expanded the French fur trade but also laid the groundwork for strategic control of the lands west of the Appalachians. Even Frontenac's frequent abuse of his position cannot diminish these achievements. He died in office at Quebec on Nov. 28, 1698.　　　　　F. J. THORPE

Bibliography: Delanglez, Jean, *Frontenac and the Jesuits* (1939); Eccles, William J., *Frontenac: The Courtier Governor* (1959).

See also: FRENCH AND INDIAN WARS.

frontier

In American history, the frontier was the westernmost area of settlement at any given time in the expansion of the nation. Historians assume that the process of extending the frontier westward began in 1607 with the settlement of Jamestown and ended around 1890, when there was no longer any new land for homesteaders. Many of the attitudes and principles associated with this process—rugged individualism, conquest and progress, law and order, free enterprise, and the right to bear arms—reinforce American ideas and myths.

THE WESTWARD MOVEMENT
Europeans traditionally thought of a frontier as a fortified boundary line that ran through densely populated regions and separated one country from another. The American frontier, on the other hand, existed near the edge of free land—"the meeting place between savagery and civilization"—and distinguished the line of most rapid and effective Americanization. Nineteenth-century U.S. census reports defined it as the outer margin of a settled area where the density of population varied from 2 to 6 people per mi².

Frontier settlers moved from the Atlantic coast across 3,000 miles (more than 4,800 km) of wilderness, deserts, and mountains until they were finally stopped by the Pacific Ocean. This advance averaged 10 mi (16 km) a year, but in actuality movement progressed by successive waves and at a very uneven rate. Geography and hostile Indians generally determined the boundaries of a particular frontier region. The fall line—the junction of the tidewater region and the piedmont—marked the frontier of the 17th century. Within the next 100 years, pioneers pushed the settlement line to the base of the Alleghenies. During the American Revolution, many settlers crossed the mountains into Kentucky and Ten-

This 19th-century allegorical painting of the westward expansion portrays Columbia's spirit inspiring the pioneers in their arduous journey across the continent. Thousands followed the trails across the Great Plains, the Rockies, and the Great Basin to the Pacific coast.

Louis de Buade, comte de Frontenac, was appointed governor of New France in 1672. Recognized as one of the major builders of New France, Frontenac sponsored much exploration and expanded the fur trade. During King William's War (1689–97) he subdued the Iroquois and repulsed a British attack on Quebec.

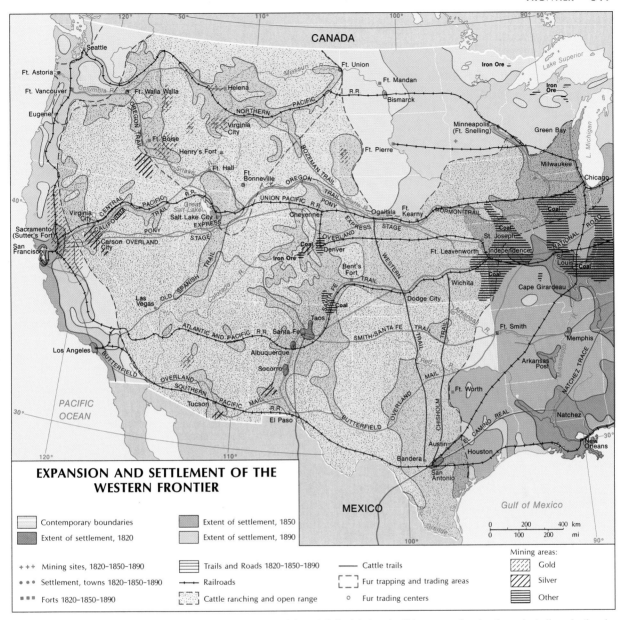

EXPANSION AND SETTLEMENT OF THE WESTERN FRONTIER

Contemporary boundaries

Extent of settlement, 1820

Extent of settlement, 1850

Extent of settlement, 1890

+ + +   Mining sites, 1820-1850-1890

• • •   Settlement, towns 1820-1850-1890

■ ■ ■   Forts 1820-1850-1890

Trails and Roads 1820-1850-1890

Railroads

Cattle ranching and open range

Cattle trails

Fur trapping and trading areas

○   Fur trading centers

Mining areas:

Gold

Silver

Other

This map illustrates the expansion of the American frontier west of the Mississippi during the 19th century, showing the major trails and railroads and settlements. The westward movement occurred in several distinct phases, characterized by fur-trading, mining, cattle-raising, and farming.

nessee and from there ventured into the Old Northwest and Old Southwest. Pioneers poured through the Cumberland Gap and down the Ohio in ever-increasing numbers. By 1820, all the lands east of the Mississippi had been carved into separate states or territories.

During the next three decades, a wave of settlers moved beyond the Mississippi to the edge of the arid plains. Near the 98th meridian, the forested area gives way to rolling prairies, and farther beyond, the prairies merge with the Great Plains. As the elevation increases, the annual rainfall gradually drops below that amount necessary for conventional agriculture. For this reason, settlement halted for a long time at the bend of the Missouri and along the eastern boundary of Indian Territory (Oklahoma), Nebraska, and Kansas. Long after Missouri, Arkansas, and Iowa had been admitted to statehood, Minnesota and Wisconsin to the north still retained their frontier characteristics.

The discovery of gold in California in 1848 altered the pattern of westward migration, as hordes of settlers and prospec-

tors passed through the Great Plains, Rocky Mountains, and Great Basin to the very edge of the Pacific Ocean. By 1860, the line separating the settled region from the unoccupied zones had moved back to the Rockies. For all practical purposes, the last remaining frontier—excluding Alaska—now lay between the mountains to the west and the prairies to the east, bordered on the north by Canada and on the south by the Rio Grande.

During the post–Civil War years, cattlemen moved onto the Great Plains from Texas, and farmers, or nesters, poured in from the Mississippi Valley. By 1880 the settled area included northern Michigan, Wisconsin, Minnesota, and the Black Hills, and the remainder of the nation's heartland was quickly being inhabited. Frontier expansion was effectively over by the end of the decade, when the superintendent of the census stated that the settlements of the West "now lie so scattered over the western half of the United States that there no longer can be said to be a frontier line."

When the good land became scarce and the population of

a particular region reached a certain level, the frontier line pushed forward. This rarely produced movement along an even north-south course, as the government perhaps would have preferred. Instead, the process more closely resembled that of water pouring through a break in a dam; settlers bypassed barriers in search of particularly attractive spots for relocation. Sometimes progress was rapid, as in the rush into Kentucky, Tennessee, Mississippi, and Alabama; but in other places movement was extremely slow. Much depended upon the transportation routes, hostility of the Indians, location of river valleys, fertility of the soil, or economic conditions at home. As the fingers of settlement pushed deeper into the wilderness, they invariably left vast unoccupied regions in between.

This irregular advance created special problems for the army, whose tasks included protecting the settlements and government surveyors and controlling the Indians. No sooner would new military posts be completed than they would be left far behind in the interior. Many pioneers, however, chose to remain near an established fort. Some took up trades, constructed mills, opened general stores, or raised crops and livestock. After the need for military protection had lessened, many such communities developed into cities—for example, Pittsburgh, Pa.; Cincinnati, Ohio; Detroit; Chicago; Minneapolis, Minn; and St. Paul, Minn.

Fur-Trade Frontier. The development of the major geographical areas from wildernesses to settled lands occurred in stages, each characterized by a distinct type of people engaged in a predominating economic activity. The patterns of development varied, but the first to enter new territory usually were the fur trappers and traders. These men moved in advance of civilization, opening new trails into the wilderness and crossing the continent decades ahead of the miners, cattlemen, and farmers. Many preferred solitude to association with other settlers; they adapted to the ways of the Indians and took Indian women for wives or concubines. Some operated as free trappers and exchanged their yearly catch of furs for guns, knives, traps, whiskey, tobacco, and other supplies at the closest trading posts. Others worked for the major companies that dominated the business before its rapid decline (see FUR TRADE).

Although the trappers and traders, known as MOUNTAIN MEN, spread disease and whiskey among the Indians and ruthlessly exploited the beaver and other furbearing animals, they played a significant role in the opening of each frontier between the Atlantic and Pacific coasts. The fur-trading business flourished during the first four decades of the 19th century; thereafter, changing styles, reduced prices, depletion of resources, and advancing civilization brought about its decline. Some fur traders and trappers later served as guides for emigrant companies; others settled down to raise livestock or to farm. Jim BRIDGER, one of the more renowned and free-spirited mountain men, operated a famous trading post near South Pass in Wyoming between 1843 and 1855. Another for-

The American artist Charles Russell captures the rugged action and spirit of cowboy life in his painting A Tight Dally and a Loose Latigo. From the 1860s onward, as ranching expanded across the plains, the romantic cowboy image came to symbolize the taming of the frontier.

mer mountain man, William Wolfskill, became one of California's most important landowners and is generally credited with being the father of that state's modern wine industry.

Cattlemen's Frontier. Each new region also had its "cowpens," or cattle-raising, stage, which usually followed that of the trappers and traders and preceded that of the farmers. In early Massachusetts, cattle raising was important in the Charles River valley; it was later established in upper New York and the Mohawk Valley. For a short time, cattlemen raised stock among the canebrakes and marshes of the tidewater region, before retreating into the piedmont and mountain valleys beyond the fall line. Having crossed the Appalachians, the raising of cattle, sheep, and swine became increasingly important as far west as the Mississippi River. It developed into a bonanza industry on the grasslands of the Great Plains, which stretched from the Rio Grande to the Canadian border. Soon after the Civil War, the practice of driving cattle from Texas to the northern markets commenced; it continued for the next 30 years, until the railroads and packinghouses had moved closer to sources of supply.

By the mid 1880s the range had become overstocked, and barbed-wire fences and railroads crisscrossed the Great Plains. By this time, homesteaders were winning the battle with the ranchers for dominance of the public domain, and ranching was changing from a frontier industry to a corporate enterprise. Then came the severe winters of 1885–86 and 1886–87, which destroyed more than three-fourths of the herds on the northern plains. Soon after, fenced pasture and farms replaced the open range, and the era of round-ups and trail drives was ended. Today legend has transformed the COWBOY of this period into the epitome of the frontier hero, and frontier buffs throughout the world try to recapture a life-style that is, in fact, largely fictitious.

Mining Frontier. The mining frontier advanced in a less orderly fashion than that of the traders and herdsmen. It sometimes lagged far behind the line of settlements, as in Georgia in the 1820s and 1830s; in other instances mining operations were begun long before communities of settlers arrived, as was the case with the lead mining in Illinois and Missouri and the goldfields of California. The California GOLD RUSH was set off by the discovery of gold on the American River in January 1848. It involved the largest migration of people over the longest distances in the briefest span of time in the history of the world. Gold seekers left scars along every stream and gulch from one end of the far West to the other. They rushed back and forth wherever opportunity beckoned—from California to Colorado and Nevada, then to New Mexico and Idaho, Montana, Wyoming, and finally, in 1876, to the Black Hills of South Dakota.

Like the fur trading of the early 19th century, mining enjoyed its greatest boom in the mountainous regions. In less than a generation it was transformed from a frontier industry to a corporate enterprise. Unlike other movements, mining assumed an urban characteristic from the beginning. Its work-

During the early 1800s, fur trappers and traders explored the American frontier in the Rocky Mountains long before the miners, cattleherders, and farmers appeared. Known as mountain men, two of these buckskin-clad traders are portrayed in this 19th-century drawing by Frederic Remington.

The discovery of gold in 1848 at Sutter's Mill in California began a series of gold and silver rushes. Simple methods and equipment were used by the prospectors, such as the sluicebox shown here. Although few were successful in their search, the miners remained and contributed greatly to the economic growth of California and the west.

ers measured property by the foot rather than by the acre or section. Their activities probably hastened the civilizing process of the American West by a quarter of a century or more.

Farming Frontier. In addition to the trappers, miners, and cattlemen, many other specific groups of people contributed to the development of the frontier—explorers; missionaries; soldiers; builders of turnpikes, railroads, and canals; land speculators; and Indians. But perhaps most significant was the farmer. Wherever farmers appeared, they changed the face of the land, destroying forever its virgin characteristics and pushing settlements to the edge of the wilderness. Whereas furs, minerals, and grass had attracted other pioneers, the rich soils of the river valleys and prairies attracted the farmers. Unlike their predecessors, they set out to conquer nature and not to compromise with it. Trees and Indians had to be eradicated like weeds and varmints, while the soil was cultivated.

For three centuries, most Americans lived within easy reach of cheap land. They often made no attempt to buy it even at $1.25 an acre, but simply built a log cabin or sod house anywhere on the public domain they chose to squat. In time they cleared a spot large enough for crops and a garden to support their families and even to produce a surplus for sale. They grubbed the stumps, built roads, laid out towns, and established churches and schools.

As the countryside began to fill up, many settlers sold their homes and land and moved farther west to start the process all over again. Six or seven moves during one's lifetime was not unusual. As one region emerged from the frontier stage, another entered it. The government of each new frontier area derived elements from the regions just left, and each move westward contributed to this process of change and growth.

THE LURE OF THE FRONTIER

A number of factors lured men and women to new frontiers: worn-out land and other economic impediments at home; available roads, canals, riverboats, and later railroads; and the dream of adventure and romance. Moving toward the setting sun became a compulsive urge, and once an individual caught the fever, no logical argument against pulling up stakes could change his mind. To millions of Americans the frontier was a place to go to simply because it was there. The fertile soil, abundant game, and lack of restrictions constituted the stuff of dreams.

Even though the frontier never quite lived up to the vision, many who arrived there felt compelled to keep the dream alive for others rather than to admit the truth. Perhaps this explains the tendency of people of the frontier to exaggerate, speaking of the good things as very good and the bad as very bad. The dime novels of Ned BUNTLINE were based upon pure fantasy, but so was much of what Capt. John SMITH wrote about the Virginia frontier three centuries earlier. What people believe to be true is often as important as the truth itself, and generations of Americans have grown up with the idea that the frontier during the closing decades of the 19th century represented this country at its most adventurous, as well as its most violent.

In its frontier days, America possessed almost limitless natural resources, and the government distributed those resources liberally. Congress set the pattern in 1796 with a minimum reserved price for land. This principle remained in effect, theoretically at least, until the PREEMPTION ACT of 1841, which allowed squatters to purchase the land they already occupied at a base price of $1.25 an acre for 160 acres (about 65 ha). The so-called log-cabin legislation eased the way for passage of the HOMESTEAD ACT of 1862. Under this act, title to a quarter section of land could be obtained by paying a small fee and establishing the claim by occupying the land for five years. With basic modifications, the act remained in effect until 1977; but it failed to create the utopia that its sponsors had promised, and it seldom gave the working man a true fresh start.

The Homestead Act has been called "a wager by the federal government of 160 acres of land against a man's ability to live and survive on it for five years." In the East, where rain is plentiful, a 160-acre farm was considered more than adequate, but a farmer on the Great Plains needed two to four times that for extensive agriculture, and he needed several thousand acres if he was a rancher. The situation was worsened by certain congressional amendments to the act; these inadvertently allowed speculators to take advantage of various loopholes and acquire extraordinarily large holdings of the best land. As a result, many settlers were forced to buy from the railroads and other speculators, and the full intent of the Homestead Act was never realized.

Because of the forbidding features of the Great Plains, farmers did not move there in large numbers until after 1870. The adaptation of the windmill, the invention of barbed wire,

(Above) *During the American Revolution, state governments issued land grants, such as this one to General George Rogers Clark, to recruit troops. Land was distributed for settlement under the Preemption (1841) and Homestead acts (1862).*

(Below) *Settlers of the treeless Great Plains built their homes, called "soddies," out of earth. The influx of farmers to the Plains states following the 1862 Homestead Act limited the previously "open" range and led to the decline of the great cattle ranches.*

In this 19th-century sketch by Seth Eastman, pioneers defend against an attack by the Comanche Indians. Wagon trains were used to transport people and goods during the westward expansion.

and the development of dry farming eventually paved the way for the most rapid land rush of all. Within two decades settlers populated Kansas and Nebraska and swarmed over the grasslands of Dakota, Wyoming, and Montana. The conquest of the Great Plains proved more difficult than previous frontier experiences because of the harsh climate and more formidable Indians. Even so, it took place in a relatively brief period of time. Between 1870 and 1900 approximately 430 million acres of public domain were occupied or brought under cultivation. This represented about 40 percent of the total land area occupied and improved since 1607.

FRONTIER LIFE

The myth of the American frontier as a bucolic place where one could do as one pleased has continued to influence popular attitudes. In reality, the process of opening a wilderness region and wresting a living from the land took a heavy toll. Pioneer women suffered especially, as the stories of Hamlin GARLAND and other writers so poignantly reveal. The incessant burden of hard work, childbearing, and sickness, as well as fear of Indian attacks, caused most women to grow old before the age of 40. Worse yet was the stupefying loneliness brought on by the lack of social contact with friends or neighbors for months at a time.

Characteristics. The raw frontier experience also fostered boisterous politics, rude manners, disregard for conventions, contempt for intellectual and cultural pursuits, mobility of population, unmitigated waste, and the exploitation of natural resources. The predominant spirit was to take while the taking was good, and frontier history includes many accounts of men who carved out empires and acquired great wealth within a few years. But the cattle kings, railroad and town builders, lumber barons, and mineowners sometimes lost fortunes as quickly as they made them. Still, there was always

Life on the frontier was rugged and, on occasion, violent. In California, for example, a period of lawlessness, characterized in part by "claim-jumping," followed the 1848 discovery of gold. In the 1850s self-appointed law-enforcement groups, or vigilance committees, were formed in San Francisco. Later, vigilante justice was also practiced in Montana and Idaho.

another tomorrow; for whatever faults the frontiersman possessed, he was usually ready to start again.

Small-mindedness and petty thievery were rare among frontier people. A stranger was considered honest until proved otherwise, and it was taken for granted that any traveler stopping at a farmhouse was welcome to have supper and to spend the night; an offer to pay for such hospitality would have been taken as an insult. Locks symbolized an impeachment of public honesty and integrity, and frontier people frequently did not secure the doors of their homes or even their places of business. A Texas historian declared that there was not one lock on a single building or office in the town of Colorado City throughout the 1880s. In warm weather a merchant frequently did not bother to close his store before going home at night.

Similarly, a man's word on the frontier was held to be as good as his bond. The owners of various mercantile enterprises at the crossing of Red River near present-day Vernon, Tex., sold supplies and clothing on credit, or advanced money without collateral, to literally hundreds of cowboys and total strangers between 1874 and 1894 without losing a dime. Some customers rode hundreds of miles out of their way to settle accounts as soon as they had the money. Like the miners in California, frontiersmen might shoot or hang a thief or murderer in short order, but they would rarely deceive him.

An admirable characteristic of Americans has been their ability to organize themselves smoothly and swiftly into a body politic. But the very ease with which town charters could be drawn up, laws passed, and officials elected sometimes fostered too much self-confidence in the community or lulled the political conscience of the ordinary person. The simplicity of frontier governmental apparatus made it easy for lawless elements to seize what government there was. When this happened, local leaders formed VIGILANTE groups to apprehend and punish the guilty and to put their weak governments back in order. But the primary danger of frontier vigilantism was that some men continued to take the law into their own hands after regular judicial processes had been instituted.

Most frontier people were friendly, hard working, and just, and for every act of violence during the frontier period, there were thousands of acts of kindness, generosity, and sacrifice. People usually worked together harmoniously for the good of the community. The majority literally practiced the biblical adage and served as their brother's keeper. They gave their time, money, and sometimes their lives in behalf of friends or total strangers in moments of misfortune or extreme danger. If a neighbor lost his crop or if sickness prevented him from planting at the proper time, the whole neighborhood donated part of their harvest or time. If a bank threatened to foreclose a mortgage or an official tried to seize a man's livestock or tools because he could not pay his taxes, friends and neighbors frequently banded together to prevent it.

The Frontier Heritage. The transition from rural to urban society has long been accomplished, but the frontier remains very much a part of the American heritage. For example, many Americans continue to keep and sometimes revere guns, even though guns have not been survival necessities for more than three generations. American folklore tends to support the image of tough, aggressive, and unafraid heros who tamed the wild frontier. This has contributed to the commonly expressed philosophy that winning is everything, whether on the football field, used car lot, or in the board room of a large corporation.

Perhaps this explains why frontier types such as the cowboy, mountain man, or outlaw have endured so long in American literature and legend. They went out and got what they wanted with their own two hands, frequently by violent means. Their deeds, real and imaginary, have served as a cultural metaphor of how Americans view themselves. However, in terms of actual frontier life, the emphasis is misleading. In many respects it is remarkable that the American frontier was settled in as orderly a fashion as it was.

TURNER'S FRONTIER THESIS

The best-known interpretation of the American frontier experience was proposed by Frederick Jackson TURNER. As a little-known historian from the University of Wisconsin, Turner read a paper, "The Significance of the Frontier in American History," at the annual meeting of the American Historical Association in Chicago in 1893. According to the 32-year-old professor, "The existence of an area of free land, its continuous recession, and the advance of American settlement westward explain American development." Turner enunciated what has been called the "safety valve" theory of U.S. history: "Whenever social conditions . . . tended to press upon labor, or political restraints to impede the freedom of the mass, there was this gate of escape to the free conditions of the frontier. . . . Men would not accept inferior wages and a permanent position of social insubordination when this promised land of freedom and equality was theirs for the taking." He also concluded that the frontier decreased American dependence on England and that the true point of view in American history of the United States "is not the Atlantic Coast, but the West."

Turner's hypothesis altered the course of American historical scholarship, which at that time was focused almost exclusively on New England and the East. Among other things, Turner suggested that in the course of the westward movement forces were created or released that shaped American ideas of government and contributed to the evolution of its economic and social institutions. For the rest of his life Turner and his students tested the application of the frontier thesis in various periods and places without serious challenge by critics. During the 1930s and 1940s, the tide ran strongly against Turner's ideas regarding the democratizing influence of the frontier. Charles Wilson Pierson and other historians criticized his thesis severely and maintained that it was an inadequate guide to American development. More recently, Ray Allen Billington, Wilbur Jacobs, and other historians have placed the thesis in better perspective. Although aware of its many faults, they nevertheless believe that it should stand upon reasonableness rather than upon proof.

Turner observed in 1893 that the open frontier was already an environment of the past and that Americans should of necessity move on to another chapter of history. Regardless of the validity of his thesis as a whole, few will quarrel with his assertion that the American frontier experience will never be repeated.

W. EUGENE HOLLON

Bibliography: Billington, R. A., *The Frontier Thesis* (1977) and *Westward to the Pacific* (1979); Clark, T. D., ed., *The Great American Frontier* (1975); Jacobs, W. R., *Frederick Jackson Turner's Legacy* (1964); Limerick, P. N., *The Legacy of Conquest* (1987); Merk, F., *History of the Westward Movement* (1975); Nash, R., *Wilderness and the American Mind*, rev. 3d ed. (1982); Ride, M., and Billington, R. A., eds., *America's Frontier Story* (1980); Taylor, G. R., ed., *The Turner Thesis* (1936); Turner, F. J., *The Frontier in American History* (1920; repr. 1985); Van Every, D., *Ark of Empire* (1988).

frontier literature: see WESTERNS.

Frontinus, Sextus Julius   [frahn-ty'-nuhs]

Sextus Julius Frontinus, AD c.35–104, was a Roman civil servant and author. He held the office of consul in 73, 98, and 100, was governor of Britain from 74 to 78, and served as superintendent of aqueducts in Rome under Emperor Nerva. Frontinus wrote two works on military strategy, but is best known for his treatise *De aquis urbis Romae* (*Concerning the Waters of the City of Rome*), which described the city's aqueducts, listed the technical and administrative staff responsible for them, and discussed problems of maintenance.

frost

Frost is a light deposit of ice that is formed by the condensation of water vapor on a surface whose temperature is below freezing (0° C/32° F) at sea level. Knowledge of when and where frost may occur is of great importance in agriculture, ecology, energy conservation, and the construction industry.

Within soils, the movement of a frost front, and the opposite process, thawing, are complex cases of heat transmission,

or conduction. At the boundary of solid and liquid, the latent heat of fusion (the additional heat at the melting point that is required to fuse a substance, approximately 80 cal/g for ice) is released if frost is forming; the latent heat is absorbed if frost is thawing.

Radiation frost, a local phenomenon, is most likely to occur during calm, clear, dry nights when rapid, long-wave radiation to the sky results in great heat loss from the surface or object. Advection frost is the result of a cold air mass moving into an area, which often produces a hard freeze. HOARFROST (white frost) is caused by the sublimation of ice crystals on objects at temperatures below freezing, whereas black frost (often called dry frost or killing frost) forms on vegetation when air is dry but at temperatures below the freezing point.

WERNER H. TERJUNG

See also: FROST ACTION; PERMAFROST.

Frost, Robert

Robert Lee Frost, b. San Francisco, Mar. 26, 1874, d. Boston, Jan. 29, 1963, was one of America's leading 20th-century poets and a four-time winner of the Pulitzer Prize. An essentially pastoral poet often associated with rural New England, Frost wrote poems whose philosophical dimensions transcend any region. Although his verse forms are traditional—he often said, in a dig at archrival Carl Sandburg, that he would as soon play tennis without a net as write free verse—he was a pioneer in the interplay of rhythm and meter and in the poetic use of the vocabulary and inflections of everyday speech. His poetry is thus both traditional and experimental, regional and universal.

After his father's death in 1885, when young Frost was 11, the family left California and settled in Massachusetts. Frost attended high school in that state, entered Dartmouth College, but remained less than one semester. Returning to Massachusetts, he taught school and worked in a mill and as a newspaper reporter. In 1894 he sold "My Butterfly: An Elegy" to *The Independent,* a New York literary journal. A year later he married Elinor White, with whom he had shared valedictorian honors at Lawrence (Mass.) High School. From 1897 to 1899 he attended Harvard College as a special student but left without a degree. Over the next ten years he wrote (but rarely published) poems, operated a farm in Derry, N.H. (purchased for him by his paternal grandfather), and supplemented his income by teaching at Derry's Pinkerton Academy.

In 1912, at the age of 38, he sold the farm and used the proceeds to take his family to England, where he could devote himself entirely to writing. His efforts to establish himself and his work were almost immediately successful. *A Boy's Will* was accepted by a London publisher and brought out in 1913, followed a year later by *North of Boston.* Favorable reviews on both sides of the Atlantic resulted in American publication of the books by Henry Holt and Company, Frost's primary American publisher, and in the establishing of Frost's transatlantic reputation.

As part of his determined efforts on his own behalf, Frost had called on several prominent literary figures soon after his

One of America's most widely read and critically acclaimed poets, Robert Frost received numerous honors for his verse, among them four Pulitzer Prizes and two unanimous resolutions of praise from the U.S. Senate. In 1961, at the inauguration of President John F. Kennedy, Frost read his poem "The Gift Outright," from the collection entitled A Witness Tree (1942).

arrival in England. One of these was Ezra Pound, who wrote the first American review of Frost's verse for Harriet Monroe's *Poetry* magazine. (Though he disliked Pound, Frost was later instrumental in obtaining Pound's release from long confinement in a Washington, D.C., mental hospital.) Frost was more favorably impressed and more lastingly influenced by the so-called Georgian poets Lascelles Abercrombie, Rupert Brooke, and T. E. Hulme, whose rural subjects and style were more in keeping with his own. While living near the Georgians in Gloucestershire, Frost became especially close to a Welshman named Edward Thomas, whom he urged to turn from prose to poetry. Thomas did so, dedicating his first and only volume of verse to Frost before his death during World War I.

The Frosts sailed for the United States in February 1915 and landed in New York City two days after the U.S. publication of *North of Boston* (the first of his books to be published in America). Sales of that book and of *A Boy's Will* enabled Frost to buy a farm in Franconia, N.H.; to place new poems in literary periodicals and publish a third book, *Mountain Interval* (1916); and to embark on a long career of writing, teaching, and lecturing. In 1924 he received a Pulitzer Prize in poetry for *New Hampshire* (1923). He was lauded again for *Collected Poems* (1930), *A Further Range* (1936), and *A Witness Tree* (1942). Over the years he received an unprecedented number of literary, academic, and public honors.

Frost's importance as a poet derives from the power and memorability of particular poems. "The Death of the Hired Man" (from *North of Boston*) combines lyric and dramatic poetry in blank verse. "After Apple-Picking" (from the same volume) is a free-verse dream poem with philosophical undertones. "Mending Wall" (also published in *North of Boston*) demonstrates Frost's simultaneous command of lyrical verse, dramatic conversation, and ironic commentary. "The Road Not Taken" and "Birches" (from *Mountain Interval*) and the oft-studied "Stopping by Woods on a Snowy Evening" (from *New Hampshire*) exemplify Frost's ability to join the pastoral and philosophical modes in lyrics of unforgettable beauty.

Frost's poetic and political conservatism caused him to lose favor with some literary critics, but his reputation as a major poet is secure. He unquestionably succeeded in realizing his life's ambition: to write "a few poems it will be hard to get rid of."

Reviewed by R. H. WINNICK

Bibliography: Brunshaw, S., *Robert Frost Himself* (1989); Gerber, P. L., ed., *Critical Essays on Robert Frost* (1982); Hall, D., *Robert Frost: Contours of Belief* (1980); Katz, S. L., *Elinor Frost* (1988); Lathem, E. C., ed., *Robert Frost's Poetry and Prose* (1984); Pritchard, W. H., *Frost: A Literary Life Reconsidered* (1984); Thompson, L., *Robert Frost*, 3 vols. (1966–76); Thompson, L., and Winnick, R. H., *Robert Frost: A Biography*, ed. by E. C. Lathem (1981); Walsh, J. E., *Into My Own: The English Years of Robert Frost, 1912–1915* (1988).

frost action

Frost action is the WEATHERING process caused by repeated cycles of freezing and thawing. Groundwater confined in pores of rock or soil expands almost 9 percent in volume upon freezing, exerting great pressure on the surrounding material and causing frost heaving in soil and frost wedging in rock.

When groundwater freezes in soil, an ice crystal grows, generally in the direction of heat loss, and pushes soil particles upward. More rapid heat loss under rock fragments results in greater growth of ice crystals beneath the fragments and causes them to surface. Uneven freezing produces mounds or other irregularities that protrude above the surface and are surrounded by circular or polygonal accumulations of large particles that have slid off (see PATTERNED GROUND).

Frost heaving occurring along a slope produces soil creep because particles rise perpendicular to the slope as the ice crystal grows, but they sink vertically upon thawing. Thawing of frozen groundwater produces a soft, spongy soil.

The expansion of water upon freezing can also cause rocks to split if the water has been confined in joints and crevices, or shatter if it has been confined in the pores. A felsenmeer is a large block field produced by frost wedging. When frost wedging occurs on a slope, TALUS, or rock debris, will occur along or at the base of the slope.

Bibliography: Berg, R., and Wright, E., eds., *Frost Action and Its Control* (1984); Williams, P., and Smith, M., *The Frozen Earth* (1991).

frostbite

Frostbite is tissue damage resulting from exposure to subfreezing temperatures. Injury to the skin, muscle, blood vessels, and nerves is caused by formation of ice crystals in these tissues and by a drastic reduction of blood flow in the frozen areas. Early signs of frostbite include a general numbness of the affected area and a skin color change from slightly flushed to white to grayish blue as the injury progresses. In mild frostbite the skin feels hard while the underlying tissue is soft. In moderate frostbite, large blisters form on the skin and underlying tissues. Severe frostbite causes major tissue damage, often resulting in GANGRENE from the loss of blood supply to the area. The frozen area should be thawed with warm water (about 37.8° C/100° F) as soon as possible and loosely bandaged until medical care is available. The area should not be massaged, since this may cause more tissue damage. For mild cases, full recovery is possible, but the affected area often has persistent numbness, sensitivity to cold, and a tendency to repeated frostbite. More severe cases may require amputation of the affected area.

Froude, William   [frood]

An English civil engineer and naval architect, William Froude, b. Nov. 28, 1810, d. May 4, 1879, pioneered in ship hydrodynamics. Educated at Oxford, Froude began his career as a railway engineer, but in 1856 he became interested in ship construction and suggested the use of the bilge keel, a finlike projection on both sides of a ship below the waterline that reduced rolling. The device was adopted by the British Navy. Froude's research with ship models showed that the primary components of resistance to motion were skin friction and the formation of waves by the ship. He also invented a hydraulic DYNAMOMETER to measure the power of large marine engines.

frozen food

Although weather freezing is an ancient technique for preserving foods in cold climates, science and engineering principles have been applied to the freezing of foods only since the late 1920s. Much of the work was directed toward perfecting methods for the fast freezing of foods, since fast freezing retains texture and flavor characteristics better than do slow-freezing methods, which result in the growth of large crystals and the concentration of solutes. Three quick-freezing methods exist: air-blast freezing; immersion freezing, using such refrigerants as brine, cryogenic liquids or gas (liquid nitrogen, carbon dioxide); and indirect contact freezing, using chilled plates (see also FREEZE DRYING). Some vitamin loss takes place during processing, varying according to the food, the type of process, and the type of packaging. Freezing may also cause a slight loss of minerals, some denaturation of protein, and some oxidation of fats. These losses may occur during the preparation, in storage, or during the thawing of the product prior to consumption.

Frozen foods of high quality are now available in the United States and in many other parts of the world. Extensive quality control measures ensure the freshness and optimal texture, color, and taste of frozen food products. In addition to subjective, or sensory evaluation, tests, a number of instruments are used to make objective measurements of freshness, tenderness, ripeness, and other characteristics of quality. At the same time, freezing technology has advanced to the point where cooked dishes—complete with their seasonings—and entire meals can be purchased frozen and heated ready-to-eat in microwave or conventional ovens.

Freezing is not a sterilization process. Even extreme cold does not prevent the growth of bacteria, yeasts, and molds or the activity of enzymes. Extreme cold does, however, slow down the growth of microorganisms, and frozen foods, if prepared in a sanitary manner and unthawed before use, are as wholesome as fresh foods.

MARTIN SEVERIN PETERSON

Bibliography: Gormley, T. R., and Zeuthen, P., eds., *Chilled Foods* (1990); Robinson, R. K., ed., *Microbiology of Frozen Foods* (1985).

fructose

Fructose, $C_6H_{12}O_6$, is an important MONOSACCHARIDE, or simple sugar, found in most fruits and in honey. It is also found in sugarcane and sugar beets, where it is chemically combined with GLUCOSE to form the disaccharide sucrose. Fructose (also called levulose) is the sweetest sugar, and like other CARBOHYDRATE molecules it can provide the body with energy. Although broken down in the body more slowly than glucose, fructose has essentially the same nutritional value.

fruit fly

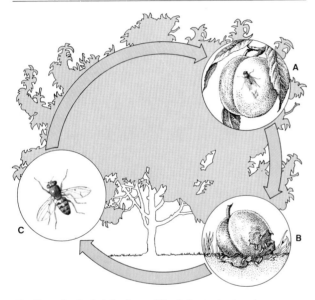

The life cycle of a fruit fly, Drosophila phalcrata, *begins when an adult female lays her eggs inside the skin of an overripe fruit still on a tree (A). Larvae hatch (B) and feed on the fruit, which drops to the ground. A developing larva leaves the rotting fruit and bores into soil, where it pupates and emerges as a mature fly (C).*

Fruit fly is the common name for a large number of small insects whose larvae typically eat their way through fruits. Vinegar, or pomace, fruit flies, classified in the family Drosophilidae, typically feed on fungi (yeasts) found on decaying fruit. All other fruit flies, members of the family Tephritidae, feed directly on fruit. Many fruit flies, including the apple maggot, cherry fruit flies, Oriental fruit fly, and Mediterranean fruit fly, are highly destructive and serious agricultural pests. One species of vinegar fruit fly—*Drosophila melanogaster*—played an important part in the development of theories of heredity and is still used for research in genetics.

The apple maggot, *Rhagoletis pomonella,* attacks apples, crab apples, pears, and plums. Females deposit the eggs under the skin of fruit. The eggs hatch into white maggots that tunnel their way through the fruit, drop to the ground, and change into puparia. New flies emerge in the spring. Adults, about 6 mm (0.2 in) long, have dark bodies with light bands on the abdomen and dark-patterned wings. Cherry fruit flies, *R. congulata* and *R. fausta,* are similar.

The Mediterranean fruit fly, or Medfly, *Ceratitus capitata,* is a major pest of citrus and other fruits. It is widespread in many areas, particularly tropical regions. In the United States strict quarantine laws and control measures had largely eradicated it, but in 1980 Medflies were spotted in California. Attempts to control the outbreak by releasing sterile males to interfere with the normal reproductive cycle were not successful, and a major outbreak in 1981 was finally controlled only by the extensive aerial spraying of the pesticide malathion.

fruits and fruit cultivation

When the proper levels of juice, sugar, and acid are reached, oranges are harvested by clipping them from the trees or by pulling them from the stems, as is done in this Florida orange grove. The fruit is then packed and shipped or processed into juice or frozen concentrate.

Apples may be harvested by hand, as in this orchard in Virginia. When the apples reach the proper size and color, they are harvested by twisting them so that the stem breaks away from the branch without damaging the tree. The apples are crated and shipped, or stored at temperatures near 0° C (32° F).

Fruit is the ripened ovary of any flowering plant, or ANGIOSPERM, and usually contains one or more seeds. No fruit occurs in the other class of seed plants, gymnosperm, which includes the fern and the conifer.

CLASSIFICATION OF FRUIT

By definition, fruit refers to such edibles as tomatoes, string beans, corn, peas, and mustard, as well as to nuts, acorns, oranges, peaches, and others. Tomatoes, string beans, and peaches, for example, are all fruits that are eaten whole; whereas peas, corn, and mustard are the seeds, or fertilized ovules, of fruits. Flour is ground from the fruit of the wheat plant, and coffee is made from the seeds of the coffee fruit, or bean.

Some fruits are partly derived from flower structures other than the ovary, and these are called accessory fruits. Most accessory fruits, such as bananas, cucumbers, and gooseberries, are fleshy throughout and are therefore called false berries. The apple and pear are accessory fruits called pomes; the edible portion is the fleshy exterior, and the true fruit forms the core.

Fruits promote seed dispersal and seed germination. Animals that eat fleshy fruits may spit out or expel undigested seeds with the feces and deposit them in a new location. Dry fruits, like nuts, may be carried about by animals such as the squirrel and left in some forgotten hiding place. Fruits with burrs, hooks, or wing blades may be scattered widely by the wind or, clinging to the pelt of a passing animal, be transported to other locations. Fruits that fall to the ground eventually decay, and this aids seed development by enriching the soil.

The nutritional value of fruits varies. Many have few calories because they are composed largely of water: a ripe tomato, for example, may be 97 percent water. Such fruits are valued in the human diet primarily for their vitamin content and their distinctive tastes and textures. Soybeans and peanuts, on the other hand, have high protein and caloric content, and valuable oils are obtained from olive and sunflower fruits and castor-oil seeds. Cereal grains are humankind's ma-

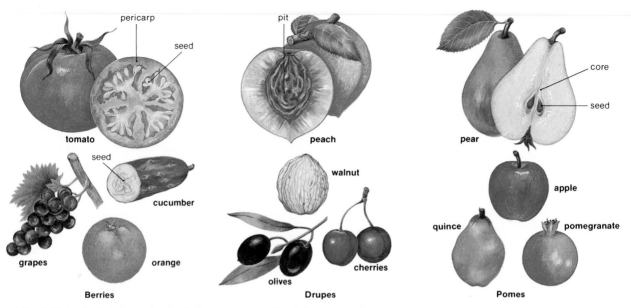

pericarp

seed

tomato

seed

cucumber

grapes

orange

Berries

pit

peach

walnut

olives

cherries

Drupes

core

seed

pear

apple

quince

pomegranate

Pomes

(Above) *Fleshy simple fruits consist of a single mature ovary with a fleshy or mostly fleshy wall, or pericarp. They are classified as berries, drupes, or pomes. Berries (left) have seeds embedded in fleshy tissue. True berries such as tomatoes and grapes have entirely fleshy pericarps. Pepos are berries with a hard rind, including watermelons and cucumbers. Hesperidiums such as oranges have leathery rinds and internal segmentation. Drupes (center) have a hard pit surrounding a single seed; the outer part of the pericarp forms a thin skin. Drupes include peaches, olives, cherries, and certain nuts. Pomes (right), such as pears and apples, have papery central cores containing several seeds.*

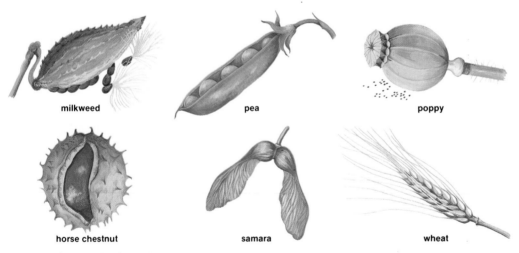

milkweed

pea

poppy

The seed follicles of dehiscent dry fruits may open along one edge (milkweed); legume follicles split along both edges (pea). The poppy sheds its seeds through pores in its seed capsule.

horse chestnut

samara

wheat

Indehiscent dry fruits include the chestnut, an achene, which has a thin, separable pericarp. The fruit of the ash tree is a samara, with a wing-shaped pericarp. Wheat is a caryopsis, with the pericarp and seed coat fused.

Aggregate fruits consist of a number of mature ovaries from a single flower; each ovary forms a complete fruit. Many so-called berries are aggregates. Each "seed" of a strawberry is a small achene. Raspberries and blackberries consist of clusters of small, individual drupes.

Multiple fruits consist of a number of mature ovaries produced by a cluster of flowers. The pineapple is produced by hundreds of flowers; each of its segments is an individual fruit. Each "seed" of a fig is also a fruit. The mulberry consists of a cluster of tiny drupes.

achene

strawberry

fruitlet

fruitlet

fig

drupe

drupe

raspberry

blackberry

pineapple

mulberry

jor food, contributing more than two-thirds of the world production of edible dry matter and half of the world's protein.

SIMPLE FRUITS

A simple fruit consists of a single ripened ovary and may be either dry or fleshy. With ripening, the walls of a simple dry fruit become leathery, papery, or woody. At maturity the walls may be dehiscent, opening to shed the seeds, or indehiscent, remaining closed and usually containing only one seed. Dehiscent fruits are further classified as follicles, legumes, or capsules. The follicle dehisces along one side only. Examples include milkweed and peony fruits. Such legumes as the pea dehisce along two sides.

The capsule, one of the commonest kinds of simple dry fruits, develops from a compound pistil, which is two or more carpels (inner flower parts) fused together. The poppy fruit is a capsule from which the seeds are released through a distal ring of pores. The large single seed of the horse-chestnut fruit, however, is released only when the thick, spiny, three-valved capsule falls apart at maturity.

Dry, Hard Fruits. Indehiscent dry fruits include the achene, grain, samara, and nut. The achene—for example, of the dandelion or buttercup—contains a single seed that almost fills the fruit cavity but is separable from the ovary wall, or pericarp. Because of their small size, achenes are frequently mistaken for seeds. The grain, or caryopsis, is the characteristic fruit of the grass family, including the cereals. It differs from the achene in that the thin seed coat is fused with the pericarp. The samara also is usually one-seeded and has a winglike outgrowth of the pericarp that facilitates its dispersal by wind. Familiar examples are the fruits of elm, sycamore, ash, and maple trees.

A nut is a drupe, which is a one-seeded fruit with a thickened pericarp that hardens upon ripening. Examples are the fruits of hazel, oak, beech, chestnut, and walnut. The term *nut* is popularly misused, often when referring to individual seeds. The so-called Brazil nut is a seed, one of 12 to 20 borne in a globular, thick-walled capsule. The peanut fruit is a legume containing edible seeds, or peanuts, and the edible parts of almond and walnuts are the seeds of drupes.

Fleshy Fruits. Fruits in which all or most of the fruit wall is fleshy at maturity are classified as simple fleshy fruits. They are further classified as berries, drupes, false berries, and pomes. The seeds escape as a result of the decomposition of the fleshy tissues. The entire ovary wall of the berry ripens into a fleshy, usually edible, pericarp. Berries include the fruits of the tomato, grape, date, aubergine, avocado, and red pepper. There may be a single seed, as in the date, or many, as in the tomato. Citrus fruits are modified berries in which the pericarp forms the peel and the edible part consists of saclike outgrowths of the carpel walls.

The pericarp of a drupe is divided into three parts: an outer exocarp, which is often a thin skin; the fleshy mesocarp; and the endocarp, which is a stone or pit enclosing the seed. Drupes include the olive, plum, cherry, and peach. In the coconut fruit the exocarp and mesocarp form the fibrous husk, while the familiar nut is a single seed enclosed in the woody endocarp.

COMPOUND FRUIT

Compound fruit is either classified as aggregate or multiple. An aggregate fruit is a cluster of ripened ovaries produced by a single flower. The individual fruits of raspberry, for example, are tiny drupes that separate as a unit from the receptacle. The strawberry, however, is both aggregate and accessory: the individual fruits are achenes, commonly called the seeds, while the fleshy edible part is the receptacle.

A multiple fruit is formed from a number of flowers grouped closely together as an inflorescence, rather than a single flower. Each flower produces a fruit, and the fruits remain together at maturity. The best example is the pineapple, which comprises fruits derived from several hundred individual flowers fused together. The fig, breadfruit, and mulberry are also multiple fruits.   A. J. WALKER

COMMERCIAL FRUIT CROPS

Horticulturally, fruit is defined as the seed-bearing product of a perennial plant. The botanical fruits of annual plants, such

as the tomato, melon, or bean, are classified as vegetables for horticultural purposes.

Geographical Distribution of Fruit Crops. Fruits are grown commercially throughout the temperate and tropical areas of the world. Tropical fruits, the banana and pineapple, for example, are mostly evergreen and are seriously damaged or killed by freezing temperatures. Those of the subtropics are also mostly evergreen, but possess some resistance to freezing injury, and benefit from seasonal changes. Commercial citrus culture, for instance, is concentrated in regions where night temperatures in winter approach freezing. The quality of the fruit and its skin color are enhanced by cool weather during the period of fruit maturation, but the trees require warm weather for proper growth.

In warm-temperate regions most fruit species are deciduous, with exceptions such as the evergreen olive. Almost all warm-temperate fruits can resist temperatures down to −7° C (19.4° F) during winter dormancy. These species cannot be grown commercially in the tropics or subtropics, because they must experience a short period of low temperature in order to flower. Because a long, warm growing season is necessary for satisfactory productivity and quality, however, they cannot be cultivated commercially in cooler regions. The grape is grown in warm-temperate areas, and in terms of total production it is the most important perennial fruit in the world. Other warm-temperate fruits include figs, olives, members of the genus *Prunus* (apricot, peach, plum, almond), and filbert, walnut, and pistachio nuts.

The cool-temperate species are characteristically deciduous and can withstand temperatures as low as −20° C (−4° F). Among the important cool-temperate fruits are species of apple, pear, cherry, strawberry, raspberry, and currant.

The Chilling Period. Temperate zone fruits and other overwintering plants have acquired the ability to resist severe freezing. In the early fall such plants go into the condition known as rest, or DORMANCY: all growth ceases and the plant becomes hardened and resistant to low winter temperatures. If the plant were to continue growing during mild autumn and early winter weather, it would be too succulent and tender to withstand the first freeze of winter.

In order to flower and fruit properly, the plant must experience a certain number of hours at temperatures below 7° C (45° F) before the dormancy period ends. This number of hours, called the chilling period, has been used as an index by horticulturalists to provide an estimate of the relative adaptability of each variety to different climatic regions. Some peach varieties require 250 hours of chilling for blossoming; others require 1,000 hours. The apple generally needs a longer chilling period than the peach, the almond requires less chilling than any other deciduous fruit species, and most cherry species have a long chilling requirement.

The symptoms of inadequate chilling vary according to the species of fruit tree but, in general, consist of the death of flower buds and the dropping of blossoms before they can open. Flowers that develop may fail to set fruit, or the fruit may be undersized because of inadequate leaf development. For temperate-zone fruit growers, the chilling period is the primary factor determining success or failure of crops.

Fruit Ripening and Storage. The onset of ripening, which marks the end of the growth of the fruit and the start of its senescence, is controlled by hormones. The fruit tissues soften as cell wall materials break down, stored starches are converted to sugar, and characteristic pigment changes take place. Ripening fruits produce minute quantities of the gas ethylene, which is used commercially to accelerate ripening of citrus and other tree fruits. Fruits that are to be harvested early are sprayed with an ethylene compound. Other chemicals can be used to retard ripening and thus to extend the harvesting season.

Harvested fruits continue to carry on most of the life processes that were predominant just before harvest. They respire, using oxygen; give off carbon dioxide; and generate heat. The process of respiration consumes food and water stored in the fruit and leads to the breakdown of fruit tissues. It is this breakdown that causes perishability in fruit. Respiration and tissue breakdown can be delayed by holding the fruit under refrigeration. Many temperate zone fruits can be stored safely at 0° to 5° C (32° to 41° F), but tropical and subtropical fruits are subject to chilling injury and must be stored at warmer temperatures.

Fruits may also be stored in refrigerated storage rooms, where the oxygen content of the atmosphere is reduced and the carbon dioxide level is increased. In this controlled atmosphere (CA), fruit respiration is reduced still further. CA storage method is becoming common for apples and pears.

Drying or dehydration of fruits is another technique for prolonging edibility. It is commonly used for dates, figs, prunes, and apricots, although the process works equally well with the more watery fruits such as apples or pears. Freezing and canning are used to preserve the more perishable berries. Most nuts are far less perishable than shell-less fruits, but even they are subject to mold and rancidity and are often kept in controlled atmosphere storage.   JEROME HULL, JR.

Bibliography: Alford, D. V., *Colour Atlas of Fruit Pests* (1984); Blackburn-Maze, P., *The Complete Guide to Fruit Growing* (1989); Childers, N. B., *Modern Fruit Science,* 9th ed. (1983); Gross, J., *Pigments in Fruits* (1987); Monselise, S. P., *CRC Handbook of Fruit Set and Development* (1986); Moore, J. N., and Janick, J., eds., *Methods in Fruit Breeding* (1983); Page, S., and Smilie, J., *The Orchard Almanac,* 2d ed. (1988); Reich, L., *Uncommon Fruits Worthy of Attention* (1991).

See also: FLOWER; HORTICULTURE; TROPICAL FRUIT.

Frumentius, Saint   [froo-men'-shuhs]

Saint Frumentius, *c.*300–*c.*380, is known as the "Apostle of the Abyssinians." A youth from Tyre, he was attacked and shipwrecked, with Saint Aedesius, on the Ethiopian coast. They were taken as captives to the royal Abyssinian court at Aksum, where they engaged in missionary work and eventually became court officials. About 340, Frumentius was consecrated a bishop at Alexandria, Egypt, by Saint Athanasius. Feast day: Aug. 1 (Ethiopian); Dec. 18 (Coptic); Nov. 30 (Greek); Oct. 27 (Roman).

Frunze   [froon'-zeh]

Frunze, also called Bishkek, or Pishpek (1989 pop., 626,000), is the capital of Kyrgyzstan. Situated at an altitude of 755 m (2,477 ft), the city lies at the foot of the Kirghiz Mountains, a range of the Tian Shan system. It is a manufacturing center and the metropolis of the Chu valley, the most densely settled area of predominantly mountainous Kyrgyzstan. Its factories, which yield about half the nation's industrial output, produce machinery, textiles, and food products. A former possession of the khanate of Kokand, it was captured by the Russians in 1862. Called Frunze (after M. V. Frunze, a local Communist leader) when Kyrgyzstan was part of the USSR, the city reverted to its traditional name, Bishkek, in 1991.

frustration

Frustration is the blocking of a person's active movement toward a goal. In psychology the term is generally applied to the emotional state that results from such blocking. Frustration is inevitable in daily life, because people must continually overcome large and small obstacles. Many, however, do not even try to achieve goals that they greatly desire because they suffer from a sense of inadequacy, which they may feel whether the inadequacy is real or imagined.

Frustration may result from the attempt to reach incompatible goals. Attractive but mutually exclusive goals cause a type of inner conflict known as approach-approach conflict. Such a conflict occurs, for example, when a person chooses one of two equally attractive jobs and, at the same time, regrets the choice that was made. In an approach-avoidance conflict, a person may simultaneously wish for and fear an action: if both tendencies are equal in strength—if, for instance, a person wishes to get married but also fears the responsibilities of marriage—he or she may become immobilized, incapable of any action. Avoidance-avoidance conflict occurs when two equally unpleasant consequences are confronted, and avoiding one

leads to the other: a person may wish to avoid being fired, but at the same time dislike the boring job.

The most positive reaction to frustration is to analyze the situation and choose the most effective way to eliminate or bypass its cause. For some people, though, the reaction to frustration is anger, often leading to AGGRESSION. This approach may produce even more frustration. Anger vented against a safe, albeit inappropriate, target is called displaced aggression. Another reaction to frustration is withdrawal into fantasy (psychologists call this withdrawal "reaction repression") or regression to methods of adjustment that were successful in childhood.

Several compensatory reactions to frustration also exist. Failure in one area of activity may result in an intense effort to succeed in another area. Experience with a low level of frustration usually enables a person to develop a tolerance for the emotion, so that other situations in which goals are blocked can be dealt with more effectively and with less trauma.
                                             KENNETH E. MOYER

Bibliography: Janis, Irving L., *Stress and Frustration* (1971); Lawson, Reed, *Frustration* (1965); Maier, N. R., *Frustration* (1966; repr. 1982); Wallace, Leon, *Pleasure and Frustration* (1984).

See also: DEFENSE MECHANISMS.

Fry, Christopher

Christopher Fry, b. Dec. 18, 1907, is an English playwright whose verse dramas, although failing to revive the use of poetry in the theater, were greatly successful in their time and include several minor classics. Fry began his career in the theater as an actor and director. His first successful play was the one-act *A Phoenix Too Frequent* (1946). Three full-length poetic comedies followed: *The Lady's Not for Burning* (1948), *Venus Observed* (1950), and *The Dark Is Light Enough* (1954). Of his religious plays, *A Sleep of Prisoners* (1951) was the most widely produced. Fry's other writing includes translations of works by the French playwrights Jean Anouilh and Jean Giraudoux, film scripts for *The Beggar's Opera* (1953), *Ben Hur* (1959), *Barabbas* (1962), *The Bible* (1966), and his family history, *Can You Find Me?* (1978).   ROBIN BUSS

Bibliography: Buning, Sietze, *More Than the Ear Discovers* (1983); Leeming, Glenda, *Christopher Fry* (1990).

Fry, Edwin Maxwell

Maxwell Fry, b. Aug. 2, 1899, d. Sept. 3, 1987, was a pioneer of modern architecture in Great Britain in the 1930s. Trained at Liverpool University, he worked in a traditional manner until about 1931, when he built Sassoon House, the first reinforced-concrete apartment building in London. When Walter GROPIUS arrived from Germany, the two formed a partnership, and although lack of funding prevented most of their designs from being built, their school at Impington in Cambridgeshire (1936) remains a landmark in British educational buildings. During World War II, Fry and his architect wife, Jane Drew, worked as town-planning advisors in West Africa, and together they produced the influential book *Tropical Architecture in the Humid Zone* (1956). From 1951 to 1954, Fry and Drew collaborated with LE CORBUSIER on designing public housing for India's new city CHANDIGARH. Fry's *Autobiographic Sketches* was published in 1975.

Fry, Elizabeth

Elizabeth Fry, b. May 21, 1780, d. Oct. 12, 1845, was an English prison reformer and philanthropist. She became a Quaker in 1798; devoted to serving the poor, she was recognized as a minister. In 1813 she started investigating prison conditions and began visiting jails to read the Bible and preach to the inmates. Appalled at the treatment of female prisoners in Newgate prison, London, she publicized abuses—asking for separation of the sexes, classification of prisoners, more food and clothing, and better supervision. She organized an association that supported religious and secular instruction for the inmates and provided clothing and other necessities for pris-

Elizabeth Fry, a British prison reformer, Quaker minister, and philanthropist, campaigned throughout Great Britain and Europe to improve prison conditions. She appears here in an engraving based on a portrait by Charles Robert Leslie.

oners. Fry wrote tracts, testified before parliamentary committees, and visited monarchs in Europe to advocate prison reform.　　　　　　　　　　　　　　　　J. WILLIAM FROST

Bibliography: Fry, Katharine, and Cresswell, Rachel, eds., *Memoir of the Life of Elizabeth Fry* (1848; repr. 1972); Rose, June, *Elizabeth Fry* (1980).

Fry, Franklin Clark

Franklin Clark Fry, b. Bethlehem, Pa., Aug. 30, 1900, d. June 6, 1968, was a Lutheran clergyman and ecumenist. The son and grandson of Lutheran ministers, he served as the pastor of Lutheran churches from 1925 to 1944 and went on to become president of the United Lutheran Church in America (1944–62) and of the Lutheran Church in America (1962–68). Fry was deeply involved in the ecumenical movement and became (1954) chairman of the central committee of the World Council of Churches.　　　　　　　　　　　　JOHN F. PIPER, JR.

Fry, Roger

Roger Eliot Fry, b. Dec. 14, 1866, d. Sept. 9, 1934, was an English art critic and artist. Fry became interested in art as a student at Cambridge University, and after a stay in Italy in 1891 he returned to England and had some success as a painter. In 1894, Fry began to lecture on art and quickly became an influential critic and author. His initial exposure to Paul Cézanne's paintings in 1906 made him an enthusiastic champion of the postimpressionists, and in November 1910 he organized a successful exhibition of their works at the Grafton Gallery, London. From 1905 to 1910, Fry was curator of paintings at the Metropolitan Museum of Art, New York City. Fry wrote on individual artists but was at his best in more general aesthetic studies, such as *Vision and Design* (1920), *Reflections on British Painting* (1934), and *Last Lectures* (1939), which he was in the course of delivering as Slade Professor of Fine Art at Cambridge University when he died.　　　　　RAYMOND LISTER

Bibliography: Woolf, Virginia, *Roger Fry, A Biography* (1940; repr. 1976).

Frye, Northrop

Herman Northrop Frye, b. Sherbrooke, Quebec, Canada, July 14, 1912, d. Jan. 23, 1991, was a literary critic known for his studies of the relationships of literature, myth, and society. His first major work, *Fearful Symmetry* (1947), which explores myth and mysticism in William Blake's works, was a pioneering work in the "mythical" school of modern criticism.

Frye's best-known work is *The Anatomy of Criticism* (1957). In this controversial study, Frye, who was ordained a minister in 1936, introduced a critical system built on the analysis of recurrent literary archetypes, especially the Judeo-Christian myths of the quest, redemption, and fall. Although Frye's reputation rests chiefly on the *Anatomy*, he wrote extensively on Shakespeare, Milton, and the English Romantics.

After receiving degrees from Toronto University's Victoria College (1933) and Oxford's Merton College (1940), Frye joined the Victoria faculty and became (1967) a professor at the University of Toronto. He gained an international reputation as a lecturer on his theories, which were further explored in *Spiritus Mundi* (1976) and in such later works as *The Great Code: The Bible and Literature* (1982) and *Words with Power* (1990).

Bibliography: Ayre, J., *Northrop Frye* (1989); Balfour, I., *Northrop Frye* (1988); Cook, D., *Northrop Frye* (1986); Denham, R. D., *Northrop Frye: An Annotated Bibliography of Primary and Secondary Sources* (1987).

FSH: see GONADOTROPHIN; HORMONES; PITUITARY GLAND.

Fu Pao-shih　(Fu Baoshi)　[foo-pow-shih]

Fu Pao-shih, 1904–65, was a traditional Chinese painter and art historian. Like many of the intellectuals of his time, Fu went abroad to further his education. His painting, however, had deep roots in traditional China. After his return from Japan in 1935, he taught art at various universities and wrote extensively on Chinese art. As a painter, he was admired for his landscapes and figures, which showed the influence of the 17th-century Individualist school.　　　LOUISA SHEN TING

Fu-Shou-Lu　(Fushoulu)　[foo-shoh'-loo]

In Chinese mythology, the Fu-Shou-Lu are the three so-called stellar gods: Fu Hsing, god of happiness; Shou Hsing, god of longevity; and Lu Hsing, god of prosperity. The most revered of the three is Shou Hsing, who is believed to determine the life span of each individual. The other two gods are deified historical figures.

Fu-shun　(Fushun)　[foo'-shoon]

Fu-shun (1988 est. pop., 1,290,000) is a city in China on the Hun River in the highly industrialized Liaoning province of Manchuria. The area's high-quality coal deposits are exploited chiefly by open-cut methods, and the mines, which extend for 16 km (10 mi), are among the largest in the world. The shale oil overlying the coal is processed in large refineries here. Fu-shun also has iron and steel mills, as well as aluminum-processing and chemical plants.

Fu-shun was settled by the 8th century but did not grow until 1905, when the Russians began to mine coal. Industrial development, expanded by the Japanese during the 1930s, has continued to grow under the present Chinese regime.

Fuad I, King of Egypt　[foo-ahd']

Fuad I, b. Mar. 26, 1868, d. Apr. 28, 1936, was the first king of modern Egypt. A son of ISMAIL PASHA, he succeeded his brother Hussein Kamil as sultan in 1917 and became king on his country's independence in 1922. His reign was marked by continued British influence in politics and by the king's struggle against the WAFD party.　　　　　　　　ROBIN BUSS

Fuchs, Daniel　[fuks]

Daniel Fuchs, b. New York City, June 25, 1909, is an American writer known especially for three novels: *Summer in Williamsburg* (1934), *Homage to Blenholt* (1936), and *Low Company* (1937), all dealing with Jewish life in Brooklyn, N.Y. In Hollywood in the 1950s, Fuchs wrote several successful screenplays including the Academy Award-winning script for *Love Me or Leave Me* (1955). His last novel, *West of the Rockies* (1971), was a bleak work about Hollywood lives and loves.　　　　　　　　　　　　F. M. PAULSEN

Fuchs, Sir Vivian

Sir Vivian Fuchs, b. Feb. 11, 1908, is a British geologist and Antarctic explorer. After serving as an officer in World War II, he headed a survey of the Falkland Islands (1947–50). During the International Geophysical Year (1957–58), he led the 12-man Commonwealth Trans-Antarctic Expedition, the first land crossing of Antarctica. Using snow tractors and dog teams, and supported by aircraft, the team made its way from the Filchner Ice Shelf to McMurdo Sound in 99 days, a feat for which Fuchs was knighted.

Bibliography: Fuchs, Vivian, and Hillary, Edmund, *The Crossing of Antarctica: The Commonwealth Trans-Antarctic Expedition, 1955-1958* (1959).

Füchsel, Georg Christian   [fuek'-suhl]

The German geologist and physician Georg Christian Füchsel, b. Feb. 14, 1722, d. June 20, 1773, was the first to recognize groupings of related strata, or rock layers, as geologic formations (see STRATIGRAPHY).

Füchsel assumed that natural processes are uniform through time. Basing his theories on studies of the Thüringen region of Germany, he distinguished different formations, each composed of the same material and formed during the same geologic time. He illustrated his discoveries in the first published geological map, showing both the distribution of the rocks and their relative ages.

Bibliography: Geikie, Archibald, *The Founders of Geology* (1905).

fuchsia   [fue'-shuh]

Fuchsias, genus *Fuchsia,* are small shrubs or trees belonging to the evening-primrose family, Onagraceae. They are native to New Zealand, Tahiti, and regions in Central and South America. The sizes of various species range from 46 cm (18 in) to more than 600 cm (20 ft) in height. Many species have hanging flowers that are brilliant red, purple, or pink in color. Hardy fuchsia, *F. magellanica,* and honeysuckle fuchsia, *F. triphylla,* are two well-known ornamentals, and their hybrids are often grown in hanging baskets and even, in warm climates, planted as hedges.

Honeysuckle fuchsia, F. triphylla, *is a decorative shrub that is native to the West Indies. Its tubular, showy flowers are borne in hanging clusters. It reaches about 60 cm (2 ft) in height.*

Fucus   [fue'-kuhs]

Fucus, or rockweed, is a genus of brown algae in the family Fucaceae, division Phaeophyta, that often grows on rocks, shells, or pilings. *Fucus* has many flattened, forked branches with swollen, terminal reproductive organs (receptacles), a disklike foot called a holdfast, and swollen air bladders. Its receptacles have tiny cavities (conceptacles) that produce the sex cells, which shed at low tide. Eggs and sperm occur on the same or separate plants, depending on the species. Alginic acid, used in ice cream and other confections as well as in paints, is derived from the algae.

fuel

Fuel is any substance used to produce heat energy through a chemical or nuclear reaction. The energy is produced by the conversion of a portion of the fuel's mass.

ORIGIN OF FUELS

The fuels used today as ENERGY SOURCES fall into two general categories: those which are photosynthetic in origin and those which make use of atomic nuclei. The process of photosynthesis harnesses solar energy to produce the chemical reactions that convert carbon dioxide and water into carbohydrates. Initially, photosynthesis leads to the growth of plants, which can be burned directly as fuel; wood, straw, and other dry vegetable remains are still used as fuel throughout the world. Alternatively, the plants may be eaten by animals, which in turn produce waste products that can be burned directly or processed in digesters to produce gas (largely methane). This gas can then be burned in the same way as any other gaseous fuel. The important feature of these fuels is that they are renewable, because the plant life will generate a new crop after some determinable period of time.

Fuel derived from photosynthesis is also produced through the accumulation of decaying animal and vegetable matter over long periods of time. PEAT, for example, accumulates in suitable boggy areas, where the conditions are such that the normal processes of decay are arrested, and the cellulose that makes up the fibrous structure of plants is converted into humus. In certain areas of the world, notably the USSR, Germany, and Ireland, peat is an important fuel used not only for domestic purposes but also on a large scale in electricity generation.

Fossil Fuels. More important is the conversion of vegetable matter into coal (see COAL AND COAL MINING), a transformation not completely understood, although the basic geological processes are known. A peatlike deposit is formed and is subsequently covered by a layer of sand and silt, which stops the processes of peat formation. Over the course of time, the thickness of the sedimentary layer of silt and sand increases, and the deposit is subjected to increasing pressure. Water and volatile components are expelled, and the remaining material becomes relatively deficient in oxygen and richer in carbon. Hydrogen ceases to combine with oxygen to form water and instead becomes attached to carbon, forming HYDROCARBONS. This process may take millions of years, but it eventually transforms the spongy, fibrous peaty material into hard, brittle coal.

The starting point for the formation of oil (see PETROLEUM; NATURAL GAS) is the decay of marine plankton that has accumulated in the sediments at the bottom of the sea. Subsequent processes basically similar to those of coal formation bring about the transformation to hydrocarbons. The formation of hard, nonporous cap rock (see SALT DOME) prevents the oil from escaping. Oil and gas deposits are smaller, relatively more isolated, and less numerous than coal deposits.

Because fossil fuels have accumulated from the remains of plants and animals that lived many millions of years ago, coal, oil, and natural gas are finite, nonrenewable resources.

Nuclear Fuels. Nuclear fuels (see NUCLEAR ENERGY) are made possible by the near instability of some heavy atomic nuclei, particularly uranium-235 and plutonium-239. When the nucleus of one of these isotopes is struck by a slow-moving neutron, it undergoes fission and splits into two separate nuclei of almost equal mass, releasing energy in the process. The energy released per unit weight is much larger than that produced by the burning of fossil fuels. Nuclear fission fuels are a legacy from the Earth's formation; they are the remnants of what was once a much more active mixture of radioactive and fissionable materials 2 billion years ago and earlier.

Energy is also released from nuclear reactions between very light nuclei, such as hydrogen isotopes, when they combine to form a heavier atom, such as helium. This is called nuclear fusion, a process that, if properly harnessed, might provide a solution to the world's long-term energy-supply problem. Unfortunately, no experimental system has yet been perfected (see FUSION, NUCLEAR; FUSION ENERGY).

HISTORY OF FUEL USE

Although time scales vary from country to country, the historical development of fuel use in the industrialized nations follows a simple basic pattern: a decline in the use of wood as fuel, the adoption of fuels with a higher energy content, and the diversification of fuels. Until the beginning of the 17th century, fire was used for cooking and heating and for smelting and firing kilns. Wood, the principal fuel, was used to produce another fuel, CHARCOAL, for smelting.

The industrial expansion that began in the 17th century caused a fuel shortage that was not alleviated until the replacement of wood by coal and of charcoal by COKE. The development of the steam engine in the late 17th century exacerbated the fuel-supply problem. The improvements by Thomas Newcomen in 1712 made the use of steam engines economical for pumping water out of mines and established coal as the primary fuel for Britain and, later, for all of Europe. Throughout the 18th century, further developments increased the efficiency of the steam engine, expanded the range of its applications in industry, and increased the rate of exploitation of coal as a primary fuel.

By the late 19th century industrialization had reached the limits of what was possible using coal and steam alone, and new energy sources and distribution systems were being developed. Clean and convenient systems for distributing gas and electricity to domestic and industrial consumers were constructed in the cities. At approximately the same time, the use of oil became feasible. The United States, with its own domestic supplies of oil and natural gas, was able to base its industrial expansion on this new fuel, while European countries, without large-scale oil and gas deposits, continued to expand their coal-based economies but began to import oil to meet demand. The rapid development of the automobile as the preferred form of transportation, especially in the United States, enormously expanded the market for liquid fuels. After World War II, oil became very cheap on the international markets, and world dependence on it for industrial development and replacement projects increased dramatically.

All the Western nations were greatly affected by the sharp price rise in petroleum products in the 1970s (see PETROLEUM), which produced a variety of responses. France, for example, pushed ahead with its rapid development of nuclear energy, while other nations made plans to fall back on the extensive coal reserves in the United States, Australia, and South Africa. The SYNTHETIC FUELS program initiated under President Jimmy Carter—a plan for the large-scale production of liquid and gaseous fuels from coal and oil shale (see SHALE, OIL)—encountered serious cost problems. It also aroused fears of environmental damage in the areas (mainly in the Southwest) where mining operations and synthesizing plants were planned.

Other experimental fuels include ethanol and methanol, produced by conversion of biomass (see GASOHOL), and METHANE, the main constituent of natural gas. The use of HYDROGEN as a fuel—perhaps in hydrogen-powered FUEL CELLS—awaits the invention of methods for producing it inexpensively, primarily by electrolysis, the passing of electricity through water. Devices for storing the fuel, either as a pressurized gas or as a very low-temperature liquid, are also being investigated. Another possibility might be the heating of stored liquid ammonia—made by combining hydrogen and nitrogen—to release its hydrogen component.

Wood made a comeback in such forested areas as New England and the Pacific Northwest, where, by the mid 1980s, wood-burning stoves and furnaces were supplying a considerable proportion of domestic heat. In 1984 nine percent of U.S. electric-generation plants were burning wood as a fuel. Air pollution from wood smoke and cheaper oil in the late 1980s combined to shrink the use of wood, however.

Many developing countries still depend almost entirely on wood for domestic fuel, even as their rapidly expanding populations consume the available wood, and deforestation creates fuel shortages and major environmental problems.

Few countries have seriously investigated the possibilities of SOLAR ENERGY, which may ultimately supply the most abundant and least polluting form of fuel, should oil and natural gas supplies be exhausted or become too costly.

FUEL PROPERTIES AND USES

The primary fuels can be processed to yield different by-products or secondary fuels. The uses to which specific fuels may

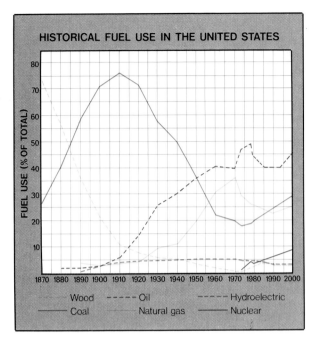

By 1890 coal had supplanted wood as the primary fuel in the United States; coal in turn had been superseded by petroleum and natural gas by 1950. In the near future the United States may once again rely on coal and wood, along with nuclear energy, as primary energy sources.

be put depend greatly on the properties of the fuel itself. Domestic fuels must be relatively clean; fuels for power generation, on the other hand, may be fairly low-grade if the equipment is available to clean them and reduce the effluents created when they are burned. Other factors, such as availability and convenience, also play an important part. The high cost of cutting and transporting peat or wood, for example, is a factor in the delivered cost.   JOHN T. McMULLAN

Bibliography: Anderson, Larry L., and Tillman, David A., *Fuels from Waste* (1977) and *Synthetic Fuels from Coal* (1979); Bisio, Attilio, *Encyclopedia of Energy Technology* (1983); Bungay, H. R., *Energy: The Biomass Options* (1981); Cannon, James S., *The Drive for Clean Air: Natural Gas and Methanol Vehicles* (1989); Leclercq, Jacques, *The Nuclear Age* (1986); McMullan, J. T., *Energy Resources and Supply* (1976); Smith, K. R., *Biofuels, Air Pollution, and Health: A Global Review* (1987); Speight, James G., *Fuel Science and Technology Handbook* (1990); Sperling, Daniel, ed., *Alternative Transportation Fuels* (1989).

See also: BUTANE; GASOLINE; KEROSENE; LIQUEFIED PETROLEUM GAS; POWER, GENERATION AND TRANSMISSION OF; PROPANE.

fuel cell

A fuel cell is a device that continuously converts chemicals into direct-current electricity through electrochemical reactions. In a typical fuel cell hydrogen combines with hydroxyl ions at one electrode to produce water and electrons. The electrons perform electrical work by flowing through an external circuit to the other electrode, where they recombine with oxygen and water to produce hydroxyl ions. The overall reaction is $2H_2 + O_2 \rightarrow 2H_2O$. The fuel cell differs from a BATTERY in that its reactants must be supplied from an outside source. Fuel cells can theoretically convert fuel to electricity with nearly 100% efficiency. By contrast, burning fuel to produce steam for electricity is 40% to 50% efficient, and internal-combustion engines are only 10% to 20% efficient.

History. The first attempt to obtain electricity directly from a fuel was probably made in 1802 by Sir Humphry Davy, who described a cell with a carbon anode and aqueous nitric acid as the cathodic reactant. The first hydrogen-oxygen cell (reported 1839) was composed of two platinum strips immersed in acidified water; the upper part of one was exposed to hydrogen, the other to oxygen. Numerous attempts were made to develop efficient fuel cells that used carbon, because a galvanic cell that produced electrical energy directly from carbon and oxygen would be an inexpensive source of energy.

Types. The most common fuel cells have used oxygen and hydrogen gas with potassium hydroxide as an electrolyte. The water produced by the reaction is carried out by circulating gases and condenses externally.

Considerable research has been done on fuel-cell systems that use the direct oxidation of hydrocarbons. One promising model, the solid-oxide (or monolithic) cell, passes fuel through a ceramic honeycomb structure that resembles corrugated cardboard. The solid-oxide cell (so called because it contains electrolytes of yttria-stabilized zirconium oxide) produces electrical energy from almost any hydrocarbon fuel, including gasoline. Moreover, it produces little pollution and maintains high efficiency even at low operating levels.

Fuel cells are at present used chiefly in space vehicles and for limited military purposes. A 4.8-megawatt plant was put into operation in Tokyo in 1984, however. In the United States it is anticipated that similar electricity-producing and COGENERATION plants will eventually be on-line. Even cars may someday be powered by economical fuel cells.

ROBERT A. POWERS AND GEOFFREY W. MELLORS

Bibliography: Appleby, John, ed., *Fuel Cells* (1987); Miller, Richard E., and Rupnow, Marcia E., *Fuel Cells* (1991).

A fuel cell produces electricity from a chemical reaction of hydrogen and oxygen. The chemical reaction forms water as a by-product. This cell is made up of two gas chambers (1), a platinum-coated wire cathode (2) and anode (3), and a very thin electrolyte-saturated membrane (4) that can pass ions but not atoms or molecules. As molecular oxygen (6) entering the cell contacts the cathodic platinum, it is split into atoms (7), which combine with electrolyte water (8) and cathode electrons to form hydroxyl ions (9), which move to the anode. At the anode, molecular hydrogen (10) is split into atoms (11) similarly. These atoms combine with the hydroxyl ions to produce water (12), which is drained periodically, and electrons, which flow through the external circuit (5) as an electric current.

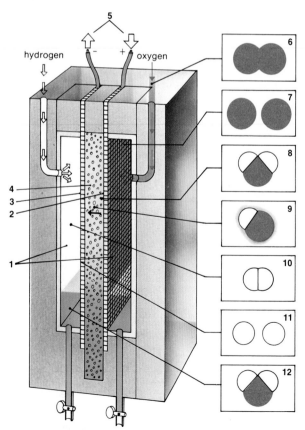

fuel injection

Fuel injection is a method of supplying a precise mixture of fuel and air—electronically measured and controlled—to the cylinders of an internal-combustion engine. With fuel injection, gasoline or diesel mixtures burn more cleanly, fuel consumption is cut, and the pollutants in the engine exhaust are reduced to a minimum amount that can be disposed of by a CATALYTIC CONVERTER. Mechanical fuel injection technology has been in use in diesel engines for many years. Although it was available for high-performance racing and sports cars from the 1950s, the technology did not come into wide use in passenger cars until the mid-1980s, when more stringent emissions-control legislation required cleaner-burning fuel-feeding methods. Fuel injection has now replaced the CARBURETOR on most new cars.

The injector system for a gasoline engine uses sensors to read the amount of oxygen in the exhaust, an indicator of how efficiently and cleanly fuel is being burned in the engine cylinders. Sensors also monitor engine speed and other significant measures of performance. All sensor signals are fed into a small computer located, usually, under the dashboard or the floor. The injector itself is a small valve powered by a solenoid switch. Gasoline is sent under pressure from the fuel pump into the valve. A signal from the computer actuates the switch, and fuel sprays out of the valve nozzle into the cylinders, where it mixes with the incoming air stream. The computer controls only one variable, the length of the injector pulse. Such factors as cold starts, a warm-running engine, or high-altitude oxygen compensation are adjusted for solely by changing the length of time the valve is open.

There are two primary systems of automobile fuel injection. Single-point, or throttle-body, injection has one or two injectors that operate from a central point. Multi-point injection uses a separate injector for each cylinder.

Bibliography: Norbye, J., *Automotive Fuel Injection Systems* (1988).

Fuentes, Carlos   [fwayn'-tays]

The 20th-century Mexican writer Carlos Fuentes uses the contemporary postrevolutionary period of his native country as a background for his writings. His novels explore the social impact of the revolution and study the Mexican people through their history and mythology.

Carlos Fuentes, b. Nov. 11, 1928, one of Mexico's leading writers, is known for his experimental novels and social criticism. A lawyer by training, Fuentes published his first work, a collection of surrealist short stories, *Los días enmascarados* (The Masked Days), in 1954. In his first novel, *Where the Air Is Clear* (1958; Eng. trans., 1960), he portrayed a cross section of Mexico City's population and the events they had lived through since the 1910 revolution. *The Death of Artemio Cruz* (1962; Eng. trans., 1964) brought Fuentes international recognition. Two later symbolic novels, *A Change of Skin* (1967; Eng. trans., 1968) and *Cumpleaños* (Birthdays, 1969), combined myth and history, two themes that have been persistent in Fuentes's work. More recent novels include *Terra Nostra* (1975; Eng. trans., 1976), *Distant Relations* (1982; Eng. trans., 1982), *The Old Gringo* (1985; Eng. trans., 1985), and *Christopher Unborn* (1989; Eng. trans., 1989). In addition, Fuentes has authored the television series "The Buried Mirror," a five-part history of Hispanic civilization.

The author of two absurdist plays, Fuentes has also published *Casa con dos puertas* (House with Two Doors, 1970) and *Tiempo mexicano* (Mexican Time, 1971), essay collections on American and Mexican writing and art. Deeply influenced by the philosopher Octavio Paz and the poet José Gorostiza, Fuentes first focused on the betrayal of the ideals of the Mexican Revolution; his later work presents a more universal examination of the human condition.   EDWARD MULLEN

Bibliography: Brody, R., and Rosman, C., eds., *Carlos Fuentes: A Critical View* (1982); Faris, W. B., *Carlos Fuentes* (1983).

Fugard, Athol [foo'-gard]

Athol Fugard, b. June 11, 1932, is internationally known as South Africa's finest producing playwright. Almost all his plays are about South Africa's black population, praising the human spirit's tenacity in the face of misery and humiliation. His powerful plays, many of which were banned by pro-apartheid South African governments, include *The Blood Knot* (1961); *Boesman and Lena* (1970; film, 1972), which won a 1972 Obie Award; and a trilogy that includes *The Island, Sizwe Banzi Is Dead* (both 1973), and *Statements after an Arrest under the Immorality Act* (1974). Of his later plays most critics single out *A Lesson from Aloes* (1978), *Master Harold . . . & the Boys* (1982), and *The Road to Mecca* (1984) as the best he has written. Fugard describes his work in *Notebooks 1960–1977* (1983).

Bibliography: Vandenbroucke, R., *Truths the Hand Can Touch: The Theatre of Athol Fugard* (1985).

Fugger (family) [fug'-ur]

The Fuggers of Augsburg, Germany, were the most successful family of merchants, mineowners, and bankers of the 16th century. Jacob Fugger (1459–1525) took control of the family firm in 1485. In return for loans to the counts of Tyrol and the Habsburg emperors, Fugger obtained monopoly concessions for the mining of Tyrolese silver, Hungarian copper, and Spanish mercury. For a time the firm's profits rose by more than 50 percent each year. The loans to the Habsburgs rose similarly, and the business became a vital part of the Habsburg government finances. Gradually the Habsburgs ruined the Fuggers by repeated failures to repay loans. The firm was finally closed in the mid-1600s.   H. G. KOENIGSBERGER

Bibliography: Ehrenberg, Richard, *Capital and Finance in the Age of the Renaissance* (1928; repr. 1985).

fuging tune [fueg'-ing]

The fuging tune was a short religious vocal composition that opened with a section in chordal style and concluded with an imitative passage, usually repeated, in which all voices entered at different times with the same thematic material. It was common in 17th- and 18th-century England and 18th- and early 19th-century America. The fuging tune was not an attempt to create a fugue in miniature, but a device to bring variety to the homophonic (chordal) psalm tune. Among the dozens of American fuging-tune composers, in addition to William BILLINGS, who is the best known, were Lewis Edson, Daniel Read, and Oliver Holden.   ELWYN A. WIENANDT

Bibliography: Lowens, I., *Music and Musicians in Early America* (1964).

Fugitive Slave Laws

The U.S. Congress legislated separate Fugitive Slave Laws in 1793 and 1850 that provided for return between states of escaped slaves. The first act was largely ineffective. As slavery was abolished in the Northern states and antislavery sentiment increased, enforcement in the North became lax. Several Northern states passed personal liberty laws that allowed fugitives a jury trial; others prohibited state officials from cooperating in the capture and return of fugitives.

As a concession to the South, Congress legislated a more stringent Fugitive Slave Law as part of the COMPROMISE OF 1850. Violent disorders broke out during the 1850s, however, when slaveholders attempted to capture runaways in the North. Northern states rendered the law useless by passing more sweeping personal liberty laws. The dispute over the Fugitive Slave laws was an important cause of conflict between North and South. On June 28, 1864, during the Civil War, Congress repealed both acts.   DOUGLAS T. MILLER

Bibliography: Campbell, Stanley W., *The Slave Catchers* (1970).

Fugitives and Agrarians

The Fugitives, also called the Agrarians, were a group of American poets and critics based at Vanderbilt University. The group included John Crowe RANSOM, Allen TATE, and Robert Penn WARREN. They defended the aristocratic heritage of the South, an agrarian society they felt was being destroyed by industrialization. They expressed these views in *I'll Take My Stand* (1930), their manifesto. They published the poetry magazine *The Fugitive* (1922–25) and contributed to *The Southern Review, The Sewanee Review*, and *The Kenyon Review*.

Bibliography: Conkin, P., *The Southern Agrarians* (1988); Cowan, L., *The Fugitive Group* (1959); Stewart, J. L., *The Burden of Time* (1965).

fugue [fueg]

The fugue is the most highly developed form of imitative COUNTERPOINT; it came to prominence in the late 17th century as the successor to the ricercar and canzona. The fugue has no strict form; rather, it is a contrapuntal style with regularly recurring features, its distinguishing character being its texture more than its shape. It is written for a given number of parts, from two to normally no more than five or six. The entire composition of a fugue is based on a theme called the "subject," which is introduced as a solo melody. The part that introduces it commonly continues with a "countersubject," while another part sounds the original theme against the countersubject as an "answer." Entries and exchanges continue until all the parts have entered with the subject theme, thus completing an "exposition." Less complex sections, called episodes (in which the subject is excluded), separate additional expositions (complete or incomplete), or "developments," from one another. Fugues often end with a stretto, in which statements of the subject overlap; that is, each entry begins before the previous one has completed its statement. Sometimes a pedal point—a sustained bass tone against which the other parts provide harmonies—precedes the closing statement of the subject.

The subject of a fugue may be modified in one or more of the following ways: augmentation, in which the subject is presented in longer notes; diminution, in which the note values are halved or quartered; inversion, in which the subject is sounded upside down; and retrograde, in which it is backward.

The rules of fugue were formulated by Johann Joseph FUX in his *Gradus ad Parnassum* (1725), a volume that served as a model text for counterpoint study until well into the next century. Johann Sebastian BACH brought the fugue to its peak of development in both instrumental and vocal music. It continued to interest later composers, especially Ludwig van Beethoven, who used it in nearly every idiom he cultivated. In the baroque period the fugue was an important component of Masses, cantatas, oratorios, and large anthems; it was used in keyboard works, more often for organ than harpsichord and piano, and in chamber and orchestral music until Beethoven's time.   ELWYN A. WIENANDT

Bibliography: Kitson, C. H., *The Elements of Fugal Construction* (1929; repr. 1981); Mann, A., *The Study of Fugue* (1958; repr. 1987); Verrall, J. W., *Fugue and Invention in Theory and Practice* (1990).

Fuji, Mount [foo'-jee]

Mount Fuji (Japanese: Fujiyama) is a dormant volcano located 112 km (70 mi) southwest of Tokyo in south central Honshu island. The highest mountain in Japan, it rises in near-perfect symmetry from a base 126 km (78 mi) in circumference to a height of 3,776 m (12,388 ft). Five interconnecting lakes, formed during earlier lava flows, ring its base. One of these lakes, Kawaguchi, is famous for the inverted image of the mountain reflected in its water. Long held sacred by Japanese Buddhists, Fuji has inspired artists and poets for centuries.

Legend maintains that Fuji was created during an earthquake in 286 BC. Geologists believe that it and the rugged peaks that stretch across Honshu from the Sea of Japan to the Pacific Ocean were created during the Tertiary Period (65–2 million years ago). The elliptical crater, now approximately 610 m (2,000 ft) in diameter, was formed during the Quaternary Period, when great quantities of lava flowed from its center. The last eruption occurred in 1707. The slopes of Fuji are seriously eroded, and rock and sand slides occur often. Concrete barriers are being constructed to slow the deterioration.

Cultivated fields ring the mountain base to a height of 365 m (1,200 ft). At higher elevations bamboo groves are superseded by pine forests, and, above 1,830 m (6,000 ft), lie snowfields. Thousands of hikers and pilgrims climb to the summit during July and August. Mount Fuji is located in Fuji-Hakone-Izu National Park.

Fujian (Fukien) [foo'-jhee-en]

Fujian, a province in southeastern China, is located on the Formosa Strait across from Taiwan. The province has an area of 123,100 km² (47,500 mi²) and a population of 30,048,224 (1990). FUZHOU (Foochow) is the capital and chief port. Except for an irregular coastal strip and the long Min River valley, most of Fujian is mountainous, reaching 1,800 m (6,000 ft) in the Wui (Wu-i) Shan in the east. Rice, fruits, sugarcane, and tea are grown at lower elevations. Coal, iron, copper, and other minerals are mined, and timber is important.

Fujian became part of China during the 2d century BC. From the 17th through the 19th century, it was the departure point for many of China's emigrants to Southeast Asia.

Fujimori, Alberto K.

Alberto Kenyo Fujimori, b. July 28, 1938, the son of Japanese immigrants, was elected president of Peru in 1990. An agronomist and radio talk show host, he won an upset victory by appealing to the country's poor. As president, Fujimori enjoyed popular support but encountered a hostile legislature. After 20 months in office he suspended the constitution and dissolved the legislature, which was replaced by an elected constituent assembly in November 1992. A year later the electorate approved a new constitution that strengthened his authority and removed a bar to his seeking reelection. His economic reforms and a successful campaign against the guerrilla SHINING PATH were rewarded in 1993 by a commitment of $2 billion in U.S. and Japanese foreign loans.

Fukien: see FUJIAN.

Fukuda Takeo [foo-koo'-dah tah-kay'-oh]

The Japanese conservative political leader Fukuda Takeo, b. Jan. 14, 1905, served as prime minister from 1976 to 1978. He studied at Tokyo Imperial University and from 1929 to 1950 worked in the Ministry of Finance. He became director of the Budget Bureau in 1947. Wrongly implicated in a financial scandal in 1950, Fukuda resigned and in 1952 entered Japan's House of Representatives. He was minister of finance in 1965–66, 1968–71, and 1973–74. In December 1976 he succeeded MIKI TAKEO as prime minister. In November 1978, Fukuda lost the leadership of the Liberal-Democratic party to OHIRA MASAYOSHI, who became premier.

Fukuoka [foo-koo'-oh-kah]

Fukuoka, the capital of Fukuoka prefecture, Japan, is located on Hakata Bay in the northern part of Kyushu island, about 100 km (62 mi) north-northeast of Nagasaki. The city has a population of 1,249,320 (1991 est.).

Fukuoka is near the western end of the east-west Tokaido megalopolis, a huge urban-industrial region. One of the leading commercial, industrial, and political centers of Kyushu,

it manufactures iron and steel, chemicals, ceramics, machinery, textiles, and processed food. Agriculture in the surrounding area is also important to the city's economy. The city is the home of Kyushu University, one of the five imperial universities of Japan, established in 1910. Fukuoka repelled two invasion attempts by Mongols in the 13th century.   JAMES CHAN

Fulani [foo-lahn'-ee]

The Fulani, also called Fulbe or Peul, are an African people widely dispersed through West Africa, from Senegal eastward to Chad and western Sudan. They number more than 7,000,000 and speak a language in the Atlantic subgroup of the Niger-Congo stock of African languages. Their physical characteristics include light copper-colored skin, straight hair, and thin nose and lips.

Some Fulani are nomadic cattle herders, others are sedentary town residents. Nomadic Fulani live in bands, move about with their herds, and are essentially egalitarian; they are pagans or indifferent Muslims. Town-dwelling Fulani live mainly by farming, trade, and the production of crafts; they are ardent Muslims and are often stratified into social classes. Both types of Fulani traditionally kept slaves. Fulani descent and residence are traced through the male line. Marriage is predominantly polygynous, with co-wives living in separate houses.

A Muslim people since the 11th century, the Fulani have played a major role in the history of West Africa. During the 1600s they became leaders in an Islamic spiritual renaissance and, beginning in the 1700s, proselytized widely in the Sudan. In 1804–10, USMAN DAN FODIO led a jihad (holy war) in which the Hausa states of northern Nigeria were conquered. From then on these states were governed by Fulani rulers and fief-holders until British conquest in 1903.   PHOEBE MILLER

Bibliography: Johnston, H. A. S., *The Fulani Empire of Sokoto* (1967); Stenning, Derrick, *Savannah Nomads* (1959; repr. 1964).

Fulbright, J. William

J. William Fulbright, a U.S. senator from Arkansas, served as chairman of the powerful Senate Foreign Relations Committee and was a chief congressional critic of American involvement in the Vietnam War. He also spoke out against U.S. military intervention in the Dominican Republic (1965) and advocated increased congressional participation in the formulation of foreign policy. In 1975, after he left the Senate, Fulbright joined a Washington law firm.

James William Fulbright, b. Sumner, Mo., Apr. 9, 1905, served for 30 years as U.S. senator from Arkansas. A Rhodes scholar, a lawyer, and a Democrat, he entered the U.S. House of Representatives in 1943 and the Senate in 1945. In 1946 he sponsored the Fulbright Act, which provided government grants for the international exchange of students and teachers.

During the cold war period following World War II, Fulbright advocated accommodation with the Communist world but at the same time pushed for a powerful nuclear deterrent and a strong alliance with the countries of Western Europe. As chairman of the Senate Committee on Foreign Relations from 1959 to 1974, he took issue with the use of executive power in determining foreign policy and argued that Congress should have greater control of decisions involving foreign aid and American military commitments overseas. He was often critical of U.S. foreign policy, speaking out against the Bay of Pigs invasion of Cuba in 1961 and the armed intervention in the Dominican Republic in 1965. In the late 1960s he became a leading opponent of the U.S. involvement in the Vietnam War. Fulbright was defeated for renomination in 1974.

Bibliography: Berman, W. C., *William Fulbright and the Vietnam War* (1988); Brown, E. J., *William Fulbright* (1985); Lynn, N. B., and Mc-Clure, A. F., *The Fulbright Premise* (1973).

Fulbright Exchange Program

The Fulbright Exchange Program, which is sponsored by the U.S. government, is designed to promote mutual understanding among nations by providing travel grants to enable graduate students and professors to engage in research, study, and teaching abroad. The program was initiated in 1946 through the efforts of Senator William Fulbright and was expanded by the Fulbright-Hays Act of 1961.

fulgurite   [ful'-guh-rite]

Fulgurite is natural silica glass (see SILICA MINERALS) fused by the heat of a lightning strike or meteorite impact. Sand fulgurites are hollow, branching tubes commonly 3–20 m (10–60 ft) long and 1 cm (0.4 in) in diameter; they form on sandy beaches, desert sand dunes, or lakeshores. The less common rock fulgurites are thin, glassy crusts on the rocky summits of some mountains. Fulgurites are composed of lechatelierite, a high-temperature quartz mineral.

Fuller, Alfred Carl

Alfred Carl Fuller, b. Nova Scotia, Jan. 13, 1885, d. Dec. 4, 1973, was the first "Fuller Brush man." In 1903 he moved to Boston and worked as a salesman for a brush company. Fuller started his own company in Hartford, Conn., in 1906, making the twisted-wire brushes himself and selling them door to door. In 1913 the firm was incorporated as the Fuller Brush Company, and its nationwide direct-sales organization eventually made Fuller products so famous they needed little advertising. The comedian Red Skelton played the title role in the 1948 movie *Fuller Brush Man.* Fuller's autobiography, *A Foot in the Door,* appeared in 1960.

Fuller, Loie

One of the instigators of modernism in the theater, the American dancer Loie Fuller (originally Mary Louise Fuller), b. Fullersburg, Ill., Jan. 22, 1862, d. Jan. 21, 1928, created a furor with her novel use of theatrical techniques in the dance. Although her influence was felt mainly in Europe, where she first appeared in 1892 (in Paris) and where she settled for the rest of her life, she helped to create an atmosphere in which such experimental dancers as her fellow American Isadora Duncan could flourish. A self-trained dancer, Loie Fuller, with her innovative ideas (above all, the manipulation of long, diaphanous skirts under continually changing lights) caused a sensation. Popular with theatergoers, she also became a cult figure for many of the artists and writers of her time—such as Auguste Rodin, Henri de Toulouse-Lautrec, and Stéphane Mallarmé—to whom she seemed the embodiment of art. She retired in 1926.   DALE HARRIS

Bibliography: Fuller, Loie, *Fifteen Years of a Dancer's Life* (1913; repr. 1976).

Fuller, Margaret

The American writer and intellectual Sarah Margaret Fuller, b. May 23, 1810, d. July 19, 1850, is generally regarded as one of America's first major woman journalists and authors and, along with Edgar Allan Poe, the best literary critic of her day.

Fuller was born near Boston, the first of nine children. Her father committed her to a complete and rigorous education

Margaret Fuller, an American editor and social critic, worked closely with Ralph Waldo Emerson and the transcendentalists before accepting Horace Greeley's invitation to write literary criticism for the New York Tribune. *Fuller's most notable essay,* Woman in the Nineteenth Century *(1845), is a powerful study of feminism.*

normally reserved for boys. Her precocious intellect soon brought her into contact with circles of young thinkers at Harvard and around Cambridge in the late 1820s. She also taught in Bronson ALCOTT's experimental Temple School (1836–37) in Boston and at her own Green Street School in Providence, R.I. (1837–39). In 1836 she met Emerson and by 1839 had become a prominent member of the transcendentalists and had published her translation of Johann Eckermann's *Conversations with Goethe* (1839). She edited the transcendentalist journal, the *Dial,* from 1840 to 1842. In Boston between 1839 and 1844 she began holding her famous Conversations, or intellectual discussions. In 1844, Fuller published the accounts of her travels to the midwest in *Summer on the Lakes, in 1843,* and that same year she went to New York to join the staff of Horace Greeley's *Tribune* as literary critic. While in New York she published *Woman in the Nineteenth Century* (1845), probably the most impressive early American feminist work, and *Papers on Literature and Art* (1846).

In 1846 she went to Europe as America's first woman foreign correspondent, reported from England and the Continent, and lived in Italy from 1847 to 1850. In Italy she met and began living with Count Giovanni Angelo Ossoli, ten years her junior. The couple had a child in 1848 and were married in 1849. Fuller became a partisan of the Roman republic led by Mazzini, a popular revolt against the dominance of the Papal States, and began to write a history of the revolution, which she thought would be her finest achievement. In 1850 she sailed for America to escape the upheavals in Italy, but she and her family died in a shipwreck off the coast of Fire Island, N.Y.

JOEL MYERSON

Bibliography: Blanchard, Paula, *Margaret Fuller* (1978); Emerson, Ralph Waldo, Channing, William Henry, and Clarke, James Freeman, *Memoirs of Margaret Fuller Ossoli,* 2 vols. (1852); Myerson, Joel, *Margaret Fuller: An Annotated Secondary Bibliography* (1977) and *Margaret Fuller: A Descriptive Bibliography* (1978); Stern, Madeleine B., *The Life of Margaret Fuller* (1942).

Fuller, Melville Weston

As the eighth chief justice of the United States (1888–1910), Melville Weston Fuller, b. Augusta, Maine, Feb. 11, 1833, d. July 4, 1910, left no distinctive legal mark. An advocate of strict construction of the Constitution, Fuller's most important opinions invalidated the Income Tax Act of 1893. He was popular, however, and a great friend of Oliver Wendell Holmes, Jr. He helped to settle the Venezuela Boundary Dispute (1899) and served on the Permanent Court of Arbitration at The Hague.

Bibliography: King, Willard L., *Melville Weston Fuller* (1950; repr. 1967).

Fuller, R. Buckminster

The futurist Richard Buckminster Fuller, b. Milton, Mass., July 12, 1895, d. July 1, 1983, achieved an international reputation as an inventor, designer, and philosopher. Although he showed inventive talent at an early age, Fuller had great diffi-

The American architect and inventor Buckminster Fuller devised some of the most original and practical designs of modern technology. Best known for his economical and ecologically conservative geodesic domes derived from his system of vectorial geometry, Fuller created houses and cars based on similar "dymaxion" principles of "more for less."

culty finding an appropriate occupation. Dropping out of Harvard after his freshman year, he educated himself while working at various industrial jobs and serving in the U.S. Navy during World War I. Fuller had no patience with the profit motive and was interested in developing new products and designs only as long as technical problems remained challenging. This trait so displeased investors in his early business ventures that in 1927 he found himself unemployed in Chicago with a family to support. He devoted the next year to formulating a philosophical approach to technological innovation.

Fuller worked from the premise that humankind's creative intelligence is limitless. Therefore, technological progress can, if unhampered by outmoded traditions and conventions, give all human beings a rich and satisfying life. The Earth's limited resources, in his view, can be overcome by inventions that provide ever-greater amenities while using ever-decreasing amounts of materials. Because Fuller was persuaded that humans' geographical mobility should also be limitless, many of his major inventions were designed to reduce or eliminate barriers to mobility. The first of these, the Dymaxion House of 1927—entirely self-contained and readily movable—hung from a central core, thereby greatly reducing its use of materials, weight, and cost. His Dymaxion Car of 1933 brought similar economies to the automobile. His GEODESIC DOME (first perfected in 1947) encloses a greater volume with less material than any alternative form and may well be the most significant structural innovation of the 20th century. The interesting large, spherical CARBON molecules that display a geodetic form have been named fullerenes, or buckminsterfullerenes, in his honor. Fuller's many design credits include the U.S. Pavilion at the Montreal world's fair (1967).

Fuller, who held more than 2,000 patents and was the author of about 25 books, including *Operating Manual for Spaceship Earth* (1969), was an enormously popular college lecturer. From 1959 until his death he was a professor at Southern Illinois University.   J. MEREDITH NEIL

Bibliography: Caspar, D. E., *R. Buckminster Fuller* (1988); Martin, W., ed., *The Artifacts of R. Buckminster Fuller*, 4 vols. (1985); Meller, J., ed., *The Buckminster Fuller Reader* (1970); Potter, R. F., *Buckminster Fuller* (1990); Seiden, L. S., *Buckminster Fuller's Universe* (1987; repr. 1989).

Fuller, Thomas

Thomas Fuller, b. June 19, 1608, d. Aug. 16, 1661, was an English historian and biographer whose best-known work is *History of the Worthies of England*, published posthumously in 1665. It contains witty character sketches, noted for their quaint style. A renowned preacher, Fuller also wrote *The Holy State and the Profane State* (1642) and an ecclesiastical history of England.

Bibliography: Addison, W., *Worthy Doctor Fuller* (1951; repr. 1971).

fullerenes: see CARBON.

fuller's earth

Fuller's earth is a mixture of clay or silt materials in which montmorillonite and attapulgite normally predominate. It has the property of adsorption and was used originally by fullers (textile workers) to remove oil from cloth. Fuller's earth is now used in oil-well drilling mud and floor-sweeping compounds, as a pesticide carrier, and to remove color from oils.

Fulton

Fulton (1990 pop., 10,033), located about 160 km (100 mi) west of St. Louis in east central Missouri, is the seat of Callaway County. Fulton serves as the commercial center for the surrounding agricultural region. Firebrick manufacturing is the principal industry, although machinery and shoes are also produced. In 1946, Sir Winston Churchill made his famous Iron Curtain speech there at Westminster College (1851). Fulton was founded in 1825.

Fulton, Robert

The American inventor, artist, and engineer Robert Fulton, b. Lancaster County, Pa., Nov. 14, 1765, d. Feb. 24, 1815, is best known for his pioneer work in the development of the STEAMBOAT. In the mid-1780s he worked as an artist in Philadelphia, and in 1786 he went to London to study painting under Benjamin West. By the early 1790s his interests had shifted to science and engineering. In 1794 he received a British patent for a double inclined plane used to raise and lower canal boats from one level to another. Two years later he published *A Treatise on the Improvement of Canal Navigation* and also submitted plans for cast-iron aqueducts.

Fulton moved to France in 1797 and in the same year submitted proposals to the French government for a submarine. His submarine, the *Nautilus*, was launched in 1800; although it proved workable, neither the French, British, nor U.S. governments demonstrated support for the project, and in 1806 he abandoned it. In the meantime Fulton agreed (1802) to design and build for Robert R. Livingston a steamboat that would operate on the Hudson River. His first steamboat was successfully tested on the Seine River in 1803. Fulton returned to the United States in 1806, and in 1807 his steamboat was launched in New York harbor. The boat, which eventually was called the CLERMONT, proved the commercial feasibility of steamboats. Fulton later constructed other steamboats, including a warship. Fulton is popularly considered the inventor of the steamship, but others had built steamships before him.

Bibliography: Hutcheon, Wallace S., Jr., *Robert Fulton: Pioneer of Undersea Warfare* (1981); Philip, Cynthia, *Robert Fulton* (1985).

fumarole   [fue'-muh-rohl]

A fumarole (from the Latin word for "smoke hole") is a small hole, vent, or fissure in the Earth from which gases and vapors escape. Most fumaroles are found in areas of recent volcanic activity, where ground temperatures are still very high. Recently erupted LAVA contains various dissolved gases that react with engulfed organic material to form water vapor, hydrogen, hydrogen fluoride, and hydrogen sulfide. In old volcanic areas where temperatures are lower, the gases given off are mostly carbon dioxide, methane, nitrogen, and oxygen. Fumaroles laden with sulfurous vapors are called solfataras.

A different type of fumarole—essentially a nearly dried-up HOT SPRING—emits mostly steam and water vapor. This kind forms in areas that are not necessarily associated with active VOLCANOES, such as Yellowstone National Park.

Fumaroles near recently active volcanoes emit very hot gases. During the 1909 eruption of Tenerife in the Canary Islands a temperature as high as 860° C (1,580° F) was recorded. Near older volcanic sites, temperatures run as low as 100° C (212° F).   JOHN S. RINEHART

Bibliography: Green, J., and Short, N., eds., *Volcanic Landforms and Surface Features* (1971); VanRose, S., and Mercer, I., *Volcanoes* (1991).

fumigation

Fumigation is the use of a gas or a volatile solid or liquid to control pests infesting buildings, foods, plants, and soil. Because of the necessity for high volatility, only about 20 chemicals are routinely used as fumigants. They include compounds of arsenic, cyanide, and chlorine. Many are highly toxic and can be used only with careful controls.

Gases are used to fumigate enclosed spaces such as buildings, grain elevators, or ships. When fumigation is carried out in the open air, the gas is confined by large sheets of plastic, which are draped over stacks of lumber or piles of hay, or even over entire structures. Safety precautions include the use of gas masks, detection devices to signal the presence of harmful concentrations or residues of fumigants, and procedures that permit delayed or remote release of the gas.

In liquid form, fumigants may be injected into the ground adjacent to roads and railroads to eradicate weeds or around houses to eliminate termites and other insects or fungi in the soil. When used as soil sterilants, fumigants must be carefully applied. The effects of some fumigant chemicals may persist in the soil for long periods: arsenic compounds, for example, may remain potent for up to 10 years.

Bibliography: Page, B. G., and Thomson, W. T., eds., *The Insecticide, Herbicide, Fungicide Quick Guide*, rev. ed. (1990); Watson, Theo F., et al., *Practical Insect Pest Management* (1977).

See also: PESTICIDES AND PEST CONTROL.

fumitory   [fue'-mi-tohr-ee]

Fumitory comprises about 19 genera and 425 species of herbs in the family Fumariaceae. Ramping fumitory, *Fumaria capreolata*, is a climbing annual herb, up to 90 cm (3 ft) long. Its leaves have segments with oblong or wedge-shaped lobes. The flowers are irregular, in dense racemes, and the petals are creamy or pinkish, but dark reddish purple at the tip. Common fumitory, *F. officinalis*, has a slender stem, finely dissected almost fernlike leaves, and slightly smaller flowers. Its fruits are rough when dry.   K. B. PAUL

Funchal   [foon-shahl']

Funchal (1981 pop., 48,638) is the capital city of Portugal's Madeira Islands in the Atlantic Ocean. Situated on the south shore of Madeira Island it is a center of commerce, communications, and industry. It is also a scenic port and a winter resort. The city was founded in 1421 by Portuguese explorers. In the old sector is the Se, a 15th-century cathedral.

function

The concept of a function is basic to almost all parts of mathematics and its applications. A specific kind of mathematical relation, it can be considered as a way of associating each element of a set A with one and only one element of a set B. For example, if A is the set $\{1, 2, 3\}$ and B is the set $\{1, 4, 9\}$, which consists of the squares of set A, then one can associate each element of set A with its square in set B. This function, called f, can be pictured as shown below.

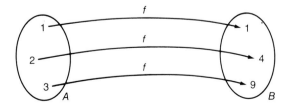

Functions are often called "mappings." Mathematicians use the terminology "f maps 1 in A into 1 in B," "f maps 2 in A into 4 in B," and "f maps 3 in A into 9 in B." Given an element a in A, the element b in B determined by f is designated by $f(a)$ (which is read "f of a") and is called a functional value. Thus for this example, $f(1) = 1$, $f(2) = 4$, and $f(3) = 9$.

The set A that is being mapped by f is called the domain of

f, and the set B, which is the set of all $f(a)$ for a in A, is called the range of f. Thus in the above example, the domain of f is $\{1, 2, 3\}$, and the range of f is $\{1, 4, 9\}$.

Functions are frequently defined by EQUATIONS. Thus one can write the function of the above example as $x \rightarrow x^2$, or as the $f{:}f(x) = x^2$, or as the function f such that $f(x) = x^2$.

Other examples of functions are the following: C: $C(r) = 2\pi r$ (the circumference of a circle of radius r); s: $s(t) = 490t^2$ (the distance in centimeters that a freely falling body will travel in t seconds); and r: $r(x) = \sqrt{x}$ (length of the side of a square whose area is x). For the functions C and r, the domain would be taken to be the set of all positive numbers, since it would make no sense to speak, for example, of a circle whose radius was 0 or -1. For the function s the domain would be taken to be the set of all non-negative numbers, that is, positive numbers and zero.

It is by no means necessary, however, that the function be defined by an equation. For example, let the domain of f be the set of natural numbers, 1, 2, 3, 4, . . ., and define $f(a) = 0$ if a is odd and $f(a) = 1$ if a is even. Thus, for example, $f(1) = f(3) = f(5) = 0$, and $f(2) = f(4) = f(6) = 1$. The range of f is then $\{0, 1\}$.

The domain or range of a function need not be a set of numbers. For example, let T be the set of all triangles and let f associate with each triangle its area. Then f is a function whose domain is T and whose range is the set of all positive real numbers. As another example, let T again be the set of all triangles and let r associate with each triangle t its reflection in a fixed line L in the plane, as shown in the figure below. Then the range of r is also T.

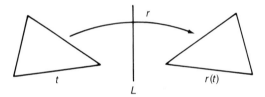

Every function f with domain D and range R determines a set of ordered pairs $(a, f(a))$, where a is in D and $f(a)$ is in R. Thus for f: $f(x) = x^2$ with $D = \{1, 2, 3\}$, the set F of ordered pairs $\{(1, 1), (2, 4), (3, 9)\}$ is obtained. It could also be said that F *defines* the function f, since if the set F is given, it could be deduced that $1 \xrightarrow{f} 1$, $2 \xrightarrow{f} 4$, and $3 \xrightarrow{f} 9$. Not every set of ordered pairs, however, will define a function. For example, suppose that the set of ordered pairs is $\{(1, 1), (1, 2)\}$. This would indicate that if f were a function defined by this set, one would have $1 \xrightarrow{f} 1$ and also $1 \xrightarrow{f} 2$. This is simply not possible, since a function must associate with each element of its domain one and only one element of its range. In order for a function f to exist it is necessary that there be a set P of ordered pairs such that if (x_1, y_1) is in P, then, if $y_2 \neq y_1$, (x_1, y_2) is not in P.

These observations lead to a formal definition of a function. A function f is a set of ordered pairs (x, y) such that if (x_1, y_1) is in f and (x_1, y_2) is in f, then $y_1 = y_2$. Note that it is permissible for a function f to have (x_1, y_1) in f and also (x_2, y_1) in f with $x_1 \neq x_2$. For example, $\{(1, 1), (-1, 1)\}$ can be described by f: $f(x) = x^2$ with domain $\{1, -1\}$ and range $\{1\}$.

Although not every set of ordered pairs describes a function, any set of ordered pairs is called a relation.   ROY DUBISCH

Bibliography: Klentos, G., and Newmyer, J., *Elementary Functions: Algebra and Analytic Geometry* (1975); Sobel, Max, and Lerner, N., *Algebra for College Students*, 3d ed. (1986); Spanier J., and Oldham, K. B., *An Atlas of Functions* (1987).

See also: SET THEORY.

functionalism   (in design)

Functionalism is the concept or doctrine that the design and form of an object should be determined by consideration of its intended function or use. Although functionalism has been a significant concept in all design since prehistoric times, it has been particularly important in the development of MODERN ARCHITECTURE. In the 19th century the American artist Horatio GREENOUGH and the French architect Eugène Emmanuel VIOLLET-LE-DUC developed in their writings the theory that architecture should express directly the structural functions of the parts of a building. The theoretical basis was thus provided for overcoming eclecticism in architecture (see ECLECTICISM, art)—the predominant tendency of the 19th and early 20th century to use historic forms to decorate most architecture.

In 1896 the American architect Louis SULLIVAN formulated the statement "form follows function," which served as a unifying thesis for the modern movement until the 1960s. Although the statement was frequently misinterpreted to imply that satisfying a building's utilitarian purposes in the most efficient manner would automatically result in beauty, Sullivan meant that form and function must be considered as one in the design process, not allowing purely aesthetic considerations to dictate a building's form.   RON WIEDENHOEFT

functionalism   (in social science)

Functionalism is a general social theory that stresses the mutual interdependence among the institutions and customs of any particular society. Functional analysis explains how social order is achieved by the functions that institutions—such as the state, religious groups, the family, schools, and markets—perform. For example, in complex societies like the United States, religion and the family support values that function to reinforce the operations of the democratic state and market economy. In simpler, tribal societies, participation in religious rituals functions to sustain social solidarity among groups related by kinship, but without centralized political institutions. Functionalist theory distinguishes between manifest and latent levels in the functioning of social institutions. In the preceding example, the manifest function of ritual, as understood by the tribe, may be to appease the gods, but its latent function, as understood by the social scientist, is to maintain group relationships.

Although basic to the writings of major 19th-century European social theorists, especially Émile DURKHEIM, functionalism was explicitly developed as a contemporary general theory by the sociologists Talcott PARSONS and Robert MERTON during the 1950s. This theory was the leading influence in Anglo-American sociology as well as in the other social sciences into the 1970s. Somewhat earlier than Parsons and Merton, Bronislaw MALINOWSKI and A. R. RADCLIFFE-BROWN, working separately, had developed a version of functionalist theory designed specifically for the research task of anthropology, focused on the study of small-scale, non-Western societies.

Since the 1970s functionalism has been modified to deal more adequately with the dynamics of social conflict. Functionalism is now cast in the sophisticated language of systems theory.   GEORGE E. MARCUS

Bibliography: Giddens, A., Central Problems in Social Theory (1979); Giddens, A., and Turner, J., eds., Social Theory Today (1987); Merton, R. K., Social Theory and Social Structure, rev. ed. (1968).

fund-raising

Fund-raising is an activity whose purpose is to encourage voluntary contributions of money to such entities as educational and religious institutions and public-interest and social-welfare organizations. (For coverage of fund-raising for political candidates, see CAMPAIGN, POLITICAL.) Many organizations seek their funds from FOUNDATIONS AND ENDOWMENTS and business corporations rather than individuals. Although organized giving takes place throughout the world, it assumes a special importance in the United States, where government plays a smaller role in supporting services than in many other countries. Subject to restrictions introduced in 1986, charitable donations may be deducted from federal income tax.

In 1989, a total $114.7 billion was given in the United States, of which $96.4 billion came from individuals; the rest was donated by businesses and foundations and through bequests. About 54% of the total was donated to religious or-

ganizations. Many donors make small contributions on a regular basis, such as weekly or monthly, a tradition that has its roots in tithing. Many religiously sponsored organizations, such as the Jewish Family Service or Church World Service, however, raise money separately for the welfare services they provide, both domestic and international. These and other humanitarian organizations mount special drives to raise relief funds for the victims of particular disasters, such as earthquakes and famines.

Education accounted for about 10.5% of total donations in 1989. Institutions of higher education often direct much of their fund-raising efforts toward alumni giving and bequests. The health-care field also received about 10% of the total; giving in this area is dominated by foundations rather than private individuals. Social-welfare groups received over 11% of the total, the largest single portion going to local agencies through avenues of the United Way (formerly the Community Chest), the umbrella organization for annual community fund drives.

About 7.5% of all donations went to arts and humanities groups. Public radio and television stations periodically broadcast their fund-raising campaigns; like many other groups, they often receive matching grants from foundations. Civic and public groups, such as the Sierra Club or the National Association for the Advancement of Colored People (NAACP), received 3.5% of the total.

Many large organizations, such as the American Cancer Society, conduct nationwide campaigns and often employ professional fund-raising staffs. Some organizations retain nonprofit fund-raising firms whose remuneration is a flat fee, based on the time necessary to raise the funds for their client organizations. Both mail and direct-contact campaigns are used by professional firms. Much fund-raising activity, however, takes place at the local level and is organized by nonprofessionals. Such activities as the fire-department breakfast, fairs, and walkathons frequently support vital local services and secondarily provide a focus for community involvement for many.   FRED SCHNAUE

Bibliography: Bayley, T. D., The Fund Raiser's Guide to Successful Campaigns (1987); Broce, T. E., Fund Raising, rev. 2d ed. (1986); Heetland, D. L., Fundamentals of Fund Raising (1990); Hopkins, B. R., Charity under Siege: Government Regulation of Fund Raising (1980); Kelly, K. S., ed., Fund Raising and Public Relations (1991); Schneiter, Paul H., The Art of Asking: How to Solicit Philanthropic Gifts (1985).

fundamental constants: see ATOMIC CONSTANTS.

fundamental interactions

All known physical interactions of matter occur through the agency of four basic, or fundamental, kinds of forces: gravitation, electromagnetism, the strong nuclear force, and the weak nuclear force. The first two are well known; because they act over long distances, it is easy to observe their effects. Strong and weak nuclear forces, on the other hand, were not discovered until the 20th century. The range of their effects is limited to subatomic distances (see FUNDAMENTAL PARTICLES); therefore, they can be studied only by using the special techniques of NUCLEAR PHYSICS. A major goal of physicists is to develop a single description of forces (UNIFIED FIELD THEORY) that will relate the four types of interactions.

Each force has a characteristic strength. If the strong nuclear force between two protons is assigned a strength of 1, then the electromagnetic, weak nuclear, and gravitational forces between the same two protons have relative strengths of 10^{-2}, 10^{-5}, and an incredibly small 10^{-40}. Thus the effect of gravity on interactions among particles of atomic size is negligible.

Gravitation. The most pervasive interaction is GRAVITATION. Every particle of matter seems to attract every other particle with a force that is proportional to the mass of each and inversely proportional to the square of their separation. This relationship was first proposed by Isaac NEWTON. Gravitational force becomes appreciable only when at least one of the attracting masses is very large, typically of planetary size. Newton's theory of gravitation is fundamental, in the sense that all motion due to the gravitational forces exerted on all objects can be described as a result of the same force. Several slight deviations from the predictions of Newton's theory are observed, and are explained by Albert EINSTEIN's general theory of RELATIVITY, a more fundamental and sweeping theory that reproduces the Newtonian results as a first approximation. A few scientists have hypothesized a fifth force—a weak, repelling force that would work against gravity—but this notion has gained little favor among physicists in general.

Electromagnetic Force. Electromagnetic forces (see ELECTRICITY; MAGNETISM) exist among particles bearing electric charge or intrinsic magnetic moments or both. These particles need not be stable, but their net electrical charge must be conserved throughout any and all reactions they undergo. All of chemistry, hence all of biology, is a direct consequence of the electromagnetic interaction of atoms and molecules.

Strong and Weak Forces. When isolated, the neutron, a fundamental particle with no electric charge and a slightly larger mass than the proton, decays very slowly, by means of a weak nuclear interaction, into a proton plus an electron-neutrino pair. Weak nuclear forces are similarly involved in many nuclear decay processes and in all interactions that involve neutrinos. On the other hand, neutrons and protons are themselves bound together over distances of the order of 10^{-12} cm by short-range strong nuclear forces to make up the nuclei of all atoms. Disintegration and transmutation of radioactive nuclei (see RADIOACTIVITY) depend on the details of the strong, weak, and electromagnetic interactions between bound nuclear particles.

Unification Attempts. Beginning in the early 20th century, scientists sought to unify, in theory, the fundamental forces. The first successful attempt was the ELECTROWEAK THEORY, which unified the electromagnetic and weak nuclear forces. Formulated in the late 1960s, it was confirmed in 1983 when experimenters observed the appropriate electroweak vector BOSONS. Present attempts (as yet unsuccessful) to unify the strong, weak, and electromagnetic forces are called GRAND UNIFICATION THEORIES.   H. M. FRIED

Bibliography: Davies, Paul, *The Forces of Nature*, 2d ed. (1986); Veltman, M. J. G., "The Higgs Particle," *Scientific American*, November 1986.

Fundamental Orders

Settlers from the first permanent Connecticut River valley towns of Hartford, Wethersfield, and Windsor met in Hartford in 1639 and adopted the Fundamental Orders of Connecticut, a written body of laws by which they would govern themselves. Thomas HOOKER and Roger LUDLOW played key roles in framing this document, sometimes called the first written constitution. It provided for a system of government similar to that of Massachusetts, except that church membership was not specified as a qualification for suffrage and the general court (legislature) could assemble without a call by the governor. Most of its principles were confirmed by the royal charter granted to Connecticut in 1662.

fundamental particles

Scientists of every period have believed that certain objects are fundamental and that others are derived, in the sense that the latter are composed of the former. In one version of this distinction, the fundamental objects are particles, or points of matter carrying such properties as mass. Although the view of which objects qualify as fundamental particles has changed several times, the notion that the world is ultimately made of such material points, moving through space, has endured in some form ever since the theory of ATOMISM was first proposed by the Greeks LEUCIPPUS and DEMOCRITUS in the 5th century BC.

The atomic theory languished until the 18th and early 19th centuries, when physicists and chemists revived it to explain the properties of gases and some of the facts of chemistry. In these theories the fundamental particles, the ATOMS, remained indivisible points. The discovery in the late 19th and the 20th century that atoms were composite, rather than indivisible, set the stage for modern discoveries.

HISTORY OF MODERN PARTICLE PHYSICS

The history of modern particle physics has gone through four stages. In the first stage, Sir Joseph J. THOMSON discovered (1897), by studying electricity passing through gases, that all atoms contain certain particles, called ELECTRONS, that carry a negative electric charge. Because atoms are electrically neutral, there must be balancing positive charges somewhere in the atom. Ernest RUTHERFORD proposed (1911), based on a series of experiments by Hans GEIGER and Ernest Marsden, that these positive charges are concentrated in a very small volume, called the ATOMIC NUCLEUS, at the center of the atom.

In the second stage, scientists recognized, through an analysis of isotopes of elements, that all atomic nuclei could be thought of as composed of two types of particles: the PROTON, which carries both mass and electric charge, and the NEUTRON, which has about the same mass as a proton but is electrically neutral. This model was confirmed through the discovery (1932) of free neutrons by Sir James CHADWICK.

The third stage of modern particle physics came with the recognition that protons, neutrons, and electrons—the constituents of ordinary matter—were but three of a vast number of similar particles, which differed only in a few properties, such as their mass, and in their stability against spontaneous decay. Experiments with particle ACCELERATORS indicated that these many subatomic particles could be readily produced from protons and neutrons, provided that enough energy was available to produce the additional mass of the new particles predicted by the rules of Albert Einstein's RELATIVITY theory. These discoveries in the 1940s and '50s indicated that the proton and neutron were not really fundamental particles and that they would have to be understood as part of a much larger family of similar objects.

In the fourth stage physicists found a successful explanation for the large number of particles. The prevailing theory is that many of these particles are combinations of QUARKS.

PROPERTIES OF PARTICLES

The subatomic particles carry two kinds of properties: those which can vary for a given particle, such as total energy, and those which remain the same for one type of particle, such as mass, spin, electric charge, and color. The combination of the latter four properties serves to define each particle type and to distinguish the particles from each other.

Mass. The mass of an object, originally thought of as an independent property of matter, is now recognized as a measure of the energy content of the object when it is at rest, according to Einstein's equation $E = mc^2$. The rest energy of a fundamental particle ranges from zero to many millions (MeV) or billions (GeV) of electron volts.

Spin. Many fundamental particles behave as if they are spinning on an internal axis, as the Earth does. According to the theories of QUANTUM MECHANICS, the angular momentum related to this spin can take on only certain values: either zero or an integer or half-integer multiple of the constant $\hbar = 1.04 \times 10^{-27}$ erg-seconds. Each particle has a specific and unchanging value of spin.

Electric Charge. All known electric and magnetic effects originate from the property of electric charge, which is carried by certain subatomic particles. All particles of one type, such as electrons, have the same charge. Further, all observed particles have either charge zero or a positive or negative integer multiple of the proton's charge, symbolized by e. Quarks, which have not been directly observed, are thought to have charges $2/3\ e$ and $-1/3\ e$.

Color. Quarks carry another property, known as color, which, like electric charge, remains constant in any particle reaction. Three forms of color exist, and each quark bears one of these. A quark of one color can convert into one of another color by emission or absorption of a type of gauge particle called a GLUON, which also must carry the color property in order that the total color remain constant.

INTERACTIONS AND CLASSIFICATION OF PARTICLES

The fundamental particles exhibit several characteristic forms of behavior that have enabled physicists to find patterns among the particles and to make successful theories of their internal structure. The most remarkable thing that particles do

FUNDAMENTAL PARTICLES

Quarks	Symbol	Mass (GeV)	Charge	Leptons	Symbol	Mass (GeV)	Charge
Up	u	.378	+2/3	Electron	e	0.511	−1
Down	d	.336	−1/3	Electron neutrino	ν_e	$<4.6 \ 10^{-5}$	0
Strange	s	.540	−1/3	Muon	μ	105.66	−1
Charmed	c	1.5	+2/3	Muon neutrino	ν_μ	<0.52	0
Bottom (or Beauty)	b	4.72	−1/3	Tau	τ	1784.2	−1
Top (or Truth)	t	30–50	+2/3	Tau neutrino	ν_τ	<250	0

Hadrons (examples)	Symbol	Quark Composition	Charge	Gauge Particles (Bosons)		Mass (GeV)	Charge
Proton	p	uud	+1	Gluon		0	0
Neutron	n	udd	0	Photon		0	0
Lambda	Λ	uds	0	W^+		79.5	+1
Omega$^-$	Ω^-	sss	−1	W^-		79.5	−1
Pion	π°	$u\bar{u}$ or $d\bar{d}$	0	Z°		91	0
J/ψ	J, ψ	$c\bar{c}$	0	Graviton		0	0

is to change into one another, either by the decay of a single particle into several others (see RADIOACTIVITY) or in a collision between two particles from which several new ones may emerge. Quantum mechanics allows only the probabilities of these transformations to be predicted.

Fundamental Interactions. Because the fundamental particles change into one another, the old notion of a force—an influence that produces physical change—is insufficient to describe their behavior. Instead physicists speak of a FUNDAMENTAL INTERACTION—any influence that causes a collection of particles to undergo some change. A measure of the strength of the interaction is the rate at which such changes take place. If other conditions are equal, then the stronger the interaction, the less time is needed for a change to occur.

Using this measure, physicists have discovered four fundamental interactions, known, in decreasing order of strength, as the strong nuclear, the electromagnetic, the weak nuclear, and the gravitational forces (see ELECTRICITY; GRAVITATION; MAGNETISM; NUCLEAR PHYSICS). Each type of fundamental particle participates in a specific subset of the four interactions. The HADRONS—which comprise MESONS, whose spin is an integer multiple of ℏ, and BARYONS, whose spin is a half-integer multiple of ℏ—can undergo all four types of interaction. Another type of particle, the charged LEPTONS, can undergo all of the interactions except the strong nuclear. Uncharged leptons, or NEUTRINOS, undergo only weak-nuclear and gravitational interactions and are little affected by other matter.

The four known interactions are generated by the exchange of gauge bosons, also called gauge particles. PHOTONS are the carriers of electromagnetic interactions, gluons carry strong interactions between quarks, and W and Z particles (first observed in the early 1980s) generate weak interactions. All of these gauge bosons have one unit of spin. The still-hypothetical graviton, which carries the gravitational force, would be a gauge boson with two units of spin.

Conservation Laws. The four interactions differ not only in strength but also in their detailed behavior, especially regarding which quantities are conserved (see CONSERVATION, LAWS OF) when the interaction operates. A quantity is said to be conserved in a process when its value remains the same throughout the process. In reactions involving fundamental particles, such quantities as energy, linear momentum, angular momentum, and electric charge are always conserved.

Until recently, scientists believed that the number of baryons in a reaction is also always conserved. This law would forbid a proton from decaying into lighter particles, and indeed such decays have never been seen. Some scientists, however, have suggested that protons do decay, if rarely, and are testing this hypothesis.

There are also conservation laws that apply for some interactions but not others. Some of the hadrons, such as the sigma-plus particle (Σ^+), are produced by strong interactions but decay only by weak interactions. Because of these circumstances, these particles, termed *metastable*, exist between

production and decay for enough time (10^{-10} seconds) to leave an observable track in a detection device (see DETECTOR, PARTICLE). The fact that metastable hadrons do not decay by strong interactions suggests that some law inhibits the decay. Because the decay does occur by weak interactions, the latter must not obey this law. Physicists assign a property called strangeness to several metastable hadrons. Strangeness is conserved in strong and electromagnetic interactions but not in weak interactions. Several other properties of particles that obey such partial conservation laws are also recognized, each with its own set of metastable particles.

Antimatter. Another important criterion for classification is the division into particles and antiparticles (see ANTIMATTER). This distinction was first theorized for electrons by Paul DIRAC in 1930 and was later extended to all other particles. According to the principles of relativity and quantum mechanics, for every type of particle there exists a corresponding antiparticle with the same spin and mass but with opposite electric charge. Such particles as the PHOTON, whose electric charge, baryon number, and strangeness are all zero, are identical to their antiparticles. Antiparticles for most of the known particles have been observed, beginning with the antielectron, or POSITRON, detected by Carl David ANDERSON in 1932. The preponderance of matter over antimatter is a result of little understood processes that occurred very early in the history of the universe (see COSMOLOGY).

Quarks and Gluons. In addition to the metastable hadrons, there are hundreds of known hadrons that are unstable and will decay by strong interactions. These unstable hadrons typically have lifetimes of 10^{-20} seconds or less. The properties of hadrons have been explained with some success by the quark-gluon theory of strong interactions. According to this theory, hadrons are composed of combinations of the various types of quarks. The quarks are held together by unbreakable bonds resulting from gluon exchange between the quarks. Baryons are each composed of three quarks; mesons are composed of a quark and an antiquark. Six different types of quarks are theorized to exist, each of which can be any of the three colors.

The quark-gluon theory also explains why quarks and gluons are never observed alone, but rather, in combinations such as the three quarks that make up a baryon. Gluon exchange induces a force between quarks, and between the gluons themselves, that remains strong even when the particles involved are relatively far apart. Because of this, it is not possible to separate the quarks and gluons of a single hadron far enough from each other so that they can be observed in isolation. This phenomenon is referred to as confinement of quarks and gluons. Certain combinations of quarks and gluons are color neutral, just as some combinations of electric charges are charge neutral. These color-neutral systems are the observed hadrons. It follows from the mathematical theory of the quark-gluon interaction that color neutrality can be achieved with three quarks, or with a quark and an antiquark.

ADVANCED THEORIES

Many aspects of fundamental particles remain to be understood. Although the photon and the W and Z particles have similar properties, their masses are very different. Theories accounting for this in terms of a breakdown of an underlying SYMMETRY have been partially successful, but it is unknown whether this breakdown arises from the interaction of W and Z with undiscovered spin-zero particles called Higgs bosons, or from some other mechanism (see HIGGS PARTICLE).

Many physicists are uncomfortable with the large number of particles. Some have devised theories describing particles as tightly bound combinations of a small number of more fundamental particles. According to the so-called Standard Model, only three foursomes, or "generations," of particles exist, each consisting of two quarks and two leptons. The first, consisting of up and down quarks, the electron, and the electron neutrino, constitutes ordinary matter. The second consists of charm and strange quarks plus the muon and muon neutrino, while the third consists of top and bottom quarks plus the tau and tau neutrino. Experiments have supported this theory.

Another approach involves a mathematical description of particles in which close relations are found between particles of different spin. These so-called supersymmetry theories imply the existence of many yet-undiscovered particles, such as spin-zero quark analogues. Many physicists think that the rest energies of such particles would be about one trillion electron volts (TeV). To produce them, accelerators of much higher energy than existing ones are needed. In order to create the hypothesized particles, accelerators would require thousands of superconducting magnets, as well as rings that are 100 km (62 mi) in circumference (see ACCELERATOR, PARTICLE). It is proposed that the collisions of protons accelerated to such energies might yield the new fundamental particles (see UNIFIED FIELD THEORY).

GERALD FEINBERG

Bibliography: Feinberg, Gerald, *What Is the World Made Of?* (1977); Feynmann, R. P., *Elementary Particles and the Laws of Physics* (1988); Fritzsche, Harald, *Quarks* (1983); Pagels, Heinz, *The Cosmic Code* (1982); Weinberg, Steve, *Subatomic Particles* (1983).

fundamentalism

Fundamentalism is a term popularly used to describe strict adherence to Christian doctrines based on a literal interpretation of the Bible. This usage derives from a late-19th- and early-20th-century transdenominational Protestant movement that opposed the accommodation of Christian doctrine to modern scientific theory and philosophy. With some differences among themselves, fundamentalists insist on belief in the inerrancy of the Bible, the virgin birth and divinity of Jesus Christ, the vicarious and atoning character of his death, his bodily resurrection, and his second coming as the irreducible minimum of authentic Christianity. This minimum was reflected in such early declarations as the 14-point creed of the Niagara Bible Conference of 1878 and the 5-point statement of the Presbyterian General Assembly of 1910.

Two immediate doctrinal sources for fundamentalist thought were MILLENARIANISM and biblical inerrancy. Millenarianism, belief in the physical return of Christ to establish a 1,000-year earthly reign of blessedness, was a doctrine prevalent in English-speaking Protestantism by the 1870s. At the same time, powerful conservative forces led by Charles Hodge and Benjamin Warfield opposed the growing use of literary and historical criticism in biblical studies, defending biblical inspiration and the inerrant authority of the Bible.

The name fundamentalist was coined in 1920 to designate those "doing battle royal for the Fundamentals." Also figuring in the name was *The Fundamentals*, a 12-volume collection of essays written in the period 1910–15 by 64 British and American scholars and preachers. Three million copies of these volumes and the founding of the World's Christian Fundamentals Association in 1919 gave sharp identity to fundamentalism as it moved into the 1920s. Leadership moved across the years from such men as A. T. Pierson and A. J. Gordon to A. C. Dixon, William Jennings BRYAN, and J. G. Machen.

As fundamentalism developed, most Protestant denominations in the United States felt the division between liberalism and fundamentalism. The Baptists, Presbyterians, and Disciples of Christ were more affected than others. Nevertheless, talk of schism was much more common than schism itself. Perhaps the lack of a central organization and a normative creed, certainly the caricature of fundamentalism arising from the SCOPES TRIAL (1925), the popularization of the liberal response by representatives like Harry Emerson FOSDICK, well-publicized divisions among fundamentalists themselves, and preoccupations with the Depression of the 1930s and World War II curtailed fundamentalism's appeal. By 1950 it was either isolated and muted or had taken on the more moderate tones of EVANGELICALISM. In the 1970s and '80s, however, fundamentalism again became an influential force in the United States. Promoted by popular television evangelists (see RELIGIOUS BROADCASTING) and represented by such groups as the MORAL MAJORITY, the new politically oriented "religious right" opposes the influence of liberalism and secularism in American life. The term *fundamentalist* has also been used to describe members of militant Islamic groups.

PAUL MERRITT BASSETT

Bibliography: Averill, L. J., *Religious Right, Religious Wrong* (1989); Cole, S. G., *History of Fundamentalism* (1931; repr. 1971); Furniss, Norman, *The Fundamentalist Controversy, 1918–1931* (1954); Lawrence, Bruce, *Defenders of God* (1989); Marsden, George, *Fundamentalism and American Culture* (1980); Sandeen, E. R., *The Roots of Fundamentalism* (1970).

Fundy, Bay of [fuhn'-dee]

The Bay of Fundy is a 240-km-long (150-mi) arm of the Atlantic Ocean that separates the Canadian provinces of Nova Scotia and New Brunswick and runs in a northeasterly direction. The bay is noted for its swift and exceptionally high tides of up to 21 m (70 ft). Serious attempts are being made to harness the tide as an alternative energy source, particularly in the Minas Basin area, where the wide bay necks sharply down to a 50-km (30-mi) width. The Petitcodiac River exhibits a TIDAL BORE, or upstream wave, and the falls at St. John are reversed as a result of the force of the tide. St. John, New Brunswick, is the largest city on the bay.

funeral customs

Funeral customs are the ceremonies connected with the disposition of the dead. Anthropologists have found that formal procedures exist for insuring proper treatments of the deceased in virtually every society, regardless of how primitive or remote. Like birth and marriage, death seems universally to be regarded as a socially significant event, marked by rituals and beliefs that dictate how the dead are to be dealt with and how the survivors are to mourn. This fact has led anthropologists to view funeral customs as the final *rite de passage* (see PASSAGE, RITES OF) in an individual's lifespan.

Rites of Separation and Transition. Funeral ceremonies generally involve events that symbolize the separation of the deceased from his or her former status, a transitional phase, and the deceased's final assumption of a new role in the afterlife. A ritual cleansing of the corpse is the typical form of expression for the rite of separation. Among many groups this involves washing the corpse in holy water and dressing the deceased in special garb; it may sometimes also include EMBALMING procedures. Like all funerary rites, these ceremonies are intimately related to the religious beliefs of the specific society in which they are practiced. Some groups remove the flesh from the skeleton, polishing the remaining bones and teeth. In traditional Tibetan culture the corpse is exposed to scavengers, birds of prey, or the elements to cleanse the skeleton.

The transitional phase, after the corpse has been prepared or cleansed but prior to its final disposition, is of variable length, depending upon the customs of the specific groups. Some societies will permit a relatively brief period to elapse, generally in the form of a WAKE. Close relatives and friends will gather to watch the closed or open coffin into which the body of the deceased has been placed for one or more nights. These may be solemn or joyous occasions; often this

The funeral procession, in which mourners escort the body to the place of interment, reflects, in either its elaboration or its simplicity, the social status of the deceased. Subdued colors are traditional expressions of mourning, although white or another light color may be worn in cultures or religions in which death is viewed as a joyous occasion.

period is accompanied by prayers. In many cases disposition is delayed for prominent persons; in Korea, for example, a delay of up to three months is permitted. Among certain groups the corpse is allowed to decompose in a shallow grave, within a tree, or upon a scaffold, thereby enabling the soul or spirit to emerge from the body. After the appropriate period of time has elapsed the corpse is recovered, prayers are said, and the remains are buried in an ordinary grave.

Modes of Disposition. Following the rites of separation and transition is the final phase of permanent disposition of the body. As with the other phases, great diversity of methods exists for disposing of the corpse. The most common form of disposition is BURIAL. The body may be interred in a simple pit or beneath a large earthen mound. The corpse may be wrapped in cloth, placed in a coffin, or buried directly in the earth. The grave may contain the body of a single deceased individual or large numbers of corpses. The dead may be placed in symbolically important positions, such as facing a given direction or in a flexed position. Segmented burials may occur in which the skull is buried separately from the rest of the body.

CREMATION is also used by numerous groups to dispose of the dead. In its simplest form, the deceased is incinerated on a pyre or in a crematory, and the ashes are disposed of ritually. Sometimes the body of the deceased is placed in a house, on a raft, or on a boat, and the entire structure is ignited. Other methods used to dispose of the dead include placing the corpse in a sarcophagus, which in turn is housed in a vault, mausoleum, or other type of TOMB. Sinking the corpse in water or permitting it to drift down a river or out to sea are other methods found.

Funeral customs reveal much about a culture's structure, values, and religion. In an egalitarian society all funerals generally involve the same degree of elaboration. In societies stratified on the basis of wealth or rank, burial in large vaults for the rich or the nobility contrast with less ornate practices for the lower classes. The inclusion of many personal possessions, like those found in the sumptuously furnished pyramid tombs of the ancient Egyptians, often reveal the nature of the afterlife anticipated by the members of a given society.

In many societies, especially in the past, funeral ceremonies were intended to ensure that the spirit of the deceased is properly treated so that it will gain admission to its final resting place. The fear that spirits of the dead will return to the living world to bestow tragedy or death upon those who do not venerate them in the prescribed manner has been the major motivation for elaborate funeral arrangements in many societies. Before it was banned in 1829 an extreme manifestation of this was found in the Hindu rite of SUTTEE, in which the widow of the deceased would voluntarily perform an act of self-immolation by throwing herself onto the funeral pyre of her husband. Should she refuse, relatives and friends of her husband often forced her to do so lest plague or death come to the village.

Bali's Hindu culture prescribes cremation as the standard method for disposal of the dead. Here, mourners torque the tower supporting the deceased into a twisted position to prevent evil forces from ascending the structure before cremation is complete.

Mourning. Many customs of mourning have been observed around the world, including isolation or marking of the bereaved (such as by the wearing of black in many Western cultures); taboos on speaking the name of the deceased; use of ritual specialists such as priests or undertakers in funeral ceremonies; and final funeral ceremonies that terminate the mourning period weeks, months, or even years after a death.

The bereaved in almost all societies cry, sometimes for long periods of time. In many societies anger and aggression are also part of grief and mourning. Funerals provide a means for the deeply grieved relatives and friends of the dead to openly display their grief and so channel their intense emotions into nondestructive paths. This therapeutic value of funerals, in providing a means of catharsis for those individuals most seriously affected by their loss, enables them to resume a more or less normal life after the appropriate period of mourning has passed.

Prehistoric Evidence. Archaeological research indicates that funeral customs have been practiced for many thousands of years. The earliest known evidence of ritual associated with death dates back to some 60,000 years ago at SHANIDAR cave in Iraq. A pollen analysis of the soil revealed that hyacinths, hollyhocks, and daisies had been strewn over the grave site of a NEANDERTHALER buried within the cave.

At La Ferassie, an archaeological site in the Dordogne area of France that dates back at least 50,000 years, a skeleton of a boy 15 or 16 years old was found, laid out with a beautifully fashioned stone axe near his hand. With the body were charred wild cattle bones, perhaps the remnants of a funeral feast. Near the same site graves of three other children and two adults, interred together in what may have been a family plot, were also discovered. MELVIN EMBER

Bibliography: Bendann, Effie, *Death Customs* (1930; repr. 1990); Berrill, Margaret, *Mummies, Masks, and Mourners* (1990); Bowman, LeRoy E., *The American Funeral* (1959; repr. 1990); Habenstein, Robert W., and Lamers, William M., *Funeral Customs the World Over* (1960); Huntington, R., and Metcalf, P., *Celebrations of Death* (1979); Puckle, Bertram S., *Funeral Customs* (1926; repr. 1990); Rosenblatt, Paul C., et al., *Grief and Mourning in Cross-Cultural Perspective* (1976); Toynbee, J. M. C., *Death and Burial in the Roman World* (1971).

funeral industry

The funeral industry is concerned with the handling and burial of the dead and, often, with arrangements for the conduct of funerals. The industry is sizable, earning an annual gross income of some $6 billion and employing 77,000 persons, many of whom are licensed funeral directors or embalmers and work primarily through the 15,000 funeral homes in the United States. (Many Western countries handle funerals through institutions analogous to those in the United States; in other parts of the world FUNERAL CUSTOMS differ widely.) For a fee that is decided on in negotiations between the bereaved family and the funeral home, the home undertakes to remove the body of the deceased from the place of death, to prepare the body for burial, to provide rooms where mourners can meet and where a service may be held, and to make the burial arrangements. Sometimes, the body will be embalmed and cosmetic attention paid to the face. The home also supplies the coffin, or "casket."

Every state enforces its own regulations governing the practices of funeral homes and the disposition of bodies. Nevertheless, the industry has been the subject of investigation by government agencies, notably the Federal Trade Commission (FTC). In 1982 the FTC issued a regulation, which became effective in mid-1983, requiring funeral directors to disclose their prices and to offer customers their choice of services. It also prohibited embalming without the family's permission, except under certain circumstances.

In recent years the increased use of CREMATION rather than burial has led to the formation of memorial societies, nonprofit membership organizations that contract for cremations at low cost to members. Many Americans now belong to these societies, prearranging their own funerals.

Bibliography: Carlson, Lisa, *Caring For Your Own Dead* (1987); Farrell, J. J., *Inventing the American Way of Death, 1830–1920* (1980); Mitford, Jessica, *The American Way of Death*, 2d ed. (1963); Shipley, R. R., *The Consumer's Guide to Death, Dying and Bereavement* (1982).

fungi [fuhn'-jy]

The fungi constitute a large and diverse group of organisms that share some characteristics with both lower plants (algae) and lower animals but are not closely related to either. They contain true mitochondria and membrane-enclosed nuclei, lack chlorophyll and chloroplasts, and reproduce by both asexual and sexual means. Most fungi grow as branched tubular systems, or mycelia, whose individual filaments or hyphae, are surrounded by rigid cell walls containing chitin, cellulose, or both, and other polysaccharides. All fungi lack photosynthetic ability and therefore require preformed organic compounds. They exist throughout the world.

INDUSTRIAL USES

The microfungi are most often used commercially because of their rapid growth. Brewer's yeast was used for brewing beer, fermenting grapes and other substances to produce wines, and starting mashes for distilled spirits long before the process of FERMENTATION was scientifically understood. Alcohol, the prod-

Many species of fungi reproduce asexually by producing spores that eventually develop into new organisms. This photomicrograph of the aquatic fungus Hesseltina vesiculosa shows unusual sporangiophores. These specialized hyphae, or elongated filaments, bear reproductive structures called sporangia—spheres in which the spores are produced.

uct of fermentation, also has chemical and medical uses. Baker's yeast is equally important in the baking industry. Camembert cheese derives its flavor from *Penicillium camemberti*, and Roquefort from *P. roqueforti*. Soy sauce is fermented with *Aspergillus oryzae* or *A. soyae*.

ANTIBIOTICS were first produced using penicillin from *P. notatum*; the antibiotic activity of this fungus was described (1929) by the British scientist Alexander Fleming. Only through a joint effort of British and American scientists during World War II, however, was industrial-scale production achieved by using better-producing mutant strains of *P. chrysogenum*. A huge antibiotic industry has since developed. Only a few of the many antibiotics now available, however, are of fungal origin: the penicillins, the cephalosporins, and gresiofulvin, which is one of the few effective antifungal antibiotics. Various microfungi are used to produce a number of organic acids—gluconic, itaconic, and citric acids, for example—and in other chemical processes. Citric acid fermentation by *Aspergillus niger* yields about 99,000 tons each year. Fungi are also grown for the production of enzymes such as the acid proteases, which are used commercially for meat tenderizing and bread making.

CLASSIFICATION OF FUNGI

Prior to the development of the microscope in the 1600s, the only fungi described were the higher fungi that have large fruiting structures, such as MORELS, MUSHROOMS, and PUFFBALLS. The first scientific description of fungi was given by Piér Antonio Micheli, an Italian botanist, in his work *Nova Plantarum Genera* (1729). In 1836 the study of fungi was termed MYCOLOGY. Because fungi and bacteria were for many years considered more similar to plants than to animals, mycology has traditionally been a branch of botany.

Evolution. Fossil records reveal that fungi occurred in the early periods; however, the record is sparse, and most phylogenetic speculations have been based on comparisons of living species. As a result, the evolutionary relationships are still not clear. It is generally accepted that fungi arose as more than one phylogenetic branch from flagellated protistan ancestors. Their evolution is most probably polyphyletic along at least three lines.

Taxonomy. Groups of fungi are classified according to their methods of sexual reproduction, types of life cycle, growth forms, and methods of asexual propagation. Because the fossil record is inadequate, no single classification scheme is accepted by all mycologists; changes continue to be made, particularly at the lower levels. It is now generally agreed, however, that the major fungi groups should be classified in a kingdom Fungi (Mycetae), separate from plants and animals. In some phylogenetic classification systems, the plasmodial fungi and the fungi that produce flagellated zoospores are grouped in the kingdom Protista (Whittaker and Margulis, 1978). Most mycologists, however, group all fungi in the same kingdom, with plasmodial organisms in the division Myxomycota (or Gymnomycota) and all others in either one division, the Eumycota (true fungi), or in two divisions, the Mastigomycota (with flagellate spores) and Amastigomycota (with non-flagellate spores). The simpler, two-division system of Ainsworth (1973) is followed below.

DESCRIPTION OF MAJOR GROUPS

Division Myxomycota. The organisms in this division grow as multinucleate amoeboid plasmodia and produce motile uninucleate amoebae, as well as biflagellate cells. Their true evolutionary relations are still not known.

Members of the class Plasmodiophoromycetes of this division parasitize the roots of plants, and some species may infect the hyphae of aquatic fungi. *Plasmodiophora brassicae* causes a disease of cabbages called clubroot.

The class Myxomycetes comprises the true, free-living plasmodial SLIME MOLDS, which range from microscopic species to those which produce very large and conspicuous plasmodia. Starvation induces the plasmodia to convert to sporangia, in which nonmotile spores are formed. They typically grow under moist conditions in or on decaying wood or other vegetation. *Physarum polycephalum* produces large, yellow plasmodia and has been used extensively for basic cell research.

Division Eumycota. The so-called true fungi are placed in this division, and all except the Oömycetes may be related as a single phyletic series.

In the subdivision Mastigomycotina, which comprises two classes, the fungi produce motile spores, called zoospores, with one or two flagella.

The class Chytridiomycetes (the chytrids, or water molds) includes three orders of fungi that produce asexual zoospores with a single posterior whiplash flagellum in a sporangium, or more specifically a zoosporangium. Most species are microscopic, and many grow as parasites within the cells of algae, other fungi, or higher plants. The cells are coenocytic (multinuclear) and enclosed in rigid walls containing chitin, except for some that grow as plasmodia within their host. The chytrids characteristically grow as sac-shaped cells with tapering, rootlike extensions, called rhizoids, that penetrate the substra-

tum or its host. In asexual reproduction part or all of the cell body is converted into zoosporangia, or sporangia-producing zoospores. Sexual reproduction leads to a thick-walled, often dormant resting spore.

The class Oömycetes, the second in the subdivision Mastigomycotina, is a group of fungi (water molds and fish molds) that typically occur in freshwater streams and ponds or as parasites of higher plants. They are economically significant in agriculture, because although many are saprobes, living off decayed matter, others cause damping-off or rotting of seedlings; downy mildews of many plants, such as potato blight; and fish diseases. Oömycetes reproduce asexually by motile biflagellate zoospores with one whiplash and one tinsel flagellum. Pathogenic species such as *Phytophthora infestans* (the cause of potato blight) and *Plasmopara viticola* (the cause of downy mildew of grape) produce zoospores on specialized branches (sporangiophores) of the mycelium. The zoosporangia break free and are carried by wind or water to new hosts, whereupon zoospores may be released to initiate new infections or, under dry conditions, the sporangia may directly produce a mycelium.

The subdivision Zygomycotina has a single class, Zygomycetes. This class includes fungi (bread molds or pin molds) that typically produce an abundant and rapidly growing aerial, coenocytic mycelium and are common causes for the decay of foods and other rich sources of organic material. The cell walls contain chitin as a primary component. They reproduce asexually by means of nonmotile spores (sporangiospores) produced in sporangia formed on branches (sporangiophores) of the mycelium. In some species, such as *Rhizopus nigricans*, the sporangia arise in clusters with rhizoids at the base and hyphal strands (stolons) interconnecting the clusters. The spores are released by breakdown of the sporangial wall and dispersed by air or water currents. They "germinate" by direct outgrowth of a hyphal tube to produce a new mycelium.

Sexual reproduction may occur between different parts of the same mycelium (homothallic mating) or between two self-sterile but cross-fertile strains of opposite mating type (heterothallic mating). The latter is regulated by a single pair of genes, or alleles. One gene is said to be of the plus mating type and the other of the minus mating type. The gamentangia, or sex organs, fuse to form a dormant, thick-walled, pigmented, and often sculptured zygote called the zygospore. The mature zygospores eventually germinate to produce a new haploid mycelium.

The genetic regulation of sexual reproduction in fungi was first discovered (1904) in the Zygomycetes by Albert Francis Blakeslee, who coined the terms *homothallism* and *heterothallism* to describe the two types of mating strains. Both are now known to be common throughout the fungi.

The subdivision Ascomycotina (formerly the class Ascomycetes) includes all true fungi in which sexual reproduction results in ascospores, produced within a specialized cell called an ascus. In many ascomycetes, male structures (antheridia) and female structures (ascogonia) are produced. The antheridia donate nuclei to the ascogonia by fusion with a receptive filament, the trichogyne. In others the same function may be accomplished by conidia (asexual spores that can also serve as fertilizing elements) or by hyphal fusion.

The parental nuclei unite in the ascogonium and enter hyphal branches that grow out from it within a developing fruiting body, the ascocarp. The paired parental nuclei divide synchronously (conjugate division) in specialized hyphae with binucleate cells (ascogenous hyphae). The tip cells of the ascogenous hyphae form a hook in which the haploid parental nuclei fuse to produce a diploid zygote nucleus. The zygote nucleus immediately undergoes meiotic (reduction) divisions to produce four haploid nuclei in the enlarging cell, called the ascus at this stage of development. In most cases a mitotic nuclear division then doubles the number of nuclei per ascus, after which each nucleus is enclosed in a cell wall to form the ascospores.

Other major features of the fungi of this subdivision are that the cell walls contain chitin; the hyphae have simple,

The life cycle of a slime mold begins when the adult fungus (A) produces spores. Upon germination (B), spores of plasmodial slime molds release one to four swarm cells (C); spores of cellular slime molds produce one to four amoebalike organisms (D), which, like the swarm cells, may then divide (E). Pairs of swarm cells (F) or amoebas (G) fuse to form binucleate zygotes (H), which then undergo mitotic cell division. Zygotes of plasmodial slime molds fuse (J) to form a multinucleate plasmodium (K), in which individual cells are not differentiated. Zygotes of cellular slime molds aggregate to form a similar mass called a pseudoplasmodium, in which individual cells do not fuse. Both masses eventually form sporangia (L), which, when they mature (M), produce new spores.

washer-shaped septa with a central pore; and asexual reproduction occurs by formation of nonmotile spores (conidia, oidia, arthrospores, and others) that are usually produced on specialized branches called conidiophores.

Several classes of ascomycetes exist. The class Hemiascomycetes includes the YEASTS; these may be unicellular or mycelial, but all lack ascogenous hyphae and fruits. Most yeasts are saprobic, commonly occurring on plant parts, in soil, and in other locations with adequate moisture and organic material. A small group is parasitic on the leaves, twigs, and branches of vascular plants, causing leaf curl and witches'-broom (tufts of branchlets resulting from repeated branching). It is unclear whether the yeasts are a primitive ascomycete type or whether they are derived from more complex forms.

Another class of ascomycetes, Plectomycetes, includes several economically important fungi that form their asci in small, simple, closed, fruiting structures (cleistothecia). The powdery MILDEWS—so named from the powdery appearance of infected leaves—are all obligate parasites of higher plants and are largely host specific. The fungus grows on the surface as a white, cottony mycelial mat and produces many simple conidiophores and ellipsoidal spores (conidia). The surface cells of the host are invaded by special extensions called haustoria. The conidia give rise to new sites of infections by germination on the surface and haustorium formation. The cleistothecia become brown or black at maturity, bear a number of characteristically shaped external appendages—hook-shaped or spearlike, for example—and overwinter on the fallen leaves. The ascospores are forcefully discharged in the spring and initiate new infections. *Erisiphe graminis* strains infect a number of grass species, including wheat and barley.

A second major group of plectomycetes includes the commercially utilized genera *Aspergillus* and *Penicillium*, as well as important pathogens of plants and humans. Sexual reproduction is relatively rare among species of *Aspergillus* and *Penicillium*. *Aspergillus* produces chains of pigmented, asexual conidia on the surface of an inflated region of a branch, called a conidiophore. Conidium formation is similar in *Penicillium*, but the conidiophore is branched to form a brushlike structure (penicillus) instead of having an inflated vesicle. The conidia are connected in chains on the conidiophores but are readily dispersed by air currents. The green, black, yellow, and gray colors of the colonies of these common microfungi are the result of the color of the huge number of pigmented conidia produced on the surface.

In addition to their roles in the decay of plant and animal residues and in food spoilage, these fungi are of great significance to humans in other ways. *Aspergillus fumagatus*, a common inhabitant of heated compost, can cause respiratory disease in humans, and a number of related species may produce aflatoxin, a tumor-inducing alkaloid, in poorly stored, moldy grain. Species of both *Penicillium* and *Aspergillus* are used extensively in commercial fermentations. This class also includes other species that cause disease in humans, animals, and plants; for example, the fungus *Ceratocystis ulmi* is responsible for DUTCH ELM DISEASE, other species cause a wilt disease in oaks, and still others reduce the quality of lumber.

All fungi in the class Pyrenomycetes produce asci and ascospores as an organized hymenial layer in a fruiting body called a perithecium. The perithecium is a small, flask-shaped structure with a thin wall that surrounds a basal tuft of asci; the opening at the top is called an ostiole. The ascospores are typically discharged violently from the tips of the asci as they sequentially protrude through the ostiole. The perithecia may form as separate structures on the mycelium, or they may lie just below the surface of a larger mass of sterile hyphae called a stroma.

This class includes a large number of fungi in several orders. Many are saprobes that grow on dung or cellulosic materials; others cause diseases of higher plants. Fungi of the genus *Neurospora* produce single, dark perithecia on the substratum and large numbers of salmon-colored, ellipsoidal conidia on the abundant aerial mycelium. These fungi are characterized by linearly arranged ascospores, minimal nutritional requirements, and a rapid growth rate—traits that make

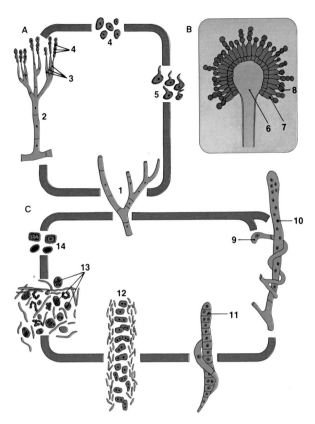

Reproduction in most species of *Penicillium* and *Aspergillus* is asexual. In *Penicillium* (A) the somatic hyphae (1) produce conidiophores (2) that branch into sterigmata (3), each of which bears a long chain of specialized spores called conidia (4). The conidia germinate (5) and produce new hyphae. In *Aspergillus* (B) a bulbous vesicle (6) forms, from which the sterigmata (7) and conidia (8) grow. Some species, however, appear to have a sexual stage (C), which presumably is similar in both genera. One hypha produces a (male) antheridium (9), which spirals around a (female) ascogonium (10) produced by another hypha. Their cells merge, and nuclei pair off (11). Fusion of nuclei (12)—forming zygotes—and meiosis occur, producing asci (13), which release ascospores (14) that germinate and produce new hyphae.

them ideal for laboratory experimentation. In the 1930s, George W. Beadle and Edward L. Tatum began experiments with *N. crassa* that led to the development of a new discipline, biochemical genetics. They demonstrated that each protein is a product of a single gene.

Xylaria species produce upright stromatic fruits 4–8 cm (1.5–3 in) tall with a dark, hard outer rind. Just below the surface large numbers of perithecia are formed, their ostioles opening to the outside. Conidia are formed on the surface of the stroma before the perithecia mature and produce ascospores. The dark ascospores are discharged in such large numbers that the area around the fruits may appear black. Other genera produce dark, cushion-shaped fruits. Most species are saprobes on dead stumps, logs, and woody branches; a few are parasitic on living trees, for example, *Daldinia concentrica* on ash.

Claviceps purpurea, which causes the disease ERGOT of rye, produces perithecia in the inflated ends of small, purple, nonwoody stromata in the spring when susceptible grasses, such as rye, are in flower. The needlelike ascospores are discharged and, if they fall on a flower, produce a mycelium that grows and invades the ovary tissue, producing large numbers of small conidiophores on the surface. The conidia are exuded in droplets of sweet material that attract insects, who carry the conidia to other flowers and start new infections. Eventu-

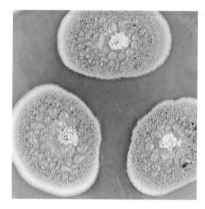

(Left) *Penicillin is produced by* Pencillium chrysogenum (shown) *and the related* P. notatum. (Center) Geastrum *fungi are called earthstars because they burst into a star shape when releasing spores.* (Right) Meripilus giganteus *grows in rosettelike clusters as wide as 70 cm (28 in).*

ally the entire ovary is replaced by tightly packed mycelium enclosed in a hard, lavender rind. This dormant stage is called a sclerotium and may be harvested along with good seed in rye grown for consumption. The sclerotia overwinter on the straw or on the ground, and in the following season they produce new stromata and infect the new crop.

The CUP FUNGI, MORELS, TRUFFLES, and earthtongues are ascomycetes in the class Discomycetes. The fertile hymenial layer of asci is exposed at maturity in all but the truffles, which are produced below ground. This layer lines various surfaces of the fruiting bodies, or apothecia; it occurs on the inner surface of cup fungi, within channels in the closed fruits of the truffle, on the outer surface in earthtongues, and on the surfaces lining the pits on the caps of morels. Parasitic species such as *Monilinia fructicola*, the cause of brown rot in peach, may produce numerous conidia, but many saprobic species do not. The morel, *Morchella esculenta*, produces rather large, tan brown, stalked fruits with a roughly conical cap that is lined with shallow pits separated by ridges. The fungi of this species grow in woodlands and fruit in the spring. They are considered excellent for eating, as are other, related species, but the false morel, *Gyromitra*, is poisonous. Some types that have cup-shaped fruits grow in similar habitats; others are commonly found growing on the dung of various herbivorous animals. Truffles, genus *Tuber*, are a popular delicacy in Europe. These fungi form dark, warty, potatolike fruits below the surface of the ground and are found in association with the roots of oak and beech trees. Several species have been found on the United States Pacific coast, but none are considered edible.

The ascomycetes of the class Loculoascomycetes include those fungi whose asci lie within a cavity (locule) in a tightly knit mass of hyphae called a stroma. These differ from stromatic species in the class Pyrenomycetes in that the fertile cavities do not have their own distinct wall layers. Ascostromatic fungi also produce asci with a double wall. The group includes a number of fungi that are saprobes or pathogenic on plants; some of them parasitize insects. The fruits may be very small and may contain either a single locule or a number of locules with individually separated asci. The ascospores are discharged through a pore formed by lysis of stromatic cells between the cavity and the surface of the stroma. *Venturia inaequalis*, of this class, causes apple scab disease in various *Malus* species, such as the apple, crab apple, and hawthorn. It infects the leaves, twigs, and fruits.

The true fungi also include the subdivision Basidiomycotina, the members of which produce haploid sexual spores (basidiospores) on a specialized cell called the basidium. Another important characteristic of the basidiomycetes is that they all produce a "primary" haploid mycelium (the monokaryon); also, as a result of crossing, a "secondary" mycelium (the dikaryon) results, which contains pairs of parental nuclei that replicate by conjugate division. The secondary hyphae usually bear tubular "clamp connections" around each cross-wall

that separates the binucleate cells. This group includes the rust and smut fungi, as well as mushrooms, puffballs, and related forms.

The rusts and smuts in the class Hemibasidiomycetes of basidiomycetes all produce basidia that are divided, or septate. The jelly fungi have rudimentary gelatinous fruiting bodies and are economically unimportant, mainly growing on decaying wood. Both the rusts and smuts produce a thick-walled spore (teliospore, or teleutospore) on the secondary mycelium, and it is this cell that produces the basidium and basidiospores. Both groups are parasites of many higher plants and do not produce fruiting bodies; they instead develop the teliospores in or on the tissues of the host plant.

The rusts are obligate parasites of plants and may have very complex life cycles, occurring in up to five different stages on two unrelated plant species. *Puccinia graminis*, the cause of wheat rust, is one such long-cycled, heteroecious (two-host) fungus. Other species may lack some stages and may parasitize only a single host (autoecious).

Smut fungi have simpler life cycles and can often be grown readily in culture, although they may not complete their life cycle in artificial media. The teliospores produce basidia that are either septate and form basidiospores as buds from each cell, or lack septa and develop several spores at the tip. The basidiospores of *Ustilago maydis*, the cause of corn smut, detach from the fruiting body and can be grown as a budding, yeastlike phase in culture.

The subdivision Basidiomycotina also includes the classes Hymenomycetes and Gasteromycetes, which comprise the mushrooms, toadstools, puffballs, and related species. They are the most advanced groups of fungi and produce the largest fruiting bodies. In the Hymenomycetes the basidia occur in a hymenium that lines the surface of gills, pores, or spines and is exposed before the basidiospores are produced. In the Gasteromycetes (puffballs) there may or may not be a true hymenial layer, and the basidiocarps either remain closed or else open after the basidiospores have been produced. Both groups lack specialized structures for sexual mating, but they have complex genetic systems that regulate sexual compatibility by means of hyphal fusion between monokaryons. Many species are edible, but others are deadly poisonous.

The subdivision Deuteromycotina includes all fungi that lack known sexual reproductive structures and thus cannot be otherwise classified. Many soil fungi, plant pathogens, and industrially useful species are included in this group.

JAMES S. LOVETT

Bibliography: Ainsworth, G. C., *Introduction to the History of Mycology* (1976); Alexopoulos, C. J., *Introductory Mycology*, 3d ed. (1979); Garraway, M. O., and Evans, R. C., *Fungal Nutrition and Physiology* (1984); Gray, W. D., and Alexopoulos, C. J., *Biology of the Myxomycetes* (1968); Hawksworth, D. L., et al., *Ainsworth and Bisby's Dictionary of the Fungi,* 7th ed. (1983); Moore-Landecker, E., *Fundamentals of the Fungi,* 3d ed. (1990); Webster, J., *Introduction to Fungi,* 2d ed. (1980).

fungus diseases

About 30 human diseases caused by fungi are known. Such fungi usually reside in soil and enter the body through a skin puncture or the lungs, but some spread between humans or from animals to humans. The INFECTIOUS DISEASES, called mycoses, develop slowly and are sometimes difficult to treat. Even diagnoses can be complicated, because few laboratory tests are specific for the organisms.

Dermatophytoses. These are mycoses of the skin, hair, or nails, but never of internal organs. Common names include RINGWORM, athlete's foot, jock itch, and nail fungus. Medically they are called tinea (Latin for "worm"); thus tinea capitis is scalp ringworm and so forth. About two dozen fungus species cause ringworms. They are grouped in three genera: *Microsporum* (hair and skin infections), *Epidermophyton* (skin and nails), and *Trichophyton* (all three). Ringworms—except certain nail infections—respond well to medication, although several weeks of treatment are usually needed; little resistance, however, develops to reinfection.

Among the more common such fungi are *M. canis,* which is acquired from cats and dogs and is a worldwide cause of scalp and body infections, and *E. floccosum,* a worldwide cause of body and foot ringworms and onychomycosis (a nail ringworm). *T. mentagrophytes* and *T. rubrum* are common causes of athlete's foot and of toenail infections that are hard to cure. A contagious body ringworm called black dot ringworm, caused by *T. tonsurans,* is common in the Pacific region and Europe and increasingly so in the United States. *T. verrucosum,* which causes large, ugly lesions on the scalp and body, is worldwide and spreads from cattle to humans.

Systemic Mycoses. These fungi can invade the internal organs, bones, and eyes. Some may exist as both spores (the infectious particles) and yeasts (the parasitic stage). The mycoses range from transient infections to fatal diseases, but the latter are rare and are usually seen in patients debilitated by other diseases such as cancer. Several drugs are effective in many cases, but diagnosis must be certain beforehand because of their varying toxicity.

About four species of ASPERGILLUS can cause the lung disease called Aspergillosis in debilitated persons, in whom the disease can be fatal. Another potentially fatal mycosis, CANDIDIASIS, is unique in being acquired from *Candida* yeasts that are normal inhabitants of the gastrointestinal tract. The term actually covers a spectrum of diseases, ranging from white patches in the mouth (thrush) to persistent vaginal infections to invasions of almost any organ. The latter are usually fatal only in persons debilitated by disease.

COCCIDIOIDOMYCOSIS, or "valley fever," infects up to 90% of the inhabitants of the southwestern United States and northern Mexico. Usually after an influenzalike episode the patient gains protection against reinfection, but in a few cases the fungi infect internal organs, often fatally. The agent, *Coccidioides immitis,* lives in desert soils.

Cryptococcosis is caused by a yeast found worldwide in pigeon droppings. It probably enters the body through the lungs, and in rare instances a fatal brain disease called cryptococcal MENINGITIS results. Cryptococcosis is usually seen in debilitated persons.

HISTOPLASMOSIS is caused by *Histoplasma capsulatum,* which occurs in bird droppings or bat guano. It is found worldwide, but in the United States the endemic area is the Mississippi River basin. Most people inhaling the spores develop lifelong immunity, but in rare cases the organism invades white blood cells and becomes a parasite of the reticuloendothelial system, the only mycosis to do so. Histoplasmosis may be fatal.

Sporotrichosis is called the gardener's disease because the fungus, *Sporothrix schenckii,* enters its host from a thorn or other vegetation scratch. Over a period of weeks or months the organism can cause lesions that progress up the lymph channels of the arm. Potassium iodide is an effective therapeutic agent. The disease occurs worldwide.

Mycotoxicosis. This is not a mycosis but, instead, the ingestions of toxins produced by any one of several fungi. Such fungi occur worldwide, usually as saprophytes on vegetation.

Aflatoxin, for example, derives from *Aspergillus flavus* infections of corn. ERGOT, a common disease of rye and other grains, is caused by fungi of the genus *Claviceps* and was once a serious problem for humans. Some mycotoxins are used therapeutically in medicine, but others are lethal in extremely small amounts.

GLENN S. BULMER

Bibliography: Ainsworth, G. C., *Introduction to the History of Medical and Veterinary Mycology* (1987); Bulmer, G. S., *Introduction to Medical Mycology* (1979); Christensen, C. M., *Molds, Mushrooms and Mycotoxins* (1975); Evans, E. G., and Richardson, M. D., *Medical Mycology* (1989); Roberts, S. O., et al., *A Clinician's Guide to Fungal Diseases* (1984).

Funk, Casimir   [funk', kaz'-ih-mir]

Casimer Funk, b. Feb. 23, 1884, d. Nov. 19, 1967, a Polish-American biochemist, was a pioneer in the study of vitamins and coined the term *vitamine,* later changed to *vitamin.* In 1911 he isolated a pure chemical from yeast and rice polishings that became known as vitamin B_1, or thiamine. Funk also contributed to an understanding of vitamin deficiency.

Funston, Frederick   [fuhns'-tuhn]

Frederick Funston, b. New Carlisle, Ohio, Nov. 9, 1865, d. Feb. 19, 1917, was an American general who, on Mar. 23, 1901, captured Emilio AGUINALDO, leader of the Filipino insurrection against U.S. occupation. After fighting from 1896 in the Cuban rebel army opposing Spanish rule, Funston was given command of a Philippines-bound Kansas volunteer regiment when the Spanish-American War began in 1898. He did not see action against Spain, but during the subsequent Filipino insurrection he won a Medal of Honor for bravery under fire at the Battle of Calumpit in the winter of 1898–99. For capturing Aguinaldo, Funston was transferred to the regular army as a brigadier general. In 1914 he commanded the U.S. troops sent by President Woodrow Wilson to occupy Veracruz, Mexico. Promoted to major general, Funston commanded the troops on the Mexican border from 1914 to 1917.

Bibliography: Funston, Frederick, *Memories of Two Wars* (1911).

Fur

The Fur are a people of western Sudan, after whom the province and former Islamic sultanate DARFUR is named. They inhabit the high country stretching south from the 3,050-m (10,000-ft) Jebel Marra Mountains and number about 1,500,000. They are generally slim and Negroid in appearance. Their language belongs to the Nilo-Scharan family and is remotely related to others in the savanna belt of the Sudan. The Fur established a dynastic Islamic state in the early 16th century. Darfur was annexed to Egyptian Sudan in 1874. It was again independent from 1888 to 1916, when an Anglo-Egyptian colonial administration was established in the area.

The Fur are sedentary farmers who rely mainly on the cultivation of millet during the rainy season; their villages range from 50 to a few thousand inhabitants. The Fur adhere to Islam and have adopted Arab names and dress. Their society is divided into wealthy landowners, lower castes of smiths, tanners, and other artisans, and serfs. Although descent is traced through the male line, residence is matrilocal, so that elders are surrounded by their daughters and their daughters' husbands. Today the traditional hierarchy of Fur chiefs is integrated into the Sudan administrative system.   BRIAN SPOONER

Bibliography: Lampen, E. D., *Sudan Notes and Records* (1950).

fur

Fur is the soft, hairy coat of an animal that is processed into a pelt and used to make wearing apparel. By definition, a true fur, such as mink, is made up of a soft, thick, insulating layer called underfur, and a top layer of longer, lustrous guard hairs. Furs such as Persian lamb lack guard hairs, however, while others such as monkey fur lack an underlayer. The quality of the pelt of any species varies according to where and when it is taken. Most furs come from cold or temperate climates, and they are usually at their prime in midwinter.

FUR SOURCES

Although some fur-bearing species such as beaver or seal are hunted or trapped, many popular furs are produced from animals that have been raised on fur farms or ranches.

Wild Furs. Commercial furs from wild sources constitute at most half of the total trade. In recent years, regulations designed to prevent the extinction of certain wild species have reduced the number of fur pelts taken in the wild. Formerly prized furs, such as those from the leopard, cheetah, or jaguar, may no longer be hunted in the countries where they are indigenous, and many other countries forbid their importation. The Federal Endangered Species Act prohibits the sale of these furs in the United States. In addition, special laws that protect certain North American species are enforced in the United States and Canada; the killing of North Pacific fur seals, which precipitated the BERING SEA CONTROVERSY, has been regulated by an international agreement among the United States, Canada, Japan, and Russia. A 1972 agreement regulates the hunting of Antarctic seals.

In the United States, those wild animals that may still be legally taken are also protected by federal and state laws that control licensing and specify the trapping methods, the seasons, and the maximum take for each species.

Fur Farming. As an industry, fur farming—the breeding and rearing of wild species for their pelts—is relatively new. The first experimental farms in the United States and Canada were established in the 1920s in order to develop techniques for breeding mink and silver fox. Breeding techniques have improved to the point where breeders are now able to develop fur mutations with specific desirable characteristics, such as quality, color, and pelt size.

The color of a silver fox pelt, with its silver-tipped, black guard hairs, is the result of a mutation of the wild red fox and was established over a period of years of controlled mating. Mink ranchers have developed a large number of mutant fur shades, and at the present time 12 color classes, each with many variations, are produced from ranch-raised mink. These range from the standard dark brown to shades of beige, blue, gray, and white. Since the 1930s, mink ranching has grown into a thriving industry in the United States. Scandinavia and Russia have their own industries, based on breeding stock sold by U.S. ranches. In addition to mink and fox, other wild species raised on ranches include chinchilla and nutria. Various species of sheep (Karakul, broadtail, Persian lamb) are reared for lamb pelts. Ranch farming of other wild species—beaver, raccoon, or skunk—is theoretically possible.

FUR MARKETING

Regularly scheduled sales for fur dealers and brokers are held, primarily in the large fur-marketing centers of New York, Montreal, London, and Saint Petersburg. There are also specialized markets for specific furs—Greenville, S.C., for sealskin, Seattle or Stockholm for rabbit skin. Offerings are sorted according to quality, color, and size and are usually sold by lot at public auction.

FUR MANUFACTURING

Dressing. In the dressing process, pelts are cleaned of animal greases and tanned to make the skin more pliable. (See LEATHER AND HIDES for a description of the tanning process.) Some furs may have the guard hairs plucked out and the underfur sheared closer to the skin, as in sheared beaver and raccoon, to create a different texture. The natural yellowish white of some furs is bleached to achieve a pure white; or a darker fur may be bleached to a lighter color and then dyed. A tip-dyed fur is one in which a dye is lightly brushed onto the fur surface. After being processed, the pelts are softened again in a revolving drum filled with sawdust. The final dressing process is glazing, where the fur is combed, the oils in the skin are brought to the surface with a padded iron, and a glazing substance, such as a liquid vegetable gum, is brushed on to increase the fur's sheen.

Garment Making. In the production of a fur garment the dressed furs are matched for uniformity. The waste parts—the head, tail, and paws—are cut away. In mink and other costly furs an additional process called letting-out is employed, whereby the skin of the pelt is cut down the center, and

each half is sliced into narrow diagonal strips ranging in width from 1.5 to 13 mm ($\frac{1}{16}$ to $\frac{1}{2}$ in). These strips are resewn to produce a longer, narrower pelt that will give the finished garment a more graceful line. The let-out fur sections are dampened, stretched, and nailed on a large board to a pattern that includes each of the garment pieces. When dry, the fur sections will conform to that pattern. They are then stitched into the complete garment, which needs only a final glazing and a lining to be finished.

The skin pieces left over from the letting-out and other manufacturing processes are matched and sewn together into plates, 0.61 m × 1.22 m (2 ft × 4 ft) rectangular sections that will be used to make other, usually less costly, garments.

In the skin-on-skin process, used primarily for small furs such as muskrat, raccoon, and rabbit, whole skins are trimmed and sewn together. Although the seams are hidden under the fur, the draping qualities of a garment produced by the skin-on-skin process are not usually as graceful, nor can the natural patterns in some furs be kept intact.   SANDY PARKER

THE FUR INDUSTRY

Of all the apparel industries, fur seems the most sensitive to changing economic and social trends. After a sharp decline

IMPORTANT COMMERCIAL FURS

Fur	Sources and Fur Qualities
Fox, especially Arctic (blue or white) fox, black fox,* cross fox,* kit fox, red fox, silver fox*	Taken wild or ranch-raised throughout the Northern Hemisphere. Fox fur has both ground and guard hair. Colors range from deep red and brown to pale gray and silver. Fox fur is often dyed.
Lamb, including broadtail, Karakul, mouton-dyed, Persian	Lamb pelts, which have only ground hair, come from Russia, China, India, Africa, regions of Turkey, Argentina, and North America. Broadtail, the pelt of the newborn or unborn Karakul lamb, has flat, wavy hair. Other lamb furs are curly, except for mouton, where the fur has been sheared to look like beaver.
Mink	Most mink is ranch-raised, with the largest numbers produced in Russia and Scandinavia. Mink has both dense ground hair and long, glossy guard hair. Many colors have been developed from mutant mink.
Nutria (coypu)	Ranch-raised in North America, taken wild in South America. Guard hairs are plucked, and the commercial fur consists of the thick, short ground hair.
Opossum	Taken wild in North and South America. The coarse fur is light brown or gray.
Rabbit (coney, lapin)	Taken wild throughout the world, although some are ranch-raised. The guard hairs are usually plucked, and the fur dyed.
Raccoon	Taken wild in North and South America. Gray or black fur with long guard hairs.
Sable	Taken wild in Siberia. Among the most valued of furs, with long lustrous guard hair, thick ground hair. Very dark brown or brownish black.
Seal, fur	Taken wild in Alaska, Siberia, South America, South Africa, and Japan. Coarse guard hairs are plucked, dense ground hair is often dyed.
Squirrel	Taken wild in Siberia. Long, glossy guard hair, long, dense ground hair. Pelts are often dyed.

*Mutant.

in the late 1960s and the 1970s, due in large part to increased environmental concerns, the industry rebounded in the early 1980s. High-priced, high-fashion coats—Russian sable and lynx, silver fox, and mink made by American craftspeople and with prestigious designer labels—sold as never before. Asia has developed its own fur industry, however, and less expensive coats, sometimes made of Asian furs (China now has its own mink ranches) captured over one-quarter of the U.S. market in the mid-1980s. Less-expensive garments are generally heavier, the skins less supple and often not precisely color-matched so that the coats must be dyed and will not always hold their color. Cheaper coats usually use fewer skins and thus tend to wear out more quickly. By the end of the decade, however, partisans of animal rights had convinced many potential buyers that the wearing of furs was morally wrong, and the fur industry dived into another decline.

Russia, the United States, and Canada are the chief fur-producing countries. Muskrat, raccoon, and beaver are the principal wild furs taken in the United States; mink and chinchilla are the main ranch-produced furs.

Bibliography: Adams, L., *Mink Raising* (1979); Bachrach, Max, *Fur—A Practical Treatise: Geography of the Fur World* (1977); Deems, Eugene F., and Pursley, Duane, *North American Fur-Bearers* (1983); Ewing, Elizabeth, *Fur in Dress* (1981); Golden, L., and Lulow, K., *How to Buy and Maintain a Fur Coat* (1986); Kaplan, D. C., *The World of Furs* (1974); Samet, A., *Pictorial Encyclopedia of Furs,* rev. ed. (1950).

fur seal: see SEAL.

fur trade

The fur trade in North America profoundly influenced the economic life, exploration, and diplomacy of the United States and Canada. The scarcity of fur-bearing animals in Europe by the 17th century encouraged English, French, and Dutch traders to look to their nations' colonies as sources of valuable animal skins. Several factors favored the development of the fur trade in the New World: the great abundance of animals in the American woodlands; the presence of Indians skilled in trapping and in the processing of pelts; and, above all, the possibility of tremendous profit. Goods bought for one livre in France could be traded to Indians for skins worth 200 livres when brought back to Paris. Consequently traders eagerly sought out the pelts of deer, otter, bear, marmot, fox, and, most important, beaver, whose fur was ideal for making the broad-brimmed hats popular in Europe.

French Trade. The French were particularly fortunate, for in the colony of NEW FRANCE the St. Lawrence River and Great Lakes gave them access to inland forests teeming with animal life. Only the land along the St. Lawrence was suited to farming, so the fur trade became the mainstay of the colony's economy. To tap the region's potential, the French explored the area around the Great Lakes and the valleys of the Ohio and Mississippi rivers and negotiated commercial and military alliances with the Hurons, Ottawas, Illinois, and many other Indian tribes.

Indians either brought furs into the settlements of Quebec, Montreal, and Three Rivers or traded with the *coureurs de bois,* Frenchmen who often would live among the Indians for months at a time. The Indians' reliance upon European utensils, weapons, and blankets revolutionized their way of life and made them increasingly dependent on those supplying these goods. To protect French interests, the French constructed a series of military posts and towns: Niagara, Detroit, Mackinac (Michilimackinac), Kaskaskia, Natchez, New Orleans, Mobile, and others. By 1715 the French had established a widespread fur-trading empire that was highly profitable under the best conditions. But its success depended upon fluctuating prices in Europe, long lines of supply, and a delicate system of Indian alliances. Moreover, the French faced increasing competition from the English colonies.

British Trade. Although all English colonies on the Atlantic coast engaged in fur trading, the enterprise was especially important in South Carolina, Pennsylvania, and, above all, New York. There the Hudson and Mohawk rivers allowed easy transport of furs from Lake Erie to the trading center of Albany and the port of New York. In the 18th century, French supremacy in the fur trade was challenged by the HUDSON'S BAY COMPANY in northeastern Canada and by New York traders in alliance with the confederation of Iroquois Indians. Bitter competition in western New York and the upper Ohio Valley led directly to the FRENCH AND INDIAN WAR of 1754–63, in which Britain wrested from France control of Canada and all the land east of the Mississippi River.

U.S. Trade. After the United States won its independence in the American Revolution, the British Hudson's Bay Company and NORTH WEST COMPANY continued to operate in Canada and in the Pacific Northwest. The U.S. government tried to discourage trade with Indians except by its own agents, but private firms eventually dominated the field. John Jacob Astor's AMERICAN FUR COMPANY controlled Great Lakes trade and later operated in the northern Rocky Mountains and far Northwest. Although Manuel Lisa had led an expedition to the upper Missouri River in 1809, the heyday of the trans-Mississippi fur trade began with the expeditions of William ASHLEY and Andrew Henry to the same area in 1822 and 1823. Ashley and Henry soon inaugurated the rendezvous system by which MOUNTAIN MEN who lived in the wilds year-round met in the mountains with representatives of trading companies each summer to exchange animal skins for goods.

While trapping proved an economic boon for the market centers of the fur trade, particularly St. Louis, Mo., and Taos, N.Mex., its impact on the national economy was not great. Far more important was the exploration of the Rocky Mountains, Great Basin, and Pacific coast by such mountain men as Jedediah SMITH, James BRIDGER, and Thomas FITZPATRICK in their search for animals. Settlers on their way west were soon taking advantage of the trappers' knowledge of the area.

By 1840 bitter competition among trappers had severely reduced the beaver population in the West. This decline in supply, along with the growing popularity of the silk hat in Europe, meant the end of the golden age of the fur trade, although some trappers and Indians continued to bring skins to trading posts on the Great Plains.   ELLIOTT WEST

Bibliography: Carlos, A. M., *The North American Fur Trade, 1804–21* (1986); Cleland, R. G., *This Reckless Breed of Men: The Trappers and Fur Traders of the Southwest* (1992); Geary, Steven, *Fur Trapping in North America,* rev. ed. (1985); Gibson, J. R., *Otter Skins, Boston Ships, and China Goods: The Maritime Fur Trade of the Northwest Coast* (1992); Innis, H. A., *The Fur Trade of Canada,* rev. ed. (1956); Irving, W., *Astoria* (1836; repr. 1967); Krech, S., ed., *Indians, Animals, and the Fur Trade* (1986); Victor, F. F., *River of the West,* 2 vols. (1983–85); Wood, W. R., and Thiessen, T. P., eds., *Early Fur Trade on the Northern Plains* (1985).

Furies

In Greek mythology, the three Furies—Tisiphone, Megaera, and Alecto—were goddesses of vengeance. Their function was to punish crimes that had escaped detection or public justice. Although their usual abode was HADES, they also pursued the living, as in the story of ORESTES. In appearance they were ugly, bat-winged, serpent-haired creatures born of the blood of URANUS when he was mutilated by the sickle of CRONUS. In the afterlife, the Furies dispensed justice from the netherworld, where, armed with scourges, they meted out the torments of remorse and other punishments. The Furies, also known as Erinyes, were called the Eumenides in later Greek literature.

Furman University

Established in 1826 and associated with the South Carolina Baptist Convention, Furman University (enrollment: 2,910; library: 325,797 volumes) is a private coeducational school in Greenville, S.C. Furman offers cooperative programs with Georgia Institute of Technology, Auburn University, and Duke University.

Furman v. Georgia

In its opinion in the case of *Furman v. Georgia* (1972), the U.S. Supreme Court invalidated the CAPITAL PUNISHMENT laws of 39 states by holding that the "imposition and carrying out of the death penalty" constituted "cruel and unusual punishment" in violation of the 8TH AMENDMENT and the 14TH AMENDMENT because it was imposed in an arbitrary and capricious manner. Each member of the Court, five in the majority and four in dissent, filed a separate opinion, but the concurrences of Justices White and Stewart were especially significant in that they left open the question whether any other system of capital punishment would be unconstitutional.

In 1976 the Court rejected the contention that the death penalty per se is cruel and unusual punishment in violation of the Constitution, as long as jury discretion in imposing a death sentence is controlled by "clear and objective standards so as to produce nondiscriminatory application." This decision led to the electrocution in Florida (May 25, 1979) of convicted murder John Spenkelink, the first execution since 1967 in which a condemned person was put to death against his will.

ROBERT J. STEAMER

furnace   [fur'-nis]

Furnaces are closed devices in which FUEL is burned to produce high temperatures. They are usually lined with fire-resistant brick insulation and metal and are not to be confused with OVENS, which are similar devices that operate at much lower temperatures.

Furnaces were known as long ago as 3000 BC, during the Bronze Age, when they were used to melt and alloy copper and tin to make bronze artifacts such as vases, urns, axes, helmets, and swords. With the advent of the IRON AGE, furnaces became more highly developed to reach the higher temperatures required to separate iron from its ores and to forge articles of commerce and war. Today, highly specialized furnaces include the BLAST FURNACE, the ELECTRIC FURNACE, the OPEN-HEARTH FURNACE, and the REVERBATORY FURNACE. The nuclear reactor may also be considered a furnace, as well as any solar energy device that concentrates solar radiation. Over the last 100 years, as the domestic hot-water space-heating boiler has gradually been displaced, the term "furnace" has also come to be applied to the forced-air furnace widely used as in-home HEATING SYSTEMS.

High-pressure, or gun-type, oil burners are used to heat many homes. Oil pumped under pressure through a nozzle is atomized into a fine mist, mixed with air, and burned in a refractory fire pot, or chamber, after ignition by a high-voltage spark generated by a transformer.

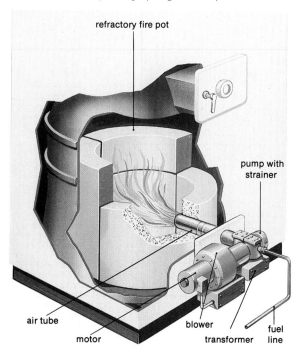

refractory fire pot

pump with strainer

air tube

blower

motor

transformer

fuel line

BASIC PRINCIPLES

If the gaseous products of fossil fuel combustion in a furnace are in direct contact with the gaseous, liquid, or solid substance to be heated, the furnace is said to be direct fired. If the heat from the products of combustion is transferred through a partition or HEAT EXCHANGER, the furnace is said to be indirect fired.

The direct-fired furnace is preferred whenever possible because it is cheaper to construct, operate, and maintain. Higher temperatures can be reached rapidly and it can also be cooled down more rapidly, but the substance being heated is contaminated by flue (combustion) gases and is subject to changing conditions of oxidation and reduction. Volatile components of the heated substance are vaporized and dissipated in the flue gases.

Indirect-fired furnaces protect the heated substance from direct contact with the flue gases by a wall division or heat exchanger. The flue charge passes on one side and the heated substance passes on the other. Although they are expensive to construct, indirect-fired furnaces permit easier control of temperatures. Moreover, an artificial atmosphere can surround the heated substance to prevent undesirable chemical reactions that might damage its integrity. For example, nitrogen is often used in furnaces to prevent the reduction and the oxidation that an air atmosphere could create.

TYPES

Furnaces may be classified according to the kind of fuel that they use.

Solid and Liquid Fuel Furnaces. Solid fuel furnaces burn their fuel on a grate, where the primary combustion occurs. Heat created by this combustion is tranferred to the substance to be heated by radiation, conduction, and convection. Major problems include maintaining a continuous, evenly fired fuel bed and removing the ash and separating it from the unburned fuel. If a coal-burning furnace is operated with too much air, for example, the coal may form clinkers, and unburned fuel falls through the grates.

Liquid fuels are much easier to transport, store, handle, and burn than solid fuels. Refineries make fuel oils in several different grades. Diesel engines and home furnaces burn the light oils. Ships and power plants use a heavy residual oil called Bunker C, which must be heated before it can be atomized and burned in the firebox of the boiler. Liquid fuels produce a very hot radiant flame.

Solid fuels such as coal and coke may be powdered and burned like liquid fuels (see COAL AND COAL MINING). They are blown into the furnace mixed with 10% to 20% excess air to assure almost complete combustion. The high cost of installing equipment to handle powdered fuels makes them impractical except for use in large utility boilers. By contrast, equipment to burn liquid fuels is cheap to install, operate, and maintain.

In some furnaces, such as blast furnaces and lime KILNS, the fuel is mixed with the heated substance so that the heat of combustion is highest at the point where it is needed. In such operations the fuel mix must remain porous, so that air can be circulated through it for combustion.

Gas-Fired Furnaces. Gas is the best possible fuel for furnaces because it burns the cleanest and is the easiest to control. Gas may be introduced at different points in the furnace to ensure an even furnace temperature or assist in secondary combustion (burning the products of incomplete combustion) where low-grade fuels are used.

The efficiency of combustion is greatly increased when gas is burned in contact with hot surfaces. This permits the gas, which is not radiant in itself, to raise the surface to incandescence and to release its heat by radiation, which is a very effective way to transfer heat.

F. T. ANDREWS

Furness, Frank   [fur'-nis]

The American architect Frank Furness, b. Philadelphia, Nov. 12, 1839, d. June 27, 1912, began his training in the Philadelphia office of John Fraser, and then entered the New York studio of Richard Morris HUNT, who was well-versed in contemporary French and English design theory. After distinguished service in the Civil War, Furness returned (1866) to Philadelphia and formed a partnership with George W. Hewitt. His reputation was firmly established by his design for the PENNSYLVANIA ACADEMY OF THE FINE ARTS (1872-76), in which he fused elements of neoclassical (see NEOCLASSICISM, art) and GOTHIC REVIVAL architecture in a manner that recalled the contemporary French fashion for the *néo Grec*. With this design Furness began a transition in American architecture away from the derivative academic buildings of the previous generation toward a highly decorated and stridently colorful Victorian style. Furness was much influenced by John Ruskin's enthusiasm for the Venetian Gothic, but he was the first American architect to put European ideas to original use in his native country.

Furness's work, which includes numerous public buildings and private houses in the Philadelphia area, had a strong effect upon the leading architect of the following generation, Louis SULLIVAN, who was employed by Furness as a draftsman in 1873.   HOWARD BATCHELOR

Bibliography: O'Gorman, James, *The Architecture of Frank Furness* (1973); Whiffen, Marcus, *American Architecture since 1780* (1969).

Furniss, Harry

Harry Furniss, b. Ireland, Mar. 26, 1854, d. Jan. 14, 1925, was a largely self-taught caricaturist who, after moving to London in 1873, became a popular cartoonist and illustrator. His political cartoons appeared frequently in such widely read periodicals as *The Illustrated London News* (1876-84) and *Punch* (1880-94). After leaving *Punch* in 1894, he turned to free-lance work; among his commissions was his famous Pear's Soap poster picturing an unwashed tramp.

Furniss's illustrations adorned Lewis Carroll's *Sylvie and Bruno* (1889) and editions of Charles Dickens (1910) and William Makepeace Thackeray (1911). Among his own books were an 1890 lampoon of highbrow art, *Royal Academy Antics*, and the 1901 memoir *Confessions of a Caricaturist*. He also wrote novels and essays.

furniture

The history of furniture and of its manufacture are the two major topics of this article. Furniture originated as utilitarian, functional objects. In prehistory there were needs to be met: something to sit on, something to sleep in, and eventually something in which to store things. The objects created to meet these needs were, by definition, utilitarian. Then, at some time so remote that it cannot be pinpointed, groups arose whose members desired objects that were both utilitarian and attractively decorated, or, in short, decorative furniture. That this transition took place thousands of years ago cannot be doubted.

DECORATIVE FURNITURE

The first sophisticated cultures of which there is any knowledge—the Chinese, the Egyptians, the Greeks, the Romans—all had highly developed forms of decorative furniture. The styles and techniques manifested in these pieces could only have been the end result of a long period of development.

Origins of Decorated Furniture. Decoration in furniture is part of the general artistic development of society, although almost certainly a later manifestation. That is, the society that has developed elaborately decorated furnishings invariably will also have a highly sophisticated tradition of painting and sculpture. Moreover, it seems quite clear that the latter developments preceded the former. For example, there is no evidence that the people who produced the cave paintings of Altamira (c.13,500 BC) or the sculptured limestone form of the Venus of Willendorf (c.30,000-25,000 BC; Naturhistorisches Museum, Vienna) ever used furniture, much less decorative furniture. Thousands of years later their descendants in Spain, France, and Germany began to make the furniture for which these areas are now famous.

It is clear, however, that early decoration was different from that of later epochs in both nature and purpose. All early art, whether a rock painting or a carved chief's stool, served a ritual, magical purpose. Even in this century the painted or carved headmen's seats of Africa and the Pacific Islands were clearly understood within the society to be more than attractive pieces of furniture. They were symbols of power, and it is safe to assume that all decoration initially was intended to reinforce this purpose—to propitiate the gods, to bring luck, or to ward off evil. Only with the development of a cultural level in which people perceive themselves as having some control over their destiny does true decoration—art for its own sake, for pleasure—begin to appear.

The role of the artist-decorator-designer is directly related to the way in which people view the resultant work. In a culture in which decoration is considered to have supernatural attributes, the designer is a priest with status and direct access to the temporal rulers. In a society in which people assume the roles of gods, the decorator serves their purposes. The artist may then be a mere anonymous artisan or such an artist may find favor in high places and become rich and powerful. Thus such designers as Juste Aurèle MEISSONNIER, a favorite of Louis XV, wielded political influence far in excess of their social status because they created styles of furniture that found favor with the ruling nobility.

What is considered decorative may vary depending upon social whim. The painted pine and fir furniture of central Europe and North America, for example, was certainly intended by its creators to be decorative, but it was many years before tastemakers in the business of antique furniture considered it anything more than a crude imitation of more costly furnishings.

Such changes in taste may have an interesting effect on the value of decorative furniture. A marquetry desk by the German designer David Roentgen (1743-1807) cost hundreds of dollars when made. Today it would cost many thousands. Yet the percentage of increase in its value cannot be compared with that of a painted Pennsylvania dower chest that might have sold in 1790 for $3.00 and which today could bring $13,000 or more.

Types and Techniques. What is called decorative furniture is found in every part of the world. In certain regions, such as the Pacific islands and the desert areas of the Near East, custom and climate have militated against the use of many types of furniture; yet those forms which do exist—small chests and low tables in Persia, for example—may be plain and functional in form but elaborately decorated.

Decoration varies from country to country. Carving is certainly one of the earliest techniques employed, and at certain times, such as during the European Gothic period, it was predominant. Painting or staining is equally pervasive. On the other hand, certain sophisticated techniques have had more limited application. The use of wood veneer and MARQUETRY (wood inlay in contrasting light and dark patterns), ormolu (the application of gilt-bronze mounts), and the use of lacquerwork imply a technical development limited primarily to the more advanced cultures of Asia and Europe. Yet in the societies where these advanced techniques do appear they are frequently of great age. Veneering and inlaying with semiprecious stones, ivory, metal, and mother-of-pearl were practiced in Egypt as long ago as the Early Dynastic Period (c.3100-2613 BC).

Egyptian Furniture. Egypt, in fact, was one of the earliest cen-

This Egyptian folding stool (4th century BC), delicately carved of acacia and ornamented with animal forms, exhibits the simple, lightweight design characteristic of much Egyptian furniture. (Metropolitan Museum of Art, New York City.)

ters for the making of decorative furnishings. The tombs of the Nile Valley have yielded a rich store of chests, tables, stools, and beds. These were embellished in many different ways. Chairs were often painted a dead white, whereas storage chests were boldly stained with bands of geometric decoration. Gilding was used extensively. Varnishes and waxed finishes were also applied to the wood, and carving was common. Chair and table legs were usually carved in the shape of a curved animal leg terminating in a bull hoof or lion paw.

Greek and Roman Furniture. Greece, between 1200 and 300 BC, produced an even greater variety of decorative furniture. Native olive, yew, and cedar wood were turned, carved, painted, and inlaid with precious stones. Cast bronze legs in animal form were applied to chairs and tables whose forms were low and curvilinear. Chests were covered with a rich gilt and inlaid with ivory, and the heavily carved couches of the period resembled elongated thrones. As in Egypt, the way of life dictated light, movable pieces; most furniture was portable or even collapsible, as illustrated by the folding X or scissors chair, a form still popular today.

A far greater variety of forms developed in ancient Rome, in part because the Romans freely adopted and modified the furnishings of Greece and Egypt. Carving was of great importance to the Roman artisan, who cut chair and settee backs to imitate the heads of mules or horses and who used the curving cabriole or animal leg freely. Many other techniques were also utilized. Beds and couches were mounted on lathe-turned legs, painted in bright colors or inlaid in contrasting woods, and mounted with brass fittings. A great many different types of chairs, tables, stools, and pedestals were created, and every type of decorative technique known at the time

(Left) *A Ming dynasty testered bed with an alcove (c.15th–16th century), of fine rosewood, illustrates the plain, boxlike design typical of Ming furniture. Chinese cabinetmakers used such decorative elements as inlay and carving very sparingly, maximizing instead the beauty of the wood through highly polished forms.*

(Right) *A Chinese armchair dating from the late Ming dynasty (16th and 17th centuries) displays the simplicity and functionalism of classic Ming furniture design. The introduction of folding stools to China during the 3rd century AD initiated the long development of these graceful armchairs.*

This detail from a Greek vase, showing a banquet scene, includes such items of furniture as couches and small tables. The Greek couch, used when eating as well as sleeping, was generally made of wood, with a raised headrest and carved or lathe-turned legs.

was employed in their manufacture. Roman style and methods were not only important at that time but also played a major role in the development of later European design.

Chinese Furniture. China was the great Eastern cabinetmaking center, although the significance of early Chinese furnishings has come to be truly appreciated in the West only within the last 100 years. No one knows when the first of these pieces was made, but miniature furniture found in tombs of the Han dynasty (202 BC–AD 220) display a wide variety of furnishings, including chairs, cupboards of several sizes, tables, and chests. These differ from occidental examples in several ways. First, they have a sophisticated flowing line not unlike that of modern bentwood and tubular-steel furniture. In this respect Chinese furniture is far more "modern" than any other found in the ancient world. Secondly, decoration is by most standards limited. The pieces are made almost exclusively of rich, fine-grained hardwoods such as ebony, rosewood, or sandalwood, polished to a high natural-color finish. Carving, when used, is generally confined to small areas; and such fittings as locks and drawer pulls (generally of brass or iron) are of much greater visual importance. Inlay in brass, copper, pew-

ter, or marble is applied to flat surfaces but never in the quantity found on Roman and Egyptian furniture.

Lacquerwork or japanning is, of course, traditionally associated with Chinese taste; but, in fact, the process of applying a lacquer finish (involving the painting on and polishing of countless layers of shellac) was so time-consuming and expensive that only in palaces would one find complete suites of lacquer furniture. Similarly, teak, regarded by many as the traditional Chinese furniture wood, was rarely used prior to the 19th century, and only then in pieces intended for export to Europe. The bulk of Chinese furniture continued to be made of the traditional materials and in traditional ways, characteristics that lingered well into this century.

Byzantine Furniture. Unlike the relatively static style of China, European furniture, in form and decoration, reflects periodic changes over the course of time. The earliest European influence was that of Greece and Rome. As mentioned above, Roman crafts had reached a high degree of sophistication well before the birth of Christ. However, following the collapse of the Western Roman Empire in the 5th century, much of this skill was lost to Europe. It persisted, however, in the East, where the ancient city of Byzantium had been designated in AD 330 as Constantinople, the capital of the Eastern Roman Empire (commonly called the Byzantine Empire).

Constantinople flourished until 1453, and Byzantine furniture forms had a profound influence on the styles of Italy and, indeed, on all of western Europe. The Byzantine style was essentially a mixture of Greco-Roman and Oriental elements, and nearly all the surviving finer furniture made in this manner was intended for royal or ecclesiastical use. The general form was Roman, but superimposed upon this was profuse ornamentation in the Eastern mode—that is, an emphasis on curvilinear and geometric forms with much mosaic inlay in gold, glass, and stone. Contrary to Roman practice, human and animal figures were less often incorporated, and decorative elements tended to be stiff and conventionalized rather than fluid.

Medieval European Furniture. Although its influence waned with time, Byzantine taste was dominant in the eastern Mediterranean until the 15th century. Farther west, however, furniture, decorated or not, became an uncommon luxury during the so-called Dark Ages in Europe. Very little has survived from the Merovingian (c.500–750), Carolingian (c.750–950), and Ottonian (c.950–1050) periods. The bronze chair known as the "Throne of Dagobert" (early 9th century; Louvre, Paris), the best-known example of Carolingian furniture, clearly reveals its Roman ancestry.

What style there was in this area came in the Romanesque period (beginning c.1050), also reflecting its origin in a debased Roman style. Furniture forms, in contrast to those of the Eastern Empire, were few—primarily, chests, tables, and stools—and decoration was almost exclusively carved, chiefly in the form of primitive, vigorous floral motifs. The wood of

This 16th-century French choir stall demonstrates the influence of Renaissance decorative motifs, seen in the back carving, upon a predominantly Gothic ecclesiastical form. As late as the 17th century, churches and monasteries remained among the principal repositories of the fine furnishings so scarce in medieval Europe. (Philadelphia Museum of Art.)

The Throne of Dagobert (early 9th century; back added 11th century), a Carolingian seat of honor crafted in bronze, follows the design of the folding stool used centuries earlier by Roman dignitaries. A symbol of authority, the ornate folding chair became an appropriate throne for medieval rulers whose courts were frequently moved from place to place. (Louvre, Paris.)

choice was oak, and furnishings were crude and heavy, reflecting the limited technical knowledge of the time.

Gothic Furniture. By the 12th century, however, conditions in western Europe had begun to improve. Nation-states started to emerge and with them a more settled life. The dominant factor in this era—which came to be known as the Gothic— was the church, and the dominant masters were the architects and stonemasons. Building on the existing Romanesque style, architects in France and later in the rest of western Europe began to construct massive churches whose form influenced nearly everything else made during the period. This was particularly true of the furniture, whose makers borrowed not only decorative details but even construction methods (the skeleton framework) from the stonemasons.

Gothic furniture is essentially rectilinear in concept, and its decorative motifs—round or pointed arches, carved tracery, pillars and buttresses—are taken directly from church architecture of the time. As in the preceding era, carving was the preferred method of embellishment, with native plant forms such as grape and maple leaves, wild cress, and parsley dominating the foliage; figural subjects, primarily birds and animals or humans in grotesque forms, were also used.

Oak and walnut, both of which lend themselves to carving, were the preferred timbers, and carving and molding often almost entirely covered the surface of a piece. Toward the end of the period painted decoration became popular, but sophis-

ticated techniques such as inlay were almost entirely absent in furniture; nor was there a great variety of forms. The greatest decorative skill was lavished on chests and coffers, but stools, benches, tables, and a very few chairs were also made. Befitting their dominant position, the clergy had a somewhat greater range of furnishings. Altars, screens, and desks (often embellished with the layered "linenfold" carving characteristic of the period) were found in churches and monasteries, but nowhere did there exist the variety of furniture that would be found in subsequent periods.

Renaissance Furniture. The Gothic mode, although exceedingly popular in northern Europe, made little headway in Italy, and by 1400 a new style was rapidly developing there. This was the Renaissance style, a mixture of native Greco-Roman forms and Eastern ideas derived from Constantinople. Renaissance decoration, far more elaborate than its Romanesque predecessor, was imposed upon furniture, which was constructed by cabinetmakers who were becoming artists.

The widespread use of mill-sawed and lathe-turned wood led to the making of lighter, well-constructed furnishings, while the range of timbers employed was expanded to include walnut, pine, ebony, and other woods. Decoration became varied and complex. To the catalog of Gothic decorative motifs were added those of the East: stars, crescents, and the intertwining scrollwork known as the arabesque. From the

An elaborately finished Spanish varqueño (17th century), a drop front writing desk resting on a chest, displays the intricate geometric decoration that distinguishes much Spanish furniture. Simply constructed, the piece reveals the influence of Islamic artistic tradition in its complex ornamentation. (Metropolitan Museum of Art, New York City.)

(Left) This 16th-century storage chest or cassone from northern Italy is richly embellished with allegorical figures and ornamental designs. The demand for fine furniture in Renaissance Italy led to the rapid development of the cassone as an elaborate artistic showpiece. (Metropolitan Museum of Art, New York City.)

(Below) A Louis XVI commode, designed by J. H. Riesener, exhibits the heavy proportions and elegant, symmetrical ornamentation characteristic of early neoclassical furniture. Riesener's union of simple form with restrained decoration made him the undisputed master of the Louis XVI style. (The Frick Collection, New York City.)

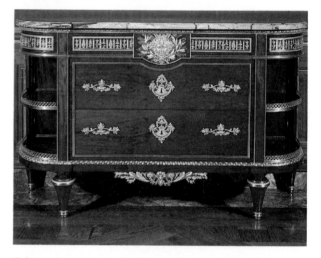

East also came intarsia, the inlay in wood of bone, shell, and metal. Gilding became popular again, as it had been in Roman times; famous painters of the day, such as PIERO DI COSIMO, vied for the opportunity to decorate the storage chests and cupboards of their royal patrons. Carving, however, continued to be popular, improving in both quality and variety as it moved from the structural rigidity of architectural forms into the province of the sculptor.

A great variety of new furnishings appeared at this time including, in Italy, the *cassone*, a very large storage chest, and, in Spain, a framed drop-front desk, the *vargueno*, which was carved, inlaid, and painted with the greatest care. Also in Spain iron and leather were first used extensively in the construction and decoration of furniture.

Baroque Furniture. By the middle of the 16th century a new style, the baroque, was emerging, first in Italy and later in France where, under Louis XIV, cabinetmaking became a recipient of royal patronage and subject to royal control. The first *ébéniste du roi* (cabinetmaker to the king) was André Charles BOULLE, appointed in 1672, whose furniture epitomizes the baroque style.

Baroque furniture is characterized by strong emphasis on decoration and a reduced concern with form. Scale is deliberately distorted, and carving grows lavish with deep moldings, sinuous twisted scrollwork, and pediments of gigantic proportions in relation to the pieces they crown.

Carving was the most important decorative technique employed in the baroque style. Veneering was also popular, however, and marquetry was practiced, as was inlay in gilt, bronze, and marble; marble inlay was used extensively for tabletops made in Italy and exported. Chairs, the forms of which were now many and varied, were also carved and frequently covered with stamped and gilded leather studded with nailheads in the Spanish manner.

Rococo Furniture. The disenchantment with form continued during the following period, the rococo (1700–75). The term *rococo* is derived from *rocaille*, the French word for shellwork in garden grottoes. Rococo furniture is typically light in weight and feeling with curving, asymmetrical forms lushly decorated with floral and animal motifs. Surface decoration, including gilding, painting, carving, and application of gilt bronze ornaments, almost totally dissolves the outline of individual furniture pieces, as in the furniture of Jean François OEBEN and Jean Henri RIESENER.

The greatest patron of the ROCOCO STYLE was Louis XV of France; French decorative furniture in the Louis XV style is scarce and costly and is considered by many to be among the finest ever made. There is no question that it is extraordinary in execution and in form. New forms, such as the slant-front desk, were invented; old forms changed their appearance, as the curved cabriole leg was applied to tables and chairs and chests of drawers assumed swelling bombé, or bulging, serpentine fronts. (See STYLES OF LOUIS XIII–XVI.)

In England a more conservative mode prevailed in the baroque and rococo periods, typified by the QUEEN ANNE STYLE— with cabriole legs, graceful curves, and opulent carving, as in

(Below) A lady's dressing table, attributed to the 18th-century cabinetmaker Jean François Oeben, displays the delicate curves, slender proportions, and detailed ornament of the Louis XV style. The fine floral marquetry and mechanical ingenuity of this piece testify to the high level of craftsmanship attained by French rococo cabinetmakers. (National Gallery of Art, Washington, D.C.)

This Louis XV armchair (c.1770), composed entirely of curving forms, epitomizes the delicate grace of French rococo furniture. It is characterized by such features as the slender frame, always visible and often accented by carved molding, and the rich floral ornamentation. (National Gallery of Art, Washington, D.C.)

(Left) The classical revival of the late 18th century returned linearity and an almost architectural monumentality to furniture forms. This 18th-century roll-top desk, designed by one of the leading cabinetmakers of the time, David Roentgen, exemplifies the neoclassic style. Intricate marquetry, compartments, and mechanical devices are typical of Roentgen's work. (Metropolitan Museum of Art, New York City.)

(Below) The Empire style of the early 19th century combined classical austerity with Napoleonic grandeur. This couch (c.1810), attributed to Duncan Phyfe, an American designer, is derived from the form of a Roman triclinium, or banquet couch. (Ford Museum, Dearborn, Mi.)

(Above) Marquetry, or inlay work, flourished during the reign of King Louis XV of France. This ornate 18th-century dressing table, seen from above, displays the elegant marquetry floral patterns and fanciful scrollings characteristic of Louis XV, or rococo, style.

the work of Grinling GIBBONS. Publication of Thomas CHIPPENDALE's Gentleman and Cabinet Maker's Directory (1754) heralded the birth of a style that owed much to the influence of imported Chinese furnishings.

The German style of baroque and rococo furniture achieved its own exuberant flowering, especially in Munich in the work of François CUVILLIÉS for the Bavarian royal family. His Reiche Zimmer (Rich Rooms, c.1750) in the Munich Residenz and his furnishings for his AMALIEN PAVILION (1734–40) in the park of NYMPHENBURG PALACE are considered the highest achievements of the German rococo style.

Neoclassic Furniture. In time the lush decoration and irregular form of the rococo went out of fashion, and after 1770 cabinetmakers sought new inspiration, which they found in the recently discovered Roman ruins at Herculaneum and Pompeii, first excavated in 1748, and in the general interest in antiquity called NEOCLASSICISM. From the architectural forms and wall paintings found in Pompeii such designers as Robert ADAM in England and David Roentgen in Germany developed a new style—the neoclassic (1770–1810).

Carving and curvilinear form, so popular in the two previous periods, now nearly disappeared and was replaced by strong vertical and horizontal lines, combined with delicate construction and flat panels decorated with contrasting veneers or painted designs. Furniture legs became long and slim with a square taper or a reeded form. Fluting and grooving emphasized the verticality of the pieces, and moldings and feet took the forms of the capitals and bases of Greek and Roman columns. Decorative devices were used more spar-

ingly, and those employed were classical in form, such as the oak leaf, the urn, and the Greek palm. Brass and gilt continued to be used but only in delicate, small-scale fittings.

Empire Furniture. Neoclassicism came late to France and was soon replaced, first by the DIRECTOIRE STYLE and soon after by Napoleon's version of the classic revival, known appropriately as the EMPIRE STYLE. Empire furniture is characterized by absolute symmetry, heavy proportions, and wide, flat surfaces, sparse molding and decoration, and veneering. Carving, except on chair arms and table legs, is rare, and ormolu is used with a certain restraint. Motifs and forms were inspired by Egyptian, Greek, and Roman furniture. The Empire style was enthusiastically adopted in England and particularly so in the United States, as in the work of Lambert HITCHCOCK and Duncan PHYFE. In Germany and Austria the Empire style formed the basis for the pervasive BIEDERMEIER style, an even simpler and heavier version of Empire.

Victorian Furniture. The Victorian era, spanning the reign of the British queen Victoria (1837–1901), spawned the greatest proliferation of decorative furniture ever seen. This was in part due to the eclectic nature of design during the era. Rather than working within a single, dominant style as had previously been the custom, furniture makers borrowed and adapted elements from numerous previous eras, using them interchangeably in bewildering combinations. The proliferation of Victorian furniture was also made possible by the mechanization of furniture manufacture, which took place in the 1840s. The development of mechanical presses and veneer-cutting machinery allowed for the rapid and inexpensive (if not always artistic) creation of decorative furniture. Moreover, improvements in transportation made the finest and most exotic woods—mahogany, rosewood, teak, ebony, and the like—readily available throughout the world in quantity.

As a consequence, a great variety of decorative furniture

(Left) *This parlor from the Colonel Robert J. Milligan house, in Saratoga, N.Y., exemplifies the Victorian style of mid-19th-century America. The curvilinear rococo was one of the most prevalent of the various revived styles popular during the Victorian era. The introduction of matching sets of furniture created harmonious and richly ornamental rooms. A parlor set was usually composed of a couch, armchair, lady's chair, and several side chairs. (Brooklyn Museum, N.Y.)*

was produced. In some pieces carving was the dominant element. The carved and pressed oak furniture of the late 19th and early 20th centuries has for some years been very popular with collectors. Intended originally as plain, inexpensive ware, such pieces are now almost luxury items. Other Victorian furnishings are more elaborate. Pieces were made of mahogany, rosewood, and walnut veneer, while other pieces were inlaid with ceramic title, colored glass, or various metals.

Stylistic adaptations hark back to other eras. Victorian Gothic is carved to imitate 14th-century church furnishings,

This richly carved bed (c.1860) of laminated rosewood characterizes the work of John Belter, an American designer. Belter devised a laminating process that enabled him to create intricate naturalistic carvings on his rococo pieces. (Brooklyn Museum, N.Y.)

(Left) *The sinuous lines of Art Nouveau appeared in the decorative as well as in the graphic arts toward the end of the 19th century. The French designer Hector Guimard's pearwood side table (c.1908) reflects the curved forms and naturalistic motifs characteristic of Art Nouveau. (Museum of Modern Art, New York City.)*

while Renaissance Revival pieces show a strong, if archaic, Italian influence. The Victorian era's final flowering was in the style called ART NOUVEAU, related to the rococo style and directly inspired by the ARTS AND CRAFTS MOVEMENT. Art Nouveau furniture is characterized by sinuous, flowing lines and rich contrasts of light and shadow, as in the desks, tables, and chairs designed by the French architect Hector GUIMARD.

In spite of all the eclectic revivals of the 19th century, certain important advances were made: the American John

BELTER created laminated wood furniture beginning about 1845; and in 1841, Michael Thonet of Vienna patented the bentwood process. These new techniques had a profound influence on later furniture design and manufacture.

Meanwhile, taste was changing once again, with a reaction to Victorian decorative excesses. Under the influence of the Arts and Crafts Movement in England, led by William Morris, and, in the United States, led by such Morris disciples as designers Elbert Hubbard (1865–1915) and Gustav Stickley (1847–1942), a new style emerged. Mission, as it was called in the United States, emphasized square-cut, heavy oak furniture upholstered in leather. Popular in the early 20th century, the style was revived beginning in the 1970s, both for collectors and for buyers of contemporary copies.

Scandinavian and Bauhaus Furniture. Early in this century, designers in Scandinavia began to employ wood and steel in a large repertoire of what is now called "modern" furniture. Such designer-architects as Alvar AALTO of Finland and Arne JACOBSEN of Denmark set style precedents that are still followed. However, the strongest influence on modern furnishings was the Paris *Exposition Universelle des Arts Decoratifs et Industriels Modernes* of 1925, at which the BAUHAUS architects Ludwig MIES VAN DER ROHE and Marcel BREUER showed the first modern nickel-plated steel furniture as well as adaptations and updated versions of Thonet's bentwood furniture. These pieces, severely elegant and simple, became 20th-century classics that influenced all subsequent designers.

The Paris Exposition also launched the style now called ART DECO, which had its roots in the Viennese SECCESSION MOVEMENT of the first decade of the 20th century. Art Deco furniture, like its architecture, is sleek, streamlined, and decorated with geometric designs and abstracted natural forms. This style was in vogue until 1939 and then experienced a revival of interest in the 1960s and '70s.

Contemporary Furniture. Many 20th-century furniture designers have been architects, including Frank Lloyd WRIGHT, Charles and Henry Greene (see GREENE AND GREENE), Eero SAARINEN, and Charles EAMES in the United States. Their furniture was usually designed for their own buildings, but much of it was capable of mass manufacture, such as Saarinen's pedestal chair of molded plastic and the so-called Eames chair (in fact designed by Eames and Saarinen) of molded plywood upholstered in leather. The popularity of the Eames and Saarinen designs was part of a shift toward simple, functional furniture, along with a revival and adaptation of earlier Scandinavian designs. Synthetic materials have been adopted rapidly in furniture design and manufacture. Line is all important, and decoration as it existed in the 19th century and before has effectively ceased to exist (except in rare and expensive pieces made by hand—and often created by artists rather than designers). In part, the disappearance of decoration is a matter of taste, but it also reflects the fact that artisans are no longer trained to do this sort of work.

Late 20th-century trends in furniture fashions show a wide-

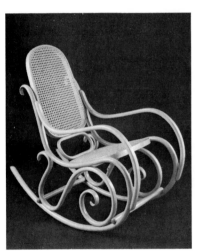

(Left) *Michael Thonet's bentwood rocking chair (c.1860), in its simple design and construction, foreshadowed the clean lines and functionalism of 20th-century furniture.*

(Right) *The comfortable sculptural designs created by Charles Eames are typified by the Eames chair and ottoman, among the most successful and most imitated works of the 20th century.*

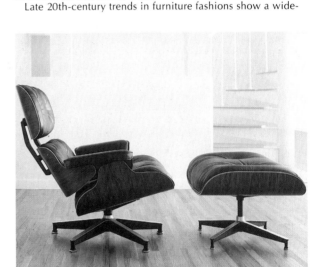

(Below) *These two examples of contemporary furniture illustrate the great range available to modern designers. (Left) The red leather chair, slung from a structure of thin metal bars, is by German designer Till Leeser, who exhibits his work as art. (Right) A table by American designer George Nakashima is typical of this famous artisan's use of solid wood and his exploitation of the natural profile of a cut of timber to dictate the shape of a piece.*

(Above) *Ludwig Mies van der Rohe's classic Barcelona chair (1929) epitomizes the spare, elegant, and functional Bauhaus designs.*

ranging eclecticism, as styles from almost every period re-emerge—although the basic, boxy Scandinavian look continues to dominate in inexpensive, mass-market furniture. Artistry and craftsmanship are still valued, however, as the works of master carpenter George Nakashima, or the Shaker-styled cabinetry of one-of-a-kind furniture makers attest.

WILLIAM C. KETCHUM, JR.

FURNITURE MANUFACTURE

Furniture making remained a handicraft until the early 19th century, when water- and steam-powered tools came into widespread use. Powered saws could cut and shape wood pieces quickly and in quantity, and large steam-driven presses made it possible to stamp decorative patterns on wood instead of laboriously carving them by hand. These labor-saving devices also reduced the role of the individual artisan. Whereas a carpenter had once undergone a long apprenticeship and had learned how to produce an entire piece of furniture from scratch, such a person was now responsible only for a single process in the production line, for example, the turning of chair legs or the gluing of drawer joints.

Early Factory Systems. The chair factory established (1818) by the American furniture maker Lambert HITCHCOCK was typical of the early factory systems. Situated on the Barkhamsted River in Connecticut, the factory was almost completely water powered, and the individual pieces of each chair were sawed, planed, and turned by machine. Assembly, painting, and the elaborate stenciling that became a Hitchcock trademark were done by hand but on a production line.

In the United States industrialization was accelerated by the expansion of migration to the West. The thousands of new settlers in the frontier territories created a huge new market for inexpensive furniture. In Grand Rapids, Mich., and in other cities on the fringes of settlement, a number of factories began to pour out furniture in unprecedented volume. Mass production cut costs so low that inexpensive pieces were offered as premiums to purchasers of soaps and perfumes. Eventually, the name *Borax* became an epithet that signified cheap, shoddy, mass-produced furniture.

By the end of the 19th century, furniture handcrafts that had once flourished were now used only by custom shops making expensive furniture to order or by people interested in the arts-and-crafts revival.

Influence of Technology on Design. Throughout the 19th century factory-made furniture imitated traditional styles. It was not until the early 20th century that designers began to consider the potential offered by mass-production techniques. In Germany the Bauhaus School (founded 1919) attempted to design objects that were attractive, simple, and reproducible in quantity, although perhaps expensive. In the United States the modernist movement achieved wide recognition beginning only in the 1930s, with designers such as Charles Eames, Paul McCobb, T. H. Robsjohn-Gibbings, and Eero Saarinen. Their designs eventually transformed the manufacture of furniture, allowing the introduction of simple, undecorated surfaces, functional shapes, and a range of new materials: glass, chrome, steel, aluminum, and plastic.

Contemporary Manufacture. Contemporary wood furniture frequently uses a combination of wood with such composite materials as Masonite and plywood. Wood surfaces are usually made of a thin veneer laid over a less expensive wood. Many veneers are made of plastic or plastic-covered wood.

Mass-produced furniture parts are machine-cut and -sanded and assembled with Powered hand tools or with mechanically applied glues. The component parts of flat-surfaced furniture, such as chests and tables, are often spray painted on a moving belt, in a completely automatic process. More complicated or expensive pieces are stained and varnished by hand.

The development of quick-setting, permanent-bonding glues and of new techniques in lamination and high-pressure processes has encouraged the creation of new furniture forms. A one-piece molded chair body, for example, can be produced by gluing many layers of thin wood veneer together, then molding the veneer block into a chair shape in a heat press. Plastic furniture shapes are molded or cast, and molded plastic or fiberglass is also used—instead of wood—for the skele-

tons of furniture to be covered by upholstery.

The cushions used on contemporary styles are usually filled with sponge rubber or plastic foam. For traditional chairs and sofas, however, traditional handcrafts are still used. Coiled steel springs are tied in a lacing of burlap webbing and attached to the furniture frame. The springs are embedded in a bulky filling material, such as foam rubber, then covered with a soft padding layered to the desired shape of the piece, and finished with upholstery fabric. The use of mechanical knives to cut many layers of fabric into the necessary shapes and the replacement of upholsterer's tacks by air-driven staples are the only modern innovations in the upholstering process.

Knockdown and Do-It-Yourself Furniture. A knockdown table or chest of drawers, purchased disassembled and packed in a flat box, can be put together with glue and a few screws. Home-assembled furniture has been made possible by modern machining methods that can produce furniture components to precise size tolerances, and by joining and finishing techniques that are so simple an amateur can easily build attractive pieces from precut components.

Bibliography: Allwood, Rosamond, *Victorian Furniture, 1837–1887* (1990); Battersby, Martin, et al., *The History of Furniture* (1976); Bavaro, Joseph, and Mossman, Thomas L., *The Furniture of Gustave Stickley* (1990); Boger, Louise A., *The Complete Guide to Furniture Styles* (1969; repr. 1982); Cheneviere, Antoine, *Russian Furniture: The Golden Age, 1780–1840* (1988); Comstock, Helen, *American Furniture: 17th, 18th, and 19th Century Styles* (1980); Darling, S. S., *Chicago Furniture* (1984); Edwards, Ralph, *Dictionary of English Furniture*, 3 vols. (1986); Eidelberg, Martin, ed., *Design 1935–1965: What Modern Was* (1991); Grant, Jerry V., and Allen, Douglas R., *Shaker Furniture Makers* (1989); Hinckley, F. Lewis, *Hepplewhite, Sheraton, and Regency Furniture* (1987); Joyce, Ernest, *Encyclopedia of Furniture Making* (1989); Ketchum, W. C., Jr., *Furniture Two: Neoclassic to the Present* (1981); Lucie-Smith, Edward, *Furniture: A Concise History* (1985); Mang, Karl, *History of Modern Furniture* (1979); Naeve, Milo, *Identifying American Furniture* (1981); Payne, C., ed., *Sotheby's Concise Encyclopedia of Furniture* (1989); Sembach, K.-J., *Contemporary Furniture* (1987); Smith, Nancy, *Old Furniture: Understanding the Craftsman's Art* (1975); Stimpson, Miriam, *Modern Furniture Classics* (1987); Vandal, Norman, *Queen Anne Furniture* (1990).

See also: ANTIQUE COLLECTING; INDUSTRIAL DESIGN; INTERIOR DESIGN.

Furtwängler, Wilhelm   [foort'-veng-glur]

Wilhelm Furtwängler, b. Jan. 25, 1886, d. Nov. 30, 1954, was perhaps the outstanding German conductor of the 20th century. He studied with Max von Schillings and Josef Rheinberger and held conducting posts in Zurich, Strasbourg, Lübeck, Mannheim, and Frankfurt am Main before succeeding Arthur Nikisch in 1922 as director of the Berlin Philharmonic and Leipzig Gewandhaus orchestras. He also became closely associated with the Vienna Philharmonic Orchestra and appeared as guest conductor with the New York Philharmonic for three seasons (1925–27). An opponent of the Hitler regime, he nonetheless remained in Germany during the Nazi years. An Allied tribunal found him innocent of collaboration.

Furtwängler was renowned for his individual yet scrupulous performances of the German repertory. His grasp of the immense musical structures of Richard Wagner and Anton Bruckner was unequaled.

LAWRENCE FUCHSBERG

Bibliography: Furtwängler, Wilhelm, *Collected Essays,* trans. by L. A. Fenn (1965), and *Concerning Music,* trans. by L. J. Lawrence (1953; repr. 1977); Gallup, Stephen, *Biography of Wilhelm Furtwängler* (1991); Geissmar, Berta, *Two Worlds of Music* (1946); Gillis, Daniel, *Furtwängler and America* (1970; repr. 1980) and, as ed., *Furtwängler Recalled* (1965).

furze   [furz]

Furze, or gorse, is the common name for a genus, *Ulex*, of about 25 species of shrubs in the pea family, Leguminosae. Furze is native to Europe and is widely cultivated; its dense branches are dark green and spiny. The principal species is *U. europaeus*, which grows up to 1.2 m (4 ft) tall or more in sunny areas with sandy or gravelly soil. Its yellow flowers are showy and are produced continuously in mild climates. The plants are sometimes used to stabilize dry banks.

fuse

The electrical fuse is a device placed in an electrical circuit to avoid overload. It usually contains a thin strip of metal that melts and breaks when a current above a certain amperage passes through it. It is important that a fuse or other CIRCUIT BREAKER control an overloaded circuit in order to avoid damage to the system (see ELECTRICAL WIRING).

Fuseli, Henry   [fue'-zil-ee]

Henry Fuseli, b. Zurich, Feb. 6, 1741, d. Apr. 16, 1825, was an artist and art historian. The son of a painter, he was educated as a theologian at the Collegium Carolinum in Zurich but had to flee from Switzerland as a result of radical views expressed in his early writings. Fuseli went to Berlin and then to London, where he settled in 1764. There he translated one of Johann Winckelmann's first essays on ancient Greek art into English and was encouraged by Sir Joshua Reynolds to become a painter. With this in mind he went (1770) to Italy for eight years, studying classical antiquity and the art of Michelangelo, two sources that were to remain permanent influences on his style. From that time on most of his energy was devoted to painting.

Fuseli's early literary and theological training remained a decisive factor throughout his career. His subject paintings were frequently drawn from a wide range of literature; Shakespeare was his favorite writer. In his choice of subjects he showed a preference for the fantastic and the horrific (for an example, see FAIRY). Much romantic art is literary in origin, and in this respect Fuseli was a key romantic painter (see ROMANTICISM, art). His paintings, although highly imaginative, were sometimes technically inept; his ideas often appear less stilted, however, in the freshness of his many drawings. He also produced paintings and drawings of women in elongated forms, sometimes with fantastic hairstyles.

As professor of painting at the Royal Academy in London from 1799 to 1805, and again from 1810 until his death, Fuseli gave the best series of discourses since those of Reynolds. He started to compile the first history of Italian art in the English language and revised the standard dictionary on art of the time.   DAVID IRWIN

Bibliography: Ganz, P., *The Drawings of Henry Fuseli* (1949); Knowles, J., *The Life and Writings of Henry Fuseli*, 3 vols. (1831; repr. 1982); Powell, N., *Fuseli: The Nightmare* (1973); Schiff, G., and Hofmann, W., *Henry Fuseli* (1977); Weinglass, H. H., ed., *The Collected English Letters of Henry Fuseli* (1982).

fusion, nuclear

Nuclear fusion is a type of nuclear reaction in which two atomic nuclei combine to form a heavier nucleus, releasing energy. For a fusion reaction to take place, the nuclei, which are positively charged, must have enough kinetic energy to overcome their electrostatic force of repulsion. This can occur either when one nucleus is accelerated to high energies by an accelerating device, or when the energies of both nuclei are raised by the application of very high temperatures. The latter method, referred to as thermonuclear fusion, is the source of the Sun's energy. If a proton is accelerated and collides with another proton, these nuclei can fuse, forming a deuterium nucleus (one proton and one neutron), a positron, a neutrino, and energy. Such a reaction is not self-sustaining because the released energy is not readily imparted to other nuclei. Thermonuclear fusion of deuterium and tritium (one proton and two neutrons) will produce a helium nucleus and an energetic neutron that can help sustain further fusion. This is one basis of the HYDROGEN BOMB, which employs a brief, uncontrolled thermonuclear fusion reaction. A great effort is now under way to harness thermonuclear fusion as a source of power (see FUSION ENERGY).

Thermonuclear fusion depends on high energies, and the possibility of low-energy, low-temperature nuclear fusion has generally been discounted. Early in 1989, however, two electrochemists startled the scientific world and aroused great public interest when they declared that they had achieved

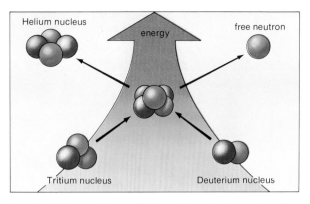

In nuclear fusion two light nuclei unite to form a heavier nucleus. The fusion of deuterium and tritium, for example, yields helium and a neutron and releases tremendous energy. The energy produced by the hydrogen bomb and by the Sun and stars results from fusion reactions.

room-temperature fusion in a simple laboratory experiment. The scientists, Stanley Pons of the University of Utah and Martin Fleischmann of the University of Southampton, England, described their experiment as involving an electrochemical cell in which palladium and platinum electrodes were immersed in heavy water (see DEUTERIUM). They claimed that the cell produced more heat than could be accounted for by a chemical reaction alone, and that they had observed certain typical fusion by-products in the course of the process. According to their theory, deuterium was absorbed by the palladium electrode and fused there, releasing the extra heat. Various laboratories around the world tried to duplicate the process, with conflicting but generally negative results. Nevertheless, scientists continued to explore this possibility of "cold" fusion.

Bibliography: Dagani, Ron, "Hopes for Cold Fusion Diminish as Ranks of Disbelievers Swell," *Chemical & Engineering News,* May 22, 1989, and "Cold Fusion Anomalies More Perplexing than Ever," *Chemical & Engineering News,* Nov. 6, 1989.

fusion energy

A fusion reaction is one in which two atomic nuclei merge to form a heavier nucleus and, in most cases, an accompanying product such as a free nucleon. In almost all types of fusion reactions between light nuclei, a portion of their rest mass is converted into KINETIC ENERGY of the reaction products, or into gamma rays. Stars produce energy through a variety of fusion reactions. In main-sequence stars such as the Sun, the net effect of these reactions is to convert hydrogen nuclei (protons) into helium nuclei. The kinetic energy and gamma rays released in the process heat the stellar interior, maintaining it at the very high temperatures (greater than 10 million K) required to continue the fusion. Such conditions, where the thermal energy of the nuclei drives them together in spite of their electrostatic repulsion, are called thermonuclear.

This process, which has been driving the stars for billions of years, has clear potential as a power source on Earth, and scientists have worked for decades toward the goal of employing thermonuclear fusion reactions to produce useful power. The two fusion reactions that are by far the most promising both involve the heavier isotopes of hydrogen: deuterium (composed of one proton and one neutron), and tritium (composed of one proton and two neutrons). Deuterium occurs naturally as a minor constituent in all hydrogen-containing materials—such as water—in quantities sufficient to meet all the energy needs of societies for many billions of years. Tritium can be bred from lithium by a neutron-induced reaction in a blanket that could conceivably surround a fusion reactor. The western United States contains large lithium deposits in the salts of dry lake beds, and much larger quantities are dissolved in the sea. The reaction that occurs with the greatest probability and at the lowest temperatures involves the fusing of a deuterium nucleus with a tritium nucleus to form a helium (He^4) nucleus and a neutron. The products contain 17.6 million electron volts (MeV) of released kinetic energy. The second promising reaction, involving the fusing of two deuterium nuclei, has two branches that occur with about equal probability. One leads to a He^3 nucleus, a neutron, and 3.2 MeV of kinetic energy; the other produces a tritium nucleus, a proton, and 4.0 MeV. While the deuterium-deuterium reaction is the one that could furnish power beyond even the expected lifetime of the Sun, it is the somewhat more easily produced deuterium-tritium reaction, which would itself be sufficient for many thousands of years, that will provide most of the energy in the next generation of research devices.

Fusion reactions can be induced easily by using a charged particle accelerator (see ACCELERATOR, PARTICLE) to bombard a solid or gaseous tritium target with energetic deuterium nuclei. This technique consumes power rather than producing it, however, because most of the accelerated nuclei lose their energy through elastic collisions with electrons and nuclei, without producing fusion reactions. A net energy gain is obtained only by mimicking the Sun and producing starlike thermonuclear conditions. Because a reactor must be much smaller than a star and must operate in a limited time frame, however, it must have a much higher power density and be several times hotter than the center of the Sun. The advantage of carrying out the reactions under thermonuclear conditions is that the energy transferred between particles in elastic collisions is not really wasted as long as it remains within the thermonuclear matter. That is, energy that is lost by one nucleus in an elastic collision is transferred to the particle it hits and is still available to eventually initiate a fusion reaction.

At thermonuclear temperatures, matter can exist only in the plasma state, consisting of electrons, positive ions, and very few neutral atoms (see PLASMA PHYSICS). Fusion reactions that occur within a plasma serve to heat it further, because the portion of the reaction energy that remains with the electrically charged reaction products is transferred to the bulk of the plasma through collisions. In the deuterium-tritium reaction the positively charged helium nucleus carries 3.5 MeV. The neutron escapes the plasma with little interaction and, in a reactor, could deposit its 14.1 MeV in a surrounding lithium blanket. That would breed tritium and also heat an exchange medium (such as helium), which would then be used to produce steam to turn generator turbines. However, the plasma also loses thermal energy through a variety of processes: conduction, convection, and bremsstrahlung (electromagnetic radiation emitted when a charged particle decelerates). Energy also escapes through line radiation from electrons undergoing level transitions in heavier impurities, and through losses of hot nuclei that capture an electron and escape any confining fields. Ignition occurs when the energy deposited within the plasma by fusion reactions equals or exceeds the energy being lost.

In order to achieve ignition, a plasma must be confined and heated. Obviously, a plasma at millions of degrees is not compatible with an ordinary confining wall, but the effect of this incompatibility is not the destruction of the wall, as might be expected. Although the temperature of a thermonuclear plasma is very high and the power flowing through it may be large, the stored energy is relatively small and would quickly be radiated away by impurities if the plasma touched a wall and began to vaporize it. A thermonuclear plasma is thus self-limiting, because any significant contact with the vessel housing it causes its extinction within a few thousandths of a second.

Magnetic Confinement. Since the early 1950s, most fusion research has used magnetic fields to confine the charged particles that constitute a plasma. The density required in magnetic-confinement fusion is much lower than atmospheric density, so the plasma vessel is evacuated and then filled with the hydrogen-isotope fuel at 0.000001 times the density of the atmosphere. Magnetic-field configurations fall into two types: open and closed. In an open configuration the charged particles, which are spiraling along magnetic field lines maintained by a SOLENOID, are reflected at each end of a cell by

stronger magnetic fields. In this simplest type of mirror machine, many particles that have most of their velocity parallel to the solenoidal magnetic field are not reflected and can escape. Present-day mirror machines retard this loss by using additional plasma cells to set up electrostatic potentials that help confine the hot ions within the central solenoidal field.

In closed configurations, the magnetic-field lines along which charged particles move are continuous within the plasma. This closure has most commonly taken the form of a torus, or doughnut shape, and the most common example is the TOKAMAK. In a tokamak the primary confining field is toroidal and is produced by coils surrounding the vacuum vessel. Other coils cause current to flow through the plasma by induction. This toroidally flowing current engenders a poloidal magnetic field, at right angles, that wraps itself around the plasma. The poloidal field and the stronger toroidal field, acting together, yield magnetic-field lines that spiral around the torus. This spiraling ensures that a particle spends equal amounts of time above and below the toroidal midplane, thus canceling the effects of a vertical drift that occurs because the magnetic field is stronger on the inside of the torus than on the outside.

Plasma Heating. Tokamak plasmas can be heated to temperatures of 10–15 million K by the current flowing in the plasma. At higher temperatures the plasma resistance becomes too low for this method to be effective, and heating is accomplished by injecting beams of very energetic neutral particles into the plasma. These ionize, become trapped, and transfer their energy to the bulk plasma through collisions. Alternatively, radiofrequency waves are launched into the plasma at frequencies that resonate with various periodic particle motions. The waves give energy to these resonant particles, which transfer it to the rest of the plasma through collisions.

Current Drive. Experiments are also under way in which radiofrequency waves are used to push electrons around the tokamak to maintain the plasma current. Such noninductive current drive allows the tokamak pulse to outlast the time limits imposed by the fact that, in a transformer-driven tokamak, the plasma current lasts only as long as the current in the secondary coils is changing. When the secondary coils reach their current limits, confinement is lost, and the plasma terminates until the transformer can be reset (a matter of at least seconds). Although the plasma in an inductively driven tokamak is pulsed, the electricity produced would not be, because the thermal inertia of the neutron-capturing blanket would sustain steam generation between pulses. By allowing longer pulse or steady-state plasma operation, however, radiofrequency current drive could lessen the thermal stresses in the fusion reactor.

Major components of the TFTR tokamak at Princeton University are shown. The toroidal field coils produce the strong (up to 50 kG) toroidal magnetic field, which, along with the poloidal field produced by the plasma current, confines the plasma. The equilibrium field coils control the plasma position. The plasma is heated by beams of energetic atoms produced from ions accelerated in the ion sources.

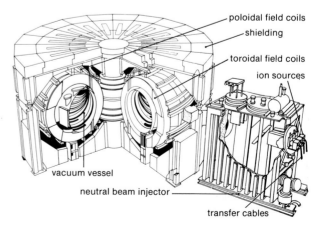

poloidal field coils

shielding

toroidal field coils

ion sources

vacuum vessel

neutral beam injector

transfer cables

Inertial Confinement. Another approach to fusion, pursued since about 1974, is termed inertial confinement. Its aim is to compress a solid pellet of frozen deuterium and tritium to very high temperatures and densities in a process analogous to what occurs in a thermonuclear (hydrogen) bomb. The compression is accomplished by bombarding the pellet from all sides, simultaneously, with an intense pulse of LASER light, ions, or electrons. The outer pellet mass vaporizes and, by mechanical reaction, imparts inwardly directed momentum to the remaining pellet core. The inertia of the inwardly driven pellet material must be sufficient to localize the resulting fusion plasma for the approximately 10^{-9} seconds required to get significant energy release. In 1988 it was learned that the U.S. government, which secretly had been using underground nuclear tests in Nevada to study inertial-confinement fusion, had achieved such fusion in 1986 by this means.

Progress toward Energy Production. The minimum confinement condition necessary to achieve energy gain in a deuterium-tritium plasma—the so-called Lawson criterion—is that the product of density in ions per cm^3 and energy containment time in seconds must exceed 6×10^{13}. This was attained in 1983 for the first time in a hydrogen plasma at the Massachusetts Institute of Technology. Further advances have since been made elsewhere. In 1991, for example, the Joint European Torus at Culham Laboratory near Oxford, England, yielded up to 2 million watts in a pulse lasting two seconds. Much research has yet to be done, however, before fusion power reactors become a reality. Japan, Russia, the European Community, and the United States agreed in 1992 to explore the feasibility of building a huge new fusion-research center.

The goal of fusion is, in effect, to make and hold a small star. Such a goal is daunting. That it is pursued even so is an indication of the magnitude of the benefits that success could bring. Besides providing an almost inexhaustible fuel supply, fusion is environmentally benign. The resulting ash is harmless, the afterheat in the reactor structure would be much less than in a fission reactor, and the heat would be distributed through a greater thermal mass. In addition, because fusion is not a chain reaction, it cannot run out of control. Any perturbation would cause the plasma to extinguish itself. It would also be difficult to produce nuclear-weapons materials surreptitiously at a fusion plant. Because no fissionable material should ordinarily be present, it would be a simple matter to detect characteristic gamma rays. Present levels of support for research are aimed at building a demonstration fusion power plant in the early 21st century.   LARRY R. GRISHAM

Bibliography: Akiyama, M., ed., *Design Technology of Fusion Reactors* (1991); Conn, R., et al., "The International Thermonuclear Experimental Reactor" *Scientific American* April 1992; Heppenheimer, T., *The Man-Made Sun* (1984); Roth, J., *Introduction to Fusion Energy* (1986).

Fust, Johann [foost]

Johann Fust, b. *c.*1400, d. Oct. 30, 1466, was a German printer and the financial backer of Johannes GUTENBERG, who is credited with the invention of movable type and the printing press. The money advanced by Fust in 1450 and an additional loan granted about 1452 enabled Gutenberg to develop his printing process and to buy the necessary materials and equipment. When Gutenberg could not repay him, Fust foreclosed and took possession of Gutenberg's press and materials. With Peter Schöffer, who had been Gutenberg's foreman, Fust published the 42-line GUTENBERG BIBLE *c.*1455 and the Psalter in 1457, the first example of color printing. Both volumes, however, had been designed and initiated by Gutenberg and are generally credited to him. Fust's firm later produced the Benedictine Psalter (1459), the 48-line Bible (1462), and an edition of Cicero's *De officiis*. Fust died on a trip to Paris, and Schöffer inherited the business.

Fustel de Coulanges, Numa Denis [fue-stel' duh koo-lahnzh', nue-mah' den-ee']

The French historian Fustel de Coulanges, b. Mar. 18, 1830, d. Sept. 12, 1889, was the first professor of medieval history at the University of Paris (1878–89). His first major work, *La Cité antique* (1864), concerned Greek and Roman institutions, but most of his studies, including *Histoire des institutions politiques de l'ancienne France* (6 vols., 1875–92), dealt with early French history. Fustel's emphasis on objectivity and primary sources had a major influence on French historiography.

Bibliography: Herrick, Jane, *The Historical Thought of Fustel de Coulanges* (1954).

Futuna Islands: see WALLIS AND FUTUNA ISLANDS.

futures

Futures are contracts describing the sale of a "commodity" scheduled to occur at a later date. No money changes hands between the buyer and seller when a trade is made, but both must post collateral ("margin") to demonstrate their good faith to fulfill their future obligations. Initial margin deposits range between 5% and 15% of contract value.

Futures contract markets are an important part of the financial system. They let businesses shift the risk of losing money to others more willing to bear it. In doing so, the futures markets provide information about the value of the items traded.

Futures markets are organized by commodity-futures exchanges. An exchange standardizes the terms of all contracts, oversees trading, and coordinates all payments. Members of an exchange gather in a "pit" or "ring" on the exchange floor and trade contracts by shouting and using hand signals.

Until the 1970s, virtually all futures contracts were written for agricultural commodities, such as wheat. Now some of the largest futures markets trade contracts on financial instruments, such as currencies, government and corporate debt, and stock indexes. In 1982, exchanges organized markets for put and call options on futures contracts (see OPTION TRADING).

The two largest U.S. futures exchanges are the Chicago Board of Trade and the Chicago Mercantile Exchange. Both have important agricultural and financial-futures markets. Some other exchanges are located in New York City, Kansas City, London, Tokyo, and Paris. In the United States the Commodity Futures Trading Commission regulates all futures trading.   JAMES F. GAMMILL, JR.

Bibliography: Hull, John C., *Introduction to Future and Options Markets* (1991).

futurism

Futurism, a movement in early-20th-century Italian painting and sculpture, was initiated by the literary manifesto of Filippo Tommaso MARINETTI, published in the French newspaper *Le Figaro* in February 1909. Marinetti extolled the dynamic energy of the modern machine, declared that classical art was less beautiful than the automobile, and proposed that art should celebrate the violence of speed and war. He simultaneously decried conventional artistic taste and its preference for the achievements of the Italian past over recent innovations of technology. In the following year a group of young painters led by Umberto BOCCIONI produced a technical manifesto that applied Marinetti's ideas to painting. Boccioni and his fellow signatories, Giacomo BALLA, Carlo CARRÀ, Gino SEVERINI, and Luigi Russolo, sought to represent the sensations of movement and used the word *dynamism* to describe the relationship between a moving object and its surroundings, as when a vehicle, speeding along a street, sets up vibrations that shake surrounding buildings.

In order to represent the movement of machines and human figures, the futurists resorted to the techniques of French CUBISM, which used fragmented images consisting of intersecting planes to impart a sense of motion to their work. Marcel DUCHAMP's celebrated *Nude Descending a Staircase* (1912; Philadelphia Museum of Art) reveals the shared characteristics of the two movements. Through a series of similar forms distributed in jerky sequence across the canvas, Duchamp finds a concrete equivalent for the idea of descent. Like Duchamp, the futurists moved toward abstraction, striving to represent the noises of a construction site, as in Boccioni's *The*

Gino Severini's Danseuse bleue (1912), in its vitality and rhythm, exemplifies the dynamic movement sought by the adherents of futurism. Severini was one of the movement's founders and leading figures and was also closely associated with cubism. (Mattiolo Collection, Milan.)

City Rises (1910–11; Museum of Modern Art, New York City), or the patterns of sound made by music, as in Russolo's *Music* (1911; private collection, London).

In a second manifesto of 1912, Boccioni applied futurist doctrine to the three-dimensional medium of sculpture, suggesting that a work of art might be set in motion by a motor and that sculpture might incorporate ready-made objects of common use. His ideas, which he did not live to put into practice, were later brought to fruition by KINETIC ART, and in the COLLAGES and assemblage of Pablo PICASSO and Duchamp.

The futurist movement lost momentum when, in 1915, many of its members joined the army. The death of Boccioni in 1916 deprived the futurists of their guiding spirit. His theories did, however, find expression in the architecture of Antonio Sant'Elia, who designed futurist cities and technical installations, perpetuating an interest in the aesthetic beauty of the machine age. Thereafter the aims of futurism were absorbed by other movements, notably by ART DECO, VORTICISM, and DADA.

HOWARD BATCHELOR

Bibliography: Baldacci, P., and Daverio, P., eds., *Futurism, 1911–18* (1991); Clough, Rosa, *Futurism* (1961); Hewitt, A., *Fascist Modernism* (1993); Lista, G., *Futurism* (1986); Perloff, Marjorie, *The Futurist Movement* (1987); Tisdall, C., and Bozzola, A., *Futurism* (1978; repr. 1985).

futurology

Futurology is the study of long-term trends in society in order to develop and promote alternative ways of dealing with future events or conditions. With the capacity to alert both governments and private industries to future problems and future opportunities, futurology is directed toward assisting in intelligent decision making. The terms *futures research, future studies, futurism,* and *forecasting* are also used to describe this field of study.

Although some of these terms date only from the 1940s in both Europe and the United States, societies throughout history have used a variety of methods for predicting the future. Early examples include Chinese ORACLE BONES, used for divination during the Shang dynasty (c.1766–c.1122 BC), and the Egyptian Book of the Dead, dating from as early as the 18th dynasty (1570–1320 BC), a collection of spells and formulas from which the Egyptians hoped to gain guidance for the afterlife.

During the modern era, with the onset of the Industrial Revolution, engineers were perceived as folk heroes, while science-fiction writers, such as Jules VERNE and Edward BELLAMY, popularized futuristic thinking. The 20th century brought H. G. WELLS to the forefront of science fiction, as a futurist who was able to blend an excellent understanding of science with imagination and profound social concerns.

World War II was the turning point for research on the fu-

ture. In 1944, Henry Harley Arnold, a general in the U.S. Air Force, initiated the first technological forecasting project, and in 1946 he was instrumental in establishing the RAND Corporation as a THINK TANK. The development and application of technological forecasting techniques accelerated in the late 1940s, 1950s, and 1960s, and other important future-oriented think tanks, such as the Stanford Research Institute (1946) and the Hudson Institute (1961), were created. In recent decades the writings of such futurists as Daniel BELL and Alvin Toffler (1928–) have dealt with the period of transformation to a highly complex, technological, global society, and the works of Buckminster FULLER and Herman Kahn (1922–83) have forecast views of possible future lifestyles and conditions.

A wide diversity of methods is used by futurists to make forecasts, ranging from simple, informed hunches to complex computer analyses. Because futurists recognize the unavoidable uncertainty inherent in forecasting, much of their work focuses on "what-if" examinations of alternatives rather than precise prediction. Two general types of forecasting methods exist, exploratory and normative. Exploratory forecasts, which begin with the past by examining historical data and move into the future by projecting probability outcomes, are labeled the "can do" type. Examples of exploratory forecasts are trend extrapolations and growth models. Normative forecasts, which include market analyses and relevance trees, imagine a desired future in order to facilitate the making of decisions that will achieve a predicted, or preferred, future.

Two other popular methods that cannot be strictly classified in one of the above categories are Delphi, an iterative and anonymous questioning process used to obtain the judgment of a panel of experts, and scenario writing, which uses a narrative to present an image of a future.

Pitfalls in forecasting include reliance on a single method, invalid underlying assumptions, and basing the forecast only on the very recent past (thus missing overriding long-term trends).

HAROLD A. LINSTONE

Bibliography: De Jouvenel, Bertrand, *The Art of Conjecture* (1964); Martino, Joseph P., *Technological Forecasting for Decision Making*, 2d ed. (1983); Coates J. F., and Jarratt, J., *What Futurists Believe* (1989).

Fux, Johann Joseph [fuks]

Johann Joseph Fux, b. 1660, d. Feb. 14, 1741, was an Austrian organist and composer famous for his skill in COUNTERPOINT. He became composer to the Austrian court in 1698 and by 1715 had risen to the position of first *Kapellmeister*. He wrote more than 400 compositions, mostly polyphonic church music. His fame, however, rests almost entirely on his treatise on musical theory, *Gradus ad Parnassum* (*Steps to Parnassus*, 1725).

WILLIAM HAYS

Bibliography: Bukofzer, M., *Music in the Baroque Era* (1947); Sadie, Julie A., ed., *Companion to Baroque Music* (1991); White, Harry, ed., *Johann Joseph Fux and the Music of the Austro-Italian* (1992).

Fuzhou

Fuzhou is the capital and largest city of Fujian (Fukien) province, China. It is located near the mouth of the Min River, about 55 km (34 mi) from the Taiwan Strait and has a population of 1,250,000 (1989 est.). Fuzhou is also known by its traditional name, Yongcheng (Yung-ch'eng; Banyan City), because its humid tropical climate favors the growth of banyan trees. Major manufactures include machinery, paper, chemicals, and textiles. The city is also noted for its traditional handicraft industries such as lacquerware and sculpture. A railroad linking it to the main Chinese rail system was opened in 1958. In the hills around Fuzhou are many historic temples. Educational institutions include Fuzhou University and Fujian Medical College.

Fuzhou was founded in the late 6th century. It was one of the five earliest treaty ports opened (1842) to international trade as a result of the Opium Wars and was particularly important for its export of tea. But it declined after 1880 as a result of silting of the river and the decreasing demand for China tea.

JAMES CHAN